THE
OFFICIAL
ACT®
PREP PACK

Start Preparing with the **ONLY** Official ACT Prep Guide Here

Use the Access Code Found on the Inside Front Cover of This Book at https://onlineprep.act.org/voucher to Get Started with ACT Online Prep™

WILEY

Published by John Wiley & Sons, Inc., Hoboken, New Jersey.

Wiley publishes in a variety of print and electronic formats and by print-on-demand. Some material included with standard print versions of this book may not be included in e-books or in print-on-demand. If this book refers to media such as a CD or DVD that is not included in the version you purchased, you may download this material at http://booksupport.wiley.com. For more information about Wiley products, visit www.wiley.com.

ACT endorses the *Code of Fair Testing Practices in Education* and the *Code of Professional Responsibilities in Educational Measurement*, guides to the conduct of those involved in educational testing. ACT is committed to ensuring that each of its testing programs upholds the guidelines in each *Code*. A copy of each *Code* may be obtained free of charge from ACT Customer Services. (70), P.O. Box 1008, Iowa City, IA 52243-1008, 319-337-1429.

ACT Publications
P.O. Box 168
Iowa City, Iowa 52243-0168

ISBN 978-1-119-58052-2

Cover design: Wiley
Printed in the United States of America
PB Printing C10008115_03152019

The Official ACT Prep Guide Contents

Preface

Thank you for choosing the The Official ACT® Prep Pack. You clearly want to do your very best on the ACT test, and this set of resources will help get you there.

The Official ACT Prep Pack includes a six-month subscription to ACT® Online Prep™, a web-based learning and practice program. Inside the front cover of this book you will find instructions on how to access the unique code that unlocks the full version of ACT Online Prep. This code will unlock both the web and mobile versions.

Together, ACT Online Prep and this printed Official ACT Prep Guide, feature six genuine ACT tests (all of which include the optional writing section), which you can use for practice. You'll also find detailed explanations of every correct question response so that you can review your progress and learn which areas need more of your attention.

Using the prep pack will help you become familiar with the following:

- The content of the ACT
- The procedures you'll follow when you're actually taking the ACT
- The types of questions you can expect to find on the ACT
- Suggestions on how to approach each type of question
- General test-taking strategies

This book was designed to help you know what to expect when you take the ACT so that you can relax and concentrate on doing your best. The more you know about what to expect on any test you take, the more likely it is that your performance on that test will accurately reflect your overall preparation and achievement in the areas it measures. Knowing what to expect can help reduce any nervousness you may feel as you approach the test.

ACT Online Prep gives you the chance to practice thousands of questions through a systematic learning process anywhere you are, across multiple mobile devices. Once you've unlocked your account, by entering your unique code, download the app for additional practice on the go.

The ACT measures your understanding of what you've been taught in core high school courses that you have likely completed by the time you finish high school. Because it has taken you years to learn all of this material, it might take you some time to review for the ACT. You can't expect to cram for the ACT in a night or two; however, any review can be helpful, even if it just makes you more comfortable when you sit down to take the ACT. We hope this prep pack helps you gauge how much review you really need and identifies the specific subject areas on which to focus your efforts.

How This Book Is Arranged

This book is divided into five parts:

Part One: **Getting Acquainted with the ACT.** Chapters in this part introduce the ACT, explain how to prepare, and present general test-taking techniques and strategies for you to consider.

Part Two: **Taking and Evaluating Your First Practice Test.** This part includes a practice test along with guidance on how to use the test to identify areas where you may need to invest more time and effort.

Part Three: **Improving Your Score.** Chapters in this part present test-taking strategies tailored for each subject test—English, math, reading, and science—along with suggestions for taking the optional writing test.

Part Four: **Taking Additional Practice Tests.** In this part, you have the opportunity to take four additional practice tests, see the results, and interpret your scores to determine how well prepared you are to take the ACT.

Part Five: **Moving Forward to Test Day.** This part prepares you for test day by explaining how to register for the ACT and describing what to expect on the day of the test, so you show up on time with everything you need.

The parts are identified by bars on the edge of their right-hand pages.

Before You Begin

There is no standardized way to prepare for the ACT. Everyone learns and prepares differently. Some people prepare best when they are by themselves. Others need to work with fellow students to do their best. Still others function best in a structured class with a teacher leading them through their work. Use whatever method works best for you. Keep in mind, though, that when you actually take the ACT, it will be just you and the test.

As you use this book and ACT Online Prep to prepare for the ACT, consider working in 1-hour segments (except when you're taking the timed practice tests, of course). If you want to invest more than 1 hour a day, that's fine, but take breaks to stretch and give your mind a chance to absorb the material. Toiling to the point of burnout is counterproductive.

Part One: Getting Acquainted with the ACT Test

In This Part

This part introduces you to the ACT, the five tests that it is composed of (English, mathematics, reading, science, and the optional writing test), and testing procedures. It also features test-taking strategies and skills that apply to all of the component tests. Specifically, you will do the following:

- Find out what is covered on the tests.
- Determine when you can use a calculator and the types of calculators you are permitted to use and prohibited from using.
- Get a preview of what you can expect on test day.
- Obtain guidance on how to prepare for test day.
- Learn test-taking strategies that may improve your scores on all of the tests.

Chapter 1: About the ACT

The ACT measures your achievement in core academic areas important for your college and career success: English, math, reading, science, and (optionally) writing. It isn't an IQ test—it doesn't measure your basic intelligence. It's an achievement test that's been carefully designed—using surveys of classroom teachers, reviews of curriculum guides for schools all over the country, and advice from curriculum specialists and college faculty members—to be one of several effective tools for evaluating your college and career readiness.

The individual tests that make up the ACT consist of questions that measure your knowledge and skills. You're not required to memorize facts or vocabulary to do well on the ACT. Of course, all the terms, formulas, and other information you learned in your classes will be useful to you when you take the ACT. However, last-minute cramming (such as memorizing 5,000 vocabulary words or the entire periodic table of elements) won't directly improve your performance on the ACT.

Description of the ACT

The ACT consists of four multiple-choice tests—English, mathematics, reading, and science—and an optional writing test. Topics covered on these five tests correspond very closely to topics covered in typical high school classes. Table 1.1 gives you a snapshot of all five tests.

Table 1.1: ACT Tests

Test	Questions	Time	Content Covered
English	75 questions	45 minutes	Measures standard written English knowledge and skills along with English language conventions
Mathematics	60 questions	60 minutes	Measures mathematical skills students have typically acquired in courses taken up to the beginning of grade 12
Reading	40 questions	35 minutes	Measures reading comprehension
Science	40 questions	35 minutes	Measures the interpretation, analysis, evaluation, reasoning, and problem-solving skills required in the natural sciences
Writing (optional)	1 prompt	40 minutes	Measures writing skills emphasized in high school English classes and in entry-level college composition courses

Questions on the tests are intended to help assess college and career readiness. The following sections provide an overview of what you should know to perform well on each test. For additional details, check out the ACT College and Career Readiness Standards presented in chapter 12.

English Test

75 questions, 45 minutes

The English test consists of five essays or passages, each of which is accompanied by a sequence of multiple-choice test questions. Different passage types are employed to provide a variety of rhetorical situations. Passages are chosen not only for their appropriateness in assessing writing skills but also to reflect students' interests and experiences.

You will receive four scores for the ACT English test: a total test score based on all 75 questions and three reporting category scores based on the following:

- Production of Writing
- Knowledge of Language
- Conventions of Standard English

Production of Writing

Production of Writing tests knowledge and skills in two areas of English composition:

- Topic development in terms of purpose and focus
- Organization, unity, and cohesion

Topic Development in Terms of Purpose and Focus

Examples of knowledge and skills tested include the following:

- Determine the relevance of material to the topic or the focus of the passage or paragraph.
- Identify the purpose of a word or phrase (for example, identify a person, define a term, or describe an object).
- Determine whether a passage has met a specific goal.
- Use a word, phrase, or sentence to accomplish a specific purpose, such as convey a feeling or attitude or illustrate a given statement.

Organization, Unity, and Cohesion

Examples of knowledge and skills tested include the following:

- Determine the need for transition words or phrases to define relationships in terms of time or logic.
- Determine the most logical place for a sentence in a paragraph.
- Provide a suitable conclusion for a paragraph or passage (for example, summarizing the main idea).
- Provide a suitable introduction for a paragraph or passage.
- Rearrange sentences in a paragraph or paragraphs in a passage to establish a logical flow.
- Determine the most logical place to divide a paragraph to achieve the stated goal.

Knowledge of Language

Knowledge of Language questions test your ability to clearly and succinctly express yourself in written English. Knowledge and skills tested include the following:

- Revise unclear, clumsy, and confusing writing.
- Delete redundant and wordy material.
- Revise an expression to make it conform to the style and tone used throughout the passage.

- Determine the need for conjunctions to create logical connections between clauses.
- Choose the most appropriate word or phrase in terms of the sentence content.

Conventions of Standard English

Conventions of Standard English questions test knowledge and skills such as the following:

- Determine the need for punctuation or conjunctions to join clauses or to correct awkward-sounding fragments, fused sentences, and faulty subordination and coordination of clauses.
- Recognize and correct inappropriate shifts in verb tense.
- Recognize and correct disturbances in sentence structure, such as faulty placement of adjectives, participial phrase fragments, missing or incorrect relative pronouns, dangling or misplaced modifiers, faulty parallelism, run-on sentences, and weak conjunctions between independent clauses.
- Maintain consistent and logical verb tense and voice and pronoun person within a paragraph or passage.

Note: Spelling, vocabulary, and rote recall of grammar rules are not tested.

Mathematics Test

60 questions, 60 minutes

The mathematics test presents multiple-choice questions that require you to use reasoning skills to solve practical math problems. The material covered on the test emphasizes the major content areas that are prerequisites to successful performance in entry-level courses in college mathematics. Some questions may belong to a set of several questions (for example, several questions about the same graph or chart).

Conceptual knowledge and computational skills are assumed as background for the problems, but recall of complex formulas and extensive computation is not required.

Nine scores are reported for the ACT mathematics test: a total test score based on all 60 questions and eight reporting category scores based on specific mathematical knowledge and skills. The reporting categories are:

- Preparing for Higher Mathematics, which includes separate scores for Number and Quantity, Algebra, Functions, Geometry, and Statistics and Probability
- Integrating Essential Skills
- Modeling

Preparing for Higher Mathematics

This category captures the more recent mathematics that students are learning, starting when they begin using algebra as a general way of expressing and solving equations. This category is divided into the following five subcategories:

- Number and Quantity
- Algebra
- Functions
- Geometry
- Statistics and Probability

Number and Quantity

Math questions in this category test your knowledge of numbers and fundamental math concepts and operations, including the following:

- Perform calculations on whole numbers and decimals.
- Recognize equivalent fractions and fractions in lowest terms.
- Locate rational numbers (whole numbers, fractions, decimals, and mixed numbers) on the number line.
- Recognize single-digit factors of a number.
- Identify a digit's place value.
- Demonstrate knowledge of elementary number concepts, including rounding, ordering of decimals, pattern identification, primes, and greatest common factor.
- Write powers of 10 using exponents.
- Comprehend the concept of length on the number line, and find the distance between two points.
- Understand absolute value in terms of distance.
- Find the distance between two points with the same x-coordinate or y-coordinate in the coordinate plane.
- Add, subtract, and multiply matrices (tables of numbers).
- Order fractions.
- Find and use the least common multiple.
- Demonstrate knowledge of complex numbers and multiply two complex numbers.

- Comprehend the concept of irrational numbers, such as π.
- Apply properties of rational exponents.
- Use relations involving addition, subtraction, and scalar multiplication of vectors and matrices.
- Analyze and draw conclusions based on number concepts.

Algebra and Functions

The mathematics test contains questions that require knowledge of and skills in algebra, functions, or both. *Algebra* involves formulas and equations in which letters and other symbols are used to represent unknown or unspecified values. A *function* is a rule, equation, or expression that produces exactly one output for any given input; for example, $2x$ is a function in that any input used for x results in an output that is twice the input's value.

Algebra

Algebra knowledge and skills tested include the following:

- Demonstrate knowledge of basic expressions, such as $b + g$ to identify a total.
- Solve equations in the form $x + a = b$, where a and b are whole numbers or decimals.
- Use substitution to evaluate mathematical expressions.
- Combine like terms, such as $2x + 5x$.
- Add and subtract algebraic expressions.
- Multiply two binomials.
- Match inequalities with their graphs on the number line.
- Demonstrate knowledge of slope.
- Solve real-world problems by using first-degree equations.
- Solve inequalities.
- Match linear or compound inequalities with their graphs on the number line.
- Add, subtract, and multiply polynomials.
- Solve quadratic equations.
- Factor quadratics.
- Work with squares/square roots and cubes/cube roots of numbers.
- Work with scientific notation.

- Solve problems involving positive integer exponents.
- Determine the slope of a line from an equation.
- Solve linear inequalities when the method involves reversing the inequality sign.
- Solve systems of two linear equations.
- Solve absolute value equations and inequalities.
- Match quadratic inequalities with their graphs on the number line.

Functions

Questions that involve functions test your ability to do the following:

- Understand the concept of a function having a well-defined output value at each valid input value.
- Extend a given pattern by a few terms for patterns that have a constant increase or decrease between terms or that have a constant factor between terms.
- Evaluate linear, quadratic, and polynomial functions expressed in function notation at the integer level.
- Interpret statements that use function notation in terms of their context.
- Find the domain of polynomial functions and rational functions.
- Find the range of polynomial functions.
- Find where a rational function's graph has a vertical asymptote.
- Use function notation for simple functions of two variables.
- Relate a graph to a situation described qualitatively in terms of faster change or slower change.
- Build functions for relations that are inversely proportional or exponential.
- Find a recursive expression for the general term in a sequence described recursively.
- Evaluate composite functions of integer values.
- Compare actual values and the values of a modeling function to judge model fit and compare models.
- Demonstrate knowledge of geometric sequences.
- Demonstrate knowledge of unit circle trigonometry.
- Match graphs of basic trigonometric functions with their equations.

- Use trigonometric concepts and basic identities to solve problems.
- Demonstrate knowledge of logarithms.
- Write an expression for the composite of two simple functions.

Algebra and Functions

Questions that involve both algebra and functions test your ability to do the following:

- Solve problems using whole numbers and decimals in the context of money.
- Solve one- or two-step arithmetic problems using positive rational numbers, such as percent.
- Relate a graph to a situation described quantitatively.
- Solve two- or three-step arithmetic problems involving concepts such as rate and proportion, sales tax, percentage off, and estimation.
- Perform word-to-symbol translations.
- Solve multistep arithmetic problems that involve planning or converting units of measure (for example, feet per second to miles per hour).
- Build functions and write expressions, equations, or inequalities with a single variable for common pre-algebra settings, such as rate and distance problems and problems that involve proportions.
- Match linear equations with their graphs in the coordinate plane.
- Solve word problems containing several rates, proportions, or percentages.
- Build functions and write expressions, equations, and inequalities for common algebra settings.
- Interpret and use information from graphs in the coordinate plane.
- Solve complex math problems involving percent of increase or decrease or requiring integration of several concepts.
- Build functions and write expressions, equations, and inequalities when the process requires planning and/or strategic manipulation.
- Analyze and draw conclusions based on properties of algebra and/or functions.
- Analyze and draw conclusions based on information from graphs in the coordinate plane.
- Identify characteristics of graphs based on a set of conditions or on a general equation such as $y = ax^2 + c$.

- Given an equation or function, find an equation or function whose graph is a translation by specified amounts up or down.

Geometry

Geometry questions are based primarily on the mathematical properties and relationships of points, lines, angles, two-dimensional shapes, and three-dimensional objects. Knowledge and skills tested include the following:

- Estimate the length of a line segment based on other lengths in a geometric figure.
- Calculate the length of a line segment based on the lengths of other line segments that go in the same direction (for example, overlapping line segments and parallel sides of polygons with only right angles).
- Perform common conversions of money and of length, weight, mass, and time within a measurement system (for example, inches to feet and hours to minutes).
- Compute the area and perimeter of triangles, rectangles, and other polygons.
- Use properties of parallel lines to find the measure of an angle.
- Exhibit knowledge of basic angle properties and special sums of angle measures (for example, 90°, 180°, and 360°).
- Use geometric formulas when all necessary information is given.
- Locate points in the coordinate plane.
- Translate points up, down, left, and right in the coordinate plane.
- Use several angle properties to find an unknown angle measure.
- Count the number of lines of symmetry of a geometric figure.
- Use symmetry of isosceles triangles to find unknown side lengths or angle measures.
- Recognize that real-world measurements are typically imprecise and that an appropriate level of precision is related to the measuring device and procedure.
- Compute the perimeter of composite geometric figures with unknown side lengths.
- Compute the area and circumference of circles.
- Given the length of two sides of a right triangle, find the length of the third side.
- Express the sine, cosine, and tangent of an angle in a right triangle as a ratio of given side lengths.
- Determine the slope of a line from points or a graph.
- Find the midpoint of a line segment.

- Find the coordinates of a point rotated 180° around a given center point.
- Use relationships involving area, perimeter, and volume of geometric figures to compute another measure (for example, surface area for a cube of a given volume and simple geometric probability).
- Use the Pythagorean theorem.
- Apply properties of 30°–60°–90°, 45°–45°–90°, similar, and congruent triangles.
- Apply basic trigonometric ratios to solve right-triangle problems.
- Use the distance formula.
- Use properties of parallel and perpendicular lines to determine an equation of a line or coordinates of a point.
- Find the coordinates of a point reflected across a vertical or horizontal line or across $y = x$.
- Find the coordinates of a point rotated 90° across a vertical.
- Recognize special characteristics of parabolas and circles (for example, the vertex of a parabola and the center or radius of a circle).
- Use relationships among angles, arcs, and distances in a circle.
- Compute the area of composite geometric figures when planning and/or visualization is required.
- Use scale factors to determine the magnitude of a size change.
- Analyze and draw conclusions based on a set of conditions.
- Solve multistep geometry problems that involve integrating concepts, planning, and/or visualization.

Statistics and Probability

Statistics is a branch of mathematics that involves the collection and analysis of large quantities of numerical data. *Probability* is a branch of mathematics that involves calculating the likelihood of an event occurring or a condition existing. Statistics and Probability questions test your ability to do the following:

- Calculate averages.
- Read and extract relevant data from a basic table or chart and use the data in a computation.
- Use the relationship between the probability of an event and the probability of its complement.

- Calculate the missing data value given the average and all other data values.
- Translate from one representation of data to another (for example, from a bar graph to a circle graph).
- Compute probabilities.
- Describe events as combinations of other events (for example, using *and*, *or*, and *not*).
- Demonstrate knowledge of and apply counting techniques.
- Calculate the average given the frequency counts of all the data values.
- Manipulate data from tables and charts.
- Use Venn diagrams in counting.
- Recognize that when data summaries are reported in the real world, results are often rounded and must be interpreted as having appropriate precision.
- Recognize that when a statistical model is used, model values typically differ from actual values.
- Calculate or use a weighted average.
- Interpret and use information from tables and charts, including two-way frequency tables.
- Recognize the concepts of conditional and joint probability and of independence expressed in real-world contexts.
- Distinguish among mean, median, and mode for a list of numbers.
- Analyze and draw conclusions based on information from tables and charts, including two-way frequency tables.
- Understand the role of randomization in surveys, experiments, and observational studies.
- Demonstrate knowledge of conditional and joint probability.
- Recognize that part of the power of statistical modeling comes from looking at regularity in the differences between actual values and model values.

Integrating Essential Skills

Students learn some of the most useful mathematics before grade 8: rates and percentages; proportional relationships; area, surface area, and volume; average and median; expressing numbers in different ways; using expressions to represent quantities and equations to capture relationships; and other topics. Each year, students should grow in what they can accomplish using learning from prior years. Students should be able to solve problems of increasing complexity, combine skills in longer chains of steps, apply skills in more varied contexts, understand more connections, and increase fluency. In order to assess whether students have had appropriate growth, all questions in this reporting category focus on the higher-level cognitive skills, such as making decisions on how to approach a problem, comparing, reasoning, planning, applying algebra strategically, drawing conclusions, solving novel problems, and the like.

Modeling

Modeling uses mathematics to represent with a model an analysis of an actual, empirical situation. Models often help us predict or understand the actual. However, sometimes knowledge of the actual helps us understand the model, such as when addition is introduced to students as a model of combining two groups. The Modeling reporting category represents all questions that involve producing, interpreting, understanding, evaluating, and improving models. Each modeling question is also counted in the other appropriate reporting categories previously identified. Thus, the Modeling reporting category is an overall measure of how well a student uses modeling skills across mathematical topics.

Reading Test

40 questions, 35 minutes

The reading test comprises four sections, each containing one long or two shorter prose passages that are representative of the level and kinds of text commonly encountered in first-year college curricula. Passages on topics in social studies, natural science, literary narrative (including prose fiction), and the humanities are included, and the passages vary in terms of how challenging and complex they are.

Four scores are reported for the ACT reading test: a total test score based on all 40 questions and three reporting category scores based on specific knowledge and skills.

The reading test measures your reading comprehension in three general areas:

- Key Ideas and Details
- Craft and Structure
- Integration of Knowledge and Ideas

Key Ideas and Details

Questions that test reading comprehension focus primarily on identifying key details in the passage and grasping the overall meaning of the passage. Reading skills tested are divided into three categories:

- Close reading
- Central ideas, themes, and summaries
- Relationships

Close Reading

Close-reading skills involve your ability to do the following:

- Locate and interpret facts or details in a passage.
- Draw logical conclusions.
- Paraphrase statements.

Central Ideas, Themes, and Summaries

Questions that focus on central ideas, themes, and summaries challenge your ability to do the following:

- Identify the topic and distinguish it from the central idea or theme.
- Identify or infer the central idea or theme of a passage.
- Summarize key supporting ideas or details.

Relationships

Relationship questions involve the ability to do the following:

- Identify the sequence of events or place events in their correct sequence.
- Identify stated or implied cause-effect relationships.
- Identify stated or implied comparative relationships.

Craft and Structure

Some reading questions go beyond the meaning of the passage to challenge your understanding of how the author crafted and structured the passage. Reading skills tested in this area are divided into three categories:

- Word meanings and word choice
- Text structure
- Purpose and point of view

Word Meanings and Word Choice

Reading questions may focus on the meaning or impact of a word or phrase, challenging your ability to do the following:

- Interpret the meaning of a word or phrase, including determining technical, academic, connotative, and figurative meanings.
- Understand the implication of a word or phrase and of descriptive language.
- Analyze how the choice of a specific word or phrase shapes the meaning or tone of a passage.

Text Structure

Text-structure questions ask you to analyze how various structural elements function to serve a specific purpose in the passage. To answer such questions, you may need to do one of the following:

- Analyze how one or more sentences in passages relate to the whole passage.
- Identify or infer the function of one or more paragraphs.
- Analyze the overall structure of a passage.

Purpose and Point of View

The reading test may include questions that challenge your ability to do the following:

- Identify or infer the author's or narrator's purpose or intent.
- Determine how an author's or narrator's purpose or intent shapes the content and style of the passage.
- Recognize an author's or narrator's point of view.

Integration of Knowledge and Ideas

Reading questions may require that you go beyond simply reading and understanding a passage to analyzing one or more passages. Reading skills tested in the area of Integration of Knowledge and Ideas are divided into two categories:

- Arguments
- Multiple texts

Arguments

Questions related to argumentative essays may test your ability to do the following:

- Identify or infer the central claim being presented in the passage.
- Analyze how one or more sentences offer reasons for or support the claim.

Multiple Texts

Multiple-text questions involve reading two passages and doing the following:

- Compare the two passages.
- Draw logical conclusions using information from the two passages.

Science Test

40 questions, 35 minutes

The science test measures the interpretation, analysis, evaluation, reasoning, and problem-solving skills required in the natural sciences: life science/biology; physical science/chemistry, physics; and earth and space science. (See chapter 12 for a more detailed breakdown of science content covered on the test.)

The test assumes that students are in the process of taking the core science course of study (three years or more) that will prepare them for college-level work and have completed a course in earth science and/or physical science and a course in biology. The test presents several sets of scientific information, each followed by a number of multiple-choice test questions. The scientific information is conveyed in the form of reading passages and graphic representations—graphs (charts), tables, and illustrations.

Four scores are reported for the ACT science test: a total test score based on all 40 questions and three reporting category scores based on scientific knowledge, skills, and practices. The reporting categories are:

- Interpretation of Data
- Scientific Investigation
- Evaluation of Models, Inferences, and Experimental Results

Interpretation of Data

Interpretation of Data involves the following skills:

- Select data from a data presentation (for example, a food web diagram, a graph, a table, or a phase diagram).
- Identify features of a table, graph, or diagram (for example, units of measurement).
- Find information in text that describes a data presentation.
- Understand scientific terminology.
- Determine how the values of variables change as the value of another variable changes in a data presentation.
- Compare or combine data from one or more data presentations (for example, order or sum data from a table).
- Translate information into a table, graph, or diagram.
- Perform a interpolation or extrapolation using data in a table or graph (for example, categorize data from a table using a scale from another table).
- Determine and/or use a mathematical relationship that exists between data.
- Analyze presented information when given new information.

Scientific Investigation

Questions that apply to scientific investigation are typically related to experiments and other research. Such questions challenge your ability to do the following:

- Find information in text that describes an experiment.
- Understand the tools and functions of tools used in an experiment.
- Understand the methods used in an experiment.
- Understand experimental design.
- Identify a control in an experiment.
- Identify similarities and differences between experiments.
- Determine which experiments use a given tool, method, or aspect of design.
- Predict the results of an additional trial or measurement in an experiment.
- Determine the experimental conditions that would produce specified results.
- Determine the hypothesis for an experiment.
- Determine an alternate method for testing a hypothesis.
- Understand precision and accuracy issues.
- Predict the effects of modifying the design or methods of an experiment.
- Determine which additional trial or experiment could be performed to enhance or evaluate experimental results.

Evaluation of Models, Inferences, and Experimental Results

Some questions on the science test challenge your ability to evaluate models, inferences, and experimental results. (A *model* is a description of an object or phenomenon intended to explain and predict its behavior.) To answer such questions, you must be able to do the following:

- Find basic information in a model.
- Identify implications in a model.
- Determine which models present certain information.
- Determine which hypothesis, prediction, or conclusion is, or is not, consistent with one or more data presentations, models, or pieces of information in text.
- Identify key assumptions in a model.
- Identify similarities and differences between models.

- Determine whether presented information or new information supports or contradicts (or weakens) a hypothesis or conclusion and why.
- Identify the strengths and weaknesses of models.
- Determine which models are supported or weakened by new information.
- Determine which experimental results or models support or contradict a hypothesis, prediction, or conclusion.
- Use new information to make a prediction based on a model.

Writing Test (Optional)

1 prompt, 40 minutes

The writing test is a 40-minute essay test that measures your writing skills—specifically those writing skills emphasized in high school English classes and in entry-level college composition courses.

The test asks you to produce an essay in response to a contemporary issue. You will be given a prompt that presents the issue and provides three different perspectives on it. Your task is to write an essay in which you develop a perspective on the issue and explore how it relates to at least one other perspective.

Trained readers will evaluate your essay for the evidence it provides of a number of core writing skills. You will receive a total of five scores for this test: a single subject-level writing score reported on a scale of 2–12 and four domain scores based on an analytic scoring rubric. The four domain scores are

- Ideas and Analysis
- Development and Support
- Organization
- Language Use and Conventions

Ideas and Analysis

Effective writing depends on effective ideas. It is important to think carefully about the issue in the prompt and compose an argument that addresses the issue meaningfully. In evaluating the ideas and analysis in your essay, readers will look for your ability to do the following:

- Generate a clear main idea that establishes your perspective on the issue.
- Engage with multiple perspectives on the issue by analyzing the relationship between your perspective and at least one other perspective.

- Clarify your understanding of the issue and differing perspectives on it by providing a relevant context for discussion.
- Analyze critical elements (e.g., implications and complexities) of the issue and perspectives under consideration.

Development and Support

Even the best ideas must be developed and supported to be effective in a written argument. By explaining and illustrating your points, you help the reader understand your thinking. In evaluating this dimension of your essay, readers will look for your ability to do the following:

- Clarify your ideas by explaining your reasoning.
- Bolster your claims with persuasive examples.
- Convey the significance of your perspective by exploring reasons why your ideas are worth considering.
- Extend your argument by considering qualifications, exceptions, counterarguments, and complicating factors.

Organization

Organizational choices are essential to effective writing. Guide the reader through your discussion by arranging your ideas according to the logic of your argument. As readers evaluate the organization of your essay, they will look for your ability to do the following:

- Unify your essay by making strategic use of a controlling idea and other organizational techniques (e.g., theme or motif).
- Group ideas clearly, with each paragraph limited to the discussion of related ideas.
- Produce a sequence of ideas that follows a clear logic, both in terms of the argument's overall structure (e.g., introduction, body, conclusion) and within the argument itself, with each point following from the last.
- Use transitions to connect ideas, both within paragraphs (e.g., relating claims to support) and across paragraphs (e.g., moving from one discussion into another).

Language Use and Conventions

Skillful language use enhances argumentative writing. Strategic choices in the vocabulary you use and the style you employ can make your essay more effective. To evaluate your use of language, readers will look for your ability to do the following:

- Make precise word choices that communicate your ideas with clarity.
- Demonstrate control over a variety of sentence structures.

- Match the style of your writing to the audience and purpose (e.g., more evocative language to convey emotional appeals versus a more neutral voice to convey an argument based on reason).
- Accurately apply the conventions of grammar, word usage, syntax, and mechanics.

The Fifth Test

ACT tries out questions on national test dates to develop future tests. Your room supervisor may ask you to take a fifth test that may be multiple-choice or one for which you will create your own answers. Please try your best on these questions because your participation can help shape the future of the ACT. The results from the fifth test will not be reflected on your reported scores. Participation on the fifth test will extend testing time by approximately 20 minutes.

ACT Test Formats: Paper and Online

The ACT is available as a paper test and as an online test in certain states and educational districts. Regardless of format, what is most important is the knowledge and skills you have developed over your course of study. If you know the material, whether you choose answers by marking them on paper or clicking an option on a computer screen will likely make little difference.

Using a Calculator

You may use a permitted calculator only on the mathematics test, but you are not required to do so. All math problems on the test can be solved without a calculator, and you may be able to perform some of the math more quickly in your head or on scratch paper.

Note: You may use any four-function, scientific, or graphing calculator as long as it is a permitted calculator modified, if necessary, as described in the following. For additional details and ACT's most current calculator policy, visit www.act.org.

Certain types of calculators, including the following, are prohibited:

- Calculators with built-in or downloaded computer algebra system (CAS) functionality, including the TI-89, TI-92, TI-Nspire CAS, HP Prime, HP 48GII, HP 40G, HP 49G, HP 50G, fx-ClassPad 400, ClassPad 300, ClassPad 330, and all Casio models that start with CFX-9970G. (Using the TI-89 is the most common reason students are dismissed from the ACT for prohibited calculator use.)
- Handheld, tablet, or laptop computers, including PDAs.
- Electronic writing pads or pen-input devices (the Sharp EL 9600 is permitted).
- Calculators built into cell phones or any other electronic communication devices.
- Calculators with a typewriter keypad (letter keys in QWERTY format, but letter keys not in QWERTY format are permitted).

The following types of calculators are permitted but only after they are modified as noted:

- Calculators that can hold programs or documents (remove all documents and all programs that have CAS functionality).
- Calculators with paper tape (remove the tape).
- Calculators that make noise (mute the device).
- Calculators with an infrared data port (completely cover the infrared data port with heavy opaque material such as duct tape or electrician's tape). These calculators include the Hewlett-Packard HP 38G series, HP 39G series, and HP 48G.
- Calculators that have power cords (remove all power and electrical cords).
- Accessible calculators (such as audio-talking or braille calculators) may be allowed under the accessibility policies for the ACT test. (Visit www.act.org for details.)

If you choose to use a calculator during the mathematics test, follow these guidelines:

- Use a calculator you are accustomed to using. A more powerful, but unfamiliar, calculator may be a disadvantage. If you are unaccustomed to using a calculator, practice using it when you take the practice tests in this book, so you are comfortable with using it in a test situation.
- Sharing calculators during the test is not permitted.
- Make sure your calculator works properly. If your calculator uses batteries, the batteries should be strong enough to last throughout the testing session.
- Bring a spare calculator and/or extra batteries.

Taking the Test

Knowing what to expect on test day can alleviate any anxiety you may feel. The following list describes the steps you will take through the testing day:

1. You must report to the test center by the reporting time.
    - If you are testing on a ***national test*** date the reporting time is 8:00 AM.
        - You will need to bring the following:
            - A printed copy of your ACT admission ticket, which contains important match information that cannot be found anywhere else. Failure to bring your admission ticket will delay your scores.

- Acceptable photo ID; if you do not bring acceptable photo ID, you will not be allowed to take the test.
- Sharpened no. 2 soft-lead pencils with good erasers (no mechanical pencils or ink pens).
- A calculator, if you would like to use one.

- If you are testing during the week day at your school through ***state and district*** testing the reporting time will be at the same time you usually report for school.
  - You will need to bring the following:
    - Acceptable photo ID
    - Sharpened no. 2 soft-lead pencils with good erasers (no mechanical pencils or ink pens)
    - A calculator, if you would like to use one

(**Note:** You will *not* be admitted to test if you are late or if your ID does not meet ACT's requirements.)

2. When all examinees present at the reporting time are checked in and seated, wait until you are notified to start the test.

3. A short break is scheduled after the first two tests. You are prohibited from using a cell phone or any electronic device during the break, and you may not eat or drink anything in the test room. (If you take the ACT with writing, you will have time before the writing test to relax and sharpen your pencils.)

4. When time has expired, tests are collected and you are dismissed.

Note: If you do not complete all your tests for any reason, tell a member of the testing staff whether or not you want your answer document scored before you leave the test center. If you do not, all tests attempted will be scored.

For more about registering for the ACT and being well prepared for test day, turn to chapter 13.

Summary

This book should help you to understand how to get ready to take the ACT. Knowing the basics should get you started. By now, you should have a fair idea of what to expect at the test center and know where to find more information: on ACT's website at www.act.org. Now that you know the basic information, you should be ready to start preparing for the ACT.

NOTES

Chapter 2: Preparation, Skills, and Strategies

Performance on the ACT is largely influenced by two factors: the knowledge and skills you acquire over your many years of formal education and your familiarity with the test format and questions.

The best preparation for the ACT is taking rigorous high school classes. If you've taken challenging courses, paid attention in class, and completed your assignments satisfactorily, you've already done much of the preparation required to do well on the ACT.

Your familiarity with the test format and questions and your comfort and confidence in tackling the ACT also play an important role in how well you do on the test. Of course, no test-taking strategy can help you choose the correct answer when you don't understand the question or don't have the knowledge and skills to answer it, but certain strategies and skills can help you avoid common mistakes that will lower your score, such as misreading an answer choice or spending too much time on any given question.

The suggestions in this chapter are designed to help you build on the preparation that you have already completed. They're taken from advice gathered over years—from education specialists, testing specialists, and people who, similar to you, have taken lots of tests. Read the advice, try it out, and see whether it helps. Realize that you can choose how you will take the ACT. Then make intelligent choices about what will work for you.

Mental Preparation

The best mental preparation for the ACT is rigorous course work, but mental preparation also involves confidence and clear thinking. The following tips will help make you feel calmer and more confident so that you'll do your very best on the ACT.

Identify Strengths and Address Areas of Improvement

One of the best ways to prepare mentally for the test is to identify your strengths and areas of improvement, then work toward addressing the areas that may hamper your performance on the test. For example, if time expires before you have a chance to answer all of the questions on a practice test, you need to work on pacing. If you struggle to comprehend word problems in math, you need to practice solving more word problems. However, if you breeze through reading comprehension questions, you might not need to spend time improving your reading comprehension skills.

The following sections explain how to identify strengths and areas of improvement and address issues that may hamper your performance on the test.

Take the First Practice Test

To evaluate your ACT readiness take the first practice test in chapter 3 and analyze the results, as instructed in chapter 4. The test-taking experience and the results will help reveal your strengths and areas of improvement. If you do well on the first practice test, you can be confident that you know the material and are comfortable with the test format. You may decide to take additional practice tests for confirmation or review the test-taking skills in this chapter and in chapters 5 through 9 to see whether they can help you do even better.

If your performance on the first practice test falls short of your goal, you may need to do additional course work in certain subject areas or invest additional time and effort developing effective test-taking strategies and skills. Do not be discouraged if you do not meet your goal on the practice test. Be thankful that your areas for improvement were identified prior to test day and that you now have the information you need to formulate your improvement plan.

Identify Subject Areas to Review

Some students do better in certain subjects than in others. The practice tests in this book will help you identify your stronger and weaker subjects. As you take and score the practice tests, create a list of the subject areas and types of questions you struggle to answer. For example, if you had trouble answering math questions about angles in a triangle, the circumference of a circle, the volume of a cube, the relationships among parallel and perpendicular lines, and so forth, you may need a refresher course in plane geometry.

Chapter 1 includes a list of subject areas covered on each portion of the ACT to help you categorize the questions you answered incorrectly and identify subject areas you need to study or review.

Plan Your Practice and Study Time

To stay on track leading up to test day, set up a reasonable schedule to practice and study for the ACT. **Set aside small amounts of time** for studying over an extended period—days, weeks, or even months—so you won't feel the need to cram in the days leading up to the test.

Make your schedule flexible enough to allow for a surprise homework assignment or some unexpected fun. And find a way to reward yourself as you get the work done, even if it's just a checklist you can mark to show your progress. A flexible schedule with regular rewards will prevent burnout while keeping you motivated.

Develop a Positive Mental Attitude

Approach the ACT confident that you will do your best. Although confidence alone obviously isn't enough to ensure good performance on a test, doubt and fear can hurt your performance. Be confident in your ability to do well on the ACT. **You will do well!** You just need to be prepared.

Some small changes can make a surprising difference. For example, how you imagine yourself taking the exam may affect how well you actually do. Negative thoughts have a way of generating negative results. So **practice positive thinking;** imagine yourself meeting the challenge of the exam with ease. The day of the test, tell yourself you intend to do your best, and believe it.

Keep the Test in Perspective

Remembering that the ACT is only one part of the process of your education and training will help you keep it in perspective. So will remembering that the ACT and tests similar to it are designed to provide you with feedback and direction. Your scores can help make decisions about your future education and career choices. Think of the test as an opportunity to get to know more about yourself, not as a potential barrier to your future plans.

Another way to keep the ACT in perspective is to use the test as an opportunity to identify careers that match your interests, abilities, and values; explore suitable college majors; and start choosing high school courses that align with your future education and career goals.

General Test-Taking Strategies and Skills

How you approach the ACT and various types of questions, how well you manage your time, whether you change answers, and other factors may affect how well you do on the ACT. The following sections present a few test-taking strategies and skills to help you perform to the best of your ability.

Remain Calm

When you're under pressure during a test, an unexpected question or a minor incident such as breaking a pencil can be very upsetting. For many students, the natural tendency at such times is to panic. Panic detracts from test performance by causing students to become confused and discouraged and to have trouble recalling information they know.

It's a good idea to have a strategy ready for dealing with incidents that might rattle your nerves. One effective strategy is to take a brief time out to center yourself. Take slow, deep breaths and let yourself relax. Put the test temporarily out of mind. Close your eyes if you want. Visualize yourself confidently resuming work on the test, turning in a completed answer document, and leaving the room with a feeling of having done your best work. Allow 20 to 30 seconds for your time out, which is probably all you'll need to regain your composure.

Pace Yourself

The ACT, similar to many tests, must be completed within a specific and limited amount of time. Working quickly and efficiently is one of the skills necessary for conveying how much you've learned in the subject area being tested.

To develop an effective, efficient pace, time yourself as you take the practice tests. If time expires before you have a chance to answer all the questions, you know that you need to work faster next time. If you rushed through the test, had time remaining at the end, and made careless mistakes, you know that you will need to work at a more relaxed pace and be more careful in answering questions.

Warning: Don't try to push yourself to work so fast that you make errors. Answering 50 questions carefully and correctly and leaving 10 unanswered is better than answering 60 questions too quickly and missing 20 because of mistakes.

Although you won't want to lose time by being distracted, you shouldn't obsess about time either. Use all of the time available so you can do your very best on the test.

Some people suggest more formal methods for pacing yourself by allocating a certain amount of time per question or set of questions, as in the following examples:

- **Divide the available time by the number of questions.** For example, on the mathematics test, divide 60 minutes by 60 questions, and you know you have 1 minute per question.
- **Divide the available time into different stages of the writing process.** If you're taking the optional writing test, you may want to allocate the time to planning, writing, and revising/editing your essay. Keep in mind that you probably won't have enough time to fully draft, revise, and then recopy your essay, so spending a few minutes planning your essay before you start writing it is usually wise.

Keep in mind that these strategies are not foolproof, that some questions will take you longer to answer than others, and that doing the math to calculate your time allocations takes time. You may be better off developing a feel for the time and occasionally checking the clock to make sure you're on track to finish, perhaps with a few minutes remaining at the end to check answers you were unsure of. If you want to keep track of your pace while taking the ACT, bring a watch. Not all testing centers have wall clocks.

Know the Directions Ahead of Time

You can save yourself precious moments on the ACT by being familiar with the directions ahead of time. Then, when taking the test, you can read the directions to refresh your memory instead of having to spend time and mind power processing those directions. For example, the ACT English, reading, and science tests ask for the "best" answer, and the mathematics test asks for the "correct" answer. This simple difference in the instructions signals an important distinction to keep in mind as you're working through those tests. Because only one answer is "correct" in the mathematics test, you'll want to be sure your understanding of the question and your calculations are precise—so that your answer matches one, and only one, of the possible answers. In the other tests, more than one of the possible answers may be correct to some degree, and you'll need to be careful to select the "best" answer among those potentially "correct" ones. You'll find the directions for each test in the practice ACT tests in this book.

The directions for the writing test are also very important, because they spell out the aspects of writing that will be evaluated. They also tell you where in the test booklet you can plan your essay and where you should write your final version. The directions for the writing test and a sample answer document appear in the practice ACT tests in this book.

Before you take the ACT, become familiar with the answer document. Knowing in advance how to use the answer document will save you time and prevent worry when you take the actual ACT.

Read Carefully and Thoroughly

Just as it's important to read and understand the directions for a test, it's also important to read and understand each question and answer choice on the test. As you've probably discovered somewhere along the line, you can miss even the simplest test question by reading carelessly and overlooking an important word or detail. Some questions on the ACT, for instance, require more than one step, and the answer to each preliminary step may be included as an answer choice. If you read these questions too quickly, you can easily make the mistake of choosing a plausible answer that relates to a preliminary step but is the incorrect answer to the question.

Take the time to read each question carefully and thoroughly before choosing your answer. Make sure you understand exactly what the question asks and what you are to do to answer it. You may want to underline or circle key words in the test booklet (see the later section "Write Notes in Your Test Booklet"). Reread the item if you are confused.

Watch the question's wording. Look for words such as *not* or *least,* especially when they are not clearly set off with underlining, capital letters, or bold type. Don't make careless errors because you only skimmed the question or the answer choices. Pay close attention to qualifying words such as *all, most, some, none; always, usually, seldom, sometimes, never; best, worst; highest, lowest; smaller, larger.* (There are many other qualifying words; these are only a few examples of related groups.) When you find a qualifier in one of the responses to a question, a good way to determine whether or not the response is the best answer is to substitute related qualifiers and see which makes the best statement. For example, if a response says, "Tests are always difficult," you might test the truth of the word *always* by substituting *sometimes* and the other words related to *always.*

If any of the words other than the one in the answer makes the best statement, then the response is not the best answer.

Pay close attention to modifying or limiting phrases in the statement. For instance, a question in the reading test might have the following as a possible answer: "Lewis and Clark, the great British explorers, began their historic trip to the West Coast by traveling up the Mississippi." The answer is incorrect because Lewis and Clark were not British but were US citizens. (You would not be expected to know from memory that Lewis and Clark were US citizens; that information would be included in the passage.)

Read all the answer choices before selecting one. Questions on the ACT often include answer choices that seem plausible but aren't quite correct. Even though the first answer choice may appeal to you, the correct or best answer may be farther down the list.

When taking the writing test, read the writing prompt carefully. Before you start to plan your essay, make sure you understand the writing prompt and the issue it asks you to respond to.

Choose Strategies for Answering Easier and More Difficult Questions

A strategy for taking the ACT is to answer the easy questions first and skip the questions you find difficult. After answering all of the easy questions, go back and answer the more difficult questions, as time permits. When you skip a question, mark it in the test booklet (but not on the answer document), so you can quickly flip back to it later. Also, make absolutely sure that on the answer document, you skip the set of answer choices that correspond to the question you skipped.

Use Logic on More Difficult Questions

When you return to more difficult questions, use logic to eliminate incorrect answer choices. Compare the remaining answer choices and note how they differ. Such differences may provide clues as to what the question requires. Eliminate as many incorrect answer choices as you can, then make an educated selection from the remaining choices. See the next section for additional guidance.

Choose a Strategy for Guessing on Multiple-Choice Questions

On some standardized tests, you're penalized for each incorrect answer. On the ACT multiple-choice tests, however, your raw score is based on the number of questions you answer correctly—nothing is deducted for wrong answers.

Because you're not penalized for guessing on the ACT, answering every question is advantageous. Here's a good way to proceed:

1. If a question stumps you, try to eliminate wrong choices. Narrowing your choices increases your odds of guessing the correct answer.
2. If you still aren't sure about the answer, take your best guess.

You don't need a perfect reason to eliminate one answer and choose another. Sometimes an intelligent guess is based on a hunch—on something you may know but don't have time to consciously recognize in a timed-test situation.

Maybe you've heard some advice about how to answer questions when you don't know the correct answer, such as "When in doubt, choose 'C,'" or "When in doubt, select the longest (or shortest) alternative," or "If 'none of the above' (or a similar response) is among the answer choices, select it." Although these bits of advice may hold true now and then, the questions on the ACT have been carefully written to make these strategies ineffective.

Choose a Strategy for Changing Answers

You think you marked the wrong answer choice on a certain question. Do you go with your original answer or change it to the new answer? Some people advise to always go with your first response. And surely everyone has had the experience of agonizing over a response, trying to decide whether to change it, then doing so only to find out later that the first answer was the correct one.

However, some research by education and testing specialists suggests that you should change your answer when you change your mind. If you're like the test-takers in the study, your second answer is more likely to be the correct one.

So, how can you decide what to do? Before you change an answer, think about how you approached the question in the first place. Give some weight to the reasons why you now believe another answer is better. Don't mechanically follow an arbitrary rule just because it works for somebody else. Know yourself; then trust yourself to make intelligent, informed decisions.

Write Notes in Your Test Booklet

You're allowed to write in the test booklet, so feel free to write notes in the test booklet to flag key details or to work out a problem on paper.

Mark Your Answers Carefully

Only answers marked on the answer document during the time allowed for a particular test will count. Carefully mark your answers on the answer document as you work through the questions on each test.

Remember that during an actual test you may not fill in answers or alter answers on your answer document after "stop" is called.

For the writing test, writing (or printing) legibly in English in the correct place in the test booklet is vital. If readers cannot read what you have written, they will be unable to score your essay. You are allowed to write or print your essay, but you must do so clearly. Keep in mind, you must write your essay **using a soft-lead pencil (not a mechanical pencil).** You must write on the lined pages in the answer folder. If you make corrections, do so thoroughly. You may write corrections or additions neatly between the lines of your essay, but you may not write in the margins.

Plan to Check Your Answers

When you reach the end of one of the ACT tests with several minutes to spare, you may feel you've done quite enough. Resist the temptation to rest. Use the remaining time to check your work, as follows:

- For the multiple-choice tests, be sure you've marked all your answers in the proper section on the answer document.
- Be certain you've answered all the questions on your answer document, even the ones you weren't sure about. (Of course, you must be very careful to stop marking ovals when time is called.)
- When you reach the end of the mathematics test, check your calculations. You may check your calculations using the test booklet or scratch paper, or using a permitted calculator (see chapter 1).
- Check your answer document for stray pencil marks that may be misread by the scoring machine. Erase any such marks cleanly and completely.
- Be sure you've marked only one answer on your answer document for each question.
- If there are too many questions for you to check all of your answers, be sure to check those that you feel most uncertain about first, then any others that you have time for on that test.
- At the end of the writing test, take a few minutes to read over your essay. Correct any mistakes in spelling, grammar, usage, or punctuation. If you see any words that are difficult to read, rewrite them so they're legible. Make any revisions neatly between the lines (but do not write in the margins).

Learn Strategies for Specific Tests

In addition to the general test-taking strategies presented in the preceding sections there are specific strategies for each of the ACT tests. For example, on the mathematics test, if a question includes an illustration, you may want to write dimensions given in the question on the illustration to help you visualize what the question is asking. In part 3 of this book, the chapters provide test-taking tips for each of the ACT tests along with additional information that reveals the types of questions you can expect to encounter on each test.

Summary

All the strategies outlined in this chapter are merely suggestions intended to give you ideas about good preparation habits and strategies for getting through the ACT in the best, most efficient manner possible. Some of the strategies will work for you, others won't. Feel free to pick and choose from among all the strategies in this chapter, and the more specific strategies in part 3, so that you have a test-taking plan that works best for you.

2 Part Two: Taking and Evaluating Your First Practice Test

In This Part

In this part, you have the opportunity to take, score, and evaluate your first practice test. This exercise enables you to identify your strengths and weaknesses, so you can develop an efficient study plan that focuses on areas where you need the most improvement. In this part, you will do the following:

Simulate testing conditions, so you become acclimated to the conditions you will experience on test day.

Take a complete practice test comprising all five ACT tests—English, mathematics, reading, science, and the optional writing test.

Score your test to gauge your overall performance.

Review explanatory answers to understand why you answered each question correctly or incorrectly.

Determine whether you need to work more on subject matter or on test-taking strategies and skills.

Analyze your performance on each test to gain better insight on the knowledge and skills in greatest need of improvement.

3 Chapter 3: Taking and Scoring Your First ACT Practice Test

In this chapter, you take the first of the four practice tests in this book, score the test, and review the answers with explanations. We encourage you to take the test under conditions similar to those you will encounter on test day and to try your very best.

After you take and score the test and review the answers, you will be well poised to analyze your performance in chapter 4. The results of this first practice test will help you identify subject areas you may need to review and test-taking strategies, such as pacing, that you may want to work on prior to test day.

Simulating Testing Conditions

Taking the practice tests can help you become familiar with the ACT. We recommend that you take the tests under conditions that are as similar as possible to those you will experience on the actual test day. The following tips will help you make the most of the practice tests:

- The four multiple-choice tests require a total of 2 hours and 55 minutes. Try an entire practice test in one sitting, with a

10-minute break between the mathematics test and the reading test. (If you are taking the writing test, you may also take a break of roughly 5 minutes after the science test.)

- Sit at a desk with good lighting. You will need sharpened no. 2 pencils with good erasers. You may not use mechanical pencils or highlight pens. Remove all books and other aids from your desk. On test day, you will not be allowed to use references or notes. Scratch paper is not needed as each page of the mathematics test has a blank column that you can use for scratch work. In some circumstances you are not permitted to write in your test booklet. In those circumstances, you'll be given scratch paper, and you can use it to jot down the numbers of the questions you skip.
- If you plan to use a calculator on the mathematics test, review the details about permissible calculators on ACT's website, www.act.org. Use a calculator with which you are familiar for both the practice test and on the test day. You may use any four-function, scientific, or graphing calculator on the mathematics test, except as specified on ACT's website and in chapter 1.
- Use a digital timer or clock to time yourself on each test. Set your timer for 5 minutes less than the allotted time for each test so you can get used to the 5-minute warning. (Students approved for self-paced extended time should set a timer for 60-minute warnings up to the total time allowed—5 hours for the multiple-choice tests. If you take the optional writing test, you will then have an additional hour to complete that test.)
- Allow yourself only the time permitted for each test.
- Detach and use one sample multiple-choice answer document.
- Read the general test directions on the first page of the practice test. After reading the directions, start your timer and begin with the English test. Continue through the science test, taking a short break between the mathematics test and the reading test. If you do not plan to take the ACT writing test, score your multiple-choice tests using the information beginning on page 101.
- If you plan to take the writing test, take a short break after the science test. Detach (or photocopy) the writing test answer document that follows the writing test planning pages. Then read the test directions on the first page of the practice ACT writing test. After reading the directions, start your timer, then carefully read the prompt. After you have considered what the prompt is asking you to do, use the pages provided to plan your essay, and then write your essay on the answer document. After you have finished, score your essay using the information beginning on page 108.

PAGE 1

The ACT® *Sample Answer Sheet*

EXAMINEE STATEMENT, CERTIFICATION, AND SIGNATURE

1. Read the following **Statement:** By submitting this answer document, I agree to comply with and be bound by the *Terms and Conditions: Testing Rules and Policies for the ACT® Test* provided in the ACT registration materials for this test, including those concerning test security, score cancellation, examinee remedies, binding arbitration, and consent to the processing of my personally identifying information, including the collection, use, transfer, and disclosure of information as described in the ACT Privacy Policy (www.act.org/privacy.html).

   I understand that ACT owns the test questions and responses and affirm that I will not share any test questions or responses with anyone by any form of communication before, during, or after the test administration. I understand that assuming anyone else's identity to take this test is strictly prohibited and may violate the law and subject me to legal penalties.

   International Examinees: By my signature, I am also providing my consent to ACT to transfer my personally identifying information to the United States to ACT, or a third-party service provider for processing, where it will be subject to use and disclosure under the laws of the United States. I acknowledge and agree that it may also be accessible to law enforcement and national security authorities in the United States.

2. Copy the **Certification** shown below (only the text in italics) on the lines provided. Write in your normal handwriting.

Certification: *I agree to the Statement above and certify that I am the person whose name and address appear on this answer document.*

Your Signature

Today's Date

Do NOT mark in this shaded area.

USE A SOFT LEAD NO. 2 PENCIL ONLY.
(Do NOT use a mechanical pencil, ink, ballpoint, correction fluid, or felt-tip pen.)

A NAME, MAILING ADDRESS, AND TELEPHONE
(Please print.)

Last Name | First Name | MI (Middle Initial)

House Number & Street (Apt. No.); or PO Box & No.; or RR & No.

City | State/Province | ZIP/Postal Code

Area Code / Number | Country

ACT, Inc.—Confidential Restricted when data present

ALL examinees must complete block A – please print.

Blocks B, C, and D are required for all examinees. Find the MATCHING INFORMATION on your ticket. Enter it EXACTLY the same way, even if any of the information is missing or incorrect. Fill in the corresponding ovals. If you do not complete these blocks to match your previous information EXACTLY, your scores will be **delayed up to 8 weeks**.

ACT

PO BOX 168, IOWA CITY, IA 52243-0168

B MATCH NAME
(First 5 letters of last name)

A B C D E F G H I J K L M N O P Q R S T U V W X Y Z

C MATCH NUMBER

1 2 3 4 5 6 7 8 9 0

D DATE OF BIRTH

Month	Day	Year
January		
February		
March	1	1
April	2	2
May	3	3
June	4	4
July	5	5
August	6	6
September	7	7
October	8	8
November	9	9
December	0	0

 A011 215 190 Rev 1 IM-(A)199526-001:654321 Printed in the US.

Your First Practice Test

PAGE 2

Marking Directions: Mark only **one** oval for each question. Fill in response completely. Erase errors cleanly without smudging.

Correct mark: ○ ● ○ ○

Do NOT use these *incorrect* or *bad* marks.

Incorrect marks:
Overlapping mark:
Cross-out mark:
Smudged erasure:
Mark is too light:

BOOKLET NUMBER

①	①	①	①	①	①
②	②	②	②	②	②
③	③	③	③	③	③
④	④	④	④	④	④
⑤	⑤	⑤	⑤	⑤	⑤
⑥	⑥	⑥	⑥	⑥	⑥
⑦	⑦	⑦	⑦	⑦	⑦
⑧	⑧	⑧	⑧	⑧	⑧
⑨	⑨	⑨	⑨	⑨	⑨
⓪	⓪	⓪	⓪	⓪	⓪

FORM

Print your 5-character **Test Form** in the boxes above and fill in the corresponding oval at the right.

BE SURE TO FILL IN THE CORRECT FORM OVAL.

○ 16MC1 ○ 18MC4
○ 16MC2 ○ 19MC5
○ 16MC3

TEST 1

1 Ⓐ Ⓑ Ⓒ Ⓓ	14 Ⓕ Ⓖ Ⓗ Ⓙ	27 Ⓐ Ⓑ Ⓒ Ⓓ	40 Ⓕ Ⓖ Ⓗ Ⓙ	53 Ⓐ Ⓑ Ⓒ Ⓓ	66 Ⓕ Ⓖ Ⓗ Ⓙ
2 Ⓕ Ⓖ Ⓗ Ⓙ	15 Ⓐ Ⓑ Ⓒ Ⓓ	28 Ⓕ Ⓖ Ⓗ Ⓙ	41 Ⓐ Ⓑ Ⓒ Ⓓ	54 Ⓕ Ⓖ Ⓗ Ⓙ	67 Ⓐ Ⓑ Ⓒ Ⓓ
3 Ⓐ Ⓑ Ⓒ Ⓓ	16 Ⓕ Ⓖ Ⓗ Ⓙ	29 Ⓐ Ⓑ Ⓒ Ⓓ	42 Ⓕ Ⓖ Ⓗ Ⓙ	55 Ⓐ Ⓑ Ⓒ Ⓓ	68 Ⓕ Ⓖ Ⓗ Ⓙ
4 Ⓕ Ⓖ Ⓗ Ⓙ	17 Ⓐ Ⓑ Ⓒ Ⓓ	30 Ⓕ Ⓖ Ⓗ Ⓙ	43 Ⓐ Ⓑ Ⓒ Ⓓ	56 Ⓕ Ⓖ Ⓗ Ⓙ	69 Ⓐ Ⓑ Ⓒ Ⓓ
5 Ⓐ Ⓑ Ⓒ Ⓓ	18 Ⓕ Ⓖ Ⓗ Ⓙ	31 Ⓐ Ⓑ Ⓒ Ⓓ	44 Ⓕ Ⓖ Ⓗ Ⓙ	57 Ⓐ Ⓑ Ⓒ Ⓓ	70 Ⓕ Ⓖ Ⓗ Ⓙ
6 Ⓕ Ⓖ Ⓗ Ⓙ	19 Ⓐ Ⓑ Ⓒ Ⓓ	32 Ⓕ Ⓖ Ⓗ Ⓙ	45 Ⓐ Ⓑ Ⓒ Ⓓ	58 Ⓕ Ⓖ Ⓗ Ⓙ	71 Ⓐ Ⓑ Ⓒ Ⓓ
7 Ⓐ Ⓑ Ⓒ Ⓓ	20 Ⓕ Ⓖ Ⓗ Ⓙ	33 Ⓐ Ⓑ Ⓒ Ⓓ	46 Ⓕ Ⓖ Ⓗ Ⓙ	59 Ⓐ Ⓑ Ⓒ Ⓓ	72 Ⓕ Ⓖ Ⓗ Ⓙ
8 Ⓕ Ⓖ Ⓗ Ⓙ	21 Ⓐ Ⓑ Ⓒ Ⓓ	34 Ⓕ Ⓖ Ⓗ Ⓙ	47 Ⓐ Ⓑ Ⓒ Ⓓ	60 Ⓕ Ⓖ Ⓗ Ⓙ	73 Ⓐ Ⓑ Ⓒ Ⓓ
9 Ⓐ Ⓑ Ⓒ Ⓓ	22 Ⓕ Ⓖ Ⓗ Ⓙ	35 Ⓐ Ⓑ Ⓒ Ⓓ	48 Ⓕ Ⓖ Ⓗ Ⓙ	61 Ⓐ Ⓑ Ⓒ Ⓓ	74 Ⓕ Ⓖ Ⓗ Ⓙ
10 Ⓕ Ⓖ Ⓗ Ⓙ	23 Ⓐ Ⓑ Ⓒ Ⓓ	36 Ⓕ Ⓖ Ⓗ Ⓙ	49 Ⓐ Ⓑ Ⓒ Ⓓ	62 Ⓕ Ⓖ Ⓗ Ⓙ	75 Ⓐ Ⓑ Ⓒ Ⓓ
11 Ⓐ Ⓑ Ⓒ Ⓓ	24 Ⓕ Ⓖ Ⓗ Ⓙ	37 Ⓐ Ⓑ Ⓒ Ⓓ	50 Ⓕ Ⓖ Ⓗ Ⓙ	63 Ⓐ Ⓑ Ⓒ Ⓓ	
12 Ⓕ Ⓖ Ⓗ Ⓙ	25 Ⓐ Ⓑ Ⓒ Ⓓ	38 Ⓕ Ⓖ Ⓗ Ⓙ	51 Ⓐ Ⓑ Ⓒ Ⓓ	64 Ⓕ Ⓖ Ⓗ Ⓙ	
13 Ⓐ Ⓑ Ⓒ Ⓓ	26 Ⓕ Ⓖ Ⓗ Ⓙ	39 Ⓐ Ⓑ Ⓒ Ⓓ	52 Ⓕ Ⓖ Ⓗ Ⓙ	65 Ⓐ Ⓑ Ⓒ Ⓓ	

TEST 2

1 Ⓐ Ⓑ Ⓒ Ⓓ Ⓔ	11 Ⓐ Ⓑ Ⓒ Ⓓ Ⓔ	21 Ⓐ Ⓑ Ⓒ Ⓓ Ⓔ	31 Ⓐ Ⓑ Ⓒ Ⓓ Ⓔ	41 Ⓐ Ⓑ Ⓒ Ⓓ Ⓔ	51 Ⓐ Ⓑ Ⓒ Ⓓ Ⓔ
2 Ⓕ Ⓖ Ⓗ Ⓙ Ⓚ	12 Ⓕ Ⓖ Ⓗ Ⓙ Ⓚ	22 Ⓕ Ⓖ Ⓗ Ⓙ Ⓚ	32 Ⓕ Ⓖ Ⓗ Ⓙ Ⓚ	42 Ⓕ Ⓖ Ⓗ Ⓙ Ⓚ	52 Ⓕ Ⓖ Ⓗ Ⓙ Ⓚ
3 Ⓐ Ⓑ Ⓒ Ⓓ Ⓔ	13 Ⓐ Ⓑ Ⓒ Ⓓ Ⓔ	23 Ⓐ Ⓑ Ⓒ Ⓓ Ⓔ	33 Ⓐ Ⓑ Ⓒ Ⓓ Ⓔ	43 Ⓐ Ⓑ Ⓒ Ⓓ Ⓔ	53 Ⓐ Ⓑ Ⓒ Ⓓ Ⓔ
4 Ⓕ Ⓖ Ⓗ Ⓙ Ⓚ	14 Ⓕ Ⓖ Ⓗ Ⓙ Ⓚ	24 Ⓕ Ⓖ Ⓗ Ⓙ Ⓚ	34 Ⓕ Ⓖ Ⓗ Ⓙ Ⓚ	44 Ⓕ Ⓖ Ⓗ Ⓙ Ⓚ	54 Ⓕ Ⓖ Ⓗ Ⓙ Ⓚ
5 Ⓐ Ⓑ Ⓒ Ⓓ Ⓔ	15 Ⓐ Ⓑ Ⓒ Ⓓ Ⓔ	25 Ⓐ Ⓑ Ⓒ Ⓓ Ⓔ	35 Ⓐ Ⓑ Ⓒ Ⓓ Ⓔ	45 Ⓐ Ⓑ Ⓒ Ⓓ Ⓔ	55 Ⓐ Ⓑ Ⓒ Ⓓ Ⓔ
6 Ⓕ Ⓖ Ⓗ Ⓙ Ⓚ	16 Ⓕ Ⓖ Ⓗ Ⓙ Ⓚ	26 Ⓕ Ⓖ Ⓗ Ⓙ Ⓚ	36 Ⓕ Ⓖ Ⓗ Ⓙ Ⓚ	46 Ⓕ Ⓖ Ⓗ Ⓙ Ⓚ	56 Ⓕ Ⓖ Ⓗ Ⓙ Ⓚ
7 Ⓐ Ⓑ Ⓒ Ⓓ Ⓔ	17 Ⓐ Ⓑ Ⓒ Ⓓ Ⓔ	27 Ⓐ Ⓑ Ⓒ Ⓓ Ⓔ	37 Ⓐ Ⓑ Ⓒ Ⓓ Ⓔ	47 Ⓐ Ⓑ Ⓒ Ⓓ Ⓔ	57 Ⓐ Ⓑ Ⓒ Ⓓ Ⓔ
8 Ⓕ Ⓖ Ⓗ Ⓙ Ⓚ	18 Ⓕ Ⓖ Ⓗ Ⓙ Ⓚ	28 Ⓕ Ⓖ Ⓗ Ⓙ Ⓚ	38 Ⓕ Ⓖ Ⓗ Ⓙ Ⓚ	48 Ⓕ Ⓖ Ⓗ Ⓙ Ⓚ	58 Ⓕ Ⓖ Ⓗ Ⓙ Ⓚ
9 Ⓐ Ⓑ Ⓒ Ⓓ Ⓔ	19 Ⓐ Ⓑ Ⓒ Ⓓ Ⓔ	29 Ⓐ Ⓑ Ⓒ Ⓓ Ⓔ	39 Ⓐ Ⓑ Ⓒ Ⓓ Ⓔ	49 Ⓐ Ⓑ Ⓒ Ⓓ Ⓔ	59 Ⓐ Ⓑ Ⓒ Ⓓ Ⓔ
10 Ⓕ Ⓖ Ⓗ Ⓙ Ⓚ	20 Ⓕ Ⓖ Ⓗ Ⓙ Ⓚ	30 Ⓕ Ⓖ Ⓗ Ⓙ Ⓚ	40 Ⓕ Ⓖ Ⓗ Ⓙ Ⓚ	50 Ⓕ Ⓖ Ⓗ Ⓙ Ⓚ	60 Ⓕ Ⓖ Ⓗ Ⓙ Ⓚ

TEST 3

1 Ⓐ Ⓑ Ⓒ Ⓓ	8 Ⓕ Ⓖ Ⓗ Ⓙ	15 Ⓐ Ⓑ Ⓒ Ⓓ	22 Ⓕ Ⓖ Ⓗ Ⓙ	29 Ⓐ Ⓑ Ⓒ Ⓓ	36 Ⓕ Ⓖ Ⓗ Ⓙ
2 Ⓕ Ⓖ Ⓗ Ⓙ	9 Ⓐ Ⓑ Ⓒ Ⓓ	16 Ⓕ Ⓖ Ⓗ Ⓙ	23 Ⓐ Ⓑ Ⓒ Ⓓ	30 Ⓕ Ⓖ Ⓗ Ⓙ	37 Ⓐ Ⓑ Ⓒ Ⓓ
3 Ⓐ Ⓑ Ⓒ Ⓓ	10 Ⓕ Ⓖ Ⓗ Ⓙ	17 Ⓐ Ⓑ Ⓒ Ⓓ	24 Ⓕ Ⓖ Ⓗ Ⓙ	31 Ⓐ Ⓑ Ⓒ Ⓓ	38 Ⓕ Ⓖ Ⓗ Ⓙ
4 Ⓕ Ⓖ Ⓗ Ⓙ	11 Ⓐ Ⓑ Ⓒ Ⓓ	18 Ⓕ Ⓖ Ⓗ Ⓙ	25 Ⓐ Ⓑ Ⓒ Ⓓ	32 Ⓕ Ⓖ Ⓗ Ⓙ	39 Ⓐ Ⓑ Ⓒ Ⓓ
5 Ⓐ Ⓑ Ⓒ Ⓓ	12 Ⓕ Ⓖ Ⓗ Ⓙ	19 Ⓐ Ⓑ Ⓒ Ⓓ	26 Ⓕ Ⓖ Ⓗ Ⓙ	33 Ⓐ Ⓑ Ⓒ Ⓓ	40 Ⓕ Ⓖ Ⓗ Ⓙ
6 Ⓕ Ⓖ Ⓗ Ⓙ	13 Ⓐ Ⓑ Ⓒ Ⓓ	20 Ⓕ Ⓖ Ⓗ Ⓙ	27 Ⓐ Ⓑ Ⓒ Ⓓ	34 Ⓕ Ⓖ Ⓗ Ⓙ	
7 Ⓐ Ⓑ Ⓒ Ⓓ	14 Ⓕ Ⓖ Ⓗ Ⓙ	21 Ⓐ Ⓑ Ⓒ Ⓓ	28 Ⓕ Ⓖ Ⓗ Ⓙ	35 Ⓐ Ⓑ Ⓒ Ⓓ	

TEST 4

1 Ⓐ Ⓑ Ⓒ Ⓓ	8 Ⓕ Ⓖ Ⓗ Ⓙ	15 Ⓐ Ⓑ Ⓒ Ⓓ	22 Ⓕ Ⓖ Ⓗ Ⓙ	29 Ⓐ Ⓑ Ⓒ Ⓓ	36 Ⓕ Ⓖ Ⓗ Ⓙ
2 Ⓕ Ⓖ Ⓗ Ⓙ	9 Ⓐ Ⓑ Ⓒ Ⓓ	16 Ⓕ Ⓖ Ⓗ Ⓙ	23 Ⓐ Ⓑ Ⓒ Ⓓ	30 Ⓕ Ⓖ Ⓗ Ⓙ	37 Ⓐ Ⓑ Ⓒ Ⓓ
3 Ⓐ Ⓑ Ⓒ Ⓓ	10 Ⓕ Ⓖ Ⓗ Ⓙ	17 Ⓐ Ⓑ Ⓒ Ⓓ	24 Ⓕ Ⓖ Ⓗ Ⓙ	31 Ⓐ Ⓑ Ⓒ Ⓓ	38 Ⓕ Ⓖ Ⓗ Ⓙ
4 Ⓕ Ⓖ Ⓗ Ⓙ	11 Ⓐ Ⓑ Ⓒ Ⓓ	18 Ⓕ Ⓖ Ⓗ Ⓙ	25 Ⓐ Ⓑ Ⓒ Ⓓ	32 Ⓕ Ⓖ Ⓗ Ⓙ	39 Ⓐ Ⓑ Ⓒ Ⓓ
5 Ⓐ Ⓑ Ⓒ Ⓓ	12 Ⓕ Ⓖ Ⓗ Ⓙ	19 Ⓐ Ⓑ Ⓒ Ⓓ	26 Ⓕ Ⓖ Ⓗ Ⓙ	33 Ⓐ Ⓑ Ⓒ Ⓓ	40 Ⓕ Ⓖ Ⓗ Ⓙ
6 Ⓕ Ⓖ Ⓗ Ⓙ	13 Ⓐ Ⓑ Ⓒ Ⓓ	20 Ⓕ Ⓖ Ⓗ Ⓙ	27 Ⓐ Ⓑ Ⓒ Ⓓ	34 Ⓕ Ⓖ Ⓗ Ⓙ	
7 Ⓐ Ⓑ Ⓒ Ⓓ	14 Ⓕ Ⓖ Ⓗ Ⓙ	21 Ⓐ Ⓑ Ⓒ Ⓓ	28 Ⓕ Ⓖ Ⓗ Ⓙ	35 Ⓐ Ⓑ Ⓒ Ⓓ	

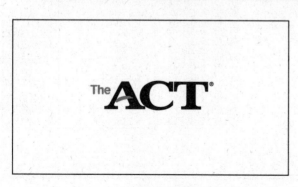

PAGE 1

The ACT® *Sample Answer Sheet*

EXAMINEE STATEMENT, CERTIFICATION, AND SIGNATURE

1. Read the following **Statement:** By submitting this answer document, I agree to comply with and be bound by the *Terms and Conditions: Testing Rules and Policies for the ACT® Test* provided in the ACT registration materials for this test, including those concerning test security, score cancellation, examinee remedies, binding arbitration, and consent to the processing of my personally identifying information, including the collection, use, transfer, and disclosure of information as described in the ACT Privacy Policy (www.act.org/privacy.html).

   I understand that ACT owns the test questions and responses and affirm that I will not share any test questions or responses with anyone by any form of communication before, during, or after the test administration. I understand that assuming anyone else's identity to take this test is strictly prohibited and may violate the law and subject me to legal penalties.

   International Examinees: By my signature, I am also providing my consent to ACT to transfer my personally identifying information to the United States to ACT, or a third-party service provider for processing, where it will be subject to use and disclosure under the laws of the United States. I acknowledge and agree that it may also be accessible to law enforcement and national security authorities in the United States.

2. Copy the **Certification** shown below (only the text in italics) on the lines provided. Write in your normal handwriting.

Certification: *I agree to the Statement above and certify that I am the person whose name and address appear on this answer document.*

Your Signature

Today's Date

Do NOT mark in this shaded area.

USE A SOFT LEAD NO. 2 PENCIL ONLY.
(Do NOT use a mechanical pencil, ink, ballpoint, correction fluid, or felt-tip pen.)

A NAME, MAILING ADDRESS, AND TELEPHONE
(Please print.)

Last Name | First Name | MI (Middle Initial)

House Number & Street (Apt. No.); or PO Box & No.; or RR & No.

City | State/Province | ZIP/Postal Code

Area Code / Number | Country

ACT, Inc.—Confidential Restricted when data present

ALL examinees must complete block A – please print.

Blocks B, C, and D are required for all examinees. Find the MATCHING INFORMATION on your ticket. Enter it EXACTLY the same way, even if any of the information is missing or incorrect. Fill in the corresponding ovals. If you do not complete these blocks to match your previous information EXACTLY, your scores will be **delayed up to 8 weeks**.

ACT

PO BOX 168, IOWA CITY, IA 52243-0168

B MATCH NAME
(First 5 letters of last name)

A B C D E F G H I J K L M N O P Q R S T U V W X Y Z

C MATCH NUMBER

1 2 3 4 5 6 7 8 9 0

D DATE OF BIRTH

Month | Day | Year

January
February
March
April
May
June
July
August
September
October
November
December

 22877 A011 215 190 Rev 1 IM-(A)199526-001:654321 Printed in the US.

Your First Practice Test

PAGE 2

Marking Directions: Mark only **one** oval for each question. Fill in response completely. Erase errors cleanly without smudging.

Correct mark: ○ ● ○ ○

Do NOT use these *incorrect* **or** *bad* **marks.**

Incorrect marks:
Overlapping mark:
Cross-out mark:
Smudged erasure:
Mark is too light:

BOOKLET NUMBER

1	1	1	1	1	1
2	2	2	2	2	2
3	3	3	3	3	3
4	4	4	4	4	4
5	5	5	5	5	5
6	6	6	6	6	6
7	7	7	7	7	7
8	8	8	8	8	8
9	9	9	9	9	9
0	0	0	0	0	0

FORM

Print your 5-character **Test Form** in the boxes above and fill in the corresponding oval at the right.

BE SURE TO FILL IN THE CORRECT FORM OVAL.

○ 16MC1 ○ 18MC4
○ 16MC2 ○ 19MC5
○ 16MC3

TEST 1

1 Ⓐ Ⓑ Ⓒ Ⓓ	14 Ⓕ Ⓖ Ⓗ Ⓙ	27 Ⓐ Ⓑ Ⓒ Ⓓ	40 Ⓕ Ⓖ Ⓗ Ⓙ	53 Ⓐ Ⓑ Ⓒ Ⓓ	66 Ⓕ Ⓖ Ⓗ Ⓙ
2 Ⓕ Ⓖ Ⓗ Ⓙ	15 Ⓐ Ⓑ Ⓒ Ⓓ	28 Ⓕ Ⓖ Ⓗ Ⓙ	41 Ⓐ Ⓑ Ⓒ Ⓓ	54 Ⓕ Ⓖ Ⓗ Ⓙ	67 Ⓐ Ⓑ Ⓒ Ⓓ
3 Ⓐ Ⓑ Ⓒ Ⓓ	16 Ⓕ Ⓖ Ⓗ Ⓙ	29 Ⓐ Ⓑ Ⓒ Ⓓ	42 Ⓕ Ⓖ Ⓗ Ⓙ	55 Ⓐ Ⓑ Ⓒ Ⓓ	68 Ⓕ Ⓖ Ⓗ Ⓙ
4 Ⓕ Ⓖ Ⓗ Ⓙ	17 Ⓐ Ⓑ Ⓒ Ⓓ	30 Ⓕ Ⓖ Ⓗ Ⓙ	43 Ⓐ Ⓑ Ⓒ Ⓓ	56 Ⓕ Ⓖ Ⓗ Ⓙ	69 Ⓐ Ⓑ Ⓒ Ⓓ
5 Ⓐ Ⓑ Ⓒ Ⓓ	18 Ⓕ Ⓖ Ⓗ Ⓙ	31 Ⓐ Ⓑ Ⓒ Ⓓ	44 Ⓕ Ⓖ Ⓗ Ⓙ	57 Ⓐ Ⓑ Ⓒ Ⓓ	70 Ⓕ Ⓖ Ⓗ Ⓙ
6 Ⓕ Ⓖ Ⓗ Ⓙ	19 Ⓐ Ⓑ Ⓒ Ⓓ	32 Ⓕ Ⓖ Ⓗ Ⓙ	45 Ⓐ Ⓑ Ⓒ Ⓓ	58 Ⓕ Ⓖ Ⓗ Ⓙ	71 Ⓐ Ⓑ Ⓒ Ⓓ
7 Ⓐ Ⓑ Ⓒ Ⓓ	20 Ⓕ Ⓖ Ⓗ Ⓙ	33 Ⓐ Ⓑ Ⓒ Ⓓ	46 Ⓕ Ⓖ Ⓗ Ⓙ	59 Ⓐ Ⓑ Ⓒ Ⓓ	72 Ⓕ Ⓖ Ⓗ Ⓙ
8 Ⓕ Ⓖ Ⓗ Ⓙ	21 Ⓐ Ⓑ Ⓒ Ⓓ	34 Ⓕ Ⓖ Ⓗ Ⓙ	47 Ⓐ Ⓑ Ⓒ Ⓓ	60 Ⓕ Ⓖ Ⓗ Ⓙ	73 Ⓐ Ⓑ Ⓒ Ⓓ
9 Ⓐ Ⓑ Ⓒ Ⓓ	22 Ⓕ Ⓖ Ⓗ Ⓙ	35 Ⓐ Ⓑ Ⓒ Ⓓ	48 Ⓕ Ⓖ Ⓗ Ⓙ	61 Ⓐ Ⓑ Ⓒ Ⓓ	74 Ⓕ Ⓖ Ⓗ Ⓙ
10 Ⓕ Ⓖ Ⓗ Ⓙ	23 Ⓐ Ⓑ Ⓒ Ⓓ	36 Ⓕ Ⓖ Ⓗ Ⓙ	49 Ⓐ Ⓑ Ⓒ Ⓓ	62 Ⓕ Ⓖ Ⓗ Ⓙ	75 Ⓐ Ⓑ Ⓒ Ⓓ
11 Ⓐ Ⓑ Ⓒ Ⓓ	24 Ⓕ Ⓖ Ⓗ Ⓙ	37 Ⓐ Ⓑ Ⓒ Ⓓ	50 Ⓕ Ⓖ Ⓗ Ⓙ	63 Ⓐ Ⓑ Ⓒ Ⓓ	
12 Ⓕ Ⓖ Ⓗ Ⓙ	25 Ⓐ Ⓑ Ⓒ Ⓓ	38 Ⓕ Ⓖ Ⓗ Ⓙ	51 Ⓐ Ⓑ Ⓒ Ⓓ	64 Ⓕ Ⓖ Ⓗ Ⓙ	
13 Ⓐ Ⓑ Ⓒ Ⓓ	26 Ⓕ Ⓖ Ⓗ Ⓙ	39 Ⓐ Ⓑ Ⓒ Ⓓ	52 Ⓕ Ⓖ Ⓗ Ⓙ	65 Ⓐ Ⓑ Ⓒ Ⓓ	

TEST 2

1 Ⓐ Ⓑ Ⓒ Ⓓ Ⓔ	11 Ⓐ Ⓑ Ⓒ Ⓓ Ⓔ	21 Ⓐ Ⓑ Ⓒ Ⓓ Ⓔ	31 Ⓐ Ⓑ Ⓒ Ⓓ Ⓔ	41 Ⓐ Ⓑ Ⓒ Ⓓ Ⓔ	51 Ⓐ Ⓑ Ⓒ Ⓓ Ⓔ
2 Ⓕ Ⓖ Ⓗ Ⓙ Ⓚ	12 Ⓕ Ⓖ Ⓗ Ⓙ Ⓚ	22 Ⓕ Ⓖ Ⓗ Ⓙ Ⓚ	32 Ⓕ Ⓖ Ⓗ Ⓙ Ⓚ	42 Ⓕ Ⓖ Ⓗ Ⓙ Ⓚ	52 Ⓕ Ⓖ Ⓗ Ⓙ Ⓚ
3 Ⓐ Ⓑ Ⓒ Ⓓ Ⓔ	13 Ⓐ Ⓑ Ⓒ Ⓓ Ⓔ	23 Ⓐ Ⓑ Ⓒ Ⓓ Ⓔ	33 Ⓐ Ⓑ Ⓒ Ⓓ Ⓔ	43 Ⓐ Ⓑ Ⓒ Ⓓ Ⓔ	53 Ⓐ Ⓑ Ⓒ Ⓓ Ⓔ
4 Ⓕ Ⓖ Ⓗ Ⓙ Ⓚ	14 Ⓕ Ⓖ Ⓗ Ⓙ Ⓚ	24 Ⓕ Ⓖ Ⓗ Ⓙ Ⓚ	34 Ⓕ Ⓖ Ⓗ Ⓙ Ⓚ	44 Ⓕ Ⓖ Ⓗ Ⓙ Ⓚ	54 Ⓕ Ⓖ Ⓗ Ⓙ Ⓚ
5 Ⓐ Ⓑ Ⓒ Ⓓ Ⓔ	15 Ⓐ Ⓑ Ⓒ Ⓓ Ⓔ	25 Ⓐ Ⓑ Ⓒ Ⓓ Ⓔ	35 Ⓐ Ⓑ Ⓒ Ⓓ Ⓔ	45 Ⓐ Ⓑ Ⓒ Ⓓ Ⓔ	55 Ⓐ Ⓑ Ⓒ Ⓓ Ⓔ
6 Ⓕ Ⓖ Ⓗ Ⓙ Ⓚ	16 Ⓕ Ⓖ Ⓗ Ⓙ Ⓚ	26 Ⓕ Ⓖ Ⓗ Ⓙ Ⓚ	36 Ⓕ Ⓖ Ⓗ Ⓙ Ⓚ	46 Ⓕ Ⓖ Ⓗ Ⓙ Ⓚ	56 Ⓕ Ⓖ Ⓗ Ⓙ Ⓚ
7 Ⓐ Ⓑ Ⓒ Ⓓ Ⓔ	17 Ⓐ Ⓑ Ⓒ Ⓓ Ⓔ	27 Ⓐ Ⓑ Ⓒ Ⓓ Ⓔ	37 Ⓐ Ⓑ Ⓒ Ⓓ Ⓔ	47 Ⓐ Ⓑ Ⓒ Ⓓ Ⓔ	57 Ⓐ Ⓑ Ⓒ Ⓓ Ⓔ
8 Ⓕ Ⓖ Ⓗ Ⓙ Ⓚ	18 Ⓕ Ⓖ Ⓗ Ⓙ Ⓚ	28 Ⓕ Ⓖ Ⓗ Ⓙ Ⓚ	38 Ⓕ Ⓖ Ⓗ Ⓙ Ⓚ	48 Ⓕ Ⓖ Ⓗ Ⓙ Ⓚ	58 Ⓕ Ⓖ Ⓗ Ⓙ Ⓚ
9 Ⓐ Ⓑ Ⓒ Ⓓ Ⓔ	19 Ⓐ Ⓑ Ⓒ Ⓓ Ⓔ	29 Ⓐ Ⓑ Ⓒ Ⓓ Ⓔ	39 Ⓐ Ⓑ Ⓒ Ⓓ Ⓔ	49 Ⓐ Ⓑ Ⓒ Ⓓ Ⓔ	59 Ⓐ Ⓑ Ⓒ Ⓓ Ⓔ
10 Ⓕ Ⓖ Ⓗ Ⓙ Ⓚ	20 Ⓕ Ⓖ Ⓗ Ⓙ Ⓚ	30 Ⓕ Ⓖ Ⓗ Ⓙ Ⓚ	40 Ⓕ Ⓖ Ⓗ Ⓙ Ⓚ	50 Ⓕ Ⓖ Ⓗ Ⓙ Ⓚ	60 Ⓕ Ⓖ Ⓗ Ⓙ Ⓚ

TEST 3

1 Ⓐ Ⓑ Ⓒ Ⓓ	8 Ⓕ Ⓖ Ⓗ Ⓙ	15 Ⓐ Ⓑ Ⓒ Ⓓ	22 Ⓕ Ⓖ Ⓗ Ⓙ	29 Ⓐ Ⓑ Ⓒ Ⓓ	36 Ⓕ Ⓖ Ⓗ Ⓙ
2 Ⓕ Ⓖ Ⓗ Ⓙ	9 Ⓐ Ⓑ Ⓒ Ⓓ	16 Ⓕ Ⓖ Ⓗ Ⓙ	23 Ⓐ Ⓑ Ⓒ Ⓓ	30 Ⓕ Ⓖ Ⓗ Ⓙ	37 Ⓐ Ⓑ Ⓒ Ⓓ
3 Ⓐ Ⓑ Ⓒ Ⓓ	10 Ⓕ Ⓖ Ⓗ Ⓙ	17 Ⓐ Ⓑ Ⓒ Ⓓ	24 Ⓕ Ⓖ Ⓗ Ⓙ	31 Ⓐ Ⓑ Ⓒ Ⓓ	38 Ⓕ Ⓖ Ⓗ Ⓙ
4 Ⓕ Ⓖ Ⓗ Ⓙ	11 Ⓐ Ⓑ Ⓒ Ⓓ	18 Ⓕ Ⓖ Ⓗ Ⓙ	25 Ⓐ Ⓑ Ⓒ Ⓓ	32 Ⓕ Ⓖ Ⓗ Ⓙ	39 Ⓐ Ⓑ Ⓒ Ⓓ
5 Ⓐ Ⓑ Ⓒ Ⓓ	12 Ⓕ Ⓖ Ⓗ Ⓙ	19 Ⓐ Ⓑ Ⓒ Ⓓ	26 Ⓕ Ⓖ Ⓗ Ⓙ	33 Ⓐ Ⓑ Ⓒ Ⓓ	40 Ⓕ Ⓖ Ⓗ Ⓙ
6 Ⓕ Ⓖ Ⓗ Ⓙ	13 Ⓐ Ⓑ Ⓒ Ⓓ	20 Ⓕ Ⓖ Ⓗ Ⓙ	27 Ⓐ Ⓑ Ⓒ Ⓓ	34 Ⓕ Ⓖ Ⓗ Ⓙ	
7 Ⓐ Ⓑ Ⓒ Ⓓ	14 Ⓕ Ⓖ Ⓗ Ⓙ	21 Ⓐ Ⓑ Ⓒ Ⓓ	28 Ⓕ Ⓖ Ⓗ Ⓙ	35 Ⓐ Ⓑ Ⓒ Ⓓ	

TEST 4

1 Ⓐ Ⓑ Ⓒ Ⓓ	8 Ⓕ Ⓖ Ⓗ Ⓙ	15 Ⓐ Ⓑ Ⓒ Ⓓ	22 Ⓕ Ⓖ Ⓗ Ⓙ	29 Ⓐ Ⓑ Ⓒ Ⓓ	36 Ⓕ Ⓖ Ⓗ Ⓙ
2 Ⓕ Ⓖ Ⓗ Ⓙ	9 Ⓐ Ⓑ Ⓒ Ⓓ	16 Ⓕ Ⓖ Ⓗ Ⓙ	23 Ⓐ Ⓑ Ⓒ Ⓓ	30 Ⓕ Ⓖ Ⓗ Ⓙ	37 Ⓐ Ⓑ Ⓒ Ⓓ
3 Ⓐ Ⓑ Ⓒ Ⓓ	10 Ⓕ Ⓖ Ⓗ Ⓙ	17 Ⓐ Ⓑ Ⓒ Ⓓ	24 Ⓕ Ⓖ Ⓗ Ⓙ	31 Ⓐ Ⓑ Ⓒ Ⓓ	38 Ⓕ Ⓖ Ⓗ Ⓙ
4 Ⓕ Ⓖ Ⓗ Ⓙ	11 Ⓐ Ⓑ Ⓒ Ⓓ	18 Ⓕ Ⓖ Ⓗ Ⓙ	25 Ⓐ Ⓑ Ⓒ Ⓓ	32 Ⓕ Ⓖ Ⓗ Ⓙ	39 Ⓐ Ⓑ Ⓒ Ⓓ
5 Ⓐ Ⓑ Ⓒ Ⓓ	12 Ⓕ Ⓖ Ⓗ Ⓙ	19 Ⓐ Ⓑ Ⓒ Ⓓ	26 Ⓕ Ⓖ Ⓗ Ⓙ	33 Ⓐ Ⓑ Ⓒ Ⓓ	40 Ⓕ Ⓖ Ⓗ Ⓙ
6 Ⓕ Ⓖ Ⓗ Ⓙ	13 Ⓐ Ⓑ Ⓒ Ⓓ	20 Ⓕ Ⓖ Ⓗ Ⓙ	27 Ⓐ Ⓑ Ⓒ Ⓓ	34 Ⓕ Ⓖ Ⓗ Ⓙ	
7 Ⓐ Ⓑ Ⓒ Ⓓ	14 Ⓕ Ⓖ Ⓗ Ⓙ	21 Ⓐ Ⓑ Ⓒ Ⓓ	28 Ⓕ Ⓖ Ⓗ Ⓙ	35 Ⓐ Ⓑ Ⓒ Ⓓ	

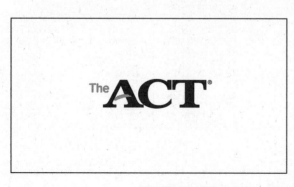

080658

Practice Test 1

EXAMINEE STATEMENT, CERTIFICATION, AND SIGNATURE

1. Read the following **Statement:** By opening this test booklet, I agree to comply with and be bound by the *Terms and Conditions: Testing Rules and Policies for the ACT® Test* provided in the ACT registration materials for this test, including those concerning test security, score cancellation, examinee remedies, binding arbitration, and consent to the processing of my personally identifying information, including the collection, use, transfer, and disclosure of information as described in the ACT Privacy Policy (www.act.org/privacy.html).

   I understand that ACT owns the test questions and responses and affirm that I will not share any test questions or responses with anyone by any form of communication before, during, or after the test administration. I understand that assuming anyone else's identity to take this test is strictly prohibited and may violate the law and subject me to legal penalties.

   International Examinees: By my signature, I am also providing my consent to ACT to transfer my personally identifying information to the United States to ACT, or a third-party service provider for processing, where it will be subject to use and disclosure under the laws of the United States. I acknowledge and agree that it may also be accessible to law enforcement and national security authorities in the United States.

2. Copy the **Certification** shown below (only the text in italics) on the lines provided. Write in your normal handwriting.

   Certification: *I agree to the Statement above and certify that I am the person whose name appears on this form.*

   ____

   ____

3. Sign your name as you would any official document, enter today's date, and print your name in the spaces provided.

   Your Signature ______ Today's Date ______ Print Your Name ______

Form 16MC1

2019 | 2020

Directions

This booklet contains tests in English, mathematics, reading, and science. These tests measure skills and abilities highly related to high school course work and success in college. **Calculators may be used on the mathematics test only.**

The questions in each test are numbered, and the suggested answers for each question are lettered. On the answer document, the rows of ovals are numbered to match the questions, and the ovals in each row are lettered to correspond to the suggested answers.

For each question, first decide which answer is best. Next, locate on the answer document the row of ovals numbered the same as the question. Then, locate the oval in that row lettered the same as your answer. Finally, fill in the oval completely. Use a soft lead pencil and make your marks heavy and black. **Do not use ink or a mechanical pencil.**

Mark only one answer to each question. If you change your mind about an answer, erase your first mark thoroughly before marking your new answer. For each question, make certain that you mark in the row of ovals with the same number as the question.

Only responses marked on your answer document will be scored. Your score on each test will be based only on the number of questions you answer correctly during the time allowed for that test. You will **not** be penalized for guessing. **It is to your advantage to answer every question even if you must guess.**

You may work on each test **only** when the testing staff tells you to do so. If you finish a test before time is called for that test, you should use the time remaining to reconsider questions you are uncertain about in that test. You may **not** look back to a test on which time has already been called, and you may **not** go ahead to another test. To do so will disqualify you from the examination.

Lay your pencil down immediately when time is called at the end of each test. You may **not** for any reason fill in or alter ovals for a test after time is called for that test. To do so will disqualify you from the examination.

Do not fold or tear the pages of your test booklet.

DO NOT OPEN THIS BOOKLET UNTIL TOLD TO DO SO.

1 ■ ■ ■ ■ ■ ■ ■ ■ ■ 1

ENGLISH TEST

45 Minutes—75 Questions

DIRECTIONS: In the five passages that follow, certain words and phrases are underlined and numbered. In the right-hand column, you will find alternatives for the underlined part. In most cases, you are to choose the one that best expresses the idea, makes the statement appropriate for standard written English, or is worded most consistently with the style and tone of the passage as a whole. If you think the original version is best, choose "NO CHANGE." In some cases, you will find in the right-hand column a question about the underlined part. You are to choose the best answer to the question.

You will also find questions about a section of the passage, or about the passage as a whole. These questions do not refer to an underlined portion of the passage, but rather are identified by a number or numbers in a box.

For each question, choose the alternative you consider best and fill in the corresponding oval on your answer document. Read each passage through once before you begin to answer the questions that accompany it. For many of the questions, you must read several sentences beyond the question to determine the answer. Be sure that you have read far enough ahead each time you choose an alternative.

PASSAGE I

What Elephants Learn

Cynthia Moss has been studying <u>elephants, since 1972</u> [1] when she started the <u>now-famous</u> [2] Amboseli Elephant Research Project in Amboseli National Park in Kenya. An author, lecturer, filmmaker, and a fierce advocate for elephants—which face a daunting array of threats to their survival, from droughts to human <u>encroachment</u> [3] Moss is widely considered an expert on the social behavior of these creatures. [4]

1. A. NO CHANGE
   B. elephants, since 1972,
   C. elephants since 1972,
   D. elephants' since 1972

2. F. NO CHANGE
   G. more-then-famous
   H. now famously
   J. famously

3. A. NO CHANGE
   B. encroachment—
   C. encroachment:
   D. encroachment,

4. At this point, the writer is considering adding the following true statement:

   Humans are among the threats to the animal's survival.

   Should the writer make this addition here?

   F. Yes, because it presents a crucial factor in determining Moss's interest in working with elephants.
   G. Yes, because it introduces the idea that becomes the focus of the rest of the essay.
   H. No, because the essay is focused on elephants and does not otherwise mention a human presence in their lives.
   J. No, because this information is already provided in the paragraph.

GO ON TO THE NEXT PAGE.

1 ■ ■ ■ ■ ■ ■ ■ ■ ■ 1

A key finding from her intensive, field, studies is the extent to which elephant survival depends on learned behavior.

As Moss has observed, however, a calf must learn how to use its trunk. At first a young elephant will drink by kneeling down at the water's edge and it sipped directly with its mouth. The habit of pulling water into its trunk. Then releasing that water into its mouth develops only after months as if witnessing other elephants doing so.

On occasion, Moss will see a calf stick its trunk into the mouth of its mother and pull out a bit of whatever plant material she is eating. In this way, the calf learns what kinds of vegetation are safe to eat on the savanna, where poisonous plants also grow.

[1] Elephants live in family groups, each one headed by a matriarch. [2] This senior female teaches adolescent females by modeling proper care of younger elephants. [3] One of Moss's most memorable observations in which this regard involved three elephants. [4] These were a matriarch, Echo, and two offspring: Enid, a ten-year-old female, and Ely, also named by Moss. [5] Echo showed Enid how to care for Ely by staying close to him when he was feeding and sleeping and by running to his aid when he signaled his distress. [6] Ely not only overcame his early limitations, but he also grew up to be a confident young bull.

5. A. NO CHANGE
B. intensive field studies
C. intensive field studies,
D. intensive, field studies

6. F. NO CHANGE
G. for instance,
H. as always,
J. by now,

7. A. NO CHANGE
B. which it sips
C. and sipping
D. that sips

8. F. NO CHANGE
G. trunk and then
H. trunk then by
J. trunk

9. A. NO CHANGE
B. when witnessing
C. of witnessing
D. then witness

10. F. NO CHANGE
G. in this regard
H. ones that
J. which

11. A. NO CHANGE
B. a baby male.
C. an elephant.
D. the third.

12. F. NO CHANGE
G. he also will have grown
H. he also had grown
J. also growing

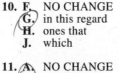

GO ON TO THE NEXT PAGE.

Your First Practice Test

1 ■ ■ ■ ■ ■ ■ ■ ■ ■ 1

[7] Ely was born with deformed feet that initially prevented him from walking. [13]

Moss has brought compelling stories and information about elephants is provided to an ever-expanding audience. She hopes others will in turn become advocates for the animals she admires and understands in ways few others do.

13. For the sake of logic and cohesion, the best placement for Sentence 7 would be:
   A. where it is now.
   B. before Sentence 1.
   C. after Sentence 3.
   D. after Sentence 4.

14. F. NO CHANGE
   G. is given by her to
   H. is reaching
   J. to

Question 15 asks about the preceding passage as a whole.

15. Suppose the writer's goal had been to write a brief essay focusing on some aspect of animal behavior in the wild. Would this essay accomplish that goal?
   A. Yes, because the essay focuses on Moss's research on how elephants on the savanna learn to identify their various family members.
   B. Yes, because the essay focuses on elephants on the savanna and some of the behaviors they display, as studied by Moss.
   C. No, because the essay focuses instead on how elephants have evolved in Kenya as compared to how they have evolved in other parts of Africa.
   D. No, because the essay focuses on elephants that Moss studies in zoos around the world.

PASSAGE II

The following paragraphs may or may not be in the most logical order. Each paragraph is numbered in brackets, and question 29 will ask you to choose where Paragraph 2 should most logically be placed.

Ghost Signs

[1]

Seeing remnants of outdoor advertisements from a bygone era, they are called "ghost signs." I search for them on city streets, in town squares, and along country roads. Some are weather-beaten billboards; others are faded murals painted years ago on the sides of old buildings. Whatever words remain *Fruiterer* . . . *Apothecary* . . . *Gramophones* . . . *Pan-Handle Coffee*—are often barely

16. F. NO CHANGE
   G. The sight of remnants
   H. To see remnants
   J. Remnants

17. A. NO CHANGE
   B. era that is no more,
   C. era of another time,
   D. era of times past,

18. F. NO CHANGE
   G. remain—
   H. remain,
   J. remain:

GO ON TO THE NEXT PAGE.

legible, pale fragments of yesterday's consumer culture should strike me as silly or sad. After all, there they are: advertising products and businesses that no longer exist. Yet, they themselves survive without apology, with instead, their simple claims and complex colors. The contrast draws me in every time.

[2]

I collect ghost signs. Not the signs themselves, but photos of them. Driving home from school one chilly October evening, my collection got its start. I had made the same drive countless times before, but I had never noticed the sign.

[3]

Then there it was, an ad for "Joe's Café," perched atop a metal pole, which was upright under a cape of kudzu vines. Maybe it was the way the setting sun's illumination of the yellowing plastic. Maybe it was the small hole, a clue to vandalism or of a hailstorm. Instead, something about the sign touched me. I pulled over. In the twilight, I got out of the car, snapped a picture with my phone, and sent it to some friends. I vowed to return with my camera to better capture the forlorn, luminous beauty of my discovery. Since that dusky evening, I have been happily haunted by ghost signs.

19. A. NO CHANGE
B. that should
C. they should
D. should they

20. F. NO CHANGE
G. products and businesses,
H. products, and businesses
J. products: businesses

21. A. NO CHANGE
B. apology, with, instead,
C. apology with instead,
D. apology with instead

22. F. NO CHANGE
G. Driving home from school one chilly October evening was the beginning of my collection.
H. I started my collection one chilly October evening, driving home from school.
J. The start of my collection came to me driving home from school one chilly October evening.

23. Given that all the choices are accurate, which one echoes a central point the writer makes about ghost signs?
A. NO CHANGE
B. was not what interested me,
C. might have been wood,
D. was disappearing

24. F. NO CHANGE
G. illuminating setting sun on
H. sun illuminated the set on
J. setting sun illuminated

25. A. NO CHANGE
B. evidence of
C. evidently
D. DELETE the underlined portion.

26. F. NO CHANGE
G. On the other hand, something
H. Meanwhile, something
J. Something

GO ON TO THE NEXT PAGE.

1          1

[4]

Once in a while, I take a friend with me on my searches. People who know of my fascination will point me to where they think they have seen a ghost sign. Favorite finds include an ad for sliced bread, one for a "modern" motel, and yet another for fountain pen repair services. As fun as it is to have company, my best hunts have been <u>solitude</u>[27] trips. I appreciate the beauty of ghost signs more when <u>I like the signs,</u>[28] am alone.

27. A. NO CHANGE
B. solitarily
C. solitaire
D. solo

28. F. NO CHANGE
G. I, like, the signs
H. I, like the signs,
J. I like, the signs,

Questions 29 and 30 ask about the preceding passage as a whole.

29. For the sake of logic and cohesion, Paragraph 2 should be placed:

A. where it is now.
B. before Paragraph 1.
C. after Paragraph 3.
D. after Paragraph 4.

30. Suppose the writer's primary purpose had been to describe starting and enjoying a new hobby. Would this essay accomplish that purpose?

F. Yes, because it presents the event that led to the narrator becoming interested in finding ghost signs and taking photographs of them.
G. Yes, because it describes the narrator's experience of learning from a friend where to find ghost signs and how much fun the search itself can be.
H. No, because it uses negative terms such as *lonely* and *forlorn* to describe the narrator's experience of collecting ghost signs.
J. No, because it instead describes two hobbies—photography and collecting ghost signs—and does not indicate which one gave the narrator more pleasure.

PASSAGE III

Blue Holes of the Bahamas

[1]

The Bahamas, a series of semitropical islands off the southeast coast of the United <u>States, which are</u>[31] home to some of the most unusual geological formations in the world: underwater caves known as blue holes. [A] These

31. A. NO CHANGE
B. States, are
C. States are
D. States,

GO ON TO THE NEXT PAGE.

vertical caves were formed over thousands of years, and their cold depths provide abundant clues to the islands' past.

[2]

32 During the formation process, tiny grains of calcium carbonate separated from the seawater. These grains built[33] up, then compacted, forming the limestone that makes up the islands. [B] Over time, rainwater permeated the porous limestone but was trapped just above sea level, buoyed by[34] the denser seawater below. Jostled back and forth by tides, the layer of slightly acidic, brackish water eroded limestone faster than either rainwater—or seawater—[35] could alone. As the limestone eroded caves[36] formed.

[3]

Over time periods in which the weather changed drastically,[37] sea levels rose and fell by hundreds of feet. This allowed the cave-creating process to be a process that repeated at different depths hundreds of feet apart.[38] The roofs of many caves collapsed, leaving the chambers beneath exposed.

32. Given that all the following statements are true, which one, if added here, would most effectively introduce the topic of this paragraph?
   - F. The Bahamas were formed from calcium carbonate, a component of seawater.
   - G. Calcium carbonate, a common rock substance, is also found in seawater.
   - H. Much of the land making up the Bahamas is still underwater.
   - J. Most types of limestone contain calcium carbonate.

33. A. NO CHANGE
   - B. are building
   - C. will build
   - D. build

34. F. NO CHANGE
   - G. being buoyed because of
   - H. it being buoyed by
   - J. buoying it was

35. A. NO CHANGE
   - B. rainwater, or seawater,
   - C. rainwater, or seawater
   - D. rainwater or seawater

36. F. NO CHANGE
   - G. limestone, eroded caves
   - H. limestone eroded, caves
   - J. limestone eroded caves,

37. Which choice most specifically illustrates how long the cave-creating process took?
   - A. NO CHANGE
   - B. Between ice ages and the more temperate eras that followed them,
   - C. During this extended time,
   - D. As time passed,

38. F. NO CHANGE
   - G. repeat again and again at various different depths.
   - H. repeat at different depths that varied.
   - J. repeat at different depths.

GO ON TO THE NEXT PAGE.

1 ■ ■ ■ ■ ■ ■ ■ ■ ■ 1

Some of these blue holes open to small contained caves [39] others open to miles-long interconnected tunnels. [40]

[4]

The telltale sign of a blue hole is a circular patch of water striking darker [41] than the water surrounding them. [42] (The darker water indicates greater depth.) [C] Divers have found the remains of turtles and alligators. Now extinct on [43] the islands, stalactites and stalagmites from a time when the caves were above sea level, and artifacts of early human inhabitants.

[5]

[D] Hundreds of blue holes can be sighted off [44] the Bahamas. So far, most remain unexplored by divers, owing in part to the danger of cave diving. Often the only clue to the mysteries below is the tantalizing sight of dark blue water leading deep into the sea.

39. **A.** NO CHANGE
B. caves that
C. caves;
D. caves,

40. At this point, the writer is considering adding the following true sentence:

> At 663 feet deep, Dean's Blue Hole in Long Island, Bahamas, is a popular cave-diving destination.

Should the writer make this addition here?

F. Yes, because it supports the preceding sentence by providing an example of a blue hole that is very deep.
G. Yes, because it allows the reader to visualize a specific blue hole in the Bahamas.
H. No, because it offers a detail that is unrelated to the paragraph's focus on the cave-creating process.
J. No, because it does not provide an adequate description of Dean's Blue Hole.

41. **A.** NO CHANGE
B. strikingly darker
C. strikingly darkly
D. striking darkly

42. **F.** NO CHANGE
G. these.
H. one.
J. it.

43. **A.** NO CHANGE
B. alligators now. Extinct on
C. alligators now extinct on
D. alligators now extinct. On

44. Which choice most effectively suggests the shape of blue holes as described earlier in the essay?

F. NO CHANGE
G. dot the waters of
H. darken parts of
J. appear in

Question 45 asks about the preceding passage as a whole.

45. The writer wants to add the following sentence to the essay:

> In these depths, fossils and ancient rock formations are incredibly well preserved.

This sentence would most logically be placed at:

A. Point A in Paragraph 1.
B. Point B in Paragraph 2.
C. Point C in Paragraph 4.
D. Point D in Paragraph 5.

GO ON TO THE NEXT PAGE.

1 ■ ■ ■ ■ ■ ■ ■ ■ ■ 1

PASSAGE IV

The Walls of Rome

[1]

Rome, founded on the banks of the Tiber River, boasts two ancient walls that, when they were built, surrounded the city. [A] Although both were built as walls intended to defend the city protectively [46] and stood ten meters tall they [47] were erected under different historical circumstances.

[2]

It's [48] thought that the Servian Wall was constructed in the early fourth century BCE and named after Servius Tullius, who was the sixth king of Rome. The eleven-kilometer wall encircled Rome's seven hills and stood entirely on the east side of the Tiber River. [B]

[3]

The Aurelian Wall, [49] built in the late third century CE by the Roman Emperor Aurelian, was more sturdier than [50] the older wall. It was nineteen kilometers long greatly expanded [51] and surrounded the city of Rome as well as a small section of the Tiber's west bank. Erected almost 600 years after the Servian Wall, the Aurelian Wall protected Rome while the army was away, defending the empire's far-flung frontiers from enemy attacks. [C] The massive wall deterred many enemies who might have been tempted to attack Rome during those intervals the city was sparsely defended.

46. F. NO CHANGE
G. defensive walls for defending the city
H. walls to provide defensive protection
J. defensive walls

47. A. NO CHANGE
B. tall. They
C. tall, they
D. tall; they

48. F. NO CHANGE
G. Among historians, its
H. Its'
J. Its

49. A. NO CHANGE
B. Wall had been
C. Wall, which,
D. Wall, was

50. F. NO CHANGE
G. much sturdier than
H. more sturdier then
J. much sturdier then

51. Which of the following placements for the underlined portion makes it most clear that it was Rome that had expanded?
A. Where it is now
B. After the words *surrounded the*
C. After the word *Rome*
D. After the words *of the*

GO ON TO THE NEXT PAGE.

Your First Practice Test

1 ■ ■ ■ ■ ■ ■ ■ ■ ■ 1

[4]

[D] The Aurelian Wall featured eighteen large gateways permitting both foot and chariot traffic in and out of the city. In other words, a series of 381 towers and eleven smaller side gates called posterns were evenly spaced along the rest of the wall. Both the posterns and the towers served as defensive positions for protecting Rome. Walkable passages lined the inner side of the wall.

52. F. NO CHANGE
G. Therefore, a
H. Instead, a
J. A

53. A. NO CHANGE
B. Both, the posterns and the towers,
C. Both the posterns, and the towers
D. Both the posterns and the towers,

54. Which choice provides the most specific information about how posterns and towers served as defensive positions?
F. NO CHANGE
G. by providing cover for armed guards during an enemy attack.
H. in that they were designed to help Rome repel enemy attacks.
J. by keeping Rome safe from invaders.

[5]

The Romans used bricks to build the Aurelian Wall. However, only small portions of the Servian Wall remains, some of which can be seen inside a chain restaurant located beneath Rome's central train station. [57] It could, perhaps, be considered ironic that remnants

55. Given that all the statements are true, which one provides the most effective transition to Paragraph 5?
A. NO CHANGE
B. Today, the Aurelian Wall continues to dominate the Roman landscape.
C. Emperor Aurelian did not survive long enough to see the completion of the Aurelian Wall.
D. Before the Servian and Aurelian Walls were built, ancient Rome was most likely protected by mounds of earth.

56. F. NO CHANGE
G. were remaining,
H. has remained,
J. remain,

57. At this point, the writer is considering adding the following true statement:

To hasten the construction of the Aurelian Wall, existing architectural features, such as aqueducts, were incorporated into the structure.

Should the statement be added here?
A. Yes, because it adds information about the Aurelian Wall that supports the main idea of the paragraph.
B. Yes, because it demonstrates how innovative and practical the Roman engineers were.
C. No, because it provides a detail that interrupts the paragraph's discussion of the Servian Wall in the present day.
D. No, because it provides a level of detail about the wall that is inconsistent with the level of detail in the rest of the essay.

GO ON TO THE NEXT PAGE.

1 ■ ■ ■ ■ ■ ■ ■ ■ ■ 1

of a wall that once protected the future[58] capital of one of the ancient world's most famous empires are now preserved and recognized as historically significant by archaeologists.[59]

58. F. NO CHANGE
G. what was yet to be appointed to the designation of
H. what would in reality become the
J. a would be but not yet

59. Which choice best completes the irony that is set up in the first part of the sentence?
A. NO CHANGE
B. as important relics of Rome's earliest boundaries.
C. within a fast-food restaurant.
D. in such varied locations.

Question 60 asks about the preceding passage as a whole.

60. The writer is considering adding the following statement to the essay:

> The two walls can be thought of as concentric circles emanating from the ancient Roman Forum.

If the writer were to add this statement, it would most logically be placed at:
F. Point A in Paragraph 1.
G. Point B in Paragraph 2.
H. Point C in Paragraph 3.
J. Point D in Paragraph 4.

PASSAGE V

James Forten, Revolutionary Sailmaker

[1]

"I have been taken prisoner for the liberties of my country, and never will prove a traitor to her interests." [A] Before entering a British-run prison during the American Revolution prisoner of war, James Forten,[61] said these words as a patriotic rejection of his British captor's offer to free him and educate him in England.

61. A. NO CHANGE
B. Revolution, prisoner of war James Forten,
C. Revolution, prisoner of war James Forten
D. Revolution prisoner of war, James Forten

[2]

[62] He knew his chance of surviving[63] imprisonment were slim.

62. Which of the following sentences, if added here, would provide the most logical transition from the preceding paragraph to this paragraph?
F. Forten was one of many to serve in the American Revolution.
G. Forten's rejection was risky.
H. Such an offer must have been unusual.
J. Many would later admire Forten's skills as an innovator.

63. A. NO CHANGE
B. chances to surviving
C. chances of surviving
D. chance to survive

GO ON TO THE NEXT PAGE.

1 ■ ■ ■ ■ ■ ■ ■ ■ ■ 1

Forten also knew that if released at the war's end or as part of an exchange, he, a free black man, might be captured and sold into slavery as he journeyed home to Philadelphia. Forten not only survived but became one of the most successful businessmen and ardent abolitionists in the United States. [65]

[3]

Forten's rise to prosperity began upon his return home when a sailmaker hired him to design, mend, and sew sails. Forten's knowledge of ships, gained from his experiences as a sailor during the war, paid off. He rose to the position of foreman, and in 1798, Forten bought the sailmaker's business. [B]

[4]

Employing thirty-eight workers, white and black, Forten held his employees to a high standard. Viewed as a professional academy, his business produced skilled apprentices who constructed sails for dozens of vessels. The bulk of Forten's business records was probably lost after the business was sold. [68] Soon, many regarded Forten as the city's premier sailmaker in Philadelphia.

64. F. NO CHANGE
G. exchange; he as
H. exchange—he
J. exchange. He

65. If the writer were to delete the preceding sentence, the paragraph would primarily lose:
A. a description of the tactics Forten used to survive imprisonment and become a successful businessman and abolitionist.
B. a transition from a discussion of the ramifications of Forten's decision to a discussion of his success as a sailmaker and abolitionist.
C. a comparison between Forten's work as a businessman and his role as an abolitionist.
D. an analysis of how Forten transitioned from a prisoner to a businessman and abolitionist.

66. F. NO CHANGE
G. had arose
H. had rose
J. raised

67. A. NO CHANGE
B. workers, whom were
C. workers:
D. workers

68. The writer is considering deleting the preceding sentence. Should the sentence be kept or deleted?
F. Kept, because it establishes a correlation between Forten's business records and the early success of Forten's business.
G. Kept, because it provides evidence to support the claim that Forten employed thirty-eight workers.
H. Deleted, because it blurs the paragraph's focus on the success of Forten's business.
J. Deleted, because it contradicts the idea that Forten had high expectations for his business.

69. A. NO CHANGE
B. foremost leading sailmaker in his native Philadelphia.
C. premier sailmaker in the city of Philadelphia.
D. premier sailmaker.

GO ON TO THE NEXT PAGE.

[5]

A savvy businessman, Forten <u>supported abolitionist causes.</u> 70 When the War of 1812 closed the port of Philadelphia, Forten used his profits in real estate and lending to support his sailmaking enterprise. When the need for <u>smaller,</u> 71 quicker vessels changed sail design, he adapted. One thing Forten refused to do, however, was fit a slave ship with sails.

[6]

In fact, historians estimate that the sailmaker invested <u>over greater than half his</u> 72 fortune in work to abolish slavery. [C] One of the wealthiest men in Philadelphia, Forten helped finance the *Liberator*, a powerful abolitionist newspaper. [D] The Revolutionary War <u>veteran, who served in this war,</u> 73 believed that the United States owed all residents the right to freedom.

70. Given that all the following choices are accurate, which one most effectively provides a transition into the next sentence of the essay?

- **F.** NO CHANGE.
- **G.** had fought for his country in the Revolutionary War.
- **H.** donated to such places as schools and hospitals.
- **J.** maintained his business during difficult times.

71.
- **A.** NO CHANGE
- **B.** smaller, and more
- **C.** smaller, more
- **D.** smaller

72.
- **F.** NO CHANGE
- **G.** over more than half of his own
- **H.** more than over half of his
- **J.** over half of his

73.
- **A.** NO CHANGE
- **B.** veteran, cultivating the sails of freedom,
- **C.** veteran, nurturing the road to reform,
- **D.** veteran

Questions 74 and 75 ask about the preceding passage as a whole.

74. The writer is considering adding the following true statement to the essay:

> Writing under a pen name, Forten himself submitted numerous articles and letters, calling for the end of slavery.

If the writer were to add this sentence to the essay, it would most logically be placed at:

- **F.** Point A in Paragraph 1.
- **G.** Point B in Paragraph 3.
- **H.** Point C in Paragraph 6.
- **J.** Point D in Paragraph 6.

75. Suppose the writer's primary purpose had been to describe in detail the daily operations of a successful business in the newly formed United States. Would this essay accomplish that purpose?

- **A.** Yes, because it describes how Forten became a successful businessman and how his business survived numerous challenges.
- **B.** Yes, because it describes the historical significance of Forten's business and how the business evolved.
- **C.** No, because it focuses more on Forten as a patriot, businessman, and abolitionist than on the daily workings of his business.
- **D.** No, because it focuses primarily on contrasting Forten's work as an abolitionist with his work as a sailmaker.

END OF TEST 1

STOP! DO NOT TURN THE PAGE UNTIL TOLD TO DO SO.

2 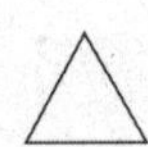         2

MATHEMATICS TEST

60 Minutes—60 Questions

DIRECTIONS: Solve each problem, choose the correct answer, and then fill in the corresponding oval on your answer document.

Do not linger over problems that take too much time. Solve as many as you can; then return to the others in the time you have left for this test.

You are permitted to use a calculator on this test. You may use your calculator for any problems you choose, but some of the problems may best be done without using a calculator.

Note: Unless otherwise stated, all of the following should be assumed.

1. Illustrative figures are NOT necessarily drawn to scale.
2. Geometric figures lie in a plane.
3. The word *line* indicates a straight line.
4. The word *average* indicates arithmetic mean.

DO YOUR FIGURING HERE.

1. Which of the following expressions is equivalent to $a(4 - a) - 5(a + 7)$?

A. $-2a - 35$
B. $-2a + 7$
C. $-a^2 - a - 35$
D. $-a^2 - a + 7$
E. $-2a^3 - 35$

2. Which of the following inequalities orders the numbers 0.2, 0.03, and $\frac{1}{4}$ from least to greatest?

F. $0.2 < 0.03 < \frac{1}{4}$
G. $0.03 < 0.2 < \frac{1}{4}$
H. $0.03 < \frac{1}{4} < 0.2$
J. $\frac{1}{4} < 0.03 < 0.2$
K. $\frac{1}{4} < 0.2 < 0.03$

3. If $x^2 + 4 = 29$, then $x^2 - 4 = ?$

A. 5
B. $\sqrt{21}$
C. 21
D. 25
E. 33

GO ON TO THE NEXT PAGE.

2 △ △ △ △ △ △ △ △ △ 2

DO YOUR FIGURING HERE.

4. The vertices of a rectangle are (−1,−2), (4,−2), (4,3), and (−1,3). When the rectangle is graphed in the standard (x,y) coordinate plane below, what percent of the total area of the rectangle lies in Quadrant III ?

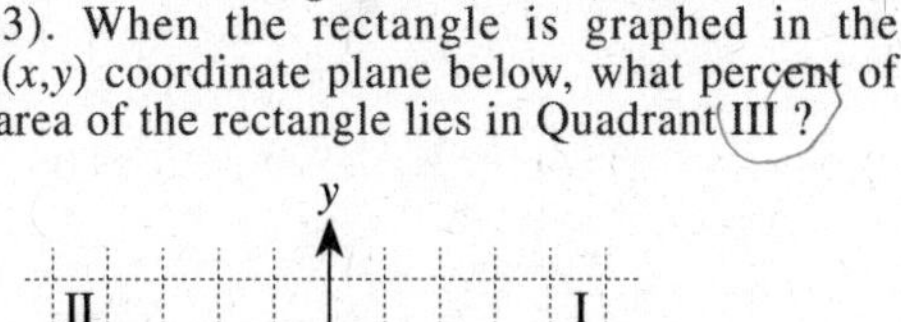

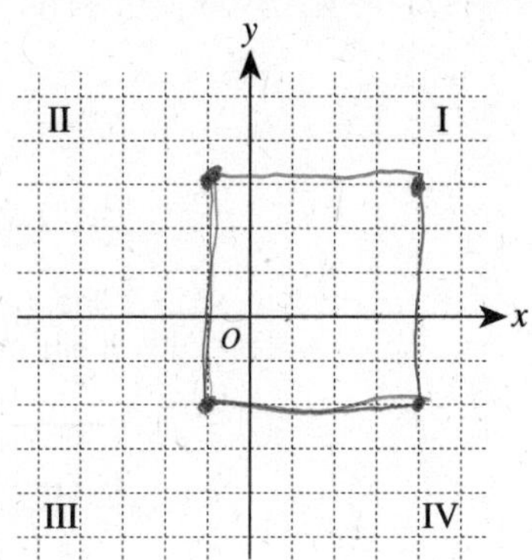

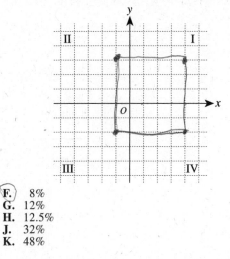

F. 8%
G. 12%
H. 12.5%
J. 32%
K. 48%

5. In 1985, the cost of clothing for a certain family was \$620. In 1995, 10 years later, the cost of clothing for this family was \$1,000. Assuming the cost increased linearly, what was the cost of this family's clothing in 1991 ?

A. \$908
B. \$848
C. \$812
D. \$810
E. \$772

6. The square root of a certain number is approximately 9.2371. The certain number is between what 2 integers?

F. 3 and 4
G. 4 and 5
H. 9 and 10
J. 18 and 19
K. 81 and 99

7. A bag contains 10 pieces of flavored candy: 4 lemon, 3 strawberry, 2 grape, and 1 cherry. One piece of candy will be randomly picked from the bag. What is the probability the candy picked is NOT grape flavored?

A. $\frac{1}{5}$

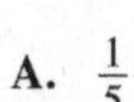

B. $\frac{1}{4}$

C. $\frac{1}{2}$

D. $\frac{3}{4}$

E. $\frac{4}{5}$

GO ON TO THE NEXT PAGE.

2 △ △ △ △ △ △ △ △ △ 2

8. When points A and $B(-3,4)$ are graphed in the standard (x,y) coordinate plane below, the midpoint of $\overline{AB}$ will be (1,2). What will be the coordinates of point A ?

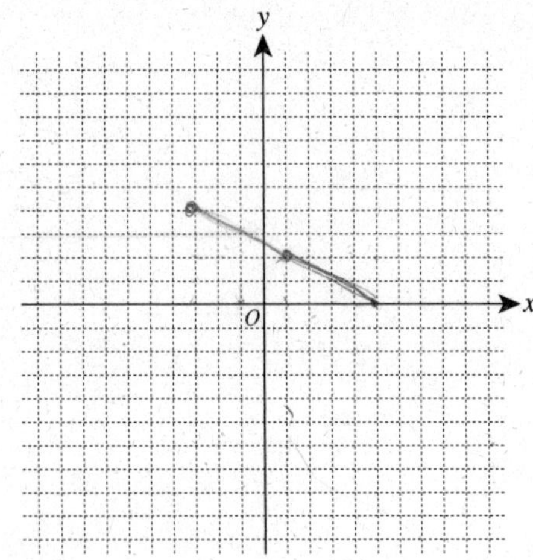

F. (−7,6)
G. (−2,1)
H. (−1,3)
J. (−1,8)
K. (5,0)

9. Andrea manages a company that currently has 116 customers, which is 8 more than twice the number of customers the company had 1 year ago. How many customers did the company have 1 year ago?

A. 50
B. 54
C. 62
D. 66
E. 100

10. Joseph will have a 200-foot-long fence installed around his yard. The A+ Fence Company charges a \$500.00 fee, plus a set amount per foot of fence. The A+ Fence Company has given Joseph an estimate of \$2,200.00 to install the fence around his yard. What is the set amount per foot of fence?

F. \$ 4.00
G. \$ 4.80
H. \$ 8.50
J. \$11.00
K. \$13.50

11. For a math homework assignment, Karla found the area and perimeter of a room of her house. She reported that the area of her rectangular living room is 180 square feet and that the perimeter is 54 feet. When drawing a sketch of her living room the next day, she realized that she had forgotten to write down the dimensions of the room. What are the dimensions of Karla's living room, in feet?

A. 9 by 20
B. 10 by 18
C. 12 by 15
D. 14 by 13
E. 16 by 11

GO ON TO THE NEXT PAGE.

2 △ △ △ △ △ △ △ △ △ 2

DO YOUR FIGURING HERE.

Use the following information to answer questions 12–14.

Carrie's Chocolate Shop and Tamika's Treat Shop both sell candy in boxes. The table below lists the price (the total amount the customer pays) of each box of candy sold at the shops. For each shop, there is a linear relationship between the price of a box of candies and the number of candies in that box. These are the only numbers of candies that can be purchased at the shops.

Candies per box (n)	Price at Carrie's Chocolate Shop (c)	Price at Tamika's Treat Shop (t)
5	\$1.50	\$2.25
10	\$2.50	\$2.75
15	\$3.50	\$3.25
20	\$4.50	\$3.75
25	\$5.50	\$4.25
30	\$6.50	\$4.75

12. Jeremy has \$10.00 in quarters to spend on candy. What is the maximum number of quarters he would have left after paying for a box of 25 candies at Tamika's Treat Shop?

(Note: Each quarter is worth \$0.25.)

F. 10
G. 17
H. 22
J. 23
K. 30

13. At Tamika's Treat Shop, what is the average price per candy in a box of 20, to the nearest \$0.01 ?

A. \$0.08
B. \$0.19
C. \$0.23
D. \$0.30
E. \$0.45

14. Which of the following equations gives the relationship between the price in dollars, c, and the number of candies, n, in a box of candies at Carrie's Chocolate Shop?

F. $c = 0.2n + 0.5$
G. $c = 0.3n$
H. $c = 0.5n + 1.5$
J. $c = \quad n - 3.5$
K. $c = 1.4n - 5.5$

GO ON TO THE NEXT PAGE.

2 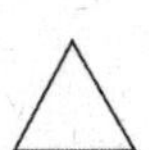      **2**

DO YOUR FIGURING HERE.

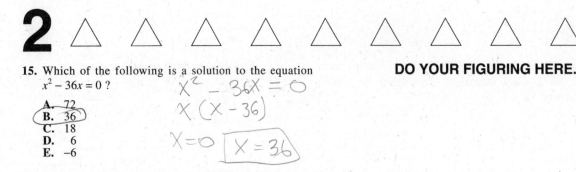

15. Which of the following is a solution to the equation $x^2 - 36x = 0$?

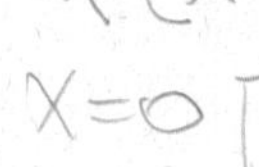

A. 72
B. 36
C. 18
D. 6
E. −6

16. In the figure below, vertices D and F of $\triangle DEF$ lie on $\overline{CG}$, the measure of $\angle CDE$ is 148°, and the measure of $\angle EFG$ is 140°. What is the measure of $\angle DEF$?

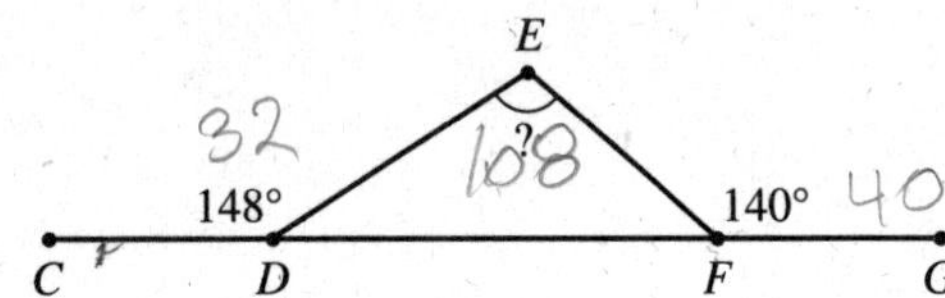

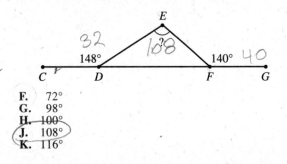

F. 72°
G. 98°
H. 100°
J. 108°
K. 116°

17. A company ships notepads in rectangular boxes that each have inside dimensions measuring 9 inches long, 9 inches wide, and 12 inches tall. Each notepad is in the shape of a cube with an edge length of 3 inches. What is the maximum number of notepads that will fit in 1 closed box?

A. 10
B. 11
C. 12
D. 22
E. 36

18. The function f is defined as $f(x) = -4x^3 - 4x^2$. What is $f(-4)$?

F. −320
G. −192
H. 16
J. 192
K. 320

19. Which of the following (x,y) pairs is the solution for the system of equations $x + 2y = 4$ and $-2x + y = 7$?

A. (−2,3)
B. (−1,2.5)
C. (1,1.5)
D. (2,1)
E. (4,0)

20. Which of the following is a value of x that satisfies $\log_x 36 = 2$?

F. 4
G. 6
H. 8
J. 16
K. 18

GO ON TO THE NEXT PAGE.

2 △ △ △ △ △ △ △ △ △ 2

DO YOUR FIGURING HERE.

21. A 5-inch-by-7-inch photograph was cut to fit exactly into a 4-inch-by-6-inch frame. What is the area, in square inches, of the part of the photograph that was cut off?

A. 2
B. 10
C. 11
D. 12
E. 24

22. A line contains the points A, B, C, and D. Point B is between points A and C. Point D is between points C and B. Which of the following inequalities *must* be true about the lengths of these segments?

F. $BC < AB$
G. $BD < AB$
H. $BD < CD$
J. $CD < AB$
K. $CD < BC$

23. If x and y are positive integers such that the greatest common factor of x^2y^2 and xy^3 is 45, then which of the following could y equal?

A. 45
B. 15
C. 9
D. 5
E. 3

24. To test a new medicine, each of 300 volunteers was assigned a distinct number from 1 to 300. Next, a calculator was used to simulate drawing 150 balls from among 300 congruent balls. The balls were numbered the same way as the volunteers so that 150 volunteers to receive the new medication would be chosen without bias. The other volunteers received a placebo. Weeks later, the 2 groups were compared. Which of the following phrases best describes the company's testing?

F. Randomized census
G. Randomized experiment
H. Nonrandomized experiment
J. Randomized sample survey
K. Nonrandomized sample survey

25. One caution sign flashes every 4 seconds, and another caution sign flashes every 10 seconds. At a certain instant, the 2 signs flash at the same time. How many seconds elapse until the 2 signs next flash at the same time?

A. 6
B. 7
C. 14
D. 20
E. 40

GO ON TO THE NEXT PAGE.

2 △ △ △ △ △ △ △ △ △ 2

DO YOUR FIGURING HERE.

26. For all nonzero values of a and b, the value of which of the following expressions is *always* negative?

F. $a - b$
G. $-a - b$
H. $|a| + |b|$
J. $|a| - |b|$
K. $-|a| - |b|$

27. Graphed in the same standard (x,y) coordinate plane are a circle and a parabola. The circle has radius 3 and center (0,0). The parabola has vertex (−3,−2), has a vertical axis of symmetry, and passes through (−2,−1). The circle and the parabola intersect at how many points?

A. 0
B. 1
C. 2
D. 3
E. 4

28. 40% of 250 is equal to 60% of what number?

F. 150
G. 160
H. $166\frac{2}{3}$
J. 270
K. 375

29. Which of the following inequalities is equivalent to $-2x - 6y > 2y - 4$?

A. $x < -4y + 2$
B. $x > -4y + 2$
C. $x < 2y + 2$
D. $x < 4y + 2$
E. $x > 4y + 2$

GO ON TO THE NEXT PAGE.

2          2

DO YOUR FIGURING HERE.

30. For an angle with measure α in a right triangle, $\sin \alpha = \frac{40}{41}$ and $\tan \alpha = \frac{40}{9}$. What is the value of $\cos \alpha$?

F. $\frac{9}{41}$
G. $\frac{41}{9}$
H. $\frac{9}{40}$
J. $\frac{9}{\sqrt{1{,}519}}$
K. $\frac{9}{\sqrt{3{,}281}}$

31. The perimeter of rectangle $ABCD$ is 96 cm. The ratio of the side lengths $AB{:}BC$ is 3:5. What is the length, in centimeters, of $\overline{AB}$?

A. 6
B. 18
C. 30
D. 36
E. 60

32. For $\triangle ABC$ shown below, base $\overline{AC}$ has a length of 16 inches and altitude $\overline{BD}$ has a length of 8 inches. The area of a certain square is equal to the area of $\triangle ABC$. What is the length, in inches, of a side of the square?

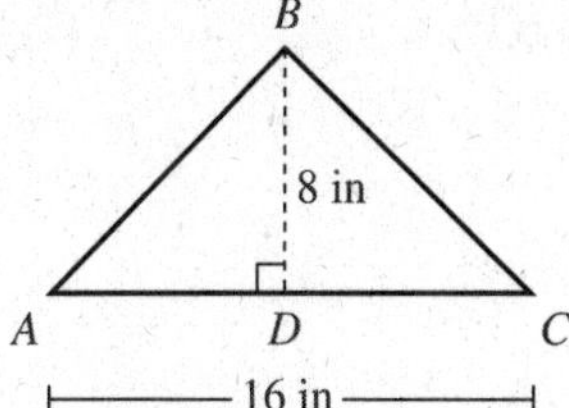

F. 6
G. 8
H. 12
J. 16
K. 32

Your First Practice Test

GO ON TO THE NEXT PAGE.

2 △ △ △ △ △ △ △ △ △ 2

DO YOUR FIGURING HERE.

Use the following information to answer questions 33–36.

In the figure shown below, $ABCD$ is a rectangle, $EFGH$ is a square, and $\overline{CD}$ is the diameter of a semicircle. Point K is the midpoint of $\overline{CD}$. Point J is the midpoint of both $\overline{AB}$ and $\overline{EF}$. Points E and F lie on $\overline{AB}$. The 3 given lengths are in meters.

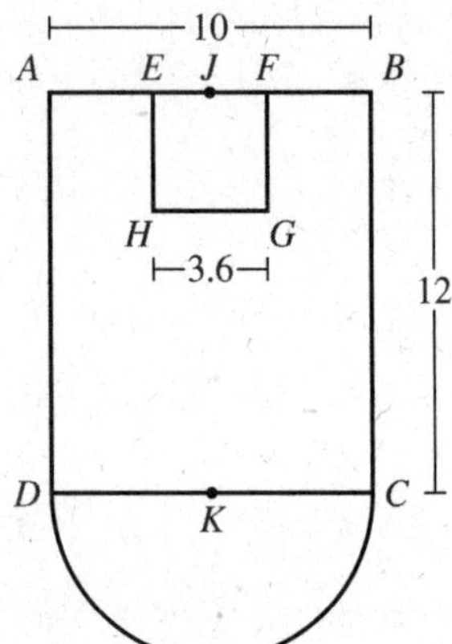

33. The length of $\overline{EH}$ is what percent of the length of $\overline{AD}$?
    - **A.** 15.6%
    - **B.** 30%
    - **C.** 36%
    - **D.** 43.2%
    - **E.** 50%

34. What is the length, in meters, of $\overline{JD}$?
    - **F.** 13
    - **G.** 15.6
    - **H.** 17
    - **J.** $\sqrt{44}$
    - **K.** $\sqrt{244}$

35. What is the length, in meters, of arc $\overset{\frown}{CD}$?
    - **A.** 2.5π
    - **B.** 5π
    - **C.** 6.25π
    - **D.** 10π
    - **E.** 25π

36. The figure will be placed in the standard (x,y) coordinate plane so that K is at the origin, $\overline{AB}$ is parallel to the x-axis, and 1 meter equals 1 coordinate unit. Which of the following values could be the y-coordinate of H ?
    - **F.** 1.8
    - **G.** 3.6
    - **H.** 8.4
    - **J.** 10
    - **K.** 12

GO ON TO THE NEXT PAGE.

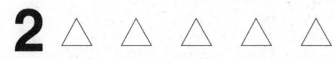

2 △ △ △ △ △ △ △ △ △ 2

DO YOUR FIGURING HERE.

37. What is the length, in coordinate units, of the altitude from C to $\overline{AB}$ in $\triangle ABC$ shown in the standard (x,y) coordinate plane below?

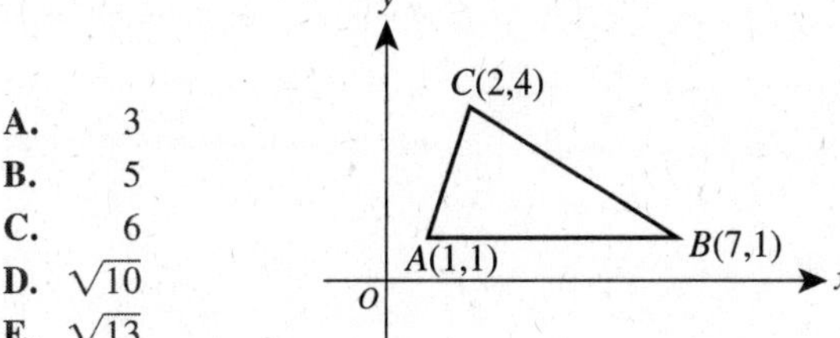

A. 3
B. 5
C. 6
D. $\sqrt{10}$
E. $\sqrt{13}$

38. At a local post office, on average, 3 customers are in line when the post office closes each day. The probability, P, that exactly n customers are in line when the post office closes can be modeled by the equation $P = \frac{3^n e^{-3}}{n!}$. Given that $e^{-3} \approx 0.05$, which of the following values is closest to the probability that exactly 2 customers are in line when the post office closes?

F. 0.08
G. 0.11
H. 0.15
J. 0.23
K. 0.45

39. What is the amplitude of the function $f(x) = \frac{1}{2}\cos(3x + \pi)$?

A. $\frac{1}{3}$
B. $\frac{1}{2}$
C. $\frac{3}{2}$
D. 2
E. 3

40. License plates on cars in a certain state consist of 3 letters taken from the 26 letters, A through Z, followed by 3 digits taken from the 10 digits, 0 through 9. Which of the following expressions gives the number of distinct license plates that are possible given that repetition of both letters and digits is allowed?

F. $10^3 \cdot 26^3$
G. $(10 + 26)^3$
H. $2(26!)^3(10!)^3$
J. $(3 + 3)^{26 + 10}$
K. $(26! \cdot 10!)^3 + (26! \cdot 10!)^3$

GO ON TO THE NEXT PAGE.

2 △ △ △ △ △ △ △ △  2

DO YOUR FIGURING HERE.

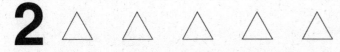

41. For 20 quiz scores in a typing class, the table below gives the frequency of the scores in each score interval. Which score interval contains the median of the scores?

Score interval	Frequency
96–100	3
91–95	1
86–90	3
81–85	4
76–80	9

A. 96–100
B. 91–95
C. 86–90
D. 81–85
E. 76–80

42. In the complex numbers, where $i^2 = -1$,
$\frac{1}{1+i} \cdot \frac{1-i}{1-i} = ?$

F. $i - 1$

G. $1 + i$

H. $1 - i$

J. $\frac{1-i}{2}$

K. $\frac{1+i}{2}$

43. Temperatures measured in degrees Fahrenheit (F) are related to temperatures measured in degrees Celsius (C) by the formula $F = \frac{9}{5}C + 32$. There is 1 value of x for which x degrees Fahrenheit equals x degrees Celsius. What is that value?

A. −72
B. −40
C. −32
D. 0
E. 32

GO ON TO THE NEXT PAGE.

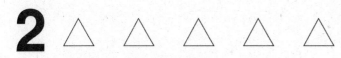

2 △ △ △ △ △ △ △ △ △ 2

44. The table below gives experimental data values for variables x and y. Theory predicts that y varies directly with x. Based on the experimental data, which of the following values is closest to the constant of variation?

(Note: The variable y varies directly with the variable x provided that $y = kx$ for some nonzero constant k, called the *constant of variation.*)

x	y
2.75	0.140
8.50	0.425
14.75	0.750
16.75	0.850
21.00	1.050

F. −2.61
G. 0.05
H. 3.61
J. 15.90
K. 20.00

DO YOUR FIGURING HERE.

Your First Practice Test

45. During a snowstorm, the relationship between the depth of accumulated snow, y inches, and the elapsed time, x hours, was modeled by the equation $2x - 5y = -5$. One of the following graphs in the standard (x,y) coordinate plane models the equation for positive values of x and y. Which one?

A.
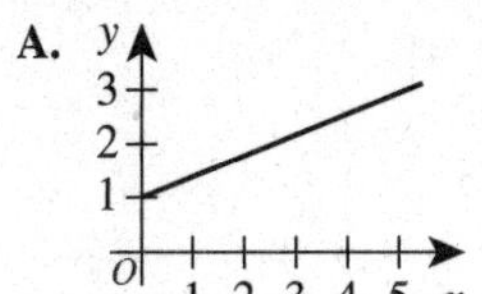

B.
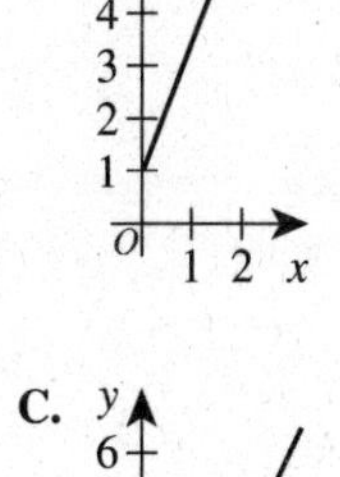

C.
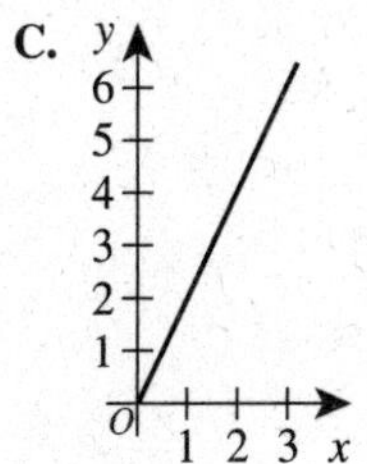

D.
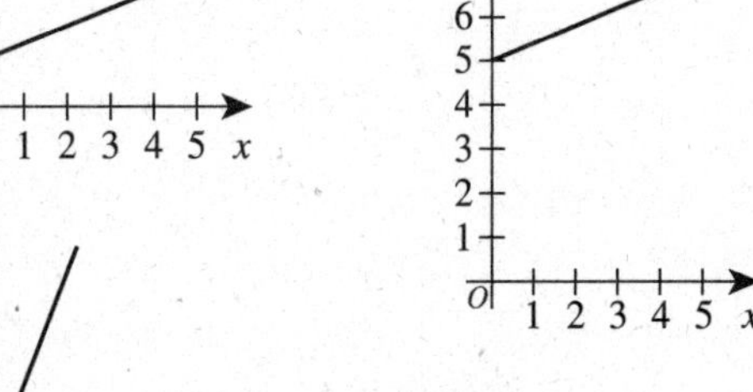

E.
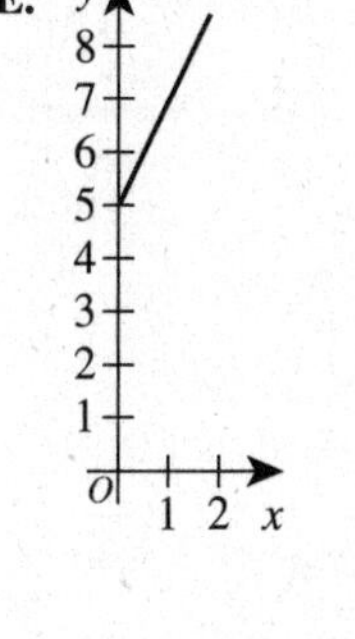

GO ON TO THE NEXT PAGE.

2 △ △ △ △ △ △ △ △ △ 2

DO YOUR FIGURING HERE.

46. Diana is baking bread, and the original recipe calls for $1\frac{1}{2}$ teaspoons of yeast and $2\frac{1}{2}$ cups of flour. Diana will use the entire contents of a packet that contains $2\frac{1}{4}$ teaspoons of yeast and will use the same ratio of ingredients called for in the original recipe. How many cups of flour will Diana use?

F. $1\frac{7}{8}$

G. $3\frac{1}{4}$

H. $3\frac{1}{2}$

J. $3\frac{3}{4}$

K. 4

47. For all nonzero values of x, $\frac{12x^6 - 9x^2}{3x^2} = ?$

A. $4x^3 - 3x$
B. $4x^3 - 3$
C. $4x^4 - 9x^2$
D. $4x^4 - 3x$
E. $4x^4 - 3$

48. Four matrices are given below.

$$W = \begin{bmatrix} 1 & 2 \\ 5 & 8 \end{bmatrix} \quad X = \begin{bmatrix} 3 & 9 \\ 7 & 4 \end{bmatrix} \quad Y = \begin{bmatrix} 1 & 3 & 7 \\ 4 & 2 & 6 \end{bmatrix} \quad Z = \begin{bmatrix} 5 & 8 \\ 2 & 9 \\ 3 & 7 \end{bmatrix}$$

Which of the following matrix products is undefined?

F. WX
G. WY
H. YZ
J. XW
K. XZ

GO ON TO THE NEXT PAGE.

2 △ △ △ △ △ △ △ △ △ 2

49. The 3 parabolas graphed in the standard (x,y) coordinate plane below are from a family of parabolas. A general equation that defines this family of parabolas contains the variable n in addition to x and y. For one of the parabolas shown, $n = 1$; for another, $n = 2$; and for the third, $n = 3$. Which of the following could be a general equation that defines this family of parabolas for all $n \geq 1$?

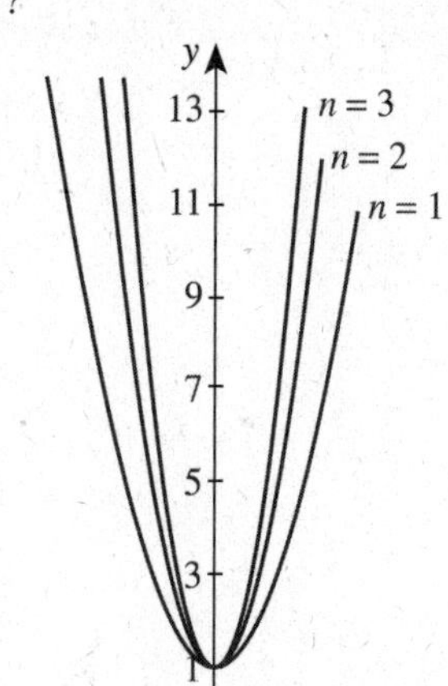

A. $y = nx^2 + 1$

B. $y = \frac{1}{n}x^2 + 1$

C. $y = x^2 + n$

D. $y = -nx^2 + 1$

E. $y = -\frac{1}{n}x^2 + 1$

DO YOUR FIGURING HERE.

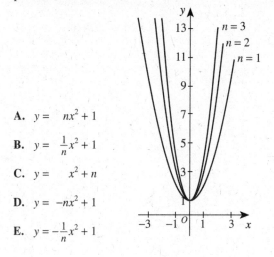

50. After polling a class of 20 music students by a show of hands, you find that 8 students play the guitar and 9 students play the piano. Given that information, what is the minimum number of students in this music class who play both the guitar and the piano?

F. 0
G. 1
H. 8
J. 9
K. 17

51. A teacher assigns each of her 18 students a different integer from 1 through 18. The teacher forms pairs of study partners by using the rule that the sum of the pair of numbers is a perfect square. Assuming the 9 pairs of students follow this rule, the student assigned which number *must* be paired with the student assigned the number 1 ?

A. 16
B. 15
C. 9
D. 8
E. 3

Your First Practice Test

GO ON TO THE NEXT PAGE.

2 △ △ △ △ △ △ △ △ △ 2

DO YOUR FIGURING HERE.

52. Lucky found \$8.25 in pennies, nickels, dimes, and quarters while walking home from school one week. When she deposited this money in the bank, she noticed that she had twice as many nickels as pennies, 1 fewer dime than nickels, and 1 more quarter than nickels. How many quarters did Lucky find that week?

F. 3
G. 9
H. 16
J. 21
K. 26

53. Given $10^{\left(\frac{2x-1}{x}\right)} = 1$, $x = ?$

A. $-\frac{1}{2}$

B. $-\frac{1}{8}$

C. $\frac{1}{2}$

D. $\frac{10}{19}$

E. 1

54. The table below shows the results of a survey of 250 people who were asked whether they like to read and whether they play a musical instrument.

	Play a musical instrument	Do NOT play a musical instrument	Total
Like to read	50	60	110
Do NOT like to read	40	100	140
Total	90	160	250

According to the results, what is the probability that a randomly selected person who was surveyed likes to read, given that the person plays a musical instrument?

F. $\frac{1}{5}$

G. $\frac{5}{9}$

H. $\frac{5}{11}$

J. $\frac{9}{25}$

K. $\frac{11}{25}$

GO ON TO THE NEXT PAGE.

2 △ △ △ △ △ △ △ △ △ 2

DO YOUR FIGURING HERE.

55. Mario was riding a bicycle with wheels 26 inches in diameter. During 1 minute of Mario's ride, the wheels made exactly 200 revolutions. At what average speed, in *feet per second*, was Mario riding during that minute?

A. $\frac{65}{9}\pi$

B. $\frac{65}{18}\pi$

C. $\frac{130}{9}\pi$

D. $\frac{845}{18}\pi$

E. $\frac{1{,}690}{9}\pi$

56. Whenever j and k are positive integers such that $(\sqrt{3})^j = 27^k$, what is the value of $\frac{j}{k}$?

F. $\frac{1}{6}$

G. $\frac{3}{2}$

H. 3

J. 4

K. 6

57. A finite arithmetic sequence has 7 terms, and the first term is $\frac{3}{4}$. What is the difference between the mean and the median of the 7 terms?

A. 0

B. $\frac{3}{4}$

C. $\frac{4}{3}$

D. 3

E. 4

GO ON TO THE NEXT PAGE.

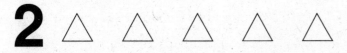

2 △ △ △ △ △ △ △ △ △ 2

DO YOUR FIGURING HERE.

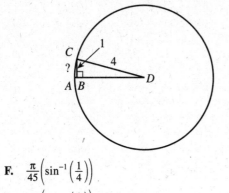

58. In the circle with center D shown below, the length of radius $\overline{CD}$ is 4 cm, the length of $\overline{BC}$ is 1 cm, and $\overline{BC}$ is perpendicular to radius $\overline{AD}$ at B. When $\angle ADC$ is measured in degrees, which of the following expressions represents the length, in centimeters, of $\overset{\frown}{AC}$?

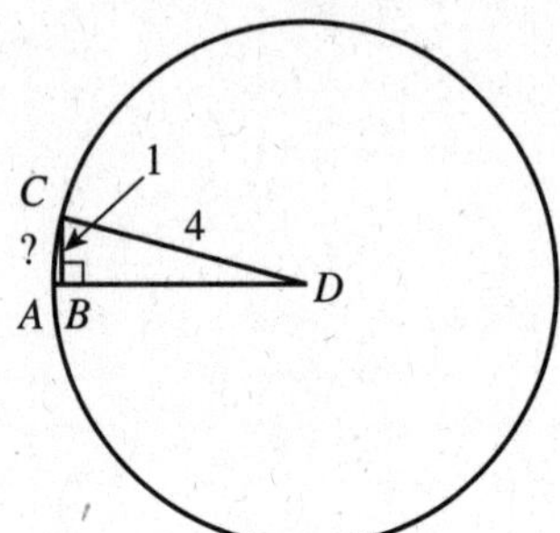

F. $\frac{\pi}{45}\left(\sin^{-1}\left(\frac{1}{4}\right)\right)$

G. $\frac{\pi}{45}\left(\cos^{-1}\left(\frac{1}{4}\right)\right)$

H. $\frac{2\pi}{45}\left(\sin^{-1}\left(\frac{1}{4}\right)\right)$

J. $\frac{2\pi}{45}\left(\cos^{-1}\left(\frac{1}{4}\right)\right)$

K. $\frac{2\pi}{45}\left(\tan^{-1}\left(\frac{1}{4}\right)\right)$

59. The lengths of the triangle shown below are rounded to the nearest 0.1 cm. What is the area, to the nearest 1 cm^2, of this triangle?

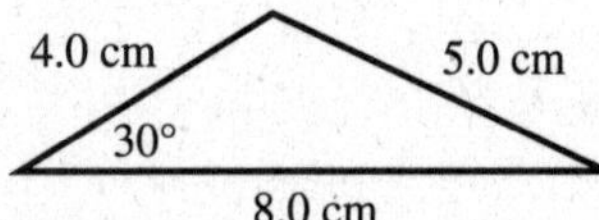

(Note: The area of any triangle with sides of length a, b, and c opposite angles of measure A, B, and C, respectively, is given by $\frac{1}{2}ab \sin C$.)

A. 4
B. 5
C. 8
D. 10
E. 14

GO ON TO THE NEXT PAGE.

2 △ △ △ △ △ △ △ △ △ 2

60. The probability distribution of the discrete random variable X is shown in the table below. What is the expected value of X ?

x	Probability $P(X = x)$
0	$\frac{1}{6}$
1	$\frac{1}{12}$
2	$\frac{1}{4}$
3	$\frac{1}{12}$
4	$\frac{1}{12}$
5	0
6	$\frac{1}{3}$

F. $\frac{1}{6}$

G. $\frac{1}{3}$

H. 1

J. 2

K. $3\frac{1}{6}$

DO YOUR FIGURING HERE.

END OF TEST 2

STOP! DO NOT TURN THE PAGE UNTIL TOLD TO DO SO.

DO NOT RETURN TO THE PREVIOUS TEST.

3 3

READING TEST

35 Minutes—40 Questions

DIRECTIONS: There are several passages in this test. Each passage is accompanied by several questions. After reading a passage, choose the best answer to each question and fill in the corresponding oval on your answer document. You may refer to the passages as often as necessary.

Passage I

LITERARY NARRATIVE: This passage is adapted from the novel *A Map of Home* by Randa Jarrar (©2008 by Randa Jarrar).

I don't remember how I came to know this story, and I don't know how I can possibly still remember it. On August 2, the day I was born, my *baba* (father) stood at the nurses' station of St. Elizabeth's Medical Center of Boston with a pen between his fingers and filled out my birth certificate. He had raced down the stairs seconds after my birth, as soon as the doctor had assured him that I was all right. While filling out my certificate, Baba realized that he didn't know my sex for sure but that didn't matter; he'd always known I was a boy, had spoken to me as a boy while I was in Mama, and as he approached the box that contained the question, NAME OF CHILD, he wrote with a quivering hand and in his best English cursive, Nidal (strife; struggle). It was not my grandfather's name, and Baba, whose name is Waheed and who was known during his childhood as Said, was the only son of the family, so the onus of renaming a son after my grandfather fell squarely upon his shoulders. It was an onus he brushed off his then-solid shoulders unceremoniously, like a piece of lint or a flake of dandruff; these are analogies my grandfather would the next day angrily pen in a letter sent from Jenin to Boston.

When he'd filled out the entire form, Baba regally relayed it to the nurse, who he remembers was called Rhonda. Then Baba, in flip-flops, turned around and raced up the white-tiled hallway, bypassed the elevator, ran up the three floors to the maternity ward, and burst into the birthing room.

"How is my queen?" said Baba, caressing my mother's face.

"She's lovely," Mama said, thinking he meant me, "and eight whole pounds, the buffalo! No wonder my back was so . . . " Baba's brow furrowed, and Mama couldn't finish her complaint, because, eager to correct his mistake, Baba was already out the door and running down the white-tiled hallway, past new mothers and their red-faced babies, past hideous robes in uncalled-for patterns, bypassing the elevator, and sliding down the banister of the staircase. He raced on, screaming for Rhonda, where is Rhonda, help me, Rhonda, an outcry that provided the staff with three weeks' worth of laughter.

Rhonda emerged with the birth certificate in hand, and Baba, who is not usually known for laziness, grabbed a pen and added at the end of my name a heavy, reflexive, feminizing, possessive, cursive "I."

Moments later, Mama, who had just been informed of my *nom de guerre*, got out of bed and walked us to the elevator, the entire time ignoring my baba, who was screaming, "Nidali is a beautiful name, so unique, come on Ruz, don't be so rash, you mustn't be walking, you need to rest!"

Mama must not have fought long, or who knows: maybe she went to the nurses' station and talked to Rhonda, and maybe Rhonda told her that the birth certificate was already sent out—that Mama would have to go to the office of the City of Boston clerk and see the registrar of vital statistics, where they keep the birth *and* death certificates—and maybe Mama, who is the most superstitious of all humans (even more than Baba, and to that she'll attest) shuddered at the thought of taking me, a newborn, through the heat and the Boston traffic to a place where, she must've imagined, people went to fill out death certificates, and she must've further imagined that going on such a trip, to such a place, would surely bring about my death—because I still have my name.

Whenever I imagined Baba running out just after my birth and sliding through the hallways like a movie star, I knew he must have embellished. Baba liked to do that: tell stories that were impossible but true all at once, especially if those stories made him look like a rock star. This is because he used to be a writer and was now an architect. Our little apartment was filled with blueprints and plastic models of houses instead of notebooks and poetry: a reality that filled him with great sadness. So Baba put that sadness into these stories.

Mama liked to expose him when he told such stories; she was his paparazzo, his story-cop. This was because she was the true rock star: a musician who no longer played music. Our house was filled with Baba's blueprints and plastic models of houses and with my schoolwork and toys and dolls and a hundred half pairs of socks instead of a piano: a reality that filled her with great sadness.

I knew from the beginning that home meant embellishing, and that's why I loved school. Teachers were there; they taught us facts based on reality.

GO ON TO THE NEXT PAGE.

3 3

1. The point of view from which the passage is told is best described as that of:
   A. a first person narrator who re-creates a story about her parents and the birth of their first child, events which happened before the narrator was born.
   B. a first person narrator who offers insight into characters' thoughts and relates actions mainly from a time she was too young to remember.
   C. an omniscient third person narrator who relates the thoughts and actions of several characters.
   D. a limited third person narrator who relates events most closely from the perspective of Nidali.

2. The narrator mentions a piece of lint and a flake of dandruff primarily to:
   F. imply that the narrator's grandfather didn't value family traditions.
   G. provide examples of movements Baba made while filling out the birth certificate.
   H. emphasize the importance of naming the baby after the baby's grandfather.
   J. illustrate the casual way in which the narrator's father ignored a tradition.

3. Based on the passage, Mama's reaction to learning the name Baba gave the baby can best be described as:
   A. disapproval followed by resignation.
   B. annoyance followed by amusement.
   C. embarrassment followed by outrage.
   D. shock followed by resentment.

4. The sequence of actions described in the seventh paragraph (lines 54–68) can best be characterized as:
   F. Baba's exaggerated account of Mama's trip to the office of the City of Boston clerk.
   G. a scenario the narrator imagines could have happened.
   H. the story of how Nidali got her name from Mama's point of view.
   J. a memory that the narrator shares to reveal more about her personality.

5. The narrator concludes that Mama didn't go to the office of the City of Boston clerk based on the fact that:
   A. Baba believed it would be unlucky to change a baby's name at that point.
   B. going there would've required taking the baby out in a severe winter storm.
   C. Mama had a tendency to change her mind quickly.
   D. the narrator still has the name Nidali.

6. In line 78, the phrase *these stories* most nearly refers to:
   F. the conflicting stories about the origins of Nidali's name.
   G. Baba's notebooks and poetry.
   H. the embellished tales Baba liked to tell.
   J. the narrator's accounts of her family's time in Boston.

7. According to the passage, which of the following emotions do Baba and Mama share regarding their professional lives?
   A. Pride
   B. Anxiety
   C. Sadness
   D. Contentment

8. Of the following characters, which one does the narrator describe as the most superstitious?
   F. Mama
   G. Baba
   H. Nidali
   J. Rhonda

9. The narrator most strongly suggests that Mama does which of the following when Baba tells stories?
   A. Yawns and rolls her eyes in mock boredom
   B. Goes about her business and ignores him
   C. Chimes in with exaggerations and white lies
   D. Corrects him about the accuracy of details

10. In the passage, the narrator makes which of the following distinctions?
   F. Home is a place of embellished stories, whereas school is a place of facts and reality.
   G. Mama is a true rock star, whereas Baba is an amateur musician.
   H. Being an architect made Baba happy, whereas being a writer made him miserable.
   J. Writing requires great imagination, whereas playing music requires great skill.

GO ON TO THE NEXT PAGE.

3 3

Passage II

SOCIAL SCIENCE: Passage A is adapted from the book *Seabiscuit: An American Legend* by Laura Hillenbrand (©2001 by Laura Hillenbrand). Passage B is adapted from the article "The Flop Heard Round the World" by Peter Carlson (©2007 by The Washington Post).

Passage A by Laura Hillenbrand

The horseless carriage was just arriving in San Francisco, and its debut was turning into one of those colorfully unmitigated disasters that bring misery to everyone but historians. Consumers were staying away from the "devilish contraptions" in droves. In San Francisco in 1903, the horse and buggy was not going the way of the horse and buggy.

For good reason. The automobile, so sleekly efficient on paper, was in practice a civic menace, belching out exhaust, kicking up storms of dust, becoming hopelessly mired in the most innocuous-looking puddles, and tying up horse traffic. Incensed local lawmakers responded with monuments to legislative creativity. The laws of at least one town required automobile drivers to stop, get out, and fire off Roman candles every time horse-drawn vehicles came into view. Massachusetts tried and, fortunately, failed to mandate that cars be equipped with bells that would ring with each revolution of the wheels. In some towns police were authorized to disable passing cars with ropes, chains, and wires. San Francisco didn't escape the legislative wave. Bitter local officials pushed through an ordinance banning automobiles from all tourist areas, effectively exiling them from the city.

Nor were these the only obstacles. The asking price for the cheapest automobile amounted to twice the $500 annual salary of the average citizen—some cost three times that much—and all that bought you was four wheels, a body, and an engine. "Accessories" like bumpers, carburetors, and headlights had to be purchased separately. Navigation was a nightmare. The first of San Francisco's road signs were only just being erected, hammered up by an enterprising insurance underwriter who hoped to win clients by posting directions into the countryside, where drivers retreated for automobile "picnic parties" held out of the view of angry townsfolk.

The first automobiles imported to San Francisco had so little power that they rarely made it up the hills. The grade of Nineteenth Avenue was so daunting for the engines of the day that watching automobiles straining for the top became a local pastime.

Passage B by Peter Carlson

In the mid-1950s, Ford Motor Company was building not one, not two, but 18 varieties of Edsel, including a convertible and a station wagon. The designers came up with some interesting ideas. They created a push-button transmission and put it in the middle of the steering wheel, where most cars have a horn. And they fiddled with the front end: Where other cars had horizontal chrome grilles, the Edsel would have a vertical chrome oval in its grille. It was new! It was different!

Unfortunately, it didn't work. It couldn't suck in enough air to cool the engine. "They had to keep opening up that oval to get more air in there," says Jim Arnold, who was a trainee in Edsel's design shop. "And it didn't look as good."

Edsel didn't have its own assembly lines, so the cars were produced in Ford and Mercury plants, which caused problems. Every once in a while, an Edsel would roll past workers who were used to Mercurys or other Fords. Confused, they sometimes failed to install all the parts before the Edsel moved on down the line. Cars without parts can be a problem, of course, but other aspects of the Edsel juggernaut worked perfectly—the hype, for instance. The Edsel PR team touted the glories of the cars, but wouldn't let anybody see them. When they finally released a photo, it turned out to be a picture of . . . the Edsel's hood ornament. And hundreds of publications actually printed it!

On September 4, 1957, proclaimed by Ford as E-Day, nearly 3 million Americans flocked to showrooms to see the Edsel. Unfortunately, very few of them bought the Edsel. "We couldn't even get people to drive it," says C. Gayle Warnock, Edsel's public relations director. "They just didn't like the car. They just didn't like the front end."

But styling was hardly the worst problem. Oil pans fell off, trunks stuck, paint peeled, doors failed to close and the much-hyped "Teletouch" push-button transmission had a distressing tendency to freeze up. People joked that Edsel stood for "Every day something else leaks."

Another major problem was caused by bad luck: The Edsel was an upscale car launched a couple months after a stock market plunge caused a recession. Sales of all premium cars plummeted.

Before E-Day, Edsel's hypemeisters promised to sell 200,000 cars the first year. Actually, they sold 63,110. Sales dropped below 45,000 the second year. And only 2,846 of the 1960 models sold before Ford pulled the plug.

GO ON TO THE NEXT PAGE.

3 3

Questions 11–13 ask about Passage A.

11. Which of the following statements about automobiles in San Francisco in 1903 is best supported by Passage A?

A. They were affordable for the average citizen but unpopular nevertheless.
B. They were used more by tourists for sightseeing purposes than by citizens for practical purposes.
C. They failed to capture the public imagination in spite of huge public relations efforts.
D. They were considered a public nuisance by all but a small segment of the population.

12. Which of the following terms in Passage A is used more figuratively than literally?

F. Puddles (line 11)
G. Monuments (line 13)
H. Bells (line 18)
J. Hills (line 39)

13. The purpose of the quotation marks around the word *accessories* in line 29 is most likely to:

A. suggest that the features were actually essentials.
B. indicate that the word appeared in legal documents.
C. emphasize that the word was widely misunderstood.
D. clarify that inexpensive automobiles had some luxury features.

Questions 14–17 ask about Passage B.

14. Which of the following statements best captures how Passage B characterizes the failure of the Edsel?

F. It happened gradually and went unnoticed at the time by the public.
G. It happened quickly despite promising initial sales.
H. It was on a huge scale, occurred swiftly, and was a public event of sorts.
J. It occurred when other automakers were doing well and therefore embarrassed Ford all the more.

15. The statement in lines 43–45 is typical of Passage B in the way it:

A. contrasts data about the Edsel with data about other cars of the 1950s.
B. conveys the obligation that Ford executives felt to involve consumers in the design of the Edsel.
C. combines an industry perspective on the Edsel with that of the typical consumer.
D. suggests the entire Edsel enterprise was marked by extremes.

16. Which of the following events referred to in Passage B occurred first chronologically?

F. E-Day ended.
G. The stock market plunged.
H. Edsel sales dropped below 45,000.
J. Edsel sales reached 2,846.

17. As it is used in the passage, the term *premium cars* (line 86) serves primarily as a:

A. reference to what Edsels have become now that they are valued antiques.
B. name for a type of car that was ushered in by the makers of the Edsel.
C. label for a category of cars that the makers of the Edsel intended it to belong to.
D. derisive term used sarcastically by Edsel owners who were disappointed in their purchase.

Questions 18–20 ask about both passages.

18. A similarity between the two passages is that they both:

F. examine their topics from a significant distance of time.
G. reveal the author's professional background as a way of lending credibility to the text.
H. assert that automobiles have contributed little that is worthwhile to society.
J. incorporate information about traffic and road conditions into a discussion of automobile design.

19. An element of Passage A that is not present in Passage B is a reference to what aspect of the automobile culture?

A. Related legislation
B. Public opinion
C. Economics
D. Quotations from industry experts

20. If publicity experts had been assigned to build enthusiasm for the cars mentioned in Passage A using the methods described in Passage B, the experts would most likely have first released photos to the press that showed:

F. cars going up Nineteenth Avenue in San Francisco.
G. a single detail such as a gleaming headlight or a polished door handle.
H. the meticulous work done along the assembly line to ensure the quality of the new car.
J. an attractive young couple smiling as they enjoy a car ride past horses grazing in pastures.

GO ON TO THE NEXT PAGE.

3 3

Passage III

HUMANITIES: This passage is adapted from the article "Winslow Homer: His Melancholy Truth" by John A. Parks (©2006 by VNU Business Media).

The images in the paintings of Winslow Homer epitomize a peculiarly American 19th-century world. Through Homer's eyes, it is a world in which people live in close contact with nature and natural forces, a world where landscape and ocean are viewed not as a paradise but as powers and presences that can be enjoyed and whose threats can sometimes be overcome. And, particularly in his later paintings, it is a world imbued with a stark and melancholy atmosphere.

In 1867, two of Homer's canvases were chosen to hang at the Great Exposition in Paris. The artist spent 10 months in the city, which later proved to have a profound effect on his art. A large display of Japanese prints was exhibited in the same building as his own paintings, and the process of simplification that it revealed and the wealth of pictorial invention it provided made a deep impression on the artist. The influence of Japanese art on Homer's painting was immediately apparent upon his return to the United States. The weakness of earlier compositions is replaced by a boldness and lucidity in which simple shapes are massed into powerful designs.

Although Homer's work of the 1870s gained strength, the artist continued to paint his genre subjects: tourist scenes, schoolchildren, and farm life. It wasn't until 1881, however, that he found the subject matter that would inspire him most. In that year, for reasons unknown, Homer went to England, where he elected to spend the summer at the town of Tynemouth on the coast of the North Sea. It is possible that he was searching for a town filled with the type of tourists and bathers that made his paintings of the Jersey shore successful back home. But Tynemouth was also a community of fishermen who wrested their livelihood from the dangerous and unpredictable waters of the North Sea. Moreover, the light and weather in that part of the world, so much farther north than Atlantic City, is much gloomier and more dramatic than that of the Jersey coast. It was there that Homer became enthralled by the dramas of the people who make their living from the ocean: the fishermen's wives staring out to sea as they wait for their men, the launch of the lifeboat to rescue sailors from a foundering ship, the agonizingly fragile fishing boats being tossed on angry waves. Here at last was a subject matter that matched the artist's deepest feelings. The dynamic and dangerous relationship between human activity and natural forces exposed in this setting would occupy Homer for many years to come. On his return to America he elected to leave New York and relocate to the rural town of Prouts Neck, Maine.

The legend of Winslow Homer is that he left New York civilization to become a recluse on the coast of Maine for the last 25 years of his life. In reality, the property at Prouts Neck—which included a large, rambling hotel building—was purchased by his brother Charles for the whole extended Homer family. The artist also built a studio with an ocean view just yards away from the family house so throughout the summers he could enjoy the company of his father, his brothers and their wives, as well as the year-round guests of the many local people whose friendship he valued. Homer continued to travel frequently, spending parts of the winter in the Caribbean. But the artist always lived alone, and when he was working, which was the large part of most of his days, he could be extremely short-tempered when interrupted.

The sea outside his window now inspired the artist to create what came to be known as his greatest paintings. The Maine coast is extremely rocky and prone to monstrous gales that—at their most powerful—can whip up the waves to 40 or 50 feet. Screaming winds can rip across the breakers, creating long horizontal trails of spray. Homer rendered this sea with all the understanding of a painter who knows to simplify and synthesize. In paintings such as *Eastern Point* and *Cannon Rock* the construction of the water has been reorganized into clear graphic shapes and strong directional lines that echo the Japanese printmaking that had such a lasting effect on his work. The rocks in the paintings are massed into powerful, almost flat, designs and the brushing has become energetic, as though feeding from the physical strength of the ocean. These paintings take on an abstract grandeur that has justly made them famous. They remain, however, haunting evocations of the eternal power of the ocean.

21. The main purpose of the passage is to:

A. describe an artist's most famous painting and the experience that inspired it.
B. explore the relationship between the natural world and the fine arts.
C. provide an overview of an artist's career and important influences on that artist's work.
D. describe the work of artists who epitomized a peculiarly American nineteenth-century world.

22. It can reasonably be inferred from the passage that which of the following scenes would most likely be the subject of a painting created by Homer late in his life?

F. A family strolling along the boardwalk in Atlantic City
G. A fishing boat being violently pitched about on a stormy ocean
H. A farm nestled in the idyllic countryside
J. A tourist sipping coffee at a Parisian café

GO ON TO THE NEXT PAGE.

23. Based on the passage, the way Homer depicted shapes in his early work and the way he depicted them in his later work is best described as shifting from:
    A. weak to powerful.
    B. sharp to rounded.
    C. dark to light.
    D. uplifting to melancholy.

24. According to the passage, Homer felt fascination for the subjects that inspired him at Tynemouth for a:
    F. short time; Homer soon abandoned them for the genre subjects he'd been painting previously.
    G. short time; Homer found little commercial success painting those subjects.
    H. long time; Homer regularly returned to Tynemouth to paint.
    J. long time; Homer continued to be inspired by what he saw there for years.

25. According to the passage, the paintings that Tynemouth inspired Homer to create mainly featured:
    A. scenes of tourists and sunbathers enjoying the beach.
    B. the interplay between the sea and the lives of fishermen and their families.
    C. the dynamic struggle between farmers and the powerful forces of nature.
    D. the soothing yet dramatic beauty of the North Sea and its rocky shoreline.

26. The passage most strongly suggests that the main turning point in the development of Homer as an artist was his:
    F. discovery of subject matter that profoundly inspired him.
    G. sense of accomplishment at having paintings displayed at the Great Exposition.
    H. decision to spend winters in the Caribbean, where he was inspired by the sea.
    J. rejection of the belief that the world was stark and melancholy.

27. The author characterizes the immediate effect of experiences in Paris upon Homer's work as:
    A. subtle; Homer continued to paint simple shapes and powerful designs but used more color.
    B. dramatic; Homer's work became bolder and clearer.
    C. imperceptible; Homer's work didn't change until several years later.
    D. significant; Homer abandoned the subjects he'd been painting before his time in Paris.

28. The main idea of the last paragraph is that:
    F. Homer's paintings of the Maine coast exhibit the culmination of his artistic skills.
    G. Homer's paintings of the sea evoke the grandeur of the human spirit in the natural world.
    H. the most effective way to depict water in a painting is to use graphic shapes and directional lines.
    J. viewing two of Homer's famous paintings of the sea had a lasting effect on the author.

29. The author speculates that Homer may have chosen to go to Tynemouth because he:
    A. wanted to return to the place that had originally inspired him to be a painter.
    B. expected to be able to work better without the distractions he struggled with in Paris.
    C. needed a break from the overcrowded Jersey coast.
    D. hoped to find the kinds of subjects he had depicted in some of his earlier popular paintings.

30. The passage states that in Prouts Neck, Homer could be irritable when:
    F. his paintings weren't selling well.
    G. storms prevented him from painting outdoors.
    H. the sea was too rough to go boating.
    J. he was interrupted while painting.

GO ON TO THE NEXT PAGE.

3 3

Passage IV

NATURAL SCIENCE: This passage is adapted from the article "Worlds Apart: Seeking New Earths" by Timothy Ferris (©2009 by National Geographic Society).

It took humans thousands of years to explore our own planet and centuries to comprehend our neighboring planets, but nowadays new worlds are being discovered every week. To date, astronomers have identified more than 370 "exoplanets," worlds orbiting stars other than the sun. Many are strange. There's an Icarus-like "hot Saturn" 260 light-years from Earth, whirling around its parent star so rapidly that a year there lasts less than three days. Circling another star 150 light-years out is a scorched "hot Jupiter," whose upper atmosphere is being blasted off to form a gigantic, comet-like tail. Three benighted planets have been found orbiting a pulsar—the remains of a once mighty star shrunk into a spinning atomic nucleus the size of a city—while untold numbers of worlds have evidently fallen into their suns or been flung out of their systems to become "floaters" that wander in eternal darkness.

Amid such exotica, scientists are eager for a hint of the familiar: planets resembling Earth, orbiting their stars at just the right distance—neither too hot nor too cold—to support life as we know it. No planets quite like our own have yet been found, presumably because they're inconspicuous. To see a planet as small and dim as ours amid the glare of its star is like trying to see a firefly in a fireworks display; to detect its gravitational influence on the star is like listening for a cricket in a tornado. Yet by pushing technology to the limits, astronomers are rapidly approaching the day when they can find another Earth and interrogate it for signs of life.

Only 11 exoplanets, all of them big and bright and conveniently far away from their stars, have as yet had their pictures taken. Most of the others have been detected by using the spectroscopic Doppler technique, in which starlight is analyzed for evidence that the star is being tugged ever so slightly back and forth by the gravitational pull of its planets. In recent years astronomers have refined the Doppler technique so exquisitely that they can now tell when a star is pulled from its appointed rounds by only one meter a second—about human walking speed. That's sufficient to detect a giant planet in a big orbit, or a small one if it's very close to its star, but not an Earth at anything like our Earth's 93-million-mile distance from its star. The Earth tugs the sun around at only one-tenth walking speed, or about the rate that an infant can crawl; astronomers cannot yet prize out so tiny a signal from the light of a distant star.

Another approach is to watch a star for the slight periodic dip in its brightness that will occur should an orbiting planet circle in front of it and block a fraction of its light. At most a tenth of all planetary systems are likely to be oriented so that these mini-eclipses, called transits, are visible from Earth, which means that astronomers may have to monitor many stars patiently to capture just a few transits. The French COROT satellite, now in the third and final year of its prime mission, has discovered seven transiting exoplanets, one of which is only 70 percent larger than Earth.

The United States' Kepler satellite is COROT's more ambitious successor. Launched from Cape Canaveral in March 2008, Kepler is essentially just a big digital camera with a .95-meter aperture and a 95-megapixel detector. It makes wide-field pictures every 30 minutes, capturing the light of more than 100,000 stars in a single patch of sky between the bright stars Deneb and Vega. Computers on Earth monitor the brightness of all those stars over time, alerting humans when they detect the slight dimming that could signal the transit of a planet.

Because that dimming can be mimicked by other phenomena, such as the pulsations of a variable star or a large sunspot moving across a star's surface, the Kepler scientists won't announce the presence of a planet until they have seen it transit at least three times—a wait that may be only a few days or weeks for a planet rapidly circling close to its star but years for a terrestrial twin. By combining Kepler results with Doppler observations, astronomers expect to determine the diameters and masses of transiting planets. If they manage to discover a rocky planet roughly the size of Earth orbiting in the habitable zone—not so close to the star that the planet's water has been baked away, nor so far out that it has frozen into ice—they will have found what biologists believe could be a promising abode for life.

31. Which of the following descriptions best reflects the way the passage is organized?

- **A.** It raises the question of whether exoplanets exist and then presents to an equal extent arguments on both sides.
- **B.** It focuses first on the search for planets, then sharpens that focus to the search for planets like our own.
- **C.** It defines planets, first those in Earth's solar system and then those familiar mostly to astronomers.
- **D.** It refers to mythology, then moves to a technical description of those exoplanets the size of Earth or smaller.

32. The passage makes use of both technical terms and:

- **F.** rhetorical questions.
- **G.** figurative language.
- **H.** excerpts from the writings of astronauts.
- **J.** excerpts from the writings of ancient astronomers.

GO ON TO THE NEXT PAGE.

3 3

33. As it is used in line 18, the term *such exotica* refers to:

A. the sophisticated equipment used to locate previously unidentified planets.
B. the contents of our solar system, in particular the planets Jupiter and Saturn.
C. overblown claims about planets far from Earth.
D. planets and solar systems vastly unlike Earth and its solar system.

34. What is the main idea of the second paragraph (lines 18–30)?

F. Recently discovered exoplanets have disappointed scientists.
G. Some exoplanets were once thought to be stars at the center of solar systems.
H. Some recently discovered exoplanets spin on their axis at the same speed that Earth spins on its axis.
J. Planets that resemble Earth are extremely hard to detect.

35. The passage's description of the spectroscopic Doppler technique indicates that it is a method used to identify the:

A. intensity of light reaching Earth from a planet outside Earth's solar system.
B. effect of a planet's gravitational pull on the sun the planet is orbiting.
C. speed at which a planet rotates on its axis.
D. distance between an exoplanet and its former sun.

36. According to the passage, in order to confirm a possible planet using the Kepler method, scientists look for:

F. evidence of water both as a solid and a liquid on the supposed planet.
G. an uninterrupted light originating from the supposed planet.
H. identical results in images of the same location taken 24 hours apart.
J. three occurrences of a slight dimming in a star that strongly indicates a planet's presence.

37. According to the passage, at the time the passage was written, how many exoplanets had had their picture taken?

A. 370
B. 95
C. 11
D. 0

38. According to the passage, which of the following is a capability of the Kepler?

F. It can capture the light of more than 100,000 stars in a single patch of sky.
G. It can determine the distance between an exoplanet and its star.
H. It can travel up to 150 light-years away from Earth.
J. It can determine the surface features of planets well enough to indicate the presence of water.

39. In the passage, Deneb and Vega are identified as:

A. stars at the edges of the area examined by the Kepler.
B. planets that are only 70 percent larger than Earth.
C. scientists pioneering in the field of planet searching.
D. former stars whose traveling light is still visible.

40. According to the passage, what do scientists expect to determine about any given transiting planet by combining Kepler results with Doppler observations?

F. The length of its year
G. Its distance from its sun
H. Its diameter and mass
J. Its distance from Earth

END OF TEST 3

STOP! DO NOT TURN THE PAGE UNTIL TOLD TO DO SO.

DO NOT RETURN TO A PREVIOUS TEST.

4 ○ ○ ○ ○ ○ ○ ○ ○ ○ 4

SCIENCE TEST

35 Minutes—40 Questions

DIRECTIONS: There are several passages in this test. Each passage is followed by several questions. After reading a passage, choose the best answer to each question and fill in the corresponding oval on your answer document. You may refer to the passages as often as necessary.

You are NOT permitted to use a calculator on this test.

Passage I

In a study of fur pigmentation in deer mice, *Peromyscus polionotus*, scientists compared the brightness of the fur of mice from populations located different distances directly inland from a coastal site. Figure 1 shows the 2 facial regions and the 2 body regions at which the fur of each mouse was evaluated (on a scale from 0 to 1.00) with respect to its brightness. Figure 1 also shows how, for each of the 4 regions, average relative brightness varied with inland distance.

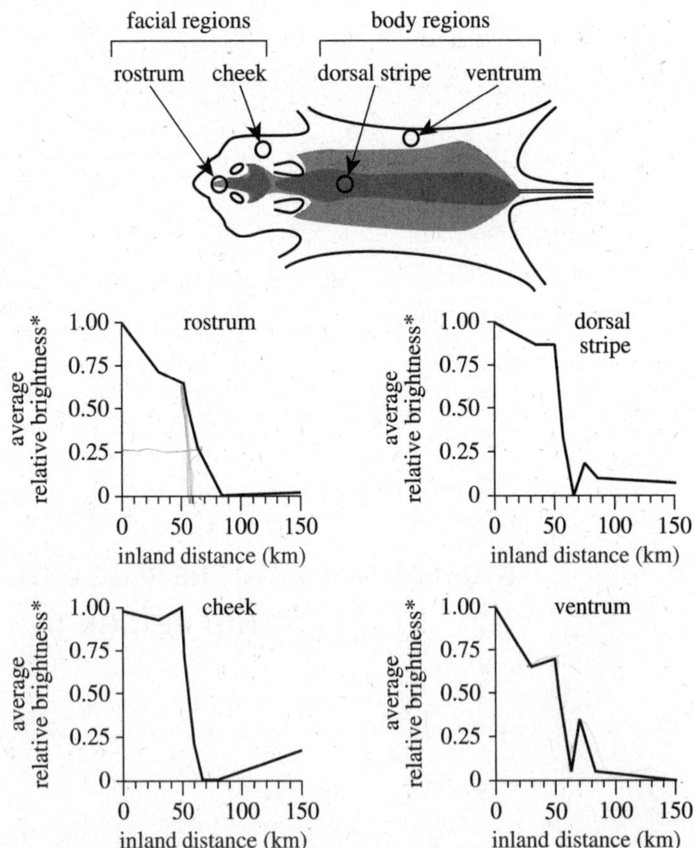

*For each facial or body region, the darkest fur pigmentation was assigned a brightness value of 0, and the lightest fur pigmentation was assigned a brightness value of 1.00.

Figure 1

GO ON TO THE NEXT PAGE.

4 ○ ○ ○ ○ ○ ○ ○ ○ ○ 4

Figure 2 shows how the average brightness of surface soil samples, given as the average percent relative reflectance, varied with inland distance.

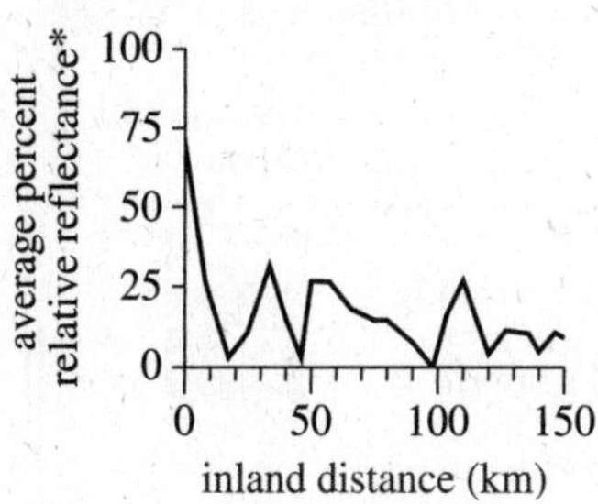

*compared to a standard that was assigned 100% reflectance

Figure 2

Figures 1 and 2 adapted from Lynne M. Mullen and Hopi E. Hoekstra. "Natural Selection Along an Environmental Gradient: A Classic Cline in Mouse Pigmentation." ©2008 by The Author(s).

1. Based on Figure 2, on average, where was the brightest surface soil found?

A. At the coastal site
B. 50 km inland
C. 100 km inland
D. 150 km inland

2. According to Figure 1, the average relative brightness of the dorsal stripe was 0.25 at an inland distance that was closest to which of the following?

F. 20 km
G. 40 km
H. 60 km
J. 80 km

3. According to Figure 1, the greatest change in the average relative brightness of the fur on the rostrum occurred between which of the following inland distances?

A. 0 km and 25 km
B. 25 km and 50 km
C. 50 km and 75 km
D. 100 km and 125 km

4. Based on Figure 1, on average, was the fur pigmentation on the ventrum of *P. polionotus* lighter or darker 150 km inland than it was at the coastal site?

F. Lighter, because the average relative brightness 150 km inland was greater.
G. Lighter, because the average relative brightness 150 km inland was less.
H. Darker, because the average relative brightness 150 km inland was greater.
J. Darker, because the average relative brightness 150 km inland was less.

5. Which of the following statements best explains the geographic variation in the fur pigmentation of *P. polionotus* ? At any given inland distance, the more closely the fur pigmentation of a *P. polionotus* mouse matches the soil, the:

A. less likely the mouse will be found by a predator, and thus the less likely it will pass its fur pigmentation traits to its offspring.
B. less likely the mouse will be found by a predator, and thus the more likely it will pass its fur pigmentation traits to its offspring.
C. more likely the mouse will be found by a predator, and thus the less likely it will pass its fur pigmentation traits to its offspring.
D. more likely the mouse will be found by a predator, and thus the more likely it will pass its fur pigmentation traits to its offspring.

6. Based on Figure 2, on average, was the surface soil at the coastal site lighter or darker than the standard that was used for the comparison?

F. Lighter; the average percent relative reflectance of the soil at the coastal site was 100%.
G. Lighter; the average percent relative reflectance of the soil at the coastal site was less than 100%.
H. Darker; the average percent relative reflectance of the soil at the coastal site was 100%.
J. Darker; the average percent relative reflectance of the soil at the coastal site was less than 100%.

Your First Practice Test

GO ON TO THE NEXT PAGE.

4 ○ ○ ○ ○ ○ ○ ○ ○ ○ 4

Passage II

A high concentration of *dissolved nickel* (Ni^{2+}) in wastewater is an environmental concern. Students studied the removal of Ni^{2+} from wastewater, using an aqueous Ni^{2+} solution as a model of wastewater.

In water, hydroxide (OH^-) reacts with Ni^{2+} to form nickel hydroxide monohydrate [$Ni(OH)_2{\cdot}H_2O$]. The balanced chemical equation for this reaction is

$$Ni^{2+} + 2OH^- + H_2O \rightarrow Ni(OH)_2{\cdot}H_2O$$

Because the monohydrate is a solid, it can be filtered from the solution. Some of the solid will eventually dissolve if it is left in contact with the solution.

The students did 2 experiments to study how reaction time and filtration method affected the removal of Ni^{2+} from the aqueous Ni^{2+} solution.

Experiment 1

In each of Trials 1–3, Steps 1–4 were performed:

1. Thirty-two mL of aqueous 1.0 mole/L OH^- solution and 260 mL of aqueous 0.060 mole/L Ni^{2+} solution were poured into the same flask.
2. The mixture was stirred at 22°C for 10 min, 3 days, or 7 days.
3. Solid monohydrate was recovered by *standard filtration* (see Figure 1).

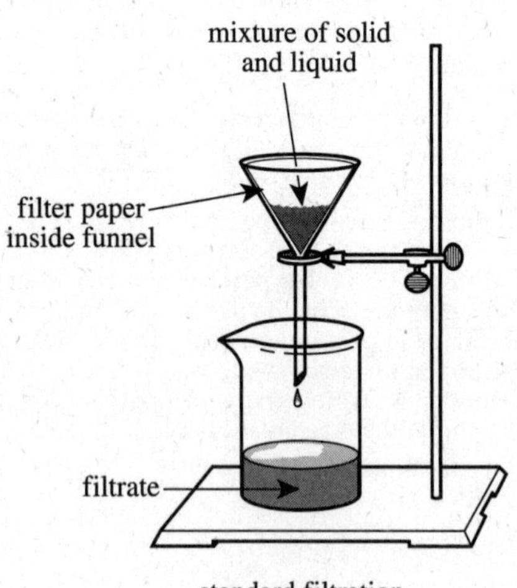

Figure 1

4. The *concentration of Ni^{2+} in the filtrate*, CNF, was determined, in milligrams of Ni^{2+} per kilogram of solution (mg/kg).

Experiment 2

In each of Trials 4–6, Steps 1–4 in Experiment 1 were performed except that in Step 3, solid monohydrate was recovered by *vacuum filtration* (see Figure 2).

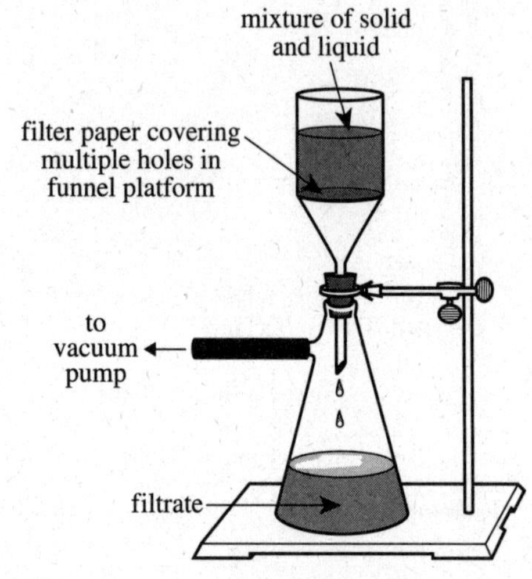

Figure 2

The results of Experiments 1 and 2 are shown in Table 1.

Table 1

Experiment	Trial	Reaction time	CNF (mg/kg)
1	1	10 min	6
	2	3 days	39
	3	7 days	42
2	4	10 min	58
	5	3 days	69
	6	7 days	73

Table 1 adapted from K. Blake Corcoran, Brian E. Rood, and Bridget G. Trogden, "Chemical Remediation of Nickel(II) Waste: A Laboratory Experiment for General Chemistry Students." ©2010 by Division of Chemical Education, Inc., American Chemical Society.

7. If a reaction time of 2 days had been tested in Experiment 1, the CNF would most likely have been:

A. less than 6 mg/kg.
B. between 6 mg/kg and 39 mg/kg.
C. between 39 mg/kg and 42 mg/kg.
D. greater than 42 mg/kg.

GO ON TO THE NEXT PAGE.

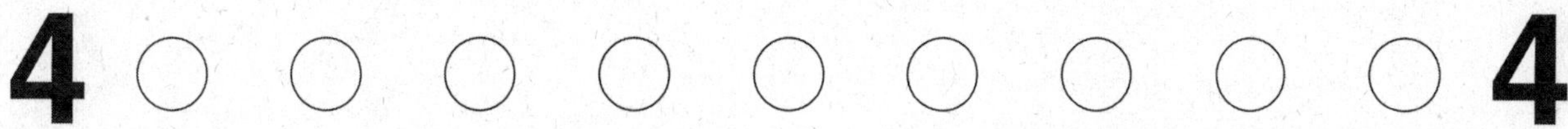

8. Based on the results of Experiments 1 and 2, what combination of reaction time and filtration method resulted in the lowest concentration of dissolved nickel in the filtrate?

	reaction time	filtration method
F.	10 min	standard
G.	7 days	standard
H.	10 min	vacuum
J.	7 days	vacuum

9. Was the net force exerted on the mixture in the funnel more likely greater in Trial 3 or in Trial 6 ?

A. Trial 3, because the filtration apparatus was connected to a vacuum pump.
B. Trial 3, because the filtration apparatus was not connected to a vacuum pump.
C. Trial 6, because the filtration apparatus was connected to a vacuum pump.
D. Trial 6, because the filtration apparatus was not connected to a vacuum pump.

10. In each trial, the students performed which of the following chronological sequences of steps?

F. Measuring the CNF; recovering the solid by filtration; mixing the Ni^{2+} and the OH^- solutions
G. Mixing the Ni^{2+} and the OH^- solutions; recovering the solid by filtration; measuring the CNF
H. Recovering the solid by filtration; measuring the CNF; mixing the Ni^{2+} and the OH^- solutions
J. Recovering the solid by filtration; mixing the Ni^{2+} and the OH^- solutions; measuring the CNF

11. A student predicted that when solid monohydrate is recovered by vacuum filtration, a greater CNF will result for a reaction time of 3 days than for a reaction time of 10 min. Do the data in Table 1 support this prediction?

A. No; Trial 1 had a greater CNF than did Trial 2.
B. No; Trial 5 had a greater CNF than did Trial 4.
C. Yes; Trial 1 had a greater CNF than did Trial 2.
D. Yes; Trial 5 had a greater CNF than did Trial 4.

12. In how many of the 6 trials was nickel hydroxide monohydrate recovered by standard filtration after OH^- and Ni^{2+} had been allowed to react for at least 3 days?

F. 1
G. 2
H. 4
J. 6

13. Based on the balanced chemical equation in the passage, as 6 OH^- ions are consumed, how many formula units of $Ni(OH)_2{\cdot}H_2O$ are produced?

A. 3
B. 6
C. 12
D. 18

Your First Practice Test

GO ON TO THE NEXT PAGE.

4 ○ ○ ○ ○ ○ ○ ○ ○ ○ 4

Passage III

Star formation begins with the gravitational collapse of matter in an interstellar gas cloud. A *protostar* (forming star) affects gas in the surrounding portions of the cloud in 2 ways:

- The protostar's gravitational field attracts gas, causing the gas to *accrete* (accumulate onto the protostar).
- *Radiation pressure* (RP) associated with the protostar's emissions causes gas to be pushed away from the protostar, inhibiting accretion.

Star formation ends when the effect of RP overcomes that of gravity. At that point, the protostar can no longer gain mass by accretion and is considered a fully formed star.

Three scientists debate whether the maximum mass that a protostar can reach by accretion is great enough to account for the most massive stars observed.

Scientist 1

The effect of RP is uniform in all directions around a protostar. As a result, the maximum mass that a protostar can reach by accretion is 20 M_S (1 M_S = mass of the Sun). Any further increase in mass requires at least 1 *stellar merger* (the combination of 2 or more fully formed stars into 1). Because stars tend to form in clusters, stellar mergers are likely.

Scientist 2

Scientist 1 is correct that stellar mergers are likely. However, because a protostar rotates about its axis, a disk of gas forms in the plane of the protostar's equator. This reduces the effect of RP in that plane, allowing gas from the disk to readily accrete. As a result, the maximum mass that a protostar can reach by accretion is 40 M_S. Any further increase in mass requires at least 1 stellar merger.

Scientist 3

Stellar mergers are very unlikely given the vast distances between stars, even within clusters. Scientist 2 is correct about the formation and the effect of the disk. In addition, a protostar produces bubble-like regions of radiation that increase the effect of RP near the protostar's poles, promoting the flow of gas into the disk. As a result, accretion continues until the surrounding portions of the cloud are nearly depleted of gas. Therefore, the maximum mass that a protostar can reach by accretion is limited only by the amount of available gas.

14. Relative to the center of the protostar, does gravity more likely accelerate gas particles inward or outward, and does RP more likely accelerate gas particles inward or outward?

	gravity	RP
F.	inward	inward
G.	inward	outward
H.	outward	inward
J.	outward	outward

15. Based on Scientist 2's argument, do gas particles more likely accrete near the equator or near the poles of a protostar with a disk?

A. Near the equator, because the effect of RP is increased there.
B. Near the equator, because the effect of RP is reduced there.
C. Near the poles, because the effect of RP is increased there.
D. Near the poles, because the effect of RP is reduced there.

GO ON TO THE NEXT PAGE.

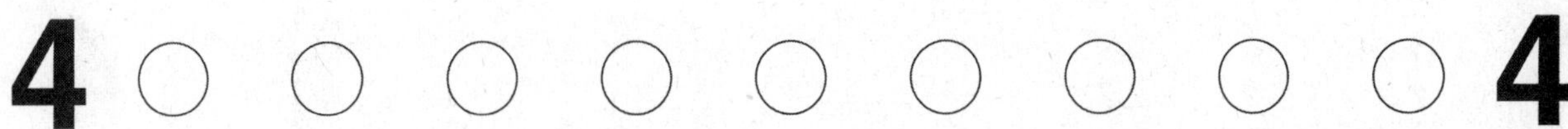

16. Detailed surveys of star clusters in and near the Milky Way have yielded no evidence of stellar mergers having occurred at any time during the galaxy's history. These results are *inconsistent* with the argument(s) of which scientist(s)?

F. Scientist 1 only
G. Scientist 3 only
H. Scientists 1 and 2 only
J. Scientists 1 and 3 only

17. One of the most massive stars known is Eta Carinae, which has an approximate mass of 120 M_S. Based on the arguments of Scientists 1, 2, and 3, respectively, what is the *minimum* number of stars, each formed entirely by accretion, that would have been required to form Eta Carinae?

	Scientist 1	Scientist 2	Scientist 3
A.	5	3	1
B.	5	4	2
C.	6	3	1
D.	6	4	2

18. When the effect of RP overcomes that of gravity, a star is said to have "emerged from its envelope," because that is the first time the star is directly observable from outside the cloud. An observation of which of the following stars emerging from its envelope would support Scientist 2's argument but weaken Scientist 1's argument?

F. A 15 M_S star
G. A 20 M_S star
H. A 30 M_S star
J. A 50 M_S star

19. Scientists 2 and 3 agree that a disk forms around a protostar as a result of the protostar's:

A. motion.
B. emission of radiation.
C. location within a star cluster.
D. merger with another star.

20. Which of the scientists, if any, would be likely to agree that the Sun could have formed entirely by accretion?

F. Scientist 1 only
G. Scientist 3 only
H. Scientists 1, 2, and 3
J. None of the scientists

GO ON TO THE NEXT PAGE.

4 ○ ○ ○ ○ ○ ○ ○ ○ ○ 4

Passage IV

Two studies were done to examine how the proportion of *vermicompost* (feces from earthworms) in a particular potting soil affects the *yield* of each of 2 plant species: *Solanum lycopersicum* (a tomato plant) and *Capsicum annuum* (a pepper plant). The yield of a plant species is the mass of fruit produced per plant of the species.

Six different mixtures (Mixtures 1–6) were prepared according to the percents listed in Table 1.

Table 1

Mixture	Percent by volume of: vermicompost	potting soil
1	0	100
2	20	80
3	40	60
4	60	40
5	80	20
6	100	0

Study 1

Equal amounts of Mixtures 1–6 were distributed among thirty-six 2 L pots in the following manner: 1.5 kg of Mixture 1 was put into each of 6 pots, 1.5 kg of Mixture 2 was put into each of 6 other pots, 1.5 kg of Mixture 3 was put into each of 6 other pots, and so on. Then, 3 *S. lycopersicum* seeds were added to each pot. For the next 158 days, all the pots received equal amounts of water and light. On Day 28 of the 158 days, all the seedlings that had emerged were removed from the pots with the exception of a single seedling in each pot. On Day 158, the yield of the remaining plant in each pot was measured. The average yield of the plants grown in each mixture was then calculated. The results are shown in Figure 1.

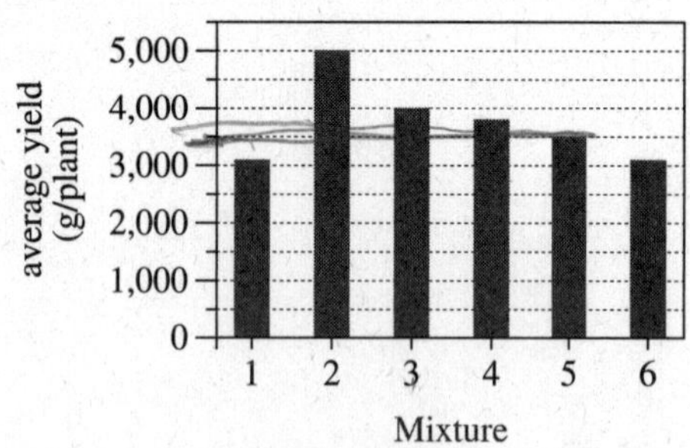

Figure 1

Figure 1 adapted from Rola M. Atiyeh et al., "Influence of Earthworm-Processed Pig Manure on the Growth and Yield of Greenhouse Tomatoes." ©2000 by Elsevier Science Ltd.

Study 2

The procedures of Study 1 were repeated, except that 5 *C. annuum* seeds instead of 3 *S. lycopersicum* seeds were added to each pot, the pots received water and light for 149 days instead of 158 days, seedling removal occurred on Day 42 of the 149 days, and plant yield was measured on Day 149. The results are shown in Figure 2.

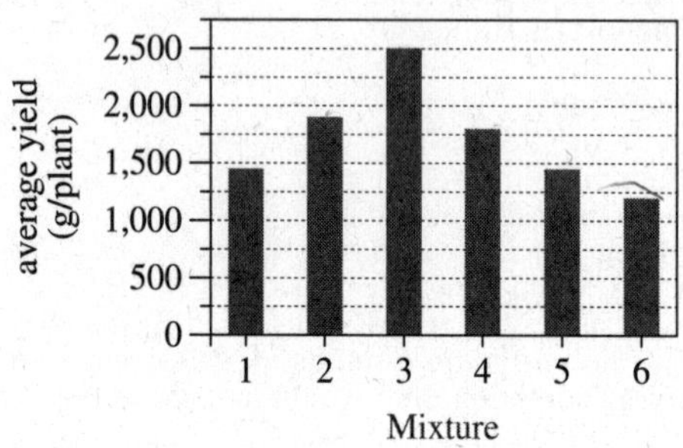

Figure 2

Figure 2 adapted from Norman Q. Arancon et al., "Effects of Vermicomposts Produced from Food Waste on the Growth and Yields of Greenhouse Peppers." ©2004 by Elsevier Science Ltd.

21. In both studies, as the percent by volume of vermicompost increased from 0% through 100%, the average yield:
   - **A.** decreased only.
   - **B.** increased only.
   - **C.** decreased, then increased.
   - **D.** increased, then decreased.

22. In Study 1, which of the following mixtures was most likely intended to serve as a control for the effect of vermicompost on plant yield?
   - **F.** Mixture 1
   - **G.** Mixture 2
   - **H.** Mixture 4
   - **J.** Mixture 5

23. Suppose that in Study 1, average yield had been calculated in *kilograms* per plant (kg/plant) instead of g/plant. The average yield for Mixture 5 would have been:
   - **A.** 1.45 kg/plant.
   - **B.** 3.50 kg/plant.
   - **C.** 14.5 kg/plant.
   - **D.** 35.0 kg/plant.

GO ON TO THE NEXT PAGE.

4 ○ ○ ○ ○ ○ ○ ○ ○ ○ 4

24. Which of the factors listed below were the same in Study 2 as they were in Study 1 ?

I. Number of pots used per mixture
II. Length of time needed to perform the study
III. Volume of each pot

F. I and II only
G. I and III only
H. II and III only
J. I, II, and III

25. Is the statement "Tomato plants require a *lower* proportion of vermicompost in the potting soil to achieve maximum yield than do pepper plants" consistent with the results of Studies 1 and 2 ?

A. Yes; in Study 1, the greatest average yield was attained with Mixture 2, whereas in Study 2, the greatest average yield was attained with Mixture 3.
B. Yes; in Study 1, the greatest average yield was attained with Mixture 3, whereas in Study 2, the greatest average yield was attained with Mixture 2.
C. No; in Study 1, the greatest average yield was attained with Mixture 2, whereas in Study 2, the greatest average yield was attained with Mixture 3.
D. No; in Study 1, the greatest average yield was attained with Mixture 3, whereas in Study 2, the greatest average yield was attained with Mixture 2.

26. In a 2 L pot, the presence of more than one plant can negatively affect the growth of all the plants in the pot, due to competition among the plants. What action was taken in the studies to prevent competition among the plants?

F. Only one seed was planted per pot.
G. Only one seedling was planted per pot.
H. After an initial period of growth, all but one seed was removed from each pot.
J. After an initial period of growth, all but one seedling was removed from each pot.

27. *S. lycopersicum* and *C. annuum* required water and light for the process represented by which of the following expressions?

A. Water + light → glucose + oxygen + carbon dioxide
B. Glucose + water + light → oxygen + carbon dioxide
C. Oxygen + water + light → glucose + carbon dioxide
D. Carbon dioxide + water + light → glucose + oxygen

Your First Practice Test

GO ON TO THE NEXT PAGE.

4 ○ ○ ○ ○ ○ ○ ○ ○ ○ 4

Passage V

A *cathode-ray tube* (CRT) is a sealed, evacuated glass tube with a filament at one end and a fluorescent screen at the other end (see Figure 1).

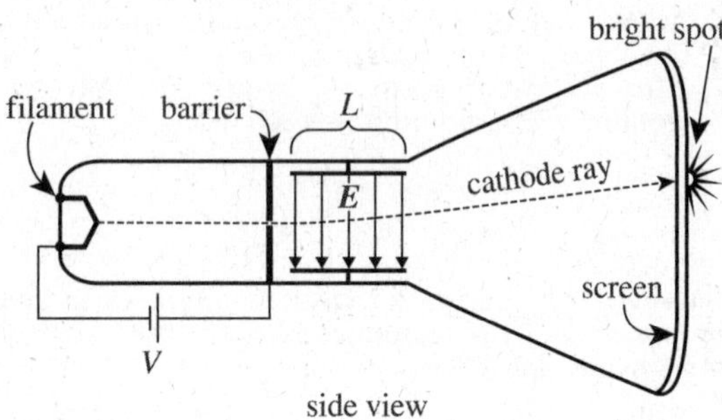

Figure 1

Figure 1 adapted from David Halliday, Robert Resnick, and Jearl Walker, *Fundamentals of Physics*, 9th ed. ©2011 John Wiley & Sons, Inc.

When heated, the filament emits cathode rays that are accelerated by an electric potential, V, toward a barrier having a pinhole. Beyond the barrier are 2 conducting plates, each of length L, that have an electric field, $\mathbf{E}$, between them. (The direction of $\mathbf{E}$ can be upward or downward; in Figure 1, it is downward.) Any rays that pass through the pinhole travel through the field and strike the screen, producing a bright spot of visible light.

A group of students performed 3 studies on various CRTs, each of which had a ruler taped to the outer surface of the screen (see Figure 2) to measure a spot's vertical location, y (in centimeters, cm).

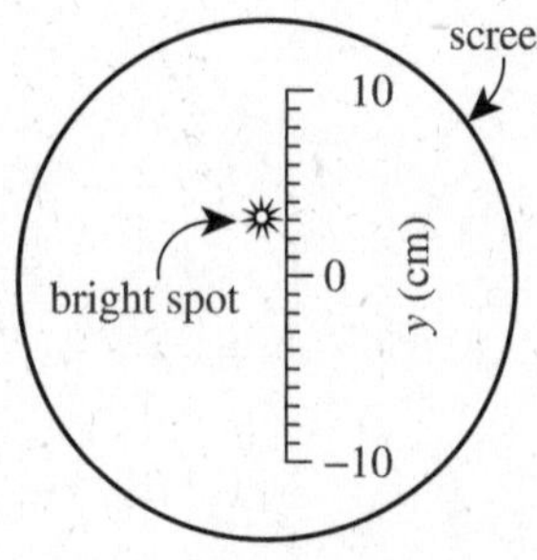

Figure 2

Study 1

The students obtained a CRT having $L = 2.5$ cm. They set V to 1.0 kilovolt (kV), varied both the direction and the magnitude (in newtons per coulomb, N/C) of $\mathbf{E}$, and recorded the resulting values of y (see Table 1).

Table 1

Trial	$\mathbf{E}$ direction*	$\mathbf{E}$ magnitude (N/C)	y (cm)
1	↑	1.0×10^4	−3.2
2	↑	2.0×10^4	−6.3
3	↑	3.0×10^4	−9.5
4	↓	1.0×10^4	3.2
5	↓	2.0×10^4	6.3
6	↓	3.0×10^4	9.5

*↑ = upward
↓ = downward

Study 2

Using the CRT from Study 1, the students set the magnitude of $\mathbf{E}$ to 1.0×10^4 N/C, varied V, and recorded the resulting values of y (see Table 2).

Table 2

Trial	V (kV)	y (cm)
7	0.5	6.3
8	1.0	3.2
9	1.5	2.1
10	2.0	1.6
11	2.5	1.3

Study 3

The students obtained various CRTs, each having a different L. For each CRT, they set V to 1.0 kV, set the magnitude of $\mathbf{E}$ to 1.0×10^4 N/C, and recorded the resulting value of y (see Table 3).

Table 3

Trial	L (cm)	y (cm)
12	1.5	−2.0
13	2.0	−2.6
14	2.5	−3.2
15	3.0	−3.8
16	3.5	−4.4

GO ON TO THE NEXT PAGE.

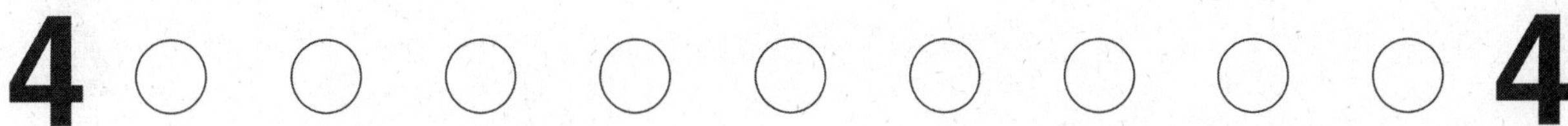

28. Studies 1 and 2 differed in which of the following ways? In Study 1, the students determined how the spot's location varied with:

F. electric potential, whereas in Study 2, they determined how the spot's location varied with the magnitude and direction of the electric field.
G. plate length, whereas in Study 2, they determined how the spot's location varied with electric potential.
H. the magnitude and direction of the electric field, whereas in Study 2, they determined how the spot's location varied with electric potential.
J. plate length, whereas in Study 2, they determined how the spot's location varied with the magnitude and direction of the electric field.

29. Suppose that the students had performed a trial in Study 2 in which y was 2.6 cm. The value of V in this trial would most likely have been:

A. less than 1.0 kV.
B. between 1.0 kV and 1.5 kV.
C. between 1.5 kV and 2.0 kV.
D. greater than 2.0 kV.

30. Figure 2 could serve as an illustration of the result(s) of which trial(s)?

F. Trial 1 only
G. Trial 8 only
H. Trials 1 and 4 only
J. Trials 4 and 8 only

31. Based on the results of Study 1, in which direction did $\mathbf{E}$ most likely point in Study 2, and in which direction did $\mathbf{E}$ most likely point in Study 3 ?

	Study 2	Study 3
A.	↑	↑
B.	↑	↓
C.	↓	↑
D.	↓	↓

32. Once a CRT is sealed, it cannot be reopened. However, because both V and $\mathbf{E}$ are controlled from the outside, a CRT can be used repeatedly under varying conditions. Based on the descriptions of Studies 1–3, what is the *minimum* number of different CRTs that the students required to complete the 3 studies?

F. 1
G. 5
H. 11
J. 16

33. Suppose that the students had performed a trial in which the cathode rays traveled all the way from the filament to the screen in a straight-line path, striking the screen at $y = 0$ cm. Based on the results of Studies 1 and 2, which of the following statements about V and the magnitude of $\mathbf{E}$ in this trial would have been true?

A. V was zero but the magnitude of $\mathbf{E}$ was nonzero.
B. V was nonzero but the magnitude of $\mathbf{E}$ was zero.
C. Both V and the magnitude of $\mathbf{E}$ were zero.
D. Both V and the magnitude of $\mathbf{E}$ were nonzero.

34. In a CRT, $\mathbf{E}$ is generated by building up equal and opposite electric charges on the 2 conducting plates. Suppose that cathode rays are negatively charged. If $\mathbf{E}$ is directed downward as shown in Figure 1, which conducting plate is more likely the negatively charged plate?

F. The top plate, because charges of like sign are attracted to each other.
G. The top plate, because charges of like sign are repelled from each other.
H. The bottom plate, because charges of like sign are attracted to each other.
J. The bottom plate, because charges of like sign are repelled from each other.

Your First Practice Test

GO ON TO THE NEXT PAGE.

4  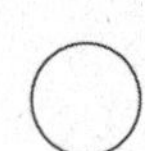 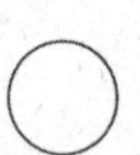  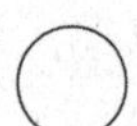     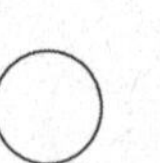 4

Passage VI

For gas atoms in a state of random motion, the *mean free path*, λ, is the average distance a gas atom will travel between collisions with other gas atoms. This distance depends upon the diameter of the gas atom, *d*, the volume of the gas, *V*, and the number of atoms of the gas, *N*. Table 1 lists the name, symbol, and value of *d* (in nanometers, nm) for each of 4 gases. Figure 1 shows, for each gas, at 293 kelvins (K), how λ (in nm) varies with *V* (in liters, L) in a sample with $N = 6 \times 10^{23}$ atoms of the gas. Figure 2 shows, for each gas, at 293 K, how λ varies with *N* in a sample with $V = 25$ L.

Table 1

Gas	Symbol	*d* (nm)
Neon	Ne	0.076
Argon	Ar	0.142
Krypton	Kr	0.176
Xenon	Xe	0.216

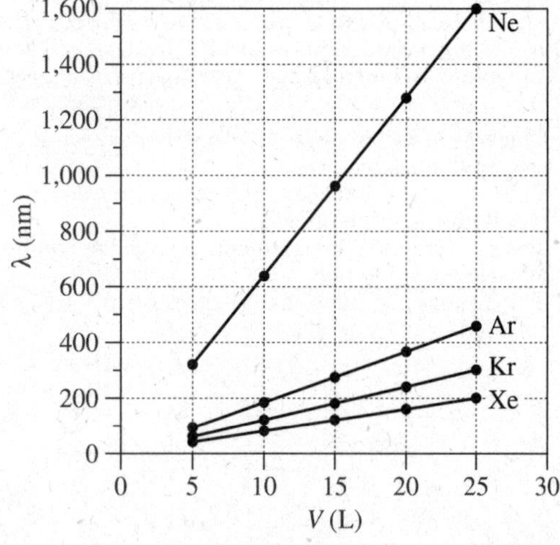

Figure 1

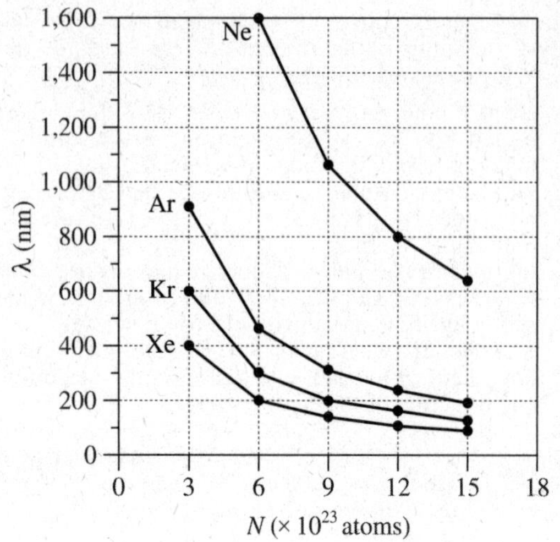

Figure 2

35. According to Figure 2, what is the order of gas samples from shortest λ to longest λ for $N = 15 \times 10^{23}$ atoms?

A. Ne, Ar, Kr, Xe
B. Ne, Kr, Ar, Xe
C. Xe, Ar, Kr, Ne
D. Xe, Kr, Ar, Ne

36. According to Figure 2, doubling the Ne sample size from 6×10^{23} atoms to 12×10^{23} atoms effectively multiplies λ for Ne by a factor of:

F. $\frac{1}{4}$.
G. $\frac{1}{2}$.
H. 2.
J. 4.

GO ON TO THE NEXT PAGE.

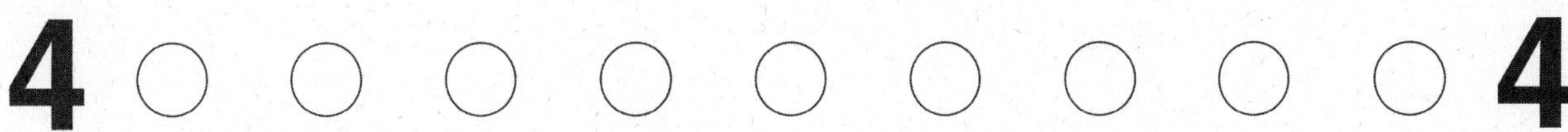

37. Consider 2 Kr samples at 293 K, each with $N = 6 \times 10^{23}$ atoms, but one with $V = 25$ L and the other with $V = 50$ L. Based on Figure 1, λ for the 50 L sample would most likely be how many times as great as λ for the 25 L sample?

A. $\frac{1}{4}$
B. $\frac{1}{2}$
C. 2
D. 4

38. Based on Figure 1, for the Xe and Ar gas samples with $V = 20$ L, compared to λ for Xe, approximately how much longer is λ for Ar ?

F. 50 nm
G. 100 nm
H. 150 nm
J. 200 nm

39. The *collision frequency* is defined as the number of collisions between gas atoms per second. Consider the 5 L and 25 L Xe samples represented in Figure 1. Assuming the Xe atoms have the same average speed in both samples, in which sample would the collision frequency more likely be higher?

A. In the 5 L sample; Xe atoms in the 5 L sample travel, on average, shorter distances between collisions and therefore collide more often.
B. In the 5 L sample; Xe atoms in the 5 L sample travel, on average, longer distances between collisions and therefore collide more often.
C. In the 25 L sample; Xe atoms in the 25 L sample travel, on average, shorter distances between collisions and therefore collide more often.
D. In the 25 L sample; Xe atoms in the 25 L sample travel, on average, longer distances between collisions and therefore collide more often.

40. For a particular sample of radon (Rn) gas in a 25 L container at 293 K, λ is approximately 320 nm. If d for Rn is 0.240 nm, then, based on Table 1 and Figure 2, approximately how many Rn atoms are most likely in this sample?

F. Less than 6×10^{23}
G. Between 6×10^{23} and 9×10^{23}
H. Between 9×10^{23} and 12×10^{23}
J. More than 12×10^{23}

END OF TEST 4

STOP! DO NOT RETURN TO ANY OTHER TEST.

You may wish to photocopy these sample answer document pages to respond to the practice ACT Writing Test.

Please enter the information at the right before beginning the writing test.

Use a soft lead No. 2 pencil only. Do NOT use a mechanical pencil, ink, ballpoint, or felt-tip pen.

WRITING TEST BOOKLET NUMBER

Print your 6-digit **Booklet Number** in the boxes at the right.

WRITING TEST FORM

Print your 5-character **Test Form** in the boxes above and fill in the corresponding oval at the right.

- 16W1A
- 16W2A
- 16W3A
- 18W4A
- 19WT5

Begin WRITING TEST here.

If you need more space, please continue on the next page.

WRITING TEST

If you need more space, please continue on the back of this page.

WRITING TEST

If you need more space, please continue on the next page.

WRITING TEST

STOP here with the writing test.

072950

Practice Writing Test Prompt 1

Your Signature: ______________________
(Do not print.)

Print Your Name Here: ______________________

Your Date of Birth:
[ ][ ] - [ ][ ] - [ ][ ][ ][ ]
Month Day Year

Form 16W1A

You must take the multiple-choice tests before you take the writing test.

Directions

This is a test of your writing skills. You will have **forty** (40) minutes to read the prompt, plan your response, and write an essay in English. Before you begin working, read all material in this test booklet carefully to understand exactly what you are being asked to do.

You will write your essay on the lined pages in the **answer document** provided. Your writing on those pages will be scored. You may use the unlined pages in this test booklet to plan your essay. Your work on these pages will not be scored.

Your essay will be evaluated based on the evidence it provides of your ability to:

- clearly state your own perspective on a complex issue and analyze the relationship between your perspective and at least one other perspective
- develop and support your ideas with reasoning and examples
- organize your ideas clearly and logically
- communicate your ideas effectively in standard written English

Lay your pencil down immediately when time is called.

DO NOT OPEN THIS BOOKLET UNTIL TOLD TO DO SO.

PO Box 168
Iowa City, IA 52243-0168

Free Music

Free music is now available through many legal sources, from streaming services to online radio stations, making it largely unnecessary to purchase an album or even a single song. As sales figures continue to drop, some musicians, both high-profile and relatively unknown, have even quit trying to sell their music altogether, choosing instead to release new material for free online. Perhaps this trend is a matter of simple economics: cheap is good, but free is better. But it is worth considering whether our apparent unwillingness to spend money on music is an indication that its value in our lives is changing.

Read and carefully consider these perspectives. Each suggests a particular way of thinking about the changing value of music in our lives.

Perspective One

Digital technologies and the Internet have changed our relationship with music. It is so plentiful and readily available now that all value has been diluted.

Perspective Two

Music competes for our attention with many other kinds of inexpensive entertainment these days. We still value it, but we also have a lot of other ways to spend our money.

Perspective Three

With so many free sources, people are listening to more music and discovering more new musicians than ever before. Wide availability has only increased our appreciation of music.

Essay Task

Write a unified, coherent essay about whether the value of music in our lives is changing. In your essay, be sure to:

- clearly state your own perspective on the issue and analyze the relationship between your perspective and at least one other perspective
- develop and support your ideas with reasoning and examples
- organize your ideas clearly and logically
- communicate your ideas effectively in standard written English

Your perspective may be in full agreement with any of those given, in partial agreement, or completely different.

Planning Your Essay

Your work on these prewriting pages will not be scored.

Use the space below and on the back cover to generate ideas and plan your essay. You may wish to consider the following as you think critically about the task:

Strengths and weaknesses of different perspectives on the issue

- What insights do they offer, and what do they fail to consider?
- Why might they be persuasive to others, or why might they fail to persuade?

Your own knowledge, experience, and values

- What is your perspective on this issue, and what are its strengths and weaknesses?
- How will you support your perspective in your essay?

If you need more space to plan, please continue on the back of this page.

Planning Your Essay

Use this page to continue planning your essay. Your work on this page will not be scored.

Scoring Your Practice Test

After taking your first ACT practice test, you are ready to score the test to see how you did overall. In this section, you learn how to determine your raw score, convert raw scores to scale scores, compute your Composite score, determine your estimated percentile ranks for each of your scale scores, and score your practice writing test.

When scoring each practice test and reviewing your scores, remember that your scores on the practice tests are only estimates of the scores that you will obtain on the ACT. If your score isn't as high as you expected, it could mean a number of things. Maybe you need to review important content and skills. Maybe you should work a little faster when taking the test. Perhaps you simply weren't doing your best work on the test. Or maybe you need to take more challenging courses to be better prepared. Keep in mind that a test score is just one indicator of your level of academic knowledge and skills. You know your own strengths and weaknesses better than anyone else, so keep them in mind as you evaluate your performance.

On each of the four multiple-choice tests (English, mathematics, reading, and science), the number of questions you answer correctly is called a *raw* score. To figure out your raw scores for the practice tests in this book count all your correct answers for each test using the scoring keys provided in the next section, "Scoring Your Multiple-Choice Practice Tests." Then you can convert your raw scores into *scale* scores.

A *scale score* is a raw score that is converted to a scale score to enhance score interpretation and allow comparability across different forms. Scale scores are the scores that ACT reports to students, high schools, colleges, and scholarship agencies. One of the reasons ACT uses scale scores is to adjust for small differences among different forms of the ACT. After you've converted your raw scores for the practice tests to scale scores, you'll want to convert your scale scores to percentile ranks. Percentile ranks, which are explained in the following pages, are useful for interpreting your scores relative to the scores of others who have taken the ACT.

If you took the optional practice writing test, the later section "Scoring Your Practice Writing Test Essay" includes an analytic rubric for evaluating your essay and estimating your writing test score. It is difficult to be objective about one's own work, and you have not had the extensive training provided to actual readers of the writing test. However, it is to your advantage to read your own writing critically. Becoming your own editor helps you grow as a writer and as a reader, so it makes sense for you to evaluate your own practice essay. That having been said, it may also be helpful for you to give your practice essay to another reader to get another perspective: perhaps that of a classmate, a parent, or an English teacher, for example. To rate your essay, you and your reader should read the analytic rubric on pages 109–110 and the examples on pages 304–328, and then assign your practice essay a score of 1 (low) through 6 (high) in each of the four writing domains (Ideas and Analysis, Development and Support, Organization, and Language Use and Conventions).

Your writing test domain scores are based on the analytic rubric used to score the essays, whereas the overall score is calculated from the four domain scores.

Finally, convert your writing test score to percentile ranks using the procedures described. Percentile ranks enable you to compare your writing test score to those of others who have taken the writing test.

Scoring Your Multiple-Choice Practice Tests

To score each of your multiple-choice practice tests, starting with the English test, follow these steps:

STEP 1. Write a "1" in the blank for each question that you answered correctly. An example is provided in the following box:

	Key		Your answer was
1.	A	___	Incorrect
2.	J	1	Correct
3.	B	1	Correct
4.	G	___	Incorrect

English ■ Scoring Key ■ Practice Test 1

	Key			Key			Key	
1.	C	___	26.	J	___	51.	B	___
2.	F	___	27.	D	___	52.	J	___
3.	B	___	28.	H	___	53.	A	___
4.	J	___	29.	A	___	54.	G	___
5.	B	___	30.	F	___	55.	B	___
6.	G	___	31.	B	___	56.	J	___
7.	C	___	32.	F	___	57.	C	___
8.	G	___	33.	A	___	58.	F	___
9.	C	___	34.	F	___	59.	C	___
10.	G	___	35.	D	___	60.	F	___
11.	B	___	36.	H	___	61.	C	___
12.	F	___	37.	B	___	62.	G	___
13.	D	___	38.	J	___	63.	C	___
14.	J	___	39.	C	___	64.	F	___
15.	B	___	40.	H	___	65.	B	___
16.	J	___	41.	B	___	66.	F	___
17.	A	___	42.	J	___	67.	A	___
18.	G	___	43.	C	___	68.	H	___
19.	B	___	44.	G	___	69.	D	___
20.	F	___	45.	C	___	70.	J	___
21.	B	___	46.	J	___	71.	A	___
22.	H	___	47.	C	___	72.	J	___
23.	D	___	48.	F	___	73.	D	___
24.	J	___	49.	A	___	74.	J	___
25.	B	___	50.	G	___	75.	C	___

STEP 2. Add the numbers you entered in step 1 and write this total in the following shaded box. This is your raw score.

Number Correct (Raw Score) for:	
English test (75 questions)	______

STEP 3. Repeat steps 1 and 2 for the ACT mathematics, reading, and science tests using the scoring keys on the following pages.

Mathematics ■ Scoring Key ■ Practice Test 1

	Key			Key			Key	
1.	C	______	21.	C	______	41.	D	______
2.	G	______	22.	K	______	42.	J	______
3.	C	______	23.	E	______	43.	B	______
4.	F	______	24.	G	______	44.	G	______
5.	B	______	25.	D	______	45.	A	______
6.	K	______	26.	K	______	46.	J	______
7.	E	______	27.	C	______	47.	E	______
8.	K	______	28.	H	______	48.	K	______
9.	B	______	29.	A	______	49.	A	______
10.	H	______	30.	F	______	50.	F	______
11.	C	______	31.	B	______	51.	B	______
12.	J	______	32.	G	______	52.	J	______
13.	B	______	33.	B	______	53.	C	______
14.	F	______	34.	F	______	54.	G	______
15.	B	______	35.	B	______	55.	A	______
16.	J	______	36.	H	______	56.	K	______
17.	E	______	37.	A	______	57.	A	______
18.	J	______	38.	J	______	58.	F	______
19.	A	______	39.	B	______	59.	C	______
20.	G	______	40.	F	______	60.	K	______

Number Correct (Raw Score) for:	
Math test (60 questions)	______

Reading ■ Scoring Key ■ Practice Test 1

	Key			Key			Key	
1.	B	______	15.	D	______	29.	D	______
2.	J	______	16.	G	______	30.	J	______
3.	A	______	17.	C	______	31.	B	______
4.	G	______	18.	F	______	32.	G	______
5.	D	______	19.	A	______	33.	D	______
6.	H	______	20.	G	______	34.	J	______
7.	C	______	21.	C	______	35.	B	______
8.	F	______	22.	G	______	36.	J	______
9.	D	______	23.	A	______	37.	C	______
10.	F	______	24.	J	______	38.	F	______
11.	D	______	25.	B	______	39.	A	______
12.	G	______	26.	F	______	40.	H	______
13.	A	______	27.	B	______			
14.	H	______	28.	F	______			

Number Correct (Raw Score) for:

Reading test (40 questions) ______

Science ■ Scoring Key ■ Practice Test 1

	Key			Key			Key	
1.	A	______	15.	B	______	29.	B	______
2.	H	______	16.	H	______	30.	J	______
3.	C	______	17.	C	______	31.	C	______
4.	J	______	18.	H	______	32.	G	______
5.	B	______	19.	A	______	33.	B	______
6.	J	______	20.	H	______	34.	J	______
7.	B	______	21.	D	______	35.	D	______
8.	F	______	22.	F	______	36.	G	______
9.	C	______	23.	B	______	37.	C	______
10.	G	______	24.	G	______	38.	J	______
11.	D	______	25.	A	______	39.	A	______
12.	G	______	26.	J	______	40.	F	______
13.	A	______	27.	D	______			
14.	G	______	28.	H	______			

Number Correct (Raw Score) for:

Science test (40 questions) ______

STEP 4. On each of the four tests, the total number of correct responses yields a raw score. Use the conversion table on the following page to convert your raw scores to scale scores. For each of the four tests, locate and circle your raw score or the range of raw scores that includes it in the conversion table. Then, read across to either outside column of the table and circle the scale score that corresponds to that raw score. As you determine your scale scores, enter them in the blanks provided below. The highest possible scale score for each test is 36. The lowest possible scale score for any of the four tests is 1.

	Your Scale Scores
English	_______
Mathematics	_______
Reading	_______
Science	_______
Sum of Scores	_______

STEP 5. Compute your Composite score by averaging the four scale scores. To do this, add your four scale scores and divide the sum by 4. If the resulting number ends in a fraction, round it off to the nearest whole number. (Round down any fraction less than one-half; round up any fraction that is one-half or more.) Enter this number in the appropriate blank below. This is your Composite score. The highest possible Composite score is 36. The lowest possible Composite score is 1.

	Your Scale Scores
English	_______
Mathematics	_______
Reading	_______
Science	_______
Sum of Scores	_______
Composite Score (sum ÷ 4)	_______

Scale Score Conversion Table: Practice Test 1

Scale Score	Raw Score				Scale Score
	English	Mathematics	Reading	Science	
36	74–75	57–60	40	39–40	**36**
35	71–73	54–56	39	38	**35**
34	70	53	38	37	**34**
33	69	52	37	36	**33**
32	68	51	36	35	**32**
31	66–67	50	35	34	**31**
30	65	49	34	–	**30**
29	64	47–48	33	33	**29**
28	62–63	45–46	32	32	**28**
27	60–61	43–44	31	31	**27**
26	58–59	40–42	29–30	29–30	**26**
25	55–57	38–39	28	27–28	**25**
24	52–54	35–37	27	25–26	**24**
23	49–51	33–34	25–26	23–24	**23**
22	46–48	32	24	21–22	**22**
21	44–45	30–31	22–23	20	**21**
20	41–43	28–29	21	18–19	**20**
19	39–40	26–27	19–20	16–17	**19**
18	37–38	24–25	17–18	15	**18**
17	35–36	21–23	16	14	**17**
16	32–34	17–20	15	12–13	**16**
15	29–31	14–16	13–14	11	**15**
14	26–28	12–13	12	10	**14**
13	24–25	9–11	10–11	9	**13**
12	22–23	8	9	8	**12**
11	19–21	6–7	7–8	7	**11**
10	17–18	5	6	6	**10**
9	14–16	4	5	5	**9**
8	12–13	–	–	4	**8**
7	10–11	3	4	3	**7**
6	8–9	2	3	–	**6**
5	6–7	–	–	2	**5**
4	5	1	2	–	**4**
3	3–4	–	1	1	**3**
2	2	–	–	–	**2**
1	0–1	0	0	0	**1**

STEP 6. Use the table on page 107 to determine your estimated percentile ranks (percent at or below) for each of your scale scores. In the far left column of the table, circle your scale score for the English test (from page 105). Then read across to the percentile rank column for that test; circle or put a checkmark beside the corresponding percentile rank. Use the same procedure for the other three tests (from page 105). Using the right-hand column of scale scores for your science test and Composite scores may be easier. As you mark your percentile ranks, enter them in the blanks provided. You may also find it helpful to compare your performance with the national mean (average) score for each of the four tests and the Composite as shown at the bottom of the table.

National Distributions of Cumulative Percents for ACT Test Scores
ACT-Tested High School Graduates from 2016, 2017, and 2018

Score	ENGLISH	MATHEMATICS	READING	SCIENCE	COMPOSITE	STEM	Score
36	100	100	100	100	100	100	36
35	99	99	99	99	99	99	35
34	97	99	97	99	99	99	34
33	95	98	95	97	98	98	33
32	93	97	93	96	97	97	32
31	92	96	90	95	95	96	31
30	91	95	88	94	93	94	30
29	88	93	85	92	91	93	29
28	87	91	83	91	89	91	28
27	85	88	80	88	86	88	27
26	82	83	77	86	82	84	26
25	79	79	74	82	78	80	25
24	75	74	71	77	74	75	24
23	70	68	66	70	69	69	23
22	64	64	60	64	63	64	22
21	59	60	54	56	58	58	21
20	53	56	48	49	51	52	20
19	47	52	43	42	45	45	19
18	43	47	37	36	39	38	18
17	39	40	31	29	32	30	17
16	35	30	27	23	26	23	16
15	29	18	22	17	20	15	15
14	23	9	17	13	14	9	14
13	18	3	12	9	8	4	13
12	14	1	8	6	4	2	12
11	10	1	4	4	1	1	11
10	6	1	2	2	1	1	10
9	3	1	1	1	1	1	9
8	2	1	1	1	1	1	8
7	1	1	1	1	1	1	7
6	1	1	1	1	1	1	6
5	1	1	1	1	1	1	5
4	1	1	1	1	1	1	4
3	1	1	1	1	1	1	3
2	1	1	1	1	1	1	2
1	1	1	1	1	1	1	1
Mean	20.2	20.6	21.3	20.8	20.9	20.9	
S.D.	6.9	5.5	6.6	5.6	5.7	5.3	

Note: These national norms are the source of U.S. ranks, for multiple-choice tests, displayed on ACT reports during the 2018–2019 testing year.

These norms with a sample size of 6,035,197, are based on 2016, 2017, and 2018 graduates.

Scoring Your Practice Writing Test Essay

To score your practice writing test essay, follow these steps:

STEP 1. Use the guidelines on the following analytic rubric to score your essay. Because many essays do not fit the exact description at each score point, read each description and try to determine which paragraph in the rubric best describes most of the characteristics of your essay.

The ACT Writing Test Analytic Rubric

	Ideas and Analysis	*Development and Support*	*Organization*	*Language Use and Conventions*
Score 6: **Responses at this scorepoint demonstrate effective skill in writing an argumentative essay.**	The writer generates an argument that critically engages with multiple perspectives on the given issue. The argument's thesis reflects nuance and precision in thought and purpose. The argument establishes and employs an insightful context for analysis of the issue and its perspectives. The analysis examines implications, complexities and tensions, and/or underlying values and assumptions.	Development of ideas and support for claims deepen insight and broaden context. An integrated line of skillful reasoning and illustration effectively conveys the significance of the argument. Qualifications and complications enrich and bolster ideas and analysis.	The response exhibits a skillful organizational strategy. The response is unified by a controlling idea or purpose, and a logical progression of ideas increases the effectiveness of the writer's argument. Transitions between and within paragraphs strengthen the relationships among ideas.	The use of language enhances the argument. Word choice is skillful and precise. Sentence structures are consistently varied and clear. Stylistic and register choices, including voice and tone, are strategic and effective. While a few minor errors in grammar, usage, and mechanics may be present, they do not impede understanding.
Score 5: **Responses at this scorepoint demonstrate well-developed skill in writing an argumentative essay.**	The writer generates an argument that productively engages with multiple perspectives on the given issue. The argument's thesis reflects precision in thought and purpose. The argument establishes and employs a thoughtful context for analysis of the issue and its perspectives. The analysis addresses implications, complexities and tensions, and/or underlying values and assumptions.	Development of ideas and support for claims deepen understanding. A mostly integrated line of purposeful reasoning and illustration capably conveys the significance of the argument. Qualifications and complications enrich ideas and analysis.	The response exhibits a productive organizational strategy. The response is mostly unified by a controlling idea or purpose, and a logical sequencing of ideas contributes to the effectiveness of the argument. Transitions between and within paragraphs consistently clarify the relationships among ideas.	The use of language works in service of the argument. Word choice is precise. Sentence structures are clear and varied often. Stylistic and register choices, including voice and tone, are purposeful and productive. While minor errors in grammar, usage, and mechanics may be present, they do not impede understanding.
Score 4: **Responses at this scorepoint demonstrate adequate skill in writing an argumentative essay.**	The writer generates an argument that engages with multiple perspectives on the given issue. The argument's thesis reflects clarity in thought and purpose. The argument establishes and employs a relevant context for analysis of the issue and its perspectives. The analysis recognizes implications, complexities and tensions, and/or underlying values and assumptions.	Development of ideas and support for claims clarify meaning and purpose. Lines of clear reasoning and illustration adequately convey the significance of the argument. Qualifications and complications extend ideas and analysis.	The response exhibits a clear organizational strategy. The overall shape of the response reflects an emergent controlling idea or purpose. Ideas are logically grouped and sequenced. Transitions between and within paragraphs clarify the relationships among ideas.	The use of language conveys the argument with clarity. Word choice is adequate and sometimes precise. Sentence structures are clear and demonstrate some variety. Stylistic and register choices, including voice and tone, are appropriate for the rhetorical purpose. While errors in grammar, usage, and mechanics are present, they rarely impede understanding.
Score 3: **Responses at this scorepoint demonstrate some developing skill in writing an argumentative essay.**	The writer generates an argument that responds to multiple perspectives on the given issue. The argument's thesis reflects some clarity in thought and purpose. The argument establishes a limited or tangential context for analysis of the issue and its perspectives. Analysis is simplistic or somewhat unclear.	Development of ideas and support for claims are mostly relevant but are overly general or simplistic. Reasoning and illustration largely clarify the argument but may be somewhat repetitious or imprecise.	The response exhibits a basic organizational structure. The response largely coheres, with most ideas logically grouped. Transitions between and within paragraphs sometimes clarify the relationships among ideas.	The use of language is basic and only somewhat clear. Word choice is general and occasionally imprecise. Sentence structures are usually clear but show little variety. Stylistic and register choices, including voice and tone, are not always appropriate for the rhetorical purpose. Distracting errors in grammar, usage, and mechanics may be present, but they generally do not impede understanding.

(continued)

The ACT Writing Test Analytic Rubric

	Ideas and Analysis	*Development and Support*	*Organization*	*Language Use and Conventions*
Score 2: **Responses at this scorepoint demonstrate weak or inconsistent skill in writing an argumentative essay.**	The writer generates an argument that weakly responds to multiple perspectives on the given issue. The argument's thesis, if evident, reflects little clarity in thought and purpose. Attempts at analysis are incomplete, largely irrelevant, or consist primarily of restatement of the issue and its perspectives.	Development of ideas and support for claims are weak, confused, or disjointed. Reasoning and illustration are inadequate, illogical, or circular, and fail to fully clarify the argument.	The response exhibits a rudimentary organizational structure. Grouping of ideas is inconsistent and often unclear. Transitions between and within paragraphs are misleading or poorly formed.	The use of language is inconsistent and often unclear. Word choice is rudimentary and frequently imprecise. Sentence structures are sometimes unclear. Stylistic and register choices, including voice and tone, are inconsistent and are not always appropriate for the rhetorical purpose. Distracting errors in grammar, usage, and mechanics are present, and they sometimes impede understanding.
Score 1: **Responses at this scorepoint demonstrate little or no skill in writing an argumentative essay.**	The writer fails to generate an argument that responds intelligibly to the task. The writer's intentions are difficult to discern. Attempts at analysis are unclear or irrelevant.	Ideas lack development, and claims lack support. Reasoning and illustration are unclear, incoherent, or largely absent.	The response does not exhibit an organizational structure. There is little grouping of ideas. When present, transitional devices fail to connect ideas.	The use of language fails to demonstrate skill in responding to the task. Word choice is imprecise and often difficult to comprehend. Sentence structures are often unclear. Stylistic and register choices are difficult to identify. Errors in grammar, usage, and mechanics are pervasive and often impede understanding.

STEP 2. Because your writing test domain scores are the sum of two readers' ratings of your essay, multiply your own 1–6 rating from step 1 by 2. Or, have both you and someone else read and score your practice essay, add those ratings together, and record the total in the Domain Score column in step 3.

STEP 3. Enter your writing test domain scores in the following box.

			Domain Score
Ideas and Analysis	________	× 2 =	________
Development and Support	________	× 2 =	________
Organization	________	× 2 =	________
Language Use and Conventions	________	× 2 =	________

STEP 4. Enter the sum of the second-column scores here ______.

STEP 5. Divide sum by 4† (range 2–12). This is your Writing Subject score.

†Round value to the nearest whole number. Round down any fraction less than one-half; round up any fraction that is one-half or more.

STEP 6. Use the table on page 112 to determine your estimated percentile rank (percent at or below) for your writing subject score.

National Distributions of Cumulative Percents Writing Score ACT-Tested High School Graduates from 2016, 2017, and 2018	
Score	**Writing**
12	22
11	18
10	15
9	12
8	7
7	5
6	4
5	3
4	3
3	2
2	2
1	1
Mean	17.8
S.D.	6.4

Note: The norms for the ACT ELA and 2–12 Writing scores are the source of U.S. and state ranks printed on ACT score reports during the 2018–2019 testing year. The norms for the ACT 1–36 Writing scores are the source of U.S. and state ranks printed on ACT supplemental score reports for test events between September 2015 and June 2017.
These norms with a sample size of 2,839,108, are based on 2016, 2017, and 2018 graduates.

Reviewing Explanatory Answers

After scoring your test, review the questions and answers to gain a better understanding of why each correct answer is correct and why the other choices for each question are wrong. We encourage you to review the explanatory answers for all questions, not just those you missed. As you read through the explanations, note any subject matter or concepts you don't fully understand, such as subject-verb agreement on the English test or how to calculate the volume of three-dimensional objects on the mathematics test.

The following sections give the correct answers for each question along with an explanation of why each correct answer is correct, why each of the other choices is wrong, and (in some cases) insight into why certain wrong answers may have been tempting choices. For more guidance on how to identify subject areas or skills you may need to work on, turn to chapter 4.

ENGLISH • PRACTICE TEST 1 • EXPLANATORY ANSWERS

Passage I

Question 1. The best answer is C because a comma is appropriate between the noun *1972* and the dependent, relative clause that begins with the word *when.*

The best answer is NOT:

A because the comma incorrectly separates the adverbial phrase "since 1972" from the main clause and the verb phrase it modifies, "has been studying."

B because the phrase "since 1972" is essential to the meaning of the main clause (restrictive). Setting the phrase off with commas indicates the phrase is nonrestrictive, resulting in an ungrammatical sentence.

D because the context of the sentence requires the word *elephants* in the main clause to be plural and non-possessive, not plural possessive.

Question 2. The best answer is F because the choice correctly forms the adjective *now-famous* to modify "Amboseli National Park," the compound noun that follows.

The best answer is NOT:

G because it incorrectly uses the adverb of time *then* rather than the conjunction *than* (used when making comparisons).

H because it incorrectly uses the adverb form *famously* to modify the noun that follows rather than the appropriate adjective form *famous.*

J because it incorrectly uses the adverb form *famously* to modify the noun that follows rather than the appropriate adjective form *famous.*

ENGLISH • PRACTICE TEST 1 • EXPLANATORY ANSWERS

Question 3. The best answer is B because the parenthetical information about the various threats to elephants' survival interrupts the main clause and needs to be set off with appropriate punctuation (commas, parentheses, or em dashes). The parenthetical is introduced with an em dash, and therefore the parenthetical must end with an em dash.

The best answer is NOT:

A because the lack of punctuation creates a run-on sentence and does not appropriately set off the parenthetical information in the middle of the main clause.

C because a colon has to have an independent clause preceding it, and what comes before this colon is not a complete thought. The colon also incorrectly implies that what follows the colon defines what comes before it.

D because the parenthetical information about the various threats to elephants' survival appears in the middle of the main clause and therefore needs to be set off with appropriate punctuation. The parenthetical is introduced with an em dash, so what follows the parenthetical must also be an em dash. This choice incorrectly uses a comma instead of a dash.

Question 4. The best answer is J because the preceding sentence mentions "human encroachment" as a threat to elephants, and inserting this sentence would add redundant information to the essay.

The best answer is NOT:

F because inserting this sentence would add redundant information, and the essay does not specify what factor determined Moss's interest in working with elephants.

G because inserting this sentence would add redundant information, and the focus of the rest of the essay is on elephants and learned behavior, not on the specific threat of humans to elephants.

H because the essay does mention the presence of humans in the lives of elephants in terms of the threat of humans to elephants' survival and in terms of Moss's study of elephants.

Question 5. The best answer is B because no punctuation is needed. The absence of punctuation creates a grammatical, clear, and understandable sentence.

The best answer is NOT:

A because the comma between the words *intensive* and *field* incorrectly separates the adjective from the noun it modifies. Furthermore, the comma between the words *field* and *studies* separates the two parts of the compound noun "field studies."

C because the comma following the word *studies* incorrectly separates the subject of the main clause from its verb.

D because the comma between the words *intensive* and *field* incorrectly separates the adjective from the noun it modifies.

ENGLISH • PRACTICE TEST 1 • EXPLANATORY ANSWERS

Question 6. The best answer is G because the phrase "for instance" offers the most logical transition from the claim about elephants and learned behavior at the end of the preceding paragraph to a specific example of learned behavior in elephants in this paragraph.

The best answer is NOT:

F because the word *however* indicates that the ideas in this paragraph will contrast with those from the preceding paragraph, which is not the case. Therefore, *however* does not offer a logical transition from the claim about elephants and learned behavior in the preceding paragraph to the example of learned behavior in elephants provided in this paragraph.

H because the phrase "as always" does not offer a logical transition from the claim about elephants and learned behavior in the preceding paragraph to an example of learned behavior in elephants in this paragraph.

J because the phrase "by now" does not offer a logical transition from the claim about elephants and learned behavior in the preceding paragraph to an example of learned behavior in elephants in this paragraph.

Question 7. The best answer is C because the gerund phrase "and sipping" maintains parallelism with the gerund *kneeling*, avoiding faulty and potentially confusing constructions within the prepositional phrase that begins with "by kneeling."

The best answer is NOT:

A because the phrase "and it sipped" is not parallel with the gerund *kneeling*, resulting in a faulty construction. This phrase would also require a comma before the word *and*, as it would end the sentence with an independent clause.

B because the phrase "which it sips" incorrectly implies that the elephant is sipping the water's edge rather than the water itself. The *which* phrase would also require a comma to precede it in order to be grammatically correct.

D because the phrase "that sips" is not parallel with the gerund *kneeling*. The phrase "that sips" also incorrectly implies that the water's edge is sipping (a misplaced modifier).

ENGLISH • PRACTICE TEST 1 • EXPLANATORY ANSWERS

Question 8. The best answer is G because the prepositional phrase that starts with "of pulling water" contains a compound object: "pulling and releasing." The phrase "trunk and then" correctly joins the two objects with a conjunction and most clearly describes the elephant's habit.

The best answer is NOT:

F because placing a period after the word *trunk* separates the compound object of the preposition and creates two sentence fragments.

H because the phrase "trunk then by" does not correctly join the compound object of the preposition and does not clearly explain the elephant's habit.

J because the word *trunk* does not correctly join the compound object of the preposition and creates a run-on sentence.

Question 9. The best answer is C because "of witnessing" creates a prepositional phrase that most clearly and logically describes what the elephant has been doing for months.

The best answer is NOT:

A because the phrase "as if witnessing" results in a faulty construction and implies that the elephant's observation was theoretical rather than actual.

B because the phrase "when witnessing" results in a faulty construction, and the combination of the adverbs *after* and *when* does not clearly explain what the elephant has spent months doing.

D because the phrase "then witness" results in a faulty construction and does not clearly describe what the elephant has spent months doing.

Question 10. The best answer is G because the phrase "in this regard" adds a prepositional phrase that creates a clear and complete sentence.

The best answer is NOT:

F because the phrase "in which this regard" is unnecessarily wordy, unclear, and creates a sentence fragment.

H because the referent for the phrase "ones that" is unclear, and its use creates a sentence fragment.

J because the word *which* creates a sentence fragment.

ENGLISH • PRACTICE TEST 1 • EXPLANATORY ANSWERS

Question 11. The best answer is B because the phrase "a baby male" is the only choice that adds new and relevant information to the sentence.

The best answer is NOT:

A because the idea that Moss named the elephants in her observations is implicit in this paragraph and is not relevant to the focus of the sentence on the age of the elephants.

C because the phrase "an elephant" adds redundant information to the paragraph.

D because the phrase "the third" adds redundant information to the paragraph.

Question 12. The best answer is F because the phrase "he also grew" avoids an unnecessary tense shift within the sentence.

The best answer is NOT:

G because the phrase "he also will have grown" unnecessarily shifts the verb tense from simple past tense (*overcame*) to future perfect tense.

H because the phrase "he also had grown" unnecessarily shifts the verb tense from simple past tense (*overcame*) to past perfect tense.

J because the phrase "also growing" creates a sentence fragment and is not clearly connected to the main, independent clause.

Question 13. The best answer is D because this placement makes it clear why Echo needed to take special care of Ely and why Ely might signal distress.

The best answer is NOT:

A because this placement does not logically connect to the idea in the preceding sentence that Ely overcame his limitations. This placement also introduces a new idea at the end of a paragraph.

B because Ely has not yet been introduced in the paragraph, so placing the information about his deformed feet at the beginning of the paragraph does not make sense.

C because Ely is not introduced until sentence 4, so placing the information about his deformed feet before sentence 4 does not make sense.

ENGLISH • PRACTICE TEST 1 • EXPLANATORY ANSWERS

Question 14. The best answer is J because all that is needed to complete the main clause of the sentence and make its meaning clear is the preposition *to* (connecting the phrase "an ever-expanding audience").

The best answer is NOT:

F because this choice adds an unnecessary verb phrase "is provided," which makes the structure of the sentence faulty and its meaning unclear.

G because this choice adds the unnecessary phrase "is given by her to," which makes the structure of the sentence faulty and its meaning unclear.

H because this choice adds an unnecessary verb phrase "is reaching," which makes the structure of the sentence faulty and its meaning unclear.

Question 15. The best answer is B because the essay does focus on Moss's observations of specific learned behavior in elephants in Kenya.

The best answer is NOT:

A because the essay focuses on Moss's observations of elephant behavior and not elephants' ability to identify various family members.

C because the essay focuses on Moss's observations of elephant behavior and not on how elephants have evolved differently throughout Africa.

D because the essay focuses on Moss's observations of behavior in elephants in Kenya and not on elephants in zoos around the world.

Passage II

Question 16. The best answer is J because the phrase "Remnants of outdoor advertisements from a bygone era" functions as an appositive, providing more information about the compound noun "ghost signs." This is an acceptable, grammatical inversion of the construction "They are called 'ghost signs,' remnants of outdoor advertisements from a bygone era."

The best answer is NOT:

F because the phrase "Seeing remnants" is a misplaced modifier that incorrectly implies *they* (the ghost signs) are seeing remnants.

G because the phrase "The sight of remnants" is a misplaced modifier that incorrectly implies that ghost signs are the "sight of remnants," not the remnants themselves.

H because the phrase "To see remnants" is a misplaced modifier that incorrectly implies that ghost signs are "to see remnants."

Your First Practice Test

ENGLISH • PRACTICE TEST 1 • EXPLANATORY ANSWERS

Question 17. The best answer is A because the phrase "bygone era" in the sentence is sufficient to express the idea that ghost signs are remnants of outdoor advertisements from an earlier time.

The best answer is NOT:

B because the phrase "era that is no more" is redundant.

C because the phrase "era of another time" is redundant.

D because the phrase "era of times past" is redundant.

Question 18. The best answer is G because the examples of words found on ghost signs interrupt the main clause and must be set off by appropriate punctuation (commas, parentheses, or em dashes). This parenthetical information ends with an em dash and, therefore, must be introduced with an em dash as well.

The best answer is NOT:

F because the lack of punctuation creates a run-on sentence that does not appropriately set off the parenthetical examples.

H because the comma after *remain* does not appropriately set off the parenthetical examples (an em dash is required).

J because the colon after *remain* does not appropriately set off the parenthetical examples (an em dash is required).

Question 19. The best answer is B because the relative pronoun *that* is required to logically and grammatically link the clause that follows to the rest of the sentence.

The best answer is NOT:

A because the word *should* results in an illogical, faulty connection between the sentence's clauses.

C because adding the word *they* makes the final clause independent, resulting in a run-on sentence.

D because the phrase "should they" results in an illogical, faulty connection between the sentence's clauses.

ENGLISH • PRACTICE TEST 1 • EXPLANATORY ANSWERS

Question 20. The best answer is F because no punctuation is necessary in order to connect compound direct object "products and businesses" to the rest of the sentence.

The best answer is NOT:

G because the comma following "products and businesses" incorrectly separates the main clause from the restrictive relative clause "that no longer exist."

H because the comma following the word *products* separates the two objects in the compound direct object "products and businesses."

J because the colon incorrectly implies that "businesses that no longer exist" is a definition of *products*.

Question 21. The best answer is B because the word *instead* is an interrupting aside that needs to be set off by commas. A comma also needs to come before the word *with* to separate the entire prepositional phrase "with, instead, their simple claims of complex colors" from the main clause.

The best answer is NOT:

A because the word *instead* is an interrupting aside that needs to be set off by commas, and this choice does not provide a comma directly before the word *instead*.

C because the word *instead* is an interrupting aside and needs to be set off by commas, and this choice does not provide a comma directly before the word *instead*. This choice also lacks a comma directly before the word *with*; this comma is required in order to correctly connect the prepositional phrase to the rest of the sentence.

D because both the word *instead* and the prepositional phrase that begins with the word *with* need to be set off by commas. This choice does not contain any punctuation.

ENGLISH • PRACTICE TEST 1 • EXPLANATORY ANSWERS

Question 22. The best answer is H because this sentence is the most logical and grammatical choice, making it clear that the narrator started her collection one October as she was driving home from school.

The best answer is NOT:

F because this choice removes the subject *I* from the sentence, creating a misplaced modifier in which the participle phrase "Driving home from school one chilly October evening" modifies the noun phrase "my collection."

G because this choice removes the subject *I* from the sentence, creating a dangling modifier in which the participle phrase "Driving home from school one chilly October evening" has no clear noun to modify. Therefore, it is possible to read this as the "beginning of my collection" was driving home.

J because the structure of this sentence is confusing and creates a misplaced modifier in which the participle phrase "driving home from school one chilly October evening" modifies "the start of my collection." Furthermore, the clause "The start of my collection came to me" is unclear and implies that the collection was moving by itself.

Question 23. The best answer is D because the idea that the ad for Joe's Café was disappearing echoes the point the narrator made earlier in the essay that ghost signs are barely legible, faded, and pale.

The best answer is NOT:

A because the idea that the ad for Joe's Café was upright does not echo a point made earlier in the essay.

B because the idea that the narrator was not interested in the ad for Joe's Café is not supported by the rest of the essay (the narrator "collects" ghosts signs as a hobby).

C because the idea that the ad for Joe's Café might have been made of wood does not echo a point made earlier in the essay.

ENGLISH • PRACTICE TEST 1 • EXPLANATORY ANSWERS

Question 24. The best answer is J because the phrase "setting sun illuminated" creates a logical and grammatical sentence.

The best answer is NOT:

F because the lack of a verb in the phrase "setting sun's illumination of" results in an incomplete, illogical sentence.

G because the lack of a verb in the phrase "illuminating setting sun on" results in an incomplete, illogical sentence.

H because this choice creates a sentence that says "the sun illuminated the set on the yellowing plastic," which is illogical.

Question 25. The best answer is B because "evidence of" is the correct, idiomatic phrase needed in order to make this sentence most understandable ("evidence of vandalism or of a hailstorm").

The best answer is NOT:

A because the phrase "a clue to vandalism" is not idiomatic, and the preposition *to* is not parallel with the preposition *of* in "of a hailstorm."

C because the adverb *evidently* results in a faulty construction when combined with the prepositional phrase "of a hailstorm."

D because deleting the underlined portion leaves a structurally flawed, illogical sentence that reads "Maybe it was the small hole, vandalism or of a hailstorm."

Question 26. The best answer is J because no transitional word or phrase is necessary in order to connect this sentence to the ideas in the rest of the paragraph.

The best answer is NOT:

F because the transitional word *Instead* implies that a contrast is being set up in this sentence. Rather, the sentence is building on the idea presented in the preceding sentence.

G because the transitional phrase "On the other hand" implies that a contrast is being set up in this sentence; instead, the sentence is building on the idea presented in the preceding sentence.

H because the transitional word *Meanwhile* incorrectly implies that the idea in this sentence is not directly connected to the idea presented in the preceding sentence.

ENGLISH • PRACTICE TEST 1 • EXPLANATORY ANSWERS

Question 27. The best answer is D because given the context of the sentence, the adjective *solo* is the most logical and precise word to modify the noun *trips*.

The best answer is NOT:

A because the phrase "solitude trips" does not make sense given the context.

B because using the adverb *solitarily* to modify the noun *trips* is not logical or grammatical.

C because the phrase "solitaire trips" doesn't make sense given the context.

Question 28. The best answer is H because the phrase "like the signs" is a nonrestrictive phrase in which the narrator compares herself to the signs. Setting off the phrase with commas prevents ambiguity when reading the sentence.

The best answer is NOT:

F because omitting the comma between the words *I* and *like* creates ambiguity and reads as though the narrator is about to describe something she likes, rather than setting up a comparison. The comma following the word *signs* also creates the fragment "am alone" at the end of the sentence.

G because setting off only the word *like* with commas creates a nonrestrictive element. If the word *like* were removed, the sentence would read "I the signs am alone," indicating that *like* is essential to the meaning of the phrase and should not be set off by commas.

J because setting off only the words "the signs" with commas creates a nonrestrictive element. If the words "the signs" were removed, the sentence would read "I like am alone," indicating that "the signs" is essential to the meaning of the entire phrase and should not be set off by commas.

Question 29. The best answer is A because the paragraph's current placement makes the most logical sense within the narrative. The narrator first introduces signs, describes generally how her collection began, describes the specific instance that first drew her to ghost signs, and then concludes the essay by describing her hunts generally.

The best answer is NOT:

B because paragraph 1 is the best and clearest introduction of ghost signs. Describing how the narrator began collecting ghost signs (paragraph 2) before describing what they actually are does not make logical sense.

C because no logical transition exists between paragraph 1 and paragraph 3 if paragraph 2 were to be moved after paragraph 3. It also doesn't make sense for the narrator to describe taking pictures of the ad for Joe's Café in paragraph 3 before she introduces the idea that she uses photography to "collect" ghost signs.

D because paragraph 2 would not serve as a logical conclusion to the essay; it introduces the main focus of the essay.

Question 30. The best answer is F because the essay describes the narrator's hobby of photographing ghost signs and how her hobby got started after she saw the sign for Joe's Café.

The best answer is NOT:

G because the essay does not indicate that the narrator learned her hobby from a friend.

H because although the essay does use the terms *lonely* and *forlorn* to describe a particular sign, her description of her hobby is positive.

J because the essay describes only one hobby: collecting ghost signs in photographs.

Passage III

Question 31. The best answer is B because "a series of semitropical islands off the southeast coast of the United States" is an appositive phrase that further describes the Bahamas. This phrase is nonrestrictive and must be set off by commas. The verb *are* is also needed to avoid a sentence fragment.

The best answer is NOT:

A because the word *which* in this choice creates a sentence fragment. If the appositive ("a series of semitropical islands off the southeast coast of the United States") were removed, the sentence would read "The Bahamas, which are home to some of the most unusual geological formations in the world: underwater caves known as blue holes."

C because this choice removes the comma between the words *States* and *are*, which does not correctly set off the appositive from the main clause of the sentence.

D because this choice removes the verb *are* from the main clause, creating a sentence fragment.

ENGLISH • PRACTICE TEST 1 • EXPLANATORY ANSWERS

Question 32. The best answer is F because this paragraph focuses on the formation of the caves, and this choice most logically introduces the topic by introducing a critical component of the formation: calcium carbonate. This choice is the only one to give us two pieces of essential information: that the Bahamas were formed from calcium carbonate and that calcium carbonate is a component of seawater.

The best answer is NOT:

G because the description of calcium carbonate is too general and is not specifically tied to the formation of the caves, which is the topic of the paragraph. Furthermore, the phrase "also found in seawater" does not connect to the preceding paragraph, since there is no mention of other components of seawater.

H because the idea that much of the land making up the Bahamas is still underwater is not immediately relevant to the topic of this paragraph, which is how the caves formed.

J because the idea that most types of limestone contain calcium carbonate is only loosely related to the focus of the paragraph and does not introduce the topic of cave formation.

Question 33. The best answer is A because the simple past tense *built* is consistent with the verb tense in the rest of the paragraph.

The best answer is NOT:

B because "are building" shifts the verb tense to present progressive tense, which is inconsistent with the verb tense in the rest of the paragraph.

C because "will build" shifts the verb tense to future tense, which is inconsistent with the verb tense in the rest of the paragraph.

D because *build* shifts the verb tense to simple present tense, which is inconsistent with the verb tense in the rest of the paragraph.

Question 34. The best answer is F because this choice presents the clearest, most concise, and most idiomatic way to say that the rainwater was buoyed by the seawater below.

The best answer is NOT:

G because this choice is unnecessarily wordy and illogical (it is not idiomatic to state that the rainwater was being buoyed because of the denser seawater below; the limestone was buoyed by the seawater).

H because the introduction of the pronoun-verb combination "it being" creates a sentence that is unnecessarily wordy and awkwardly constructed.

J because switching to the passive construction here is not only awkward but also results in an illogical sentence (the rainwater, trapped just below sea level, could not have buoyed the denser seawater below).

ENGLISH • PRACTICE TEST 1 • EXPLANATORY ANSWERS

Question 35. The best answer is D because the word *either* in the sentence indicates that the brackish water is being compared to two things at the same time: rainwater and seawater. The omission of punctuation is appropriate and indicates that these two nouns are parallel elements in the construction "either rainwater or seawater."

The best answer is NOT:

A because setting off the phrase "or seawater" with dashes separates the parallel elements (rainwater or seawater). Without further explanation, this separation is unnecessary and illogical.

B because setting off the phrase "or seawater" with commas separates the parallel elements (rainwater or seawater) and also incorrectly implies that seawater is acting as an appositive for rainwater.

C because placing a comma after rainwater incorrectly separates the parallel elements (rainwater or seawater).

Question 36. The best answer is H because the introductory adverb clause "As the limestone eroded" must be separated from the main clause ("caves formed") by a comma.

The best answer is NOT:

F because the introductory adverb clause "As the limestone eroded" must be followed by a comma; the omission of punctuation creates ambiguity and results in a run-on sentence.

G because inserting a comma after the word *limestone* interrupts the introductory adverb clause "As the limestone eroded" and creates an incomplete thought. Moreover, *eroded* incorrectly refers to caves instead of limestone.

J because inserting a comma after the word *caves* incorrectly implies that the limestone eroded the caves and makes the meaning of the sentence ambiguous. The comma also leaves the verb *formed* without a subject.

Question 37. The best answer is B because this choice provides the most specific indication of time. Both "ice ages" and "temperate eras" speak to large swaths of time and indicate that a great deal of time passed during the cave-formation process.

The best answer is NOT:

A because "time periods in which the weather changed drastically" is vague and does not indicate a specific length of time. Weather can change drastically over short periods of time; therefore, "time periods" does not do enough to illustrate a specific length of time.

C because this choice is not as specific as B; "extended time" could be interpreted differently by different readers.

D because "As time passed" does not indicate a specific length of time.

Your First Practice Test

ENGLISH • PRACTICE TEST 1 • EXPLANATORY ANSWERS

Question 38. The best answer is J because the phrase "repeat at different depths" is the clearest and most concise choice in this context.

The best answer is NOT:

F because this choice is unnecessarily wordy and redundant. The preceding sentence already tells us that sea levels rose and fell by 100s of feet; "process to be a process" is also redundant.

G because "repeat again and again" and "various different" are both redundant.

H because "different depths that varied" is unnecessarily wordy and redundant.

Question 39. The best answer is C because the semicolon correctly separates the two independent clauses.

The best answer is NOT:

A because omitting punctuation between these two independent clauses creates a run-on sentence.

B because *that* doesn't make sense in context and creates a run-on sentence.

D because inserting a comma after the word *caves*, without adding a coordinating conjunction, creates a comma splice.

Question 40. The best answer is H because the specific information about Dean's Blue Hole as a popular cave-diving destination is not related to the focus of the paragraph, which is on cave formation in general.

The best answer is NOT:

F because the information about Dean's Blue Hole is only tangentially related to the preceding sentence.

G because the sentence does not provide enough information about Dean's Blue Hole to help the reader visualize this particular underwater cave. Even if the sentence did provide sufficient description, this information wouldn't be relevant because it is not related to the paragraph's focus on cave formation.

J because the sentence should not be added because the information about Dean's Blue Hole isn't related to the paragraph's focus on cave formation, not because the sentence doesn't provide an adequate description of Dean's Blue Hole.

ENGLISH • PRACTICE TEST 1 • EXPLANATORY ANSWERS

Question 41. The best answer is B because the noun *water* must be modified by the adjective *darker*, and the adjective *darker* should be modified by the adverb *strikingly*. This is the only choice that uses the correct adjective and adverb forms of these words.

The best answer is NOT:

A because the sentence is setting up a comparison between the appearance of the water of the blue hole and the water surrounding it; given this context, the correct adverb form to modify *darker* is *strikingly*.

C because the noun *water* must be modified by an adjective; this choice incorrectly modifies *water* with the adverb *darkly*.

D because the sentence sets up a comparison between the appearance of the water of the blue hole and the water surrounding it; therefore, the verb *striking* doesn't make sense here. Furthermore, the noun *water* must be modified by an adjective; this choice incorrectly modifies *water* with the adverb *darkly*.

Question 42. The best answer is J because the pronoun *it* is appropriate given the context and agrees in number with its antecedent "a circular patch of water."

The best answer is NOT:

F because the pronoun *them* does not agree in number with its singular antecedent "blue hole."

G because the pronoun *these* does not agree in number with its singular antecedent "blue hole."

H because the pronoun *one* is a confusing pronoun choice for the antecedent "a circular patch of water." *One* implies that the focus is on a particular circular patch of water, whereas the sentence is describing a feature of blue holes in general.

Question 43. The best answer is C because the sentence presents a list of three findings of divers, the first of which is "remains of turtles and alligators now extinct on the island."

The best answer is NOT:

A because adding a period between *alligators* and *Now* creates a sentence fragment and interrupts the list of the findings of divers.

B because adding a period between *now* and *Extinct* creates a sentence fragment and interrupts the list of the findings of divers.

D because adding a period between *extinct* and *On* creates a sentence fragment and interrupts the list of the findings of divers.

Question 44. The best answer is G because the essay tells us that the telltale sign of a blue hole is a "circular patch of water." The word *dot* (a small round mark) indicates the circular shape of the blue holes and is the only choice that suggests a shape.

The best answer is NOT:

F because the phrase "can be sighted off" does not indicate shape in any way.

H because the phrase "darken parts of" speaks to color, not shape.

J because the phrase "appear in" does not indicate shape.

Question 45. The best answer is C because this placement most logically connects "these depths" in the added sentence to the first two sentences of paragraph 4 in which the depths of the water are described. The information about the well-preserved fossils and rock formations also helps introduce other discoveries made by divers in the caves.

The best answer is NOT:

A because the depths and exploration of the blue holes have not yet been introduced in paragraph 1, making this placement of the added sentence illogical.

B because this placement interrupts the description of cave formation in paragraph 2.

D because the added sentence does not logically introduce paragraph 5, which describes unexplored caves more generally. Moreover, the information about fossils and rock formations being well preserved should come before the list of examples in the previous sentence.

Passage IV

Question 46. The best answer is J because the phrase "defensive walls" is itself sufficient to express the original purpose of the ancient walls.

The best answer is NOT:

F because the word *protectively* is not needed here. The sentence's idea—that the walls were defensive—would be clear simply with "walls intended to defend."

G because the phrase "defensive walls for defending the city" is also redundant. Either "defensive walls" or "for defending the city" would be appropriate, not both.

H because the phrase "walls to provide defensive protection" is unnecessarily wordy; "defensive protection" is somewhat redundant.

ENGLISH • PRACTICE TEST 1 • EXPLANATORY ANSWERS

Question 47. The best answer is C because the introductory adverb clause that starts with *Although* must be followed by a comma, and this choice correctly places a comma following the word *tall*.

The best answer is NOT:

A because the introductory adverb clause that starts with *Although* must be followed by a comma, and the omission of punctuation between *tall* and *they* creates a run-on sentence.

B because adding a period between *tall* and *They* creates a sentence fragment ("Although both were built as defensive walls and stood ten meters tall.").

D because a semicolon is used to separate two independent clauses, and placing a semicolon here would split a dependent clause ("Although both were built as defensive walls and stood ten meters tall") and an independent clause ("they were erected under different historical circumstances").

Question 48. The best answer is F because the word *It's* is correctly used in its contraction form to create a sentence that begins "It is thought that . . ."

The best answer is NOT:

G because this choice offers the possessive pronoun *its* rather than the contraction *it's*.

H because this choice also attempts a possessive pronoun. The use of the pronoun is incorrect, as is the placement of the apostrophe.

J because this choice places the possessive pronoun *its* into the sentence rather than the contraction *it's*.

Question 49. The best answer is A because the comma following "Aurelian Wall" correctly sets off the nonrestrictive appositive phrase "built in the late third century CE by the Roman Emperor Aurelian," which further describes the Aurelian Wall.

The best answer is NOT:

B because adding the verb phrase "had been" creates a sentence with two predicates. In order to be grammatically correct, the sentence would have to read "the Aurelian Wall had been built in the late third century CE *and* was much sturdier than the older wall."

C because the word *which* is unnecessary before the appositive "built in the late third century CE by the Roman Emperor Aurelian" and separates the appositive from its noun.

D because adding the verb *was* creates a sentence with two predicates and results in a run-on.

ENGLISH • PRACTICE TEST 1 • EXPLANATORY ANSWERS

Question 50. The best answer is G because the phrase "much sturdier than" uses the correct comparative adjective *much* and the correct use of the subordinating conjunction *than* to compare the Aurelian Wall with the older wall.

The best answer is NOT:

F because the phrase "more sturdier" is an incorrect use of the comparative adjective *more* in combination with *sturdier.*

H because the phrase "more sturdier" is an incorrect use of the comparative adjective *more* in combination with *sturdier.* Furthermore, the subordinating conjunction *than* must be used to set up the comparison in the sentence, not the adverb *then.*

J because the subordinating conjunction *than* must be used to set up the comparison in the sentence, not the adverb *then.*

Question 51. The best answer is B because the meaning of the phrase "greatly expanded" is most clear in this case when it is placed directly before the noun it modifies: "city of Rome." When we read "surrounded the greatly expanded city of Rome," it is obvious that Rome itself, rather than the wall or the river, had expanded.

The best answer is NOT:

A because this placement of "greatly expanded" results in an unclear sentence; no noun directly precedes or follows the phrase. It sounds as if the wall itself has expanded, which doesn't make sense.

C because the phrase "greatly expanded" does not make sense grammatically or logically when it follows directly after the noun *Rome.*

D because this placement of the phrase "greatly expanded" incorrectly indicates that it was the Tiber's west bank that was greatly expanded, not the city of Rome.

Question 52. The best answer is J because no transition is needed between these two sentences, both of which describe the physical features of the Aurelian Wall.

The best answer is NOT:

F because the transitional phrase "in other words" implies that the ideas presented in this sentence are a restatement of the ideas in the preceding sentence, which isn't the case.

G because *Therefore* implies a cause-effect relationship between this sentence and the preceding sentence, and there is no obvious cause-effect here.

H because *Instead* implies that a contrast is being made between this sentence and the preceding sentence, and there is no contrast being made between the physical features of the wall.

ENGLISH • PRACTICE TEST 1 • EXPLANATORY ANSWERS

Question 53. The best answer is A because no punctuation is necessary within the phrase "Both the posterns and the towers." The conjunction *both* at the beginning of the phrase indicates that the two things that follow equally served as defensive positions.

The best answer is NOT:

B because putting commas around the phrase "the posterns and the towers" incorrectly separates the conjunction *both* from the two nouns that follow. Placing commas around the phrase also signals that the phrase is nonrestrictive; in fact, the information is essential to understanding the sentence.

C because placing a comma after *posterns* incorrectly separates the two parallel nouns ("the posterns and the towers").

D because placing a comma after the word *towers* incorrectly separates the subject of the sentence ("the posterns and towers") from the verb (*served*).

Question 54. The best answer is G because this is the only choice that specifically indicates how the posterns and towers were used as defensive positions. They provided cover during an enemy attack.

The best answer is NOT:

F because the phrase "for protecting Rome" does not add any new information to the sentence, nor does it provide specific information about how the posterns and towers served as defensive positions.

H because the phrase does not add any new information about how the posterns and towers served as defensive positions; "to help Rome repel against enemy attacks" stops short of providing specific information. How did they help repel enemy attacks? That information can be found in **G**.

J because "by keeping Rome safe from invaders" does not add specific information about how the posterns and towers actually kept Rome safe from invaders. Again, see **G**.

ENGLISH • PRACTICE TEST 1 • EXPLANATORY ANSWERS

Question 55. The best answer is B because the information about the Aurelian Wall continuing to dominate the Roman landscape most logically introduces the focus of paragraph 5 on what remains of the walls today. It also creates the best contrast between the well-preserved Aurelian Wall and the scant remains of the Servian Wall, a contrast demanded by the word *however.*

The best answer is NOT:

A because the information about the materials Romans used to build the Aurelian Wall does not logically introduce the focus of paragraph 5, which is on what remains of the walls today, and there is no clear connection between this information and the *however* in the next sentence.

C because there is no logical connection between the information about Emperor Aurelian and the information that follows in the paragraph.

D because the information about mounds of earth serving as protection prior to the construction of the walls is unrelated to the main focus of the essay and does not logically introduce the focus of paragraph 5, which is on what remains of the walls today.

Question 56. The best answer is J because the plural verb *remain* agrees in number with its plural subject *portions.* (The verb must agree with *portions,* not with *wall.*)

The best answer is NOT:

F because the singular verb *remains* does not agree in number with the plural subject *portions.*

G because the verb phrase "were remaining" shifts the verb tense in the sentence and is inconsistent with the verb tense in the rest of the paragraph.

H because the singular verb phrase "has remained" does not agree in number with the plural subject *portions.*

Question 57. The best answer is C because the information about architectural features of the Aurelian Wall is out of place and is unrelated to the discussion of the Servian Wall in the present day.

The best answer is NOT:

A because at this point the paragraph's focus is on the Servian Wall in the present day; this sentence is neither related nor does it support the main idea.

B because the innovations and practicality of Roman engineers is irrelevant to the focus of the paragraph on the Servian Wall in the present day.

D because the level of detail is irrelevant; the sentence should not be added because it provides details that are unrelated to the topic at this point in the paragraph. Moreover, the level of detail itself is actually consistent with the level of detail in the rest of the essay.

ENGLISH • PRACTICE TEST 1 • EXPLANATORY ANSWERS

Question 58. The best answer is F because "the future" provides the clearest and most concise description of the capital.

The best answer is NOT:

G because "what was yet to be appointed to the designation of" is unnecessarily wordy and somewhat unclear.

H because "what would in reality become the" is unnecessarily wordy; there is no reason to stress *reality* here at all.

J because "a would-be but not yet" is exceedingly awkward phrasing. A clearer way to express the idea of "future" is simply to say "the future."

Question 59. The best answer is C because the preservation of the remnants of the Servian Wall in a location that is commonplace and average, such as a fast-food restaurant, can be considered ironic given the prestige and distinction originally associated with the wall and the city in which it resided. Moreover, the idea of a centuries-old wall being preserved in a fast-food restaurant—where food is designed to be served and eaten quickly and which are often temporary themselves—might also be considered ironic.

The best answer is NOT:

A because the detail that the importance of the wall is recognized by archaeologists simply builds on the idea about the prestige of the wall and Rome in the first part of the sentence. No irony is created with this choice.

B because this idea builds on the idea about the prestige of the wall and Rome in the first part of the sentence. It makes sense that a wall that once protected the future capital of one of the ancient world's most famous empires would be preserved as an important relic, and therefore no irony is created with this choice.

D because "such varied locations" is vague in comparison to **C**, and the essay only provides one location before this point. Any resulting irony is unclear at best; the irony is best completed with "fast-food restaurant" in **C**.

ENGLISH • PRACTICE TEST 1 • EXPLANATORY ANSWERS

Question 60. The best answer is F because the description of the walls as two concentric circles most logically connects to the general introduction of the walls in the first paragraph, in which the walls are described as surrounding the city and serving as protective barriers.

The best answer is NOT:

G because paragraph 2 only describes the construction of the Servian Wall, so the information about how the two walls look together does not logically fit here.

H because paragraph 3 only describes the construction of the Aurelian Wall, so the information about how the two walls look together does not logically fit here.

J because paragraph 4 continues the description of the Aurelian Wall, so the information about how the two walls look together does not logically fit here.

Passage V

Question 61. The best answer is C because the comma following the introductory adverb clause ("Before entering a British-run prison during the American Revolution") is appropriate. Both the phrase "prisoner of war" and the name "James Forten" are restrictive in the sentence, so neither should be set off or interrupted by commas.

The best answer is NOT:

A because the name *James Forten* is restrictive (essential to the meaning of the sentence) and should not be set off by commas. Furthermore, a comma is required following the introductory adverb clause ("Before entering a British-run prison during the American Revolution").

B because the comma following the name *Forten* incorrectly separates the subject of the sentence (*James Forten*) from its verb (*said*).

D because placing a comma after the word *war* separates the descriptor "prisoner of war" from the noun it modifies (*James Forten*), and eliminating the comma after the word *Revolution* introduces ambiguity ("American Revolution prisoner of war").

ENGLISH • PRACTICE TEST 1 • EXPLANATORY ANSWERS

Question 62. The best answer is G because this choice best introduces the focus of the paragraph, which is on the risks Forten faced by rejecting the British captor's offer and choosing to stay in the United States.

The best answer is NOT:

F because the detail that Forten was one of many to serve in the American Revolution is unrelated to the main focus of the essay and does not introduce the focus of this paragraph, which is on the risks Forten faced by staying in the United States.

H because this sentence is unrelated to the focus of the paragraph. The information in this sentence relates to the British captor's offer instead of to the risk Forten took in refusing the offer; the focus of the paragraph is not on the offer but on the potential consequences for Forten in rejecting it.

J because this information is both vague and out of place at this point in the essay, and this choice does not logically introduce the focus of the paragraph (Forten's decision to stay in the United States and the risks he faced as a result).

Question 63. The best answer is C because the plural noun *chances* agrees in number with the plural verb *were*, and the choice correctly uses the preposition *of* in the idiomatic phrase "chances of surviving."

The best answer is NOT:

A because the singular noun *chance* does not agree in number with the plural verb *were.*

B because "chances to surviving" contains an incorrect use of the preposition *to* in the idiomatic phrase "chances of surviving."

D because the singular noun *chance* does not agree in number with the plural verb *were.*

Question 64. The best answer is F because a comma is required both following the dependent adverbial clause "if released at the war's end or as part of an exchange" and following the noun *he* (to separate the noun from its appositive "a free black man").

The best answer is NOT:

G because a semicolon should be used to separate two independent clauses; in this case, the semicolon after the word *exchange* separates a dependent and independent clause.

H because a comma should be used following the dependent adverbial clause "if released at the war's end or as part of an exchange," not a dash. Furthermore, omitting a comma between the word *he* and the phrase "a free black man" does not set off the appositive from its noun.

J because placing a period between the words *exchange* and *he* creates a sentence fragment.

ENGLISH • PRACTICE TEST 1 • EXPLANATORY ANSWERS

Question 65. The best answer is B because the sentence demonstrates that Forten did make the right choice, despite the risks, and became successful as a result. Without this sentence, the essay lacks a clear transition to paragraph 3.

The best answer is NOT:

A because this sentence does not give any information about the tactics Forten used to survive imprisonment, and the essay has not yet described how he became a successful businessman.

C because this sentence does not compare or give any specifics about Forten's work as a businessman or abolitionist.

D because this sentence does not analyze or provide specific information about how Forten transitioned from a prisoner to a businessman and abolitionist.

Question 66. The best answer is F because the simple past tense *rose* is consistent with the verb tense in the rest of the paragraph.

The best answer is NOT:

G because *arose* is the wrong verb in context, and *had arose* is an incorrect formation (the correct past perfect form of *arose* is *had arisen*).

H because the shift to past perfect tense is inconsistent with the verb tense in the rest of the paragraph, and the correct past perfect tense form of the verb *rise* is *had risen,* not *had rose.*

J because the transitive verb *raised* is used incorrectly here since there is no direct object. Instead, the sentence calls for the intransitive verb *rose.*

Question 67. The best answer is A because the appositive phrase "white and black" further describes the workers. Because it is nonrestrictive, this phrase needs to be set off with commas.

The best answer is NOT:

B because the relative pronoun *whom* is used incorrectly here; *whom* is an object pronoun, but the sentence requires a subject pronoun (*who*).

C because an independent clause must precede a colon; in this choice, the colon is preceded by a dependent clause.

D because the appositive phrase "white and black" needs to be offset from its noun *workers* with commas; the omission of a comma following *workers* is incorrect.

ENGLISH • PRACTICE TEST 1 • EXPLANATORY ANSWERS

Question 68. The best answer is H because the focus of the paragraph is on how Forten's sailmaking business became a success; the information about his lost business records is unrelated to this focus.

The best answer is NOT:

F because the loss of Forten's business records is not related to the success of his business; the sentence does not establish a correlation. The sentence is also unrelated to the paragraph's focus on the success of Forten's business.

G because the loss of Forten's business records does not reveal specific information about how many workers Forten employed. The sentence does not provide evidence, nor is it related to the paragraph's focus on the success of Forten's business.

J because the sentence does not contradict the idea that Forten had high expectations for his workers; the information about the loss of business records is unrelated to Forten's high expectations. Although the sentence should be deleted, the reason this choice offers for deleting it is inaccurate.

Question 69. The best answer is D because it is the most concise, least redundant choice. The phrase "premier sailmaker" by itself is sufficient to express the high regard people had for Forten's sailmaking business.

The best answer is NOT:

A because "premier sailmaker in Philadelphia" is redundant; the essay has already mentioned what city Forten worked in.

B because *foremost* and *leading* are redundant, and "in his native Philadelphia" repeats information the essay has already provided.

C because "premier sailmaker in the city of Philadelphia" is unnecessarily wordy and unnecessarily repeats information about the city in which Forten works.

Your First Practice Test

ENGLISH • PRACTICE TEST 1 • EXPLANATORY ANSWERS

Question 70. The best answer is J because the paragraph provides two examples of Forten overcoming hardships in his business: the closing of the port of Philadelphia during the War of 1812 and changing demands in sail design, both of which he adapted to. Therefore, this choice most logically introduces the focus of this paragraph.

The best answer is NOT:

F because the information about Forten sustaining his business during wartime hardships and meeting changing demands, which is the focus of the paragraph, is not related to abolitionist causes, so this choice does not logically introduce this paragraph.

G because this choice repeats information about Forten's service during the Revolutionary War and is unrelated to the focus of the paragraph on Forten's ability to adapt to changing circumstances.

H because the information about Forten sustaining his business during wartime hardships and meeting changing demands, which is the focus of the paragraph, is not related to the information about Forten's donations to schools and hospitals. This choice does not logically introduce this paragraph.

Question 71. The best answer is A because the coordinate adjectives *smaller* and *quicker* both modify the noun *vessels*, and therefore a comma is needed to separate the two adjectives. The order of the adjectives could be swapped to say "quicker, smaller vessels," and it would not change the meaning of the sentence. Likewise, the sentence could say "smaller and quicker" or "quicker and smaller."

The best answer is NOT:

B because the coordinating conjunction *and* is incorrect when used with a comma between two coordinating adjectives (either a comma or the word *and* would be appropriate, not both), and the word *more* is incorrectly used with the comparative adjective *quicker*.

C because the word *more* is incorrectly used with the comparative adjective *quicker.*

D because a comma is needed to separate a pair of coordinate adjectives, or adjectives that both modify the same noun and not each other. In this case *smaller* and *quicker* both modify *vessels*; *smaller* does not modify *quicker.*

ENGLISH • PRACTICE TEST 1 • EXPLANATORY ANSWERS

Question 72. The best answer is J because the phrase "over half of his" is the clearest and most concise choice to express how much money Forten invested in abolitionist causes.

The best answer is NOT:

F because the phrase "over greater than half" is unnecessarily wordy; *over* and *greater* mean the same thing.

G because the phrase "over more than half" is unnecessarily wordy and redundant.

H because the phrase "more than over half" is redundant; either "more than half" or "over half" would have been acceptable, but not both.

Question 73. The best answer is D because it is the most logical and concise choice to conclude the essay.

The best answer is NOT:

A because the phrase "who served in this war" is redundant following the noun *veteran.*

B because the phrase "cultivating the sails of freedom" presents a vague and confusing metaphor (what exactly does "the sails of freedom" mean or refer to?), and the repetition of the word *freedom* in the sentence is a questionable stylistic choice.

C because "nurturing the road to reform" is a phrase that, like "cultivating the sails of freedom," might sound good at first but actually presents a vague and confusing metaphor. "Nurturing the road" is not idiomatic and doesn't make much sense in context.

Question 74. The best answer is J because the information about the articles Forten submitted under a pen name makes logical sense only if placed after the sentence that introduces his financing of the newspaper *Liberator.*

The best answer is NOT:

F because this sentence does not logically fit at this point in the essay; Forten has not yet been introduced or credited with the quotation in the first sentence. The information about his submission of articles under a pen name is also out of chronological order in the essay.

G because the information about his submission of articles under a pen name is not related to the focus of paragraph 3, which outlines how Forten got involved in the sailmaking business.

H because it does not make logical sense to describe how Forten submitted articles to a publication under a pen name before introducing the newspaper itself.

ENGLISH • PRACTICE TEST 1 • EXPLANATORY ANSWERS

Question 75. The best answer is C because the focus of the essay is on Forten and the significant roles he played (patriot, businessman, abolitionist) and not on the more specific daily operations of his successful business.

The best answer is NOT:

A because the essay does not describe in detail the daily operations of a successful business. Although the essay does describe how Forten became a successful businessman and survived numerous challenges, the focus of the essay is on Forten's significance in other aspects as well.

B because although the essay does, to a degree, indicate the historical significance of Forten's business and the various ways it evolved, the main purpose of the essay is to describe Forten's significance more generally.

D because the essay does not contrast Forten's work as an abolitionist with his work as a sailmaker but instead shows how his success in business was beneficial to and worked in tandem with his work as an abolitionist.

MATHEMATICS • PRACTICE TEST 1 • EXPLANATORY ANSWERS

Question 1. The correct answer is C. The correct approach for this problem is to first distribute a and then combine the two a-terms. Doing so, we get $a(4 - a) - 5(a + 7) = 4a - a^2 - 5a - 35 = -a^2 - a - 35$. If you chose **A**, you may have thought that $a \cdot a = a$ and did not get the a^2-term when you distributed. If you chose **B**, you may have made the same error as above but also forgotten to distribute −5 over *both terms* of $(a + 7)$. If you chose **D**, you may have forgotten to distribute −5 over *both terms* of $(a + 7)$. If you chose **E**, you may have incorrectly combined like terms by thinking $4a - a^2 - 5a = (4 - 1 - 5)a^3$. Remember, you can only combine terms with identical variable parts.

Question 2. The correct answer is G. You can order the numbers by considering the decimal equivalent of $\frac{1}{4} = 0.25$ and writing each fraction in an equivalent form with 100 as the denominator: $0.2 = \frac{20}{100}$, $0.03 = \frac{3}{100}$, and $\frac{1}{4} = \frac{25}{100}$. The fractions can then be ordered based on the magnitude of the numerator: $\frac{3}{100} < \frac{20}{100} < \frac{25}{100}$ or $0.03 < 0.2 < \frac{1}{4}$. If you chose **F**, you may have incorrectly used $2 < 3 < 4$. If you chose **H** or **J**, you may not have considered that $\frac{1}{4} = 0.25$. If you chose **K**, you may have incorrectly given the order from *greatest* to *least.*

Question 3. The correct answer is C. Because $x^2 + 4 = 29$, you can solve the equation for x^2, $x^2 + 4 = 29 \Leftrightarrow x^2 = 25$. Substitute the value of x^2 into the expression $x^2 - 4$ to calculate the value the expression is equal to $x^2 - 4 = 25 - 4 = 21$.

If you chose **A**, you might have solved $x^2 + 4 = 29$ for the principal square root of x, $x^2 + 4 = 29 \Leftrightarrow x^2 = 25 \Leftrightarrow \sqrt{x^2} = \sqrt{25} \Leftrightarrow x = 5$ and neglected to evaluate the expression $x^2 - 4$. If you chose **B**, you might have incorrectly combined $x^2 + 4 = 29$ with $x^2 - 4$ and solved for x, $x^2 + 4 = 29 - 4 \Leftrightarrow x^2 = 29 - 4 - 4 \Leftrightarrow x^2 = 21 \Leftrightarrow x = \sqrt{21}$. If you chose **D**, you might have only solved $x^2 + 4 = 29$ for x^2, $x^2 + 4 = 29 \Leftrightarrow x^2 = 25$. If you chose **E**, you might have incorrectly manipulated $x^2 + 4 = 29$ and only solved for x^2, $x^2 + 4 = 29 \Leftrightarrow x^2 = 29 + 4 \Leftrightarrow x^2 = 33$.

Question 4. The correct answer is F. As shown in the following figure, the given vertices form a 5-unit-by-5-unit rectangle (or square), which has an area of $5 \times 5 = 25$ square coordinate units. The portion of that square lying in Quadrant III is shown in the figure as the 2-unit-by-1-unit shaded rectangle, which has an area of $2 \times 1 = 2$ square coordinate units. Therefore, the percent of the total area of the square lying in

Quadrant III $= \frac{\text{the area of the shaded rectangle}}{\text{the area of the square}} \times 100\% = \frac{2}{25} \times 100\% = 8\%$.

Your First Practice Test

MATHEMATICS • PRACTICE TEST 1 • EXPLANATORY ANSWERS

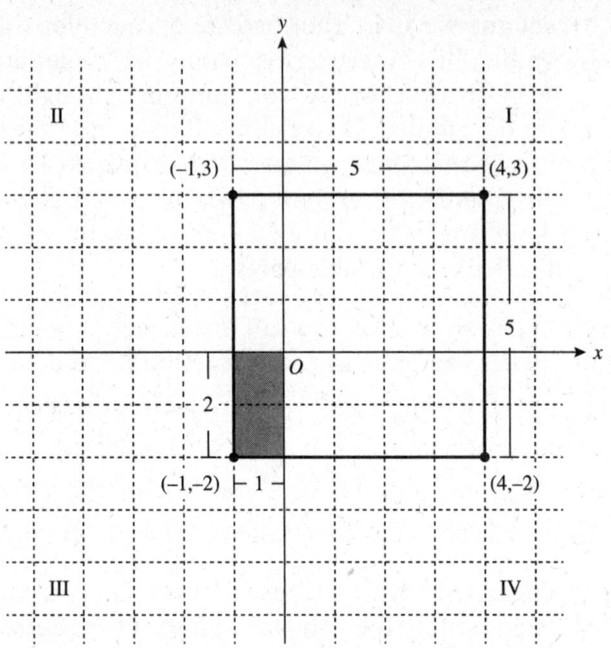

Question 5. The correct answer is B. Assuming the cost increased *linearly* is equivalent to assuming the cost increased *at a constant rate.* Because the cost of the clothing increased from \$620 to \$1,000 in 10 years, the constant rate is equal to $\frac{\$1{,}000-\$620}{10 \text{ years}}$, or \$38 per year.

Therefore, the cost of the family's clothing in 1991 (6 years after 1985) is:

\$620 + (6 years)(\$38 per year) = \$620 + \$228 = \$848.

Question 6. The correct answer is K. You can let x represent the certain number so that $\sqrt{x} = 9.2371$ or $x = 9.2371^2$ after squaring both sides of the equation. Now, $9^2 < x < 9.5^2 \rightarrow 81 < x < 90.25$ and $90.25 < 99$, so x is between 81 and 99. If you chose **F**, you could have incorrectly thought that $x^2 = 9.2371$ and used the fact that $3^2 = 9$ and $4^2 = 16$. If you chose **G**, you could have incorrectly thought that $2x = 9.2371$ or $x = \frac{9.2371}{2}$, which is between $\frac{8}{2} = 4$ and $\frac{10}{2} = 5$. If you chose **H**, you could have incorrectly thought that $x = 9.2371$, which is between 9 and 10. If you chose **J**, you could have incorrectly thought that $\frac{x}{2} = 9.2371$ or $x = 2(9.2371)$, which is between $2(9) = 18$ and $2(9.5) = 19$.

MATHEMATICS • PRACTICE TEST 1 • EXPLANATORY ANSWERS

Question 7. The correct answer is E. There are $10 - 2 = 8$ pieces of candy that are NOT grape, and $\frac{8}{10} = \frac{4}{5}$. If you chose **A**, you may have incorrectly found the probability that the candy randomly picked IS grape. If you chose **B**, you may have incorrectl[illegible]d the probability of *grape* out of the four flavors. If you chose **C**, you may have inco[illegible]ught that the candy randomly picked is either grape or *not grape*, so there is a 50% cha[illegible] *grape*. If you chose **D**, you may have incorrectly found the probability of *not grape* o[illegible] four flavors.

Question 8. The correct answer is K. The coordinates of the midpoint, (x_m,y_m), of a segment with endpoints (x_1,y_1) and (x_2,y_2) are $\left(\frac{x_1+x_2}{2},\frac{y_1+y_2}{2}\right)$. Substituting, we get $1 = \frac{x_1+(-3)}{2} \Leftrightarrow 2 = x_1 - 3 \Leftrightarrow x_1 = 5$, and $2 = \frac{y_1+4}{2} \Leftrightarrow 4 = y_1 + 4 \Leftrightarrow y_1 = 0$. Therefore the midpoint is (5,0), **K**. An alternative approach to this problem would be to plot point *B* and the midpoint and then use the concept of displacement to find the coordinates of *A*. Because point *B* is 4 coordinate units *left* and 2 coordinate units *up* from the midpoint, point *A* must be 4 coordinate units *right* and 2 coordinate units *down* from the midpoint, (1,2). So, once again, we find the coordinates of point *A* to be $(1 + 4,2 - 2) = (5,0)$. If you chose **F**, you may have used the correct midpoint formula but interchanged the coordinates of the midpoint and point *B*. If you chose **G**, you may have incorrectly written minus signs in the formula where there should be plus signs and used (1,2) and point *B* as the 2 endpoints. If you chose **H**, you found the midpoint of the segment with endpoints (1,2) and point *B*. If you chose **J**, you may have incorrectly written minus signs in the formula where there should be plus signs.

Question 9. The correct answer is B. Let x represent the number of customers Andrea's company had 1 year ago. Paraphrasing, the 116 customers are 8 more than twice the number of customers the company had 1 year ago. Replacing the "are" with "=" and translating both halves of the sentence into symbols, we get $116 = 2x + 8$. Solving this equation, we get $x = 54$, which is **B**. If you chose **A**, you may have added 8 to x rather than to $2x$, giving you the incorrect equation $116 = 2(x + 8)$. If you chose **C**, you may have subtracted 8 from $2x$ rather than adding it, giving you the incorrect equation $116 = 2x - 8$. If you chose **D**, you may have subtracted 8 from x and then doubled that, obtaining the incorrect equation $116 = 2(x - 8)$. If you chose **E**, you may have written the incorrect equation $116 = x + 2(8)$. Please remember that "8 more than" means to add 8 to something. Add it to what? Add it to "twice the number of customers the company had 1 year ago," which is $2x$.

Question 10. The correct answer is H. You can find the set amount per foot of fence by subtracting the \$500.00 fee from the estimate given: \$2,200.00 – \$500.00 = \$1,700 and dividing that result by 200 ft: $\frac{\$1{,}700}{200\text{ ft}} = \$8.50$ per foot of fence. If you chose **F**, you may have incorrectly subtracted 200 from 2,200 and divided that result by 500. If you chose **G**, you may have incorrectly added 200 to 2,200 and divided that result by 500. If you chose **J**, you may have forgotten to subtract 500 from 2,200 before dividing by 200. If you chose **K**, you may have incorrectly used the sum of 500 and 2,200 divided by 200.

MATHEMATICS • PRACTICE TEST 1 • EXPLANATORY ANSWERS

Question 11. The correct answer is C. You can solve this problem numerically by considering all the possible pairs of integer values representing the width and length of the room for which the area equals 180 ft^2. Then you can find the pair of values for which the perimeter equals 54 ft (that pair of values is 12 ft and 15 ft in the shaded region of the following table).

Width (ft)	1	2	3	4	5	6	9	10	12
Length (ft)	180	90	60	45	36	30	20	18	15
Area (ft^2)	180	180	180	180	180	180	180	180	180
Perimeter (ft)	362	184	126	98	82	72	58	56	54

You can also approach this problem analytically by solving the system of equations $2w + 2l = 54$ and $wl = 180$, which result from using the perimeter and the area formulas, respectively.

Notice that $2w + 2l = 54$ is equivalent to $w + l = 27$, and solving $wl = 180$ for l gives $l = \frac{180}{w}$. Substituting this value for l, you obtain $w + \frac{180}{w} = 27$; multiplying both sides by w and then subtracting $27w$ from both sides leads to $w^2 - 27w + 180 = 0$. Factoring the quadratic gives the equivalent equation $(w - 12)(w - 15) = 0$, with solutions $w = 12$ or $w = 15$; the corresponding solutions for l are $\frac{180}{w} = 15$ and $\frac{180}{w} = 12$.

You may notice that the work involved in factoring is essentially the same work required in the numerical method, so the analytical method is a little less efficient. You may also notice that the system of equations is symmetric in w and l, so that the solutions for *either w or l* give the dimensions of the living room.

Question 12. The correct answer is J. You can consider that \$10.00 – \$4.25 = \$5.75 and $\frac{\$5.75}{\$0.25} = 23$ quarters. If you chose **F**, you may have found the number of quarters in \$25.00 and divided that number by 10. If you chose **G**, you may have incorrectly considered the number of quarters in \$4.25 only. If you chose **H**, you may have incorrectly used the price of 25 candies at Carrie's Chocolate Shop. If you chose **K**, you may have incorrectly divided the number of quarters in \$25 by 10 and subtracted that result from the number of quarters in \$10.00.

Question 13. The correct answer is B. The average price per candy is the total price divided by the number of candies. This is equal to $\frac{\$3.75}{20} = \$0.1875$ or \$0.19 when rounded to the nearest \$0.01. If you chose **A**, you may have incorrectly found the change in price from 5 candies to 20 candies and divided that result by 20. If you chose **C**, you may have incorrectly used the price of 20 candies at Carrie's Chocolate Shop. If you chose **D**, you may have incorrectly multiplied the cost of 5 candies at Carrie's Chocolate Shop by 4 and divided that result by 20. If you chose **E**, you may have incorrectly multiplied the cost of 5 candies at Tamika's Treat Shop by 4 and divided that result by 20.

MATHEMATICS • PRACTICE TEST 1 • EXPLANATORY ANSWERS

Question 14. The correct answer is F. You can verify that the relationship is linear by noting that each increase of 5 candies results in an increase of \$1.00 in price so that the slope of the line is $m = \frac{1.00}{5} = 0.20$. The equation can then be written in the form $c = 0.20n + b$. You can solve for the value of b by substituting any one of the (n,c) ordered pairs for Carrie's Chocolate Shop into the equation. Using (5,1.50), we have $b = 1.50 - 0.20(5) = 0.50$. Therefore, the correct equation is $c = 0.20n + 0.50$. If you chose **G**, you may have incorrectly thought that the slope of the line would be $\frac{1.50}{5}$ and $b = 0$. If you chose **H**, you may have incorrectly found the slope to be the change in price at Tamika's Treat Shop relative to the change in price at Carrie's Chocolate Shop and the value of b as the price for 5 candies at Carrie's Chocolate Shop. If you chose **J**, you may have incorrectly thought the \$1.00 increase in price is because of an increase of 1 piece of candy and solved for b using the equation $b = 1.50 - 5(1)$. If you chose **K**, you may have incorrectly found the slope by dividing the difference in price of 30 candies at the 2 shops by the difference in price of 25 candies at the 2 shops and using an ordered pair from Carrie's Chocolate Shop to find the value of b.

Question 15. The correct answer is B. To solve the quadratic equation $x^2 - 36x = 0$ for x, you would factor the left side to apply the zero product rule to $x(x - 36) = 0$. Thus, $x = 0$ or $x - 36 = 0$ implies $x = 0$ or 36. The solution given as an answer choice is 36.

If you chose **C**, you probably divided 36 by 2. If you chose **D**, you probably dropped the x in the second term and solved $x^2 = 36$ for a positive value. If you chose **E**, you probably dropped the x in the second term and solved $x^2 = 36$ for negative value because there was a negative sign in the original equation.

Question 16. The correct answer is J. Using the properties of supplementary angles, we find the measures of $\angle EDF = 180° - 148° = 32°$and $\angle EFD = 180° - 140° = 40°$. Then, by the 180° rule for triangles, the measure of $\angle DEF = 180° - 32°- 40° = 108°$. If you chose **F**, you may have forgotten to subtract the measures of $\angle EDF$ and $\angle EFD$ from 180° (180° rule for triangles). If you chose **G**, you may have incorrectly subtracted 140° from 148° and added that result to 90°. If you chose **H**, you may have incorrectly subtracted 140° rather than 148° from 180° for angle $\angle EDF$. If you chose **K**, you may have incorrectly subtracted 148° rather than 140° from 180° for angle $\angle EFD$.

Question 17. The correct answer is E. Assume the base of the box is 9 inches by 9 inches. Because both dimensions are divisible by 3, 3 rows with 3 notepads in each row placed edge to edge will exactly cover the base. We can call this 1 layer. Because the box is 12 inches high, it will hold exactly 4 such layers. Therefore, 4 layers with 9 notepads in each layer will result in 36 notepads in the box, **E.** Because all 3 dimensions of the box are evenly divisible by the edge length of the cubical notepads, this can also be thought of as $\frac{9}{3} = 3$ notepads wide, $\frac{9}{3} = 3$ notepads long, and $\frac{12}{3} = 4$ notepads high, and $3 \times 3 \times 4 = 36$. If you chose **A**, you may have obtained 3 notepads long by 3 notepads wide by 4 notepads high but then added instead of multiplying. Because there will be no gaps or overlap of the notepads in the box, another method would be to divide the volume of the box by the volume of a single notepad. Using

Your First Practice Test

MATHEMATICS • PRACTICE TEST 1 • EXPLANATORY ANSWERS

the formula for the volume of rectangular prism, $V = l \times w \times h$, we get $\frac{\text{Volume of the box}}{\text{Volume of a notepad}} = \frac{9(9)(12)}{3(3)(3)} = 36$. If you chose **B**, you may have been thinking this way but incorrectly used the area of $\frac{1}{2}$ of the faces of the box instead of volume of the box. If you chose **C**, you may have thought the box could hold only one layer 3 notepads long by 4 notepads high, and you did not consider how many notepads it could hold widthwise. If you chose **D**, you may have been trying to divide the volume of the box by the volume of a single notepad, but you incorrectly found the volume of the box to be $2(9 \times 9 + 9 \times 12 + 9 \times 12)$, which is the surface area instead.

Question 18. The correct answer is J. Evaluate the function f for $x = -4$, $f(-4) = -4(-4)^3 - 4(-4)^2 = -4(-64) - 4(16) = 256 - 64 = 192$. If you chose **F**, you might have dropped the negative sign on the first 4 in the function: $4(-4)^3 - 4(-4)^2$. If you chose **G**, you might have dropped the negative signs on both 4s in the function: $4(-4)^3 + 4(-4)^2$. If you chose **H**, you might have dropped the negative on the first 4, evaluated the function at $x = 4$, and incorrectly calculated the exponents in the function: $4(4)3 - 4(4)2$. If you chose **K**, you might have dropped the negative sign on the second 4 in the function: $-4(-4)^3 + 4(-4)^2$.

Question 19. The correct answer is A. Solving the first equation for x gives you $x = 4 - 2y$. Plugging in the expression that x equals into the second equation gives you $-2(4 - 2y) + y = 7$. You can solve for y as follows $-8+4y+y=7 \Leftrightarrow -8+5y=7 \Leftrightarrow 5y=15 \Leftrightarrow y=3$ Now, take the value for y and plug it in for y in one of the original equations and solve for x, $x+2(3)=4 \Leftrightarrow x+6=4 \Leftrightarrow x=-2$. Therefore, $(-2,3)$ is the solution for this system of equations.

If you chose **B**, you might have plugged -1 in for x in the first equation and solved for y without checking to see if those values hold for the second equation, $-1+2y=4 \Leftrightarrow 2y=5 \Leftrightarrow y=2.5$. If you chose **C**, you might have plugged 1 in for x in the first equation and solved for y without checking to see if those values hold for the second equation, $1+2y=4 \Leftrightarrow 2y=3 \Leftrightarrow y=1.5$. If you chose **D**, you might have plugged 1 in for y in the first equation and solved for x without checking to see if those values hold for the second equation, $x+2(1)=4 \Leftrightarrow x+2=4 \Leftrightarrow x=2$. If you chose **E**, you might have plugged 0 in for y in the first equation and solved for x without checking to see if those values hold for the second equation, $x+2(0)=4 \Leftrightarrow x+0=4 \Leftrightarrow x=4$.

Question 20. The correct answer is G. By definition, $\log_x 36$ is the power of x that it would take to be 36. That power is 2 from the right side of the equation. So, $x^2 = 36$. This equation is satisfied when $x = 6$.

The most common wrong answer is **K**, which is the solution to $x \cdot 2 = 36$.

Question 21. The correct answer is C. The area of a rectangle is given by area = length × width, or $A = lw$. The area of the picture before cutting is $A = 7(5) = 35$ square inches. The area enclosed by the frame is $A = 6(4) = 24$ square inches. Subtracting, we see $35 - 24 = 11$ square inches must be cut off the picture to make it exactly

MATHEMATICS • PRACTICE TEST 1 • EXPLANATORY ANSWERS

fit into the frame. That is **C.** If you chose **A**, you may have incorrectly thought that because the picture is 1 inch longer and 1 inch wider than the frame, a total of 2 inches must be cut off the picture. Please note that the problem asks for how much *area* must be cut off the picture. If you chose **B**, you may have incorrectly thought that because the picture is 1 inch longer and 1 inch wider than the frame, and the frame is 4 inches by 6 inches, the total area cut off must be $1(6) + 1(4)$ square inches. If you chose **D**, you may have incorrectly thought that because the picture is 1 inch longer and 1 inch wider than the frame, and the picture is 5 inches by 7 inches, the total area cut off must be $1(5) + 1(7)$ square inches. If you chose **E**, you may have incorrectly thought that because the picture is 1 inch longer and 1 inch wider than the frame, the amount of area that needs to cut off is $1 \times 1 \times$ the area of the frame.

Question 22. The correct answer is K. As the following diagrams show, there are many different arrangements of points that satisfy the conditions. But, in all of these, the order of points starting from point *A* is *A*, *B*, *D*, *C*.

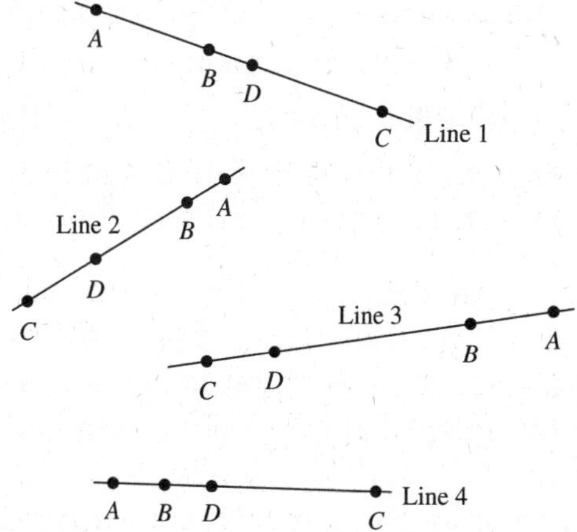

Because *D* is between *C* and *B* distance *CD* is always shorter than distance *BC*. So, answer choice **K** is always true.

The other answer choices can each be true for particular arrangements of the points, but they can also each be false for particular arrangements. Line 1 shows that **F** is sometimes false, Line 2 that **G** is sometimes false, Line 3 that **H** is sometimes false, and Line 4 that **J** is sometimes false. If you got an incorrect answer, you probably did not consider enough cases.

Question 23. The correct answer is E. If you find which of the following integers could be y when the greatest common factor of x^2y^2 and xy^3 is 45, then you first recognize that the greatest common factor of x^2y^2 and xy^3 is xy^2, which equals 45. Because x and y are both positive integers and $45 = 3^2 5$, there are two possibilities for x, 5 or 45. If x is 45, then y is 1. If x is 5, then $y = 3$. Thus, 3 is the answer choice.

If you chose **B**, you probably found x rather than y. If you chose **C**, you probably found y^2 rather than y. If you chose **D**, you probably found xy rather than y.

Your First Practice Test

MATHEMATICS • PRACTICE TEST 1 • EXPLANATORY ANSWERS

Question 24. The correct answer is G. The company's testing was randomized because the 150 volunteers were chosen without bias. The testing was also an experiment because the results from a control group (the group that received the placebo) and a treatment group (the group that received the new medication) were compared. If you chose **F**, you might not have realized that a census is a survey of a population and does not involve testing medicine. If you chose **H**, you might not have realized that the experiment was randomized by the simulation described, which is similar to the randomized selection of a marble from a bag of marbles. If you chose **J** or **K**, you might not have realized that, for a sample survey, all the volunteers would have received the same survey or test—there would be no control group or treatment group.

Question 25. The correct answer is D. The two signs will flash at the same time when the elapsed time is a common multiple of the signs' flash intervals, 4 seconds and 10 seconds. The least common multiple of 4 and 10 is 20, so the signs will flash at the same time after 20 seconds elapse.

If you chose **A**, you might have subtracted the 4-second flash interval from the 10-second flash interval $10 - 4 = 6$. If you chose **B**, you might have divided the sum of the 4-second flash interval and the 10-second flash interval by 2, $\frac{4+10}{2} = \frac{14}{2} = 7$. If you chose **C**, you might have added the 4-second flash interval to the 10-second flash interval. If you chose **E**, you might have multiplied the 4-second flash interval and the 10-second flash, $4(10) = 40$.

Question 26. The correct answer is K. Please recall that $|x|$ means the *absolute value of* x and, by definition, $|x| = x$ if $x \geq 0$ and $|x| = -x$ if $x < 0$. In any case, $|x|$ is positive for all nonzero values of x. Because the sum of 2 positive numbers is positive, $|a| + |b| > 0$. Multiplying both sides of this inequality by -1 and remembering to switch the direction of the inequality sign, we get $-(|a| + |b|) = -|a| - |b| < -0 = 0$. Therefore, the expression in **K** is *always* negative. We now show by example that the expressions in **F**, **G**, and **J** *can be* positive and that the expression in **H** is *always* positive. If you let $a = b = -1$, then $-a - b = -(-1) - (-1) = 1 + 1 = 2$. Hence, the expression in **G** can be positive. If you let $a = 2$ and $b = 1$, then $a - b = 2 - 1 = 1$, so the expression in **F** can be positive. Using those same two values for a and b, $|a| - |b| = |2| - |1| = 2 - 1 = 1$, so the expression in **J** can be positive. Finally, because the sum of two positive numbers is positive, $|a| + |b|$ is positive, so the expression in **H** is *always* positive.

Question 27. The correct answer is C. You can sketch the graphs of the two conics to determine the number of points of intersection. The circle is centered at the origin and has a radius of 3. The vertex of the parabola is $(-3,-2)$, and passes through $(-2,-1)$ so that the parabola turns upward. The vertex of the parabola is at a distance of $\sqrt{(-3)^2 + 2^2} = \sqrt{13}$ coordinate units from the origin and all points on the circle are at a distance of 3 coordinate units from the origin, so the vertex lies outside the circle. Thus, for $x < -3$, the parabola will not intersect the circle in any points. For $x > 3$, the parabola intersects the circle at two distinct points, one on the lower semicircle and one on the upper

MATHEMATICS • PRACTICE TEST 1 • EXPLANATORY ANSWERS

semicircle. If you chose **A**, you may have considered the portion of the parabola determined only by $x < -3$. If you chose **B**, you may have considered only where the parabola intersects the upper semicircle. If you chose **D**, you may have thought the parabola intersects the circle at the y-intercept of the lower semicircle and passed through the upper semicircle at two distinct points. If you chose **E**, you may have thought the vertex of the parabola lies below the y-intercept of the lower semicircle circle and thus intersects both the lower semicircle and the upper semicircle in two distinct points.

Question 28. The correct answer is H. Using *of* as times and *is* as equals, you can write $0.4(250) = 0.6x$ so that $x = \frac{0.4(250)}{0.6} = 166\frac{2}{3}$. If you chose **F**, you may have incorrectly found 60% of 250. If you chose **G**, you may have incorrectly found 160% of 40% of 250. If you chose **J**, you may have incorrectly subtracted 40 from 250 and then added 60. If you chose **K**, you may have solved the incorrect equation, $0.6(250) = 0.4x$.

Question 29. The correct answer is A. We will write this inequality equivalently, with x on the left, in two steps. First, we add $6y$ to both sides and obtain $-2x > 8y - 4$. Then we divide both sides by -2, remembering to reverse the direction of the inequality sign when we do so. Doing this, we get the inequality $x < -4y + 2$, which is **A**. If you chose **B**, you probably forgot to reverse the direction of the inequality sign when you divided both sides by a negative number. If you chose **C**, you may have subtracted $6y$ from both sides instead of adding it in the first step. If you chose **D**, you may have obtained $-2x > 8y - 4$ but then missed the sign on y when you divided $8y$ by -2. If you chose **E**, you may have missed the sign on y when you divided $8y$ by -2 and also not reversed the direction of the inequality sign when you divided both sides by a negative number.

Question 30. The correct answer is F. You can use the identity $\tan\alpha = \frac{\sin\alpha}{\cos\alpha}$ or $\cos\alpha = \frac{\sin\alpha}{\tan\alpha}$ to find that $\cos\alpha = \frac{\left(\frac{40}{41}\right)}{\left(\frac{40}{9}\right)} = \frac{9}{41}$. Alternatively, you can use the ratios $\sin\alpha = \frac{\text{opposite}}{\text{hypotenuse}} = \frac{40}{41}$, $\tan\alpha = \frac{\text{opposite}}{\text{adjacent}} = \frac{40}{9}$, and $\cos\alpha = \frac{\text{adjacent}}{\text{hypotenuse}} = \frac{9}{41}$. If you chose **G**, you may have incorrectly used $\frac{\tan\alpha}{\sin\alpha}$. If you chose **H**, you may have incorrectly used $\frac{1}{\tan\alpha}$. If you chose **J** or **K**, you may have attempted to calculate the length of the hypotenuse of the triangle using the given values.

Question 31. The correct answer is B. You can use the formula for the perimeter of a rectangle, $P = 2(w + l)$ with $P = 96$, $AB = w$, and $BC = l$, to find that $w + l = \frac{96}{2} = 48$. Using this equation and the given ratio with k as the constant of proportionality, we have $w = 3k$ and $l = 5k$, so that the equation becomes $3k + 5k = 48$ or $8k = 48$. Solving for k gives $k = 6$ so that $w = AB = 3(6) = 18$ cm. If you chose **A**, you may have incorrectly thought that the length is given by the constant of proportionality. If you chose **C**, you may have incorrectly found BC rather than AB. If you chose **D**, you may have incorrectly thought the perimeter is given by $P = (w + l)$ and used this result to find AB. If you chose **E**, you may have incorrectly thought the perimeter is given by $P = (w + l)$ and used this result to find BC.

MATHEMATICS • PRACTICE TEST 1 • EXPLANATORY ANSWERS

Question 32. The correct answer is G. The area of a triangle is found by multiplying $\frac{1}{2}$ by the length of its altitude, h, and by the length of its base, b, $\frac{1}{2}hb$. For ΔABC, the length of the altitude is 8 inches and the length of the base is 16 inches. Therefore, the area of ΔABC is 64 square inches, $\frac{1}{2}(8)(16) = \frac{1}{2}(128) = 64$. The area, in square inches, of a square with side length x inches is x^2, $x^2 = 64 \Leftrightarrow x = \sqrt{64} \Leftrightarrow x = 8$. Thus the length of a side of the square is 8 inches.

If you chose **F**, **H**, **J**, or **K**, you might be misremembering the formulas for calculating the areas of a triangle and a square. If you chose **F**, you might have divided the sum of the lengths of the base and the altitude by 4, $(8 + 16) \div 4$. If you chose **H**, you might have divided the product of the length of the base and 3 by 4, $(16)(3) \div 4$. If you chose **J**, you might have correctly calculated the area of the triangle but then divided the area by 4 rather than calculating the square root, $\frac{1}{2}(8)(16) \div 4$. If you chose **K**, you might have divided the product of the lengths of the base and altitude by 4, $(8)(16) \div 4$.

Question 33. The correct answer is B. You can use the fact that $EFGH$ is a square so $HG = EF = 3.6$ meters, and $ABCD$ is a rectangle with $\overline{AD}$ and $\overline{BC}$ as opposing sides so $AD = BC = 12$ meters. The ratio of the length of $\overline{EH}$ to the length of $\overline{AD}$ is $\frac{3.6}{12} = 0.3$, so the length of $\overline{EH}$ is $0.3(100)\% = 30\%$ percent of the length of $\overline{AD}$. If you chose **A**, you may have incorrectly added the two lengths and written the result as a percent. If you chose **C**, you may have incorrectly used the ratio of the length of $\overline{EH}$ to the length of $\overline{AB}$. If you chose **D**, you may have incorrectly multiplied the two lengths and written the result as a percent.

Question 34. The correct answer is F. You can form a right triangle using $\overline{AD}$ and $\overline{AJ}$ as the legs and $\overline{JD}$ as the hypotenuse. The length of $\overline{AD}$ is 12 meters, and the length of $\overline{AJ}$ is $\frac{10}{2} = 5$ meters. By the Pythagorean theorem, $AD = \sqrt{12^2 + 5^2} = 13$ meters. If you chose **G**, you may have incorrectly added the two lengths 12 meters and 3.6 meters. If you chose **H**, you may have incorrectly added the two lengths $\frac{10}{2} = 5$ meters and 12 meters. If you chose **J**, you may have incorrectly used 12 and 10 for the lengths of the two legs and then subtracted their squares instead of adding them when using the Pythagorean theorem. If you chose **K**, you may have incorrectly used 12 and 10 for the lengths of the two legs.

Question 35. The correct answer is B. Using the fact that the circumference of a circle is π times the diameter of the circle, you can compute the length of arc $\widehat{CD}$ by finding $\frac{1}{2}$ of the circumference of the circle centered at K with radius $CK = \frac{10}{2} = 5$ meters: $\frac{1}{2}(10\pi) = 5\pi$ meters. If you chose **A**, you may have incorrectly used the radius of the circle instead of its diameter in the formula for the circumference. If you chose **C**, you may have incorrectly attempted to use the formula for the area of the circle. If you chose **D**, you may have forgotten to divide the circumference by 2. If you chose **E**, you may have incorrectly used the area of the circle.

MATHEMATICS • PRACTICE TEST 1 • EXPLANATORY ANSWERS

Question 36. The correct answer is H. You can note that the y-coordinate of E is 12 because E lies on $\overline{AB}$, and $\overline{AB}$ lies on the line $y = 12$. Segment $\overline{EH}$ is perpendicular to $\overline{AB}$ and has length 3.6 coordinate units. Therefore, H has y-coordinate $12 - 3.6 = 8.4$. If you chose **F**, you may have incorrectly used $\frac{1}{2}$ of the length of $\overline{EH}$. If you chose **G**, you may have incorrectly used the length of $\overline{EH}$. If you chose **J**, you may have incorrectly used the length of $\overline{AB}$. If you chose **K**, you may have incorrectly thought that H is on the line $y = 12$.

Question 37. The correct answer is A. The length can be found by finding the positive difference in the y-coordinate at C, 4, and the y-coordinate of the point where the altitude intersects $\overline{AB}$. All ordered pairs on $\overline{AB}$ have y-coordinate 1, so the length of the altitude is $4 - 1 = 3$ coordinate units. If you chose **B**, you may have incorrectly subtracted the x-coordinate at C from the x-coordinate at B. If you chose **C**, you may have incorrectly used the length of $\overline{AB}$. If you chose **D**, you may have incorrectly used the length of $\overline{AC}$. If you chose **E**, you may have incorrectly used the midpoint of $\overline{AB}$ and found the distance from this point to C.

Question 38. The correct answer is J. The correct approach for this item is to substitute 2 for n in the formula $P = \dfrac{3^n e^{-3}}{n!}$ and then evaluate. Substituting, we get $P = \dfrac{3^2 e^{-3}}{2!}$. Because $3^2 = 9$, $2! = 2$, and $e^{-3} \approx 0.05$, we get $P \approx \frac{9(0.05)}{2} = 0.225$. The *closest* choice is **J**, 0.23. If you chose **F**, you may have forgotten to square the 3 when you evaluated. If you chose **G**, you may have thought $2! = 2^2 = 4$. Remember, by definition, $k! = 1 \times 2 \times 3 \times \cdots \times (k-1) \times k$. If you chose **H**, you may have substituted 1 for n in the formula and forgotten to square 3. Please note that the question asks for the probability that exactly 2 customers are in line, so n is 2. If you chose **K**, you may have thought $2! = 1$. Please see the previously given definition of $k!$.

Question 39. The correct answer is B. You can use the fact that the amplitude of a function of the form $g(x) = A\cos(Bx + C)$ is $|A|$. Alternatively, you can use the fact that $-1 \le \cos(3x + \pi) \le 1$ so that $-\frac{1}{2} \le \frac{1}{2}\cos(3x + \pi) \le \frac{1}{2}$. The amplitude is then given by $\frac{\text{maximum} - \text{minimum}}{2} = \dfrac{\frac{1}{2} - \left(-\frac{1}{2}\right)}{2} = \frac{1}{2}$. If you chose **A**, perhaps you incorrectly thought the amplitude of $g(x) = A\cos(Bx + C)$ is given by $\left|\frac{1}{B}\right|$. If you chose **C**, you may have incorrectly thought the amplitude of $g(x) = A\cos(Bx + C)$ is given by $|AB|$. If you chose **D**, perhaps you incorrectly thought the amplitude of $g(x) = A\cos(Bx + C)$ is given by $\left|\frac{1}{A}\right|$. If you chose **E**, you may have incorrectly thought the amplitude of $g(x) = A\cos(Bx + C)$ is given by $|B|$.

Question 40. The correct answer is F. The Fundamental Counting Principle states that if event A can occur in m ways, and for each of these m ways event B can occur in n ways, there are exactly $m \times n$ ways both events can occur together. In making a license plate for this state, we have to make six decisions. We have to choose a letter, another letter, another letter, a digit, another digit, and one more digit. There are 26 ways to choose a letter. Because

Your First Practice Test

MATHEMATICS • PRACTICE TEST 1 • EXPLANATORY ANSWERS

duplications are allowed, there are 26 ways to choose the second letter, and 26 ways to choose the third letter. Similarly, there are 10 ways to choose the first digit, 10 ways to choose the second digit, and, finally, 10 ways to choose the third digit. Using the Fundamental Counting Principle, there will then be $(26)(26)(26)(10)(10)(10) = 10^3 \cdot 26^3$ distinct license plates in this state. That is **F**. **G** would be the number of ways to choose a letter *or* a digit 3 times. If you chose **H**, you might not have remembered that $k! = 1 \cdot 2 \cdot 3 \cdot 4 \cdot \ldots \cdot k$. **J** would be the number of ways of choosing 1 out of 6 items 36 times. Many permutation problems have factorials in their solutions (**K**), but 26! would mean we are arranging all 26 letters of the alphabet without allowing duplications. Similarly, 10! would mean we are arranging all 10 digits without allowing duplications.

Question 41. The correct answer is D. The median of a data set is the middle term when the set is arranged in numerical order. The 20 quiz scores are placed in score intervals that are in numerical order. Because there are 20 quiz scores, the median of the scores will be between the 10th and 11th quiz scores. There are 9 quiz scores in the 76–80 score interval, which means the 10th and 11th quiz scores occur in the 81–85 score interval. Therefore, the median of the scores is contained in the 81–85 score interval.

If you chose **A**, you might have thought the median of the scores was contained in the highest score interval. If you chose **B**, you might have thought the median of the scores was contained in the interval with the lowest frequency of scores. If you chose **C**, you might have thought the median of the scores was the middle score interval. If you chose **E**, you might have thought the median of the scores was contained in the score interval with the highest frequency of scores.

Question 42. The correct answer is J. To find an equivalent expression for $\frac{1}{1+i} \cdot \frac{1-i}{1-i}$, you multiply and get $\frac{1(1-i)}{(1+i)(1-i)} = \frac{1-i}{1-i^2} = \frac{1-i}{2}$.

If you chose **G**, you probably thought $\frac{1}{1+i}$ was equivalent to $1 + i$ and canceled $(-i)$ in both places. If you chose **H**, you probably simplified $1 - i^2$ as 1 and got $\frac{1-i}{1}$ or $1 - i$.

Question 43. The correct answer is B. For the temperature we are looking for, $F = C = x$. Substituting x for both C and F into the given formula, we get $x = \frac{9}{5}x + 32$. Multiplying both sides of this equation by 5, combining like terms, and solving for x, we get $5x = 9x + 160 \Leftrightarrow -4x = 160 \Leftrightarrow x = -40$, **B**. If you chose **A**, you may have incorrectly thought that $\frac{9}{5}$ must be distributed over $x + 32$. If you chose **C**, you may have incorrectly thought the respective freezing temperatures of water must give the desired value of x. Because water freezes at 32°F, or 0°C, you may have concluded that x must be 32°F lower than the freezing temperature in degrees Celsius. If you chose **D**, you may have tried to solve the equation $x = \frac{9}{5}x + 32$ by inspection and incorrectly thought that because there is an x-term on both sides, $x = 0$ must be the solution. If you chose **E**, you may have incorrectly thought the desired value for x is the value of F when $C = 0$.

MATHEMATICS • PRACTICE TEST 1 • EXPLANATORY ANSWERS

Question 44. The correct answer is G. You can find the value closest to k by considering that the ratio of y to x is approximately k, or $\frac{y}{x} \approx k$. As can be verified, you can choose any two of the xy-pairs to find the value among the choices closest to k. For example, $\frac{0.425}{8.50} = 0.05$. If you chose **F** or **J**, you may have incorrectly found the difference in an xy-pair. If you chose **H**, you may have incorrectly multiplied an xy-pair. If you chose **K**, you may have incorrectly divided x by y.

Question 45. The correct answer is A. The correct graphical model can be identified by considering the slope and the y-intercept of the graph of the equation $2x - 5y = -5$. Writing this equation in slope-intercept form, we get $y = \frac{2}{5}x + 1$. From this, we see the slope is $\frac{2}{5}$ and the y-intercept is 1. From the y-intercept alone, we can rule out **C**, **D**, and **E** because the y-intercepts of those graphs appear to be 0, 5, and 5, respectively. The graph in **B** appears to pass close to the point (2,6). Using that point and (0,1), along with slope in terms of the change in y over the change in x, the slope of the graph in **B** is approximately $\frac{6-1}{2-0} = \frac{5}{2}$. However, the graph in **A** appears to pass close to the point (5,3). Again, using that point and (0,1), along with slope in terms of the change in y over the change in x, the slope of the graph in **A** is approximately $\frac{3-1}{5-0} = \frac{2}{5}$. Because one of the graphs must be the correct model, it must be the graph in **A**.

Question 46. The correct answer is J. To figure out how many cups of flour Diana will use, you can set up a proportion (note: $1\frac{1}{2} = 1.5$, $2\frac{1}{2} = 2.5$, and $2\frac{1}{4} = 2.25$):
$\frac{\text{teaspoons of yeast in the recipe}}{\text{cups of flour in the recipe}} = \frac{\text{teaspoons of yeast to be used}}{\text{cups of flour to be used } (x)} \Leftrightarrow$
$\frac{1.5}{2.5} = \frac{2.25}{x} \Leftrightarrow 1.5x = 2.25(2.5) \Leftrightarrow 1.5x = 5.625 \Leftrightarrow x = 3.75$. Therefore, Diana will use $3\frac{3}{4}$ cups of flour.

If you chose **F**, you might have thought the difference between the amount of yeast the recipe calls for and the amount of yeast Diana will use should be multiplied by the amount of flour the recipe calls for, $(2\frac{1}{4} - 1\frac{1}{2})(2\frac{1}{2}) = (\frac{3}{4})(\frac{5}{2}) = \frac{15}{8}$. If you chose **G**, you might have thought the difference between the amount of yeast the recipe calls for and the amount of yeast Diana will use should be added to amount of flour the recipe calls for, $(2\frac{1}{4} - 1\frac{1}{2}) + 2\frac{1}{2} = \frac{3}{4} + 2\frac{1}{2} = 3\frac{1}{4}$. If you chose **H**, you might have thought the quotient of dividing the amount of yeast Diana will use by the amount of yeast the recipe calls for should be multiplied by 2 and added to $\frac{1}{2}$, $(2\frac{1}{4} \div 1\frac{1}{2})(2) + \frac{1}{2} = (1\frac{1}{2})(2) + \frac{1}{2} = 3 + \frac{1}{2} = 3\frac{1}{2}$. If you chose **K**, you might have thought the quotient of dividing the amount of yeast Diana will use by the amount of yeast the recipe calls for should be added to the amount of flour the recipe calls for, $(2\frac{1}{4} \div 1\frac{1}{2}) + 2\frac{1}{2} = 1\frac{1}{2} + 2\frac{1}{2} = 4$.

Your First Practice Test

MATHEMATICS • PRACTICE TEST 1 • EXPLANATORY ANSWERS

Question 47. The correct answer is E. There are two good approaches to this problem. We will show both. First, we factor the greatest common factor out of the numerator and then cancel factors of the numerator with identical factors of the denominator. Doing so, we get $\frac{12x^6-9x^2}{3x^2}=\frac{3x^2(4x^4-3)}{3x^2}=\frac{\cancel{3x^2}(4x^4-3)}{\cancel{3x^2}}=4x^4-3$. A second approach is to use the property that states $\frac{a+b}{c}=\frac{a}{c}+\frac{b}{c}$ and then reduce both rational expressions individually. Using this approach and remembering to subtract exponents when reducing a quotient of powers, we get $\frac{12x^6-9x^2}{3x^2}=\frac{12x^6}{3x^2}-\frac{9x^2}{3x^2}=\frac{\cancel{12}}{\cancel{3}}x^{6-2}-\frac{\cancel{9}}{\cancel{3}}x^{2-2}=4x^4-3$. In either case, the correct answer is **E**. If you chose **A**, you may have used the second approach shown previously but incorrectly divided the exponents rather than subtracting them. If you chose **B**, you may have used the second approach shown previously but incorrectly divided the exponents rather than subtracting them in the first term. If you chose **C**, you may have tried the first approach but incorrectly canceled the $3x^2$ in the denominator with the identical factors of the *first term* in the numerator. Remember, you must factor the numerator first and then cancel identical factors. If you chose **D**, you may have used the second approach shown but incorrectly thought $x^{2-2}=x^0=x$. Remember, any nonzero value raised to the zero power is equal to 1.

Question 48. The correct answer is K. The dimensions of a matrix can be written as $(r \times c)$, where r is the number of rows of the matrix and c is the number of columns of the matrix. To find the element in the ith row and the jth column of the product of two matrices, one must multiply the elements of the ith row of the matrix on the left with the corresponding elements in the jth column of the matrix on the right and then add those products together. For this reason, in order for the matrix product AB to be defined, the number of columns of matrix A must be equal to the number of rows of matrix B. Another way of saying that is the product of an $(r \times c)$-matrix (on the left) and an $(m \times n)$-matrix (on the right) is defined if and only if $c = m$. (Please remember that *left* and *right* are important here because matrix multiplication is not commutative.) The dimensions of W and X are (2×2), the dimensions of Y are (2×3), and the dimensions of Z are (3×2). Because X is a (2×2)-matrix and W is a (2×2)-matrix, the matrix product XW is defined (**J**). Because X is a (2×2)-matrix and Z is a (3×2)-matrix, the matrix product XZ is undefined (**K**). Because W is a (2×2)-matrix and X is a (2×2)-matrix, the matrix product WX is defined (**F**). Because W is a (2×2)-matrix and Y is a (2×3)-matrix, the matrix product WY is defined (**G**). Because Y is a (2×3)-matrix and Z is a (3×2)-matrix, the matrix product YZ is defined (**H**). Therefore, we see that XZ, **K**, is the only indicated matrix product that is undefined.

MATHEMATICS • PRACTICE TEST 1 • EXPLANATORY ANSWERS

Question 49. The correct answer is A. All the parabolas open upward. This rules out answer choices **D** and **E**. All the parabolas have the same y-intercept, (0,1). This rules out answer choice **C**, which has y-intercept equal to n, which varies. The parabolas in the family go up more quickly as the value of n increases. This means the coefficient of x must get larger as n gets larger. That happens in **A** but not in **B**.

The most common incorrect answer is **C**. A graph of that family is shown in the following figure:

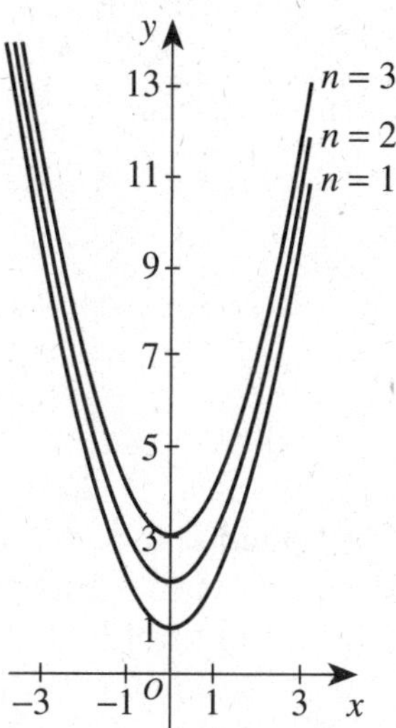

Question 50. The correct answer is F. To find the minimum number of students in a class of 20 who play both guitar and piano when 8 play guitar and 9 play piano, you must look at the range for which the guitar and piano players may overlap. For instance, all 8 who play guitar could also play piano; that's the maximum. The minimum would be the smallest overlap they can have. In this case, there are 20 total; the two groups could be disjoint because 9 + 8 or 17 is less than 20. Thus, the minimum is 0.

If you chose **G**, you probably found the difference between 9 and 8. If you chose **H**, you probably found the maximum rather than the minimum number. If you chose **K**, you probably added 9 and 8.

Question 51. The correct answer is B. The sum of any two different numbers between 1 and 18 must be between 3 and 35. The only perfect squares between 3 and 35 are 4, 9, 16, and 25. Therefore the sum of each of the nine pairs must be 4, 9, 16, or 25. So far, we know the possible pairs for 1 are 3, 8, or 15 and must consider each case.

Because 16, 17, and 18 are each greater than or equal to 16, we must pair them with a number so that the sum is 25. Therefore, 16 must be paired with 9, 17 with 8, and 18 with 7. After pairing these, we are left with 1 – 6 and 10 – 15.

MATHEMATICS • PRACTICE TEST 1 • EXPLANATORY ANSWERS

We now must consider what happens if 1 is paired with 3 or with 15.

If 1 is paired with 3, then 15 would have to pair with 10, 2 would have to pair with 14, 11 with 5, and 12 with 4. We'd then be left with 13 and 6 which CANNOT be paired. For that reason 1 CANNOT be paired with 3. Thus 1 *must* be paired with 15.

When 1 is paired with 15, the pairs are as follows:

$18 + 7 = 25$

$17 + 6 = 25$

$16 + 5 = 25$

$15 + 1 = 16$

$14 + 2 = 16$

$13 + 3 = 16$

$12 + 4 = 16$

$11 + 5 = 16$

$10 + 6 = 16$

If you chose **A**, you might have multiplied 1 and 16 rather than adding them together. If you chose **C**, you might have multiplied 1 and 9 and not considered that you need 9 pairs of numbers. If you chose **D** or **E**, you might not have considered that you need 9 pairs of numbers.

Question 52. The correct answer is J. Let p = the number of pennies, n = the number of nickels, d = the number of dimes, and q = the number of quarters. Each of these variables can be expressed in terms of a common variable—in this case, p.

Lucky had p pennies, so the value of the pennies was p cents. Because she had twice as many nickels as pennies, $n = 2p$, and the value of the nickels was $5(2p)$ cents. She had 1 fewer dime than nickels, so $d = n - 1 = 2p - 1$, and the value of the dimes was $10(2p - 1)$ cents. Finally, she had 1 more quarter than nickels, so $q = n + 1 = 2p + 1$, and the value of the quarters was $25(2p + 1)$ cents.

Because the total value of the coins is \$8.25, or 825 cents, p satisfies the following equation:

$$p + 5(2p) + 10(2p - 1) + 25(2p + 1) = 825$$

Multiplying out each factor on the left-hand side and collecting like terms, you can see that $81p + 15 = 825$, so $81p = 810$. Therefore, $p = 10$ and $q = 2p + 1 = 2(10) + 1 = 21$ quarters.

MATHEMATICS • PRACTICE TEST 1 • EXPLANATORY ANSWERS

Question 53. The correct answer is C. Solve for x:

$$10^{\left(\frac{2x-1}{x}\right)}=1$$

$$\Leftrightarrow \log\left(10^{\left(\frac{2x-1}{x}\right)}\right)=\log 1$$

$$\Leftrightarrow \frac{(2x-1)}{x}=0$$

$$\Leftrightarrow x\left(\frac{(2x-1)}{x}\right)=0\cdot x$$

$$\Leftrightarrow 2x-1=0$$

$$\Leftrightarrow 2x=1$$

$$\Leftrightarrow x=\frac{1}{2}$$

If you chose **A**, **B**, **D**, or **E**, you might have performed an incorrect algebraic manipulation and neglected to test your calculated value of x in the equation to see if it held.

For **A**, you might have correctly manipulated the expression except for incorrectly keeping the negative on the 1:

$$10^{\left(\frac{2x-1}{x}\right)}=1$$

$$\Leftrightarrow \log\left(10^{\left(\frac{2x-1}{x}\right)}\right)=\log 1$$

$$\Leftrightarrow \frac{(2x-1)}{x}=0$$

$$\Leftrightarrow x\left(\frac{(2x-1)}{x}\right)=0\cdot x$$

$$\Leftrightarrow 2x-1=0$$

$$\Leftrightarrow 2x=-1$$

Your First Practice Test

MATHEMATICS • PRACTICE TEST 1 • EXPLANATORY ANSWERS

For **B**, you might have incorrectly tried to solve the exponential equation by multiplying both sides by 10 rather than taking the log of both sides:

$$10^{\left(\frac{2x-1}{x}\right)}=1$$

$$\Leftrightarrow 10\left(10^{\left(\frac{2x-1}{x}\right)}\right)=1\cdot 10$$

$$\Leftrightarrow \frac{(2x-1)}{x}=10$$

For **D**, you might have incorrectly tried to solve the exponential equation by dividing both sides by 10 rather than taking the log of both sides:

$$10^{\left(\frac{2x-1}{x}\right)}=1$$

$$\Leftrightarrow \left(10^{\left(\frac{2x-1}{x}\right)}\right)\div 10=1\div 10$$

$$\Leftrightarrow \frac{(2x-1)}{x}=\frac{1}{10}$$

For **E**, you might have incorrectly thought $\log 1 = 1$ rather than 0:

$$10^{\left(\frac{2x-1}{x}\right)}=1$$

$$\Leftrightarrow \log\left(10^{\left(\frac{2x-1}{x}\right)}\right)=\log 1$$

$$\Leftrightarrow \frac{(2x-1)}{x}=1$$

Question 54. The correct answer is G. According to the table, 90 people play an instrument but only 50 of those 90 people like to read. Therefore, the desired probability is $\frac{50}{90} = \frac{5}{9}$.

If you chose **F**, you calculated the probability that a person randomly selected out of *the total people surveyed* both likes to read and plays a musical instrument, $\frac{50}{250}$, rather than the probability that a person randomly selected out of *the total people that play an instrument* likes to read. If you chose **H**, you calculated the probability that a person randomly selected out of *the total people that like to read* plays a musical instrument, $\frac{50}{110}$, rather than the probability that a person randomly selected out of *the total people that play an instrument* likes to read. If you chose **J**, you calculated the probability that a person randomly selected out of *the total people surveyed* plays a musical instrument, $\frac{90}{250}$, rather than the probability that a person randomly selected out of *the total people that play an instrument* likes to read. If you chose **K**, you calculated the probability that a person randomly selected out of *the total people surveyed* likes to read, $\frac{110}{250}$, rather than the probability that a person randomly selected out of *the total people that play an instrument* likes to read.

Question 55. The correct answer is A. Mario will travel a distance equal to 1 circumference of the wheel for each complete revolution of the wheel. So first, we must find the circumference of Mario's wheel. The formula for the circumference of a circle is $C = \pi D$, where D is the diameter of the circle. Hence, $C = 26\pi$ inches. Using unit multipliers to find Mario's speed in *feet per second*, we get $\left(\frac{200 \text{ rev}}{1 \text{ min}}\right)\left(\frac{1 \text{ min}}{60 \text{ sec}}\right)\left(\frac{26\pi \text{ in}}{1 \text{ rev}}\right)\left(\frac{1 \text{ ft}}{12 \text{ in}}\right) = \frac{65\pi \text{ ft}}{9 \text{ sec}}$. Therefore, the correct answer is **A**. If you chose **B**, you may have used the radius rather than the diameter when you found the circumference. If you chose **C**, you may have had an extra factor of 2 in the formula for circumference. If you chose **D**, you may have used the formula for area of a circle rather than the formula for circumference. If you chose **E**, you may have used the formula for area of a circle with an incorrect value for the radius rather than the formula for circumference.

Question 56. The correct answer is K. You can use properties of exponents and the fact that for $b > 0$, $b \neq 1$, $b^x = b^y \rightarrow x = y$ to solve for the value of $\frac{j}{k}$. Because $(\sqrt{3})^j = (3^{\frac{1}{2}})^j = 3^{\frac{j}{2}}$ and $27^k = (3^3)^k = 3^{3k}$, you can rewrite the equation as $3^{\frac{j}{2}} = 3^{3k} \rightarrow \frac{j}{2} = 3k$ so that $\frac{j}{k} = 3(2) = 6$. If you chose **F**, you may have incorrectly thought that $\left(\sqrt{3}\right)^j = 3^{2j}$ and $27^k = 3^{\frac{k}{3}}$ and solved $2j = \frac{k}{3}$. If you chose **G**, you may have incorrectly thought that $\left(\sqrt{3}\right)^j = 3^{2j}$ and solved $2j = 3k$. If you chose **H**, you may have ignored $\sqrt{3}$ to get $3^j = 3^{3k}$ and solved $j = 3k$. If you chose **J**, you may have incorrectly written 27^k as 3^{2k} and solved $\frac{j}{2} = 2k$.

MATHEMATICS • PRACTICE TEST 1 • EXPLANATORY ANSWERS

Question 57. The correct answer is A. $\frac{3}{4}$, $\frac{3}{4}+d$, $\frac{3}{4}+2d$, $\frac{3}{4}+3d$, $\frac{3}{4}+4d$, $\frac{3}{4}+5d$, $\frac{3}{4}+6d$. The median of these is the middle term, $\frac{3}{4}+3d$. The mean is the sum of all the terms divided by 7. We can quickly find the sum of these terms using the formula $S_n = \frac{n(a_1+a_n)}{2}$ where a_1 is the first term, a_n is the nth term, and n is the number of terms. The sum is thus: $S_7 = \frac{7(a_1+a_7)}{2} = \frac{7(\frac{3}{4}+\frac{3}{4}+6d)}{2} = \frac{7(\frac{6}{4}+6d)}{2} = 7(\frac{3}{4}+3d)$. Now that you have the sum, you can divide it by 7 to get the mean of the 7 terms, $\frac{7(\frac{3}{4}+3d)}{7} = \frac{3}{4}+3d$. Because the mean and the median are both $\frac{3}{4}+3d$, their difference is 0.

If you chose **B**, you might have selected the first term of the sequence. If you chose **C**, you might have taken the reciprocal of the first term. If you chose **D**, you might have thought the mean of the 7 terms was 4 and the median of the 7 terms was 7, 7 – 4 = 3. If you chose **E**, you might have thought the mean of the 7 terms was 3 and the median of the 7 terms was 7, 7 – 3 = 4.

Question 58. The correct answer is F. Arc length can be thought of as a fractional part of the circumference. That fraction is given by $\frac{\theta}{360}$, where θ is the measure of the central angle, in degrees, intercepting the desired arc. So first we must find the measure of $\angle D$. Using the sine ratio, we see $\sin \angle D = \frac{1}{4}$, making the measure of $\angle D$ equal to $(\sin^{-1}(\frac{1}{4}))°$. The circumference of the circle is $2\pi r = 2\pi(4) = 8\pi$ cm. Therefore, the length of $\overset{\frown}{AC}$ is $\frac{\sin^{-1}(\frac{1}{4})}{360} \times (8\pi)$. Reducing $\frac{8}{360}$, we get $\frac{\pi}{45}(\sin^{-1}(\frac{1}{4}))$, which is **F**. If you chose **G**, you may have incorrectly thought that the cosine ratio, not the sine ratio, is given by the length of the opposite leg over the length of the hypotenuse. If you chose **H**, you may have incorrectly used the formula for the area of the circle rather than the formula for the circumference of the circle. If you chose **J**, you may have made *both* of the described errors. If you chose **K**, you may have incorrectly thought that the tangent ratio, not the sine ratio, is given by the length of the opposite leg over the length of the hypotenuse *and* also incorrectly used the formula for the area of the circle rather than the formula for the circumference of the circle.

MATHEMATICS • PRACTICE TEST 1 • EXPLANATORY ANSWERS

Question 59. The correct answer is C. The area of the triangle can be found by using the given formula, $\frac{1}{2}ab \sin C$. Since only one angle measure is given in the triangle, use that for C in the formula: $\frac{1}{2}ab \sin 30°$. The length of the side opposite from angle C, the 30° angle, is 5.0 cm and must correspond to side c. That means that the other side lengths, 8.0 cm and 4.0 cm, correspond to sides a and b and can be plugged into the formula: $\frac{1}{2}(8.0)(4.0)(\sin 30°)$. Since the sine of 30° is $\frac{1}{2}$, $\frac{1}{2}(8.0)(4.0)(\sin 30°) = \frac{1}{2}(8.0)(4.0)(\frac{1}{2})$, which results in 8 cm^2, the area of the triangle. If you chose **A**, you may have incorrectly thought the area of the triangle was equal to $8.0(\sin 30°)$. If you chose **B**, you may have used the given formula but incorrectly used 4.0 and 5.0 for the side lengths of a and b rather than 4.0 and 8.0. If you chose **D**, you may have incorrectly thought the given triangle was a right triangle and calculated the area using $\frac{1}{2}(5.0)(4.0)$, or you may have used the given formula but incorrectly used 5.0 and 8.0 for the side lengths of a and b rather than 4.0 and 8.0. If you chose **E**, you may have incorrectly used the cosine of 30° rather than the sine of 30°.

Question 60. The correct answer is K. The expected value of a random variable is its theoretical long-run average value. We find this by $E(X) = \sum_{x_i} x_i P(X = x_i) = \frac{1}{6}(0) + \frac{1}{12}(1) + \frac{1}{4}(2) + \frac{1}{12}(3) + \frac{1}{12}(4) + 0(5) + \frac{1}{3}(6)$.

You may have gotten **F** if you did $(\frac{1}{6} + \frac{1}{12} + \frac{1}{4} + \frac{1}{12} + \frac{1}{12} + \frac{1}{3}) \div 6$. You may have gotten **G** if you recorded the last entry in the table. You may have gotten **H** if you did $\frac{1}{6} + \frac{1}{12} + \frac{1}{4} + \frac{1}{12} + \frac{1}{12} + 0 + \frac{1}{3}$. You may have gotten **J** if you did $\frac{1}{3}(6)$.

Your First Practice Test

READING • PRACTICE TEST 1 • EXPLANATORY ANSWERS

Passage I

Question 1. The best answer is B because the story is narrated by Nidali, who, in telling the story of how she came to get her name, offers perceived insights into her parents' thoughts and actions from a time she was too young to remember. First-person narration can be seen by the use of *I* throughout the passage.

The best answer is NOT:

A because even though the story is in first person, it is not about events that happened before the narrator was born; the events are the very story of the narrator being born.

C because although the story does address the thoughts and actions of several characters, those thoughts and actions are filtered through Nidali's perspective; an omniscient third-person narrator would be wholly outside the story.

D because the story is told from the perspective of *I* and *me* and *my*, indicating that this story is told by Nidali herself rather than from a third-person narrator.

Question 2. The best answer is J because Nidali describes how easily her father ignored the tradition of naming a child after the grandfather: "It was an onus he brushed off his then-solid shoulders unceremoniously" (lines 19–20). This implies Baba made this decision quite nonchalantly and without giving it a great deal of thought, brushing it off just as one would a piece of lint or dandruff.

The best answer is NOT:

F because while Baba was casual about disregarding this tradition, the grandfather "angrily" penned a letter to Nidali's father when he found out what had happened (lines 22–24); the grandfather was clearly upset that the tradition wasn't honored.

G because the lint and dandruff were explicitly called "analogies" (line 21), provided by the grandfather to describe how easily the father ignored tradition; they were not literal.

H because the lint and dandruff were not evidence of the importance of family naming traditions but rather of the ease with which the father ignored those traditions. We know the importance of this tradition from lines 15–19: "Baba, whose name is Waheed and who was known during his childhood as Said, was the only son of the family, so the onus of renaming a son after my grandfather fell squarely upon his shoulders."

READING • PRACTICE TEST 1 • EXPLANATORY ANSWERS

Question 3. The best answer is A because when Mama found out about the baby's name, even though she'd just given birth, she immediately "got out of bed and walked us to the elevator, the entire time ignoring my baba" (lines 49–50). Baba was yelling at Mama, encouraging her not to be rash, stressing that Nidali was a beautiful name. Mama's immediate action, combined with Baba's pleading, suggests her obvious disapproval. However, even though she disapproved of the name, she soon let it go; the narrator says, "Mama must not have fought long" (line 54) because she realized she couldn't change the name without having to go to a place full of death certificates. Moreover, the narrator kept the name Nidali, which means Mama eventually accepted the name.

The best answer is NOT:

B because although Mama's reaction to the name (as described above) could be interpreted to contain at least some "annoyance," she is clearly more disapproving than annoyed. Furthermore, there is no evidence in the story to suggest that she is ever amused by the situation.

C because Mama is never shown to be embarrassed, and her secondary feeling about the name is resignation, not outrage. If she were outraged, it's fair to assume she would not have given up the fight, and Nidali's name may have actually been changed.

D because even if it could be said that Mama was "shocked" by the baby's name, that shock could not be said to turn into resentment; rather, the fact Mama stops fighting about it and lets the baby keep the name makes clear that she is resigned to the name, not resentful about it.

Question 4. The best answer is G because the scene in the seventh paragraph (lines 54–68) did not really occur; it is a fictitious scene the narrator imagines could have happened had Mama pursued her quest to change the name. The narrator sets up the imagined scene by using "who knows" in the first line of the paragraph. She also repeatedly uses "maybe" to imagine the way events *might have* unfolded.

The best answer is NOT:

F because even though Baba is said to be a purveyor of exaggerated tales, this paragraph is the narrator's imagining of a scene, not Baba's telling of a story.

H because this paragraph is not told from Mama's point of view but rather comes from the perspective of Nidali, the narrator.

J because this paragraph is not a memory at all; it is a scenario that *could have* happened, as evidenced by the narrator's use of "who knows" and "maybe." The narrator could not have remembered events immediately following her own birth, and she is more concerned with the personalities of Baba and Mama than with her own.

READING • PRACTICE TEST 1 • EXPLANATORY ANSWERS

Question 5. The best answer is D because although lines 48–53 reveal that Mama is unhappy with the baby's new name, the next paragraph states that Mama "must not have fought long." The paragraph imagines everything Mama might have done if she had fought the name, including taking a trip to the clerk's office, and the narrator concludes that the trip didn't happen "because I still have my name" (lines 67–68). It is clear that if Mama had actually gone to the clerk's office, the narrator's name would have been changed.

The best answer is NOT:

A because Baba never wanted to change the name he had given the baby. That can be seen clearly in lines 51–52, when he pleads with the disapproving mother: "Nidali is a beautiful name, so unique, come on Ruz, don't be so rash . . ."

B because it is not a winter storm but summer heat that Nidali imagined might be problematic: Mama "shuddered at the thought of taking me, a newborn, through the heat" (lines 62–63).

C because the story never states or implies anything about how easily Mama might or might not change her mind.

Question 6. The best answer is H because there is an earlier reference to "these stories," where Nidali says of her father, "I knew he must have embellished. Baba liked to do that: tell stories that were impossible but true all at once, especially if those stories made him look like a rock star" (71–74).

The best answer is NOT:

F because there are no "conflicting" stories about the origins of Nidali's name; there is simply one story about where her name came from, even if that might be an elaborate or embellished story.

G because the "notebooks and poetry" mentioned in the story are what Baba would have written had he still been a writer, but their subject is not explained in this story; it's impossible to tell whether they would have been filled with sadness or not.

J because the narrator's account of her family's time in Boston isn't necessarily sad, whereas lines 71–78 make it clear that Baba places his sadness in the stories he tells, and those stories are his famously embellished ones.

READING • PRACTICE TEST 1 • EXPLANATORY ANSWERS

Question 7. The best answer is C because the narrator says the fact that her father was an architect instead of a writer was "a reality that filled him with great sadness" (lines 77–78); in addition, the narrator notes that the fact the house was filled with toys and dirty socks instead of a piano was something that caused her mother, a musician, "great sadness" (line 86).

The best answer is NOT:

A because the passage gives no indication that either feels particular pride in their professional lives. Baba is sad that he is a writer instead of an architect, and Mama is sad that she is a musician "who no longer played music" (lines 81–82).

B because although Baba and Mama are clearly sad about their professional lives, the passage does not link that sadness to anxiety in any way.

D because lines 77–78 and 85–86 make it clear the parents each feel sadness over their professional lives, and sadness does not suggest contentment.

Question 8. The best answer is F because the narrator states that Mama is "the most superstitious of all humans (even more than Baba, and to that she'll attest)" (lines 60–62).

The best answer is NOT:

G because lines 60–62 make clear that Mama was more superstitious than Baba.

H because the narrator states that Mama is "the most superstitious of all humans," which indicates she is more superstitious than Nidali herself.

J because the narrator states that Mama is "the most superstitious of all humans," which indicates she is more superstitious than Rhonda.

Question 9. The best answer is D because the narrator states that "Mama liked to expose him when he told such stories; she was his paparazzo, his story-cop" (lines 79–80). As a story-cop, Mama would be paying attention to the accuracy of details and correcting Baba.

The best answer is NOT:

A because by calling Mama a "story-cop," Nidali is implying that Mama was actively involved in pointing out Baba's mistruths, not that she was bored by his stories. There is nothing in the passage to indicate that she either yawns or rolls her eyes.

B because Mama couldn't "expose" Baba or serve as his "story-cop" if she were ignoring him.

C because there is nothing in the passage to suggest Mama participates in Baba's exaggerations and embellishments; as a "story-cop," she does the opposite.

Your First Practice Test

READING • PRACTICE TEST 1 • EXPLANATORY ANSWERS

Question 10. The best answer is F because in the last paragraph, we see a contrast between home and school: "I knew from the beginning that home meant embellishing, and that's why I loved school. Teachers were there; they taught us facts based on reality" (lines 87–89).

The best answer is NOT:

G because when the narrator describes Mama as the "true rock star," it is not to draw a distinction between Mama's musical skills and Baba's; instead, the narrator is asserting that although Baba liked to tell stories that made him *feel* like a rock star, Mama was actually an accomplished musician. The passage makes no claims about Baba being an amateur musician.

H because it inverts what makes Baba happy and sad. Lines 77–78 say he feels a "great sadness" that he is now an architect instead of a writer, not the other way around.

J because it is not text-based; the story never discusses what is required to either write or make music.

Passage II

Question 11. The best answer is D because the entire second paragraph of the passage (lines 8–24) provides examples of all the different laws that were passed to limit automobile use, including those in San Francisco. In addition, lines 4–5 state that "consumers were staying away from the 'devilish contraptions' in droves." All this indicates a great deal of displeasure regarding automobiles and very little support for them.

The best answer is NOT:

A because cars were not affordable at all; lines 25–27 actually state that "the asking price for the cheapest automobile amounted to twice the $500 annual salary of the average citizen."

B because the passage doesn't make this assertion. In fact, the passage states that cars were banned from "all tourist areas, effectively exiling them from the city" (lines 23–24).

C because passage A does not detail any public-relations efforts. (Public-relations efforts regarding the Edsel are detailed in passage B.)

READING • PRACTICE TEST 1 • EXPLANATORY ANSWERS

Question 12. The best answer is G because lines 12–13 state that "incensed local lawmakers responded with monuments to legislative creativity": these "monuments" were elaborate legislation, not actual statues or buildings constructed to commemorate something.

The best answer is NOT:

F because the "puddles" mentioned in line 11 are actual puddles cars were getting stuck in.

H because the "bells" mentioned in line 18 were real bells that rang as a warning to alert passersby to the arrival of automobiles.

J because the "hills" cited in line 39 are actual inclines automobiles were having a hard time climbing, not figurative hills the cars were unable to overcome.

Question 13. The best answer is A because the word *accessories* appears in front of a list of car parts that includes such things as bumpers and headlights, parts most consumers would deem essential. The cheapest automobiles were just four wheels, a body, and an engine; everything else was sold separately—including those parts most people would view as essential.

The best answer is NOT:

B because although the previous paragraph mentions legislation, this paragraph is primarily concerned with a different obstacle: price. The point is that even essential car parts cost extra; there is no indication that the word *accessories* appeared in legal documents.

C because the passage makes it clear that essentials were deliberately labeled as accessories, which drove up the price for the average citizen. There is no suggestion that those citizens misunderstood these essential car parts to be accessories.

D because none of the car parts listed would be considered a luxury feature. The point is that even the most basic automobiles were prohibitively expensive.

READING • PRACTICE TEST 1 • EXPLANATORY ANSWERS

Question 14. The best answer is H because the passage indicates that Ford Motor Company put a lot into the Edsel (18 varieties and a great deal of advertising hype), and lines 70–73 indicate how spectacularly the car failed. "On September 4, 1957, proclaimed by Ford as E-Day, nearly 3 million Americans flocked to showrooms to see the Edsel. Unfortunately, very few of them bought the Edsel." This indicates the failure happened on a huge scale, while the fact that Ford "pulled the plug" (line 91) on the Edsel after only a few years indicates the failure happened quickly.

The best answer is NOT:

F because only 3 years occurred between the launch of the Edsel and when Ford "pulled the plug" (line 91), which wasn't gradual but quick; in addition, the failure of the Edsel was big news, not something that went unnoticed.

G because the car didn't sell well initially. Lines 87–89 state that Ford predicted 200,000 car sales but only managed 63,110.

J because it is not text-based; the passage does not discuss other automakers.

Question 15. The best answer is D because launching "not one, not two, but 18 varieties of Edsel" (line 44) implies that one or two models might have been reasonable, but eighteen is extreme. Such grandiosity reflects the story of the Edsel overall.

The best answer is NOT:

A because these lines contain no information about any car other than the Edsel.

B because the passage does not reveal any "obligation" on the part of Ford executives to involve consumers; had they done so, perhaps those executives would have found out earlier just how unpopular the new design would be.

C because neither these lines nor the passage as a whole focus on the thoughts of the typical consumer; they focus instead on the thoughts and plans of Ford planners and designers.

READING • PRACTICE TEST 1 • EXPLANATORY ANSWERS

Question 16. The best answer is G because lines 84–85 state, "The Edsel was an upscale car launched a couple months after a stock market plunge." It is clear that the stock market plunge happened before E-Day and the car sales that followed.

The best answer is NOT:

F because E-Day was the day the Edsel was launched. According to lines 84–85, the car was launched *after* a stock market plunge.

H because the sales numbers of 45,000 and 2,846 happened in the second and third years of the Edsel's existence, which obviously happened after its launch on E-Day and the preceding stock market plunge.

J because as in **H**, the sales numbers of 45,000 and 2,846 happened in the second and third years of the Edsel's existence, which obviously happened after its launch on E-Day and the preceding stock market plunge.

Question 17. The best answer is C because the passage indicates that the Edsel was an "upscale car" (line 84) launched during a recession. The passage goes on to say that "sales of all premium cars plummeted" (lines 85–86) after the stock market plunge led to a recession, with the implication being that upscale and premium cars belonged to the same category and didn't sell well when much of the country was cutting back on luxuries.

The best answer is NOT:

A because the term *premium* is not being used to discuss the value of the Edsel today but how the car was marketed at the time of its launch.

B because the word *premium* was not invented by the makers of Edsel but was used to denote a general class of car, similar to *luxury.*

D because there is no indication in the passage that this term was used sarcastically by Edsel owners. People did joke that Edsel stood for "Every day something else leaks" (lines 81–82), so it is not unreasonable to think they might have scoffed at the term *premium.* But there is no specific textual support for D.

READING • PRACTICE TEST 1 • EXPLANATORY ANSWERS

Question 18. The best answer is F because passage A focuses on automobiles in San Francisco at the turn of the twentieth century, and passage B focuses on the history of the Ford Edsel, which debuted and died around 1960. Both happened a considerable time ago.

The best answer is NOT:

G because neither passage reveals anything about the author's experience; both are written in the third person and virtually nothing is known about the writers or their professional backgrounds.

H because neither passage makes an assertion about the automobile's overall functionality. Passage A focuses on the problems with the first cars in San Francisco, and passage B focuses on the great failure of the Ford Edsel, but neither passage implies cars have contributed little worthwhile throughout their existence.

J because passage A does discuss traffic and road conditions in San Francisco around 1903, but passage B makes no mention of those things in its look at the Ford Edsel.

Question 19. The best answer is A because in passage A, lines 12–13 mention that "incensed local lawmakers responded with monuments to legislative creativity" and the rest of the paragraph highlights various laws passed to deal with the early days of automobiles. Passage B, however, does not address legislation at all.

The best answer is NOT:

B because both passages do discuss the feelings of the general public, including passage A's emphasis on the antipathy evoked by the first automobiles in San Francisco and passage B's discussion of the Edsel's unpopularity with consumers.

C because economics are mentioned in both passages, including the cost of cars in passage A (lines 25–27) and the "stock market plunge" in line 85 of passage B.

D because passage B cites industry experts regarding the problems with the Ford Edsel, but passage A has no such quotations.

READING • PRACTICE TEST 1 • EXPLANATORY ANSWERS

Question 20. The best answer is G because lines 65–68 state, "The Edsel PR team touted the glories of the cars, but wouldn't let anybody see them. When they finally released a photo, it turned out to be a picture of . . . the Edsel's hood ornament." This illustrates how the Ford people used just a single detail in their marketing. A comparable example would be a picture of a gleaming headlight or a polished door handle.

The best answer is NOT:

F because Ford actually showed almost nothing of the car in advertisements, and their ads certainly would not have drawn attention to a potential problem with the car. The cars in passage A had problems getting up the steep Nineteenth Avenue, a detail that publicity experts likely would have wanted to keep hidden.

H because as stated, Ford's marketing for the Edsel consisted of talking up the car but actually showing very little of it. Showing the meticulousness of the assembly line would reveal too much of the car.

J because even if it seems an intelligent way to market the cars in passage A, such positive marketing was not evidenced in passage B. The lines cited above indicate the Edsel was marketed based on a single detail and an air of mystery; pictures of an attractive young couple out for a ride would run counter to that "mystery."

Passage III

Question 21. The best answer is C because this passage explores Homer's development as an artist and the various influences on his work, such as the time he spent in Paris ("the artist spent 10 months in the city, which later proved to have a profound effect on his art" (lines 11–13)) and his time in Tynemouth ("he found the subject matter that would inspire him most" (lines 26–27)).

The best answer is NOT:

A because the passage is not focused on a single painting. A few paintings are mentioned as illustrations of Homer's influences, but the passage as a whole is a broader look at Homer's work.

B because although the passage discusses the effect nature had on Homer's work, it never discusses an overall relationship between nature and the fine arts. This choice is too broad and leaves out Homer entirely.

D because the passage does not describe "artists" in the plural at all; it focuses exclusively on Homer.

READING • PRACTICE TEST 1 • EXPLANATORY ANSWERS

Question 22. The best answer is G because the passage states that Homer "found the subject matter that would inspire him most" in 1881, when he spent the summer in a coastal town and "became enthralled by the dramas of the people who make their living from the ocean" (see lines 25–44). He then spent the last 25 years of his life in Maine, where "the sea outside his window now inspired the artist to create what came to be known as his greatest paintings" (lines 68–70). It is clear that the sea and the people working on the sea most interested Homer later in his life.

The best answer is NOT:

F because it was in the 1870s that Homer was painting "his genre subjects: tourist scenes, schoolchildren, and farm life" (lines 24–25). Later in his life, beginning with his move to Tynemouth in 1881, Homer became more interested in the lives of people working on the ocean.

H because Homer might have painted something like this earlier in his career, before the sea became his primary focus.

J because after 1881 Homer became more interested in the lives of people working on the ocean; he might have painted a tourist scene like this earlier in his career.

Question 23. The best answer is A because lines 20–22 state that after Homer returned from Paris, "the weakness of earlier compositions is replaced by a boldness and lucidity in which simple shapes are massed into powerful designs."

The best answer is NOT:

B because the passage never discusses Homer's shapes as being particularly "sharp" or "rounded."

C because the passage does not indicate a shift from dark shapes to light shapes; the passage discusses Homer's themes as being "dark" but not his shapes.

D because Homer's later work is described as frequently having "a stark and melancholy atmosphere" (line 9), but his shapes are not described thus, and his earlier works are never described as particularly "uplifting."

READING • PRACTICE TEST 1 • EXPLANATORY ANSWERS

Question 24. The best answer is J because regarding what Homer found in Tynemouth, lines 46–49 state that "the dynamic and dangerous relationship between human activity and natural forces exposed in this setting would occupy Homer for many years to come." This makes clear that Homer would care about this subject for a long time, which can also be seen in the fact he moved to a similar area in Maine when he returned to the United States.

The best answer is NOT:

F because the passage explicitly states that Homer would focus on these things "for many years to come" (lines 48–49).

G because the passage makes it clear that Homer's time in Tynemouth influenced the work he did for the rest of his life.

H because even if Homer did feel a fascination for what he found at Tynemouth for "a long time," the passage never mentions whether Homer returned there.

Question 25. The best answer is B because lines 39–46 explain that what "enthralled" Homer in Tynemouth was "the fishermen's wives staring out to sea as they wait for their men, the launch of the lifeboat to rescue sailors from a foundering ship, the agonizingly fragile fishing boats being tossed on angry waves." Those scenes featuring the interplay between the sea and the lives of fishermen and their families thus became the inspiration for his works.

The best answer is NOT:

A because though lines 30–33 state that Homer may have gone to Tynemouth to look for the sorts of tourists and bathers he'd successfully painted back in New Jersey, the rest of the paragraph makes it clear that he ultimately was inspired by something else in Tynemouth.

C because Homer's time in Tynemouth had little to do with farmers but a great deal to do with fisherman.

D because in Tynemouth, Homer was said to have found a "dynamic and dangerous" (line 46) relationship between humans and the sea, not anything particularly "soothing."

READING • PRACTICE TEST 1 • EXPLANATORY ANSWERS

Question 26. The best answer is F because it's clear that Homer enjoyed some success before moving to Tynemouth (for example, his work had already been displayed in Paris at the Great Exposition in 1867), but what he found there obviously became the foundation for the rest of his career. "Here at last was a subject matter that matched the artist's deepest feelings" (lines 44–46). It was this subject matter that most moved him and led to his greatest success.

The best answer is NOT:

G because the passage never discusses Homer's feelings about his work being displayed in Paris.

H because Homer's visiting the Caribbean later in life is mentioned as being evidence that he continued to travel; along with the information about his family, this is meant to show that Homer was not a recluse. The passage does not mention what effect, if any, the Caribbean might have had on his work.

J because the passage suggests that Homer never got over his sense of melancholy about the world; as lines 8–9 state, even his later work was "imbued with a stark and melancholy atmosphere."

Question 27. The best answer is B because lines 17–22 state that Homer's viewing of Japanese art in Paris had an immediate effect on him. When he returned to the United States, the "weakness of earlier compositions [was] replaced by a boldness and lucidity . . ."

The best answer is NOT:

A because lines 17–22 indicate the changes Homer made were dramatic, not subtle.

C because lines 17–22 indicate the changes Homer made were dramatic and immediate, not imperceptible.

D because though Homer's work got stronger after Paris, his subject matter didn't change until he went to Tynemouth (lines 23–27).

Question 28. The best answer is F because lines 68–70 state that "the sea outside his window now inspired the artist to create what came to be known as his greatest paintings," with the remainder of the final paragraph emphasizing this acme in Homer's career, which occurred when he was living on the Maine coast.

The best answer is NOT:

G because the last paragraph focuses not on the grandeur of humans but the grandeur of nature, what lines 85–86 describe as "haunting evocations of the eternal power of the ocean."

H because the paragraph does not specifically discuss the best way to paint water. It is instead a broader look at the culmination of Homer's influences and skills.

J because the effect these paintings had on the author is not clear; the passage does not include the thoughts or feelings of the author.

READING • PRACTICE TEST 1 • EXPLANATORY ANSWERS

Question 29. The best answer is D because lines 30–33 state that, regarding Homer's decision to go to Tynemouth, "It is possible that he was searching for a town filled with the type of tourists and bathers that made his paintings of the Jersey shore successful back home."

The best answer is NOT:

A because there is no indication in the passage that Homer was "returning" to Tynemouth at all; it's not clear from the passage whether he'd ever been there. The passage does not specify what inspired Homer to become a painter in the first place.

B because it is not text-based. The passage makes no mention of "distractions" Homer faced in Paris.

C because lines 30–33 make clear that in Tynemouth Homer was looking for a place similar to the Jersey shore, not that he needed a break from it.

Question 30. The best answer is J because lines 66–67 are explicit about what could irk Homer when he was painting: "he could be extremely short-tempered when interrupted."

The best answer is NOT:

F because lines 66–67 clearly state that Homer could get annoyed if he was interrupted, but the passage says nothing about him being bothered by how well his paintings were or were not selling.

G because it is inconsistent with the passage to imply Homer would be upset by storms; storms at sea were the very subjects he came to love painting. Moreover, there is no evidence in the passage that Homer painted outside.

H because it is inconsistent with the passage to imply Homer would be upset by the rough sea; it was one of the subjects he loved painting later in life.

Passage IV

Question 31. The best answer is B because the first paragraph describes the discovery of planets in general, while the second paragraph switches focus to scientists' search for "a hint of the familiar: planets resembling Earth" (lines 18–19). This is the focus of the rest of the passage.

The best answer is NOT:

A because the passage does not actually "raise the question" about whether exoplanets exist. The second sentence clearly explains that they do: "To date, astronomers have identified more than 370 'exoplanets'" (lines 4–5).

C because though the passage describes the search for planets, no such definition of the term *planets* is provided, and no distinction is made between planets in Earth's solar system and more distant planets that might be familiar only to astronomers.

D because the passage doesn't really refer to mythology at all, beyond a passing mention of Icarus.

Your First Practice Test

Question 32. The best answer is G because the passage is peppered with figurative language. For example, lines 23–27 state, "To see a planet as small and dim as ours amid the glare of its star is like trying to see a firefly in a fireworks display; to detect its gravitational influence on the star is like listening for a cricket in a tornado."

The best answer is NOT:

F because there are no rhetorical questions in the passage.

H because no such excerpts are found in the passage.

G because none of these excerpts are found in the passage either.

Question 33. The best answer is D because the first paragraph mentions a number of such worlds, including "an Icarus-like 'hot Saturn'" (lines 6–7) whose year is only three days long and the many "floaters" (line 17) that languish in space. It is amid this exotica, these planets so unlike our own, that scientists search for "the familiar: planets resembling Earth" (line 19).

The best answer is NOT:

A because the term *exotica* is part of the larger phrase "amid such exotica" in line 18, thus referring back to the worlds mentioned in the first paragraph. At this point, there has been no discussion of the technology used to identify these planets.

B because the planets mentioned in the first paragraph (the "exotica") orbit stars "other than the sun" (lines 5–6). These are planets outside our solar system.

C because there are no such overblown claims in this passage; although the passage makes statements about distant worlds that could be considered strange or unusual, nothing in the passage indicates those claims are exaggerated or untrue.

Question 34. The best answer is J because the second paragraph makes clear just how difficult it would be to find a planet like Earth, equating that task to seeing a "firefly in a fireworks display" (line 25) or hearing a "cricket in a tornado" (lines 26–27). Although the remainder of the passages focuses on those efforts, this paragraph emphasizes just how difficult the task itself is.

The best answer is NOT:

F because there is no evidence in the second paragraph to support the idea that scientists were disappointed by recently discovered exoplanets.

G because the paragraph doesn't actually mention exoplanets that were once thought to be stars at the center of solar systems.

H because there is no evidence in the second paragraph to support a claim about such a discovery; in fact, it is reasonable to infer the opposite from this paragraph because planets resembling Earth are so difficult to detect.

READING • PRACTICE TEST 1 • EXPLANATORY ANSWERS

Question 35. The best answer is B because lines 33–37 state, "Most of the others [exoplanets] have been detected by using the spectroscopic Doppler technique, in which starlight is analyzed for evidence that the star is being tugged ever so slightly back and forth by the gravitational pull of its planets."

The best answer is NOT:

A because lines 33–37 make it clear that it is "gravitational pull" that the Doppler technique detects, not light intensity.

C because lines 33–37 make it clear that the Doppler technique detects gravitational pull, not rotational speed.

D because lines 33–37 make it clear that the Doppler technique detects gravitational pull, rather than directly measuring the distance between an exoplanet and its former sun.

Question 36. The best answer is J because according to lines 74–76, "Kepler scientists won't announce the presence of a planet until they have seen it transit at least three times," meaning confirmation doesn't occur until they've seen the slight dimming three times.

The best answer is NOT:

F because lines 62–63 state that "Kepler is essentially just a big digital camera," and lines 65–66 say that the camera works by "capturing the light of more than 100,000 stars in a single patch of sky." This makes clear that Kepler focuses on light, not on water in any form.

G because the Kepler does not look for uninterrupted light; it instead looks for interrupted light, including "the slight dimming that could signal the transit of a planet" (lines 69–70).

H because the passage indicates scientists will announce the presence of a planet when they see it transit at least three times, "a wait that may be only a few days or weeks" (line 76).

Question 37. The best answer is C because lines 31–33 explicitly answer this question: "Only 11 exoplanets, all of them big and bright and conveniently far away from their stars, have as yet had their pictures taken."

The best answer is NOT:

A because lines 4–5 say that 370 exoplanets have been "identified," but lines 31–33 make it clear that only 11 have been photographed.

B because 95 is the number in the passage associated with the capabilities of the Kepler camera; it has nothing to do with the number of exoplanets that have been photographed.

D because lines 31–33 clearly state that 11 exoplanets have been photographed.

READING • PRACTICE TEST 1 • EXPLANATORY ANSWERS

Question 38. The best answer is F because lines 64–67 explain that the Kepler "makes wide-field pictures every 30 minutes, capturing the light of more than 100,000 stars in a single patch of sky between the bright stars Deneb and Vega."

The best answer is NOT:

G because the Kepler doesn't determine the distance between an exoplanet and its stars, just the possible existence of such an exoplanet by any "slight dimming" (line 69) of light in space.

H because it is not text-based. The passage mentions the "hot Jupiter" (line 10) that is 150 light years from Earth but never uses that distance in any discussion of the Kepler.

J because the passage discusses the Kepler's ability to detect the possible presence of exoplanets through pictures that reveal a slight dimming of light in space; there is no indication that the Kepler can identify the presence of water on the surface of these planets.

Question 39. The best answer is A because lines 64–67 explain that the Kepler "makes wide-field pictures every 30 minutes, capturing the light of more than 100,000 stars in a single patch of sky between the bright stars Deneb and Vega," marking these stars as the edges of the examined area.

The best answer is NOT:

B because Deneb and Vega are identified as stars, not planets. The figure 70% relates to the exoplanets discovered by the French COROT satellite ("seven transiting exoplanets, one of which is only 70% larger than Earth").

C because lines 64–67 are explicit that Deneb and Vega are stars in space, not scientists.

D because there is no indication in the passage that Deneb and Vega are "former" stars.

Question 40. The best answer is H because lines 78–80 state, "By combining Kepler results with Doppler observations, astronomers expect to determine the diameters and masses of transiting planets."

The best answer is NOT:

F because lines 78–80 are explicit that it is "diameters and masses" those combined technologies can find, not the length of its year.

G because lines 78–80 are explicit that it is "diameters and masses" those combined technologies can find, not the distance from its sun.

J because lines 78–80 are explicit that it is "diameters and masses" those combined technologies can find, not its distance from Earth.

SCIENCE • PRACTICE TEST 1 • EXPLANATORY ANSWERS

Passage I

1. **The best answer is A.** According to the passage, the percent relative reflectance shown in Figure 2 is based on a comparison to a standard with 100% reflectance. The higher the percent reflectance, the brighter the soil. According to Figure 2, the highest average percent relative reflectance was 70% measured at an inland distance of 0 km. In other words, this measurement was made at the coastal site, so **A** is correct. **B** is incorrect; 50 km inland the percent reflectance was less than 25%. **C** is incorrect; 100 km inland the percent reflectance was near 0%. **D** is incorrect; 150 km inland the percent reflectance was close to 10%.

2. **The best answer is H.** According to Figure 1, the average relative brightness of the dorsal stripe was 0.25 at an inland distance of approximately 60 km. **F** is incorrect; 20 km inland the brightness was greater than 0.75. **G** is incorrect; 40 km inland the brightness was greater than 0.75. **H** is correct; 60 km inland the brightness was 0.25. **J** is incorrect; 80 km inland the brightness was less than 0.25.

3. **The best answer is C.** According to Figure 1, on the graph representing the brightness of the fur on the rostrum, the line is steepest between inland distances of 50 km and 65 km, indicating that this is where there was the greatest change in the average relative brightness of the fur on the rostrum. **A** is incorrect; between 0 km and 25 km inland, the brightness decreased by a little less than 0.25. **B** is incorrect; between 25 km and 50 km inland, the brightness decreased by less than 0.25. **C** is correct; between 50 km and 75 km inland, the brightness decreased by approximately 0.50. **D** is incorrect; between 100 km and 125 km inland, the brightness increased very slightly.

4. **The best answer is J.** According to Figure 1, 150 km inland the average relative brightness of the ventrum fur was 0 whereas at the coastal site it was 1.00. The fur was brighter at the coastal site than 150 km inland. The fur was darker 150 km inland. **F** and **G** are incorrect; the fur was darker 150 km inland. **H** is incorrect; the relative brightness 150 km inland was less. **J** is correct.

5. **The best answer is B.** In order to answer this item, the examinee must know that natural selection is the survival and reproduction of organisms because of environmental forces that result in favorable adaptations. If the fur pigmentation matches the soil, then it will increase the chances of the mouse's survival, and it will be more likely to pass these traits on to its offspring. **A** is incorrect; the mouse will be more likely to pass its fur pigmentation traits to its offspring. **B** is correct. **C** and **D** are incorrect; the mouse would be less likely to be found by a predator.

6. **The best answer is J.** According to Figure 2, the standard had 100% reflectance. Because the soil at the coastal site had an average percent relative reflectance of 70%, the soil was darker than the standard. **F** and **G** are incorrect; the surface soil at the coastal site was darker than the standard. **H** is incorrect; the average percent relative reflectance of the soil at the coastal site was 70%. **J** is correct.

SCIENCE • PRACTICE TEST 1 • EXPLANATORY ANSWERS

Passage II

7. **The best answer is B.** According to Table 1, in Experiment 1, as the reaction time increased, the CNF also increased. When the reaction time was 10 min, the CNF was 6 mg/kg, and when the reaction time was 3 days, the CNF was 39 mg/kg. If a reaction time of 2 days had been tested, then the CNF would most likely have been between 6 mg/kg and 39 mg/kg. **A** is incorrect; the CNF would have been greater than 6 mg/kg. **B** is correct. **C** and **D** are incorrect; the CNF would have been less than 39 mg/kg.

8. **The best answer is F.** According to Table 1, the lowest concentration of dissolved nickel in the filtrate was found in Trial 1 (CNF = 6 mg/kg). In Trial 1, the reaction time was 10 min and the standard filtration method was used. **F** is correct. **G** is incorrect; a CNF of 42 mg/kg was measured when the reaction time was 7 days and the standard filtration method was used. **H** is incorrect; a CNF of 58 mg/kg was measured when the reaction time was 10 min and the vacuum filtration method was used. **J** is incorrect; a CNF of 73 mg/kg was measured when the reaction time was 7 days and the vacuum filtration method was used.

9. **The best answer is C.** In order to answer this item, the examinee must know that applying a vacuum will increase the net force on the mixture in the funnel. The net force exerted on the mixture was greater in Trial 6 than in Trial 3, because the vacuum filtration technique was used in Trial 6. **A** and **B** are incorrect; the net force exerted on the mixture in the funnel was most likely less in Trial 3. **C** is correct. **D** is incorrect; the filtration apparatus was connected to a vacuum pump in Trial 6.

10. **The best answer is G.** According to the passage, the solutions were mixed, the mixture was stirred, the solid was recovered by filtration, and then the CNF was measured. **F** is incorrect; measuring the CNF was the last step. **G** is correct. **H** and **J** are incorrect; mixing the solutions was the first step.

11. **The best answer is D.** According to Table 1, when the reaction time was 3 days and vacuum filtration was used, the CNF was 69 mg/kg (Trial 5). When the reaction time was 10 min and vacuum filtration was used, the CNF was 58 mg/kg (Trial 4). The data do support the student's prediction that the CNF will be greater for 3 days and vacuum filtration than for 10 min and vacuum filtration. **A** and **B** are incorrect; the data do support the student's prediction. **C** is incorrect; Trials 1 and 2 both involved standard filtration, not vacuum filtration. **D** is correct.

12. **The best answer is G.** According to the passage, only Trials 1, 2, and 3 used standard filtration. In Trial 2, the reaction time was 3 days, and in Trial 3, the reaction time was 7 days. The reaction time for Trial 1 was only 10 min. **F** is incorrect; in both Trials 2 and 3 the solid was recovered by standard filtration after a reaction time of at least 3 days. **G** is correct. **H** and **J** are incorrect; in only 2 trials was the solid recovered by standard filtration after a reaction time of at least 3 days.

SCIENCE • PRACTICE TEST 1 • EXPLANATORY ANSWERS

13. **The best answer is A.** In order to answer this item, the examinee must recognize that the stoichiometry of the balanced chemical equation shows that 2 hydroxide ions are needed to produce 1 formula unit of the monohydrate. If 6 hydroxide ions are used, then 3 formula units of the monohydrate will be produced. **A** is correct. **B**, **C**, and **D** are incorrect; there is a 2:1 ratio between hydroxide and the product. If 6 hydroxide ions are used, then 3 monohydrates will be produced.

Passage III

14. **The best answer is G.** According to the passage, the protostar's gravitational field attracts gas. This indicates that gravity accelerates gas particles inward, toward the center of the protostar. The passage also states that RP causes gas to be pushed away. This indicates that RP will accelerate gas particles outward, relative to the center of the protostar. **F** is incorrect; RP will accelerate gas particles outward. **G** is correct. **H** is incorrect; gravity will accelerate particles inward, and RP will accelerate particles outward. **J** is incorrect; gravity will accelerate particles inward.

15. **The best answer is B.** According to Scientist 2, a disk of gas that forms at the protostar's equator reduces the effect of RP in that plane, allowing gas to accrete. This gas will therefore accrete near the equator. **A** is incorrect; the effect of RP is decreased there. **B** is correct. **C** and **D** are incorrect; the gas particles will likely accrete near the equator.

16. **The best answer is H.** According to the passage, Scientist 1 and Scientist 2 both think that stellar mergers are likely and use these to explain how certain size protostars form. Scientist 3 claims that stellar mergers are very unlikely. The lack of evidence of stellar mergers is most inconsistent with the arguments of Scientists 1 and 2. **F** is incorrect; the information is also inconsistent with the argument of Scientist 2. **G** is incorrect; the information is consistent with the argument of Scientist 3. **H** is correct. **J** is incorrect; the information is also inconsistent with the argument of Scientist 2 and is consistent with the argument of Scientist 3.

17. **The best answer is C.** According to the passage, Scientist 1 states that the maximum mass of a star formed by accretion is 20 M_S. It would take six of these stars to make Eta Carinae. Scientist 2 states that the maximum mass of a star formed by accretion is 40 M_S. It would take three of these stars to make Eta Carinae. Scientist 3 states that the maximum size is limited only by the amount of gas available; therefore, Eta Carinae could have been formed entirely by accretion. **A** and **B** are incorrect; Scientist 1 would say that 5 stars would merge to form a star with a maximum mass of only $5 \times 20\ M_S = 100\ M_S$. **C** is correct. Scientist 1 would say that 6 stars would merge to form a star with a maximum mass of $6 \times 20\ M_S = 120\ M_S$. Scientist 2 would say that 3 stars would merge to form a star with a maximum mass of $3 \times 40\ M_S = 120\ M_S$. Scientist 3 would say that 1 star could form Eta Carinae if there was enough gas available. **D** is incorrect; Scientist 2 would say that the minimum number of stars that could merge to form Eta Carinae is 3.

Your First Practice Test

SCIENCE • PRACTICE TEST 1 • EXPLANATORY ANSWERS

18. **The best answer is H.** According to the passage, Scientist 1 states that the most massive star that can form from accretion would have a mass of 20 M_S. Scientist 2 states that the most massive star that can form from accretion would have a mass of 40 M_S. A star with a mass that is greater than 20 M_S but less than or equal to 40 M_S would support Scientist 2's argument, but weaken Scientist 1's argument. **F** and **G** are incorrect; observations of these stars would not weaken the arguments of either Scientist 1 or Scientist 2. **H** is correct. **J** is incorrect; an observation of this star would weaken the arguments of both Scientist 1 and Scientist 2.

19. **The best answer is A.** According to the passage, both Scientists 2 and 3 agree that a disk of gas forms because the protostar rotates about its axis. **A** is correct; the protostar's motion (rotation) is responsible for the formation of the disk. **B** is incorrect; the emission of radiation does not cause the formation of the disk. **C** is incorrect; the location within a star cluster might affect the likelihood of a stellar merger but will not cause the formation of the disk. **D** is incorrect; a stellar merger will create a more massive star but is not responsible for the formation of the disk.

20. **The best answer is H.** According to the passage, 1 M_S is the mass of the Sun. Scientist 1 states that the maximum mass of a star formed by accretion is 20 M_S. Scientist 2 states that the maximum mass of a star formed by accretion is 40 M_S. Scientist 3 claims that the maximum mass of a star depends on the amount of available gas. All three scientists would agree that a star with a mass of 1 M_S could form entirely by accretion, assuming enough gas is present to form the sun. **F, G,** and **J** are incorrect; all three scientists would agree. **H** is correct.

Passage IV

21. **The best answer is D.** According to Figure 1, as the percent vermicompost increased, the average yield for *S. lycopersicum* increased and then decreased. Figure 2 shows that as the percent vermicompost increased, the average yield for *C. annuum* also increased and then decreased. **A, B,** and **C** are incorrect; the yield for both increased and then decreased. **D** is correct.

22. **The best answer is F.** According to Table 1, Mixture 1 had 0% compost. This mixture would serve as a control so that the scientists could determine the effect that vermicompost had on the yield. **F** is correct. **G** is incorrect; Mixture 2 was 20% vermicompost and would not serve as the control. **H** is incorrect; Mixture 4 was 60% vermicompost and would not serve as the control. **J** is incorrect; Mixture 5 was 80% vermicompost and would not serve as the control.

23. **The best answer is B.** In order to answer this item, the examinee must know how to convert units. According to Figure 1, in Study 1, the average yield for Mixture 5 was 3,500 g/plant. This is equal to 3,500 g/plant × $\frac{1\text{ kg}}{1{,}000\text{ g}}$ = 3.5 kg/plant. **A, C,** and **D** are incorrect; **B** is correct.

SCIENCE • PRACTICE TEST 1 • EXPLANATORY ANSWERS

24. **The best answer is G.** According to the passage, both studies used thirty-six 2 L pots. The type and number of seeds used in each study was different, and the amounts of time that the plants were allowed to grow were different. The number of pots used per mixture and the volume of each pot were the same in both studies. **F**, **H**, and **J** are incorrect; the length of time needed to perform Study 1 was 158 days, and the length of time needed to perform Study 2 was 149 days. **G** is correct; the number of pots used per mixture and the volume of each pot were the same in both studies.

25. **The best answer is A.** According to Figure 1, *S. lycopersicum*, a tomato plant, had its greatest average yield in Mixture 2, which was 20% vermicompost. According to Figure 2, *C. annuum*, a pepper plant, had its greatest average yield in Mixture 3, which was 40% vermicompost. The statement is consistent with the results of the studies. **A** is correct. **B** is incorrect; in Study 1 the greatest average yield was attained with Mixture 2. **C** and **D** are incorrect; the statement is consistent with the results of Studies 1 and 2.

26. **The best answer is J.** According to the passage, in Study 1, after 28 days all the seedlings except 1 were removed from each pot. In Study 2, the seedlings were removed after 42 days. **F** is incorrect; more than one seed was planted per pot in both studies. **G** is incorrect; the seedlings were not planted. **H** is incorrect; all but one *seedling* was removed from each pot. **J** is correct.

27. **The best answer is D.** In order to answer this item, the examinee must know the overall chemical reaction for photosynthesis. Carbon dioxide, water, and sunlight are used to produce oxygen and glucose. **A** is incorrect; carbon dioxide is a reactant. **B** is incorrect; glucose is a product. **C** is incorrect; oxygen is a product. **D** is correct.

Passage V

28. **The best answer is H.** According to the passage, in Study 1, the students varied the direction and magnitude of **E** (the electric field). In Study 2, the students varied V (electric potential). **F** is incorrect; electric potential was varied in Study 2. **G** is incorrect; plate length was varied in Study 3. **H** is correct. **J** is incorrect; plate length was varied in Study 3.

29. **The best answer is B.** According to Table 2, as V increased, y decreased. When $y = 3.2$ cm, $V = 1.0$ kV and when $y = 2.1$ cm, $V = 1.5$ kV. It follows that if $y = 2.6$ cm, then V would have some value between 1.0 kV and 1.5 kV. **A** is incorrect; V would have been greater than 1.0 kV. **B** is correct. **C** and **D** are incorrect; V would have been less than 1.5 kV.

30. **The best answer is J.** In Figure 2, the spot was located at approximately +3 cm. According to Tables 1 and 2, the trials with spots in this position were Trial 4 and Trial 8 (both at +3.2 cm). **F** is incorrect; $y = -3.2$ cm in Trial 1. **G** is incorrect; Trial 4 also had $y = +3.2$ cm. **H** is incorrect; $y = -3.2$ cm in Trial 1. **J** is correct.

Your First Practice Test

SCIENCE • PRACTICE TEST 1 • EXPLANATORY ANSWERS

31. **The best answer is C.** According to Table 1, when ***E*** had an upward direction, *y* was negative; when ***E*** had a downward direction, *y* was positive. Table 2 shows that in Study 2, *y* was positive, indicating that ***E*** had a downward direction. Table 3 shows that in Study 3, *y* was negative, indicating that ***E*** had an upward direction. **A**, **B**, and **D** are incorrect; **E** most likely pointed downward in Study 2 and upward in Study 3. **C** is correct.

32. **The best answer is G.** According to the passage, in Studies 1 and 2 only, *V* and ***E*** were varied and therefore one CRT with $L = 2.5$ cm could be used. In Study 3, *L* was varied, including one trial with $L = 2.5$ cm. Because five different *L* values were tested and because *L* cannot be varied from outside the tube, five different CRTs must have been used. **F**, **H**, and **J** are incorrect; a minimum of five CRTs were required. **G** is correct.

33. **The best answer is B.** According to the results of Study 1, as the magnitude of ***E*** increased, the farther the spot was from $y = 0$ cm. According to the results of Study 2, as *V* increased, *y* decreased. In order to have $y = 0$ cm, *V* should be nonzero and the magnitude of ***E*** should be zero. **A** is incorrect; *V* should be nonzero. **B** is correct. **C** is incorrect; *V* should be nonzero. **D** is incorrect; the magnitude of ***E*** should be zero.

34. **The best answer is J.** In order to answer this item, the examinee should know that charges of like sign repel each other and charges of opposite sign attract each other. According to Figure 1, the cathode ray is deflected upward (toward the top plate and away from the bottom plate). Because like charges repel one another and because the cathode ray is negatively charged, the bottom plate must be negatively charged. **F** and **G** are incorrect; the cathode ray is deflected toward the top plate and therefore the top plate must be positively charged. **H** is incorrect; charges of like sign repel one another. **J** is correct.

Passage VI

35. **The best answer is D.** According to Figure 2, when $N = 15 \times 10^{23}$ atoms, Xe had the shortest λ, followed by Kr, Ar, and Ne. **A** and **B** are incorrect; Ne had the longest λ. **C** is incorrect; Kr had the second shortest λ. **D** is correct.

36. **The best answer is G.** According to Figure 2, when *N* for Ne was equal to 6×10^{23} atoms, $\lambda = 1{,}600$ nm and when *N* for Ne was equal to 12×10^{23} atoms, $\lambda = 800$ nm. When the Ne sample size doubled, λ was reduced by half. **F**, **H**, and **J** are incorrect; λ was multiplied by ½. **G** is correct.

37. **The best answer is C.** According to Figure 1, as *V* increases, λ also increases. When $V = 5$ L, λ was approximately 50 nm and when $V = 10$ L, λ was approximately 100 nm. Based on this trend, if *V* is doubled from 25 L to 50 L, then λ should also double. **A** and **B** are incorrect; λ for the 50 L sample should be greater than λ for the 25 L sample. **C** is correct. **D** is incorrect; λ only increases by 2 times when *V* is doubled.

SCIENCE • PRACTICE TEST 1 • EXPLANATORY ANSWERS

38. **The best answer is J.** According to Figure 1, when $V = 20$ L, λ for Xe is approximately 175 nm and λ for Ar is approximately 375 nm. Thus, λ for Ar is approximately 200 nm longer than λ for Xe. **F**, **G**, and **H** are incorrect; the difference is closest to 200 nm. **J** is correct.

39. **The best answer is A.** If the atoms have the same average speed, then the sample with the shortest λ (distance between collisions) will have the highest collision frequency. Figure 1 shows that Xe atoms in the 5 L sample have a shorter λ than atoms in the 25 L sample. **A** is correct; the atoms in the 5 L sample travel a shorter distance between collisions. **B** is incorrect; the atoms in the 5 L sample travel a shorter distance between collisions. **C** and **D** are incorrect; the atoms in the 25 L sample would have a lower collision frequency.

40. **The best answer is F.** According to Figure 2, for any given λ, the lower the value of *d*, the greater the value of *N*. When λ = 320 nm for Xe, there are fewer than 6×10^{23} atoms of Xe present. Because *d* for Rn is greater than that for Xe, it follows that there are also fewer than 6×10^{23} atoms of Rn present. **F** is correct. **G**, **H**, and **J** are incorrect; there will be fewer than 6×10^{23} atoms of Rn present.

4

Chapter 4: Identifying Areas for Improvement

Your practice test scores alone provide very little insight into what you need to do to improve your score. For example, you may have missed a certain math question because you haven't yet taken trigonometry or because you misread the question or the answer choices or because you were anxious about finishing the test on time.

When evaluating your performance on any of the practice tests in this book or elsewhere, examine not only *whether* you answered a question correctly or incorrectly but also *why* you answered it correctly or incorrectly. Recognizing why you chose the correct or incorrect answer sheds light on what you need to do to improve your score on future practice tests and on the ACT. Perhaps you need to review certain subjects, take a particular course, develop a better sense of how much time to spend on each question, or read questions and answer choices more carefully.

In this chapter, we offer guidance on how to evaluate your performance on ACT Practice Test 1 in order to identify subject areas and test-taking strategies and skills that you may need to work on. Take a similar approach to evaluate your performance on subsequent practice tests.

Reviewing Your Overall Performance

After you have determined your scores, consider the following questions as you evaluate how you did on the practice tests. Keep in mind that many of these questions require you to make judgment calls based on what you were thinking or the steps you took to decide on the answer choice you selected. The answer explanations in chapter 4 may help you make these determinations, but ultimately you are the only one who can determine why or how you chose the correct or incorrect answer.

Did you run out of time before you completed a test?

If so, read the sections in this book on pacing yourself. See chapter 2 for general advice that applies to all tests, and see chapters 5 through 9 for advice specific to each test. Perhaps you need to adjust the way you use your time in responding to the questions. Remember, there is no penalty for guessing, so try to answer all questions, even if you have to make an educated guess.

Did you spend too much time trying to understand the directions to the tests?

Make sure you understand them now, so you won't have to spend too much time reading them when you take the test.

Did you rush through the test and make mistakes?

People tend to make mistakes when they are in a hurry. If you had plenty of time remaining at the end of the test but made mistakes, you probably hurried through the test and made errors such as these:

- Misreading a passage
- Misreading a question
- Not reading or considering all answer choices
- Selecting a response that was an incomplete answer
- Selecting an answer that did not directly respond to the question

Did a particular type of question confuse you?

Use the explanatory answers following each practice test to help you identify any mistakes you may have made regarding certain question types or answer choices. The explanatory answers can help you understand why you may have chosen the incorrect answer and avoid making that same mistake again.

Highlighting Strengths and Areas for Improvement on the English Test

The process of scoring your English practice test and reviewing the answer explanations should reveal the reason you chose the correct or incorrect answer for each question. If you struggled to answer questions on the test because you have not yet acquired certain English language knowledge and skills review the questions and your answers closely to determine more specifically what you need to work on.

The English test requires knowledge and skills in several areas. The best way to raise your score is to improve your English language skills, which you can accomplish in the following ways:

- Take an English composition course. Such a course will help you write more clearly, logically, and concisely while developing a better understanding of English punctuation, grammar, and usage conventions.
- Practice your writing skills in other courses. In most courses, including English literature, social studies, speech, and perhaps even science, you have opportunities to practice your writing skills and receive feedback.
- Read well-written publications in the form of books, magazine articles, and online content from reputable sources—material that has been professionally edited. As you read, pay attention to punctuation, grammar, usage, sentence structure, writing strategy, organization, and style to see how a variety of writers express themselves while adhering to the same conventions.
- Practice writing and having your writing edited by an English teacher or someone else who is qualified to provide feedback.

Test-Taking Errors

A low test score does not necessarily mean that you lack the English language knowledge and skills required to do well on the test. It may indicate that you rushed through the test and made mistakes, spent too much time on certain questions that you didn't finish, or committed some other test-taking error(s). As you evaluate your answers to determine *why* you missed certain questions, consider your test-taking strategies and skills. Place a checkmark next to each of the following common test-taking errors you think you need to work on eliminating:

Worked too slowly: You may need to improve your reading speed and comprehension or try answering the easy questions first and then returning to the harder questions if time remains.

Rushed through the test: If you finished with plenty of time remaining but made mistakes, you may need to spend more time reading and understanding the passages, reading the questions, or carefully considering all of the answer choices.

Misread passages: If you missed questions because of misreading or misinterpreting passages, work on your reading comprehension. Try reading more carefully and rereading when you do not fully understand a passage.

Misread questions: Every question points to the correct answer, so read questions carefully and make sure you understand what a question is asking before you choose your answer.

Did not consider all answer choices: If you tend to select the first answer choice that seems to be correct, try considering all answer choices before making your final selection. A good way to double-check an answer is to find reasons to eliminate the other three choices.

Did not consider the writing style: The entire passage conveys the author's overall writing style, which you may need to consider when answering certain style-related questions.

Did not consider a question's context: Writing strategy and organization questions often require consideration of surrounding text. You may need to skim the passage first before answering these questions or read one or two sentences before or after the sentence in question.

Did not account for a word's connotations: Many words have a *denotation* (a literal meaning or dictionary definition) and a *connotation* (a thought or emotion that the word evokes from the reader or listener). To answer some usage questions, you must consider what the word means in the context in which it is used.

Did not connect an underlined portion of text with its corresponding question: The underlined portion of the text and the corresponding question work together to point to the correct answer choice, so be sure to consider them both when selecting your answer.

Overlooked differences in the answer choices: Answer choices may differ so subtly that you overlook the differences, so be sure to recognize what's different about each choice before selecting your answer.

Chose an answer that introduced a new error: Some answer choices correct the error in the underlined text but introduce a new error. Do not fall for this common trap.

Did not choose the best answer: Two or more answers may be correct, but the English test requires that you choose the *best* answer. Again, consider all answer choices before selecting an answer.

Did not reread the sentence using the selected answer: A great way to double-check an answer is to insert it in place of the underlined text and then reread the sentence to make sure it makes sense.

Missed a two-part question: With a two-part question, each of the answer choices typically starts with "yes" or "no" followed by a reason, so you must determine first whether the answer is yes or no and then why. Carefully compare and consider the reasons before making your selection.

Did not consider interrelated questions: A question may be easier to answer after you have answered the next question, so consider skipping back to a question if you feel that answering the current question has given you new insight.

See chapter 5 for in-depth coverage of test-taking strategies and skills that may help to raise your English test score.

Highlighting Strengths and Areas for Improvement on the Mathematics Test

The process of scoring your mathematics practice test and reviewing the answer explanations should reveal your strengths and any areas for improvement. You may discover that you are a whiz at algebra and geometry but are in dire need of a refresher course in trigonometry. Or, you may find that your math knowledge and skills are sound in all areas but you need to work on test-taking strategies to ensure that your test results accurately reflect your knowledge and skills.

Use the checklists in the following sections to flag subject areas and test-taking skills you may need to focus on.

Math Subject Areas

If you struggled to answer questions on the test because you have not yet acquired the requisite math language knowledge and skills, review the questions and your answers closely to determine more specifically what you need to work on.

Your performance on the ACT mathematics test may be affected by your ability to handle certain types of questions. For example, you may breeze through straightforward, basic math questions but get tripped up by word problems. As you evaluate your performance on mathematics in Practice Test 1, try to identify the types of questions you struggle with most:

Basic math: These questions are straightforward with very little text. You just need to do the math.

Basic math in settings: These are word problems that challenge your ability to translate the problem into one or more mathematical equations and then solve those equations.

Very challenging math problems: These can be basic math or basic math in settings questions that challenge your ability to reason mathematically and perhaps draw from your knowledge of more than one math subject area to solve them. In addition to the differences in how math problems are presented, you may encounter *question sets*—two or more sequential math problems related to the same information.

Test-Taking Errors

Incorrect or unanswered questions on the practice test may be less of a reflection of your math knowledge and skills and more a reflection of your test-taking strategies and skills. As you review your scores and answers, try to determine whether you committed any of the following common test-taking errors:

Worked too slowly: If you answered questions correctly but your score suffered from unanswered questions because you ran out of time, you may simply need more practice to improve your speed.

Rushed through the test: If you finished with plenty of time remaining but made mistakes, you may need to spend more time reading and understanding the questions and doing the math before selecting an answer.

Got stuck on a very challenging question: Answering the easy questions first and then returning to the harder questions later may help you address this issue.

Misread the question: The question contains all information you need to answer it. Misreading the question may cause you to extract and use the wrong information in your calculations or calculate an answer for something other than what the question directed.

Overlooked information in the answer choices: Answer choices often provide clues as to what form the answer is in. A glance at the answer choices can often clarify what the question is asking for.

Overlooked or misinterpreted information in an image: Many math questions include an image, table, or graph that provides key information. Misreading an image will lead you to select the wrong answer choice.

Did not use logic to solve a problem: Math questions, especially the very challenging ones, often test your ability to reason through problems.

Not doing the math: Although you are not required to show your work on the test, consider writing out your calculations to double-check your reasoning and avoid mental errors. Also, when a question includes an image, consider writing any dimensions provided in the question on to the image so that the image contains all of the measurements you have to work with.

Not double-checking your answers: For many questions, you can insert the answer you think is correct into the equation provided and do the math to double-check the answer choice. Take the opportunity to double-check answers when given the opportunity.

For math test strategies and tips, turn to chapter 6.

Highlighting Strengths and Areas for Improvement on the Reading Test

The process of scoring the reading practice test and reviewing the answer explanations should reveal the reason you chose the correct or incorrect answer for each question. Reasons for choosing wrong answers or struggling with certain questions can be classified in three categories:

Subject matter

The type of passage—prose fiction, humanities, social studies, or science—may affect your ability to read and comprehend the passage and answer questions about it. For example, you may have no trouble answering questions about fact-based passages in social studies and science but struggle reading and understanding prose fiction.

Reading skills

The reading test is designed to evaluate numerous skills, including the ability to identify details in the text, draw generalizations about those details, and understand the meaning of a word or phrase based on how it is used in a sentence. In addition, each passage challenges you to read quickly and with understanding.

Test-taking strategies and skills

Not reading the entire passage, misreading the question or answer choices, and not verifying an answer choice with the passage can all lead to careless mistakes.

Use the checklists in the following sections to flag the types of reading passages, reading skills, and test-taking strategies and skills you may need to focus on.

Types of Reading Passages

Your ability to comprehend reading passages and answer questions about them may vary based on the type of passage. For example, if you are accustomed to reading science books and articles, you are probably familiar with many of the concepts and vocabulary in the science passages on the test; therefore, you might expect to have no trouble reading, comprehending, and answering questions about such passages. However, if you have read very little fiction, you may find it challenging to identify the plot (sequence of events), draw conclusions about characters, or sense the mood that a passage is intended to evoke. In short, you may struggle more with certain types of reading passages than with others.

As you score your reading test and review the answer explanations, use the following checklist to flag any types of reading passages you found particularly challenging (the passage type is indicated at the beginning of each passage on the test):

Prose fiction: Passages from short stories or novels

Social studies: Passages that cover topics such as anthropology, archaeology, biography, business, economics, education, geography, history, political science, psychology, and sociology

Humanities: Articles about topics including architecture, art, dance, ethics, film, language, literary criticism, memoir, music, personal essays, philosophy, radio, television, and theater

Natural science: Passages related to subjects such as anatomy, astronomy, biology, botany, chemistry, ecology, geology, medicine, meteorology, microbiology, natural history, physiology, physics, technology, and zoology

Reading Skills Tested

The ability to read, comprehend, and answer questions about passages involves numerous skills. Questions on the test are written specifically to evaluate these skills. As you review the answer explanations, place a checkmark next to any of the following skills you think you need to develop more fully:

Identify and interpret details: Nearly all questions require an ability to identify and interpret details from the passage that supports whichever answer choice you select. Many questions specifically state, "According to the passage, …" This skill is essential for performing well on the reading test.

Determine the main idea of a paragraph(s) or passage: A few questions may require an ability to recognize the general meaning or point of one or more paragraphs.

Understand comparative relationships (comparison and contrast): Questions may ask about comparisons and contrasts made in the passage.

Understand cause-effect relationships: Some reading passages explore cause-effect relationships. Others are accompanied by questions that more subtly test your ability to identify cause-effect relationships.

Make generalizations: To answer many reading questions, you must be able to draw conclusions from or make generalizations about details provided in the passage.

Determine the meaning of words or phrases from context: You are likely to encounter several questions on the ACT reading test that challenge you to determine the meaning of a word or phrase based on the context in which it is used.

Understand sequences of events: A few reading test questions may require an ability to read and comprehend a series of events.

Draw conclusions about the author's voice and method: You may be asked to get into the mind of the author and figure out what his or her attitude, purpose, or method is.

For more about reading skills tested, including examples of the types of questions used to evaluate these skills, turn to chapter 7.

Test-Taking Errors

Even if your reading speed and comprehension are solid, you may miss questions by committing one or more of the following common test-taking errors. Place a checkmark next to each error you think you may be susceptible to making:

Read too slowly or too quickly: By reading too slowly, you may not have sufficient time to read all passages and answer all questions. However, reading too quickly may result in errors or having to return to a passage several times to locate the evidence needed to decide which answer choice is correct.

Did not read the entire passage: Skim-reading a passage is useful for understanding what a passage is about, but it often results in overlooking the details required to answer specific questions. Read the entire passage word for word.

Misread the question: Questions, especially those that contain the word *NOT*, can be tricky. Make sure you understand what a question is asking as you evaluate the various answer choices.

Misread or overlooked an answer choice: Misreading an answer choice or not considering all answer choices can result in mistakes. Consider all answer choices and read them carefully.

Did not verify an answer choice with the passage: If time allows, try to verify every answer choice by locating details in the passage that support it. Use the same technique to rule out other answer choices when necessary.

For additional reading test strategies and tips, turn to chapter 7.

Highlighting Strengths and Areas for Improvement on the Science Test

The process of scoring the science practice test and reviewing the answer explanations should reveal the reason you chose the correct or incorrect answer for each question. Reasons for choosing wrong answers or struggling with certain questions can be classified into three categories:

Subject matter

The science test does not require in-depth knowledge of biology, chemistry, earth science, space science, or physics. Nor does it require you to memorize formulas or solve complex math problems. However, questions are presented in the context of these subject areas, and you may need some knowledge of scientific terms or concepts to answer some of the questions.

Question type

Science test questions are presented in three different formats: Data Representation (graphs, tables, illustrations); Research Summaries (from experiments); and Conflicting Viewpoints (alternative theories and hypotheses). You may struggle more with one type of question than with the others.

Test-taking strategies and skills

The science test evaluates your ability to extract and use information presented in a variety of formats to solve problems and answer questions. Even if you are highly skilled and knowledgeable in all science subject areas, your score will suffer if you make careless mistakes or are so careful that you run out of time before answering all of the questions.

Use the checklists in the following sections to flag the subject areas, question types, and test-taking strategies and skills you may need to focus on.

Science Subject Areas

You may benefit from identifying subject areas in which you struggle. Use the following checklist to flag subject matter you may need to review:

Biology: Cell biology, botany, zoology, microbiology, ecology, genetics, and evolution

Chemistry: Properties of matter, acids and bases, kinetics and equilibria, thermo-chemistry, organic chemistry, biochemistry, and nuclear chemistry

Earth science: Geology, meteorology, oceanography, and environmental science

Physics: Mechanics, thermodynamics, electromagnetism, fluids, solids, and optics

Space science: Formerly known as *astronomy*

Types of Science Questions

As you review answer explanations and evaluate your performance on the science test, check to see whether you had more trouble with certain types of science questions than with others. Place a checkmark next to any question types that you found particularly challenging:

Data Representation requires you to understand, evaluate, and interpret information presented in graphs, tables, and illustrations.

Research Summary requires you to understand, analyze, and evaluate the design, execution, and results of one or more experiments.

Conflicting Viewpoints requires you to compare and evaluate alternative theories, hypotheses, or viewpoints on a specific observable phenomenon.

For more about these different question types and guidance on how to approach them effectively, turn to chapter 8.

Test-Taking Errors

As mentioned previously, the science test does not require in-depth scientific knowledge. It relies more on your ability to understand and identify detailed information presented in a variety of formats—text, graphs, tables, and diagrams. If your science test score is lower than you had hoped, you may have committed one or more test-taking errors. Place a checkmark next to each of the following test-taking errors that you think you need to work on avoiding:

Worked too slowly: If time expired before you had a chance to answer all 40 questions, you need to pick up the pace.

Worked too quickly: If you finished with plenty of time remaining but made mistakes, you need to practice slowing down and reading the science passages, questions, and answer choices more carefully.

Misread or misinterpreted text: If you missed questions because you misread a passage, question, or answer choice, check this box.

Misread or misinterpreted a graph or table: Graphs, tables, and images contain much of the information required to answer the science test questions.

Misread or misinterpreted a research summary: You may need to develop a better understanding of the scientific method for designing and conducting experiments.

Did not use reason effectively to find the answer: Most of the questions on the science test challenge your ability to think and reason. If you struggled to understand questions, check this box. You may be able to improve your score by adopting a problem-solving strategy that steps you through the question, as discussed in chapter 8.

For science test-taking strategies that will help you avoid these common mistakes and others, turn to chapter 8.

Highlighting Strengths and Areas for Improvement on the Writing Test

The optional writing test is designed to evaluate your ability to write at a level expected of students entering first-year college English composition courses. A solid essay demonstrates your ability to clearly state your perspective on a complex issue and analyze the relationship between your perspective and at least one other perspective, develop and support your ideas with reasoning and examples, organize your ideas clearly and logically, and communicate your ideas effectively in standard written English.

After scoring your writing practice test, use the checklists in the following sections to highlight writing skills you may need to develop more fully and to avoid errors related to writing strategy and process.

Writing Skills Tested

As you evaluate your writing practice test, consider not only your scores but also, more importantly, which skills contributed to your scores. You may be able to improve your scores significantly by more fully developing only one or two of the following skills. Place a checkmark next to each skill you think you need to work on:

Clearly state your own perspective on a complex issue and analyze the relationship between your perspective and at least one other perspective: If your essay did not establish a clear perspective, practice formulating thesis statements. Whenever you write an essay, practice stating your thesis in the first few sentences of the essay. By presenting your perspective in the introduction, you not only state your main idea clearly but also give your essay a focal point.

If you had trouble analyzing the relationship between your perspective and at least one other perspective, practice writing counterarguments. Pick a debatable issue and choose a stance. Now, imagine what someone who disagrees with you might say, and practice writing paragraphs that first present the other person's side of the issue. Then offer your response. Next, imagine a perspective that is in general agreement with yours but differs in some important ways. How do you respond to this perspective? As you think and write, ask yourself: What accounts for the similarities and differences among your perspective and others you can imagine? Where are the strengths and weaknesses in these other perspectives, and where are the strengths and weaknesses in your own? Most importantly, ask yourself how engaging with another view—whether it generally agrees or disagrees with your own—can help you advance an argument. Considering these questions as you practice can help you learn to analyze and engage with different perspectives.

Develop and support your ideas with reasoning and examples: Failure to support your assertions can result in a lower score. Remember that every claim you make should be backed up with good supporting evidence. As you explain the reasoning behind your argument, remember that logical fallacies, including overgeneralization and moral equivalence (associating minor offenses with moral atrocities), can weaken your ideas.

Organize your ideas clearly and logically: An essay should flow directly from point A to point B and not circle back or wander off track. (Prewriting, discussed in the next section, can help ensure that your essay is well organized.)

Communicate your ideas effectively in standard written English: Here is where your mastery of punctuation, grammar, usage, sentence structure, and style applies.

You can develop all of these skills in high school English classes and other classes that require you to write essays and where you receive feedback that targets these skills. For more about improving your writing test score, along with sample essays that demonstrate the differences between high-scoring and lower-scoring essays, turn to chapter 9.

Writing Strategy or Process Errors

When scoring an essay, the focus is on the product, but the score may be a reflection of the process used to produce that essay. For example, prewriting (planning) can help you think of good ideas, ensure that your ideas are presented logically, and remind you to provide evidence to support your ideas. After scoring your practice essay, think back to when you wrote the essay and place a checkmark next to any of these writing strategy or process errors you may have committed:

Poor pacing: Writing too quickly may result in careless errors, whereas writing too slowly results in an incomplete essay or insufficient time to review and correct errors.

Insufficient prewriting (planning): It is hard to write an effective essay if you don't have much to say. If you had trouble generating critical ideas, consider using the guided prewriting section found in the test booklet. The questions presented in this section are intended to help you produce a perspective and analyze its relationships with other points of view. They are also useful as you think about how you will support your ideas. It can also be difficult to organize your ideas as you write. You may instead consider using the prewriting space to write an outline. You do not need a detailed outline, but starting with a thesis and mapping a structure to support it can help you define the logic of your argument before you begin to write it.

Not reviewing or editing: If you completed your essay with time to spare, did not review or edit it, and lost points because of grammar, usage, sentence structure, or style errors, check this box. And next time you write an essay, be sure to read and edit it as time allows.

Insufficient practice: Producing well-written essays requires practice and feedback, which you often receive only in a formal English composition course. The practice writing tests in this book provide additional opportunities, but we strongly recommend that you have your practice writing tests evaluated by a qualified third party—perhaps an English teacher or a fellow student who is a strong writer.

For additional tips on improving your writing test score, turn to chapter 9.

NOTES

3 Part Three: Improving Your Score

In This Part

This part features various ways to improve your scores on the English, mathematics, reading, science, and optional writing tests. Here, you get a preview of the types of questions you can expect on each test, along with test-taking strategies and skills that apply specifically to each test:

English: Find out more about test content, look at sample questions, and develop strategies for choosing the best answer.

Mathematics: Learn about the subject areas covered on the test, the types of math problems you will encounter, and strategies for improving your speed and accuracy in answering questions.

Reading: Discover the types of reading passages you will encounter on the test, the types of questions you will need to answer, and strategies for improving your reading speed and comprehension.

Science: Identify the areas of science covered on the test, the types of questions you will encounter, and test-taking strategies and skills for extracting information from passages and using it to reason your way to the correct answers.

Writing: Check out a sample writing prompt, find out what the people scoring your essay will be looking for, read sample scored essays from poor to excellent, and pick up a few strategies that may help to raise your writing score.

Chapter 5: Improving Your English Score

On the ACT English test, you have 45 minutes to read five passages, or essays, and answer 75 multiple-choice questions about them—an average of 15 questions per essay. The essays on the English test cover a variety of subjects; the sample passages that follow this discussion range from a personal essay about the different ways of figuring one's age to an informative essay about the legal history of school dress codes.

Content of the ACT English Test

The ACT English test is designed to measure your ability to make the wide variety of decisions involved in revising and editing a given piece of writing. The test measures your understanding of the Conventions of Standard English (punctuation, usage, and sentence structure); Production of Writing (topic development, organization, unity, and cohesion); and Knowledge of Language (word choice, style, and tone). Although you may use more informal or conversational language in your own writing, the test emphasizes the standard written English that is taught in schools around the country.

Different passage types are used to provide a variety of rhetorical situations. Passages are chosen not only for their appropriateness in assessing writing skills but also to reflect students' interests and experiences.

Questions on the English test fall into three categories:

- **Production of Writing** (topic development, organization, unity, and cohesion)
- **Knowledge of Language** (precision and concision in word choice, consistency in style and tone)
- **Conventions of Standard English** (sentence structure and formation, punctuation, and usage)

You will receive four scores for the ACT English test: a total test score based on all 75 questions and three reporting category scores based on specific knowledge and skills in the categories previously described. If you choose to take the writing test, you will also receive an English Language Arts (ELA) score based on an average of your English, reading, and writing test scores.

You will **not** be tested on spelling, vocabulary, or on rote recall of the rules of grammar. Grammar and usage are tested only within the context of the essay, not by questions such as "Must an appositive always be set off by commas?" Likewise, you won't be tested directly on your vocabulary, although the better your vocabulary is, the better equipped you'll be to comprehend the reading passages and answer questions that involve choosing the most appropriate word.

The English test doesn't require you to memorize what you read. The questions and essays are side-by-side for easy reference. This is **not** a memorization test.

The questions discussed on the following pages are taken from the sample passages and questions that follow on pages 221–227. If you prefer, you can work through the sample passages and questions before you read the rest of this discussion. However, to better understand the English test, you may want to first read the discussion, then work through the sample passages and questions.

Types of Questions on the ACT English Test

Many questions refer to an underlined portion of the essay. You must decide on the best alternative for that underlined portion. Usually, your options include NO CHANGE, which means that the essay is best as it's written. Sometimes, you'll also have the option of deleting the underlined portion. For example, the following question (from Sample Passage II on pages 223–225) offers you the option of removing the word *to* from the sentence.

Otherwise, this difference points (21)
to (22) significant underlying cultural values.

22. **F.** NO CHANGE
G. on
H. at
J. OMIT the underlined portion.

In this example, the best answer is not to delete the underlined portion but to leave it as it is (**F**).

Other questions on the English test may ask about a section of the essay or an aspect of the essay as a whole. For example, in the following question (from Sample Passage I on pages 221–223), you're given a sentence to be added to the essay, then you're asked to decide the most logical place in the essay to add that sentence.

15. Upon reviewing this essay and finding that some information has been left out, the writer composes the following sentence incorporating that information:

> Those same German influences helped spawn a similar musical form in northern Mexico known as *norteño*.

The sentence would most logically be placed after the last sentence in Paragraph:

A. 1.
B. 2.
C. 3.
D. 4.

In this example, the best answer is **C**, because paragraph 3 focuses on the European musical influences on the O'odham people of Arizona, and the last sentence of the paragraph specifically refers to the musical influences of German immigrants.

Let's look at some additional examples of the kinds of questions you're likely to find on the ACT English test. If you want to know what an individual question looks like in the context of the passage in which it appears, turn to the pages indicated. You can also use those sample passages and questions for practice, either before or after reading this discussion.

Conventions of Standard English

Conventions of Standard English questions focus on the conventions of punctuation, grammar and usage, and sentence structure and formation.

Punctuation questions involve identifying and correcting the following misplaced, missing, or unnecessary punctuation marks:

- Commas
- Apostrophes
- Colons, semicolons, and dashes
- Periods, question marks, and exclamation points

These questions address not only the rules of punctuation but also the use of punctuation to express ideas clearly. For example, you should be prepared to show how punctuation can be used to indicate possession or to set off a parenthetical element.

In many punctuation questions, the words in every choice will be identical, but the commas or other punctuation will vary. It's important to read the choices carefully in order to notice the presence or absence of commas, semicolons, colons, periods, and other punctuation. The following example of a punctuation question comes from Sample Passage I on pages 221–223.

Around this time the polka music and button accordion played by German immigrant railroad workers; left their mark on waila. [14: "workers;"]

14. F. NO CHANGE
G. workers
H. workers:
J. workers,

It may help you to read through this sentence without paying attention to the punctuation so you can identify its grammatical construction. The subject of this sentence is "the polka music and button accordion." What follows that subject might seem like the predicate verb of the sentence, but it's not. The phrase "played by German immigrant railroad workers" is a participle phrase (a phrase formed with the past participle "played"). This participle phrase functions as an adjective because it modifies the nouns it follows ("the polka music and button accordion").

After the participle phrase is the predicate verb of the main clause, "left." Then comes a phrase that explains what was left (the direct object "their mark") and a prepositional phrase that explains where it was left ("on waila").

Now we can deal with the question about what kind of punctuation should follow that participle phrase. Sometimes, these phrases are set off from the main clause with commas to indicate that the phrase is parenthetical or provides information not essential to the meaning of the sentence. That's not the case here for two reasons. First, there's no comma at the beginning of the participle phrase. Second, the phrase is essential to the sentence; the sentence is not referring to just any polka music and button accordion but to the music and accordion played by those German immigrant railroad workers (presumably, not while they were working on the railroad).

Ignoring the participle phrase for a minute, we need to ask ourselves what kind of punctuation we would usually place between the subject "the polka music and button accordion" and the predicate "left." Our answer should be no punctuation at all, making **G** the best answer. Of course, you could answer this question without this rather tedious analysis of the parts of the sentence. You might simply decide that because the sentence contains no other punctuation, you would never insert a single punctuation mark between the subject and the predicate of the main clause. Or you might just plug in each of the four punctuation choices—semicolon, no punctuation, colon, comma—and choose the one that looks or sounds best to you.

Grammar and usage questions involve choosing the best word or words in a sentence based on grammar and usage conventions. Some examples of poor and better phrases are given in the following.

- Grammatical agreement

  (Subject and verb)

  "The owner of the bicycles *are* going to sell them."
  should be:
  "The owner of the bicycles *is* going to sell them."

  * * *

  (Pronoun and antecedent)

  "Susan and Mary left *her* briefcases in the office."
  should be:
  "Susan and Mary left *their* briefcases in the office."

  * * *

  (Adjectives and adverbs with corresponding nouns and verbs)

  "Danielle spread frosting *liberal* on the cat."
  should be:
  "Danielle spread frosting *liberally* on the cat."

- Verb forms

  "Fritz had just *began* to toast Lydia's marshmallows when the rabbits stampeded."
  should be:
  "Fritz had just *begun* to toast Lydia's marshmallows when the rabbits stampeded."

- Pronoun forms and cases

  "Seymour and Svetlana annoyed *there* parents all the time."
  should be:
  "Seymour and Svetlana annoyed *their* parents all the time."

  * * *

  "After the incident with the peanut butter, the zebra and *me* were never invited back."
  should be:
  "After the incident with the peanut butter, the zebra and *I* were never invited back."

- Comparative and superlative modifiers

  "My goldfish is *more smarter* than your brother."
  should be:
  "My goldfish is *smarter* than your brother."

  * * *

"Your brother, however, has the *cuter* aardvark that I've ever seen."
should be:
"Your brother, however, has the *cutest* aardvark that I've ever seen."

- Idioms

  "The definition of a word can be looked *down* in the dictionary."
  should be:
  "The definition of a word can be looked *up* in the dictionary."

Questions dealing with pronouns often have to do with using the proper form and case of the pronoun. Sometimes they address a pronoun's agreement with its antecedent, or referent. In such cases, consider the entire sentence, and sometimes the preceding sentence, to make sure you know what the antecedent is. Consider the following question (from Sample Passage I on pages 221–223).

As the dancers step to the music, they <u>were also stepping</u> (8) in time to a sound that embodies <u>their</u> (9) unique history and suggests the influence of outside cultures on their music.

9. **A.** NO CHANGE
B. they're
C. it's
D. its'

Here, the possessive pronoun in question refers back to the subject of the main clause ("they"), which in turn refers back to the subject of the introductory subordinate clause ("the dancers"). Thus, the best answer is the third-person plural possessive pronoun ("their," **A**). Choice **B** might seem like a possibility because *they're* sounds like *their* (that is, they're homonyms). However, *they're* is a contraction for *they are.* We can rule out **C** and **D** because of the pronoun-antecedent agreement problem and also because *it's* is not a possessive pronoun but a contraction for *it is,* and *its'* is not even a word.

Sentence structure questions involve the effective formation of sentences, including dealing with relationships between and among clauses, placement of modifiers, and shifts in construction. Following are some examples:

- Subordinate or dependent clauses and participle phrases

  "These hamsters are excellent pets *because providing* hours of cheap entertainment."

  This sentence could be rewritten as:

  "These hamsters are excellent pets providing hours of cheap entertainment." (participle phrase)

  It could also be revised as:

  "These hamsters are excellent pets because they provide hours of cheap entertainment." (subordinate/dependent clause)

- Run-on or fused sentences

  "We discovered that the entire family had been devoured by *anteaters it* was horrible."

  This sentence should actually be two:

  "We discovered that the entire family had been devoured by *anteaters. It* was horrible."

- Comma splices

  "The anteaters had terrible *manners, they* just ate and ran."

  This sentence could be rewritten as:

  "The anteaters had terrible *manners. They* just ate and ran."

  Because a semicolon can serve as a "soft" period, the sentence could also be rewritten as:

  "The anteaters had terrible *manners; they* just ate and ran."

- Sentence fragments

  "*When he* found scorpions in his socks."

  This needs a subject to let us know who "he" is and what he did:

  "*Julio didn't lose his temper when he* found scorpions in his socks."

- Misplaced modifiers

  "*Snarling and snapping, Juanita* attempted to control her pet turtle."

  Unless Juanita was doing the snarling and snapping, the sentence should be rewritten:

  "*Snarling and snapping, the pet turtle* resisted Juanita's attempt to control it." It could also be rewritten this way:

  "Juanita attempted to control her *pet turtle, which snarled and snapped.*"

- Shifts in verb tense or voice

  "We sat down to the table to eat, but before we began, John *says* grace."

  This should be rewritten as:

  "We sat down to the table to eat, but before we began, John *said* grace."

- Shifts in pronoun person or number

  "Hamsters should work at the most efficient pace that *one* can."

  This should be rewritten as:

  "Hamsters should work at the most efficient pace that *they* can."

Many questions about sentence structure and formation will ask you about how clauses and phrases are linked. This means that you may have to consider punctuation or the lack of punctuation, which can create problems such as comma splices, run-on sentences, or sentence fragments. You also may have to consider various words that can be used to link clauses and phrases: conjunctions such as *and, but, because,* and *when,* and pronouns such as *who, whose, which,* and *that.* The following question (from Sample Passage I on pages 221–223) is a good example of a sentence structure question.

It is a social music that performed at weddings, birthday parties, and feasts. [underlined: music that performed; 4]

4. F. NO CHANGE
   G. music in which it is performed
   H. music, performing
   J. music, performed

What would be the best way to link the clause "It is a social music" and the phrase "performed [or performing] at weddings, birthday parties, and feasts"? Relative pronouns such as *that* and *which* stand in for the noun that the relative clause modifies. (They relate the clause to the noun.) One way to try out choices such as **F** and **G** is to replace the relative pronoun with the noun and then decide if the resulting statement makes sense:

Social music performed at weddings, birthday parties, and feasts. **(F)**

This does not make sense. Musicians perform, but the music itself does not. Music *is* performed.

In social music it is performed at weddings, birthday parties, and feasts. **(G)**

This also seems nonsensical. What does *it* refer to—social music?

The other two choices offer a different approach to connecting information in a sentence. The phrases "performing at weddings, birthday parties, and feasts" **(H)** and "performed at weddings, birthday parties, and feasts" **(J)** are participial phrases. Similar to adjective clauses, these phrases modify a noun. We can rule out **H** for the same reason that we rejected **F**: It doesn't make sense to think of "social music" as "performing." However, it sounds fine to refer to "social music" as "performed" **(J)**.

Production of Writing

Production of Writing questions focus on writing strategy, organization, and style.

Topic development questions focus on the choices made and strategies used by a writer in the act of composing or revising an essay. These questions may ask you to make decisions concerning the appropriateness of a sentence or essay in relation to purpose, audience, unity, or focus, or the effect of adding, revising, or deleting supporting material.

The following question (from Sample Passage I on pages 221–223) is a fairly typical example of the kinds of writing decisions that strategy questions ask you to make.

In the early 1900s the O'odham became acquainted with marching bands and woodwind instruments (which explains the presence of saxophones in waila). [13]	13. Given that all of the choices are true, which one is most relevant to the focus of this paragraph? A. NO CHANGE B. (although fiddles were once widely used in waila bands). C. (even though they're now often constructed of metal). D. (which are frequently found in jazz bands also).

It's important to read these questions carefully and, sometimes, to reread the essay or parts of the essay. This question is fairly clear-cut, but it does suggest that you need a pretty good sense of what paragraph 3 is about. A quick review of the paragraph indicates that it is focused on how the O'odham and their music were influenced by the musical styles and instrumentation of the European immigrants they encountered.

Which of these parenthetical statements is most relevant to that focus? Choice **D**, which states that woodwind instruments are frequently found in jazz bands, is not. Likewise, choice **C**, which indicates that woodwind instruments are now often constructed of metal, strays from the paragraph's topic. Choice **B**, which points out that fiddles were once widely used in waila bands, is getting closer, but this too seems a diversion, unconnected to the other information in this paragraph. Guitars, woodwinds, and button accordions are mentioned but not fiddles or violins.

Choice **A**, however, provides an appropriate and relevant elaboration. It draws the connection between the O'odhams' introduction to marching bands and woodwinds in the early 1900s and the eventual inclusion of saxophones in a typical waila band.

Organization questions deal with the order and coherence of ideas in an essay and the effective choice of opening, transitional, and closing statements. For example, you may be asked about the organization of ideas (the most logical order for sentences within a paragraph or paragraphs within an essay) or about the most logical transitional phrase or statement.

The following question (from Sample Passage II on pages 223–225) is a good example of the kind of organization question you might encounter.

Today, after many birthdays and New Year's Days, I now find meaningful the difference I once found confusing. <u>Otherwise,</u> (21) this difference points <u>to</u> (22) significant underlying cultural values.

21. **A.** NO CHANGE
B. Though,
C. In fact,
D. Then,

The choices in this question are sometimes referred to as conjunctive adverbs or transitional words or phrases because their main job is to connect or link the statement in one sentence with the statement in a preceding sentence. These are often little words—*so, thus, soon, yet, also*—that do a lot of work to make an essay logical.

In order to answer such questions correctly, it helps to think about the logical relationship between the sentences, as well as the logical relationships expressed by the choices. The main statement of the opening sentence of this paragraph is "I now find meaningful the difference [in computing one's age] I once found confusing." The second sentence states, "This difference points to significant underlying cultural values." The writer then goes on to explain those cultural values.

Which of these four choices enables readers to move most easily from the opening sentence into the rest of this paragraph? Choice **A** suggests that the second statement contrasts with the first statement. A typical dictionary definition for *Otherwise* is "in different circumstances." Similarly, choice **B**, *Though,* suggests that the statement to follow is contrary to or in opposition to the preceding statement. Neither of those adverbs works well here. Nor does *Then* (choice **D**), which usually expresses a time relationship—meaning "next" or "soon after in time."

The best choice here is **C**. The phrase "In fact" is often used to introduce a statement that builds on the preceding statement. We can pare down these opening sentences to their bare essentials to show that the phrase works well here: "I now find the difference in computing one's age meaningful. In fact, the difference points to important cultural values about life experience and longevity."

Knowledge of Language

These questions involve effective word choices in terms of writing style, tone, clarity, and economy. Sometimes, a phrase or sentence that isn't technically ungrammatical is nevertheless confusing because it's poorly written. Sometimes, a word or phrase clashes with the tone of the essay. Good writing also involves eliminating ambiguous pronoun references, excessively wordy or redundant material, and vague or awkward expressions.

Similar to most writing strategy and organization questions, style questions require a general understanding of the essay as a whole. The following style question (from Sample Passage III on pages 225–227) focuses on the issues of economy and consistency of tone.

The school board members believed that wearing "play clothes" to school made the students inefficient toward [32] their school work, while more formal attire established a positive educational climate.	**32. F.** NO CHANGE **G.** lazy and bored to tears with **H.** blow off **J.** lax and indifferent toward

You will be better able to recognize the appropriateness of choice **J** if you know that *lax* means "lacking necessary strictness, severity, or precision" and *indifferent* means "lacking interest, enthusiasm, or concern." These terms touch on two related but distinct concerns—academic laziness and apathy. One could imagine school board members using these very words in their meetings. And the words are consistent with the overall style and tone of this straightforward, informative essay about a legal case.

Choices **G** and **H** are fairly easy to rule out if you think about the generally formal tone of the essay. It's not that one should never use slang phrases such as "bored to tears" or "blow off" in one's writing; it's just that this particular essay is not the place to use them. When we consider that this statement is describing the school board members' belief, these phrases are even more inappropriate.

It seems more in character for school board members to be concerned about student inefficiency, but **F** is a weak choice because the phrase "inefficient toward their school work" sounds odd or awkward. Perhaps it's the preposition that trips us up. The word *toward* works fine in **J** when describing attitudes ("lax," "indifferent") toward school work, but the word *inefficient* is describing an ability or skill.

* * *

The questions provided here are a small sample of the kinds of questions that might be on the test. The previous question, for example, is only one kind of style question; it doesn't cover all the territory of style that might be addressed on the test. The sample passages and questions at the end of this section have all the examples referred to in this chapter as they would appear in a test. These sample passages and questions and the later practice tests will provide you with a thorough understanding of the ACT English test.

Strategies for Taking the ACT English Test

Pace Yourself

The ACT English test contains 75 questions to be completed in 45 minutes, which works out to exactly 36 seconds per question. Spending 1½ minutes skimming through each essay leaves you about 30 seconds to respond to each question. If you spend less time than that on each question, you can use the remaining time allowed for this test to review your work and to return to the questions that were most difficult for you. Another way to think of it is that you have 45 minutes to read and answer the questions for five essays, giving you a maximum of 9 minutes for each essay and its questions.

Be Aware of the Writing Style Used in the Essay

The five essays cover a variety of topics and are written in a variety of styles. It's important that you take into account the writing style used in each essay as you respond to the questions.

Some of the essays will be anecdotes or narratives written from an informal, first-person point of view. Others will be more formal essays, scholarly or informative in nature, often written in the third person. Some questions will ask you to choose the best answer based not on its grammatical correctness but on its consistency with the style and tone of the essay as a whole. For example, an expression that's too breezy for an essay on the life of President Herbert Hoover might be just right for a personal narrative about a writer's attempt at learning to skateboard.

Consider a Question's Context before Choosing an Answer

Some people find it helpful to skim an essay and its questions before trying to answer those questions. Having a general sense of the essay in mind before you begin to answer questions involving writing strategy or style can help. If you encounter questions about the order of sentences within a paragraph, or the order of paragraphs within an essay, or where to add a sentence in an essay, you may want to answer those questions first to make sure that the major elements of the essay are arranged logically. Understanding the order of the passage may make it easier for you to answer some of the other questions.

As you're answering each question, be sure to read at least a sentence or two beyond the sentence containing the portion being questioned. You may need to read even more than that to understand what the writer is trying to say.

Be Aware of the Connotations of Words

Vocabulary isn't tested in an isolated way on the ACT English test. Nevertheless, a good vocabulary and an awareness of not only the dictionary definitions of words but also the connotations (feelings and associations) suggested by those words will help you do well on the test.

The following question (from Sample Passage II on pages 223–225) asks you to think about how certain words and their connotations can function in terms of the rest of the essay.

Many people might be surprised to learn that the American way of computing a person's age differs from the traditional Korean way. In Korean tradition, a person is considered to be already one year old at the time of his or her birth.

As a child growing up in two cultures, I found this contest a bit confusing.
16

16. **F.** NO CHANGE
G. change
H. dispute
J. difference

Which word best captures or summarizes what has been described in the preceding paragraph? The word *contest* (**F**) doesn't seem right because it suggests a competition between opposing sides or teams. In a similar vein, the word *dispute* (**H**) doesn't fit here because it generally refers to a verbal debate or argument. The word *change* (**G**) is a little off because it expresses the idea of transformation, making something or someone different, which doesn't accurately summarize that opening paragraph. The word *difference* (**J**), however, seems just right. It echoes the verb in the first sentence of the preceding paragraph, but more important, it accurately reflects the writer's perspective up to this point in the essay that the American way and the Korean way of computing a person's age are not competing or arguing with each other. They are simply unlike each other (and because of that mismatch, a bit confusing).

In questions such as this one, you have to focus on what the words mean and what associations the words have for the typical reader.

Look for a Stated Question

Before responding to a question identified by an underlined portion, check for a stated question preceding the options. If there is one, it will provide you with some guidelines for deciding on the best choice. Some questions will ask you to choose the alternative to the underlined portion that is NOT or LEAST acceptable. Here's an example from Sample Passage I on pages 221–223.

The music is mainly instrumental—the bands generally consist of guitar, bass guitar, saxophones, accordion, and drums. [3]

3. Which of the following alternatives to the underlined portion would NOT be acceptable?
   A. instrumental; in general, the bands
   B. instrumental, the bands generally
   C. instrumental. The bands generally
   D. instrumental; the bands generally

For these types of questions, look closely at the underlined portion, because the question has told you that it *is* acceptable. Likewise, three of the alternative choices are acceptable. The best answer, in this case, is the one that is *not* acceptable. In the underlined portion, a dash is used between two independent clauses: "The music is mainly instrumental" and "the bands generally consist of guitar, bass guitar, saxophones, accordion, and drums." The dash is sometimes thought of as a less formal type of punctuation, but it can work quite well to provide emphasis or to signal that an explanation will follow.

Placing a period (**C**) or a semicolon (**D**) between these two independent clauses would also be acceptable. Likewise, choice **A** is acceptable because it too places a semicolon between the two clauses, using the phrase "in general" rather than the adverb "generally." Choice **B** is not acceptable and is, therefore, the best answer. A comma is not usually a strong enough punctuation mark between two independent clauses not joined by a conjunction. Notice that this sentence has other commas, used to distinguish nouns in a series. How would a reader know that the comma between the clauses is a much stronger break than those other commas?

Whether a stated question is presented or not, you should carefully examine what is underlined in the essay. Consider the features of writing that are included in the underlined portion. The options for each question will contain changes in one or more aspects of writing.

Note the Differences in the Answer Choices

Many of the questions that refer to underlined portions will involve more than one aspect of writing. Examine each choice and note how it differs from the others. Consider all the features of writing that are included in each option.

Avoid Making New Mistakes

Beware of correcting mistakes in the essay and, in your haste, picking a response that creates a new mistake. Be observant, especially in questions where the responses have similar wording. One comma or apostrophe can make all the difference, as the following question (from Sample Passage III on pages 225–227) illustrates.

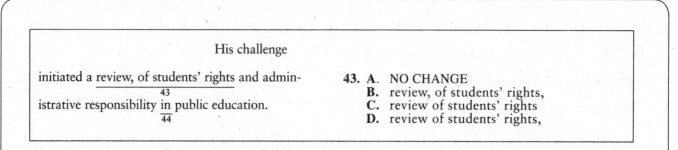

His challenge initiated a review, of students' rights and administrative responsibility in public education.
43 44

43. A. NO CHANGE
B. review, of students' rights,
C. review of students' rights
D. review of students' rights,

Perhaps you took only a moment to reject choice **A** because of the unnecessary comma between the noun *review* and the prepositional phrase "of students' rights." And if you were able to make that call, you may have ruled out choice **B** for the same reason. It is probably more difficult to recognize that the comma between the noun *rights* and the conjunction *and* (**D**) is unnecessary and misleading. Because you were thinking about how the underlined portion should be punctuated, you may also have wondered about the plural apostrophe in the word *students'* but then realize that the apostrophe is in the same place in all four choices. (The best answer is **C**.)

Determine the Best Answer

There are at least two approaches you can take to determine the best answer to a question about an underlined portion. One approach is to reread the sentence or sentences containing the underlined portion, substitute each of the answer choices in turn, and decide which is best. Another approach is to decide how the underlined portion might best be phrased and then look for your phrasing among the choices offered. If the underlined portion is correct as it is, select the NO CHANGE option.

If you can't decide which option is best, you may want to mark the question in your test booklet so you can return to it later. Remember: You're not penalized for guessing, so after you've eliminated as many options as you can, take your best guess.

Reread the Sentence Using Your Selected Answer

After you have selected the answer you feel is best, reread the corresponding sentence or sentences in the essay, substituting the answer you've selected for the underlined portion or for the boxed numeral. Sometimes an answer that sounds fine out of context doesn't fit within the sentence or essay. Be sure to keep in mind both the punctuation marks and words in each possible response; sometimes just the omission of a comma can make an important difference.

Watch for Questions about the Entire Essay or a Section of the Essay

Some questions ask about a section of the essay. They are identified by a question number in a box at the appropriate point in the essay, rather than by an underlined portion. Here's an example from Sample Passage II on pages 223–225.

Perhaps the celebration of New Year's Day in Korean culture is heightened (19) because it is thought of as everyone's birthday party. [20]

20. Upon reviewing this paragraph, the writer considers deleting the preceding sentence. If the writer were to delete the sentence, the paragraph would primarily lose:
    - **F.** a comment on the added significance of the Korean New Year celebration.
    - **G.** a repetitive reminder of what happens every birthday.
    - **H.** a defense of the case for celebrating every birthday.
    - **J.** an illustration of the Korean counting system.

This question asks you to think about the role this sentence plays in terms of the paragraph as a whole. If the sentence were deleted, the paragraph would lose the elaboration on the point that Korean tradition indicates that everyone becomes a year older on New Year's Day, regardless of when they were actually born. Without the sentence, the point about the "added significance of the Korean New Year celebration" (**F**) would have been unstated.

Some other questions ask about an aspect of the essay as a whole. These are placed at the end of the essay, following boxed instructions like these:

> Question 15 asks about the preceding passage as a whole.

You may want to read any questions that ask about the essay as a whole first so you can keep them in mind while you're reading through the essay. For questions about a section of the essay or the essay as a whole, you must decide the best answer on the basis of the particular writing or revision problem presented in the question.

Be Careful with Two-Part Questions

Some questions require extra thought because you must decide not only which option is best but also which supporting reason for an option is most appropriate or convincing. The following question occurs at the end of Sample Passage III on pages 225–227. Each option begins with either a yes or no response, followed by a supporting reason for that response.

Question 45 asks about the preceding passage as a whole.

45. Suppose the writer's goal had been to write a brief persuasive essay urging students to exercise their constitutional rights. Would this essay fulfill that goal?

A. Yes, because the essay focuses on how Kevin encouraged other students to exercise their constitutional rights.
B. Yes, because the essay focuses on various types of clothing historically worn by students as a freedom of expression.
C. No, because the essay suggests that the right to wear blue jeans was not a substantial constitutional right in the 1970s.
D. No, because the essay objectively reports on one case of a student exercising a particular constitutional right.

Once you decide whether the essay would or would not fulfill the writer's goal, as described in the question, you need to decide which reason or explanation provides the most appropriate support for the answer and is most accurate in terms of the essay. Sometimes, the supporting reason does not accurately reflect the essay (the explanations in **B** and **C**, for example). Sometimes, the reason accurately reflects the essay but doesn't logically support the answer to the question. And sometimes, the reason might logically support the question (that is, the writer's goal) but that reason overstates the focus of the essay. It may be fair to say that Kevin Bannister's case led to a review of student rights, but this essay does not at any point describe Kevin encouraging other students to exercise their rights, as **A** states. The best answer is **D;** this essay is more an objective reporting on a legal case about student rights (and that case's historical significance) than it is a persuasive argument or call to students to exercise those rights.

Watch for Interrelated Questions

As pointed out previously, you'll sometimes find that the best way to answer questions about a passage is not necessarily in their numbered order. Occasionally, answering a question after you've answered the one that follows it is easier. Or you might find two questions about different elements of the same sentence, in which case considering them both together may be helpful.

In the following example (from Sample Passage III on pages 225–227), considering questions 40 and 41 together may be helpful, because they're contained in the same sentence. First, answer the question that seems easier to you. Once you've solved that problem in the sentence, turn to the other question.

The court remained unconvinced, therefore, that [40]	**40. F.** NO CHANGE **G.** thus, **H.** moreover, **J.** however,
when wearing jeans [41] would actually impair the learning process of Kevin or of his fellow classmates.	**41. A.** NO CHANGE **B.** by wearing **C.** wearing **D.** having worn

Questions 40 and 41 deal with different kinds of writing problems. Question 40 is about choosing the most logical transitional word, and question 41 is about the correct use in this sentence of the gerund (a verb form with an *-ing* ending that's used as a noun). You might find that answering question 41 helps you to figure out the answer to question 40. The best answer to question 41 is **C**—the noun phrase "wearing jeans" works as the subject of the dependent clause "wearing jeans would actually impair the learning process of Kevin or of his fellow classmates." Try penciling in your answer choice for 41 (that is, edit the essay) so that you can more easily read the sentence while responding to question 40. Does this approach make it easier for you to decide that the most logical answer to question 40 is **J** ("however")?

* * *

Remember that this section is only an overview of the English test. Directly or indirectly, a question may test you in more than one of the areas mentioned, so do not become overly concerned with categorizing a question before you answer it. And, although awareness of the types of questions can help you be a more critical and strategic test-taker, just remember: the type of question you're answering isn't important. Most important, focus on what the question asks and do your best to pick the best answer based on evidence provided in the passage.

SAMPLE PASSAGE I

The Music of the O'odham

[1]

For some people, traditional American Indian music is associated and connected [1] with high penetrating vocals accompanied by a steady drumbeat. In tribal communities in the southwestern United States, however, one is likely to hear something similar to the polka-influenced dance music of northern Mexico. The music is called "waila." Among the O'odham tribes of Arizona, waila has been popular for [2] more than a century. The music is mainly instrumental—the bands generally [3] consist of guitar, bass guitar, saxophones, accordion, and drums.

[2]

Unlike some traditional tribal music, waila does not serve a religious or spiritual purpose. It is a social music that performed [4] at weddings, birthday parties, and feasts. The word itself [5] comes from the Spanish word for dance, *baile.* Cheek to cheek, the dance is performed to the relaxed two-step tempo, [6] and the bands often play long past [7] midnight. As the dancers step to the music, they were also stepping [8] in time to a sound that

1. A. NO CHANGE
   B. connected by some of them
   C. linked by association
   D. associated

2. F. NO CHANGE
   G. popular, one might say, for
   H. really quite popular for
   J. popular for the duration of

3. Which of the following alternatives to the underlined portion would NOT be acceptable?
   A. instrumental; in general, the bands
   B. instrumental, the bands generally
   C. instrumental. The bands generally
   D. instrumental; the bands generally

4. F. NO CHANGE
   G. music in which it is performed
   H. music, performing
   J. music, performed

5. A. NO CHANGE
   B. word, itself,
   C. word, itself
   D. word itself,

6. F. NO CHANGE
   G. Couples dance cheek to cheek to the relaxed two-step tempo,
   H. A relaxed two-step tempo, the couples dance cheek to cheek,
   J. Cheek to cheek, the two-step tempo relaxes dancing couples,

7. A. NO CHANGE
   B. play long, past,
   C. play, long past,
   D. play, long past

8. F. NO CHANGE
   G. are also stepping
   H. have also stepped
   J. will also step

embodies their unique history and suggests the influence
9

of outside cultures on their music. [10]

[3]

The O'odham in the 1700s first encountered the
11
guitars of Spanish missionaries. In the 1850s the O'odham have borrowed from the waltzes and mazurkas of
12
people of European descent on their way to California.

In the early 1900s the O'odham became acquainted with marching bands and woodwind instruments (which explains the presence of saxophones in waila).
13
Around this time the polka music and button accordion played by German immigrant railroad workers; left their
14
mark on waila.

9. A. NO CHANGE
   B. they're
   C. it's
   D. its'

10. At this point, the writer is considering adding the following true statement:

    The agricultural practices of the O'odham are similar to those of the Maya.

    Should the writer make this addition here?

    F. Yes, because the sentence establishes that the O'odham often borrowed ideas from other groups.
    G. Yes, because the sentence provides important information about the O'odham people.
    H. No, because the sentence is not supported by evidence of a connection between the O'odham and the Maya.
    J. No, because the sentence distracts from the paragraph's focus on waila's uses and influences.

11. All of the following would be acceptable placements for the underlined portion EXCEPT:
    A. where it is now.
    B. at the beginning of the sentence (revising the capitalization accordingly).
    C. after the word *guitars.*
    D. after the word *missionaries* (ending the sentence with a period).

12. F. NO CHANGE
    G. have been borrowing
    H. were borrowed
    J. borrowed

13. Given that all of the choices are true, which one is most relevant to the focus of this paragraph?
    A. NO CHANGE
    B. (although fiddles were once widely used in waila bands).
    C. (even though they're now often constructed of metal).
    D. (which are frequently found in jazz bands also).

14. F. NO CHANGE
    G. workers
    H. workers:
    J. workers,

[4]

It should be no surprise that musicians these days are adding touches of rock, country, and reggae to waila. Some listeners fear that an American musical form may soon be lost. But the O'odham are playing waila with as much energy and devotion as ever. A unique blend of traditions, waila will probably continue changing for as long as the O'odham use it to express their own sense of harmony and tempo.

Question 15 asks about the preceding passage as a whole.

15. Upon reviewing this essay and finding that some information has been left out, the writer composes the following sentence incorporating that information:

> Those same German influences helped spawn a similar musical form in northern Mexico known as *norteño.*

This sentence would most logically be placed after the last sentence in Paragraph:

A. 1.
B. 2.
C. 3.
D. 4.

SAMPLE PASSAGE II

How Old Am I?

Many people might be surprised to learn that the American way of computing a person's age differs from the traditional Korean way. In Korean tradition, a person is considered to be already one year old at the time of his or her birth.

As a child growing up in two cultures, I found this contest [16] a bit confusing. When I was in the fifth grade, was I ten or eleven years old? To add to the confusion, every New Year's Day a person [17] according to this Korean counting system, becomes a year older, regardless of his or her actual birthday. Birthdays are important throughout the world. [18] A person who is sixteen years old on his or her birthday in March would become seventeen years old on the following New Year's Day, even though he or she isn't expected to turn seventeen (in "American" years) until that next birthday in March. Perhaps the celebration of New Year's Day in Korean culture is heightened [19] because it is thought of as

16. F. NO CHANGE
G. change
H. dispute
J. difference

17. A. NO CHANGE
B. person,
C. person;
D. person who,

18. F. NO CHANGE
G. Most cultures celebrate birthdays.
H. Birthdays focus attention on a culture's youth.
J. OMIT the underlined portion.

19. A. NO CHANGE
B. raised
C. lifted
D. lighted

everyone's birthday party. [20]

Today, after many birthdays and New Year's Days, I now find meaningful the difference I once found confusing. Otherwise, [21] this difference points to [22] significant underlying cultural values. The practice of advancing a person's age [23] seems to me to reflect the value a society places on life experience and longevity. Their [24] idea was demonstrated often when [25] my elderly relatives, who took pride in reminding younger folk of their "Korean age." With great enthusiasm, [26] they added on a year every New Year's Day. By contrast American society has often been described as one that [27] values the vibrant energy of youth over the wisdom and experience gained with age. [28] After a certain age, many Americans I know would balk, refuse, and hesitate [29] at the idea of adding a year or two to what they regard as their actual age.

20. Upon reviewing this paragraph, the writer considers deleting the preceding sentence. If the writer were to delete the sentence, the paragraph would primarily lose:

F. a comment on the added significance of the Korean New Year celebration.
G. a repetitive reminder of what happens every birthday.
H. a defense of the case for celebrating every birthday.
J. an illustration of the Korean counting system.

21. A. NO CHANGE
B. Though,
C. In fact,
D. Then,

22. F. NO CHANGE
G. on
H. at
J. OMIT the underlined portion.

23. A. NO CHANGE
B. persons' age
C. persons age
D. person's age,

24. F. NO CHANGE
G. One's
H. Its
J. This

25. A. NO CHANGE
B. by
C. while
D. as if

26. Which choice would most clearly communicate the elderly relatives' positive attitude toward this practice?

F. NO CHANGE
G. Duplicating an accepted practice,
H. Living with two birthdays themselves,
J. Obligingly,

27. A. NO CHANGE
B. whose
C. this
D. whom

28. If the writer were to delete the phrases "the vibrant energy of" and "the wisdom and experience gained with" from the preceding sentence, the sentence would primarily lose:

F. its personal and reflective tone.
G. an element of humor.
H. details that illustrate the contrast.
J. the preference expressed by the writer.

29. A. NO CHANGE
B. balk and hesitate
C. refuse and balk
D. balk

Even something as visibly simple or natural as computing a person's age can prove to be not so clear-cut. Traditions like celebrating birthdays reveal how deeply we are affected by the culture we live in.

30. F. NO CHANGE
G. apparently
H. entirely
J. fully

SAMPLE PASSAGE III

Wearing Jeans in School

In 1970, the school board in Pittsfield, New Hampshire, approved a dress code that prohibited students from wearing certain types of clothing. The school board members believed that wearing "play clothes" to school made the students inefficient toward their school work, while more formal attire established a positive educational climate. When twelve-year-old Kevin Bannister wore a pair of blue jeans to school, he was sent home for violating the dress code.

Kevin and his parents believed that his constitutional rights had been violated. The United States District Court of New Hampshire; agreed to hear Kevin's case. His claim was based on the notion of personal liberty—the right of every individual to the control of his or her own

31. Given that all of the choices are true, which one would best illustrate the term *dress code* as it is used in this sentence?
A. NO CHANGE
B. clothing that was inappropriate.
C. clothing, including sandals, bell-bottom pants, and "dungarees" (blue jeans).
D. clothing that is permitted in some schools today.

32. F. NO CHANGE
G. lazy and bored to tears with
H. blow off
J. lax and indifferent toward

33. Given that all of the choices are true, which one would most effectively introduce the main idea of this paragraph?
A. NO CHANGE
B. The principal said dungarees and blue jeans were the same thing, so Kevin should have known better.
C. If Kevin's jeans had been dirty and torn, the principal might have been justified in expelling him.
D. These events occurred in a time of social unrest, and emotions were running high.

34. F. NO CHANGE
G. Court, of New Hampshire
H. Court of New Hampshire
J. Court of New Hampshire,

Improving Your Score

person—protected by the Constitution's Fourteenth Amendment. The court agreed with Kevin that a person's right <u>for wearing</u>[35] clothing of his or her own choosing is, in fact, protected by the Fourteenth Amendment.

35. A. NO CHANGE
B. of wearing
C. to wear
D. wearing

The <u>court noted, however</u>[36] that restrictions may be justified in some circumstances, such as in the school setting.

36. F. NO CHANGE
G. court noted, however,
H. court, noted however,
J. court noted however,

So did Kevin have a right to wear blue jeans to school? The court determined that the school board had failed to show that wearing jeans actually inhibited the educational <u>process, which is guided by authority figures.</u>[37]

37. A. NO CHANGE
B. process, which has undergone changes since the 1970s.
C. process, a process we all know well.
D. process.

Furthermore, the board offered no evidence to back up <u>it's</u>[38] claim <u>that</u>[39] such clothing created a negative educational environment.

38. F. NO CHANGE
G. they're
H. its
J. ones

39. A. NO CHANGE
B. where
C. which
D. in which

Certainly the school board would be justified in prohibiting students from wearing clothing that was unsanitary, revealing, or obscene. The court remained unconvinced, <u>therefore,</u>[40] that <u>when wearing</u>[41] jeans would actually impair the learning process of Kevin or of his fellow classmates.

40. F. NO CHANGE
G. thus,
H. moreover,
J. however,

41. A. NO CHANGE
B. by wearing
C. wearing
D. having worn

<u>Kevin Bannister's case was significant in that it was the first in the United States to address clothing prohibitions of a school dress code.</u>[42] His challenge

42. Which choice would most effectively open this paragraph and convey the importance of this case?
F. NO CHANGE
G. Therefore, Kevin's case reminds us that you should stand up for your rights, no matter how old you are.
H. The case for personal liberty means the right to speak up must be taken seriously by the courts.
J. All in all, clothing is an important part of our identity.

initiated a review, of students' rights and administrative [43]

43. A. NO CHANGE
B. review, of students' rights,
C. review of students' rights
D. review of students' rights,

responsibility in public education. [44]

44. F. NO CHANGE
G. on
H. with
J. about

Question 45 asks about the preceding passage as a whole.

45. Suppose the writer's goal had been to write a brief persuasive essay urging students to exercise their constitutional rights. Would this essay fulfill that goal?
A. Yes, because the essay focuses on how Kevin encouraged other students to exercise their constitutional rights.
B. Yes, because the essay focuses on various types of clothing historically worn by students as a freedom of expression.
C. No, because the essay suggests that the right to wear blue jeans was not a substantial constitutional right in the 1970s.
D. No, because the essay objectively reports on one case of a student exercising a particular constitutional right.

Answer Key for English Test Sample Questions

1.	D	16.	J	31.	C
2.	F	17.	B	32.	J
3.	B	18.	J	33.	A
4.	J	19.	A	34.	H
5.	A	20.	F	35.	C
6.	G	21.	C	36.	G
7.	A	22.	F	37.	D
8.	G	23.	A	38.	H
9.	A	24.	J	39.	A
10.	J	25.	B	40.	J
11.	C	26.	F	41.	C
12.	J	27.	A	42.	F
13.	A	28.	H	43.	C
14.	G	29.	D	44.	F
15.	C	30.	G	45.	D

Chapter 6: Improving Your Math Score

The ACT mathematics test asks you to answer 60 multiple-choice questions in 60 minutes. The questions are designed to measure your mathematical achievement—the knowledge, skills, and reasoning techniques that are taught in mathematics courses through the beginning of grade 12 and that are prerequisites for college mathematics courses. Therefore, the questions cover a wide variety of concepts, techniques, and procedures. Naturally, some questions will require computation, but you are allowed to use a calculator on the mathematics test. You'll need to understand basic mathematical terminology and to recall some basic mathematical principles and formulas. However, the questions on the test are designed to emphasize your ability to reason mathematically, not to focus on your computation ability or your ability to recall definitions, theorems, or formulas.

Content of the ACT Mathematics Test

The ACT mathematics test emphasizes the major content areas that are prerequisites to successful performance in entry-level courses in college mathematics.

Nine scores are reported for the ACT mathematics test: a total test score based on all 60 questions and eight reporting category scores based on specific mathematical knowledge and skills. The reporting categories are: Preparing for Higher Mathematics (which includes separate scores for Number and Quantity, Algebra, Functions, Geometry, and Statistics and Probability); Integrating Essential Skills; and Modeling. Descriptions follow.

Preparing for Higher Math

This category captures the more recent mathematics that students are learning, starting when they begin using algebra as a general way of expressing and solving equations. This category is divided into the following five subcategories:

- **Number and Quantity:** Demonstrate knowledge of real and complex number systems. You will understand and reason with numerical quantities in many forms, including integer and rational exponents, and vectors and matrices.
- **Algebra:** Solve, graph, and model multiple types of expressions. You will employ many different kinds of equations, including but not limited to linear, polynomial, radical, and exponential relationships. You will find solutions to systems of equations, even when represented by simple matrices, and apply your knowledge to applications.
- **Functions:** The questions in this category test knowledge of function definition, notation, representation, and application. Questions may include, but are not limited to, linear, radical, piecewise, polynomial, and logarithmic functions. You will manipulate and translate functions, as well as find and apply important features of graphs.
- **Geometry:** Define and apply knowledge of shapes and solids, such as congruence and similarity relationships or surface area and volume measurements. Understand composition of objects and solve for missing values in triangles, circles, and other figures, including using trigonometric ratios and equations of conic sections.
- **Statistics and Probability:** Describe center and spread of distributions, apply and analyze data collection methods, understand and model relationships in bivariate data, and calculate probabilities, including the related sample spaces.

Integrating Essential Skills

These questions address concepts typically learned before grade 8, such as rates and percentages; proportional relationships; area, surface area, and volume; average and median; and expressing numbers in different ways. You will solve problems of increasing complexity, combine skills in longer chains of steps, apply skills in more varied contexts, understand more connections, and become more fluent.

Modeling

This category represents all questions that involve producing, interpreting, understanding, evaluating, and improving models. Each question is also counted in the other previously identified appropriate reporting categories. This category is an overall measure of how well you use modeling skills across mathematical topics.

Types of Questions on the ACT Mathematics Test

The questions on the ACT mathematics test differ in terms of content and complexity. The rest of this section gives you examples of questions—of various types and complexities from all content areas. All of the questions used in the examples are from actual ACT mathematics tests that have been taken by students from across the country. A solution strategy is given for each question. As you read and work through each example, please keep in mind that the strategy given is just one way to solve the problem. Other strategies may work even better for you.

Basic Math Problems

The type of question you're probably the most familiar with (and probably find the easiest) is the stripped-down, bare-bones, basic math problem. Problems of this type are simple and straightforward. They test readily identifiable skills in the content areas, usually have very few words and no extra information, ask the very question you'd expect them to ask, and usually have a numeric answer.

Question 1 is a good example of a basic math problem.

1. What is 4% of 1,100 ?

A. 4
B. 4.4
C. 40
D. 44
E. 440

This problem has very few words, asks a direct question, and has a numeric answer. The solution is simple: Convert 4% to a decimal and multiply by 1,100 to get (0.04)(1,100) = 44, choice **D**. You probably wouldn't need your calculator on this problem, but remember that you may use it if you wish. If you chose answer **B** or **E**, you may have used rules about moving decimal points and moved the wrong number of places.

Question 2 is a basic algebra problem.

2. For all x, $(x + 4)(x - 5) = ?$

F. $x^2 - 20$
G. $x^2 - x - 20$
H. $2x - 1$
J. $2x^2 - 1$
K. $2x^2 - x + 20$

You should know what to do to answer the question the instant you read the problem—use the distributive property (FOIL—first, outside, inside, last) and get $x(x - 5) + 4(x - 5) = x^2 - 5x + 4x + 4(-5) = x^2 - x - 20$, choice **G**. On this problem, you probably wouldn't use your calculator. If you chose **F**, you probably just multiplied the first terms and the last terms. Check your answer by substituting a number (try 6) into the original expression and into your answer. If the results are not equal, then the expressions cannot be equivalent.

Question 3 is an example of a basic problem from algebra.

3. If $x + y = 1$, and $x - y = 1$, then $y = ?$

A. -1
B. 0
C. $\frac{1}{2}$
D. 1
E. 2

This problem gives you a system of linear equations with unknowns x and y and asks for the value of y. You might be able to solve this problem intuitively—the only number that can be added to and subtracted from another number and give the same result for the problem ($x + y$ and $x - y$ both give 1) is 0, so y must be 0, choice **B**. Or, you could use algebra and reason that, because $x + y$ and $x - y$ both equal 1, they equal each other, and $x + y = x - y$ gives $2y = 0$, so $y = 0$. Although some calculators have graphing or matrix functions for solving problems of this type, using a calculator on this problem would probably take most students longer than solving it with one of the strategies given here. If you chose answer **D**, you probably found the value of x rather than the value of y.

Question 4 is an example of a basic problem in geometry.

4. What is the slope of the line containing the points (–2,7) and (3,–3) ?

F. 4

G. $\frac{1}{4}$

H. 0

J. $-\frac{1}{2}$

K. –2

This problem has a few more words than some of the other examples of basic problems you've seen so far, but the most important word is *slope.* Seeing that you are given two points, you would probably think of the formula that defines the slope of a line through two points:

$$\frac{y_1 - y_2}{x_1 - x_2}.$$

Applying the formula gives 7 – (–3)/–2 –3 = 10/–5 = –2, choice **K**. If you chose answer **J,** you probably got the expression for slope upside down. The change in *y* goes on top.

Here is another basic geometry problem from the ACT mathematics test.

5. If the measure of an angle is $37\frac{1}{2}°$, what is the measure of its supplement, shown in the figure below?

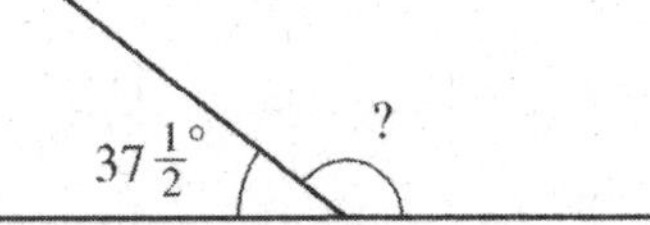

A. $52\frac{1}{2}°$

B. $62\frac{1}{2}°$

C. $127\frac{1}{2}°$

D. $142\frac{1}{2}°$

E. Cannot be determined from the given information

Similar to many geometry problems, this problem has a figure. The figure tells you what you are given (an angle of 37½°) and what you're asked to find (its supplement, marked by "?"). You need not mark anything on the figure, because all the important information is already there. If you know that the sum of the measure of an angle and the measure of its supplement equals 180°, a simple subtraction gives the correct answer (180° – 37½° = 142½°), choice **D**. If you chose **A,** you found the complement, not the supplement.

A word of caution is in order here. You probably noticed that "Cannot be determined from the given information" is one of the options for question 5. Statistics gathered over the years for the ACT mathematics test show that many students choose "Cannot be determined from the given information" even when the answer can be determined. You should not think that whenever "Cannot be determined from the given information" is an option, it is automatically the correct answer. It isn't, as question 5 demonstrates. Later in this section is a question for which the correct answer is "Cannot be determined from the given information." Be sure to think carefully about problems with this answer choice.

You'll also find basic problems, such as question 6, on the ACT mathematics test.

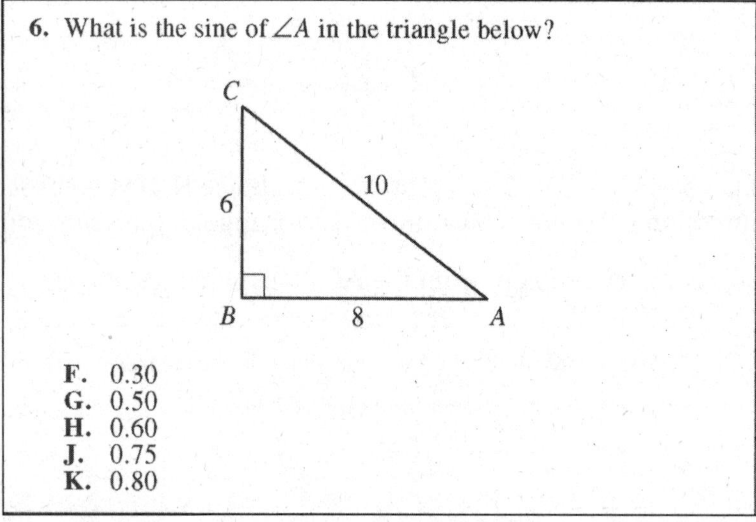

6. What is the sine of $\angle A$ in the triangle below?

F. 0.30
G. 0.50
H. 0.60
J. 0.75
K. 0.80

This question asks you to find the sine of ∠A in the triangle shown in the figure. If you have studied trigonometry, you've seen questions similar to this before. The lengths of all three sides of the triangle are given on the figure, even though only two are actually needed for finding sin ∠A. The extra information is there not to confuse you but rather to test your ability to sort out the information you need from the information you are given. Picking 6 (the length of the side opposite ∠A) and 10 (the length of the hypotenuse) and forming the ratio gives the correct answer, 0.60, choice **H**. The cosine and the tangent of ∠A are also present in the answer choices. In order to do well on problems such as this one, you need to be able to tell which trigonometric function is which.

Basic Math Problems in Settings

Basic math problems in settings are what people often call *word problems* or *story problems.* They typically describe situations from everyday life in which you need to apply mathematics in order to answer a real-life question. The major difference between this type of problem and the basic math problems that you've seen in the examples so far is that the problem isn't set up for you—you have to set it up yourself. Most people find this to be the most difficult part of word problems. The key steps are reading the problem carefully, deciding what you're trying to find, sorting out what you really need from what's given, and then devising a strategy for finding the answer. Once the problem is set up, finding the answer is not much different from solving a basic math problem.

You can find basic math problems in settings in all of the content areas. Question 7 is an example.

7. What is the total cost of 2.5 pounds of bananas at \$0.34 per pound and 2.5 pounds of tomatoes at \$0.66 per pound?

A. \$1.00
B. \$2.40
C. \$2.50
D. \$3.50
E. \$5.00

Here, you're asked to find the total cost of some bananas and tomatoes. The important information is that the total cost includes 2.5 pounds of bananas at \$0.34 per pound and 2.5 pounds of tomatoes at \$0.66 per pound. A straightforward solution strategy would be to multiply to find the cost of the bananas and the cost of the tomatoes and then add to find the total cost. Now, the problem you're left with is very basic—calculating 2.5(0.34) + 2.5(0.66). Using your calculator might save time and avoid computation errors, but if you see that 2.5(0.34) + 2.5(0.66) = 2.5(0.34 + 0.66) = 2.5(1.00) = 2.50, answer **C**, you might be able to do the computation more quickly in your head.

Basic algebra problems also can be in settings. Question 8 is an example.

8. The relationship between temperature expressed in degrees Fahrenheit (F) and degrees Celsius (C) is given by the formula

$$F = \frac{9}{5}C + 32$$

If the temperature is 14 degrees Fahrenheit, what is it in degrees Celsius?

F. −10°
G. −12°
H. −14°
J. −16°
K. −18°

Improving Your Score

In this problem, you're given a relationship (in the form of an equation) between temperatures expressed in degrees Fahrenheit (F) and degrees Celsius (C). You're also given a temperature of 14 degrees Fahrenheit and asked what the corresponding temperature would be in degrees Celsius. Your strategy would probably be to substitute 14 into the equation in place of the variable F. This leaves you with a basic algebra problem—solving the equation $14 = 9/5\,C + 32$ for C. Before going on to the next problem, checking your answer would probably be a good idea. If you chose $-10°$ (answer choice **F**), substitute -10 for C, multiply by 9/5, and add 32 to see if the result is $14°F$ and confirm that your answer choice was indeed correct. Checking doesn't take long, and you might catch an error.

Question 9 is an example of an algebra problem in a setting.

9. Amy drove the 200 miles to New Orleans at an average speed 10 miles per hour faster than her usual average speed. If she completed the trip in 1 hour less than usual, what is her usual driving speed, in miles per hour?

A. 20
B. 30
C. 40
D. 50
E. 60

After reading the problem, you know that it is about travel and that the basic formula "distance equals the rate multiplied by the time" ($D = rt$) or one of its variations $\left(r = \frac{D}{t} \text{ or } t = \frac{D}{r}\right)$ will probably be useful. For travel problems, a table is often an efficient way to organize the information. Because the problem asks for Amy's usual speed (rate), it would probably be wise to let the variable r represent her usual speed in miles per hour (mph). You might organize your table like this:

	Distance (miles)	Rate (mph)	Time (hours)
Usual trip	200	r	$\frac{200}{r}$
This trip	200	$r + 10$	$\frac{200}{(r+10)}$

Then, because the time for this trip $\left(\frac{200}{(r+10)}\right)$ is 1 hour less than the time for the usual trip $\left(\frac{200}{r}\right)$, solving $\frac{200}{(r+10)} = \frac{200}{r} - 1$ will give the answer. Solving this equation is a matter of using routine algebra skills and procedures. The solution, $r = 40$, choice **C**, answers the question, "What is her usual driving speed?" A quick check shows that driving 200 miles at 40 mph takes 5 hours and that driving 200 miles at 50 mph (which is 10 mph faster) takes 4 hours (which is 1 hour less). This quick check should convince you that your answer is correct.

Geometry problems can be in settings, too. Question 10 is an example.

10. A map is laid out in the standard (x,y) coordinate plane. How long, in units, is an airplane's path on the map as the airplane flies along a straight line from City A located at (20,14) to City B located at (5,10) ?

F. $\sqrt{1{,}201}$
G. $\sqrt{241}$
H. $\sqrt{209}$
J. 7
K. $\sqrt{19}$

In this problem, you're told that you will be working with the standard (x,y) coordinate plane and that you will need to find a distance. The distance formula should immediately come to mind. All you need is two points, and those are given. The problem now becomes a basic math problem—applying the distance formula:

$$\sqrt{(x_1-x_2)^2+(y_1-y_2)^2}=\sqrt{(20-5)^2+(14-10)^2}=\sqrt{241}\,(\mathbf{G}).$$

Your calculator might be useful in finding $(20 - 5)^2 + (14 - 10)^2$, but you should not press the square root key because most of the answer choices are in radical form.

A geometry problem in a setting is illustrated by question 11.

11. A person 2 meters tall casts a shadow 3 meters long. At the same time, a telephone pole casts a shadow 12 meters long. How many meters tall is the pole?

A. 4
B. 6
C. 8
D. 11
E. 18

Question 11 has no figure, which is sometimes the case with geometry problems. It might be wise to draw your own figure and label it with the appropriate numbers from the problem. "A person 2 meters tall casts a shadow 3 meters long" is a pretty good clue that you should draw a right triangle with the vertical leg labeled 2 and the horizontal leg labeled 3. And, "a telephone pole casts a shadow 12 meters long" suggests that you should draw another right triangle with the horizontal leg labeled 12. Finding the height of the pole amounts to finding the length of the other leg of your second triangle, which you would label with a variable, say h. Your figure would be similar to this:

Improving Your Score

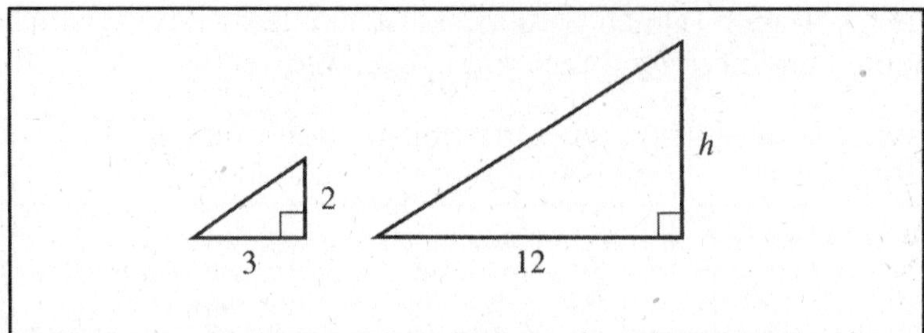

The triangles are similar (they're both right triangles and the angle that the sun's rays make with the ground is the same for both because the shadows were measured at the same time), so finding the height of the pole amounts to setting up and solving a proportion between corresponding sides of the triangles—a basic math problem. Your proportion might be $\frac{3}{12} = \frac{2}{h}$. Cross multiply—that is, multiply the numerator of each (or one) side by the denominator of the other side—to get $3(h) = 12(2)$, or $3h = 24$, and solve to get $h = 8$, choice **C.** Because the numbers are quite simple to work with, you probably wouldn't use your calculator on this problem.

Last (but not least) of the basic math questions, question 12 shows an example of a trigonometry problem in a setting.

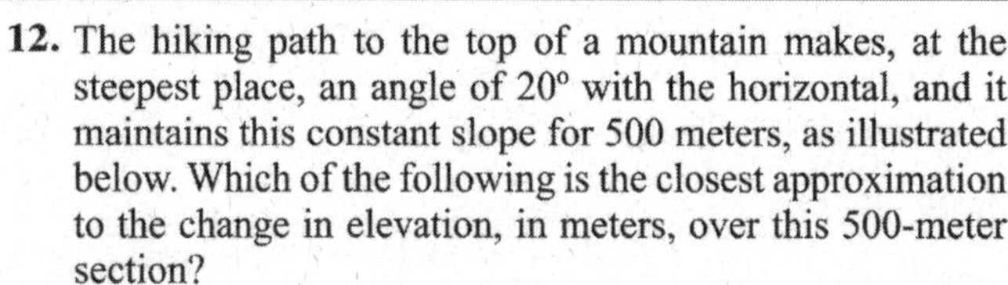

12. The hiking path to the top of a mountain makes, at the steepest place, an angle of 20° with the horizontal, and it maintains this constant slope for 500 meters, as illustrated below. Which of the following is the closest approximation to the change in elevation, in meters, over this 500-meter section?

(Note: You may use the following values, which are correct to 2 decimal places:
$\cos 20° \approx 0.94$; $\sin 20° \approx 0.34$; $\tan 20° \approx 0.36$)

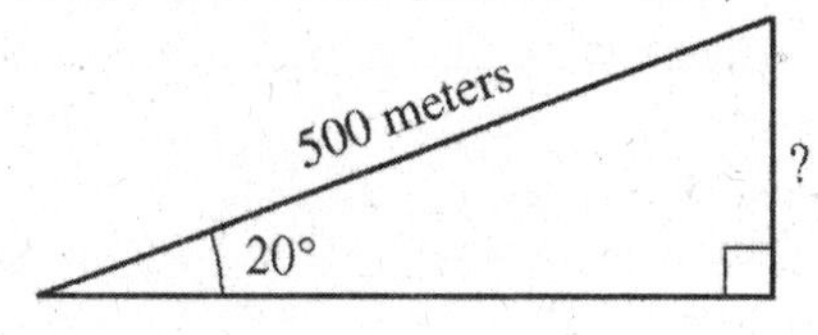

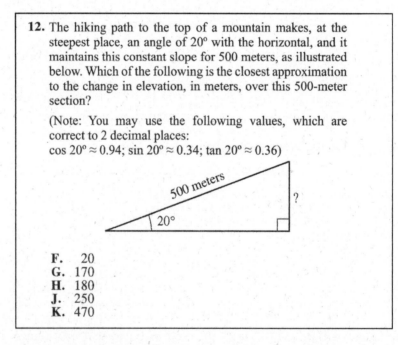

F. 20
G. 170
H. 180
J. 250
K. 470

This problem has a figure, and the figure is labeled with all the necessary information, including a question mark to tell you what you need to find. To set up the problem, you need to decide which of the trigonometric ratios involves the hypotenuse and the side opposite the given angle of a right triangle. Once you decide that the sine ratio is appropriate, you have only a basic trigonometry problem to solve: $\sin 20° = \frac{h}{500}$, or $500 \sin 20° = h$. Then, using the approximation for sin 20° given in the note, calculate $h \approx 500(0.34) = 170$, choice **G.** You may want to use your calculator to avoid computation errors. If you chose **K**, then you probably used the value for cosine rather than sine. Answer **H** comes from using tangent rather than sine.

Very Challenging Problems

The ACT mathematics test emphasizes reasoning ability, so it naturally has problems that can be very challenging. Because these problems are designed to test your understanding of mathematical concepts and your ability to pull together what you have learned in your math classes, they will probably be unlike problems you usually see. Some will be in settings, and some won't. Some will have figures, and some won't. Some will have extra information that you should ignore, and some won't have enough information, so the correct answer will be "Cannot be determined from the given information." Some will have numeric answers, some will have answers that are expressions or equations that you have to set up, and some will have answers that are statements for you to interpret and judge. On some questions your calculator will be helpful, and on others it will be better not to use it. All of the questions will share one important characteristic, however—they will challenge you to think hard and plan a strategy before you start to solve them.

Question 13 is a challenging problem.

13. If 537^{102} were calculated, it would have 279 digits. What would the digit farthest to the right be (the ones digit)?

A. 1
B. 3
C. 4
D. 7
E. 9

You certainly wouldn't want to calculate 537^{102} by hand, and your calculator doesn't display enough digits for you to be able to read off the ones digit for this very large number, so you have to figure out another way to see the ones digit. A good place to start might be to look at the ones digit for powers of 7 because 7 is the ones digit of 537. Maybe there will be a pattern: $7^0 = 1$, $7^1 = 7$, $7^2 = 49$, $7^3 = 343$, $7^4 = 2{,}401$, $7^5 = 16{,}807$, $7^6 = 117{,}649$, $7^7 = 823{,}543$. It looks like the pattern of the ones digits is 1, 7, 9, 3, 1, 7, 9, 3, . . ., with the sequence of these 4 digits repeating over and over. Now, if you can decide where in this pattern the ones digit of 537^{102} falls, you'll have the problem solved. You might organize a chart like this:

Ones digit	1	7	9	3
Power of 7	0 4	1 5	2 6	3 7

Improving Your Score

The next row would read "8 9 10 11" to show that the ones digits of 7^8, 7^9, 7^{10}, and 7^{11}, respectively, are 1, 7, 9, and 3. You could continue the chart row after row until you got up to 102, but that would take a lot of time. Instead, think about where 102 would fall. The numbers in the first column are the multiples of 4, so 100 would fall there because it is a multiple of 4. Then 101 would be in the second column, and 102 would fall in the third column. Therefore, the ones digit of 537^{102} is 9, choice **E.**

Question 14 is an algebra problem designed to challenge your ability to think mathematically and use what you've learned.

14. If $a < -1$, which of the following best describes a general relationship between a^3 and a^2 ?

F. $a^3 > a^2$

G. $a^3 < a^2$

H. $a^3 = a^2$

J. $a^3 = -a^2$

K. $a^3 = \frac{1}{a^2}$

Here you are told that $a < -1$. Then you are asked for the relationship between a^3 and a^2. By stopping to think for a moment before trying to manipulate the given inequality or experimenting with numbers plugged into the answer choices, you might realize that if $a < -1$, then a is a negative number, so its cube is a negative number. Squaring a negative number, however, gives a positive number. Every negative number is less than every positive number, so the correct relationship between a^3 and a^2 is $a^3 < a^2$, choice **G.** Of course, there are other ways to approach the problem.

For another very challenging algebra problem, look at question 15.

15. If $\left(\frac{4}{5}\right)^n = \sqrt{\left(\frac{5}{4}\right)^3}$, then n = ?

A. $-\frac{3}{2}$

B. -1

C. $-\frac{2}{3}$

D. $\frac{2}{3}$

E. $\frac{3}{2}$

In this problem, you're asked to find the value of a variable, but the variable is in the exponent. After some thought you might decide to try to rewrite $\sqrt{\left(\frac{5}{4}\right)^3}$ so that it is $\frac{5}{4}$ raised to a power. You should remember that the square root is the same as the $\frac{1}{2}$ power, so, after using some properties of exponents, $\sqrt{\left(\sqrt{\frac{5}{4}}\right)^3} = \left(\left(\sqrt{\frac{5}{4}}\right)^3\right)^{\frac{1}{2}} = \left(\frac{5}{4}\right)^{\frac{3}{2}}$. Now at least the left side and the right side of the equation have the same form, but the bases of the two expressions aren't the same—they're reciprocals. In thinking about the connection between reciprocals and exponents, it is good to realize that taking the opposite of the exponent (that is, making it have the opposite sign) will flip the base, because $a^{-k} = \frac{1}{a^k}$. That means $\left(\frac{5}{4}\right)^{\frac{3}{2}} = \left(\frac{4}{5}\right)^{-\frac{3}{2}}$. So now, with $\left(\frac{4}{5}\right)^n = \left(\frac{4}{5}\right)^{-\frac{3}{2}}$, $n = -\frac{3}{2}$, choice **A**.

Geometry problems can also be very challenging. Question 16 is an example.

16. In the standard (x,y) coordinate plane, the triangle with vertices at $(0,0)$, $(0,k)$, and $(2,m)$, where m is constant, changes shape as k changes. What happens to the triangle's area, expressed in square coordinate units, as k increases starting from 2 ?

F. The area increases as k increases.
G. The area decreases as k increases.
H. The area always equals 2.
J. The area always equals m.
K. The area always equals $2m$.

This problem might seem confusing at first because it contains two different variables and no figure to clarify. You're told that m is a constant but k changes. So, to get started, you could pick a value for m, say $m = 1$. Then, at least you can start sketching a figure. The point $(0,k)$ is on the y-axis and k increases starting with 2, so you could start by drawing a figure similar to this:

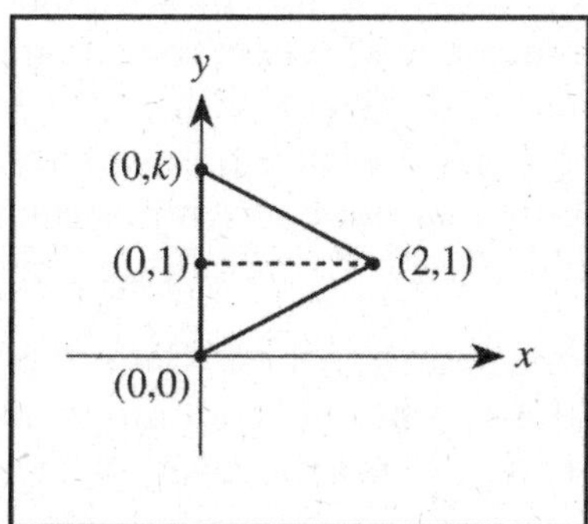

You can see the triangle that the problem mentions. If you think of the line segment from (0,0) to (0,k) as the base and the line segment from (2,1) to (0,1) as the height, you can see that as k increases, the base of the triangle gets longer but the height remains the same. From geometry, you know that the area of a triangle is given by ½(base)(height). Therefore, the area will increase as the base gets longer. So, the area will increase as k increases, choice **F**. You should be able to

Improving Your Score

reason that for any value of m, the result would have been the same, and you can feel confident that the correct answer is the first answer choice.

Question 17 is an example of a very challenging geometry problem.

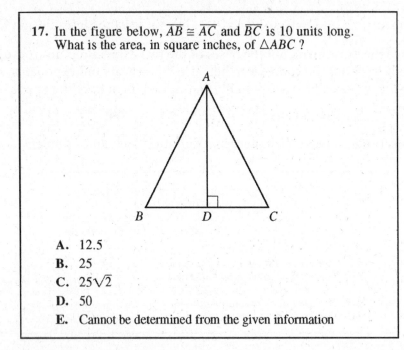

17. In the figure below, $\overline{AB} \cong \overline{AC}$ and $\overline{BC}$ is 10 units long. What is the area, in square inches, of $\triangle ABC$?

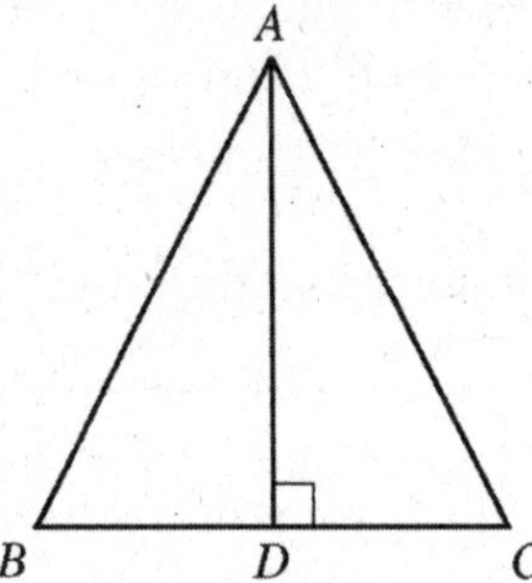

A. 12.5
B. 25
C. $25\sqrt{2}$
D. 50
E. Cannot be determined from the given information

This problem has a figure, but none of the information given is marked on the figure. A wise move is to mark the figure yourself to indicate which sides are congruent and which side is 10 units long. You need to find the area of ΔABC, and you know that the base $\overline{BC}$ is 10 units long. You need the measure of the height $\overline{AD}$ before you can apply the formula for the area of a triangle. You might ask yourself, "Is there any way to get the height?" If you were given the measure of one of the angles or the measure of one of the congruent sides, you might be able to find the height, but no other information is given. With a little more thought, you should realize that the height can be any positive number because there are infinitely many isosceles triangles with bases 10 units long. You conclude that not enough information is given to solve this problem, and the correct answer choice is **E**: "Cannot be determined from the given information."

This is the example that was mentioned earlier when "Cannot be determined from the given information" is the correct answer. Remember not to jump to a hasty conclusion when "Cannot be determined from the given information" is an answer choice. Sometimes it is the right answer, but sometimes it isn't.

Very challenging problems can be in settings, too. Question 18 is an example.

18. A bag of pennies could be divided among 6 children, or 7 children, or 8 children, with each getting the same number, and with 1 penny left over in each case. What is the smallest number of pennies that could be in the bag?

F. 22
G. 43
H. 57
J. 169
K. 337

In this problem, whenever the pennies in the bag (which contains an unknown number of pennies) are divided evenly among 6 children, 7 children, or 8 children, 1 penny is always left over. This means that if you take the extra penny out of the bag, then the number of pennies left in the bag will be divisible (with no remainder) by 6, 7, and 8. You should ask yourself, "What is the smallest number that is divisible by 6, 7, and 8?" In mathematical terminology, you're looking for the least common multiple of 6, 7, and 8. One way to find the least common multiple is to use the prime factorizations of the three numbers and to find the product of the highest power of each prime that occurs in one or more of the three numbers. This process will yield $2^3 \cdot 3 \cdot 7 = 168$. (As a check: $168 \div 6 = 28$, $168 \div 7 = 24$, and $168 \div 8 = 21$.) But wait! You're not quite finished. Remember to add back in the penny that you took out of the bag originally to make the divisions come out even. Thus, your answer is 169, choice **J**.

Question 19 is an example of an algebra word problem that is very challenging.

19. There are n students in a class. If, among those students, p% play at least 1 musical instrument, which of the following general expressions represents the number of students who play NO musical instrument?

A. np

B. $.01np$

C. $\frac{(100-p)n}{100}$

D. $\frac{(1-p)n}{.01}$

E. $100(1-p)n$

This is an example of a problem that has a mathematical expression as its answer. Finding an expression to answer a question usually makes you think more than finding a numerical answer because the variables require you to think abstractly. In this problem, you are told that out of a class of n students, p% play 1 or more musical instruments. Finding the percent of students who play no musical instrument is simple: $(100 - p)$%. To find the number of students who play no musical instrument, you'd probably want to convert $(100 - p)$% to a decimal and multiply by n. If $100 - p$ were a number you'd automatically move the decimal point two places to the left. But,

Improving Your Score

because there's no decimal point to move in 100 – p, you have to think about what you need to do to convert (100 – p)% to a decimal. Moving the decimal point two places to the left is the same as dividing by 100, so (100 – p)% as a decimal is $\frac{100-p}{100}$, and the number of students who play no musical instrument is $\frac{(100-p)n}{100}$, choice **C.**

Question 20 is an example of a very challenging geometry problem in a setting.

20. Starting at her doorstep, Ramona walked down the sidewalk at 1.5 feet per second for 4 seconds. Then she stopped for 4 seconds, realizing that she had forgotten something. Next she returned to her doorstep along the same route at 1.5 feet per second. The graph of Ramona's distance (d) from her doorstep as a function of time (t) would most resemble which of the following?

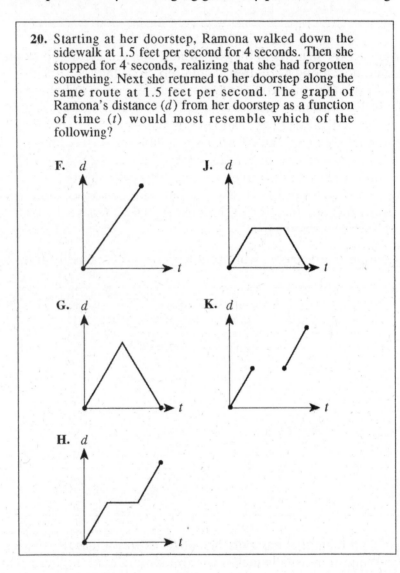

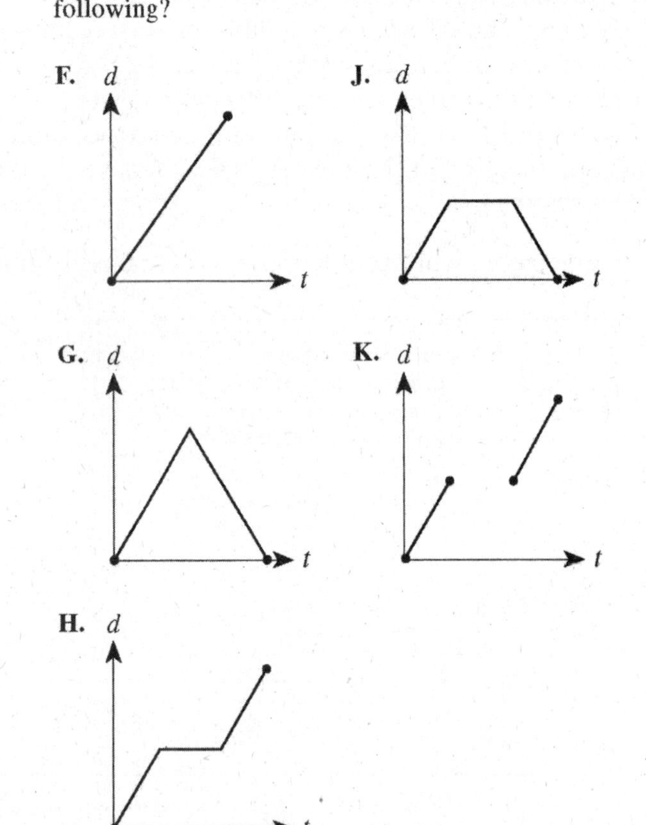

This problem is different from any of the problems you've seen so far because its answer is a graph. And, instead of giving you an equation and asking you to identify the equation's graph, this problem describes a situation and asks you to decide which graph represents the situation. You need to think about what the description of each of Ramona's activities says in terms of distance as a function of time and what each activity would translate into graphically. For example, at first, Ramona walked at a constant rate down the sidewalk. Therefore, she moved farther away from her doorstep as time elapsed, and her distance from her doorstep increased at a constant rate as time increased. So, the first part of the graph should be a line segment with a positive slope. Unfortunately, all five graphs start out this way, so none of the options can be eliminated at this point. The next thing Ramona did was stop for 4 seconds. If she stood still, her distance from her doorstep would not change even though time was still elapsing. This part of the graph should then reflect a constant value for d as time increases. It should be a horizontal line segment. This information allows you to eliminate options **F**, **G**, and **K**, because they do not have a horizontal line segment. Ramona's next activity helps you decide between **H** and **J**. Ramona walked back home at the same rate along the same route as before. On her way back home, her distance from her doorstep decreased at a constant rate as elapsed time increased. This would be graphed as a line segment with a negative slope, and therefore **J** is the correct graph.

Another word problem that challenges you to think mathematically is question 21.

21. An object detected on radar is 5 miles to the east, 4 miles to the north, and 1 mile above the tracking station. Among the following, which is the closest approximation to the distance, in miles, that the object is from the tracking station?

A. 6.5
B. 7.2
C. 8.3
D. 9.0
E. 10.0

This problem is about computing a distance, but it's a distance in three-dimensional space without a picture to help you. For this problem, drawing a sketch of the situation might help. Your sketch might be a "box" such as this:

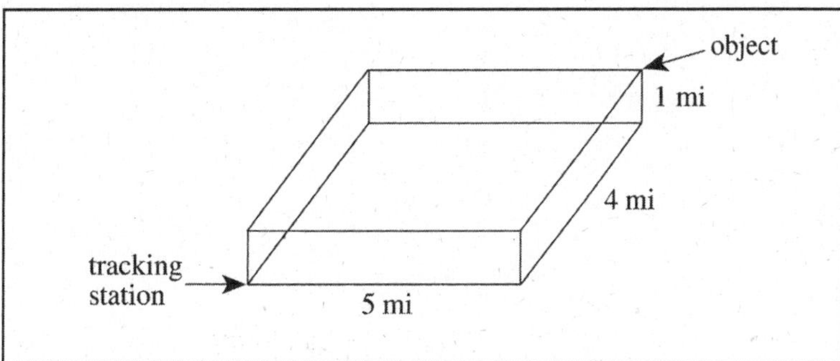

You need to find the length of the diagonal from the lower left corner of the front of the box to the top right corner of the back of the box. This is the hypotenuse of a right triangle (ΔOBT on the figure redrawn in the following) that has its right angle at B. One leg of this triangle has length 1, but the other leg is $\overline{BT}$, and you don't know the length of $\overline{BT}$.

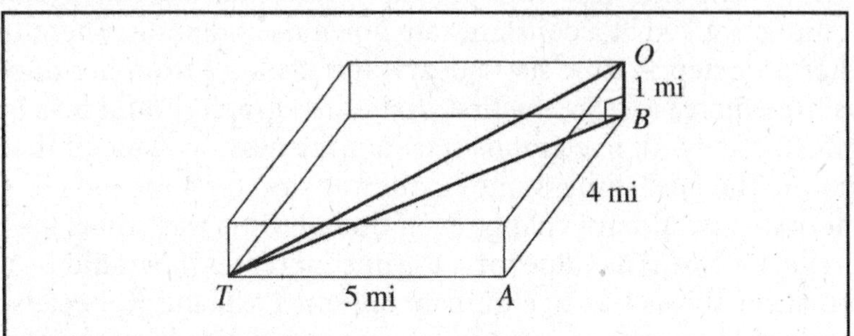

A closer look shows that $\overline{BT}$ is the hypotenuse of ΔTAB, which has its right angle at A and legs that measure 5 and 4. Using the Pythagorean theorem gives $BT = \sqrt{5^2 + 4^2} = \sqrt{41}$.

Now you can use the Pythagorean theorem again to get $OT = \sqrt{BT^2 + OB^2} = \sqrt{(\sqrt{41})^2 + 1^2} = \sqrt{42}$ which is about 6.5, choice **A**.

Question Sets

The mathematics test generally contains sets of questions that all relate to the same information. Questions 22–24 illustrate a question set that relates to information from a paragraph and a graph. The mathematics test typically contains two question sets with two to four questions per set.

Use the following information to answer questions 22–24.

At both Quick Car Rental and Speedy Car Rental, the cost, in dollars, of renting a full-size car depends on a fixed daily rental fee and a fixed charge per mile that the car is driven. However, the daily rental fee and the charge per mile are not the same for the 2 companies. In the graph below, line *Q* represents the total cost for Quick Car Rental and line *S* represents the total cost for Speedy Car Rental.

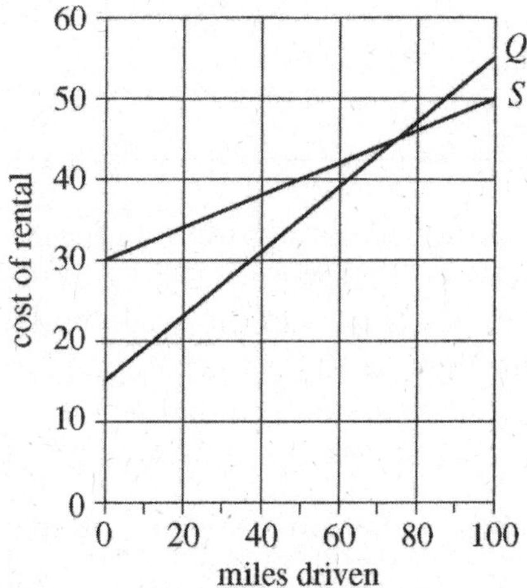

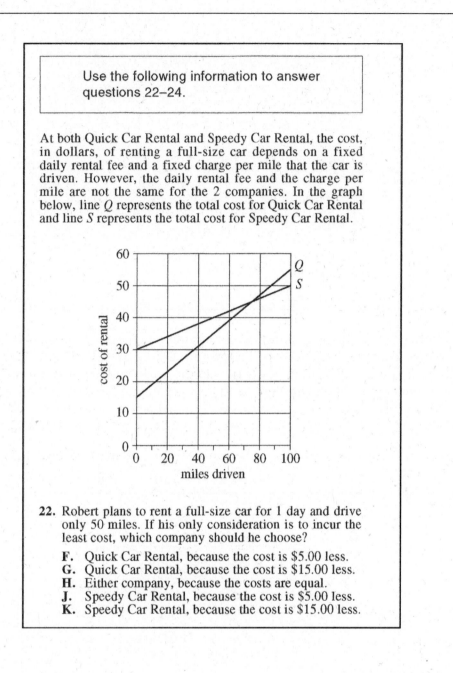

22. Robert plans to rent a full-size car for 1 day and drive only 50 miles. If his only consideration is to incur the least cost, which company should he choose?

F. Quick Car Rental, because the cost is \$5.00 less.
G. Quick Car Rental, because the cost is \$15.00 less.
H. Either company, because the costs are equal.
J. Speedy Car Rental, because the cost is \$5.00 less.
K. Speedy Car Rental, because the cost is \$15.00 less.

23. If you rent a full-size car from Quick Car Rental for 1 day, how much more would the total rental cost be if you drove the car 78 miles than if you drove it 77 miles?

A. $0.10
B. $0.15
C. $0.20
D. $0.40
E. $0.55

24. What would be the total cost of renting a full-size car from Speedy Car Rental for 1 day and driving the car 150 miles?

F. $ 60
G. $ 75
H. $ 85
J. $ 90
K. $120

Once you've looked at the information given for a group of questions, you can use the same sorts of strategies to answer the questions that you would use on any question on the ACT mathematics test. Question 22 requires you to read the graph and compare the costs of renting a car from the two companies, assuming that the car is going to be driven 50 miles. From the graph, the cost for Speedy Car Rental appears to be about $40, and the cost of Quick Car Rental appears to be about $35. These points are marked on the graph that is redrawn in the following.

So Robert will incur the least cost if he rents from Quick Car Rental because that cost is $5 less, choice **F**.

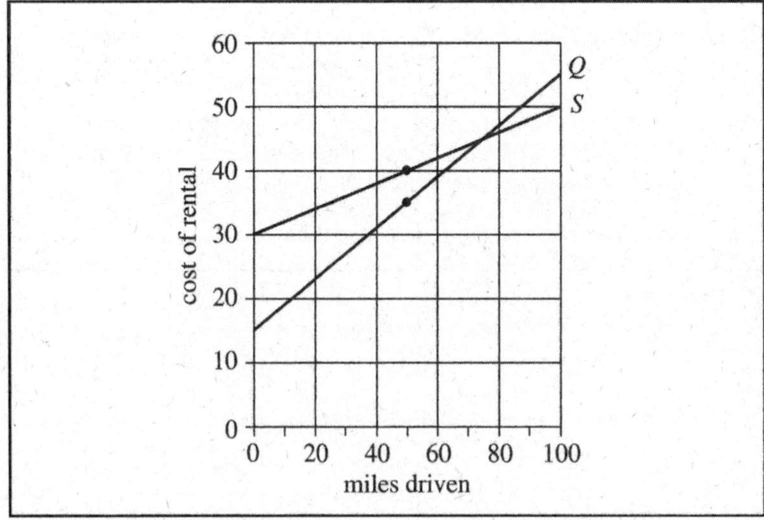

Question 23 requires you to determine how much more Robert would pay if he rented a car from Quick Car Rental and drove 78 miles than if he drove 77 miles. Using mathematical concepts might be a better approach than trying to read the graph, because you might not be able to read the graph accurately enough. You know from coordinate geometry that, in the standard (x,y) coordinate plane, the slope of a line gives the rate of change in y per unit change in x, which is exactly what you want to find in this problem—how much the cost at Quick Car Rental changes when the car is driven 1 more mile.

The formula to determine the slope of a line is $m = \frac{(y_2 - y_1)}{(x_2 - x_1)}$, where m is the slope, (x_1,y_1) are the coordinates of one point, and (x_2,y_2) are the coordinates of the other. Two points that are easy to read accurately off the graph are (0,15) and (50,35), labeled on the redrawn following graph. Plug the coordinates into the equation to get $m = \frac{(\$35 - \$15)}{(50 \text{ miles} - 0 \text{ miles})} = \frac{(\$20)}{(50 \text{ miles})} = 0.40 \text{ mile}$. So, the difference for driving 78 miles instead of 77 miles (that is, for driving 1 more mile) is \$0.40, choice **D**.

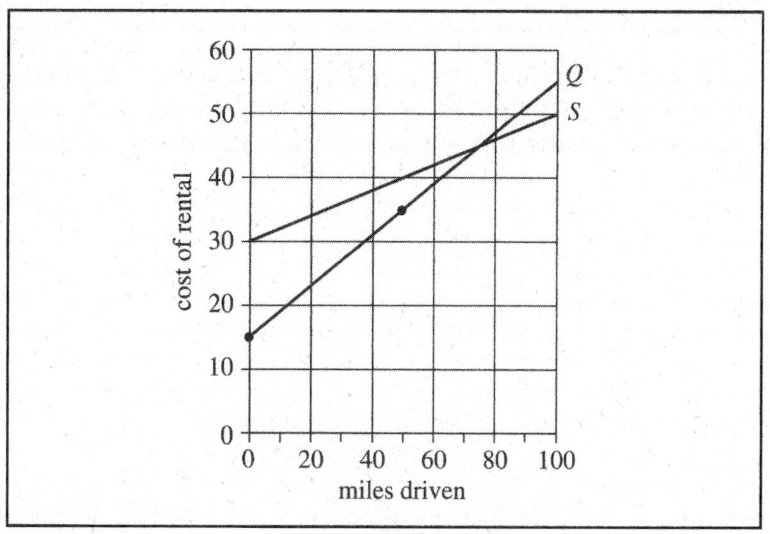

In question 24, you are asked for the cost of renting a car from Speedy Car Rental and driving it 150 miles. You can't simply read the cost off the graph, because 150 isn't on the graph, but you can find an equation of the line for Speedy Car Rental and then plug 150 into the equation. Recall that a line is determined by any two points on the line, call them (x_1,y_1) and (x_2,y_2), and that one way of finding an equation of the line is by first finding slope with $m = \frac{y_2 - y_1}{x_2 - x_1}$ and then using the two-point form of the equation of a line, $(y - y_1) = m(x - x_1)$. Here, you can use two points that are easy to read off the graph for Speedy Car Rental, such as (0,30) and (100,50), shown on the redrawn graph on the next page. The slope through any two points on this line is $m = \frac{50-30}{100-0} = \frac{20}{100} = 0.2$, and the equation $(y - 30) = 0.2(x - 0)$ fits all of the points on the line. This equation can be rewritten as $(y - 30) = 0.2x$. So, when $x = 150$, that means $(y - 30) = 0.2(150)$ and then $y - 30 = 30$ and then $y = 60$. The cost is \$60, choice **F**.

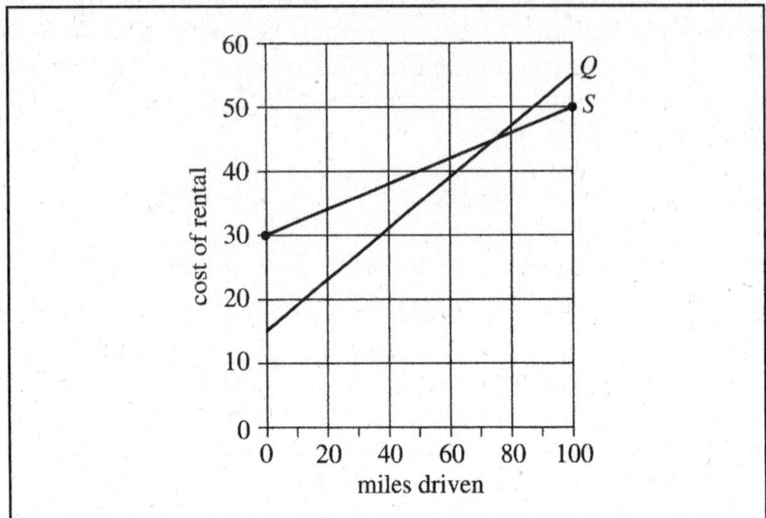

As you have seen in the sample questions in this section, the mathematics test includes many types of questions. Some will be easy for you, and some will be hard. They all will require you to demonstrate as much as possible about what you know and can do in mathematics.

Answer Key for Mathematics Test Sample Questions		
1. D	9. C	17. E
2. G	10. G	18. J
3. B	11. C	19. C
4. K	12. G	20. J
5. D	13. E	21. A
6. H	14. G	22. F
7. C	15. A	23. D
8. F	16. F	24. F

Strategies for Taking the ACT Mathematics Test

Pace Yourself

You have 60 minutes to answer 60 questions, which gives you an average of 1 minute per problem. Some problems will take you less than 1 minute, and some will take you more. Don't spend too much time on any one question. You should keep a close eye on your watch to make sure you work at a pace that will enable you to finish the test in the 60 minutes allotted. When determining your pace, be aware that the questions are arranged approximately in order of difficulty: easier questions first and hardest last.

Answer All Questions

Answer all questions even if you have no idea how to solve some of them. If you're stumped and have time, eliminate as many of the options as you can and then guess from among the remaining choices. If time is running out and you don't have time to eliminate any of the options, guess anyway. Even a wild guess has a 20% chance of being correct, but a blank has no chance of being correct. Remember, your score is based solely on the number of questions you answer correctly—there is no penalty for guessing and no penalty for wrong answers. Scores are most comparable if everyone answers every question.

Answer All the Easy Questions First, Then Go Back to Answer the Hard Ones

Easy and *hard* are relative terms. What might be easy for one student might be hard for another. You know which math topics are easy for you and which are hard. Answer all the questions that are easy for you and then go back to the hard ones. Remember that you don't get more points for answering hard questions. All questions, no matter how easy or hard, count equally toward your mathematics total score. If you don't see a way to solve a problem, or if the method you're using seems to be taking a lot of time, take your best guess (as explained in the previous section) or skip the question and move on to questions that you can answer more easily. If you skip the question, don't forget to mark in the test booklet (never on the answer document) all those questions that you skip so that you can easily return to them later.

Note: In some circumstances you are not permitted to write in your test booklet. In those circumstances, you'll be given scratch paper, and you can use it to jot down the numbers of the questions you skip.

Read Each Problem Carefully

Read carefully enough so you know what you're trying to find before you start looking for it and so you know what you have to work with to help you find it. Remember that questions may contain extraneous details you will need to ignore or insufficient information to solve the problem. Think twice before choosing "Cannot be determined from the given information," because test-takers often choose this option when the answer, in fact, can be determined from the information given. Make sure you are not overlooking a key piece of information provided or an alternate strategy for solving the problem.

Look for Information in the Answer Choices

Sometimes looking at the answer choices provides valuable information about the form of the answer. For example, you might be able to judge whether your answer should be left in radical form or converted to a decimal approximation, whether your polynomial answer should be left in factored form or multiplied out, or whether you should spend time reducing a probability to lowest terms. For some problems, you have to analyze the options as part of your solution strategy. For example, when a question asks, "Which of the following statements is true?" and the statements are the five options, you probably need to examine each option in turn. Sometimes, using the options gives you an alternate way to solve a problem. For example, suppose you're trying to solve a quadratic equation and you can't get the quadratic expression to factor and can't remember the quadratic formula. You might be able to get the correct answer by substituting the options, in turn, into the equation until one works. This strategy should be used very sparingly, however, because it can be more time-consuming than other strategies.

Use Illustrations Wisely and Whenever You Can

The old saying “A picture is worth a thousand words” holds true on the mathematics test:

- Refer to illustrations whenever they are provided.
- If no illustration is provided and one might be useful, draw your own illustration in the test booklet. This can be especially helpful in solving word problems.
- Transfer information from the question to the illustration, if you think it might be helpful. For example, you might write dimensions on the figure that are given in the question but aren’t shown on the figure or that you calculate in the process of solving the problem, or you might add marks to show congruences or draw auxiliary lines such as perpendiculars and diagonals.

Note: In some circumstances you are not permitted to write in your test booklet. In those circumstances, you’ll be given scratch paper to use.

Use Your Calculator Wisely

Each problem on the mathematics test can be solved in a reasonable amount of time without a calculator. A calculator is most helpful if you are very familiar with the one you bring to the test and you use it wisely during the test. Experimenting with the capabilities of a new calculator during the testing session or using a calculator in situations when a non-calculator approach would be better can cost you precious time. Bring the calculator that you are most familiar with—the one you use in your math classes or at home—but make sure it is an ACT-permitted calculator (visit www.actstudent.org for details). Don’t worry that other students have more sophisticated calculators than yours; the type of calculator that students use should not make a difference in their scores. Use your calculator wisely; remember that a non-calculator strategy is often better than a calculator strategy. And don’t believe everything your calculator tells you. Make sure the numbers it gives you are reasonable and make sense.

Think!

Your head is by far a more powerful and efficient problem-solving tool than a pencil or a calculator. Think before you plunge in and begin working on a problem. Don’t panic if you suddenly can’t remember a formula or all of the steps of a procedure you’ve been taught. You can often find another way to do a problem that will work just as well. For example, you don’t have to write and solve an equation for every algebra word problem. You might be able to reason through such a problem and get the correct answer without an equation. Sometimes the best option is to let your common sense about numbers take over.

Show Your Work

You have certainly heard this before—probably in every math class you've ever taken. Of course, you're not going to have time during the test to write down every step for every problem the way you might on a homework assignment, but writing down at least some of what you are thinking and doing as you solve a problem will be worth the time it takes. If you're using a calculator, you can write down the numbers that you plug into it and the intermediate results it gives you, to keep a running record of what you did. If you don't write anything down and your answer for a problem doesn't match any of the answer choices, your only alternative is to start over. But, if you have at least something written down, you may be able to go back over your work and find your mistake. Also, if you have time at the end of the test to go back and check your answers, having something written down will enable you to check your work more quickly.

Check Your Answers

Before you leave a question, make sure your answer makes sense. Don't believe everything your calculator tells you; make sure that the answer your calculator displays makes sense to you and that your answer actually answers the question. For example, if a problem about oranges and apples asks for the number of apples, make sure your answer doesn't give the number of oranges, or if a problem asks for the altitude of a triangle, make sure your answer isn't the hypotenuse. Remember, if you have time remaining after answering all of the questions, use it wisely and go back and check your work. That's a skill that will help you in college and career, too.

Chapter 7: Improving Your Reading Score

Designed to measure your reading comprehension, the ACT reading test comprises four sections, three of which contain one long prose passage and one that contains two shorter prose passages that are on the same topic. Each passage or passage set is followed by 10 multiple-choice questions, for a total of 40 questions. You are given 35 minutes to complete the test. The passages on the reading test come from published materials, such as books and magazines, written at a level that a first-year college student can expect to read for a class.

Content of the ACT Reading Test

The ACT reading test contains passages from each of the following categories:

- **Prose fiction** or **literary narrative** (literary passages from short stories, novels, memoirs, and personal essays)
- **Humanities** (informational passages on topics in architecture, art, dance, ethics, film, language, literary criticism, music, philosophy, radio, television, and theater)

- **Social science** (anthropology, archaeology, biography, business, economics, education, geography, history, political science, psychology, sociology)
- **Natural science** (anatomy, astronomy, biology, botany, chemistry, ecology, geology, medicine, meteorology, microbiology, natural history, physiology, physics, technology, zoology)

Each passage is preceded by a heading that identifies what type of passage it is (for example, "Literary Narrative"), names the author, and may include a brief note that helps in understanding the passage. Each section contains a set of multiple-choice test questions. These questions do not test the rote recall of facts from outside the passage, isolated vocabulary items, or rules of formal logic. In sections that contain two short passages, some of the questions involve both of the passages in the section.

You will receive four scores for the ACT reading test: a total test score based on all 40 questions and three reporting category scores based on the following specific knowledge and skills.

Key Ideas and Details

Read texts closely to determine central ideas and themes. Summarize information and ideas accurately. Read closely to understand relationships and draw logical inferences and conclusions including understanding sequential, comparative, and cause-effect relationships.

Craft and Structure

Determine word and phrase meanings, analyze an author's word choice rhetorically, analyze text structure, understand authorial purpose and perspective, and analyze characters' points of view. You will interpret authorial decisions rhetorically and differentiate between various perspectives and sources of information.

Integration of Knowledge and Ideas

Understand authors' claims, differentiate between facts and opinions, and use evidence to make connections between different texts that are related by topic. Some questions will require you to analyze how authors construct arguments, evaluating reasoning and evidence from various sources.

If you choose to take the writing test, you will also receive an English Language Arts (ELA) score based on an average of your English, reading, and writing test scores.

Types of Questions on the ACT Reading Test

On the reading test, the questions fall into one of the three reporting categories previously described. You shouldn't worry about these categories while you're taking the reading test. It's most important that you focus on the questions themselves and on what they ask you about a given passage. Because each passage is different, the kinds of questions will vary from passage to passage. Still, there are some general types of questions you're likely to encounter. Most questions will ask you to do one of the following:

- Identify and interpret details.
- Determine the main idea of a paragraph, paragraphs, or a passage.
- Understand comparative relationships (comparisons and contrasts).
- Understand cause-effect relationships.
- Make generalizations.
- Determine the meaning of words from context.
- Understand sequences of events.
- Analyze the author's voice and method.

Sometimes, the reading test contains other types of questions, but don't worry. Just make sure you read each passage and its questions carefully. You'll find that the information you need to determine the best answer for a question is always available in the passage. Questions that illustrate each of the most common types of questions on the reading test follow.

Representative ACT Reading Test Questions

Details. Some test questions ask you to pick out a detail from a passage. A detail can be something as seemingly simple as a characteristic of a person, place, or thing, or a particular date. Other questions of this type require you to do a bit more interpreting of minor or subtly stated details, as in the following example, based on a social studies passage on Eleanor Roosevelt (ER), which is found on page 272:

1. The passage states that ER believed the relationship between a people and their government should be:

   A. begun and carried out as if it were an isolated, individualist adventure.
   B. formed and modeled by the White House.
   C. based on organized, widespread citizen participation.
   D. controlled through radio broadcasts and formal channels.

You'll have to look around the passage for the information you need—not unusual for this kind of question. According to the author, ER's "abiding conviction . . . was that nothing good would happen to promote the people's interest unless the people themselves organized to demand government responses" (lines 55–58). Because ER felt "a people's movement required active citizen participation" (lines 58–59), it's clear that **C** is the best answer. **A**, **B**, and **D** violate the spirit of the quoted lines: ER wanted collective action and active citizen participation, not isolated individualism (**A**), White House domination (**B**), or control through radio broadcasts and formal channels (**D**).

Questions about details sometimes ask you to find the one detail that does *not* support a particular point. Such questions are usually signaled by words such as *NOT* and *EXCEPT.* Pay careful attention to these questions. When you answer them, remember that the usual question format is being reversed. Here's an example of this kind of reverse question, based on a prose fiction passage about a girl and her friend Eugene (page 270):

2. Which of the following questions is NOT answered by information in the passage?
   - **F.** Has the narrator ever walked around inside Eugene's house?
   - **G.** What hobby or interest do Eugene and the narrator share?
   - **H.** What makes Eugene's house different from other houses on the block?
   - **J.** What careers other than teaching has the narrator considered pursuing?

Three of the questions presented in the answer choices are answered by the passage, and the fourth one—the one you're looking for—isn't. Of the four, the only question not answered by the passage is **J:** we never learn what other careers besides teaching the narrator has considered pursuing. All three of the other questions are answered in the passage. We learn from lines 81–82 that although the narrator has watched the house "for so many years," she only dreams about going inside, ruling out **F.** We know from lines 39–40 and lines 63–66 that Eugene and the narrator are both interested in books, so **G** is out. According to the narrator, Eugene's house is "the only house on the block that had a yard and trees" (lines 5–6), so **H**, too, is incorrect.

Detail questions aren't the only kind of question that can make use of the reverse format. Don't worry, though—just watch for words such as *NOT* and *EXCEPT* in questions, and you'll be fine.

Main Ideas. To answer this kind of question, you need to be able to determine the focus of a passage or of a paragraph or paragraphs in a passage. You shouldn't count on finding this information summed up in the first paragraph of a passage or in the first sentence of a paragraph. You may have been advised to make the first sentence of each paragraph the topic sentence in your own writing, but not every writer does that. You'll need to figure out what the author's main point is in one or more paragraphs or in an entire passage by reading the paragraph(s) or passage carefully.

Main idea questions can be fairly straightforward. The following question, based on a social studies passage about the development of perceptual abilities (page 273), is pretty direct:

3. The main point of the passage is that:
   - **A.** during the first four to seven months of life, babies learn at an accelerated pace.
   - **B.** organisms deprived of critical life experiences may or may not develop normal sensory performance.
   - **C.** the development of perceptual abilities is the result of the interaction between nature and experience.
   - **D.** research concerned with physical skills and abilities adds little to our knowledge of the growth of the mind.

The idea that the interaction between nature and experience shapes the development of perceptual abilities (**C**) is the clear focus of the entire passage. In the first paragraph, the author states that "the ancient central question of psychology" is "how much is due to nature and how much to nurture (or, in developmental terms, to maturation and to learning)" (lines 5–8). The second through eighth paragraphs (lines 9–85) describe research designed to help answer this question as it relates to the development of perceptual abilities in children. The last paragraph sums up the passage by saying that this research helps us "catch the first glimpse of how mind is constructed out of matter by experience" (lines 88–89). Though in lines 50–53 the author describes the rapid development of infants between four and seven months old, this is only a minor part of the passage, so **A** is incorrect. The seventh paragraph (lines 61–73) does mention that organisms can be permanently harmed if they miss critical life experiences, but this, also, isn't the main point of the passage, making **B** incorrect. Choice **D** is just plain wrong: the whole passage deals with how research on physical skills and abilities has added to our knowledge of the growth of the mind.

As that example shows, you may have to rule out answer choices that either are supporting (rather than main) ideas or simply misstate what the passage says. Both types of wrong answers appear in this next example, based on the natural science passage about lightning and fire (page 275):

4. One of the main points of the third paragraph (lines 41–61) is that:

- **F.** Arizona researchers record tree mortality by volume.
- **G.** tree mortality rates fail to capture the true extent of lightning-inflicted damage.
- **H.** ponderosa pine trees are resistant to secondary diseases.
- **J.** pine tree forests draw fewer lightning strikes than many other habitat types in Arizona.

Choice **G** is the best answer here. Tree mortality rates "describe only direct injury" to trees (line 56), but lightning can also kill trees indirectly by making them vulnerable to insects, wind, and mistletoe and by causing fires. Although **F** is true, according to lines 54–56, the fact that Arizona researchers record tree mortality by volume is a minor point. The paragraph never claims that ponderosa pine trees are resistant to secondary diseases or that pine tree forests draw fewer lightning strikes than do many other habitat types in Arizona, so both **H** and **J** are incorrect.

Some questions for prose fiction or humanities passages will use phrases such as *main conflict* or *main theme* instead of *main idea*, but you should approach the questions in the same way as you would other main idea questions. Here's an example based on a prose fiction passage about a young woman, Cally Roy (page 271):

5. The main conflict in this passage could best be described as the:

- **A.** tension between the narrator's mother and Frank.
- **B.** hostility expressed between the narrator and her mother.
- **C.** narrator's efforts to break her ties to her mother and grandmothers.
- **D.** narrator's internal struggle to connect with her past and find her future.

Improving Your Score

You have to read the whole passage carefully to sort out what the main conflict is because there's at least some truth to all of the answer choices. Choice **D** turns out to be the best of the four choices because the main conflict is within the narrator herself. She journeys away from home and "into the city's bloody heart" (lines 18–19), she wonders "about the meaning of [her] spirit name" (line 22), she feels out of place in her too-big "Frankenstein body" (line 76), and she ends the passage torn between her "city corner" and her life "back home" (lines 82–83). The narrator says her mother loves Frank "too much to live with" him (lines 36–37) and also that Frank "can't drag himself away from the magnetic field of mother's voice" (lines 68–69), but the tension between the narrator's mother and Frank isn't the main conflict of the passage, making **A** wrong. There could be some hostility between the narrator and her mother because the narrator doesn't seem to want to go to the tribal college like her mother wants her to (see lines 79–82), but the narrator also wants to "curl next to her and be a small girl again" (lines 74–75), so mother-daughter hostility isn't the main conflict, either, ruling out **B**. Choice **C** misses the mark because although the narrator has left her home and her mother, her grandmothers are only briefly talked about in the passage (see lines 24–33), so the main conflict can't revolve around them.

Comparative Relationships. You're likely to find questions asking you to make comparisons and contrasts in passages that contain a lot of information or that feature multiple characters or points of view. This kind of test question can make you process a lot of information—you may be asked to weigh one concept against another and identify a significant difference between the two. But comparison and contrast questions aren't always overly complicated. In the following example, based on a humanities passage about the nature of work (page 274), the comparison is directly made in a few lines in the passage:

6. According to the author, the significant difference between a bread-maker and a bread pan is that only one:

- **F.** was used by previous generations.
- **G.** came on the market in recent years.
- **H.** goes in the oven when the dough is prepared.
- **J.** diminishes the human role in making bread.

Lines 1–3 state, "The difference between a machine and a tool—between a bread-maker and a bread pan—is that a tool extends human skills, a machine replaces them." Thus, **J** is the best answer. None of the other three answer choices is mentioned in the passage: The author never claims that the significant difference between a bread-maker and a bread pan is that one was used by previous generations (**F**), came on the market in recent years (**G**), or goes in the oven when the dough is prepared (**H**).

Not all comparative relationships questions are this direct, however. This next example, based on the same passage, shows that this type of question can get more complicated, especially when the question is in the reverse format discussed in the Details section:

7. In the third paragraph (lines 24–42), the author alludes to but apparently does NOT share the point of view of which of the following?

   A. Neighbors who live as if work is a kind of celebration
   B. The official who wants to shrink welfare rolls
   C. Those who believe that "the creation is a sacred gift"
   D. One who mends rather than replaces torn clothing

Here you have to not only determine the author's point of view but also compare his perspective to those of other people mentioned in the third paragraph. The author thinks that the idea of a work ethic "has lost its edge from tumbling over the lips of too many cynical bosses and politicians" (lines 26–27). It's reasonable to conclude that the author doesn't agree with these bosses and politicians, including "the official who wants to shrink the welfare rolls" (lines 30–31), so **B** is the best answer. It's also reasonable to conclude from the paragraph that the author shares the point of view of the people mentioned in **A**, **C**, and **D**. In lines 34–39, the author identifies himself with neighbors and others who share "a belief that the creation is a sacred gift, and that by working we express our gratitude and celebrate our powers" (**A** and **C**). In lines 39–42, he says that part of honoring that gift is "patching clothes" (**D**).

Cause-Effect Relationships. Cause-effect questions can be asked about prose fiction passages—sometimes one character's actions cause another character to react a certain way. Cause-effect questions also can arise in natural science passages in which a process is described. Sometimes the answer to a cause-effect question is stated in the passage; sometimes you have to piece together the information you've read and work out the answer on your own.

Here's an example of a fairly direct cause-effect question, based on the prose fiction passage about Cally Roy:

8. The narrator implies that losing her indis has caused her to:

   F. cling to her family.
   G. leave her home.
   H. remember its every detail.
   J. fight with her family.

The information needed to answer this question is in the first paragraph: once the narrator lost her indis, she says, she "began to wander from home, first in my thoughts, then my feet took after" (lines 11–13). Choice **G** is therefore the best answer. Choice **F** is pretty much the opposite of the truth, in the sense that the narrator decided to leave home. Although the narrator claims she "remember[s] every detail" of her indis (line 5), this isn't because she lost it but because "the turtle hung near my crib, then off my belt, and was my very first play toy" (lines 5–7). So **H** can't be the best answer. Choice **J** is incorrect because the narrator never really implies that losing her indis has caused her to fight with her family. Although her mother was "in a panic" (line 27) over the narrator's decision to leave, this seems more out of concern for the narrator than the result of a fight.

Following is an example of a somewhat more complex cause-effect question, this time based on the natural science passage on lightning and fire:

9. The third paragraph (lines 41–61) suggests that if lightning did not fix atmospheric nitrogen, then:

A. rain could not fall to Earth, leaving nitrogen in the atmosphere.
B. less nitrogen would be found on Earth.
C. electrical current could not be conducted by air.
D. lightning bolts would strike the earth with less frequency.

Although the question lets you know to look in the third paragraph, the wording of that paragraph is subtle and requires close reading. The relevant information is in lines 45–46: "Lightning helps to fix atmospheric nitrogen into a form that rain can bring to Earth." This matches nicely with **B**, which says that less nitrogen would be found on Earth. Although nitrogen would remain in the atmosphere if lightning didn't fix it, the paragraph never suggests that rain wouldn't fall to Earth, making **A** tempting but wrong. The paragraph doesn't suggest that if lightning didn't fix atmospheric nitrogen, electrical current couldn't be conducted by air or that lightning bolts would strike the earth with less frequency, making **C** and **D** incorrect.

Generalizations. This type of question usually asks you to take a lot of information—sometimes the whole passage—and boil it down into a more concise form. A generalization question may involve interpreting mood, tone, or character, or it may ask you to make some kind of general observation or draw a conclusion about the nature of an argument the author is making. The following example, based on the social studies passage about Eleanor Roosevelt, focuses on personality or character:

10. As she is revealed in the passage, ER is best described as:

F. socially controversial but quietly cooperative.
G. politically courageous and socially concerned.
H. morally strong and deeply traditional.
J. personally driven but calmly moderate.

This question requires you to sum up the complex personality of Eleanor Roosevelt in just a few short words. The best answer is **G**, because examples of ER being politically courageous and socially concerned are found throughout the passage. The fourth paragraph (lines 20–25), for instance, reveals that as First Lady, "she upset race traditions, championed a New Deal for women, and on certain issues actually ran a parallel administration" to the one her husband, Franklin Delano Roosevelt, ran as president of the United States. Although ER "is the most controversial First Lady in United States history" (lines 1–2) and though she believed in collective action and "united democratic movements for change" (lines 61–62), it would be wrong to say, as **F** does, that "socially controversial but quietly cooperative" is the best description of ER. The passage implies that there was very little quiet about ER. She clearly wasn't deeply traditional, so **H** is out. Similar to **F**, choice **J** is tempting because it's in some ways true but, again, not the best description of ER. Although she was personally driven and supported the idea of a "middle way" (line 54) between fascism and communism, **J** wrongly states that ER was calmly moderate. She was, in fact, someone who challenged long-held traditions and created great controversy by doing so.

Meanings of Words. Questions about meanings of words ask you to determine from context what a particular word, phrase, or statement most nearly means. In some cases, the word or words will probably be unfamiliar to you, but even when familiar words are tested, you'll have to look at the context in which they appear to determine the closest synonym or paraphrase. Sometimes, looking at a single sentence of the passage is enough to figure this out, but other times, you'll have to look at sentences before or after the given word, phrase, or statement in order to determine the closest meaning.

Many meanings-of-words questions will focus on a single word or a short phrase. The answer choices will include synonyms for the word or phrase that you might find in a dictionary or thesaurus, but only one of the choices will truly reflect how the word or phrase is used in this particular case. Look at the following example, based on the natural science passage about lightning and fire:

11. The *process of "electrocution"* mentioned in line 62 most nearly refers to:

- **A.** the ignition of rotten wood and pine needles.
- **B.** accidental death by electrical current.
- **C.** a lightning strike of a tree.
- **D.** the scorching of plants by lightning.

If you merely looked at the question without looking at the passage, **B** might he an attractive choice because this is how the word *electrocution* is often used in everyday life. But **B** makes little sense in the context of the fourth paragraph (lines 62–70), which discusses how lightning scorches plants, so the best answer is **D**. Scorching isn't the same thing as igniting, and the paragraph doesn't mention rotten wood or pine needles, so **A** is incorrect. Choice **C** isn't the best answer, either, because lines 64–65 state that the process of "electrocution" isn't "limited to trees."

Sometimes meanings-of-words questions will ask you to paraphrase an entire statement, as in the following example, taken from the prose fiction passage about a girl and her friend Eugene:

12. When the narrator says, "I begin to think of the present more than of the future" (lines 80–81), she most likely means that meeting Eugene led her to:

- **F.** shift some of her attention away from her career plans and onto the developing friendship.
- **G.** think more about her own work interests than about the career her parents thought she should pursue.
- **H.** put off her plans of returning to Puerto Rico or a visit in favor of continuing to prepare for college.
- **J.** want to spend more time with him instead of helping her parents plan a vacation to Puerto Rico.

All of the answer choices describe possible shifts from the future to the present, but only one, **F**, fits the context of the passage. Although in the sixth paragraph (lines 67–79) the narrator discusses her parents' dreams and her own plans to go to college and become a teacher ("the future"), the last paragraph shows the narrator shifting some of her attention to her friendship with Eugene ("the present"). She wants to go into Eugene's house and sit at the kitchen table with him "like two adults" (lines 85–86). Choice **G** is wrong because she's shifting attention away from her work interests and because we don't know what career her parents thought she should pursue. Choice **H**, too, is incorrect: the narrator doesn't say she's had plans to return to Puerto Rico, and she's thinking less, not more, about preparing for college. Although the narrator does want to spend more time with Eugene, she hasn't been helping her parents plan a vacation to Puerto Rico—the sixth paragraph only says that her parents would like to retire there someday—so **J** is incorrect.

Sequence of Events. In some passages, the order, or sequence, in which events happen is important. Sequence-of-events questions ask you to determine when, for example, a character in a prose fiction passage did something or to figure out the order in which the researchers described in a natural science passage performed certain steps in a biology experiment.

Speaking of natural science, the following question, based on a passage about the small-comet theory (page 276), requires a fairly straightforward ordering of events:

13. According to the passage, the research that led to the development of the small-comet theory began with a project originally intended to study:

A. the electrical activity accompanying sunspots.
B. water entering Earth's upper atmosphere.
C. static in satellite transmissions.
D. specks in satellite images.

The author indicates that Frank and Sigwarth were analyzing "photos of the electrical phenomena that accompany sunspots" when "they noted dark specks appearing in several images from NASA's *Dynamics Explorer 1* satellite" (lines 46–48). These specks started Frank and Sigwarth toward their small-comet theory, as the rest of the passage reveals. Thus, **A** is the best answer. The other answer choices are related to Frank and Sigwarth's research, but none of them names the original study. Lines 55–58 show that **B** is incorrect: The two scientists decided that water was entering Earth's upper atmosphere in the form of small comets only after they'd examined photos of the electrical phenomena accompanying sunspots. The author says that static in the satellite transmission was the first hypothesis Frank and Sigwarth came up with to explain the dark specks (lines 49–50), but the photos in which the specks appeared were originally taken to study sunspot-related activity, so **C** is incorrect. Choice **D** is likewise incorrect because the specks Frank and Sigwarth found were in photos originally taken as part of a study of sunspot-related activity.

The social studies passage on the development of perceptual abilities is challenging in part because you have to keep clear in your mind when certain abilities develop in infants. The following question, based on that passage, deals with that very point:

14. It is reasonable to infer from the passage that one-month-old babies will demonstrate which of the following skills?

- **F.** Noticing the difference between a pale yellow rattle and a bright yellow rattle
- **G.** Recognizing each of their older brothers and sisters as individuals
- **H.** Glancing from their father's face to their mother's face and back to their father again
- **J.** Following a wooden butterfly on a slow-moving mobile hanging above their bed

What makes this question harder is that the examples provided in the answer choices aren't specifically found in the passage. You have to infer from the information given in the passage which of the four answer choices is most likely, given the age of the child. In this case, the best answer is **J**. Lines 39–40 state that "during the first month [infants] begin to track slowly moving objects." It's reasonable to infer from this that a one-month-old baby would be able to follow a wooden butterfly on a slow-moving mobile hanging above his or her head. Choices **F**, **G**, and **H** are perceptual abilities that develop later. The ability to "differentiate among hues and levels of brightness" (lines 42–43) doesn't begin to develop until "the second month" (lines 40–41), meaning a one-month-old is unlikely to be able to note the difference between a pale yellow rattle and a bright yellow rattle (**F**). The ability to "glance from one object to another, and distinguish among family members" (lines 44–45) doesn't emerge until three months, so a one-month-old couldn't recognize each of his or her older siblings as individuals (**G**) or glance from father to mother and back again (**H**).

Author's Voice and Method. Finally, some questions deal with the author's voice and method. *Voice* relates to such things as the author's style, attitude, and point of view, whereas *method* focuses on the craft of writing—the main purpose of a passage, what role parts of a passage (such as a paragraph) play in the whole work, and so on.

A couple of examples should help clear up what this category is about. The first, taken from the social studies passage on Eleanor Roosevelt, asks you to consider what hypothetical statement the author would most likely agree with:

15. According to the last paragraph, which of the following statements would the author most likely make with regard to ER's vision and ideals?

- **A.** ER considered politics a game and played only when she knew she could win.
- **B.** ER worked with agitators and remained dedicated to the pursuit of justice and peace in victory and defeat.
- **C.** ER placed herself in the position of president, making decisions that determined White House policy.
- **D.** ER saw herself as the country's role model and personally responsible for bringing about change.

All of the ideas in **B**—though not quite in those words—can be found in the last paragraph: ER "brought her network of agitators and activists into the White House" (lines 90–91), "worked with movements for justice and peace" (lines 87–88), and "never considered a political setback a

Improving Your Score

permanent defeat" (lines 91–92). Choice **A** is incorrect because although ER "enjoyed the game" (line 93), she saw defeat as only temporary, meaning she stuck with politics, win or lose. Choice **C** goes well beyond what the last paragraph (or the rest of the passage, for that matter) says about ER. She never placed herself in the position of the president, even if, as the author pointed out earlier, "ER made decisions and engineered policy" (line 25) in some areas. Choice **D** is incorrect for the same kind of reason: neither the last paragraph nor the passage as a whole states that ER saw herself as the country's role model and as personally responsible for bringing about change. Though she lobbied for her views "in countless auditoriums, as a radio broadcaster, and in monthly, weekly, and, by 1936, daily columns" (lines 41–43), she also strongly believed in "active citizen participation" (line 59) in government.

A second example, based on the prose fiction passage about a girl and her friend Eugene, deals with the contribution two paragraphs make to the story:

16. In terms of developing the narrative, the last two paragraphs (lines 67–87) primarily serve to:

- **F.** provide background details about the narrator and her family in order to highlight the narrator's unique and shifting perspective.
- **G.** describe the narrator's family in order to establish a contrast between her parents and Eugene's parents.
- **H.** portray the narrator's family in order to show how her friendship with Eugene affected the various members of her family.
- **J.** depict the hopes and dreams of the narrator's parents in order to show how her parents' aspirations changed over time.

To answer this question correctly, consider not only what the last two paragraphs of the passage say but also their role in advancing the story. Choice **F** is the best answer here. We learn in the sixth paragraph (lines 67–79) about how the parents' dreams and the narrator's plans (going to college and becoming a teacher) differ, suggesting she has a unique perspective. The last paragraph emphasizes how the narrator's perspective has shifted from focusing on "the future" to focusing on "the present." Choice **F** is easier to see when you consider the place of the last two paragraphs in the whole passage; lines 67–87 help shift the focus from the narrator's meetings with Eugene to her reflection on how her friendship with Eugene has changed her life. Choice **G** is incorrect because although the second paragraph (lines 27–42) describes Eugene's parents and the sixth paragraph describes the narrator's parents, no direct contrast is made between the two sets of parents. The passage also contains no indication that the narrator's friendship with Eugene affects her family at all (or that they even know about it), making **H** a poor option. Choice **J** is wrong because the only discussion of the narrator's parents' aspirations is in the sixth paragraph, and nothing suggests that these aspirations changed over time.

Answer Key for Reading Test Sample Questions

1. C	7. B	13. A
2. J	8. G	14. J
3. C	9. B	15. B
4. G	10. G	16. F
5. D	11. D	
6. J	12. F	

Strategies for Taking the ACT Reading Test

Performance on the ACT reading test relies not only on reading speed and comprehension but also on test-taking strategies and skills. The following sections describe strategies and skills specifically for improving your ACT reading test score.

Pace Yourself

Before you read the first passage of the reading test, you may want to take a quick look through the entire reading test. If you choose to do this, flip through the pages and look at each of the passages and their questions. (Note that the passages begin on the pages to your left, and the questions follow.) You don't need to memorize anything—you can look at any of the reading test passages and questions during the time allotted for that test.

Some readers find that looking quickly at the questions first gives them a better idea of what to look for as they're reading the passage. It you're a slow reader, though, this may not be a good strategy. If you do decide to preview the questions, don't spend too much time on them—just scan for a few key words or ideas that you can watch for when you read the passage. To see what approach works best for you, you might want to try alternating between previewing the questions and not previewing the questions as you work through the practice tests in this book. Remember that when you take the ACT for real, a clock will be running. Plan your approach for the reading test before you take the actual ACT.

Use the Time Allotted

You have 35 minutes to read four passages and answer 40 questions. You'll want to pace yourself so you don't spend too much time on any one passage or question. If you take 2 to 3 minutes to read each passage, you'll have about 35 seconds to answer each question associated with the passage. Some of the questions will take less time, which will allow you more time for the more challenging ones.

Because time is limited, you should be very careful in deciding whether to skip more difficult questions. If you skip the difficult questions from the first passage until you work through the entire reading test, for example, you may find that you've forgotten so much of the first passage that you have to reread it before you can answer the questions that puzzled you the first time through. It will probably work better for you to think of the test as four 8-minute, 30-second units and to try to complete all the questions for a passage within its allotted time. Answer all the questions; you're not penalized for guessing.

Think of an Overall Strategy That Works for You

Are you the kind of person who likes to get the big picture first, then carefully go over your work? Do you like to answer the questions you're sure of right away and then go back and puzzle out the tougher ones? Or are you something of a perfectionist? (Do you find it hard to concentrate on a question until you know you got the one before it right?) There isn't any right way or wrong way to approach the reading test—just make sure the way you choose is the way that works best for you.

Keep the Passage as a Whole in Mind

Your initial look at the whole reading test should give you some ideas about how to approach each passage. Notice the subject heading and short paragraph before each passage. These "advance organizers" tell you the subject matter of the passage, where the passage comes from, who wrote it, and sometimes a little information about the passage. Occasionally, an advance organizer will define a difficult word, explain a concept, or provide background information. Reading the advance organizers carefully should help you be more prepared as you approach each passage.

Always remember that the reading test asks you to refer and reason on the basis of the passage. You may know a lot about the subject of some of the passages you read, but try not to let what you already know influence the way you answer the questions, because the author's perspective may differ from yours. There's a reason why many questions begin with "According to the passage" or "It can reasonably be inferred from the passage." If you read and understand the passage well, your reasoning ability will help you to figure out the correct answer. During the reading test, you can refer back to the passages as often as you like.

Find a Strategy for Approaching Each Question

First, read each question carefully so you know what it asks. Look for the best answer, but read and consider all the options, even though you may feel you've identified the best one. Ask yourself whether you can justify your choice as the best answer.

Some people find it useful to answer the easy questions first and skip the difficult ones (being careful, of course, to mark the answer document correctly and to mark in the test booklet the questions they skipped). Then they go back and consider the difficult questions. When you're working on a test question and aren't certain about the answer, try to eliminate choices you're sure are incorrect. If you can rule out a couple of choices, you'll improve your chances of selecting the correct answer. Keep referring back to the passage for information.

Reading Strategies Summary

The sample passages used as examples in this section can be found on the following pages. They come from ACTs that thousands of students have already taken. Remember, the passages in this section don't represent every type you're likely to see, but they should give you a good idea of the kinds of questions you'll encounter when you take the ACT reading test. For a more complete picture of what the ACT reading test will look like, five complete reading tests are included in the five practice ACTs in chapters 3 and 10. And remember that the best way to do well on the ACT reading test is to have a solid understanding of each passage—so read quickly but carefully.

Sample Passage I

PROSE FICTION: This passage is adapted from the short story "American History" by Judith Ortiz-Cofer (©1992 by Judith Ortiz-Cofer). The story appeared in the anthology *Iguana Dreams: New Latino Fiction.*

There was only one source of beauty and light for me my ninth grade year. The only thing I had anticipated at the start of the semester. That was seeing Eugene. In August, Eugene and his family had moved into the only house on the block that had a yard and trees. I could see his place from my bedroom window in El Building. In fact, if I sat on the fire escape I was literally suspended above Eugene's backyard. It was my favorite spot to read my library books in the summer. Until that August the house had been occupied by an old couple. Over the years I had become part of their family, without their knowing it, of course. I had a view of their kitchen and their backyard, and though I could not hear what they said, I knew when they were arguing, when one of them was sick, and many other things. I knew all this by watching them at mealtimes. I could see their kitchen table, the sink, and the stove. During good times, he sat at the table and read his newspapers while she fixed the meals. If they argued, he would leave and the old woman would sit and stare at nothing for a long time. When one of them was sick, the other would come and get things from the kitchen and carry them out on a tray. The old man had died in June. The house had stood empty for weeks. I had had to resist the temptation to climb down into the yard and water the flowers the old lady had taken such good care of.

By the time Eugene's family moved in, the yard was a tangled mass of weeds. The father had spent several days mowing, and when he finished, from where I sat, I didn't see the red, yellow, and purple clusters that meant flowers to me. I didn't see this family sit down at the kitchen table together. It was just the mother, a red-headed tall woman who wore a white uniform; the father was gone before I got up in the morning and was never there at dinner time. I only saw him on weekends when they sometimes sat on lawn-chairs under the oak tree, each hidden behind a section of the newspaper; and there was Eugene. He was tall and blond, and he wore glasses. I liked him right away because he sat at the kitchen table and read books for hours. That summer, before we had even spoken one word to each other, I kept him company on my fire escape.

Once school started I looked for him in all my classes, but P. S. 13 was a huge place and it took me days and many discreet questions to discover Eugene. After much maneuvering I managed "to run into him" in the hallway where his locker was—on the other side of the building from mine—and in study hall at the library where he first seemed to notice me, but did not speak; and finally, on the way home after school one day when I decided to approach him directly, though my stomach was doing somersaults.

I was ready for rejection, snobbery, the worst. But when I came up to him and blurted out: "You're Eugene. Right?" he smiled, pushed his glasses up on his nose, and nodded. I saw then that he was blushing deeply. Eugene liked me, but he was shy. I did most of the talking that day. He nodded and smiled a lot. In the weeks that followed, we walked home together. He would linger at the corner of El Building for a few minutes then walk down to his house.

I did not tell Eugene that I could see inside his kitchen from my bedroom. I felt dishonest, but I liked my secret sharing of his evenings, especially now that I knew what he was reading since we chose our books together at the school library.

I also knew my mother was unhappy in Paterson, New Jersey, but my father had a good job at the blue-jeans factory in Passaic and soon, he kept assuring us, we would be moving to our own house there. I had learned to listen to my parents' dreams, which were spoken in Spanish, as fairy tales, like the stories about life in Puerto Rico before I was born. I had been to the island once as a little girl. We had not been back there since then, though my parents talked constantly about buying a house on the beach someday, retiring on the island—that was a common topic among the residents of El Building. As for me, I was going to go to college and become a teacher.

But after meeting Eugene I began to think of the present more than of the future. What I wanted now was to enter that house I had watched for so many years. I wanted to see the other rooms where the old people had lived, and where the boy spent his time. Most of all, I wanted to sit at the kitchen table with Eugene like two adults, like the old man and his wife had done, maybe drink some coffee and talk about books.

Sample Passage II

PROSE FICTION: This passage is adapted from *The Antelope Wife* by Louise Erdrich (©1998 by Louise Erdrich).

My mother sewed my birth cord, with dry sage and sweet grass, into a turtle holder of soft white buckskin. She beaded that little turtle using precious old cobalts and yellows and Cheyenne pinks and greens in a careful design. I remember every detail of it, me, because the turtle hung near my crib, then off my belt, and was my very first play toy. I was supposed to have it on me all my life, bury it with me on reservation land, but one day I came in from playing and my indis was gone. I thought nothing of it, at first and for many years, but slowly over time the absence . . . it will tell. I began to wander from home, first in my thoughts, then my feet took after, so at last at the age of eighteen, I walked the road that led from the front of our place to the wider spaces and then the country beyond that, where that one road widened into two lanes, then four, then six, past the farms and service islands, into the dead wall of the suburbs and still past that, finally, into the city's bloody heart.

My name is Cally Roy. Ozhawashkwamashkodeykway is what the spirits call me. All my life so far I've wondered about the meaning of my spirit name but nobody's told it, seen it, got ahold of my history flying past. Mama has asked, she has offered tobacco, even blankets, but my grandmas Mrs. Zosie Roy and Mary Shawano only nod at her, holding their tongues as they let their eyes wander. In a panic, once she knew I was setting out, not staying home, Mama tried to call up my grandmas and ask if I could live at their apartment in the city. But once they get down to the city, it turns out they never stop moving. They are out, and out again. Impossible to track down. It's true, they are extremely busy women.

So my mom sends me to Frank.

Frank Shawano. Famous Indian bakery chef. My Mama's eternal darling, the man she loves too much to live with.

I'm weary and dirty and sore when I get to Frank's bakery shop, but right away, walking in and the bell dinging with a cheerful alertness, I smell those good bakery smells of yeasty bread and airy sugar. Behind the counter, lemony light falls on Frank. He is big, strong, pale brown like a loaf of light rye left to rise underneath a towel. His voice is muffled and weak, like it is squeezed out of the clogged end of a pastry tube. He greets me with gentle pleasure.

"Just as I'm closing." His smile is very quiet. He cleans his hands on a towel and beckons me into the back of the bakery shop, between swinging steel doors. I remember him as a funny man, teasing and playing games and rolling his eyes at us, making his pink sugar-cookie dogs bark and elephants trumpet. But now he is serious, and frowns slightly as I follow him up the back stairs and into the big top-floor apartment with the creaky floors, the groaning pipes, odd windows that view the yard. My little back room, no bigger than a closet, overlooks this space.

I'm so beat, though, I just want to crawl into my corner and sleep.

"Not too small, this place?" He sounds anxious.

I shake my head. The room seems okay, the mattress on the floor, the blankets, and the shelves for my things.

"Call your mom?" Frank gives orders in the form of a question. He acts all purposeful, as though he is going back downstairs to close up the store, but as I dial the number on the kitchen wall phone he lingers. He can't drag himself away from the magnetic field of my mother's voice, muffled, far off, but on the other end of the receiver. He stands in the doorway with that same towel he brought from downstairs, folding and refolding it in his hands.

"Mama," I say, and her voice on the phone suddenly hurts. I want to curl next to her and be a small girl again. My body feels too big, electric, like a Frankenstein body enclosing a tiny child's soul.

We laugh at some corny joke and Frank darts a glance at me, then stares at his feet and frowns. Reading between my Mama's pauses on the phone, I know she is hoping I'll miss the real land, and her, come back and resume my brilliant future at the tribal college. In spite of how I want to curl up in my city corner, I picture everything back home. On the wall of my room up north, there hang a bundle of sage and Grandma Roy's singing drum. On the opposite wall, I taped up posters and photos. Ever since I was little, I slept with a worn bear and a new brown dog. And my real dog, too, curled at my feet sometimes, if Mama didn't catch us. I never liked dolls. I made good scores in math. I get to missing my room and my dog and I lose track of Mama's voice.

Sample Passage III

SOCIAL STUDIES: This passage is adapted from volume 2 of Blanche Wiesen Cook's biography *Eleanor Roosevelt* (©1999 by Blanche Wiesen Cook).

Eleanor Roosevelt [ER] is the most controversial First Lady in United States history. Her journey to greatness, her voyage out beyond the confines of good wife and devoted mother, involved determination and amazing courage. It also involved one of history's most unique partnerships. Franklin Delano Roosevelt [FDR] admired his wife, appreciated her strengths, and depended on her integrity.

However, ER and FDR had different priorities, occasionally competing goals, and often disagreed. In the White House they ran two distinct and separate courts.

By 1933 [her first year as First Lady], ER was an accomplished woman who had achieved several of her life's goals. With her partners, ER was a businesswoman who co-owned the Val-Kill crafts factory, a political leader who edited and copublished the *Women's Democratic News,* and an educator who co-owned and taught at a New York school for girls.

As First Lady, Eleanor Roosevelt did things that had never been done before. She upset race traditions, championed a New Deal for women, and on certain issues actually ran a parallel administration. On housing and the creation of model communities, for example, ER made decisions and engineered policy.

At the center of a network of influential women who ran the Women's Committee of the Democratic Party led by Molly Dewson, ER worked closely with the women who had dominated the nation's social reform struggles for decades. With FDR's election, the goals of the great progressive pioneers, Jane Addams, Florence Kelley, and Lillian Wald, were at last at the forefront of the country's agenda. ER's mentors since 1903, they had battled on the margins of national politics since the 1880s for public health, universal education, community centers, sanitation programs, and government responsibility for the welfare of the nation's poor and neglected people.

Now their views were brought directly into the White House. ER lobbied for them personally with her new administrative allies, in countless auditoriums, as a radio broadcaster, and in monthly, weekly, and, by 1936, daily columns. Called "Eleanor Everywhere," she was interested in everyone.

Every life was sacred and worthy, to be improved by education, employment, health care, and affordable housing. Her goal was simple, a life of dignity and decency for all. She was uninterested in complex theories, and demanded action for betterment. She feared violent revolution, but was not afraid of socialism—and she courted radicals.

As fascism and communism triumphed in Europe and Asia, ER and FDR were certain that there was a middle way, what ER called an American "revolution without bloodshed." Her abiding conviction, however, was that nothing good would happen to promote the people's interest unless the people themselves organized to demand government responses. A people's movement required active citizen participation, and ER's self-appointed task was to agitate and inspire community action, encourage united democratic movements for change.

Between 1933 and 1938, while the Depression raged and the New Deal unfolded, ER worked with the popular front. She called for alliances of activists to fight poverty and racism at home, and to oppose isolationism internationally.

Active with the women's peace movement, ER spoke regularly at meetings of the Women's International League for Peace and Freedom, and the Conference on the Cause and Cure of War. She departed, however, from pacifist and isolationist positions and encouraged military preparedness, collective security, and ever-widening alliances.

Between 1933 and 1938 ER published countless articles and six books. She wrote in part for herself, to clear her mind and focus her thoughts. But she also wrote to disagree with her husband. From that time to this, no other First Lady has actually rushed for her pen to jab her husband's public decisions. But ER did so routinely, including in her 1938 essay *This Troubled World,* which was a point-by-point rejection of FDR's major international decisions.

To contemplate ER's life of example and responsibility is to forestall gloom. She understood, above all, that politics is not an isolated individualist adventure. She sought alliances, created community, worked with movements for justice and peace. Against great odds, and under terrific pressure, she refused to withdraw from controversy. She brought her network of agitators and activists into the White House, and never considered a political setback a permanent defeat. She enjoyed the game, and weathered the abuse.

Sample Passage IV

SOCIAL STUDIES: This passage is adapted from Morton Hunt's *The Story of Psychology* (©1993 by Morton Hunt). In the passage, the term *maturation* refers to the process of growth and development, and the term *perceptual ability* refers to the capacity to recognize something through the senses (sight, smell, touch, etc.).

Much maturation research is concerned with physical skills and physical attributes, and adds little to our knowledge of the growth of the mind. But research on the development of perceptual abilities begins to provide solid factual answers to the ancient central question of psychology: How much is due to nature and how much to nurture (or, in developmental terms, to maturation and to learning)?

The work has been focused on early infancy, when perceptual abilities evolve rapidly; its aim is to discover when each new ability first appears, the assumption being that at its first appearance, the new ability arises not from learning but from maturation of the optic nervous structures and especially of that part of the brain cortex where visual signals are received and interpreted.

Much has been learned by simply watching infants. What, exactly, do very young infants see? Since we cannot ask them what they see, how can we find out?

In 1961, the psychologist Robert Fantz devised an ingenious method of doing so. He designed a stand in which, on the bottom level, the baby lies on her back, looking up. A few feet above is a display area where the experimenter puts two large cards, each containing a design—a white circle, a yellow circle, a bull's-eye, a simple sketch of a face. The researcher, peering down through a tiny peephole, can watch the movement of the baby's eyes and time how long they are directed at one or the other of each pair of patterns. Fantz found that at two months babies looked twice as long at a bull's-eye as at a circle of solid color, and twice as long at a sketch of a face as at a bull's-eye. Evidently, even a two-month-old can distinguish major differences and direct her gaze toward what she finds more interesting.

Using this technique, developmental psychologists have learned a great deal about what infants see and when they begin to see it. In the first week infants distinguish light and dark patterns; during the first month they begin to track slowly moving objects; by the second month they begin to have depth perception, coordinate the movement of the eyes, and differentiate among hues and levels of brightness; by three months they can glance from one object to another, and can distinguish among family members; by four months they focus at varying distances, make increasingly fine distinctions, and begin to recognize the meaning of what they see (they look longer at a normal sketch of a face than at one in which the features have been scrambled); and from four to seven months they achieve stereopsis, recognize that a shape held at different angles is still the same shape, and gain near-adult ability to focus at varying distances.

Exactly how maturation and experience interact in the brain tissues to produce such developmental changes is becoming clear from neuroscience research. Microscopic examination of the brains of infants shows that as the brain triples in size during the first two years of life, a profusion of dendrites (branches) grow from its neurons and make contact with one another.

By the time a human is twelve, the brain has an estimated hundred trillion synapses (connections between nerve cells). Those connections are the wiring plan that establishes the brain's capabilities. Some of the synaptic connections are made automatically by chemical guidance, but others are made by the stimulus of experience during the period of rapid dendrite growth. Lacking such stimulus, the dendrites wither away without forming the needed synapses. Mice reared in the dark develop fewer dendritic spines and synaptic connections in the visual cortex than mice reared in the light, and even when exposed to light never attain normal vision.

Why should nature have done that? Why should perceptual development be possible only at a critical period and not later? It does not make evolutionary sense for the organism to be permanently impaired in sensory performance just because it fails to have the proper experiences at specific times in its development. But some brain researchers say that there is an offsetting advantage: the essential experiences are almost always available at the right time, and they fine-tune the brain structure so as to provide far more specific perceptual powers than could result from genetic control of synapse formation.

With that, the vague old terms nature and nurture take on precise new meaning. Now, after so many centuries of speculation, we catch the first glimpse of how mind is constructed out of matter by experience.

Sample Passage V

HUMANITIES: This passage is adapted from the essay "Faith and Work" by Scott Russell Sanders (©1995 by Scott Russell Sanders).

The difference between a machine and a tool—between a bread-maker and a bread pan—is that a tool extends human skills, a machine replaces them. When the freedom and craft have been squeezed out of work it becomes toil, without mystery or meaning, and that is why many people hate their jobs. You can measure the drudgery of a job by the number of layers of supervision required to keep the wheels spinning or the cash registers ringing. Toil drains us; but good work may renew us, by giving expression to our powers.

A generation or two ago it would have seemed less strange to relish hard work. My grandparents might smile at the laziness of Tom Sawyer, who fooled others into doing his chores, but they would remind you that Tom was a child. Grown-ups do their own chores, unless they are idlers, good-for-nothings, ne'er-do-wells. Grown-ups look after their own needs, provide for their families, help their neighbors, do something useful. So my grandparents taught by word and example. Any job worth doing is worth doing right, they used to say. To try sliding by with the least effort, my grandparents believed, was to be guilty of a sin called sloth.

I knew this cluster of values by experience long before I heard it referred to as the work ethic, a phrase that has lost its edge from tumbling over the lips of too many cynical bosses and politicians. Whatever happened to the work ethic? laments the manager who wishes to squeeze more profit from his employees. Whatever happened to the work ethic? groans the official who wants to shrink the welfare rolls. As I understand it, a regard for the necessity and virtue of work has nothing to do with productivity or taxes, and everything to do with fulfilling one's humanity. As I have seen it embodied in the lives not only of grandparents but of parents and neighbors and friends, this ethic arises from a belief that the creation is a sacred gift, and that by working we express our gratitude and celebrate our powers. To honor that gift, we should live simply, honestly, conservingly, saving money and patching clothes and fixing what breaks, sharing what we have.

Those values are under assault every minute of the day in a consumer economy—from advertising, from the glittering goodies in stores, from the luxurious imagery of television, magazines, and films, and from a philosophy that views the universe not as a gift to be honored but as a warehouse to be ransacked. If money is meaning, if winning the lottery or beating the stock market defines success, if the goal of life is easy sensation, then why lift a finger so long as you can force someone or something else to do it for you?

I can think of many reasons to lift a finger, among them the delight in exercising skill, in sharing labor with companions, in planning a task and carrying it through, in bringing some benefit to the world. But the chief reason for relishing work is that it allows us to practice our faith, whatever that faith may be. The Buddha advised his followers to seek right livelihood, to provide for their needs in a modest and responsible manner, with respect for other creatures, in harmony with the way of things. We show our understanding of the way of things by the quality of our work, whether or not we have heard the Buddha's teachings. The old theological debate as to whether salvation is to be gained by works or by faith begins from a false dichotomy. Faith concerns our sense of what is real, what is valuable, what is holy; work is how we act out that faith.

The Shakers condensed their faith into the maxim, "Hands to work, hearts to God." Anyone who has looked at their furniture or buildings can sense the clarity of their vision. "One feels that for the Shaker craftsmen," Thomas Merton observed, "love of God and love of truth in one's own work came to the same thing, and that work itself was a prayer, a communion with the inmost spiritual reality of things and so with God." Mother Ann Lee, who launched the Shaker movement, counseled her followers to "Do all your work as if you had a thousand years to live, and as you would if you knew you must die tomorrow."

If the purpose of life is not to acquire but to *in*quire, to seek understanding, to discover all we can about ourselves and the universe, to commune with the source of things, then we should care less about what we earn—money, prestige, salvation—and more about what we learn. In light of all we have to learn, the difference between dying tomorrow and a hundred years from tomorrow is not very great.

Sample Passage VI

NATURAL SCIENCE: This passage is adapted from *Fire in America: A Cultural History of Wildland and Rural Fire* by Stephen J. Pyne (©1982 by Princeton University Press).

Lightning affects electrical equilibrium on the earth. Air is a poor conductor, but some electricity constantly leaks to the atmosphere, creating an electrical potential. Electricity moves back according to the gradient [change in potential with distance]. During a thunderstorm, the gradient becomes very steep, and the electrical potential discharges as lightning. The discharge may move between any oppositely charged regions—from cloud to earth, from earth to cloud, or from cloud to cloud. It was calculated as early as 1887 that the earth would lose almost all its charge in less than an hour unless the supply were replenished; that is, on a global scale, lightning will discharge to the earth every hour a quantity of electricity equal to the earth's entire charge. Thunderstorms are thus an electromagnetic as well as a thermodynamic necessity. It has been reckoned that the earth experiences some 1,800 storms per hour, or 44,000 per day. Collectively, these storms produce 100 cloud-to-ground discharges per second, or better than 8 million per day globally. And these estimates are probably low. The total energy in lightning bolts varies greatly, but about 250 kilowatt hours of electricity are packed into each stroke. Almost 75 percent of this total energy is lost to heat during discharge.

Two types of discharge patterns are commonly identified: the cold stroke, whose main return [ground-to-cloud] stroke is of intense current but of short duration, and the hot stroke, involving lesser currents of longer duration. Cold lightning, with its high voltage, generally has mechanical or explosive effects; hot lightning is more apt to start fires. Studies in the Northern Rockies suggest that about one stroke in 25 has the electrical characteristics needed to start a fire. Whether it does or not depends strongly on the object it strikes, the fuel properties of the object, and the local weather. Ignition requires both heat and kindling. Lightning supplies the one with its current and occasionally finds the other among the fine fuels of rotten wood, needles, grass, or dustlike debris blown from a tree by the explosive shock of the bolt itself.

The consequences of lightning are complex. Any natural force of this magnitude will influence the biological no less than the geophysical environment, and the secondary effects of lightning are significant to life. Lightning helps to fix atmospheric nitrogen into a form that rain can bring to earth. In areas of heavy thunderstorm activity, lightning can function as a major predator on trees, either through direct injury or by physiological damage. In the ponderosa pine forests of Arizona, for example, one forester has estimated that lightning mortality runs between 0.7 and 1.0 percent per year. Other researchers have placed mortality as high as 25–33 percent. For southern pines, the figure may be even steeper. A study in Arkansas calculated that 70 percent of mortality, by volume, was due to lightning. These figures describe only direct injury, primarily the mechanical destruction of branches and bole; the other major causes of mortality—insects, wind, and mistletoe—are likely secondary effects brought about in trees weakened by lightning. All of these effects, in turn, may be camouflaged by fire induced by lightning.

The process of "electrocution" is increasingly recognized. Lightning scorch areas of between 0.25 and 25 acres have been identified. Nor is the process limited to trees: it has been documented for grasses, tomatoes, potatoes, cabbages, tea, and other crops. Long attributed to inscrutable "die-offs" or to infestation by insects or diseases (often a secondary effect), such sites are now recognized worldwide as a product of physiological trauma caused by lightning.

The most spectacular product of lightning is fire. Except in tropical rain forests and on ice-mantled land masses, lightning fire has occurred in every terrestrial environment on the globe, contributing to a natural mosaic of vegetation types. Even in tropical landscapes lightning bombardment by itself may frequently be severe enough to produce a mosaic pattern similar to that resulting from lightning fire. Lightning fires have ignited desert grasslands, tundra, chaparral, swamplands, marshes, grasslands, and, of course, forests. Though the intensity and frequency of these fires vary by region, their existence is undeniable.

Sample Passage VII

NATURAL SCIENCE: This passage is adapted from "Publish and Punish: Science's Snowball Effect" by Jon Van (©1997 by The Chicago Tribune Company).

It's a scientific finding so fundamental that it certainly will make the history books and maybe snag a Nobel Prize if it pans out, but the notion that cosmic snowballs are constantly pelting Earth is something Louis Frank just as soon would have ducked.

Frank is the University of Iowa physicist whose research led him to declare more than a decade ago that Earth is being bombarded by hundreds of house-sized comets day after day that rain water on our planet and are the reason we have oceans. That weather report caused the widely respected scientist to acquire a certain reputation among his colleagues as a bit unstable, an otherwise estimable fellow whose hard work may have pushed him over the edge.

Frank and his associate, John Sigwarth, probably went a way toward salvaging their reputations when they presented new evidence that leaves little doubt Earth is indeed being bombarded by *something* in a manner consistent with Frank's small-comet theory. Rather than gloating or anticipating glory, Frank seemed relieved that part of a long ordeal was ending. "I knew we'd be in for it when we first put forth the small-comet theory," Frank conceded, "but I was naive about just how bad it would be. We were outvoted by about 10,000 to 1 by our colleagues. I thought it would have been more like 1,000 to 1."

To the non-scientist this may seem a bit strange. After all, the point of science is to discover information and insights about how nature works. Shouldn't every scientist be eager to overturn existing ideas and replace them with his or her own? In theory, that is the case, but in practice, scientists are almost as loath to embrace radically new ideas as the rest of us.

"Being a scientist puts you into a constant schizophrenic existence," contends Richard Zare, chairman of the National Science Board. "You have to believe and yet question beliefs at the same time. If you are a complete cynic and believe nothing, you do nothing and get nowhere, but if you believe too much, you fool yourself."

It was in the early 1980s when the small-comet theory started to haunt Frank and Sigwarth, who was Frank's graduate student studying charged particles called plasmas, which erupt from the sun and cause the aurora borealis (northern lights). As they analyzed photos of the electrical phenomena that accompany sunspots, they noted dark specks appearing in several images from NASA's Dynamics Explorer 1 satellite. They assumed these were caused by static in the transmission.

After a while their curiosity about the dark spots grew into a preoccupation, then bordered on obsession. Try as they did, the scientists couldn't find any plausible explanation of the pattern of dark spots that appeared on their images. The notion that the equipment was picking up small amounts of water entering Earth's upper atmosphere kept presenting itself as the most likely answer.

Based on their images, the Iowa scientists estimated 20 comets an hour—each about 30 feet or so across and carrying 100 tons of water—were bombarding the Earth. At that rate, they would produce water vapor that would add about an inch of water to the planet every 10,000 years, Frank concluded. That may not seem like much, but when talking about a planet billions of years old, it adds up.

Such intimate interaction between Earth and space suggests a fundamentally different picture of human evolution—which depends on water—than is commonly presented by scientists. Frank had great difficulty getting his ideas into a physics journal 11 years ago and was almost hooted from the room when he presented his theory at scientific meetings. Despite the derision, colleagues continued to respect Frank's mainstream work on electrically charged particles in space and the imaging cameras he designed that were taken aboard recent NASA spacecraft to explore Earth's polar regions.

Unbeknown to most, in addition to gathering information on the northern lights, Frank and Sigwarth designed the equipment to be able to snatch better views of any small comets the spacecraft might happen upon. It was those images from the latest flights that caused even harsh critics of the small-comet theory to concede that some water-bearing objects appear to be entering Earth's atmosphere with regularity.

To be sure, it has not been proved that they are comets, let alone that they have anything to do with the oceans. But Frank's evidence opens the matter up to study. Had he been a researcher of lesser standing, his theory probably would have died long ago.

Chapter 8: Improving Your Science Score

The ACT science test asks you to answer 40 multiple-choice questions in 35 minutes. The questions measure the interpretation, analysis, evaluation, and problem-solving skills associated with science. The science test is made up of several passages, each of which is followed by multiple-choice questions.

Content of the ACT Science Test

The content areas of the ACT science test parallel the content of courses commonly taught in grades 7 through 12 and in entry-level college courses. Passages on the test represent the following content areas (examples of subjects included in each content area are given in parentheses):

- **Biology** (botany, cell biology, ecology, evolution, genetics, microbiology, zoology)
- **Chemistry** (acids and bases, biochemistry, kinetics and equilibria, nuclear chemistry, organic chemistry, properties of matter, thermo-chemistry)

- **Earth/space sciences** (astronomy, environmental science, geology, meteorology, oceanography)
- **Physics** (electromagnetism, fluids, mechanics, optics, thermodynamics, solids)

Advanced knowledge in these areas is not required, but background knowledge acquired in general, introductory science courses may be needed to correctly respond to some of the items.

The science test stresses science skills and practices over recall of scientific content, complex mathematics skills, and reading ability. The science skills and practices fall into three reporting categories. A brief description of each reporting category is as follows.

- **Interpretation of Data:** Manipulate and analyze scientific data presented in tables, graphs, and diagrams (e.g., recognize trends in data, translate tabular data into graphs, interpolate and extrapolate, and reason mathematically).
- **Scientific Investigation:** Understand experimental tools, procedures, and design (e.g., identify variables and controls) and compare, extend, and modify experiments (e.g., predict the results of additional trials).
- **Evaluation of Models, Inferences, and Experimental Results:** Judge the validity of scientific information and formulate conclusions and predictions based on that information (e.g., determine which explanation for a scientific phenomenon is supported by new findings).

The use of calculators is not permitted on the science test but should also not be needed.

Format of the ACT Science Test

The scientific information presented in each passage of the ACT science test is conveyed in one of three different formats:

- The **Data Representation** format requires you to understand, evaluate, and interpret information presented in graphic or tabular form.
- The **Research Summaries** format requires you to understand, evaluate, analyze, and interpret the design, execution, and results of one or more experiments.
- The **Conflicting Viewpoints** format requires you to evaluate several alternative theories, hypotheses, or viewpoints on a specific observable phenomenon.

Turn to chapter 1 to find out the approximate proportion of the ACT science test devoted to each of these three different passage formats.

You'll find examples of the kinds of passages that you're likely to find in each of the formats in the pages that follow.

The sample ACT science test passages and questions in this section are representative of those you'll encounter in the actual ACT. The following chart illustrates the content area, format, and topic covered by each sample passage given in the remainder of this section:

Passage	Content area	Format	Topic of passage
I	Chemistry	Data Representation	Calorimetry
II	Physics	Research Summaries	Illuminance
III	Biology	Conflicting Viewpoints	Conjugation

Data Representation Format

This type of format presents scientific information in charts, tables, graphs, and diagrams similar to those found in science journals and texts. Examples of tables used in an actual Data Representation passage administered to students are found in Sample Passage I that follows.

The questions you'll find in the Data Representation format ask you to interpret charts and tables, read graphs, evaluate scatterplots, and analyze information presented in diagrams. There are five sample questions presented with the sample Data Representation passage.

Sample Passage I

A *bomb calorimeter* is used to determine the amount of heat released when a substance is burned in oxygen (Figure 1). The heat, measured in kilojoules (kJ), is calculated from the change in temperature of the water in the bomb calorimeter. Table 1 shows the amounts of heat released when different foods were burned in a bomb calorimeter. Table 2 shows the amounts of heat released when different amounts of sucrose (table sugar) were burned. Table 3 shows the amounts of heat released when various chemical compounds were burned.

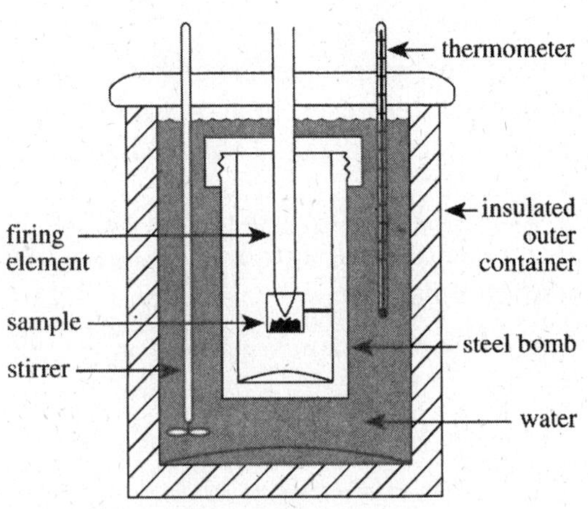

Figure 1

Figure 1 adapted from Antony C. Wilbraham, Dennis D. Staley, and Michael S. Matta, *Chemistry*. ©1995 by Addison-Wesley Publishing Company, Inc.

Table 1

Food	Mass (g)	Change in water temperature (°C)	Heat released (kJ)
Bread	1.0	8.3	10.0
Cheese	1.0	14.1	17.0
Egg	1.0	5.6	6.7
Potato	1.0	2.7	3.2

Table 1 adapted from American Chemical Society, *ChemCom: Chemistry in the Community*. ©1993 by American Chemical Society.

Table 2

Amount of sucrose (g)	Heat released (kJ)
0.1	1.6
0.5	8.0
1.0	16.0
2.0	32.1
4.0	64.0

Table 3

Chemical compound	Molecular formula	Mass (g)	Heat released (kJ)
Methanol	CH_3OH	0.5	11.4
Ethanol	C_2H_5OH	0.5	14.9
Benzene	C_6H_6	0.5	21.0
Octane	C_8H_{18}	0.5	23.9

1. According to Tables 1 and 2, as the mass of successive sucrose samples increased, the change in the water temperature produced when the sample was burned most likely:

   A. increased only.
   B. decreased only.
   C. increased, then decreased.
   D. remained the same.

2. Which of the following graphs best illustrates the relationship between the heat released by the foods listed in Table 1 and the change in water temperature?

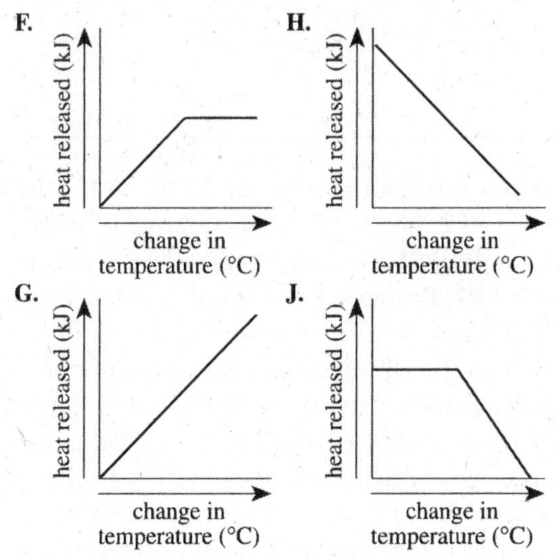

3. Based on the data in Table 2, one can conclude that when the mass of sucrose is decreased by one-half, the amount of heat released when it is burned in a bomb calorimeter will:
   A. increase by one-half.
   B. decrease by one-half.
   C. increase by one-fourth.
   D. decrease by one-fourth.

4. Which of the following lists the foods from Tables 1 and 2 in increasing order of the amount of heat released per gram of food?
   F. Potato, egg, bread, sucrose, cheese
   G. Sucrose, cheese, bread, egg, potato
   H. Bread, cheese, egg, potato, sucrose
   J. Sucrose, potato, egg, bread, cheese

5. Based on the information in Tables 1 and 2, the heat released from the burning of 5.0 g of potato in a bomb calorimeter would most likely be closest to which of the following?
   A. 5 kJ
   B. 10 kJ
   C. 15 kJ
   D. 20 kJ

Discussion of Sample Passage I (Data Representation)

According to this Data Representation passage, the amount of heat generated when a material is burned in oxygen can be determined using a *bomb calorimeter.* The bomb calorimeter has an outer shell made of an insulating material. Inside this shell is a *bomb* (steel casing) immersed in a fixed amount of water. When a material is burned inside the bomb, the water absorbs heat generated by the combustion, causing the temperature of the water to increase. The amount of the increase in water temperature depends on the amount of heat absorbed by the water. So, if we measure the increase in water temperature, we can calculate the amount of heat released when a material is burned inside the bomb.

Note that the passage contains three tables. Table 1 lists the temperature change of the water and the amount of heat generated when 1 g of each of four foods is burned in the calorimeter. Table 2 lists the amounts of heat released when various quantities of the sugar sucrose are burned. Table 3 lists several chemical compounds and their chemical formulas, as well as the amount of heat released for each compound when 0.5 g of the compound is burned in the calorimeter.

1. According to Tables 1 and 2, as the mass of successive sucrose samples increased, the change in the water temperature produced when the sample was burned most likely:

   A. increased only.
   B. decreased only.
   C. increased, then decreased.
   D. remained the same.

Question 1 asks you to determine how the change in water temperature varied as the amount of sucrose burned increased, based on the data in Tables 1 and 2. Notice that the change in water temperature and the amount of heat released are listed in Table 1 for each material burned. In Table 2, the amount of sucrose burned and the amount of heat released are listed, but the change in water temperature is not listed. Let us assume that the relationship between the amount of heat released and the change in water temperature for sucrose is the same as the relationship between the amount of heat released and the change in water temperature for the materials listed in Table 1. According to Table 2, as the amount of sucrose burned increased, the amount of heat released steadily increased. According to Table 1, as the amount of heat released increased, the magnitude of the change in water temperature steadily increased. Therefore, as the amount of sucrose burned increased, the magnitude of the change in the water temperature steadily increased. The best answer is **A**.

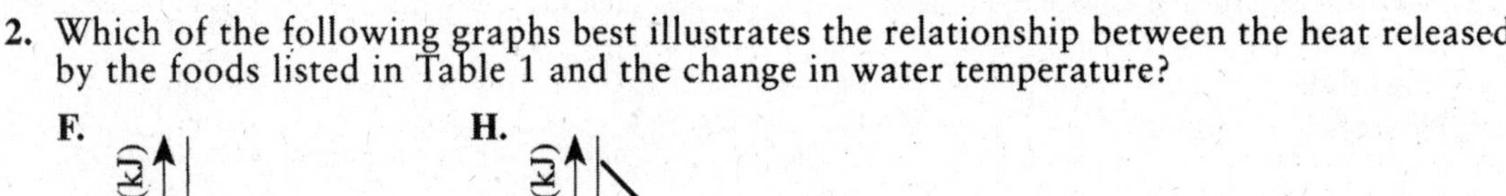

2. Which of the following graphs best illustrates the relationship between the heat released by the foods listed in Table 1 and the change in water temperature?

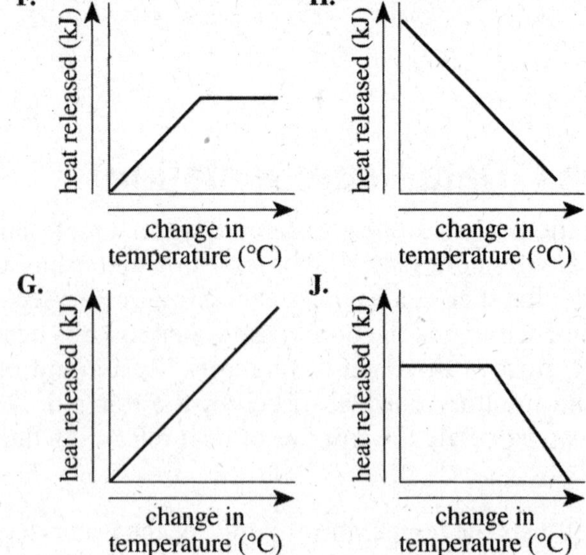

Question 2 asks you to choose a graph that best illustrates the relationship between the amount of heat released and the change in water temperature for the four substances listed in Table 1. According to the data in Table 1, as the change in water temperature increased, the amount of heat released steadily increased. No data in Table 1 supports the conclusion that as the change in water temperature increased the amount of heat released decreased or remained constant. Therefore, **G** is the best answer.

3. Based on the data in Table 2, one can conclude that when the mass of sucrose is decreased by one-half, the amount of heat released when it is burned in a bomb calorimeter will:

A. increase by one-half.
B. decrease by one-half.
C. increase by one-fourth.
D. decrease by one-fourth.

Question 3 asks you to predict, based on the data in Table 2, the fractional change in the amount of heat released by sucrose when the amount of sucrose burned is decreased by half. An examination of the data in Table 2 shows that when the amount of sucrose burned was decreased by half, the amount of heat released decreased by half. For example, when the amount of sucrose burned was decreased from 4.0 g to 2.0 g, the amount of heat released decreased from 64.0 kJ to 32.1 kJ; that is, the amount of heat released also decreased by half. (The amount of heat released actually decreased by 31.9 kJ, which is not exactly half of 64.0 kJ, but the 0.1 kJ difference between 31.9 kJ and 32.0 kJ can be attributed to limitations in the precision of the measurements [the amount of heat released is rounded off to the nearest 0.1 kJ] and can be ignored.) The amount of heat released was also decreased by half when the amount of sucrose burned was decreased from 2.0 g to 1.0 g and again when the amount of sucrose burned was decreased from 1.0 g to 0.5 g. Therefore, one can conclude that when the amount of sucrose burned is decreased by half, the amount of heat released during the burning of sucrose is decreased by half, so **B** is the best answer.

4. Which of the following lists the foods from Tables 1 and 2 in increasing order of the amount of heat released per gram of food?

F. Potato, egg, bread, sucrose, cheese
G. Sucrose, cheese, bread, egg, potato
H. Bread, cheese, egg, potato, sucrose
J. Sucrose, potato, egg, bread, cheese

Question 4 asks you to list the foods from Tables 1 and 2 in increasing order, from the food that releases the least amount of heat per gram of food to the food that releases the greatest amount of heat per gram of food. According to Table 1, the amount of heat released was determined for 1 g samples of each of the foods listed. Therefore, the amount of heat listed in Table 1 for each food item is the amount of heat released per gram of food. In Table 2, the amount of heat released is given for various masses of sucrose. To get the amount of heat released per gram of sucrose we can divide the amount of heat released by the mass of sucrose that was burned. However, an easier method is to notice that a trial was conducted using 1.0 g of sucrose, and during that trial, the amount of heat released was 16.0 kJ. Therefore, the amount of heat released per g of sucrose was 16.0 kJ/g. An inspection of the heat released by the combustion of the foods in Table 1 shows

Improving Your Score

that the potato sample released the least amount of heat (3.2 kJ/g), followed by the egg sample (6.7 kJ/g), the bread sample (10.0 kJ/g), and the cheese sample (17.0 kJ/g). The amount of heat per g released by sucrose, 16.0 kJ/g, places sucrose between the cheese sample and the bread sample. Therefore, the correct order is potato, egg, bread, sucrose, cheese. The best answer is **F**.

5. Based on the information in Tables 1 and 2, the heat released from the burning of 5.0 g of potato in a bomb calorimeter would be closest to which of the following?

A. 5 kJ
B. 10 kJ
C. 15 kJ
D. 20 kJ

Question 5 asks you to use Tables 1 and 2 to estimate the amount of heat released when 5.0 g of potato is burned. Notice that Table 1 provides you with the amount of heat released (3.2 kJ) when 1.0 g of potato is burned. You might guess that burning 5.0 g of potato in the calorimeter would cause the release of five times the amount of heat released when 1.0 g of potato is burned. Do you have any evidence to support this guess? Table 1 only lists the amount of heat released when 1.0 g of potato is burned. Table 2 provides the amount of heat released from various amounts of sucrose, but not potatoes. In the absence of information to the contrary, you can assume that the relationship between the amount of potato burned and the amount of heat released is similar to the relationship between the amount of sucrose burned and the amount of heat released. According to Table 2, the heat released in kJ equals 16 times the mass of sucrose burned in grams. Note that this relationship holds whether 0.1 g of sucrose is burned or 4.0 g of sucrose is burned. For example, if 0.1 g of sucrose is burned, 0.1 g × 16 kJ released per g of sucrose = 1.6 kJ of heat released. If 4.0 g of sucrose is burned, 4.0 g × 16 kJ released per g of sucrose = 64 kJ of heat released. This relationship is a linear relationship. If the relationship between the amount of potato burned and the amount of heat released is also linear, then burning five times the amount of potato will release five times the amount of heat. Because 3.2 kJ of heat was released when 1.0 g of potato was burned, 5 × 3.2 kJ = 16 kJ will be released when 5.0 g of potato is burned. The answer closest to 16 kJ is 15 kJ, choice **C**.

Research Summaries Format

This type of format provides descriptions of one or more related experiments or studies similar to those conducted by researchers or science students. The descriptions typically include the design, procedures, and results of the experiments or studies. The results are often depicted in graphs or tables. Sample Passage II provides an example of the Research Summaries format that shows the results of two different experiments with light bulbs. The questions you'll find in the Research Summaries format ask you to understand, evaluate, and interpret the design and procedures of the experiments or studies and to analyze the results. There are five sample questions presented with this sample Research Summaries passage.

Sample Passage II

A student studied illumination using the following equipment:

- 6 identical light bulbs (Bulbs A–F)
- Fixture 1, light fixture for Bulbs A–E
- Fixture 2, light fixture for Bulb F
- 2 identical paraffin blocks
- A sheet of aluminum foil having the same length and width as a paraffin block
- A meterstick

Light could pass through each paraffin block, and each block glowed when light passed through it. The aluminum foil was placed between the 2 blocks. The light fixtures, light bulbs, blocks, foil, and the meterstick were arranged as shown in Figure 1.

aluminum foil
Fixture 1
paraffin blocks
Fixture 2
A
B
C
D
E
F
meterstick
← L →← 0.200 m →

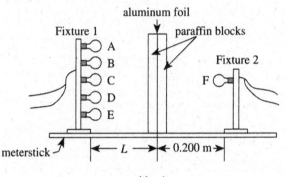

side view

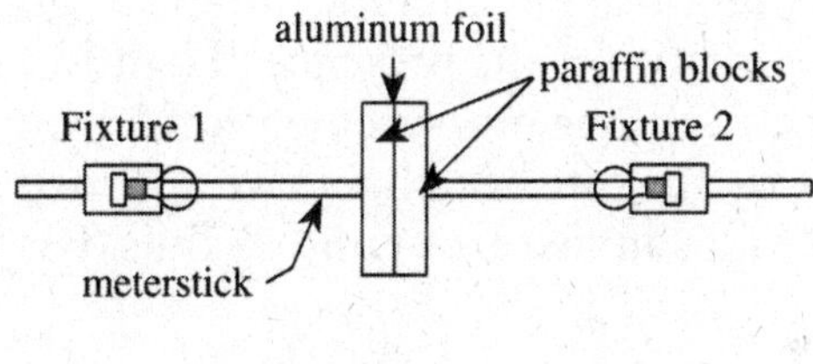

top view

Figure 1

In the following experiments, the base of Fixture 2 was always 0.200 m from the aluminum foil, and L was the distance from the base of Fixture 1 to the aluminum foil. The distance between adjacent bulbs in Fixture 1 was the same for all of the bulbs.

Bulb F was always lit.

Experiment 1

The student turned the room lights off, lit Bulb A, and varied L until the 2 blocks looked equally bright. This process was repeated using Bulbs B–E. The results are shown in Table 1.

Table 1

Bulb lit (in addition to Bulb F)	L (m) when the blocks looked equally bright
A	0.198
B	0.203
C	0.205
D	0.195
E	0.199

Experiment 2

The procedure from Experiment 1 was repeated using various combinations of Bulbs A–E. The results are shown in Table 2.

Table 2

Bulbs lit (in addition to Bulb F)	L (m) when the blocks looked equally bright
A and B	0.281
A, B, and C	0.347
A, B, C, and D	0.400
A, B, C, D, and E	0.446

Discussion of Sample Passage II (Research Summaries)

This Research Summaries passage describes two experiments in which a student uses two identical paraffin blocks to compare the brightness of the light from one source (Fixture 1) with the brightness of the light from another source (Fixture 2). Fixture 1 contains five light bulbs, Bulbs A through E, and Fixture 2 contains only one light bulb, Bulb F (see Figure 1 in the passage). The two paraffin blocks are set between the fixtures. The two blocks are separated by a sheet of aluminum foil, so that the block on the left is illuminated only by bulbs in Fixture 1, and the block on the right is illuminated only by Bulb F in Fixture 2. The distance, *L*, between Fixture 1 and the aluminum foil can be varied, but the distance between Fixture 2 and the foil, 0.200 m, is fixed.

In Experiment 1, one bulb at a time is lit in Fixture 1, and Bulb F is lit in Fixture 2. For each combination of lit bulbs, *L* is varied until the two blocks glow equally brightly. This value of *L* is recorded in Table 1 along with the combination of lit bulbs used to obtain this value of *L*. In Experiment 2, two or more bulbs at a time are lit in Fixture 1, and Bulb F is lit in Fixture 2. For each combination of lit bulbs, *L* is varied until the two blocks glow equally brightly. This value of *L* is recorded in Table 2 along with the combination of lit bulbs.

6. Which of the following best explains why the student turned off the room lights?

F. To ensure that only the light from Bulbs A–F illuminated the 2 paraffin blocks
G. To ensure that light from outside the room illuminated the 2 paraffin blocks unequally
H. To keep the 2 paraffin blocks from casting shadows, because shadows would make the meterstick harder to read
J. To keep the 2 light fixtures from casting shadows, because shadows would make the meterstick harder to read

Question 6 asks you why the student turned off the room lights before measuring *L*. Recall that the student was to compare the brightness of the light produced by Fixture 1 to the brightness of the light produced by Fixture 2 under a variety of conditions. The presence of light sources other than Fixtures 1 and 2 could have introduced error into the measurements of *L* by making one fixture or the other seem brighter than it really was. The overhead lights were turned off so that all of the light on the blocks came from the light bulbs in Fixtures 1 and 2. Thus, **F** is the best answer.

7. During Experiment 2, suppose the student replaced Fixture 1 with a new fixture. The new fixture held 6 light bulbs, each bulb identical to Bulb F. When all 6 bulbs in the new fixture were lit and the paraffin blocks looked equally bright, *L* would probably have been closest to:

A. 0.262 m.
B. 0.331 m.
C. 0.415 m.
D. 0.490 m.

Question 7 proposes that Fixture 1 be replaced by a different fixture holding six light bulbs instead of five. Each of the light bulbs in the new fixture is identical to Bulb F. The question asks you to estimate L for the case that all six light bulbs in the new fixture, as well as Bulb F, are lit. According to Table 2, as the number of lit bulbs in Fixture 1 increased from two to five, L increased. So if the new fixture is used, increasing the number of lit bulbs from five to six, one would expect L to be greater than the value of L given in Table 2 for five lit bulbs in Fixture 1, 0.446 m. Only **D** contains a value for L exceeding 0.446 m, so **D** is the best answer.

8. The main purpose of Experiment 1 was to:

F. calibrate the meterstick.
G. determine the relationship between L and the number of lit bulbs.
H. determine if L depended on a lit bulb's position in Fixture 1.
J. find the brightness of Bulb F.

Question 8 asks you to determine the main purpose of Experiment 1. In Experiment 1, one bulb at a time was lit in Fixture 1, but the location of the lit bulb in Fixture 1 was varied. Thus, the main purpose of Experiment 1 must have been to determine the effect, if any, that the location of the lit bulb had on the value of L. Only **H** states that the purpose of Experiment 1 was to determine if the position of the lit bulb within Fixture 1 affected L, so **H** must be the best answer.

9. Suppose that all of the light bulbs in Fixture 1 were replaced with a single bulb. Based on Experiments 1 and 2, if the 2 paraffin blocks looked equally bright when Fixture 2 was 0.200 m from the aluminum foil and $L = 0.446$ m, the brightness of the new light bulb was most likely:

A. $\frac{1}{6}$ the brightness of one of the original bulbs.
B. $\frac{1}{5}$ the brightness of one of the original bulbs.
C. 5 times the brightness of one of the original bulbs.
D. 6 times the brightness of one of the original bulbs.

Question 9 proposes that the five light bulbs in Fixture 1 be replaced with a single light bulb, and that when the new bulb and Bulb F are lit, for the two blocks to glow equally brightly, L must equal 0.446 m. You are asked to compare the brightness of the new bulb to the brightness of one of the original bulbs in Fixture 1. According to Table 2, the two paraffin blocks glowed equally brightly when all five bulbs in Fixture 1 were lit and L was 0.446 m, the same as the L obtained with the new bulb. Thus, the brightness of the new bulb would have to equal the sum of the brightness of the five original bulbs. Because each of the five original bulbs had the same brightness, the new bulb would have to be five times as bright as one of the original bulbs. Only **C** is consistent with this conclusion, so the best answer is **C**.

10. In Experiment 2, suppose the student had replaced Bulb F with a much brighter light bulb, Bulb G. Compared to *L* when Bulb F was used, *L* when Bulb G was used would have been:

F. greater for every combination of lit bulbs.
G. smaller for every combination of lit bulbs.
H. smaller when Bulbs A–E were simultaneously lit and greater when other combinations of light bulbs were lit.
J. greater when both Bulbs A and B were simultaneously lit and smaller when other combinations of light bulbs were lit.

Question 10 proposes that in Experiment 2, Bulb F be replaced by a much brighter bulb, Bulb G. For each combination of lit bulbs in Fixture 1 and Bulb G lit in Fixture 2, when the two paraffin blocks are equally bright, how would the value of *L* compare to that obtained when Bulb F was used in Fixture 2? Because Bulb G is brighter than Bulb F and would be the same distance (0.200 m) away from the aluminum foil as Bulb F, the paraffin block closer to Bulb G would glow more brightly than it glowed when Bulb F was used. Thus, for each combination of lit bulbs in Fixture 1, to make the two blocks glow with equal brightness, Fixture 1 would have to be closer to the blocks than when Bulb F was used. That is, when Bulb G was used, *L* for each combination of lit bulbs in Fixture 1 would have to be less than when Bulb F was used for the two blocks to glow with equal brightness. Only choice **G** is consistent with this conclusion. The best answer is **G**.

Conflicting Viewpoints Format

This type of format provides several alternative theories, hypotheses, or viewpoints on a specific observable phenomenon. These conflicting viewpoints are based on differing premises or on incomplete data and are inconsistent with one another. Sample Passage III, a biology passage on gene replication, is an example of the Conflicting Viewpoints format. Notice that this passage presents the theories of four different students.

The questions you'll find in the Conflicting Viewpoints format ask you to understand, analyze, evaluate, and compare several competing theories, hypotheses, or viewpoints. Five sample questions are presented with this sample Conflicting Viewpoints passage.

Sample Passage III

Many bacteria contain *plasmids* (small, circular DNA molecules). Plasmids can be transferred from 1 bacterium to another. For this to occur, the plasmid *replicates* (produces a linear copy of itself). The relative position of the genes is the same on the original plasmid and on the linear copy, except that the 2 ends of the linear copy do not immediately connect.

While replication is occurring, 1 end of the linear copy leaves the donor bacterium and enters the recipient bacterium. Thus, the order in which the genes are replicated is the same as the order in which they are transferred. Unless this process is interrupted, the entire plasmid is transferred, and its 2 ends connect in the recipient bacterium.

Four students studied the way in which 6 genes (F, X, R, S, A, and G) on a specific plasmid were donated by a type of bacterium (see the figure). The students determined that the entire plasmid is transferred in 90 min and that the rate of transfer is constant. They also determined that the genes are evenly spaced around the plasmid, so 1 gene is transferred every 15 min. They disagreed, however, about the order in which the genes are replicated and thus transferred. Four models are presented.

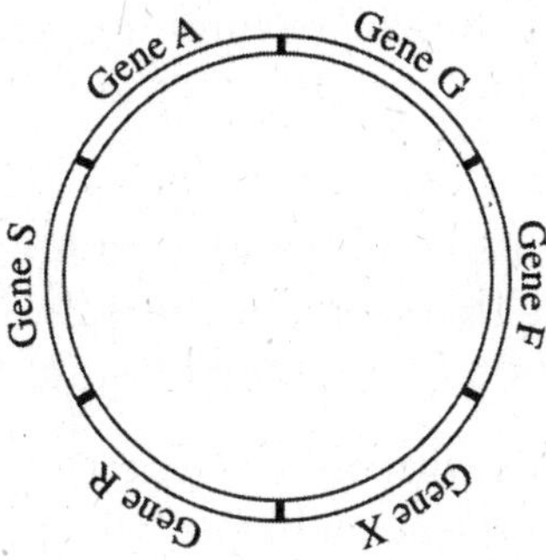

Student 1

Replication always begins between Gene F and Gene X. Gene X is replicated first and Gene F is replicated last.

Student 2

Replication always begins between Gene F and Gene X. However, the direction of replication varies. If Gene F is replicated first, Gene X is replicated last. Conversely, if Gene X is replicated first, Gene F is replicated last.

Student 3

Replication can begin between any 2 genes. Replication then proceeds around the plasmid in a clockwise direction (with respect to the figure). Thus, if Gene S is replicated first, Gene A is replicated second, and Gene R is replicated last.

Student 4

Replication can begin between any 2 genes. Likewise, replication can proceed in either direction. So the order of replication varies.

11. Based on the information presented, if the transfer of the linear copy was interrupted 50 min after transfer began, how many complete genes would have been transferred to the recipient bacterium?

A. 2
B. 3
C. 4
D. 5

12. Based on the model presented by Student 3, if all 6 genes are replicated and the first gene replicated is Gene G, the third gene replicated would be:

F. Gene F.
G. Gene A.
H. Gene S.
J. Gene X.

13. Which students believe that any of the 6 genes on the plasmid can be the first gene transferred to a recipient bacterium?

A. Students 2 and 3
B. Students 2 and 4
C. Students 3 and 4
D. Students 2, 3, and 4

14. Suppose that Student 2's model is correct and that the transfer of genes between 2 bacteria was interrupted after 30 min. Under these conditions, which of the following genes would definitely NOT be transferred from the donor bacterium to the recipient bacterium?

F. Gene A
G. Gene R
H. Gene G
J. Gene X

15. Suppose that the transfer of genes between 2 bacteria was interrupted, that the last gene transferred was Gene A, and that no incomplete copies of a gene were transferred. Based on this information, Student 1 would say that transfer was most likely interrupted how many minutes after the transfer began?

A. 15
B. 30
C. 45
D. 60

Discussion of Sample Passage III (Conflicting Viewpoints)

According to this Conflicting Viewpoints passage, plasmids (small DNA molecules, each molecule consisting of genes arranged in a circle) are found in bacteria. While a plasmid is replicating (producing an identical copy of itself) in one bacterium, the gene copies are being transferred to a second bacterium, the recipient bacterium, eventually forming a complete copy of the plasmid in the recipient bacterium.

Notice the diagram of a plasmid in the passage. The plasmid in the diagram contains six genes. The passage tells us that when the plasmid replicates, it produces a linear copy of itself; that is, the six genes in the copy are arranged in the same order as in the original plasmid, but the genes in the copy are first arranged in a row rather than in a circle. The plasmid copies one gene at a time, and, according to the passage, the gene copies are transferred to the recipient bacterium one at a time in the order in which the copies are produced. For example, if the plasmid copies Gene F, followed by Gene X, Gene F will be transferred to the recipient bacterium first, followed by Gene X. Once all of the genes of the original plasmid have been copied and transferred to a recipient bacterium, the two ends of the linear plasmid copy connect to each other, forming a circle just like the one in the passage.

Four students agree that the rate of gene transfer between bacteria is constant and occurs at the rate of one gene every 15 minutes, so a complete plasmid is transferred between the bacteria in $6 \times 15 = 90$ minutes. However, the identity of the first gene to be replicated and the direction (clockwise or counterclockwise around the circle) in which replication proceeds are subjects of disagreement among the four students.

- According to Student 1, Gene X is always replicated and transferred first, and Gene F is always replicated and transferred last. That is, replication always starts with Gene X and proceeds in a clockwise direction around the plasmid.
- According to Student 2, replication always begins with either Gene F or Gene X. If Gene F is first, then Gene X is last; that is, if replication begins with Gene F, then replication proceeds in a counterclockwise direction around the plasmid. If Gene X is first, then Gene F is last; that is, if replication begins with Gene X, then replication proceeds in a clockwise direction around the plasmid.
- According to Student 3, replication can start with any gene but always proceeds in a clockwise direction around the plasmid.
- According to Student 4, replication can start with any gene and can proceed in either direction around the plasmid.

11. Based on the information presented, if the transfer of the linear copy was interrupted 50 min after transfer began, how many complete genes would have been transferred to the recipient bacterium?

A. 2
B. 3
C. 4
D. 5

Question 11 asks you to predict how many complete genes would have been transferred to the recipient bacterium if gene transfer had been interrupted 50 minutes after transfer had begun. According to the passage, one gene was transferred every 15 minutes. Therefore, three genes would have been transferred in $3 \times 15 = 45$ minutes. A partial gene transfer would have occurred in the remaining 5 minutes, but the question asks about complete gene transfers, so you can ignore the partial gene transfer. The answer is three genes. Therefore, the best choice is **B**.

12. Based on the model presented by Student 3, if all 6 genes are replicated and the first gene replicated is Gene G, the third gene replicated would be:

F. Gene F.
G. Gene A.
H. Gene S.
J. Gene X.

Question 12 asks you to suppose that all six genes in a plasmid are replicated and that Gene G is the first gene replicated. You are asked to predict the third gene replicated, assuming that Student 3's model is correct. According to Student 3's model, replication can start with any gene but always proceeds around the plasmid in a clockwise direction. Therefore, starting with Gene G and proceeding in a clockwise direction, Gene F would be the second gene replicated and Gene X would be the third gene replicated. The best answer is **J**.

13. Which students believe that any of the 6 genes on the plasmid can be the first gene transferred to a recipient bacterium?

A. Students 2 and 3
B. Students 2 and 4
C. Students 3 and 4
D. Students 2, 3, and 4

Question 13 asks which students believe that any of the six genes on the plasmid can be the first gene transferred to a recipient bacterium. According to the passage, the order in which genes are transferred is the same as the order in which genes are replicated. Student 1 asserts that replication always begins with Gene X, so Student 1 would *disagree* with the statement that any of the six genes on the plasmid can be the first gene transferred. Student 2 asserts that replication always begins with either Gene X or Gene F, so Student 2 would *disagree* with the statement that any of the six genes on the plasmid can be the first gene transferred.

According to Students 3 and 4, replication can begin between any two genes on the plasmid, so they *agree* that any of the six genes on the plasmid can be the first gene transferred to a recipient bacterium. Because only Students 3 and 4 agree that any gene on the plasmid can be the first gene transferred, the best answer is **C**.

14. Suppose that Student 2's model is correct and that the transfer of genes between 2 bacteria was interrupted after 30 min. Under these conditions, which of the following genes would definitely NOT be transferred from the donor bacterium to the recipient bacterium?

F. Gene A
G. Gene R
H. Gene G
J. Gene X

Question 14 asks you to suppose that the transfer of genes between two bacteria was interrupted 30 minutes after the transfer began. You are asked to select from among a list of genes (A, R, G, and X) the gene that could NOT have been transferred to the recipient bacterium within the allotted 30 minutes, assuming that Student 2's model is correct. According to the passage, one complete gene transfer occurs every 15 minutes. Therefore, two complete gene transfers would have occurred after $2 \times 15 = 30$ minutes. Based on Student 2's model, gene transfer can start with Gene X and proceed around the plasmid in a clockwise direction, or transfer can start with Gene F and proceed around the plasmid in a counterclockwise direction. If transfer had started with Gene X, Gene R would have been the second gene transferred. If transfer had started with Gene F, Gene G would have been the second gene transferred. Therefore, we conclude Genes X, R, F, and G could have been transferred. The only gene in the list that could not have been transferred is Gene A. Based on Student 2's model, if Gene X had been the first gene transferred, then $4 \times 15 = 60$ minutes would have been required for Gene A to be transferred, because Gene A is the fourth gene in the clockwise direction from Gene X. If Gene F had been the first gene transferred, $3 \times 15 = 45$ minutes would have been required for Gene A to be transferred, because Gene A is the third gene in the counterclockwise direction from Gene F. The best answer is **F**.

15. Suppose that the transfer of genes between 2 bacteria was interrupted, that the last gene transferred was Gene A, and that no incomplete copies of a gene were transferred. Based on this information, Student 1 would say that transfer was most likely interrupted how many minutes after the transfer began?

A. 15
B. 30
C. 45
D. 60

Question 15 asks you to suppose that the transfer of genes between two bacteria was interrupted after the transfer of Gene A had been completed, and that no incomplete transfer of a gene occurred after the transfer of Gene A. You are asked to determine the number of minutes between the time that gene transfer began and the time at which gene transfer was interrupted, assuming that Student I's model is correct. According to Student 1, Gene X is always transferred first, and Gene F is always transferred last. That is, transfer always starts with Gene X and proceeds in a clockwise direction around the plasmid. If we count genes in the clockwise direction, starting with Gene X, we find that Gene A is the fourth gene, so Gene A would have been the fourth gene transferred. According to the passage, each complete transfer of a gene requires 15 minutes. Thus, the number of minutes between the time at which the transfer of Gene X began and the time at which the transfer of Gene A was completed would have been 4 × 15 = 60 minutes. The best answer is **D**.

Answer Key for Science Test Sample Questions

1.	A	6.	F	11.	B
2.	G	7.	D	12.	J
3.	B	8.	H	13.	C
4.	F	9.	C	14.	F
5.	C	10.	G	15.	D

Strategies for Taking the ACT Science Test

Performance on the ACT science test relies mainly on the ability to understand and process scientific information presented in various formats but can also be affected by problem-solving strategies and skills. The following sections describe strategies and skills specifically for improving your ACT science score.

Develop a Problem-Solving Method

Because you have only a limited time in which to take the science test, you may find it helpful to work out a general problem-solving method that you can use for all or most of the questions. The method described here is certainly not the only way to solve the problems, but it is one that works for most science problems. Whether you see a way to adapt this method, or you work out your own approach, use the method that works best for you.

One approach to solving problems is to break the process into a series of smaller steps, such as these:

1. Restate the problem in your own words.
2. Decide what information is needed to solve the problem.
3. Extract the needed information from the passage. Information may include data, concepts, or even conclusions you've been able to draw from the information provided.

4. Consider any additional scientific knowledge (terms or concepts) you may have.
5. Organize the information and use reason to arrive at the answer.
6. Compare your answer to the answer choices and choose the option you think is correct.

Take Notes

As you read a question, take notes in the test booklet or on scratch paper to record what the question is asking and what information you have at your disposal to answer the question. (In some circumstances you are not permitted to write in your test booklet. In those circumstances, you'll be given scratch paper to use.) Sometimes, the process of writing down or reviewing notes reveals the answer or helps you develop an effective approach to finding the answer.

Pace Yourself

Remember, you have 35 minutes to read several passages and their accompanying questions (40 questions altogether). That's about 5 minutes for each passage and the accompanying questions. You can think of it as 40 questions in 35 minutes, or a little less than a minute per question. If you're like most people, you'll find some of the passages more familiar and probably easier than some of the others, so it's a good idea to try to work fast enough to allow yourself time to come back to any questions you have trouble answering the first time.

Practice Interpreting Graphs, Tables, and Diagrams

Much of the information you need to answer the science test questions is presented graphically in the form of graphs, tables, and diagrams. Practice interpreting tables and different types of graphs, including pie charts, line charts, bar or column charts, and scatter charts, especially those included in science articles. Examine graphs and tables closely until you understand the data and can pick out specific pieces of data.

Tip: Pay attention to any and all text in graphs, tables, or diagrams, because any of this text is likely present to serve as instruction for how to interpret the data:

Graphs

Read the axis labels and the labels for any lines (curves) present. Typically, the *y*-axis indicates what is being measured (the dependent variable) and the *x*-axis most often indicates what is being manipulated (the independent variable). Some graphs may have a legend (labeled *Key*) that identifies line styles and the quantities they represent. Graphs may also have notes at the bottom of the graph to supply additional information.

Tables

Look at the column and row headings, which will identify quantities and their units of measure. Often (but not always) manipulated variables (independent variables) will be on the left side of the graph and the measured quantity (the dependent variable) will be to the right of the graph. Some tables will have notes at the bottom that provide vital information for interpreting the data.

Diagrams

Diagrams often contain labeled parts and could represent everything from a food web to a laboratory setup or show the cross-section of an object, such as the layers of Earth or of Earth's atmosphere. Diagrams generally contain more text than numbers. Look for a title (above the diagram) or a caption (below the diagram) and for labels on the diagram itself. The diagram may not have a title, but parts of it may be labeled, as in a diagram of a laboratory setup that sheds light on how an experiment works.

Give yourself some time to figure out what the graph, table, or diagram is showing you in general. You can always look at these graphic representations more closely when answering questions, but having a general idea of what they show may shed light on what the questions are asking.

Make the Most of the Information in Graphs

Graphs illustrate data in ways that can be very useful if you follow a few rules. First, it's important to identify what is being displayed in the graph (e.g., mass, volume, velocity). What unit or units of measurement is (are) used (e.g., grams, liters, kilometers per hour)? Graphs usually have axis labels that provide this information and some will have a key or legend or other short explanation of the information presented. Many graphs consist of two axes (horizontal and vertical), both of which will be labeled, and some may have dual axes with more than one curve. Remember, the first thing to find out about any graph is exactly what the numbers represent.

Once you've identified what is being presented in a graph, you can begin to look for trends in the data. The main reason for using a graph is to show how one characteristic of the data tends to influence other characteristics.

For a coordinate graph, notice how a change on the horizontal axis (or x-axis) relates to the position of the variable on the vertical axis (or y-axis). If the curve shows angles upward from lower left to upper right (as in Figure 1a), then, as the variable shown on the x-axis increases, so does the variable on the y-axis (a *direct relationship*). An example of a direct relationship is that a person's weight increases as his or her height increases. If the curve goes from the upper left to the lower right (as in Figure 1b), then, as the variable on the x-axis increases, the variable on the y-axis decreases (an *inverse relationship*). An example of an inverse relationship is that the more players there are on a soccer team, the less time each of them gets to play (assuming everyone gets equal playing time). If the graph shows a vertical or horizontal line (as in Figure 1c), the variables are probably unrelated.

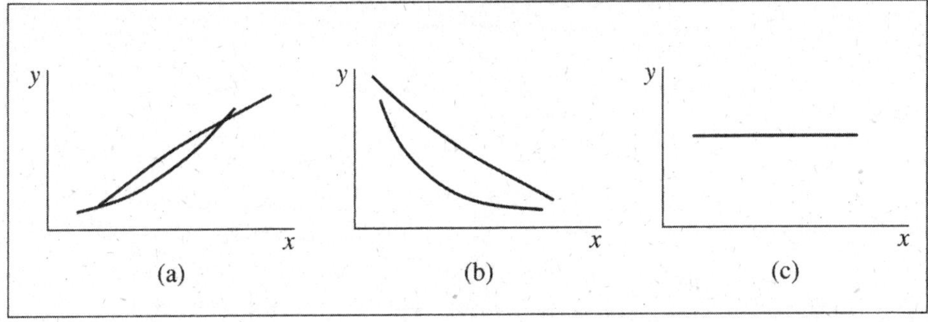

Figure 1

Improving Your Score

Sometimes, a question will ask you to estimate a value for one characteristic based on a given value of another characteristic that is beyond the limits of the curve shown on the graph. In this case, the solution will require you to *extrapolate,* or extend, the graph. If the curve is a relatively straight line, just use your pencil to extend that line far enough for the value called for to be included. If the graphed line is a curve, use your best judgment to extend the line to follow the apparent pattern. Figure 2 shows how to extend both types of graphs.

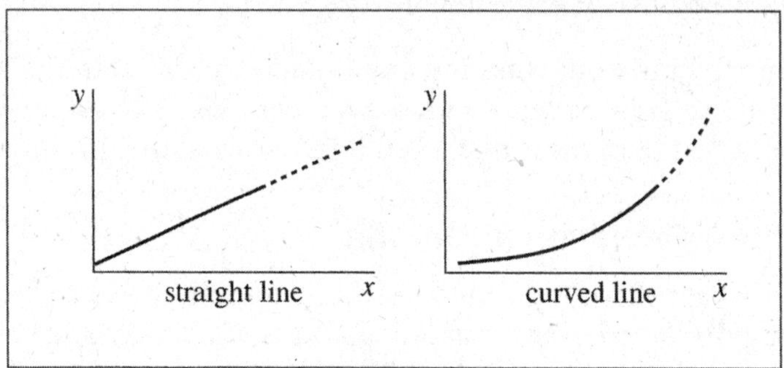

Figure 2

Another type of graph problem asks you to estimate a value that falls between two known values on a curve. This process is called *interpolation.* If the curve is shown, it amounts to finding a point on the curve that corresponds to a given value for one characteristic and reading the value for the other characteristic. (For example, "For a given *x*, find *y.*") If only scattered points are shown on the graph, draw a "best-fit line," a line that comes close to all of the points. Use this line to estimate the middle value. Figure 3 shows a best-fit line.

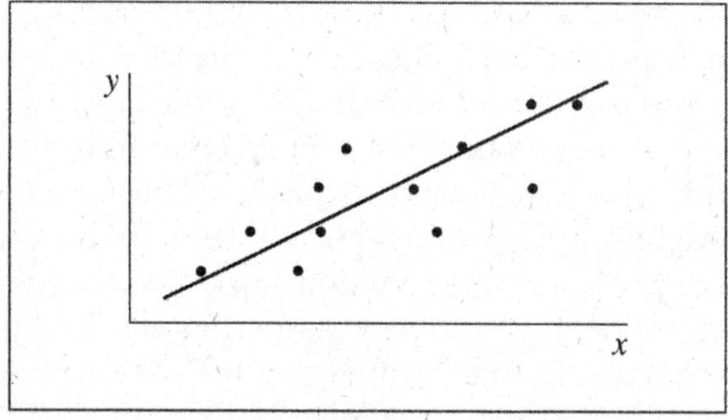

Figure 3

One very useful kind of graph shows more than one curve on the same pair of axes. Such a graph might be used when the results of a number of experiments are compared or when an experiment involves more than two variables. Analysis of this sort of graph requires that you determine the relationship shown by each curve and then determine how the curves are related to one another. Figure 4 shows a graph with multiple curves.

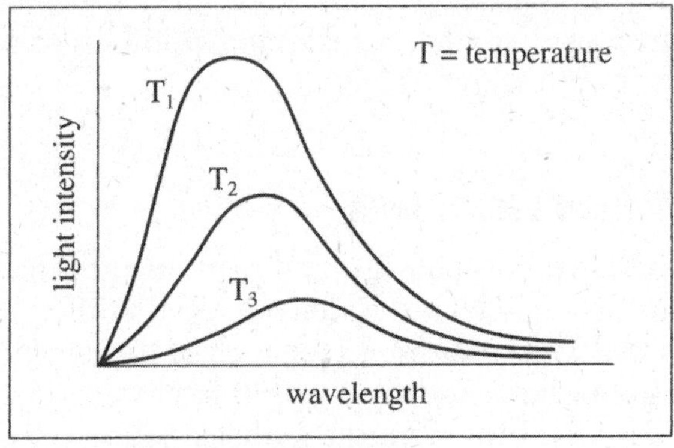

Figure 4

Make the Most of the Information in Tables

To understand what a table is showing you, you need to identify the information or data presented. You need to know two things about the information or data: the purpose it serves in the experiment and the unit (or units) of measurement used to quantify it. Generally, experiments intentionally vary one characteristic (the independent variable) to see how it affects another (the dependent variable). Tables may report results for either or both.

Once you have identified the variables, it might be helpful to sketch a graph to illustrate the relationship between them. You might sketch an *x*-axis and a *y*-axis next to the table and decide which variable to represent on each axis. Mark off the axes with evenly spaced intervals that enable all of the numbers for a category to fit along each axis. Plot some points. Again, draw a best-fit line and characterize the relationship shown.

As with graphs and diagrams, you may be asked to look for trends in the data. For example, do the numbers representing the dependent variable increase or decrease as the numbers representing the independent variable increase or decrease? If no pattern is clear, you may want to sketch a rough graph as discussed above. You may also need to make predictions about values of quantities between the data points shown (interpolation) or beyond the limits of those shown on the table (extrapolation). Another type of problem may require you to compare data from multiple columns of a table or between two or more graphs or tables. A simple examination of the numbers may be enough to see a relationship, but you may find it helpful to sketch a graph containing a curve for each category. The curves may be compared as described previously in "Make the Most of the Information in Graphs."

Develop an Understanding of Scientific Investigations

When working with a Research Summaries passage, you should be able to understand scientific processes. This includes identifying the designs of experiments, identifying assumptions and hypotheses underlying the experiments, identifying controls and variables, determining the effects of altering the experiments, identifying similarities and differences between the experiments, identifying the strengths and weaknesses of the experiments, developing other experiments that will test the same hypothesis, making hypotheses or predictions from research results, and creating models from research results.

Carefully Analyze Conflicting Viewpoints

When reading a Conflicting Viewpoints passage, first read the introductory information. This describes the phenomena about which the viewpoints will differ. It may also present a graph, table, or diagram, as well as discuss aspects that all of the viewpoints share. Then, read each viewpoint closely and note what is the same and different in each. Note each viewpoint's strengths and weaknesses. Use your own scientific knowledge and common sense to draw conclusions about each viewpoint. Which viewpoint sounds most credible? Which has the most evidence to back it up? With an understanding of and opinion about each viewpoint, you are better equipped to understand and answer questions about them.

9 Chapter 9: Improving Your Score on the Optional Writing Test

On the ACT writing test, you have 40 minutes to read a prompt and to plan and write an essay in response to it. The prompts on the writing test cover a variety of subjects intended to reflect engaging conversations about contemporary issues, and they are designed to be appropriate for response in a 40-minute timed test.

The writing test is an optional test on the ACT. Should you decide to take the writing test, it will be administered after the multiple-choice tests. Taking the writing test will not affect your scores on any of the multiple-choice tests or the Composite score. Rather, *in addition* to your scores from the multiple-choice tests and your Composite score, you will receive a writing score and may receive an English Language Arts (ELA) score.

You will have a short break between the end of the last multiple-choice test and the beginning of the writing test.

Content of the ACT Writing Test

The test consists of one writing prompt that describes a complex issue and provides three different perspectives on the issue. You are asked to read the prompt and write an essay in which you develop your own perspective on the issue. Your essay must analyze the relationship between your perspective and one or more perspectives. You may adopt one of the perspectives given in the prompt as your own, or you may introduce one that is completely different from those given. The test offers guidance and structure for planning and prewriting, but planning and prewriting are optional and do not count toward the score. Your score will also not be affected by the perspective you take on the issue. Your essay will be evaluated based on the evidence that it provides of your ability to do the following:

- Clearly state your own perspective on a complex issue and analyze the relationship between your perspective and at least one other perspective.
- Develop and support your ideas with reasoning and examples.
- Organize your ideas clearly and logically.
- Communicate your ideas effectively in standard written English.

How Your Essay Will Be Scored

Your essay will be scored analytically using a rubric with four domains that correspond to different writing skills (turn to chapter 3 for a copy of the actual analytic rubric for the ACT writing test). Two trained readers will separately score your essay, giving it a rating from 1 (low) to 6 (high) in each of the following four domains: Ideas and Analysis, Development and Support, Organization, and Language Use and Conventions. Each domain score represents the sum of the two readers' scores using the ACT Writing Test Analytic Rubric in chapter 3. If the readers' ratings differ by more than one point, a third reader will evaluate the essay and resolve the discrepancy. Your writing score is calculated from your domain scores and is reported on a scale of 2 to 12.

The readers take into account that you had merely 40 minutes to compose and write your essay. Within that time limit, polish your essay as best as you can. Make sure that all words are written clearly and neatly. Although handwriting is not scored, it could negatively affect your score if the readers can't decipher it. With careful planning, you should have time to briefly review and edit your essay after you have finished writing it. Keep in mind that you probably will not have time to rewrite or even recopy your essay. Instead, you should take a few minutes to think through your essay and jot preliminary notes on the planning pages in the scoring booklet before you begin to write. Prewriting (planning) helps you organize your ideas, manage your time, and keep you on track as you compose your essay.

Sample Prompt and Essays

In preparation for the ACT writing test, examine the sample writing prompt, essays, and scoring explanations in the following sections. The sample prompt shows what you can expect to encounter on test day; the sample essays serve as models of low-, medium-, and high-scoring essays; and the scoring explanations provide insight into the criteria the readers will use to score your essay.

Sample ACT Writing Test Prompt

Writing test prompts are similar to the following example. The standard directions in the second paragraph are a part of all prompts used in the writing test. You might want to practice by writing in response to this prompt for 40 minutes before you look ahead to the sample responses from other writers. Note that readers who have already taken the practice test in chapter 3 do not need to do so here.

Free Music

Free music is now available through many legal sources, from streaming services to online radio stations, making it largely unnecessary to purchase an album or even a single song. As sales figures continue to drop, some musicians, both high-profile and relatively unknown, have even quit trying to sell their music altogether, choosing instead to release new material for free online. Perhaps this trend is a matter of simple economics: cheap is good, but free is better. But it is worth considering whether our apparent unwillingness to spend money on music is an indication that its value in our lives is changing.

Read and carefully consider these perspectives. Each suggests a particular way of thinking about the changing value of music in our lives.

Perspective One

Digital technologies and the Internet have changed our relationship with music. It is so plentiful and readily available now that all value has been diluted.

Perspective Two

Music competes for our attention with many other kinds of inexpensive entertainment these days. We still value it, but we also have a lot of other ways to spend our money.

Perspective Three

With so many free sources, people are listening to more music and discovering more new musicians than ever before. Wide availability has only increased our appreciation of music.

Essay Task

Write a unified, coherent essay about whether the value of music in our lives is changing. In your essay, be sure to:

- clearly state your own perspective on the issue and analyze the relationship between your perspective and at least one other perspective
- develop and support your ideas with reasoning and examples
- organize your ideas clearly and logically
- communicate your ideas effectively in standard written English

Your perspective may be in full agreement with any of those given, in partial agreement, or completely different.

Sample Essay Responses

The essays that follow are sample essays produced in response to the given writing prompt. The essays illustrate how writing at different levels is evaluated and scored for the ACT writing test. The essays in no way represent a full range of ideas, approaches, or styles that could be used. Although we all can learn from reading other people's writing, you are encouraged to bring your own distinct voice and writing skills to the test. You want to produce your own best essay for the writing test—not an imitation of someone else's essay writing.

The following essays have been evaluated using the analytic rubric for the ACT writing test (see chapter 3). This same rubric will be used to score the response that you write for the ACT writing test. Each essay is followed by a scoring explanation that comments on the essay.

PAGE 3

Please enter the information at the right before beginning the Writing Test. Use a soft lead No. 2 pencil only. Do NOT use a mechanical pencil, ink, ballpoint, or felt-tip pen.	WRITING TEST BOOKLET NUMBER	WRITING TEST FORM
	238577	AC42
	Print your 6-digit **Booklet Number** in the boxes above.	Print your 4-character **Test Form** in the boxes above and fill in the corresponding oval at the right.
	First Test	

AA11 AA12 AA13 AA14 AA15 AA16 AA17 AA18 AA19 AA20 AA21 AA22 AA23 AA24 AA25 AA26 AA27 AA28 AA29 AA30 AA31 AA32 AA33 AA34 AA35 AA36 AA37 AA38 AA39 AA40 AA41 AA42 AA43 AA44 AA45 AA46 AA47 AA48 AA49 AA50 AA51 AA52 AA53 AA54 AA55 AA56 AA57 AA58 AA59 AA60 AB91 AC11 AC12 AC13 AC14 AC15 AC16 AC17 AC18 AC19 AC20 AC21 AC22 AC23 AC24 AC25 AC26 AC27 AC28 AC29 AC30 AC31 AC32 AC33 AC34 AC35 AC36 AC37 AC38 AC39 AC40 AC41 AC42 AC43 AC44 AC45 AC46 AC47 AC48 AC49 AC50 AC51 AC52 AC53 AC54 AC55 AC56 AC57 AC58 AC59 AC60 AD91 EH10 EH11 EH12 EH13 EH14

Begin WRITING TEST here.

I say three because with so many sources the people are listening more an more music and it is discovering more with new musicians than they ever before. And they said a matter of simple economics; cheap is good, but free is better.
Free music is to online music and radio stations and choosing instead to release new music.

If you need more space, please continue on the back of this page.

PLEASE DO NOT WRITE IN THIS AREA.

533921

EM-269803-203B:65432

Sample Essay 1 (Score: 1111)

Score Explanation

The writer's attempt to rearrange the prompt does not demonstrate skill in writing an argumentative essay.

Ideas and Analysis (1): The writer's intentions are hard to discern. Although the first sentence suggests that the essay will argue in favor of Perspective Three, there is no analysis to help shape or clarify the main idea of this essay. Instead, there is a confusing attempt to piece together ideas from the prompt. It is difficult to determine what this writer is trying to convey, and thus it is difficult to identify an intelligible argument.

Development and Support (1): Reasoning and illustration are unclear. Instead of elaborating on the idea that Perspective Three is favorable ("I say three"), the writer simply repeats the perspective ("because with so many sources the people are listening more an more music and [...] discovering more with new musicians than they ever before"). Attempts to develop this point further are incoherent, because subsequent explanations do not clearly relate to a main idea ("And they said a matter of simple economics; cheap is good, but free is better," "Free music is to online music and radio stations and choosing instead to release new music").

Organization (1): This response does not exhibit an organizational structure. Although the piece does assume the appearance of a paragraph, the presentation of ideas within this paragraph is disorderly. Because these ideas do not clearly relate to one another, they cannot be logically grouped. Although the writer uses transitional language ("because," "And they said"), the transitions fail to logically connect ideas.

Language Use and Conventions (1): This essay is unsuccessful in communicating a larger idea, and many of its shortcomings can be attributed to poor language control. Even though this response is heavily dependent on language drawn from the prompt, usage errors are abundant ("people are listening more an more music and it is discovering more with new musicians than they ever before") and sentences are poorly formed ("And they said a matter of simple economics; cheap is good, but free is better"). As a result, the writer fails to demonstrate skill in using language to convey an argument.

PAGE 3

Please enter the information at the right before beginning the Writing Test.

Use a soft lead No. 2 pencil only. Do NOT use a mechanical pencil, ink, ballpoint, or felt-tip pen.

WRITING TEST BOOKLET NUMBER

229953

Print your 6-digit Booklet Number in the boxes above.

First Test

WRITING TEST FORM

AC42

Print your 4-character Test Form in the boxes above and fill in the corresponding oval at the right.

AA11	AA25	AA39	AA53	AC16	AC30	AC44	AC58
AA12	AA26	AA40	AA54	AC17	AC31	AC45	AC59
AA13	AA27	AA41	AA55	AC18	AC32	AC46	AC60
AA14	AA28	AA42	AA56	AC19	AC33	AC47	AD91
AA15	AA29	AA43	AA57	AC20	AC34	AC48	EH10
AA16	AA30	AA44	AA58	AC21	AC35	AC49	EH11
AA17	AA31	AA45	AA59	AC22	AC36	AC50	EH12
AA18	AA32	AA46	AA60	AC23	AC37	AC51	EH13
AA19	AA33	AA47	AB91	AC24	AC38	AC52	EH14
AA20	AA34	AA48	AC11	AC25	AC39	AC53	
AA21	AA35	AA49	AC12	AC26	AC40	AC54	
AA22	AA36	AA50	AC13	AC27	AC41	AC55	
AA23	AA37	AA51	AC14	AC28	AC42	AC56	
AA24	AA38	AA52	AC15	AC29	AC43	AC57	

Begin WRITING TEST here.

What makes you appreciate music? Is it the many ways you can get access to it, how about being able to get it free. Also their are so many different genres of music that you could choose from. Everyday their are so many new artist catching peoples eyes now and days that, they give you a huge variety to choose from.

There are so many ways you can get music. Such as computers, phones, radio's and CD's. There are so many sources to get music from that almost anyone can listen to it. Every where you see Students listen to music in School and at college. So many young people listen to it.

Who can beat free? No one; thats the best it can get free!

If you need more space, please continue on the back of this page.

PLEASE DO NOT WRITE IN THIS AREA.

515907

EM-283603-203B:65432

PAGE 4

WRITING TEST

Music is so wide spread that people don't have to pay for music anymore. You can get it free anywhere except from one brand online music store. Who would pay for music besides those who live to have CD albums? Thats the only case I see that people would pay for their music.

To add there are so many artist and genres out in the music world that anyone can pick to listen to. Its an easy way to listen to anyone person you want to. Such a gallery to pick from. Some people believe getting music for free make music value go way down. People go to concerts and buy tickets and memorbilia that it make them artists money.

To bundle everything together having free music is awesome. You have access anywhere and every where. Having free music gives folks unlimit supply to any artist and genre they want to listen to. Although some feel it decreases the value of music. There are concerts and places you can go to and buy tickets, and artist supply.

If you need more space, please continue on the next page.

2

Do not write in this shaded area.

Sample Essay 2 (Score: 2222)

Score Explanation

The writer generates an argument in response to the task, but the argument is imprecise in its focus and inconsistent in its execution.

Ideas and Analysis (2): The writer generates an argument that weakly responds to multiple perspectives on the issue. Although something of a thesis is evident—"free music is awesome" because of the benefits to music lovers—it is only loosely related to the prompt's question of whether the value of music in our lives is changing. Analysis of the issue and its perspectives is incomplete and, in some respects, irrelevant. For example, it is unclear how the writer's point that "there are so many ways you can get music [...] you see students listen to music in school and at college" is related to the thesis or even to the concept of free music. The writer's critique of the idea that free music causes the value we place on music to decline is similarly imprecise ("Some people believe [free music] make music value go way down. People go to concerts and buy tickets and memorbila that it make them atists money").

Development and Support (2): Development and support fail to fully clarify the argument and contribute to the inconsistent sense of purpose exhibited by this response. In many cases, reasoning and illustration are circular ("There are so many ways you can get music. Such as computers, phones, radios and CD's. There are so many sources to get music from that almost anyone can listen to it") and redundant ("Who can beat free? No one; that's the best it can get free! Music is so wide spread that people don't have to pay for music anymore. You can get it free anywhere except from name brand online music store").

Organization (2): This response does exhibit an organizational structure. The writer offers an introduction and conclusion, and the body paragraphs in between are each seemingly dedicated to a main idea. A closer examination of this structure, however, reveals a number of inconsistencies. Grouping of ideas, for example, is somewhat unclear—the final body paragraph includes a counterargument that doesn't seem to address the main point of the paragraph. Furthermore, the absence of transitions within paragraphs contributes to the repetitive quality of the development.

Language Use and Conventions (2): Imprecise word choices, repetitive phrasing, unclear sentence structures, and grammatical errors: these are the markers of inconsistent skill in using language, and these markers are prevalent in this essay. A number of phrases appear multiple times throughout the essay ("their/there are so many," in particular), reflecting imprecision in vocabulary and word choice; a number of fragments and run-on sentences reveal weak mechanical control. Although the writer's exuberant voice ("that's the best it can get free!") is generally appropriate for the rhetorical purpose—after all, the argument is that free music is awesome—this relative strength does not outweigh the essay's many weaknesses in the use of language.

PAGE 3

Please enter the information at the right before beginning the Writing Test.

Use a soft lead No. 2 pencil only. Do NOT use a mechanical pencil, ink, ballpoint, or felt-tip pen.

WRITING TEST BOOKLET NUMBER

232769

Print your 6-digit Booklet Number in the boxes above.

First Test

WRITING TEST FORM

AC42

Print your 4-character Test Form in the boxes above and fill in the corresponding oval at the right.

AA11 AA12 AA13 AA14 AA15 AA16 AA17 AA18 AA19 AA20 AA21 AA22 AA23 AA24 AA25 AA26 AA27 AA28 AA29 AA30 AA31 AA32 AA33 AA34 AA35 AA36 AA37 AA38 AA39 AA40 AA41 AA42 AA43 AA44 AA45 AA46 AA47 AA48 AA49 AA50 AA51 AA52 AA53 AA54 AA55 AA56 AA57 AA58 AA59 AA60 AB91 AC11 AC12 AC13 AC14 AC15 AC16 AC17 AC18 AC19 AC20 AC21 AC22 AC23 AC24 AC25 AC26 AC27 AC28 AC29 AC30 AC31 AC32 AC33 AC34 AC35 AC36 AC37 AC38 AC39 AC40 AC41 AC42 AC43 AC44 AC45 AC46 AC47 AC48 AC49 AC50 AC51 AC52 AC53 AC54 AC55 AC56 AC57 AC58 AC59 AC60 AD91 EH10 EH11 EH12 EH13 EH14

Begin WRITING TEST here.

Over the past years music has become easier and cheaper to listen to than ever before. While people have began spending less money on music, its value has not gone down. People are still willing to pay for music. However, there has been a big decline in the amount of music bought. With music becoming free more people are able to listen and the value of music continues to go up.

The decreasing price of music has had many positive effects. Before, it was hard to listen to a lot of music because the price was too high. Now people are able to listen to music and spend their money on other things. Some think that the value of music has gone down because people aren't willing to spend money on it. However, this is not true. People are still willing to pay for some music and to go to concerts. The lowered price of music has caused music to be available to more people and has not caused the value to go down.

The fact that music has become free has had some negative effects as well. Since people are able to get music for free they spend much less money for the music. Some artists have decided to stop selling their music and just putting it out for free. This causes a decline in all music sales. Instead of spending money on music people have began to spend it on other things.

If you need more space, please continue on the back of this page.

1

PLEASE DO NOT WRITE IN THIS AREA.

525721

EM-289803-203B:65432

Improving Your Score

PAGE 4

WRITING TEST

The price people are willing to pay continues to drop. Although there have been negative effects of free music the value of music has not gone down. Overall the positive effects are much higher than the negative ones.

Even though the prices of music have dropped, its value has went up. More musicians are being discovered and our appreciation of music has only become higher. With its availability more people are able to hear the music, which causes people to spend their money on concerts. People are still willing to pay to see music, but now they have more money, so they are able to spend it on other things as well. As more music continues to be free, more people will continue to listen to it. Without music becoming free its value would have gone down because it was too expensive. The rise of free music has increased its value.

Throughout time music has become more inexpensive than ever. Now more people can hear and appreciate it while having money left over. While there are some negative effects, the positive effects are higher. While people aren't spending as much money on music, the value has gone up. People everywhere are now able to listen. Free music has made a big impact on the world of music forever.

2

If you need more space, please continue on the next page.

Do not write in this shaded area.

PAGE 5

WRITING TEST

If you need more space, please continue on the back of this page.

3

PLEASE DO NOT WRITE IN THIS AREA.

525721

EM-289803-203C:65432

PAGE 6

WRITING TEST

STOP here with the Writing Test.

4

Do not write in this shaded area.

Sample Essay 3 (Score: 3333)

Score Explanation

The writer generates an analytical argument that considers other perspectives, but the essay exhibits lapses in clarity that keep it from achieving a higher score.

Ideas and Analysis (3): The writer generates the thesis that, despite the trend toward free music, the value of music is rising. Although this idea reflects a clear focus on the issue, its execution reveals lapses in thought and purpose. In analyzing the issue and its perspectives, the writer discusses the positive and negative effects of free music. This contextual framework proves to be limited, because it results in simplistic analysis of the perspectives (see, for example, the writer's rebuttal of Perspective One and the writer's affirmation of Perspective Two). Furthermore, the negative effects the writer articulates occasionally contradict the positive effects: in the second paragraph, the writer claims that people still pay for music, but the third paragraph states that "[i]nstead of spending money on music people have began to spend it on other things." Finally, it is not always clear how the positive and negative effects the writer outlines are intended to relate to the question of the value we place on music and thus to the thesis. Though the writer attempts to make these connections ("Although there have been negative effects of free music the value of music has not gone down"), the juxtaposition of positive and negative effects, as an analytical technique, is only somewhat clear in this argument.

Development and Support (3): The argument's thesis takes shape through reasoning and illustration, which offer clarifying explanations of the positive and negative effects the writer perceives. However, this development, although relevant, is overly general ("People are still willing to pay to see music, but now they have more money, so they are able to spend it on other things as well. As more music continues to be free, more people will continue to listen to it. Without music becoming free its value would have gone down because it was too expensive"), and key ideas go unsupported ("Overall the positive effects are much higher than the negative ones").

Organization (3): The positive-negative framework provides a basic organizational structure, allowing the ideas in this response to cohere as an argument. Transitions, particularly in the topic sentences of the body paragraphs, signal shifts in the discussion and are somewhat successful in connecting ideas across the essay. Despite these strengths, however, the piece falls short of adequacy in the Organization domain. The thesis is intended to control the argument but is unable to do so; the question of the value we place on music falls in and out of focus. Furthermore, the arrangement of the discussions on positive and negative effects is a bit haphazard; the writer jumps back and forth between these discussions without an evident purpose in doing so.

Language Use and Conventions (3): The use of language exhibits basic clarity. Sentence structures are clear; errors, although distracting, rarely impede understanding; and the writer's voice and tone are appropriate for the purpose. However, as in the other three domains, language use demonstrates only developing skill. Though the writer makes reasonable word choices, vocabulary and phrasing are often overly general ("The lowered price of music has caused music to be available to more people and has not caused the value to go down," "Throughout time music has become more inexpensive than ever"), leading to imprecision in expression.

PAGE 3

Please enter the information at the right before beginning the Writing Test.

Use a soft lead No. 2 pencil only. Do NOT use a mechanical pencil, ink, ballpoint, or felt-tip pen.

WRITING TEST BOOKLET NUMBER

2	0	3	9	4	9

Print your 6-digit Booklet Number in the boxes above.

First Test

WRITING TEST FORM

A	C	4	2

Print your 4-character Test Form in the boxes above and fill in the corresponding oval at the right.

AA11 AA12 AA13 AA14 AA15 AA16 AA17 AA18 AA19 AA20 AA21 AA22 AA23 AA24
AA25 AA26 AA27 AA28 AA29 AA30 AA31 AA32 AA33 AA34 AA35 AA36 AA37 AA38
AA39 AA40 AA41 AA42 AA43 AA44 AA45 AA46 AA47 AA48 AA49 AA50 AA51 AA52
AA53 AA54 AA55 AA56 AA57 AA58 AA59 AA60 AB91 AC11 AC12 AC13 AC14 AC15
AC16 AC17 AC18 AC19 AC20 AC21 AC22 AC23 AC24 AC25 AC26 AC27 AC28 AC29
AC30 AC31 AC32 AC33 AC34 AC35 AC36 AC37 AC38 AC39 AC40 AC41 AC42 AC43
AC44 AC45 AC46 AC47 AC48 AC49 AC50 AC51 AC52 AC53 AC54 AC55 AC56 AC57
AC58 AC59 AC60 AD91 EH10 EH11 EH12 EH13 EH14

Begin WRITING TEST here.

Music has played a constant role in society throughout time. It has adapted to the circumstances, whether it be as a way of expressing oneself or as a way to revolt or stand against something. But one thing has changed about music in more recent times: the cost. Music has always cost something whether it meant buying it online or from a store. However, recently it has been becoming more available for no price at all. Many people see this as a bad this as it dilutes our values of music and others feel that it actually has broadened our appreciation of music. In reality, it is actually ~~it~~ a mix between both views.

By having music be available for free, it has made discovery of new musicians, styles, and thus new cultures more attainable. Money often is a limitation on what people can buy. Since music is now more often free, people from all areas in the economic status can listen and expand their realm of experiences. People are more likely to try out new music styles or artists because it is there and there is nothing stopping them from listening. If they have to pay money for music they aren't sure they are going to like, then people will not be willing to take a risk and try something new. To go along with taking risks, if a person does decide to listen to new music due to it being free, they are then able to

If you need more space, please continue on the back of this page.

PLEASE DO NOT WRITE IN THIS AREA.

474275

EH-269603-203B:654321

PAGE 4

WRITING TEST

immerse themselves in different cultures. This will help broaden their knowledge of music and things that effect it thus increasing their appreciation of it. It allows for exploration.

However, free music does dilute the values of it. By having it be available to everyone whenever they want, it does decrease the sacredness of it. People are more apt to take it for granted because it is there and always will be. When music wasn't free, people treasured the music they did have and when they aquired more, they tended to treasure and understand the value of their music. This is because, to get it, they had to work for it and really try to obtain it. Now, it is also available to anyone and for no price, making it not as special. They did not have to work for it and therefore, don't have the same protective feeling as they would have if they paid for it.

Music offers people a way of escape and a way of expression. While a few people may think that there are better things to spend money on, music is a great source of entertainment that offers a journey through time and experiences that other things don't offer like videogames.

If you need more space, please continue on the next page.

Do not write in this shaded area.

PAGE 5

WRITING TEST

3

If you need more space, please continue on the back of this page.

PLEASE DO NOT WRITE IN THIS AREA.

474275

EM-289803-203C:654321

PAGE 6

WRITING TEST

STOP here with the Writing Test.

Do not write in this shaded area.

Sample Essay 4 (Score: 4444)

Score Explanation

This argument engages with multiple perspectives on the issue in the prompt, building its case around the implications of two conflicting views.

Ideas and Analysis (4): This argument recognizes a complexity inherent to the issue and its perspectives: it may be possible that the availability of free music allows us to build a greater appreciation for music *and* causes music to lose some of its value. The writer makes this argument by analyzing Perspectives One and Three, touching on implications of both ("When music wasn't free, people treasured the music they did have and when they aquired more, they tended to treasure and understand the value of their music [...] Now, it is available to anyone and for no price, making it not as special," "Since music is now more often free, people from all areas in the economic status can listen and expand their realm of experiences. People are more likely to try out new music styles or artists because it is there and there is nothing stopping them from listening"). Had the writer pursued this apparent contradiction further, the argument would have become more complex, perhaps receiving a higher score. Even so, ideas and analysis in this response exhibit a degree of clarity and sophistication that are absent in the previous responses, earning the essay a score of 4 in this domain.

Development and Support (4): Lines of clear reasoning and illustration clarify meaning and purpose as the writer develops the thesis. The second paragraph, for example, provides clear reasoning to support the idea that free music builds our appreciation for music; similarly, the third paragraph rationalizes the idea that we don't value music as much as we used to. Although the writer is able to provide support for the argument, anticipating and addressing questions from the reader—How can it be that the value of music is both appreciating *and* depreciating? Is it possible that we're talking about more than one type of value?—would have brought these lines of reasoning together and strengthened the argument by considering factors that may complicate it.

Organization (4): The shape of this argument reflects its controlling idea, which is first presented in the introduction. Ideas are grouped and sequenced: within paragraphs, ideas unfold logically, and the two premises of the argument are connected clearly, with a transition to move the reader from the first premise into the second ("However, free music does dilute the value of it"). The sequence of ideas does not conclude logically; the final paragraph seems to summarize a discussion that was never carried out. Perhaps this was an attempt to leave the reader with an interesting idea to consider, but the relevance of this idea (music offers experiences other forms of entertainment cannot match) to the larger argument is entirely unclear.

Language Use and Conventions (4): Some precise word choices ("dilute," "sacredness," "treasure," "limitation," "realm of experiences") underscore the meaning of the argument. However, this precision is counterbalanced by awkward phrasing ("However, recently it has been becoming more available for no price at all") and many vague and ambiguous pronouns ("By having it be available to everyone whenever they want, it does decrease the sacredness of it"). Although these issues and errors don't always impede understanding, they negatively affect the overall quality of expression.

PAGE 9

Please enter the information at the right before beginning the Writing Test.

Use a soft lead No. 2 pencil only. Do NOT use a mechanical pencil, ink, ballpoint, or felt-tip pen.

WRITING TEST BOOKLET NUMBER

2 4 3 5 0 5

Print your 6-digit Booklet Number in the boxes above.

Second Test

WRITING TEST FORM

A C 4 2

Print your 4-character Test Form in the boxes above and fill in the corresponding oval at the right.

AA11	AA25	AA39	AA53	AC16	AC30	AC44	AC58
AA12	AA26	AA40	AA54	AC17	AC31	AC45	AC59
AA13	AA27	AA41	AA55	AC18	AC32	AC46	AC60
AA14	AA28	AA42	AA56	AC19	AC33	AC47	AD91
AA15	AA29	AA43	AA57	AC20	AC34	AC48	EH10
AA16	AA30	AA44	AA58	AC21	AC35	AC49	EH11
AA17	AA31	AA45	AA59	AC22	AC36	AC50	EH12
AA18	AA32	AA46	AA60	AC23	AC37	AC51	EH13
AA19	AA33	AA47	AB91	AC24	AC38	AC52	EH14
AA20	AA34	AA48	AC11	AC25	AC39	AC53	
AA21	AA35	AA49	AC12	AC26	AC40	AC54	
AA22	AA36	AA50	AC13	AC27	AC41	AC55	
AA23	AA37	AA51	AC14	AC28	● AC42	AC56	
AA24	AA38	AA52	AC15	AC29	AC43	AC57	

Begin WRITING TEST here.

Free music is so universal that people may no longer need to actually purchase music. However, this does not mean that people do not value or appreciate it. In fact, the lowering of the financial barrier to accessing music may have only caused music to be more prevalent in our society, exposing more people to it, and allowing those who create music to recieve attention more quickly. The value of music in our society in not decreasing, we still view music as a vital aspect in our lives.

Digital techonologies have caused music to become cheaper, because it is now so plentiful; however, a decrease in monetary value of individual songs, does not mean that we now view music with less appreciation. Much of today's music can be viewed or listened to online for free, but this is just a means for artists to more easily to allow more people to review their work. By releasing free online editions of their music, many artists have become far more well-known than they would have otherwise. For example, the Korean pop star Psy, who has released several songs barely containing any English, has become an international celebrity through the viewing of his work for free on the internet. This can be seen from the hundreds of millions of views that his music videos on Youtube recieved; without this free platform to connect the Korean rapper

If you need more space, please continue on the back of this page.

1

PLEASE DO NOT WRITE IN THIS AREA.

463309

EM-259803-203E:654321

PAGE 10

WRITING TEST

to the rest of the world, it is uncertain whether he could have attained fame so quickly. After the release of his videos, the videos went viral, quickly becoming the center of attention for the media for weeks. Psy recieved and accepted numerous requests to sing and perform from many different places including television shows in Australia. where thousands of people flocked to see his performances. Though music may be free, we still greatly appreciate music and it continues to have a profound impact on our lives.

In today's society, there are also many other relatively inexpensive forms of entertainment aside from music that compete for our attention.such as movies, TV shows, just to name a few. However, the vast majority of these kinds of entertainment also includes music. No movie today is produced without a Soundtrack, possibly consisting of the work of multiple artists. Nearly all forms of digital entertainment include music to make the experience more enjoyable, showing that music continues to hold great value in all forms of entertainment, and our society as well.

The ubiquitous and affordable nature of music in today's society has only increased our appreciation of music and allowed the discovery of many new musicians. A personal example would be my discovery of the band 5 seconds of Summer. Through online and free sources, I discovered their music and enjoyed the upbeat rythme and cheerful mood in many of their songs. If I had to spend money on an expensive album to get access to their music, it is likely that I would never have gotten the satisfaction

If you need more space, please continue on the next page.

Do not write in this shaded area.

PAGE 11

WRITING TEST

of listening to their work, and the band would have been deprived of another person who appreciates their music.

Though we may be spending less on music, we still appreciate it and acknowledge that it occupies a vital position in entertainment. Through digital technology, music has been connected with an even larger audience.

3

If you need more space, please continue on the back of this page.

PLEASE DO NOT WRITE IN THIS AREA.

463309

EM-299803-203F:654321

Improving Your Score

PAGE 12

WRITING TEST

STOP here with the Writing Test.

Do not write in this shaded area.

Sample Essay 5 (Score: 5555)

Score Explanation

The writer uses an extended example to analyze and evaluate multiple perspectives on the issue, addressing implications and critiquing underlying values.

Ideas and Analysis (5): The argument productively engages with multiple perspectives. For example, the writer uses Perspective Three as a basis for analyzing and evaluating Perspective One. In doing so, the writer addresses Perspective One's assumption that "a decrease in monetary value of individual songs" also means that "we now view music with less appreciation." This analysis serves to refine and advance a precise thesis: the value of music in our society is not decreasing; instead, by making music more accessible, we are only growing in our appreciation of music, and artists are benefitting as a result. Subsequent analysis is not quite as critical—the second point, that many other kinds of entertainment include music, is of a lower order, and the personal example does not meaningfully contribute to the discussion that precedes it. Even so, this thoughtful argument is worthy of a 5 in the Ideas and Analysis domain.

Development and Support (5): Development and support deepen understanding. Although some of the details in this example are probably unnecessary, the treatment as a whole is channeled toward conveying and bolstering the significance of the idea that free music affords musicians greater exposure, which is an important piece of the thesis. Other ideas are not developed quite so thoroughly, and the argument as a whole would be considerably stronger were it to consider complicating factors, such as objections that might be raised by someone with an opposing viewpoint on the issue. On balance, however, this is a well-developed essay.

Organization (5): Although this response does not achieve the unity and coherence required of a 6, it does exhibit the markers of a productive organizational strategy. The introduction presents the controlling idea, and the argument takes its shape around this idea, with all the writer's points working to advance and support the larger argument. A logical sequence of ideas contributes to the effectiveness of the argument; the discussion on our appreciation of music (paragraph two) is followed with a discussion on the role of music in other forms of entertainment (paragraph three), and these discussions work together to build and refine the idea that free music is not causing us to lose appreciation for music. Unfortunately, the momentum of the argument is halted by the fourth paragraph, which introduces a personal example that does not differ meaningfully from the discussion carried out in paragraph two.

Language Use and Conventions (5): Advanced sentence structures convey ideas with precision ("No movie today is produced without a soundtrack, possibly consisting of the work of several artists"), and word choice is precise ("this free platform," "caused music to be more prevalent in our society, "financial barrier"). Although the response does exhibit some clunky syntax ("After the release of his videos, the videos went viral") and a few minor usage errors ("the vast majority of these kinds of entertainment also includes music"), meaning is never in doubt.

PAGE 3

Please enter the information at the right before beginning the Writing Test.

Use a soft lead No. 2 pencil only. Do NOT use a mechanical pencil, ink, ballpoint, or felt-tip pen.

WRITING TEST BOOKLET NUMBER

387430

Print your 6-digit **Booklet Number** in the boxes above.

First Test

WRITING TEST FORM

AC42

Print your 4-character **Test Form** in the boxes above and fill in the corresponding oval at the right.

AA11 AA12 AA13 AA14 AA15 AA16 AA17 AA18 AA19 AA20 AA21 AA22 AA23 AA24 AA25 AA26 AA27 AA28 AA29 AA30 AA31 AA32 AA33 AA34 AA35 AA36 AA37 AA38 AA39 AA40 AA41 AA42 AA43 AA44 AA45 AA46 AA47 AA48 AA49 AA50 AA51 AA52 AA53 AA54 AA55 AA56 AA57 AA58 AA59 AA60 AB91 AC11 AC12 AC13 AC14 AC15 AC16 AC17 AC18 AC19 AC20 AC21 AC22 AC23 AC24 AC25 AC26 AC27 AC28 AC29 AC30 AC31 AC32 AC33 AC34 AC35 AC36 AC37 AC38 AC39 AC40 AC41 AC42 AC43 AC44 AC45 AC46 AC47 AC48 AC49 AC50 AC51 AC52 AC53 AC54 AC55 AC56 AC57 AC58 AC59 AC60 AD91 EH10 EH11 EH12 EH13 EH14

Begin WRITING TEST here.

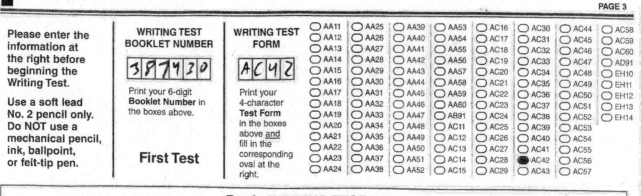

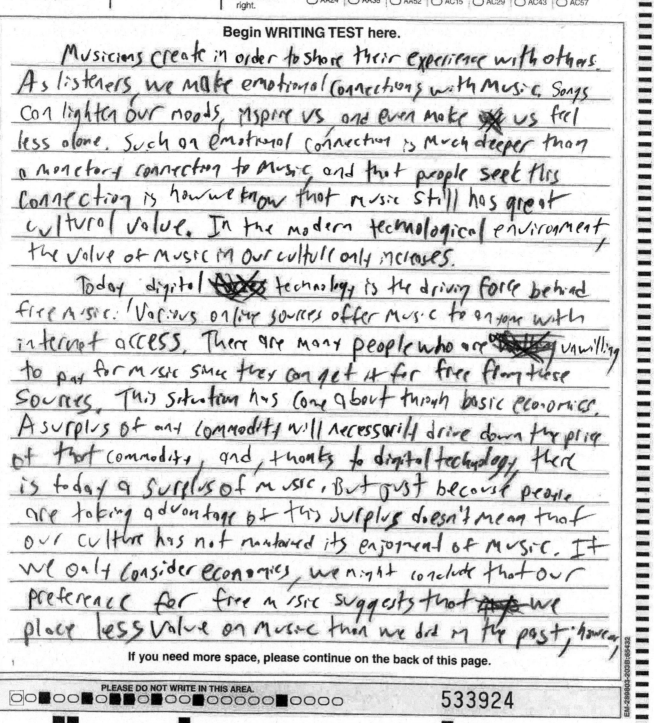

Musicians create in order to share their experience with others. As listeners, we make emotional connections with music. Songs can lighten our moods, inspire us, and even make us feel less alone. Such an emotional connection is much deeper than a monetary connection to music, and that people seek this connection is how we know that music still has great cultural value. In the modern technological environment, the value of music in our culture only increases.

Today, digital technology is the driving force behind free music. Various online sources offer music to anyone with internet access. There are many people who are unwilling to pay for music since they can get it for free from these sources. This situation has come about through basic economics. A surplus of any commodity will necessarily drive down the price of that commodity, and, thanks to digital technology, there is today a surplus of music. But just because people are taking advantage of this surplus doesn't mean that our culture has not maintained its enjoyment of music. If we only consider economics, we might conclude that our preference for free music suggests that we place less value on music than we did in the past; however,

If you need more space, please continue on the back of this page.

PLEASE DO NOT WRITE IN THIS AREA.

533924

EM-289803-2038:65432

PAGE 4

WRITING TEST

a look at the role music plays in our culture suggests that we value it as much as ever.

Think of how often we encounter music in our daily lives. We carry music with us in our pockets, wherever we go. Music plays at the grocery store, at the coffee shop, at the mall. Advertisements rely on music, baseball players have "walk-up" songs, and people spend outrageous amounts of money on customized stereo systems for their cars. Students use music for school projects, teachers use songs to help kids learn. Then, of course, there are our more direct experiences with music, like attending a concert or even making music ourselves. The prevelance of music has not diminished; if anything it has increased. Even the fact that we take advantage of all the free music available demonstrates how much we value music!

Even though economics have caused the monetary value of music to decline, its cultural value remains strong. People have shared experiences with each other through song for thousands of years, and for much of this time, free music has been readily available. Though its monetary value may shift across time, the cultural value of music is consistent.

If you need more space, please continue on the next page.

2

Do not write in this shaded area.

Improving Your Score

Sample Essay 6 (Score: 6666)

Score Explanation

This argument earns the highest scores because of a sustained, critical examination of the implications of the issue and its perspectives.

Ideas and Analysis (6): This argument is driven by a nuanced, precise thesis: shifting economic circumstances may have changed our purchasing habits when it comes to music, but these changes in consumption do not reflect a change in the value our culture places on music. By viewing the issue and its perspectives through the lens of culture and economics, the writer has employed an insightful context for analysis. Within this context, the writer is able to examine the implications of Perspective Two (the discussion on surplus) while critiquing Perspective One's assumption that this economic phenomenon is also a cultural matter. In doing so, the writer has generated an argument that critically engages with multiple perspectives on the issue.

Development and Support (6): In developing and supporting the argument, the writer keeps the thesis in full focus and thus produces an integrated line of reasoning and illustration. A concise explanation of the concept of surplus deepens the argument's insights, and the importance of this concept to the larger argument is made clear by way of an important qualification—this *is* an economic issue, but it is *also* a cultural matter—that enriches and bolsters the thesis ("If we only consider economics, we might conclude that our preference for free music suggests that we place less value on music than we did in the past; however, a look at the role music plays in our culture suggests that we value it as much as ever"). In supporting the idea that our culture has not devalued music, the writer makes skillful use of a list of examples that, in their accumulation, fortify the claim that "[t]he prevelance of music has not diminished; if anything it has increased." In these ways, reasoning and illustration are effective in conveying the meaning and importance of this argument.

Organization (6): The precise thesis brings unity and cohesion to this argument. The thesis guides a logical progression of ideas: the piece begins by introducing the main idea before discussing its central premises in turn. An effective conclusion reinforces the thesis and even manages to advance the discussion further by making efficient use of a historical context ("People have shared experiences with each other through song for thousands of years, and for much of this time, free music has been readily available. Though its monetary value may shift across time, the cultural value of music is consistent"). Transitions, both within paragraphs ("Then, of course, there are our more direct experiences with music") and between them ("however, a look at the role music plays in our culture suggests that we value it as much as ever/Think of how often we encounter music in our daily lives") form strong connections between ideas and make for smooth movement across the argument's premises.

Language Use and Conventions (6): The use of language enhances this argument. Precise word choices communicate the conceptual understanding on which this argument depends ("surplus," "commodity") and the fine distinctions on which it rests ("Such an emotional connection is much deeper than a monetary connection"). Stylistic choices are strategic and effective, as the writer shifts from a more formal register when discussing economic considerations ("A surplus of any commodity will necessarily drive down the price of that commodity") to a more informal register when discussing culture ("We carry music with us, in our pockets, wherever we go. Music plays at the grocery store, at the coffee shop, at the mall"). Errors in grammar, usage, and mechanics are virtually nonexistent.

Strategies for Taking the ACT Writing Test

Although your writing score reflects the quality of the product (the essay) you write, the writing process you follow can have a major impact on your score. For example, if you do not spend a few minutes prewriting (planning) before you start writing, you could "paint yourself into a corner" by following a line of logic that leads to an illogical conclusion and have no time left to start over.

The following sections present a few writing, prewriting, and postwriting strategies to improve the process you follow when writing your essay. Of course, no writing process can make up for a lack of knowledge and skill, which take years of study and practice to develop. If you need to sharpen your writing skills, we recommend that you take a course in English composition and practice writing and studying others' writing frequently.

Prewrite

Some writers like to plunge right in, but this is seldom a good way to do well on a timed essay. Prewriting gets you acquainted with the issue, suggests patterns for presenting your thoughts, and gives you a little breathing room to come up with interesting ideas for introducing and concluding your essay. Before writing, then, carefully consider the prompt and make sure you understand it—reread it if you aren't sure. Decide how you want to answer the question in the prompt. Then jot down your ideas on the topic: this might simply be a list of ideas, reasons, and examples that you will use to explain your point of view on the issue. Write down what you think someone might say in opposition to your point of view, and think about how you would refute their argument. Think of how best to organize the ideas in your essay. You should do your prewriting on the pages provided in your writing test booklet. You can refer back to these notes as you write the essay itself on the lined pages in your answer document.

Write

When you're ready to write your essay, proceed with the confidence that you have prepared well and that you will have attentive and receptive readers who are interested in your ideas. At the beginning of your essay, make sure readers will see that you understand the issue. Explain your point of view in a clear and logical way. If possible, discuss the issue in a broader context or evaluate the implications or complications of the issue. Address other perspectives presented in the prompt. Also consider what others might say to refute your point of view and present a counterargument. Use specific examples to explain and illustrate what you're saying. Vary the structure of your sentences, and choose varied and precise words. Make logical relationships clear by using transitional words and phrases. Don't wander off the topic. End with a strong conclusion that summarizes or reinforces your position.

Is it advisable to organize the essay by using a formula, such as "the five-paragraph essay"? Points are neither awarded nor deducted for following familiar formulas, so feel free to use one or not as best suits your preference. Some writers find formulas stifling, other writers find them a solid basis on which to build a strong argument, and still other writers just keep them handy to use when needed. The exact numbers of words and paragraphs in your essay are less important than the clarity and development of your ideas. Writers who have something to say usually find that their ideas have a way of sorting themselves out at reasonable length and in an appropriate number of paragraphs.

Review Your Essay

Take a few minutes at the end of the testing session to read over your essay. Correct any mistakes in grammar, usage, punctuation, and spelling. If you find any words that are hard to read, recopy them so your readers can read them easily. Make any corrections and revisions neatly, between the lines (but not in the margins). Your readers take into account that you had merely 40 minutes to compose and write your essay. Within that time limit, try to make your essay as polished as you can.

Practice

There are many ways to prepare for the ACT writing test. You may be surprised that these include reading newspapers and magazines, listening to news analysis on television or radio, and participating in discussions and debates about issues and problems. These activities help you become more familiar with current issues, with different perspectives on those issues, and with strategies that skilled writers and speakers use to present their points of view and respond to a range of viewpoints.

Of course, one of the best ways to prepare for the ACT writing test is to practice writing. Practice writing different kinds of texts, for different purposes, with different audiences in mind. The writing you do in your English classes will help you. So will practice in writing essays, stories, poems, plays, editorials, reports, letters to the editor, a personal journal, or other kinds of writing that you do on your own. Strive for your writing to be well developed and well organized, using precise, clear, and concise language. Because the ACT writing test asks you to explain your perspective on an issue in a convincing way, writing opportunities such as editorials or letters to the editor of a newspaper are especially helpful. Practicing a variety of different kinds of writing will help make you a versatile writer able to adjust to different writing occasions and assignments.

Share your writing with others and get feedback. Feedback helps you anticipate how readers might interpret your writing and what types of questions they might have. It will also help you identify your strengths and weaknesses as a writer. Also, keep in mind what the ACT readers will be looking for as they score your essay by examining the analytic rubric for the ACT writing test (in chapter 3). Make sure your writing meets the criteria described for the high-scoring essays.

You should also get some practice writing within a time limit. This will help build skills that are important in college and career. Taking the practice ACT writing tests in this book will give you a good idea of what timed writing is like and how much additional practice you may need.

Part Four: Taking Additional Practice Tests

In This Part

This part features four additional practice tests. Here, you take and score the tests and look at your scores from a number of different perspectives, so you can use the results more effectively in your educational and career planning. Specifically, this part gives you the opportunity to do the following:

- Take four additional practice tests.
- Score your practice tests to determine your raw score, scaled scores (similar to the scores the ACT reports), and your estimated percentage rank (how well you did compared to other students who took the tests).
- Evaluate your ACT scores from different perspectives to gain insight into what your scores mean in terms of college and career planning.

10 Chapter 10: Taking Additional Practice Tests

In this chapter, you'll find four additional practice ACT tests, copies of real answer documents for recording your answers, and explanatory answers for the questions on all of the multiple-choice tests.

Each practice test features the contents of the tests in the same order as they will be on the ACT: the English test, the mathematics test, the reading test, the science test, and the optional writing test. Following each complete practice test, you will find the explanatory answers for the multiple-choice questions on that test in the same pattern as the individual tests (English, mathematics, reading, and science).

Two copies of the answer documents that you can tear out and use to record your answers for the multiple-choice tests precede each practice test. (Two copies of these answer documents have been provided in case you make errors or if you would like to retake a practice test. When you take the actual ACT test, however, only one answer document will be provided.) One copy of the writing test answer document, which you can tear out (or photocopy) and use to write your essay, is provided for each practice writing test.

Simulating Testing Conditions

We recommend that you take all practice tests under conditions similar to those you will experience on test day. See chapter 3 for instructions.

PAGE 1

The ACT® *Sample Answer Sheet*

EXAMINEE STATEMENT, CERTIFICATION, AND SIGNATURE

1. Read the following **Statement:** By submitting this answer document, I agree to comply with and be bound by the *Terms and Conditions: Testing Rules and Policies for the ACT® Test* provided in the ACT registration materials for this test, including those concerning test security, score cancellation, examinee remedies, binding arbitration, and consent to the processing of my personally identifying information, including the collection, use, transfer, and disclosure of information as described in the ACT Privacy Policy (www.act.org/privacy.html).

   I understand that ACT owns the test questions and responses and affirm that I will not share any test questions or responses with anyone by any form of communication before, during, or after the test administration. I understand that assuming anyone else's identity to take this test is strictly prohibited and may violate the law and subject me to legal penalties.

   International Examinees: By my signature, I am also providing my consent to ACT to transfer my personally identifying information to the United States to ACT, or a third-party service provider for processing, where it will be subject to use and disclosure under the laws of the United States. I acknowledge and agree that it may also be accessible to law enforcement and national security authorities in the United States.

2. Copy the **Certification** shown below (only the text in italics) on the lines provided. Write in your normal handwriting.

Certification: *I agree to the Statement above and certify that I am the person whose name and address appear on this answer document.*

Your Signature

Today's Date

Do NOT mark in this shaded area.

USE A SOFT LEAD NO. 2 PENCIL ONLY.
(Do NOT use a mechanical pencil, ink, ballpoint, correction fluid, or felt-tip pen.)

A **NAME, MAILING ADDRESS, AND TELEPHONE (Please print.)**

Last Name | First Name | MI (Middle Initial)

House Number & Street (Apt. No.); or PO Box & No.; or RR & No.

City | State/Province | ZIP/Postal Code

Area Code / Number | Country

ACT, Inc.—Confidential Restricted when data present

ALL examinees must complete block A – please print.

Blocks B, C, and D are required for all examinees. Find the MATCHING INFORMATION on your ticket. Enter it EXACTLY the same way, even if any of the information is missing or incorrect. Fill in the corresponding ovals. If you do not complete these blocks to match your previous information EXACTLY, your scores will be **delayed up to 8 weeks**.

ACT

PO BOX 168, IOWA CITY, IA 52243-0168

B **MATCH NAME** (First 5 letters of last name)

A B C D E F G H I J K L M N O P Q R S T U V W X Y Z

C **MATCH NUMBER**

1 2 3 4 5 6 7 8 9 0

D **DATE OF BIRTH**

Month	Day	Year
January		
February		
March		
April		
May		
June		
July		
August		
September		
October		
November		
December		

 A011 215 190 Rev 1 IM-(A)199526-001:654321 Printed in the US.

PAGE 2

Marking Directions: Mark only **one** oval for each question. Fill in response completely. Erase errors cleanly without smudging.

Correct mark:

Do NOT use these ***incorrect*** **or** ***bad*** **marks.**

Incorrect marks:
Overlapping mark:
Cross-out mark:
Smudged erasure:
Mark is too light:

BOOKLET NUMBER

1	1	1	1	1	1
2	2	2	2	2	2
3	3	3	3	3	3
4	4	4	4	4	4
5	5	5	5	5	5
6	6	6	6	6	6
7	7	7	7	7	7
8	8	8	8	8	8
9	9	9	9	9	9
0	0	0	0	0	0

FORM

Print your 5-character **Test Form** in the boxes above and fill in the corresponding oval at the right.

BE SURE TO FILL IN THE CORRECT FORM OVAL.

- 16MC1
- 16MC2
- 16MC3
- 18MC4
- 19MC5

TEST 1

1 A B C D	14 F G H J	27 A B C D	40 F G H J	53 A B C D	66 F G H J
2 F G H J	15 A B C D	28 F G H J	41 A B C D	54 F G H J	67 A B C D
3 A B C D	16 F G H J	29 A B C D	42 F G H J	55 A B C D	68 F G H J
4 F G H J	17 A B C D	30 F G H J	43 A B C D	56 F G H J	69 A B C D
5 A B C D	18 F G H J	31 A B C D	44 F G H J	57 A B C D	70 F G H J
6 F G H J	19 A B C D	32 F G H J	45 A B C D	58 F G H J	71 A B C D
7 A B C D	20 F G H J	33 A B C D	46 F G H J	59 A B C D	72 F G H J
8 F G H J	21 A B C D	34 F G H J	47 A B C D	60 F G H J	73 A B C D
9 A B C D	22 F G H J	35 A B C D	48 F G H J	61 A B C D	74 F G H J
10 F G H J	23 A B C D	36 F G H J	49 A B C D	62 F G H J	75 A B C D
11 A B C D	24 F G H J	37 A B C D	50 F G H J	63 A B C D	
12 F G H J	25 A B C D	38 F G H J	51 A B C D	64 F G H J	
13 A B C D	26 F G H J	39 A B C D	52 F G H J	65 A B C D	

TEST 2

1 A B C D E	11 A B C D E	21 A B C D E	31 A B C D E	41 A B C D E	51 A B C D E
2 F G H J K	12 F G H J K	22 F G H J K	32 F G H J K	42 F G H J K	52 F G H J K
3 A B C D E	13 A B C D E	23 A B C D E	33 A B C D E	43 A B C D E	53 A B C D E
4 F G H J K	14 F G H J K	24 F G H J K	34 F G H J K	44 F G H J K	54 F G H J K
5 A B C D E	15 A B C D E	25 A B C D E	35 A B C D E	45 A B C D E	55 A B C D E
6 F G H J K	16 F G H J K	26 F G H J K	36 F G H J K	46 F G H J K	56 F G H J K
7 A B C D E	17 A B C D E	27 A B C D E	37 A B C D E	47 A B C D E	57 A B C D E
8 F G H J K	18 F G H J K	28 F G H J K	38 F G H J K	48 F G H J K	58 F G H J K
9 A B C D E	19 A B C D E	29 A B C D E	39 A B C D E	49 A B C D E	59 A B C D E
10 F G H J K	20 F G H J K	30 F G H J K	40 F G H J K	50 F G H J K	60 F G H J K

TEST 3

1 A B C D	8 F G H J	15 A B C D	22 F G H J	29 A B C D	36 F G H J
2 F G H J	9 A B C D	16 F G H J	23 A B C D	30 F G H J	37 A B C D
3 A B C D	10 F G H J	17 A B C D	24 F G H J	31 A B C D	38 F G H J
4 F G H J	11 A B C D	18 F G H J	25 A B C D	32 F G H J	39 A B C D
5 A B C D	12 F G H J	19 A B C D	26 F G H J	33 A B C D	40 F G H J
6 F G H J	13 A B C D	20 F G H J	27 A B C D	34 F G H J	
7 A B C D	14 F G H J	21 A B C D	28 F G H J	35 A B C D	

TEST 4

1 A B C D	8 F G H J	15 A B C D	22 F G H J	29 A B C D	36 F G H J
2 F G H J	9 A B C D	16 F G H J	23 A B C D	30 F G H J	37 A B C D
3 A B C D	10 F G H J	17 A B C D	24 F G H J	31 A B C D	38 F G H J
4 F G H J	11 A B C D	18 F G H J	25 A B C D	32 F G H J	39 A B C D
5 A B C D	12 F G H J	19 A B C D	26 F G H J	33 A B C D	40 F G H J
6 F G H J	13 A B C D	20 F G H J	27 A B C D	34 F G H J	
7 A B C D	14 F G H J	21 A B C D	28 F G H J	35 A B C D	

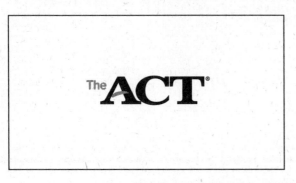

PAGE 1

The ACT® *Sample Answer Sheet*

EXAMINEE STATEMENT, CERTIFICATION, AND SIGNATURE

1. Read the following **Statement:** By submitting this answer document, I agree to comply with and be bound by the *Terms and Conditions: Testing Rules and Policies for the ACT® Test* provided in the ACT registration materials for this test, including those concerning test security, score cancellation, examinee remedies, binding arbitration, and consent to the processing of my personally identifying information, including the collection, use, transfer, and disclosure of information as described in the ACT Privacy Policy (www.act.org/privacy.html).

   I understand that ACT owns the test questions and responses and affirm that I will not share any test questions or responses with anyone by any form of communication before, during, or after the test administration. I understand that assuming anyone else's identity to take this test is strictly prohibited and may violate the law and subject me to legal penalties.

   International Examinees: By my signature, I am also providing my consent to ACT to transfer my personally identifying information to the United States to ACT, or a third-party service provider for processing, where it will be subject to use and disclosure under the laws of the United States. I acknowledge and agree that it may also be accessible to law enforcement and national security authorities in the United States.

2. Copy the **Certification** shown below (only the text in italics) on the lines provided. Write in your normal handwriting.

Certification: *I agree to the Statement above and certify that I am the person whose name and address appear on this answer document.*

Your Signature

Today's Date

Do NOT mark in this shaded area.

USE A SOFT LEAD NO. 2 PENCIL ONLY.
(Do NOT use a mechanical pencil, ink, ballpoint, correction fluid, or felt-tip pen.)

A NAME, MAILING ADDRESS, AND TELEPHONE (Please print.)

Last Name | First Name | MI (Middle Initial)

House Number & Street (Apt. No.); or PO Box & No.; or RR & No.

City | State/Province | ZIP/Postal Code

Area Code / Number | Country

ACT, Inc.—Confidential Restricted when data present

ALL examinees must complete block A – please print.

Blocks B, C, and D are required for all examinees. Find the MATCHING INFORMATION on your ticket. Enter it EXACTLY the same way, even if any of the information is missing or incorrect. Fill in the corresponding ovals. If you do not complete these blocks to match your previous information EXACTLY, your scores will be **delayed up to 8 weeks**.

ACT®

PO BOX 168, IOWA CITY, IA 52243-0168

B MATCH NAME (First 5 letters of last name)

A B C D E F G H I J K L M N O P Q R S T U V W X Y Z

C MATCH NUMBER

1 2 3 4 5 6 7 8 9 0

D DATE OF BIRTH

Month	Day	Year
January		
February		
March		
April		
May		
June		
July		
August		
September		
October		
November		
December		

 22877 A011 215 190 Rev 1 IM-(A)199526-001:654321 Printed in the US.

PAGE 2

Marking Directions: Mark only **one** oval for each question. Fill in response completely. Erase errors cleanly without smudging.

Correct mark:

Do NOT use these *incorrect* **or** *bad* **marks.**

Incorrect marks:
Overlapping mark:
Cross-out mark:
Smudged erasure:
Mark is too light:

BOOKLET NUMBER

1	1	1	1	1	1
2	2	2	2	2	2
3	3	3	3	3	3
4	4	4	4	4	4
5	5	5	5	5	5
6	6	6	6	6	6
7	7	7	7	7	7
8	8	8	8	8	8
9	9	9	9	9	9
0	0	0	0	0	0

FORM

Print your 5-character **Test Form** in the boxes above and fill in the corresponding oval at the right.

BE SURE TO FILL IN THE CORRECT FORM OVAL.

○ 16MC1
○ 16MC2
○ 16MC3
○ 18MC4
○ 19MC5

TEST 1

1 A B C D	14 F G H J	27 A B C D	40 F G H J	53 A B C D	66 F G H J
2 F G H J	15 A B C D	28 F G H J	41 A B C D	54 F G H J	67 A B C D
3 A B C D	16 F G H J	29 A B C D	42 F G H J	55 A B C D	68 F G H J
4 F G H J	17 A B C D	30 F G H J	43 A B C D	56 F G H J	69 A B C D
5 A B C D	18 F G H J	31 A B C D	44 F G H J	57 A B C D	70 F G H J
6 F G H J	19 A B C D	32 F G H J	45 A B C D	58 F G H J	71 A B C D
7 A B C D	20 F G H J	33 A B C D	46 F G H J	59 A B C D	72 F G H J
8 F G H J	21 A B C D	34 F G H J	47 A B C D	60 F G H J	73 A B C D
9 A B C D	22 F G H J	35 A B C D	48 F G H J	61 A B C D	74 F G H J
10 F G H J	23 A B C D	36 F G H J	49 A B C D	62 F G H J	75 A B C D
11 A B C D	24 F G H J	37 A B C D	50 F G H J	63 A B C D	
12 F G H J	25 A B C D	38 F G H J	51 A B C D	64 F G H J	
13 A B C D	26 F G H J	39 A B C D	52 F G H J	65 A B C D	

TEST 2

1 A B C D E	11 A B C D E	21 A B C D E	31 A B C D E	41 A B C D E	51 A B C D E
2 F G H J K	12 F G H J K	22 F G H J K	32 F G H J K	42 F G H J K	52 F G H J K
3 A B C D E	13 A B C D E	23 A B C D E	33 A B C D E	43 A B C D E	53 A B C D E
4 F G H J K	14 F G H J K	24 F G H J K	34 F G H J K	44 F G H J K	54 F G H J K
5 A B C D E	15 A B C D E	25 A B C D E	35 A B C D E	45 A B C D E	55 A B C D E
6 F G H J K	16 F G H J K	26 F G H J K	36 F G H J K	46 F G H J K	56 F G H J K
7 A B C D E	17 A B C D E	27 A B C D E	37 A B C D E	47 A B C D E	57 A B C D E
8 F G H J K	18 F G H J K	28 F G H J K	38 F G H J K	48 F G H J K	58 F G H J K
9 A B C D E	19 A B C D E	29 A B C D E	39 A B C D E	49 A B C D E	59 A B C D E
10 F G H J K	20 F G H J K	30 F G H J K	40 F G H J K	50 F G H J K	60 F G H J K

TEST 3

1 A B C D	8 F G H J	15 A B C D	22 F G H J	29 A B C D	36 F G H J
2 F G H J	9 A B C D	16 F G H J	23 A B C D	30 F G H J	37 A B C D
3 A B C D	10 F G H J	17 A B C D	24 F G H J	31 A B C D	38 F G H J
4 F G H J	11 A B C D	18 F G H J	25 A B C D	32 F G H J	39 A B C D
5 A B C D	12 F G H J	19 A B C D	26 F G H J	33 A B C D	40 F G H J
6 F G H J	13 A B C D	20 F G H J	27 A B C D	34 F G H J	
7 A B C D	14 F G H J	21 A B C D	28 F G H J	35 A B C D	

TEST 4

1 A B C D	8 F G H J	15 A B C D	22 F G H J	29 A B C D	36 F G H J
2 F G H J	9 A B C D	16 F G H J	23 A B C D	30 F G H J	37 A B C D
3 A B C D	10 F G H J	17 A B C D	24 F G H J	31 A B C D	38 F G H J
4 F G H J	11 A B C D	18 F G H J	25 A B C D	32 F G H J	39 A B C D
5 A B C D	12 F G H J	19 A B C D	26 F G H J	33 A B C D	40 F G H J
6 F G H J	13 A B C D	20 F G H J	27 A B C D	34 F G H J	
7 A B C D	14 F G H J	21 A B C D	28 F G H J	35 A B C D	

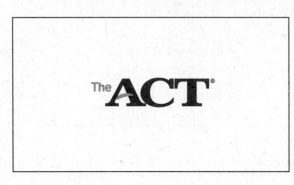

080659

Practice Test 2

EXAMINEE STATEMENT, CERTIFICATION, AND SIGNATURE

1. Read the following **Statement:** By opening this test booklet, I agree to comply with and be bound by the *Terms and Conditions: Testing Rules and Policies for the ACT® Test* provided in the ACT registration materials for this test, including those concerning test security, score cancellation, examinee remedies, binding arbitration, and consent to the processing of my personally identifying information, including the collection, use, transfer, and disclosure of information as described in the ACT Privacy Policy (www.act.org/privacy.html).

   I understand that ACT owns the test questions and responses and affirm that I will not share any test questions or responses with anyone by any form of communication before, during, or after the test administration. I understand that assuming anyone else's identity to take this test is strictly prohibited and may violate the law and subject me to legal penalties.

   International Examinees: By my signature, I am also providing my consent to ACT to transfer my personally identifying information to the United States to ACT, or a third-party service provider for processing, where it will be subject to use and disclosure under the laws of the United States. I acknowledge and agree that it may also be accessible to law enforcement and national security authorities in the United States.

2. Copy the **Certification** shown below (only the text in italics) on the lines provided. Write in your normal handwriting.

   Certification: *I agree to the Statement above and certify that I am the person whose name appears on this form.*

   ____

   ____

3. Sign your name as you would any official document, enter today's date, and print your name in the spaces provided.

   Your Signature ______ Today's Date ______ Print Your Name ______

Form 16MC2

2019 | 2020

Directions

This booklet contains tests in English, mathematics, reading, and science. These tests measure skills and abilities highly related to high school course work and success in college. **Calculators may be used on the mathematics test only.**

The questions in each test are numbered, and the suggested answers for each question are lettered. On the answer document, the rows of ovals are numbered to match the questions, and the ovals in each row are lettered to correspond to the suggested answers.

For each question, first decide which answer is best. Next, locate on the answer document the row of ovals numbered the same as the question. Then, locate the oval in that row lettered the same as your answer. Finally, fill in the oval completely. Use a soft lead pencil and make your marks heavy and black. **Do not use ink or a mechanical pencil.**

Mark only one answer to each question. If you change your mind about an answer, erase your first mark thoroughly before marking your new answer. For each question, make certain that you mark in the row of ovals with the same number as the question.

Only responses marked on your answer document will be scored. Your score on each test will be based only on the number of questions you answer correctly during the time allowed for that test. You will **not** be penalized for guessing. **It is to your advantage to answer every question even if you must guess.**

You may work on each test **only** when the testing staff tells you to do so. If you finish a test before time is called for that test, you should use the time remaining to reconsider questions you are uncertain about in that test. You may **not** look back to a test on which time has already been called, and you may **not** go ahead to another test. To do so will disqualify you from the examination.

Lay your pencil down immediately when time is called at the end of each test. You may **not** for any reason fill in or alter ovals for a test after time is called for that test. To do so will disqualify you from the examination.

Do not fold or tear the pages of your test booklet.

DO NOT OPEN THIS BOOKLET UNTIL TOLD TO DO SO.

1 ■ ■ ■ ■ ■ ■ ■ ■ ■ 1

ENGLISH TEST

45 Minutes—75 Questions

DIRECTIONS: In the five passages that follow, certain words and phrases are underlined and numbered. In the right-hand column, you will find alternatives for the underlined part. In most cases, you are to choose the one that best expresses the idea, makes the statement appropriate for standard written English, or is worded most consistently with the style and tone of the passage as a whole. If you think the original version is best, choose "NO CHANGE." In some cases, you will find in the right-hand column a question about the underlined part. You are to choose the best answer to the question.

You will also find questions about a section of the passage, or about the passage as a whole. These questions do not refer to an underlined portion of the passage, but rather are identified by a number or numbers in a box.

For each question, choose the alternative you consider best and fill in the corresponding oval on your answer document. Read each passage through once before you begin to answer the questions that accompany it. For many of the questions, you must read several sentences beyond the question to determine the answer. Be sure that you have read far enough ahead each time you choose an alternative.

PASSAGE I

The Kam Wah Chung & Co. Museum

To the casual observer, the Kam Wah Chung & Co. building, located in the eastern Oregon community of John Day, that is,[1] simply a small, unassuming structure made of rock and wood. To those with an interest in history, however, it's a unique building that preserves a part of the legacy of the Chinese community in the nineteenth-century American West.[2]

Built in the 1860s, the Kam Wah Chung building first served as a trading post for travelers who attract[3] to the land east of the Cascade Mountains by news of gold strikes there.

1. A. NO CHANGE
   B. is
   C. it's
   D. DELETE the underlined portion.

2. Given that all the choices are true, which one most effectively introduces the historical and cultural significance of the Kam Wah Chung & Co. building?
   F. NO CHANGE
   G. has seven rooms: a front room, an herb shop, two bedrooms, a stockroom, a general store, and a kitchen and bunk room.
   H. is cooperatively preserved and operated by the Oregon Parks and Recreation Department and the City of John Day.
   J. has a kitchen that holds antique tables, a large woodstove, and a variety of Chinese teas and cooking utensils.

3. A. NO CHANGE
   B. will be attracted
   C. were attracted
   D. are attracted

GO ON TO THE NEXT PAGE.

In 1887, the original owner sold the building [4]. The men combined their skills, organized a group of investors, and <u>remains</u> (5) in business together for more than fifty years.

Educated in the Chinese classics and fluent in English, Lung On was a skilled merchant who built a successful textile and import business. He also sold food and supplies to local miners. His partner, Doc Hay, established an herbal medicine clinic. Hay became famous throughout central and eastern Oregon <u>when he would make</u> (6) perceptive diagnoses and curing patients <u>whose previous treatments</u> (7) had failed. [8] Over time, the partners' building evolved into a social, medical, and supply center, as well as a post office, library, and herb shop. [9]

4. At this point, the writer is considering adding the following accurate information:

   to two enterprising young Chinese immigrants, Ing "Doc" Hay and Lung On

   Should the writer make this addition here?

   F. Yes, because it builds upon a claim made about Hay and On in the preceding sentence.
   G. Yes, because it provides a logical link to the information that follows in the essay.
   H. No, because it unnecessarily states information that's implied later in the essay.
   J. No, because it provides little information about Hay and On's partnership.

5. A. NO CHANGE
   B. has remained
   C. have remain
   D. remained

6. F. NO CHANGE
   G. for making
   H. as he made
   J. and made

7. A. NO CHANGE
   B. who experienced that their previous treatments
   C. being previous treatments which
   D. of whom previous treatments

8. The writer is considering deleting the preceding sentence. Should the sentence be kept or deleted?

   F. Kept, because it provides information that suggests why Hay's work was particularly noteworthy.
   G. Kept, because it presents examples of Hay's most challenging and successful diagnoses.
   H. Deleted, because it doesn't make clear whether On was involved with Hay's herbal medicine clinic.
   J. Deleted, because it doesn't fit logically in this paragraph about On's accomplishments.

9. If the writer were to delete the preceding sentence, the paragraph would primarily lose a statement that:

   A. demonstrates the scope of services eventually provided in the Kam Wah Chung & Co. building.
   B. makes clear that the social aspect of Kam Wah Chung & Co. was most important to visitors.
   C. provides a summary of one regular visitor's experiences at Kam Wah Chung & Co.
   D. indicates for how long Hay and On's businesses prospered.

GO ON TO THE NEXT PAGE.

1 ■ ■ ■ ■ ■ ■ ■ ■ ■ 1

[1] Hay and On's businesses prospered through the turn of the century, during the Great Depression, and beginning[10] the 1940s. [2] Because the climate in eastern Oregon is semi-arid, the artifacts left inside—including gold-mining tools, rare antique furniture, financial documents, and a thousand different herbs—were preserved. [3] Although On died in 1940, Hay continued to run Kam Wah Chung & Co. until 1948. [4] After Hay's death, his nephew inherited the building and donated it to the city of John Day. [5] For almost twenty years, it remained locked. [6] The building was restored by the state of Oregon in the 1970s and has became[11] the Kam Wah Chung & Co. Museum. [7] Designated as being called a[12] National Historic Landmark in 2005, besides,[13] it encapsulates an era. [14]

10. F. NO CHANGE
G. as it entered
H. becoming
J. into

11. A. NO CHANGE
B. have become
C. became
D. become

12. F. NO CHANGE
G. with the appropriation of
H. in being identified as a
J. a

13. A. NO CHANGE
B. in conclusion,
C. in time,
D. DELETE the underlined portion.

14. For the sake of the logic and coherence of this paragraph, Sentence 2 should be placed:
F. where it is now.
G. before Sentence 1.
H. after Sentence 3.
J. after Sentence 5.

Question 15 asks about the preceding passage as a whole.

15. Suppose the writer's goal had been to write a brief essay that outlined the steps the state of Oregon took to restore the Kam Wah Chung & Co. building. Would this essay accomplish that goal?
A. Yes, because it makes clear that the Kam Wah Chung & Co. building was renovated in the 1970s.
B. Yes, because it explains why the artifacts that were inside the Kam Wah Chung & Co. building were preserved.
C. No, because it instead focuses on describing the history of the Kam Wah Chung & Co. building and the building's uses.
D. No, because it instead focuses on critiquing both On's business philosophies and Hay's medical diagnoses and treatments.

GO ON TO THE NEXT PAGE.

PASSAGE II

One Fair Season

At first glance a Renaissance fair, looks a lot like a theme park. Crowds of people mill about, moseying they're way past costumed characters and colorful booths. Being that roller coasters and Ferris wheels, the fair's attractions are the sights, sounds, and tastes inspired by sixteenth-century England. Musicians, magicians, and archers demonstrate their talents to curious fairgoers. Horses carrying knights to a jousting match walk along the streets. Vendors, ranging from king-sized turkey legs to suits of armor, peddle wares.

I've always enjoyed attending Renaissance fairs, and I found out just how interesting they are. Those of us working at the fair spent weeks perfecting our characters' accents and mannerisms. We also incorporated sixteenth-century English vocabulary into our speech. Substituting *good morrow* for "good morning" and *gramercy* for "thank you." In my role

16. F. NO CHANGE
    G. glance, a Renaissance fair,
    H. glance, a Renaissance fair
    J. glance a Renaissance fair;

17. A. NO CHANGE
    B. they're way passed
    C. their way passed
    D. their way past

18. F. NO CHANGE
    G. Yet instead of
    H. Because of
    J. Given that

19. A. NO CHANGE
    B. Horses, carrying knights,
    C. Horses carrying knights,
    D. Horses, carrying knights

20. Which choice best conveys the horses' movement in a way that adds a sensory detail to the description of the fair?
    F. NO CHANGE
    G. clip-clop
    H. move
    J. travel

21. A. NO CHANGE
    B. Peddling wares, ranging from king-sized turkey legs to suits of armor are vendors.
    C. Ranging from king-sized turkey legs to suits of armor, vendors peddle wares.
    D. Vendors peddle wares ranging from king-sized turkey legs to suits of armor.

22. Which choice best introduces the subject of the paragraph and the rest of the essay?
    F. NO CHANGE
    G. but it wasn't until I spent a summer working at one that I understood how much effort went into re-creating the past.
    H. and I knew that getting a job at one would be the easiest way to experience one and have fun at the same time.
    J. so one summer's day, some friends and I decided to attend a nearby fair.

23. A. NO CHANGE
    B. speech, we substituted
    C. speech, substituting
    D. speech; substituting

GO ON TO THE NEXT PAGE.

1          1

as a lady-in-waiting, I often used the sixteenth-century expressions while I served the queen's meals or introduced [24] her to guests.

It was exhausting to spend every day in the hot summer temperatures while pretending to be a person whom had lived [25] in a different country and century. The physical demands were especially strenuous for the queen and us ladies-in-waiting because our costumes, they [26] consisted of confining corsets, several scratchy petticoats, and heavy velvet gowns. [27]

We strove to make the fairgoers' experience as authentic as possible. Things that had come into existence more recently [28] after the sixteenth century had to be explained in Renaissance terms. However, [29] when a guest wished to take a photograph, we would marvel at the camera and ask how such lifelike paintings were created inside the tiny box.

After three tiring months of rehearsals and performances, the fair closed for the season, and I bade *fare thee well* to my Renaissance character when the summer months were over. [30] Although it had been a wonderful trip back in time, it was a relief to return to the comforts of my own century.

24. **F.** NO CHANGE
G. to introduce
H. introducing
J. introduce

25. **A.** NO CHANGE
B. who were to live
C. whom lived
D. who lived

26. **F.** NO CHANGE
G. of our costumes, they
H. of our costumes
J. our costumes

27. At this point, the writer is considering adding the following sentence:

Many theme park characters have to wear uncomfortable costumes.

Should the writer make this addition here?

A. Yes, because it develops the essay's earlier comparison between Renaissance fairs and theme parks.
B. Yes, because it elaborates on the preceding sentence's point about costumes.
C. No, because it adds a comment that's only loosely related at this point in the essay.
D. No, because it repeats information stated elsewhere in the essay.

28. **F.** NO CHANGE
G. Any kind of object or type of item created and introduced for use
H. Anything invented
J. Stuff from

29. **A.** NO CHANGE
B. For example,
C. One time,
D. Instead,

30. **F.** NO CHANGE
G. when the fair closed down.
H. at the end of the summer.
J. DELETE the underlined portion and end the sentence with a period.

GO ON TO THE NEXT PAGE.

PASSAGE III

Uncovered at Johnson's Shut-Ins

In Reynolds County, Missouri, a one-billion-gallon blast of water caused by [31] a breach of the Taum Sauk reservoir roared down Proffit Mountain into the east fork of the Black River on December 14, 2005. They [32] ripped a channel through Johnson's Shut-Ins, one of Missouri's most popular state parks. Though flood damage marred the parks beauty for a time, [33] the scar the raging water left in its wake specifically [34] revealed over a billion years' worth of Earth's geologic history.

The area known today as Johnson's Shut-Ins State Park had began to develop [35] 1.5 billion years ago. When [36] the volcanoes that created the St. Francois Mountains exploded. Slow-moving magma cooled down its temperature [37] and crystallized to form silica-rich rhyolite [38] rock. Over time sedimentary rock such as limestone and shale, formed from material deposited by shallow inland seas, buried the rhyolite. After the seas had receded, gravel-rich rivers and streams eventually chipped away the soft sedimentary rock in some areas,

31. A. NO CHANGE
    B. water caused by,
    C. water caused, by
    D. water, caused by

32. F. NO CHANGE
    G. That they
    H. Which
    J. It

33. A. NO CHANGE
    B. park's beauty for a time,
    C. parks' beauty for a time,
    D. park's beauty for a time

34. F. NO CHANGE
    G. ultimately
    H. instead
    J. thus

35. A. NO CHANGE
    B. begun developing
    C. began to develop
    D. begun to develop

36. F. NO CHANGE
    G. ago; when
    H. ago when
    J. ago

37. A. NO CHANGE
    B. cooled down to a lower temperature
    C. lowered its temperature to cool
    D. cooled

38. F. NO CHANGE
    G. form silica-rich, rhyolite,
    H. form silica-rich rhyolite,
    J. form, silica-rich rhyolite

Taking Additional Practice Tests

GO ON TO THE NEXT PAGE.

1 ■ ■ ■ ■ ■ ■ ■ ■ ■ 1

exposing the erosion-resistant rhyolite rock and creating pockets and pits. In low places, the Black River was confined (or "shut in") [39] by the rhyolite and creating [40] the natural waterslides and canyon-like gorges that have become a summer playground for thousands of visitors.

Although the flood left the shut-ins unscathed, the surge of water that tore through the park in 2005 stripped away all trees, soil, and sedimentary rock in its [41] path. Left behind is a channel that is composed of granite—and previously unexposed rhyolite rock—and contain [42] rocks from at least three other geological eras. The menacing floodwaters also revealed a half-billion-year-old beach made of both sand and gravel.

Five years of work has restored most of the park surrounding the shut-ins. Some [43] have returned back. [44] Geologists from around the world visit to get a close look at the ancient volcanic rock along what has been named the "Scour Channel." The "Scour Channel" now rivals the park's other geologic curiosities for most frequently visited site.

39. The writer is considering deleting the underlined portion. Should the underlined portion be kept or deleted?
- **A.** Kept, because it describes how people feel when they visit the park.
- **B.** Kept, because it suggests the inspiration for the park's name.
- **C.** Deleted, because it makes an informal observation that is not consistent with the essay's tone.
- **D.** Deleted, because it interrupts the sentence's description of the Black River.

40.
- **F.** NO CHANGE
- **G.** rhyolite; creating
- **H.** rhyolite, creating
- **J.** rhyolite, created

41.
- **A.** NO CHANGE
- **B.** on their
- **C.** in their
- **D.** on its

42.
- **F.** NO CHANGE
- **G.** have contained
- **H.** are containing
- **J.** contains

43.
- **A.** NO CHANGE
- **B.** Those who are nuts about the outdoors
- **C.** Swimmers, hikers, and campers
- **D.** All types of outdoorsy people

44.
- **F.** NO CHANGE
- **G.** by coming back to the park.
- **H.** to revisit the park.
- **J.** DELETE the underlined portion and end the sentence with a period.

GO ON TO THE NEXT PAGE.

PASSAGE IV

A Birthplace of Stars

The winter night I attempted to see the famed Orion Nebula, I didn't expect to succeed. I was an inexperienced astronomer peering through [45] light-polluted skies. But I was eager to test my new telescope's capabilities, and the nebula being [46] one of the greatest sights in the night sky. So I bundled up, set out my scope to cool down (its mirrors must adjust to the cold air for optimal viewing), and scanned for the constellation Orion.

45. A. NO CHANGE
    B. astronomer, peering through,
    C. astronomer: peering through
    D. astronomer peering through,

46. F. NO CHANGE
    G. is by them said to be
    H. is said to be
    J. having been

I had prepared for this night by studying constellations in my astronomy books. Orion appears as a hunter who, in some mythologies, [47] is fighting Taurus the Bull, another constellation. [A] Even in bright skies, the telltale three stars marking Orion's belt has been [48] easy to spot. [B] I knew to follow the belt to Orion's sword, a dim line of stars extending south. [C] The middle of these is actually not a star but a nebula, the Great Orion Nebula, a birthplace of stars. [D] When gravity causes the gas and dust to collapse, forming stars. [49]

47. A. NO CHANGE
    B. hunter, who in some mythologies,
    C. hunter who, in some mythologies
    D. hunter who in, some mythologies,

48. F. NO CHANGE
    G. were being
    H. are
    J. is

49. A. NO CHANGE
    B. collapse to form stars.
    C. collapse, stars form.
    D. collapse and form stars.

The nebula, is home to thousands of young stars, [50] is often called a galactic "nursery." [51]

50. F. NO CHANGE
    G. nebula is home to thousands of young stars, and
    H. nebula, home to thousands of young stars, and
    J. nebula, home to thousands of young stars,

51. The writer wants to add the following sentence to the preceding paragraph:

    Located 1,300 light-years from Earth, the nebula is a massive cloud of gas and dust.

    This sentence would most logically be placed at:

    A. Point A.
    B. Point B.
    C. Point C.
    D. Point D.

Taking Additional Practice Tests

GO ON TO THE NEXT PAGE.

1 ■ ■ ■ ■ ■ ■ ■ ■ ■ 1

I centered my scope where the nebula should be, inserted my lowest-powered eyepiece, and leaned in to look. I just made out a dull smudge. I couldn't get much improvement even when I adjusted the focuser. Coincidentally, [52] I switched to a higher-powered eyepiece and tried a trick I'd [53] read about for viewing faint objects: using averted vision.

The principle of averted vision states that the eye can often see distant objects better by looking to their one side [54] rather than directly at them. [55] I focused my eye on an area beside the smudge, and, sure enough, my peripheral vision yielded far more of a [56] better view of the nebula's swirling clouds. I even saw the Trapezium star cluster, illuminated [57] by four bright young stars nestled in the nebula like birds' eggs [58]

52. F. NO CHANGE
    G. Similarly,
    H. Besides,
    J. So,

53. A. NO CHANGE
    B. tried a trick I'd have
    C. try a trick I'd
    D. try a trick I

54. F. NO CHANGE
    G. one side of them
    H. they're side
    J. one's side

55. The writer is considering deleting the preceding sentence. Should the sentence be kept or deleted?
    A. Kept, because it elaborates on why the narrator is capable of using averted vision when looking at the night sky.
    B. Kept, because it explains the principle that allowed the narrator to see the nebula more clearly.
    C. Deleted, because it adds a level of technical detail that is inappropriate for the tone of the essay.
    D. Deleted, because it digresses from the main point of the paragraph.

56. F. NO CHANGE
    G. a farther,
    H. a far
    J. a far,

57. A. NO CHANGE
    B. emanated
    C. emulated
    D. eliminated

58. F. NO CHANGE
    G. bird's eggs
    H. birds eggs
    J. bird eggs'

GO ON TO THE NEXT PAGE.

in a nest. [59]

59. Given that all the following statements are true, which one, if added here, would best conclude the paragraph and the essay by referring back to the opening paragraph?
    - **A.** Observing these features made my winter trek outdoors worthwhile, teaching me that a change in focus is sometimes helpful to see more clearly.
    - **B.** In addition to averted vision, it is also important to eliminate stray light and use the correct magnification when observing the night sky.
    - **C.** Although my initial goal was to observe Orion's belt and sword, the constellation is also very useful as an aid to locating other constellations such as Taurus and Gemini.
    - **D.** The Trapezium star cluster was originally discovered in 1617 by Galileo, whom I'd read about extensively in my astronomy books.

Question 60 asks about the preceding passage as a whole.

60. Suppose the writer's goal had been to write an essay about a personal experience with astronomy. Would this essay accomplish that goal?
    - **F.** Yes, because the narrator recounts several past adventures and challenges of using the telescope to view the night sky.
    - **G.** Yes, because the narrator describes a stargazing session from start to finish, from setting up the telescope to observing an actual constellation.
    - **H.** No, because it primarily focuses on the Orion Nebula and its process of star formation.
    - **J.** No, because it describes a universally used technique for viewing distant objects in the night sky.

PASSAGE V

Chords of Color

Some viewers see the paintings of abstract artist James Little as impersonal, discordant rainbows. Others see them as minimalistic distillations of <u>emotion, in other words, they are</u> [61] metaphors for Little's feelings about social issues and historical events. He paints large-scale patterns of <u>shapes—mostly triangles and narrow rectangles in vibrant</u> [62] contrasting hues.

61. **A.** NO CHANGE
    B. emotion, they see the paintings as
    C. emotion the works offer
    D. emotion,

62. Which choice is correctly punctuated and makes clear that all the shapes that Little paints are painted in vibrant and contrasting hues?
    F. NO CHANGE
    G. shapes—mostly triangles and narrow rectangles—in vibrant,
    H. shapes—mostly triangles—and narrow rectangles in vibrant,
    J. shapes, mostly triangles and narrow rectangles in vibrant

GO ON TO THE NEXT PAGE.

Taking Additional Practice Tests

1 ■ ■ ■ ■ ■ ■ ■ ■ ■ 1

His paintings explore the ambiguity of space, the energy of movement, and the coming together of unlikely elements. <u>But his subject he says is</u> [63] color. [64]

63. A. NO CHANGE
B. But his subject, he says,
C. But, his subject, he says
D. But his subject, he says

64. At this point, the writer is considering adding the following true statement:

> Little also says that Syracuse University, where he earned his MFA in 1976, was a "beacon for abstract painting."

Should the writer make this addition here?

F. Yes, because it provides a smooth transition to the biographical focus of the paragraph that follows.
G. Yes, because it indicates where Little first became focused on working with color.
H. No, because it adds information that is tangentially related to the essay but blurs the focus of the first paragraph.
J. No, because it causes unnecessary confusion concerning the essay's assertion that Little works with geometric figures.

In 2011, working out of his studio in Brooklyn, New York, Little is painting on canvas using his own blends of beeswax and oil paint. He applies at least fifteen layers of <u>these paints that he blended himself</u> [65] to achieve a thick, smooth, color-soaked, luminescent surface. Most of his paintings are <u>voluminous,</u> [66] about six feet by eight feet. To create sharp visual breaks and clean edges of color in these expansive works, he paints slashing diagonal lines and rays.

65. A. NO CHANGE
B. paint, which is of his own making, and does so
C. his own blends that he made
D. these blends

66. F. NO CHANGE
G. immeasurable,
H. mountainous,
J. large,

In his 2005 painting *Bittersweet Victory*, <u>by all means,</u> [67] the canvas is <u>bisected by a vertical, beige</u> [68] line. On the left half, three orange triangles in a row, each one <u>which stretched</u> [69] from the bottom to the top of the <u>canvas's left half,</u> [70] angle slightly to the right on a purple

67. A. NO CHANGE
B. for example,
C. in contrast,
D. thereafter,

68. Which of the following alternatives to the underlined portion would NOT be acceptable?

F. vertically bisected by a beige
G. bisected by a vertically beige
H. bisected vertically by a beige
J. bisected by a beige, vertical

69. A. NO CHANGE
B. which by stretching
C. stretching
D. stretches

70. F. NO CHANGE
G. canvas, on the left half,
H. left half of the canvas,
J. canvas,

GO ON TO THE NEXT PAGE.

background. On the right half, three vertical bands of dark green, one edge of each band slanting to create a point that touches the top of the canvas, cuts through a lime-green background. Little explains that the internal spaces in his paintings (created by lines and blocks of color) need to play off of each other in a way that lends rhythm and unity to the whole work. The effect is much like something that would remind you of a perfect jazz collaboration. [74]

One of Little's favorite assessments of his work came from a woman who told him that his paintings are optimistic. Little believes the bold, positive energy infusing his work comes from what he observes around him. His paintings reflect what he considers the essence of our experiences as human beings. The malleable nature of space, the surprising shifts, but, in the end, a balance.

71. A. NO CHANGE
B. cuts crossed
C. cut through
D. cut crossed

72. F. NO CHANGE
G. on the entirety of the
H. into the whole
J. with the entire

73. A. NO CHANGE
B. reminiscent of something that echoes
C. much like that of
D. being like

74. If the writer were to delete the preceding sentence, the paragraph would primarily lose a description of Little's work that:
F. builds on the subtle musical reference in the paragraph to create a comparison between Little's paintings and jazz.
G. indicates the popularity of Little's paintings by drawing a comparison between his work and jazz collaborations.
H. provides a transition to the following paragraph's focus on several assessments of Little's work by art critics.
J. emphasizes the idea that Little's methods allowed him to reach the goals he uniquely set for his piece *Bittersweet Victory*.

Question 75 asks about the preceding passage as a whole.

75. Suppose the writer's primary purpose had been to describe how an artist uses simple elements to convey large ideas. Would this essay accomplish that purpose?
A. Yes, because it focuses primarily on one viewer's conclusion that the lines of color in Little's *Bittersweet Victory* communicate the idea of optimism.
B. Yes, because it conveys that Little uses shapes and color to capture what he sees as the movement and rhythm of the human experience.
C. No, because it focuses too heavily on describing the metaphor that Little hoped to create with *Bittersweet Victory* but does not explain what that painting looked like.
D. No, because it indicates that Little focuses on color in his work but does not suggest the effect that his work achieves.

END OF TEST 1

STOP! DO NOT TURN THE PAGE UNTIL TOLD TO DO SO.

2 △ △ △ △ △ △ △ △ △ 2

MATHEMATICS TEST

60 Minutes—60 Questions

DIRECTIONS: Solve each problem, choose the correct answer, and then fill in the corresponding oval on your answer document.

Do not linger over problems that take too much time. Solve as many as you can; then return to the others in the time you have left for this test.

You are permitted to use a calculator on this test. You may use your calculator for any problems you choose, but some of the problems may best be done without using a calculator.

Note: Unless otherwise stated, all of the following should be assumed.

1. Illustrative figures are NOT necessarily drawn to scale.
2. Geometric figures lie in a plane.
3. The word *line* indicates a straight line.
4. The word *average* indicates arithmetic mean.

DO YOUR FIGURING HERE.

1. A restaurant occupying the top floor of a skyscraper rotates as diners enjoy the view. Ling and Sarah notice that they began their meal at 7:00 p.m. looking due north. At 7:45 p.m. they had rotated 180° to a view that was due south. At this rate, how many degrees will the restaurant rotate in 1 hour?

A. 90°
B. 180°
C. 240°
D. 270°
E. 400°

2. The cost of a gym membership is a onetime fee of $140, plus a monthly fee of $40. Brendan wrote a $500 check to pay his gym membership for a certain number of months, including the onetime fee. How many months of membership did he pay for?

F. 3
G. 4
H. 9
J. 12
K. 13

3. A museum offers a 2-hour guided group tour. For groups with fewer than 25 people the cost is $9.25 per person; for groups with 25 people or more the cost is $8.50 per person. The 27 people in the 9:00 a.m. tour group each paid $9.25 in advance. What is the total refund that the museum owes the 9:00 a.m. group?

A. $12.50
B. $13.00
C. $18.75
D. $20.25
E. $25.00

GO ON TO THE NEXT PAGE.

2 △ △ △ △ △ △ △ △ △ 2

DO YOUR FIGURING HERE.

4. The 13-member math club needs to choose a student government representative. They decide that the representative, who will be chosen at random, CANNOT be any of the 3 officers of the club. What is the probability that Samara, who is a member of the club but NOT an officer, will be chosen?

F. 0

G. $\frac{1}{13}$

H. $\frac{1}{10}$

J. $\frac{3}{13}$

K. $\frac{1}{3}$

5. Mele earned scores of 75, 70, 92, 95, and 97 points (a total of 429 points) on the first 5 tests in Economics II. Solving which of the following equations for s gives the score he needs to earn on the 6th test to average exactly 85 points for all 6 tests?

A. $\frac{429}{5} + s = 85$

B. $\frac{429}{6} + s = 85$

C. $\frac{s + 429}{5} = 85$

D. $\frac{s + 429}{6} = 85$

E. $\frac{s + 429}{6} = \frac{85}{100}$

6. The figure below shows quadrilateral $ABCD$. What is the measure of $\angle C$?

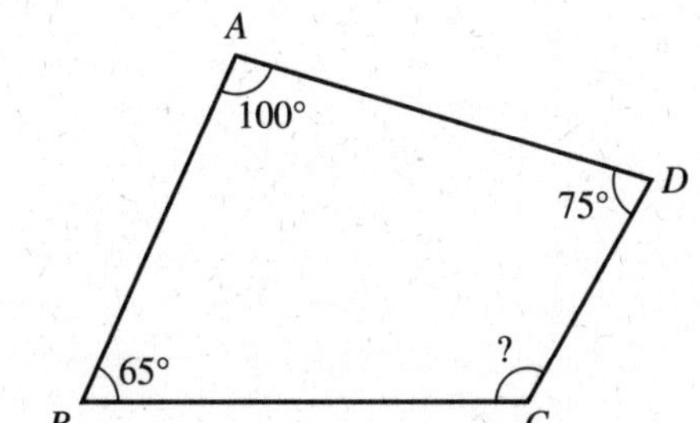

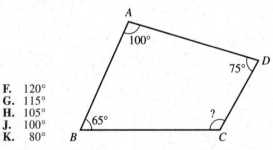

F. 120°
G. 115°
H. 105°
J. 100°
K. 80°

7. In the figure below, $\triangle ABC$ and $\triangle DEF$ are similar triangles with the given side lengths in meters. What is the perimeter, in meters, of $\triangle DEF$?

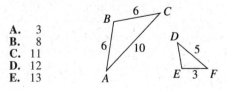

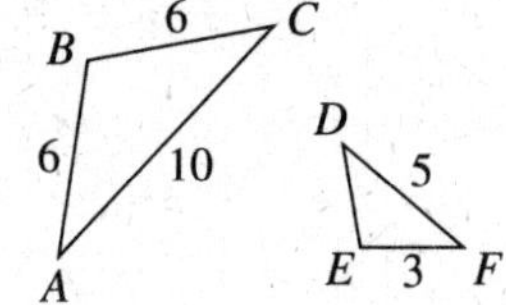

A. 3
B. 8
C. 11
D. 12
E. 13

GO ON TO THE NEXT PAGE.

2         2

DO YOUR FIGURING HERE.

8. $|3(-2) + 4| = ?$

F. −2
G. 2
H. 5
J. 9
K. 10

9. What are the values for x that satisfy the equation $(x + a)(x + b) = 0$?

A. $-a$ and $-b$
B. $-a$ and b
C. $-ab$
D. a and $-b$
E. a and b

10. In the figure below, G is the center of the circle, $\overline{LK}$ is a diameter, H lies on the circle, J lies outside the circle on $\overleftrightarrow{LK}$, and $\overleftrightarrow{JM}$ is tangent to the circle at M. Which of the following angles or minor arcs has the greatest degree measure?

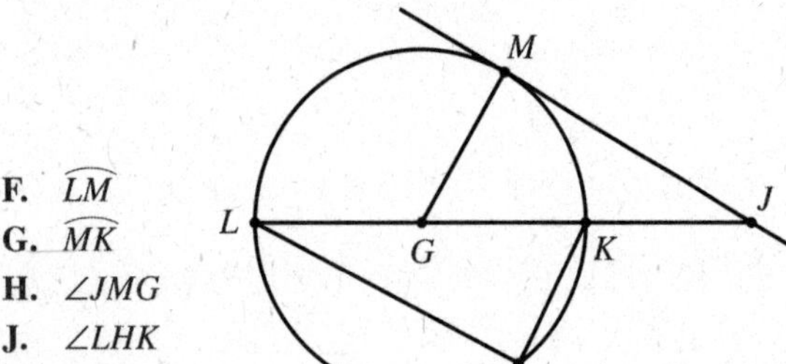

F. $\overset{\frown}{LM}$
G. $\overset{\frown}{MK}$
H. $\angle JMG$
J. $\angle LHK$
K. $\angle MJL$

11. Points B and C lie on $\overline{AD}$ as shown below. The length of $\overline{AD}$ is 30 units; $\overline{AC}$ is 16 units long; and $\overline{BD}$ is 20 units long. How many units long, if it can be determined, is $\overline{BC}$?

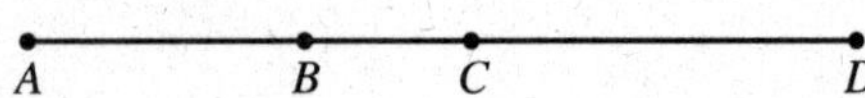

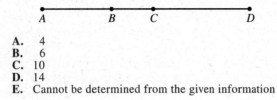

A. 4
B. 6
C. 10
D. 14
E. Cannot be determined from the given information

12. If $12x = -8(10 - x)$, then $x = ?$

F. 20
G. 8
H. $7\frac{3}{11}$
J. $6\frac{2}{13}$
K. −20

GO ON TO THE NEXT PAGE.

2 △ △ △ △ △ △ △ △ △ 2

DO YOUR FIGURING HERE.

Use the following information to answer questions 13–15.

Ken baked, frosted, and decorated a rectangular cake for the last Math Club meeting. The cake was 3 inches high, 12 inches wide, and 16 inches long. He centered the cake on a piece of cardboard whose rectangular top surface had been covered with aluminum foil, as shown in the figure below.

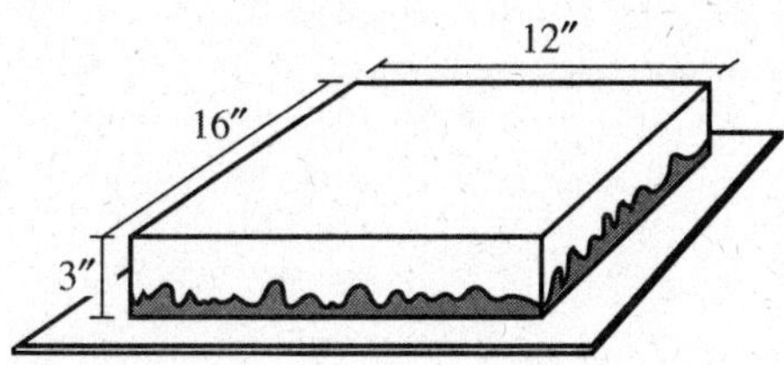

13. Ken used a piece of cardboard large enough to allow the cardboard to extend 2 inches beyond the cake on all sides. What is the area, in square inches, of the aluminum foil that is exposed on the top surface of the cardboard?

A. 60
B. 64
C. 88
D. 96
E. 128

14. At the Math Club meeting, Principal Gonzales cut the entire cake into pieces. Each piece is 2 inches wide, 2 inches long, and 3 inches high. What is the number of pieces Principal Gonzales cut the cake into?

F. 16
G. 20
H. 28
J. 48
K. 96

15. The Math Club will pay Ken \$5.00 for preparing the cake and will also pay him for the cost of the cake mix at \$1.73, the frosting mix at \$2.67, and the sales tax of 5% on these 2 items. What is the total amount the Math Club will pay Ken?

A. \$4.67
B. \$9.40
C. \$9.45
D. \$9.62
E. \$9.87

GO ON TO THE NEXT PAGE.

2 △ △ △ △ △ △ △ △ △ 2

DO YOUR FIGURING HERE.

16. What is the y-intercept of the line in the standard (x,y) coordinate plane that goes through the points $(-3,6)$ and $(3,2)$?

F. 0
G. 2
H. 4
J. 6
K. 8

17. A machine part is diagrammed in the figure below with the dimensions given in inches. If the centers of the circles lie on the same line parallel to the bottom of the part, what is the distance, in inches, between the centers of the 2 holes in the machine part?

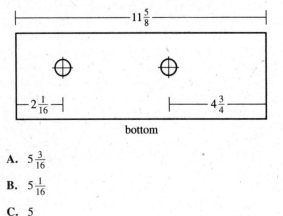

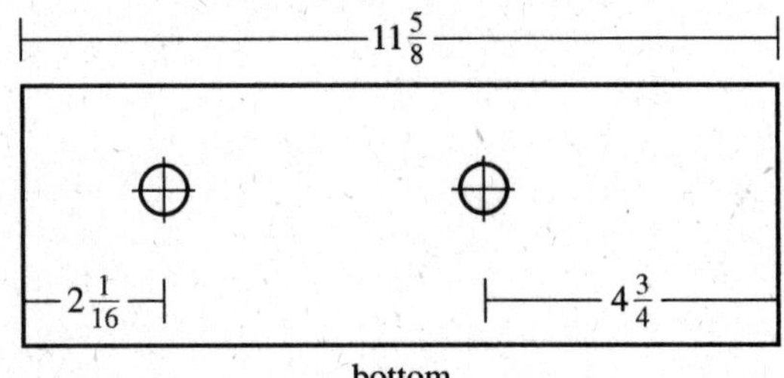

A. $5\frac{3}{16}$

B. $5\frac{1}{16}$

C. 5

D. $4\frac{13}{16}$

E. $4\frac{3}{16}$

18. The depth of a pond is 180 cm and is being reduced by 1 cm per week. The depth of a second pond is 160 cm and is being reduced by $\frac{1}{2}$ cm per week. If the depths of both ponds continue to be reduced at these constant rates, in about how many weeks will the ponds have the same depth?

F. 10
G. 20
H. 40
J. 80
K. 140

GO ON TO THE NEXT PAGE.

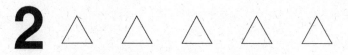

2          2

DO YOUR FIGURING HERE.

19. When graphed in the standard (x,y) coordinate plane, which of the following equations does NOT represent a line?

A. $x = 4$

B. $3y = 6$

C. $x - y = 1$

D. $y = \frac{3}{4}x - 2$

E. $x^2 + y = 5$

20. In the right triangle shown below, which of the following statements is true about $\angle A$?

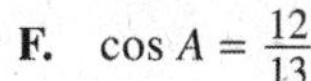

F. $\cos A = \frac{12}{13}$

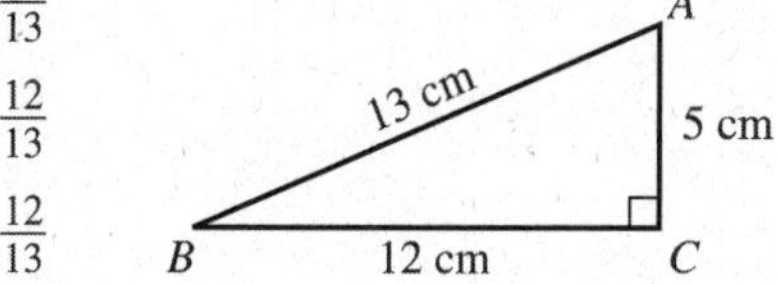

G. $\sin A = \frac{12}{13}$

H. $\tan A = \frac{12}{13}$

J. $\cos A = \frac{13}{12}$

K. $\sin A = \frac{13}{12}$

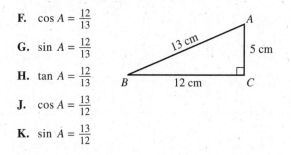

21. A park has the shape and dimensions in blocks given below. A water fountain is located halfway between point B and point D. Which of the following is the location of the water fountain from point A ?

(Note: The park's borders run east-west or north-south.)

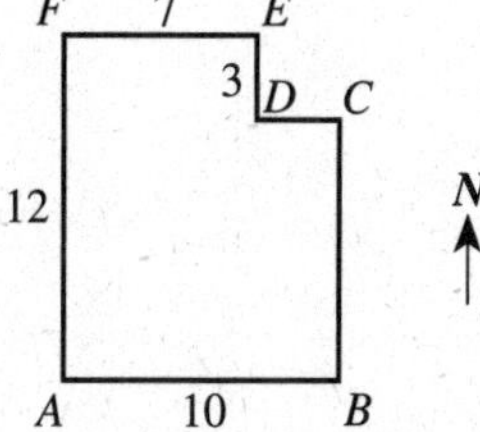

A. $3\frac{1}{2}$ blocks east and 6 blocks north

B. 5 blocks east and $4\frac{1}{2}$ blocks north

C. 5 blocks east and 6 blocks north

D. $8\frac{1}{2}$ blocks east and $4\frac{1}{2}$ blocks north

E. 9 blocks east and $7\frac{1}{2}$ blocks north

GO ON TO THE NEXT PAGE.

2 △ △ △ △ △ △ △ △ △ 2

DO YOUR FIGURING HERE.

22. The braking distance, y feet, for Damon's car to come to a complete stop is modeled by $y = \frac{3(x^2 + 10x)}{40}$, where x is the speed of the car in miles per hour. According to this model, which of the following is the maximum speed, in miles per hour, Damon can be driving so that the braking distance is less than or equal to 150 feet?

F. 10
G. 30
H. 40
J. 50
K. 60

23. If $f(x) = x^2 + x + 5$ and $g(x) = \sqrt{x}$, then what is the value of $\frac{g(4)}{f(1)}$?

A. $\frac{2}{7}$

B. $\frac{25}{7}$

C. $\frac{2}{25}$

D. 2

E. 4

24. At a school picnic, 1 junior and 1 senior will be selected to lead the activities. If there are 125 juniors and 100 seniors at the picnic, how many different 2-person combinations of 1 junior and 1 senior are possible?

F. 25
G. 100
H. 125
J. 225
K. 12,500

GO ON TO THE NEXT PAGE.

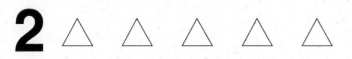

2 △ △ △ △ △ △ △ △ △ 2

DO YOUR FIGURING HERE.

25. The scatterplot in the standard (x,y) coordinate plane below contains data points showing a strong linear correlation between the variables x and y. Mia drew the line shown to model the data. One of the following equations represents Mia's line. Which one?

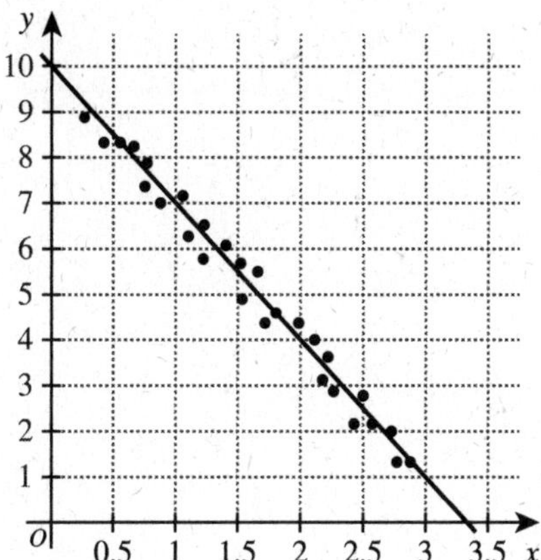

A. $y = -3x + 8$
B. $y = -3x + 10$
C. $y = -2x + 10$
D. $y = 2x + 10$
E. $y = 2x + 8$

26. The temperature, t, in degrees Fahrenheit, in a certain town on a certain spring day satisfies the inequality $|t - 24| \leq 30$. Which of the following temperatures, in degrees Fahrenheit, is NOT in this range?

F. -10
G. -6
H. -5
J. 0
K. 54

27. If 5 times a number n is subtracted from 15, the result is negative. Which of the following gives the possible value(s) for n ?

A. 0 only
B. 3 only
C. 10 only
D. All $n > 3$
E. All $n < 3$

28. For all $x > 21$, $\dfrac{(x^2 + 8x + 7)(x - 3)}{(x^2 + 4x - 21)(x + 1)} = ?$

F. 1

G. $\dfrac{9}{7}$

H. $\dfrac{x-3}{x+3}$

J. $\dfrac{2(x-3)}{x+1}$

K. $-\dfrac{4(x-3)}{x+1}$

GO ON TO THE NEXT PAGE.

Taking Additional Practice Tests

DO YOUR FIGURING HERE.

29. The median of a set of data containing 9 items was found. Four data items were added to the set. Two of these items were greater than the original median, and the other 2 items were less than the original median. Which of the following statements *must* be true about the median of the new data set?

A. It is the average of the 2 new lower values.
B. It is the same as the original median.
C. It is the average of the 2 new higher values.
D. It is greater than the original median.
E. It is less than the original median.

30. The figure below shows 2 tangent circles such that the 10-centimeter diameter of the smaller circle is equal to the radius of the larger circle. What is the area, in square centimeters, of the shaded region?

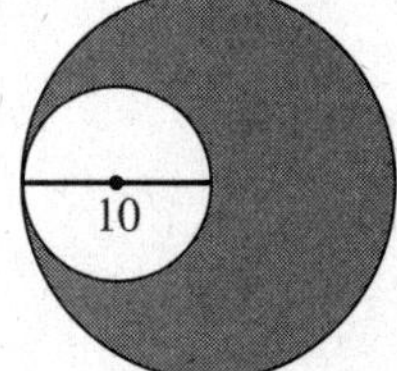

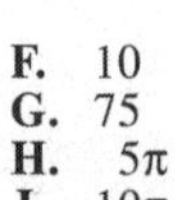

F. 10
G. 75
H. 5π
J. 10π
K. 75π

31. The sign of a is positive. The sign of b is negative. If it can be determined, what is the sign of the mean of a and b ?

A. Positive
B. Negative
C. Both positive and negative
D. Neither positive nor negative
E. Cannot be determined from the given information

> Use the following information to answer questions 32–34.

The curve $y = 0.005x^2 - 2x + 200$ for $0 \leq x \leq 200$ and the line segment from $F(0,200)$ to $G(200,0)$ are shown in the standard (x,y) coordinate plane below.

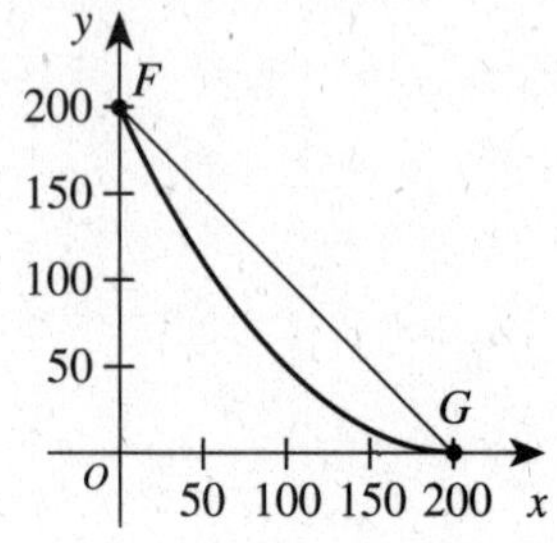

GO ON TO THE NEXT PAGE.

2 △ △ △ △ △ △ △ △ △ 2

DO YOUR FIGURING HERE.

32. What is the y-coordinate for the point on the curve with x-coordinate 20 ?

F. 160
G. 162
H. 164
J. 166
K. 168

33. The length of this curve is longer than $\overline{FG}$. About how many coordinate units long is $\overline{FG}$?

A. 20
B. 141
C. 200
D. 283
E. 400

34. Tran wants to approximate the area underneath the curve $y = 0.005x^2 - 2x + 200$ for $0 \le x \le 200$, shown shaded in the graph below.

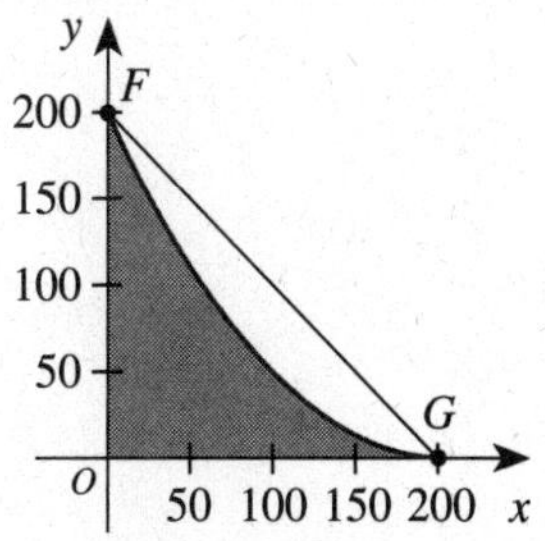

He finds an initial estimate, A, for the shaded area by using $\overline{FG}$ and computing $A = \frac{1}{2}(200 \text{ units})(200 \text{ units}) = 20{,}000$ square units. The area of the shaded region is:

F. less than 20,000 square units, because the curve lies under $\overline{FG}$.
G. less than 20,000 square units, because the curve lies over $\overline{FG}$.
H. equal to 20,000 square units.
J. greater than 20,000 square units, because the curve lies under $\overline{FG}$.
K. greater than 20,000 square units, because the curve lies over $\overline{FG}$.

GO ON TO THE NEXT PAGE.

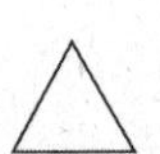        

DO YOUR FIGURING HERE.

35. A cargo ship is 4.2 miles from a lighthouse, and a fishing boat is 5.0 miles from the lighthouse, as shown below. The angle between the straight lines from the lighthouse to the 2 vessels is 5°. The approximate distance, in miles, from the cargo ship to the fishing boat is given by which of the following expressions?

(Note: The law of cosines states that for any triangle with vertices A, B, and C and the sides opposite those vertices with lengths a, b, and c, respectively, $c^2 = a^2 + b^2 - 2ab\cos C$.)

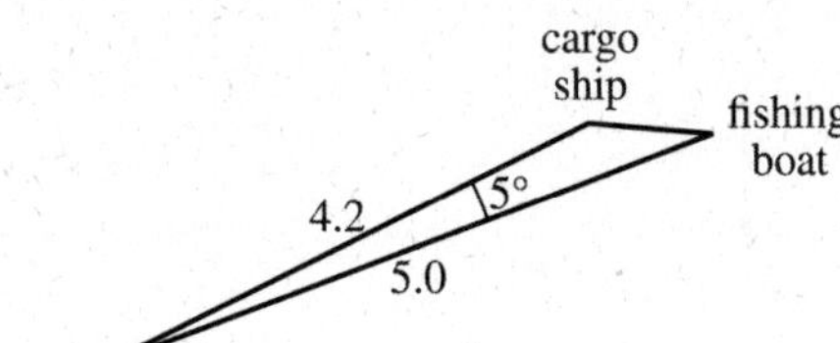

A. $\sqrt{(5.0)^2 - (4.2)^2}$
B. $\sqrt{(4.2)^2 + (5.0)^2 - 2 \cdot 4.2 \cdot 5.0 \cos 5°}$
C. $\sqrt{(4.2)^2 + (5.0)^2 + 2 \cdot 4.2 \cdot 5.0 \cos 5°}$
D. $\sqrt{(4.2)^2 + (5.0)^2 - 2 \cdot 4.2 \cdot 5.0 \cos 85°}$
E. $\sqrt{(4.2)^2 + (5.0)^2 + 2 \cdot 4.2 \cdot 5.0 \cos 85°}$

36. Which of the following equations expresses c in terms of a for all real numbers a, b, and c such that $a^3 = b$ and $b^2 = c$?

F. $c = a^6$

G. $c = a^5$

H. $c = 2a^3$

J. $c = \frac{1}{2}a$

K. $c = a$

37. After visiting Florida State University during spring break, Francisco rents a car for 2 days to travel around Florida. He has $255 to spend on car rental for the 2 days. Sea Horse Car Rental charges $50 per day and $0.25 per mile. Ocean Blue Car Rental charges $60 per day and $0.20 per mile. Which company, if either, allows him to travel more miles for the 2 days, and how many miles more?

(Note: Taxes are already included in the rental charges.)

A. Sea Horse, 20
B. Ocean Blue, 55
C. Ocean Blue, 100
D. Sea Horse, 135
E. Francisco would get the same maximum number of miles from each company.

GO ON TO THE NEXT PAGE.

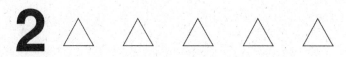

2 △ △ △ △ △ △ △ △ △ 2

DO YOUR FIGURING HERE.

38. In the standard (x,y) coordinate plane below, the points (0,0), (10,0), (13,6), and (3,6) are the vertices of a parallelogram. What is the area, in square coordinate units, of the parallelogram?

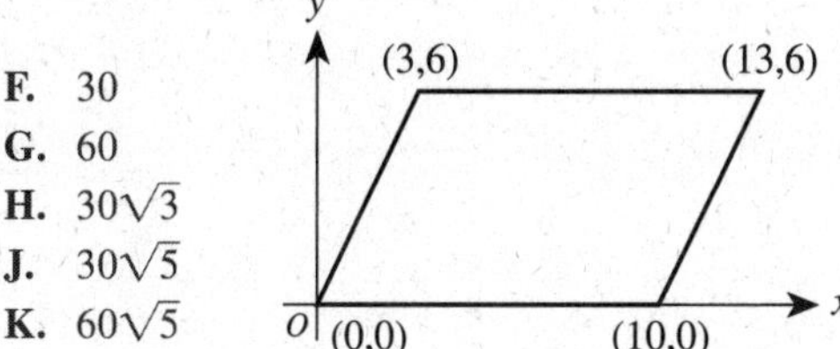

F. 30
G. 60
H. $30\sqrt{3}$
J. $30\sqrt{5}$
K. $60\sqrt{5}$

39. For every pair of natural numbers n and m, to which of the following sets must $n + m$ belong?

I. The natural numbers
II. The integers
III. The rational numbers
IV. The real numbers
V. The complex numbers

A. I, II, and III only
B. II, III, and IV only
C. III, IV, and V only
D. II, III, IV, and V only
E. I, II, III, IV, and V

40. A certain perfect square has exactly 4 digits (that is, it is an integer between 1,000 and 9,999). The positive square root of the perfect square must have how many digits?

F. 1
G. 2
H. 3
J. 4
K. Cannot be determined from the given information

41. A certain hotel has 80 rooms. Based on many previous years' occupancy rates, the owners of the hotel constructed the table below showing the daily occupancy rates and their probabilities of occurring for the coming summer season. Based on the probability distribution in the table, to the nearest whole number, what is the expected number of rooms that will be occupied on any day during the coming summer season?

Occupancy rate	Probability
0.60	0.20
0.70	0.40
0.80	0.30
0.90	0.10

A. 20
B. 25
C. 58
D. 60
E. 75

GO ON TO THE NEXT PAGE.

2 △ △ △ △ △ △ △ △ △ 2

DO YOUR FIGURING HERE.

42. What is the matrix product $\begin{bmatrix} a \\ 2a \\ 3a \end{bmatrix}\begin{bmatrix} 1 & 0 & -1 \end{bmatrix}$?

F. $\begin{bmatrix} a & 0 & -a \\ 2a & 0 & -2a \\ 3a & 0 & -3a \end{bmatrix}$

G. $\begin{bmatrix} a & 2a & 3a \\ 0 & 0 & 0 \\ -a & -2a & -3a \end{bmatrix}$

H. $\begin{bmatrix} 2a & 0 & -2a \end{bmatrix}$

J. $\begin{bmatrix} 6a & 0 & -6a \end{bmatrix}$

K. $\begin{bmatrix} 0 \end{bmatrix}$

43. What is the degree measure of the smaller of the 2 angles formed by the line and the ray shown in the figure below?

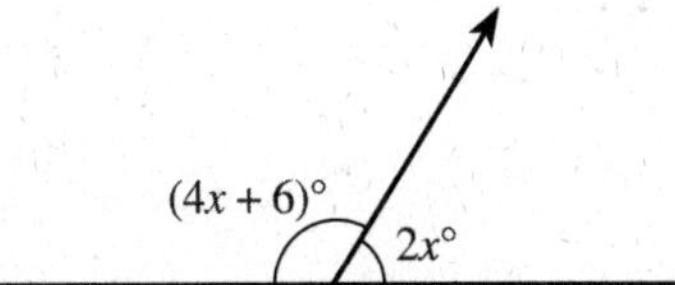

A. 14°
B. 28°
C. 29°
D. 58°
E. Cannot be determined from the given information

44. Let a equal $2b + 3c - 5$. What happens to the value of a if the value of b decreases by 1 and the value of c increases by 2 ?

F. It increases by 4.
G. It increases by 2.
H. It increases by 1.
J. It is unchanged.
K. It decreases by 2.

45. Shima will mix 1 fluid ounce of fertilizer in water for every 40 square feet of soil. At this rate, which of the following expressions gives the number of gallons of fertilizer that Shima will mix in water for 0.5 acres of soil?

(Note: 1 acre = 43,560 square feet;
1 gallon = 128 fluid ounces)

A. $\frac{0.5(40)(128)}{43{,}560}$

B. $\frac{40(128)}{0.5(43{,}560)}$

C. $\frac{0.5(43{,}560)}{40(128)}$

D. $\frac{43{,}560}{0.5(40)(128)}$

E. $\frac{0.5(43{,}560)(40)}{128}$

GO ON TO THE NEXT PAGE.

2 △ △ △ △ △ △ △ △ △ 2

DO YOUR FIGURING HERE.

46. A restaurant has 10 booths that will seat up to 4 people each. If 20 people are seated in booths, and NO booths are empty, what is the greatest possible number of booths that could be filled with 4 people?

F. 0
G. 1
H. 2
J. 3
K. 5

47. Let A and B be independent events. Denote $P(\text{A})$ as the probability that Event A will occur, and denote $P(\text{A} \cap \text{B})$ as the probability that Events A *and* B will both occur. Which of the following equations *must* be true?

A. $P(\text{A}) = P(\text{B})$
B. $P(\text{A}) = 1 - P(\text{B})$
C. $P(\text{A} \cap \text{B}) = P(\text{A}) + P(\text{B})$
D. $P(\text{A} \cap \text{B}) = P(\text{A}) \cdot P(\text{B})$
E. $P(\text{A} \cap \text{B}) = P(\text{A}) + P(\text{B}) - (P(\text{A}) \cdot P(\text{B}))$

48. In the standard (x,y) coordinate plane below, an angle is shown whose vertex is the origin. One side of this angle with measure θ passes through $(4,-3)$, and the other side includes the positive x-axis. What is the cosine of θ ?

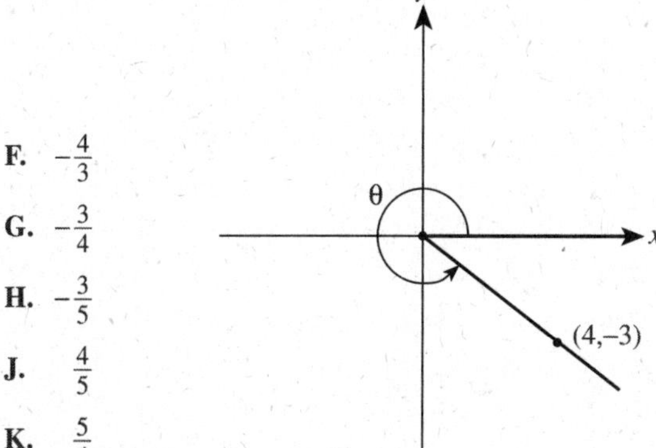

F. $-\frac{4}{3}$
G. $-\frac{3}{4}$
H. $-\frac{3}{5}$
J. $\frac{4}{5}$
K. $\frac{5}{4}$

49. Which of the following expressions, if any, are equal for all real numbers x ?

I. $\sqrt{(-x)^2}$
II. $|-x|$
III. $-|x|$

A. I and II only
B. I and III only
C. II and III only
D. I, II, and III
E. None of the expressions are equivalent.

GO ON TO THE NEXT PAGE.

2           2

DO YOUR FIGURING HERE.

50. In the figure below, A, C, F, and D are collinear; B, C, and E are collinear; and the angles at A, E, and F are right angles, as marked. Which of the following statements is NOT justifiable from the given information?

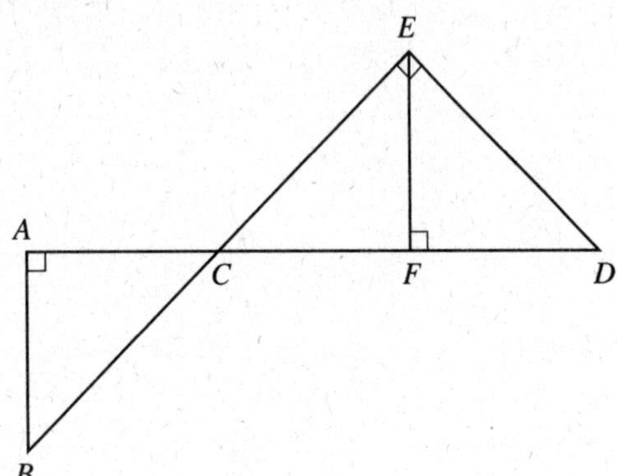

F. $\overleftrightarrow{AB}$ is parallel to $\overleftrightarrow{EF}$.
G. $\overline{DE}$ is perpendicular to $\overline{BE}$.
H. $\angle ACB$ is congruent to $\angle FCE$.
J. $\triangle BAC$ is similar to $\triangle EFC$.
K. $\overline{CE}$ is congruent to $\overline{ED}$.

51. In the figure below, all line segments are either horizontal or vertical and the dimensions given are in inches. What is the perimeter, in inches, of the figure?

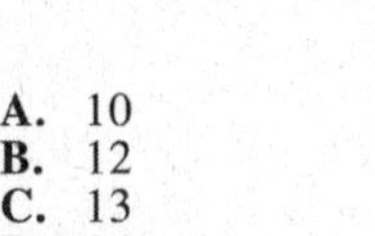

A. 10
B. 12
C. 13
D. 14
E. 16

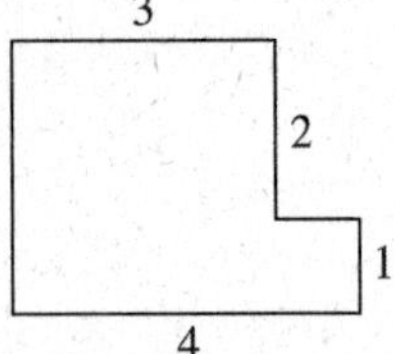

52. Triangle $\triangle ABC$ has vertices $A(8,2)$, $B(0,6)$, and $C(-3,2)$. Point C can be moved along a certain line, with points A and B remaining stationary, and the area of $\triangle ABC$ will not change. What is the slope of that line?

F. 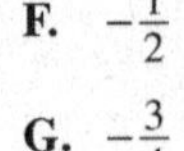 $-\frac{1}{2}$

G. $-\frac{3}{4}$

H. 0

J. 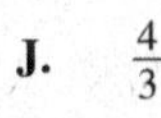 $\frac{4}{3}$

K. 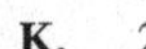 2

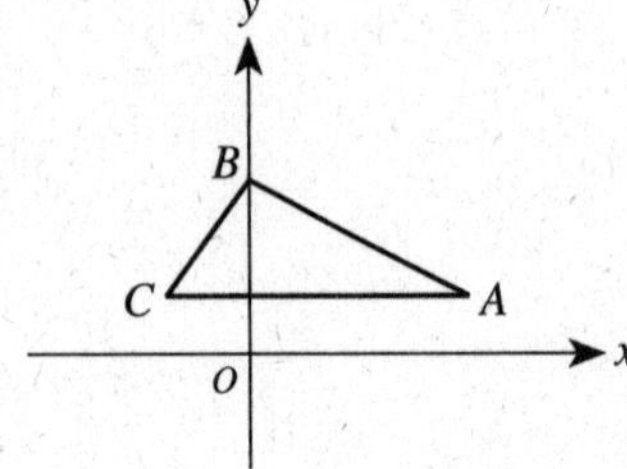

GO ON TO THE NEXT PAGE.

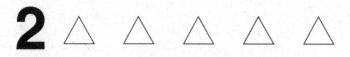

2        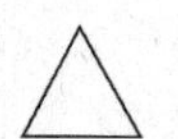 2

DO YOUR FIGURING HERE.

53. On his first day as a telemarketer, Marshall made 24 calls. His goal was to make 5 more calls on each successive day than he had made the day before. If Marshall met, but did not exceed, his goal, how many calls had he made in all after spending exactly 20 days making calls as a telemarketer?

A. 670
B. 690
C. 974
D. 1,430
E. 1,530

54. Which of the following is the graph of the function $f(x)$ defined below?

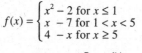

$$f(x) = \begin{cases} x^2 - 2 \text{ for } x \le 1 \\ x - 7 \text{ for } 1 < x < 5 \\ 4 - x \text{ for } x \ge 5 \end{cases}$$

F. 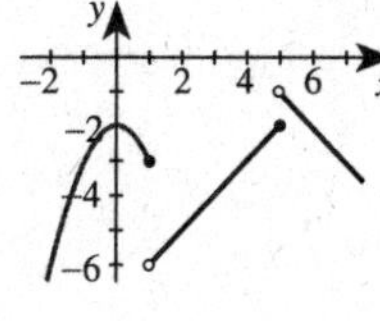

J. 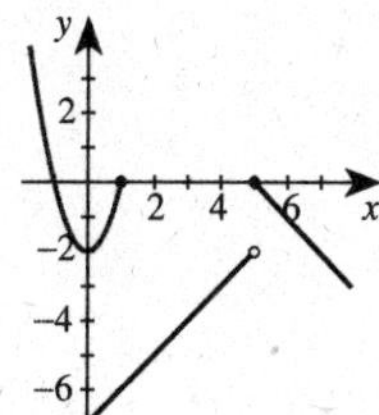

G. 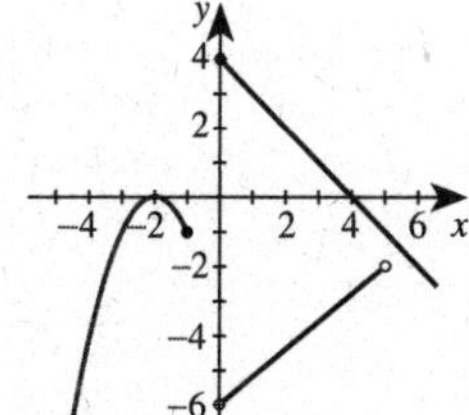

K. 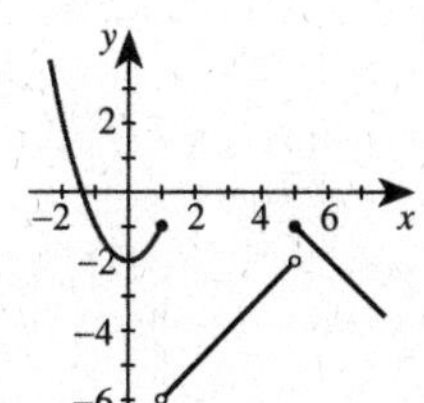

H. 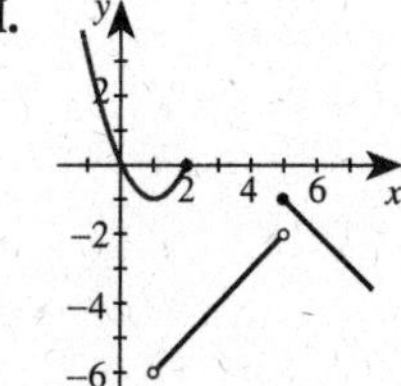

55. Which of the following expressions gives the number of permutations of 15 objects taken 5 at a time?

A. 15(5)

B. $(15 - 5)!$

C. $\frac{15!}{5!}$

D. $\frac{15!}{(15-5)!}$

E. $\frac{15!}{(5!)(15-5!)}$

Taking Additional Practice Tests

GO ON TO THE NEXT PAGE.

2          **2**

DO YOUR FIGURING HERE.

56. For all $x > 0$, which of the following expressions is equivalent to $\frac{i}{\sqrt{x} - i}$, where $i = \sqrt{-1}$?

F. i

G. $\frac{\sqrt{x}}{x}$

H. $\frac{\sqrt{x} - 1}{x + 1}$

J. $\frac{i\sqrt{x} + 1}{x - 1}$

K. $\frac{i\sqrt{x} - 1}{x + 1}$

57. Vectors $\overrightarrow{AB}$ and $\overrightarrow{CD}$ are shown in the standard (x,y) coordinate plane below. One of the following is the unit vector notation of the vector $\overrightarrow{AB} + \overrightarrow{CD}$. Which one?

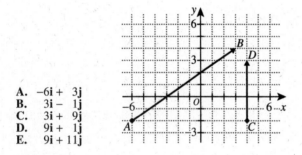

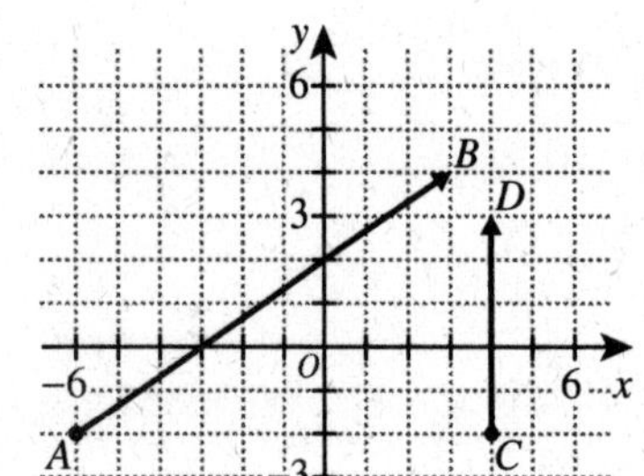

A. −6i + 3j
B. 3i − 1j
C. 3i + 9j
D. 9i + 1j
E. 9i + 11j

58. A simple pendulum consists of a small mass suspended from a string that is fixed at its upper end and has negligible mass. The length of time, t seconds, for a complete swing of a simple pendulum can be modeled by the equation $t = 2\pi\sqrt{\frac{L}{32}}$, where L is the length, in feet, of the string. If the time required for a complete swing of Pendulum 1 is triple the time required for a complete swing of Pendulum 2, the length of Pendulum 1's string is how many times the length of Pendulum 2's string?

F. $\frac{1}{3}$

G. 3

H. 6

J. 9

K. 27

GO ON TO THE NEXT PAGE.

2 △ △ △ △ △ △ △ △ △ 2

59. If $\log_a x = s$ and $\log_a y = t$, then $\log_a (xy)^2 = $?

A. $2(s + t)$
B. $s + t$
C. $4st$
D. $2st$
E. st

DO YOUR FIGURING HERE.

60. Jennifer's best long jump distance increased by 10% from 1990 to 1991 and by 20% from 1991 to 1992. By what percent did her best long jump distance increase from 1990 to 1992 ?

F. 32%
G. 30%
H. 20%
J. 15%
K. 2%

END OF TEST 2

STOP! DO NOT TURN THE PAGE UNTIL TOLD TO DO SO.

DO NOT RETURN TO THE PREVIOUS TEST.

3 READING TEST 3

35 Minutes—40 Questions

DIRECTIONS: There are several passages in this test. Each passage is accompanied by several questions. After reading a passage, choose the best answer to each question and fill in the corresponding oval on your answer document. You may refer to the passages as often as necessary.

Passage I

LITERARY NARRATIVE: This passage is adapted from the novel *Homeland* by John Jakes (©1993 by John Jakes).

Joseph Emanuel Crown, owner of the Crown Brewery of Chicago, was a worried man. Worried on several counts, the most immediate being a civic responsibility he was scheduled to discuss at an emergency meeting this Friday, the fourteenth of October; a meeting he had requested.

Joe Crown seldom revealed inner anxieties, and that was the case as he worked in his office this morning. He was a picture of steadiness, rectitude, prosperity. He wore a fine suit of medium gray enlivened by a dark red four-in-hand tied under a high collar. Since the day was not yet too warm, he kept his coat on.

Joe's hair was more silver than white. He washed it daily, kept it shining. His eyes behind spectacles with silver wire frames were dark brown, rather large, and alert. His mustache and imperial showed careful attention; he had an appointment at twelve for the weekly trim. His hands were small but strong. He wasn't handsome, but he was commanding.

Three principles ruled Joe Crown's business and personal life, of which the most important was order. In German, *Ordnung*. Without order, organization, some rational plan, you had chaos.

The second principle was accuracy. Accuracy was mandatory in brewing, where timing and temperatures were critical. But accuracy was also the keystone of any business that made money instead of losing it. The primary tool for achieving accuracy was mathematics. Joe Crown had a towering belief in the potency of correct information, and the absolute authority of numbers which provided it.

In Germany, he'd learned his numbers before he learned to read. Though a mediocre student in most school subjects, at ciphering he was a prodigy. He could add a column of figures, or do calculations in his head, with astonishing speed. In Cincinnati, his first stop in America, he'd begged the owner of a Chinese laundry to teach him to use an abacus. One of these ancient counting devices could be found in his office, sitting on a low cabinet, within reach. Money measured success; counting measured money.

Questions he asked of his employees often involved numbers. "What is the exact temperature?" "How large is the population in that market?" "How many barrels did we ship last week?" "What's the cost, per square foot, of this expansion?"

As for his third principle, modernity, he believed that, too, was crucial in business. Men who said the old ways were the best ways were fools, doomed to fall behind and fail. Joe was always searching for the newest methods to improve the brewery's product, output, efficiency, cleanliness. He hadn't hesitated to install expensive pasteurization equipment when he opened his first small brewery in Chicago. He'd been among the first to invest heavily in refrigerated freight cars. He insisted that modern machines be used in the office. From his desk he could hear the pleasing ratchet noise of a mechanical adding machine. This blended with the clicking keys and pinging bell on the black iron typewriter used for correspondence by his chief clerk, Stefan Zwick.

Originally Stefan had resisted Joe's suggestion that he learn to operate a typewriter. "Sir, I respectfully decline, a quill pen suits me perfectly."

"But Stefan," Joe said to him in a friendly but firm way, "I'm afraid it doesn't suit me, because it makes Crown's look old-fashioned. However, I'll respect your feelings. Please place a help wanted advertisement. We'll hire one of those young women who specialize in using the machines. I believe they too are called typewriters."

Zwick blanched. "A woman? In my office?"

"I'm sorry, Stefan, but you leave me no choice if you won't learn to typewrite."

Stefan Zwick learned to typewrite.

Every solid house or building was supported by a strong foundation; and so there was a foundation on which Joe Crown's three principles rested. It was not unusual, or peculiar to him. It was the cheerful acceptance, not to say worship, of hard work. Among other

GO ON TO THE NEXT PAGE.

3 3

artifacts, advertising sheets, flags and fading brown photographs of annual brewery picnics decorating his office there was a small framed motto which his wife had done colorfully in cross-stitch and put into a frame of gilded wood. *Ohne Fleiss, kein Preis*, it said. In rough translation, this reminded you that without industry there was no reward. From his desk Joe Crown couldn't see the gold-framed motto; it hung on the wall behind him, slightly to his right. But he didn't need to see it. Its truth was in him deeper than the marrow of his bones. He was a German.

1. If a stereotype of Germans is that they are tidy, meticulous, and industrious, does the characterization of Crown in this passage reinforce or weaken this stereotype?

A. It firmly reinforces the stereotype.
B. It initially reinforces and subsequently weakens the stereotype.
C. It reinforces the meticulous aspect of the stereotype but weakens the industrious aspect.
D. It weakens the stereotype in that Crown likes his surroundings tidy but expects others to do the tidying up.

2. It can reasonably be inferred that in relation to the appointment referred to in the third paragraph (lines 13–19), the meeting referred to in the first paragraph occurs:

F. on the same day.
G. several days earlier.
H. several days later.
J. several years later.

3. The passage's description of Zwick reveals that compared to Crown, he is:

A. equally fastidious about meeting a deadline.
B. less inclined to embrace new technology.
C. less afraid to state his preferences to his superiors.
D. more concerned with the company's public image.

4. The dialogue in line 72 reveals Zwick's:

F. indignation over Crown's proposed solution to the problem the two men are discussing.
G. panic over having a surprise visitor to his office.
H. excitement over meeting a new employee of Crown Brewery.
J. insensitivity to his recently hired female coworker.

5. At the time described in the passage's opening, what is Crown's most immediate preoccupation?

A. Whether he will be on time for his weekly trim
B. Whether to install expensive pasteurization equipment at his brewery
C. Zwick's impertinent behavior
D. A civic responsibility

6. The passage states that Crown was what kind of student?

F. Exceptionally gifted, especially in ciphering
G. Mediocre, except in ciphering
H. Successful when he applied himself, otherwise poor
J. Increasingly successful as he gained the use of counting aids

7. Based on the passage, which of the following questions would be most characteristic of the kind Crown typically asked his employees?

A. "Was your weekend a most pleasant one?"
B. "Have you had a chance to repair that old typewriter?"
C. "By what figure will our sales increase if we advertise in that publication?"
D. "Who among you has a better idea for how we can work well as a team?"

8. At the time in which the passage is set, which of the following devices are still apparently being used in offices in the United States even as those same devices are, in Crown's view, becoming increasingly obsolete?

F. Typewriters
G. Mechanical adding machines
H. Quill pens
J. Abacuses

9. The metaphor the author uses to help describe Crown's three principles primarily draws upon imagery from what discipline?

A. Architecture
B. Business
C. Astronomy
D. Education

10. Which of the following is a detail from the passage that indicates the length of time Crown has been in the brewery business?

F. Some outdated refrigerators from when he first opened his business
G. A newly hung cross-stitched phrase framed and placed on his office wall
H. Photographs of annual company picnics decorating his office
J. A bell, the ringing of which has marked the start of his workday for the last twenty years

GO ON TO THE NEXT PAGE.

3 3

Passage II

SOCIAL STUDIES: This passage is adapted from the book *The Age of Wonder* by Richard Holmes (©2008 by Richard Holmes).

In the summer of 1785 astronomer William Herschel embarked on his revolutionary new project to observe and resolve the heavens with a telescope more powerful than ever previously attempted.

What he intended to build was a telescope 'of the Newtonian form, with an octagon tube 40 foot long and five feet in diameter; the specula [mirrors] of which it would be necessary to have at least two, or perhaps three'. The telescope would have to be mounted in an enormous wooden gantry, capable of being turned safely on its axis by just two workmen, but also susceptible to the finest fingertip adjustments by the observing astronomer.

The forty-foot would be higher than a house. The astronomer (William) would be required to climb a series of ladders to a special viewing platform perched at the mouth of the telescope. The assistant (William's sister, Caroline) would have to be shut in a special booth below to avoid light pollution, where she would have her desk and lamp, celestial clocks, and observation journals. Astronomer and assistant would be invisible to each other for hours on end, shouting commands and replies, although eventually connected by a metal speaking-tube.

William had decided that his grand project required a new house with larger grounds for constructing and erecting the telescope. On 3 April 1786 they moved to 'The Grove', a quite small and rather dilapidated country house on the edge of the tiny village of Slough, England.

The house itself was not large, but it had sheds and stables which were gradually converted into workshops and laboratories. Above the stables were a series of haylofts which could be converted into a separate apartment. Caroline claimed these for her own. A small outside staircase led up to a flat roof from which she hoped to carry out her comet 'sweeps' in security and independently. She would check over the calculations of William's nebulae by day, and make her own sweeps up on the roof by night.

William had built Caroline a special two-foot Newtonian reflector. Because of its large aperture, its tube appeared much fatter, heavier and stubbier than normal reflectors of this type. Suspended from a pivot at the top of the box-frame, the telescope could be precisely raised or lowered by a system of pulleys operated by a winding handle. These adjustments were easy to make, and extremely fine.

This beautiful instrument was designed specifically for its huge light-gathering power and its wide angle of vision. The magnification was comparatively low at twenty-four times. As with modern binoculars, this combination of low power with a large viewing field allowed the observer to see faint stellar objects very brightly, while placing them within a comparatively wide context of surrounding stars. The telescope was perfectly designed to spot any strange or unknown object moving through the familiar field of 'fixed stars'. In other words, to catch new planets or new comets.

On 1 August 1786, only two nights after starting her new sweeps, Caroline thought she had spotted an unknown stellar object moving through Ursa Major (the Great Bear constellation). It appeared to be descending, but barely perceptibly, towards a triangulation of stars in the beautifully named constellation Coma Berenices. To find something so quickly, and in such a familiar place (the Great Bear or Big Dipper being the first stop of every amateur stargazer wanting to locate the Pole Star), seemed wildly unlikely. Caroline's Observation Book conveys meticulous caution, but also remarkable certainty.

Unable to calculate the mathematical coordinates of the object, she accompanied her observations with a series of three neat drawings or 'figures', over an eighty-minute time lapse. These showed the circular viewing field of her telescope, with an asterisk shape very slightly changing position relative to three known fixed stars. The account written into her 'Book of Work Done' catches something of her growing excitement.

> August 1st. I have calculated 100 nebulae today, and this evening I saw an object which I believe will prove tomorrow night to be a Comet. August 2nd. 1 o'clock. the object of last night IS A COMET. August 3rd. I did not go to rest till I had written to Dr Blagden [at the Royal Society] and Mr Aubert to announce the Comet.

The verification of Caroline's comet was achieved much more rapidly than William's discovery of the planet Uranus had been. Its movement through Coma Berenices was relatively easy to ascertain, and its fine hazy tail or coma was unmistakable.

11. Which of the following statements best describes how the passage characterizes William's response to Caroline's discovery of a comet?

A. The passage makes it clear that although William applauded Caroline's discovery, he was disappointed that Caroline wasn't looking for nebulae.
B. The passage claims that William supported Caroline's discovery by verifying the comet himself.
C. The passage suggests that William resented the fact that Caroline's comet was recognized so quickly.
D. The passage does not give a clear indication of how William felt about Caroline's discovery.

GO ON TO THE NEXT PAGE.

3 3

12. In the passage, the author emphasizes the large size of William's powerful telescope's octagon tube by comparing the tube's height to that of a:

F. series of ladders.
G. wooden gantry.
H. hayloft.
J. house.

13. The primary function of the fifth paragraph (lines 31–40) is to:

A. explain the methods Caroline used to perform her comet sweeps.
B. shift the passage's focus from William's project to Caroline's own astronomical work.
C. describe the renovations Caroline made to the stables in order to accommodate William's telescope.
D. introduce the passage's discussion of how Caroline's observation techniques compared to William's.

14. In the context of the passage, the excerpt from Caroline's "Book of Work Done" primarily serves to:

F. outline the process by which Caroline determined her finding was a comet.
G. provide an example of the types of observation notes Caroline made for William.
H. illustrate Caroline's growing sense of excitement about her discovery.
J. explain Dr. Blagden's and Mr. Aubert's role in verifying Caroline's discovery.

15. As it is used in line 12, the word *finest* most nearly means:

A. slightest.
B. fairest.
C. thinnest.
D. greatest.

16. The passage most strongly suggests that while William operated his telescope, Caroline would have to work below in a special booth because:

F. she would be relaying William's instructions to the workmen who turned the telescope.
G. she preferred seclusion when working on calculations.
H. the telescope's viewing platform would not be large enough to hold both William and Caroline.
J. the light from her lamp would interfere with William's view of the night sky.

17. Which of the following questions is most directly answered by the passage?

A. What inspired William to embark on his project to observe and resolve the heavens?
B. Why did Caroline and William move to "The Grove"?
C. Why couldn't Caroline calculate the coordinates of the comet she discovered?
D. How long did it take the Royal Society to confirm Caroline's discovery was a new comet?

18. It can most reasonably be inferred from the passage that compared to normal telescopes of its type, the two-foot Newtonian reflector William built had:

F. a larger aperture.
G. a smaller box-frame.
H. more magnifying power.
J. less light-gathering power.

19. According to the passage, when Caroline first saw her comet, it appeared to be moving through:

A. Coma Berenices and descending toward the Pole Star.
B. Coma Berenices and descending toward stars in the Big Dipper.
C. Ursa Major and descending toward stars in Coma Berenices.
D. a triangulation of stars, which included the Pole Star, and descending toward Coma Berenices.

20. The passage indicates that Caroline's discovery of a new comet was unlikely because Caroline:

F. found the comet quickly in a part of the sky that was familiar to astronomers and stargazers.
G. knew more about nebulae than she knew about comets.
H. had already discovered a planet while performing observations with William.
J. had little experience calculating the mathematical coordinates of stellar objects.

GO ON TO THE NEXT PAGE.

Passage III

HUMANITIES: Passage A is adapted from the essay "Truth in Personal Narrative" by Vivian Gornick (©2008 by University of Iowa Press). Passage B is adapted from the article "Fact and Fiction in *A Moveable Feast*" by Jacqueline Tavernier-Courbin (©1984 by Hemingway Review).

Passage A by Vivian Gornick

Once, in Texas, I gave a reading from my memoir *Fierce Attachments*. No sooner had I finished speaking than a woman in the audience asked a question: "If I come to New York, can I take a walk with your mama?" I told her that, actually, she wouldn't want to take a walk with my mother, it was the woman in the book she wanted to walk with. They were not exactly the same.

Shortly afterwards, I attended a party in New York where, an hour into the evening, one of the guests blurted out in a voice filled with disappointment, "Why, you're nothing like the woman who wrote *Fierce Attachments*!" At the end of the evening she cocked her head at me and said, "Well, you're *something* like her." I understood perfectly. She had come expecting to have dinner with the narrator of the book, not with me; again, not exactly the same.

On both occasions, what was desired was the presence of two people who existed only between the pages of a book. In our actual persons, neither Mama nor I could give satisfaction. We ourselves were just a rough draft of the written characters. Moreover, these characters could not live independent of the story which had called them into life, as they existed for the sole purpose of serving that story. In the flesh, neither Mama nor I were serving anything but the unaesthetic spill of everyday thought and feeling that routinely floods us all, only a select part of which, in this case, invoked the principals in a tale of psychological embroilment that had as its protagonist neither me nor my mother but rather our "fierce attachment."

At the heart of my memoir lay a revelation: I could not leave my mother because I had become my mother. This complicated insight was my bit of wisdom, the history I wanted badly to trace out. The context in which the book is set—our life in the Bronx in the 1950s, alternating with walks taken in Manhattan in the 1980s—was the situation; the story was the insight. What mattered most to me was not the literalness of the situation, but the emotional truth of the story. What actually happened is only raw material; what matters is what the memoirist makes of what happened.

Memoirs belong to the category of literature, not of journalism. It is a misunderstanding to read a memoir as though the writer owes the reader the same record of literal accuracy that is owed in newspaper reporting or historical narrative. What is owed the reader is the ability to persuade that the narrator is trying, as honestly as possible, to get to the bottom of the tale at hand.

Passage B by Jacqueline Tavernier-Courbin

The dividing line between fiction and autobiography is often a very fine and shaky one, and Ernest Hemingway's autobiography of the artist as a young man is a case in point. As nearly all readers know, Hemingway's fiction contains numerous autobiographical elements, and his protagonists are often conscious projections and explorations of the self. At the same time, Hemingway's openly autobiographical writings, *Green Hills of Africa* and *A Moveable Feast*, are barely more autobiographical than his fiction, and, in many ways, just as fictional.

A Moveable Feast is particularly complex because Hemingway was clearly conscious that it would be his literary testament. Thus, in writing it, he dealt with issues which had been important to him and he settled old scores. Among the reasons which motivated his portrayal of self and others were the need to justify himself, for he felt that he had been unfairly portrayed by some of his contemporaries, the desire to present his own version of personal relationships as well as the desire to get back at people against whom he held a grudge, the need to relive his youth in an idealized fashion, and the wish to leave to the world a flattering self-portrait. Thus, *A Moveable Feast* could hardly be an objective portrayal of its author and his contemporaries, and the accuracy of the anecdotes becomes an issue that can never be entirely resolved.

While it is impossible to verify everything Hemingway wrote in *A Moveable Feast*, one might conclude that he invented and lied relatively seldom about pure facts. When he did so, it was usually in order to reinforce the pattern he had created—i.e., a negative portrayal of literary competitors and an idealized self-portrayal. He clearly overlooked a great deal of material, distorted some, and generally selected the episodes so that they would show him as innocent, honest, dedicated, and thoroughly enjoying life. *A Moveable Feast*, in fact, appears as a fascinating composite of relative factual accuracy and clear dishonesty of intent.

Questions 21–24 ask about Passage A.

21. The main purpose of the first two paragraphs of Passage A (lines 1–16) is to:

A. establish the popularity of Gornick's book by indicating that people wanted to meet her after reading the book.
B. introduce the idea that the characters in Gornick's memoir are not exactly like their real-life counterparts.
C. illustrate Gornick's frustration with some of her readers.
D. suggest that Gornick's memoir should be classified as fiction, not as nonfiction.

GO ON TO THE NEXT PAGE.

3 3

22. Which of the following quotations from Passage A most directly relates to the party guest's disappointment upon meeting the author of *Fierce Attachments* ?
   F. "We ourselves were just a rough draft of the written characters" (lines 20–21).
   G. "I had become my mother" (line 32).
   H. "This complicated insight was my bit of wisdom" (line 33).
   J. "The story was the insight" (line 37).

23. According to Passage A, Gornick believes the heart of her memoir to be:
   A. the walks she took with her mother in Manhattan.
   B. the revelation that she had become her mother.
   C. her childhood experiences in the Bronx.
   D. her shared history with her mother.

24. According to Passage A, Gornick believes that memoirs belong to the category of:
   F. journalism.
   G. personal diaries.
   H. historical narratives.
   J. literature.

Questions 25–27 ask about Passage B.

25. According to Passage B, the protagonists in Hemingway's fiction are often:
   A. composites of Hemingway's friends.
   B. based on Hemingway's family members.
   C. projections of Hemingway himself.
   D. completely made-up characters.

26. Based on Passage B, the question of accuracy in *A Moveable Feast* is particularly difficult because:
   F. Hemingway used the book to create a particular portrait of himself and his contemporaries.
   G. Hemingway's contemporaries were writing conflicting memoirs during the same time period.
   H. Hemingway could not produce any documents to support his stories.
   J. Hemingway said his memory was excellent, but others doubt this.

27. Which of the following statements best expresses the opinion the author of Passage B seems to have about *A Moveable Feast* ?
   A. It stands alongside Hemingway's fiction as one of his best works.
   B. It is a complex example of a book that combines fact and fiction.
   C. It provides an accurate look at a specific time in Hemingway's life.
   D. It should be read with other books from the same time period.

Questions 28–30 ask about both passages.

28. Based on the passages, Gornick's and Hemingway's approaches to writing their memoirs are similar in that both writers:
   F. put real characters into wholly fictional situations.
   G. wanted to portray themselves in a flattering way.
   H. were motivated to settle old scores and present their own versions of personal relationships.
   J. used only material from their lives that served the story they each wanted to tell.

29. Based on the passages, it can most reasonably be inferred that Gornick and Hemingway would agree that when it comes to a writer's responsibility to be truthful in a memoir:
   A. the degree of truthfulness should be the same as that for fiction.
   B. if a writer can't remember the exact details of a certain event, that event should be left out of the memoir.
   C. it is more important to create an artistic whole than to relate only facts.
   D. the writer should only include incidents that have documented evidence to support them.

30. Another author wrote the following about the role of truth in memoir:

   > A memoir is a story, not a history, and real life doesn't play out as a story.

   Which passage most closely echoes the view presented in this quotation?
   F. Passage A, because it offers a story about what happens when you meet someone who doesn't live up to your expectations.
   G. Passage A, because it stresses that what happens in life is only raw material for a memoirist.
   H. Passage B, because it states that Hemingway viewed *A Moveable Feast* as his literary testament.
   J. Passage B, because it states that Hemingway seldom lied about pure facts.

GO ON TO THE NEXT PAGE.

3 3

Passage IV

NATURAL SCIENCE: This passage is adapted from the article "The Next Wave: What Makes an Invasive Species Stick?" by Robert R. Dunn (©2010 by Natural History Magazine, Inc.).

Like many biologists, Andrew V. Suarez struggled for years with the question of which colonizing organisms fail and which succeed. He studied it the hard way—with fieldwork and lab experiments—until 1999, when he found some brown jars. He had gone to the Smithsonian Institution National Museum of Natural History's National Insect Collection to look for early samples of Argentine ants collected in the United States or at its borders. He hoped to find out how vintage specimens of Argentine ants were related to the existing populations.

At the museum, among many thousands of jars of insects labeled with taxonomic notes, locations, and dates, Suarez ultimately found relatively few samples of Argentine ants. But what he found besides them was, to his mind, far more interesting: some of the ethanol-filled jars were jammed with vials of ants collected at ports of entry in the eastern U.S. from 1927 to 1985. They were ants that border agents had picked from plants being shipped into the U.S. Could those ants be identified as members of species that had failed or succeeded as colonists, and if so, could the specimens be used to compare the two groups?

In the jars and vials were 394 separate samples of ants. Suarez solicited the help of two friends, ant ecologist David A. Holway of the University of California, San Diego, and Philip S. Ward, guru of ant gurus, at the University of California, Davis. Altogether they identified 232 distinct species.

Suarez considered the traits possessed by each of the ant species in an attempt to see what might have predisposed some of them to survival. He measured whether they were big or small. He examined whether each lived in the canopy or on the ground, and whether they were from one subfamily or another. He also looked at a simpler possibility: that "survivor species" tended to be those introduced more than once. The evidence in the jars showed, for example, that Argentine ants had arrived at least twice. Were successes just a consequence of the number of tries?

When a pioneering group sets up camp and starts living in a new place, possible futures diverge. One species might be wiped out within a generation or two. A second might survive, but never become common. Yet another species might thrive, eventually spreading across states, continents, and even the world! Even if surviving in a new environment is sometimes a matter of being introduced again and again, thriving is a different story. Relatively few invasive species truly prevail.

One curious thing about Argentine ants is that they are, despite their apparent meekness, ecologically dominant. They are squishy, small, stingless wimps, as ants go, yet somehow they have managed to overpower the big, tough native ants.

There's another strange thing about Argentine ants. If you take an Argentine ant from what looks like one colony and put it together with one from a distant colony, they accept each other. In fact, you can perform that trick over much of California and very few of the ants will fight. It is as though all of the Argentine ants in California are part of a few huge colonies—"supercolonies," they've come to be called.

Biologist Ted Case joined forces with Holway and Suarez for an experiment to test whether the lack of aggression among those ant colonies somehow helped them to compete with other species. Might it simply be that by not fighting with their neighbors, the Argentine ants wasted less energy on war and could spend more time on the good stuff? It turned out that, yes, aggressive ants wasted energy fighting (and dying), and so gathered less food and fared poorly, in general. Peace pays (at least peace with one's kin), and so Argentine ants have made bank everyplace they have moved.

In fact, it isn't just for the Argentine ant that peace seems to pay. Supercolonies and the unicolonial populations they create look to be common among invasive ants.

Ants flash chemical badges identifying their home nest. Without such markers, no one knows who is friend or foe. When the clarity of "us versus them" breaks down, peace breaks out among colonies of an ant species. Different nests swap workers and queens, and the term "colony" becomes fuzzy. Experiments seemed to show that one conglomeration of Argentine ants stretched the length of California, another from Italy to Portugal . . . until, in 2009, workers from those two "colonies" (along with a third from Japan) were put together, and they didn't fight. Thus, across the entire globe, a few peaceful supercolonies could exist and expand.

31. The main purpose of this passage is to:

A. describe events that led to the discovery of Argentine ants in the United States.
B. examine the physical differences between Argentine ants and other insects.
C. highlight the technology that scientists used to determine the size of supercolonies.
D. discuss factors that contribute to a colonizing organism's success as an invasive species.

32. The author makes repeated use of which of the following in order to help establish the passage's somewhat casual tone?

F. Personal anecdotes
G. Idiomatic expressions
H. Humorous quotations
J. Self-critical asides

GO ON TO THE NEXT PAGE.

3 3

33. Which of the following events mentioned in the passage occurred first chronologically?

A. Case joined Holway and Suarez to assist them with an experiment.
B. Workers from three Argentine ant supercolonies in different parts of the world were brought together.
C. Suarez found samples of Argentine ants in the Smithsonian insect collection.
D. Holway and Ward were recruited by Suarez to assist with his research.

34. The main purpose of the fifth paragraph (lines 41–49) is to:

F. explain how Argentine ants are able to survive in new areas and discuss their spread throughout the world.
G. describe possible outcomes for a pioneering species and stress the improbability that the species will thrive.
H. define the concept of invasive species as it relates to ants.
J. compare the behaviors of Argentine ants to those of other, more successful pioneering species.

35. The author's claim that the Argentine ant behavior described in lines 56–58 is unusual is based upon which of the following assumptions?

A. Supercolonies are common among several species of ants.
B. Argentine ants in California are less aggressive than Argentine ants elsewhere.
C. California's ecosystem is especially suited for Argentine ants.
D. Ants from different colonies typically fight one another.

36. According to the passage, the question of which colonizing organisms fail and which succeed is one that has been studied by:

F. many biologists for a number of years.
G. many biologists beginning in 1999.
H. the Smithsonian exclusively.
J. Suarez exclusively.

37. The passage makes clear which of the following about the ant samples Suarez found in the Smithsonian insect collection?

A. Most of the samples were of Argentine ants.
B. Ward and Holway had collected the samples as part of a larger study of US insect populations.
C. Suarez discovered that most of the samples were of previously undiscovered species of ants.
D. Suarez was most interested in the samples that had been collected at eastern US ports of entry.

38. According to the passage, which of the following is true of Argentine ants?

F. They are stingless.
G. They are physically dominant.
H. They were first discovered in the United States by Suarez.
J. They have failed to thrive in Japan.

39. The passage indicates that compared to peaceful ants, aggressive ants:

A. live in larger colonies.
B. spend less time gathering food.
C. are less likely to live in a colony.
D. are more likely to be a "survivor species."

40. The passage most clearly establishes which of the following facts about ants?

F. In order for ant colonies to combine to form supercolonies, the colonies must have identical chemical badges.
G. Ants identify their home nests by flashing chemical badges.
H. Ant colonies from different species commonly swap workers and queens.
J. The largest supercolony of ants in the world stretches from Italy to Portugal.

END OF TEST 3

STOP! DO NOT TURN THE PAGE UNTIL TOLD TO DO SO.

DO NOT RETURN TO A PREVIOUS TEST.

4 ○ ○ ○ ○ ○ ○ ○ ○ ○ 4

SCIENCE TEST

35 Minutes—40 Questions

DIRECTIONS: There are several passages in this test. Each passage is followed by several questions. After reading a passage, choose the best answer to each question and fill in the corresponding oval on your answer document. You may refer to the passages as often as necessary.

You are NOT permitted to use a calculator on this test.

Passage I

The figure below is a pedigree that shows the inheritance of a trait, Trait G, in a family. The presence of Trait G in an individual is determined entirely by Gene G. Gene G has 2 alleles: *G*, which is dominant, and *g*, which is recessive.

Each individual represented in the pedigree was assigned a number (shown below the symbol for the individual) for reference. Scientists determined that the Gene G genotype of Individual 20 is *gg* and that the Gene G genotype of Individual 21 is *Gg*. Based on this information, the scientists concluded that Trait G is a recessive trait.

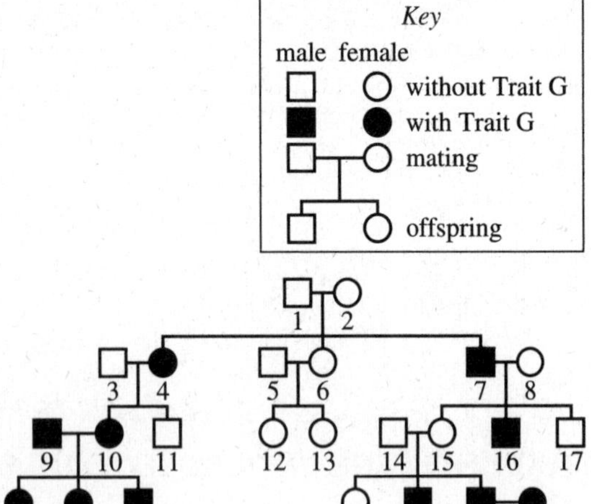

1. How many generations are shown in the figure?
   A. 3
   B. 4
   C. 22
   D. 24

2. Based on the figure, the 2 individuals in which of the following pairs most likely have the greatest genetic similarity across their genomes?
   F. Individual 3 and Individual 4
   G. Individual 12 and Individual 13
   H. Individual 16 and Individual 24
   J. Individual 18 and Individual 21

3. Suppose that Individual 23 and Individual 24 have 4 biological children. Based on the figure, how many of the children, if any, have Trait G ?
   A. 0
   B. 1
   C. 3
   D. 4

4. According to the figure, how many of the grandchildren of Individual 1 and Individual 2, if any, have Trait G ?
   F. 0
   G. 1
   H. 2
   J. 7

GO ON TO THE NEXT PAGE.

4 ○ ○ ○ ○ ○ ○ ○ ○ ○ 4

5. Based on the figure, is it likely that Trait G is a sex-linked trait?

A. Yes, because mothers with Trait G always passed Trait G to their sons.
B. Yes, because mothers with Trait G did not always pass Trait G to their sons.
C. No, because mothers with Trait G always passed Trait G to their sons.
D. No, because mothers with Trait G did not always pass Trait G to their sons.

6. Based on the information provided, will an individual with the Gene G genotype *Gg* have Trait G ?

F. Yes, because Trait G is a dominant trait.
G. Yes, because Trait G is a recessive trait.
H. No, because Trait G is a dominant trait.
J. No, because Trait G is a recessive trait.

GO ON TO THE NEXT PAGE.

4 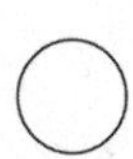 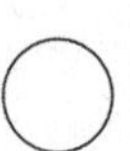   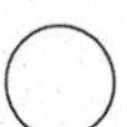  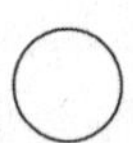 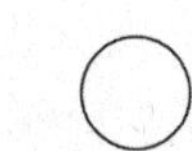 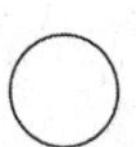 4

Passage II

Heliconia metallica is a plant found in the understory of tropical rain forests. (The *understory* is the area below the forest canopy.) *H. metallica* flowers are normally pollinated by hummingbirds. The flowers can be *self-pollinated* (egg and pollen are from the same *H. metallica* plant) or *cross-pollinated* (egg and pollen are from different *H. metallica* plants). The following study was conducted to investigate the effects of different pollination treatments on fruit production and seed mass in a population of *H. metallica*.

Study

Before pollination could occur, the *anthers* (pollen-producing structures) were removed from each of 400 *H. metallica* flowers. Then, the flowers were covered with nylon bags to prevent the normal pollinators from pollinating the flowers. The covered flowers were divided equally into 4 groups (Groups 1–4), and each group received a different pollination treatment (see Table 1). Four weeks after the pollination treatments, the percent of flowers that produced fruit and the average mass per seed were determined for each group (see Figures 1 and 2, respectively).

Table 1

Group	Pollination treatment
1	self-pollination*
2	cross-pollination with pollen collected from a single donor *H. metallica* plant
3	cross-pollination with a mixture of pollen collected from 6 donor *H. metallica* plants
4	no pollination

*Each flower was pollinated with pollen from its removed anthers.

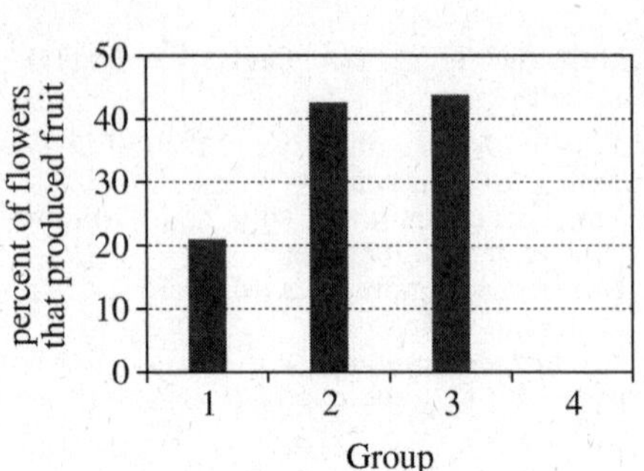

Figure 1

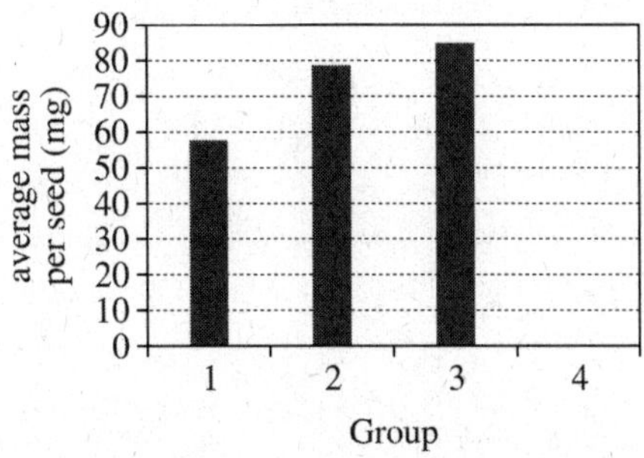

Figure 2

Table and figures adapted from Matthias Schleuning et al., "Effects of Inbreeding, Outbreeding, and Supplemental Pollen on the Reproduction of a Hummingbird-pollinated Clonal Amazonian Herb." ©2010 by The Author(s).

GO ON TO THE NEXT PAGE.

4 ○ ○ ○ ○ ○ ○ ○ ○ ○ 4

7. The data that were averaged to produce the results shown in Figure 2 were most likely collected using which of the following pieces of equipment?

A. Balance
B. pH meter
C. Telescope
D. Thermometer

8. One of the questions about *H. metallica* plants that the study was designed to answer was which of the following?

F. Does the location of the plants in the understory of tropical rain forests determine whether the flowers are self-pollinated or cross-pollinated?
G. Are the percent of flowers that produce fruit and the average mass per seed different when flowers are self-pollinated than when flowers are cross-pollinated?
H. How long after the plants are pollinated does the fruit ripen?
J. Are the flowers normally pollinated by hummingbirds?

9. The pollination treatments received by Groups 1 and 2 differed in which of the following ways? The pollen received by each Group 1 flower was:

A. from the same plant as the flower, whereas the pollen received by each Group 2 flower was from a different plant than the flower.
B. from a different plant than the flower, whereas the pollen received by each Group 2 flower was from the same plant as the flower.
C. collected from 1 plant, whereas the pollen received by each Group 2 flower was collected from 6 plants.
D. collected from 6 plants, whereas the pollen received by each Group 2 flower was collected from 1 plant.

10. For any group, the value shown in Figure 1 was most likely calculated using which of the following expressions?

F. $\frac{\text{number of seeds}}{\text{total seed mass}} \times 100$

G. $\frac{\text{total seed mass}}{\text{number of seeds}} \times 100$

H. $\frac{\text{number of flowers producing fruit}}{\text{total number of flowers}} \times 100$

J. $\frac{\text{total number of flowers}}{\text{number of flowers producing fruit}} \times 100$

11. The anthers were most likely removed from the flowers for the purpose of ensuring that the flowers:

A. would spontaneously self-pollinate.
B. would not spontaneously self-pollinate.
C. would be pollinated by hummingbirds.
D. would not be pollinated by hummingbirds.

12. Do the results of the study indicate that the nylon bags successfully prevented the normal pollinators from pollinating the *H. metallica* flowers?

F. Yes; only 20% of the flowers receiving the self-pollination treatment produced fruit.
G. Yes; none of the flowers receiving the no pollination treatment produced fruit.
H. No; only 20% of the flowers receiving the self-pollination treatment produced fruit.
J. No; none of the flowers receiving the no pollination treatment produced fruit.

13. What was the total mass of the seeds produced by the Group 3 flowers?

A. 0 mg
B. 45 mg
C. 85 mg
D. Cannot be determined from the given information

GO ON TO THE NEXT PAGE.

Passage III

When 2 types of bacteria found in the soil of a *wetland* (land having a high water table) break down organic matter, gases are generated. *Aerobic bacteria*, which require O_2, generate CO_2. *Anaerobic bacteria*, which require little or no O_2, generate CH_4.

bog soil

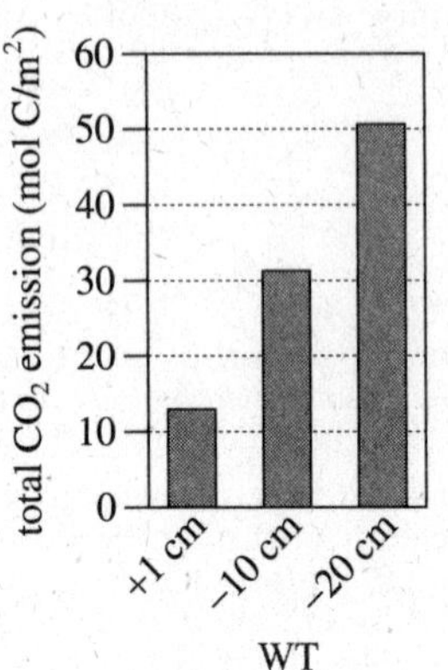

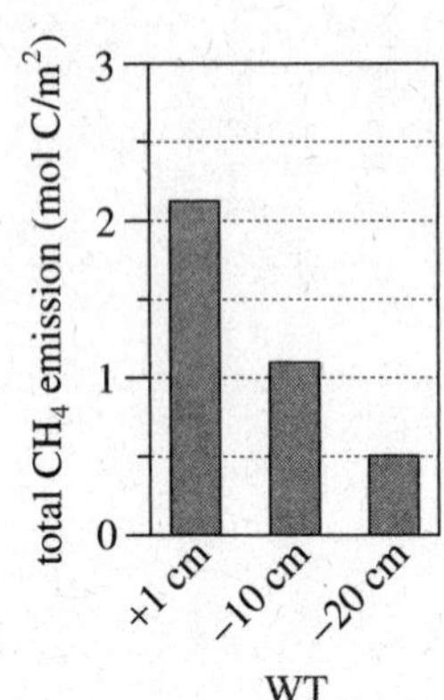

Figure 1

Study

At the beginning of a particular summer, 3 soil sections, each 1.5 m long, 1 m wide, and 0.6 m deep, were removed intact from the surface of each of 2 wetlands—a *bog* and a *fen*—after all live plants had been removed from the sections. Each section was placed in a separate 100 L tank having sides and a lid made entirely of glass. An instrument to measure gas emissions was mounted on the underside of the lid, above the soil. All the tanks were placed at an outdoor site near the wetlands.

Different amounts of water were added to the 3 tanks containing bog soil sections to produce a water table (WT) 1 cm above the surface (+1 cm) of the first soil section, a WT 10 cm below the surface (−10 cm) of the second soil section, and a WT 20 cm below the surface (−20 cm) of the third soil section. This procedure was repeated for the 3 tanks containing fen soil sections. All the lids were then closed.

Over the next 3 months, gas emissions from each soil section were measured, in moles of carbon per square meter (mol C/m^2). Throughout this period, the temperature inside the tanks was kept the same as the outdoor temperature. Figure 1 shows the total emission of CO_2 and the total emission of CH_4 from each bog soil section due to bacterial activity; Figure 2 does the same for each fen soil section.

fen soil

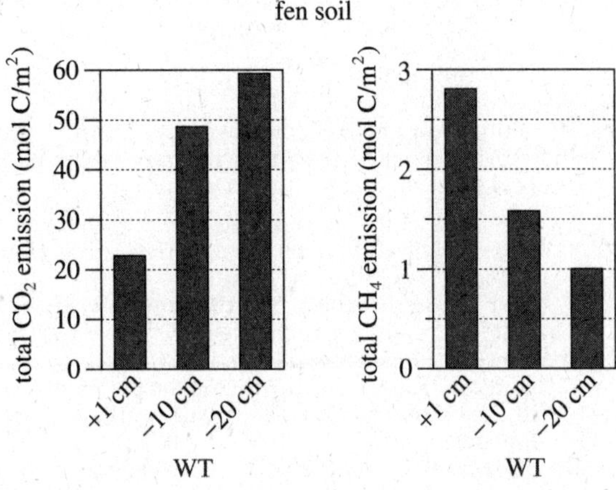

Figure 2

Figures adapted from Karen Updegraff et al., "Response of CO_2 and CH_4 Emissions from Peatlands to Warming and Water Table Manipulations." ©2001 by the Ecological Society of America.

GO ON TO THE NEXT PAGE.

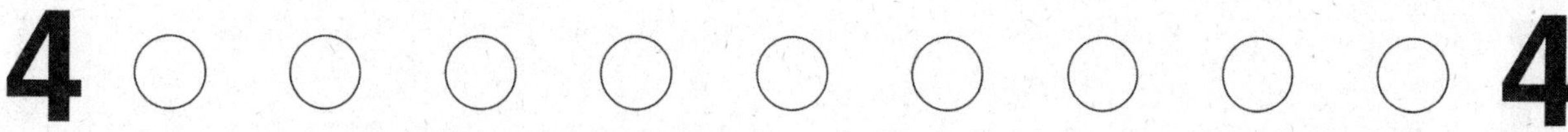

14. The researchers who conducted the study most likely chose to conduct it during the summer rather than during the winter because organic matter in soil is broken down:

F. in the summer by aerobic bacteria only and in the winter by anaerobic bacteria only.
G. in the summer by anaerobic bacteria only and in the winter by aerobic bacteria only.
H. by both aerobic and anaerobic bacteria more rapidly in the summer than in the winter.
J. by both aerobic and anaerobic bacteria less rapidly in the summer than in the winter.

15. According to the results of the study, as the water table for the bog soil sections and the fen soil sections became progressively lower, did the total CO_2 emission increase or decrease, and did the total CH_4 emission increase or decrease?

	total CO_2 emission	total CH_4 emission
A.	increased	decreased
B.	decreased	increased
C.	increased	increased
D.	decreased	decreased

16. One of the reasons that the lid on each tank was kept closed for the 3-month period was to:

F. minimize the amount of emitted gas that exited the tank.
G. maximize the amount of atmospheric gas that entered the tank.
H. prevent bacteria from leaving the tank.
J. prevent sunlight from entering the tank.

17. The 2 types of wetland investigated in this study—bogs and fens—have different levels of the nutrients that sustain bacterial growth. Do the results of the study suggest that the levels of the nutrients that sustain aerobic bacteria are higher in bogs or in fens, and do the results of the study suggest that the levels of the nutrients that sustain anaerobic bacteria are higher in bogs or in fens?

	higher nutrients for aerobic bacteria	higher nutrients for anaerobic bacteria
A.	bogs	bogs
B.	bogs	fens
C.	fens	bogs
D.	fens	fens

18. Based on the results of the study for the 2 soil sections that were completely submerged in water, were aerobic bacteria present in those sections?

F. Yes; CO_2 was emitted from those sections.
G. Yes; CH_4 was emitted from those sections.
H. No; only CO_2 was emitted from those sections.
J. No; only CH_4 was emitted from those sections.

19. Consider the total CO_2 emission from the fen soil section having a WT of -10 cm. Based on that result, over the 3 months, the average CO_2 emission from that soil section *per month* would have been closest to which of the following?

A. 10 mol C/m^2
B. 13 mol C/m^2
C. 16 mol C/m^2
D. 19 mol C/m^2

20. The study was conducted at an outdoor site near the wetlands to ensure that the tanks would be nearly identical to the wetlands with respect to which of the following conditions?

F. Amount of precipitation
G. Types of plants present
H. Volume of soil
J. Hours of daylight

GO ON TO THE NEXT PAGE.

4 ○ ○ ○ ○ ○ ○ ○ ○ ○ 4

Passage IV

Physics students performed 3 studies to determine the forces that several doors exerted on their hinges. The doors had various weights, W, and widths, D. Each door had 2 hinges; the hinges could be moved to vary the distance, S, between them. None of the doors had a doorknob.

The 2 hinges on each door were equidistant from the center of mass of the door (see the diagram).

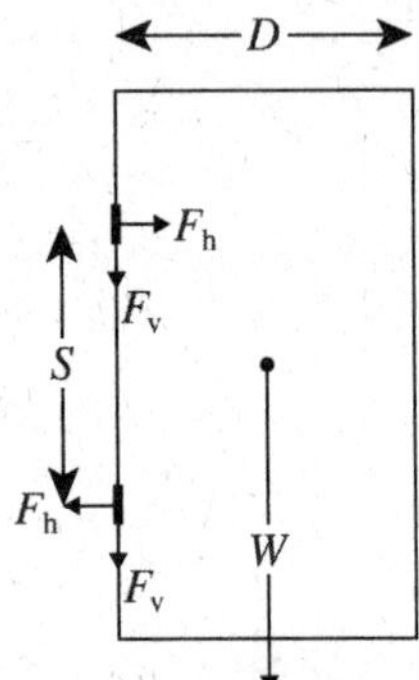

diagram of door

Each hinge was fitted with 2 force sensors. With the door attached to a door frame, one of the sensors detected the *horizontal force* exerted by the door on the hinge, F_h, and the other sensor detected the *vertical force* exerted by the door on the hinge, F_v. Once F_h and F_v were determined for each hinge, F_h was averaged over the 2 hinges, yielding the average horizontal force per hinge, $F_{h, av}$, and F_v was averaged over the 2 hinges, yielding the average vertical force per hinge, $F_{v, av}$. From $F_{h, av}$ and $F_{v, av}$, the average net force per hinge, $F_{n, av}$, could be calculated.

In the 3 studies, all forces were recorded in pounds (lb) and all lengths were recorded in inches (in).

Study 1

For a door with $W = 61$ lb and $D = 30$ in, the students determined $F_{h, av}$ and $F_{v, av}$ at various S. The results are shown in Figure 1.

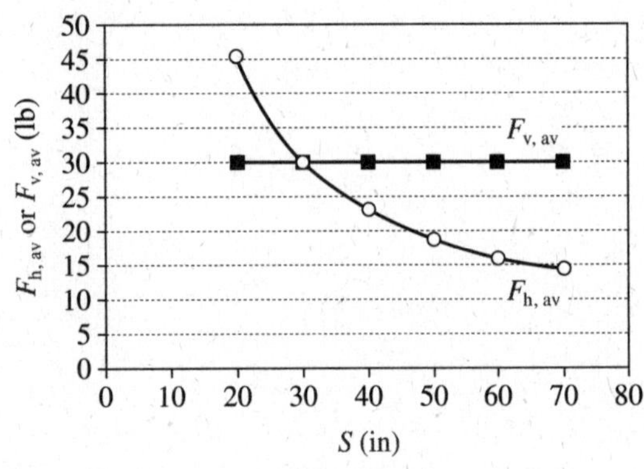

Figure 1

Study 2

For 3 doors, each with $D = 30$ in but a different W, the students determined $F_{n, av}$ at various S. The results are shown in Figure 2.

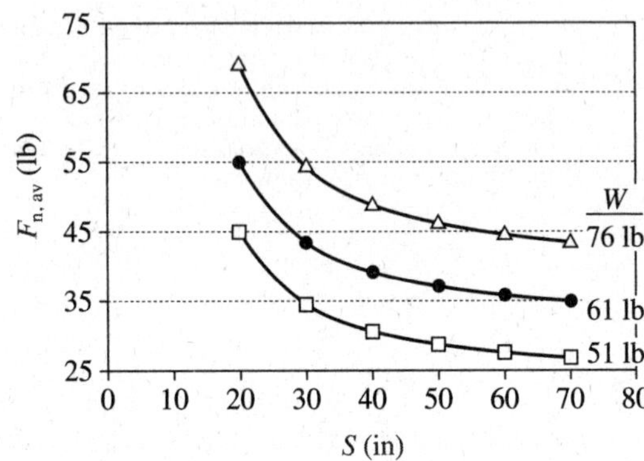

Figure 2

Study 3

For 3 doors, each with $W = 61$ lb but a different D, the students determined $F_{n, av}$ at various S. The results are shown in Figure 3.

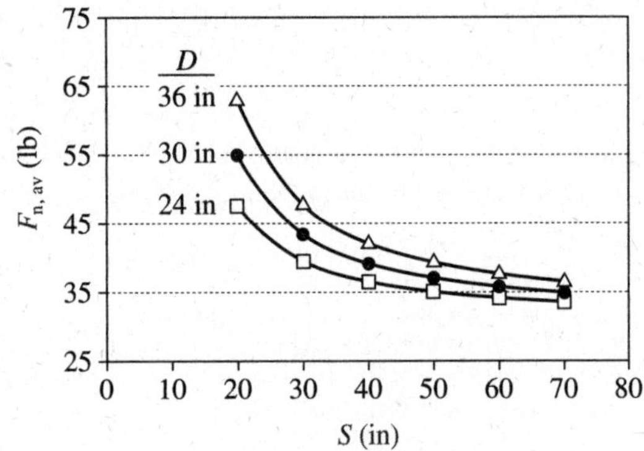

Figure 3

21. In which study, if any, was the door with the greatest mass tested?

A. Study 1
B. Study 2
C. Study 3
D. None of the studies; all the doors tested in the 3 studies had the same mass.

GO ON TO THE NEXT PAGE.

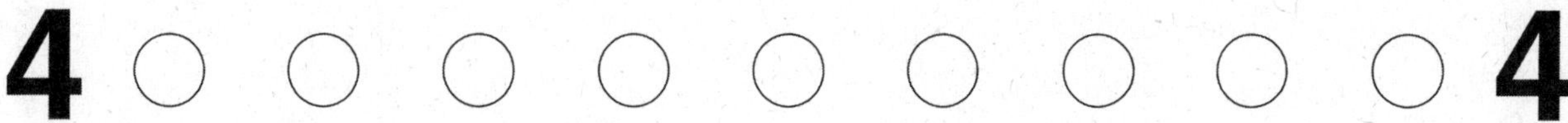

22. Which of the following statements regarding W and D best describes a difference between Study 2 and Study 3 ? In Study 2:

F. W was varied while D was held constant, whereas in Study 3, W was held constant while D was varied.
G. W was held constant while D was varied, whereas in Study 3, W was varied while D was held constant.
H. both W and D were varied, whereas in Study 3, both W and D were held constant.
J. both W and D were held constant, whereas in Study 3, both W and D were varied.

23. If a door having $W = 90$ lb, $D = 30$ in, and $S = 50$ in had been tested in Study 2, $F_{n,\,av}$ for this door would most likely have been:

A. less than 20 lb.
B. between 20 lb and 30 lb.
C. between 30 lb and 45 lb.
D. greater than 45 lb.

24. For the door tested in Study 1, when S was less than 30 in, was $F_{h,\,av}$ less than $F_{v,\,av}$ or greater than $F_{v,\,av}$, and when S was greater than 30 in, was $F_{h,\,av}$ less than $F_{v,\,av}$ or greater than $F_{v,\,av}$?

	S less than 30 in	S greater than 30 in
F.	less	less
G.	less	greater
H.	greater	less
J.	greater	greater

25. In Studies 2 and 3, which combination of W, D, and S resulted in the *lowest* $F_{n,\,av}$?

	W (lb)	D (in)	S (in)
A.	51	30	20
B.	51	30	70
C.	61	24	20
D.	61	24	70

26. In Study 1, which average force, $F_{h,\,av}$ or $F_{v,\,av}$, was independent of S ?

F. $F_{h,\,av}$, because as S increased, $F_{h,\,av}$ decreased.
G. $F_{h,\,av}$, because as S increased, $F_{h,\,av}$ remained constant.
H. $F_{v,\,av}$, because as S increased, $F_{v,\,av}$ decreased.
J. $F_{v,\,av}$, because as S increased, $F_{v,\,av}$ remained constant.

27. Suppose that, due to a manufacturing defect, a particular pair of hinges will break when a net force greater than 57 lb is exerted on each hinge. Based on Study 3, the hinges will most likely break if used on a 61 lb door with which of the following combinations of D and S ?

	D (in)	S (in)
A.	30	20
B.	30	70
C.	36	20
D.	36	70

Taking Additional Practice Tests

GO ON TO THE NEXT PAGE.

4 ○ ○ ○ ○ ○ ○ ○ ○ ○ 4

Passage V

In a chemistry class, the teacher placed 0.5 g of porous steel wool, composed mostly of iron (Fe), inside a small heat-resistant quartz tube. She then used silicone hoses to connect the quartz tube to 2 airtight glass syringes (see figure). Each syringe contained 8 mL of air, and the total volume of air in the closed apparatus was 20 mL.

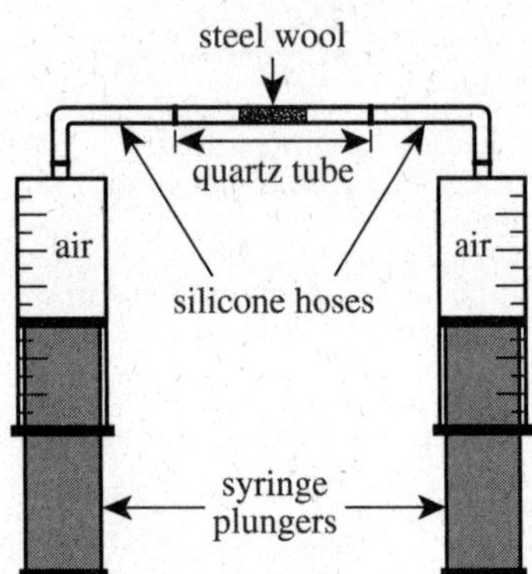

Figure adapted from Francisco Vera, Rodrigo Rivera, and César Núñez, "A Simple Experiment to Measure the Content of Oxygen in the Air Using Heated Steel Wool." ©2011 by Division of Chemical Education, Inc., American Chemical Society.

A Bunsen burner was then used to heat the contents of the quartz tube for 2 min. During heating, the plungers were moved up and down to pass the air back and forth through the steel wool. The total volume of gas in the apparatus steadily declined over the 2 min. Once the apparatus and its contents returned to room temperature, the total volume of gas in the apparatus was 16 mL.

The teacher asked each of 4 students to explain what occurred during the demonstration.

Student 1

During heating, the Fe in the steel wool reacted with all the N_2 in the air to form solid iron nitride (FeN), which was deposited on the steel wool. Air contains about 20% N_2 by volume. As a result of the reaction, the total volume of gas in the apparatus decreased by about 20%, so almost all the gas remaining in the apparatus was O_2.

Student 2

During heating, the Fe in the steel wool reacted with some of the O_2 in the air to form solid iron oxide (Fe_2O_3), which was deposited on the steel wool. Air contains about 80% O_2 by volume. As a result of the reaction, the total volume of gas in the apparatus decreased by about 20%. Almost all the gas remaining in the apparatus was a mixture of about 75% O_2 and 25% N_2 by volume.

Student 3

Student 2 is correct, except that (1) the Fe in the steel wool reacted with all the O_2 in the air and (2) air contains about 20% O_2 by volume. After the reaction, almost all the gas remaining in the apparatus was N_2.

Student 4

During heating, the Fe in the steel wool reacted with all the CO_2 in the air to form solid iron carbonate ($FeCO_3$), which was deposited on the steel wool. Air contains about 20% CO_2 by volume. As a result of the reaction, the total volume of gas in the apparatus decreased by about 20%, so almost all the gas remaining in the apparatus was O_2.

GO ON TO THE NEXT PAGE.

4 ○ ○ ○ ○ ○ ○ ○ ○ ○ 4

28. Air contains less than 1% argon by volume. This information *weakens* the explanations given by which of the students, if any?

F. Students 1 and 2 only
G. Students 3 and 4 only
H. All of the students
J. None of the students

29. Silicone hoses were most likely used to connect the quartz tube to the syringes because silicone has which of the properties listed below?

I. Strong resistance to heat
II. Low chemical reactivity
III. High solubility in water

A. I and II only
B. I and III only
C. II and III only
D. I, II, and III

30. Based on Student 4's explanation, during the demonstration, did the percent CO_2 by volume in the apparatus increase or decrease, and did the percent O_2 by volume in the apparatus increase or decrease?

	percent CO_2 by volume	percent O_2 by volume
F.	increase	increase
G.	increase	decrease
H.	decrease	decrease
J.	decrease	increase

31. Which of the students would be likely to agree that, by volume, air contains more O_2 than N_2 ?

A. Students 1 and 2 only
B. Students 1 and 3 only
C. Students 1, 2, and 4 only
D. Students 1, 3, and 4 only

32. Based on Student 3's explanation, the reaction that occurred during the demonstration would be represented by which of the following balanced chemical equations?

F. $2Fe_2O_3 \rightarrow 4Fe + 3O_2$
G. $2FeN \rightarrow 2Fe + N_2$
H. $4Fe + 3O_2 \rightarrow 2Fe_2O_3$
J. $2Fe + N_2 \rightarrow 2FeN$

33. Which of the students, if any, would be likely to agree that at the end of the demonstration, the gas remaining in the apparatus was at least 20% N_2 by volume?

A. Student 2 only
B. Students 2 and 3 only
C. All of the students
D. None of the students

34. In a chemical reaction, the *limiting reactant* is the reactant that is in the shortest supply and thus limits the amount of product that can be produced. Which student would be the most likely to agree that the limiting reactant during the demonstration was the iron in the steel wool?

F. Student 1
G. Student 2
H. Student 3
J. Student 4

GO ON TO THE NEXT PAGE.

4 ○ ○ ○ ○ ○ ○ ○ ○ ○ 4

Passage VI

Quarks constitute 1 of the 3 classes of elementary particles that form all matter in the universe. Three quarks bound together form a type of particle called a *baryon*. A quark's *effective mass* (mass when bound to other quarks) is greater than its *single-quark mass* (mass when unbound). In addition, all quarks possess a property called *spin*. A quark's spin can be oriented in 1 of 2 directions, *spin-up* (↑) or *spin-down* (↓).

Table 1 lists the symbol, electric charge, and approximate single-quark mass for each of the 6 quarks.

Table 1

Quark	Symbol	Electric charge	Single-quark mass (MeV*)
Down	*d*	$-\frac{1}{3}$	5
Up	*u*	$+\frac{2}{3}$	3
Strange	*s*	$-\frac{1}{3}$	104
Charm	*c*	$+\frac{2}{3}$	1,270
Bottom	*b*	$-\frac{1}{3}$	4,200
Top	*t*	$+\frac{2}{3}$	171,200

*million electron volts

Table 2 gives the symbol, mass, quark content, and quark spins for several baryons.

Table 2

Baryon	Symbol	Mass (MeV)	Quark content	Quark spins
Proton	p	938	*uud*	↑↓↑
Neutron	n	939	*udd*	↑↓↑
Lambda-zero	Λ^0	1,115	*uds*	↑↓↑
Delta-zero	Δ^0	1,233	*udd*	↑↑↑
Delta-minus	Δ^-	1,234	*ddd*	↑↑↑
Omega-minus	Ω^-	1,673	*sss*	↑↑↑

Tables adapted from C. Amsler et al., "Review of Particle Physics." ©2008 by Elsevier B.V.

GO ON TO THE NEXT PAGE.

4 ○ ○ ○ ○ ○ ○ ○ ○ ○ 4

35. For all quarks, the amount of spin is always $\frac{1}{2}\hbar$, where $\hbar$ is a constant. A spin-up quark has spin $+\frac{1}{2}\hbar$, and a spin-down quark has spin $-\frac{1}{2}\hbar$. Given that the spin of a baryon equals the sum of its quark spins, what are the spins of the Λ^0 and Δ^0 baryons listed in Table 2 ?

	Λ^0	Δ^0
A.	$-\frac{1}{2}\hbar$	$-\frac{3}{2}\hbar$
B.	$-\frac{1}{2}\hbar$	$-\frac{1}{2}\hbar$
C.	$+\frac{1}{2}\hbar$	$+\frac{3}{2}\hbar$
D.	$+\frac{3}{2}\hbar$	$+\frac{3}{2}\hbar$

36. Which of the following diagrams represents the quark content and quark spins for an electrically neutral baryon having only 2 quark spins oriented in the same direction?

F.

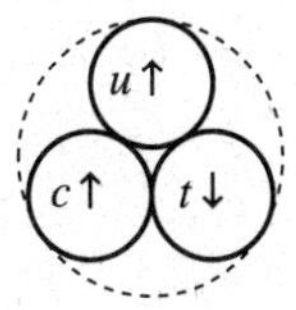

H.

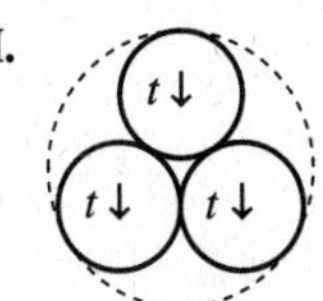

G.

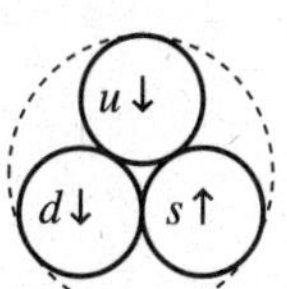

J.

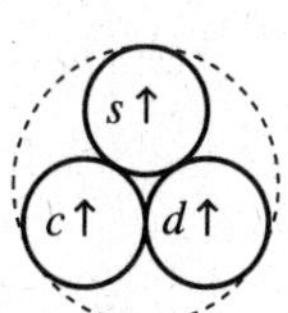

37. Is the information in Tables 1 and 2 consistent with the known electric charge for the proton?

A. No, because Tables 1 and 2 indicate the proton has an electric charge of 0.
B. No, because Tables 1 and 2 indicate the proton has an electric charge of +1.
C. Yes, because Tables 1 and 2 indicate the proton has an electric charge of 0.
D. Yes, because Tables 1 and 2 indicate the proton has an electric charge of +1.

38. Based on Tables 1 and 2, the Ω^- baryon has the same electric charge as a baryon containing which of the following quark combinations?

F. *dsb*
G. *ssc*
H. *sst*
J. *usc*

39. Based on Tables 1 and 2, atomic nuclei are made up of which types of quarks?

A. *u* and *d* only
B. *d* and *s* only
C. *u* and *s* only
D. *u*, *d*, and *s* only

40. The 6 quarks are grouped into 3 generations as shown in the table below.

Generation	Quarks
1	*d*, *u*
2	*s*, *c*
3	*b*, *t*

For which generation, if any, is the statement "Positively charged quarks are more massive than negatively charged quarks" NOT true?

F. Generation 1
G. Generation 2
H. Generation 3
J. None of the generations; the statement is true for all 3 generations.

END OF TEST 4

STOP! DO NOT RETURN TO ANY OTHER TEST.

You may wish to photocopy these sample answer document pages to respond to the practice ACT Writing Test.

Please enter the information at the right before beginning the writing test.

Use a soft lead No. 2 pencil only. Do NOT use a mechanical pencil, ink, ballpoint, or felt-tip pen.

WRITING TEST BOOKLET NUMBER

Print your 6-digit **Booklet Number** in the boxes at the right.

WRITING TEST FORM

Print your 5-character **Test Form** in the boxes above and fill in the corresponding oval at the right.

- 16W1A
- 16W2A
- 16W3A
- 18W4A
- 19WT5

Begin WRITING TEST here.

If you need more space, please continue on the next page.

WRITING TEST

If you need more space, please continue on the back of this page.

WRITING TEST

If you need more space, please continue on the next page.

WRITING TEST

STOP here with the writing test.

072951

Practice Writing Test Prompt 2

Your Signature: ____________________
(Do not print.)

Print Your Name Here: ____________________

Your Date of Birth:

Month - Day - Year

Form 16W2A

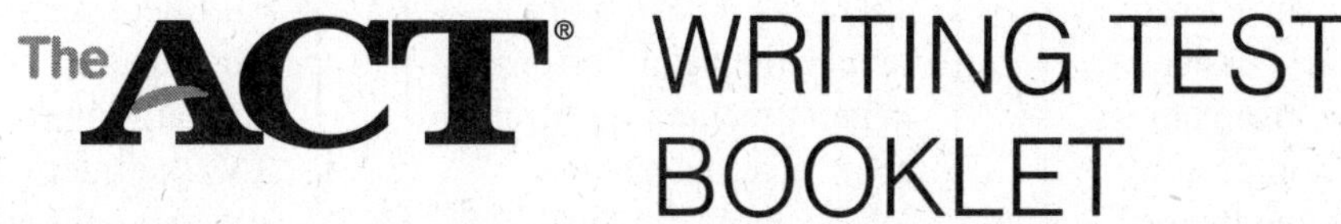

You must take the multiple-choice tests before you take the writing test.

Directions

This is a test of your writing skills. You will have **forty** (40) minutes to read the prompt, plan your response, and write an essay in English. Before you begin working, read all material in this test booklet carefully to understand exactly what you are being asked to do.

You will write your essay on the lined pages in the **answer document** provided. Your writing on those pages will be scored. You may use the unlined pages in this test booklet to plan your essay. Your work on these pages will not be scored.

Your essay will be evaluated based on the evidence it provides of your ability to:

- clearly state your own perspective on a complex issue and analyze the relationship between your perspective and at least one other perspective
- develop and support your ideas with reasoning and examples
- organize your ideas clearly and logically
- communicate your ideas effectively in standard written English

Lay your pencil down immediately when time is called.

DO NOT OPEN THIS BOOKLET UNTIL TOLD TO DO SO.

PO Box 168
Iowa City, IA 52243-0168

Declining Event Attendance

For many years, the only way to see a large public event—a concert, a movie, a baseball game—was to attend in person. More than just a function of necessity, though, physically attending a large event was seen as an opportunity to build community and fellowship through shared experience. In recent years, however, attendance at public events has declined steadily. Given the long-standing cultural role of public events, it is worth considering what declining attendance might indicate about our shifting cultural values.

Read and carefully consider these perspectives. Each suggests a particular way of thinking about declining event attendance as a reflection of shifting cultural values.

Perspective One	Perspective Two	Perspective Three
People these days value convenience over community. It's easier to watch a game from home than to attend in person, so we do it, even though it keeps us isolated from one another.	For many people, attending an event is a luxury they can't afford. When time and resources are scarce, we choose what's most practical first, even if that means sacrificing community participation.	Today, physical presence isn't necessary for participating in an event and building community. TV, the Internet, and social media offer shared experience to more people than large public events ever could before.

Essay Task

Write a unified, coherent essay about declining event attendance as a reflection of shifting cultural values. In your essay, be sure to:

- clearly state your own perspective on the issue and analyze the relationship between your perspective and at least one other perspective
- develop and support your ideas with reasoning and examples
- organize your ideas clearly and logically
- communicate your ideas effectively in standard written English

Your perspective may be in full agreement with any of those given, in partial agreement, or completely different.

Planning Your Essay

Your work on these prewriting pages will not be scored.

Use the space below and on the back cover to generate ideas and plan your essay. You may wish to consider the following as you think critically about the task:

Strengths and weaknesses of different perspectives on the issue

- What insights do they offer, and what do they fail to consider?
- Why might they be persuasive to others, or why might they fail to persuade?

Your own knowledge, experience, and values

- What is your perspective on this issue, and what are its strengths and weaknesses?
- How will you support your perspective in your essay?

If you need more space to plan, please continue on the back of this page.

Planning Your Essay

Use this page to continue planning your essay. Your work on this page will not be scored.

Scoring Your Practice Tests

How to score Practice Tests 2, 3, 4, and 5 is covered in chapter 11.

Explanatory Answers

ENGLISH • PRACTICE TEST 2 • EXPLANATORY ANSWERS

Passage I

Question 1. The best answer is B because it uses a simple present tense singular verb that agrees with the singular noun *building*. It also creates a complete sentence.

The best answer is NOT:

A because it attaches the main verb *is* to the relative pronoun *that*, creating a clause that interrupts the sentence and creates a sentence fragment (an incomplete sentence).

C because the contraction *it's* (meaning "it is") creates a faulty conjunction resulting in a fragment connected to an independent clause.

D because it removes the main verb from the sentence, resulting in a sentence fragment.

Question 2. The best answer is F because it mentions the "legacy of the Chinese community," which refers to the cultural significance of the building, and "the nineteenth-century American West," which refers to the building's historical significance.

The best answer is NOT:

G because it names specific features of the building. The features themselves do not introduce the building's historical and cultural significance.

H because it identifies the groups responsible for preserving and operating the building today but does not introduce the historical and cultural significance of the building.

J because it mentions some of the contents of the building's kitchen. The contents of the kitchen do not introduce the historical and cultural significance of the building.

Question 3. The best answer is C because it correctly uses the past tense verb *were attracted*, which is consistent with *served.*

The best answer is NOT:

A because it uses the present tense in a sentence that requires the past tense. Also, it creates an illogical thought regarding what travelers might have been attracted to the land.

B because it uses the future tense in a sentence that requires the past tense.

D because it uses the present tense in a sentence that requires the past tense.

ENGLISH • PRACTICE TEST 2 • EXPLANATORY ANSWERS

Question 4. The best answer is G because it provides a link to the information that follows by providing the names of the two young Chinese men who are referred to in the next sentence and the rest of the essay.

The best answer is NOT:

F because the preceding sentence does not make a claim about Hay and On.

H because the introduction of the men's names is necessary. Knowing that Hay and On are the men who bought the building is necessary for understanding the essay at this point.

J because it incorrectly suggests that this part of the essay focuses on Hay and On's partnership rather than on introducing Hay and On as the men who bought the building.

Question 5. The best answer is D because it uses a plural past tense verb *remained.* The essay's content calls for the past tense, and the sentence's verb must agree with its subject, *men.*

The best answer is NOT:

A because it uses a present tense verb *remains*, which does not agree with the sentence's subject. Also, it is not parallel with the other verbs in the sentence (*combined* and *organized*).

B because it uses the auxiliary verb *has*, which does not agree in number with the sentence's subject and is not parallel with the other verbs in the sentence.

C because it combines the correct auxiliary verb *have* with the incorrect verb *remain*, resulting in an improperly formed verb. Also, it is not parallel with the other verbs in the sentence.

Question 6. The best answer is G because it creates a parallel structure in which *making* and *curing* (used later in the sentence) are in the same form. The preposition *for* correctly applies to both verbs.

The best answer is NOT:

F because it inserts a dependent clause, creating a sentence in which the verbs are not parallel.

H because it inserts a dependent clause that isn't parallel with the verb *curing.*

J because it makes the latter half of the sentence into a compound predicate, which creates a problem with parallelism with the verb *curing.*

ENGLISH • PRACTICE TEST 2 • EXPLANATORY ANSWERS

Question 7. The best answer is A because it uses the possessive pronoun *whose*, which clearly explains that the treatments were those of the patients.

The best answer is NOT:

B because it is unnecessarily wordy and redundant; the idea of previous treatments explains that the treatments were already experienced.

C because it illogically indicates that the patients were the previous treatments.

D because the phrase "of whom" creates an illogical sentence with an unclear meaning.

Question 8. The best answer is F because the preceding sentence discusses Hay's medical expertise as the reason for his fame and noteworthiness.

The best answer is NOT:

G because the sentence does not mention any specific examples of Hay's diagnoses.

H because the resulting paragraph would be unevenly weighted toward On when the essay describes the two men as partners. The information about Hay is important regardless of On's involvement with the medical clinic.

J because the paragraph is about both Hay and On, not On only.

Question 9. The best answer is A because the preceding sentence lists six services that the building eventually provided. If the sentence were deleted, the paragraph would lose the details that indicate the scope of services.

The best answer is NOT:

B because the sentence provides no claims about which aspect of Kam Wah Chung & Co. was most important to visitors.

C because the sentence does not provide a summary of one visitor's experiences at Kam Wah Chung & Co.

D because the sentence provides no indication of how long Kam Wah Chung & Co. was prosperous.

ENGLISH • PRACTICE TEST 2 • EXPLANATORY ANSWERS

Question 10. The best answer is J because the word *into* is grammatical and clearly indicates a transition from the Great Depression to the 1940s.

The best answer is NOT:

F because *beginning* is a present participle, not a preposition. The sentence has a series of prepositional phrases ("through the turn of the century" and "during the Great Depression"). This final phrase needs to match the structure of the two preceding phrases.

G because the pronoun *it* is singular and cannot refer to the plural *businesses*. This *it* has no clear referent. The resulting sentence does not make clear what entered the 1940s.

H because it creates an illogical statement; *businesses* cannot become the 1940s.

Question 11. The best answer is C because the past tense is called for in the sentence, and the verb form *became* aligns with *was restored*, a past tense verb used previously in the sentence.

The best answer is NOT:

A because *has became* is an incorrect verb form.

B because the auxiliary verb *have* does not agree in number with the singular subject of the sentence, *building*.

D because *become* is a present tense verb form; the context and structure of the sentence call for a past tense verb.

Question 12. The best answer is J because it is the only option that does not introduce a redundancy into the sentence.

The best answer is NOT:

F because it is unnecessarily wordy and redundant. The word *designated* already conveys the idea that the museum was called a National Historic Landmark.

G because it is redundant; *designated* already conveys the idea of having the appropriation *of*.

H because it is redundant; *designated* already conveys the idea of being identified as.

ENGLISH • PRACTICE TEST 2 • EXPLANATORY ANSWERS

Question 13. The best answer is D because no transitional word or phrase is needed in the sentence.

The best answer is NOT:

A because the word *besides* indicates that a previous idea is being added onto, which isn't the case.

B because the phrase "in conclusion" does not offer a logical transition from the idea of the museum being designated a national landmark to the idea that the museum encapsulates an era.

C because the sentence gives an exact year when the building became a National Historic Landmark (2005), so "in time" is illogical here.

Question 14. The best answer is J because sentence 2 explains why the artifacts left inside the building were preserved. It is logical to infer that they wouldn't need to be preserved unless the building had been closed for a long time, which is exactly what sentence 5 states. Placing sentence 2 after sentence 5 makes the paragraph logical by putting the events in chronological order.

The best answer is NOT:

F because as it is now, sentence 2 interrupts the historical discussion of how Kam Wah Chung & Co. prospered and shifted in leadership over the years.

G because placing sentence 2 before sentence 1 illogically presents the information about the preservation of artifacts prior to mentioning the closing of Kam Wah Chung & Co.

H because placing sentence 2 after sentence 3 interrupts the historical discussion of how Kam Wah Chung & Co. shifted in leadership.

Question 15. The best answer is C because the focus of the essay is on the historical role of the Kam Wah Chung & Co. building. The essay details how the building was founded, who used it, and for what purposes. The essay does not outline the steps the state of Oregon took to restore the building.

The best answer is NOT:

A because although the essay mentions the restoration of the building, it primarily offers an overview of the building's historical role rather than explaining the steps the state of Oregon took to restore the building.

B because although the essay mentions how the artifacts were preserved, it primarily offers an overview of the building's historical role rather than explaining the steps the state of Oregon took to restore the building.

D because the essay does not critique On's business philosophies or Hay's medical diagnoses and treatments.

ENGLISH • PRACTICE TEST 2 • EXPLANATORY ANSWERS

Passage II

Question 16. The best answer is H because it correctly inserts a comma only after the prepositional phrase that begins the sentence.

The best answer is NOT:

F because it incorrectly inserts a comma between the subject (*fair*) and the verb (*looks*).

G because it incorrectly inserts a comma between the subject (*fair*) and the verb (*looks*) and sets off the subject ("a Renaissance fair") as nonessential information.

J because it incorrectly adds a semicolon after *fair.* A semicolon must separate two independent clauses. In this case, it separates two fragments (incomplete sentences).

Question 17. The best answer is D because it correctly uses the possessive pronoun *their* and the preposition *past* to explain the direction of movement; the people are passing by costumed characters and colorful booths.

The best answer is NOT:

A because it uses the contraction *they're* (they are) in place of *their* (possessive).

B because it uses the contraction *they're* (they are) in place of *their* (possessive) and the past tense verb *passed* in place of the preposition *past.*

C because it uses the past tense verb *passed* in place of the preposition *past.*

Question 18. The best answer is G because it creates a logical sentence that contrasts theme parks and Renaissance fairs. This comparison makes sense in the paragraph, which has been describing how theme parks and Renaissance fairs are similar up to this point.

The best answer is NOT:

F because it illogically suggests that roller coasters and Ferris wheels are the reason why Renaissance fair attractions are inspired by sixteenth-century England.

H because it creates an illogical cause-effect relationship between the roller coasters and Ferris wheels of theme parks and the sixteenth-century inspirations of Renaissance fairs.

J because it creates an illogical cause-effect relationship. Roller coasters and Ferris wheels are not the reason why Renaissance fair attractions are inspired by sixteenth-century England.

ENGLISH • PRACTICE TEST 2 • EXPLANATORY ANSWERS

Question 19. The best answer is A because no punctuation is needed here. The absence of punctuation creates the clearest indication that the sentence is referring to the horses that are carrying knights.

The best answer is NOT:

B because it makes "carrying knights" appear as nonessential information and results in a clause that lacks a verb: Horses to a jousting match.

C because it incorrectly places a comma between the subject ("horses carrying knights") and the prepositional phrase that explains where they are going ("to a jousting match").

D because it offers the beginning of a nonessential phrase ("carrying knights to . . .") that has no second comma later in the sentence to close it. This creates an ungrammatical sentence.

Question 20. The best answer is G because the verb *clip-clop* provides the sound the horses' hooves make on the streets, which is a sensory detail about the horses' movement.

The best answer is NOT:

F because the verb *walk* does not provide a sensory detail that clearly conveys the horses' movement.

H because the verb *move* only conveys the vague idea of movement without providing any sensory details.

J because the verb *travel* only conveys the vague idea of movement from one place to another without providing any sensory details.

Question 21. The best answer is D because it correctly positions the phrase "ranging from king-sized turkey legs to suits of armor" so that it modifies *wares*. The wares are the things that vary in this way.

The best answer is NOT:

A because it incorrectly suggests that the vendors are what range from turkey legs to suits of armor.

B because it offers the action ("peddling wares") before the subject (*vendors*) and separates the two with the modifier about the types of wares. The result is an unclear sentence.

C because it incorrectly modifies *vendors*, suggesting that the vendors range from turkey legs to suits of armor.

ENGLISH • PRACTICE TEST 2 • EXPLANATORY ANSWERS

Question 22. The best answer is G because it effectively introduces the subject that is developed in the paragraph and in the rest of the essay: the hard work that goes into re-creating the past at the Renaissance fair.

The best answer is NOT:

F because it misleads the reader into thinking that what follows will be about how interesting Renaissance fairs are instead of about the challenges of working at a Renaissance fair.

H because it suggests that what follows will focus on the fun of working at the Renaissance fair instead of on the challenges of working there.

J because it suggests that the paragraph and essay will focus on a specific day when the narrator attended a Renaissance fair whereas the paragraph and essay explain the challenges of working at a Renaissance fair.

Question 23. The best answer is C because it results in a complete sentence with a comma separating the main clause from the participial phrase that begins with *substituting.*

The best answer is NOT:

A because it improperly has *substituting* as the beginning of a sentence, which results in a sentence fragment.

B because it creates a comma splice (two or more complete sentences separated by only a comma). The two complete sentences joined by the comma both begin with the subject *we.*

D because it incorrectly places a semicolon between a main clause and a participial phrase. A semicolon must separate two independent clauses.

Question 24. The best answer is F because it uses the past tense verb *introduced,* which is parallel with the verb *served* (the other verb in the sentence's compound predicate). The past tense is used in most of the essay.

The best answer is NOT:

G because it incorrectly uses the infinitive *to introduce* when the past tense is needed. Also, it is not parallel with the verb *served.*

H because it incorrectly uses the participle *introducing* when the past tense is called for. Like **G**, it isn't parallel with *served.*

J because it shifts the tense from the past to the present and, similar to **G** and **H**, isn't parallel with *served.*

ENGLISH • PRACTICE TEST 2 • EXPLANATORY ANSWERS

Question 25. The best answer is D because it correctly uses the pronoun *who* to introduce the clause that describes the person the narrator was pretending to be. In this sentence, *who* is required because it functions as the subject of the clause.

The best answer is NOT:

A because it uses the object pronoun *whom* instead of the subject pronoun *who.*

B because by using the verb *were* in this sentence, the writer is incorrectly describing a past event as if it were a hypothetical future one.

C because it, like **A**, uses the object pronoun *whom* instead of the subject pronoun *who.*

Question 26. The best answer is J because no punctuation is needed here. The absence of punctuation creates the clearest and most understandable sentence that links the subject *costumes* to the verb *consisted.*

The best answer is NOT:

F because it creates the nonessential clause "they consisted of confining corsets." The resulting sentence lacks a necessary verb between *costumes* and the attributes of the costumes (confining corsets, several scratchy petticoats, and heavy velvet gowns).

G because it creates a comma splice (two or more complete sentences separated by only a comma). The word *they* becomes the subject of the second complete sentence.

H because it inserts the preposition *of*, which creates the ungrammatical phrase "because of our costumes consisted."

Question 27. The best answer is C because the sentence about the costumes theme park characters wear isn't very relevant in an essay about working at a Renaissance fair, especially given that the first paragraph makes a distinction between Renaissance fairs and theme parks.

The best answer is NOT:

A because although Renaissance fairs and theme parks are compared earlier in the essay, this sentence doesn't pertain to this paragraph's discussion of the costumes the narrator wore at the Renaissance fair.

B because although the preceding sentence does discuss uncomfortable costumes, it relates to the narrator's experience at a Renaissance fair, not at a theme park.

D because the information about costumes worn by characters at theme parks is not found elsewhere in the essay.

ENGLISH • PRACTICE TEST 2 • EXPLANATORY ANSWERS

Question 28. The best answer is H because it most clearly and concisely refers to all manner of inventions. It does not repeat the same idea, and it does not add unnecessary words to the sentence.

The best answer is NOT:

F because it is redundant and wordy. The phrase "after the sixteenth century" already conveys the idea of things that had come into existence more recently.

G because it adds wordiness and redundancy. The phrase "any kind of object or type of item" is redundant, as is the phrase "created and introduced for use."

J because it creates a notable shift in tone. "Stuff from" is more informal than the tone in the rest of the essay.

Question 29. The best answer is B because the phrase "for example" serves as a transition from the preceding sentence, which discusses describing things in Renaissance terms, to this sentence, which has the narrator describing a photograph as a small painting in a tiny box.

The best answer is NOT:

A because the adverbial conjunction *however* implies that the ideas in this sentence contrast with the ideas in the preceding sentence, which isn't the case.

C because the phrase "one time" suggests that the incident with the camera happened only once, an idea that is contradicted by the sentence's use of the auxiliary verb *would*, which suggests that the event happened more than once.

D because *instead* suggests that this event happened in place of what was described in the previous sentence. This isn't the case since the sentence offers an idea that is in line with the preceding sentence.

Question 30. The best answer is J because it removes unnecessary and redundant phrases from the sentence.

The best answer is NOT:

F because it is redundant. The essay makes clear that the narrator worked at the Renaissance fair during summer and that the fair closed once the three months were over.

G because it needlessly repeats the idea that the narrator's work ended when the fair closed.

H because it is redundant; the essay has already made clear that the fair took place during the summer.

Passage III

Question 31. The best answer is A because no punctuation is needed here. The absence of punctuation creates the clearest and most understandable sentence explaining that the blast of water was caused by a breach in the reservoir.

The best answer is NOT:

B because it adds an unnecessary and confusing comma between *by* and *a breach.*

C because it adds an unnecessary and confusing comma between *caused* and *by.*

D because it adds an unnecessary and confusing comma between *water* and *caused.* This comma sets up the information about the cause as nonessential, but it leaves the first part of the sentence as a fragment.

Question 32. The best answer is J because it begins the sentence with the pronoun *it*, which agrees in number with the singular noun *blast*, to which *it* refers.

The best answer is NOT:

F because it begins the sentence with the plural pronoun *they*, which does not agree in number with the noun *blast*, which is singular.

G because it begins the sentence with the subordinating conjunction *that*, which results in a sentence fragment (an incomplete sentence).

H because it begins the sentence with a subordinating conjunction *which* and therefore results in a sentence fragment.

Question 33. The best answer is B because the singular possessive form *park's* is the correct punctuation here. In addition, a comma is required after the word *time* in order to set off the dependent clause that begins the sentence from the main clause of the sentence.

The best answer is NOT:

A because it uses the plural *parks* rather than the possessive *park's*, which would correctly show possession.

C because it incorrectly uses the plural possessive *parks'*. The phrase "one of Missouri's most popular state parks" clearly identifies Johnson's Shut-Ins as one state park.

D because it fails to include a comma after *time*, which is required to set off the dependent clause that begins the sentence from the main clause of the sentence.

ENGLISH • PRACTICE TEST 2 • EXPLANATORY ANSWERS

Question 34. The best answer is G because the word *ultimately* is logical and indicates chronology. Despite the marred beauty, over a billion years' worth of history was revealed in the end (or, *ultimately*).

The best answer is NOT:

F because the word *specifically* calls for one or more precise examples. The sentence instead mentions a large swath of history without specific examples.

H because the word *instead* signals a change from what was expected, which doesn't make sense in the context of the sentence.

J because the word *thus* indicates a cause-effect relationship between the marred beauty and the revealing of over a billion years' worth of Earth's geologic history. No such cause-effect relationship exists.

Question 35. The best answer is C because it uses the verb *began*, which is the appropriate tense and verb form in this sentence.

The best answer is not:

A because *had began* is an incorrect verb form.

B because the verb *begun* needs an auxiliary verb, such as *had*, in order to be correct.

D because it uses the verb *begun* without an accompanying auxiliary verb.

Question 36. The best answer is H because no punctuation is needed here. The dependent clause that begins with *when* should follow immediately after the main clause.

The best answer is NOT:

F because adding a period after *ago* results in a sentence fragment (incomplete sentence) beginning with the word *when.*

G because it incorrectly adds a semicolon after *ago*, separating a dependent clause from an independent clause. A semicolon must separate two independent clauses.

J because it removes the subordinating conjunction *when*, resulting in a run-on, or fused, sentence.

ENGLISH • PRACTICE TEST 2 • EXPLANATORY ANSWERS

Question 37. The best answer is D because it is the only concise and clear option that presents the idea of cooling without being redundant.

The best answer is NOT:

A because it is unnecessarily wordy; *cooling* already encapsulates the idea of temperature.

B because "cooled down" means to come to a lower temperature; the phrase is redundant.

C because "lowered its temperature" means to cool; the phrase is redundant.

Question 38. The best answer is F because no punctuation is needed here. The absence of punctuation creates the clearest and most understandable sentence about the substance that was formed, rhyolite.

The best answer is NOT:

G because the punctuation suggests that the word *rhyolite* provides a definition or clarification about silica-rich. As a noun (rather than an adjective), *rhyolite* cannot serve this function.

H because it suggests that *rock* (all rock) is silica-rich rhyolite formed by the cooling and crystallizing of slow-moving magma, which is illogical.

J because it adds an unnecessary and confusing comma between the verb *form* and the noun indicating what was formed, silica-rich rhyolite rock.

Question 39. The best answer is B because it provides information that helps explain the park's name (*Johnson's Shut-Ins*), which otherwise might confuse readers.

The best answer is NOT:

A because the essay provides no evidence that people feel shut in when visiting the park.

C because the phrase does not depart from the overall tone of the essay, which is neither formal or informal. Rather, the phrase has a direct relationship to the park's name and should be included.

D because the phrase contributes to, rather than interrupts, the description of the Black River.

ENGLISH • PRACTICE TEST 2 • EXPLANATORY ANSWERS

Question 40. The best answer is H because it places a comma between the main clause and the explanatory participial phrase that follows it.

The best answer is NOT:

F because it inserts the conjunction *and* before the word *creating*. This creates a compound predicate wherein the two verbs must be parallel. In this case, *creating* is not parallel with *confined*.

G because it incorrectly places a semicolon between a main clause and a participial phrase. A semicolon must separate two independent clauses.

J because it places a comma between the two verbs in a compound predicate. A conjunction is needed to make this construction grammatical.

Question 41. The best answer is A because it uses the singular possessive pronoun *its*, which agrees with the singular noun *surge*, and it uses the preposition *in* to clearly describe the water cutting a path through the region.

The best answer is not:

B because it uses the preposition *on*, which suggests that the surge of water followed a path that was already there. It also uses the plural possessive pronoun *their*, which does not agree in number with the singular noun *surge*.

C because it uses the plural possessive pronoun *their*, which does not agree in number with the singular noun *surge*.

D because it uses the preposition *on*, which suggests that the path was already there. *In* more clearly indicates that the surge of water created the path.

Question 42. The best answer is J because it uses the singular verb *contains*, which agrees in number with the subject of the sentence, *channel*, which is also singular.

The best answer is NOT:

F because it uses the plural verb *contain*, which does not agree in number with subject of the sentence, *channel*.

G because it uses the verb *have*, which does not agree in number with the sentence's subject, *channel*.

H because *are* does not agree in number with the sentence's subject, *channel*.

Question 43. The best answer is C because it is clearest about who is returning to the park (swimmers, hikers, and campers), and its tone is consistent with the rest of the essay.

The best answer is NOT:

A because it uses the vague pronoun *some*, which does not clearly explain who or what has returned to the park.

B because it features an informal tone that departs from the tone of the rest of the essay.

D because it features an informal tone that doesn't fit in the essay.

Question 44. The best answer is J because it is the only option that does not introduce a redundancy into the sentence.

The best answer is NOT:

F because it is redundant; the idea contained in the word *back* is already conveyed by *returned.*

G because it is redundant; the idea of coming back to the park is already conveyed by *returned.*

H because it is redundant; to revisit the park is already conveyed by *returned.*

Passage IV

Question 45. The best answer is A because no punctuation is needed here. The absence of punctuation creates the clearest and most understandable sentence explaining that the narrator was peering through light-polluted skies.

The best answer is NOT:

B because it incorrectly sets off "peering through" as nonessential information and leaves the main clause incomplete: "inexperienced astronomer light-polluted skies."

C because it incorrectly places a colon after *astronomer*, suggesting that the phrase "peering through light-polluted skies" defines the term "inexperienced astronomer."

D because it incorrectly uses a comma to separate the preposition *through* from the noun *light-polluted skies.*

ENGLISH • PRACTICE TEST 2 • EXPLANATORY ANSWERS

Question 46. The best answer is H because it correctly creates an independent clause, which is necessary following a comma plus *and* construction.

The best answer is NOT:

F because it has the participle *being*, which cannot function as a main verb. The result is that the second part of the sentence is not an independent clause.

G because it includes the pronoun *them*, which does not clearly refer to a noun previously mentioned in the paragraph. Also, "by them" interrupts the verb phrase "is said to be."

J because it uses the participle *having* in place of a main verb, which means that the second part of the sentence is not an independent clause.

Question 47. The best answer is A because it correctly uses commas to set off the phrase "in some mythologies." In this sentence, the phrase is nonessential information, so using commas around the phrase is appropriate.

The best answer is NOT:

B because it sets off the phrase "who in some mythologies" from the rest of the sentence and results in a confusing sentence that suggests Orion and the hunter are separate figures and that Orion only appears when a hunter fights Taurus the Bull: "Orion appears as a hunter is fighting Taurus the Bull, another constellation."

C because it indicates that the phrase "in some mythologies is fighting Taurus the Bull" is nonessential information. Setting off the phrase in this way results in an ungrammatical sentence: "Orion appears as a hunter who another constellation."

D because it sets off the phrase "some mythologies" as nonessential and results in an ungrammatical sentence: "Orion appears as a hunter who in is fighting Taurus the Bull, another constellation."

Question 48. The best answer is H because it uses the plural verb *are*, which agrees in number with the plural subject of the sentence, *stars*. In addition, the verb form *are* is in the present tense, as are the verbs in the preceding sentence.

The best answer is NOT:

F because it uses the singular verb *has*, which does not agree in number with the sentence's subject, *stars*.

G because it uses the past progressive *were being* when the context of this sentence and the preceding sentence call for the present tense.

J because it uses the singular verb *is*, which does not agree in number with the sentence's subject, *stars*.

ENGLISH • PRACTICE TEST 2 • EXPLANATORY ANSWERS

Question 49. The best answer is C because it is the only option that contains a main clause and, therefore, is the only one that is a complete sentence.

The best answer is NOT:

A because it does not contain a main clause. The dependent clause "when gravity causes gas and dust to collapse" is followed by a participial phrase that lacks a subject, "forming stars."

B because it lacks a main clause. This option is one long dependent clause.

D because it lacks a main clause, consisting instead of one dependent clause.

Question 50. The best answer is J because it correctly punctuates the appositive phrase "home to thousands of young stars" by putting commas around it. This phrase adds nonessential information that helps define nebula.

The best answer is NOT:

F because it offers two phrases that begin with the verb *is* and connects those phrases only with a comma; this sentence structure would require the linking word *and* in place of the comma.

G because it incorrectly connects the two phrases beginning with *is* with a comma and the linking word *and* (rather than with the linking word alone).

H because it correctly sets off "home to thousands of young stars" as nonessential but incorrectly adds the conjunction *and*, which results in an ungrammatical sentence: "The nebula and is often called a 'galactic nursery.'"

Question 51. The best answer is D because the Great Orion Nebula is introduced in the sentence preceding Point D. The added sentence expands on the discussion of that nebula.

The best answer is NOT:

A because the nebula has not yet been mentioned at this point in the paragraph, so placing the sentence here is illogical and confusing.

B because the nebula has not yet been mentioned at this point in the paragraph.

C because the nebula has not yet been mentioned at this point in the paragraph.

ENGLISH • PRACTICE TEST 2 • EXPLANATORY ANSWERS

Question 52. The best answer is J because the word *so* serves as a logical transition from the preceding sentence, which discusses the narrator's struggle to get the nebula in focus, to this sentence, which explains that the narrator switches to a higher-powered eyepiece. The word *so* conveys the idea of intent or purpose; the narrator switches the eyepiece in an attempt to bring the nebula into focus.

The best answer is NOT:

F because the narrator purposely switches to a higher-powered eyepiece to bring the nebula into focus. The switch is not coincidental.

G because the word *similarly* indicates a comparison; no comparison is stated or implied in the paragraph.

H because the word *besides* indicates that a previous idea is being added onto, which isn't the case.

Question 53. The best answer is A because it correctly uses the past tense verbs *tried* and *had* (I'd). At this point in the essay, the narrator is describing a past event, so the past tense is called for.

The best answer is NOT:

B because the contraction "I'd have" suggests the conditional "I would have." This shifts the meaning to a hypothetical situation in the past that is not supported by the essay.

C because it uses the present tense *try* rather than the past tense *tried.*

D because it uses the present tense *try* rather than the past tense *tried.*

Question 54. The best answer is G because it correctly uses the word *them* to refer to the distant objects, whereas the phrase "one side of them" clearly explains that the viewer is looking to one side of the distant objects.

The best answer is NOT:

F because it is unclear and illogically suggests that objects have only one side.

H because it incorrectly substitutes the contraction *they're* for the possessive pronoun *their.*

J because *one's* is ambiguous in meaning. This could mean a distant object's side or a viewer's side.

ENGLISH • PRACTICE TEST 2 • EXPLANATORY ANSWERS

Question 55. The best answer is B because the sentence explains how averted vision works. Deleting the sentence would result in an essay that is less clear.

The best answer is NOT:

A because it does not elaborate on why the narrator was capable of using averted vision. Rather, the sentence explains how averted vision works.

C because the level of technical detail is not out of place in this essay, which describes details about using a telescope to view a nebula.

D because the main point of the paragraph is to explain how the narrator was able to view the nebula. Using the principle of averted vision was the key strategy for the narrator. Rather than digressing from the main point, it helps explain the main point.

Question 56. The best answer is H because it correctly establishes the comparison the narrator is making. The view with averted vision is far better than the view when looking directly at the nebula.

The best answer is NOT:

F because it indicates the wrong comparison. This phrase suggests that both averted and direct vision resulted in a better view, but averted vision permitted more of that same better view. The essay does not support this comparison.

G because it suggests that averted vision resulted in a farther view and incorrectly adds a comma between the modifier (*farther*) and the object it modifies (*view*). This is confusing in meaning and is not supported by the essay.

J because it indicates that *far* and *better* are coordinate adjectives (adjectives that can be switched without affecting the meaning of the sentence). The idea of a better, far view is unclear and unsupported by the essay.

Question 57. The best answer is A because the word *illuminated* makes sense in this context. The four bright stars help reveal the Trapezium star cluster.

The best answer is NOT:

B because the word *emanated* suggests that the cluster was spread out by or flowed from the bright stars. The bright stars are part of the cluster; the cluster does not emanate from them and is not emanated by them.

C because the word *emulated* suggests the idea of copying; the four bright stars are not copying the star cluster.

D because the word *eliminated* suggests that the bright stars are destroying the cluster. This is not supported by the essay.

ENGLISH • PRACTICE TEST 2 • EXPLANATORY ANSWERS

Question 58. The best answer is F because the plural possessive *birds'* and the plural *eggs* correctly convey that the stars look like eggs laid by birds in a nest.

The best answer is NOT:

G because it uses the singular possessive *bird's* instead of the plural possessive. To be correct, the pronoun would need to be preceded by an article such as *a*, but no such article is present.

H because the noun *birds* lacks the apostrophe that is necessary to convey the idea of possession.

J because it lacks an apostrophe with *birds* and uses an erroneous apostrophe after *eggs*, suggesting that the eggs possess something. No such possession is supported by the essay.

Question 59. The best answer is A because it concludes the essay by referring back to an idea presented in the first paragraph of the essay, as required by the stem. The sentence refers to the narrator's trek outside during the winter, which is mentioned in the first paragraph of the essay.

The best answer is NOT:

B because it introduces additional tips for using telescopes rather than referring back to the first paragraph of the essay.

C because it suggests that the narrator's goal was to view Orion's belt and sword and explains that Orion is useful in locating other constellations. Orion's sword and belt and any relationship between Orion and other constellations are not mentioned in the first paragraph of the essay.

D because it introduces more information about the Trapezium star cluster and the narrator's reading. These ideas do not have any connection to the first paragraph of the essay.

Question 60. The best answer is G because the essay focuses on one particular experience of viewing the constellation Orion, from setting up the telescope to focusing on one specific part of the constellation, the nebula.

The best answer is NOT:

F because it states that the essay recounts several past events, yet only one experience is discussed in the essay.

H because it indicates that the essay focuses on the Orion Nebula and its process of star formation are the focus of the essay. Although the Orion Nebula is a significant part of the essay, the essay does not discuss the process of star formation in the nebula. Rather, it focuses on the narrator's experience.

J because it implies that averted vision is the main subject of the essay, which isn't the case. Additionally, the fact that the narrator describes the averted vision technique in brief does not demonstrate that the essay is about a personal experience with astronomy.

ENGLISH • PRACTICE TEST 2 • EXPLANATORY ANSWERS

Passage V

Question 61. The best answer is D because it results in a complete sentence with a comma separating the main clause from the appositive phrase "metaphors for Little's feelings about social issues and historical events."

The best answer is NOT:

A because it creates a comma splice (two or more complete sentences separated by only a comma). The word *they* becomes the subject of the second complete sentence. The sentence requires a conjunction after the comma in order to be grammatical. The phrase "in other words" cannot function as a conjunction.

B because it creates a comma splice with the second sentence beginning with *they.*

C because it creates a run-on, or fused, sentence (two complete sentences with no punctuation between them).

Question 62. The best answer is G because it meets both criteria of the question. It is punctuated correctly with dashes that set off the phrase "mostly triangles and rectangles." This punctuation also indicates that all Little's shapes, not just his triangles and rectangles, are painted in vibrant and contrasting hues.

The best answer is NOT:

F because although the punctuation is acceptable, the resulting sentence suggests that only the triangles and rectangles are painted in vibrant and contrasting hues.

H because it is not correctly punctuated. The phrase "and narrow rectangles" should be included in the dashes along with "mostly triangles." Also, it is unclear whether all the shapes (or only the rectangles) are painted in vibrant and contrasting hues.

J because although the punctuation is acceptable, the resulting sentence suggests that only the triangles and rectangles are painted in vibrant and contrasting hues.

Question 63. The best answer is B because it correctly sets off the nonessential phrase "he says" using commas.

The best answer is NOT:

A because it fails to use punctuation to set off the phrase "he says" from the rest of the sentence.

C because it incorrectly sets off his subject as nonessential information, creating an ungrammatical sentence: "But he says is color."

D because it lacks the necessary comma after *says* that closes the nonessential phrase "he says."

ENGLISH • PRACTICE TEST 2 • EXPLANATORY ANSWERS

Question 64. The best answer is H because the sentence, although informative, is not strongly related to the paragraph's general discussion of Little's art. Adding information about Syracuse University would blur the focus of the first paragraph.

The best answer is NOT:

F because the sentence does not contain the kind of biographical information that would clearly connect to the paragraph that follows and therefore would not make for a smooth transition.

G because the sentence does not state that Little first became focused on color at Syracuse University.

J because the sentence does not create confusion about Little's work with geometric figures; it simply offers a detail about the school where Little earned his MFA, Syracuse University.

Question 65. The best answer is D because it is the only option that does not introduce a redundancy into the sentence.

The best answer is NOT:

A because it repeats the idea that Little blends his own paint, which is mentioned in the previous sentence.

B because it repeats the idea from the previous sentence that Little blends his own paint. Also, the idea that Little does so is already conveyed in the action word *applies*.

C because it repeats the idea that Little makes his own blends of paint. This is mentioned in the previous sentence. Also, the phrase "his own blends that he made" is redundant; it is unnecessary to state that his own blends are those that he made.

Question 66. The best answer is J because it most clearly and logically conveys the idea that Little's paintings are big, as the measurements (6 feet by 8 feet) make clear.

The best answer is NOT:

F because *voluminous* would convey an idea about how much something can hold or about a three-dimensional aspect; this is an illogical descriptor for a painting and is not supported by the two-dimensional measurements that follow in the sentence.

G because it contradicts other information in the sentence. The measurements of the paintings are provided in the sentence, so it clearly cannot be immeasurable.

H because *mountainous* suggests a three-dimensional shape that is neither conveyed nor supported by the two-dimensional measurements that follow in the sentence.

Question 67. The best answer is B because the phrase "for example" serves as a transition from the preceding sentence, which discusses Little's use of color and lines, to this paragraph, which provides a specific description of one of Little's paintings that uses lines.

The best answer is NOT:

A because the phrase "by all means" doesn't make sense in this context. This idiomatic expression has no connection to the sentence in which it is placed. On a literal level, the lines do not bisect the painting in all directions or by all methods.

C because the phrase "in contrast" suggests that *Bittersweet Victory* differs from Little's other work. Yet the essay explains that Little often uses lines and then focuses on the lines in *Bittersweet Victory* as a specific example.

D because the word *thereafter* doesn't make sense in this context, especially because *Bittersweet Victory* was painted before the work discussed in the preceding paragraph.

Question 68. The best answer is G because it is the only unacceptable alternative to the underlined phrase. The phrase "vertically beige" offers a misplaced modifier; something cannot be beige in a vertical way.

The best answer is NOT:

F because it conveys the same idea as the underlined phrase. The canvas is bisected in a vertical direction by a beige line.

H because it conveys the same idea as the underlined phrase, that the canvas is bisected by a vertical, beige line.

J because it conveys the same idea as the underlined phrase, that the canvas is bisected by a vertical, beige line.

Question 69. The best answer is C because the participle *stretching* creates a grammatical sentence that also makes sense.

The best answer is NOT:

A because it inserts the subordinating *which* into this clause, which was already subordinated from the main clause. This creates a confusing sentence structure. This option also shifts verb tense from the present to the past.

B because it inserts the subordinating *which*, creating multiple and confusing levels of subordinating clauses.

D because it creates an independent clause ("each one stretches from the bottom to the top of the canvas") in the middle of another independent clause ("three orange triangles angle slightly to the right"). The result is an unclear sentence created from a series of phrases that are spliced together.

ENGLISH • PRACTICE TEST 2 • EXPLANATORY ANSWERS

Question 70. The best answer is J because it is the only option that does not introduce a redundancy into the sentence.

The best answer is NOT:

F because it mentions that the orange triangles are on the canvas's left half, which is a detail that appears previously in the sentence.

G because it repeats the idea that the triangles are on the left half of the canvas.

H because it repeats the idea, stated previously in the sentence, that the triangles appear on the left half of the canvas.

Question 71. The best answer is C because it uses the plural verb *cut,* which agrees in number with the plural subject of the sentence, *bands.* It also uses the preposition *through,* which makes sense in the sentence.

The best answer is NOT:

A because it uses the singular verb *cuts,* which does not agree in number with the plural subject of the sentence, *bands.*

B because it uses the singular verb *cuts,* which does not agree in number with the plural *bands.* It also uses the past tense verb *crossed* as if it were a preposition, which is incorrect.

D because it uses the past tense verb *crossed* as if it were a preposition, which is incorrect.

Question 72. The best answer is F because it attaches the preposition *to* to the verb *lends,* which creates a correct idiomatic expression.

The best answer is NOT:

G because it uses the preposition *on* with *lends,* which isn't a correct idiomatic expression. It also doesn't make sense logically.

H because it uses the preposition *into* with *lends,* which creates an incorrect idiomatic expression. Also, this phrase doesn't make logical sense.

J because it uses the preposition *with* with *lends,* which creates an incorrect idiomatic expression.

ENGLISH • PRACTICE TEST 2 • EXPLANATORY ANSWERS

Question 73. The best answer is C because it conveys the comparison between the effect of Little's work and a jazz collaboration in the most clear and concise way. It does not repeat the same idea, and it does not add unnecessary words to the sentence.

The best answer is NOT:

A because the idea that something is like something else already conveys the idea that it might remind you of something else.

B because *reminiscent of* and *echoes* are redundant, making the phrase itself unnecessarily wordy.

D because it appears to be more concise, but the meaning is unclear. It could suggest that the effect of Little's work is like a jazz collaboration, that Little's work makes the viewer feel like he or she is in a jazz collaboration, or that Little's work makes it seem like he is part of a jazz collaboration.

Question 74. The best answer is F because it builds on the paragraph's previous reference to rhythm and unity by mentioning a perfect jazz collaboration and offers a comparison between Little and this jazz collaboration.

The best answer is NOT:

G because the comparison to jazz does not indicate anything about the popularity of Little's paintings.

H because the following paragraph mentions one person's assessment of Little's work, not several people's.

J because the essay does not suggest that Little had any unique goals for *Bittersweet Victory*. Rather, the paragraph about *Bittersweet Victory* provides a specific example of the ideas the essay presents about Little's work in general.

Question 75. The best answer is B because the essay discusses how Little uses bright colors and shapes to convey energy and the essence of people's experiences as human beings.

The best answer is NOT:

A because the essay does not focus on one viewer's conclusion that the lines in *Bittersweet Victory* communicate optimism.

C because the essay does not focus on what Little hoped to create with *Bittersweet Victory*, and it does explain what the painting looks like.

D because the essay does in fact suggest some of the effects Little's work achieves.

MATHEMATICS • PRACTICE TEST 2 • EXPLANATORY ANSWERS

Question 1. The correct answer is C. The restaurant is rotating 180° in 45 minutes. That is 60° every 15 minutes. That is 240° every 60 minutes. You might want to sketch something similar to the following drawing:

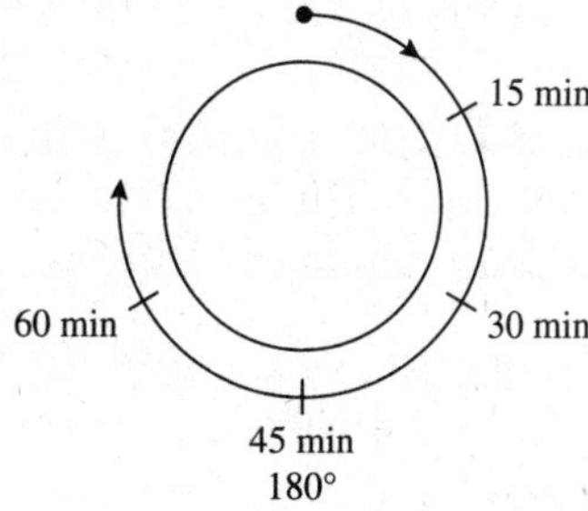

If you like an algebraic solution, you can set up a proportion $\frac{180°}{45\text{ min}} = \frac{x°}{60\text{ min}}$ and solve it:

$x = \left(\frac{180}{45}\right)60 = 4 \cdot 60 = 240.$

Most people who do not get this right choose **D**, which is a reasonable approximation.

Question 2. The correct answer is H. After subtracting the onetime fee from the amount on Brendan's check (\$500 – \$140), the remaining \$360 goes toward the amount spent on monthly fees. You can find the number of months of membership covered by the check by dividing the remaining \$360 by the monthly fee of \$40 per month, giving 9 months as the result.

You could also solve this problem by setting up and solving the equation $140 + 40m = 500$, where the expression $140 + 40m$ represents the cost of a gym membership for m months.

Question 3. The correct answer is D. The group of 27 people paid a total of \$249.75 (27 × \$9.25 per person) in advance. Because the group consisted of more than 25 people, the actual cost was \$229.50 (\$27 × \$8.50 per person). The refund is the difference between the amount paid and the actual cost, which is \$249.75 – \$229.50 = \$20.25. If you chose **C**, you could have failed to read the problem carefully and figured the refund for a group of 25 people.

Question 4. The correct answer is H. The number of possible outcomes (that is, the total number of members eligible to be chosen as representative) is 13 – 3 = 10, and the number of favorable outcomes (choosing Samara only) is 1. The probability of the favorable outcomes is equal to $\frac{\text{the number of favorable outcomes}}{\text{the number of possible outcomes}}$. So, the probability of Samara being chosen as representative would be $\frac{1}{10}$. Careful reading is essential; if you chose **G**, you may have overlooked the words CANNOT and NOT.

MATHEMATICS • PRACTICE TEST 2 • EXPLANATORY ANSWERS

Question 5. The correct answer is D. Let s represent the score on the sixth test. Then the average score on the 6 tests is equal to $\frac{75 + 70 + 92 + 95 + 97 + s}{6}$, or equivalently $\frac{s + 429}{6}$. Be sure to read carefully: the average is 85 *points*, not *percent*. Interpreting the average as a percent leads to **E** (the most common incorrect answer), rather than the correct answer of $\frac{s + 429}{6} = 85$.

Question 6. The correct answer is F. The sum of the measures of all four interior angles in any quadrilateral is always 360°. The given three angle measures add up to 65° + 100° + 75° = 240°, so the missing angle measure is 360° – 240° = 120°.

If $\overline{AB}$ was parallel to $\overline{CD}$, then the measure of $\angle B$ and the measure of $\angle C$ would add up to 180° and the answer would be **G**. But the problem does not say that those sides are parallel, and it turns out that they are not parallel.

If you chose **K**, you may have calculated the average of the three given angle measures.

Question 7. The correct answer is C. The shorter two sides are the same length in ΔABC, so the same thing has to happen in any triangle similar to it. That means that $\overline{DE}$ is the same length as $\overline{EF}$, which is 3 meters. Then, the perimeter of ΔDEF is 3 + 3 + 5 = 11 meters.

The most common incorrect answer is **A**, correctly finding the length of $\overline{DE}$ and stopping there.

Question 8. The correct answer is G. Follow the correct order of operations to simplify the expression. $|3(-2) + 4| = |-6 + 4| = |-2| = 2$. Keep in mind that absolute value of a rational number is its distance from 0 on the number line.

You may have chosen **F** if you did not take the absolute value of –2. You may have chosen **H** if you did $|3 - 2 + 4|$. You may have chosen **J** if you did $|3 + 2 + 4|$. You may have chosen **K** if you did $|3(2) + 4|$.

Question 9. The correct answer is A. This problem is asking you to figure out when two quantities multiplied together can be zero. The only way two quantities can be multiplied together to get an answer of zero is if at least one of the quantities is zero. So, either $(x + a) = 0$ or $(x + b) = 0$. The first of these equations is true when $x = -a$ and the second when $x = -b$. These are the two solution values for x.

As a check, substitute $-a$ in for x. The original equation becomes $(-a + a)(-a + b)$, which simplifies to $(0)(-a + b)$, and zero times anything is zero, so the original equation holds when $x = -a$. You could check $x = -b$ in the same manner.

If you chose **E**, you may have solved the two equations incorrectly, or you may have just looked at the quantities and chosen the $+a$ and $+b$ that appeared in the problem.

If you missed this problem, you might try substituting a value of x from your answer into the original equation to see what happens.

MATHEMATICS • PRACTICE TEST 2 • EXPLANATORY ANSWERS

Question 10. The correct answer is F. Because $m\widehat{LM} > 90°$ and $m\widehat{MK}$, $m\angle JMG$, $m\angle LHK$, $m\angle MJL$ are all less than or equal to 90°, $\widehat{LM}$ has the greatest degree measure.

We know that $m\angle JMG = 90°$ (**H** is NOT correct) because the tangent to a circle is always perpendicular to the radius drawn to the point of tangency. Because ΔMGJ is a right triangle with right angle $\angle JMG$, the other angles in the triangle, $\angle MJG$ and $\angle MGJ$, are acute. This means that $m\angle MJL < 90°$ (**K** is NOT correct) and $m\angle MGJ < 90°$. Because the degree measure of an arc of a circle is equal to the measure of the central angle that intercepts that arc, $m\angle MGJ = m\widehat{MK}$. Therefore, $m\widehat{MK} < 90°$ (**G** is NOT correct). Because $\widehat{LM}$ and $\widehat{MK}$ form a semicircle, $m\widehat{LM} + m\widehat{MK} = 180°$ and because $m\widehat{MK} < 90°$, $m\widehat{LM} > 90°$. Because $\angle LHK$ is inscribed in semicircle $\widehat{LHK}$, $m\angle LHK = 90°$ (**J** is NOT correct).

Question 11. The correct answer is B. To find BC when AD is 30 units, AC is 16 units, BD is 20 units, and the points are along $\overline{AD}$ as shown in the following, you must notice that $\overline{BC}$ is the intersection of $\overline{AC}$ and $\overline{BD}$.

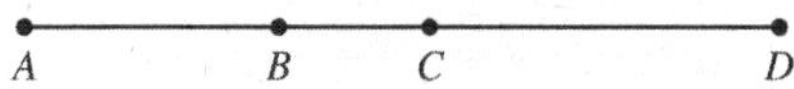

So the sum of the lengths of $\overline{AC}$ and $\overline{BD}$ would be the same as the sum of the lengths of $\overline{AD}$ and $\overline{BC}$, because $AC = AB + BC$, $BD = BC + CD$, and $AD = AB + BC + CD$. By substitution, $AC + BD = AB + BC + BC + CD = AB + BC + CD + BC = AD + BC$.

By substituting lengths $AD + BC = AC + BD$, or $30 + BC = 16 + 20$, or $30 + BC = 36$. Subtracting 30 from both sides yields $BC = 6$.

If you chose **A**, you probably subtracted 16 from 20. If you chose **E**, you probably thought you needed more information to solve the problem.

Question 12. The correct answer is K. There are many ways to solve this equation. One solution is the following:

start with		$12x$	$= -8(10 - x)$
divide both sides by −8	$\Rightarrow$	$-\frac{3}{2}x$	$= 10 - x$
add x to both sides	$\Rightarrow$	$-\frac{1}{2}x$	$= 10$
multiply both sides by −2	$\Rightarrow$	x	$= -20$

Another solution method would be to graph $y = 12x$ and $y = -8(10 - x)$ and see where the two graphs intersect. A calculator would produce these graphs, and you could find an approximate solution. That is good enough for this problem because the answer choices are spread apart.

This is a problem in which checking your answer is easy and can pay off. When $x = -20$, the left side of the original equation is 12(–20), which is –240. The right side is –8(10 – (–20)), which simplifies to –8(10 + 20), then to –8(30), and then to –240. This solution checks. No other answer choice would satisfy the equation.

If you chose **H** or **J**, you may have multiplied out $-8(10 - x)$ to get $-80 + x$ or $-80 - x$ and done the rest of the steps correctly. You could have caught this by checking your answer. If you made an error with minus signs, you may have chosen one of the other answer choices.

Question 13. The correct answer is E. Because the cardboard extends 2 inches beyond the cake on all sides, the cardboard forms a rectangle whose length and width are each 4 inches longer than the length and width of the rectangular cake, as shown in the following figure. The area of aluminum foil that is exposed (the shaded region in the figure) equals the area of the foil covering the entire cardboard surface (or area of the cardboard) minus the area of the foil covered by the cake. So the area, in square inches, of aluminum foil exposed equals 20(16) – 16(12) = 320 – 192 = 128.

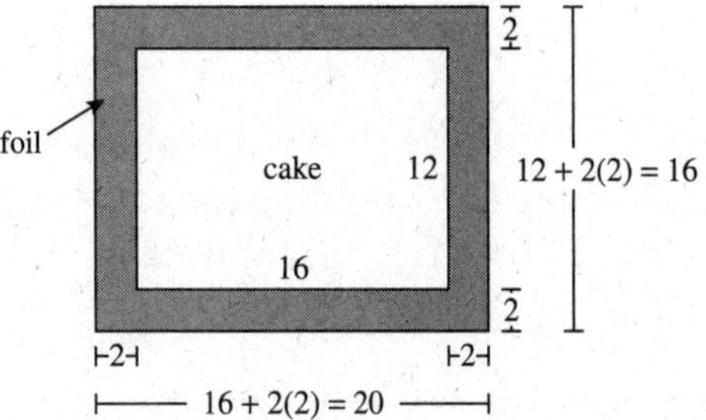

Question 14. The correct answer is J. The following figure shows the cake after it has been cut. The length of the cut cake is (16 inches) ÷ (2 inches per piece) = 8 pieces. The width of the cut cake is (12 inches) ÷ (2 inches per piece) = 6 pieces. Because the cake has 6 rows each containing 8 pieces, the cake was cut into 6(8) = 48 pieces.

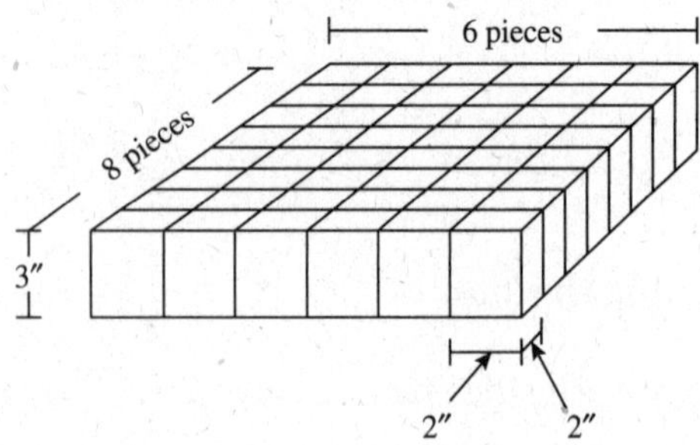

MATHEMATICS • PRACTICE TEST 2 • EXPLANATORY ANSWERS

Question 15. The correct answer is D. The following table lists all expenses for Ken's cake that were given in the problem.

	Expenses for cake	cost
	Cake preparation	\$5.00
Items purchased {	Cake mix	\$1.73
	Frosting mix	\$2.67
	Tax on items purchased	0.05(\$1.73 + \$2.67) = \$0.22

The total amount the Math Club will pay Ken is the sum of the costs shown in the table, \$5.00 + \$1.73 + \$2.67 + \$0.22 = \$9.62.

Question 16. The correct answer is H. Sketching a picture can be helpful.

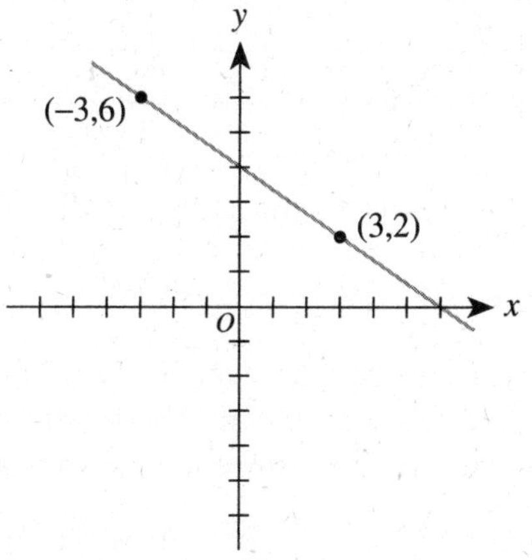

These points are on opposite sides of the y-axis, and an equal distance away from the y-axis, because the x-coordinates are 3 and –3. So, the midpoint will be the y-intercept of the line. The y-coordinate of the midpoint is $\frac{6+2}{2}$, which is 4.

If the points were not so nicely spaced with the y-axis, you could find the equation of the line through the two points and use it to identify the y-intercept. The slope of the line would be the change in y divided by the change in x, $\frac{6-2}{-3-3}=-\frac{2}{3}$. The point-slope form of the equation is then $y-2=-\frac{2}{3}(x-3)$. Next, put this into slope-intercept form $y-2=-\frac{2}{3}\cdot x-\left(-\frac{2}{3}\right)\cdot 2 \Rightarrow y-2=-\frac{2}{3}x+2 \Rightarrow y=-\frac{2}{3}x+2+2 \Rightarrow y=-\frac{2}{3}x+4$, and the 4 is the y-intercept.

From the picture alone, you could deduce that the line had to cross the y-axis between 2 and 6. This observation eliminates all the answer choices except the correct one.

MATHEMATICS • PRACTICE TEST 2 • EXPLANATORY ANSWERS

Question 17. The correct answer is D. Let x (shown in the following figure) represent the distance between the centers of the 2 holes. Because the 3 segments with lengths $2\frac{1}{16}$ inches, x inches, and $4\frac{3}{4}$ inches are collinear, the sum of their lengths must be $11\frac{5}{8}$. Therefore, $x = 11\frac{5}{8} - 2\frac{1}{16} - 4\frac{3}{4} = \frac{93}{8} - \frac{33}{16} - \frac{19}{4} = \frac{186}{16} - \frac{33}{16} - \frac{76}{16} = \frac{77}{16} = 4\frac{13}{16}$ inches.

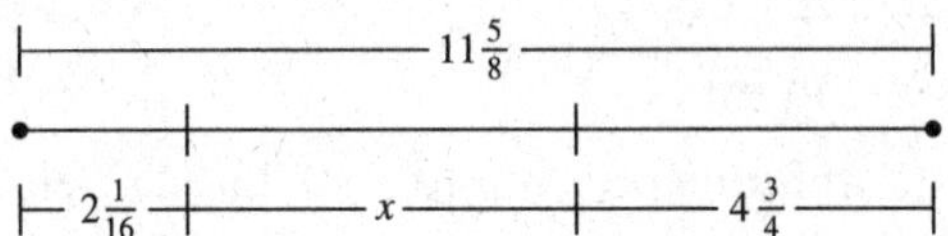

Question 18. The correct answer is H. Each week, both ponds get shallower. The following table shows what happens for the first few weeks.

	Now	1 week	2 weeks	3 weeks	4 weeks
First pond	180 cm	179 cm	178 cm	177 cm	176 cm
Second pond	160 cm	159.5 cm	159 cm	158.5 cm	158 cm
Difference	20 cm	19.5 cm	19 cm	18.5 cm	18 cm

The ponds are getting closer and closer to the same depth, at the rate of 0.5 cm per week. Because the ponds started out 20 cm different, it will take $20 \div 0.5 = 40$ weeks to bring them to the same depth.

You could also check the answer choices. Answer **F** is not correct because, after 10 weeks, the first pond would be $180 - 10 = 170$ cm deep, and the second pond would be $160 - 5 = 155$ cm deep. The other incorrect answers can be eliminated in the same way.

The most common incorrect answer was **G**. If you chose that answer, you may have reasoned that it would take 20 weeks for the first pond to get down to the level of the second pond. And that is correct, except that the second pond has become shallower during those 20 weeks, so the ponds are not the same depth.

Question 19. The correct answer is E. A line will always have an equation of the form $x = a$ or $y = mx + b$, for suitable constants a, m, and b. And, if a graph has an equation that can be put into one of these forms, the graph is a line.

Equation **A** is already in the first form, where $a = 4$.

Starting with Equation **B**, divide both sides by 3 and you will get $y = 2$. This is the second form, with $m = 0$ and $b = 2$.

Equation **C** can be manipulated into the second form as follows: $x - y = 1 \Rightarrow -y = 1 - x \Rightarrow +y = -1 + x \Rightarrow y = x - 1$, which has $m = 1$ and $b = -1$.

Equation **D** is already in the second form, with $m = \frac{3}{4}$ and $b = -2$.

MATHEMATICS • PRACTICE TEST 2 • EXPLANATORY ANSWERS

Equation **E** can be written as $y = -x^2 + 5$. This is the equation of a parabola, shown below. It is the only one of the equations that is not a line.

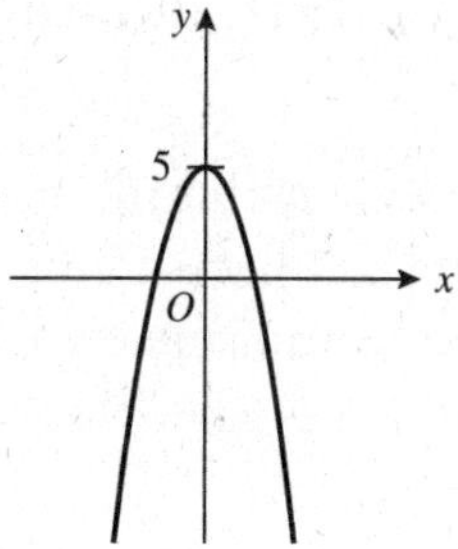

Question 20. The correct answer is G. All the answer choices are in terms of $\angle A$. Many people remember the trigonometric functions in the context of a right triangle, in terms of the lengths of the side opposite the angle, the side adjacent to the angle, and the hypotenuse. For the triangle given in the problem, the side opposite $\angle A$ has length 12 cm, the side adjacent to $\angle A$ has length 5 cm, and the hypotenuse has length 13 cm. The values of the trig functions are $\cos A = \frac{\text{adjacent}}{\text{hypotenuse}} = \frac{5}{13}$, $\sin A = \frac{\text{opposite}}{\text{hypotenuse}} = \frac{12}{13}$, and $\tan A = \frac{\text{opposite}}{\text{adjacent}} = \frac{5}{12}$.

The only answer choice that gives one of these is **G**.

If you chose **F**, you may have been expecting the angle to be at one end of the horizontal base of the triangle. The value of $\cos B$ is $\frac{12}{13}$. Triangles can be rotated to any position. The terms *opposite*, *adjacent*, and *hypotenuse* are chosen to apply when the triangle is in an arbitrary position.

Question 21. The correct answer is D. To find the location of the water fountain located halfway between points B and D, it makes sense to give coordinates to the points relative to point A (see the following diagram). The first coordinate is the number of blocks east, and the second coordinate is the number of blocks north.

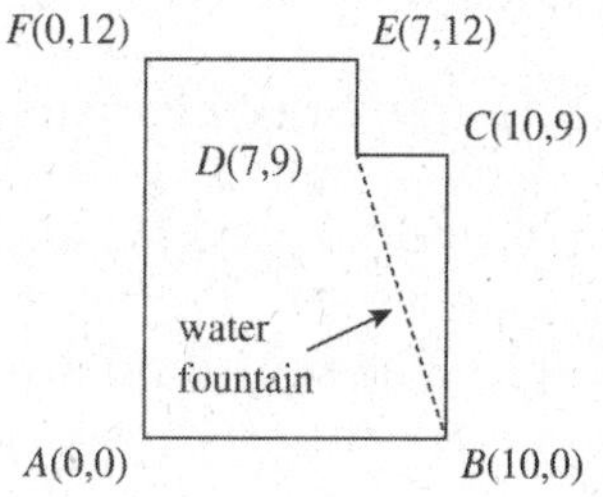

The water fountain is at the midpoint of $\overline{BD}$, and so the midpoint formula applies. For points with coordinates (x_1,y_1) and (x_2,y_2), the midpoint has coordinates $\left(\frac{x_1+x_2}{2}, \frac{y_1+y_2}{2}\right)$. For B (10,0) and D (7,9), the midpoint is $\left(\frac{10+7}{2}, \frac{0+9}{2}\right) \Rightarrow \left(\frac{17}{2}, \frac{9}{2}\right) \Rightarrow \left(8\frac{1}{2}, 4\frac{1}{2}\right)$.

Taking Additional Practice Tests

MATHEMATICS • PRACTICE TEST 2 • EXPLANATORY ANSWERS

B is halfway between A and C. Choice **C** is halfway between B and F. If you chose **E**, you may have found the wrong coordinates for C, D, or E.

Once you put coordinates on the picture, you can see that only one answer choice is reasonable.

Question 22. The correct answer is H. Although it may not be worth your time to sketch a graph during the ACT, you should at least have a general idea of the situation in your mind. This is the equation of a parabola. Common sense will tell you that if the car is going faster, it will take a longer distance to brake to a stop. So the parabola is opening upward.

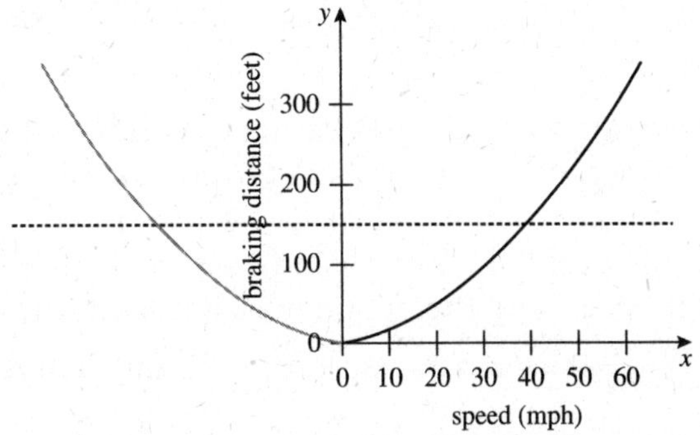

The horizontal dashed line on the graph is where the braking distance is 150 feet. Only half of the parabola is shown. There are two points where the parabola intersects this line. One would be to the left of the y-axis, which represents a negative speed for the car. If you solve an equation to find the intersection points, you will have to discard the intersection point with a negative speed.

If you took the time to create a graph, perhaps even on a graphing calculator, you might be able to estimate closely enough to choose among the answer choices. The desired speed is the x-coordinate of the intersection point.

To get this speed algebraically, the desired braking distance is 150 feet, and the equation $y=\dfrac{3(x^2+10x)}{40}$ gives the relation between speed (x) and braking distance (y). So you can solve the equation $150=\dfrac{3(x^2+10x)}{40}$. One solution path starts by multiplying both sides by 40 and continues as follows:
$150\cdot 40=3(x^2+10x)\Rightarrow \frac{6{,}000}{3}=x^2+10x\Rightarrow x^2+10x-2{,}000=0\Rightarrow (x+50)(x-40)=0\Rightarrow x=-50$ or $x=40$. You must discard the first solution. The only remaining solution is $x=40$, which represents a speed of 40 miles per hour.

MATHEMATICS • PRACTICE TEST 2 • EXPLANATORY ANSWERS

If you chose **J**, you may have done everything correctly except that when you solved $(x + 50)(x - 40) = 0$, you thought $x = 50$ was a solution. If you substitute 50 for x in the equation $(x + 50)(x - 40) = 0$, you will see that it is not a solution.

If you chose **F**, you may have made a numerical mistake when you substituted $x = 10$ into the breaking-distance equation. The value is $\frac{3(10^2 + 10 \cdot 10)}{40} = \frac{3(200)}{40}$. It might be tempting to reduce $\frac{200}{40}$ to 50 and then get $3(50) = 150$, which is what you are looking for. But $\frac{200}{40}$ is 5, not 50.

Substituting the answer choices into the equation is a reasonable strategy for this problem. You can use the results from one of the answer choices to help you choose the next one to substitute, because you probably know that it takes longer to stop if you are going faster. The results of these substitutions are given in the following:

	Speed (mph)	Calculations	Braking distance (ft)
F	10	$\frac{3(200)}{40} = 3(5)$	15
G	30	$\frac{3(1{,}200)}{40} = 3(30)$	90
H	40	$\frac{3(2{,}000)}{40} = 3(50)$	150
J	50	$\frac{3(3{,}000)}{40} = 3(75)$	225
K	60	$\frac{3(4{,}200)}{40} = 3(105)$	315

Question 23. The correct answer is A. Substitution gives $g(4) = \sqrt{4} = 2$ and $f(1) = 1^2 + 1 + 5 = 7$. Then $\frac{g(4)}{f(1)} = \frac{2}{7}$.

If you chose **C**, you may have started substituting 4 in function g and then continued substituting 4 into function f. The value of $\frac{g(4)}{f(4)}$ is $\frac{2}{25}$.

Question 24. The correct answer is K. There are 125 juniors who could be chosen. For *each* of those 125 juniors, there are 100 seniors who could be chosen. That makes $125 \cdot 100 = 12{,}500$ different pairs of students who could be chosen.

If you chose **J**, you probably added 125 and 100. If you chose **G**, perhaps you were figuring that once 100 pairs were formed, there would be no seniors left to put into another pair. Only one pair will be chosen, but there are many more than 100 pairs that are possible choices.

Question 25. The correct answer is B. The line on the graph has a negative linear correlation because as x increases y decreases. The line Mia drew goes through the points (0,10) and (3,1). To find the slope, m, we use $m = \frac{y_1 - y_2}{x_1 - x_2}$, and we get $m = \frac{10-1}{0-3} = \frac{9}{-3} = -3$. The y-intercept, where the line crosses the y-axis, is at positive 10. Inserted into $y = mx + b$, where

MATHEMATICS • PRACTICE TEST 2 • EXPLANATORY ANSWERS

b is the y-intercept, we get the equation $y = -3x + 10$. If you thought **A**, you did not determine the correct y-intercept. If you thought **C** or **D**, you did not determine the correct slope. If you thought **E**, you did not determine the correct y-intercept or slope.

Question 26. The correct answer is F. You could certainly test all of the answer choices to solve this problem. The first choice, -10, leaves the left side of the relation as $|-10 - 24|$, which simplifies to $|-34|$, which is 34. And $34 \leq 30$ is false, so this is the correct answer.

Another way to solve this problem is to think about the interpretation of absolute value as a distance: $|t - 24| \leq 30$ means that the distance on the number line between t and 24 is at most 30 units. This distance would be greater than 30 only when t was more than 30 above 24 or more than 30 below 24. That is when t is more than 54, or t is less than -6. Answer choices **G–K** are all closer to 24 than this.

The most common wrong answer is 54 (**K**), which is right at the limit of how far away it can get from 24. Still, -10 is farther away from 24 than 54 is.

Question 27. The correct answer is D. The phrase "5 times a number n" can be represented as $5n$. If this is subtracted from 15, the expression $15 - 5n$ represents the result. Saying that this result is negative can be represented as $15 - 5n < 0$. Subtracting 15 from both sides gives $-5n < -15$, and then dividing both sides by -5 gives $n > 3$ (remember to reverse the direction of the inequality).

Most people who missed this chose **E**. This could come from not reversing the inequality in the last step of the solution, or it could come from subtracting 15 from $5n$ rather than subtracting $5n$ from 15.

Answer choice **B** is the result of solving $15 - 5n = 0$. This would give the boundary where the expression changes from positive to negative, so it's closely related to the problem you were asked to solve. If you chose this, you would still need to find the values of n where the expression is negative, knowing that $n = 3$ is the only place the expression is zero.

Question 28. The correct answer is F. Because $(x^2 + 8x + 7) = (x + 7)(x + 1)$, you can factor the numerator further into the product $(x + 1)(x + 7)(x - 3)$. Similarly, because $(x^2 + 4x - 21) = (x + 7)(x - 3)$, you can factor the denominator further into the product $(x + 7)(x - 3)(x + 1)$. Then, as long as the denominator is not zero (that is, as long as x is not equal to -7, 3, or -1, which is guaranteed by the requirement that $x > 21$), you can write the given rational function as $\frac{(x+1)(x+7)(x-3)}{(x+7)(x-3)(x+1)}$. Using the commutative property for multiplication, the factors in the numerator can be reordered, producing the equivalent expression $\frac{(x+7)(x-3)(x+1)}{(x+7)(x-3)(x+1)}$. Because the numerator and denominator are equal, this rational expression is equal to 1.

MATHEMATICS • PRACTICE TEST 2 • EXPLANATORY ANSWERS

Question 29. The correct answer is B. Imagine the original 9 data items in order from smallest to largest. You might sketch a picture something like that shown in the following. The median is the fifth item in this list, because it is the middle value in the set.

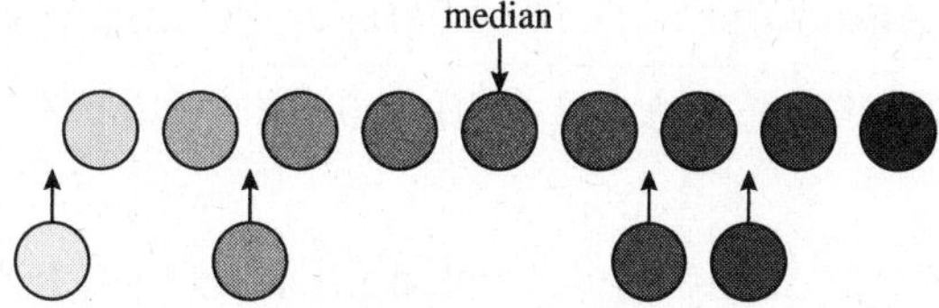

When the additional 4 data items are put into the list, there are 9 + 4 = 13 items on the list. Because 2 of these items are greater than the original median and 2 of these items are less than the original median, the original median is the middle value in the new set. That makes the original median the new median.

Question 30. The correct answer is K. The shaded area is the area of the larger circle minus the area of the smaller circle. The area of the larger circle is $\pi r^2 = \pi(10)^2 = 100\pi$ square centimeters. The area of the smaller circle is $\pi(5)^2 = 25\pi$ square centimeters. The difference is 75π square centimeters.

If you chose **J**, you probably found the difference in the perimeters of the two circles. You may have used the perimeter formula rather than the area formula. Another possibility is that you calculated 10^2 as $2 \cdot 10$ and 5^2 as $2 \cdot 5$. But 10^2 is $10 \cdot 10$, and 5^2 is $5 \cdot 5$.

Question 31. The correct answer is E. The mean of a and b is $\frac{a+b}{2}$. Because a is positive and b is negative $\frac{a+b}{2} = \frac{|a|-|b|}{2}$. If $|a| > |b|$, then the mean is positive. If $|a| < |b|$, then the mean is negative. If $|a| = |b|$, then the mean is 0. Because we only know the sign of a and b and NOT their magnitudes, we cannot determine if the mean is positive, negative, or 0.

If you chose **A**, you might not have realized that if $a = 3$ and $b = -4$, the mean of a and b is a negative number: $\frac{a+b}{2} = \frac{3+(-4)}{2} = -\frac{1}{2}$. If you chose **B**, you might not have realized that if $a = 4$ and $b = -4$, the mean of a and b is 0: $\frac{a+b}{2} = \frac{4+(-4)}{2} = 0$. If you chose **C**, you might not have realized that every number is positive (greater than 0), negative (less than 0), or neither (equal to 0). If you chose **D**, you might not have realized that the mean could be a positive number or a negative number: if $a = 4$ and $b = -2$, $\frac{a+b}{2} = \frac{4+(-2)}{2} = \frac{2}{2} = 1$; if $a = 3$ and $b = -4$, $\frac{a+b}{2} = \frac{3+(-4)}{2} = -\frac{1}{2}$.

Question 32. The correct answer is G. If the x-coordinate is 20, then the y-coordinate can be found by substituting 20 for x.

$0.005(20)^2 - 2(20) + 200 = 0.005(400) - 40 + 200 = 0.5(4) + 160 = 2 + 160.$

In theory, you could read the value off the graph, but you would not be able to read it accurately enough.

Taking Additional Practice Tests

MATHEMATICS • PRACTICE TEST 2 • EXPLANATORY ANSWERS

Many incorrect answers are caused by mistakes with the first term, $0.005x^2$. If you chose **F**, you may have made a decimal error calculating $0.005(20)^2$ and gotten 0.2 rather than 2.0. Other errors in calculating this term lead to **H**, **J**, and **K**.

Question 33. The correct answer is D. The distance formula (or the Pythagorean theorem) gives this distance directly. It is $\sqrt{(200-0)^2+(0-200)^2}=\sqrt{200^2+200^2}=\sqrt{2\cdot 200^2}=200\sqrt{2}\approx$ $200(1.414)=282.8$

Another way to solve this is to notice that the length of $\overline{FO}$ is 200 units, and $\overline{FG}$ is longer. Also, the path from F to O to G is 400 units long, and the direct path along $\overline{FG}$ is shorter than this path. So **D** is the only reasonable answer among those given.

Question 34. The correct answer is F. The shaded region is entirely contained in the given triangle because the curve is below the hypotenuse of the triangle, $\overline{FG}$. The area of the triangle is made up of the shaded area plus the unshaded area above the curve and inside the triangle. So the shaded area is less than the area of the triangle.

Question 35. The correct answer is B. With $a = 4.2$, $b = 5.0$, and a 5° measure for $\angle C$, then the law of cosines gives the length of the third side of the triangle (the distance between the cargo ship and the fishing boat) as $\sqrt{(4.2)^2+(5.0)^2-2\cdot 4.2\cdot 5.0\cos 5^\circ}$.

If you chose **C**, you probably missed the minus sign in the middle of the expression. About half the students who do not get the correct answer choose **C**.

The 85° angle in answer choices **D** and **E** would be the angle measure by the fishing boat, but only if the angle by the cargo ship was a right angle. It turns out that it isn't a right angle.

Question 36. The correct answer is F. Because $a^3 = b$, then $b^2 = (a^3)^2$. Substituting this into the equation $c = b^2$ gives $c = (a^3)^2$. Because $(a^3)^2 = a^6$, the result is $c = a^6$.

The most common incorrect answer is **G**. If you chose that answer, you probably wrote $(a^3)^2$ as a^5. If you write $(a^3)^2$ out as $(a^3)(a^3)$ and then $(a \cdot a \cdot a)(a \cdot a \cdot a)$, you can see that it is a^6.

If you chose **H**, you probably wrote $(a^3)^2$ as $2(a^3)$.

Question 37. The correct answer is B. The cost of renting a car from Sea Horse for 2 days is $2(50) + 0.25m$ where m is the number of miles driven. Because Francisco has \$255 to spend, the maximum number of miles he can drive if he rents from Sea Horse is the solution to the equation $100 + 0.25m = 255$, or $m = 160$.

Similarly, the maximum number of miles Francisco can drive if he rents from Ocean Blue is the solution to $2(60) + 0.20m = 255$, or $m = 675$, because $675 - 620 = 55$. If Francisco rents from Ocean Blue, he can travel 55 miles more than if he rents from Sea Horse. If you chose **A**, you may have made an error when solving $100 + 0.25m = 255$ and $2(60) + 0.20m = 255$. If you chose **C**, you may have divided cost per day by the cost per mile for each company, and then subtracted those quotients; Ocean Blue Car Rental has the greater quotient. If you

MATHEMATICS • PRACTICE TEST 2 • EXPLANATORY ANSWERS

chose **D**, you may have subtracted the daily cost of rental from Ocean Blue Car Rental from the total allotted amount. If you chose **E**, you may have found that each car rental would give Francisco the same number of miles.

Question 38. The correct answer is G. The area of a parallelogram is given by bh, where b is the length of the base and h is the height (here, the distance between the bottom and the top). It sometimes helps to picture this formula geometrically.

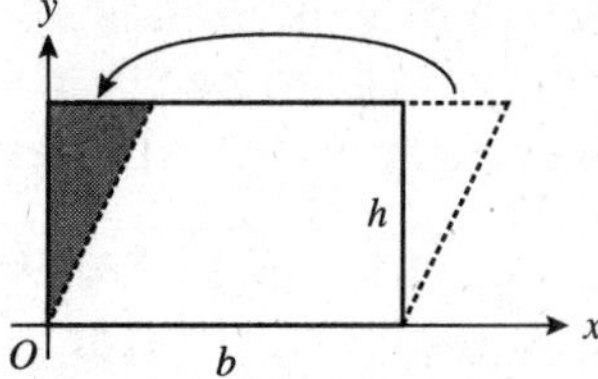

If you cut off the right triangle from the right side, it fits exactly onto the left side to form a rectangle. The rectangle has the same area as the parallelogram. The rectangle's area is bh, where b is the length of the base and h is the height. This is even the same formula as for the parallelogram. The difference is that h is the length of a side of the rectangle, but it is not the length of a side of the parallelogram.

And so, for either the rectangle or the parallelogram, $b = 10$ coordinate units and $h = 6$ coordinate units, making the area $bh = 10 \cdot 6 = 60$ square coordinate units.

The distance from (0,0) to (3,6) is $\sqrt{3^2+6^2} = 3\sqrt{1^2+2^2} = 3\sqrt{5}$ coordinate units. If you chose **J**, you probably multiplied this side length by the length of the base, 10 coordinate units. This is the stereotypical mistake when figuring the area of a parallelogram. The picture shows why the height is the right thing to use, not the length of the side.

If you chose **H**, you may have calculated the length from (0,0) to (3,6) as $\sqrt{6^2-3^2} = 3\sqrt{2^2-1^2} = 3\sqrt{3}$ and multiplied by the length of the base.

Question 39. The correct answer is E. Because n and m are both natural numbers, the sum of n and m is another natural number, $n + m$. Natural numbers are a subset of integers, integers are a subset of rational numbers, rational numbers are a subset of real numbers, and real numbers are a subset of complex numbers. Therefore, $n + m$ belongs to the sets found in I, II, III, IV, and V. If you chose **A**, you might not have realized that rational numbers are a subset of real numbers and therefore a subset of complex numbers. If you chose **B**, you might not have realized that the sum of two natural numbers is another natural number, and that real numbers are a subset of complex numbers. If you chose **C**, you might not have realized that the sum of two natural numbers is another natural number, which is also an integer. If you chose **D**, you might not have realized that sum of two natural numbers is another natural number.

MATHEMATICS • PRACTICE TEST 2 • EXPLANATORY ANSWERS

Question 40. The correct answer is G. If you don't see a way to approach this problem right off, a useful general technique is to look for some concrete numbers that illustrate the conditions. One thought is to start checking numbers from 1,000 on up to find a perfect square. A calculator would be a good idea. $\sqrt{1{,}000} \approx 31.62$, $\sqrt{1{,}001} \approx 31.64$, $\sqrt{1{,}002} \approx 31.65$, oh, this will take a while. A perfect square between 1,000 and 9,999 would have to have its square root between $\sqrt{1{,}000}$ and $\sqrt{9{,}999}$ because the square root function is an increasing function. This will help you find examples more quickly: $25^2 = 625$ is too low; $35^2 = 1{,}225$ is in the interval. The smallest perfect square in this interval is $32^2 = 1{,}024$. Because $100^2 = 10{,}000$, the largest perfect square in this interval has to be $99^2 = 9{,}801$. The square roots of all these perfect squares are the integers from 32 up to 99. All these square roots have 2 digits.

A quicker way is to find $\sqrt{1{,}000} \approx 31.62$ and $\sqrt{9{,}999} \approx 99.99$, which is a range that contains all possible square roots of the perfect squares. Any integer in this range has 2 digits.

The most common incorrect answer is **K**. If you chose this answer, perhaps you made a calculation error that led you to believe you'd found a perfect square between 1,000 and 9,999 whose square root had 3 digits. And then you correctly found one whose square root had 2 digits. Your logic was correct. Some students probably choose **K** because they do not know how to solve the problem. Maybe that's as good a guess as any, but looking for concrete numbers would be a good strategy if you have time.

Question 41. The correct answer is C. The expected occupancy rate is the sum of the products of each occupancy rate and its corresponding probability: $0.6(0.2) + 0.7(0.4) + 0.8(0.3) + 0.9(0.1) = 0.73$. To calculate the expected number of rooms that will be occupied during the coming summer season, multiply the expected occupancy rate by the total number of rooms: $0.73(80) \approx 58$.

If you chose **A**, you might have calculated the average of the probabilities and multiplied that by the total number of rooms: $\left(\frac{0.2 + 0.4 + 0.3 + 0.1}{4}\right)(80)$. If you chose **B**, you might have converted the probabilities in the table to percentages and then found the average percentage: $\frac{20 + 40 + 30 + 10}{4}$. If you chose **D**, you might have calculated the average of the complement probabilities and multiplied that by the total number of rooms: $\left(\frac{0.8 + 0.6 + 0.7 + 0.9}{4}\right)(80)$. If you chose **E**, you might have calculated the complement of the probabilities, converted those complement probabilities to percentages, and then found the average complemented probability: $\frac{60 + 70 + 80 + 90}{4}$.

Question 42. The correct answer is F. To calculate a matrix product, you go across each row in the first matrix and down each column in the second matrix. You multiply the terms from a row by the corresponding terms from the column, and you add all those terms together for the row-column combination and put the sum in that row-column of the result matrix. You do this for each row-column combination.

MATHEMATICS • PRACTICE TEST 2 • EXPLANATORY ANSWERS

That explanation is correct but pretty abstract. Your math text might have some examples that you can look over to make things more concrete.

In this case, there is only 1 element in each row of the first matrix, and 1 element in each column in the second matrix. The matrix product is:

$$\begin{bmatrix} a \\ 2a \\ 3a \end{bmatrix} \begin{bmatrix} 1 & 0 & -1 \end{bmatrix} = \begin{bmatrix} a\cdot 1 & a\cdot 0 & a\cdot(-1) \\ 2a\cdot 1 & 2a\cdot 0 & 2a\cdot(-1) \\ 3a\cdot 1 & 3a\cdot 0 & 3a\cdot(-1) \end{bmatrix} = \begin{bmatrix} a & 0 & -a \\ 2a & 0 & -2a \\ 3a & 0 & -3a \end{bmatrix}$$

The computations in **G** are basically correct, but the terms were put in the wrong places.

If you chose **K**, you may have reasoned that whatever role the 1 played in the second matrix, the –1 would cancel it out, and the 0 would not change that. If all the terms were combined, that would be the case. But a matrix can keep the terms separate.

Question 43. The correct answer is D. Because the base is a straight line, these two angle measures add up to 180°. In the language of algebra, this can be represented as $(4x + 6) + (2x) = 180$. Solving this for x gives $6x + 6 = 180$, then $x + 1 = 30$, then $x = 29$. This makes one angle measure $4(29) + 6 = 122$ degrees and the other angle measure $2(29) = 58$ degrees. (Check: Is 122° + 58° equal to 180°? Yes.)

The problem asks for the measure of the smallest of these two angles. That is 58°.

If you chose **C**, you probably just stopped as soon as you found the value of x. The problem asks for something different. The other popular incorrect answer is **E**.

Question 44. The correct answer is F. The new value of b is $(b - 1)$, and the new value of c is $(c + 2)$. Substituting into the expression for a gives $2(b - 1) + 3(c + 2) - 5$, which simplifies to $2b - 2 + 3c + 6 - 5$. Because you are looking for the change in a, try to write this expression in terms of the original expression for a. You can do this as $(2b + 3c - 5) - 2 + 6$, which simplifies to $(2b + 3c - 5) + 4$. And that is the old value of a increased by 4.

If you chose **H**, you may have expanded $2(b - 1) + 3(c + 2)$ to $2b - 1 + 3c + 2$.

Question 45. The correct answer is C. We want to find the number of gallons of fertilizer, x, for which the rate $\frac{x}{0.5\text{ acre}}$ is equal to $\frac{1\text{ fl.oz}}{40\text{ sq.ft}}$. We do this by solving for x: $x = \frac{1\text{ fl.oz}}{40\text{ sq.ft}} \times \frac{0.5\text{ acre}}{1}$ and then multiplying by the conversion factor given in the item. We want to eliminate all units besides gallons to get the answer: $x = \frac{1\text{ fl.oz}}{40\text{ sq.ft}} \times \frac{0.5\text{ acre}}{1} \times \frac{43{,}650\text{ sq.ft}}{1\text{ acre}} \times \frac{1\text{ gal}}{128\text{ fl.oz}} = \frac{0.5(43{,}560)}{40(128)}$ gallons. You may have gotten **A** if your conversion setup did not eliminate acres in the numerator and had gallon in the denominator, so you got acre per gallon.

MATHEMATICS • PRACTICE TEST 2 • EXPLANATORY ANSWERS

You may have gotten **B** if your conversions were inverted and you found per gallon. You may have gotten **D** if you divided by 0.5 acre instead of multiplying by 0.5 acre and therefore got gallon per acre. You may have gotten **E** if your conversion did not eliminate square feet in the numerator and fluid ounces in the denominator and got square feet times gallon per fluid ounce.

Question 46. The correct answer is J.

Because no booths can be empty, imagine 1 person sitting in each booth. That leaves 10 people standing around waiting for you to tell them where to sit. How many booths can you fill up with another 3 people each? Well, you can get 3 groups of 3 people from the 10 who are still standing, with 1 person left over. That means that you can fill at most 3 booths with 4 people. There will be 1 booth with 2 people, and the other 6 booths will have 1 person. (Check: Are there 20 people? $3(4) + 0(3) + 1(2) + 6(1) = 12 + 2 + 6 = 20$. Yes. Are there 10 booths? $3 + 0 + 1 + 6 = 10$. Yes.)

MATHEMATICS • PRACTICE TEST 2 • EXPLANATORY ANSWERS

If you chose **K**, you filled up 5 booths with 4 people each. But, you left the other 5 booths with no one sitting there. The problem specified that NO booths are empty. (This is the most common wrong answer.)

If you chose **G**, you may have just miscounted. Make sure you check your work. You might want to draw a diagram for problems like this so that you can check your work more easily.

Question 47. The correct answer is D. You can calculate the chances of Events A and B both occurring by multiplying the probability of each event occurring. That means that the correct expression is $P(\text{A} \cap \text{B}) = P(\text{A}) \cdot P(\text{B})$.

If you chose **A**, you might have thought the probability of Event A occurring is the same as the probability of Event B occurring. If you chose **B**, you might have thought the probability of Event A occurring is the complement of the probability of Event B occurring. If you chose **C**, you might have thought that the probability of Event A occurring and the probability of Event B occurring should be added together rather than multiplied. If you chose **E**, you might have confused the formula for the probability of A and B both occurring with the formula for the probability of A *or* B occurring, $P(\text{A} \cup \text{B}) = P(\text{A}) + P(\text{B}) - (P(\text{A}) \cdot P(\text{B}))$.

Question 48. The correct answer is J. The following figure shows the 3-4-5 right triangle with sides formed by the x-axis, the vertical line through (4,–3), and the terminal side of θ. The angle, α, formed by the terminal side and the x-axis is called the *reference angle* of θ. The relationship between θ and α is $\cos\alpha = |\cos\theta|$. From the figure, you can see that $\cos\alpha = \frac{\text{the length of the side adjacent to } \angle\alpha}{\text{the length of the hypotenuse}} = \frac{4}{5} = |\cos\theta|$. Because the terminal side of θ lies in Quadrant IV, $\cos\theta$ is positive. Therefore, $\cos\theta = \frac{4}{5}$.

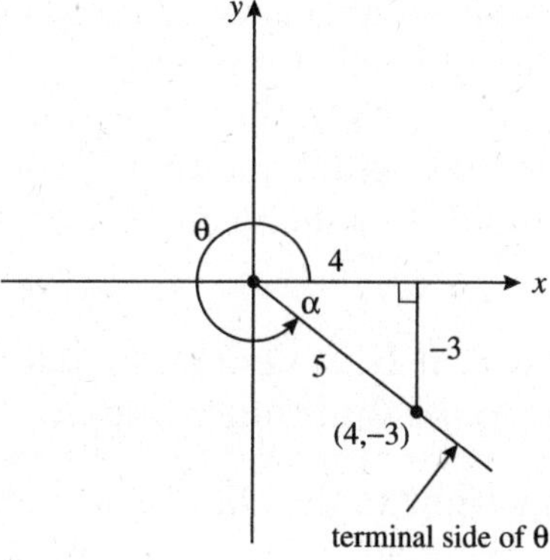

Taking Additional Practice Tests

MATHEMATICS • PRACTICE TEST 2 • EXPLANATORY ANSWERS

Question 49. The correct answer is A. If x is a negative number, then let $y = -x$, where y is a positive number. Then $\sqrt{y^2}$ is just y. In terms of x, this says $\sqrt{(-x)^2} = -x$. For example, let x be -5. The left side is $\sqrt{(-(-5))^2}$, which simplifies to $\sqrt{(5)^2}$, and then to 5. The right side is $-(-5)$, which is also 5.

For any number x, its square and the square of its opposite are equal: $(x)^2 = (-x)^2$. For example, $(5)^2 = (-5)^2$. This shows that $\sqrt{(-x)^2} = \sqrt{x^2}$. When x is a positive number, or zero, then $\sqrt{x^2} = x$. Putting these last two statements together, $\sqrt{(-x)^2} = x$ whenever x is a positive number or zero. For example, when $x = 5$, $\sqrt{(-5)^2} = 5$.

Summarizing, you now know that $\sqrt{(-x)^2} = -x$ whenever x is a negative number, and $\sqrt{(-x)^2} = x$ whenever x is positive or zero. Another way of saying this is $\sqrt{(-x)^2} = |x|$.

Because $|x| = |-x|$ for all values of x, the paragraphs above show that I and II are saying the same thing—they're equivalent.

However, II is always positive or zero, and III is always negative or zero, so the only time they are equal is when x is zero. For example, when $x = 1$, $|-1| = 1$ but $-|1| = -1$. So II and III are not equivalent.

The most common incorrect answer is **C**. Even though statements II and III look a lot alike—they have the exact same symbols in almost the same order—they are not equivalent. One is never negative and one is never positive.

If you answered **E**, you probably saw that II and III are not equivalent. Expression I looks so much different than either of the others that it is tempting to just say it can't be the same. One approach would be to test a few numbers in the expressions. Be sure that one is positive and one is negative. If you substitute these into I and into II correctly, you will find they match. Then, you should suspect that I and II could be equivalent and look for a way to convince yourself of this.

Question 50. The correct answer is K. Statement **F**, that $\overleftrightarrow{AB}$ and $\overleftrightarrow{EF}$ are parallel, is true because both are perpendicular to the same other line, $\overleftrightarrow{AD}$.

Because $\angle DEB$ is marked with a right angle, $\overline{DE}$ is perpendicular to $\overline{BE}$, and so **G** is true.

The two angles, $\angle ACB$ and $\angle FCE$, are vertical angles, so **H** is true.

Statement **J** is true because the angles in ΔBAC are congruent to the angles in ΔEFC. First, $\angle A$ is congruent to $\angle F$ because they are both right angles. Next, $\angle ACB$ and $\angle FCE$ are vertical angles. And third, the remaining angles must have the same measure because the sum of the interior angle measures in any triangle is 180°.

MATHEMATICS • PRACTICE TEST 2 • EXPLANATORY ANSWERS

Because all of the other statements are true, you would expect statement **K** to be false. The following diagram shows such a case. Only if $\angle ECF$ is congruent to $\angle EDF$ can $\overline{CE}$ be congruent to $\overline{DE}$.

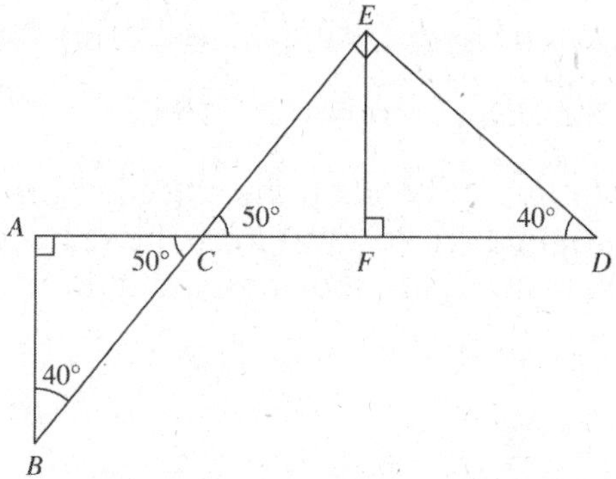

Question 51. The correct answer is D. This geometric figure has six sides, but you are only given the length of four of those sides. One of the slickest ways to find the perimeter is to move two of the sides to form a rectangle with the same perimeter. The following drawing shows the new rectangle:

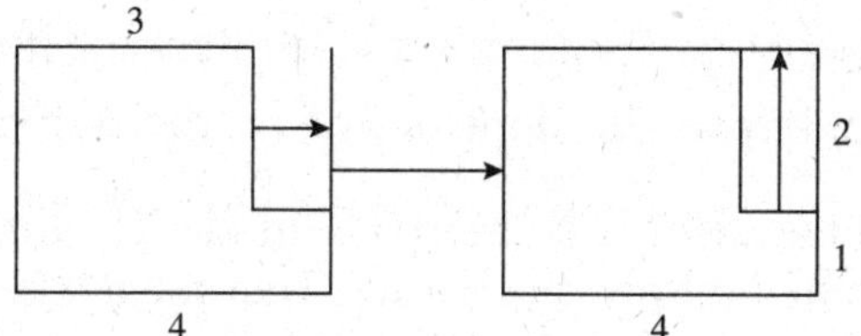

The bottom of this rectangle is 4 inches long, and the right side is 3 inches long. So, the perimeter is $4 + 3 + 4 + 3 = 14$ inches.

An alternate method is to deduce that the left side is 3 inches long because it is the same length as the vertical sides on the right. And the last unknown side is 1 inch long because it is the difference between the horizontal 4-inch side on the bottom and the horizontal 3-inch side on the top. Then the perimeter (going clockwise) is $4 + 3 + 3 + 2 + 1 + 1 = 14$ inches.

If you chose **C**, you may have forgotten to add in the horizontal side that connects the vertical 2-inch side and the vertical 1-inch side.

If you chose **A**, you may have added just the numbers given directly on the figure. Or you may have calculated the area instead of the perimeter.

Question 52. The correct answer is F. Because points A and B are stationary, the side $\overline{AB}$ of ΔABC will not change in length or direction. The *altitude* of ΔABC with respect to side $\overline{AB}$ is the segment having one endpoint at point C that is perpendicular to $\overleftrightarrow{AB}$. The area of ΔABC, in square coordinate units, can be found using the following formula:

area = $\frac{1}{2}(AB)$(the length of the altitude from C to $\overline{AB}$)

Because the length AB must remain constant, the altitude from C of any new triangle whose area is equal to that of the original ΔABC must have the same length. Three of these new triangles (and their altitudes from C) are shown in the following figures:

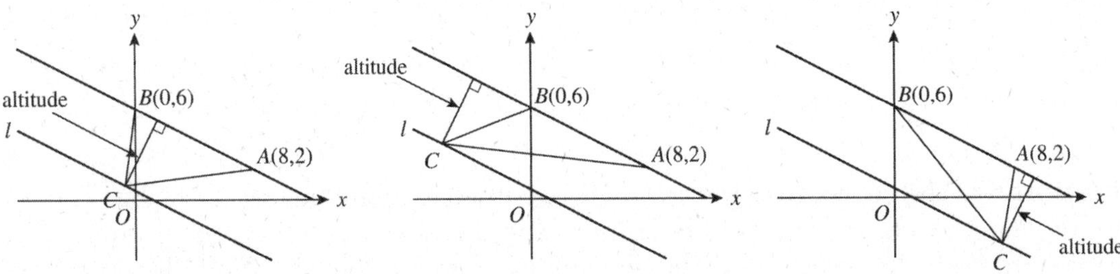

In order that all altitudes from the moving point C have equal lengths, C must lie on the line l (shown in each figure), where line l is parallel to $\overleftrightarrow{AB}$. Because line l is parallel to $\overleftrightarrow{AB}$, the lines must have equal slopes. Therefore, the slope of line l = the slope of $\overleftrightarrow{AB} = \frac{6-2}{0-8} = \frac{4}{-8} = -\frac{1}{2}$.

Question 53. The correct answer is D. Marshall made 24 calls on the first day. He makes 5 more calls each day than he had the day before. That means he made 29 calls on the second day. The following table shows the number of calls he made on each of the 20 days:

Day	1	2	3	4	5	6	7	8	9	10
No. calls	24	29	34	39	44	49	54	59	64	69

Day	11	12	13	14	15	16	17	18	19	20
No. calls	74	79	84	89	94	99	104	109	114	119

You could try to add all of these up. You might make a mistake, even with a calculator but that method is straightforward and would work.

Another approach is to notice that the number of calls for the first day and the last day add up to 143, as do the number of calls for Day 2 and Day 19, as do the number for Day 3 and Day 18, as do all the other pairs of days, working forward from the beginning and backward from the end. There are 10 pairs of days, each with 143 calls. That is 1,430 calls for the 20 days.

MATHEMATICS • PRACTICE TEST 2 • EXPLANATORY ANSWERS

A third approach is to notice that this is an arithmetic series, where each term is 24 + 5k, where k represents the numbers from 0 to 19. When k is 0, then it is Day 1,and there are 24 + 0 calls. With sigma notation, the sum of all the calls on the 20 days can be represented as $\sum_{k=0}^{19}(24+5k)$. This is equivalent to $\left(\sum_{k=0}^{19}24\right)+\left(\sum_{k=0}^{19}5k\right)$, which is equivalent to $\left(\sum_{k=0}^{19}24\right)+5\left(\sum_{k=0}^{19}k\right)$. The first summation is saying to add 24 + 24 + · · · 24, where there are 20 of the 24s added together. That is just 24 · 20 = 480. The second summation is a common one and simplifies to $\frac{(19)(19+1)}{2}=190$. That makes the series sum to 480 + 5(190) = 480 + 950 = 1,430 calls.

A fourth approach relies on accurately remembering the following formula for the sum of an arithmetic series: $S_n=\frac{n}{2}[2a+(n-1)d]$, where the first term in the series is a, the common difference between terms is d, there are n terms in the series, and the sum is S_n. Substituting the quantities you know gives $\frac{20}{2}[2\cdot24+(20-1)\cdot5]=10[48+95]=10[143]=1{,}430$ calls.

If you used the summation approach and got **C**, you may have simplified $\sum_{k=0}^{19}(24+5k)$ to $24+5\left(\sum_{k=0}^{19}k\right)$, leaving out the multiplier of 24.

If you chose **B**, you may have simplified the summation to $(24)(20)+\left(\sum_{k=0}^{19}k\right)$, leaving out the factor of 5. Or, you may have calculated the number of calls for Day 10 and multiplied this by 10.

Question 54. The correct answer is K. This is called a piecewise-defined function because it is pieces of different functions put together to form a single function. When $x \le 1$, the equation is $f(x) = x^2 - 2$, so $f(1) = 1^2 - 2 = -1$ and $f(0) = 0^2 - 2 = -2$. (Actually, this information is enough to eliminate all the graphs except the correct one. But you might want to read the rest of this explanation anyhow.)

The graph of $y = x^2 - 2$ is a parabola, opening upward. Its graph is shown on page 444. The only part of the graph that applies for this piecewise-defined function is the part where $x \le 1$. The rest of the graph is represented with dashes.

MATHEMATICS • PRACTICE TEST 2 • EXPLANATORY ANSWERS

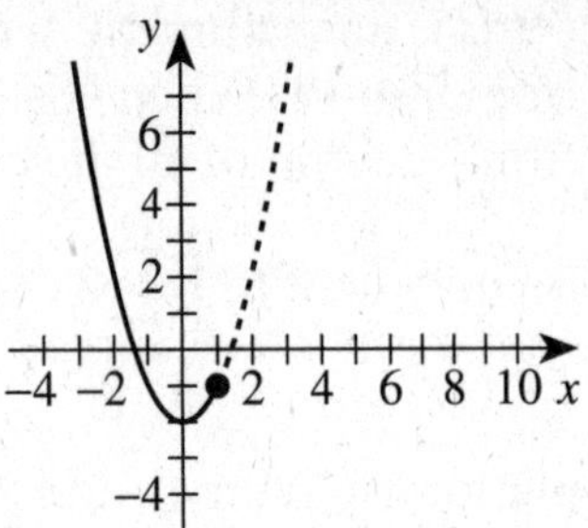

When $1 < x < 5$, then $f(x) = x - 7$, so $f(2) = 2 - 7 = -5$ and $f(4) = 4 - 7 = -3$. This is a straight line. A graph is shown in the following, with the parts outside $1 < x < 5$ shown with dashes.

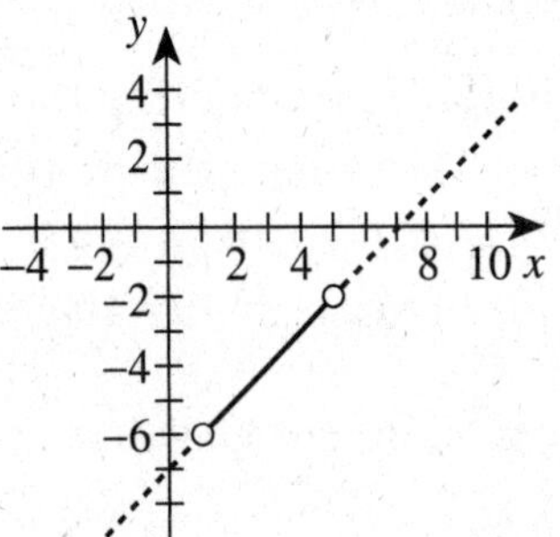

When $x \geq 5$, the equation is $f(x) = 4 - x$, so $f(5) = 4 - 5 = -1$ and $f(6) = 4 - 6 = -2$. This is also a straight line. Its graph is shown in the following, with the part outside $x \geq 5$ shown with dashes.

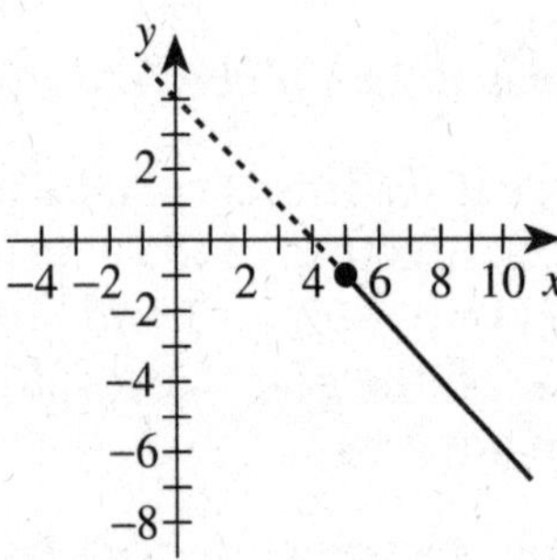

K puts all these pieces together.

MATHEMATICS • PRACTICE TEST 2 • EXPLANATORY ANSWERS

Question 55. The correct answer is D. The formula for calculating the number of permutations of n objects taken r at a time is $\frac{n!}{(n-r)!}$. Therefore, the correct expression is $\frac{15!}{(15-5)!}$. If you chose **A, B, C,** or **E**, you may have used the incorrect formula. The expression in **A** gives 5 times the number of objects. The expression in **B** gives the total permutations for 10 objects. The expression in **C** gives the number of permutations for 15 objects taken 10 at a time. The expression in **E** gives the number of combinations of 15 objects taken 5 at a time.

Question 56. The correct answer is K. To find an equivalent expression, you could simplify the expression by multiplying the numerator and denominator by the complex conjugate of the denominator, $\sqrt{x}+i$.

$\frac{i}{\sqrt{x}-i}\cdot\frac{\sqrt{x}+i}{\sqrt{x}+i}=\frac{i\sqrt{x}+i^2}{(\sqrt{x})(\sqrt{x})+i\sqrt{x}-i\sqrt{x}-i^2}=\frac{i\sqrt{x}+(\sqrt{-1})^2}{x-(\sqrt{-1})^2}=\frac{i\sqrt{x}-1}{x-(-1)}=\frac{i\sqrt{x}-1}{x+1}$. If you chose **F**, you might have incorrectly thought that you could eliminate the x's and the 1's in the expression $\frac{i\sqrt{\not x}+\not 1}{\not x-\not 1}$. If you chose **G**, you might have incorrectly thought that you could eliminate the i's in the expression $\frac{\not i}{\sqrt{x}-\not i}$. If you chose **H**, you might have incorrectly multiplied the expression by its complex conjugate. If you chose **J**, you might have incorrectly thought that $i^2=1$.

Question 57. The correct answer is E. You can use the fact that Point A has coordinates (–6,–2) and Point B has coordinates (3,4), so the component form of $\overrightarrow{AB}$ is $\langle 3-(-6), 4-(-2)\rangle=\langle 9,6\rangle$. Point C has coordinates (4,–2) and Point D has coordinates (4,3), so the component form of $\overrightarrow{CD}$ is $\langle 4-4, 3-(-2)\rangle=\langle 0,5\rangle$. Writing $\overrightarrow{AB}$ and $\overrightarrow{CD}$ in terms of the unit vectors, $\mathbf{i}=\langle 1,0\rangle$ and $\mathbf{j}=\langle 0,1\rangle$ results in $\overrightarrow{AB}=9\mathbf{i}+6\mathbf{j}$ and $\overrightarrow{CD}=0\mathbf{i}+5\mathbf{j}$. Therefore, vector $\overrightarrow{AB}+\overrightarrow{CD}=(9+0)\mathbf{i}+(6+5)\mathbf{j}=9\mathbf{i}+11\mathbf{j}$.

If you chose **A**, you may have incorrectly thought that $\overrightarrow{AB}=\langle -6,-2\rangle$. If you chose **B**, you may have incorrectly thought that $\overrightarrow{AB}=\langle 3,4\rangle$ and $\overrightarrow{CD}=\langle 0,-5\rangle$. If you chose **C**, you may have incorrectly thought that $\overrightarrow{AB}=\langle 3,4\rangle$. If you chose **D**, you may have incorrectly thought that $\overrightarrow{CD}=\langle 0,-5\rangle$.

Question 58. The correct answer is J. Let L_1 feet be the length of Pendulum 1 and t_1 seconds be the time for a complete swing of Pendulum 1. Let L_2 and t_2 describe Pendulum 2 in the same way. The time for a complete swing of Pendulum 1 is triple the time required for a complete swing of Pendulum 2. This means that $t_1 = 3t_2$.

The most common approaches to solving problems like this involve finding an equation that contains the two variables the question asks about, here L_1 and L_2, and solving for one variable or solving for the ratio of the variables.

MATHEMATICS • PRACTICE TEST 2 • EXPLANATORY ANSWERS

By the equation that relates L to t, the equation $t_1 = 3t_2$ becomes $2\pi\sqrt{\frac{L_1}{32}} = 3 \cdot 2\pi\sqrt{\frac{L_2}{32}}$ (which is an equation that contains both L_1 and L_2). Dividing both sides by 2π gives the equation $\sqrt{\frac{L_1}{32}} = 3\sqrt{\frac{L_2}{32}}$. Squaring both sides gives $\frac{L_1}{32} = 9 \cdot \frac{L_2}{32}$. Multiplying both sides by 32 gives $L_1 = 9L_2$. So, Pendulum 1's string is 9 times the length of Pendulum 2's string.

The most common incorrect answer is **G**. If you chose that, you might have reasoned that if one variable triples, then any other variable must also triple. This happens for some functions, notably linear functions, but the function in this problem is not linear. The value of L must go up by a factor of 9 so that the square root will go up by a factor of 3.

If you chose **H**, you may have reasoned that, in order for the square root to go up by a factor of 3, the quantity under the square root must go up by a factor of 6. That would mean that L would go up by a factor of 6. This turns out not to be enough, because if L goes up by a factor of 6, the square root will only go up by a factor of $\sqrt{6}$, which is less than 3.

Question 59. The correct answer is A. By properties of logarithms, $\log_a(xy)^2 = 2\log_a(xy) = 2(\log_a x + \log_a y) = 2(s + t)$.

If you chose **D**, you may have done all of the previous steps correctly, except for thinking that $\log_a(xy) = \log_a x \cdot \log_a y$ (using multiplication rather than addition on the right side).

Answer **C** could come from thinking that $\log_a(xy)^2 = \log_a(x^2y^2) = \log_a x^2 \cdot \log_a y^2 = 2\log_a x \cdot 2\log_a y$. The first and last steps are correct, but not the middle one.

Question 60. The correct answer is F. Let d be her distance in 1990. Her distance in 1991 would be $1.1 \cdot d$. And her distance in 1992 would be $1.2(1.1 \cdot d)$, which simplifies to $1.32 \cdot d$. This represents an increase of 32% from 1990 to 1992.

The most common incorrect answer is **G**. If you chose this, you probably added the 10% and the 20% to get 30%. This would work fine if the percents were percents of the same thing. But the first increase is a percent of the 1990 distance, while the second is a percent of the 1991 distance.

One good strategy for investigating problems like this is to choose a specific number to represent the initial distance. Say you choose 10 feet for her 1990 distance. The 1991 distance would be the original 10 feet plus a 10% increase, which is 1 more foot, for a total of 11 feet. To find the 1992 distance, take the 11 feet and add 20% of this amount, which is 2.2 feet. Then, the 1992 distance is 11 + 2.2 = 13.2 feet. The percent increase from the original 10 feet is $\left(\frac{13.2-10}{10}\right)(100\%) = (0.32)(100\%) = 32\%$. These are the same operations done in the first method, but the calculations are done with concrete numbers rather than abstract variables.

READING • PRACTICE TEST 2 • EXPLANATORY ANSWERS

Passage I

Question 1. The best answer is A because throughout the passage Crown is explicitly characterized as industrious and fastidious; his life and business are described as being ruled by the three tenets of order, accuracy, and modernity, all of which are grounded in his reverence for hard work. This description and characterization firmly reinforce the stereotype that Germans are tidy, meticulous, and industrious.

The best answer is NOT:

B because Crown is characterized consistently throughout the passage as adhering to the principles of order and industry in all aspects of his life and work; there is no evidence in the passage that he weakens the German stereotype.

C because Crown is explicitly described as accepting and even revering the principle of hard work. His personal philosophy that "without industry there was no reward" (lines 86–87) is described as being ingrained in him "deeper than the marrow of his bones" (lines 90–91). This clearly does not weaken the industrious aspect of the German stereotype.

D because there is no evidence in the passage that Crown expects others to do the tidying up for him.

Question 2. The best answer is H because it can most reasonably be inferred that the "appointment at twelve" referred to in line 17 would occur that day, whereas the "emergency meeting" referred to in lines 4–5 is scheduled to take place "this Friday" (line 5), indicating that the meeting would happen in the near future.

The best answer is NOT:

F because "this Friday" in line 5 indicates that the meeting will happen on a day in the near future, whereas the appointment is indicated as being scheduled for that day. If the meeting and the appointment were meant to happen on the same day, the narrator likely would have said "today" instead of "this Friday."

G because the passage makes it clear that the meeting "this Friday" has not yet occurred, especially considering it is described as an immediate concern of Crown's.

J because the passage makes it clear that the meeting is an immediate concern of Crown's, and that the meeting will happen "this Friday," indicating the near future, not years in the future.

Question 3. The best answer is B because lines 47–57 describe the principle of modernity to which Crown unwaveringly subscribes, giving examples of how quickly he embraces new technology. Zwick, however, is reluctant to move from using an old-fashioned quill pen to a modern typewriter (lines 62–64), learning to typewrite only when he is compelled to.

The best answer is NOT:

A because there is no clear evidence in the passage that Zwick adheres to a certain level of fastidiousness regarding the meeting of deadlines.

C because the passage characterizes Zwick as being clearly unafraid to state his preferences to his superior (Crown), but there is no evidence in the passage that Crown is afraid to state his preferences to his superiors. Indeed, there is no suggestion in the passage that Crown *has* superiors.

D because there is no evidence in the passage that Zwick holds concern about the company's public image; Crown, however, is clearly concerned with the company's image, as evidenced in lines 66–67, when he says that using quill pens instead of typewriters "makes Crown's look old-fashioned."

Question 4. The best answer is F because when Zwick is said to have "blanched" in line 72, it is in response to Crown's proposal that a woman be hired as a typewriter if Zwick refuses to learn typewriting. Zwick's indignation is expressed in the rest of line 72: "A woman? In my office?"

The best answer is NOT:

G because the passage makes clear that the woman is a theoretical employee, not an actual visitor in the office.

H because the passage makes clear from context that Zwick is not excited about the prospect of a female employee; the passage also makes clear that the female employee being discussed is theoretical.

J because the passage makes clear that Crown will hire a female employee only if Zwick continues to refuse to learn to typewrite; Crown has not actually hired anyone.

READING • PRACTICE TEST 2 • EXPLANATORY ANSWERS

Question 5. The best answer is D because lines 2–5 clearly state that Crown's "most immediate" worry was a "civic responsibility" that he would soon be discussing at a meeting.

The best answer is NOT:

A because there is no evidence in the passage that Crown is preoccupied with whether he will be on time for his weekly trim; the appointment for the trim is only mentioned as a passing matter of fact.

B because the passage makes clear in lines 52–54 that Crown had no hesitation in installing expensive pasteurization equipment in his brewery; the passage also makes clear that this is not a preoccupation of his at the time described in the passage's opening.

C because the passage does not indicate that Crown is at all preoccupied with Zwick's behavior, and the passage also indicates that Crown's exchange with Zwick in lines 62–74 took place before the time described in the passage's opening.

Question 6. The best answer is G because the passage states that Crown was "a mediocre student in most school subjects" but that "at ciphering he was a prodigy" (lines 33–34).

The best answer is NOT:

F because the passage states that Crown was a "mediocre student in most school subjects" (lines 33–34); he was exceptionally gifted only at ciphering.

H because there is no evidence in the passage that Crown was a successful student whether he applied himself or not; he is simply described as being a mediocre student outside of his talent at ciphering.

J because there is no evidence in the passage that Crown's success as a student increased as he mastered counting aids.

Question 7. The best answer is C because the passage characterizes Crown in lines 42–46 as prone to asking questions of his employees that would elicit a specific answer, likely one that involved numbers. The question about sales figures in **C** best fits these characteristics.

The best answer is NOT:

A because there is no evidence in the passage supporting the idea that Crown is likely to ask an open-ended, personal question of his employees.

B because the passage most strongly suggests in lines 42–46 that Crown's questions to his employees most likely involve numbers, and a question about repairing old equipment does not involve numbers.

D because there is no evidence in the passage supporting the idea that Crown is concerned about team dynamics among his employees to the point where he would ask such a question of them. Lines 42–46 also most strongly suggest that Crown's questions to his employees involve numbers, and the question about team-building does not involve numbers.

READING • PRACTICE TEST 2 • EXPLANATORY ANSWERS

Question 8. The best answer is H because the passage describes Crown as subscribing to the principle of modernity, and his exchange with Zwick in lines 62–74 most nearly suggests that quill pens were the status quo in offices in the United States at the time the passage was set, though more advanced technology was beginning to become available. To Crown, who wanted his business to use the "newest methods" (line 51) of technology, such as typewriters and mechanical adding machines, these quill pens seemed "old-fashioned" (line 67).

The best answer is NOT:

F because the passage indicates that the typewriter is among the "modern machines" (line 56) that Crown insists be used in his office.

G because the passage indicates in lines 56–58 that the mechanical adding machine is one of the "modern machines" (line 56) that Crown insists be used in his office.

J because the passage gives no clear evidence that abacuses are widely used in US offices at the time the passage is set. The abacus mentioned in the passage is described as an ancient counting device (line 39) that Crown keeps in his office, "within reach" (line 40). Presumably such an ancient counting device is not widely used in US offices at the time the passage is set, but Crown does not necessarily seem to see the abacus as becoming increasingly obsolete.

Question 9. The best answer is A because the metaphor used in the passage to describe Crown's three principles primarily includes language about building, which is a fundamental part of architecture as a discipline. Line 26 describes Crown's second principle of accuracy as a "keystone," and lines 76–78 compare Crown's three principles to a "solid house or building" that is "supported by a strong foundation": Crown's attitude toward hard work.

The best answer is NOT:

B because business is only mentioned in the passage in the very literal sense of Crown's brewery business and its operations.

C because astronomy is not mentioned in the passage.

D because education is mentioned in the passage only in the literal sense of Crown's education as a student.

READING • PRACTICE TEST 2 • EXPLANATORY ANSWERS

Question 10. The best answer is H because the passage describes the photographs of annual brewery picnics decorating Crown's office as "fading" and "brown" (line 81), indicating that they have hung on the wall of his office (and thus that Crown has been in the brewery business) for a length of time.

The best answer is NOT:

F because the passage makes no mention of outdated refrigerators; it only mentions that Crown invested in "refrigerated freight cars" (lines 55–56), which represented a new technology at the time.

G because the passage makes no mention of how long the cross-stitch made by Crown's wife has been hanging on his office wall.

J because there is no mention of such a bell in the passage; it only mentions the "pinging bell on the black iron typewriter" (lines 59–60).

Passage II

Question 11. The best answer is D because there is no mention in the passage of William's response to Caroline's discovery, thus there is no clear indication of how he felt about her discovery.

The best answer is NOT:

A because there is no evidence in the passage that William either applauded Caroline's discovery or was disappointed that she wasn't looking for nebulae.

B because there is no evidence in the passage that William either supported Caroline's discovery or verified it himself.

C because there is no evidence in the passage that William resented how quickly Caroline's discovery was verified.

Question 12. The best answer is J because the passage states that "the forty-foot [octagon tube] would be higher than a house" (line 14). This is a direct comparison used to emphasize the enormous size of the "octagon tube 40 foot long" (line 6).

The best answer is NOT:

F because the series of ladders mentioned in line 16 is a description of part of the telescope itself; the telescope is not being compared to the ladders.

G because the wooden gantry mentioned in line 10 is described as something the telescope would have to be mounted in; the telescope itself isn't compared to the gantry.

H because the haylofts mentioned in line 34 are described as part of the stables that could be converted into an apartment; the telescope is not compared to the haylofts.

READING • PRACTICE TEST 2 • EXPLANATORY ANSWERS

Question 13. The best answer is B because the first four paragraphs in the passage focus on William Herschel and his telescope project, but the remainder of the passage focuses primarily on his sister Caroline and her astronomical work; the fifth paragraph serves as a transition, moving the passage's discussion from details about William's telescope project to details about Caroline's work.

The best answer is NOT:

A because the passage does not explain any specific methods Caroline used to perform her comet sweeps.

C because the passage does not say that Caroline herself made renovations to the stables, nor does it specify that the renovations would be done to accommodate William's telescope.

D because the passage does not compare Caroline's observation techniques with William's; at this point, the passage shifts to a discussion of Caroline's astronomical work.

Question 14. The best answer is H because the passage says in lines 79–80 that "The account written into [Caroline's] 'Book of Work Done' catches something of her growing excitement." This statement is then supported and illustrated by the excerpt from Caroline's "Book of Work Done" that immediately follows. Her writing "IS A COMET" in capital letters (line 85), and the statement that she "did not go to rest" until she had written to the Royal Society about the comet (lines 85–88), also reveal her enthusiasm about her discovery.

The best answer is NOT:

F because though the excerpt in the passage indicates that it took Caroline a bit of time to verify that her finding was a comet, the passage contains no clear outline of the process by which Caroline determined her finding was a comet.

G because the passage indicates that the excerpt contains notes from Caroline's own work, not that the notes were made for William in particular.

J because though the passage implies that Dr. Blagden and Mr. Aubert were points of authority regarding astronomical discovery at the time, it does not explain the role they may have had in verifying Caroline's discovery.

READING • PRACTICE TEST 2 • EXPLANATORY ANSWERS

Question 15. The best answer is A because in the context of lines 9–13, it is clear that the word *finest* is being used in juxtaposition with the description of the enormous telescope and its workings. The telescope was so massive that it would have to be mounted in an enormous gantry and turned by two workmen, but it would be so intricate and precise that it could be adjusted in "fine," or "slight," ways by the astronomer.

The best answer is NOT:

B because the word *fairest* generally denotes either lightness in complexion or appearance, or it pertains to justice and equity. However, the word *finest* in the context of lines 9–13 is meant to indicate precision, not any of the concepts associated with fairness.

C because the context of lines 9–13 indicates that the word *finest* is being used in the sense of precision, and it would be inaccurate to describe precise or exact fingertip adjustments as *thin.*

D because the word *greatest* denotes either size or level of excellence. The word *finest* in the context of lines 9–13 is clearly meant to indicate the precision involved in the adjustments, not any of the concepts associated with greatness.

Question 16. The best answer is J because the sentence in lines 17–21 states that Caroline would have to be in the special booth below William "to avoid light pollution, where she would have her desk and lamp, celestial clocks, and observation journals," meaning that the light from her lamp (which she needed to record her observations) would have affected William's ability to observe the night sky though the telescope.

The best answer is NOT:

F because the passage states that both Caroline and William would be "shouting commands and replies" (lines 22–23); there is no evidence that Caroline would be relaying William's instructions to workmen.

G because there is no evidence in the passage that Caroline preferred seclusion when working on calculations; the passage states that she would work in the booth "to avoid light pollution" (line 19), not because she wanted to be alone.

H because the passage does not indicate the size of the viewing platform or the number of people it could hold, so there is no evidence in the passage to support the idea that the platform wouldn't be large enough to hold both William and Caroline.

READING • PRACTICE TEST 2 • EXPLANATORY ANSWERS

Question 17. The best answer is B because lines 25–27 directly answer the question of why William and Caroline moved to "The Grove": "William had decided that his grand project required a new house with larger grounds for constructing and erecting the telescope." They moved to "The Grove," which is described as meeting these requirements.

The best answer is NOT:

A because the passage makes no mention of what motivated William to embark on his project; it only mentions when he was inspired to begin the project ("in the summer of 1785" (line 1)).

C because the passage mentions that Caroline was "unable to calculate the mathematical coordinates" of the comet she discovered, but it does not give any reason as to why she was unable to do so.

D because the passage does say that "the verification of Caroline's comet was achieved much more rapidly than William's discovery of the planet Uranus" (lines 89–91), but it does not directly specify how long it took the Royal Society to verify that Caroline's discovery was a comet.

Question 18. The best answer is F because the passage states that because of the reflector's "large aperture, its tube appeared much fatter, heavier and stubbier than normal reflectors of this type" (lines 42–44). Thus it can most reasonably be inferred that the reflector's aperture was larger than those of typical telescopes of that type at the time.

The best answer is NOT:

G because there is no mention in the passage of the size of the reflector's box-frame.

H because the passage states that the reflector's magnification was "comparatively low at twenty-four times" (lines 51–52), meaning that it had less magnifying power compared to similar telescopes at the time.

J because the passage states that the reflector was "designed specifically for its huge light-gathering power" (lines 49–50), indicating that, if anything, it likely had more light-gathering power than similar telescopes at that time, not less.

READING • PRACTICE TEST 2 • EXPLANATORY ANSWERS

Question 19. The best answer is C because the passage states in lines 62–66 that "Caroline thought she had spotted an unknown stellar object moving through Ursa Major" which "appeared to be descending, but barely perceptibly, towards a triangulation of stars in the beautifully named constellation Coma Berenices."

The best answer is NOT:

A because lines 62–66 clearly state that the comet was moving "towards" the stars in Coma Berenices, not through Coma Berenices or toward the Pole Star.

B because lines 62–66 clearly state that the comet was moving "towards" the stars in Coma Berenices, not through Coma Berenices or toward the Big Dipper.

D because lines 62–66 clearly state that the comet was moving "through" Ursa Major and "towards" the triangulation of stars in Coma Berenices, not through them.

Question 20. The best answer is F because the passage states in lines 67–70 that "to find something so quickly, and in such a familiar place (the Great Bear or Big Dipper being the first stop of every amateur stargazer wanting to locate the Pole Star), seemed wildly unlikely." Thus the passage indicates that Caroline's find was unlikely because she found the comet quickly in a part of the sky that was very familiar to stargazers.

The best answer is NOT:

G because there is no evidence in the passage that Caroline had more knowledge of nebulae than she did of comets.

H because the passage mentions in lines 90–91 "William's discovery of the planet Uranus," but there is no mention of Caroline being involved in that discovery.

J because the passage indicates that Caroline had plenty of experience with mathematical calculations in astronomy, and though line 73 does state that she was "unable to calculate the mathematical coordinates" of her comet, the passage gives no indication that her discovery was unlikely because she had little experience with such calculations.

READING • PRACTICE TEST 2 • EXPLANATORY ANSWERS

Passage III

Question 21. The best answer is B because the first paragraph of passage A reveals Gornick's belief that her mother and the character of her mother in her memoir are not exactly the same; the second paragraph reveals Gornick's belief that, similarly, the narrator of the memoir and her actual self are not quite the same. Together, in the context of the passage as a whole, these paragraphs serve to introduce the idea that the characters in Gornick's memoir differ from the people they are based on.

The best answer is NOT:

A because though the paragraphs provide a few details implying a measure of popularity for Gornick's book, the main purpose of these two paragraphs, especially in the context of the passage as a whole, is to establish the idea in **B**, not to establish her book's popularity.

C because there is no indication in the passage that Gornick is overly frustrated with her readers' questions and comments.

D because Gornick argues in line 42 that "memoirs belong to the category of literature," but she is not suggesting that memoirs are fiction and should be classified as such. Her argument is that "emotional truth" is more important in memoirs than are completely literal and accurate details.

Question 22. The best answer is F because lines 8–16 explain that the party guest was disappointed because she felt Gornick was "nothing like the woman who wrote *Fierce Attachments*!" The quotation "We ourselves were just a rough draft of the written characters" (lines 20–21) exemplifies the discrepancy between an actual person and a character depicted in a memoir that led to the guest's disappointment.

The best answer is NOT:

G because the party guest's disappointment had nothing to do with Gornick's perceived similarity to Gornick's mother. The guest's disappointment stemmed from the fact that the narrator of the book and Gornick herself were "not exactly the same" (line 16).

H because the quotation in question refers to the idea that Gornick had hoped to express in her memoir, whereas the party guest's disappointment had to do with the unexpected difference between the narrator in the book and Gornick herself.

J because the quotation in question refers to the insight that Gornick had hoped to express in her memoir, whereas the party guest's disappointment had to do with the unexpected difference between the narrator in the book and Gornick herself.

READING • PRACTICE TEST 2 • EXPLANATORY ANSWERS

Question 23. The best answer is B because Gornick identifies the heart of her memoir in lines 31–32: the revelation that "I could not leave my mother because I had become my mother."

The best answer is NOT:

A because the author indicates that the walks she took with her mother in Manhattan in the 1980s are part of "the context in which the book is set" (lines 34–35), but the passage does not indicate that Gornick believes them to be the heart of her memoir.

C because the author indicates that her childhood experiences in the Bronx in the 1950s are part of "the context in which the book was set" (lines 34–35), but the passage does not indicate that Gornick believes them to be the heart of her memoir.

D because the author states in lines 31–32 that she believes the heart of her memoir is the revelation she had about having become her mother, not just that they had a shared history.

Question 24. The best answer is J because the author claims in lines 42–43 that "memoirs belong to the category of literature, not of journalism."

The best answer is NOT:

F because the author explicitly states in lines 42–43 that memoirs do not belong to the category of journalism.

G because the author explicitly claims in line 42 that "memoirs belong to the category of literature"; personal diaries are not mentioned in the passage.

H because the author explicitly claims in line 42 that "memoirs belong to the category of literature"; she also goes on to say that memoirs need not be as literally accurate as historical narrative (lines 43–46).

Question 25. The best answer is C because the first paragraph asserts that Hemingway's fiction contained autobiographical elements and his "protagonists are often conscious projections and explorations of the self" (lines 55–56).

The best answer is NOT:

A because the passage states in lines 53–56 that Hemingway's fictional protagonists are often projections of the self; there is no mention in the passage of Hemingway basing his protagonists on composites of his friends.

B because the passage states in lines 53–56 that Hemingway's fictional protagonists are often projections of the self; there is no mention in the passage of Hemingway basing his protagonists on family members.

D because the passage states in lines 53–56 that Hemingway's fictional protagonists are often projections of the self; there is no mention in the passage of Hemingway's protagonists being completely made-up characters.

Question 26. The best answer is F because the passage explains in lines 61–73 that "*A Moveable Feast* is particularly complex because Hemingway was clearly conscious that it would be his literary testament" and that he thus used the book to portray himself and his contemporaries in a certain light. Lines 73–76 state that "*A Moveable Feast* could hardly be an objective portrayal of its author and his contemporaries, and the accuracy of the anecdotes becomes an issue that can never be entirely resolved."

The best answer is NOT:

G because though the passage mentions that Hemingway "felt that he had been unfairly portrayed by some of his contemporaries" (lines 67–68), the passage indicates that the question of accuracy has to do with Hemingway's own writing, not with the writings of others.

H because the passage makes no mention of Hemingway being unable to produce documents to support his stories.

J because the passage makes no mention of Hemingway claiming the excellence of his memory or of others doubting such a claim.

Question 27. The best answer is B because the author of passage B states that "*A Moveable Feast* is particularly complex" (line 61) and that it "appears as a fascinating composite of relative factual accuracy and clear dishonesty of intent" (lines 87–88). These statements, in addition to details the author provides throughout the passage about Hemingway's purposeful blurring of fact and fiction, support the idea that the passage author believes *A Moveable Feast* to be a complex example of a book that combines fact and fiction.

The best answer is NOT:

A because the passage author makes no particular claim about the quality of any of Hemingway's other works, nor does she compare *A Moveable Feast* to any of Hemingway's other works.

C because the passage author makes clear that she believes the accuracy of *A Moveable Feast* is in question and "an issue that can never be entirely resolved" (lines 75–76).

D because the passage author does not suggest anywhere in the passage that *A Moveable Feast* should be read alongside other books from the time period; her argument pertains primarily only to *A Moveable Feast.*

READING • PRACTICE TEST 2 • EXPLANATORY ANSWERS

Question 28. The best answer is J because in passage A, Gornick's point is that her memoir was not necessarily literally true; what mattered to her was portraying "not the literalness of the situation, but the emotional truth of the story" (lines 38–39). She explains that the characters in her memoir differed from the actual people they were based on in that "these characters could not live independent of the story which had called them into life, as they existed for the sole purpose of serving that story" (lines 21–24). Similarly, throughout passage B, Hemingway is described as selectively using material from his life and blurring fact and fiction in order to best serve the story he wanted to tell: "He clearly overlooked a great deal of material, distorted some, and generally selected the episodes so that they would show him as innocent, honest, dedicated, and thoroughly enjoying life" (lines 83–86).

The best answer is NOT:

F because the passages indicate that both Gornick and Hemingway may not have been completely literally accurate in their memoirs, but their stories were based on a foundation of real-life situations—not wholly fictional ones.

G because though passage B states that Hemingway wanted "to leave to the world a flattering self-portrait" (lines 72–73), nowhere in passage A does Gornick indicate that she was concerned with portraying herself in a flattering way in her memoir.

H because though passage B states that Hemingway wanted to "present his own version of personal relationships" (lines 68–69) and "get back at people against whom he held a grudge" (lines 70–71), nowhere in passage A does Gornick indicate that she was motivated to write her memoir to "settle old scores."

READING • PRACTICE TEST 2 • EXPLANATORY ANSWERS

Question 29. The best answer is C because in passage A, Gornick explains her belief that, in memoir, complete literal accuracy is not necessary but that the point is to convey the "emotional truth of the story" (line 39), "trying, as honestly as possible, to get at the bottom of the tale at hand" (lines 48–49). She states that "what actually happened is only raw material; what matters is what the memoirist makes of what happened" (lines 39–41). Similarly, in passage B, Hemingway is portrayed as focusing on the particular stories he wanted to portray rather than focusing on factual accuracy: "He invented and lied relatively seldom about pure facts. When he did so, it was usually in order to reinforce the pattern he had created . . ." (lines 79–81). Thus it seems that both Gornick and Hemingway would agree that creating a cohesive, meaningful, and artistic whole is more important than detailing plain facts in a memoir.

The best answer is NOT:

A because there is no evidence in either passage that Gornick or Hemingway would believe that a writer has as much license to create when writing memoir as he or she does when writing fiction.

B because both passages indicate that the exact details of events are less important than the story the memoirist wants to tell that is based on memories of events. There is no evidence in either passage that Gornick or Hemingway would believe a writer should exclude an event entirely from a memoir if he or she cannot remember the exact details of the event.

D because there is no evidence in either passage that either Gornick or Hemingway would believe memoirists should write only about incidents that have documented evidence supporting their stories; neither author is concerned with evidence as fact.

Question 30. The best answer is G because the main idea expressed in passage A is that Gornick believes that "what actually happened is only raw material; what matters is what the memoirist makes of what happened" (lines 39–41). This idea echoes the quotation, which indicates that there is necessarily a difference between a memoir, which is a story, and the details and facts of real life.

The best answer is NOT:

F because though there is an anecdote about Gornick not meeting a particular reader's expectation, that story is simply supporting Gornick's point that characters in memoirs differ from real people; the anecdote does not relate to the quotation's claim that a memoir is a story and not a history.

H because the statement in passage B about Hemingway viewing *A Moveable Feast* as his literary testament explains only his motivation for writing the story the way he did; it doesn't relate to the quotation's claim that a memoir is a story and not a history.

J because the statement in passage B claiming that Hemingway seldom lied about pure facts focuses on the factual accuracy of his memoir or how much it reflected history, and this idea stands in contrast to the quotation's claim that memoir is in fact a story and not a history.

READING • PRACTICE TEST 2 • EXPLANATORY ANSWERS

Passage IV

Question 31. The best answer is D because the passage focuses on Suarez's research on colonizing ants and his conclusions about what enables some species to survive over others.

The best answer is NOT:

A because the passage makes clear that Argentine ants living in the United States had already been discovered; in order to examine why some colonizing organisms fail and some succeed, Suarez hoped to examine "early samples of Argentine ants collected in the United States" (lines 7–8).

B because the passage primarily focuses on ant species and does not compare the physical characteristics of ants to other insects. The passage also focuses more exclusively on the behavior of ants rather than their physical characteristics.

C because the passage makes no mention of the technology scientists use to determine the size of supercolonies.

Question 32. The best answer is G because peppered throughout this passage are certain colloquial phrases not often seen in scientific tracts, including that a scientist did it "the hard way" (lines 3–4), that one scientist was the "guru of ant gurus" (line 27), that Argentine ants were "wimps" (line 52), and that certain species always "made bank" (line 73). The use of such relaxed language helps create a casual tone for the reader.

The best answer is NOT:

F because the passage includes no personal anecdotes, never even mentioning the author's life or incorporating the use of the word *I*.

H because the passage author uses informal language at times but includes no quotations that are humorous.

J because the passage includes no "self-critical" asides, as again the author does not place himself in the passage in any way other than through his use of colloquial language.

READING • PRACTICE TEST 2 • EXPLANATORY ANSWERS

Question 33. The best answer is C because the first paragraph tells readers that Suarez "found some brown jars" at the Smithsonian in 1999, meaning this event occurred before the turn of the century, well before the other choices.

The best answer is NOT:

A because lines 63–66 state that "Case joined forces with Holway and Suarez" to study ant aggression but that happened only after Suarez and Holway had been classifying the ants (lines 28–29), which happened only after Suarez found the jars.

B because line 86 states that those ants were brought together "in 2009," a full decade after Suarez first found the brown jars.

D because lines 25–28 state that Holway and Ward were "solicited" to help Suarez with classifying the jars Suarez had previously found in the Smithsonian, which couldn't have happened until Suarez found the jars.

Question 34. The best answer is G because the opening sentence of the fifth paragraph states the focus of the paragraph: that when a group moves to a new area, "possible futures diverge" (line 42). What follows in the paragraph are examples of these possible futures and the indication that it's unlikely for a species to survive, let alone thrive in a new area.

The best answer is NOT:

F because the paragraph is not focused specifically on Argentine ants but discusses pioneering species in general and the likelihood that they will survive.

H because the paragraph does not provide a definition of invasive species, nor does the paragraph specifically mention ants.

J because the paragraph does not mention or focus on Argentine ants specifically, nor does it compare their survival rates with those of other species.

Question 35. The best answer is D because lines 56–58 state that if Argentine ants from different colonies are placed together, "they accept each other." This is noted directly after line 55 describes this as "strange" behavior, so it can be assumed that in most similar situations ants would fight one another, not accept one another.

The best answer is NOT:

A because the lines in question have nothing to do with the prevalence of supercolonies among ant species but with the trait of Argentine ants to accept each other.

B because the passage does not differentiate in these lines between California's Argentine ants and the same ants in other places.

C because the lines in question don't discuss California's ecosystem in any way.

READING • PRACTICE TEST 2 • EXPLANATORY ANSWERS

Question 36. The best answer is F because lines 1–3 state that Suarez was "like many biologists" who "struggled for years with the question of which colonizing organisms fail and which succeed."

The best answer is NOT:

G because lines 1–3 make it clear that Suarez was one of many; no dates are attached to the work done by the others.

H because lines 1–3 make it clear that many biologists struggled with this question. Moreover, there is no indication in the passage that Suarez was affiliated with the Smithsonian, and he worked alongside others—Holway and Ward—who were affiliated with different universities.

J because lines 1–3 state that Suarez was "like many biologists."

Question 37. The best answer is D because lines 15–18 state that what Suarez found in the brown jars other than Argentine ants was "far more interesting: some of the ethanol-filled jars were jammed with vials of ants collected at ports of entry in the eastern U.S. from 1927 to 1985." Those ants provided the basis for Suarez's research.

The best answer is NOT:

A because lines 14–15 state that "Suarez ultimately found relatively few samples of Argentine ants," meaning they were not "most of the samples" at all.

B because lines 25–28 state that Suarez recruited Ward and Holway to help him, not that they had accrued all these samples.

C because line 24 states that the brown jars revealed "394 separate samples" which line 29 explains were "232 distinct species," but the passage otherwise does not say how many of those ants might have been previously "undiscovered."

READING • PRACTICE TEST 2 • EXPLANATORY ANSWERS

Question 38. The best answer is F because line 52 clearly states Argentine ants are "squishy, small, stingless wimps."

The best answer is NOT:

G because lines 51–53 describe those ants as "ecologically dominant," yet small and not physically dominant.

H because the passage makes clear Suarez found samples of the ants in the Smithsonian, not that he discovered the species himself.

J because lines 84–88 state that "one conglomeration of Argentine ants stretched the length of California, another from Italy to Portugal . . . until, in 2009, workers from those two "colonies" (along with a third from Japan) were put together . . ." Thus, the passage makes clear that Argentine ants existed in Japan to such a degree that they could form with other colonies to create a supercolony. There is no indication in the passage that the species did not thrive in Japan.

Question 39. The best answer is B because lines 69–71 say that studies show that "aggressive ants wasted energy fighting (and dying), and so gathered less food and fared poorly."

The best answer is NOT:

A because the passage does not indicate that aggressive ants live in larger colonies than do peaceful ants.

C because the passage does not indicate that aggressive ants are more likely than peaceful ants to live in a colony.

D because the passage does not indicate that aggressive ants are more likely than peaceful ants to be a "survivor species." In fact, lines 69–71 state that aggressive ants spend more time "dying" because they fight so much.

Question 40. The best answer is G because this fact is stated clearly in lines 78–79: "Ants flash chemical badges identifying their home nest."

The best answer is NOT:

F because this idea is not supported by the passage, as lines 79–80 indicate that without those chemical markers, "no one knows who is friend or foe," with the end result of that being that peace breaks out. When peace breaks out, the term *colony* gets muddied and supercolonies form, with nests exchanging workers and queens.

H because the passage makes clear that supercolonies form only when chemical markers are absent and that swapping ants between colonies is not normal.

J because the passage discusses conglomerations of Argentine ants in supercolonies that go "the length of California, another from Italy to Portugal" (lines 85–86), but the passage doesn't indicate which of those is bigger or if one of those is the "largest" supercolony in the world.

SCIENCE • PRACTICE TEST 2 • EXPLANATORY ANSWERS

Passage I

1. **The best answer is B.** The figure shows the first generation (Individuals 1 and 2), the second generation (Individuals 4, 6, and 7), the third generation (Individuals 10, 11, 12, 13, 15, 16, and 17), and the fourth generation (Individuals 18–23). **A**, **C**, and **D** are incorrect; the figure shows four generations. **B** is correct.

2. **The best answer is G.** In order to answer this item, the examinee must know that the more closely related two individuals are to each other, the greater the genetic similarity is likely to be. According to the figure, Individuals 12 and 13 are sisters and would likely have the greatest genetic similarity. **F** is incorrect; individuals 3 and 4 are mates, not siblings. **G** is correct; Individuals 12 and 13 are sisters and would have the greatest genetic similarity. **H** is incorrect; Individuals 16 and 24 are not blood relatives. **J** is incorrect; Individuals 18 and 21 are second cousins.

3. **The best answer is D.** In order to answer this item, the examinee must know how to work a genetic cross. According to the figure, both Individuals 23 and 24 have Trait G. According to the passage, Trait G is recessive. It follows that Individuals 23 and 24 both have the *gg* genotype and that all their children will also have the *gg* genotype. All their children will therefore have Trait G. **A**, **B**, and **C** are incorrect; all four of the children will have Trait G. **D** is correct.

4. **The best answer is H.** According to the figure, the grandchildren of Individuals 1 and 2 are Individuals 10, 11, 12, 13, 15, 16, and 17. According to the key for the figure, a black circle and black square represent individuals with Trait G. Of the grandchildren, only Individuals 10 and 16 have Trait G. **F**, **G**, and **J** are incorrect; two of the grandchildren have Trait G. **H** is correct.

5. **The best answer is D.** In order to answer this item, the examinee should know that with a sex-linked trait, an affected female passes the trait to all her sons. According to the figure, Individuals 4 and 10 were the only females with Trait G who had a son. Individual 4's son, Individual 11, did not have Trait G. It follows that Trait G is not a sex-linked trait. **A** and **B** are incorrect; Trait G is not a sex-linked trait. **C** is incorrect; Individual 4 did not pass Trait G to her son. **D** is correct.

6. **The best answer is J.** According to the passage, Individual 21 has the Gene G genotype *Gg*. According to the figure, Individual 21 does not have Trait G. The passage states that Trait G is the recessive trait. An individual with the *Gg* genotype will have the dominant trait. **F** and **G** are incorrect; an individual with the *Gg* genotype will not have Trait G. **C** is incorrect; Trait G is a recessive trait. **J** is correct; the individual will not have Trait G, the recessive trait.

SCIENCE • PRACTICE TEST 2 • EXPLANATORY ANSWERS

Passage II

7. **The best answer is A.** In order to answer this item, the examinee must know that a balance is used to determine mass. Figure 2 gives the average mass per seed for each group. In order to determine the average mass per seed, the scientists would have to measure the mass of the seeds using a balance. **A** is correct. **B** is incorrect; the pH was not measured in this experiment. **C** is incorrect; a telescope is typically used for viewing distant objects and would not have been needed for this experiment. **D** is incorrect; a thermometer is used to measure temperature.

8. **The best answer is G.** According to the passage, the experiment was conducted to investigate the effects of different pollination treatments on fruit production and seed mass. **F** is incorrect; the location of the plants was not a variable in the experiment. **G** is correct; the experiment investigated different types of pollination. **H** is incorrect; the experiment did not measure the amount of time until fruit ripened. **J** is incorrect; the scientists did not question whether or not the flowers were typically pollinated by hummingbirds.

9. **The best answer is A.** According to Table 1, the flowers in Group 1 were self-pollinated whereas the flowers in Group 2 were cross-pollinated, using pollen from a single donor. **A** is correct. **B** is incorrect; the pollen used for Group 1 was from the same plant as the flowers in Group 1. **C** is incorrect; the pollen received by each Group 2 flower was collected from a single donor. **D** is incorrect; the pollen used for Group 1 was from a single plant.

10. **The best answer is H.** Figure 1 shows the percent of flowers that produced fruit. In order to calculate this percentage, the examinee must divide the number of flowers that produced fruit by the total number of flowers. **F** and **G** are incorrect; the number and mass of seeds is not relevant. **H** is correct. **J** is incorrect; the number of flowers producing fruit should be in the numerator, and the total number of flowers should be in the denominator.

11. **The best answer is B.** According to the passage, the anthers are the pollen-producing structures in the flower. By removing the anthers, the flower would not be able to spontaneously self-pollinate. **A** is incorrect; without the anthers present, the flowers would not be able to spontaneously self-pollinate. **B** is correct. **C** and **D** are incorrect; the presence or absence of anthers would not affect the ability of the flowers to be pollinated by hummingbirds.

12. **The best answer is G.** According to Figure 1, 0% of the flowers in Group 4 produced fruit. This suggests that the nylon bags successfully prevented the normal pollinators from pollinating the flowers, because none of the flowers in Group 4 were pollinated. **F** is incorrect; 20% of the flowers receiving self-pollination treatments produced fruit. **G** is correct; 0% of the flowers in Group 4 produced fruit, indicating that the nylon bags prevented normal pollinators from pollinating the flowers. **H** and **J** are incorrect; the data suggest that the bags did prevent the normal pollinators from pollinating the flowers.

SCIENCE • PRACTICE TEST 2 • EXPLANATORY ANSWERS

13. **The best answer is D.** The results given indicate the average mass per seed but not the number of seeds. Without knowing the number of seeds, one cannot figure out the total mass of the seeds. **A**, **B**, and **C** are incorrect; there is not enough information to determine the total mass of the seeds produced by the flowers. **D** is correct.

Passage III

14. **The best answer is H. F** and **G** are incorrect; both CH_4 and CO_2 were produced indicating that the organic matter was being broken down by both aerobic and anaerobic bacteria. **H** is correct; the organic material was most likely broken down more rapidly during the warmer summer months. **J** is incorrect; the organic material was most likely broken down less rapidly in the winter.

15. **The best answer is A.** According to Figures 1 and 2, for both bog soil and fen soil, as the water table levels decreased from +1 cm to −20 cm, the total CO_2 emissions increased. The figures also show that for both bog soil and fen soil, as the water table levels decreased, the total CH_4 emissions also decreased. **A** is correct. **B** is incorrect; the total CO_2 emissions increased. **C** is incorrect; the total CH_4 emissions decreased. **D** is incorrect; the total CO_2 emissions increased.

16. **The best answer is F.** According to the passage, gas emissions for each soil section were measured. By keeping a lid on each tank, the scientists would have been able to collect and measure all the gases emitted by each section. **F** is correct; the scientists would get a better measurement if none of the emitted gases were lost from the tank. **G** is incorrect; the scientists' results would be incorrect if atmospheric gases entered the tank. **H** is incorrect; the bacteria were in the soil and were not likely to leave the tanks. **J** is incorrect; the tanks were made of glass allowing sunlight to enter the tanks.

17. **The best answer is D.** According to Figures 1 and 2, the amount of CO_2 emitted from the fen soil at each WT level was greater than the amount emitted from the bog soil. The amount of CH_4 emitted from the fen soil at each WT level was also greater than the amount emitted from the bog soil. One may conclude that the levels of nutrients that sustain both types of bacteria are greater in the fen soil than in the bog soil. **A** is incorrect; the data suggest that the fen soil contains higher levels of nutrients for both aerobic and anaerobic bacteria. **B** is incorrect; the data suggest that there are higher levels of nutrients for aerobic bacteria in fen soil. **C** is incorrect; the data suggest that there are higher levels of nutrients for anaerobic bacteria in fen soil. **D** is correct.

18. **The best answer is F.** According to the passage, aerobic bacteria generate CO_2. The results illustrated in Figures 1 and 2 show that CO_2 was produced in both types of soil at all WT levels, indicating that aerobic bacteria were present in the soil sections that were completely submerged in water. **F** is correct. **G** is incorrect; CO_2 was also emitted from those sections. **H** and **J** are incorrect; the results indicate that aerobic bacteria were present in all the sections.

SCIENCE • PRACTICE TEST 2 • EXPLANATORY ANSWERS

19. **The best answer is C.** According to Figure 2, the fen soil section with a WT of −10 cm had a total CO_2 emission of 48 mol C/m^2 over the 3-month period. The average CO_2 emission per month is 48/3 = 16 mol C/m^2. **A** is incorrect; an average CO_2 emission of 10 mol C/m^2 would result in a total emission of 30 mol C/m^2. **B** is incorrect; an average CO_2 emission of 13 mol C/m^2 would result in a total emission of 39 mol C/m^2. **C** is correct; an average CO_2 emission of 16 mol C/m^2 would result in a total emission of 48 mol C/m^2. **D** is incorrect; an average CO_2 emission of 19 mol C/m^2 would result in a total emission of 57 mol C/m^2.

20. **The best answer is J. F** is incorrect; because the tanks were covered, no precipitation would fall on the samples. **G** is incorrect; all live plants were removed from the sections. **H** is incorrect; the volume of each sample was much less than the wetlands. **J** is correct; because the tanks were made of glass, the samples would be exposed to the same amount of daylight as the wetlands.

Passage IV

21. **The best answer is B.** Because the weight of an object is related to its mass, the door with the greatest mass is the door with the greatest weight. According to the passage, the door with the greatest weight had a weight of 76 lb and was used in Study 2. **A** is incorrect; the door used in Study 1 had a weight of 61 lb. **B** is correct; doors with weights of 51 lb, 61 lb, and 76 lb were used in Study 2. **C** is incorrect; the doors used in Study 3 each had a weight of 61 lb. **D** is incorrect; the doors tested in Study 2 had different masses.

22. **The best answer is F.** According to the passage, in Study 2, D was held constant, and W and S were varied. In Study 3, W was held constant, and D and S were varied. **F** is correct. **G** is incorrect; W was varied in Study 2. **H** is incorrect; W was varied in Study 2 only. **J** is incorrect; W was held constant in Study 3 only.

23. **The best answer is D.** According to the results of Study 2, when $D = 30$ in and $S = 50$ in, $F_{n,av}$ increases as W increases. When $W = 76$ lb, $F_{n,av} = 46$ lb. If an additional door with $W = 90$ lb had been tested, $F_{n,av}$ would most likely have been greater than 46 lb. **A**, **B**, and **C** are incorrect; $F_{n,av}$ would have been greater than 45 lb. **D** is correct.

24. **The best answer is H.** Figure 1 shows that $F_{v,av}$ remained constant at all values of S. Figure 1 also shows that $F_{h,av}$ was greater than $F_{v,av}$ for all $S < 30$ in, equal to $F_{v,av}$ for $S = 30$ in, and less than $F_{v,av}$ for all $S > 30$ in. **F** and **G** are incorrect; $F_{h,av}$ was greater than $F_{v,av}$ for all $S < 30$ in. **H** is correct; $F_{h,av}$ was greater than $F_{v,av}$ for all $S < 30$ in, and less than $F_{v,av}$ for all $S > 30$ in. **J** is incorrect; $F_{h,av}$ was less than $F_{v,av}$ for all $S > 30$ in.

SCIENCE • PRACTICE TEST 2 • EXPLANATORY ANSWERS

25. **The best answer is B.** According to Figure 2, in Study 2, the lowest $F_{n,av}$ was 27 lb. According to Figure 3, in Study 3, the lowest $F_{n,av}$ was 33 lb. The lowest value for $F_{n,av}$ of 27 lb was measured when $W = 51$ lb, $D = 30$ in, and $S = 70$ in. **A** is incorrect; under these conditions, $F_{n,av} = 45$ lb. **B** is correct; under these conditions, $F_{n,av} = 27$ lb. **C** is incorrect; under these conditions, $F_{n,av} = 48$ lb. **D** is incorrect; under these conditions, $F_{n,av} = 33$ lb.

26. **The best answer is J.** Figure 1 shows that as *S* was varied, there was no change in $F_{v,av}$, while $F_{h,av}$ decreased as *S* increased. $F_{v,av}$ was independent of *S*.**F** is incorrect; this shows that $F_{h,av}$ was dependent on *S*.**G** is incorrect; $F_{h,av}$ did not remain constant as *S* increased. **H** is incorrect; $F_{v,av}$ did not decrease as *S* increased. **J** is correct; $F_{v,av}$ remained constant as *S* increased.

27. **The best answer is C. A** is incorrect; according to Figure 3, under these conditions, the net force on each hinge was 55 lb and the hinge would not break. **B** is incorrect; under these conditions, the net force on each hinge was 35 lb and the hinge would not break. **C** is correct; under these conditions, the net force on each hinge was 62 lb and the hinge would break. **D** is incorrect; under these conditions, the net force on each hinge was 37 lb and the hinge would not break.

Passage V

28. **The best answer is J.** According to the passage, none of the students mentioned argon. All four students referred to "almost all the gas remaining . . .," which suggests that other gases, such as argon, could be present. The fact that air contains less than 1% argon by volume does not weaken the explanation given by any of the students. **F**, **G**, and **H** are incorrect; the information does not weaken any of the explanations. **J** is correct.

29. **The best answer is A.** Because the quartz tube was heated with a Bunsen burner, it was important that the silicone hoses had a strong resistance to heat. Because a chemical reaction was taking place when the steel wool was heated, it was important that the silicone hoses have a low chemical reactivity. No water was used in the experiment, nor was water generated, and therefore the solubility of the silicone hoses in water would not be important. **A** is correct; it is most important that the silicone hoses be resistant to heat and have a low chemical reactivity. **B** is incorrect; the hoses should also have low chemical reactivity, and the water solubility of the hoses is not relevant. **C** is incorrect; the hoses should also have strong resistance to heat, and the water solubility of the hoses is not relevant. **D** is incorrect; the water solubility of the hoses is not relevant.

SCIENCE • PRACTICE TEST 2 • EXPLANATORY ANSWERS

30. **The best answer is J.** According to Student 4, the Fe reacted with CO_2 in the air, and after the reaction, almost all the remaining gas was O_2. Because the CO_2 was used up, the percent CO_2 by volume decreased. Because the remaining gas was nearly all O_2, the percent O_2 by volume increased as the CO_2 reacted. **F** is incorrect; the percent CO_2 decreased as the CO_2 reacted with the Fe. **G** is incorrect; the percent CO_2 decreased and the percent O_2 increased. **H** is incorrect; the percent O_2 increased as the amount of CO_2 decreased. **J** is correct.

31. **The best answer is C.** According to Student 1, air contains 20% N_2 by volume, and after the N_2 reacted with the Fe, almost all the gas remaining was O_2. It follows that Student 1 believes air is approximately 80% O_2. Student 2 states that air contains about 80% O_2. Student 3 states that air contains 20% O_2 by volume, and after the O_2 reacted with the Fe, almost all the gas remaining was N_2. It follows that Student 3 believes air is approximately 80% N_2. According to Student 4, air contains about 20% CO_2 by volume, and after the CO_2 reacted with the Fe, almost all the gas remaining was O_2. It follows that Student 4 believes air is approximately 80% O_2. Students 1, 2, and 4 all believe that air contains approximately 80% O_2 by volume and therefore would agree that, by volume, air contains more O_2 than N_2. **A**, **B**, and **D** are incorrect; Students 1, 2, and 4 would agree that, by volume, air contains more O_2 than N_2. Student 3 states that air is approximately 80% N_2. **C** is correct.

32. **The best answer is H.** In order to answer this item, the examinee needs to understand how reactants and products are placed in chemical equations. According to Student 3, the Fe reacted with the O_2 to form Fe_2O_3. Fe and O_2 are reactants and will appear on the left side of the equation. Fe_2O_3 is the product and will appear on the right side of the equation. **F** is incorrect; the reactants and product are on the wrong sides of this equation. **G** is incorrect; N_2 and FeN are not involved in the reaction. **H** is correct. **J** is incorrect; N_2 and FeN are not involved in the reaction.

33. **The best answer is B.** According to the passage, Students 1 and 4 claim that almost all the gas remaining is O_2. Student 2 claims that almost all the remaining gas is a mixture of about 75% O_2 and 25% N_2. Student 3 claims that almost all the remaining gas is N_2. Students 2 and 3 would agree that the gas remaining was at least 20% N_2 by volume. **A** is incorrect; Student 3 would also agree. **B** is correct. **C** is incorrect; Students 1 and 4 would not agree. **D** is incorrect; Students 2 and 3 would agree.

34. **The best answer is G.** According to Student 1, the Fe reacted with *all* the N_2, indicating that N_2 is the limiting reagent, and Fe is present in excess. Student 2 stated that the Fe reacted with *some* of the O_2, indicating the Fe is the limiting reagent and O_2 is present in excess. Student 3 stated that the Fe reacted with *all* the O_2, indicating that O_2 is the limiting reagent and Fe is present in excess. Student 4 stated that the steel wool reacted with *all* the CO_2, indicating that CO_2 was the limiting reagent and Fe was present in excess. Only Student 2 would likely agree that Fe was the limiting reagent. **F**, **H**, and **J** are incorrect; only Student 2 would agree that Fe was the limiting reagent. **G** is correct.

SCIENCE • PRACTICE TEST 2 • EXPLANATORY ANSWERS

Passage VI

35. **The best answer is C.** According to Table 2, the Λ^0 baryon contains 2 spin-up quarks and 1 spin-down quark. The sum of those spins is therefore $+\frac{1}{2}\hbar$. The Δ^0 baryon contains 3 spin-up quarks. The sum of those spins is therefore $+\frac{3}{2}\hbar$. A, B, and D are incorrect; the spin of the Λ^0 baryon is $+\frac{1}{2}\hbar$, and the spin of the Δ^0 baryon is $+\frac{3}{2}\hbar$. **C** is correct.

36. **The best answer is G.** In order to answer this item, the examinee needs to know that an "electrically neutral" particle has an electric charge of 0. The quark charges are given in Table 1. **F** is incorrect; *u, c,* and *t* quarks each have a charge of $+\frac{2}{3}$ so the net charge is +2. **G** is correct; a *u* quark has a charge of $+\frac{2}{3}$ and the *d* and *s* quarks each have a charge of $-\frac{1}{3}$, so the net charge is 0. **H** is incorrect; this baryon has 3 spin-down quarks. **J** is incorrect; this baryon has 3 spin-up quarks.

37. **The best answer is D.** In order to answer this item, the examinee needs to know that the charge on a proton is +1. According to Table 2, the quark content of a proton is *uud*. According to Table 1, a *u* quark has a charge of $+\frac{2}{3}$ and each *d* quark has a charge of $-\frac{1}{3}$, so the net charge is +1, which is consistent with the known charge of a proton. **A, B,** and **C** are incorrect. **D** is correct.

38. **The best answer is F.** According to Table 2, the quark content of a Ω^- baryon is *sss*. According to Table 1, each *s* quark has a charge of $-\frac{1}{3}$ and, therefore, the net charge of a Ω^- baryon is −1. **F** is correct; the *d, s,* and *b* quarks each have a charge of $-\frac{1}{3}$, so the net charge is −1. **G** is incorrect; each *s* quark has a charge of $-\frac{1}{3}$ and the *c* quark has a charge of $+\frac{2}{3}$, so the net charge is 0. **H** is incorrect; each *s* quark has a charge of $-\frac{1}{3}$ and the *t* quark has a charge of $+\frac{2}{3}$, so the net charge is 0. **J** is incorrect; the *u* and *c* quarks each have a charge of $+\frac{2}{3}$ and the *s* quark has a charge of $-\frac{1}{3}$, so the net charge is +1.

39. **The best answer is A.** In order to answer this item, the examinee must know that nucleons are limited to protons and neutrons. According to Table 2, the quark content of a proton is *uud*, and the quark content of a neutron is *udd*. Based on this information, one can conclude that nuclei are made up of *u* and *d* quarks. **A** is correct. **B, C,** and **D** are incorrect; there are only *u* and *d* quarks in protons and neutrons.

40. **The best answer is F.** The masses and charges for the quarks are given in Table 1. **F** is correct; the *d* quark has a mass of 5 MeV and a negative charge. The *u* quark has a mass of 3 MeV and a positive charge. The quark with a positive charge is *not* more massive than the quark with the negative charge. **G** is incorrect; the *s* quark has a mass of 104 MeV and a negative charge. The *c* quark has a mass of 1,270 MeV and a positive charge. The positively charged quark *is* more massive than the negatively charged quark. **H** is incorrect; the *b* quark has a mass of 4,200 MeV and a negative charge. The *t* quark has a mass of 171,200 MeV and a positive charge. The positively charged quark *is* more massive than the negatively charged quark. **J** is incorrect; the statement is not true for Generation 1.

PAGE 1

The ACT® *Sample Answer Sheet*

EXAMINEE STATEMENT, CERTIFICATION, AND SIGNATURE

1. Read the following **Statement:** By submitting this answer document, I agree to comply with and be bound by the *Terms and Conditions: Testing Rules and Policies for the ACT® Test* provided in the ACT registration materials for this test, including those concerning test security, score cancellation, examinee remedies, binding arbitration, and consent to the processing of my personally identifying information, including the collection, use, transfer, and disclosure of information as described in the ACT Privacy Policy (www.act.org/privacy.html).

   I understand that ACT owns the test questions and responses and affirm that I will not share any test questions or responses with anyone by any form of communication before, during, or after the test administration. I understand that assuming anyone else's identity to take this test is strictly prohibited and may violate the law and subject me to legal penalties.

   International Examinees: By my signature, I am also providing my consent to ACT to transfer my personally identifying information to the United States to ACT, or a third-party service provider for processing, where it will be subject to use and disclosure under the laws of the United States. I acknowledge and agree that it may also be accessible to law enforcement and national security authorities in the United States.

2. Copy the **Certification** shown below (only the text in italics) on the lines provided. Write in your normal handwriting.

Certification: *I agree to the Statement above and certify that I am the person whose name and address appear on this answer document.*

Your Signature

Today's Date

Do NOT mark in this shaded area.

USE A SOFT LEAD NO. 2 PENCIL ONLY.
(Do NOT use a mechanical pencil, ink, ballpoint, correction fluid, or felt-tip pen.)

A NAME, MAILING ADDRESS, AND TELEPHONE (Please print.)

Last Name | First Name | MI (Middle Initial)

House Number & Street (Apt. No.); or PO Box & No.; or RR & No.

City | State/Province | ZIP/Postal Code

Area Code / Number | Country

ACT, Inc.—Confidential Restricted when data present

ALL examinees must complete block A – please print.

Blocks B, C, and D are required for all examinees. Find the MATCHING INFORMATION on your ticket. Enter it EXACTLY the same way, even if any of the information is missing or incorrect. Fill in the corresponding ovals. If you do not complete these blocks to match your previous information EXACTLY, your scores will be **delayed up to 8 weeks.**

ACT®

PO BOX 168, IOWA CITY, IA 52243-0168

B MATCH NAME (First 5 letters of last name)

A B C D E F G H I J K L M N O P Q R S T U V W X Y Z

C MATCH NUMBER

1 2 3 4 5 6 7 8 9 0

D DATE OF BIRTH

Month	Day	Year
January	0 1 2 3	0 1 2 3 4 5 6 7 8 9
February		
March		
April		
May		
June		
July		
August		
September		
October		
November		
December		

 22877 A011 215 190 Rev 1 IM-(A)199526-001:654321 Printed in the US.

PAGE 2

Marking Directions: Mark only **one** oval for each question. Fill in response completely. Erase errors cleanly without smudging.

Correct mark: ◯ ⬤ ◯ ◯

Do NOT use these *incorrect* or *bad* marks.

Incorrect marks:
Overlapping mark:
Cross-out mark:
Smudged erasure:
Mark is too light:

BOOKLET NUMBER

①	①	①	①	①	①
②	②	②	②	②	②
③	③	③	③	③	③
④	④	④	④	④	④
⑤	⑤	⑤	⑤	⑤	⑤
⑥	⑥	⑥	⑥	⑥	⑥
⑦	⑦	⑦	⑦	⑦	⑦
⑧	⑧	⑧	⑧	⑧	⑧
⑨	⑨	⑨	⑨	⑨	⑨
⓪	⓪	⓪	⓪	⓪	⓪

FORM

Print your 5-character **Test Form** in the boxes above and fill in the corresponding oval at the right.

BE SURE TO FILL IN THE CORRECT FORM OVAL.

◯ 16MC1 ◯ 18MC4
◯ 16MC2 ◯ 19MC5
◯ 16MC3

TEST 1

1 Ⓐ Ⓑ Ⓒ Ⓓ	14 Ⓕ Ⓖ Ⓗ Ⓙ	27 Ⓐ Ⓑ Ⓒ Ⓓ	40 Ⓕ Ⓖ Ⓗ Ⓙ	53 Ⓐ Ⓑ Ⓒ Ⓓ	66 Ⓕ Ⓖ Ⓗ Ⓙ
2 Ⓕ Ⓖ Ⓗ Ⓙ	15 Ⓐ Ⓑ Ⓒ Ⓓ	28 Ⓕ Ⓖ Ⓗ Ⓙ	41 Ⓐ Ⓑ Ⓒ Ⓓ	54 Ⓕ Ⓖ Ⓗ Ⓙ	67 Ⓐ Ⓑ Ⓒ Ⓓ
3 Ⓐ Ⓑ Ⓒ Ⓓ	16 Ⓕ Ⓖ Ⓗ Ⓙ	29 Ⓐ Ⓑ Ⓒ Ⓓ	42 Ⓕ Ⓖ Ⓗ Ⓙ	55 Ⓐ Ⓑ Ⓒ Ⓓ	68 Ⓕ Ⓖ Ⓗ Ⓙ
4 Ⓕ Ⓖ Ⓗ Ⓙ	17 Ⓐ Ⓑ Ⓒ Ⓓ	30 Ⓕ Ⓖ Ⓗ Ⓙ	43 Ⓐ Ⓑ Ⓒ Ⓓ	56 Ⓕ Ⓖ Ⓗ Ⓙ	69 Ⓐ Ⓑ Ⓒ Ⓓ
5 Ⓐ Ⓑ Ⓒ Ⓓ	18 Ⓕ Ⓖ Ⓗ Ⓙ	31 Ⓐ Ⓑ Ⓒ Ⓓ	44 Ⓕ Ⓖ Ⓗ Ⓙ	57 Ⓐ Ⓑ Ⓒ Ⓓ	70 Ⓕ Ⓖ Ⓗ Ⓙ
6 Ⓕ Ⓖ Ⓗ Ⓙ	19 Ⓐ Ⓑ Ⓒ Ⓓ	32 Ⓕ Ⓖ Ⓗ Ⓙ	45 Ⓐ Ⓑ Ⓒ Ⓓ	58 Ⓕ Ⓖ Ⓗ Ⓙ	71 Ⓐ Ⓑ Ⓒ Ⓓ
7 Ⓐ Ⓑ Ⓒ Ⓓ	20 Ⓕ Ⓖ Ⓗ Ⓙ	33 Ⓐ Ⓑ Ⓒ Ⓓ	46 Ⓕ Ⓖ Ⓗ Ⓙ	59 Ⓐ Ⓑ Ⓒ Ⓓ	72 Ⓕ Ⓖ Ⓗ Ⓙ
8 Ⓕ Ⓖ Ⓗ Ⓙ	21 Ⓐ Ⓑ Ⓒ Ⓓ	34 Ⓕ Ⓖ Ⓗ Ⓙ	47 Ⓐ Ⓑ Ⓒ Ⓓ	60 Ⓕ Ⓖ Ⓗ Ⓙ	73 Ⓐ Ⓑ Ⓒ Ⓓ
9 Ⓐ Ⓑ Ⓒ Ⓓ	22 Ⓕ Ⓖ Ⓗ Ⓙ	35 Ⓐ Ⓑ Ⓒ Ⓓ	48 Ⓕ Ⓖ Ⓗ Ⓙ	61 Ⓐ Ⓑ Ⓒ Ⓓ	74 Ⓕ Ⓖ Ⓗ Ⓙ
10 Ⓕ Ⓖ Ⓗ Ⓙ	23 Ⓐ Ⓑ Ⓒ Ⓓ	36 Ⓕ Ⓖ Ⓗ Ⓙ	49 Ⓐ Ⓑ Ⓒ Ⓓ	62 Ⓕ Ⓖ Ⓗ Ⓙ	75 Ⓐ Ⓑ Ⓒ Ⓓ
11 Ⓐ Ⓑ Ⓒ Ⓓ	24 Ⓕ Ⓖ Ⓗ Ⓙ	37 Ⓐ Ⓑ Ⓒ Ⓓ	50 Ⓕ Ⓖ Ⓗ Ⓙ	63 Ⓐ Ⓑ Ⓒ Ⓓ	
12 Ⓕ Ⓖ Ⓗ Ⓙ	25 Ⓐ Ⓑ Ⓒ Ⓓ	38 Ⓕ Ⓖ Ⓗ Ⓙ	51 Ⓐ Ⓑ Ⓒ Ⓓ	64 Ⓕ Ⓖ Ⓗ Ⓙ	
13 Ⓐ Ⓑ Ⓒ Ⓓ	26 Ⓕ Ⓖ Ⓗ Ⓙ	39 Ⓐ Ⓑ Ⓒ Ⓓ	52 Ⓕ Ⓖ Ⓗ Ⓙ	65 Ⓐ Ⓑ Ⓒ Ⓓ	

TEST 2

1 Ⓐ Ⓑ Ⓒ Ⓓ Ⓔ	11 Ⓐ Ⓑ Ⓒ Ⓓ Ⓔ	21 Ⓐ Ⓑ Ⓒ Ⓓ Ⓔ	31 Ⓐ Ⓑ Ⓒ Ⓓ Ⓔ	41 Ⓐ Ⓑ Ⓒ Ⓓ Ⓔ	51 Ⓐ Ⓑ Ⓒ Ⓓ Ⓔ
2 Ⓕ Ⓖ Ⓗ Ⓙ Ⓚ	12 Ⓕ Ⓖ Ⓗ Ⓙ Ⓚ	22 Ⓕ Ⓖ Ⓗ Ⓙ Ⓚ	32 Ⓕ Ⓖ Ⓗ Ⓙ Ⓚ	42 Ⓕ Ⓖ Ⓗ Ⓙ Ⓚ	52 Ⓕ Ⓖ Ⓗ Ⓙ Ⓚ
3 Ⓐ Ⓑ Ⓒ Ⓓ Ⓔ	13 Ⓐ Ⓑ Ⓒ Ⓓ Ⓔ	23 Ⓐ Ⓑ Ⓒ Ⓓ Ⓔ	33 Ⓐ Ⓑ Ⓒ Ⓓ Ⓔ	43 Ⓐ Ⓑ Ⓒ Ⓓ Ⓔ	53 Ⓐ Ⓑ Ⓒ Ⓓ Ⓔ
4 Ⓕ Ⓖ Ⓗ Ⓙ Ⓚ	14 Ⓕ Ⓖ Ⓗ Ⓙ Ⓚ	24 Ⓕ Ⓖ Ⓗ Ⓙ Ⓚ	34 Ⓕ Ⓖ Ⓗ Ⓙ Ⓚ	44 Ⓕ Ⓖ Ⓗ Ⓙ Ⓚ	54 Ⓕ Ⓖ Ⓗ Ⓙ Ⓚ
5 Ⓐ Ⓑ Ⓒ Ⓓ Ⓔ	15 Ⓐ Ⓑ Ⓒ Ⓓ Ⓔ	25 Ⓐ Ⓑ Ⓒ Ⓓ Ⓔ	35 Ⓐ Ⓑ Ⓒ Ⓓ Ⓔ	45 Ⓐ Ⓑ Ⓒ Ⓓ Ⓔ	55 Ⓐ Ⓑ Ⓒ Ⓓ Ⓔ
6 Ⓕ Ⓖ Ⓗ Ⓙ Ⓚ	16 Ⓕ Ⓖ Ⓗ Ⓙ Ⓚ	26 Ⓕ Ⓖ Ⓗ Ⓙ Ⓚ	36 Ⓕ Ⓖ Ⓗ Ⓙ Ⓚ	46 Ⓕ Ⓖ Ⓗ Ⓙ Ⓚ	56 Ⓕ Ⓖ Ⓗ Ⓙ Ⓚ
7 Ⓐ Ⓑ Ⓒ Ⓓ Ⓔ	17 Ⓐ Ⓑ Ⓒ Ⓓ Ⓔ	27 Ⓐ Ⓑ Ⓒ Ⓓ Ⓔ	37 Ⓐ Ⓑ Ⓒ Ⓓ Ⓔ	47 Ⓐ Ⓑ Ⓒ Ⓓ Ⓔ	57 Ⓐ Ⓑ Ⓒ Ⓓ Ⓔ
8 Ⓕ Ⓖ Ⓗ Ⓙ Ⓚ	18 Ⓕ Ⓖ Ⓗ Ⓙ Ⓚ	28 Ⓕ Ⓖ Ⓗ Ⓙ Ⓚ	38 Ⓕ Ⓖ Ⓗ Ⓙ Ⓚ	48 Ⓕ Ⓖ Ⓗ Ⓙ Ⓚ	58 Ⓕ Ⓖ Ⓗ Ⓙ Ⓚ
9 Ⓐ Ⓑ Ⓒ Ⓓ Ⓔ	19 Ⓐ Ⓑ Ⓒ Ⓓ Ⓔ	29 Ⓐ Ⓑ Ⓒ Ⓓ Ⓔ	39 Ⓐ Ⓑ Ⓒ Ⓓ Ⓔ	49 Ⓐ Ⓑ Ⓒ Ⓓ Ⓔ	59 Ⓐ Ⓑ Ⓒ Ⓓ Ⓔ
10 Ⓕ Ⓖ Ⓗ Ⓙ Ⓚ	20 Ⓕ Ⓖ Ⓗ Ⓙ Ⓚ	30 Ⓕ Ⓖ Ⓗ Ⓙ Ⓚ	40 Ⓕ Ⓖ Ⓗ Ⓙ Ⓚ	50 Ⓕ Ⓖ Ⓗ Ⓙ Ⓚ	60 Ⓕ Ⓖ Ⓗ Ⓙ Ⓚ

TEST 3

1 Ⓐ Ⓑ Ⓒ Ⓓ	8 Ⓕ Ⓖ Ⓗ Ⓙ	15 Ⓐ Ⓑ Ⓒ Ⓓ	22 Ⓕ Ⓖ Ⓗ Ⓙ	29 Ⓐ Ⓑ Ⓒ Ⓓ	36 Ⓕ Ⓖ Ⓗ Ⓙ
2 Ⓕ Ⓖ Ⓗ Ⓙ	9 Ⓐ Ⓑ Ⓒ Ⓓ	16 Ⓕ Ⓖ Ⓗ Ⓙ	23 Ⓐ Ⓑ Ⓒ Ⓓ	30 Ⓕ Ⓖ Ⓗ Ⓙ	37 Ⓐ Ⓑ Ⓒ Ⓓ
3 Ⓐ Ⓑ Ⓒ Ⓓ	10 Ⓕ Ⓖ Ⓗ Ⓙ	17 Ⓐ Ⓑ Ⓒ Ⓓ	24 Ⓕ Ⓖ Ⓗ Ⓙ	31 Ⓐ Ⓑ Ⓒ Ⓓ	38 Ⓕ Ⓖ Ⓗ Ⓙ
4 Ⓕ Ⓖ Ⓗ Ⓙ	11 Ⓐ Ⓑ Ⓒ Ⓓ	18 Ⓕ Ⓖ Ⓗ Ⓙ	25 Ⓐ Ⓑ Ⓒ Ⓓ	32 Ⓕ Ⓖ Ⓗ Ⓙ	39 Ⓐ Ⓑ Ⓒ Ⓓ
5 Ⓐ Ⓑ Ⓒ Ⓓ	12 Ⓕ Ⓖ Ⓗ Ⓙ	19 Ⓐ Ⓑ Ⓒ Ⓓ	26 Ⓕ Ⓖ Ⓗ Ⓙ	33 Ⓐ Ⓑ Ⓒ Ⓓ	40 Ⓕ Ⓖ Ⓗ Ⓙ
6 Ⓕ Ⓖ Ⓗ Ⓙ	13 Ⓐ Ⓑ Ⓒ Ⓓ	20 Ⓕ Ⓖ Ⓗ Ⓙ	27 Ⓐ Ⓑ Ⓒ Ⓓ	34 Ⓕ Ⓖ Ⓗ Ⓙ	
7 Ⓐ Ⓑ Ⓒ Ⓓ	14 Ⓕ Ⓖ Ⓗ Ⓙ	21 Ⓐ Ⓑ Ⓒ Ⓓ	28 Ⓕ Ⓖ Ⓗ Ⓙ	35 Ⓐ Ⓑ Ⓒ Ⓓ	

TEST 4

1 Ⓐ Ⓑ Ⓒ Ⓓ	8 Ⓕ Ⓖ Ⓗ Ⓙ	15 Ⓐ Ⓑ Ⓒ Ⓓ	22 Ⓕ Ⓖ Ⓗ Ⓙ	29 Ⓐ Ⓑ Ⓒ Ⓓ	36 Ⓕ Ⓖ Ⓗ Ⓙ
2 Ⓕ Ⓖ Ⓗ Ⓙ	9 Ⓐ Ⓑ Ⓒ Ⓓ	16 Ⓕ Ⓖ Ⓗ Ⓙ	23 Ⓐ Ⓑ Ⓒ Ⓓ	30 Ⓕ Ⓖ Ⓗ Ⓙ	37 Ⓐ Ⓑ Ⓒ Ⓓ
3 Ⓐ Ⓑ Ⓒ Ⓓ	10 Ⓕ Ⓖ Ⓗ Ⓙ	17 Ⓐ Ⓑ Ⓒ Ⓓ	24 Ⓕ Ⓖ Ⓗ Ⓙ	31 Ⓐ Ⓑ Ⓒ Ⓓ	38 Ⓕ Ⓖ Ⓗ Ⓙ
4 Ⓕ Ⓖ Ⓗ Ⓙ	11 Ⓐ Ⓑ Ⓒ Ⓓ	18 Ⓕ Ⓖ Ⓗ Ⓙ	25 Ⓐ Ⓑ Ⓒ Ⓓ	32 Ⓕ Ⓖ Ⓗ Ⓙ	39 Ⓐ Ⓑ Ⓒ Ⓓ
5 Ⓐ Ⓑ Ⓒ Ⓓ	12 Ⓕ Ⓖ Ⓗ Ⓙ	19 Ⓐ Ⓑ Ⓒ Ⓓ	26 Ⓕ Ⓖ Ⓗ Ⓙ	33 Ⓐ Ⓑ Ⓒ Ⓓ	40 Ⓕ Ⓖ Ⓗ Ⓙ
6 Ⓕ Ⓖ Ⓗ Ⓙ	13 Ⓐ Ⓑ Ⓒ Ⓓ	20 Ⓕ Ⓖ Ⓗ Ⓙ	27 Ⓐ Ⓑ Ⓒ Ⓓ	34 Ⓕ Ⓖ Ⓗ Ⓙ	
7 Ⓐ Ⓑ Ⓒ Ⓓ	14 Ⓕ Ⓖ Ⓗ Ⓙ	21 Ⓐ Ⓑ Ⓒ Ⓓ	28 Ⓕ Ⓖ Ⓗ Ⓙ	35 Ⓐ Ⓑ Ⓒ Ⓓ	

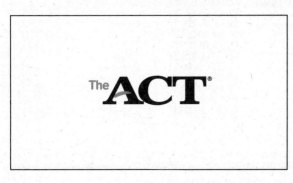

PAGE 1

The ACT® *Sample Answer Sheet*

EXAMINEE STATEMENT, CERTIFICATION, AND SIGNATURE

1. Read the following **Statement:** By submitting this answer document, I agree to comply with and be bound by the *Terms and Conditions: Testing Rules and Policies for the ACT® Test* provided in the ACT registration materials for this test, including those concerning test security, score cancellation, examinee remedies, binding arbitration, and consent to the processing of my personally identifying information, including the collection, use, transfer, and disclosure of information as described in the ACT Privacy Policy (www.act.org/privacy.html).

   I understand that ACT owns the test questions and responses and affirm that I will not share any test questions or responses with anyone by any form of communication before, during, or after the test administration. I understand that assuming anyone else's identity to take this test is strictly prohibited and may violate the law and subject me to legal penalties.

   International Examinees: By my signature, I am also providing my consent to ACT to transfer my personally identifying information to the United States to ACT, or a third-party service provider for processing, where it will be subject to use and disclosure under the laws of the United States. I acknowledge and agree that it may also be accessible to law enforcement and national security authorities in the United States.

2. Copy the **Certification** shown below (only the text in italics) on the lines provided. Write in your normal handwriting.

Certification: *I agree to the Statement above and certify that I am the person whose name and address appear on this answer document.*

____

____

____

Your Signature Today's Date

Do NOT mark in this shaded area.

USE A SOFT LEAD NO. 2 PENCIL ONLY.
(Do NOT use a mechanical pencil, ink, ballpoint, correction fluid, or felt-tip pen.)

A NAME, MAILING ADDRESS, AND TELEPHONE (Please print.)

Last Name First Name MI (Middle Initial)

House Number & Street (Apt. No.); or PO Box & No.; or RR & No.

City State/Province ZIP/Postal Code

/

Area Code Number Country

ACT, Inc.—Confidential Restricted when data present

ALL examinees must complete block A – please print.

Blocks B, C, and D are required for all examinees. Find the MATCHING INFORMATION on your ticket. Enter it EXACTLY the same way, even if any of the information is missing or incorrect. Fill in the corresponding ovals. If you do not complete these blocks to match your previous information EXACTLY, your scores will be **delayed up to 8 weeks.**

ACT®

PO BOX 168, IOWA CITY, IA 52243-0168

B MATCH NAME (First 5 letters of last name)

A B C D E F G H I J K L M N O P Q R S T U V W X Y Z

C MATCH NUMBER

1 2 3 4 5 6 7 8 9 0

D DATE OF BIRTH

Month	Day	Year
January	1 2 3 0	1 2 3 4 5 6 7 8 9 0
February		
March		
April		
May		
June		
July		
August		
September		
October		
November		
December		

A011 215 190 Rev 1

IM-(A)199526-001:654321 Printed in the US.

PAGE 2

Marking Directions: Mark only **one** oval for each question. Fill in response completely. Erase errors cleanly without smudging.

Correct mark:

Do NOT use these *incorrect* **or** *bad* **marks.**

Incorrect marks:
Overlapping mark:
Cross-out mark:
Smudged erasure:
Mark is too light:

BOOKLET NUMBER

1	1	1	1	1	1
2	2	2	2	2	2
3	3	3	3	3	3
4	4	4	4	4	4
5	5	5	5	5	5
6	6	6	6	6	6
7	7	7	7	7	7
8	8	8	8	8	8
9	9	9	9	9	9
0	0	0	0	0	0

FORM

Print your 5-character **Test Form** in the boxes above and fill in the corresponding oval at the right.

BE SURE TO FILL IN THE CORRECT FORM OVAL.

- 16MC1
- 16MC2
- 16MC3
- 18MC4
- 19MC5

TEST 1

1 A B C D	14 F G H J	27 A B C D	40 F G H J	53 A B C D	66 F G H J
2 F G H J	15 A B C D	28 F G H J	41 A B C D	54 F G H J	67 A B C D
3 A B C D	16 F G H J	29 A B C D	42 F G H J	55 A B C D	68 F G H J
4 F G H J	17 A B C D	30 F G H J	43 A B C D	56 F G H J	69 A B C D
5 A B C D	18 F G H J	31 A B C D	44 F G H J	57 A B C D	70 F G H J
6 F G H J	19 A B C D	32 F G H J	45 A B C D	58 F G H J	71 A B C D
7 A B C D	20 F G H J	33 A B C D	46 F G H J	59 A B C D	72 F G H J
8 F G H J	21 A B C D	34 F G H J	47 A B C D	60 F G H J	73 A B C D
9 A B C D	22 F G H J	35 A B C D	48 F G H J	61 A B C D	74 F G H J
10 F G H J	23 A B C D	36 F G H J	49 A B C D	62 F G H J	75 A B C D
11 A B C D	24 F G H J	37 A B C D	50 F G H J	63 A B C D	
12 F G H J	25 A B C D	38 F G H J	51 A B C D	64 F G H J	
13 A B C D	26 F G H J	39 A B C D	52 F G H J	65 A B C D	

TEST 2

1 A B C D E	11 A B C D E	21 A B C D E	31 A B C D E	41 A B C D E	51 A B C D E
2 F G H J K	12 F G H J K	22 F G H J K	32 F G H J K	42 F G H J K	52 F G H J K
3 A B C D E	13 A B C D E	23 A B C D E	33 A B C D E	43 A B C D E	53 A B C D E
4 F G H J K	14 F G H J K	24 F G H J K	34 F G H J K	44 F G H J K	54 F G H J K
5 A B C D E	15 A B C D E	25 A B C D E	35 A B C D E	45 A B C D E	55 A B C D E
6 F G H J K	16 F G H J K	26 F G H J K	36 F G H J K	46 F G H J K	56 F G H J K
7 A B C D E	17 A B C D E	27 A B C D E	37 A B C D E	47 A B C D E	57 A B C D E
8 F G H J K	18 F G H J K	28 F G H J K	38 F G H J K	48 F G H J K	58 F G H J K
9 A B C D E	19 A B C D E	29 A B C D E	39 A B C D E	49 A B C D E	59 A B C D E
10 F G H J K	20 F G H J K	30 F G H J K	40 F G H J K	50 F G H J K	60 F G H J K

TEST 3

1 A B C D	8 F G H J	15 A B C D	22 F G H J	29 A B C D	36 F G H J
2 F G H J	9 A B C D	16 F G H J	23 A B C D	30 F G H J	37 A B C D
3 A B C D	10 F G H J	17 A B C D	24 F G H J	31 A B C D	38 F G H J
4 F G H J	11 A B C D	18 F G H J	25 A B C D	32 F G H J	39 A B C D
5 A B C D	12 F G H J	19 A B C D	26 F G H J	33 A B C D	40 F G H J
6 F G H J	13 A B C D	20 F G H J	27 A B C D	34 F G H J	
7 A B C D	14 F G H J	21 A B C D	28 F G H J	35 A B C D	

TEST 4

1 A B C D	8 F G H J	15 A B C D	22 F G H J	29 A B C D	36 F G H J
2 F G H J	9 A B C D	16 F G H J	23 A B C D	30 F G H J	37 A B C D
3 A B C D	10 F G H J	17 A B C D	24 F G H J	31 A B C D	38 F G H J
4 F G H J	11 A B C D	18 F G H J	25 A B C D	32 F G H J	39 A B C D
5 A B C D	12 F G H J	19 A B C D	26 F G H J	33 A B C D	40 F G H J
6 F G H J	13 A B C D	20 F G H J	27 A B C D	34 F G H J	
7 A B C D	14 F G H J	21 A B C D	28 F G H J	35 A B C D	

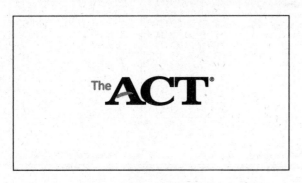

080660

Practice Test 3

EXAMINEE STATEMENT, CERTIFICATION, AND SIGNATURE

1. Read the following **Statement:** By opening this test booklet, I agree to comply with and be bound by the *Terms and Conditions: Testing Rules and Policies for the ACT® Test* provided in the ACT registration materials for this test, including those concerning test security, score cancellation, examinee remedies, binding arbitration, and consent to the processing of my personally identifying information, including the collection, use, transfer, and disclosure of information as described in the ACT Privacy Policy (www.act.org/privacy.html).

   I understand that ACT owns the test questions and responses and affirm that I will not share any test questions or responses with anyone by any form of communication before, during, or after the test administration. I understand that assuming anyone else's identity to take this test is strictly prohibited and may violate the law and subject me to legal penalties.

   International Examinees: By my signature, I am also providing my consent to ACT to transfer my personally identifying information to the United States to ACT, or a third-party service provider for processing, where it will be subject to use and disclosure under the laws of the United States. I acknowledge and agree that it may also be accessible to law enforcement and national security authorities in the United States.

2. Copy the **Certification** shown below (only the text in italics) on the lines provided. Write in your normal handwriting.

   Certification: *I agree to the Statement above and certify that I am the person whose name appears on this form.*

   ____

   ____

3. Sign your name as you would any official document, enter today's date, and print your name in the spaces provided.

   ______________________ Your Signature ______ Today's Date ______________________ Print Your Name

Form 16MC3

2019|2020

Directions

This booklet contains tests in English, mathematics, reading, and science. These tests measure skills and abilities highly related to high school course work and success in college. **Calculators may be used on the mathematics test only.**

The questions in each test are numbered, and the suggested answers for each question are lettered. On the answer document, the rows of ovals are numbered to match the questions, and the ovals in each row are lettered to correspond to the suggested answers.

For each question, first decide which answer is best. Next, locate on the answer document the row of ovals numbered the same as the question. Then, locate the oval in that row lettered the same as your answer. Finally, fill in the oval completely. Use a soft lead pencil and make your marks heavy and black. **Do not use ink or a mechanical pencil.**

Mark only one answer to each question. If you change your mind about an answer, erase your first mark thoroughly before marking your new answer. For each question, make certain that you mark in the row of ovals with the same number as the question.

Only responses marked on your answer document will be scored. Your score on each test will be based only on the number of questions you answer correctly during the time allowed for that test. You will **not** be penalized for guessing. **It is to your advantage to answer every question even if you must guess.**

You may work on each test **only** when the testing staff tells you to do so. If you finish a test before time is called for that test, you should use the time remaining to reconsider questions you are uncertain about in that test. You may **not** look back to a test on which time has already been called, and you may **not** go ahead to another test. To do so will disqualify you from the examination.

Lay your pencil down immediately when time is called at the end of each test. You may **not** for any reason fill in or alter ovals for a test after time is called for that test. To do so will disqualify you from the examination.

Do not fold or tear the pages of your test booklet.

DO NOT OPEN THIS BOOKLET UNTIL TOLD TO DO SO.

1 ■ ■ ■ ■ ■ ■ ■ ■ ■ 1

ENGLISH TEST

45 Minutes—75 Questions

DIRECTIONS: In the five passages that follow, certain words and phrases are underlined and numbered. In the right-hand column, you will find alternatives for the underlined part. In most cases, you are to choose the one that best expresses the idea, makes the statement appropriate for standard written English, or is worded most consistently with the style and tone of the passage as a whole. If you think the original version is best, choose "NO CHANGE." In some cases, you will find in the right-hand column a question about the underlined part. You are to choose the best answer to the question.

You will also find questions about a section of the passage, or about the passage as a whole. These questions do not refer to an underlined portion of the passage, but rather are identified by a number or numbers in a box.

For each question, choose the alternative you consider best and fill in the corresponding oval on your answer document. Read each passage through once before you begin to answer the questions that accompany it. For many of the questions, you must read several sentences beyond the question to determine the answer. Be sure that you have read far enough ahead each time you choose an alternative.

PASSAGE I

Miami Time

My family is part of the Miami tribe a Native American people,[1] with strong ties to territory in present-day Ohio, Indiana, and Illinois. Growing up in the Midwest, I often heard my grandmother talk about "Miami time." When she was doing something she loved, whether it was making freezer jam or researching tribal history,[2] she refused to be rushed in a hurry.[3] "I'm on Miami time today," she would say. Conversely, if we were running late for an appointment. She[4] would chide us by saying, "Get a move on. We're not running on Miami time today, you know."

1. A. NO CHANGE
   B. tribe, a Native American, people
   C. tribe, a Native American people
   D. tribe; a Native American people

2. At this point, the writer would like to provide a glimpse into the grandmother's interests. Given that all the choices are true, which one best accomplishes this purpose?
   F. NO CHANGE
   G. being actively involved in her pursuits,
   H. things I really hope she'll teach me one day,
   J. historical research as well as domestic projects,

3. A. NO CHANGE
   B. hurried or rushed.
   C. made to go faster or rushed.
   D. rushed.

4. F. NO CHANGE
   G. appointment; she
   H. appointment and she
   J. appointment, she

GO ON TO THE NEXT PAGE.

It was a difficult concept for me to grasp. My grandmother tried to explain that "Miami time" referred to those moments, when time seemed to slow down or stand still. Recently, the meaning of her words started to sink in. One morning, my son and I will inadvertently slip out of the world measured in seconds, minutes, and hours, and into one measured by curiosity and sensation.

[1] On a familiar trail near our house, I was pushing Jeremy in his stroller and were thinking of the day ahead and the tasks I had to complete. [2] Suddenly, he squealed with pure delight and pointed toward a clearing. [3] There, two does and three fawns stood watching us. [4] Five pairs of ears flicked like antennae seeking a signal. [5] After a few moments, the deer lowered their heads and began to eat, as if they had decided we were harmless. [6] By then, my son's face was full of wonder. [11]

We spent the rest of the morning veering from the trail to investigate small snatches of life. Lizards lazing in the sun and quail rustled through grasses surprised us. Wild blackberries melted on our tongues. For example, the aroma of crushed eucalyptus leaves tingled in our noses.

5. Given that all the choices are true, which one provides the best opening to this paragraph?
   A. NO CHANGE
   B. I remember being late for a doctor's appointment one day.
   C. My grandmother lived with us, and as a result she and I became close over the years.
   D. My son asks me about my grandmother, whom he never met.

6. F. NO CHANGE
   G. moments when
   H. moments, as if
   J. moments, because

7. A. NO CHANGE
   B. spoken statements to my ears
   C. expressed opinions on the matter
   D. verbal remarks in conversation

8. F. NO CHANGE
   G. inadvertently slip
   H. are inadvertently slipping
   J. inadvertently slipped

9. A. NO CHANGE
   B. were having thoughts
   C. thinking
   D. DELETE the underlined portion.

10. F. NO CHANGE
    G. does, and three fawns
    H. does and three fawns,
    J. does and, three fawns

11. For the sake of the logic and coherence of this paragraph, Sentence 3 should be placed:
    A. where it is now.
    B. before Sentence 1.
    C. after Sentence 1.
    D. after Sentence 4.

12. F. NO CHANGE
    G. rustling
    H. were rustling
    J. DELETE the underlined portion.

13. A. NO CHANGE
    B. On the other hand, the
    C. Just in case, the
    D. The

Taking Additional Practice Tests

GO ON TO THE NEXT PAGE.

1 ■ ■ ■ ■ ■ ■ ■ ■ ■ 1

By the time we found our way back to the car, the sun was high in the sky. We had taken three hours to complete a hike we usually finished in forty-five minutes. Yet the hike felt shorter then [14] ever. As we drove off, I remembered something else my grandmother used to say: "Miami time passes all too quickly."

14. F. NO CHANGE
G. more shorter then
H. the shortest than
J. shorter than

Question 15 asks about the preceding passage as a whole.

15. Suppose the writer's goal had been to write a brief essay conveying a personal experience with "Miami time." Would this essay successfully fulfill that goal?
A. Yes, because it presents the narrator's firsthand experience of a morning spent in Miami time.
B. Yes, because it reveals that after a conversation with the grandmother, the narrator decided to live in Miami time.
C. No, because it shares the views of more than one person with regard to the meaning of Miami time.
D. No, because the term "Miami time" belonged to the grandmother, not to the narrator.

PASSAGE II

Faith Ringgold's Quilting Bee

The artist Faith Ringgold has made a name for herself with her "story quilts," lively combinations of painting, quilting, and storytelling. Each artwork consists of a painting framed by quilted squares of fabric and story panels. One of these artworks, *The Sunflowers Quilting Bee at Arles*, depicts a scene of women at work on a quilt in a field of towering yellow flowers that eight [16] African American women sit around the quilt that covers their laps. Who are these people stitching among the flowers? What brings them so close that their shoulders touch?

16. F. NO CHANGE
G. flowers and eight
H. flowers. Eight
J. flowers, eight

GO ON TO THE NEXT PAGE.

Thus, the answers to these questions can be found in the artwork itself. Ringgold has told the story of this gathering on two horizontal panels of text. One panel is sewn into the piece's top border, the other into it's bottom border. These eight women the story explains, strove in their various ways to support the cause of justice in the world.

In reality, these women never met to piece together a quilt. The scene comes out of the artists imagination as a statement of the unity of purpose that she perceives in their lives. Sojourner Truth and Harriet Tubman fought to abolish slavery and, later, was active in the crusade for suffrage. Newspaper journalist Ida B. Wells courageously spoke out for social and racial justice in the late nineteenth and early twentieth centuries.

17. A. NO CHANGE
    B. Instead, the
    C. Furthermore, the
    D. The

18. F. NO CHANGE
    G. of this gathering the story on two horizontal panels of text.
    H. on two horizontal panels the story of this gathering of text.
    J. the story on two horizontal panels of text of this gathering.

19. A. NO CHANGE
    B. its'
    C. its
    D. their

20. F. NO CHANGE
    G. women, the story explains—
    H. women the story explains—
    J. women, the story explains,

21. The underlined phrase could be placed in all the following locations EXCEPT:
    A. where it is now.
    B. after the word *support.*
    C. after the word *cause.*
    D. after the word *world* (ending the sentence with a period).

22. F. NO CHANGE
    G. summary,
    H. addition,
    J. contrast,

23. A. NO CHANGE
    B. artist's imagination
    C. artists' imagination
    D. artists imagination,

24. F. NO CHANGE
    G. was actively engaged
    H. was engaged
    J. were active

25. Given that all the choices are true, which one provides the most relevant information at this point in the essay?
    A. NO CHANGE
    B. married Ferdinand Barnett, editor of the first Black newspaper in Chicago, the *Chicago Conservator.*
    C. wrote for newspapers in Memphis, New York City, and finally, Chicago.
    D. was born in Holly Springs, Mississippi, in 1862, the eldest of eight children.

GO ON TO THE NEXT PAGE.

1 ■ ■ ■ ■ ■ ■ ■ ■ ■ 1

Establishing her own hair products business, herself [26] in the first decade of the twentieth century, millions of dollars were later bequeathed by Madam C. J. Walker to charities and educational institutions. [27] Among the schools that benefited from this generosity, were [28] those that Mary McLeod Bethune opened and ran in order to provide a better education for Black students. And Fannie Lou Hamer, Ella Baker, and Rosa Parks showed leadership and strength during the civil rights movement, it happened in [29] the 1950s and 1960s.

In the artwork, Ringgold has surrounded these women with bright sunflowers. The flowers seem to celebrate the women's accomplishments and the beauty of their shared vision. [30]

26. F. NO CHANGE
G. business belonging to her
H. business, herself,
J. business

27. A. NO CHANGE
B. Madam C. J. Walker later bequeathed millions of dollars to charities and educational institutions.
C. charities and educational institutions later received millions of dollars from Madam C. J. Walker.
D. millions of dollars were later bequeathed to charities and educational institutions by Madam C. J. Walker.

28. F. NO CHANGE
G. generosity; were
H. generosity were
J. generosity were:

29. A. NO CHANGE
B. movement, it took place in
C. movement, that happened in
D. movement of

30. If the writer were to delete the preceding sentence, the essay would primarily lose:
F. an interpretation of the artwork that serves to summarize the essay.
G. a reflection on the women depicted in the artwork that compares them to Ringgold.
H. a description of a brushwork technique that refers back to the essay's opening.
J. an evaluation of Ringgold's artistic talent that places her in a historical context.

PASSAGE III

1902: A Space Odyssey

Our technologically advanced times has allowed [31] filmmakers to create spectacular science fiction films to intrigue us with worlds beyond our experience. Imagine the excitement in 1902 when [32] audiences first saw *Le Voyage dans la lune (A Trip to the Moon)*, a groundbreaking movie produced by Georges Méliès.

31. A. NO CHANGE
B. have allowed
C. allows
D. was allowing

32. F. NO CHANGE
G. 1902, and when
H. 1902, which
J. 1902, where

GO ON TO THE NEXT PAGE.

[1] Undaunted, Méliès honed his photographic skills to tell fantasy stories instead. [2] Méliès, a French magician, was fascinated by the workings of the new motion picture camera. [3] Specializing in stage illusions, he thought the camera offered potential to expand its[33] spectacular magic productions. [4] By 1895, he was working with the new invention. [5] He found out, however,[34] that the public preferred live magic acts to filmed versions. [35]

Méliès's magician's eye led him to discover the basics of special effects. [36] He experimented with effects such as speeding up and slowing down the action, reversing it for backward movement, and superimposing images of fantastic creatures over real people. Using overhead pulleys and trapdoors, he was able to do interesting things.[37]

Aware of the popularity of Jules Verne's science fiction novels, Méliès saw exciting possibilities in filming a space odyssey. The interplanetary travel film that he created, *A Trip to the Moon*, had production costs of $4,000, highly excessively[38] for its time. In this film, a space capsule that is fired and thereby launched and projected[39] from a cannon lands in the eye of the Man in the Moon.

33. A. NO CHANGE
B. their
C. his
D. it's

34. F. NO CHANGE
G. out, however;
H. out, however
J. out however,

35. For the sake of the logic and coherence of this paragraph, Sentence 1 should be placed:
A. where it is now.
B. after Sentence 2.
C. after Sentence 3.
D. after Sentence 5.

36. The writer is considering deleting the preceding sentence from the essay. The sentence should NOT be deleted because it:
F. describes Méliès's ability as a magician, which is important to understanding the essay.
G. begins to explain the techniques of trick photography that Méliès eventually learned.
H. creates a transition that provides a further connection between Méliès the magician and Méliès the filmmaker.
J. indicates that Méliès's interest in learning about trick photography existed before his interest in magic.

37. Given that all the choices are true, which one would best conclude this sentence so that it illustrates Méliès's skill and inventiveness?
A. NO CHANGE
B. he used effects commonly seen in his stage productions.
C. his actors could enter and leave the scene.
D. he perfected eerie film entrances and exits.

38. F. NO CHANGE
G. exceeding highly
H. high excessively
J. exceedingly high

39. A. NO CHANGE
B. fired
C. fired from and consequently projected
D. fired and thereby propelled

Taking Additional Practice Tests

GO ON TO THE NEXT PAGE.

1 ■ ■ ■ ■ ■ ■ ■ ■ ■ 1

In a strange terrain filled with hostile <u>creatures,</u>[40] the space travelers experience many adventures. They escape back to Earth in the capsule by falling off the edge of the <u>moon, landing</u>[41] in the ocean, they bob around until a passing ship finally rescues them.

Producing the film long before interplanetary explorations <u>had began,</u>[42] Méliès could <u>arouse</u>[43] his audience's curiosity with unconstrained fantasy. <u>People are still going to theaters to see science fiction films.</u>[44]

40. **F.** NO CHANGE
G. creatures, who they now realize live there,
H. creatures, whom they are encountering,
J. creatures who are found there,

41. **A.** NO CHANGE
B. moon after landing
C. moon. Landing
D. moon, after landing

42. **F.** NO CHANGE
G. would of begun,
H. have began,
J. had begun,

43. Which of the following alternatives to the underlined word would be LEAST acceptable?

A. whet
B. stimulate
C. awaken
D. disturb

44. Given that all the choices are true, which one would most effectively express the writer's viewpoint about Méliès's role in science fiction filmmaking?

F. NO CHANGE
G. This first space odyssey provided the genesis for a film genre that still packs theaters.
H. Méliès made an important contribution to filmmaking many years ago.
J. In Méliès's production even the film crew knew a lot about space.

Question 45 asks about the preceding passage as a whole.

45. Suppose the writer's goal had been to write a brief essay highlighting the contributions a single artist can make to a particular art form. Would this essay fulfill that goal?

A. Yes, because the essay asserts that Méliès's work as a magician never would have succeeded without the contributions of the artists in the film industry.
B. Yes, because the essay presents Méliès as a magician who used his talents and curiosity to explore and excel in the film world.
C. No, because the essay focuses on the process of making science fiction films, not on a single artist's work.
D. No, because the essay suggests that it took many artists working together to create the success that Méliès enjoyed.

GO ON TO THE NEXT PAGE.

PASSAGE IV

Nancy Drew in the Twenty-First Century

I thought the Nancy Drew mystery series had went out of style. I was sure that girls growing up today would have more up-to-date role models and my generation's favorite sleuth would of been retired to the library's dusty, back rooms. I was wrong.

Nancy Drew, the teenaged heroine of heaps of young adult mystery novels, is alive and well and still on the job. I know because my niece, Liana, and her friends were reading that all summer long. By the time Liana went back to school and had followed Nancy Drew on a safari to solve *The Spider Sapphire Mystery* and had explored Incan ruins for clues to *The Secret of the Crossword Cipher.* With Nancy's help, Liana had read about different places and various cultures all over the world.

46. F. NO CHANGE
    G. gone out of
    H. went from
    J. gone from

47. A. NO CHANGE
    B. would have been
    C. would of
    D. DELETE the underlined portion.

48. F. NO CHANGE
    G. libraries dusty,
    H. libraries dusty
    J. library's dusty

49. Which choice provides the most specific information?
    A. NO CHANGE
    B. a high number
    C. hundreds
    D. plenty

50. F. NO CHANGE
    G. novels, is alive,
    H. novels is alive,
    J. novels is alive

51. A. NO CHANGE
    B. the mysteries
    C. up on that
    D. it over

52. F. NO CHANGE
    G. school, she had
    H. school, having
    J. school, she

53. A. NO CHANGE
    B. solve:
    C. solve;
    D. solve,

54. Given that all the choices are true, which one best illustrates the variety of settings for the Nancy Drew mysteries and also expresses Liana's interest in these books?
    F. NO CHANGE
    G. Along with Nancy, Liana had many breathtaking adventures involving all sorts of colorful characters.
    H. With Nancy in the lead, Liana had chased suspects from Arizona to Argentina, from Nairobi to New York.
    J. Through her exposure to Nancy, Liana learned about many new places around the world.

Taking Additional Practice Tests

GO ON TO THE NEXT PAGE.

1 ■ ■ ■ ■ ■ ■ ■ ■ ■ 1

When I was a girl in the 1960s, my friends and I loved Nancy Drew. [55] We loved her loyal companions, her bravado, and there was a love for her freedom to do what she wanted. [56]

We also [57] loved how smart she was and how pretty, how confident and successful. We were surprised and delighted that eighteen-year-old Nancy was so accomplished at so many things. She was able to solve crimes, [58] win golf tournaments, kick bad guys in the shins, and impress her father's distinguished clients. She did it all—and without scuffing her shoes or losing her supportive boyfriend, Ned.

Liana and her friends don't seem to care that Nancy is pretty or popular. They laugh, mockingly I think, at Nancy's friend Bess, who squeals at spiders. They prefer her other girlfriend George, the judo expert and computer whiz. They skip over the long descriptions of outfits and fashion accessories. According to Liana, they just want to get on with the story.

55. At this point, the writer is thinking about adding the following true statement:

> One of a number of series that have featured the young female detective, the Nancy Drew Mystery Story series was begun in 1930 and now totals 173 books.

Should the writer make this addition here?

- **A.** Yes, because it supports statements about the longevity and popularity of this series.
- **B.** Yes, because it helps to explain why the narrator "loved Nancy Drew."
- **C.** No, because it distracts the reader from the main focus of this paragraph.
- **D.** No, because it fails to include relevant information about the author of the series.

56.
- **F.** NO CHANGE
- **G.** a love for her freedom to do what she wanted.
- **H.** her freedom to do what she wanted.
- **J.** the freedom to do as one wants.

57. Which of the following alternatives to the underlined portion would be LEAST acceptable?

- **A.** furthermore
- **B.** therefore
- **C.** likewise
- **D.** DELETE the underlined portion.

58.
- **F.** NO CHANGE
- **G.** was capable of solving crimes,
- **H.** was good at crime solving,
- **J.** solved crimes,

GO ON TO THE NEXT PAGE.

Perhaps I am overly optimistic, but I'd like to believe that Liana's generation doesn't love Nancy Drew because she's a successful girl detective. They don't need to be reminded that girls can be successful they know that. [59] What these girls need and love are the stories themselves: those exciting adventure tales spiced with mystery. [60]

59. A. NO CHANGE
B. successful they already know
C. successful; they know
D. successful, knowing

60. Which choice most effectively supports the point being made in the first part of this sentence?
F. NO CHANGE
G. the answers to the mysteries of their lives.
H. a strong role model for their generation.
J. the ability to overcome obstacles.

PASSAGE V

Visiting Mars on a Budget

With its distinctive red tint and its polar ice caps, the planet Mars has fascinated humans for thousands of years. There were [61] ancient Babylonian astronomers who associated Mars with their war god Negral, to twentieth-century science fiction writers whose works become best-sellers, [62] this planet has often been a symbol of ill will and danger.

61. A. NO CHANGE
B. When
C. From
D. Those

62. Given that all the choices are true, which one is most relevant to the statement that follows in this sentence?
F. NO CHANGE
G. with their wild imaginations about outer space,
H. who penned spine-tingling stories of "little green men from Mars,"
J. who created images of Mars in literature,

The United States has competed with other countries to explore space. [63] By 2003, the National Aeronautics and Space Administration (NASA) would of sent [64] thirty spacecraft to the red planet, speculation has been prompted [65] that a human voyage may no longer be the stuff of fiction.

63. Given that all the choices are true, which one best leads from the preceding paragraph to the subject of this paragraph?
A. NO CHANGE
B. Today, such negative associations seem to be dissipating.
C. In 1958, the United States founded an agency to run its space program.
D. Earth and Mars are both planets in the inner solar system.

64. F. NO CHANGE
G. had sent
H. send
J. have sent

65. A. NO CHANGE
B. to which speculation has prompted
C. prompting speculation
D. which is speculation

GO ON TO THE NEXT PAGE.

1 ■ ■ ■ ■ ■ ■ ■ ■ ■ 1

Few would deny that the idea of a human mission to Mars is exciting, who is ready to pay for such an expedition?
66

Recent reports suggest that the cost of a human voyage to Mars could run as high as 100 billion dollars. This is a startling number, especially in light of the fact that the International Space Station, the most ambitious NASA project yet, carried a projected price tag of "only" 17 billion dollars. In the end, NASA overspent on the International Space Station. [68] One can only imagine if the final price of a human voyage to Mars would be.
67 ... 69

In contrast, the two Mars Rovers—robotic spacecraft launched in 2003—carried a combined price tag of less than one billion dollars. These Rovers are sophisticated pieces of technology, with the capacity and ability to examine soil and rocks. Their equipment may answer questions that have long been posed about the presence of water and life on Mars.
70 ... 71

66. F. NO CHANGE
G. Maybe a few
H. Although few
J. Few, if any,

67. A. NO CHANGE
B. yet
C. yet:
D. yet—

68. The writer is considering adding the following true information to the end of the preceding sentence (placing a comma after the word *Station*):

with a final construction cost of almost 30 billion dollars.

Should the writer make this addition?

F. Yes, because it strengthens the assertion made in this sentence by adding explicit detail.
G. Yes, because it proves space flight will be more affordable in the future.
H. No, because it weakens the point made in the paragraph about the cost of human flight to Mars.
J. No, because it detracts from the essay's focus on the human experience in travel to Mars.

69. A. NO CHANGE
B. what
C. how
D. DELETE the underlined portion.

70. Given that all the choices are true, which one most effectively describes what the Mars Rovers are?
F. NO CHANGE
G. which captured the imagination of the general public—
H. the products described at length in the media—
J. familiar to many who watched the news coverage at the time—

71. A. NO CHANGE
B. genuine capacity
C. potential capacity
D. capacity

GO ON TO THE NEXT PAGE.

Sending machines unaccompanied by humans to Mars does drain some of the romance out of <u>aging or older</u> [72] visions of space travel. <u>In other words,</u> [73] we need to keep in mind that the right equipment can accomplish as much as any crew of scientists, if not more—<u>such as</u> [74] a fraction of the cost. Before any astronaut boards a spacecraft for that distant planet, the staggering expense of such a mission should be carefully considered. [75]

72. **F.** NO CHANGE
G. old age
H. aging old
J. age-old

73. **A.** NO CHANGE
B. For that reason alone,
C. In that time frame,
D. Even so,

74. **F.** NO CHANGE
G. at
H. but only
J. DELETE the underlined portion.

75. The writer is considering ending the essay with the following statement:

> With the passage of time, humans will continue to gaze in awe toward the heavenly skies as a source of inspiration and mystery.

Should the writer add this sentence here?

A. Yes, because it captures the emotion that is the basis for the space exploration described in the essay.
B. Yes, because it invites the reader to reflect on the insignificance of money in relation to the mystery of space.
C. No, because it does not logically follow the essay's chronological history of people who traveled in space.
D. No, because it strays too far from the essay's focus on Mars and the cost of sending humans there.

END OF TEST 1

STOP! DO NOT TURN THE PAGE UNTIL TOLD TO DO SO.

2 △ △ △ △ △ △ △ △ △ 2

MATHEMATICS TEST

60 Minutes—60 Questions

DIRECTIONS: Solve each problem, choose the correct answer, and then fill in the corresponding oval on your answer document.

Do not linger over problems that take too much time. Solve as many as you can; then return to the others in the time you have left for this test.

You are permitted to use a calculator on this test. You may use your calculator for any problems you choose, but some of the problems may best be done without using a calculator.

Note: Unless otherwise stated, all of the following should be assumed.

1. Illustrative figures are NOT necessarily drawn to scale.
2. Geometric figures lie in a plane.
3. The word *line* indicates a straight line.
4. The word *average* indicates arithmetic mean.

DO YOUR FIGURING HERE.

1. On level ground, a vertical rod 12 feet tall casts a shadow 4 feet long, and at the same time a nearby vertical flagpole casts a shadow 12 feet long. How many feet tall is the flagpole?

A. 4
B. 8
C. 12
D. 20
E. 36

2. Kalino earned 85, 95, 93, and 80 points on the 4 tests, each worth 100 points, given so far this term. How many points must he earn on his fifth test, also worth 100 points, to average 90 points for the 5 tests given this term?

F. 87
G. 88
H. 90
J. 92
K. 97

3. If $x = -5$, what is the value of $\frac{x^2 - 1}{x + 1}$?

A. -6
B. -4
C. 4
D. $5\frac{4}{5}$
E. 19

GO ON TO THE NEXT PAGE.

2 △ △ △ △ △ △ △ △ △ 2

DO YOUR FIGURING HERE.

4. Kaya ran $1\frac{2}{5}$ miles on Monday and $2\frac{1}{3}$ miles on Tuesday. What was the total distance, in miles, Kaya ran during those 2 days?

F. $3\frac{2}{15}$

G. $3\frac{3}{8}$

H. $3\frac{2}{5}$

J. $3\frac{7}{15}$

K. $3\frac{11}{15}$

5. Consider the 3 statements below to be true.

All insects that are attracted to honey are ants.
Insect I is not an ant.
Insect J is attracted to honey.

Which of the following statements is necessarily true?

A. Insect I is an ant not attracted to honey.
B. Insect I is an ant attracted to honey.
C. Insect I is attracted to honey.
D. Insect J is not attracted to honey.
E. Insect J is an ant.

6. What is the value of the expression $\sqrt{\frac{m}{x-3}}$ when $x = -1$ and $m = -16$?

F. -2

G. 2

H. $2\sqrt{2}$

J. $2i$

K. $2i\sqrt{2}$

7. Tickets for a community theater production cost \$6 each when bought in advance and \$8 each when bought at the door. The theater group's goal is at least \$2,000 in ticket sales for opening night. The theater group sold 142 opening-night tickets in advance. What is the minimum number of tickets they need to sell at the door on opening night to make their goal?

A. 143
B. 144
C. 192
D. 250
E. 357

Taking Additional Practice Tests

GO ON TO THE NEXT PAGE.

2 △ △ △ △ △ △ △ △ △ 2

DO YOUR FIGURING HERE.

8. Mark and Juanita own a sandwich shop. They offer 3 kinds of bread, 5 kinds of meat, and 3 kinds of cheese. Each type of sandwich has a combination of exactly 3 ingredients: 1 bread, 1 meat, and 1 cheese. How many types of sandwiches are possible?

F. 11
G. 15
H. 30
J. 45
K. 120

9. If $12(x - 11) = -15$, then $x = ?$

A. $-\frac{49}{4}$

B. $-\frac{13}{6}$

C. $-\frac{5}{4}$

D. $-\frac{1}{3}$

E. $\frac{39}{4}$

10. In the figure below, A, D, C, and E are collinear. $\overline{AD}$, $\overline{BD}$, and $\overline{BC}$ are all the same length, and the angle measure of $\angle ABD$ is as marked. What is the degree measure of $\angle BCE$?

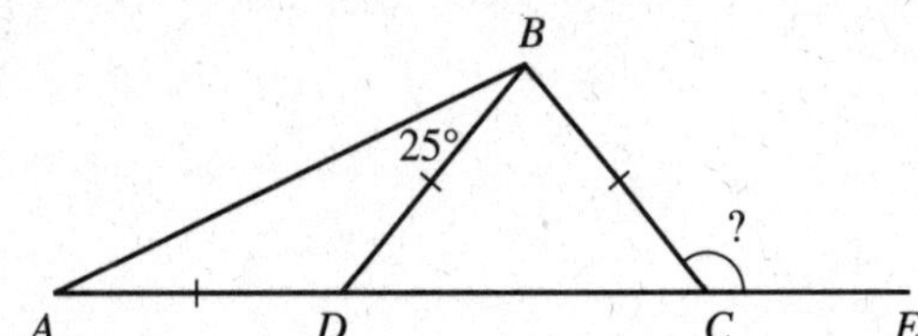

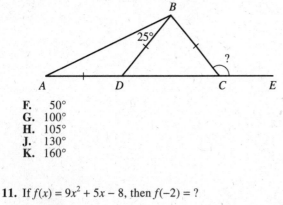

F. 50°
G. 100°
H. 105°
J. 130°
K. 160°

11. If $f(x) = 9x^2 + 5x - 8$, then $f(-2) = ?$

A. −54
B. −18
C. 18
D. 36
E. 38

12. What is the least common multiple of 30, 20, and 70 ?

F. 40
G. 42
H. 120
J. 420
K. 42,000

GO ON TO THE NEXT PAGE.

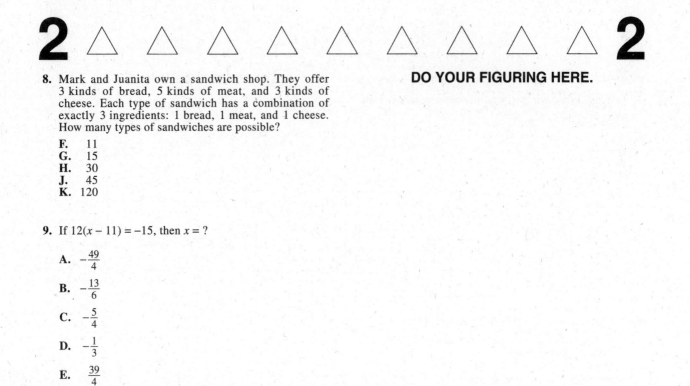

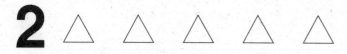

2 △ △ △ △ △ △ △ △ △ 2

13. While doing a problem on his calculator, Tom meant to divide a number by 2, but instead he accidentally multiplied the number by 2. Which of the following calculations could Tom then do to the result on the calculator screen to obtain the result he originally wanted?

A. Subtract the original number
B. Multiply by 2
C. Multiply by 4
D. Divide by 2
E. Divide by 4

DO YOUR FIGURING HERE.

14. The 8-sided figure below is divided into 5 congruent squares. The total area of the 5 squares is 125 square inches. What is the perimeter, in inches, of the figure?

F. 25
G. 60
H. 80
J. 100
K. 125

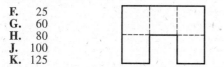

15. Hai has \$100 available to buy USB drives to back up data for his business computers. Each USB drive has a price of \$8, and Hai will pay a sales tax of 7% of the total price of the USB drives. What is the maximum number of USB drives Hai can buy?

A. 11
B. 12
C. 13
D. 14
E. 15

16. A certain computer performs 1.5×10^8 calculations per second. How many seconds would it take this computer to perform 6.0×10^{16} calculations?

F. 2.5×10^{-9}
G. 9.0×10^0
H. 4.0×10^2
J. 4.0×10^8
K. 9.0×10^{24}

17. One of the following is an equation of the linear relation shown in the standard (x,y) coordinate plane below. Which equation is it?

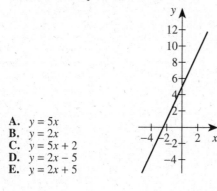

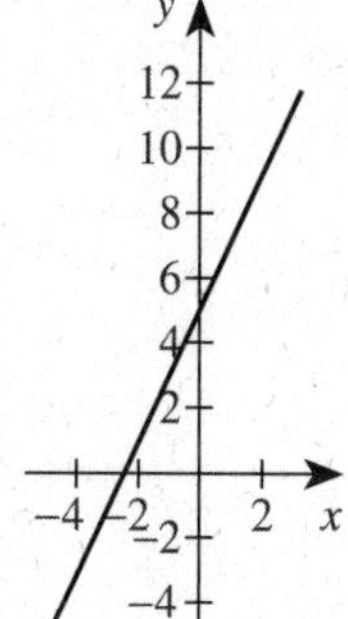

A. $y = 5x$
B. $y = 2x$
C. $y = 5x + 2$
D. $y = 2x - 5$
E. $y = 2x + 5$

Taking Additional Practice Tests

GO ON TO THE NEXT PAGE.

2 △ △ △ △ △ △ △ △ △ 2

DO YOUR FIGURING HERE.

18. A square is circumscribed about a circle of 7-foot radius, as shown below. What is the area of the square, in square feet?

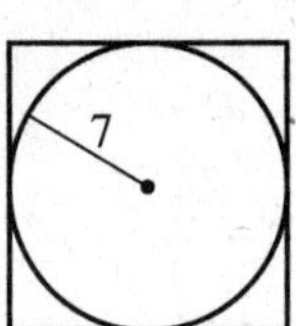

F. 49
G. 56
H. 98
J. 49π
K. 196

19. Two workers were hired to begin work at the same time. Worker A's contract called for a starting salary of \$20,000 with an increase of \$800 after each year of employment. Worker B's contract called for a starting salary of \$15,200 with an increase of \$2,000 after each year of employment. If x represents the number of full years' employment (that is, the number of yearly increases each worker has received), which of the following equations could be solved to determine the number of years until B's yearly salary equals A's yearly salary?

A. $20{,}000 + 800x = 15{,}200 + 2{,}000x$
B. $20{,}000 + 2{,}000x = 15{,}200 + 800x$
C. $(20{,}000 + 800)x = (15{,}200 + 2{,}000)x$
D. $(2{,}000 + 800)x = 20{,}000 - 15{,}200$
E. $(2{,}000 - 800)x = 20{,}000 + 15{,}200$

20. A ramp for loading trucks is 13 feet long and covers 12 feet along the level ground, as shown below. How many feet high is the highest point on the ramp?

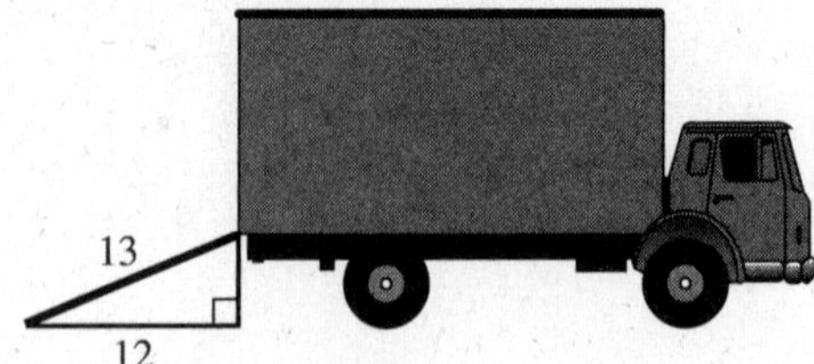

F. 1
G. 2
H. 4
J. 5
K. $6\frac{1}{4}$

GO ON TO THE NEXT PAGE.

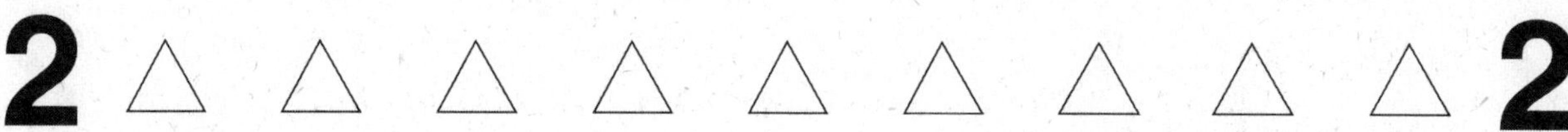

21. The expression $7(x + 3) - 3(2x - 2)$ is equivalent to:

A. $x + 1$
B. $x + 15$
C. $x + 19$
D. $x + 23$
E. $x + 27$

DO YOUR FIGURING HERE.

22. If 115% of a number is 460, what is 75% of the number?

F. 280
G. 300
H. 320
J. 345
K. 400

23. When $(2x - 3)^2$ is written in the form $ax^2 + bx + c$, where a, b, and c are integers, $a + b + c = ?$

A. -17
B. -5
C. 1
D. 13
E. 25

24. What is the area, in square feet, of the figure below?

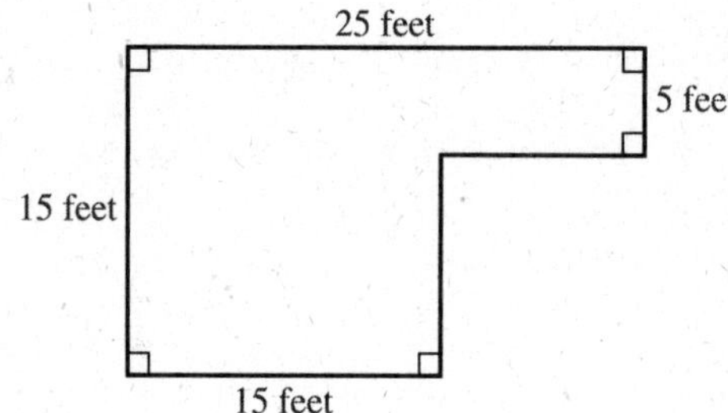

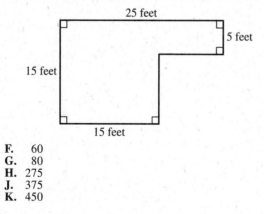

F. 60
G. 80
H. 275
J. 375
K. 450

GO ON TO THE NEXT PAGE.

2 △ △ △ △ △ △ △ △ △ 2

DO YOUR FIGURING HERE.

25. Barb is going to cover a rectangular area 8 feet by 10 feet with rectangular paving blocks that are 4 inches by 8 inches by 2 inches to make a flat patio. What is the minimum number of paving blocks she will need if all the paving blocks will face the same direction?

(Note: Barb will not cut any of the paving blocks.)

A. 80
B. 360
C. 601
D. 960
E. 1,213

26. What is the slope of the line represented by the equation $6y - 14x = 5$?

F. -14

G. $\frac{5}{6}$

H. $\frac{7}{3}$

J. 6

K. 14

27. Let m and n be 2 positive integers, such that $m < n$. Which of the following compound inequalities *must* be true?

A. $0 < \sqrt{mn} < m$
B. $1 < \sqrt{mn} < m$
C. $m < \sqrt{mn} < n$
D. $\sqrt{m} < \sqrt{mn} < \sqrt{n}$
E. $\sqrt{m-n} < \sqrt{mn} < \sqrt{m+n}$

28. Two similar triangles have perimeters in the ratio 3:5. The sides of the smaller triangle measure 3 cm, 5 cm, and 7 cm, respectively. What is the perimeter, in centimeters, of the larger triangle?

F. 15
G. 18
H. 20
J. 25
K. 36

GO ON TO THE NEXT PAGE.

2 △ △ △ △ △ △ △ △ △ 2

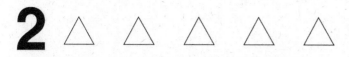

29. Thomas and Jonelle are playing darts in their garage using the board with the point values for each region shown below. The radius of the outside circle is 10 inches, and each of the other circles has a radius 2 inches smaller than the next larger circle. All of the circles have the same center. Thomas has only 1 dart left to throw and needs at least 30 points to win the game. Assuming that his last dart hits at a random point within a single region on the board, what is the percent chance that Thomas will win the game?

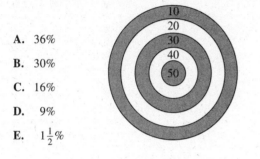

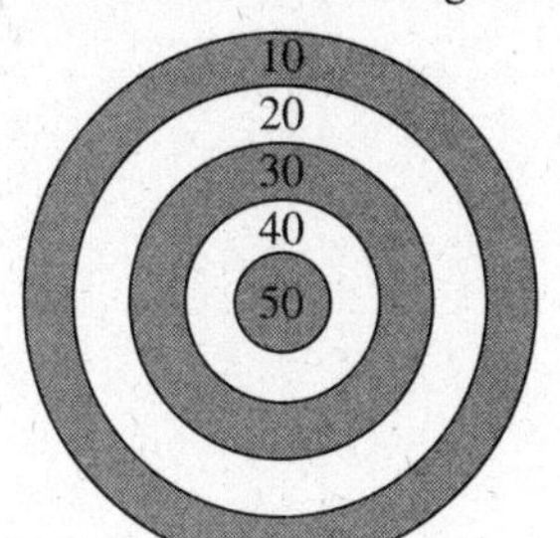

A. 36%
B. 30%
C. 16%
D. 9%
E. $1\frac{1}{2}$%

DO YOUR FIGURING HERE.

30. When asked his age, the algebra teacher said, "If you square my age, then subtract 23 times my age, the result is 50." How old is he?

F. 23
G. 25
H. 27
J. 46
K. 50

31. The distance, d, an accelerating object travels in t seconds can be modeled by the equation $d = \frac{1}{2}at^2$, where a is the acceleration rate, in meters per second per second. If a car accelerates from a stop at the rate of 20 meters per second per second and travels a distance of 80 meters, about how many seconds did the car travel?

A. Between 1 and 2
B. Between 2 and 3
C. Between 3 and 4
D. 4
E. 8

32. Which of the following is the set of all real numbers x such that $x + 3 > x + 5$?

F. The empty set
G. The set containing all real numbers
H. The set containing all negative real numbers
J. The set containing all nonnegative real numbers
K. The set containing only zero

Taking Additional Practice Tests

GO ON TO THE NEXT PAGE.

2 △ △ △ △ △ △ △ △ △ 2

DO YOUR FIGURING HERE.

Use the following information to answer questions 33–35.

A survey in a study skills class asked the 20 students enrolled in the class how many hours (rounded to the nearest hour) they had spent studying on the previous evening. The 20 responses are summarized by the histogram below.

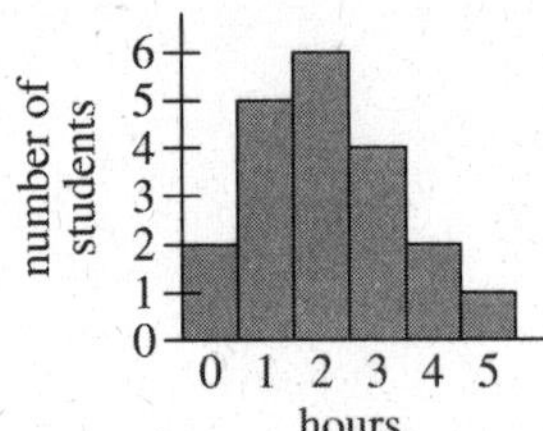

33. What fraction of the students responded that they had spent less than 3 hours studying?

A. $\frac{13}{100}$

B. $\frac{1}{5}$

C. $\frac{3}{10}$

D. $\frac{13}{20}$

E. $\frac{17}{20}$

34. The teacher decides to show the data in a circle graph (pie chart). What should be the measure of the central angle of the sector for 3 hours?

F. 18°
G. 20°
H. 36°
J. 72°
K. 90°

35. To the nearest tenth of an hour, what is the average number of hours for the 20 survey responses?

A. 2.0
B. 2.1
C. 2.3
D. 2.5
E. 3.0

GO ON TO THE NEXT PAGE.

2 △ △ △ △ △ △ △ △ △ 2

36. Pentagons have 5 diagonals, as illustrated below.

DO YOUR FIGURING HERE.

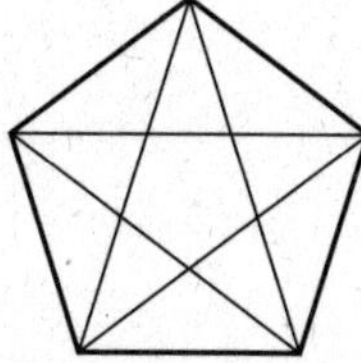

How many diagonals does the octagon below have?

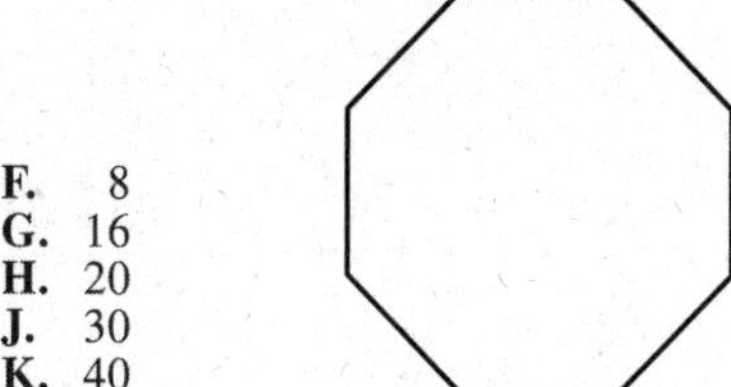

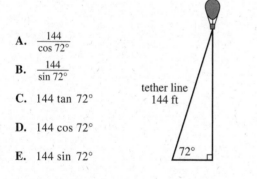

F. 8
G. 16
H. 20
J. 30
K. 40

37. The bottom of the basket of a hot-air balloon is parallel to the level ground. One taut tether line 144 feet long is attached to the center of the bottom of the basket and is anchored to the ground at an angle of 72°, as shown in the figure below. Which of the following expressions gives the distance, in feet, from the center of the bottom of the basket to the ground?

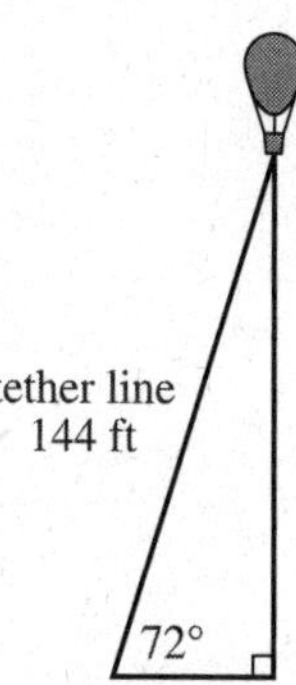

A. 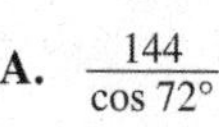 $\frac{144}{\cos 72°}$

B. $\frac{144}{\sin 72°}$

C. 144 tan 72°

D. 144 cos 72°

E. 144 sin 72°

38. The coordinates of the endpoints of $\overline{GH}$, in the standard (x,y) coordinate plane, are $(-8,-3)$ and $(2,3)$. What is the x-coordinate of the midpoint of $\overline{GH}$?

F. −6
G. −3
H. 0
J. 3
K. 5

GO ON TO THE NEXT PAGE.

2          2

DO YOUR FIGURING HERE.

39. Let $2x + 3y = 4$ and $5x + 6y = 7$. What is the value of $8x + 9y$?

A. −10
B. −1
C. 2
D. 7
E. 10

40. What are the values of θ, between 0 and 2π, when $\tan \theta = -1$?

F. $\frac{\pi}{4}$ and $\frac{3\pi}{4}$ only

G. $\frac{3\pi}{4}$ and $\frac{5\pi}{4}$ only

H. $\frac{3\pi}{4}$ and $\frac{7\pi}{4}$ only

J. $\frac{5\pi}{4}$ and $\frac{7\pi}{4}$ only

K. $\frac{\pi}{4}$, $\frac{3\pi}{4}$, $\frac{5\pi}{4}$, and $\frac{7\pi}{4}$

41. For the complex number i and an integer x, which of the following is a possible value of i^x ?

A. 0
B. 1
C. 2
D. 3
E. 4

42. A can of soda pop has the shape of a right circular cylinder with an inside height of 6 inches and an inside diameter of 2 inches. When you pour the soda pop from the full can into a cylindrical glass with an inside diameter of 3 inches, about how many inches high is the soda pop in the glass?
(Note: The volume of a right circular cylinder is $\pi r^2 h$.)

F. $2\frac{2}{3}$

G. 4

H. 5

J. $6\frac{2}{3}$

K. 8

GO ON TO THE NEXT PAGE.

2 △ △ △ △ △ △ △ △ △ 2

DO YOUR FIGURING HERE.

43. The height and radius of the right circular cylinder below are given in meters. What is the volume, in cubic meters, of the cylinder?

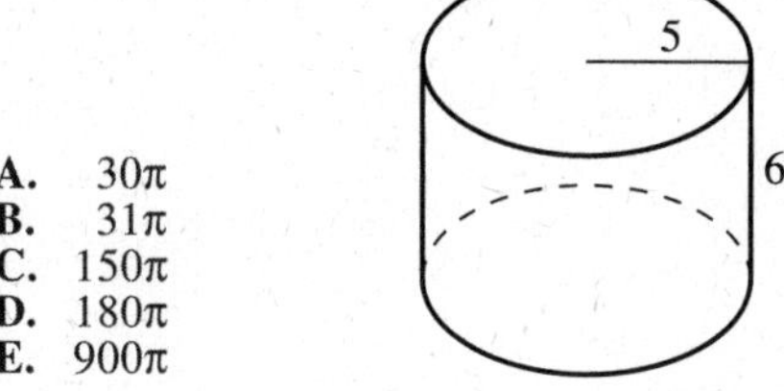

A. 30π
B. 31π
C. 150π
D. 180π
E. 900π

44. Lines l_1 and l_2 intersect each other and 3 parallel lines, l_3, l_4, and l_5, at the points shown in the figure below. The ratio of the perimeter of $\triangle ABC$ to the perimeter of $\triangle AFG$ is 1:3. The ratio of DE to FG is 2:3. What is the ratio of AC to CE ?

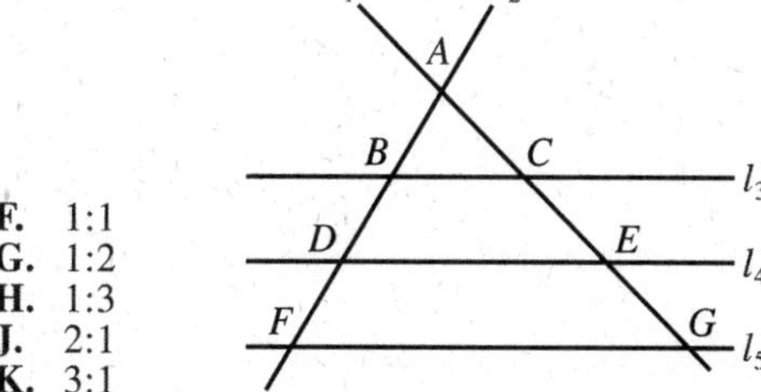

F. 1:1
G. 1:2
H. 1:3
J. 2:1
K. 3:1

45. A rocket lifted off from a launch pad and traveled vertically 30 kilometers, then traveled 40 kilometers at 30° from the vertical, and then traveled 100 kilometers at 45° from the vertical, as shown in the figure below. At that point, the rocket was how many kilometers above the height of the launch pad?

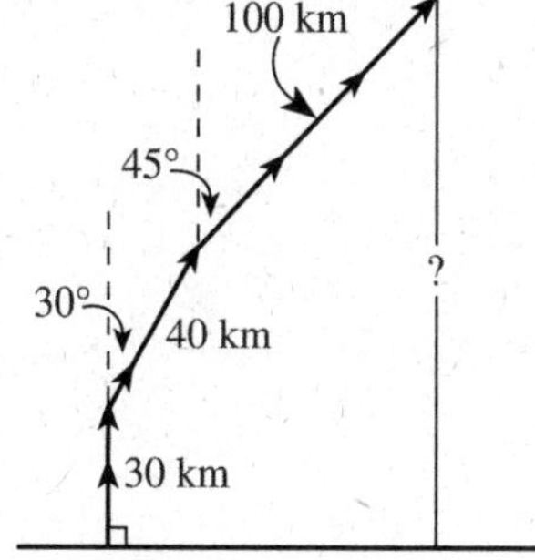

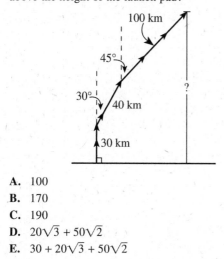

A. 100
B. 170
C. 190
D. $20\sqrt{3} + 50\sqrt{2}$
E. $30 + 20\sqrt{3} + 50\sqrt{2}$

GO ON TO THE NEXT PAGE.

2 △ △ △ △ △ △ △ △ △ 2

DO YOUR FIGURING HERE.

46. Machine A produces 500 springs a day. The number of *defective* springs produced by this machine each day is recorded for 60 days. Based on the distribution given below, what is the expected value of the number of *defective* springs produced by Machine A in any single day?

Number, n, of defective springs produced	Probability that n defective springs are produced in any single day
0	0.70
1	0.20
2	0.05
3	0.05

F. 0.00
G. 0.45
H. 0.70
J. 1.00
K. 1.50

47. The height above the ground, h units, of an object t seconds after being thrown from the top of a building is given by the equation $h = -2t^2 + 10t + 48$. An equivalent factored form of this equation shows that the object:

A. starts at a point 2 units off the ground.
B. reaches a maximum height of 3 units.
C. reaches a maximum height of 8 units.
D. reaches the ground at 3 seconds.
E. reaches the ground at 8 seconds.

48. For all positive values of g and h, which of the following expressions is equivalent to $g^2\sqrt{g^5} \cdot h^2\sqrt[4]{h^5}$?

F. $g^2h^2\sqrt[5]{g^2h^2}$
G. $g^3h\sqrt[4]{g^2h^3}$
H. $g^4h^3\sqrt[4]{g^2h}$
J. $g^4h^4\sqrt{gh}$
K. g^7h^7

49. The value of $\log_5\left(5^{\frac{13}{2}}\right)$ is between which of the following pairs of consecutive integers?

A. 0 and 1
B. 4 and 5
C. 5 and 6
D. 6 and 7
E. 9 and 10

GO ON TO THE NEXT PAGE.

2 △ △ △ △ △ △ △ △ △ 2

Use the following information to answer questions 50–52.

DO YOUR FIGURING HERE.

A storage facility is currently offering a special rate to customers who sign contracts for 6 months or more. According to this special rate, the first month's rent is \$1, and for each month after the first month, customers pay the regular monthly rental rate. The table below shows the storage unit sizes available, the floor dimensions, and the regular monthly rental rate. All the units have the same height.

Size	Floor dimensions, in meters	Regular monthly rental rate
1	2 × 4	\$ 30
2	4 × 4	\$ 60
3	4 × 8	\$100
4	8 × 8	\$150
5	8 × 16	\$200

50. Daria will sign a contract to rent a Size 3 unit for 12 months at the current special rate. The amount Daria will pay for 12 months at the current special rate represents what percent decrease from the regular rental rate for 12 months?

F. 8.25%
G. 8.33%
H. 8.42%
J. 9.00%
K. 9.09%

51. Size 5 units can be subdivided to form other sizes of units. What is the greatest number of Size 1 units that can be formed from a single Size 5 unit?

A. 2
B. 4
C. 8
D. 10
E. 16

52. Janelle, the owner of the storage facility, is considering building new units that have floor dimensions larger than Size 5 units. She will use the floor area to determine the heating requirements of these larger units. For this calculation, Janelle will use the same relationship between the unit size number and the respective floor area for Sizes 1 through 5. Which of the following expressions gives the floor area, in square meters, of a Size x storage unit?

F. $2^3 \cdot x$
G. 2^{3x}
H. $2^{(2+x)}$
J. $2(x+1)^2$
K. $(x+2)^2$

GO ON TO THE NEXT PAGE.

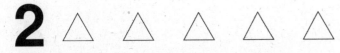

2 △ △ △ △ △    △ 2

DO YOUR FIGURING HERE.

53. A trigonometric function with equation $y = a \sin(bx + c)$, where a, b, and c are real numbers, is graphed in the standard (x,y) coordinate plane below. The *period* of this function $f(x)$ is the smallest positive number p such that $f(x + p) = f(x)$ for every real number x. One of the following is the period of this function. Which one is it?

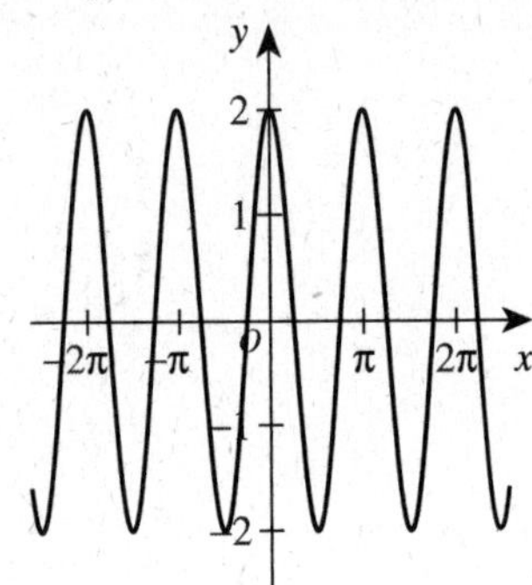

A. $\frac{\pi}{2}$

B. π

C. 2π

D. 4π

E. 2

54. The component forms of vectors **u** and **v** are given by $\mathbf{u} = \langle 5,3 \rangle$ and $\mathbf{v} = \langle 2,-7 \rangle$. Given that $2\mathbf{u} + (-3\mathbf{v}) + \mathbf{w} = \mathbf{0}$, what is the component form of **w** ?

F. $\langle -16, 15 \rangle$
G. $\langle -4, -27 \rangle$
H. $\langle 3, 10 \rangle$
J. $\langle 4, 27 \rangle$
K. $\langle 16, -15 \rangle$

55. For how many integers x is the equation $3^{x+1} = 9^{x-2}$ true?

A. 0
B. 1
C. 2
D. 3
E. An infinite number

GO ON TO THE NEXT PAGE.

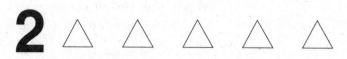

2 △ △ △ △ △ △ △ △ △ 2

56. In $\triangle ABC$ shown below, the length of $\overline{AC}$ and the measure of θ will remain constant. The length of $\overline{AC}$ is 20 inches and the measure of $\angle C$ is equal to θ. Initially, the length of $\overline{BC}$ is 15 inches, and the length of $\overline{BC}$ is the function given by $f(t) = 15 - 2t$, where t is time, in seconds, since the length of $\overline{BC}$ began to decrease. What is the time, t, at which the resulting triangle will have an area that is $\frac{1}{2}$ the area of the original triangle?

(Note: The area of a triangle is $\frac{1}{2}ab \sin x$, where a and b are the lengths of the sides that form the interior angle with measure x.)

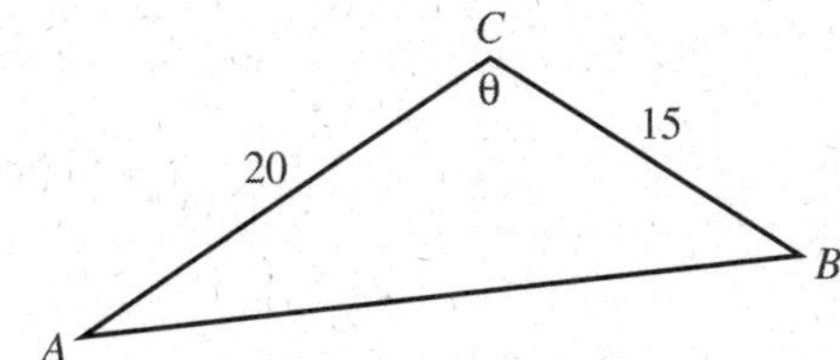

F. 0

G. $\frac{15}{8}$

H. $\frac{15}{4}$

J. $\frac{45}{8}$

K. $\frac{45}{4}$

57. Which of the following expressions gives the number of distinct permutations of the letters in PEOPLE ?

A. 6!

B. 4(4!)

C. $\frac{6!}{4!}$

D. $\frac{6!}{2!}$

E. $\frac{6!}{(2!)(2!)}$

DO YOUR FIGURING HERE.

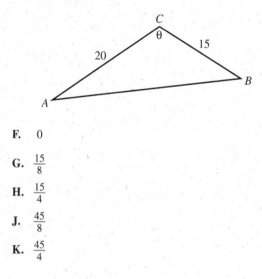

Taking Additional Practice Tests

GO ON TO THE NEXT PAGE.

2 △ △ △ △ △ △ △ △ 2

58. Which of the following expressions is equivalent to $49x^2 + 81$?

F. $(7x + 9)^2$
G. $(7x + 9i)^2$
H. $(7x - 9i)^2$
J. $(7x - 9)(7x + 9)$
K. $(7x - 9i)(7x + 9i)$

DO YOUR FIGURING HERE.

59. A bivariate data set of observed values along with a line of best fit for the data set are shown in the standard (x,y) coordinate plane below. The set of 4 residuals for the model is given by $y_i - y(x_i)$, for $i = 1, 2, 3, 4$, where y_i is the observed y-value corresponding to the input x_i, and $(x_i, y(x_i))$ is on the line of best fit. What is the absolute value of the largest residual for this model?

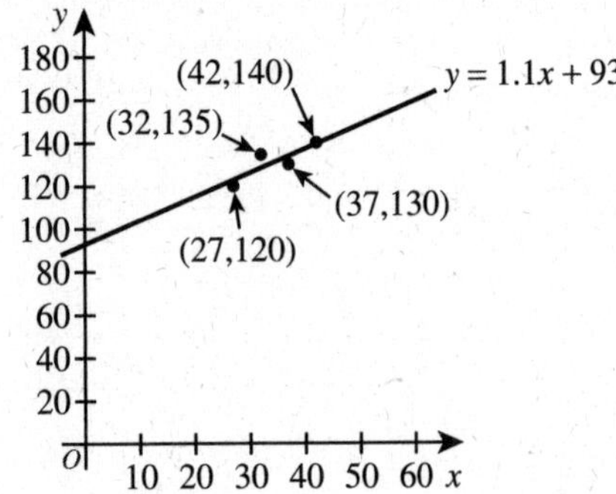

A. 2.5
B. 6.8
C. 15.0
D. 20.0
E. 42.0

GO ON TO THE NEXT PAGE.

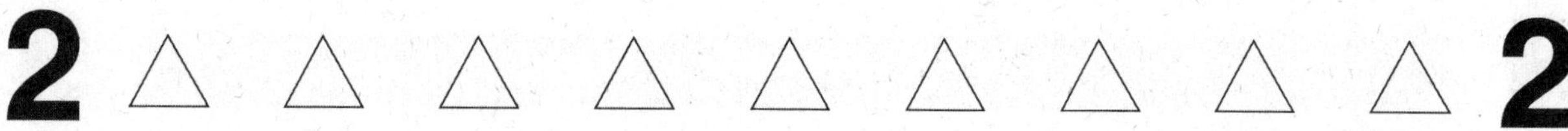

60. For the first 5 possible values of x, the table below gives the probability, $P(x)$, that a certain factory machine will make x errors on any given workday.

x errors	$P(x)$
0	0.0823
1	0.2185
2	0.2712
3	0.2046
4	0.1238

Which of the following values is closest to the probability that this machine will make at least 1 error on any given workday?

F. 0.2185
G. 0.5996
H. 0.6992
J. 0.8181
K. 0.9177

DO YOUR FIGURING HERE.

END OF TEST 2

STOP! DO NOT TURN THE PAGE UNTIL TOLD TO DO SO.

DO NOT RETURN TO THE PREVIOUS TEST.

3 3

READING TEST

35 Minutes—40 Questions

DIRECTIONS: There are several passages in this test. Each passage is accompanied by several questions. After reading a passage, choose the best answer to each question and fill in the corresponding oval on your answer document. You may refer to the passages as often as necessary.

Passage I

PROSE FICTION: This passage is adapted from the novel *The Fisher King* by Paule Marshall (©2000 by Paule Marshall).

It was nearing the end of the second set, the jazz show winding down when Hattie heard Abe Kaiser at the microphone call Everett Payne's name. Heard his name and, to her surprise, saw him slowly stand up in the bullpen up front. She hadn't seen him join the other local musicians, including Shades Bowen with his tenor sax, in what was called the bullpen, which was simply a dozen or so chairs grouped near the bandstand. The young locals gathered there each Sunday evening, hoping for a chance to perform. Because toward the end of the final set, the custom was to invite one or two of them to sit in with the band. They sometimes even got to choose the tune they wanted to play.

This Sunday, Everett Payne, not long out of the army, was the one being invited to sit in.

Breath held, Hattie watched him separate himself from the hopefuls and approach the stand, taking his time, moving with what almost seemed a deliberate pause between each step. The crowd waiting.

That was his way, Hattie knew. His body moving absentmindedly through space, his head, his thoughts on something other than his surroundings, and his eyes like a curtain he occasionally drew aside a fraction of an inch to peer out at the world. A world far less interesting than the music inside his head.

She watched now as he slowly mounted the bandstand and conferred with the bassist and drummer, those two were all he would need. Then, without announcing the name of the tune he intended playing, without in any way acknowledging the audience, he sat down at the piano and brought his hands—large hands, the fingers long and splayed and slightly arched—down on the opening bars of "Sonny Boy Blue."

"Sonny Boy Blue!" That hokey-doke tune!

Around her, the purists looked askance at each other from behind their regulation shades and slouched deeper in their chairs in open disgust.

At first, hokey though it was, he played the song straight through as written, the rather long introduction, verse, and chorus. And he did so with great care, although at a slower tempo than was called for and with a formality that lent the Tin Pan Alley tune a depth and thoughtfulness no one else would have accorded it.

Quickly taking their cue from him, the bassist reached for his bow, the drummer for his brushes, the two of them also treating the original as if it were a serious piece of music.

Everett Payne took his time paying his respects to the tune as written, and once that was done, he hunched closer to the piano, angled his head sharply to the left, completely closed the curtain of his gaze, and with his hands commanding the length and breadth of the keyboard he unleashed a dazzling pyrotechnic of chords (you could almost see their colors), polyrhythms, seemingly unrelated harmonies, and ideas—fresh, brash, outrageous ideas. It was an outpouring of ideas and feelings informed by his own brand of lyricism and lit from time to time by flashes of the recognizable melody. He continued to acknowledge the little simple-minded tune, while at the same time furiously recasting and reinventing it in an image all his own.

A collective in-suck of breath throughout the club.

Where, Hattie wondered, did he come by the dazzling array of ideas and wealth of feeling? What was the source? It had to do, she speculated, listening intently, with the way he held his head, angled to the left like that, tilted toward both heaven and earth. His right side, his right ear directed skyward, hearing up there, in the Upper Room among the stars Mahalia sang about, a new kind of music: splintered, atonal, profane, and possessing a wonderful dissonance that spoke to him, to his soul-case. For him, this was the true music of the spheres, of the maelstrom up there. When at the piano, he kept his right ear tuned to it at all times, letting it guide him, inspire him. His other ear? It remained earthbound, trained on the bedrock that for him was Bach and the blues.

Again and again he took them on a joyous, terrifying roller coaster of a ride it seemed to Hattie, and when he finally deposited them on terra firma after close to twenty minutes, everyone in Putnam Royal

GO ON TO THE NEXT PAGE.

3 3

could only sit there as if they were in church and weren't supposed to clap. Overcome. Until finally Alvin Edwards, who lived on Decatur Street and played trumpet in the school band, leaped to his feet and renamed him.

Alvin brought everyone up with him. Including the purists who normally refused to applaud even genius. They too stood up in languid praise of him.

1. It can reasonably be inferred from the passage that Shades Bowen:

A. did not accompany Everett Payne as he played "Sonny Boy Blue."
B. had been in the army with Everett Payne.
C. was the oldest musician in the bullpen.
D. did not usually allow the local musicians to play with the band.

2. The main purpose of the statement in line 62 is to:

F. illustrate the high expectations the audience initially had for Everett Payne's performance.
G. inform the reader of the audience's reaction to Everett Payne's performance.
H. counteract the narrator's description of Everett Payne's performance.
J. provide proof that Everett Payne was well known to the audience.

3. The passage most strongly suggests that the second set of the jazz shows at the club is:

A. the final set.
B. much longer than the first set.
C. followed by a third set on Sunday nights.
D. performed solely by the musicians in the bullpen.

4. Which of the following details is used in the passage to indicate how the purists in the audience initially reacted to Everett Payne's choice of music?

F. The overall silence of the audience, including the purists
G. The description of the audience's collective in-suck of breath
H. The posture the purists assumed in their seats
J. The fact that the purists stood up

5. According to the narrator, what did Hattie see Everett Payne do prior to playing "Sonny Boy Blue"?

A. Move quickly from his seat to the bandstand
B. Study the audience around him
C. Confer with the bassist and the drummer
D. Announce the name of the tune he was going to play

6. The passage initially portrays the purists most nearly as:

F. knowledgeable and open minded.
G. snobbish and intolerant.
H. rational and well educated.
J. inexperienced and uninhibited.

7. It can reasonably be inferred from the passage that Hattie believed Bach and the blues were the:

A. musical influences that Everett Payne tried to avoid representing when he played piano.
B. foundation of Everett Payne's inventive piano playing.
C. true music of the heavens that inspired Everett Payne's creativity as a piano player.
D. reason why Everett Payne's piano-playing abilities limited him to Tin Pan Alley tunes.

8. According to the passage, when Everett Payne first played "Sonny Boy Blue" straight through, he did so:

F. more slowly than was intended by the composer.
G. after it had been suggested by Abe Kaiser.
H. against the wishes of the bassist and drummer.
J. without following the original tune.

9. According to the passage, Hattie speculated that the source of Everett Payne's musical ideas and feelings during "Sonny Boy Blue" was in:

A. the way he tilted his head.
B. the simplemindedness of the song.
C. his ability to play with great formality.
D. his connection with the silent audience.

10. The narrator states that to Hattie, Everett Payne's performance was:

F. overly slow and formal.
G. deliberate yet absentminded.
H. like a song played in a church.
J. a roller coaster of a ride.

GO ON TO THE NEXT PAGE.

3 3

Passage II

SOCIAL STUDIES: This passage is adapted from Richard Moe's article "Mindless Madness Called Sprawl," based on a speech he gave on November 30, 1996, in Fresno, California (©1996 by Richard Moe).

At the time he gave the speech, Moe was president of the National Trust for Historic Preservation.

Drive down any highway leading into any town in the country, and what do you see? Fast-food outlets, office parks and shopping malls rising out of vast barren plains of asphalt. Residential subdivisions spreading like inkblots obliterating forests and farms in their relentless march across the landscape. Cars moving sluggishly down the broad ribbons of pavement or halting in frustrated clumps at choked intersections. You see communities drowning in a destructive, soulless, ugly mess called sprawl.

Many of us have developed a frightening form of selective blindness that allows us to pass by the appalling mess without really seeing it. We've allowed our communities to be destroyed bit by bit, and most of us have shrugged off this destruction as "the price of progress."

Development that destroys communities isn't progress. It's chaos. And it isn't inevitable, it's merely easy. Too many developers follow standard formulas, and too many government entities have adopted laws and policies that constitute powerful incentives for sprawl.

Why is an organization like the National Trust for Historic Preservation so concerned about sprawl? We're concerned because sprawl devastates older communities, leaving historic buildings and neighborhoods underused, poorly maintained or abandoned. We've learned that we can't hope to revitalize these communities without doing something to control the sprawl that keeps pushing further and further out from the center.

But our concern goes beyond that, because preservation today is about more than bricks and mortar. There's a growing body of grim evidence to support our belief that the destruction of traditional downtowns and older neighborhoods—places that people care about—is corroding the very sense of community that helps bind us together as a people and as a nation.

One form of sprawl—retail development that transforms roads into strip malls—is frequently spurred on by discount retailers, many of whom are now concentrating on the construction of superstores with more than 200,000 square feet of space. In many small towns, a single new superstore may have more retail space than the entire downtown business district. When a store like that opens, the retail center of gravity shifts away from Main Street. Downtown becomes a ghost town.

Sprawl's other most familiar form—spread-out residential subdivisions that "leapfrog" from the urban fringe into the countryside—is driven largely by the American dream of a detached home in the middle of a grassy lawn. Developers frequently claim they can build more "affordable" housing on the edge of town—but "affordable" for whom?

The developer's own expenses may be less, and the home buyer may find the prices attractive—but who picks up the extra costs of fire and police protection, new roads and new utility infrastructure in these outlying areas? We all do, in the form of higher taxes for needless duplication of services and infrastructure that already exist in older parts of our cities and towns.

People who say that sprawl is merely the natural product of marketplace forces at work fail to recognize that the game isn't being played on a level field. Government at every level is riddled with policies that mandate or encourage sprawl.

By prohibiting mixed uses and mandating inordinate amounts of parking and unreasonable setback requirements, most current zoning laws make it impossible—even illegal—to create the sort of compact walkable environment that attracts us to older neighborhoods and historic communities all over the world. These codes are a major reason why 82 percent of all trips in the United States are taken by car. The average American household now allocates more than 18 percent of its budget to transportation expenses, most of which are auto-related. That's more than it spends for food and three times more than it spends for health care.

Our communities should be shaped by choice, not by chance. One of the most effective ways to reach this goal is to insist on sensible land-use planning. The way we zone and design our communities either opens up or forecloses alternatives to the automobile. Municipalities should promote downtown housing and mixed-use zoning that reduce the distances people must travel between home and work. The goal should be an integrated system of planning decisions and regulations that knit communities together instead of tearing them apart. We should demand land-use planning that exhibits a strong bias in favor of existing communities.

11. The principal aim of the passage can best be classified as:

A. persuasive.
B. explanatory.
C. descriptive.
D. narrative.

GO ON TO THE NEXT PAGE.

3 3

12. Among the following quotations from the passage, the one that best summarizes what the author would like to see happen is:
   F. "laws and policies that constitute powerful incentives for sprawl" (lines 20–22).
   G. "the destruction of traditional downtowns" (line 34).
   H. "'affordable' housing on the edge of town" (line 53).
   J. "an integrated system of planning decisions and regulations" (lines 87–88).

13. The last paragraph differs from the first paragraph in that in the last paragraph the author:
   A. asks a question and then answers it.
   B. uses more statistics to support his arguments.
   C. incorporates more emotional language.
   D. offers solutions rather than stating a problem.

14. In the passage, the author answers all of the following questions EXCEPT:
   F. How long has sprawl been happening in US cities?
   G. Is development synonymous with progress?
   H. What is one major reason that people in the United States use automobiles so much?
   J. What should communities do to combat sprawl?

15. The author states that one superstore may do all of the following EXCEPT:
   A. have more retail space than an entire downtown.
   B. lead to serious downtown renovations.
   C. make the downtown area into a ghost town.
   D. shift the center of gravity away from downtown.

16. The statistics cited by the author in the tenth paragraph (lines 67–79) are used to illustrate the concept that:
   F. allowing mixed uses of land leads to environmental destruction.
   G. current zoning laws help create a compact, walkable environment.
   H. land-use regulations now in effect increase the overall costs of transportation.
   J. Americans spend too much of their budgets on food and health care.

17. One form of sprawl the author describes is retail development that:
   A. adjoins existing downtown areas.
   B. utilizes historic buildings.
   C. turns roads into strip malls.
   D. promotes a sense of community around a superstore.

18. As it is used in line 51, the word *detached* most nearly means:
   F. objective.
   G. set apart.
   H. broken apart.
   J. taken away.

19. The author uses the statement "The game isn't being played on a level field" (line 64) most nearly to mean that:
   A. cities needlessly duplicate essential services.
   B. higher taxes for some people make their lives more difficult.
   C. marketplace forces are at work.
   D. governmental decisions influence marketplace forces.

20. The phrase *mixed uses* (line 67) most likely refers to:
   F. having large parking lots around even larger stores.
   G. preserving and restoring historic neighborhoods.
   H. ensuring that automobiles cannot be driven to the various local businesses.
   J. allowing one area to contain various types of development.

GO ON TO THE NEXT PAGE.

3 3

Passage III

HUMANITIES: This passage is adapted from the essay "My Life with a Field Guide" by Diana Kappel-Smith (©2002 by Phi Beta Kappa Society).

I was seventeen when it started. My family was on vacation, and one day we went on a nature walk led by a young man a few years older than I. Probably I wanted to get his attention—I'm sure I did—so I pointed to a flower and asked, "What's that?"

"Hmmm? Oh, just an aster," he said.

Was there a hint of a sniff as he turned away? There was! It was just an aster and I was just a total ignoramus!

And I remember the aster. Its rays were a brilliant purple, its core a dense coin of yellow velvet. It focused light as a crystal will. It faced the sun; it was the sun's echo.

Later that day, a book with a green cover lay on the arm of a chair under an apple tree. It was the same volume that our guide had carried as he marched us through the woods. The book had been left there, by itself. It was a thing of power. In the thin summer shadow of the tree, quivering, like a veil, the book was revealed, and I reached for it. A FIELD GUIDE TO WILD FLOWERS—PETERSON & McKENNY, its cover said. Its backside was ruled like a measuring tape, its inside was full of drawings of flowers. By the end of that week I had my own copy. I have it still.

Over the next several years this field guide would become my closest companion, a slice of worldview, as indispensable as eyes or hands. I didn't arrive at this intimacy right away, however. This wasn't going to be an easy affair for either of us.

I'll give you an example of how it went. After I'd owned the Peterson's for about a week, I went on a hike with some friends up a little mountain, taking the book along. Halfway up the mountain, there by the trailside was a yellow flower, a nice opportunity to take my new guide for a test drive. "Go on ahead!" I said to my hiking companions, "I'll be a minute . . ." Famous last words.

I had already figured out the business of the book's colored tabs. I turned in an authoritative way to the Yellow part and began to flip through. By the time the last of my friends had disappeared up the trail, I'd arrived at a page where things looked right. Five petals? Yes. Pinnate leaves? Whatever. Buttercup? There are, amazingly, *eleven* buttercups. Who would have thought? However hard I tried to make it so, my item was not one of them. Next page. Aha! this looked more like it. Bushy cinquefoil? Nope, leaves not *quiiite* right, are they? As the gnats descended, I noticed that there were six more pages ahead, each packed with five-petaled yellow flowers—St. John's wort loosestrifes, puccoons.

Why I persisted in carrying it around and consulting its crowded pages at every opportunity, I have no idea. The book was stubborn; well, I was stubborn, too; that was part of it. And I had no choice, really, not if I wanted to *get in*. A landscape may be handsome in the aggregate, but this book led to the particulars, and that's what I wanted. A less complete guide would have been easier to start with, but more frustrating in the end. A more complete book would have been impossible for me to use. So I persisted in wrestling with the Peterson's, and thus by slow degrees the crowd of plant stuff in the world became composed of individuals. As it did, the book changed: its cover was stained by water and snack food, the spine grew invitingly lax, and some of the margins sprouted cryptic annotations.

By the time the next summer came, I had fully discovered the joy of the hunt, and every new species had its trophy of data—name and place and date—to be jotted down. If I'd found a flower before, I was happy to see it again. I often addressed it with enthusiasm: *Hi there, Solidago hispida!* I discovered early on that a plant's Latin name is a name of power by which the plant can be uniquely identified among different spoken tongues, across continents, and through time. The genus name lashes it firmly to its closest kin, while its species name describes a personal attribute—*rubrum* meaning red, *officinale* meaning medicinal, *odoratus* meaning smelly, and so on. It all makes such delightful sense!

My friend Julie and I identified individual plants in our rambles, but from the particulars we began to know wholes. Bogs held one community, montane forests held another, and the plants they held in common were clues to intricate dramas of climate change and continental drift. So from plant communities it followed that the grand schemes of things, when they came our way, arrived rooted in real place and personal experience: quaternary geology, biogeography, evolutionary biology all lay on the road that we had begun to travel.

21. The passage is best described as being told from the point of view of someone who is:

A. tracing her developing interest in identifying flowers and in the natural world.
B. reexamining the event that led her to a lifelong fascination with asters.
C. reviewing her relationships with people who have shared her interest in flowers.
D. describing how her hobby of identifying flowers became a profitable career.

GO ON TO THE NEXT PAGE.

3 3

22. As portrayed by the author, the young man responded to her question about the flower with what is best described as:

F. acceptance.
G. surprise.
H. condescension.
J. anger.

23. What name, if any, does the author report assigning to the yellow flower she came across during a mountain hike?

A. St. John's wort
B. Loosestrife
C. Puccoon
D. The passage doesn't name the flower.

24. Looking back at her early experiences with the Peterson's, the author most strongly implies that the guide was:

F. daunting at first, but in retrospect preferable to either a more or a less complete guide.
G. easy to use in the beginning, but more frustrating in the end than a more complete guide would have been.
H. impossible for her to follow until she started pairing it with a different guide written for beginners.
J. appealing initially until she realized how poorly illustrated its crowded pages were.

25. As it is used in line 56, the phrase *get in* most nearly means:

A. arrive at a physical location.
B. be chosen for group membership.
C. truly understand the subject.
D. be friendly with someone.

26. The passage best supports which of the following conclusions about Julie?

F. She has more experience than the author has in identifying flowers.
G. She owns a house that's close to either a bog or a montane forest.
H. She sees value in understanding the various communities of plants.
J. She stopped using the Peterson's as her primary source of flower information.

27. The author states that the Peterson's became her closest companion over a period of several:

A. days.
B. weeks.
C. months.
D. years.

28. In the context of the passage, the author's statement in lines 56–58 most nearly means that she:

F. learned to understand landscapes by looking at their overall patterns rather than their details.
G. found that landscapes lost their appeal the more she tried to understand them logically.
H. hoped to paint attractive portraits of landscapes by paying careful attention to details.
J. sought a deeper knowledge of landscapes through learning about their individual parts.

29. The details in lines 64–66 primarily serve to suggest the:

A. poor craftsmanship the publishing company used in producing the Peterson's.
B. transformation the author's copy of the Peterson's underwent as a result of heavy use.
C. strange writing the author often encountered in reading the Peterson's.
D. carelessness with which the author used the Peterson's, much to her later regret.

30. The author refers to *Solidago hispida* as an example of a flower that she:

F. had great trouble identifying the first time she stumbled upon it.
G. hopes to finally come across on one of her nature walks.
H. was pleased to encounter again after she had learned to identify it.
J. feels has an inappropriate name given the plant's characteristics.

GO ON TO THE NEXT PAGE.

3 3

Passage IV

NATURAL SCIENCE: This passage is adapted from the article "When Research Is a Snow Job" by Sarah Boyle (©2002 by National Wildlife).

The figure is beyond comprehension: Every year, 1,000,000,000,000,000,000,000,000 (1 septillion) snowflakes fall worldwide. As the crystals fall, they encounter different atmospheric conditions that produce flakes with unique attributes. The more complex those conditions are, the more elaborate the crystals.

Kenneth Libbrecht is a physicist at the California Institute of Technology. Along with the work of scientists at the U.S. Department of Agriculture's Agricultural Research Service (ARS), his research is uncovering new information about the magical world of snow crystals—information that has practical applications in such diverse areas as agriculture and the production of electricity.

Snow crystals are individual crystals—usually in a hexagonal form—while snowflakes are collections of two or more snow crystals. Beginning as condensed water vapor, a crystal typically grows around a nucleus of dust. Its shape depends on how the six side facets—or faces—grow in relation to the top and bottom facets. If they grow relatively tall, the crystal appears column-like; if the side facets are short compared to the length of the bottom and top facets, the crystal looks platelike.

Currently Libbrecht is trying to crack the problem of why the crystal facets' growth varies with temperature. He believes this may have something to do with the ice surface's "quasi-liquid" layer, which affects how water molecules stick to the surface.

By manipulating the temperature and humidity within an incubation chamber (and by adding an electric current or various gases at times), Libbrecht creates "designer" snowflakes in his lab. Such experiments are helping him determine how crystals form.

William Wergin, a retired ARS research biologist, and a colleague, Eric Erbe, were using scanning electron microscopy to look at biological problems relating to agriculture. To avoid the laborious procedure that using such equipment usually entails, the two scientists decided to freeze the tissue they were working with and look at it in the frozen state.

"One day it happened to be snowing," says Wergin, "and we were looking for a specimen. We imaged some snowflakes and were very surprised to see what we did." It was the first time anyone had attempted to image snow crystals with scanning electron microscopy, which provides precise detail about the crystals' shape, structural features and metamorphosed conditions (crystals often change once on the ground depending on the surrounding environment).

Wergin called another ARS colleague, hydrologist Albert Rango, to see if the snow crystal magnifications had any applications for his research. Rango now uses Wergin's electron microscopy data, along with microwave satellite data, in the Snowmelt Runoff Model to predict the amount of water available in a winter snowpack. For western states such as Colorado, Montana, Utah and Wyoming, about 75 percent of the annual water supply comes from snowmelt. Snowmelt water is critical to crop irrigation and hydroelectric power, as well as recreation and domestic water supplies, fisheries management and flood control.

Before employing the scanning electron microscopy results, the forecasted amounts of snowpack water were inaccurate whenever the size and shape of the snow crystals varied much from the norm. "The more we know about crystals," notes Rango, "the easier it will be to use microwave satellite data for predictions of the snow water equivalent."

Currently, forecasts using the model are about 90 percent accurate. A 1980 study estimated that improving the prediction by 1 percent would save $38 million in irrigation and hydropower in the western United States.

Rango is also looking ahead at climate change predictions. "Following the estimates that have been made about what will happen by 2100, things are definitely warming up," he says. Temperature increases will likely result in a reduction in stream flow as overall snow accumulation decreases, winter precipitation runs off as rain, and water evaporates at a quicker rate. The gap between water supply and demand will magnify even more, greatly increasing water's economic value, anticipates Rango.

Not only does the crystal research help gauge snowmelt, it is also useful in predicting avalanches, designing artificial snow, and, perhaps in the near future, examining air pollution. "You can put snow in a scanning electron microscope and tell which elements are present, such as sulfur and nitrogen," says Wergin. "You can then see what kind of pollution is in the area and possibly track the source."

31. It can reasonably be inferred from the passage that the information about the scientific study of snow is presented primarily to:

A. emphasize the importance of communication among scientists.
B. explain how snow crystal facets influence the snowpack in some western states.
C. showcase the varied uses of the scanning electron microscope.
D. demonstrate some of the practical applications of the study of snow crystals.

GO ON TO THE NEXT PAGE.

3 3

32. According to the passage, the use of scanning electron microscopy can save money by:
   F. encouraging scientists to make estimates of water requirements far into the future.
   G. allowing forecasters to predict more accurately the quantity of water in the snowpack.
   H. helping agricultural researchers to identify biological problems.
   J. increasing the water supply for Colorado, Montana, Utah, and Wyoming by 75 percent.

33. It can reasonably be inferred that the phrase *metamorphosed conditions* (lines 47–48) refers to the:
   A. temperature and humidity at which crystals form.
   B. process by which snow crystals develop from a speck of dust and water vapor.
   C. state of snow crystals after they reach the ground.
   D. major changes in environmental conditions.

34. According to the passage, the addition of electron microscopy data to the Snowmelt Runoff Model allows scientists using the model to include in their predictions detailed information about:
   F. microwave satellite data.
   G. structural variations of snow crystals.
   H. locations having the most snowfall.
   J. biological problems related to agriculture.

35. According to Rango, one reason that water's economic value is likely to increase by the year 2100 is that:
   A. more water will be polluted by then.
   B. less water will be wasted due to more accurate predictions of the water supply.
   C. the sulfur and nitrogen content in snow is likely to increase.
   D. predicted climate changes will reduce overall snow accumulation.

36. According to the passage, snowflakes have infinite variety because:
   F. enormous numbers of snow crystals fall worldwide.
   G. falling snow crystals meet with varied atmospheric conditions.
   H. snow crystals fall at various rates, creating unique snowflakes.
   J. complexities in the atmosphere slow snow crystal development.

37. The passage states that snowflakes differ from snow crystals in that snowflakes:
   A. grow around a nucleus of dust.
   B. combine to form snow crystals.
   C. grow in relation to top and bottom facets.
   D. are composed of more than one crystal.

38. The term *"designer" snowflakes* (line 32) refers directly to the fact that:
   F. no two snowflakes are alike.
   G. Libbrecht produces the snowflakes in his lab.
   H. snowflakes are part of the grand design of nature.
   J. Libbrecht's snowflakes exhibit special beauty.

39. As it is used in line 59, the word *critical* most nearly means:
   A. evaluative.
   B. faultfinding.
   C. vital.
   D. acute.

40. The passage states that research about snow crystals has helped scientists do all of the following EXCEPT:
   F. extract pollutants from snow.
   G. gauge snowmelt.
   H. design artificial snow.
   J. predict avalanches.

END OF TEST 3

STOP! DO NOT TURN THE PAGE UNTIL TOLD TO DO SO.

DO NOT RETURN TO A PREVIOUS TEST.

4 ○ ○ ○ ○ ○ ○ ○ ○ ○ 4

SCIENCE TEST

35 Minutes—40 Questions

DIRECTIONS: There are several passages in this test. Each passage is followed by several questions. After reading a passage, choose the best answer to each question and fill in the corresponding oval on your answer document. You may refer to the passages as often as necessary.

You are NOT permitted to use a calculator on this test.

Passage I

Two measures of water quality are the number of *Escherichia coli* bacteria present and the *biotic index*, BI (a numerical value based on the type, diversity, and pollution tolerance of aquatic invertebrate animals). Both of these measures can be affected by water flow.

E. coli levels that are above 100 colonies formed per 100 mL of water indicate reduced water quality. Figure 1 shows the *E. coli* levels on 5 collection days at Sites 1 and 2 in a river.

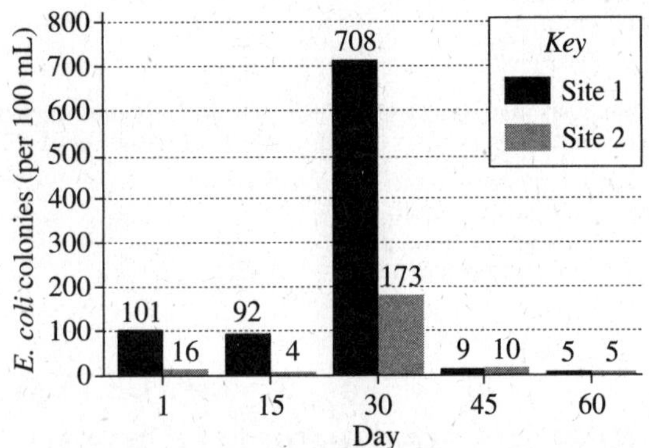

Figure 1

Table 1 shows how water quality rating varies with BI. Table 2 shows the average BI of each site during the collection period.

Table 1

BI	Water quality rating
≥ 3.6	excellent
2.6 to 3.5	good
2.1 to 2.5	fair
1.0 to 2.0	poor

Table 2

Location	Average BI
Site 1	6.3
Site 2	2.5

Figure 2 shows the water flow at each site on the 5 collection days.

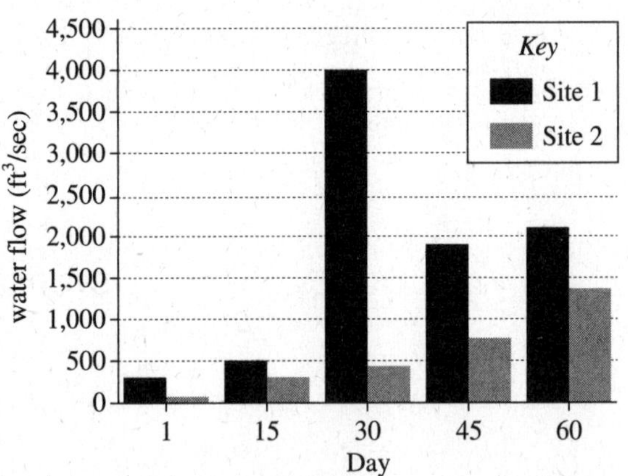

Figure 2

Figures adapted from Stephen C. Landry and Michele L. Tremblay, "State of the Upper Merrimack 1995–1997: A River Quality Report." ©2000 by Upper Merrimack River Local Advisory Committee.

GO ON TO THE NEXT PAGE.

1. If an *E. coli* level of over 400 colonies formed per 100 mL of water is unsafe for swimming, on which of the following collection days and at which site would it have been unsafe to swim?
   A. Day 1 at Site 1
   B. Day 30 at Site 1
   C. Day 1 at Site 2
   D. Day 30 at Site 2

2. Based on Figures 1 and 2, consider the average water flow and the average *E. coli* level for Site 1 and Site 2 over the collection period. Which site had the higher average water flow, and which site had the higher average *E. coli* level?

	Higher water flow	Higher *E. coli* level
F.	Site 1	Site 1
G.	Site 1	Site 2
H.	Site 2	Site 1
J.	Site 2	Site 2

3. According to Table 1, what is the relationship between water quality and biotic index?
   A. As water quality improves, biotic index increases.
   B. As water quality improves, biotic index remains the same.
   C. As water quality degrades, biotic index increases.
   D. As water quality degrades, biotic index remains the same.

4. As water quality improves, the number of *stone fly larvae* (a type of aquatic invertebrate) increases. Students hypothesized that more stone fly larvae would be found at Site 1 than at Site 2. Are the data presented in Table 2 consistent with this hypothesis?
   F. Yes; based on BI, Site 1 had a water quality rating of good and Site 2 had a water quality rating of poor.
   G. Yes; based on BI, Site 1 had a water quality rating of excellent and Site 2 had a water quality rating of fair.
   H. No; based on BI, Site 1 had a water quality rating of poor and Site 2 had a water quality rating of good.
   J. No; based on BI, Site 1 had a water quality rating of fair and Site 2 had a water quality rating of excellent.

5. Which set of data best supports the claim that Site 1 has *lower* water quality than Site 2 ?
   A. Figure 1
   B. Figure 2
   C. Table 1
   D. Table 2

6. Suppose large amounts of fertilizer from adjacent fields begin to enter the river at Site 1. The BI of this site will most likely change in which of the following ways? The BI will:
   F. increase, because water quality is likely to increase.
   G. increase, because water quality is likely to decrease.
   H. decrease, because water quality is likely to increase.
   J. decrease, because water quality is likely to decrease.

GO ON TO THE NEXT PAGE.

4 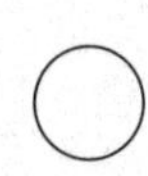 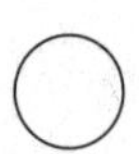   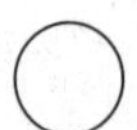 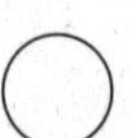 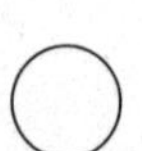  4

Passage II

Aluminum water-based paints (AWPs) contain aluminum (Al) flakes that give surfaces a shiny, metallic appearance. If the flakes corrode, a dull coating of aluminum hydroxide forms on them:

$$2Al + 6H_2O \rightarrow 2Al(OH)_3 + 3H_2$$

Table 1 shows the volume of H_2 gas produced over time (at 25°C and 1 atm) from 100 mL samples of freshly made AWPs 1–3 in 3 separate trials. AWPs 1–3 were identical except that each had a different concentration of DMEA, an AWP ingredient that increases pH.

Table 1

AWP	pH of AWP	Volume (mL) of H_2 produced by:			
		Day 2	Day 4	Day 6	Day 8
1	8	4	33	81	133
2	9	21	187	461	760
3	10	121	1,097	2,711	4,480

The AWP 3 trial was repeated 4 times, but for each trial, the sample had the same concentration of 1 of 4 corrosion inhibitors (see Figure 1).

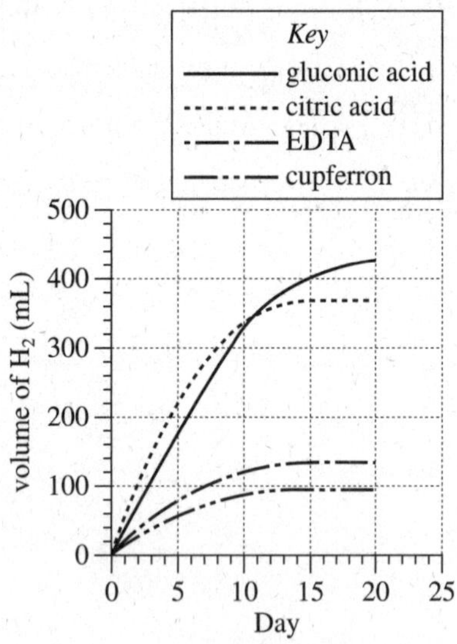

Figure 1

Figure 1 adapted from Bodo Müller, "Corrosion Inhibitors for Aluminum." ©1995 by Division of Chemical Education, Inc., American Chemical Society.

7. Based on Table 1, which of the following graphs best shows how the volume of H_2 produced by AWP 2 changed over time?

A. 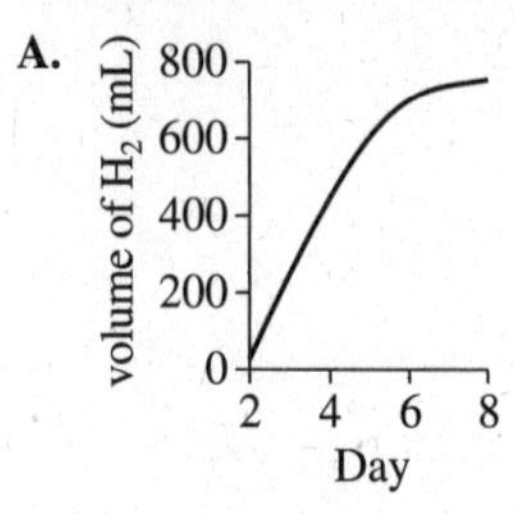

C. 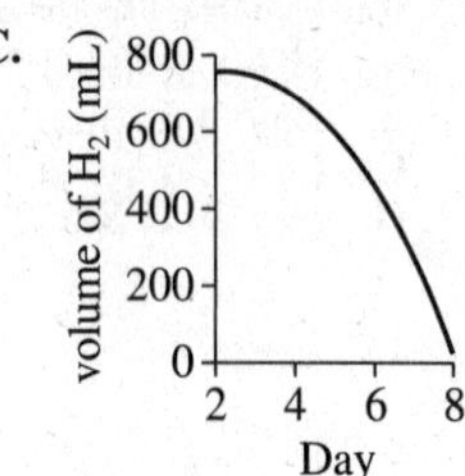

B. 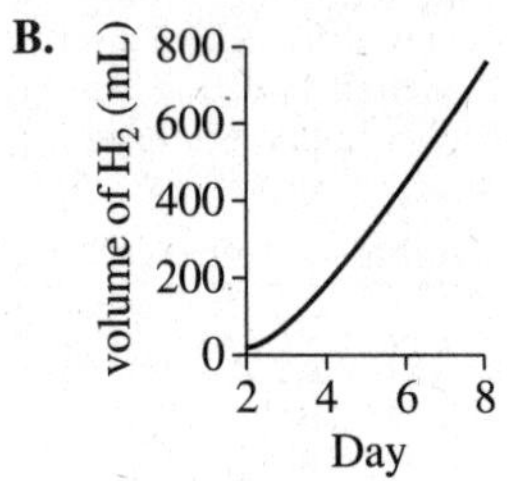

D. 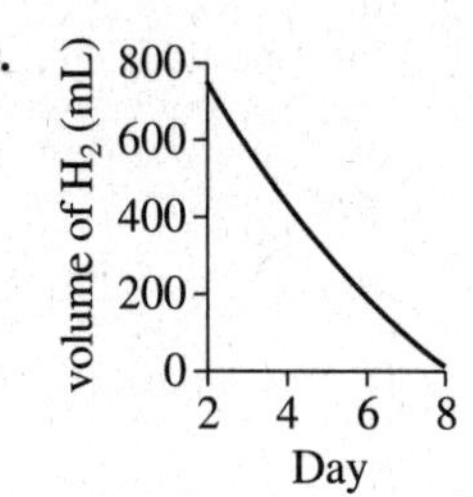

8. Based on Table 1, if the volume of H_2 produced by Day 10 from the AWP 1 sample had been measured, it would most likely have been:

F. less than 133 mL.
G. between 133 mL and 461 mL.
H. between 461 mL and 760 mL.
J. greater than 760 mL.

9. According to Table 1, what volume of H_2 was produced by AWP 1 from the time the volume was measured on Day 6 until the time the volume was measured on Day 8 ?

A. 52 mL
B. 81 mL
C. 133 mL
D. 214 mL

10. In the trials represented in Table 1 and Figure 1, by measuring the volume of H_2, the experimenters were able to monitor the rate at which:

F. H_2O is converted to Al.
G. Al is converted to H_2O.
H. Al is converted to $Al(OH)_3$.
J. $Al(OH)_3$ is converted to Al.

GO ON TO THE NEXT PAGE.

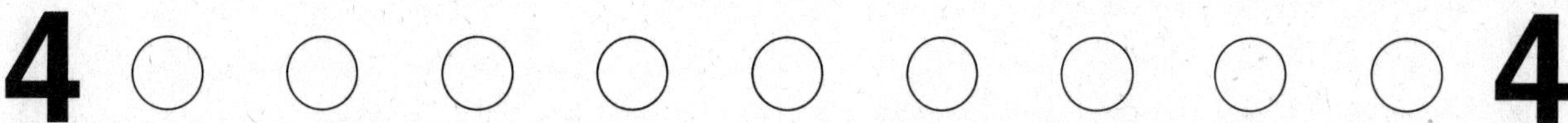

11. Based on the passage, is DMEA most likely an acid or a base?

A. An acid, because DMEA decreases pH.
B. An acid, because DMEA increases pH.
C. A base, because DMEA decreases pH.
D. A base, because DMEA increases pH.

12. Consider the volume of H_2 produced by Day 2 from the AWP 3 sample that contained no corrosion inhibitor. Based on Table 1 and Figure 1, the AWP 3 sample containing EDTA produced approximately the same volume of H_2 by which of the following days?

F. Day 1
G. Day 4
H. Day 7
J. Day 10

GO ON TO THE NEXT PAGE.

4 ○ ○ ○ ○ ○ ○ ○ ○ ○ 4

Passage III

Students studied forces by using 2 identical platform scales, Scale A and Scale B, one of which is shown in Figure 1.

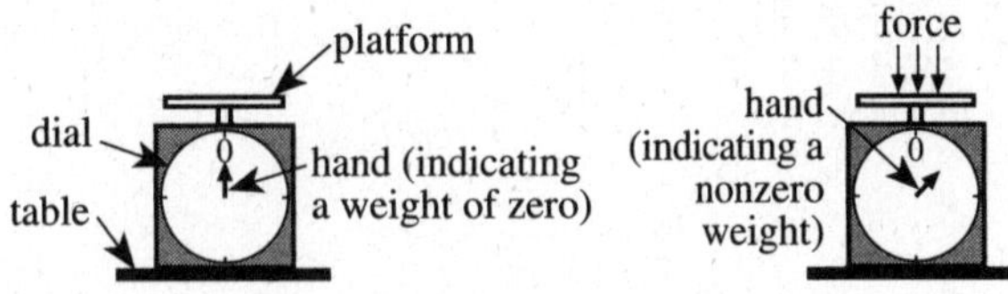

Figure 1

The weight of the platform of each scale was insignificant. When a force (such as that produced by a weight) was exerted on the surface of the platform, the hand rotated clockwise away from the zero point on the dial. The amount of rotation was directly proportional to the strength of the force.

Study 1

Prior to each of Trials 1–3, the students set the dial readings of both Scales A and B to zero. In each of these 3 trials, Scale A was stacked on top of Scale B (see Figure 2). In Trial 1, no weight was placed on the platform of Scale A; in Trial 2, a 5.0 newton (N) weight was placed on the platform of Scale A; and in Trial 3, a 10.0 N weight was placed on the platform of Scale A. The dial readings for the 3 trials are also shown in Figure 2.

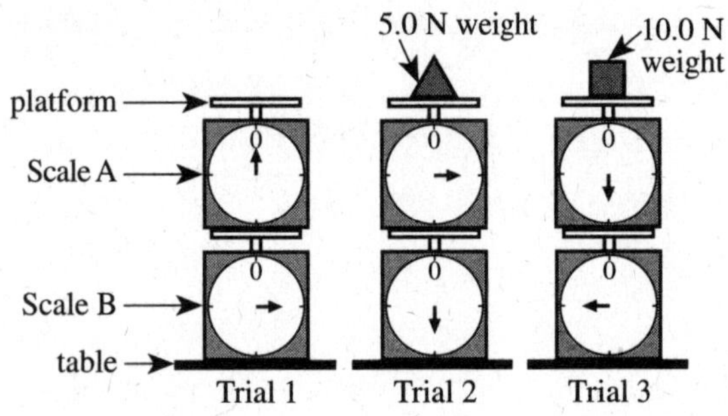

Figure 2

Study 2

The students placed a pencil on the platform of each scale and positioned on top of the pencils a board that spanned the 0.40 m distance between the 2 scales. Prior to each of Trials 4–6, the students set the dial readings of Scales A and B to zero (see Figure 3).

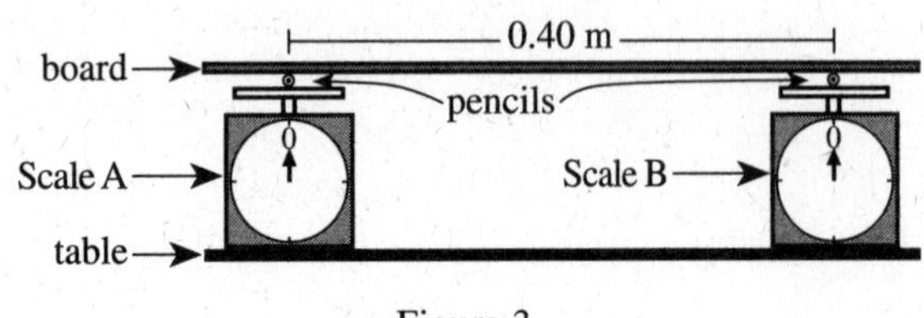

Figure 3

In each of these 3 trials, a 10.0 N weight was placed on the board at various distances from the pencil on Scale B (see Figure 4). In Trial 4, the weight was 0.10 m from the pencil; in Trial 5, the weight was 0.20 m from the pencil; and in Trial 6, the weight was 0.30 m from the pencil. The dial readings for the 3 trials are also shown in Figure 4.

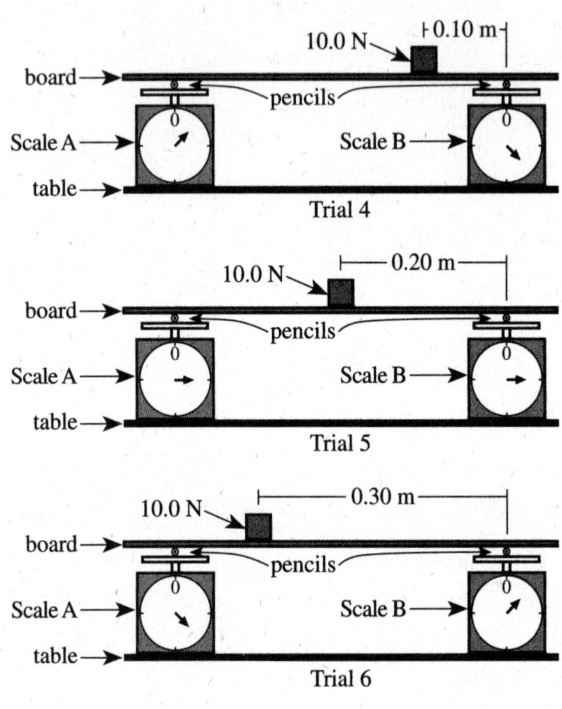

Figure 4

13. In which of the trials in Study 2, if any, was the force of the 10.0 N weight equally distributed between Scales A and B ?

A. Trial 4
B. Trial 5
C. Trial 6
D. None of the trials

14. Based on the results of Trials 1 and 2, Scale A and Scale B each weighed:

F. 2.5 N.
G. 5.0 N.
H. 7.5 N.
J. 10.0 N.

GO ON TO THE NEXT PAGE.

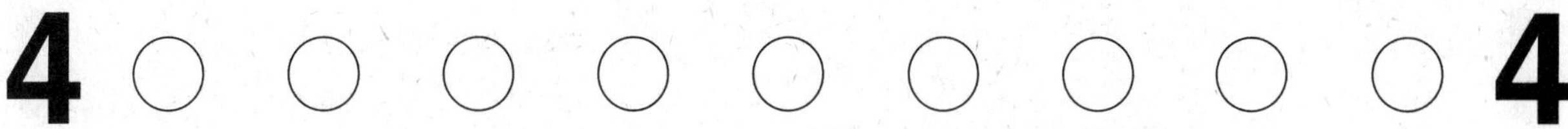

15. Assume that whenever a weight was placed on a scale's platform, a spring inside the scale was compressed. Assume also that the greater the added weight, the greater the amount of compression. Was the amount of potential energy stored in Scale A's spring greater in Trial 1 or in Trial 3 ?

A. In Trial 1, because the amount of weight on the platform of Scale A was greater in Trial 1.
B. In Trial 1, because the amount of weight on the platform of Scale A was less in Trial 1.
C. In Trial 3, because the amount of weight on the platform of Scale A was greater in Trial 3.
D. In Trial 3, because the amount of weight on the platform of Scale A was less in Trial 3.

16. In a new study, suppose Scale A were placed upside down atop Scale B, so that the platform of Scale A rested directly on the platform of Scale B. Which of the following drawings best represents the results that would most likely be obtained for this arrangement?

F.

H.

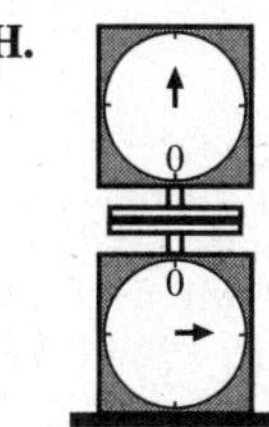

G.

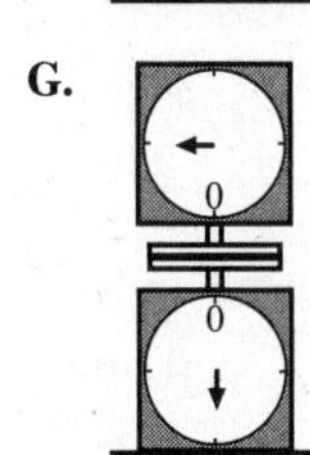

J.

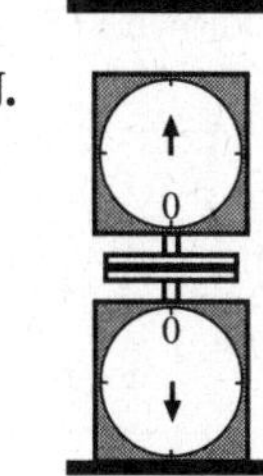

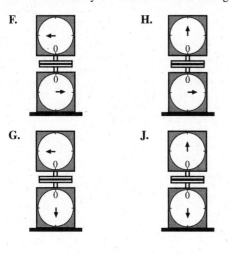

17. The main reason the pencils were placed on the scales in Study 2 was most likely:

A. so that the line of contact between each pencil and its platform could be used as a reference line for distance measurements.
B. so that the board would roll from side to side, rather than sliding from side to side over the scales' platforms.
C. to add additional weight to the scales.
D. to provide extra room for air above each scale's platform, so that the air pressure would be the same above and below the platform.

18. In Study 2, as the distance between the 10.0 N weight and the pencil on Scale B increased, the amount of force exerted on the surface of Scale B's platform:

F. remained the same.
G. increased only.
H. decreased only.
J. varied, but with no general trend.

19. Which of the following statements most likely describes an important reason for setting the dial readings of both scales to zero after Study 1, prior to each of Trials 4–6 ?

A. To add the weights of the scales to each weight measurement
B. To add the weights of the board and pencils to each weight measurement
C. To subtract the weights of the scales from each weight measurement
D. To subtract the weights of the board and pencils from each weight measurement

GO ON TO THE NEXT PAGE.

4 ○ ○ ○ ○ ○ ○ ○ ○ ○ 4

Passage IV

The *octane number* of a fuel is a measure of how smoothly the fuel burns in a gasoline engine. Lower octane fuels *knock* (explode) when burned, which lowers fuel efficiency and can cause engine damage. Heptane knocks considerably when burned and is given an octane number of 0. Isooctane knocks very little and is given an octane number of 100.

Different proportions of heptane and isooctane were mixed to obtain mixtures with octane numbers between 0 and 100 (see Table 1).

Table 1

Volume of heptane (mL)	Volume of isooctane (mL)	Octane number
0	100	100
10	90	90
25	75	75
50	50	50
90	10	10
100	0	0

Experiment 1

A sample of each fuel mixture listed in Table 1 was burned in a test engine at an engine speed of 600 revolutions per minute (rpm). The number of knocks per minute was determined for each mixture. This was done so that an octane number could be assigned to any fuel by measuring its knock rate.

Experiment 2

Adding tetraethyllead (TEL) to a fuel changes its octane number. Different amounts of TEL were added to 1,000 mL samples of isooctane. Each fuel mixture was tested under the same conditions used in Experiment 1, and the measured knock rate was used to determine the octane number (see Figure 1).

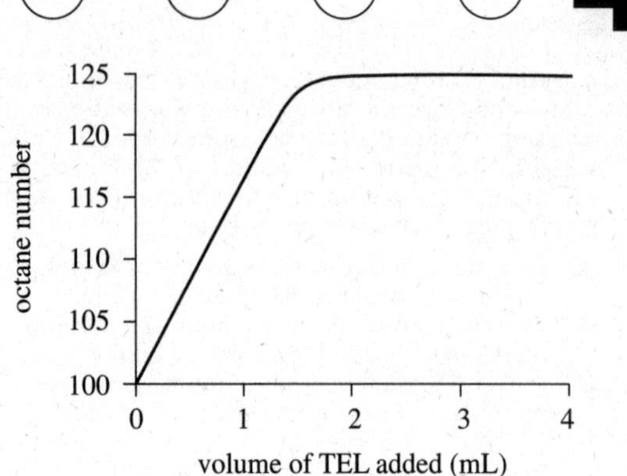

Figure 1

Experiment 3

The *engine octane requirement* (EOR) is the minimum octane number of a fuel required for an engine to operate without becoming damaged. Fuels A and B were burned separately in an engine at different speeds. Table 2 shows the octane number determined for each fuel at each engine speed and the known EOR of the engine at each speed.

Table 2

Engine speed (rpm)	EOR	Octane number in engine of:	
		Fuel A	Fuel B
1,500	97.4	98.4	96.7
2,000	95.3	96.6	96.1
2,500	93.5	95.0	95.4
3,000	91.9	92.3	93.8
3,500	90.6	90.9	92.5

GO ON TO THE NEXT PAGE.

4 ○ ○ ○ ○ ○ ○ ○ ○ ○ 4

20. Based on Experiment 3, as engine speed increases, the minimum octane number of fuel required for an engine to operate without becoming damaged:

F. increases only.
G. decreases only.
H. increases, then decreases.
J. decreases, then increases.

21. Suppose a trial had been performed in Experiment 3 at an engine speed of 2,200 rpm. At this engine speed, which of the following sets of octane numbers would most likely have been determined for Fuel A and Fuel B ?

	Fuel A	Fuel B
A.	95.0	95.4
B.	96.1	95.8
C.	96.6	96.1
D.	97.6	96.4

22. Which of the following expressions is equal to the octane number of each fuel mixture listed in Table 1 ?

F. $\frac{\text{volume of isooctane}}{\text{volume of heptane}} \times 100$

G. $\frac{\text{volume of heptane}}{\text{volume of isooctane}} \times 100$

H. $\frac{\text{volume of isooctane}}{\text{(volume of heptane + volume of isooctane)}} \times 100$

J. $\frac{\text{volume of heptane}}{\text{(volume of heptane + volume of isooctane)}} \times 100$

23. Based on Table 1 and Experiment 2, if 3 mL of TEL were added to a mixture of 100 mL of heptane and 900 mL of isooctane, the octane number of the resulting fuel would most likely be:

A. less than 55.
B. between 55 and 90.
C. between 90 and 125.
D. greater than 125.

24. Which of the 2 fuels from Experiment 3 would be better to use in an engine that will run at all engine speeds between 1,500 rpm and 3,500 rpm ?

F. Fuel A, because its octane number was lower than the EOR at each of the engine speeds tested.
G. Fuel A, because its octane number was higher than the EOR at each of the engine speeds tested.
H. Fuel B, because its octane number was lower than the EOR at each of the engine speeds tested.
J. Fuel B, because its octane number was higher than the EOR at each of the engine speeds tested.

25. Based on Table 1, if 2 mL of heptane were mixed with 8 mL of isooctane, the octane number of this mixture would be:

A. 2.
B. 8.
C. 20.
D. 80.

26. Suppose that 1 mL of TEL is added to 1,000 mL of heptane. Based on Experiment 2, one would predict that the octane number of the TEL/heptane mixture would be:

F. higher than the octane number of pure heptane, but lower than 115.
G. higher than the octane number of pure heptane, and higher than 115.
H. lower than the octane number of pure heptane, but higher than 115.
J. lower than octane number of pure heptane, and lower than 115.

GO ON TO THE NEXT PAGE.

4 ○ ○ ○ ○ ○ ○ ○ ○ ○ 4

Passage V

Introduction

Comets are complex mixtures of ices and dust that orbit the Sun. They can be classified by orbital period as either *long-period comets* or *short-period comets*.

Long-period comets have orbital periods of more than 200 yr and originate within our solar system in the *Oort Cloud*, a spherical shell of many icy bodies located at an average distance of 40,000 A.U. from the Sun (1 A.U. = average distance of Earth from the Sun). Long-period comets approach the Sun from all directions.

Short-period comets have orbital periods of 200 yr or less, and their orbital planes have *inclinations* 30° or less with respect to the *ecliptic plane*, the plane of Earth's orbit around the Sun. Portions of these planes are shown in Figure 1.

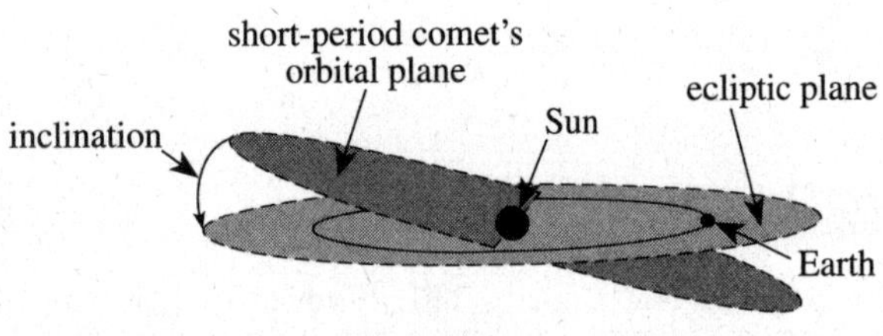

Figure 1

Two scientists present their viewpoints about the origin of short-period comets.

Scientist A

Short-period comets in our solar system originate within a thin ring-shaped region called the *Kuiper Belt* (KB). The KB has a small inclination with respect to the ecliptic plane and is located in the solar system between 30 A.U. and 50 A.U. from the Sun. The KB contains billions of icy bodies with diameters between 10 km and 30 km. These comet-size objects are too small to be clearly discerned at that distance with telescopes located on Earth's surface. Such telescopes have gathered indirect evidence, but not clear images, of much larger icy bodies that are part of the KB. The small inclinations of short-period comets' orbital planes with respect to the ecliptic plane are consistent with an origin in the KB. It has been discovered that other nearby stars have similar regions of icy bodies surrounding them.

Scientist B

The KB does not exist. Short-period comets were once long-period comets. Some long-period comets pass close enough to the giant planets (for example, Jupiter) to be influenced by the gravitational fields of the giant planets and are forced into orbits with orbital periods less than 200 yr. These altered orbits have orbital planes that have small inclinations with respect to the ecliptic plane. Also, most of the studied short-period comets have orbital planes with small inclinations with respect to the orbital planes of the giant planets, which, in turn, have small inclinations with respect to the ecliptic plane.

GO ON TO THE NEXT PAGE.

4 ○ ○ ○ ○ ○ ○ ○ ○ ○ 4

27. Which of the following generalizations about comets is most consistent with Scientist B's viewpoint?

A. Long-period comets cannot become short-period comets.
B. Short-period comets cannot become long-period comets.
C. Long-period comets can become short-period comets.
D. No long-period comets or short-period comets orbit the Sun.

28. Scientist A would most likely suggest that a new telescope more powerful than previous telescopes be used to search which of the following regions of space for objects in the KB ?

F. The region 100,000 A.U. beyond our solar system
G. The region 30 A.U. to 50 A.U. from the Sun at an angle of 90° with respect to the ecliptic plane
H. The region 30 A.U. to 50 A.U. from the Sun at angles of 0° to 30° with respect to the ecliptic plane
J. The region closely surrounding the planet Jupiter

29. Given the information about short-period comets in the introduction, which of the following inclinations with respect to the ecliptic plane would most likely NOT be observed for the orbital planes of short-period comets?

A. 5°
B. 15°
C. 30°
D. 45°

30. According to Scientist B, which of the following planets in our solar system is most likely capable of changing the orbit of a long-period comet over time?

F. Mercury
G. Earth
H. Mars
J. Saturn

31. Comet Halley currently has an orbital period of 76 yr. According to the information provided, Scientist B would most likely currently classify Comet Halley as a:

A. short-period comet that originated in the Oort Cloud.
B. short-period comet that originated in the KB.
C. long-period comet that originated in the Oort Cloud.
D. long-period comet that originated in the KB.

32. Based on Scientist A's viewpoint, the "much larger icy bodies" in the KB most likely have diameters of:

F. less than 10 km.
G. between 10 km and 20 km.
H. between 20 km and 30 km.
J. greater than 30 km.

33. Suppose a study of 1 nearby star revealed that it had no spherical shell of material similar to the Oort Cloud surrounding it. How would this discovery most likely affect the scientists' viewpoints, if at all?

A. It would weaken Scientist A's viewpoint only.
B. It would strengthen Scientist B's viewpoint only.
C. It would strengthen both scientists' viewpoints.
D. It would have no effect on either scientist's viewpoint.

GO ON TO THE NEXT PAGE.

Passage VI

Tomato plants grow poorly in high-salt environments. This effect is caused by 2 processes:

- A net movement of H_2O between the cytoplasm of the plants' cells and the environment via osmosis
- An increase in the cytoplasmic Na^+ concentration

The plant *Arabidopsis thaliana* carries a gene, *AtNHX1*. The product of this gene, *VAC*, facilitates uptake of cytoplasmic Na^+ by the plant's vacuoles.

A researcher created 4 genetically identical lines of tomato plants (L1–L4). An *AtNHX1* gene from *Arabidopsis thaliana* was isolated and 2 identical copies of this gene were incorporated into L1's genome. This process was repeated with L2 and L3 using a different *AtNHX1* allele for each line, so that L1, L2, and L3 had different genotypes for *AtNHX1*. The researcher then did an experiment.

Experiment

Fifty seedlings from each of the 4 lines were grown in 10 L of nutrient solution for 80 days. The 10 L nutrient solution contained H_2O, 12 g of fertilizer, and 3 g of NaCl. The nutrient solution was replaced every 5 days. After 80 days, average height, average mass (without fruit), and average fruit mass (per plant) were measured (see Table 1).

Table 1

3 g of NaCl/10 L nutrient solution

Line	Height (cm)	Mass (kg)	Fruit mass (kg)
L1	124	1.2	2.1
L2	128	1.2	2.0
L3	120	1.2	2.1
L4	124	1.2	2.0

This process was repeated except the 10 L nutrient solution contained 60 g of NaCl instead of 3 g of NaCl (see Table 2).

Table 2

60 g of NaCl/10 L nutrient solution

Line	Height (cm)	Mass (kg)	Fruit mass (kg)
L1	119	1.1	1.9
L2	121	1.1	1.9
L3	61	0.4	1.1
L4	63	0.5	1.0

The process was repeated again except the 10 L nutrient solution contained 120 g of NaCl instead of 3 g of NaCl (see Table 3).

Table 3

120 g of NaCl/10 L nutrient solution

Line	Height (cm)	Mass (kg)	Fruit mass (kg)
L1	118	1.0	1.8
L2	115	1.0	1.7
L3	34	0.2	0
L4	36	0.3	0

Tables 1–3 adapted from Hong-Xia Zhang and Eduardo Blumwald, "Transgenic Salt-Tolerant Tomato Plants Accumulate Salt in Foliage But Not in Fruit." ©2001 by Nature Publishing Group.

GO ON TO THE NEXT PAGE.

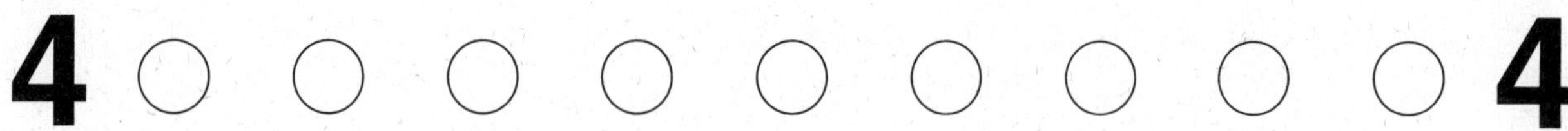

34. One plant produced no fruit and had a height of 21 cm. Which of the following most likely describes this plant?

F. It was from L2 and was grown in a 10 L nutrient solution containing 60 g of NaCl.
G. It was from L2 and was grown in a 10 L nutrient solution containing 120 g of NaCl.
H. It was from L4 and was grown in a 10 L nutrient solution containing 60 g of NaCl.
J. It was from L4 and was grown in a 10 L nutrient solution containing 120 g of NaCl.

35. During osmosis, water migrates through a semipermeable barrier. The osmosis referred to in the passage occurs through which of the following structures?

A. Chromosomes
B. Nuclear envelope
C. Cell membrane
D. Rough endoplasmic reticulum

36. For each line, as the concentration of salt in the nutrient solutions increased, average plant mass:

F. increased only.
G. decreased only.
H. increased, then decreased.
J. decreased, then increased.

37. Which of the following was an independent variable in the experiment?

A. Whether a line received *AtNHX1*
B. Whether a tomato plant was used
C. Plant mass without fruit
D. Plant height

38. Which of the following best characterizes the genotype of L1 for *AtNHX1* after L1 was genetically modified?

F. It was heterozygous, since its 2 *AtNHX1* alleles were different.
G. It was heterozygous, since its 2 *AtNHX1* alleles were identical.
H. It was homozygous, since its 2 *AtNHX1* alleles were different.
J. It was homozygous, since its 2 *AtNHX1* alleles were identical.

39. Suppose the data for all of the plants were plotted on a graph with height on the *x*-axis and mass (without fruit) on the *y*-axis. Suppose also that the best-fit line for these data was determined. Which of the following would most likely characterize the slope of this line?

A. The line would not have a slope, because the line would be vertical.
B. The slope of the line would be zero.
C. The slope of the line would be negative.
D. The slope of the line would be positive.

40. The researchers included 1 of the 4 lines to serve as a control. This line was most likely which one?

F. L1
G. L2
H. L3
J. L4

END OF TEST 4

STOP! DO NOT RETURN TO ANY OTHER TEST.

You may wish to photocopy these sample answer document pages to respond to the practice ACT Writing Test.

Please enter the information at the right before beginning the writing test.

Use a soft lead No. 2 pencil only. Do NOT use a mechanical pencil, ink, ballpoint, or felt-tip pen.

WRITING TEST BOOKLET NUMBER

Print your 6-digit **Booklet Number** in the boxes at the right.

WRITING TEST FORM

Print your 5-character **Test Form** in the boxes above and fill in the corresponding oval at the right.

- ◯ 16W1A
- ◯ 16W2A
- ◯ 16W3A
- ◯ 18W4A
- ◯ 19WT5

Begin WRITING TEST here.

If you need more space, please continue on the next page.

WRITING TEST

If you need more space, please continue on the back of this page.

WRITING TEST

If you need more space, please continue on the next page.

WRITING TEST

STOP here with the writing test.

072952

Practice Writing Test Prompt 3

Your Signature: ______________________
(Do not print.)

Print Your Name Here: ______________________

Your Date of Birth:

☐☐ - ☐☐ - ☐☐☐☐
Month Day Year

Form 16W3A

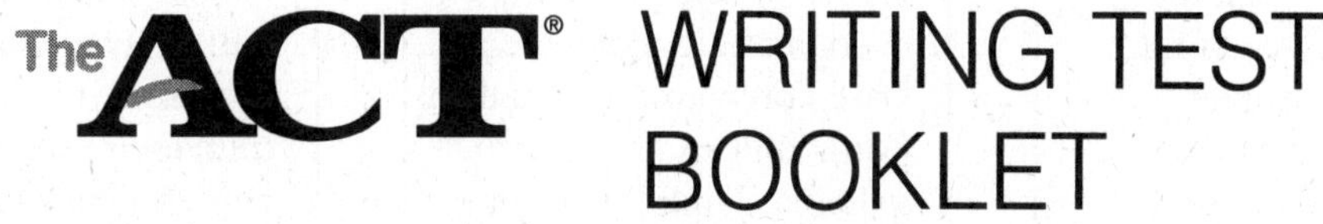

You must take the multiple-choice tests before you take the writing test.

Directions

This is a test of your writing skills. You will have **forty** (40) minutes to read the prompt, plan your response, and write an essay in English. Before you begin working, read all material in this test booklet carefully to understand exactly what you are being asked to do.

You will write your essay on the lined pages in the **answer document** provided. Your writing on those pages will be scored. You may use the unlined pages in this test booklet to plan your essay. Your work on these pages will not be scored.

Your essay will be evaluated based on the evidence it provides of your ability to:

- clearly state your own perspective on a complex issue and analyze the relationship between your perspective and at least one other perspective
- develop and support your ideas with reasoning and examples
- organize your ideas clearly and logically
- communicate your ideas effectively in standard written English

Lay your pencil down immediately when time is called.

DO NOT OPEN THIS BOOKLET UNTIL TOLD TO DO SO.

PO Box 168
Iowa City, IA 52243-0168

Vocational Education

For many years, public high schools in the United States emphasized vocational skills—the skills students would need to learn a trade and get a job. Classes in auto repair, office skills, and woodworking, for example, were common. The last few decades have seen career and technical training fall out of favor in public education, replaced gradually by additional academic courses. While many schools maintain a vocational program, these programs are often threatened with elimination when school budgets are strained. Given its uncertain status in many schools, it is worth considering what value vocational training adds to education.

Read and carefully consider these perspectives. Each suggests a particular way of thinking about the value of vocational training in education.

Perspective One

Schools must seek to prepare all students for their futures. Career training provides focus for many students and helps schools reach those who don't excel in academic subjects.

Perspective Two

In every field, the skills workers need today are based on knowledge and communication. As such, schools should focus on academic subjects only.

Perspective Three

No one knows what jobs will be available in the future, so it is not wise to train today's students for any specific career.

Essay Task

Write a unified, coherent essay about the value of vocational training in education. In your essay, be sure to:

- clearly state your own perspective on the issue and analyze the relationship between your perspective and at least one other perspective
- develop and support your ideas with reasoning and examples
- organize your ideas clearly and logically
- communicate your ideas effectively in standard written English

Your perspective may be in full agreement with any of those given, in partial agreement, or completely different.

Planning Your Essay

Your work on these prewriting pages will not be scored.

Use the space below and on the back cover to generate ideas and plan your essay. You may wish to consider the following as you think critically about the task:

Strengths and weaknesses of different perspectives on the issue

- What insights do they offer, and what do they fail to consider?
- Why might they be persuasive to others, or why might they fail to persuade?

Your own knowledge, experience, and values

- What is your perspective on this issue, and what are its strengths and weaknesses?
- How will you support your perspective in your essay?

If you need more space to plan, please continue on the back of this page.

Planning Your Essay

Use this page to continue planning your essay. Your work on this page will not be scored.

Scoring Your Practice Tests

Scoring Practice Practice Tests 2, 3, 4, and 5 is covered in chapter 11.

Explanatory Answers

ENGLISH • PRACTICE TEST 3 • EXPLANATORY ANSWERS

Passage I

Question 1. The best answer is C because the comma after *tribe* sets off what follows as a nonrestrictive appositive that describes what "the Miami tribe" is: "a Native American people with strong ties to territory in present-day Ohio, Indiana, and Illinois."

The best answer is NOT:

A because it is missing the comma needed after *tribe* to set off the following nonrestrictive appositive from the noun *tribe* and because it places an unnecessary and confusing comma between the noun *people* and the series of prepositional phrases starting with "with strong ties" that follows and describes *people.*

B because it pointlessly separates with a comma the adjective *Native American* from the noun *people.*

D because it misuses the semicolon. The semicolon inappropriately implies that what will follow is an independent clause, as in "My family is part of the Miami tribe; we are a Native American people. . ."

Question 2. The best answer is F because "making freezer jam or researching tribal history" gives the most specific and vivid glimpse of what the grandmother was interested in.

The best answer is NOT:

G because "being actively involved in her pursuits" is vague and gives no suggestion of what those pursuits are.

H because "things I really hope she'll teach me one day" gives no suggestion of what those things are.

J because "historical research as well as domestic projects" offers only a general notion of the interests that are more pointedly described in **F.**

Question 3. The best answer is D because the word *rushed* by itself is sufficient to express the idea "urged to hasten."

The best answer is not:

A because the word *rushed* and the phrase "in a hurry" are redundant.

B because the words *hurried* and *rushed* are redundant.

C because the phrase "made to go faster" and the word *rushed* are redundant.

ENGLISH • PRACTICE TEST 3 • EXPLANATORY ANSWERS

Question 4. The best answer is J because a comma is appropriate between the long introductory adverbial clause "if we were running late for an appointment" and the sentence's main clause, which begins with *she.*

The best answer is NOT:

F because placing a period after the word *appointment* makes the introductory adverbial clause (subordinated by the conjunction *if*) into a sentence fragment and because doing so obscures how the ideas are related.

G because placing a semicolon after the word *appointment* makes the introductory adverbial clause into a sentence fragment and obscures how the ideas are related.

H because the coordinating conjunction *and* should not be used to join two unequal sentence elements, such as a subordinate clause and a main clause, as would be the case here.

Question 5. The best answer is A because it opens this paragraph with a general statement about the concept of Miami time and serves as the most logical link between the preceding paragraph and the subject of this paragraph.

The best answer is NOT:

B because the reference to the doctor's appointment is only loosely related to the end of the preceding paragraph and to the subject of this paragraph, which is defining and describing the concept of Miami time.

C because the general reference to the relationship between the narrator and the grandmother is only loosely related to the subject of this paragraph, which is defining and describing the concept of Miami time.

D because the general reference to the son being curious about and having never met the grandmother is only loosely related to the subject of this paragraph, which is defining and describing the concept of Miami time.

ENGLISH • PRACTICE TEST 3 • EXPLANATORY ANSWERS

Question 6. The best answer is G because the dependent clause "when time seemed to slow down or stand still" is necessary information to explain which moments are being referred to and thus should not be set off from the rest of the sentence by a comma.

The best answer is NOT:

F because the comma between the words *moments* and *when* identifies the information in the dependent clause "when time seemed to slow down or stand still" as unnecessary information when, in fact, the clause is vital to defining the moments of Miami time.

H because the comma between the words *moments* and *as if* identifies the information in the dependent clause "as if time seemed to slow down or stand still" as unnecessary information and because the conjunction *as if* does not appropriately link the ideas in this sentence.

J because the comma between the words *moments* and *because* identifies the information in the dependent clause "because time seemed to slow down or stand still" as unnecessary information and because the conjunction *because* does not appropriately link the ideas in this sentence.

Question 7. The best answer is A because the word *words* by itself is a sufficient, clear, and appropriate way to refer to what the grandmother had said.

The best answer is NOT:

B because the phrase "spoken statements to my ears" is clumsy, wordy, and overly formal for the tone of the essay.

C because the phrase "expressed opinions on the matter" is wordy and overly formal for the tone of the essay.

D because the phrase "verbal remarks in conversation" is wordy, redundant, and overly formal for the tone of the essay.

Question 8. The best answer is J because the past tense verb *slipped* appropriately describes an event that occurred in the past and is consistent with the other past tense verbs used throughout the essay.

The best answer is NOT:

F because the verb *will slip* describes a past event in future tense.

G because the verb *slip* describes a past event in present tense.

H because the verb *are slipping* describes a past event in present progressive tense.

ENGLISH • PRACTICE TEST 3 • EXPLANATORY ANSWERS

Question 9. The best answer is C because *thinking* is the second half of a compound verb (*was pushing and . . . thinking*). The words *I was* are implied in front of *thinking.*

The best answer is NOT:

A because the plural verb *were thinking* doesn't agree with the singular subject *I.*

B because the plural verb *were having* doesn't agree with the singular subject *I.*

D because deleting the underlined portion would leave the second part of the sentence without a verb ("I was pushing Jeremy in his stroller and of the day ahead . . .").

Question 10. The best answer is F because no punctuation should interrupt the compound subject "two does and three fawns" or separate it from the rest of the sentence.

The best answer is NOT:

G because it places an unnecessary comma between parts of the compound subject.

H because it places an unnecessary comma between the compound subject and the verb *stood.*

J because it places an unnecessary comma between parts of the compound subject.

Question 11. The best answer is A because sentence 3, which introduces the deer, fits logically between sentence 2's reference to Jeremy squealing and pointing at the clearing and sentence 4's reference to the movement of the deer's ears.

The best answer is NOT:

B because the word *there* in sentence 3 would have no logical antecedent, leaving unclear where the deer are. Also, the setting for the paragraph, revealed in Sentence 1 ("a familiar trail near our house"), would not yet have been established.

C because the narration in the first part of the paragraph involves a surprise: the pair are out for a walk (sentence 1), then Jeremy suddenly squeals and points (sentence 2), and then the surprise is explained (sentence 3). Placing the revelation in sentence 3 ahead of what happens "suddenly" in sentence 2 removes the surprise.

D because the word *there* in sentence 3 would have no logical antecedent in sentence 4, leaving unclear what *there* refers to. Also, the more general introduction to the deer in sentence 3 ("two does and three fawns") should occur before the more specific reference to the deer in sentence 4 ("five pairs of ears").

ENGLISH • PRACTICE TEST 3 • EXPLANATORY ANSWERS

Question 12. The best answer is G because the word *rustling* is parallel in form to *lazing* earlier in the sentence. Together, these two words help form the compound subject of the verb *surprised* ("Lizards lazing . . . and quail rustling . . . surprised us").

The best answer is NOT:

F because *rustled* isn't parallel in form to *lazing* previously in the sentence, and this lack of parallelism creates an ungrammatical sentence ("Lizards lazing in the sun and quail rustled through grasses surprised us").

H because *were rustling* isn't parallel in form to *lazing* previously in the sentence, and this lack of parallelism creates an ungrammatical sentence ("Lizards lazing in the sun and quail were rustling through grasses surprised us").

J because deleting the underlined portion creates an ungrammatical, nonsensical sentence ("Lizards lazing in the sun and quail through grasses surprised us").

Question 13. The best answer is D because no transition word or phrase is necessary here to make the sentence part of a list of sensory experiences the narrator and son had: seeing lizards and quail, eating wild blackberries, and smelling crushed eucalyptus leaves.

The best answer is NOT:

A because the phrase "For example" illogically suggests that the aroma of crushed eucalyptus leaves is an example of the taste of wild blackberries rather than being the third item in a list of sensory experiences.

B because the phrase "On the other hand" illogically suggests that the aroma of crushed eucalyptus leaves is somehow in opposition to the taste of wild blackberries rather than being the third item in a list of sensory experiences.

C because the phrase "Just in case" makes no sense in this context; it is unclear what smelling the aroma of crushed eucalyptus leaves would be designed to prevent.

Question 14. The best answer is J because "shorter than" is the correct comparative form to use to contrast how long the 3-hour hike seemed to take with how long the normal-length hike usually seemed.

The best answer is NOT:

F because the adverb *then* is incorrectly used instead of the preposition *than* to introduce the second part of the comparison.

G because *more shorter* is an incorrectly formed comparative term and because the adverb *then* is incorrectly used instead of the preposition *than* to introduce the second part of the comparison.

H because *shortest* is a superlative term used here incorrectly to compare two things.

ENGLISH • PRACTICE TEST 3 • EXPLANATORY ANSWERS

Question 15. The best answer is A because most of the essay narrates a hike that took a long time but seemed short, the rhetorical aim being to illustrate one of the narrator's personal experiences with Miami time because that concept is defined in the early part of the essay.

The best answer is NOT:

B because although the essay has met the goal specified in the question, which was to convey a personal experience with Miami time, the reason given here is inaccurate. The essay doesn't reveal whether the narrator decided to live in Miami time, nor is it clear that one can actually choose to live always in Miami time.

C because the essay has met the goal specified in the question, which was to convey a personal experience with Miami time. That the grandmother's view of Miami time is represented doesn't detract from the fact that the essay still relates the narrator's personal experience.

D because the essay has met the goal specified in the question, which was to convey a personal experience with Miami time. It is unclear what it would mean for the term *Miami time* to *belong* to the grandmother; in any case, the essay indicates that the narrator and the grandmother came to share a similar sense of Miami time.

Passage II

Question 16. The best answer is H because the meaning here is clearest when the ideas are divided into two sentences, with the first sentence giving a general description of the artwork and the second describing the eight women in the artwork more specifically.

The best answer is NOT:

F because the relative pronoun *that* should be used to connect an adjectival clause to a main clause, not two main clauses. *That* in this position would logically refer to the immediately preceding noun, *flowers*, which makes no sense here.

G because the coordinating conjunction *and* creates a rambling sentence in which it's difficult to tell where one thought ends and the next begins, especially without a comma before *and*.

J because using only the comma after the word *flowers* to join two independent clauses creates a comma splice.

Question 17. The best answer is D because no transition word is necessary here to link the two questions posed at the end of the essay's first paragraph with the answers that unfold beginning in the second paragraph.

The best answer is NOT:

A because the word *thus* illogically suggests that the fact that the answers to the questions posed at the end of the essay's first paragraph can be found in the artwork itself is a result of the questions being posed.

B because the word *instead* illogically sets up a contrast between the questions posed at the end of the essay's first paragraph and the fact that the answers can be found in the artwork itself.

C because the word *furthermore* illogically suggests that something additional but similar to the questions posed at the end of the essay's first paragraph is coming next (mostly likely, more questions), when, in fact, the essay switches to discussing the answers to the questions.

Question 18. The best answer is F because the word order creates a clear, understandable sentence.

The best answer is NOT:

G because the placement of the phrase "the story" creates a nonsensical statement.

H because the placement of the phrase "of text" creates a nonsensical expression ("this gathering of text").

J because the placement of the phrase "on two horizontal panels of text" divides the phrase "the story" from the prepositional phrase that describes the story, "of this gathering."

Question 19. The best answer is C because *its* is the correct form of the singular possessive pronoun and agrees with its singular antecedent, understood to be the noun *piece.*

The best answer is NOT:

A because *it's* is a contraction meaning "it is" rather than the singular possessive pronoun *its*, which is needed here.

B because *its'* is an incorrect form of the singular possessive pronoun *its*, which is needed here.

D because *their* is the plural possessive pronoun, which doesn't agree with its singular antecedent, understood to be the noun *piece.*

ENGLISH • PRACTICE TEST 3 • EXPLANATORY ANSWERS

Question 20. The best answer is J because the interposed explanatory phrase "the story explains" is properly set off from the rest of the sentence by two commas, indicating that the phrase could be omitted without changing the basic meaning of the sentence.

The best answer is NOT:

F because the interposed explanatory phrase "the story explains" is not preceded by a comma, which would be needed to set the phrase off properly from the rest of the sentence.

G because the interposed explanatory phrase "the story explains" is improperly set off from the rest of the sentence by a comma before the phrase and a dash after the phrase. Either two commas or two dashes would be appropriate, but not one of each.

H because the interposed explanatory phrase "the story explains" is not preceded by a dash, which would be needed to set the phrase off properly from the rest of the sentence.

Question 21. The best answer is C because placing the underlined portion after the word *cause* is the only one of the four choices that wouldn't be acceptable. This placement of the phrase "in their various ways" divides the phrase "the cause" from the prepositional phrase that describes the cause, "of justice." Therefore, all of the choices would be acceptable EXCEPT **C**.

The best answer is NOT:

A because keeping the underlined portion where it is now creates a clear and correct sentence in English.

B because placing the underlined portion after the word *support* creates a clear and correct sentence in English.

D because placing the underlined portion after the word *world* (and before the period) creates a clear and correct sentence in English.

Question 22. The best answer is F because the rest of the paragraph explains that the women depicted in the artwork lived at different times and so couldn't have sat together and made a quilt.

The best answer is NOT:

G because the phrase "in summary" illogically suggests that the sentence summarizes the preceding text, which it does not do.

H because the phrase "in addition" illogically suggests that the sentence directly adds to the preceding text, which it does not do.

J because the phrase "in contrast" illogically suggests that the sentence provides a direct contrast to the preceding text, which it does not do.

ENGLISH • PRACTICE TEST 3 • EXPLANATORY ANSWERS

Question 23. The best answer is B because Ringgold is the only artist being referred to at this point; the singular possessive form of the noun *artist's* is therefore required.

The best answer is NOT:

A because *artists* is a plural noun, not the singular possessive form of the noun *artist's* that is required.

C because *artists'* is a plural possessive form of the noun, not the singular possessive form *artist's* that is required.

D because the phrase "artists imagination" uses the plural form of the noun *artists* instead of the singular possessive, *artist's*, that is required, and because **D** includes an unnecessary comma after the word *imagination.*

Question 24. The best answer is J because the plural verb *were* agrees with the plural compound subject, "Sojourner Truth and Harriet Tubman."

The best answer is NOT:

F because the singular verb *was* doesn't agree with the plural compound subject "Sojourner Truth and Harriet Tubman."

G because the singular verb *was* doesn't agree with the plural compound subject "Sojourner Truth and Harriet Tubman."

H because the singular verb *was* doesn't agree with the plural compound subject "Sojourner Truth and Harriet Tubman."

Question 25. The best answer is A because information about Wells speaking out for social and racial justice is highly relevant, given that the paragraph focuses on the causes championed by the women, including Wells, depicted in Ringgold's artwork.

The best answer is NOT:

B because information about the man Wells married is only marginally relevant to the topic of the paragraph: the historical reality behind Ringgold's artwork.

C because information about which newspapers Wells wrote for isn't as relevant to the topic of the paragraph as the information in **A**.

D because information about Wells's birthplace, birth year, and siblings is only marginally relevant to the topic of the paragraph.

ENGLISH • PRACTICE TEST 3 • EXPLANATORY ANSWERS

Question 26. The best answer is J because the word *business* is sufficient, together with the words *her own* earlier in the sentence, to indicate that Madam C. J. Walker established her own business.

The best answer is NOT:

F because the intensive pronoun *herself* is awkward and redundant with *her own* and because the comma between the noun *business* and the intensive *herself* is unnecessary and confusing.

G because the phrase "belonging to her" is awkward and redundant with "her own."

H because the intensive pronoun *herself* is awkward and redundant with "her own" and because an intensifier, even when appropriate in a sentence, doesn't need to be set off by commas from the rest of the sentence.

Question 27. The best answer is B because this sentence structure makes "Madam C. J. Walker" the subject of the sentence, which is necessary in order to have the introductory participial phrase "establishing her own hair products business in the first decade of the twentieth century" refer clearly to Walker.

The best answer is NOT:

A because this sentence structure makes the introductory participial phrase a dangling modifier that refers to "millions of dollars," which doesn't make sense.

C because this sentence structure makes the introductory participial phrase a dangling modifier that refers to "charities and educational institutions," which doesn't make sense.

D because this sentence structure makes the introductory participial phrase a dangling modifier that refers to "millions of dollars," which doesn't make sense.

ENGLISH • PRACTICE TEST 3 • EXPLANATORY ANSWERS

Question 28. The best answer is H because no punctuation is warranted in this underlined portion. "Among the schools that benefited from this generosity" is an introductory adverbial phrase that, because it immediately precedes the verb it modifies, should not be set off by a comma. Had the sentence elements been arranged in the more typical subject-verb-object order ("Those [schools] that Mary McLeod Bethune opened and ran in order to provide a better education for Black students were among the schools that benefited from this generosity"), it would've been more obvious that no internal punctuation is required.

The best answer is NOT:

F because the comma after the word *generosity* is an unwarranted break between the prepositional phrase and the verb it modifies.

G because the semicolon after the word *generosity* creates two inappropriate sentence fragments, as neither what precedes nor what follows the semicolon is an independent clause.

J because the colon after the word *were* is unwarranted; what follows the colon is not a series, a list, an explanation, or a clarification.

Question 29. The best answer is D because the phrase "movement of" creates a clear, complete sentence, with the preposition *of* heading the phrase *of the 1950s and 1960s.*

The best answer is NOT:

A because "movement, it happened in" forms a second independent clause in the sentence joined to the original independent clause by only a comma, creating a comma splice.

B because "movement, it took place in" forms a second independent clause in the sentence joined to the original independent clause by only a comma, creating a comma splice.

C because "movement, that happened in" forms a second independent clause in the sentence joined to the original independent clause by only a comma, creating a comma splice.

Question 30. The best answer is F because the sentence under consideration interprets what the flowers represent ("seem to celebrate") and makes a concluding reference to the main focus of the essay ("the women's accomplishments and the beauty of their shared vision").

The best answer is NOT:

G because the sentence under consideration makes no comparison of Ringgold to the women depicted in the artwork.

H because the sentence under consideration says nothing about a brushwork technique.

J because the sentence under consideration offers no evaluation of Ringgold's artistic talent, only an interpretation of what the flowers represent ("seem to celebrate").

ENGLISH • PRACTICE TEST 3 • EXPLANATORY ANSWERS

Passage III

Question 31. The best answer is B because the plural present perfect verb *have allowed* agrees with the plural subject *times* and indicates appropriately that the creation of spectacular science fiction films continues.

The best answer is NOT:

A because the singular present perfect verb *has allowed* doesn't agree with the plural subject *times.*

C because the singular verb *allows* doesn't agree with the plural subject *times.*

D because the singular past progressive verb *was allowing* doesn't agree with the plural subject *times* and incorrectly indicates that the creation of spectacular science fiction films ended in the past.

Question 32. The best answer is F because the relative adverb *when* is appropriately used to follow a time expression ("in 1902"); no punctuation is needed.

The best answer is NOT:

G because the coordinating conjunction *and* treats a dependent clause ("when audiences first saw . . .") as a second independent clause, creating a nonsensical sentence.

H because the relative pronoun *which* logically refers to *1902*, both implying that audiences first saw the year 1902 (rather than first seeing a groundbreaking movie) and creating a garbled sentence.

J because the relative adverb *where* doesn't fit logically into this context, since *1902* refers to time rather than place.

Question 33. The best answer is C because *his* is the appropriate masculine singular pronoun to refer to the male magician Méliès.

The best answer is NOT:

A because the singular pronoun *its* refers to things, not people, and in the sentence would illogically refer to the camera rather than Méliès.

B because the plural pronoun *their* has no logical antecedent in the sentence.

D because *it's* is a contraction meaning "it is," which makes no sense in the sentence.

ENGLISH • PRACTICE TEST 3 • EXPLANATORY ANSWERS

Question 34. The best answer is F because when a conjunctive adverb such as *however* is used in the middle of a sentence, it needs to be set off by commas.

The best answer is NOT:

G because the semicolon after the word *however* creates an abbreviated main clause ("he found out, however;") followed by an inappropriate sentence fragment ("that the public preferred live magic acts to filmed versions").

H because the phrase "out, however" lacks the comma after the word *however* needed to set off the conjunctive adverb from the rest of the sentence.

J because the phrase "out however," lacks the comma after the word *out* needed to set off the conjunctive adverb from the rest of the sentence.

Question 35. The best answer is D because sentence 1 explains what Méliès did after he was *undaunted* by the discovery that people didn't like filmed magic acts (sentence 5). He began *instead* to tell fantasy stories.

The best answer is NOT:

A because keeping sentence 1 where it is now would weaken the logic and coherence of the paragraph. The paragraph would begin with a reference to Méliès being *undaunted* and turning to fantasy stories *instead* before Méliès had been formally described in sentence 2 and before the incident that caused him to turn away from filmed magic acts had been related (sentences 3 to 5).

B because placing sentence 1 after sentence 2 would weaken the logic and coherence of the paragraph. The words *undaunted* and *instead* in sentence 1 would make no sense, because there's nothing in sentence 2 to suggest that Méliès had met with any problems.

C because placing sentence 1 after sentence 3 would weaken the logic and coherence of the paragraph. The words *undaunted* and *instead* in sentence 1 would make no sense, because there's nothing in sentences 2 or 3 to suggest that Méliès had met with any problems.

ENGLISH • PRACTICE TEST 3 • EXPLANATORY ANSWERS

Question 36. The best answer is H because the sentence under consideration should NOT be deleted; it creates a transition between the preceding paragraph, about Méliès the magician, and this paragraph, which focuses on Méliès's exploration of special film effects.

The best answer is NOT:

F because the sentence under consideration mentions Méliès's "magician's eye" but doesn't otherwise describe his ability as a magician.

G because the sentence under consideration mentions "the basics of special effects" but doesn't begin to explain any of the techniques of trick photography.

J because the sentence under consideration doesn't indicate "that Méliès's interest in learning about trick photography existed before his interest in magic." The preceding paragraph, in fact, describes Méliès's interests as beginning with magic, then moving into filmmaking.

Question 37. The best answer is D because perfecting "eerie film entrances and exits" is a specific example of Méliès's skill and inventiveness.

The best answer is NOT:

A because the clause "he was able to do interesting things" is vague and doesn't give any specific illustration of Méliès's skill and inventiveness.

B because the clause "he used effects commonly seen in his stage productions" doesn't suggest that Méliès was particularly skillful or inventive; on the contrary, it suggests that the best Méliès could do as a filmmaker was to copy himself.

C because "his actors could enter and leave the scene" shifts the focus away from Méliès to his actors, which doesn't effectively highlight Méliès's skill and inventiveness and because relative to **D**, **C** is imprecise.

Question 38. The best answer is J because the phrase "exceedingly high" appropriately uses the adverb *exceedingly* in front of the adjective it modifies, *high*, which in turn modifies the noun *costs*.

The best answer is NOT:

F because an adjective is needed to modify the noun *costs*, whereas the phrase "highly excessively" consists of two adverbs.

G because an adjective is needed to modify the noun *costs*, whereas the phrase "exceeding highly" consists of a participle and an adverb.

H because the phrase "high excessively" reverses conventional word order.

ENGLISH • PRACTICE TEST 3 • EXPLANATORY ANSWERS

Question 39. The best answer is B because the verb *fired* is sufficient to indicate the action clearly.

The best answer is NOT:

A because the words *fired*, *launched*, and *projected* mean essentially the same thing in this context, making the phrasing redundant.

C because the words *fired* and *projected* mean essentially the same thing in this context, making the phrasing redundant.

D because the words *fired* and *propelled* mean essentially the same thing in this context, making the phrasing redundant.

Question 40. The best answer is F because the noun *creatures* is sufficient to indicate clearly what the terrain was filled with.

The best answer is NOT:

G because the clause "who they now realize live there" adds only wordiness to the sentence, which already strongly implies that the space travelers realize that the hostile creatures they encounter live in the strange terrain.

H because the clause "whom they are encountering" adds only wordiness to the sentence, which already clearly indicates that the space travelers encounter hostile creatures in the strange terrain.

J because the clause "who are found there" adds only wordiness to the sentence, which already clearly indicates that hostile creatures are found in the strange terrain.

Question 41. The best answer is C because for clarity this sequence of events should be divided into two sentences, the first indicating that the travelers fall off the edge of the moon to escape and the second establishing that the travelers land in the ocean and are eventually rescued.

The best answer is NOT:

A because using only a comma after the word *moon* to join two independent clauses creates a comma splice. (Alternatively, it's possible to see the error here as a comma splice created by the comma after the word *ocean*.)

B because the phrase "moon after landing" creates a fused sentence. (Alternatively, it's possible to see the error here as a comma splice created by the comma after the word *ocean*, with the sentence then suggesting illogically that the space travelers fell off the edge of the moon after landing in the ocean.)

D because using only a comma after the word *moon* to join two independent clauses creates a comma splice. (Alternatively, it's possible to see the error here as a comma splice created by the comma after the word *ocean*.)

ENGLISH • PRACTICE TEST 3 • EXPLANATORY ANSWERS

Question 42. The best answer is J because the past perfect verb *had begun* is made up of the past tense form *had* and the past participle *begun.* Past perfect is called for here because Méliès produced *A Trip to the Moon* long before interplanetary explorations had taken place.

The best answer is NOT:

F because *had began* is an improperly formed past perfect verb that uses the past tense form *began* instead of the past participle *begun.*

G because *would of begun* is an improperly formed verb that uses the word *of* instead of *have.*

H because *have began* is an improperly formed present perfect verb that uses the past tense form *began* instead of the past participle *begun.* (Even if the present perfect verb had been formed properly, it still wouldn't work in this context because the past perfect is needed to indicate that producing *A Trip to the Moon* occurred before interplanetary explorations had taken place.)

Question 43. The best answer is D because *disturb* is the only one of the four alternatives that, in the context of the sentence, can't reasonably be used as a substitute for the underlined word (*arouse*). "Disturb his audience's curiosity" is neither a conventional expression in standard English nor an appropriate innovation here. Therefore, *disturb* is the LEAST acceptable alternative to *arouse.*

The best answer is NOT:

A because the word *whet*, meaning here to stimulate or excite curiosity, is an acceptable, idiomatically appropriate alternative to the word *arouse.*

B because the word *stimulate*, meaning here to encourage or increase curiosity, is an acceptable, idiomatically appropriate alternative to the word *arouse.*

C because the word *awaken*, meaning here to stir up or stimulate curiosity, is an acceptable, idiomatically appropriate alternative to the word *arouse.*

ENGLISH • PRACTICE TEST 3 • EXPLANATORY ANSWERS

Question 44. The best answer is G because the writer's assertion that *A Trip to the Moon* "provided the genesis for a film genre"—science fiction—"that still packs theaters" is both specific and consistent with the writer's point, made throughout the essay, that Méliès produced a landmark movie.

The best answer is NOT:

F because the assertion that "People are still going to theaters to see science fiction films" has no clear tie to Méliès's role in science fiction filmmaking.

H because the assertion that "Méliès made an important contribution to filmmaking many years ago" is vague and doesn't clearly express the writer's viewpoint about Méliès's role in science fiction filmmaking.

J because the assertion that "In Méliès's production even the film crew knew a lot about space" shifts the focus away from Méliès's own role in science fiction filmmaking.

Question 45. The best answer is B because the essay fulfills the specified goal by focusing on a single artist, Méliès, and explaining how he used his talents as a magician and filmmaker to produce the landmark film *A Trip to the Moon* and thereby inaugurated the genre of science fiction films.

The best answer is NOT:

A because although the essay fulfills the goal specified in the question, which was to highlight the contributions a single artist can make to a particular art form, the essay doesn't assert that Méliès's work as a magician never would have succeeded without the contributions of the artists in the film industry. Instead, the essay indicates that Méliès was a successful magician prior to having any association with film and filmmaking.

C because the essay fulfills the goal specified in the question and because the main focus of the essay is on a single artist, Méliès, and a specific film, *A Trip to the Moon*, not on the general process of making science fiction films.

D because the essay fulfills the goal specified in the question and because the essay doesn't suggest that it took many artists working together to create Méliès's success. Rather, the essay stresses Méliès's accomplishments as a magician and his central role in creating the film *A Trip to the Moon*.

ENGLISH • PRACTICE TEST 3 • EXPLANATORY ANSWERS

Passage IV

Question 46. The best answer is G because the past perfect verb *had gone* is made up of the past tense form *had* and the past participle *gone.* Past perfect is called for here because if the Nancy Drew mystery series had gone out of style, it would have occurred prior to the events narrated here in past tense ("I thought . . ."). Furthermore, "gone out of style" is a conventional, idiomatic expression indicating that something has become unfashionable.

The best answer is NOT:

F because *had went* is an improperly formed past perfect verb that uses the past tense form *went* instead of the past participle *gone.*

H because *had went* is an improperly formed past perfect verb that uses the past tense form *went* instead of the past participle *gone* and because "went from style" isn't a conventional, idiomatic expression in standard English.

J because "gone from style" isn't a conventional, idiomatic expression in standard English.

Question 47. The best answer is B because the context calls for the auxiliary verb *would* to express the presumption expressed by "I was sure" (and to parallel *would have* earlier in the sentence) and calls for the present perfect verb *have been retired* in the passive voice to indicate the idea that the "sleuth" received the action of being "retired" to the library's back rooms.

The best answer is NOT:

A because *would of been* is an improperly formed verb that uses the word *of* instead of *have.*

C because *would of* is an improperly formed verb that uses the word *of* instead of *have.*

D because deleting the underlined portion leaves just the simple past tense verb *retired*, which isn't parallel to the other verb in the sentence, *would have.*

ENGLISH • PRACTICE TEST 3 • EXPLANATORY ANSWERS

Question 48. The best answer is J because the possessive form of the word *library* (*library's*) is needed to indicate "the dusty back rooms of the library" and because no comma is needed between the words *dusty* and *back* since *back rooms* functions as a single unit (a compound noun) and *dusty* and *back* aren't coordinate adjectives.

The best answer is NOT:

F because the comma between *dusty* and *back* is unnecessary since *back rooms* functions as a single unit (a compound noun) and *dusty* and *back* aren't coordinate adjectives. (You couldn't say "the library's dusty *and* back rooms," for example.)

G because the plural form *libraries* is incorrectly used in place of the possessive form *library's* and because the comma between *dusty* and *back* is unnecessary since *back rooms* functions as a single unit (a compound noun) and *dusty* and *back* aren't coordinate adjectives.

H because the plural form *libraries* is incorrectly used in place of the possessive form *library's*.

Question 49. The best answer is C because of the four choices, the word *hundreds* provides the most specific information about the number of Nancy Drew novels in existence.

The best answer is NOT:

A because the word *heaps* is vague and too informal for the style and tone of the essay.

B because the phrase "a high number" is vague.

D because the word *plenty* is vague.

Question 50. The best answer is F because the comma after the word *novels* is needed to finish setting off the nonrestrictive appositive "the teenaged heroine of hundreds of young adult mystery novels" from *Nancy Drew*, the noun the appositive describes.

The best answer is NOT:

G because the comma after the word *alive* is unnecessary since the list of adjectives "alive and well and still on the job" is already linked by the coordinating conjunction *and*.

H because a comma is needed after the word *novels* to finish setting off the nonrestrictive appositive "the teenaged heroine of hundreds of young adult mystery novels" from *Nancy Drew*, the noun the appositive describes, and because the comma after the word *alive* is unnecessary since the list of adjectives "alive and well and still on the job" is already linked by the coordinating conjunction *and*.

J because a comma is needed after the word *novels* to finish setting off the nonrestrictive appositive "the teenaged heroine of hundreds of young adult mystery novels" from *Nancy Drew*, the noun the appositive describes.

ENGLISH • PRACTICE TEST 3 • EXPLANATORY ANSWERS

Question 51. The best answer is B because the phrase "the mysteries" makes clear that the girls were reading Nancy Drew novels all summer long.

The best answer is NOT:

A because the pronoun *that* has no clear, logical antecedent. Though *that* is obviously intended to refer to the Nancy Drew novels the girls were reading all summer long, *that* is singular and *novels* is plural.

C because the pronoun *that* has no clear, logical antecedent. Though *that* is obviously intended to refer to the Nancy Drew novels the girls were reading all summer long, *that* is singular whereas *novels* is plural. Furthermore, "reading up on that" is an idiomatic phrase but one that doesn't work in this context. To "read up on" something means to learn about a topic, not to read a number of novels for pleasure.

D because "Liana and her friends were reading it over all summer long" is confusing in more than one way. First, we again have to ask what they were reading, because *it* doesn't logically refer to anything in the preceding sentence. Then "over all summer long" is a redundant phrase, with *over* being an extra, or superfluous, word.

Question 52. The best answer is G because the main clause of the sentence must have a subject (*she*) and a verb (*had followed*), and the verb must be in past perfect tense to indicate that Liana had already read the Nancy Drew novels *The Spider Sapphire Mystery* and *The Secret of the Crossword Cipher* before she went back to school.

The best answer is NOT:

F because "school and had" leaves the sentence without a main clause, creating an inappropriate sentence fragment.

H because "school, having" leaves the sentence without a main clause, creating an inappropriate sentence fragment.

J because "school, she" creates an inappropriate verb tense shift. The words "By the time" and "went back" signal that the past perfect verb *had followed*, rather than the simple past form *followed*, is needed to indicate that Liana had already read the Nancy Drew novels *The Spider Sapphire Mystery* and *The Secret of the Crossword Cipher* before she went back to school.

Question 53. The best answer is A because no punctuation is warranted between the verb *solve* and its direct object, *The Spider Sapphire Mystery.*

The best answer is NOT:

B because the colon between the verb *solve* and its direct object, *The Spider Sapphire Mystery*, is unnecessary and confusing.

C because the semicolon between the verb *solve* and its direct object, *The Spider Sapphire Mystery*, is unnecessary and confusing.

D because the comma between the verb *solve* and its direct object, *The Spider Sapphire Mystery*, is unnecessary and confusing.

Question 54. The best answer is H because this sentence names some specific settings for the Nancy Drew novels (Arizona, Argentina, Nairobi, New York) and uses the verb *had chased*, which suggests that Liana was so caught up in what she was reading that she felt like she was solving the mysteries along with Nancy Drew.

The best answer is NOT:

F because this sentence refers generally to "different places and various cultures all over the world" but doesn't specify any settings for the Nancy Drew novels and because the verb *had read* doesn't make clear that Liana was particularly interested in the novels.

G because this sentence refers generally to "many breathtaking adventures involving all sorts of colorful characters" but doesn't specify any settings for the Nancy Drew novels.

J because this sentence refers generally to "many new places around the world" but doesn't specify any settings for the Nancy Drew novels and because the phrases *through her exposure to* and *learned about* don't make clear that Liana was particularly interested in the novels.

ENGLISH • PRACTICE TEST 3 • EXPLANATORY ANSWERS

Question 55. The best answer is C because the proposed sentence, concerning how many books are in one of the series featuring Nancy Drew, shouldn't be added at this point in the essay because it distracts the reader from the main point of the paragraph, which is about why the narrator and her childhood friends loved Nancy Drew so much.

The best answer is NOT:

A because while the proposed sentence does attest to the longevity and popularity of the Nancy Drew Mystery Story series, the sentence is out of place and largely irrelevant at this point in a paragraph mainly about the place Nancy Drew held in the narrator's childhood and that of her friends.

B because the proposed sentence, with its facts and figures, addresses the history of the Nancy Drew Mystery Story series, not why the narrator loved Nancy Drew, which is why the sentence is out of place and largely irrelevant at this point in a paragraph mainly about the place Nancy Drew held in the narrator's childhood and that of her friends.

D because while the proposed sentence shouldn't be added at this point, adding in information about the author of the Nancy Drew Mystery Story series would only make the sentence more out of place and irrelevant, given that the paragraph is mainly about the place Nancy Drew held in the narrator's childhood and that of her friends.

Question 56. The best answer is H because "her freedom to do what she wanted" is clear and is parallel with "her loyal companions" and "her bravado," used previously in the sentence to identify two other things the narrator and her friends loved about Nancy Drew.

The best answer is NOT:

F because "there was a love for her freedom to do what she wanted" is not parallel with the two similar structures in the sentence ("her loyal companions," "her bravado") and is awkward, wordy, and redundant with "we loved."

G because "a love for her freedom to do what she wanted" is not parallel with the two similar structures in the sentence ("her loyal companions," "her bravado") and is awkward and redundant with "we loved."

J because "the freedom to do as one wants" is not parallel with the two similar structures in the sentence ("her loyal companions," "her bravado") and because the impersonal and rather formal pronoun *one* is stilted and out of place in a sentence focused on Nancy Drew's qualities.

ENGLISH • PRACTICE TEST 3 • EXPLANATORY ANSWERS

Question 57. The best answer is B because the word *therefore* is the only one of the four alternatives that, in the context of the sentence, can't reasonably be used as a substitute for the underlined portion (*also*). *Therefore* introduces something that is a result of something else, but *also* only signals the addition of one or more things. Thus, *therefore* is the LEAST acceptable alternative to *also.*

The best answer is NOT:

A because the word *furthermore*, meaning "in addition," is an acceptable alternative to the word *also*, as the two mean essentially the same thing in this context.

C because the word *likewise*, meaning "in a similar manner," is an acceptable alternative to the word *also*, as the two mean essentially the same thing in this context.

D because deleting the underlined portion doesn't change the meaning of the sentence much if at all. Even without the word *also*, the sentence is clearly adding to the list of qualities that the narrator and her friends loved about Nancy Drew.

Question 58. The best answer is F because the phrase "was able to solve crimes" effectively sets up a grammatically parallel list of notable things Nancy Drew was able to do: "solve crimes," "win golf tournaments," "kick bad guys in the shins," and "impress her father's distinguished clients."

The best answer is NOT:

G because the phrase "was capable of solving crimes" doesn't set up a parallel list of notable things Nancy Drew was able to do, as *solving* isn't parallel with *win*, *kick*, and *impress*, nor is it standard to say that Drew "was capable of . . . win golf tournaments," and so on.

H because the phrase "was good at crime solving" doesn't set up a parallel list of notable things Nancy Drew was able to do, as *solving* isn't parallel with *win*, *kick*, and *impress*, nor is it standard to say that Drew "was good at . . . win golf tournaments," and so on.

J because the phrase "solved crimes" doesn't set up a parallel list of notable things Nancy Drew was able to do, as *solved* isn't parallel with *win*, *kick*, and *impress.*

ENGLISH • PRACTICE TEST 3 • EXPLANATORY ANSWERS

Question 59. The best answer is C because the semicolon after the word *successful* is appropriately used to divide this sentence into two closely related independent clauses.

The best answer is NOT:

A because the lack of appropriate punctuation and/or a conjunction between the words *successful* and *they* creates a fused sentence.

B because the lack of appropriate punctuation and/or a conjunction between the words *successful* and *they* creates a fused sentence.

D because "successful, knowing" creates a confusing, possibly redundant sentence, as it's not clear who knows what.

Question 60. The best answer is F because the phrase "those exciting adventure tales spiced with mystery" effectively supports the point in the first part of the sentence that what the girls in Liana's generation "need and love" is entertaining fiction ("the stories themselves").

The best answer is NOT:

G because the phrase "the answers to the mysteries of their lives" suggests that what the girls in Liana's generation "need and love" are stories that teach the girls about themselves, whereas "the stories themselves," used in the first part of the sentence, suggests that what the girls really want is entertaining fiction.

H because the phrase "a strong role model for their generation" suggests that what the girls in Liana's generation "need and love" are stories that inspire them, whereas "the stories themselves," used in the first part of the sentence, suggests that what the girls really want is entertaining fiction. The preceding two sentences in the paragraph also make the point that girls today don't need a "successful girl detective" as a role model.

J because the phrase "the ability to overcome obstacles" clumsily suggests that what the girls in Liana's generation "need and love" are stories that show a "successful girl detective" rising above adversity, whereas "the stories themselves," used in the first part of the sentence, suggests that what the girls really want is entertaining fiction. The preceding two sentences in the paragraph also make the point that girls today don't need a "successful girl detective" as a role model.

Passage V

Question 61. The best answer is C because the preposition *from* effectively sets up the long introductory phrase "From ancient Babylonian astronomers . . . to twentieth-century science fiction writers" that begins the sentence.

The best answer is NOT:

A because the words "there were" introduce another independent clause into the sentence, resulting in ungrammatical and confusing sentence structure.

B because the subordinating conjunction *when* creates a nonsensical introductory phrase and an ungrammatical sentence.

D because the adjective *those* creates a nonsensical introductory phrase and an ungrammatical sentence.

Question 62. The best answer is H because the clause "who penned spine-tingling stories of 'little green men from Mars'" is the most relevant to helping make the point that Mars "has often been a symbol of ill will and danger."

The best answer is NOT:

F because the fact that there are twentieth-century science fiction writers "whose works become best-sellers" isn't relevant to making the point that Mars "has often been a symbol of ill will and danger."

G because the comment that there are twentieth-century science fiction writers who have "wild imaginations about outer space" is too vague to help explain why Mars "has often been a symbol of ill will and danger."

J because the fact that there are twentieth-century science fiction writers "who created images of Mars in literature" doesn't say anything specific about the nature of those images or help explain why Mars "has often been a symbol of ill will and danger."

ENGLISH • PRACTICE TEST 3 • EXPLANATORY ANSWERS

Question 63. The best answer is B because this sentence effectively ties together the bad reputation Mars has often had ("such negative associations"), described in the preceding paragraph, and the more recent interest in robotic and human missions to Mars, discussed in this paragraph.

The best answer is NOT:

A because this sentence about the United States competing with other countries to explore space is at best only loosely relevant to the topic of this paragraph, which is recent interest in robotic and human missions to Mars, and is unconnected to the topic of the preceding paragraph, which is Mars's impact on thought and culture.

C because this sentence about which year the United States founded its space agency is loosely relevant to the topic of this paragraph, which is recent interest in robotic and human missions to Mars, but is unconnected to the topic of the preceding paragraph, which is Mars's impact on thought and culture.

D because this sentence about Earth and Mars being planets in the inner solar system offers encyclopedia- or textbook-style information that is only loosely related to the topic of this paragraph, which is recent interest in robotic and human missions to Mars, and the topic of the preceding paragraph, which is Mars's impact on thought and culture.

Question 64. The best answer is G because the past perfect tense verb *had sent* is made up of the past tense form *had* and the past participle *sent.* Past perfect is called for here to indicate that one event in the past (NASA sending its thirtieth spacecraft to Mars) took place before another past event ("By 2003").

The best answer is NOT:

F because *would of sent* is an improperly formed verb that uses the word *of* instead of *have.*

H because the simple past tense verb *send* is inappropriate given that a past perfect verb is needed to make clear that NASA had already sent its thirtieth spacecraft to Mars "by 2003."

J because the present perfect tense verb *have sent* is inappropriate given that a past perfect verb is needed to make clear that NASA had already sent its thirtieth spacecraft to Mars "by 2003."

ENGLISH • PRACTICE TEST 3 • EXPLANATORY ANSWERS

Question 65. The best answer is C because the participial phrase "prompting speculation" modifies in a clear way the preceding clause: by sending thirty spacecraft to Mars by 2003, NASA had led people to think seriously about the possibility of a human mission to Mars.

The best answer is NOT:

A because the subject *speculation* and the verb *has been prompted* begin a second independent clause joined to the first by only the comma after the word *planet*, creating a comma splice.

B because the words "to which speculation has prompted" create a confusing and ungrammatical construction, partly because "speculation has prompted" isn't a conventional, idiomatic expression and partly because the pronoun *which* has no logical antecedent.

D because the words "which is speculation" create a confusing construction because the pronoun *which* has no logical antecedent.

Question 66. The best answer is H because the phrase "Although few" begins a subordinate introductory clause that is set off from the sentence's main clause with a comma, resulting in a complete and logical sentence.

The best answer is NOT:

F because the lack of a subordinating conjunction in front of the word *Few* turns the introductory clause into an independent clause joined to the sentence's main clause by only the comma after the word *exciting.* The result is a comma splice.

G because the lack of a subordinating conjunction in front of the words "Maybe a few" turns the introductory clause into an independent clause joined to the sentence's main clause by only the comma after the word *exciting.* The result is a comma splice.

J because the lack of a subordinating conjunction in front of the words "Few, if any," turns the introductory clause into an independent clause joined to the sentence's main clause by only the comma after the word *exciting.* The result is a comma splice.

ENGLISH • PRACTICE TEST 3 • EXPLANATORY ANSWERS

Question 67. The best answer is A because the nonrestrictive appositive "the most ambitious NASA project yet" is nonessential explanatory information that needs to be set off by commas from the rest of the sentence.

The best answer is NOT:

B because a comma is needed after the word *yet* to finish setting off the nonrestrictive appositive "the most ambitious NASA project yet" from the rest of the sentence.

C because a comma, not a colon, is needed after the word *yet* to finish setting off the nonrestrictive appositive "the most ambitious NASA project yet" from the rest of the sentence.

D because a comma, not a dash, is needed after the word *yet* to finish setting off the nonrestrictive appositive "the most ambitious NASA project yet" from the rest of the sentence. Although a pair of dashes could have been used to set off the nonrestrictive appositive, the writer uses a comma after the word *Station*, so parallelism requires that a second comma follow the word *yet*.

Question 68. The best answer is F because the information should be added to the sentence; the explicit detail about the amount of money actually spent on constructing the space station—nearly double the already high projected cost of $17 billion—strengthens the sentence's assertion that "NASA overspent on the International Space Station."

The best answer is NOT:

G because although the information should be added to the sentence, nothing in the information suggests, let alone proves, that space flight will be more affordable in the future.

H because the information would strengthen, rather than weaken, the point made in the paragraph about the high cost of human flight to Mars. If the actual cost of constructing the International Space Station was almost double the projected cost, it's reasonable to worry about the accuracy of the already high projections of the cost of sending humans to Mars. Thus, the information should be added to the sentence.

J because the essay's focus isn't on the human experience in travel to Mars but rather on the costs of manned and unmanned missions to the planet. The information isn't a digression but instead strengthens the point made in the paragraph about the high cost of human flight to Mars. Thus, the information should be added to the sentence.

Question 69. The best answer is B because *what* is the logical introductory word in the noun clause functioning as the direct object of the verb *imagine*, resulting in "what the final price of a human voyage to Mars would be." Turning this clause around reinforces the idea that *what* is the best answer: "The final price of a human voyage to Mars would be *what*?"

The best answer is NOT:

A because *if* is an illogical introductory word in the noun clause functioning as the direct object of the verb *imagine.* Turning the clause around makes this clear: "The final price of a human voyage to Mars would be *if*?"

C because *how* is an illogical introductory word in the noun clause functioning as the direct object of the verb *imagine.* Turning the clause around makes this clear: "The final price of a human voyage to Mars would be *how*?"

D because deleting the underlined portion results in an illogical, incomplete-sounding sentence: "One can only imagine the final price of a human voyage to Mars would be."

Question 70. The best answer is F because "robotic spacecraft launched in 2003" offers an effective description of the Mars Rovers.

The best answer is NOT:

G because "which captured the imagination of the general public" doesn't offer any specific description of the Mars Rovers.

H because "the products described at length in the media" doesn't offer any specific description of the Mars Rovers.

J because "familiar to many who watched the news coverage at the time" doesn't offer any specific description of the Mars Rovers.

Question 71. The best answer is D because the word *capacity* is sufficient to refer to the capability of the Mars Rovers to examine soil and rocks.

The best answer is NOT:

A because the words *capacity* and *ability* are redundant; they mean basically the same thing in this context.

B because the adjective *genuine* in the phrase "genuine capacity" creates a confusing expression; *genuine* suggests there might be some doubt about the Rovers' capability, but no doubts have been raised.

C because the phrase "potential capacity" is a confusing expression; *potential* suggests there might be some conditions or limits on the Rovers' capability, but no conditions or limits have been mentioned.

ENGLISH • PRACTICE TEST 3 • EXPLANATORY ANSWERS

Question 72. The best answer is J because *age-old*, which means having been around for a long time, is a conventional, idiomatic expression that makes sense in this context.

The best answer is NOT:

F because the words *aging* and *older* are redundant; they mean basically the same thing in this context. "Aging or older visions" is also not likely what the writer intends to say here, because the writer suggests in the essay that there's a timeless appeal to the notion of human spaceflight.

G because "old age" creates a silly expression ("old age visions") that implies that visions of human space travel are held only by old people.

H because "aging old" creates a nonsensical expression ("aging old visions").

Question 73. The best answer is D because the phrase "Even so," meaning "despite that," effectively signals the contrast between the preceding sentence, which says that using only machines to explore Mars may take some of the romance out of space travel, and this sentence, which says that we nevertheless need to remember that the right machines can do as much as if not more than humans can and at a fraction of the cost.

The best answer is NOT:

A because the phrase "In other words" incorrectly indicates that this sentence restates or summarizes the preceding sentence. Instead, this sentence offers a contrast to the preceding one.

B because the phrase "For that reason alone" incorrectly indicates that this sentence offers a consequence following from a circumstance identified in the preceding sentence. Instead, this sentence offers a contrast to the preceding one.

C because the phrase "In that time frame" makes no sense in context, as no time frame is indicated in the preceding sentence. Instead, this sentence offers a contrast to the preceding one.

ENGLISH • PRACTICE TEST 3 • EXPLANATORY ANSWERS

Question 74. The best answer is G because the word *at* creates a conventional, idiomatic expression ("at a fraction of the cost") that makes sense in the context of the writer identifying an additional consideration (machines doing as much as if not more than humans *and* at a much lower cost).

The best answer is NOT:

F because the phrase *such as* creates a nonsensical expression ("such as a fraction of the cost").

H because the phrase "but only" is missing the word *at* that would make it a conventional, idiomatic expression ("but only at a fraction of the cost") and because *but* suggests a contrast with what precedes it in the sentence when what follows is an additional consideration (machines doing as much as if not more than humans and at a much lower cost). (The writer here might have used "at only," for example, but not "but only.")

J because deleting the underlined portion creates a nonsensical expression. "A fraction of the cost" suggests that what precedes it in the sentence identifies a cost (e.g., ". . . less than one billion dollars—a fraction of the cost [of a human mission]"), but this isn't the case.

Question 75. The best answer is D because concluding the essay with the proposed sentence would blur the essay's focus on Mars and the cost of sending humans there.

The best answer is NOT:

A because although the proposed sentence may capture the emotion that is the basis for the space exploration described in the essay, the sentence is out of place as a conclusion to an essay focused mainly on the expense of a human mission to Mars.

B because although the proposed sentence may invite the reader to reflect on the insignificance of money in relation to the mystery of space, the sentence is out of place as a conclusion to a paragraph and essay on the expense of a human mission to Mars.

C because although the proposed sentence shouldn't be added at this point, the essay doesn't contain a chronological history of people who traveled in space.

MATHEMATICS • PRACTICE TEST 3 • EXPLANATORY ANSWERS

Question 1. The correct answer is E. You may want to make a sketch of this situation in your mind or, better yet, in the space in your test booklet. A sample sketch is shown in the following:

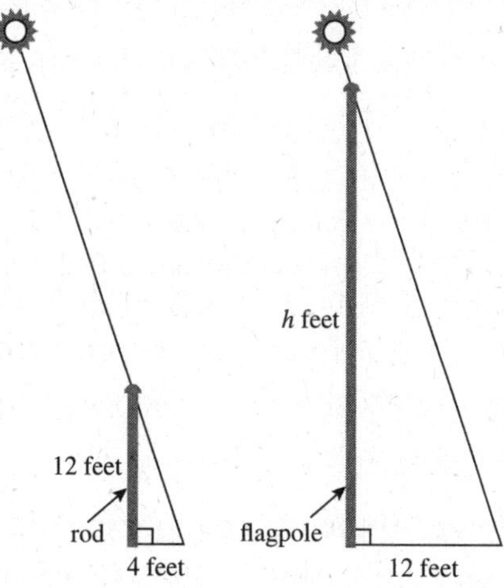

The vertical rod and the vertical flagpole each form a right angle with the level ground, resulting in two right triangles. The smaller right triangle (at left) is composed of the rod, the rod's shadow, and the line of sight of the sun through the top of the rod. The larger right triangle (at right) is composed of the flagpole, the flagpole's shadow, and the line of sight of the sun through the top of the flagpole. Because the angle of elevation of the sun is the same for each triangle, the two triangles are similar by the angle-angle similarity property. Using the ratios of corresponding sides of the similar triangles, the proportion $\frac{12}{h}=\frac{4}{12}$ is solved to find the height of the flagpole, $h = 36$ feet.

Common errors in this problem result from relying on an incorrect mental image or labeling the dimensions on the sketch incorrectly. If you chose **A**, you might have set up and solved the proportion $\frac{h}{12}=\frac{4}{12}$.

Question 2. The correct answer is K. If you knew the unknown score, you could check to see that it was correct by adding up all five scores, dividing by 5 to get the average, and checking to see that the result was 90. Let x be the unknown score. Then the sum of all the scores is $85 + 95 + 93 + 80 + x$, and the average is $\frac{85+95+93+80+x}{5}$. For the average to be 90, that means $\frac{85+95+93+80+x}{5}=90$. To solve that equation, you can multiply both sides by 5 to get $85 + 95 + 93 + 80 + x = 450$ and then subtract 353 from both sides to get $x = 97$.

G is closest to the average of the four given scores, $\frac{85+95+93+80}{4}=88.25$. To raise an average of 88.25 up to 90 would take an increase of about 2 points, but a single new score of 92 (answer choice **J**) would not raise the average much. You can check your answer to see that it is too low: $\frac{85+95+93+80+92}{5}=\frac{445}{5}=89$. You can check any answer choice to see whether it is correct.

MATHEMATICS • PRACTICE TEST 3 • EXPLANATORY ANSWERS

Question 3. The correct answer is A. Substituting –5 for x produces a numerator equal to $(-5)^2 - 1 = 25 - 1 = 24$ and a denominator equal to $-5 + 1 = -4$. Therefore, $\frac{x^2 - 1}{x + 1} = \frac{24}{-4} = -6$. The most common wrong answer is **C**, which comes from forgetting the negative sign in the given x-value: $\frac{5^2 - 1}{5 + 1} = \frac{24}{6} = 4$.

Question 4. The correct answer is K. To find the total distance, in miles, Kaya ran, you need the sum of $1\frac{2}{5}$ and $2\frac{1}{3}$. To add mixed numbers together, each fraction must have a common denominator. Because 3 and 5 do not have any common factors besides 1, the least common denominator is 3(5), or 15. To convert $\frac{2}{5}$, you multiply by $\frac{3}{3}$. The result is $\frac{6}{15}$. To convert $\frac{1}{3}$, you multiply by $\frac{5}{5}$. The result is $\frac{5}{15}$. To add $1\frac{6}{15}$ and $2\frac{5}{15}$, you first add 1 and 2 and then $\frac{6}{15} + \frac{5}{15}$. The result is $3\frac{6+5}{15}$, or $3\frac{11}{15}$.

If you chose **F**, you probably added the whole number parts and multiplied the fractions. If you chose **G**, you probably added the whole number parts and added the numerators and the denominators separately: $\frac{2+1}{5+3}$. If you chose **J**, you probably converted $\frac{2}{5}$ to $\frac{2}{15}$ incorrectly and then added 1 + 2 and $\frac{2}{15} + \frac{5}{15}$.

Question 5. The correct answer is E. Although you could try out various combinations of the given three statements and try to make a conclusion, it might be more straightforward to look at each of the answer choices to see whether it contradicts one of the given three statements or whether it could be deduced from the given three statements.

A and **B** each say that Insect I is an ant. This directly contradicts the second given statement, so **A** and **B** are false.

Consider **C**: if it is true (Insect I is attracted to honey), then the first given statement implies that Insect I is an ant. This contradicts the second given statement, so **C** is false.

D directly contradicts the third given statement, so **D** is false.

For **E**, consider Insect J. The third given statement tells you that Insect J is attracted to honey, and the first given statement tells you that, because all insects attracted to honey are ants, Insect J must be an ant. So **E** must be true.

Question 6. The correct answer is G. You can find the value of this expression by substituting the given values of x and m into the expression and then simplifying: $\sqrt{\frac{-16}{-4}} = \sqrt{4}$.

You may have gotten **F** if you did $\sqrt{\frac{-16}{4}} \Rightarrow -\sqrt{4}$.

You may have gotten **H** if you did $\sqrt{\frac{-16}{-2}} = \sqrt{8}$. You may have gotten **J** if you did $\sqrt{\frac{-16}{4}} = \sqrt{-4}$.

You may have gotten **K** if you did $\sqrt{\frac{-16}{4}} = \sqrt{-4}$.

MATHEMATICS • PRACTICE TEST 3 • EXPLANATORY ANSWERS

Question 7. The correct answer is B. The amount collected from the sale of 142 tickets bought in advance is equal to ($6 per ticket)(142 tickets) = $852. The amount collected from the sale of d tickets bought at the door is equal to ($8 per ticket)($d$ tickets) = 8d$. The total amount collected from all ticket sales is $852 + 8d$. To determine the minimum number of tickets to produce $2,000 in ticket sales, you can set up an inequality: $852 + 8d \geq 2{,}000$. Subtracting 852 from both sides and then dividing by 8 produces the equivalent inequality $d \geq 143.5$. Keep in mind, however, that d must be a whole number of tickets, so you must select the whole number d to satisfy the inequality. This means you must round 143.5 *up* to obtain the correct answer. If you chose **A**, you probably rounded *down* to 143. If you chose **D**, you might have divided 2,000 by 8 without thinking carefully about what the numbers represent. If you chose **C** or **E**, you probably set up the inequality incorrectly.

Question 8. The correct answer is J. For each kind of bread, there are 5 kinds of meat, so that is $3 \cdot 5$ combinations of bread and meat. For each of these 15 combinations of bread and meat, there are 3 kinds of cheese. That makes $15 \cdot 3 = 45$ combinations of bread, meat, and cheese.

The tree diagram on page 572 shows all 45 combinations. It would take a lot of time to list all these cases, but you can imagine what the tree looks like without having to write it all out. You can see that parts of the tree repeat many times, and so you can use multiplication to help you count.

MATHEMATICS • PRACTICE TEST 3 • EXPLANATORY ANSWERS

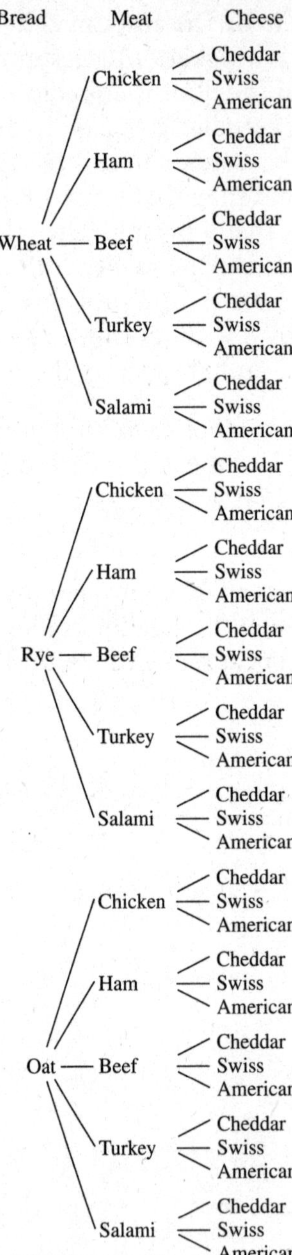

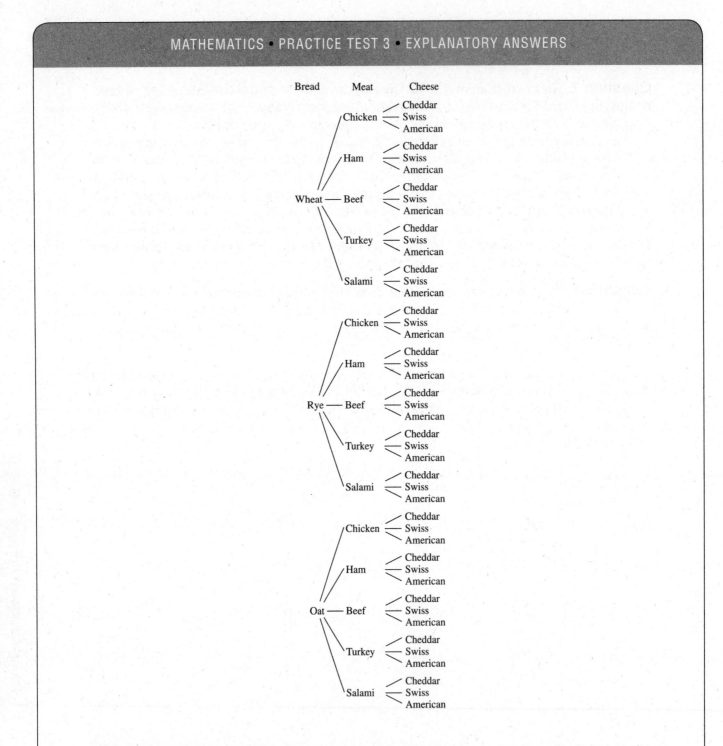

Question 9. The correct answer is E. Use of the distributive property gives the equivalent equation $12x - 132 = -15$. Adding 132 to both sides of the equation results in the equation $12x = 117$, implying that the solution is $x = \frac{117}{12}$, or $\frac{39}{4}$ when reduced to lowest terms. If you distributed 12 to *only* the first term, x, but forgot to distribute 12 to the second term, you probably got an answer of $-\frac{1}{3}$.

MATHEMATICS • PRACTICE TEST 3 • EXPLANATORY ANSWERS

Question 10. The correct answer is J. The following figure illustrates the progression of angle measures found in determining the measure of $\angle BCE$.

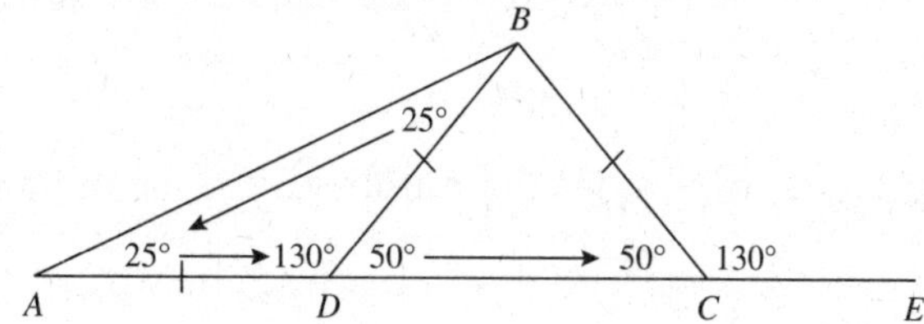

Because $\overline{BD} \cong \overline{AD}, \Delta ABD$ is isosceles, so its base angles are congruent. Therefore, $m\angle BAD = m\angle ABD = 25°$. Because the sum of the angle measures in ΔABD must equal $180°$, $m\angle ADB = 180° - (25° + 25°) = 130°$. Because $\angle ADB$ and $\angle BDC$ are a linear pair, $m\angle BDC = 180° - 130° = 50°$. Because $\overline{BD} \cong \overline{BC}$, ΔDBC is isosceles, so *its* base angles are congruent: $m\angle BCD = m\angle BDC = 50°$. Finally, $\angle BCD$ and $\angle BCE$ are a linear pair, so $m\angle BCE = 180° - 50° = 130°$.

Question 11. The correct answer is C. When you substitute –2 for x, you get $9(-2)^2 + 5(-2) - 8 = 9(4) + (-10) - 8 = 18$. If you chose **A**, you probably evaluated $9(-2)^2$ as –36. If you chose **E**, you probably evaluated $5(-2)$ as 10.

Question 12. The correct answer is J. One efficient way to solve this problem numerically is by listing the multiples of the largest of the 3 numbers (70) as a sequence and determining whether or not each succeeding term in the sequence is a multiple of *both* 20 and 30.

70 (multiple of neither)
140 (multiple of 20 only)
210 (multiple of 30 only)
280 (multiple of 20 only)
350 (multiple of neither)
420 (multiple of both 20 and 30)

The first term in the sequence that is a multiple of both 20 and 30 is 420, which is the least common multiple of 20, 30, and 70. You can also find the least common multiple by expressing each of the three numbers as a product of primes (with exponents), listing all bases of exponential expressions shown, and choosing for each base listed the highest-valued exponent shown.

$$30 = 2^1 \times \mathbf{3^1} \times \mathbf{5^1}$$
$$20 = \mathbf{2^2} \times 5^1$$
$$70 = 2^1 \times 5^1 \times \mathbf{7^1}$$

The least common multiple is $2^2 \times 3^1 \times 5^1 \times 7^1 = 420$.

Taking Additional Practice Tests

MATHEMATICS • PRACTICE TEST 3 • EXPLANATORY ANSWERS

Question 13. The correct answer is E. You may want to choose an even integer as Tom's initial number, follow his steps in obtaining the *incorrect* answer, and then determine *what* operation using *what* number is needed to obtain the desired number. For example:

1. Choose the integer 6 as the initial number.
2. When Tom "accidentally multiplies the number by 2," he obtains an incorrect answer of 12.
3. Had Tom correctly divided the initial number by 2, he would have obtained 3 as the answer.
4. To convert his incorrect answer of 12 to the desired answer of 3, he must divide by 4.

You may want to confirm that **E** is the correct answer by choosing a different initial number and repeating the steps.

Question 14. The correct answer is G. The 8-sided figure in the problem consists of 5 congruent squares whose areas total 125 square inches. Therefore, each congruent square has an area of $125 \div 5 = 25$ square inches, so each side of each square is $\sqrt{25} = 5$ inches long. The perimeter of the 8-sided figure is composed of 12 of these sides, each of length 5 inches, as shown in the following figure. Therefore, the 8-sided figure has a perimeter of $12 \times 5 = 60$ inches.

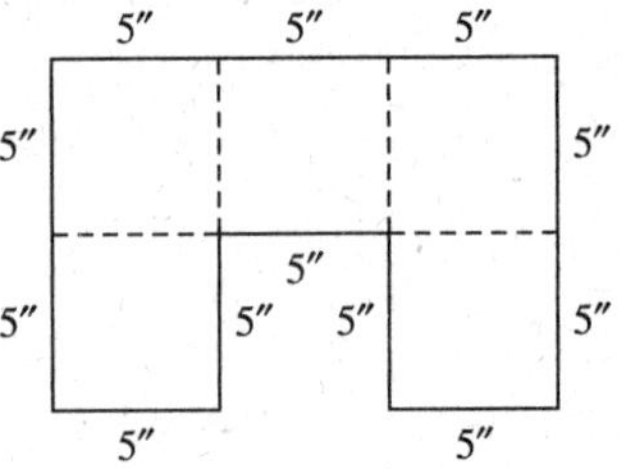

Question 15. The correct answer is A. You can find the total number of USBs Hai can buy by dividing the total cost of \$100 by the cost of 1 USB plus tax for 1 USB, $\$8 \times (1 + 0.07)$: $\frac{100}{1.07(8)}$. You cannot buy a partial USB; therefore, you must round down to 11 whole USBs. You may have gotten **B** if you did $\frac{100}{1.07(8)}$ and rounded up. You may have gotten **C** if you did $\frac{100}{1.08(7)}$ and rounded down. You may have gotten **D** if you did $\frac{100}{1.08(7)}$ and rounded up. You may have gotten **E** if you did $\frac{100+8}{7}$ and rounded down.

MATHEMATICS • PRACTICE TEST 3 • EXPLANATORY ANSWERS

Question 16. The correct answer is J. Because the item gives a unit rate, you can set up a proportional relationship and solve for x: $\frac{1.5\times10^8 \text{ calculations}}{1 \text{ second}}=\frac{6.0\times10^{16}}{x}$, $x=\frac{6.0\times10^{16}}{1.5\times10^8}$. You divide the coefficients and subtract the exponents because the bases are the same in each expression: $4.0 \times 10^{16-8} = 4.0 \times 10^8$.

You may have gotten **F** if you did $\frac{1.5\times10^8}{6.0\times10^{16}} = 0.25 \times 10^{-8}$. You may have gotten **G** if you did $6.0(1.5) \times 10$. You may have gotten **H** if you incorrectly simplified $\frac{6.0\times10^{16}}{1.5\times10^8}$ to be $4.0 \times 10^{\frac{16}{8}}$. You may have gotten **K** if you did $(1.5 \times 10^8)(6.0 \times 10^{16})$.

Question 17. The correct answer is E. Each answer choice is a linear equation in *slope-intercept form*; that is, $y = mx + b$, where the value of m gives the slope of the line and the value of b gives the y-intercept of the line. Only the equation shown in **E** represents a line having a y-intercept ($b = 5$), that matches the value of the y-intercept indicated by the given graph.

Question 18. The correct answer is K. To find the area of a square circumscribed about a circle with a radius of 7 feet, you would need to find the side length of the square. Because the diameter of the circle is the distance between 2 opposite sides of the square, the side length of the square is twice the radius, 2(7), or 14 feet. To find the area of the square, you square the side length, 14^2, to get 196 square feet.

If you chose **F**, you probably thought 7 feet was the side length and squared 7 to get 49 square feet. If you chose **J**, you probably used the formula for the area of a circle, πr^2, where r is the radius, to get πr^2, or 49π square feet.

Question 19. The correct answer is A. For x years of full years' employment after being hired, Worker A's starting salary ($20,000) increases by $800 per year and Worker B's starting salary ($15,200) increases by $2,000 per year. After x years, Worker A's salary has increased by 800x$ and Worker B's salary has increased by $2,000$x$. So, for x years of full years' employment after being hired, Worker A's yearly salary is represented by the expression $20{,}000 + 800x$ and Worker's B's salary is represented by the expression $15{,}200 + 2{,}000x$. These 2 yearly salaries are equal at the value of x for which the equation $20{,}000 + 800x = 15{,}200 + 2{,}000x$ is true.

Question 20. The correct answer is J. The figure shows a right triangle with two given side measures. To find the length of the third side, use the Pythagorean theorem:

$$(\text{length of the hypotenuse})^2 = (\text{length of one side of the triangle})^2 + (\text{length of the other side of the triangle})^2$$

In this problem, the 13-foot measure represents the length of the hypotenuse. So the formula gives the equation $13^2 = 12^2 + x^2$, where x feet is the length of the missing side. To find x^2, subtract 12^2 from each side of the equation. The subtraction results in the equivalent equation $25 = x^2$, resulting in the solution $x = \pm 5$. Because the side length of a triangle must be positive, you can ignore the negative solution. If you chose **F**, you probably took the length of the hypotenuse and subtracted the length of the given leg, without applying the Pythagorean theorem at all. If you chose **G**, you probably *doubled* the lengths, rather than *squaring* them.

Question 21. The correct answer is E. To simplify this expression, use the distributive property: $7(x + 3) - 3(2x - 2) = 7x + (7)(3) + (-3)(2x) + (-3)(-2) = 7x + 21 + (-6x) + 6$. Then combine like terms to obtain $x + 27$. If you chose **B**, perhaps you forgot that $a - b = a + (-b)$, and so you distributed 3 rather than -3 to the -2 term in $(2x - 2)$. If you chose **A**, perhaps you forgot to distribute the 7 and the -3 to the second term in each set of grouping symbols, setting $7(x + 3)$ equal to $7x + 3$ and $-3(2x - 2)$ equal to $-6x - 2$.

Question 22. The correct answer is G. To find 75% of a number, n, for which 115% of n is 460, you first set up an equation to find n using the fact that 115% of n is 460, or $1.15n = 460$. After dividing by 1.15, you find $n = 400$. Then, 75% of 400 is 400(0.75), or 300.

If you chose **J**, you probably found 75% of 460 as 460(0.75), or 345. If you chose **K**, you probably found n using the equation $1.15n = 460$ by dividing by 1.15 and getting 400.

Question 23. The correct answer is C. This problem tests your knowledge of how to square a binomial. The expression $(2x - 3)^2$ can be expanded into the $ax^2 + bx + c$ form using the distributive property as shown in the following:

$$\begin{aligned}(2x - 3)^2 &= (2x - 3)(2x - 3) = (2x)(2x) + (2x)(-3) + (-3)(2x) + (-3)(-3)\\ &= 4x^2 - 6x - 6x + 9 = 4x^2 - 12x + 9\end{aligned}$$

When the coefficients of $4x^2 - 12x + 9$ are matched with the coefficients of $ax^2 + bx + c$, you can see that $a = 4$, $b = -12$, and $c = 9$, and that $a + b + c = 4 + (-12) + 9 = 1$.

When you square a binomial, you must multiply two binomial expressions using the distributive property. Common errors result from reasoning that $(2x - 3)^2$ is equivalent to $(2x)^2 + (-3)^2$ or $(2x)^2 - (3)^2$, resulting in **B** or **D**.

Question 24. The correct answer is H. Two common approaches are often used in solving this problem.

In the first approach, the polygon can be divided into a 15 ft by 15 ft square and a 10 ft by 5 ft rectangle (see the following Figure 1). The area of the polygon is equal to the sum of the areas of the rectangle and the square: (15)(15) + (10)(5) = 275 square feet.

In the second approach, you take the rectangle formed by the 15 ft and 25 ft sides of the polygon and "cut away" a 10 ft by 10 ft square (see the following Figure 2). In this case, the area of the polygon is equal to the difference of the areas of the rectangle and the square: (15)(25) − (10)(10) = 275 square feet.

MATHEMATICS • PRACTICE TEST 3 • EXPLANATORY ANSWERS

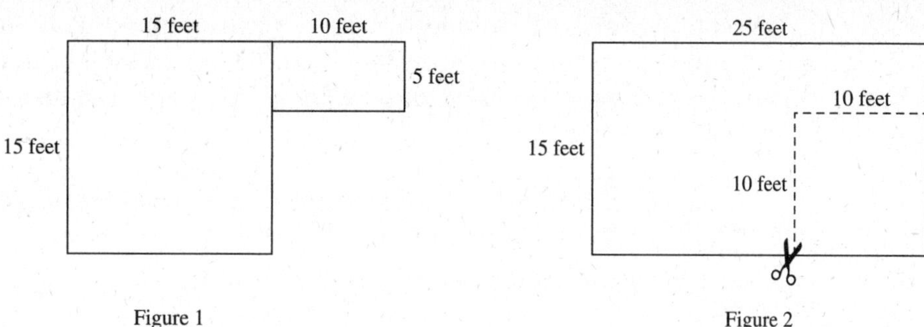

Figure 1

Figure 2

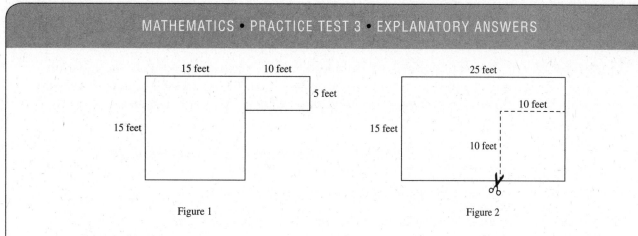

Question 25. The correct answer is B. The way to use the minimum number of blocks is to have a side of the block with the largest area face upward. That is the side that is 4″ by 8″. The 4″ width of the blocks will fit 3 to each foot. The 8″ length of the blocks will fit 3 to each 2 feet. The blocks could be arranged as shown, with 24 block widths in one direction and 15 block lengths in the other direction. That makes $15 \cdot 24 = 360$ blocks. The blocks could be arranged in different patterns, but the top area of all the blocks has to equal the $(8)(10) = 80$-square-foot area Barb is covering.

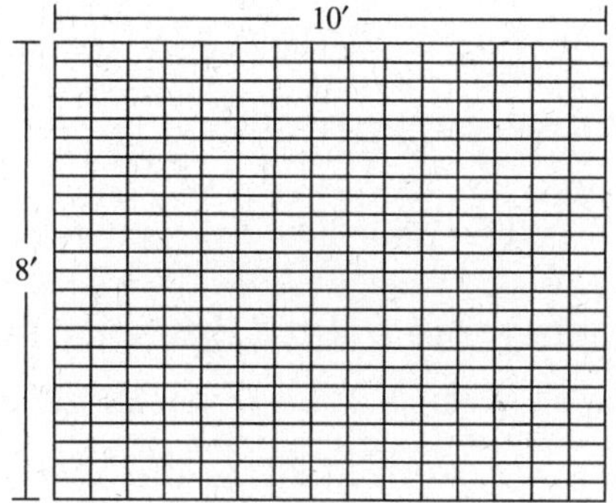

An alternate way to work this problem is to calculate the total area, 80 square feet, and divide by the largest area a single block can cover, 32 square inches. The area to be covered is $(8)(12) = 96$ inches in one direction and $(10)(12) = 120$ inches in the other direction, which makes the total area $(96)(120) = 11{,}520$ square inches. If you divide this by the area of a single block, 32 square inches, you will get $\frac{11{,}520}{32} = 360$ blocks.

If you got answer **A**, you may have calculated the area of the patio in square feet.

Taking Additional Practice Tests

MATHEMATICS • PRACTICE TEST 3 • EXPLANATORY ANSWERS

Question 26. The correct answer is H. To find the slope, you can manipulate the equation $6y - 14x = 5$ algebraically in order to find its equivalent equation expressed in *slope-intercept form*, which is $y = mx + b$, where m is the slope and b is the y-intercept. The manipulations are shown in the following:

$$6y-14x=5 \Rightarrow 6y=14x+5 \Rightarrow y=\frac{14}{6}x+\frac{5}{6}$$

The slope of the line equals $\frac{14}{6}$, or $\frac{7}{3}$ when reduced to lowest terms.

Question 27. The correct answer is C. First we will show that $m < \sqrt{mn}$:

Because m and n are positive integers such that $m < n$, $n = m + k$ where k is a positive integer and $m \geq 1$. For this reason, we know $\sqrt{mn} = \sqrt{m(m+k)} = \sqrt{m^2+km}$. Because the square root function increases as its input increases and $m^2+km > m^2$, $\sqrt{m^2+km} > \sqrt{m^2}$, and $\sqrt{m^2} = m$. Thus, $\sqrt{mn} > m$.

Then, we will show that $\sqrt{mn} < n$ by a similar argument:

Start by solving $n = m + k$ for m: $n - k = m$. Then write $\sqrt{mn} = \sqrt{(n-k)n} = \sqrt{n^2-kn}$. Because $n^2 - kn < n^2$, $\sqrt{(n-k)n} < \sqrt{n^2}$, and $\sqrt{n^2} = n$. Thus, $\sqrt{mn} < n$.

We have shown $m < \sqrt{mn}$ and $\sqrt{mn} < n$; thus, $m < \sqrt{mn} < n$.

If you chose **A** or **B**, you might have not realized that $\sqrt{mn}$ must be larger than m. Notice that for $m = 1$ and $n = 4$, $\sqrt{1(4)} > 1$ because $2 > 1$. If you chose **D**, you might have not considered cases such as when $m = 1$ and $n = 2$. Notice that for this case $\sqrt{mn} = \sqrt{n}$; thus, $\sqrt{mn} < \sqrt{n}$ is false. If you chose **E**, you might have not considered cases such as when $m = 3$ and $n = 4$. Notice that for this case $\sqrt{mn} > \sqrt{m+n}$ because $\sqrt{12} > \sqrt{7}$; thus, $\sqrt{mn} < \sqrt{m+n}$ is false.

Question 28. The correct answer is J. Similar triangles are triangles whose corresponding sides are proportional. The solution, x, is found by setting up the following proportion:

$$\frac{\text{the perimeter of the smaller triangle}}{\text{the perimeter of the larger triangle}} = \frac{3}{5} = \frac{(3+5+7)\text{ cm}}{x\text{ cm}}$$

To solve $\frac{3}{5} = \frac{15}{x}$ for x, cross-multiply to obtain the equivalent equation $3x = 75$, and divide by 3 to obtain $x = 25$.

Question 29. The correct answer is A. The area of the whole board is $\pi r^2 = \pi \cdot 10^2 = 100\pi$ square inches. The radius of the outside of the 20 ring is $10 - 2 = 8$ inches. The radius of the outside of the 30 ring is $8 - 2 = 6$ inches, so the area of the circle that includes 30, 40, and 50 points is $\pi \cdot 6^2 = 36\pi$ square inches. If a dart hits at a random spot on the board, the chance of it hitting in a certain region is proportional to the area of that region. So, the percent chance of hitting inside a region that is worth at least 30 points is $\frac{36\pi}{100\pi} \cdot 100\% = 36\%$.

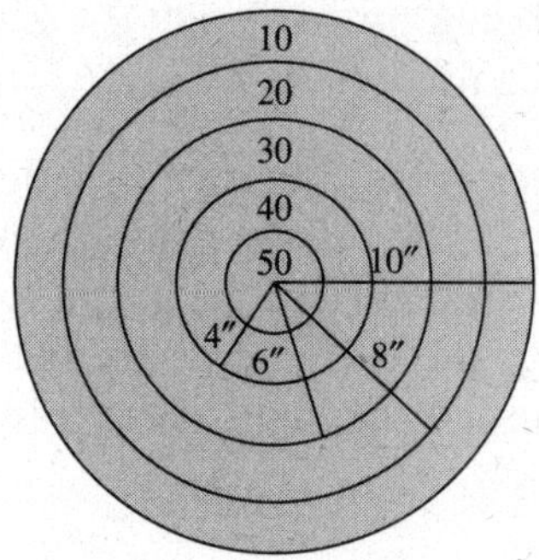

C is the percent chance of getting *more* than 30 points, using the 4-inch radius of the inside of the 30 ring.

Question 30. The correct answer is G. You can use translation skills to set up an algebraic equation that, when solved, yields the solution to the problem.

1. Let the variable a represent the teacher's age.
2. "If you *square* my age" translates into "a^2."
3. "23 *times* my age" translates into "$23a$."
4. "then *subtract* 23 times my age" translates into "$a^2 - 23a$." Because the words *than* and *from* do not appear in the sentence, the order of the terms "a^2" and "$23a$" is NOT reversed when translated into mathematical language.
5. "the result is 50" translates into "= 50."

Therefore, the translation gives the equation $a^2 - 23a = 50$, which you may solve by subtracting 50 from both sides and factoring.

The equation $a^2 - 23a - 50 = 0$ is true, provided that $(a + 2)(a - 25) = 0$, which happens if $a = -2$ (but age cannot be negative) or $a = 25$.

Question 31. The correct answer is B. "If a car accelerates from a stop at the *rate* of 20 meters per second per second" implies that $a = 20$, and "travels a *distance* of 80 meters" implies that $d = 80$. Substituting these values into the equation $d = \frac{1}{2}at^2$ gives the equation $80 = \frac{1}{2}(20)t^2$ or, equivalently, $80 = 10t^2$, or $8 = t^2$. Therefore, $t = \sqrt{8} \approx 2.8$ seconds.

MATHEMATICS • PRACTICE TEST 3 • EXPLANATORY ANSWERS

Question 32. The correct answer is F. To find the real numbers x such that $x + 3 > x + 5$, you would subtract x and 3 from both sides. The result is $0 > 2$, but that inequality is never true, so there is no solution for x. It is the empty set.

If you chose **G**, you probably switched the inequality and got $0 < 2$ after you subtracted x and 3 from both sides. If you chose **H**, you probably got $0 > 2$ and then thought that a negative value for x would change the inequality.

Question 33. The correct answer is D. You must first determine from the frequency bar graph the number of students in the class responding that they spent 0, 1, or 2 hours studying on the previous evening. The bars in the graph indicate that 2 students studied 0 hours, 5 students studied 1 hour, and 6 students studied 2 hours. Therefore, the fraction of students in the class that responded they had spent less than 3 hours studying is equal to $\frac{\text{the number of students studying less than 3 hours}}{\text{the number of students in the class}} = \frac{2+5+6}{20} = \frac{13}{20}$.

If you chose **B** (the most common incorrect answer), perhaps you overlooked the phrase "less than" and selected the number of students studying exactly 3 hours as the numerator, obtaining the fraction $\frac{4}{20}$, or $\frac{1}{5}$.

Question 34. The correct answer is J. In the following figure, the shaded sector represents the 3-hour group:

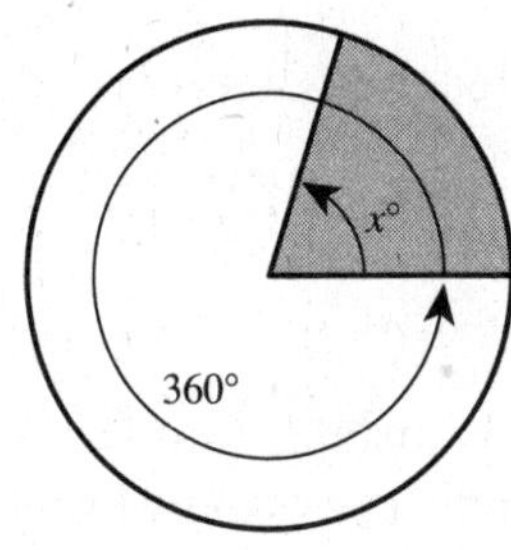

For this circle graph, the ratio $\frac{\text{the area of the shaded sector}}{\text{the area of the circle}}$ is equivalent to the ratio $\frac{\text{the number of students in the 3-hour group}}{\text{the number of students in the class}}$. These ratios, in turn, are equivalent to the ratio $\frac{\text{the measure of the central angle of the sector representing the 3-hour group}}{\text{the measure of the angle covered by 1 complete circle}}$. Letting the numerator of this last ratio equal $x°$, and using the fact that the denominator of this ratio is 360°, you obtain the proportions $\frac{4}{20} = \frac{\text{the number of students studying 3 hours}}{\text{the number of students in the class}} = \frac{x°}{360°}$, so $x = 72$.

MATHEMATICS • PRACTICE TEST 3 • EXPLANATORY ANSWERS

Question 35. The correct answer is B. Because this frequency bar graph gives the number of times each response was given, the frequency bar graph was constructed from the following 20 data values:

$$0, 0, 1, 1, 1, 1, 1, 2, 2, 2, 2, 2, 2, 3, 3, 3, 3, 4, 4, 5$$

The average number of hours for the 20 responses is equal to the average of the data values, which is defined to be $\frac{\text{the sum of the data values}}{\text{the number of data values}}$.

This is equal to $\frac{0+0+1+1+1+1+1+2+2+2+2+2+2+3+3+3+3+4+4+5}{20}$, or, equivalently, $\frac{2(0)+5(1)+6(2)+4(3)+2(4)+1(5)}{20} = \frac{42}{20} = 2.1$.

Question 36. The correct answer is H. To find the number of diagonals the octagon has, you would label the 8 vertices as endpoints. Those segments (which are the diagonals) are $\overline{AC}$, $\overline{AD}$, $\overline{AE}$, $\overline{AF}$, $\overline{AG}$, $\overline{BD}$, $\overline{BE}$, $\overline{BF}$, $\overline{BG}$, $\overline{BH}$, $\overline{CE}$, $\overline{CF}$, $\overline{CG}$, $\overline{CH}$, $\overline{DF}$, $\overline{DG}$, $\overline{DH}$, $\overline{EG}$, $\overline{EH}$, and $\overline{FH}$. There are 20 diagonals.

If you chose **F**, you probably just found the number of vertices in an octagon. If you chose **G**, you probably just multiplied the number of vertices by the number of endpoints of a diagonal, $8(s)$, or 16.

Question 37. The correct answer is E. As shown in the following figure, the tether line, the level ground, and a line segment representing the altitude of the bottom of the basket form a right triangle.

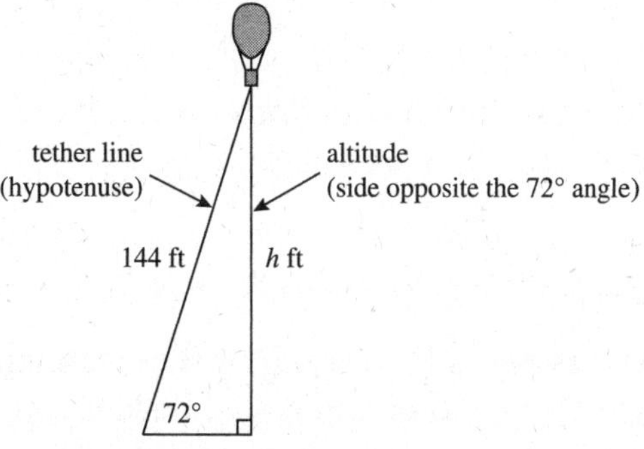

Let the length of the altitude equal h feet. You can use a trigonometric ratio to find h. The tether line forms the hypotenuse of the right triangle, and the line segment representing the altitude is the side opposite the 72° angle. Therefore, the trigonometric ratio to be used with respect to the 72° angle is the sine ratio, which gives the following equation:

$$\sin 72^\circ = \frac{\text{the length of the side opposite the } 72^\circ \text{ angle}}{\text{the length of the hypotenuse}} = \frac{h}{144}$$

Multiplying both sides of the equation $\frac{h}{144} = \sin 72^\circ$ by 144 yields the value of h, which is $144 \sin 72^\circ$.

MATHEMATICS • PRACTICE TEST 3 • EXPLANATORY ANSWERS

Question 38. The correct answer is G. The midpoint of a line segment is the point halfway between the two endpoints of the line segment. A formula for finding the midpoint (x_m,y_m) of two points (x_1,y_1) and (x_2,y_2) in the standard (x,y) coordinate plane is $(x_m,y_m)=\left(\frac{x_1+x_2}{2},\frac{y_1+y_2}{2}\right)$. The x-coordinate of the midpoint, x_m, is the *average* of the x-coordinates of the endpoints of the line segment. In the case of $\overline{GH}$, $x_m=\left(\frac{x_1+x_2}{2}=\frac{-8+2}{2}\right)=-3$.

Question 39. The correct answer is E. To determine the value of $8x + 9y$, find the solution (x,y) to the system of two equations given in the problem. This system can be solved using an elimination method. First, determine which of the two variables would be easiest to eliminate. For this system, eliminating the y-variable would be easier. In order to eliminate the y-variable, the y-coefficients in each equation (or equivalent equation) must be opposite numbers (–6 and 6 would be the best choice). Therefore, all terms in the upper equation should be multiplied by –2 (Step 1 following) to form an equivalent equation with –6 as the y-coefficient. Now the two equations have y-coefficients of –6 and 6, respectively, so adding the equations will eliminate the y-variable (Step 2 following).

		Step 1		**Step 2**
$2x+3y=4$	$\Rightarrow$	$-2(2x+3y)=-2(4)$	$\Rightarrow$	$-4x-6y=-8$
$5x+6y=7$		$5x+6y=7$		$5x+6y=\ 7$
				$x \quad =-1$

Substituting into either of the two initial equations produces an equation that can be solved for y; for example, letting $x = -1$ in $2x + 3y = 4$ gives $2(-1) + 3y = 4$. Solving for y, $-2 + 3y = 4$, so $3y = 6$. Therefore, $y = 2$.

Substituting $x = -1$ and $y = 2$ into $8x + 9y$ yields $8(-1) + 9(2) = -8 + 18 = 10$.

Question 40. The correct answer is H. If we draw θ in standard position and its terminal side intersects the unit circle at (x,y), then $\tan\theta=\frac{y}{x}$. Because we want to solve $\tan\theta=-1$, we want the ratio $\frac{y}{x}=-1$. This only happens when $\theta=\frac{3\pi}{4}$ or $\theta=\frac{7\pi}{4}$. Recall that $\tan\theta<0$ only when the terminal side of θ is in Quadrants II or IV.

You may have gotten **K** if you solved $\tan\theta=\pm1$. You may have gotten **F** if you thought the tangent of an angle was negative when its terminal side was in Quadrants I and II. You may have gotten **G** if you thought the tangent of an angle was negative when its terminal side was in Quadrants II and III. You may have gotten **J** if you thought the tangent of an angle was negative when its terminal side was in Quadrants III and IV.

MATHEMATICS • PRACTICE TEST 3 • EXPLANATORY ANSWERS

Question 41. The correct answer is B. By definition, $i^2 = -1$, so $i^4 = (i^2)^2 = (-1)^2 = 1$. Therefore, $i^x = 1$ for $x = 4$, so 1 is a possible value of i^x when x is an integer. More generally, when x is an integer, the only values of i^x possible are i, -1, $-i$, and 1, as shown in the following table:

...	i^{-3}	i^{-2}	i^{-1}	i^0	i^1	i^2	i^3	i^4	i^5	i^6	i^7	i^8	i^9	i^{10}	i^{11}	i^{12}	...
...	i	-1	$-i$	1	i	-1	$-i$	1	i	-1	$-i$	1	i	-1	$-i$	1	...

This rules out **A**, **C**, **D**, and **E.**

Question 42. The correct answer is F. Because the diameter of the can is 2 inches and the diameter of the glass is 3 inches, the radius of the can is 1 inch and the radius of the glass is 1.5 inches. Therefore, using $\pi r^2 h$, the volume of the can is $\pi(1^2)(6)$, or 6π, and the volume of the glass is $\pi(1.5^2)h$, or $2.25\pi h$. Because the volume of the soda pop can and the volume of the glass are equal, $6\pi = 2.25\pi h$. Solving for h gives us $h = 2\frac{2}{3}$.

You may have gotten **G** if you thought that height and diameter were directly proportional: $2(6) = 3h$. You may have gotten **H** if you thought that because the radius increased by 1 inch, then the height should decrease by 1 inch. You may have gotten **J** if you added all the values in the stem. You may have gotten **K** if you did $\frac{6\pi}{\frac{3}{4}\pi}$.

Question 43. The correct answer is C. The volume in cubic meters, V, of a right circular cylinder of radius r meters and height h meters is given by the formula $V = \pi r^2 h$. For the cylinder in this problem, $r = 5$ and $h = 6$. Therefore, $V = \pi(5^2)(6) = 150\pi$ cubic meters.

Question 44. The correct answer is F. The three triangles in the given figure (ΔABC, ΔADE, and ΔAFG) can be shown to be similar by use of the angle-angle similarity property.

Because $\Delta ABC \sim \Delta AFG$, the statement "The ratio of the perimeter of ΔABC to the perimeter of ΔAFG is 1:3" implies that the ratio of AC to AG is 1:3. So if $AC = 1$ unit, then $AG = 3$ units (see the following Figure 1).

Because $\Delta ADE \sim \Delta AFG$, the statement "The ratio of DE to FG is 2:3" implies that the ratio of AE to AG is 2:3. So if $AG = 3$ units, then $AE = 2$ units (see the following Figure 2).

This means that $AE = 2$ units when $AC = 1$ unit, implying that $CE = 1$ unit (see the following Figure 3). Therefore, the ratio of AC to CE is 1:1.

MATHEMATICS • PRACTICE TEST 3 • EXPLANATORY ANSWERS

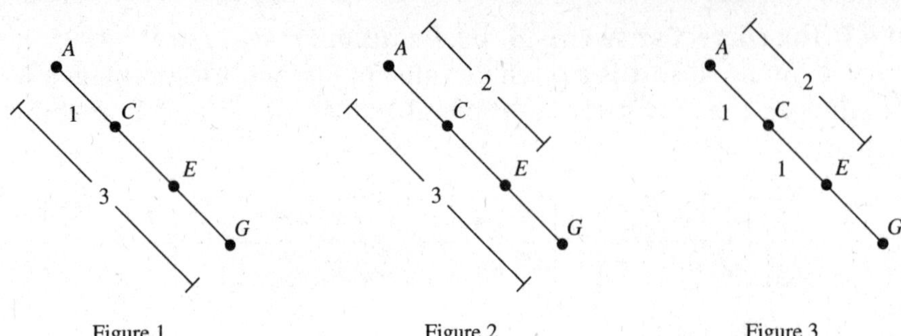

Figure 1 Figure 2 Figure 3

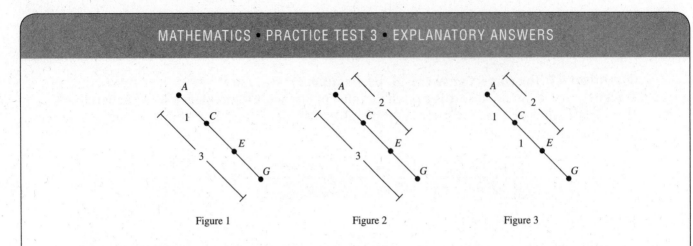

Question 45. The correct answer is E. The following Figure 1 shows the first phase, when the rocket traveled vertically for 30 kilometers.

Figure 2 shows the second phase, when the rocket traveled 40 km at 30° from the vertical. The three distances shown in Figure 2 are in the ratio $1{:}\sqrt{3}{:}2$, a characteristic of 30°-60°-90° triangles. The vertical distance covered in the second phase is $20\sqrt{3}$ km.

Figure 3 shows the third phase, when the rocket traveled 100 km at 45° from the vertical. The three distances shown in Figure 3 are in the ratio $1{:}1{:}\sqrt{2}$, a characteristic of 45°-45°-90° triangles. The vertical distance covered in the third phase is $50\sqrt{2}$ km.

Taking the sum of the vertical distances covered by each of the three phases gives the vertical distance of the rocket above the launch pad after the third phase.

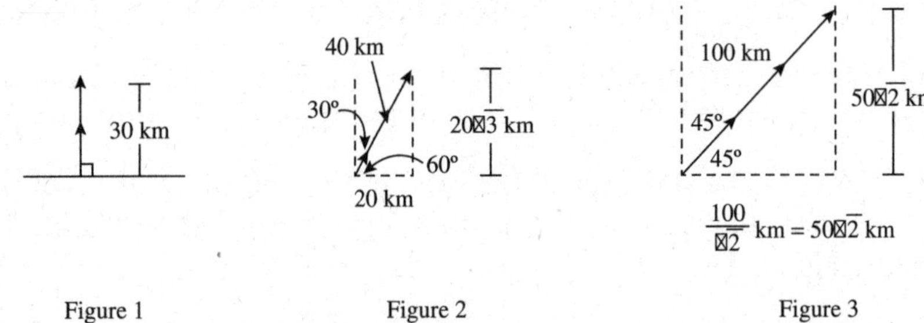

Figure 1 Figure 2 Figure 3

Question 46. The correct answer is G. Let X be a random variable that can take on all and only the values of $x_1, x_2, x_3, \cdots x_n$. The expected value of X is defined by $EV(X) = x_1p_1 + x_2p_2 + \cdots + x_np_n$, where, for $k = 1, 2, 3, \cdots n$, X takes the value of x_k with a probability of p_k. Using this formula, we see $EV(n) = 0(0.70) + 1(0.20) + 2(0.05) + 3(0.05) = 0.45$, **G.** If you chose either **F** or **H**, you probably did not recall the definition of the expected value of a random variable. If you chose **J**, you added the probabilities of the four possible values of n. If you chose **K**, you found the mean of the four possible values of n. In all four of these incorrect cases, please see the previously given definition of expected value.

MATHEMATICS • PRACTICE TEST 3 • EXPLANATORY ANSWERS

Question 47. The correct answer is E. We can find the factored form of the equation by first factoring out a GCF of –2, $h = -2(t^2 - 5t - 24)$, and then further factoring the quadratic to $h = -2(t + 3)(t - 8)$. The object reaches the ground when $h = 0$ and time is positive. By the zero product property, $0 = -2(t + 3)(t - 8)$ when $t = -3$ or $t = 8$. Because 8 is the positive value of t that is the solution to $h = 0$, the object will hit the ground at 8 seconds.

If you chose **D**, you might have picked the negative value of t in the solution to $0 = -2(t + 3)(t - 8)$ and then taken the absolute value. If you chose **B** or **C**, you might have confused the factored form of a quadratic equation with the vertex form. This equation can be written as $h = -2(x - 2.5)^2 + 60.5$, so the maximum height is 60.5 units. If you chose **A**, you might have not realized that the starting point is the value of h when $t = 0$, which is 48.

Question 48. The correct answer is H. Rewrite the values in the radicand as exponents, and then simplify.

$$g^2\sqrt{g^5} \cdot h^2\sqrt[4]{h^5}$$

$$g^2 g^{\frac{5}{2}} \cdot h^2 h^{\frac{5}{4}}$$

$$g^{2+\frac{5}{2}} \cdot h^{2+\frac{5}{4}}$$

$$g^{\frac{9}{2}} \cdot h^{\frac{13}{4}}$$

$$g^{4\frac{1}{2}} \cdot h^{3\frac{1}{4}}$$

$$g^4 h^3 \sqrt[4]{g^2 h}$$

You probably got **F** if you did $g^{2+\frac{2}{5}} \cdot h^{2+\frac{2}{5}}$. You probably got **G** if you did $g^{\frac{2+5}{2}} \cdot h^{\frac{2+5}{4}}$. You probably got **J** if you did $g^{2+\frac{5}{2}} \cdot h^{2+\frac{5}{2}}$. You probably got **K** if you did $g^{2+5} \cdot h^{2+5}$.

Question 49. The correct answer is D. The value of $\log_5(5^{\frac{13}{2}})$ is found by solving the equation $\log_5(5^{\frac{13}{2}}) = x$. By definition of logarithm to the base 5, this equation is equivalent to the equation $5^x = 5^{\frac{13}{2}}$. The equation $5^x = 5^{\frac{13}{2}}$ is equivalent to the equation $x = \frac{13}{2}$, whose value is between 6 and 7.

Question 50. The correct answer is F. We need to find the percent decrease, which is found by using the formula for percent change.

$$\text{percent change} = \frac{|\text{original cost} - \text{new cost}|}{\text{original cost}} \times 100$$

Taking Additional Practice Tests

MATHEMATICS • PRACTICE TEST 3 • EXPLANATORY ANSWERS

The Size 3 unit is \$100 per month, and the special rate is \$1 for the first month. The original cost would have been 12(100), but because there is a special rate of \$1 for the first month, Daria only needs to pay the original monthly fee for 11 months, 11(100) + 1. Use the formula to find the percent decrease.

$$\frac{|12(100) - (11(100)+1)|}{12(100)} \times 100 = \frac{|99|}{12(100)} \times 100$$

You may have gotten **G** if you did $\frac{100}{12(100)} \times 100$. You may have gotten **H** if you did $\frac{100+1}{12(100) - 1} \times 100$. You may have gotten **J** if you did $\frac{100 - 1}{11(100)} \times 100$. You may have gotten **K** if you did $\frac{100}{11(100)} \times 100$.

Question 51. The correct answer is E. The Size 5 unit is 8×16, and the Size 1 unit is 2×4. One way to solve is to divide the width by width and length by length, if width × length. We can see that the Size 1 unit's width of 2 can fit into the Size 5 unit's width of 8 four times, or $\frac{8}{2}$. Similarly, we see that Size 1 unit's length of 4 can fit into Size 5 unit's length of 16 four times, or $\frac{16}{4}$. Because we are dealing with area, we multiply $\frac{8}{2}(\frac{16}{4})$, or 4×4, to get the maximum number of Size 1 units into Size 5 units. A drawing would also help you see this answer. A possible drawing:

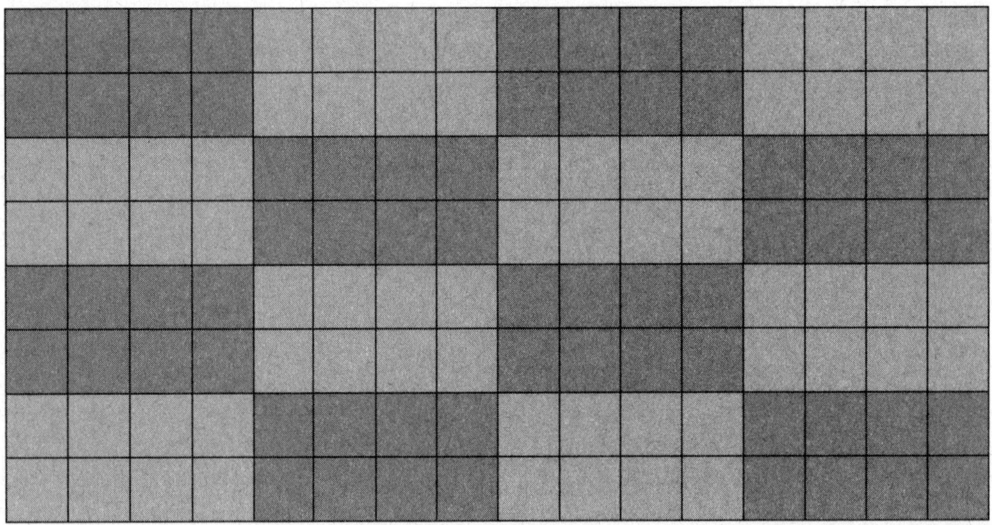

You may have gotten **A** if you divided length from the Size 1 unit and width from the Size 5 unit as $\frac{8}{4}$. You may have gotten **B** if you divided only the widths as $\frac{8}{2}$. You may have gotten **C** if you did $\frac{8}{2} + \frac{16}{4}$. You may have gotten **D** if you did $\frac{16}{2} + \frac{8}{4}$.

MATHEMATICS • PRACTICE TEST 3 • EXPLANATORY ANSWERS

Question 52. The correct answer is H. x = unit size number. The relationship between the unit size number and the area of each unit is as follows:

x	Area	Pattern
1	8	8×2^0
2	16	8×2^1
3	32	8×2^2
4	64	8×2^3
5	128	8×2^4

Notice as the unit size number increases, the area increases exponentially. The pattern is shown in the table.

The expression that summarizes this pattern is $8 \times 2^{(x-1)}$ or $2^3 \times 2^{(x-1)}$. Using properties of exponents, the simplest form is $2^{(2+x)}$. You may have gotten **F** if you thought the pattern was $8 \times$ unit size number. You may have gotten **G, J,** or **K** if you did not understand the pattern.

Question 53. The correct answer is B. The graph of any trigonometric function of the form $y = a\sin(bx + c)$ is cyclical. That is, the graph is composed of repeating, identical *cycles*. The shaded region in the following graph shows one such cycle. The *period* of the function is the width of the smallest interval of x on which one of these cycles appears. In the following graph, the period is the width of the shaded region, given by $2\pi - \pi = \pi$.

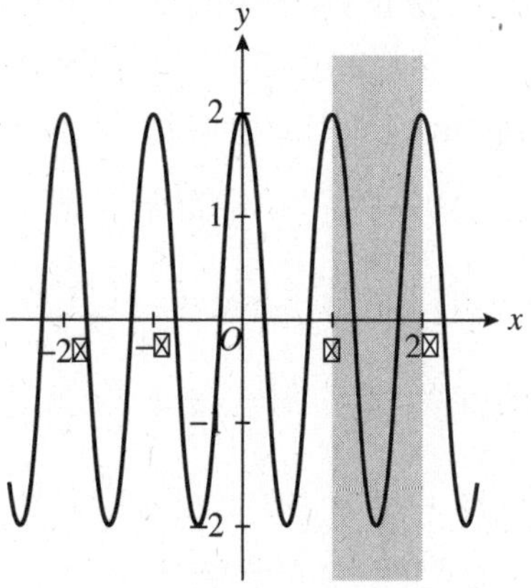

The period of $y = \sin x$ is 2π, which is **C**, the most common incorrect answer. If you chose **E**, you may have confused *period* with *amplitude*.

MATHEMATICS • PRACTICE TEST 3 • EXPLANATORY ANSWERS

Question 54. The correct answer is G. The component form of w can be found by adding the opposite of the scalar horizontal components together and the opposite of the scalar vertical components together: $-2\langle 5,3\rangle + 3\langle 2,-7\rangle = \langle -10 + 6, -6 - 21\rangle$.
If you got **F**, you may have done $-2\langle 5,3\rangle - 3\langle 2,-7\rangle = \langle -10 - 6, -6 + 21\rangle$.
If you got **H**, you may have done $\langle 5,3\rangle - \langle 2,-7\rangle = \langle 5 - 2, 3 + 7\rangle$.
If you got **J**, you may have done $2\langle 5,3\rangle - 3\langle 2,-7\rangle = \langle 10 - 6, 6 + 21\rangle$.
If you got **K**, you may have done $2\langle 5,3\rangle + 3\langle 2,-7\rangle = \langle 10 + 6, 6 - 21\rangle$.

Question 55. The correct answer is B. We can rewrite the bases as powers of a common base. The common base here is 3, because $3^1 = 3$, and $3^2 = 9$.

$$3^{x+1} = 3^{2(x-2)}$$
$$3^{x+1} = 3^{2x-4}$$
$$x + 1 = 2x - 4$$
$$x = 5$$

This is the one and only solution that makes the equation true.

If you chose **A**, you may have set the exponents equal to each other before finding a common base and found there was no solution, OR you may have not found a common base and tried instead to solve for x. If you chose **C**, you may have rewritten 9 as 3^2 and misinterpreted the squared for two solutions. If you chose **D**, you may have done $\frac{9}{3}$. If you chose **E**, you thought the exponential equation had an infinite number of solutions.

Question 56. The correct answer is H. The area of the original triangle is $\frac{1}{2}(20)(15)\sin\theta$. The area of the resulting triangle is $\frac{1}{2}(20)(15 - 2t)\sin\theta$. To find the time, t, when the resulting triangle has an area that is $\frac{1}{2}$ the area of the original triangle, you need to set the area of the resulting triangle equal to $\frac{1}{2}$ the area of the original triangle and solve for t:

$$\tfrac{1}{2}(20)(15 - 2t)\sin\theta = \tfrac{1}{2}\left(\tfrac{1}{2}(20)(15)\sin\theta\right)$$
$$\Leftrightarrow (20)(15 - 2t)\sin\theta = \tfrac{1}{2}(20)(15)\sin\theta$$
$$\Leftrightarrow (15 - 2t)\sin\theta = \tfrac{1}{2}(15)\sin\theta$$
$$\Leftrightarrow 15 - 2t = \tfrac{1}{2}(15)$$
$$\Leftrightarrow 30 - 4t = 15$$
$$\Leftrightarrow -4t = -15$$
$$\Leftrightarrow t = \tfrac{15}{4}$$

MATHEMATICS • PRACTICE TEST 3 • EXPLANATORY ANSWERS

If you chose **F**, you might have incorrectly set the area of the original triangle equal to the area of the resulting triangle and solved for t: $\frac{1}{2}(20)(15)\sin\theta = \frac{1}{2}(20)(15 - 2t)\sin\theta$. If you chose **G**, **J**, or **K**, you might have set up the problem correctly but made a mistake in your algebra. For **G**, you might not have distributed the four correctly:

$$\frac{1}{2}(20)(15 - 2t)\sin\theta = \frac{1}{2}\left(\frac{1}{2}(20)(15)\sin\theta\right)$$

$$\Leftrightarrow \frac{1}{2}(15 - 2t) = \frac{1}{4}(15)$$

$$\Leftrightarrow 4\left(\frac{1}{2}(15 - 2t)\right) = 4\left(\frac{1}{4}(15)\right)$$

$$\Leftrightarrow 2(15) - 8t = 15$$

For **J**, you might have dropped the $\frac{1}{2}$ in the area of the original triangle:

$$\frac{1}{2}(20)(15 - 2t)\sin\theta = \frac{1}{2}\left(\frac{1}{2}(20)(15)\sin\theta\right)$$

$$\Leftrightarrow (15 - 2t) = \frac{1}{4}(15)$$

For **K**, you might have thought $\frac{1}{2} \cdot \frac{1}{2}$ canceled out, incorrectly distributed the $\frac{1}{2}$ in the area of the resulting triangle, and then dropped the negative:

$$\frac{1}{2}(20)(15 - 2t)\sin\theta = \frac{1}{2}\left(\frac{1}{2}(20)(15)\sin\theta\right)$$

$$\Leftrightarrow \frac{1}{2}(15 - 2t) = 15$$

$$\Leftrightarrow \frac{1}{2}(15) - 2t = 30$$

$$\Leftrightarrow 15 - 4t = 60$$

$$\Leftrightarrow 4t = 45$$

Question 57. The correct answer is E. Distinct permutations are permutations without repetition. We want to find how many unique orderings there are of the letters PEOPLE. The number of ways to order 6 different letters would be 6!. Because the P and the E are repeated twice, we must divide by 2! to account for the repeated P and again by 2! to account for the repeated E. Thus we get $\frac{6!}{(2!)(2!)}$.

If you got **A** you probably didn't account for letters P and E that cannot be repeated. If you got **B** you probably didn't understand distinct permutations. If you got **C** you probably

MATHEMATICS • PRACTICE TEST 3 • EXPLANATORY ANSWERS

considered the 6 letters in the word and 4 different letters in the word. If you got **D** you probably considered the 6 different letters in the word and that only 1 letter repeated.

Question 58. The correct answer is K. Complex conjugate pairs can be written in the form $(a + bi)(a - bi)$, which when simplified equals $a^2 - b^2i^2 = a^2 + b^2$.

The value of $i^2 = -1$; therefore, when $(7x - 9i)(7x + 9i)$ is simplified, it equals $49x^2 - 81i^2 = 49x^2 - 81(-1) = 49x^2 + 81$. You may have gotten **F** if you took the square root of $49x^2$ and 81. Notice that $(7x + 9)^2 = 49x^2 + 126x + 81$. You may have gotten **G** or **H** if you forgot that a complex conjugate pair consists of one expression with an addition and its conjugate pair has subtraction. You may have gotten **J** if you forgot the i in the conjugate pairs.

Question 59. The correct answer is B. Given an input x_i, the absolute value of the residual gives the vertical distance between the observed y_i-value and the $y(x_i)$-value predicted by the line of best fit. By inspecting the graph, the ordered pair (32, 135) appears to have the greatest vertical distance from the line of best fit. The absolute value of this residual is given by $|135 - y(32)| = |135 - (1.1(32) + 93)| = |135 - 128.2| = 6.8$. The remaining residuals are $|120 - y(27)| = |127 - (1.1(27) + 93)| = 2.7$, $|140 - y(42)| = |140 - (1.1(42) + 93)| = 0.8$, and $|130 - y(37)| = |130 - (1.1(37) + 93)| = 3.7$. If you chose **A**, you may have chosen the correct ordered pair (32, 135) but incorrectly computed the absolute value by adding 32 and 93 before multiplying by 1.1. If you chose **C**, you probably computed the difference in the 2 y_i-values 135 and 120. If you chose **D**, you may have incorrectly thought that the residual is the absolute value of the difference in the largest and smallest y_i-values, 140 and 120. If you chose **E**, you may have correctly identified the point farthest from the line but computed the vertical distance between 135 and the y-intercept of the line, 93.

Question 60. The correct answer is K. Making at least 1 error on any given day and making no errors are complementary events. Hence,

$$P(x \geq 1) = 1 - P(x = 0)$$
$$\Leftrightarrow P(x \geq 1) = 1 - 0.0823$$
$$\Leftrightarrow P(x \geq 1) = 0.9177$$

If you chose **F**, you might have thought that the probability of *at least* 1 error is the same as the probability of *exactly* 1 error, $P(1)$. If you chose **G** or **J**, you might have thought that the table shows the probabilities for making any number of errors possible on a given day and not realized that it only shows the probabilities for making 0–4 errors. For **G**, you might have thought that the probability of at least 1 error is the same as the sum of the probabilities of 2–4 errors, $P(2)+P(3)+P(4)$. For **J**, you might have thought that the probability of at least 1 error is the same as the sum of the probabilities of 1–4 errors, $P(1)+P(2)+P(3)+P(4)$. If you chose **H**, you might have thought that the probability of making at least 1 error is equal to the complement of the sum of the probability of 1 error and the probability of no errors, $1-(P(1)+P(0))=1-P(1)-P(0)$.

READING • PRACTICE TEST 3 • EXPLANATORY ANSWERS

Passage I

Question 1. The best answer is A because the passage identifies Shades Bowen as one of the other local musicians in the "bullpen" (lines 5–6) and goes on to state that, of those local musicians, Everett Payne "was the one being invited to sit in" (line 15) and play with the band that night. In this context, "the one" indicates that only Everett was sitting in, and no mention is made in the passage of any other musician sitting in.

The best answer is NOT:

B because although the passage indicates that Everett Payne is "not long out of the army" (lines 14–15), the passage makes no mention of Shades Bowen having been in the army as well.

C because although the passage refers to all the people in the "bullpen" as "young locals" (line 9), the passage makes no mention of Shades Bowen's age.

D because the passage states that Everett Payne joined Shades Bowen in the "bullpen" (lines 5–7) where "young locals gathered . . . each Sunday evening, hoping for a chance to perform" (lines 9–10). This indicates that Shades Bowen was a local musician himself, and there is no indication in the passage that Shades Bowen had any role in deciding which other local musicians were allowed to play with the band.

Question 2. The best answer is G because the statement in question (line 62) describes the audience's physical reaction to Everett Payne's performance. This performance is described in great detail in the preceding paragraph (lines 48–61) as being impressive enough to warrant such a reaction.

The best answer is NOT:

F because the statement in question (line 62) refers to the audience's physical reaction to the improvisational passages that Payne played after he had taken his time "paying his respects to the tune as written" (lines 48–49). This indicates that the audience reaction was not based on "initial expectations" but rather on later developments in the playing of the song "Sonny Boy Blue."

H because the statement in question (line 62) supports, rather than counteracts, the narrator's description of Payne's performance.

J because there is no mention in the passage that Payne is well known by the audience.

READING • PRACTICE TEST 3 • EXPLANATORY ANSWERS

Question 3. The best answer is A because the passage describes the jazz show as "winding down" (lines 1–2) near the end of the second set. This implies that the second set is the final set of the show.

The best answer is NOT:

B because there is no description in the passage of the first set or of the length of either the first or the second set.

C because the narrator mentions that the show is "winding down" (lines 1–2), which suggests that there will be no third set.

D because the passage states that the jazz show is "nearing the end of the second set" (line 1) when the musicians in the "bullpen" were called up to play. If the *entire* second set was performed solely by musicians from the "bullpen," then they would not be "called up to play" only toward the end of that set.

Question 4. The best answer is H because the passage states that when the purists first heard Payne's choice of music, they "slouched deeper in their chairs in open disgust" (lines 36–37).

The best answer is NOT:

F because although the passage mentions the silence following Payne's performance (lines 81–83), there is no specific mention of the audience reacting to Payne's choice of music with silence.

G because the audience's in-suck of breath (line 62) is in response to Payne's performance, not to his choice of music.

J because the purists stood up at the end of Payne's performance "in languid praise" (line 88) of Payne, not as a reaction to Payne's choice of music.

Question 5. The best answer is C because the narrator describes how she watched as Payne "slowly mounted the bandstand and conferred with the bassist and drummer" (lines 26–27).

The best answer is NOT:

A because Payne did not move quickly to the bandstand. Rather, the narrator describes him as moving with "a deliberate pause between each step" (lines 18–19).

B because the narrator describes Payne as sitting down to play "without in any way acknowledging the audience" (line 30).

D because the narrator says that Payne sat down at the piano "without announcing the name of the tune he intended playing" (lines 28–29).

READING • PRACTICE TEST 3 • EXPLANATORY ANSWERS

Question 6. The best answer is G because the purists are described as reacting negatively to Payne because of his choice of song (lines 35–37), suggesting intolerance. They are also described as usually refusing "to applaud even genius" (line 88), implying snobbishness.

The best answer is NOT:

F because although the term *purist* in the context of a jazz audience suggests that they may be knowledgeable about jazz music, the purists in this audience are described as reacting negatively to Payne because of his choice of song (lines 35–37), suggesting that they are intolerant rather than open-minded.

H because the passage makes no mention of whether or not the purists are educated. Additionally, the purists are not portrayed as rational, as they usually refuse to acknowledge a praiseworthy performance (lines 87–88).

J because although the purists may be "uninhibited" in that they visibly react or do not react to performances as they please, the passage makes no mention of their "inexperience" regarding jazz. In fact, the opposite impression is created by the purists' initial disgust at the prospect of hearing a "hokey" (line 38), or old-fashioned, tune such as "Sonny Boy Blue." Moreover, the term *purist* in general denotes someone devoted to the most essential or "pure" expression of a particular idea or practice, and such devotion usually indicates a deep familiarity with the object of their devotion rather than "inexperience."

Question 7. The best answer is B because the narrator refers to Bach and the blues as being the "bedrock" on which Payne had been trained (lines 76–77).

The best answer is NOT:

A because there is nothing in the passage to suggest that Everett did anything to avoid representing Bach and the blues when he played piano.

C because the narrator describes Bach and the blues as being "earthbound" (line 76) and "the bedrock" (line 76) of Payne's musical inspiration. Moreover, the narrator contrasts these influences, which Payne hears through "his other ear" (line 75) with "the true music of the spheres" (lines 72–73), which he hears through "his right ear directed skyward" (line 68).

D because the passage does not imply that Everett is limited to "Tin Pan Alley" tunes. Rather, the passage states that Everett "recast" and "reinvented" the Tin Pan Alley tune "Sonny Boy Blue" "in an image all his own" (lines 60–61).

Question 8. The best answer is F because the passage indicates that Payne first played the song "at a slower tempo than was called for" (line 41).

The best answer is NOT:

G because there is no indication in the passage that Payne spoke with anyone other than the bassist and the drummer.

H because although the passage states that Payne conferred with the bassist and the drummer (line 27), there is no mention in the passage that either the bassist or the drummer had any reaction to what Payne said to them.

J because when Payne first played "Sonny Boy Blue," he played the song "straight through as written" (line 39). The passage also states that throughout Payne's performance, he "continued to acknowledge the little simple-minded tune" (lines 59–60).

Question 9. The best answer is A because Hattie speculates that Payne's talent "had to do . . . with the way he held his head . . . tilted" (lines 65–67).

The best answer is NOT:

B because the narrator never mentions the simplemindedness of the tune as being related to Payne's musical ideas and feelings. Rather, the characterization of "Sonny Boy Blue" as a "little simple-minded tune" (lines 59–60) creates a contrast between Payne's elaborate and inventive improvisations and the simple and overly familiar song that he chooses as a vehicle for those improvisations.

C because although the narrator mentions Payne's formality in playing through the parts of "Sonny Boy Blue" the first time (lines 42–43), the narrator does not identify this formality as the source of the musical ideas and feelings showcased in Payne's improvisations.

D because the passage makes no mention of any connection Payne feels with his audience. Rather, the passage states that Payne does not even acknowledge his audience before playing (line 30).

Question 10. The best answer is J because the passage states that Payne's performance seemed to Hattie "a joyous, terrifying roller coaster of a ride" (lines 78–79).

The best answer is NOT:

F because although the passage states that Payne's rendition of the song began slowly and formally (lines 41–43), the passage goes on to contrast this beginning with a lengthy improvisational section described in terms that indicate that Hattie found the performance as a whole anything but formal (lines 48–61).

G because there is no indication in the passage that Hattie considers Payne's musical performance absent-minded. Instead, she describes his body "moving absentmindedly through space" as he approaches the bandstand to play (lines 20–21).

H because the narrator does not describe Payne's performance of "Sonny Boy Blue" as resembling a song played in church. Rather, she describes the audience reacting to Payne's performance "as if they were in church and weren't supposed to clap" (lines 82–83).

Passage II

Question 11. The best answer is A because the passage as a whole presents a cohesive argument that sprawl is both unpleasant and harmful (lines 9–10, 25–27, 33–37, 44–47, 59–61, 74–79); that its destructive effects are too often ignored (lines 11–16); that characterizations of sprawl as either inevitable or desirable are flawed (lines 17–19, 52–54, 62–66); that policies currently in place encourage sprawl to continue (lines 19–22, 66–74); and that there are a set of alternative policies that, if adopted, would resist sprawl and reduce these harmful effects (lines 80–91). The overall effect of these linked propositions is to persuade the reader that a choice must be made between a proven harm and a beneficial alternative. Moreover, the language used to describe sprawl throughout the passage is consistently negative, including, for example, the initial identification of sprawl as a "destructive, soulless, ugly mess" (lines 9–10). In contrast to these descriptions, communities without sprawl are described as "places that people care about" (line 35) or characterized as representing a "compact walkable environment" (70–71). Drawing a contrast between attractive and unattractive descriptions, as this passage does, is a common tactic of persuasive rhetoric.

The best answer is NOT:

B because although the author explains what sprawl is, the main purpose of the passage is not merely to explain what sprawl is but to argue for measures that would control sprawl and "knit communities together" (line 89).

C because although the author does describe sprawl throughout the passage, these descriptions are more often colorful and emotional than they are precise and exact. For example, sprawl is initially characterized as a "destructive, soulless mess" (lines 9–10). By contrast, communities without sprawl are described as "places that people care about" (line 35) or characterized as representing a "compact walkable environment" (lines 70–71). Drawing a contrast between attractive and unattractive descriptions, as this passage does, is a common tactic of persuasive rather than descriptive rhetoric. Therefore the principal aim of the passage is persuasive rather than descriptive.

D because the passage does not tell a story. Rather, it informs the reader of a problem and urges the reader not only to see sprawl as a problem as well but also to take measures to solve the problem.

READING • PRACTICE TEST 3 • EXPLANATORY ANSWERS

Question 12. The best answer is J because after describing the effect of sprawl on communities, and criticizing policies that encourage sprawl, the author proposes the adoption of policies that discourage sprawl, such as "downtown housing and mixed-use zoning" (lines 85–86) and goes on to explain that "the goal should be an integrated system of planning decisions and regulations that knit communities together instead of tearing them apart" (lines 87–90). Therefore, in the context of the sentence in which it appears and in the context of the entire passage, the establishment of "an integrated system of planning decisions and regulations" is clearly something that the author would like to see happen.

The best answer is NOT:

F because the full sentence in question reads "Too many developers follow standard formulas, and too many government entities have adopted laws and policies that constitute powerful incentives for sprawl" (lines 19–22). The author's opposition to the laws in question is signaled within the sentence by the assertion that "too many government entities" enact them. In the context of the sentence in which it appears and in the context of the author's criticism of sprawl throughout the passage, the enactment of "laws . . . that provide powerful incentives for sprawl" is not something that the author would like to see happen.

G because "the destruction of traditional downtowns" (line 34) is presented as an end result of sprawl and as something that "is corroding the very sense of community that helps bind us together as a people and as a nation" (lines 35–37). In the context of the sentence in which it appears and in the context of the author's criticism of sprawl throughout the passage, "the destruction of traditional downtowns" is not something that the author would like to see happen.

H because the author explains that "'affordable' housing on the edge of town" (line 53) is only more affordable for developers (line 55), and that the construction of this housing, which is a familiar form of sprawl (lines 48–50), requires "higher taxes for needless duplication of services and infrastructure" (lines 59–60). In the context of the sentence in which it appears and in the context of the author's criticism of sprawl throughout the passage, construction of this housing is not something that the author would like to see happen.

READING • PRACTICE TEST 3 • EXPLANATORY ANSWERS

Question 13. The best answer is D because in the first paragraph the author defines sprawl as a problem, and in the last paragraph, the author offers possible solutions to this problem, including "sensible land-use planning" (line 82), "mixed-use zoning" (lines 85–86), and "an integrated system of planning decisions and regulations" (lines 87–88).

The best answer is NOT:

A because the author does not ask a question at any point in the final paragraph. Rather, the author offers solutions to the problem explained throughout the passage.

B because the author mentions no specific statistics in the final paragraph.

C because the final paragraph does not incorporate more emotional language than the first. If anything, the opposite may be true. In the first paragraph, the author uses emotionally loaded language to encourage the reader to agree that the "destructive, soulless, ugly mess called sprawl" (lines 9–10) is a serious problem. By contrast, the last paragraph, while arguing that "our communities should be shaped by choice, not by chance" (lines 80–81), uses more precise and less emotional language to describe possible solutions to the problem of sprawl, such as "an integrated system of planning decisions and regulations" (lines 87–88). This less emotional language encourages the reader to agree that these solutions may be effective.

Question 14. The best answer is F because the passage makes no mention of how long the problem of sprawl has been happening in US cities.

The best answer is NOT:

G because the author answers this question in lines 17–18: "Development that destroys communities isn't progress. It's chaos."

H because the author argues that current zoning laws, which make construction of a "walkable environment" impossible, "are a major reason why 82 percent of all trips taken in the United States are taken by car" (lines 69–74).

J because the author offers solutions to the problem of what to do to combat sprawl in the final paragraph in the passage.

READING • PRACTICE TEST 3 • EXPLANATORY ANSWERS

Question 15. The best answer is B because the passage does not support the idea that the opening of a superstore leads to downtown renovations. Rather, the passage states that, after a superstore opens in a small town, "downtown becomes a ghost town" (lines 46–47).

The best answer is NOT:

A because the author states that "in many small towns, a single new superstore may have more retail space than the entire downtown business district" (lines 42–44).

C because the author states that, after a superstore opens in a small town, "downtown becomes a ghost town" (lines 46–47).

D because the author states that, when a superstore opens in a small town, "the retail center of gravity shifts away from Main Street" (lines 45–46).

Question 16. The best answer is H because the statistics in question (lines 73–76) show that a significant majority of all trips taken in the United States are taken by car, and that American families spend a significant portion of their budget on transportation expenses. The author argues that these statistics regarding automobile transportation and its costs represent the effects of land use regulations that make it impossible to construct a "compact walkable environment" (lines 69–71).

The best answer is NOT:

F because the statistics in question (lines 73–76) do not support the idea that mixed-use zoning leads to environmental destruction. Rather, they show that a significant majority of all trips taken in the United States are taken by car, and that American families spend a significant portion of their budget on transportation. According to the author, the dependence on automobile transportation is a result of current zoning laws "prohibiting mixed uses" (line 67). Because this dependence on automobile transportation is associated with sprawl, which is associated with environmental destruction throughout the passage, the statistics in question support the argument that it is the prohibition of mixed-use zoning, rather than mixed-use zoning itself, that creates environmental destruction (line 67).

G because the statistics in question (lines 73–76) show that a significant majority of all trips taken in the United States are taken by car, and that American families spend a significant portion of their budget on transportation expenses. The author argues that these statistics regarding automobile transportation and its costs represent the effects of land-use regulations that make it impossible to construct a "compact walkable environment" (lines 69–71).

J because the statistics in question do not support the idea that Americans spend too much of their budgets on food and health care. Rather, the passage states that "the average American household now allocates more than 18 percent of its budget to transportation expenses" and that this is "more than it spends for food and three times more than it spends for health care" (lines 74–79). This strongly suggests that Americans spend too much on transportation, rather than suggesting that they spend too much on food and health care.

READING • PRACTICE TEST 3 • EXPLANATORY ANSWERS

Question 17. The best answer is C because the passage refers to "retail development that transforms roads into strip malls" (lines 38–39).

The best answer is NOT:

A because the author discusses the type of sprawl that develops far away from town centers (line 30), not adjacent to them.

B because the author argues that the development of sprawl leads to the neglect of historic buildings in towns (lines 26–27), not that sprawl leads to the utilization of these buildings.

D because the author argues that the construction of superstores is part of a process whereby "the retail center of gravity shifts away from Main Street" and "downtown becomes a ghost town" (lines 45–47). This strongly suggests that superstores are associated with the destruction, rather than the promotion, of a sense of community in the towns in which they are constructed.

Question 18. The best answer is G because the sentence is describing how residential subdivisions are driven "by the American dream of a detached home in the middle of a grassy lawn" (lines 50–52). Since a grassy lawn surrounds the home being referred to, it is reasonable to assume there is space between the home and other structures. In other words, the home is "set apart."

The best answer is NOT:

F because although the word *detached* can indicate an objective point of view, *detached* is used in this context to describe a house, which does not have a point of view.

H because the passage does not provide a clear sense of what "broken apart" would mean in the context of this sentence.

J because there is nothing in the passage to suggest that the home being referred to was "taken away" from another location.

READING • PRACTICE TEST 3 • EXPLANATORY ANSWERS

Question 19. The best answer is D because the statement in question is preceded by, and is intended to counter, the claim made by some people that "sprawl is merely the natural product of marketplace forces at work" (lines 62–63). Therefore, the author is arguing that people who make this claim "fail to recognize" (line 63) that those market forces are influenced by governmental decisions. The author's rhetoric here assumes that the reader will recognize "a level playing field" as a popular expression for conditions governed purely by market forces, and will understand that a playing field that "isn't level" (line 64) refers to conditions in which governmental decisions *do* influence market forces.

The best answer is NOT:

A because the "needless duplication of services and infrastructure" (line 60) referred to in the passage is identified as a *result* of sprawl, whereas the phrase "the game isn't being played on a level field" (line 64) is used to identify the influence of governmental decisions on market forces, and not market forces alone, as a *cause* of sprawl.

B because the "higher taxes" (line 59) referred to in the passage are identified as a *result* of sprawl, whereas the phrase "the game isn't being played on a level field" (line 64) is used to identify the influence of governmental decisions on market forces, and not market forces alone, as a *cause* of sprawl.

C because the phrase "the game isn't being played on a level field" (line 64) is used to identify the influence of governmental decisions on market forces, and not market forces alone, as a cause of sprawl. The author's rhetoric here assumes that the reader will recognize "a level playing field" as a popular expression for conditions governed purely by market forces, and will understand that a playing field that "isn't level" (line 64) refers to conditions in which governmental decisions do influence market forces.

READING • PRACTICE TEST 3 • EXPLANATORY ANSWERS

Question 20. The best answer is J because the passage identifies zoning laws that prohibit "mixed uses" (line 67) as a primary cause of the separation of urban commercial zones and residential subdivisions described in the three paragraphs that immediately precede the sentence in question (lines 48–66). That separation of commercial and residential land use is contrasted, in the following sentences, with "the sort of compact walkable environment that attracts us to older neighborhoods and historic communities all over the world" (lines 70–72). Therefore the phrase "mixed uses" can be understood as referring to zoning that allows one area to contain various types of development.

The best answer is NOT:

F because the passage identifies both large parking lots (lines 3–4) and large retail stores (lines 38–42) as being characteristic of sprawl, which is encouraged by the prohibition of "mixed uses" (line 67). Furthermore, parking lots and retail stores are both understood to be commercial uses of land, and therefore the phrase "mixed uses" is unlikely to refer to them.

G because although the passage states that the prohibition of "mixed uses" (line 67) makes it "impossible—even illegal—to create the sort of compact walkable environment that attracts us to older neighborhoods and historic communities" (lines 69–72), the phrase "mixed uses" itself is not directly associated with historic preservation in any way. Rather, "mixed uses" refers to the designation of land use as residential, commercial, or industrial under zoning laws.

H because although "mixed uses" (line 67) are understood within the context of the passage as encouraging the creation of a "walkable environment" (line 71), there is no association between the phrase "mixed uses" and the prohibition of driving or parking.

READING • PRACTICE TEST 3 • EXPLANATORY ANSWERS

Passage III

Question 21. The best answer is A because the passage begins with the narrator's description of an incident in which she first became interested in identifying flowers and in the natural world (lines 1–24), and the remainder of the passage describes how this early interest developed into a larger part of her life.

The best answer is NOT:

B because although the identification of an aster is part of the incident (lines 1–24) that leads to the narrator's lifelong interest in flowers and the natural world, there is no mention in the passage of the author having a lifelong fascination for asters in particular. Rather, the incident in question leads to a lifelong fascination with identifying flowers in general.

C because although the author briefly mentions hiking with companions (lines 31–32) and identifying flowers with a friend (lines 81–82), the primary focus of the passage is on the author's individual interest in flowers and how that interest developed.

D because the author does not discuss her career in the passage.

Question 22. The best answer is H because the author describes the young man's answer to her question as containing "the hint of a sniff" (line 7), which indicates that she detected disdain or condescension in the tone of the young man's answer.

The best answer is NOT:

F because there is nothing in the passage to suggest that the guide treated the author with acceptance. Rather, his reaction to her question about the flower is described as containing "the hint of a sniff" (line 7), which indicates disdain or condescension, qualities that are incompatible with acceptance.

G because there is no mention in the passage of the guide being surprised by the author's question. Rather, his reaction is described as containing "the hint of a sniff" (line 7), which indicates disdain or condescension and not surprise.

J because there is no mention in the passage of the guide becoming angry with the author. Rather, his reaction to her question about the flower is described as containing "the hint of a sniff" (line 7), which indicates disdain or condescension and not anger.

READING • PRACTICE TEST 3 • EXPLANATORY ANSWERS

Question 23. The best answer is D because although the author describes her efforts to identify a yellow flower on a particular hike (lines 30–51), she does not name the flower in question. Rather, she uses the description of this incident to explain her developing "intimacy" (line 28) with the book *A Field Guide to Wild Flowers.*

The best answer is NOT:

A because although the author mentions St. John's wort, loosestrife, and puccoon as "five-petaled yellow flowers" (lines 50–51) similar to the one she is trying to identify, she does not identify the flower in question as St. John's wort.

B because although the author mentions St. John's wort, loosestrife, and puccoon as "five-petaled yellow flowers" (lines 50–51) similar to the one she is trying to identify, she does not identify the flower in question as loosestrife.

C because although the author mentions St. John's wort, loosestrife, and puccoon as "five-petaled yellow flowers" (lines 50–51) similar to the one she is trying to identify, she does not identify the flower in question as puccoon.

Question 24. The best answer is F because the author states that though daunting at first, the book was neither too frustrating as a more basic book would have become nor too daunting as a more complex one would have been (lines 58–61).

The best answer is NOT:

G because the author indicates that the book was not easy to use in the beginning. Rather, it was difficult for her, but she "persisted in wrestling" (line 61) with the book until it became easier.

H because the author makes no mention in the passage of any other guide she used.

J because the author makes no negative statements about the illustrations in the guide.

READING • PRACTICE TEST 3 • EXPLANATORY ANSWERS

Question 25. The best answer is C because the sentence in question reads "I had no choice, really, not if I wanted to *get in*" (lines 55–56), and the surrounding sentences indicate that the matter she had no choice in was the use of the field guide, which "led to the particulars" (line 57), or deepened her understanding, of the landscape. Therefore, in this context, to "get in" to a subject can be understood as meaning to fully understand that subject.

The best answer is NOT:

A because the sentence in question reads "I had no choice, really, not if I wanted to *get in*" (lines 55–56), and there is no indication in the surrounding lines that the matter she has no choice in is her arrival in a specific location. Rather, she wants to figuratively, and not literally, arrive at a deeper understanding of the landscape, and she has no choice but to use the field guide in order to do so (lines 55–58).

B because the sentence in question reads "I had no choice, really, not if I wanted to *get in*" (lines 55–56), and there is no indication in the surrounding lines or the passage as a whole that the matter she has no choice in has anything to do with membership in any group. Rather, she wants to figuratively, and not literally, "get in" to a deeper understanding of the landscape, and she has no choice but to use the field guide in order to do so (lines 55–58).

D because the sentence in question reads "I had no choice, really, not if I wanted to *get in*" (lines 55–56), and there is no indication in the surrounding lines or the passage as a whole that the matter she has no choice in has anything to do with being friendly with someone. Rather, she wants to figuratively, and not literally, "get in" to a deeper understanding of the landscape, and she has no choice but to use the field guide in order to do so (lines 55–58).

Question 26. The best answer is H because the author states that she and Julie began to see that their understanding of plant communities was valuable because it led to a greater understanding of larger issues such as "climate change and continental drift" (lines 85–86).

The best answer is NOT:

F because there is no information in the passage about Julie's level of experience in identifying plant life.

G because there is no information in the passage about Julie owning a house near a bog.

J because there is no information in the passage about whether or not Julie used the Peterson's guide.

READING • PRACTICE TEST 3 • EXPLANATORY ANSWERS

Question 27. The best answer is D because the author states that "over the next several years this field guide would become my closest companion" (lines 25–26), specifying that she measures the period in question in "years."

The best answer is NOT:

A because the author states that "over the next several years this field guide would become my closest companion" (lines 25–26), specifying "years" and not days as the way in which she measures the period in question.

B because the author states that "over the next several years this field guide would become my closest companion" (lines 25–26), specifying "years" and not weeks as the way in which she measures the period in question.

C because the author states that "over the next several years this field guide would become my closest companion" (lines 25–26), specifying "years" and not months as the way in which she measures the period in question.

Question 28. The best answer is J because the author's statement that "a landscape may be handsome in the aggregate, but this book led to the particulars, and that's what I wanted" (lines 56–58) contrasts the surface appeal of a landscape seen at a distance with the deeper knowledge of a landscape that only comes from familiarity with the "particulars," or individual parts, and specifies that this deeper knowledge of the landscape is what she sought.

The best answer is NOT:

F because the author's statement that "a landscape may be handsome in the aggregate, but this book led to the particulars, and that's what I wanted" (lines 56–58) specifies that she was more interested in the deeper knowledge of the landscape that comes from familiarity with the "particulars," or individual parts, than she was in an understanding of a landscape that might come from looking at its overall patterns.

G because although the passage does relate the way in which the field guide helps the author break landscapes down logically into their "particulars" (line 57), or individual parts, there is no indication that this made landscapes lose their appeal. Rather, she states that this kind of understanding was "what [she] wanted" (line 58) and that the logically ordered classifications in the field guide all made "such delightful sense" (lines 79–80).

H because there is no indication in the passage that the deeper understanding of landscapes that she sought through knowledge of their "particulars" (line 57), or individual parts, was in any way related to painting portraits of those landscapes.

READING • PRACTICE TEST 3 • EXPLANATORY ANSWERS

Question 29. The best answer is B because the details in question describe the ways in which the field guide "changed" (line 64) as she figuratively, and not literally, "persisted in wrestling" (line 61) with it "by slow degrees" (line 62). In this context, these details indicate that this transformation occurred because of heavy use over a long period of time.

The best answer is NOT:

A because there is no indication that the transformation of the book described by the details in question (lines 64–66) takes place because of poor craftsmanship. Rather, the details in question describe the ways in which the field guide "changed" (line 64) as she, figuratively and not literally "persisted in wrestling" (line 61) with it "by slow degrees" (line 62). In this context, these details indicate that this transformation occurred because of heavy use over a long period of time.

C because the passage implies that the "cryptic annotations" (line 66) in the guide were made by the author herself.

D because the details in question describe the ways in which the field guide "changed" (line 64) as she, figuratively and not literally "persisted in wrestling" (line 61) with it "by slow degrees" (line 62). Although this indicates that the book's condition was transformed because of heavy use, there is no specific indication of carelessness and no mention anywhere in the passage of any regret the author has regarding her use of the field guide.

Question 30. The best answer is H because the author mentions *Solidago hispida* in order to exemplify her practice of addressing flowers that she has encountered before by their Latin name after she has learned to identify them (lines 70–72).

The best answer is NOT:

F because the passage makes no mention of any trouble the author had initially identifying *Solidago hispida*.

G because the author mentions *Solidago hispida* as an example of a flower she has addressed in the past with great enthusiasm, meaning she has already come across the flower in her nature walks.

J because there is no indication anywhere in the passage that the author feels the name *Solidago hispida* is inappropriate. Rather, the author mentions *Solidago hispida* only in order to exemplify her practice of addressing flowers by their Latin name (lines 70–72).

READING • PRACTICE TEST 3 • EXPLANATORY ANSWERS

Passage IV

Question 31. The best answer is D because the passage states that information gained from the study of snow crystals "has practical applications in such diverse areas as agriculture and the production of electricity" (lines 12–14). Specific details about these practical applications are presented in the final five paragraphs (lines 50–91) of the passage.

The best answer is NOT:

A because although the passage does mention the fact that scientists have communicated with each other during the course of studying snow crystals (lines 50–54), communication is secondary to the main point of the passage, which is to explain the practical applications of such a study.

B because although the passage does discuss the role of snow crystal facets in the formation of snow crystals (lines 19–23) and also discusses the winter snowpack in some Western states (lines 56–61), the passage makes no specific connection between the snow crystal facets and the snowpack and does not indicate that either one is the primary reason for presenting information about the scientific study of snow.

C because although the passage does tell the story of the first time a scanning electron microscope was used in the scientific study of snow (lines 34–49), it tells this story in the context of presenting information about the practical applications of the scientific study of snow and does not explicitly discuss the varied uses of the scanning electron microscope.

Question 32. The best answer is G because the passage states that "before employing the scanning electron microscopy results, the forecasted amounts of snowpack water were inaccurate" (lines 62–64) and that "improving the prediction [of snowpack water] by 1 percent would save $38 million" in costs (lines 71–72). Improving a prediction can be understood as making that prediction more accurate, which establishes a connection between the use of the scanning electron microscope and saving money.

The best answer is NOT:

F because although the passage mentions future predictions in the context of less snowfall expected (lines 75–80), those future predictions are not linked to any money saved.

H because as the passage states, the two scientists (who were looking at biological problems) froze the tissue they were using in order "to avoid the laborious procedure" (lines 37–38) that the use of scanning electron microscopes usually entailed. The passage does not state that the scientists were saving money by using these microscopes when looking for these biological problems.

J because although the passage states that snowmelt accounts for 75 percent of the annual water supply of these western states (lines 56–58), the passage mentions nothing about increasing the water supply of these states as a means of saving money.

READING • PRACTICE TEST 3 • EXPLANATORY ANSWERS

Question 33. The best answer is C because the phrase in question is immediately followed by a statement in parentheses explaining that "crystals often change once on the ground depending on the surrounding environment" (lines 48–49). Because *metamorphosed* means "changed," and *conditions* and *environment* have similar meanings, we can read the parenthetical statement as clarifying the fact that "metamorphosed conditions" refers to the state of snow crystals after they reach the ground.

The best answer is NOT:

A because the passage does not establish a direct connection between the phrase "metamorphosed conditions" (lines 47–48) and the temperature and humidity at which crystals form. Rather, the phrase in question is immediately followed by a statement in parentheses explaining that "crystals often change once on the ground depending on the surrounding environment" (lines 48–49). Read in context, the parenthetical statement, which makes no mention of the temperature and humidity at which crystals form, can be understood as defining the phrase "metamorphosed conditions."

B because the passage does not establish a direct connection between the phrase "metamorphosed conditions" (lines 47–48) and the process by which snow crystals develop from a speck of dust and water vapor. Rather, the phrase in question is immediately followed by a statement in parentheses explaining that "crystals often change once on the ground depending on the surrounding environment" (lines 48–49). Read in context, the parenthetical statement, which makes no mention of the formation of snow crystals, can be understood as defining the term "metamorphosed conditions."

D because the phrase in question (lines 47–48) is immediately followed by a statement in parentheses explaining that "crystals often change once on the ground depending on the surrounding environment" (lines 48–49). This clarification indicates that the phrase "metamorphosed conditions" refers to changes in the snowflake that occur as a result of changes in the environment and not directly to changes in the environment.

READING • PRACTICE TEST 3 • EXPLANATORY ANSWERS

Question 34. The best answer is G because the passage explains that "before employing the scanning electron microscopy results, the forecasted amounts of snowpack water were inaccurate whenever the size and shape of the snow crystals varied much from the norm" (lines 62–65). This indicates that the addition of scanning electron microscopy data allowed scientists using the model to include more detailed information about structural variations in snow crystals in their predictions, making those predictions more accurate.

The best answer is NOT:

F because the passage does not specify that the addition of scanning microscopy data allowed scientists using the Snowmelt Runoff Model to include more detailed information about microwave satellite data. Rather, the passage states that Albert Rango "now uses Wergin's electron microscopy data, along with microwave satellite data, in the Snowmelt Runoff Model to predict the amount of water available in a winter snowpack" (lines 52–56). This indicates that scanning electron microscopy data and microwave satellite data are used in conjunction with each other, not that one allows the inclusion of more detailed information about the other.

H because the passage makes no mention of electron microscopy in helping provide detailed information about locations having the highest amount of snowfall.

J because although the passage mentions that William Wergin and Eric Erbe were looking for biological problems related to agriculture (lines 34–37), there is no mention of biological problems in the discussion of the Snowmelt Runoff Model, which occupies the last five paragraphs of the passage (lines 50–91).

Question 35. The best answer is D because the passage states that, because of temperature increases, less snow will fall, thus "greatly increasing water's economic value" (lines 77–82).

The best answer is NOT:

A because although the passage mentions an increased ability to track water pollution via the use of crystal research (lines 90–91), the passage makes no mention of an increase of pollution as a cause of an increase in water's value.

B because the passage makes no mention of water conservation leading to an increase in water's value.

C because although the passage mentions the ability of scanning electron microscopes to detect sulfur and nitrogen in snow (lines 87–89), the passage makes no mention of a predicted increase in sulfur and nitrogen levels in snow.

READING • PRACTICE TEST 3 • EXPLANATORY ANSWERS

Question 36. The best answer is G because the passage states that "as the crystals fall, they encounter different atmospheric conditions that produce flakes with unique attributes" (lines 3–5).

The best answer is NOT:

F because although the passage does state that 1 septillion snowflakes fall worldwide each year (lines 1–3), the passage does not make any connection between that enormous number and the infinite variety of snowflakes. Rather, the passage states that "as the crystals fall, they encounter different atmospheric conditions that produce flakes with unique attributes" (lines 3–5).

H because the passage makes no connection between the rate at which snowflakes fall and the infinite variety of snowflakes. Rather, the passage states that "as the crystals fall, they encounter different atmospheric conditions that produce flakes with unique attributes" (lines 3–5).

J because although the passage does state that more complex atmospheric conditions produce more elaborate and therefore more varied snow crystals (lines 5–6), the passage makes no connection between those complex atmospheric conditions and the speed at which snow crystals develop, and the passage makes no connection between the speed at which snow crystals develop and the infinite variety of snowflakes.

Question 37. The best answer is D because the passage states that "snowflakes are collections of two or more snow crystals" (lines 16–17).

The best answer is NOT:

A because the passage does not state that snowflakes grow around a nucleus of dust. Rather, the passage states that "snowflakes are collections of two or more snow crystals" (lines 16–17) and that a crystal "typically grows around a nucleus of dust" (lines 18–19).

B because the snowflakes do not combine to form snow crystals. Rather, according to the passage, the opposite is true: snow crystals combine to form snowflakes (lines 16–17).

C because although the passage states that the shape of a snow crystal "depends on how the six side facets—or faces—grow in relation to the top and bottom facets" (lines 19–20), there is no mention of any direct relation between top and bottom facets and the growth of snowflakes.

READING • PRACTICE TEST 3 • EXPLANATORY ANSWERS

Question 38. The best answer is G because the passage specifies that the physicist Kenneth Libbrecht "creates 'designer' snowflakes in his lab" (lines 31–32).

The best answer is NOT:

F because the passage makes no connection between the term "'designer' snowflakes" (line 32) and the fact that no two snowflakes are alike. Rather, the passage specifies that the physicist Kenneth Libbrecht "creates 'designer' snowflakes in his lab" (lines 31–32).

H because the passage makes no mention of the grand design of nature. Rather, the passage specifies that the physicist Kenneth Libbrecht "creates 'designer' snowflakes in his lab" (lines 31–32).

J because although the passage does state that the physicist Kenneth Libbrecht "creates 'designer' snowflakes in his lab" (lines 31–32), the passage makes no mention of the beauty of Libbrecht's snowflakes.

Question 39. The best answer is C because the sentence in question states that "snowmelt water is critical to crop irrigation and hydroelectric power, as well as recreation and domestic water supplies, fisheries management and flood control" (lines 58–61). In context, this is understood to mean that snowmelt water is vital, or very important, to these processes and practices.

The best answer is NOT:

A because the sentence in question states that "snowmelt water is critical to crop irrigation and hydroelectric power, as well as recreation and domestic water supplies, fisheries management and flood control" (lines 58–61). In this context *critical* cannot be read as meaning "evaluative" because snowmelt water cannot evaluate anything or anyone.

B because the sentence in question states that "snowmelt water is critical to crop irrigation and hydroelectric power, as well as recreation and domestic water supplies, fisheries management and flood control" (lines 58–61). In this context *critical* cannot be read as meaning "faultfinding" because snowmelt water cannot find fault with anything or anyone.

D because the sentence in question states that "snowmelt water is critical to crop irrigation and hydroelectric power, as well as recreation and domestic water supplies, fisheries management and flood control" (lines 58–61). In context, the adjective *critical* is understood to mean that snowmelt water is vital, or very important, to these processes and practices. Although it is also an adjective and can sometimes be understood to mean vital or important, *acute* cannot be substituted for *critical* in this sentence because it would be neither grammatical nor logical to say "water is *acute* to crop irrigation."

READING • PRACTICE TEST 3 • EXPLANATORY ANSWERS

Question 40. The best answer is F because although the passage does state that research about snow crystals has helped scientists to identify and possibly track the source of pollutants in snow (lines 90–91), the passage does not make any connection between research about snow crystals and the extraction of pollutants *from* snow.

The best answer is NOT:

G because one meaning of *gauge* is "to measure," and the term *snowmelt* refers to water generated by a melting snowpack; therefore, when the passage states that research about snow crystals has helped scientists to "predict the amount of water available in a winter snowpack" (lines 55–56), that statement means that research about snow crystals has helped scientists to gauge (measure) the probable amount of snowmelt. Lines 84–85 specifically state that "the crystal research help[s] gauge snowmelt."

H because the passage states that, in the process of conducting research about snow crystals, physicist Kenneth Libbrecht "creates 'designer' snowflakes in his lab" (lines 31–32).

J because the passage states that research about snow crystals "is also useful in predicting avalanches" (line 85).

SCIENCE • PRACTICE TEST 3 • EXPLANATORY ANSWERS

Passage I

1. **The best answer is B.** According to Figure 1, the only site with *E. coli* levels above 400 colonies per 100 mL was Day 30 at Site 1. **A** is incorrect; the *E. coli* level on Day 1 at Site 1 was 101 colonies formed per 100 mL. **B** is correct; the *E. coli* level on Day 30 at Site 1 was 708 colonies formed per 100 mL. **C** is incorrect; the *E. coli* level on Day 1 at Site 2 was 16 colonies formed per 100 mL. **D** is incorrect; the *E. coli* level on Day 30 at Site 2 was 173 colonies formed per 100 mL.

2. **The best answer is F.** According to Figure 1, the *E. coli* levels were much higher at Site 1 than Site 2 on 3 of the five days measured and nearly the same on the other two days measured, indicating that the average *E. coli* levels were higher at Site 1 than at Site 2 over the collection period. According to Figure 2, the water flow was greater for Site 1 than Site 2 on all five days that measurements were taken, indicating that the average water flow was higher for Site 1 than Site 2 over the collection period. **F** is correct; both the water flow and *E. coli* levels were greater for Site 1 than Site 2. **G, H,** and **J** are incorrect.

3. **The best answer is A.** According to Table 1, the better the water quality rating, the greater the value for BI. Therefore, **A** is correct. **B, C,** and **D** are incorrect; biotic index is neither independent of water quality nor does it increase as water quality degrades.

4. **The best answer is G.** According to Table 2, the average BI for Site 1 was 6.3, indicating that the water quality rating for Site 1 was excellent. The average BI for Site 2 was 2.5, indicating that the water quality rating for Site 2 was fair. One would expect more stone fly larvae at the site with the higher water quality, which is Site 1. The results are consistent with the students' hypothesis. **F** is incorrect; Site 1 had a water quality rating of excellent, and Site 2 had a water quality rating of fair. **G** is correct. **H** and **J** are incorrect; Site 1 had a better water quality rating.

5. **The best answer is A.** According to the passage, *E. coli* levels above 100 colonies formed per 100 mL indicate reduced water quality. According to Figure 1, on Days 1 and 30, Site 1 had *E. coli* levels above 100 colonies formed per 100 mL. **A** is correct; Figure 1 contains the information about *E. coli* levels. **B** is incorrect; Figure 2 contains information about water flow, and no relationship is given between water flow and water quality. **C** is incorrect; Table 1 shows how water quality rating varies with BI. Table 1 contains no information about Sites 1 or 2. **D** is incorrect; according to Table 2, Site 1 has a higher water quality rating than does Site 2.

SCIENCE • PRACTICE TEST 3 • EXPLANATORY ANSWERS

6. **The best answer is J.** In order to answer this item, the examinee must know that the introduction of large amounts of fertilizer may cause eutrophication, leading to reduction in water quality. A higher BI corresponds to a higher water quality rating. A reduction in water quality after the introduction of the fertilizer would therefore cause a decrease in the BI. **F** and **G** are incorrect; the BI will decrease, not increase. **H** is incorrect; the water quality will decrease. **J** is correct.

Passage II

7. **The best answer is B.** According to Table 1, AWP 2 produced 21 mL of H_2 by Day 2, 187 mL by Day 4, 461 mL by Day 6, and 760 mL by Day 8. **A** is incorrect; this figure shows the production of more than 200 mL of H_2 by Day 4. **B** is correct. **C** and **D** are incorrect; both show a decrease in the volume of H_2 over time.

8. **The best answer is G.** According to Table 1, AWP 1 produced 4 mL of H_2 in the first 2 days, 29 mL of H_2 in the next 2 days, 48 mL of H_2 in the next 2 days, and 52 mL of H_2 in the last 2 days. If the volume had been measured on Day 10, it is likely that the additional amount of H_2 produced would have been no more than 50–60 mL. This would have resulted in a total volume of no more than 200 mL H_2 produced. **F** is incorrect; 133 mL of H_2 had been produced by Day 8. **G** is correct. **H** and **J** are incorrect; a total volume of H_2 greater than 461 mL would require the formation of 328 mL from Day 8 to Day 10, which is very unlikely based on the rate of H_2 formation seen in Days 2–8.

9. **The best answer is A.** According to Table 1, 133 mL of H_2 was produced by AWP 1 on Day 8, and 81 mL of H_2 was produced by AWP 1 on Day 6. The amount produced between those measurements was 133 – 81 = 52 mL. **A** is correct. **B**, **C**, and **D** are incorrect; 52 mL of H_2 was produced.

10. **The best answer is H.** In order to answer this item, the examinee must have a basic understanding of chemical equations. H_2 is one of the reaction products and is formed at half the rate that $Al(OH)_3$ is formed. Measuring the volume of H_2 that forms would therefore give information about the rate of formation of $Al(OH)_3$. **F** and **G** are incorrect; H_2O and Al are both reactants and are not converted into one another. **H** is correct; Al is converted to $Al(OH)_3$. **J** is incorrect; Al is converted to $Al(OH)_3$.

11. **The best answer is D.** In order to answer this item, the examinee must understand that a base will increase the pH of water (and realize that the passage states that AWPs are water-based). The passage states that DMEA is an AWP ingredient that increases pH. Therefore, DMEA is a base. **A**, **B**, and **C** are incorrect; DMEA is a base because it increases pH. **D** is correct.

SCIENCE • PRACTICE TEST 3 • EXPLANATORY ANSWERS

12. **The best answer is J.** According to Table 1, on Day 2 the AWP 3 sample had produced 121 mL of H_2. According to Figure 1, the sample containing EDTA produced 121 mL of H_2 on approximately Day 10. **F** and **G** are incorrect; the volume of H_2 was not greater than 100 mL until Day 7. **H** is incorrect; only 100 mL of H_2 had been produced on Day 7. **J** is correct; on Day 10 approximately 121 mL of H_2 had been produced.

Passage III

13. **The best answer is B.** Figure 4 shows that for Trial 5 both scales had equal readings, indicating that the weight was equally distributed. **A** is incorrect; in Trial 4, Scale B had a higher reading than did Scale A. **B** is correct; in Trial 5, both scales had equal readings. **C** is incorrect; in Trial 6, Scale A had a higher reading than did Scale B. **D** is incorrect; the weight was equally distributed in Trial 5.

14. **The best answer is G.** Figure 2 (Trial 1) shows that Scale A caused the hand on Scale B to move ¼ of the way around the dial. Figure 2 (Trial 2) shows that a 5.0 N weight causes the hand on Scale A to move ¼ of the way around the dial. Scale B has a weight of 5.0 N. **F**, **H**, and **J** are incorrect; the scales have a weight of 5.0 N. **G** is correct.

15. **The best answer is C.** In order to answer this item, the examinee must know that as a spring is compressed, the potential energy stored in the spring increases. The stored potential energy would therefore be greatest when the spring is compressed the most, and the spring would be compressed the most when the heaviest weight is placed on the scale. In Trial 1, there is no weight on Scale A; thus the spring would not be compressed at all. In Trial 3, there is a 10.0 N weight on Scale A, and the spring would be compressed. **A** and **B** are incorrect; the potential energy stored in the spring of Scale A would be greater in Trial 3. **C** is correct. **D** is incorrect; the amount of weight was greater in Trial 3.

16. **The best answer is F.** According to Figure 2, the weight of Scale A is 5.0 N (the hand on the scale moves ¼ of the way around the dial). Scale B should read 5.0 N whether Scale A is right side up or upside down. When Scale A is upside down, the spring in Scale A is also compressed by the weight of Scale A; therefore, Scale A should also read 5.0 N. **F** is correct; both scales read 5.0 N with the hands ¼ of the way around the dials. **G** is incorrect; Scale B reads 10.0 N with the hand ½ of the way around the dial. **H** is incorrect; Scale A reads 10.0 N with the hand ½ of the way around the dial. **J** is incorrect; both scales read 10.0 N.

SCIENCE • PRACTICE TEST 3 • EXPLANATORY ANSWERS

17. **The best answer is A.** The description of Study 2 states that the distance between Scale B and the 10.0 N weight was measured from the pencil to the weight. Therefore, the pencils were most likely intended to be used as a convenient visual reference from which to measure distance, so **A** is correct. **B** is incorrect; any side-to-side motion of the board would have been contrary to the design of Study 2. **C** is incorrect; the students intentionally zeroed out the weights of the pencils and the board. **D** is incorrect; air pressure would have been equal above and below each platform regardless of whether the pencils had been included or not.

18. **The best answer is H.** According to Figure 4, when the distance between the weight and the pencil on Scale B was 0.10 m, Scale B read approximately 7.5 N. When the distance between the weight and the pencil was 0.20 m, Scale B read 5.0 N, and when the distance was 0.30 m, Scale B read 2.5 N. As the distance increased, the amount of force exerted on Scale B decreased. **F**, **G**, and **J** are incorrect. **H** is correct.

19. **The best answer is D.** In Trials 4–6, pencils were placed on each scale and a board was placed on top. In order to measure only the amount of force exerted by the weight and not the force exerted by the pencils and the board, the scales were zeroed. **A** is incorrect; setting the dial readings to zero would not add in the weights of the scales. **B** is incorrect; the weights of the board and pencils were subtracted, not added. **C** is incorrect; setting the dial readings to zero would not subtract the weights of the scales. **D** is correct; the students were interested only in the force exerted by the weight and not the pencils and board.

Passage IV

20. **The best answer is G.** According to the passage, the EOR is the minimum octane number of a fuel required for an engine to operate without becoming damaged. According to Table 2, as engine speed increases the EOR decreases. **F**, **H**, and **J** are incorrect. **G** is correct.

21. **The best answer is B.** According to Table 2, as the engine speed increases, the octane numbers for each fuel decrease. At an engine speed of 2,000 rpm, the octane number for Fuel A was 96.6, and the octane number for Fuel B was 96.1. At an engine speed of 2,500 rpm, the octane number for Fuel A was 95.0, and the octane number for Fuel B was 95.4. At an engine speed of 2,200 rpm the octane number for Fuel A should be between 95.0 and 96.6, and the octane number for Fuel B should be between 95.4 and 96.1. **A** is incorrect; the octane numbers for both fuels should be higher. **B** is correct. **C** and **D** are incorrect; the octane numbers for both fuels should be lower.

SCIENCE • PRACTICE TEST 3 • EXPLANATORY ANSWERS

22. **The best answer is H.** According to Table 1, the octane number is equal to the percent isooctane in the mixture. The percent isooctane for a given mixture is:

$$\frac{\text{volume of isooctane}}{\text{volume of isooctane} + \text{volume of heptane}} \times 100$$

F is incorrect; taking the first entry in the table as an example, $100 \div 0 \neq 0$. **G** is incorrect; taking the first entry in the table as an example, $0 \div 100 \neq 100$. **H** is correct; taking the first entry in the table as an example, $(100 \div 100) \times 100 = 100$. **J** is incorrect; taking the first entry in the table as an example, $(0 \div 100) \times 100 \neq 100$.

23. **The best answer is C.** Based on the information in Table 1, a mixture containing 100 mL of heptane and 900 mL of isooctane would have an octane number of 90. According to the results of Experiment 2, adding 4 mL of TEL to 1,000 mL of isooctane increased the octane number from 100 to 125. One would predict that adding 3 mL of TEL to the heptane/isooctane mixture would increase the octane number to some value greater than 90 but less than 125. **A** and **B** are incorrect; the octane number would be increased to a value greater than 90. **C** is correct. **D** is incorrect; upon addition of the TEL, the octane number of pure isooctane was increased to 125; the octane number of the mixture containing 90% isooctane would not be greater than 125.

24. **The best answer is G.** According to the passage, the minimum octane number of a fuel required for an engine to run without being damaged is the EOR. The best fuel would be that which has an octane number greater than the EOR at all engine speeds between 1,500 rpm and 3,500 rpm. Fuel A has an octane number greater than the EOR at all engine speeds. The octane number for Fuel B at 1,500 rpm is 96.7, and the EOR is 97.4. Fuel A would be the best choice. **A** is incorrect; the octane number for Fuel A is higher than the EOR at each engine speed tested. **G** is correct. **H** and **J** are incorrect; the octane number for Fuel B at 1,500 rpm is lower than the EOR.

25. **The best answer is D.** In order to answer this item, the examinee should understand solution properties. According to Table 1, the octane number decreases as the percentage of isooctane in the mixture decreases. A solution containing 80% isooctane should have an octane number between those of a solution containing 90% isooctane (90) and 75% isooctane (75). **A**, **B**, and **C** are incorrect; the octane number should be between 75 and 90. **D** is correct; a solution that is 80% isooctane would have an octane number of 80.

SCIENCE • PRACTICE TEST 3 • EXPLANATORY ANSWERS

26. **The best answer is F.** The results of Experiment 2 indicate that adding 1 mL of TEL to 1,000 mL of isooctane increased the octane number from 100 to 115. It is reasonable to predict that if 1 mL of TEL were added to 1,000 mL of heptane, the octane number would likewise increase. However, because Table 1 indicates that pure heptane has an octane number of zero, the addition of such a small volume of TEL is unlikely to increase the octane number to 115 or greater. Therefore, it is most reasonable to predict that a mixture of 1 mL of TEL and 1,000 mL of heptane would have an octane number that is higher than that of pure heptane but lower than 115. **F** is correct. **G**, **H**, and **J** are incorrect; it is unlikely that adding 1 mL of TEL to 1,000 mL of heptane would result in the octane number either decreasing to less that of pure heptane or increasing to greater than 115.

Passage V

27. **The best answer is C.** Scientist B argues that short-period comets were once long-period comets. **A** is incorrect; Scientist B claims that long-period comets do become short-period comets. **B** is incorrect; Scientist B does not discuss whether or not short-period comets can become long-period comets. **C** is correct. **D** is incorrect; Scientist B agrees that both long-period and short-period comets orbit the Sun.

28. **The best answer is H.** Scientist A states that the KB is 30 AU to 50 AU from the Sun and has a small inclination with respect to the ecliptic plane. Scientists should search this region of space for objects in the KB. **F** is incorrect; this region would be too far away to find objects in the KB. **G** is incorrect; the region at smaller angles with respect to the ecliptic plane should be searched. **H** is correct. **J** is incorrect; Scientist A does not suggest that the region surrounding Jupiter would be part of the KB.

29. **The best answer is D.** According to the introduction, the orbital planes of short-period comets have inclinations of 30° or less with respect to the ecliptic plane. **A**, **B**, and **C** are incorrect; one would expect short-period comets to have orbital planes with inclinations of 30° or less with respect to the ecliptic plane. **D** is correct; one would not expect the orbital plane of a short-period comet to be as large as 45° with respect to the ecliptic plane.

30. **The best answer is J.** In order to answer this item, the examinee should know that Saturn is one of the "giant planets" of our solar system. Scientist B states that the orbits of long-period comets are affected by the gravitational fields of the giant planets. **F**, **G**, and **H** are incorrect; these are smaller planets and may not be large enough to affect the orbits of the long-period comets. **J** is correct; Saturn is a giant planet.

SCIENCE • PRACTICE TEST 3 • EXPLANATORY ANSWERS

31. **The best answer is A.** According to the introduction, short-period comets have orbital periods of 200 years or less. Scientist B claims that short-period comets were once long-period comets. The introduction states that long-period comets originate in the Oort Cloud. Scientist B would most likely agree that Comet Halley is a short-period comet that originated in the Oort Cloud. **A** is correct. **B** is incorrect; Scientist B claims that the KB does not exist. **C** is incorrect; because the orbital period of Comet Halley is less than 200 years, it is a short-period comet. **D** is incorrect; Comet Halley is a short-period comet, and Scientist B claims that the KB does not exist.

32. **The best answer is J.** Scientist A states that the icy bodies in the KB with diameters between 10 km and 30 km are too small to be seen with telescopes on Earth's surface. The much larger icy bodies must have diameters greater than 30 km. **F**, **G**, and **H** are incorrect; the diameters should be greater than 30 km. **J** is correct.

33. **The best answer is D.** The two scientists do not dispute the presence of the Oort Cloud around our solar system. The absence of a spherical shell similar to the Oort Cloud near a similar star would not affect either viewpoint. **A**, **B**, and **C** are incorrect. **D** is correct.

Passage VI

34. **The best answer is J.** The plant in question has a height of only 21 cm, and it produced no fruit. According to the results of the experiment, these properties are most consistent with the data shown for the L4 plants that were grown in a nutrient solution containing 120 g of NaCl. The L2 and L4 plants grown in nutrient solutions containing 60 g of NaCl had both greater average plant heights and non-zero average fruit masses. Likewise, for the L2 plants grown in a nutrient solution containing 120 g of NaCl. Therefore, **F**, **G**, and **H** are incorrect. **J** is correct.

35. **The best answer is C.** In order to answer this item, the examinee must know that the cell membrane separates the cell's cytoplasm from the environment. According to the passage, the H_2O moved between the cytoplasm of the plants' cells and the environment. If the H_2O was passing from the cell to the environment, then it passed through the cell membrane. **A**, **B**, and **D** are incorrect; in order for water to pass between the cytoplasm into the environment, it must pass through the cell membrane. **C** is correct.

36. **The best answer is G.** In order to answer this item, the examinee must know that NaCl is a salt. According to Tables 1, 2, and 3, as the amount of NaCl added to the nutrient solution increased, the plant mass decreased. **F** is incorrect; the mass did not increase. **G** is correct. **H** and **J** are incorrect; the plant mass decreased only.

SCIENCE • PRACTICE TEST 3 • EXPLANATORY ANSWERS

37. **The best answer is A.** The researchers controlled which lines received the *AtNHX1* gene. **A** is correct. **B** is incorrect; only tomato plants were used, so this was not a variable. **C** is incorrect; the plant mass was a dependent variable. **D** is incorrect; the plant height was a dependent variable.

38. **The best answer is J.** In order to answer this item, the examinee must understand the concept of an allele and the relationship between homozygosity and genotype. The passage indicates that two identical alleles of the *AtNHX1* gene were incorporated into L1's genome. An organism that has two identical alleles for a given gene is homozygous for that gene. Therefore, **F**, **G**, and **H** are incorrect. **J** is correct.

39. **The best answer is D.** According to the information in Tables 1, 2, and 3, as the height decreased, the mass decreased. A plot of this data would result in a line with a positive slope. **A** and **B** are incorrect; the line would have a slope because the mass changed as the height changed. **C** is incorrect; the line would have a positive slope because the mass increased as the height increased. **D** is correct.

40. **The best answer is J.** L1, L2, and L3 all had *AtNHX1* introduced. L4 did not have *AtNHX2* introduced; L4 was the control. **F**, **G**, and **H** are incorrect; L1, L2, and L3 all contained different genotypes for *AtNHX1*. **J** is correct; L4 was not altered.

PAGE 1

The ACT® *Sample Answer Sheet*

EXAMINEE STATEMENT, CERTIFICATION, AND SIGNATURE

1. Read the following **Statement:** By submitting this answer document, I agree to comply with and be bound by the *Terms and Conditions: Testing Rules and Policies for the ACT® Test* provided in the ACT registration materials for this test, including those concerning test security, score cancellation, examinee remedies, binding arbitration, and consent to the processing of my personally identifying information, including the collection, use, transfer, and disclosure of information as described in the ACT Privacy Policy (www.act.org/privacy.html).

   I understand that ACT owns the test questions and responses and affirm that I will not share any test questions or responses with anyone by any form of communication before, during, or after the test administration. I understand that assuming anyone else's identity to take this test is strictly prohibited and may violate the law and subject me to legal penalties.

   International Examinees: By my signature, I am also providing my consent to ACT to transfer my personally identifying information to the United States to ACT, or a third-party service provider for processing, where it will be subject to use and disclosure under the laws of the United States. I acknowledge and agree that it may also be accessible to law enforcement and national security authorities in the United States.

2. Copy the **Certification** shown below (only the text in italics) on the lines provided. Write in your normal handwriting.

Certification: *I agree to the Statement above and certify that I am the person whose name and address appear on this answer document.*

____

____

____

Your Signature ________________ Today's Date __________

Do NOT mark in this shaded area.

USE A SOFT LEAD NO. 2 PENCIL ONLY.
(Do NOT use a mechanical pencil, ink, ballpoint, correction fluid, or felt-tip pen.)

A NAME, MAILING ADDRESS, AND TELEPHONE
(Please print.)

Last Name | First Name | MI (Middle Initial)

House Number & Street (Apt. No.); or PO Box & No.; or RR & No.

City | State/Province | ZIP/Postal Code

Area Code / Number | Country

ACT, Inc.—Confidential Restricted when data present

ALL examinees must complete block A – please print.

Blocks B, C, and D are required for all examinees. Find the MATCHING INFORMATION on your ticket. Enter it EXACTLY the same way, even if any of the information is missing or incorrect. Fill in the corresponding ovals. If you do not complete these blocks to match your previous information EXACTLY, your scores will be **delayed up to 8 weeks**.

ACT

PO BOX 168, IOWA CITY, IA 52243-0168

B MATCH NAME
(First 5 letters of last name)

A B C D E F G H I J K L M N O P Q R S T U V W X Y Z

C MATCH NUMBER

1 2 3 4 5 6 7 8 9 0

D DATE OF BIRTH

Month	Day	Year
January	1	1
February	2	2
March	3	3
April	4	4
May	5	5
June	6	6
July	7	7
August	8	8
September	9	9
October	0	0
November		
December		

 A011 215 190 Rev 1 IM-(A)199526-001:654321 Printed in the US.

PAGE 2

Marking Directions: Mark only **one** oval for each question. Fill in response completely. Erase errors cleanly without smudging.

Correct mark:

Do NOT use these ***incorrect*** **or** ***bad*** **marks.**

Incorrect marks:
Overlapping mark:
Cross-out mark:
Smudged erasure:
Mark is too light:

BOOKLET NUMBER

1	1	1	1	1	1
2	2	2	2	2	2
3	3	3	3	3	3
4	4	4	4	4	4
5	5	5	5	5	5
6	6	6	6	6	6
7	7	7	7	7	7
8	8	8	8	8	8
9	9	9	9	9	9
0	0	0	0	0	0

FORM

Print your 5-character **Test Form** in the boxes above and fill in the corresponding oval at the right.

BE SURE TO FILL IN THE CORRECT FORM OVAL.

- 16MC1
- 16MC2
- 16MC3
- 18MC4
- 19MC5

TEST 1

1 A B C D	14 F G H J	27 A B C D	40 F G H J	53 A B C D	66 F G H J
2 F G H J	15 A B C D	28 F G H J	41 A B C D	54 F G H J	67 A B C D
3 A B C D	16 F G H J	29 A B C D	42 F G H J	55 A B C D	68 F G H J
4 F G H J	17 A B C D	30 F G H J	43 A B C D	56 F G H J	69 A B C D
5 A B C D	18 F G H J	31 A B C D	44 F G H J	57 A B C D	70 F G H J
6 F G H J	19 A B C D	32 F G H J	45 A B C D	58 F G H J	71 A B C D
7 A B C D	20 F G H J	33 A B C D	46 F G H J	59 A B C D	72 F G H J
8 F G H J	21 A B C D	34 F G H J	47 A B C D	60 F G H J	73 A B C D
9 A B C D	22 F G H J	35 A B C D	48 F G H J	61 A B C D	74 F G H J
10 F G H J	23 A B C D	36 F G H J	49 A B C D	62 F G H J	75 A B C D
11 A B C D	24 F G H J	37 A B C D	50 F G H J	63 A B C D	
12 F G H J	25 A B C D	38 F G H J	51 A B C D	64 F G H J	
13 A B C D	26 F G H J	39 A B C D	52 F G H J	65 A B C D	

TEST 2

1 A B C D E	11 A B C D E	21 A B C D E	31 A B C D E	41 A B C D E	51 A B C D E
2 F G H J K	12 F G H J K	22 F G H J K	32 F G H J K	42 F G H J K	52 F G H J K
3 A B C D E	13 A B C D E	23 A B C D E	33 A B C D E	43 A B C D E	53 A B C D E
4 F G H J K	14 F G H J K	24 F G H J K	34 F G H J K	44 F G H J K	54 F G H J K
5 A B C D E	15 A B C D E	25 A B C D E	35 A B C D E	45 A B C D E	55 A B C D E
6 F G H J K	16 F G H J K	26 F G H J K	36 F G H J K	46 F G H J K	56 F G H J K
7 A B C D E	17 A B C D E	27 A B C D E	37 A B C D E	47 A B C D E	57 A B C D E
8 F G H J K	18 F G H J K	28 F G H J K	38 F G H J K	48 F G H J K	58 F G H J K
9 A B C D E	19 A B C D E	29 A B C D E	39 A B C D E	49 A B C D E	59 A B C D E
10 F G H J K	20 F G H J K	30 F G H J K	40 F G H J K	50 F G H J K	60 F G H J K

TEST 3

1 A B C D	8 F G H J	15 A B C D	22 F G H J	29 A B C D	36 F G H J
2 F G H J	9 A B C D	16 F G H J	23 A B C D	30 F G H J	37 A B C D
3 A B C D	10 F G H J	17 A B C D	24 F G H J	31 A B C D	38 F G H J
4 F G H J	11 A B C D	18 F G H J	25 A B C D	32 F G H J	39 A B C D
5 A B C D	12 F G H J	19 A B C D	26 F G H J	33 A B C D	40 F G H J
6 F G H J	13 A B C D	20 F G H J	27 A B C D	34 F G H J	
7 A B C D	14 F G H J	21 A B C D	28 F G H J	35 A B C D	

TEST 4

1 A B C D	8 F G H J	15 A B C D	22 F G H J	29 A B C D	36 F G H J
2 F G H J	9 A B C D	16 F G H J	23 A B C D	30 F G H J	37 A B C D
3 A B C D	10 F G H J	17 A B C D	24 F G H J	31 A B C D	38 F G H J
4 F G H J	11 A B C D	18 F G H J	25 A B C D	32 F G H J	39 A B C D
5 A B C D	12 F G H J	19 A B C D	26 F G H J	33 A B C D	40 F G H J
6 F G H J	13 A B C D	20 F G H J	27 A B C D	34 F G H J	
7 A B C D	14 F G H J	21 A B C D	28 F G H J	35 A B C D	

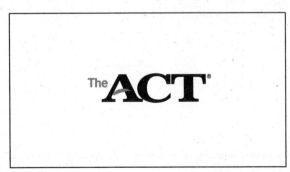

PAGE 1

The ACT® *Sample Answer Sheet*

EXAMINEE STATEMENT, CERTIFICATION, AND SIGNATURE

1. Read the following **Statement:** By submitting this answer document, I agree to comply with and be bound by the *Terms and Conditions: Testing Rules and Policies for the ACT® Test* provided in the ACT registration materials for this test, including those concerning test security, score cancellation, examinee remedies, binding arbitration, and consent to the processing of my personally identifying information, including the collection, use, transfer, and disclosure of information as described in the ACT Privacy Policy (www.act.org/privacy.html).

   I understand that ACT owns the test questions and responses and affirm that I will not share any test questions or responses with anyone by any form of communication before, during, or after the test administration. I understand that assuming anyone else's identity to take this test is strictly prohibited and may violate the law and subject me to legal penalties.

   International Examinees: By my signature, I am also providing my consent to ACT to transfer my personally identifying information to the United States to ACT, or a third-party service provider for processing, where it will be subject to use and disclosure under the laws of the United States. I acknowledge and agree that it may also be accessible to law enforcement and national security authorities in the United States.

2. Copy the **Certification** shown below (only the text in italics) on the lines provided. Write in your normal handwriting.

Certification: *I agree to the Statement above and certify that I am the person whose name and address appear on this answer document.*

Your Signature

Today's Date

Do NOT mark in this shaded area.

USE A SOFT LEAD NO. 2 PENCIL ONLY.
(Do NOT use a mechanical pencil, ink, ballpoint, correction fluid, or felt-tip pen.)

A NAME, MAILING ADDRESS, AND TELEPHONE
(Please print.)

Last Name | First Name | MI (Middle Initial)

House Number & Street (Apt. No.); or PO Box & No.; or RR & No.

City | State/Province | ZIP/Postal Code

/

Area Code | Number | Country

ACT, Inc.—Confidential Restricted when data present

ALL examinees must complete block A – please print.

Blocks B, C, and D are required for all examinees. Find the MATCHING INFORMATION on your ticket. Enter it EXACTLY the same way, even if any of the information is missing or incorrect. Fill in the corresponding ovals. If you do not complete these blocks to match your previous information EXACTLY, your scores will be **delayed up to 8 weeks.**

ACT®

PO BOX 168, IOWA CITY, IA 52243-0168

B MATCH NAME
(First 5 letters of last name)

A B C D E F G H I J K L M N O P Q R S T U V W X Y Z

C MATCH NUMBER

1 2 3 4 5 6 7 8 9 0 — 1 2 3 4 5 6 7 8 9 0

D DATE OF BIRTH

Month	Day	Year
January		
February		
March	1 1	1 1
April	2 2	2 2
May	3 3	3 3
June	4	4 4
July	5	5 5
August	6	6 6
September	7	7 7
October	8	8 8
November	9	9 9
December	0 0	0 0

 22877 A011 215 190 Rev 1 IM-(A)199526-001:654321 Printed in the US.

PAGE 2

Marking Directions: Mark only **one** oval for each question. Fill in response completely. Erase errors cleanly without smudging.

Correct mark:

Do NOT use these *incorrect* or *bad* marks.

Incorrect marks:
Overlapping mark:
Cross-out mark:
Smudged erasure:
Mark is too light:

BOOKLET NUMBER

1	1	1	1	1	1
2	2	2	2	2	2
3	3	3	3	3	3
4	4	4	4	4	4
5	5	5	5	5	5
6	6	6	6	6	6
7	7	7	7	7	7
8	8	8	8	8	8
9	9	9	9	9	9
0	0	0	0	0	0

FORM

Print your 5-character **Test Form** in the boxes above and fill in the corresponding oval at the right.

BE SURE TO FILL IN THE CORRECT FORM OVAL.

- 16MC1
- 16MC2
- 16MC3
- 18MC4
- 19MC5

TEST 1

1 A B C D	14 F G H J	27 A B C D	40 F G H J	53 A B C D	66 F G H J
2 F G H J	15 A B C D	28 F G H J	41 A B C D	54 F G H J	67 A B C D
3 A B C D	16 F G H J	29 A B C D	42 F G H J	55 A B C D	68 F G H J
4 F G H J	17 A B C D	30 F G H J	43 A B C D	56 F G H J	69 A B C D
5 A B C D	18 F G H J	31 A B C D	44 F G H J	57 A B C D	70 F G H J
6 F G H J	19 A B C D	32 F G H J	45 A B C D	58 F G H J	71 A B C D
7 A B C D	20 F G H J	33 A B C D	46 F G H J	59 A B C D	72 F G H J
8 F G H J	21 A B C D	34 F G H J	47 A B C D	60 F G H J	73 A B C D
9 A B C D	22 F G H J	35 A B C D	48 F G H J	61 A B C D	74 F G H J
10 F G H J	23 A B C D	36 F G H J	49 A B C D	62 F G H J	75 A B C D
11 A B C D	24 F G H J	37 A B C D	50 F G H J	63 A B C D	
12 F G H J	25 A B C D	38 F G H J	51 A B C D	64 F G H J	
13 A B C D	26 F G H J	39 A B C D	52 F G H J	65 A B C D	

TEST 2

1 A B C D E	11 A B C D E	21 A B C D E	31 A B C D E	41 A B C D E	51 A B C D E
2 F G H J K	12 F G H J K	22 F G H J K	32 F G H J K	42 F G H J K	52 F G H J K
3 A B C D E	13 A B C D E	23 A B C D E	33 A B C D E	43 A B C D E	53 A B C D E
4 F G H J K	14 F G H J K	24 F G H J K	34 F G H J K	44 F G H J K	54 F G H J K
5 A B C D E	15 A B C D E	25 A B C D E	35 A B C D E	45 A B C D E	55 A B C D E
6 F G H J K	16 F G H J K	26 F G H J K	36 F G H J K	46 F G H J K	56 F G H J K
7 A B C D E	17 A B C D E	27 A B C D E	37 A B C D E	47 A B C D E	57 A B C D E
8 F G H J K	18 F G H J K	28 F G H J K	38 F G H J K	48 F G H J K	58 F G H J K
9 A B C D E	19 A B C D E	29 A B C D E	39 A B C D E	49 A B C D E	59 A B C D E
10 F G H J K	20 F G H J K	30 F G H J K	40 F G H J K	50 F G H J K	60 F G H J K

TEST 3

1 A B C D	8 F G H J	15 A B C D	22 F G H J	29 A B C D	36 F G H J
2 F G H J	9 A B C D	16 F G H J	23 A B C D	30 F G H J	37 A B C D
3 A B C D	10 F G H J	17 A B C D	24 F G H J	31 A B C D	38 F G H J
4 F G H J	11 A B C D	18 F G H J	25 A B C D	32 F G H J	39 A B C D
5 A B C D	12 F G H J	19 A B C D	26 F G H J	33 A B C D	40 F G H J
6 F G H J	13 A B C D	20 F G H J	27 A B C D	34 F G H J	
7 A B C D	14 F G H J	21 A B C D	28 F G H J	35 A B C D	

TEST 4

1 A B C D	8 F G H J	15 A B C D	22 F G H J	29 A B C D	36 F G H J
2 F G H J	9 A B C D	16 F G H J	23 A B C D	30 F G H J	37 A B C D
3 A B C D	10 F G H J	17 A B C D	24 F G H J	31 A B C D	38 F G H J
4 F G H J	11 A B C D	18 F G H J	25 A B C D	32 F G H J	39 A B C D
5 A B C D	12 F G H J	19 A B C D	26 F G H J	33 A B C D	40 F G H J
6 F G H J	13 A B C D	20 F G H J	27 A B C D	34 F G H J	
7 A B C D	14 F G H J	21 A B C D	28 F G H J	35 A B C D	

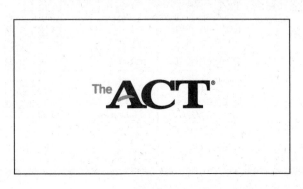

080661

Practice Test 4

EXAMINEE STATEMENT, CERTIFICATION, AND SIGNATURE

1. Read the following **Statement:** By opening this test booklet, I agree to comply with and be bound by the *Terms and Conditions: Testing Rules and Policies for the ACT® Test* provided in the ACT registration materials for this test, including those concerning test security, score cancellation, examinee remedies, binding arbitration, and consent to the processing of my personally identifying information, including the collection, use, transfer, and disclosure of information as described in the ACT Privacy Policy (www.act.org/privacy.html).

   I understand that ACT owns the test questions and responses and affirm that I will not share any test questions or responses with anyone by any form of communication before, during, or after the test administration. I understand that assuming anyone else's identity to take this test is strictly prohibited and may violate the law and subject me to legal penalties.

   International Examinees: By my signature, I am also providing my consent to ACT to transfer my personally identifying information to the United States to ACT, or a third-party service provider for processing, where it will be subject to use and disclosure under the laws of the United States. I acknowledge and agree that it may also be accessible to law enforcement and national security authorities in the United States.

2. Copy the **Certification** shown below (only the text in italics) on the lines provided. Write in your normal handwriting.

   Certification: *I agree to the Statement above and certify that I am the person whose name appears on this form.*

   ____

   ____

3. Sign your name as you would any official document, enter today's date, and print your name in the spaces provided.

   Your Signature ______ Today's Date ______ Print Your Name ______

Form 18MC4

2019 | 2020

Directions

This booklet contains tests in English, mathematics, reading, and science. These tests measure skills and abilities highly related to high school course work and success in college. **Calculators may be used on the mathematics test only.**

The questions in each test are numbered, and the suggested answers for each question are lettered. On the answer document, the rows of ovals are numbered to match the questions, and the ovals in each row are lettered to correspond to the suggested answers.

For each question, first decide which answer is best. Next, locate on the answer document the row of ovals numbered the same as the question. Then, locate the oval in that row lettered the same as your answer. Finally, fill in the oval completely. Use a soft lead pencil and make your marks heavy and black. **Do not use ink or a mechanical pencil.**

Mark only one answer to each question. If you change your mind about an answer, erase your first mark thoroughly before marking your new answer. For each question, make certain that you mark in the row of ovals with the same number as the question.

Only responses marked on your answer document will be scored. Your score on each test will be based only on the number of questions you answer correctly during the time allowed for that test. You will **not** be penalized for guessing. **It is to your advantage to answer every question even if you must guess.**

You may work on each test **only** when the testing staff tells you to do so. If you finish a test before time is called for that test, you should use the time remaining to reconsider questions you are uncertain about in that test. You may **not** look back to a test on which time has already been called, and you may **not** go ahead to another test. To do so will disqualify you from the examination.

Lay your pencil down immediately when time is called at the end of each test. You may **not** for any reason fill in or alter ovals for a test after time is called for that test. To do so will disqualify you from the examination.

Do not fold or tear the pages of your test booklet.

DO NOT OPEN THIS BOOKLET UNTIL TOLD TO DO SO.

ENGLISH TEST

45 Minutes—75 Questions

DIRECTIONS: In the five passages that follow, certain words and phrases are underlined and numbered. In the right-hand column, you will find alternatives for the underlined part. In most cases, you are to choose the one that best expresses the idea, makes the statement appropriate for standard written English, or is worded most consistently with the style and tone of the passage as a whole. If you think the original version is best, choose "NO CHANGE." In some cases, you will find in the right-hand column a question about the underlined part. You are to choose the best answer to the question.

You will also find questions about a section of the passage, or about the passage as a whole. These questions do not refer to an underlined portion of the passage, but rather are identified by a number or numbers in a box.

For each question, choose the alternative you consider best and fill in the corresponding oval on your answer document. Read each passage through once before you begin to answer the questions that accompany it. For many of the questions, you must read several sentences beyond the question to determine the answer. Be sure that you have read far enough ahead each time you choose an alternative.

PASSAGE I

The Object of Love

[1]

[A] I was waiting at the veterinarian's office recently with my cat when a young woman came in.(1) After she sat down next to me, she asked if I would mind if she took her pet iguana out of its carrier. It was just a baby, she said, and it liked being held. [B]

[2]

Now, I'm not fond of iguanas. [C] They're strange, unpredictable creatures that belong deep in a rain forest, walking on the ground(2) or resting high in the trees, which are(3) hidden in the canopy.

1. A. NO CHANGE
   B. into the veterinarian's office where I was.
   C. in, and there I was, waiting in the office.
   D. in while I was waiting there.

2. Which choice provides the most vivid description of iguanas on the floor of a rain forest?
   F. NO CHANGE
   G. scuttling through dank undergrowth
   H. living underneath the treetops
   J. moving about down low

3. A. NO CHANGE
   B. trees, they are
   C. trees,
   D. trees;

GO ON TO THE NEXT PAGE.

Wishing to be polite, but with reluctance in my voice, [4] I told the woman that I didn't mind. She thanked me as she popped open the plastic carrier and pulled the iguana out, onto her lap.

[3]

I guardedly examined the animal: A dinosaur-like thing, it was the size of a cat but armored in gray-green scales, with a black-striped, whiplike tail two feet long. It had a spine with tiny spikes, [5] and its muscular limbs ended with what resembled crinkly leather gloves drawn tightly over fine-boned human hands. When I looked more closely, I saw a tiny claw at the tip of each slender finger.

[4]

The woman began to pet the iguana under its chin, and the little dragon arched its neck and closed its eyes. The reptile's calmness amazed me, as did the caress that was given tenderly from the woman to her pet [6] and watched it peacefully rest. With a twinge of pity, I thought how sad it was for us [7] to lavish so much affection on something that couldn't love her back.

[5]

At that moment, the iguana slowly opened its eyes, which shone large and bright, from [8] its scaly face. [D] Head slightly cocked, it regarded [9] me, steadily and fixedly, like a judge delivering [10] a verdict.

4. The writer is considering deleting the underlined portion. Should the underlined portion be kept or deleted?
   - **F.** Kept, because it suggests that the narrator had previously sat next to an iguana, out of its carrier, at the veterinarian's office.
   - **G.** Kept, because it emphasizes the narrator's feelings about the iguana being taken out of its carrier.
   - **H.** Deleted, because it characterizes the narrator in a manner that's inconsistent with how the narrator is characterized in the rest of the essay.
   - **J.** Deleted, because it detracts from the paragraph's purpose of providing background information about iguanas.

5. Given that all the choices are accurate, which one provides the most precise description of the pattern of spikes on the iguana's spine?
   - **A.** NO CHANGE
   - **B.** I saw spikes that looked like they were just beginning to develop,
   - **C.** There were small spikes on its armored back,
   - **D.** Rows of budding spikes lined its spine,

6. **F.** NO CHANGE
   - **G.** tenderness with which the woman caressed her pet
   - **H.** woman caressing her pet tenderly
   - **J.** tenderness the woman showed

7. **A.** NO CHANGE
   - **B.** the woman
   - **C.** people
   - **D.** you

8. **F.** NO CHANGE
   - **G.** large and bright from,
   - **H.** large, and bright from
   - **J.** large and bright from

9. Which of the following alternatives to the underlined portion would NOT be acceptable?
   - **A.** scrutinized
   - **B.** supposed
   - **C.** appraised
   - **D.** considered

10. **F.** NO CHANGE
    - **G.** having a delivery of
    - **H.** in deliverance with
    - **J.** deliver

GO ON TO THE NEXT PAGE.

Taking Additional Practice Tests

1 ■ ■ ■ ■ ■ ■ ■ ■ ■ 1

[6]

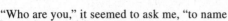

"Who are you," it seemed to ask me, "to name the proper object of love?"

[7]

The veterinary assistant called for my <u>cat, and me from the hallway</u>[11] that leads to the examination area. A bit unsettled, I rose and picked up my cat carrier. As I walked from the waiting room into the hall, I glanced back and saw the iguana snuggle down into the young woman's lap, <u>looking</u>[12] as content as a kitten, and close its eyes again.

11. **A.** NO CHANGE
B. cat, and me from the hallway,
C. cat and me from the hallway,
D. cat and me from the hallway

12. **F.** NO CHANGE
G. like as if it was giving off the impression of being
H. appearing something like
J. sort of like it was

Questions 13 and 14 ask about the preceding passage as a whole.

13. Upon reviewing the essay and finding that some information has been left out, the writer composes the following sentence incorporating that information:

> She told me that her iguana especially liked attention when it was in unfamiliar surroundings, and that this was its first trip to the veterinarian.

If the writer were to add this sentence to the essay, it would most logically be placed at:

A. Point A in Paragraph 1.
B. Point B in Paragraph 1.
C. Point C in Paragraph 2.
D. Point D in Paragraph 5.

14. Suppose the writer's primary purpose had been to describe a moment in which a person notices something unexpected while observing his or her surroundings. Would this essay accomplish that purpose?

F. Yes, because it describes what the narrator, while waiting at the vet, perceived to be a surprising bond between a woman and her pet iguana.
G. Yes, because it recounts a moment when the narrator, while waiting at the vet, realized people often don't know when they're being impolite.
H. No, because it instead tells the story of why the narrator doesn't like iguanas.
J. No, because it instead focuses on providing information about the physical characteristics of iguanas and their habitat.

GO ON TO THE NEXT PAGE.

PASSAGE II

Billy Mills Takes the Gold

[1] Runner Billy Mills qualified to run in the 10,000-meter race in the 1964 Tokyo Olympics, but he was a long shot. [2] In Tokyo, however, Mills became the first to win an Olympic gold medal for the United States in this event. [3] His qualifying entry time lagged almost a full minute above the world-record time held by Australian Ron Clarke. [18]

15. A. NO CHANGE
    B. nonetheless,
    C. in fact,
    D. DELETE the underlined portion.

16. F. NO CHANGE
    G. Olympic gold medal,
    H. Olympic gold, medal,
    J. Olympic, gold medal

17. A. NO CHANGE
    B. around
    C. behind
    D. from

18. Which of the following sequences of sentences makes this paragraph most logical?
    F. NO CHANGE
    G. 1, 3, 2
    H. 2, 1, 3
    J. 2, 3, 1

Mills, an Oglala Lakota, spent his childhood on the Pine Ridge Reservation in South Dakota. He started long-distance running while attending boarding school in Kansas. Initially, running was part of his training regimen for boxing, his first love. Mills had dreamed of being a boxer since he was a child.

19. A. NO CHANGE
    B. Mills an Oglala Lakota
    C. Mills an Oglala Lakota,
    D. Mills, an Oglala Lakota

20. Given that all the choices are true, which one most effectively concludes this paragraph and provides a transition to the following paragraph?
    F. NO CHANGE
    G. Yet Mills didn't quite make it as a boxer.
    H. Mills soon realized that he had greater potential as a runner than as a boxer.
    J. Mills also tried playing basketball and football, although he didn't excel at them.

Mills broke numerous high school track records, earning himself an athletic scholarship to the University of Kansas. With Mills as a star runner, Kansas won the 1959 and 1960 NCAA Outdoor Track and Field Championships. After graduation, he became an officer in the Marines and assumed the duties of military life. However, Mills was soon drawn back to the track, and, while still in the Marines, races became part of his life again.

21. A. NO CHANGE
    B. his talent raced back to him
    C. he began racing
    D. racing was in his life

GO ON TO THE NEXT PAGE.

1 ■ ■ ■ ■ ■ ■ ■ ■ ■ 1

<u>At an important point in his training,</u> [22] Mills wrote the words "Gold Medal" in his journal. He was determined to win, despite being rather unknown as an athlete. [23] Because of his unremarkable qualifying time, the US Olympic shoe sponsor didn't even send him running shoes for the race. <u>Luckily,</u> [24] Mills borrowed a pair and was ready to run when he hit the starting line. [25]

All eyes were on the <u>overseers,</u> [26] Mohamed Gammoudi of Tunisia and Ron Clarke, as they began the last lap of the race. Suddenly, <u>Mills, who had been in third place,</u> [27] broke from the pack, sprinted ahead, and won the race. Before a

22. Given that all the choices are accurate, which one most effectively introduces the paragraph by returning to the topic of the essay's opening paragraph?

F. NO CHANGE
G. A future inductee into the US Track and Field Hall of Fame,
H. Three weeks before the 1964 Olympics,
J. Committed to success,

23. If the writer were to delete the word *rather* from the preceding sentence, the sentence would primarily lose a word that:

A. implies that some people were already aware of Mills's talent.
B. helps describe Mills's approach to motivating himself for a race.
C. explains why Mills decided to take on the challenge of running in the Olympics.
D. emphasizes that Mills needed more training before he could win the race.

24. Which choice best emphasizes Mills's commitment to winning the gold medal?

F. NO CHANGE
G. Eventually,
H. Undeterred,
J. Concentrating,

25. At this point, the writer is considering adding the following true statement:

> Bob Hayes, another US runner in the Tokyo Olympics, ran with a borrowed shoe after realizing he only had one of his two shoes with him; he then won the 100-meter race.

Should the writer make this addition here?

A. Yes, because it adds important details about two US track and field gold medalists in 1964.
B. Yes, because it reveals that two runners used other people's shoes to win their races.
C. No, because it shifts the essay's focus from the US track team members to their shoes.
D. No, because it interrupts the essay's discussion of Mills preparing for and running the 10,000-meter race.

26. F. NO CHANGE
G. rulers,
H. authorities,
J. leaders,

27. A. NO CHANGE
B. Mills who had been in third place,
C. Mills, who had been in third place
D. Mills who had been in third place

GO ON TO THE NEXT PAGE.

stunned crowd, Mills had run the 10,000 meters 45 seconds faster than his qualifying time. He set an Olympic record of 28 minutes 24 seconds, finishing ahead of Mohamed Gammoudi and Ron Clarke. As of 2014, he remained the only US runner to have won an Olympic gold medal in the 10,000-meter race.

28. F. NO CHANGE
G. has ran
H. has run
J. had ran

29. The writer is considering deleting the underlined portion (adjusting the punctuation as needed). Should the underlined portion be kept or deleted?
A. Kept, because it effectively connects the closing paragraph to the essay's opening paragraph.
B. Kept, because it adds a detail to the essay's retelling of Mills's victory.
C. Deleted, because it repeats a point already made clear by the paragraph.
D. Deleted, because it strays from the main point of the paragraph.

PASSAGE III

Hearing Is Believing

The movie scene unfolds, a boy out exploring trudges across the snow and arrives at a boarded-up house. As the lad knocks on the door, it slowly opens. Inside, dim light from a cracked and dusty window reveals an old man descending a staircase. Part of what draws an audience into scenes like this, with that in mind, is the sounds that accompany the images. The crunch, the knock, the squeak, the creak.

In most films, such sounds are recorded after the cameras have stopped rolling, a practice named for Jack Foley, who was working in Hollywood in the late 1920s when "talkies" swept silent movies off the screen. It was Foley whom figured out that squeezing a sock full of cornstarch, a sound like that of footsteps in the snow. He put an old rocking chair to work to create the creaking of

30. F. NO CHANGE
G. unfolds a boy,
H. unfolds. A boy
J. unfolds a boy

31. A. NO CHANGE
B. this, for the time being,
C. this, nevertheless,
D. this

32. Which choice best suggests that talkies swiftly and dramatically put an end to the silent-movie era?
F. NO CHANGE
G. invited the beginning of what would one day become a new era in the film industry.
H. stirred up the movie industry and delighted the general public.
J. began their entrance onto the screens of Hollywood.

33. A. NO CHANGE
B. himself whom
C. who
D. he

34. F. NO CHANGE
G. cornstarch, which makes
H. cornstarch produces
J. cornstarch to get

GO ON TO THE NEXT PAGE.

stairs. When a scene called for the sound of more than one person walking, Foley grabbed a cane to generate the allusion of many people on foot. Low-budget solutions to big problems that eventually earned him the status of a Hollywood legend. Movies with sound were in their infancy at the time.

The need for "Foley" arises from the sound clutter of real life. The job of the sound technician (whose role is distinct from that of the "Foley artist") is to record dialogue without capturing all the distracting background noise. An airplane flying overhead. A phone ringing. A door. Then, while viewing the film in a Foley studio: a small room with a screen, a microphone, and countless props—the Foley artist re-creates the sounds of the actors' actions. It was Jack Foley who pioneered this process.

Directors adored him. To re-create the audible ruckus of Caesar's army for the movie *Spartacus*, Foley jangled a set of keys in front of the microphone. That simple act, a Jack Foley classic, cut the movie's budget by untold thousands of dollars.

35. **A.** NO CHANGE
B. produce the elusion
C. create the illusion
D. make the allusion

36. **F.** NO CHANGE
G. about which they eventually
H. that eventually even so
J. eventually

37. **A.** NO CHANGE
B. A cane was one of the props Foley used to achieve the desired sound effects.
C. The process he pioneered is one that takes place after the actors have been filmed for the movie.
D. DELETE the underlined portion.

38. **F.** NO CHANGE
G. aroused from
H. arises
J. arise

39. If the writer were to delete the underlined portion, the essay would primarily lose information that:
A. establishes what the role of a sound technician is in making a movie.
B. clarifies the origin of the term "Foley artist."
C. indicates that various occupations were highly influenced by the work of Jack Foley.
D. reduces the chance of confusion about whether "sound technician" means "Foley artist."

40. **F.** NO CHANGE
G. The slamming door, which is not part of the scene.
H. The sound of a door.
J. A door slamming.

41. **A.** NO CHANGE
B. studio—
C. studio,
D. studio

42. **F.** NO CHANGE
G. unspeakable
H. speechless
J. endless

GO ON TO THE NEXT PAGE.

The director had planned to ship actors and horses, an army's worth headed to a battlefield overseas to get an authentic sound recording. Instead, they all stayed home, and the audience never knew the difference. [44]

43. A. NO CHANGE
 B. worth, were headed to
 C. worth, to
 D. worth

44. The writer is considering deleting the preceding sentence. Should the sentence be kept or deleted?
 F. Kept, because it suggests that audiences eventually came to know about Foley's work.
 G. Kept, because it ends the essay with a detail that suggests the impact of Foley's work on both the makers and viewers of movies.
 H. Deleted, because it shifts the focus of the paragraph from Foley to the movie's director, making a weak ending to an essay about Foley.
 J. Deleted, because it suggests that Foley's work was insignificant to the public.

PASSAGE IV

Talking Bacteria

In her lab at Princeton University, molecular biologist, Bonnie Bassler leans over a collection of petri dishes; her face illuminated by an aquamarine glow. The glow, caused by a particular species, of bacteria is confirmation of a phenomenon Bassler has been investigating for years. Bacteria, the simplest forms of life, have the ability to communicate with each other.

As a student in graduate school, Bassler became intrigued with other researchers' and their discoveries involving *Vibrio fischeri*; a luminescent marine bacteria. Researchers found that these bacteria only begin to glow once they have formed a group. A series of experiments revealed that each bacterial cell releases an autoinducer,

45. A. NO CHANGE
 B. University, molecular biologist Bonnie Bassler,
 C. University, molecular biologist Bonnie Bassler
 D. University molecular biologist Bonnie Bassler

46. F. NO CHANGE
 G. dishes and her face is
 H. dishes, her face is
 J. dishes, her face

47. A. NO CHANGE
 B. species, of bacteria,
 C. species of bacteria,
 D. species of bacteria

48. F. NO CHANGE
 G. researcher's and their
 H. researchers'
 J. researchers

49. A. NO CHANGE
 B. *fischeri* which is
 C. *fischeri*,
 D. *fischeri*

GO ON TO THE NEXT PAGE.

1           1

a type of chemical signal. A sensory protein allowed [50] other bacteria to "hear" this molecular message. Once the bacteria have released a high enough concentration of autoinducer, they [51] assemble and begin to glow. This "quorum sensing" enables the bacteria to coordinate their actions and perform their specific function.

On the contrary, [52] in her own lab, Bassler found evidence of quorum sensing in a related bacterial species called [53] *Vibrio harveyi*. She also discovered that *V. harveyi* release a second autoinducer, or AI-2. This AI-2, which Bassler has described as a chemical "trade language," makes it possible for bacteria to communicate with other species of bacteria in the same neck of the woods. [54] She found that each of the species she studied, including ones [55] that live in humans, releases AI-2.

After her 2002 discovery, Bassler began using information from her quorum-sensing studies to understand how virulent strains of bacteria found in humans communicate. [56] These disease-spreading bacteria [57] rely on quorum sensing to spread disease. Bassler is hopeful that her ongoing studies of AI-2 will enable she and her team [58] to disrupt

50. F. NO CHANGE
G. would have allowed
H. has allowed
J. allows

51. A. NO CHANGE
B. autoinducer—they
C. autoinducer. They
D. autoinducer they

52. F. NO CHANGE
G. Eventually,
H. Ordinarily,
J. Namely,

53. A. NO CHANGE
B. related, bacterial species, called
C. related, bacterial species called
D. related bacterial species called,

54. F. NO CHANGE
G. neighboring proximity.
H. surrounding locale.
J. vicinity.

55. Which of the following alternatives to the underlined portion would NOT be acceptable?
A. the kinds
B. species
C. those
D. them

56. F. NO CHANGE
G. has been communicating.
H. is communicating.
J. communicates.

57. A. NO CHANGE
B. bacteria that Bassler has studied
C. bacteria that live in humans
D. bacteria

58. F. NO CHANGE
G. her and her team
H. herself and them
J. her and them

GO ON TO THE NEXT PAGE.

quorum sensing [59].

59. At this point, the writer is considering adding the following information:

> and ultimately develop new methods for treating bacterial infections

Given that the information is accurate, should the writer make this addition here?

A. Yes, because it clarifies that Bassler and her team are focusing their research on bacteria that live in humans.
B. Yes, because it specifies how Bassler's research could directly affect humans.
C. No, because it fails to specify which strains of bacteria are prone to attacking humans' immune systems.
D. No, because it fails to explain how Bassler and her team plan to disrupt quorum sensing.

PASSAGE V

Mapping the London Underground

[1]

Soon after the London Underground subway lines were introduced in the late 1800s, a system for mapping these <u>vicinities creeping beneath</u> [60] was needed so that travelers could navigate this new mode of transportation. <u>As a result, early</u> [61] maps relied on a geographically accurate scale that simply superimposed the twisting subway lines over standard maps of the city streets above. [A] These maps clearly depicted the few subway lines that extended into suburban London, but they compressed and <u>obscured</u> [62] the compact, heavily trafficked routes

60. F. NO CHANGE
G. subterranean routes
H. submerged zones
J. low-down alleys

61. A. NO CHANGE
B. To provide an example, early
C. Secondly, early
D. Early

62. Which choice is clearest and suggests the highest degree of failure of early maps to legibly depict the subway routes directly under central London?

F. NO CHANGE
G. in general were disappointing about
H. made indecipherable
J. didn't fully capture

Taking Additional Practice Tests

GO ON TO THE NEXT PAGE.

1 ■ ■ ■ ■ ■ ■ ■ ■ ■ 1

that converged directly under central London. [63]

[2]

In the 1930s, electrical engineer Harry Beck proposed a solution that would eliminate the need for geographical accuracy. He created a map that was a scaled-down linear diagram of the subway lines. More a stylistic outline of the routes <u>besides</u> [64] a true-to-life <u>sketch; it</u> [65] did not represent actual distances between points. [B] Beck's map, modeled after electrical wiring diagrams, had a clean, grid-like structure <u>having also</u> [66] color-coded routes. Focusing on creating the simplest possible schema <u>to show</u> [67] travelers how to get from one station to another, he <u>did away with all references to city streets above.</u> [68]

[3]

[1] The London Passenger Transport Board, which represented the subway lines, initially resisted Beck's map. [2] Still, willing to try anything to <u>rise</u> [69] subway ridership and therefore revenues, <u>a limited number of copies were printed.</u> [70] [3] Beck's map became a huge success.

63. At this point, the writer is considering adding the following true statement:

> Today, the Tube, as the London Underground subway is called, covers approximately 250 miles of trackway.

Should the writer make this addition here?

A. Yes, because it provides details about the London Underground that explain the significance of the subway's modern name.
B. Yes, because it suggests the need for clear, accurate maps of the expansive London Underground.
C. No, because it is only loosely related to the information about the London Underground that is provided in the first paragraph.
D. No, because it blurs the focus of the first paragraph, which is about the most recent maps of the London Underground.

64. F. NO CHANGE
G. than
H. instead
J. into

65. A. NO CHANGE
B. sketch, and it
C. sketch, it
D. sketch. It

66. F. NO CHANGE
G. additionally included
H. and featuring
J. and

67. A. NO CHANGE
B. would show
C. had shown
D. showed

68. Given that all the choices are accurate, which one gives the clearest example of how Beck created the "simplest possible schema" in his map for subway passengers?
F. NO CHANGE
G. had been irritated with the curving lines on early maps of the London Underground.
H. knew that if his map were to become popular, it had to be easy to use.
J. created a map that has iconic status today.

69. A. NO CHANGE
B. increase
C. enlarge
D. upend

70. F. NO CHANGE
G. the board printed a limited number of copies.
H. copies in a limited number were printed.
J. copies printed in a limited number.

GO ON TO THE NEXT PAGE.

[4] Over a million copies were in circulation within six months. [5] Board members felt that not showing relative distances between stations was too radical. [71]

[4]

For most of his life, Beck continued to make small refinements to "the diagram," as he called his map, but he retained it's basic elements. [C] His deceptively simple diagrammatic approach to mapping, remains standard in the field of information design not only in London but also around the world. From Sydney, Australia, to Chicago, Illinois, urban transit maps continue to model this to navigate the spaces below. [D]

71. For the sake of logic and cohesion, Sentence 5 should be placed:

A. where it is now.
B. after Sentence 1.
C. after Sentence 2.
D. after Sentence 3.

72. F. NO CHANGE
G. their
H. its
J. its'

73. A. NO CHANGE
B. diagrammatic, approach to mapping,
C. diagrammatic approach to mapping
D. diagrammatic approach, to mapping,

74. F. NO CHANGE
G. this means Beck created, which remains standard in the field,
H. Beck's deceptively simple approach to mapping
J. Beck's innovative method

Question 75 asks about the preceding passage as a whole.

75. The writer is considering adding the following sentence to the essay:

> Actual distances shouldn't matter to subway passengers, he believed, because they didn't have to make navigational decisions, such as choosing when to turn.

If the writer were to add this sentence, it would most logically be placed at:

A. Point A in Paragraph 1.
B. Point B in Paragraph 2.
C. Point C in Paragraph 4.
D. Point D in Paragraph 4.

END OF TEST 1

STOP! DO NOT TURN THE PAGE UNTIL TOLD TO DO SO.

2 △ △ △ △ △ △ △ △ △ 2

MATHEMATICS TEST

60 Minutes—60 Questions

DIRECTIONS: Solve each problem, choose the correct answer, and then fill in the corresponding oval on your answer document.

Do not linger over problems that take too much time. Solve as many as you can; then return to the others in the time you have left for this test.

You are permitted to use a calculator on this test. You may use your calculator for any problems you choose, but some of the problems may best be done without using a calculator.

Note: Unless otherwise stated, all of the following should be assumed.

1. Illustrative figures are NOT necessarily drawn to scale.
2. Geometric figures lie in a plane.
3. The word *line* indicates a straight line.
4. The word *average* indicates arithmetic mean.

DO YOUR FIGURING HERE.

1. The top surface of a rectangular table has an area of 100 square feet and a width of 5 feet. What is the length, in feet, of the surface?

A. 10
B. 15
C. 20
D. 95
E. 500

2. A wallet containing 2 five-dollar bills, 9 ten-dollar bills, and 5 twenty-dollar bills is found and returned to its owner. The wallet's owner will reward the finder with 1 bill drawn randomly from the wallet. What is the probability that the bill drawn will be a twenty-dollar bill?

F. $\frac{1}{16}$
G. $\frac{1}{10}$
H. $\frac{1}{5}$
J. $\frac{5}{16}$
K. $\frac{5}{11}$

3. In his costume supplies, Elmo the clown has 4 noses, 3 pairs of lips, and 2 wigs. A clown costume consists of 1 nose, 1 pair of lips, and 1 wig. How many different clown costumes can Elmo make?

A. 3
B. 9
C. 12
D. 14
E. 24

GO ON TO THE NEXT PAGE.

2 △ △ △ △ △ △ △ △ △ 2

DO YOUR FIGURING HERE.

4. Esteban and his family are making care packages to send to children at summer camp. Each complete care package contains 5 pens, 2 notebooks, 3 envelopes, 12 cookies, and 5 candy bars. Esteban and his family have already made 7 complete care packages and the following materials remain:

3 boxes of pens (10 pens per box)

4 boxes of notebooks (5 notebooks per box)

2 boxes of envelopes (12 envelopes per box)

84 cookies

$4\frac{1}{2}$ boxes of candy bars (10 candy bars per box)

How many additional complete care packages can Esteban and his family make with the remaining materials?

F. 6
G. 7
H. 8
J. 10
K. 15

5. A formula for the volume of a right circular cone is $V = \frac{1}{3}\pi r^2 h$, where r is the radius of the base and h is the height of the cone. Using $\frac{22}{7}$ as an approximate value for π, which of the following values is closest to the volume, in cubic inches, of a cone with height 28 inches and radius 6 inches?

A. 264
B. 352
C. 1,056
D. 4,224
E. 4,928

6. In $\triangle ACD$ below, B is on $\overline{AC}$, E is on $\overline{AD}$, the measure of $\angle CAD$ is 28°, and $\overline{AD}$ is perpendicular to both $\overline{BE}$ and $\overline{CD}$. What is the measure of $\angle CBE$?

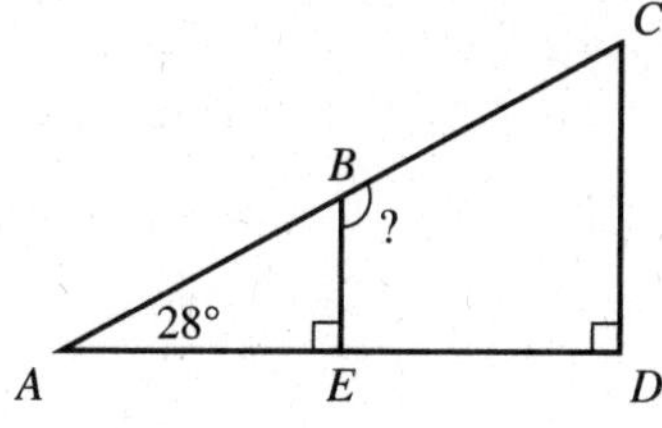

F. 104°
G. 118°
H. 124°
J. 146°
K. 152°

GO ON TO THE NEXT PAGE.

2 △ △ △ △ △ △ △ △ △ 2

DO YOUR FIGURING HERE.

7. What is the sum of $0.1x^2 + 3x + 80$ and $0.5x^2 - 2x + 60$ for all x ?

A. $-0.4x^2 + 5x + 20$
B. $0.6x^2 + x + 140$
C. $0.6x^2 + 5x + 140$
D. $x^2 + 5x + 140$
E. $5.6x^2 + 140$

8. Students studying motion observed a cart rolling at a constant rate along a straight line. The table below gives the distance, d feet, the cart was from a reference point at 1-second intervals from $t = 0$ seconds to $t = 5$ seconds.

t	0	1	2	3	4	5
d	15	18	21	24	27	30

Which of the following equations represents this relationship between d and t ?

F. $d = t + 15$
G. $d = 3t + 12$
H. $d = 3t + 15$
J. $d = 15t + 3$
K. $d = 33t$

9. Dmitry bought a pair of pants at the discounted price of \$30. The original price of the pants was \$40. What was the percent of the discount?

A. 4%
B. 10%
C. 25%
D. $33\frac{1}{3}\%$
E. 75%

10. What is the value of $|-6| - |7 - 41|$?

F. -40
G. -28
H. 28
J. 40
K. 54

11. Samantha, Nyla, and Jerry own shares of stock in the Triumph Hotels company. The shares of stock that they own have a combined value of \$6,880. Samantha owns 70 shares, Nyla owns 50 shares, and Jerry owns 40 shares. What is the value of the shares Samantha owns?

A. \$ 98
B. \$ 301
C. \$3,010
D. \$4,816
E. \$5,351

GO ON TO THE NEXT PAGE.

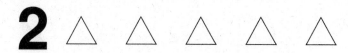

2 △ △ △ △ △ △ △ △ △ 2

12. A new club wants to attract customers who are at least 18 but less than 30 years of age. One of the number lines below illustrates the range of ages, in years, of the customers the club wants to attract. Which number line is it?

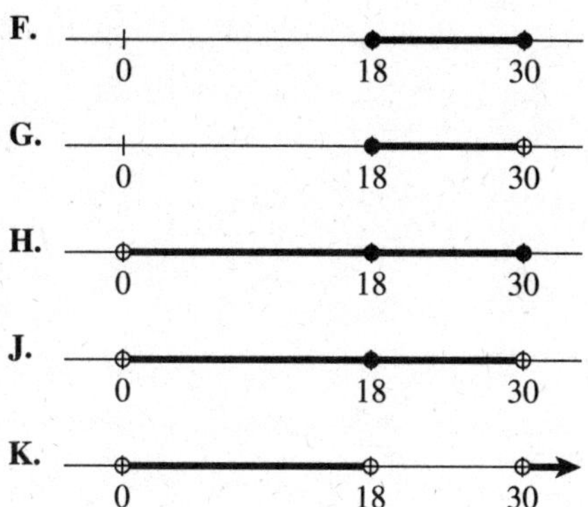

13. In the figure shown below, E and G lie on $\overline{AC}$, D and F lie on $\overline{AB}$, $\overline{DE}$ and $\overline{FG}$ are parallel to $\overline{BC}$, and the given lengths are in feet. What is the length of $\overline{AC}$, in feet?

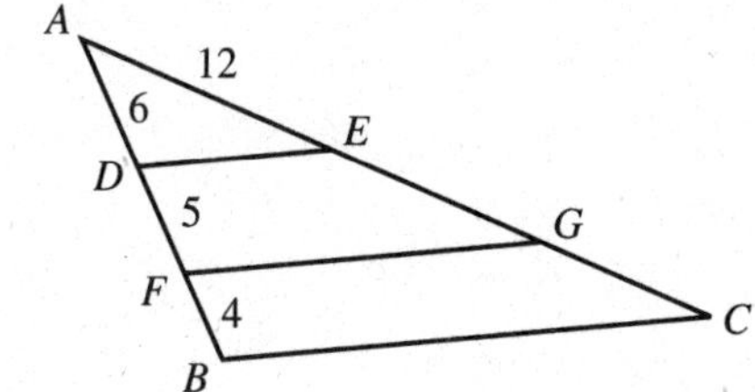

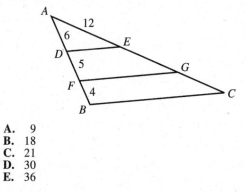

A. 9
B. 18
C. 21
D. 30
E. 36

14. Which of the following integers is closest to $\frac{\sqrt{50}}{2}$?

F. 3
G. 4
H. 5
J. 13
K. 14

15. The ratio of Jane's age to her daughter's age is 9:2. The sum of their ages is 44. How old is Jane?

A. 22
B. 33
C. 35
D. 36
E. 40

DO YOUR FIGURING HERE.

Taking Additional Practice Tests

GO ON TO THE NEXT PAGE.

2          2

DO YOUR FIGURING HERE.

16. For the next school year, a college will use $\frac{1}{9}$ of the money in its operating budget for library books and $\frac{1}{6}$ of the money in its operating budget for scholarships. What fraction of the operating budget remains for other uses?

F. $\frac{1}{18}$
G. $\frac{5}{18}$
H. $\frac{13}{18}$
J. $\frac{20}{27}$
K. $\frac{8}{9}$

17. What value of x makes the proportion below true?

$$\frac{10}{10+x} = \frac{35}{42}$$

A. 2
B. 7
C. 12
D. 17
E. 32

18. The rectangle shown in the figure below is partitioned into 3 triangles, 2 of which are shaded. What is the total area, in square inches, of the 2 shaded regions?

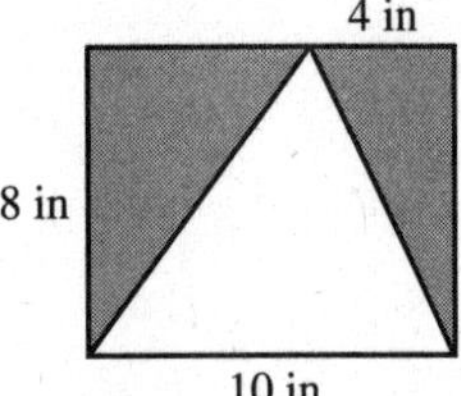

F. 20
G. 24
H. 32
J. 40
K. 80

19. Which of the following ordered pairs in the standard (x,y) coordinate plane satisfies the system of inequalities below?

$$x > 2$$
$$y > 0$$
$$x + y < 5$$

A. (1,3)
B. (2,2)
C. (3,1)
D. (3,2)
E. (4,0)

GO ON TO THE NEXT PAGE.

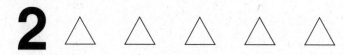

2 △ △ △ △ △ △ △ △ △ 2

DO YOUR FIGURING HERE.

20. The graph of $y = 3 - 5\sin(x - \pi)$ is shown in the standard (x,y) coordinate plane below. What is the range of y ?

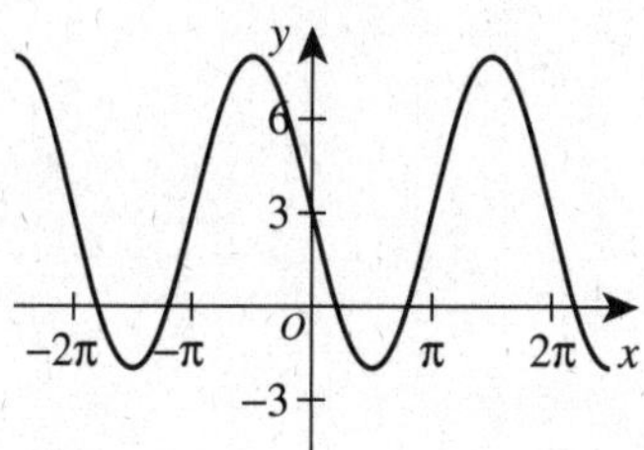

F. $-5 \le y \le 5$
G. $-2 \le y \le 2$
H. $-2 \le y \le 8$
J. $3 \le y \le 8$
K. $3 \le y \le 10$

21. Given functions $f(x) = 2x + 1$ and $g(x) = x^2 - 4$, what is the value of $f(g(-3))$?

A. −29
B. −25
C. −19
D. 11
E. 21

22. A fabric store sells flannel and calico fabrics. Joan pays $25 for 3 yards of flannel and 4 yards of calico. Chris pays $11 for 1 yard of flannel and 2 yards of calico. What is the price of 1 yard of calico?

F. $3
G. $4
H. $5
J. $6
K. $7

23. The scores given below were earned by 10 students on a recent biology test. What is the median score?

71, 94, 86, 77, 88, 94, 88, 80, 78, 94

A. 85
B. 86
C. 87
D. 88
E. 91

24. A parallelogram has a perimeter of 84 inches, and 1 of its sides measures 16 inches. If it can be determined, what are the lengths, in inches, of the other 3 sides?

F. 16, 16, 36
G. 16, 18, 18
H. 16, 26, 26
J. 16, 34, 34
K. Cannot be determined from the given information

GO ON TO THE NEXT PAGE.

2          2

DO YOUR FIGURING HERE.

25. In the figure below, all of the small squares are equal in area, and the area of rectangle $ABCD$ is 1 square unit. Which of the following expressions represents the area, in square units, of the shaded region?

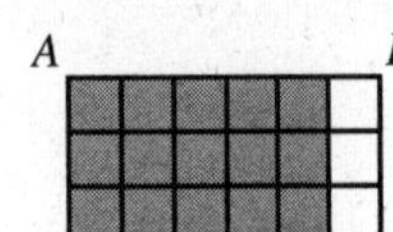

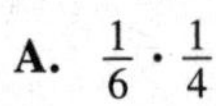

A. $\frac{1}{6} \cdot \frac{1}{4}$

B. $\frac{1}{6} \cdot \frac{3}{4}$

C. $\frac{1}{6} \cdot \frac{5}{6}$

D. $\frac{5}{6} \cdot \frac{1}{4}$

E. $\frac{5}{6} \cdot \frac{3}{4}$

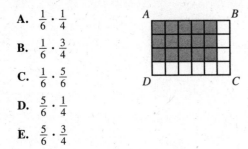

26. A bag contains 16 red marbles, 7 yellow marbles, and 19 green marbles. How many additional red marbles must be added to the 42 marbles already in the bag so that the probability of randomly drawing a red marble is $\frac{3}{5}$?

F. 18
G. 23
H. 37
J. 42
K. 52

27. For all $a > 0$, which of the following expressions is equal to a^{-2} ?

A. $-2a$

B. $-a^2$

C. $\frac{1}{2a}$

D. $\frac{1}{\sqrt{a}}$

E. $\frac{1}{a^2}$

28. Jamie claims, "If a triangle is in Set A, then it is not isosceles." Later, Jamie discovers that $\triangle MNP$ is a counterexample proving this claim false. Which of the following statements *must* be true about $\triangle MNP$?

F. It is isosceles and in Set A.
G. It is scalene and in Set A.
H. It is obtuse and not in Set A.
J. It is scalene and not in Set A.
K. It is isosceles and not in Set A.

GO ON TO THE NEXT PAGE.

2 △ △ △ △ △ △ △ △ △ 2

DO YOUR FIGURING HERE.

Use the following information to answer questions 29–32.

Parallelogram *ABCD* is graphed in the standard (x,y) coordinate plane below. Sides $\overline{AB}$ and $\overline{CD}$ are each $\sqrt{10}$ coordinate units long. Sides $\overline{AD}$ and $\overline{BC}$ are each 5 coordinate units long. The distance between $\overline{AD}$ and $\overline{BC}$ is 3 coordinate units.

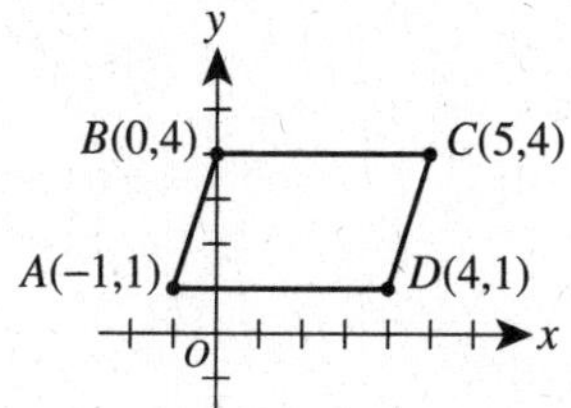

29. What is the area, in square coordinate units, of *ABCD* ?

A. 5
B. 7.5
C. 10
D. 15
E. 20

30. What is the distance, in coordinate units, from *B* to *D* ?

F. 3
G. 4
H. 5
J. 7
K. 8

31. What is the slope of $\overleftrightarrow{BC}$?

A. 0
B. 1
C. 4
D. 5
E. Undefined

32. Parallelogram *ABCD* will be reflected over the *y*-axis. What will be the coordinates of the image of *A* ?

F. (−4, 1)
G. (−1,−1)
H. (1,−1)
J. (1, 1)
K. (4,−1)

---

33. Which of the following is equivalent to $8^2 \cdot 4^{0.5}$?

A. 2^7
B. $4^{4.5}$
C. $8^{2.5}$
D. 16^2
E. 32

GO ON TO THE NEXT PAGE.

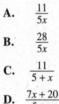

2 △ △ △ △ △ △ △ △ △ 2

DO YOUR FIGURING HERE.

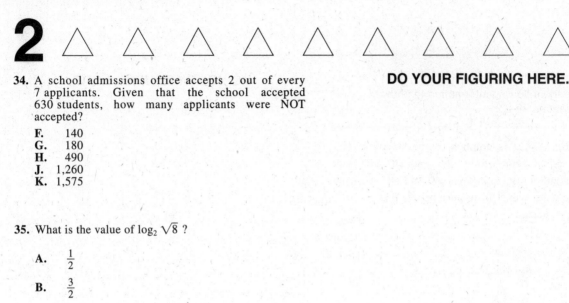

34. A school admissions office accepts 2 out of every 7 applicants. Given that the school accepted 630 students, how many applicants were NOT accepted?

F. 140
G. 180
H. 490
J. 1,260
K. 1,575

35. What is the value of $\log_2 \sqrt{8}$?

A. $\frac{1}{2}$

B. $\frac{3}{2}$

C. $\sqrt{2}$

D. 1

E. 3

36. Jie asked 90 students to choose 1 favorite fruit from 4 options. Jie has begun to represent the results in the circle graph below. Peaches were chosen as the favorite of 15 students. Apples, bananas, and strawberries were each chosen as favorites by an equal number of the remaining students. What must be the measure of the central angle in the circle graph for bananas?

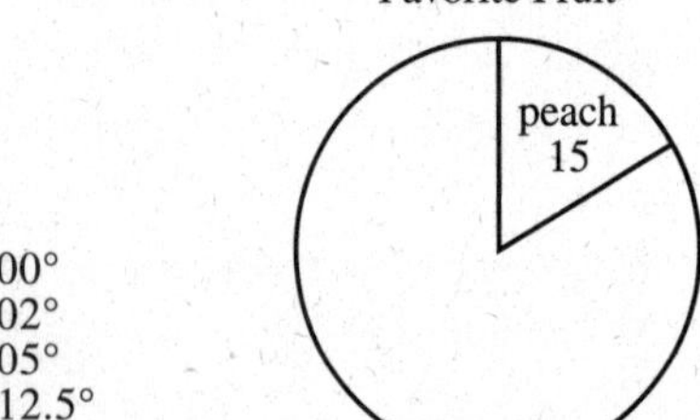

F. 100°
G. 102°
H. 105°
J. 112.5°
K. 115°

37. For all real numbers x such that $x \neq 0$, $\frac{4}{5} + \frac{7}{x} = ?$

A. $\frac{11}{5x}$

B. $\frac{28}{5x}$

C. $\frac{11}{5+x}$

D. $\frac{7x+20}{5+x}$

E. $\frac{4x+35}{5x}$

GO ON TO THE NEXT PAGE.

2 △ △ △ △ △ △ △ △ △ 2

Use the following information to answer questions 38–40.

DO YOUR FIGURING HERE.

The Harrisburg Recreation Center recently changed its hours to open 1 hour later and close 3 hours later than it had previously. Residents of Harrisburg age 16 or older were given a survey, and 560 residents replied. The survey asked each resident his or her student status (high school, college, or nonstudent) and what he or she thought about the change in hours (approve, disapprove, or no opinion). The results are summarized in the table below.

Student status	Approve	Disapprove	No opinion
High school	30	4	11
College	14	10	6
Nonstudent	85	353	47
Total	129	367	64

38. What fraction of these nonstudent residents replied that they disapproved of the change in hours?

F. $\frac{1}{3}$

G. $\frac{4}{45}$

H. $\frac{14}{75}$

J. $\frac{353}{367}$

K. $\frac{353}{485}$

39. Suppose a person will be chosen at random from these 560 residents. Which of the following values is closest to the probability that the person chosen will NOT be a high school student and will NOT have replied with no opinion?

A. 0.06
B. 0.09
C. 0.44
D. 0.83
E. 0.98

40. After constructing the table, it was discovered that the student status of 15 residents who replied that they approved had been incorrectly classified as nonstudents. After correcting the errors, exactly 60% of the college students had replied that they approved. To the nearest 1%, what percent of high school students replied that they approved?

F. 60%
G. 67%
H. 70%
J. 75%
K. 82%

GO ON TO THE NEXT PAGE.

2 △ △ △ △ △ △ △ △ △ 2

41. Set A and Set B each consist of 5 distinct numbers. The 2 sets contain identical numbers with the exception of the number with the least value in each set. The number with the least value in Set B is greater than the number with the least value in Set A. The value of which of the following measures *must* be greater for Set B than for Set A ?

A. Mean only
B. Median only
C. Mode only
D. Mean and median only
E. Mean, median, and mode

DO YOUR FIGURING HERE.

42. For all x such that $0 \le x \le 90$, which of the following expressions is NOT equal to $\sin x°$?

F. $-\sin(-x°)$

G. $\sin(-x°)$

H. $\cos(90 - x)°$

J. $\cos(x - 90)°$

K. $\sqrt{1 - (\cos x°)^2}$

43. A 3-inch-tall rectangular box with a square base is constructed to hold a circular pie that has a diameter of 8 inches. Both are shown below. What is the volume, in cubic inches, of the smallest such box that can hold this pie?

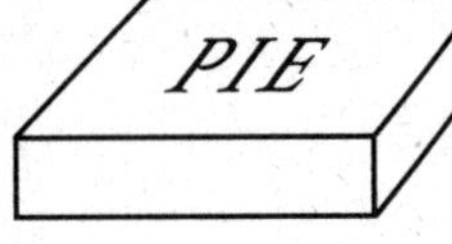

8

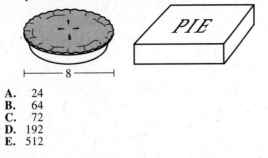

A. 24
B. 64
C. 72
D. 192
E. 512

44. Quadrilateral $ABCD$ is shown in the figure below with the lengths of the 4 sides given in meters. The measure of $\angle C$ is 90°. What is $\tan A$?

B, 4, 13, C, A, 3, 12, D

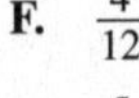

F. $\frac{4}{12}$

G. $\frac{5}{12}$

H. $\frac{4}{13}$

J. $\frac{5}{13}$

K. $\frac{12}{13}$

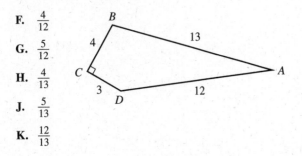

GO ON TO THE NEXT PAGE.

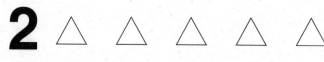

2 △ △ △ △ △ △ △ △ △ 2

45. Given today is Tuesday, what day of the week was it 200 days ago?

A. Monday
B. Tuesday
C. Wednesday
D. Friday
E. Saturday

DO YOUR FIGURING HERE.

46. In the figure below, line m is perpendicular to line n, and both lines intersect line q at the same point. The measure of $\angle 1$ is $(3x - 10)°$, and the measure of $\angle 2$ is $(2x + 10)°$. What is the measure of $\angle 3$?

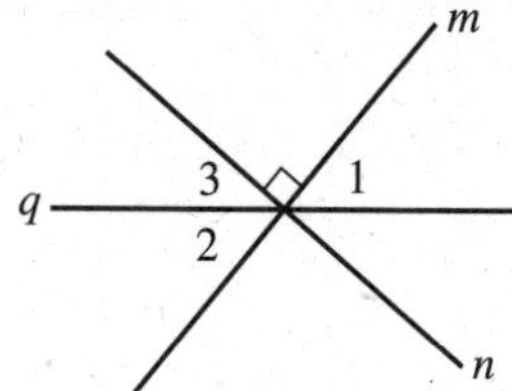

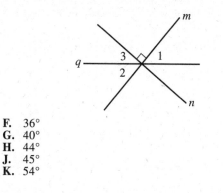

F. 36°
G. 40°
H. 44°
J. 45°
K. 54°

47. The greatest common factor of 2 whole numbers is 10. The least common multiple of these same 2 numbers is 120. What are the 2 numbers?

A. 6 and 20
B. 10 and 12
C. 10 and 20
D. 20 and 60
E. 30 and 40

48. The side lengths of a certain triangle are 4, 5, and 7 centimeters. Which of the following descriptions best classifies this triangle?

F. Scalene acute
G. Scalene right
H. Scalene obtuse
J. Isosceles obtuse
K. Isosceles right

49. A professional baseball team will play 1 game Saturday and 1 game Sunday. A sportswriter estimates the team has a 60% chance of winning on Saturday but only a 35% chance of winning on Sunday. Using the sportswriter's estimates, what is the probability that the team will *lose* both games?

(Note: Neither game can result in a tie.)

A. 14%
B. 21%
C. 25%
D. 26%
E. 39%

Taking Additional Practice Tests

GO ON TO THE NEXT PAGE.

2        2

50. The graph of $f(x) = \dfrac{x-3}{x^2-2x-3}$ is shown below. What is the domain of $f(x)$?

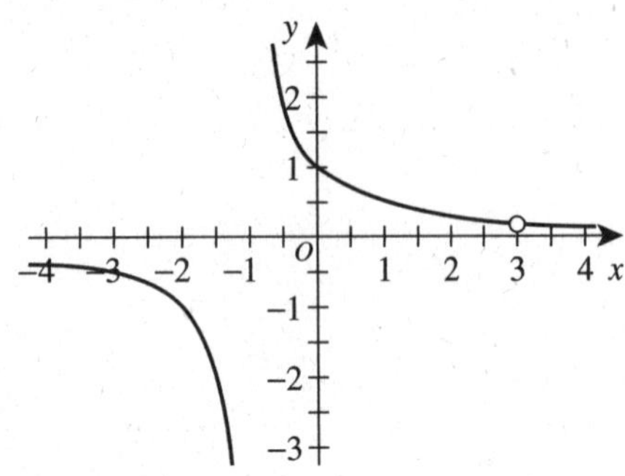

F. $\{x \mid x \neq -1\}$
G. $\{x \mid x \neq 2\}$
H. $\{x \mid x \neq 3\}$
J. $\{x \mid x \neq -1 \text{ and } x \neq 3\}$
K. $\{x \mid x \neq 0 \text{ and } x \neq 2\}$

51. Get-A-Great-Read Books is adding a new phone line. The phone company says that the first 3 digits of the phone number must be 555, but the remaining 4 digits, where each digit is a digit from 0 through 9, can be chosen by Get-A-Great-Read Books. How many phone numbers are possible?

A. $5(9^4)$
B. $5^3(9^4)$
C. $5^3(10^4)$
D. 9^4
E. 10^4

52. In the standard (x,y) coordinate plane, the circle centered at (1,3) that passes through (4,7) is the set of all points that are:

F. 5 coordinate units from (1,3).
G. 5 coordinate units from both (1,3) and (4,7).
H. 5 coordinate units from the line segment with endpoints (1,3) and (4,7).
J. equidistant from (1,3) and (4,7).
K. equidistant from the line segment with endpoints (1,3) and (4,7).

53. Which of the following values is the x-coordinate of the point in the standard (x,y) coordinate plane where the graph of the line $y = 7$ intersects the graph of the function $y = \ln(x-2) + 3$?

A. 6
B. $e^4 + 2$
C. $4e + 2$
D. $\ln(4) + 2$
E. $\ln(5) + 3$

GO ON TO THE NEXT PAGE.

2 △ △ △ △ △ △ △ △ △ 2

54. Three copy machines—A, B, and C—copy at the same rate and will all be used to make copies of a report. At 8:00 a.m., all 3 machines begin copying. Machine A breaks down at 10:00 a.m. and is back in service at 1:00 p.m. Machine B breaks down at 12:00 p.m. (noon) and begins copying again at 3:00 p.m. All 3 machines finish copying at 5:00 p.m. when the copying of the report is complete. One of the following graphs shows n, the number of copies made, as a function of t, the time at any given point during the copying. Which graph is it?

DO YOUR FIGURING HERE.

F. 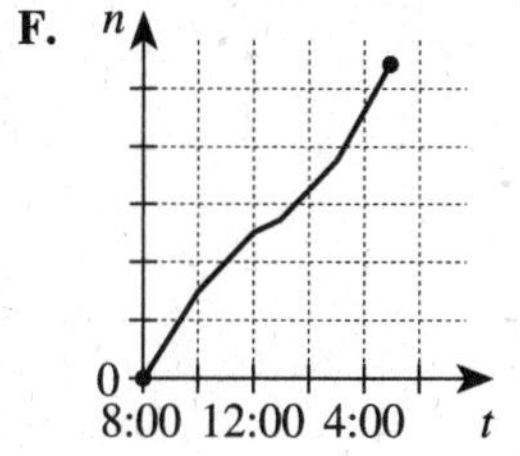

J. 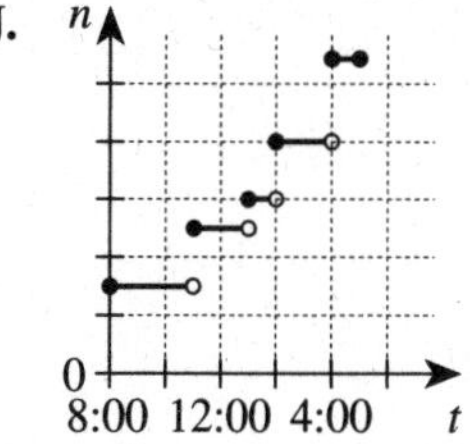

G. 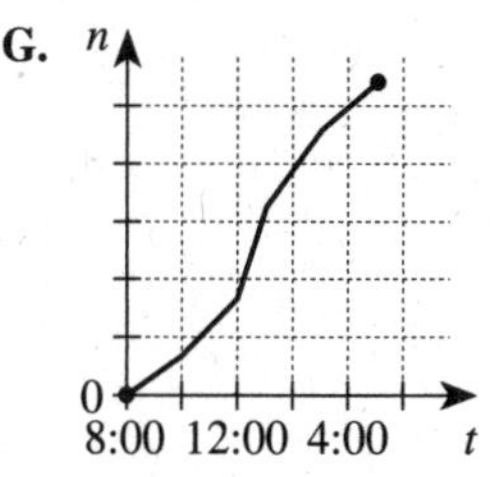

K. 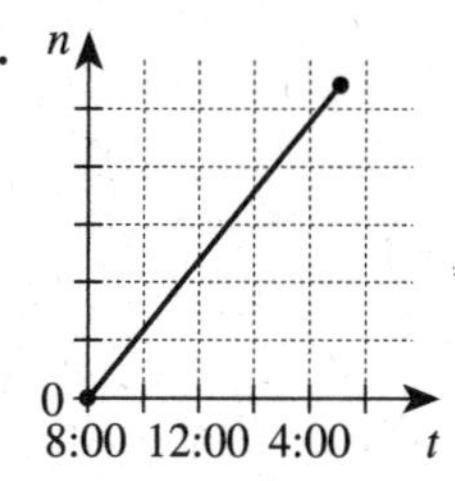

H. 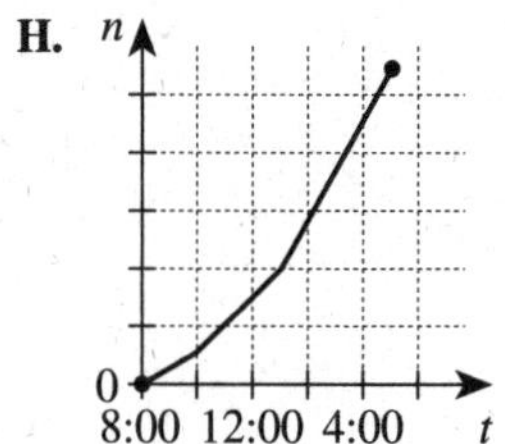

55. A sporting-goods store sells baseball caps for \$22 each. At this price, 40 caps are sold per week. For every \$1 decrease in price, the store will sell 4 more caps per week. The store will adjust the price to maximize revenue. What will be the maximum possible revenue for 1 week?

(Note: The revenue equals the number of caps sold times the price per cap.)

A. \$ 880
B. \$ 882
C. \$ 924
D. \$ 960
E. \$1,024

Taking Additional Practice Tests

GO ON TO THE NEXT PAGE.

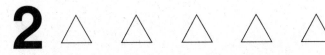

2 △ △ △ △ △ △ △ △ △ 2

56. Each of the following graphs in the standard (x,y) coordinate plane has the same scale on both axes. One graph is the graph of $ax + by \le c$, where $0 < a < b < c$. Which one is it?

DO YOUR FIGURING HERE.

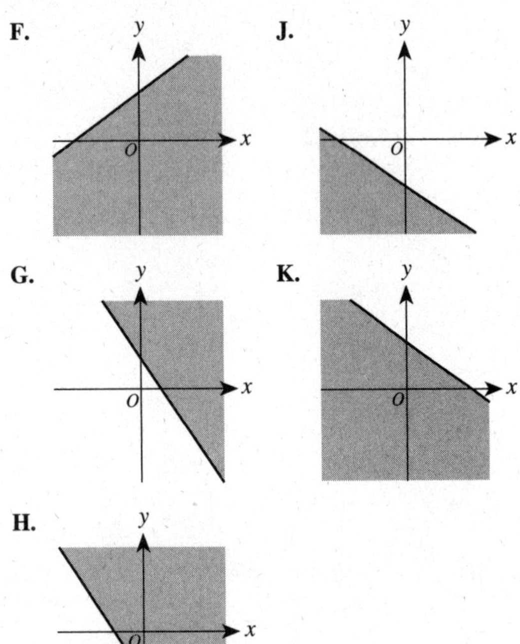

57. The art club designed and made banners of the school colors, blue and white, for their fund-raiser. Each banner required $\frac{1}{4}$ yard of blue material and $\frac{3}{8}$ yard of white material. The club originally planned to purchase exactly enough material to make 500 banners, but found the material to be cheaper if purchased in full bolts—the blue material in 10-yard bolts and the white material in 12-yard bolts. How many extra banners was the club able to make if they purchased enough full bolts to make at least 500 banners?

A. 12
B. 13
C. 15
D. 16
E. 20

GO ON TO THE NEXT PAGE.

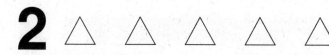

2 △ △ △ △ △ △ △ △ △ 2

DO YOUR FIGURING HERE.

58. For all real numbers x and the imaginary number i, which of the following expressions is equivalent to $(x - 3i)^3$?

F. $x^3 - 9x^2i - 27x + 27i$
G. $x^3 + 9x^2i - 27x - 27i$
H. $x^3 + 3x^2i - 9x - 27i$
J. $x^3 - 3x^2i - 9x + 27i$
K. $x^3 + 27i$

59. The graph in the standard (x,y) coordinate plane below is the graph of one of the following functions. Which one?

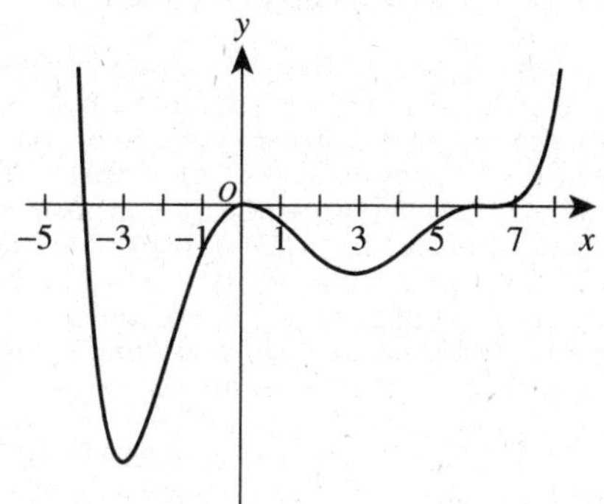

A. $g(x) = x(x - 6)(x + 4)$
B. $h(x) = x^2(x + 6)(x - 4)$
C. $n(x) = x^2(x + 6)^3(x - 4)$
D. $p(x) = x^2(x - 6)^3(x + 4)$
E. $q(x) = x^3(x - 6)^2(x + 4)$

60. The table below shows the numbers of rows and columns in each of 5 matrices.

Matrix	Number of rows	Number of columns
A	m	n
B	m	m
C	k	n
D	m	k
E	n	m

For distinct values of k, m, and n, which of the following matrix products is NOT possible?

F. ED
G. DC
H. CE
J. AE
K. AC

Taking Additional Practice Tests

END OF TEST 2

STOP! DO NOT TURN THE PAGE UNTIL TOLD TO DO SO.

DO NOT RETURN TO THE PREVIOUS TEST.

3 3

READING TEST

35 Minutes—40 Questions

DIRECTIONS: There are several passages in this test. Each passage is accompanied by several questions. After reading a passage, choose the best answer to each question and fill in the corresponding oval on your answer document. You may refer to the passages as often as necessary.

Passage I

LITERARY NARRATIVE: Passage A is adapted from the short story "Leaving Memphis" by Lauren Birden (©2008 by Narrative Magazine, Inc.). Passage B is adapted from the short story "Mandarins" by Ryunosuke Akutagawa (©2006 by Fiction, Inc.).

Passage A by Lauren Birden

You see her first in the Memphis bus station on a two-hour layover. You pretend you haven't because she looks ready to talk. "Stonewashed jeans," you think, watching her tap her platform sandals at the front of the boarding line. When she catches you staring, you pull your lips tight and stare at the floor in front of her. She starts toward you anyway. She plops down in the hard plastic seat next to you, moving her purse to her lap. You motion to your open novel and shrug as if to say, "Can't stop now," but she asks, "Where you from?" and now you can't shake her.

You're not a bad person. You just wish Greyhound assigned seating. It's not the straw-blond hair teased up around her face, not even the sad, neglected teeth that make you want to turn off the overhead reading lamp and smile at her in the dark. "I have a sneaking suspicion that we're the same person," she says, and you say, "That's funny," because you know you've been inventing yourself this whole time. She smiles and waits for you to agree how similar the two of you are.

She tells you about the man she's taking the bus to see. "Left for a construction job in Palm Beach. Says my eyes are as blue as the Atlantic Ocean, and he can't bear to look at the thing but one more time if I'm not there with him. You can't trust a man with a gun or a heart, but he swears he loves me." She waits for you to tell her of a better love. You can't think of a story to compare.

She says, "We're the same person." She's waiting for you to tell her yes, that you both have had the same heartache and know about scars and love the same. But you're thinking at the window again as a radio tower passes that reminds you of the Eiffel Tower.

Firefly porch lights are perched, fat and throbbing, outside every occasional home you pass. You say, "You know, you're so very right," and then, nothing more. The woman resigns herself to turning away in the quiet. You're telling the truth for once.

Passage B by Ryunosuke Akutagawa

Evening was falling one cloud-covered winter's day, as I boarded a Tokyo-bound train departing from Yokosuka. I found a seat in the corner, sat down, and leaned my head back against the window frame, half-consciously watching for the station to recede slowly into the distance. But then I heard coming from the ticket-gate the clattering of dry-weather clogs, followed immediately by the cursing of the conductor. The door of the second-class carriage was flung open, and a 13- or 14-year-old girl came bursting in.

At that moment, with a shudder, the train began to lumber slowly forward. I raised my eyes to look for the first time at the girl seated now on the opposite side. She wore her lusterless hair drawn up into a bun, in the traditional shape of a gingko leaf. Apparently from constant rubbing of her nose and mouth with the back of her hand, her cheeks were chapped and red. A grimy woolen scarf of yellowish green hung loosely down to her knees, on which she held a large bundle wrapped in cloth. To blot her existence, I took out my newspaper, and began to read.

The girl feverishly endeavored to open the window, the glass apparently proving to be too heavy for her. Gazing coldly at her desperate struggle as she fought with chilled hands, I hoped that she would fail, and at that very moment, the window at last came down with a thud. I would surely have barked at this unknown girl to reclose the window, had it not been for the outside view, which was now growing ever brighter, and for the smell, borne in on the cold air, of earth, dry grass, and water.

Just then I saw standing behind the barrier of a desolate crossing three red-cheeked boys. Looking up to see the train as it passed, they raised their hands as one and let out with all the strength of their young voices a high pitched cheer. And at that instant the girl, the full upper half of her body leaning out of the window, abruptly extended her hands and began moving them briskly left and right. Five or six mandarin oranges, radiating the color of the warm sun and filling my heart with sudden joy, descended on the children standing there to greet the passing train.

I knew immediately the meaning of it all. This girl, perhaps leaving home now to go into service as a

GO ON TO THE NEXT PAGE.

3 3

maid or an apprentice, had been carrying in her bundle these oranges and tossed them to her younger brothers as a token of gratitude for coming to see her off.

Elated, I raised my head and gazed at the girl with very different eyes. For the first time I was able to forget, at least for a moment, my unspeakable fatigue and this tedious life.

Questions 1–3 ask about Passage A.

1. Which of the following questions is specifically answered in Passage A?

A. Why is the character referred to as "you" leaving Memphis?
B. Why is the blond woman traveling to Palm Beach?
C. What is the blond woman thinking about at the end of the passage?
D. Where is the blond woman from originally?

2. As they are used in line 24, what do the words *the thing* refer to?

F. A construction job
G. The blond woman's eyes
H. The Atlantic Ocean
J. A bus

3. As it is used in line 35, the phrase "every occasional home" most nearly suggests that on the bus trip, the main characters of Passage A are passing through an area in which:

A. the porches of some homes intermittently glow from the light of fireflies.
B. most homes do not have a porch light on.
C. particularly large and bright fireflies swarm around a few of the homes.
D. the few homes built there are situated far apart.

Questions 4–7 ask about Passage B.

4. Throughout Passage B, the girl's reaction to the narrator is to:

F. pay no attention to him.
G. engage him in conversation.
H. view him as an annoying intruder.
J. express surprise to discover she's not alone.

5. The narrator of Passage B hopes that the girl will fail at opening the window. Based on Passage B as a whole, this hope most strongly captures the:

A. girl's helplessness and her uncertain future.
B. narrator's typical foul mood and dark state of mind.
C. three young boys' pleasure in seeing their sister off.
D. train conductor's impatience with the girl's behavior.

6. It can most reasonably be inferred from Passage B that the girl frantically tries to open the window because she needs to:

F. be able to throw oranges to her brothers.
G. prove to herself that she would be able to open the heavy window in an emergency.
H. create space between herself and the narrator.
J. freshen the stagnant air in the train with a cool breeze.

7. In Passage B, which of the following pairs of actions most clearly cues the narrator that someone is about to board the train at the last minute?

A. The cursing of the conductor and the screech of the train's brakes
B. The bursting open of the second-class-carriage door and the rustle of paper parcels
C. The clattering of clogs and the cursing of the conductor
D. The shouting of a young girl and the clattering of clogs

Questions 8–10 ask about both passages.

8. Which of the following elements is most clearly similar in the two passages?

F. The occasional use of the second person point of view
G. The time period in which each passage is set
H. The inclusion of key bits of dialogue between characters
J. The situational premise of the plot

9. Among the characters in both passages, which one is portrayed as being most interested in having a conversation?

A. "You"
B. The 13- or 14-year-old girl
C. The narrator of Passage B
D. The blond woman

10. Which of the following statements best describes how both "you" of Passage A and the narrator of Passage B react when they first see the blond woman and the young girl, respectively?

F. They consider the other character to be somewhat pitiful looking.
G. They are angry that the other character has delayed their departure.
H. They are surprised by the other character's reason for traveling.
J. They believe the other character is enviable because life seems so easy for her.

GO ON TO THE NEXT PAGE.

3 3

Passage II

SOCIAL SCIENCE: This passage is adapted from the article "Travels with R.L.S." by James Campbell (©2000 by The New York Times Company).

Robert Louis Stevenson (1850–1894) preferred to circumnavigate civilization, with its increasing reliance on contraptions, and steer toward the rougher fringes. He self-consciously turned his back on the Victorian idol, progress. In similar spirit, he chose the past more often than the present as a setting for fiction. His most popular novels—*Treasure Island, Kidnapped, The Master of Ballantrae*—are set in a semimythical realm, where the fire of adventure catches on every page. Stevenson loved the sound of clashing swords; he didn't want them getting tangled up in telephone wires overhead.

Stevenson, though, was destined to be a modern man. He was born into a Scottish family of civil engineers, esteemed for its technological genius. His grandfather, also Robert, was Britain's greatest builder of lighthouses, and his graceful towers continue to guide sailors today. Three of Robert's sons followed him into the profession, including Robert Louis Stevenson's father, Thomas, who made his own mark in the field of optics—his louvre-boarded screens for the protection of thermometers are still in use today.

It was expected that Robert Louis would enter the family business in turn, and a great wringing of hands greeted his announcement to the contrary. He told his father that he wanted to be a writer, which Thomas Stevenson regarded as no profession at all. We can imagine the consternation when Stevenson's letters arrived bearing pleas such as "Take me as I am . . . I *must* be a bit of a vagabond." And a vagabond was precisely what he set out to be: longhaired, careless about food, walking through France or planning an epic ocean voyage, a far cry from the offices of D. & T. Stevenson, Engineers. He was forging the template for generations of college-educated adventurers to come. "I travel not to go anywhere, but to go," he wrote in *Travels With a Donkey* (1879). "I travel for travel's sake. The great affair is to move."

Stevenson would not be an engineer, but he left his own lights, in Scotland and across the world, by which it is possible to trace his unceasing movement. No other writer, surely, is as much memorialized by the words "lived here" as he is. There are five houses with Stevenson associations in Edinburgh alone, not to mention the little schoolhouse he attended as a child and the lavish gardens opposite the family home in Heriot Row, where he played and, the fanciful will have you believe, first acted out the quest for Treasure Island. I have shadowed Stevenson up to the northeast of Scotland, where he tried his hand at being an apprentice engineer, back down to the Hawes Inn at South Queensferry, where David Balfour is tricked into going to sea in *Kidnapped*. There are landmarks in Switzerland, France and on the Pacific Islands where the adventure of his final years took place.

Recently, I stumbled across Abernethy House where Stevenson lived briefly in London when he was 23. It stands in a secluded corner of Hampstead, high up on a hill, and separated from foggy London by farms and heath. It was while standing on Hampstead Hill one night that he gazed down on London and imagined a technological miracle of the future, "when in a moment, in the twinkling of an eye, the design of the monstrous city flashes into vision—a glittering hieroglyph." He is anticipating the effects of electricity and a time when the streetlamps would be lighted "not one by one" by the faithful old lamplighter, but all at once, by the touch of a button. Not for him improvements in optics; give him the flickering gas lamp and the "skirts of civilization" any day.

Lamps occur frequently in Stevenson's writing. There are the essays "A Plea for Gas Lamps" and "The Lantern Bearers," and his poem for children, "The Lamplighter," which celebrates an old custom: "For we are very lucky, with a lamp before the door, / And Leerie stops to light it as he lights so many more." Then there is his memoir in which he describes how, when a child and sick, his nurse would take him to the window, "whence I might look forth into the blue night starred with street lamps, and see where the gas still burned behind the windows of other sickrooms." And the lights shine again, with a subdued glow, in the obituary he wrote of his father. Thomas Stevenson's name may not have been widely known, yet "all the time, his lights were in every part of the world, guiding the mariner."

A year later, Stevenson chartered a schooner and became a mariner himself, sailing circuitously through the South Seas. He had, in a sense, entered the family business at last.

11. As it is used in line 3, the phrase "the rougher fringes" most nearly means the same as which of the following phrases?

A. "The fire of adventure" (line 9)
B. "An epic ocean voyage" (lines 32–33)
C. "A glittering hieroglyph" (line 64)
D. "Skirts of civilization" (lines 69–70)

12. It can reasonably be concluded that the passage author is a credible source of biographical information about Stevenson because the passage author:

F. traveled to several towns and countries where Stevenson lived and worked to research him.
G. has read Stevenson's two most popular novels, *Kidnapped* and *Treasure Island*.
H. worked for a time in the offices of D. & T. Stevenson, Engineers, as Stevenson had.
J. comes from Edinburgh, where the adventure of Stevenson's final years took place.

GO ON TO THE NEXT PAGE.

3 3

13. The main idea of the second paragraph (lines 13–22) is that:

A. Stevenson's grandfather insisted his sons become educated in civil engineering.
B. Stevenson was a modern man whose engineering talents were suppressed by his desire to be a writer.
C. Stevenson's father earned greater esteem for his louvre-boarded screens than Stevenson's grandfather did for his lighthouses.
D. Stevenson was the grandson, son, and nephew of men respected for their technological genius.

14. The main idea of the fifth paragraph (lines 56–70) is that:

F. the plot of one of Stevenson's books was inspired by his vision of electric lights in London.
G. Stevenson envisioned the use of electric streetlights in London before they became reality.
H. Stevenson longed for a time when electricity would replace flickering gas lamps.
J. Stevenson realized that his father's improvements in optics would become the "technological miracle of the future."

15. According to the passage, which of the professions listed below did Stevenson enter into?

I. Apprentice engineer
II. Lamplighter
III. Mariner
IV. Writer
V. Builder

A. IV only
B. I, II, and IV only
C. I, III, and IV only
D. III, IV, and V only

16. The passage author most likely uses the description in lines 10–12 in order to:

F. emphasize how little technological progress had taken place during Stevenson's lifetime.
G. stress that Stevenson was increasingly dependent on modern inventions.
H. create a visual image that helps make Stevenson's opinion about progress more vivid.
J. illustrate that Stevenson was an avid sword fighter.

17. As it is used in line 24, the phrase "a great wringing of hands" most nearly refers to the Stevenson family's:

A. dismay over Stevenson's announcement that he wasn't joining the family business.
B. disapproval of Stevenson's slovenly appearance and poor diet.
C. humiliation at Stevenson publicly renouncing the family business in favor of traveling.
D. consternation at receiving Stevenson's letters pleading to have his family accept his choice.

18. It can most reasonably be inferred from the passage that as a traveler, Stevenson:

F. thought reaching the destination was what made the trip worthwhile.
G. encouraged other young men to take up traveling rather than pursue an education.
H. was searching for a model for the character David Balfour in *Kidnapped*.
J. was happiest when he was on an adventure with no itinerary.

19. As it is used in line 56, the phrase *stumbled across* most nearly means:

A. found by accident.
B. staggered toward.
C. unearthed.
D. tripped over.

20. According to the passage, at the time of his death, Thomas Stevenson was:

F. estranged from Robert Louis, who had refused to join the family business.
G. unaware that his name would become associated with lighthouses.
H. more famous than his son, who was by that time a popular author.
J. not widely known himself, but the results of his work were familiar the world over.

GO ON TO THE NEXT PAGE.

3 3

Passage III

HUMANITIES: This passage is adapted from the article "Proceed with Caution: Using Native American Folktales in the Classroom" by Debbie Reese (©2007 by the National Council of Teachers of English).

Traditional stories include myths, legends, and folktales rooted in the oral storytelling traditions of a given people. Through story, people pass their religious beliefs, customs, history, lifestyle, language, values, and the places they hold sacred from one generation to the next. As such, stories and their telling are more than simple entertainment. They matter—in significant ways—to the well-being of the communities from which they originate. Acclaimed Laguna Pueblo writer Leslie Marmon Silko writes that the oral narrative, or story, was the medium by which the Pueblo people transmitted "an entire culture, a worldview complete with proven strategies for survival." In her discussion of hunting stories, she says:

> These accounts contained information of critical importance about the behavior and migration patterns of mule deer. Hunting stories carefully described key landmarks and locations of fresh water. Thus, a deer-hunt story might also serve as a map. Lost travelers and lost piñon-nut gatherers have been saved by sighting a rock formation they recognize only because they once heard a hunting story describing this rock formation.

Similarly, children's book author Joseph Bruchac writes,

> . . . rather than being 'mere myths,' with 'myth' being used in the pejorative sense of 'untruth,' those ancient traditional tales were a distillation of the deep knowledge held by the many Native American nations about the workings of the world around them.

Thus, storytelling is a means of passing along information, but it does not mean there is only one correct version of any given story. During a telling, listeners can speak up if they feel an important fact or detail was omitted, or want to offer a different version of the story. In this way, the people seek or arrive at a communal truth rather than an absolute truth. A storyteller may revise a story according to his or her own interpretation, or according to the knowledge of the audience, but in order for it to be acceptable to the group from which the story originated, it should remain true to the spirit and content of the original.

Traditional stories originate from a specific people, and we expect them to accurately reflect those people, but do they? As a Pueblo Indian woman, I wonder, what do our stories look like when they are retold outside our communities, in picture book format, and marketed as "Native American folktales" for children? Are our religious, cultural, and social values presented accurately? Are children who read these folktales learning anything useful about us?

Much of what I bring to bear on my research emanates from my cultural lens and identity as a Pueblo Indian woman from Nambe Pueblo. I was born at the Indian hospital in Santa Fe, New Mexico, and raised on our reservation. As a Pueblo Indian child, I was given a Tewa (our language) name and taught to dance. I went to religious ceremonies and gatherings, and I learned how to do a range of things that we do as Pueblo people. This childhood provided me with "cultural intuition." Cultural intuition is that body of knowledge anyone acquires based upon their lived experiences in a specific place. As a scholar in American Indian studies, I know there are great distinctions between and across American Indian tribal nations. For instance, my home pueblo is very different from the other pueblos in New Mexico, among which there are several different language groups.

I draw upon both my cultural intuition and knowledge when reading a book about Pueblo Indians. For example, when I read Gerald McDermott's *Arrow to the Sun: A Pueblo Indian Tale* (1974), I wondered what Pueblo the book is about. There are 19 different Pueblos in New Mexico, and more in Arizona. In which Pueblo did this story originate? That information is not included anywhere in the book, and there are other problems as well. In the climax of the story, the boy must prove himself by passing through "the Kiva of Lions, the Kiva of Serpents, the Kiva of Bees, and the Kiva of Lightning" where he fights those elements. McDermott's kivas are frightening places of trial and battle, but I know kivas are safe places of worship and instruction.

Depictions that are culturally acceptable at one Pueblo are not necessarily acceptable at a different Pueblo. As such, elders at one Pueblo would say the book could be used with their children, while elders at another Pueblo would disagree. This is not a question of cultural authenticity; it is one of appropriateness in teaching, given a specific audience.

21. The passage author's reaction to which of the following experiences best exemplifies the point that she brings her own cultural intuition to her reading and research?

A. Learning about Bruchac's perspective on ancient traditional tales
B. Reading a portrayal of kivas in a Pueblo book
C. Presenting her research to a Pueblo community other than her own
D. Discussing the oral narrative with Silko

GO ON TO THE NEXT PAGE.

3 3

22. The main purpose of the first paragraph (lines 1–24) is to:
    F. explain how traditional stories change as they are passed from one generation to the next.
    G. discuss the value of traditional stories and their functions within a community.
    H. contrast the purposes of folktales with those of myths and legends.
    J. demonstrate that folktales measure how a culture's worldview has changed over time.

23. The passage author most strongly suggests that a particular group would deem one of its own stories to be unacceptable if, during a telling, the storyteller:
    A. incorporated new details into the story.
    B. used his or her own experiences to interpret one event in the story.
    C. agreed with an audience member's adding a detail to the story.
    D. significantly changed the spirit of the story.

24. One function of the passage author's statement that her home pueblo is very different from the other pueblos in New Mexico is to:
    F. describe the culture and traditions of her home pueblo.
    G. help support her later analysis and critique of McDermott's book.
    H. directly compare the stories of several American Indian tribal nations to those of her tribe.
    J. list the criteria she uses to evaluate books marketed as "Native American folktales."

25. The passage author most strongly implies that whether Pueblo elders will approve a book for the children of their community depends on the book's:
    A. entertainment value compared to similar books.
    B. popularity among other tribal members.
    C. appropriateness and relevance to that community's cultural values.
    D. successful representation of the worldview of many cultural groups.

26. As she is presented in the passage, Silko indicates that one purpose of Laguna Pueblo hunting stories was to help hunters:
    F. locate and rescue lost hunters from other tribes.
    G. document the number of successful hunts from one season to the next.
    H. identify the behavior and migration patterns of game.
    J. find caches of food by following trails made by piñon-nut gatherers.

27. The passage author most directly connects her knowledge of the distinctions between and across American Indian tribal nations to her experiences as:
    A. a scholar in American Indian studies.
    B. a friend of McDermott.
    C. an editor of picture books marketed as "Native American folktales."
    D. an elder in her Nambe Pueblo community.

28. As it is used in line 66, the word *great* most nearly means:
    F. excessive.
    G. significant.
    H. exuberant.
    J. splendid.

29. Which of the following characteristics among the several Pueblo communities in New Mexico does the passage author most directly use as evidence of their diversity?
    A. Their vast geographic differences
    B. Their disparity in resources
    C. Their varied approaches to parenting
    D. Their several different language groups

30. The passage author states that kivas are places she associates with:
    F. fear and trial.
    G. mystery and excitement.
    H. rest and healing from illness.
    J. worship and instruction.

GO ON TO THE NEXT PAGE.

3 3

Passage IV

NATURAL SCIENCE: This passage is adapted from the article "The Asphalt Jungle" by Peter Del Tredici (©2010 by Natural History Magazine, Inc.).

The ecology of the city is defined not only by the cultivated plants that require maintenance and the protected remnants of natural landscapes, but also by the spontaneous vegetation that dominates the neglected interstices. Greenery fills the vacant spaces between our roads, homes, and businesses; lines ditches and chain-link fences; sprouts in sidewalk cracks and atop neglected rooftops. Some of those plants, such as box elder, quaking aspen, and riverside grape, are native species present before humans drastically altered the land. Others, including chicory, Japanese knotweed, and Norway maple, were brought in intentionally or unintentionally by people. And still others—among them common ragweed, path rush (*Juncus tenuis*), and tufted lovegrass (*Eragrostis pectinacea*)—arrived on their own, dispersed by wind, water, or wild animals. Such species grow and reproduce in many American cities without being planted or cared for. They can provide important ecological services at very little cost to taxpayers, and if left undisturbed long enough they may even develop into mature woodlands.

There is no denying that most people consider many such plants to be "weeds." From a utilitarian perspective, a weed is any plant that grows on its own where people do not want it to grow. From the biological perspective, weeds are opportunistic plants that are adapted to disturbance in all its myriad forms, from bulldozers to acid rain. Their pervasiveness in the urban environment is simply a reflection of the continual disruption that characterizes that habitat—they are not its cause. In an agricultural context, the competition of weeds with economic crops is the primary reason for controlling them. In an urban area, a weed is any plant growing where people are trying to cultivate something else, or keep clear of vegetation altogether. The complaints of city dwellers are usually based on aesthetics (the plants are perceived as ugly, or as signs of blight and neglect) or on security concerns (they shield human activity or provide habitat for vermin).

From a plant's perspective, it is not the density of the human population that defines the urban environment, but the abundance of paving (affecting access to soil and moisture) and prevalence of disturbance. In other words, a sidewalk crack is a sidewalk crack whether it is in a city or a suburb. Urbanization is a process, not a place—a process that tends to leave the soil in a compacted, impoverished, and often contaminated state.

The plants that grow and survive in derelict urban wastelands are famous (or infamous) for their ability to grow under extremely harsh conditions. Through a quirk of evolutionary fate, they developed traits in their native habitats that seem to have "preadapted" them to flourish in cities. One study, by biologist Jeremy T. Lundholm of St. Mary's University in Halifax, Nova Scotia, and his then student Ashley Marlin, concluded that many successful urban plants are native to exposed cliffs, disturbed rock outcrops, or dry grasslands, all of which are characterized by soils with a relatively high pH. Cities, with their tall, granite-faced buildings and concrete foundations, are in a sense the equivalent of the natural limestone cliff habitats where those species originated. Similarly, as the British ecologist and "lichen hunter" Oliver L. Gilbert noted in his classic book *The Ecology of Urban Habitats*, the increased use of deicing salts on our roads and highways has resulted in the development of microhabitats along their margins that are typically colonized by calcium-loving grassland species adapted to limestone soils or by salt-loving plants from coastal habitats.

In general, the successful urban plant needs to be *flexible* in all aspects of its life history, from seed germination through flowering and fruiting; *opportunistic* in its ability to take advantage of locally abundant resources that may be available for only a short time; and *tolerant* of the stressful growing conditions caused by an abundance of pavement and a paucity of soil. The plants that grow in our cities managed to survive the transition from one land use to another as cities developed. The sequence starts with native species adapted to ecological conditions before the city was built. Those are followed, more or less in order, by species preadapted to agriculture and pasturage, to pavement and compacted soil, to lawns and landscaping, to infrastructure edges and environmental pollution—and ultimately to vacant lots and rubble.

31. The passage as a whole can best be described as:

A. an argument for eradicating weeds in urban areas.
B. a discussion of the factors that contribute to the survival of weeds in urban environments.
C. a report on the need for increased vegetation in cities and suburbs.
D. a discussion of how environmentalists are changing their attitudes toward so-called weeds.

32. Based on how the following four perspectives are outlined in the second paragraph (lines 22–39), which one would the author most likely share?

F. A utilitarian perspective
G. An agricultural perspective
H. A biological perspective
J. A city dweller's perspective

33. It is reasonable to infer that, in the author's opinion, *spontaneous vegetation* (line 4) is most unlike which of the following types of plants mentioned in the passage?

A. Common ragweed (line 14)
B. Economic crops (line 32)
C. Urban plants (line 57)
D. Calcium-loving grassland species (lines 68–69)

GO ON TO THE NEXT PAGE.

3 3

34. Which of the following opinions regarding weeds adapting to rather than causing a changing habitat is most clearly implied by the passage?

F. Removing weeds from places they are considered undesirable is simpler than people realize.
G. Weeds have wrongly been blamed for contributing to certain kinds of deterioration in urban areas.
H. Changing people's minds about weeds has caused a pervasive acceptance of them in urban areas.
J. City vegetation reflects that the life cycle of weeds is simpler than that of cultivated plants.

35. As it is used in line 5, the word *greenery* most nearly refers to:

A. cultivated plants.
B. protected natural landscapes.
C. weeds.
D. crops.

36. Based on the passage, in comparison to Gilbert's observation in his book, the scientific study by Lundholm and Marlin can best be described as:

F. complementary; Gilbert reached a conclusion similar to the one reached by Lundholm and Marlin.
G. contrasting; Lundholm and Marlin conducted a more recent study that questions the note in Gilbert's book.
H. interdependent; Lundholm and Marlin used Gilbert's book as a foundation for their study.
J. irrelevant; Gilbert was studying the ecology of urban habitats, while Lundholm and Marlin studied natural environments with high pH soils.

37. The last paragraph most strongly suggests that the author's attitude toward so-called weeds in urban areas is one of:

A. alarm due to the threat they pose to native plants.
B. concern as he fears they will not survive in their new habitat.
C. annoyance over the manner in which they contribute to urban decay.
D. respect for their ability to adapt to a wide array of challenging conditions.

38. According to the passage, Norway maple was first brought into the urban environment by:

F. people.
G. wind.
H. water.
J. birds.

39. As it is used in lines 15–16, the phrase *on their own* most nearly means:

A. one at a time.
B. without human aid.
C. in a self-propelled fashion.
D. voluntarily.

40. According to the passage, if people stopped disturbing weeds in an urban environment, eventually the weeds might:

F. compete for space and start to die out.
G. enhance landscaped gardens.
H. dry out the soil.
J. develop into woodlands.

END OF TEST 3

STOP! DO NOT TURN THE PAGE UNTIL TOLD TO DO SO.

DO NOT RETURN TO A PREVIOUS TEST.

4 ○ ○ ○ ○ ○ ○ ○ ○ ○ 4

SCIENCE TEST

35 Minutes—40 Questions

DIRECTIONS: There are several passages in this test. Each passage is followed by several questions. After reading a passage, choose the best answer to each question and fill in the corresponding oval on your answer document. You may refer to the passages as often as necessary.

You are NOT permitted to use a calculator on this test.

Passage I

A teacher asked each of 4 students to describe the *molecular shape* (the geometrical arrangement of the atoms in a molecule) of each of 4 molecules: arsenic trifluoride (AsF_3), arsenic trichloride ($AsCl_3$), arsenic tribromide ($AsBr_3$), and arsenic triiodide (AsI_3).

Student 1

An AsF_3 molecule is *T-shaped*, with the As atom in the center. All the atoms in AsF_3 lie in the same plane, and there are 2 unique angles—90° and 180°—between adjacent As–F bonds (see Figure 1).

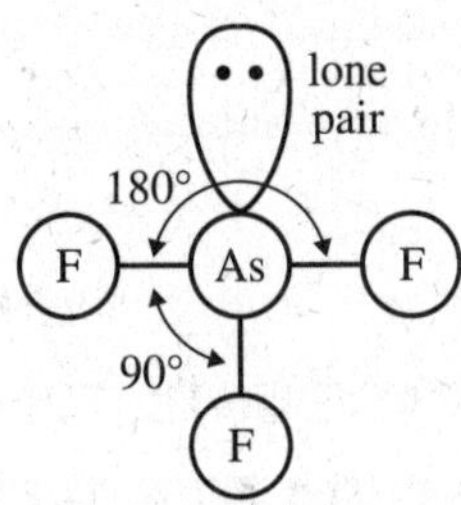

Figure 1

The As atom has a *lone pair* (an outer pair of electrons not involved in chemical bonding) that lies in the same plane as the As and F atoms. These electrons strongly repel the 3 As–F bonds, resulting in the 2 unique bond angles of 90° and 180°.

$AsCl_3$, $AsBr_3$, and AsI_3 are also T-shaped.

Student 2

The shape of an AsF_3 molecule is *trigonal planar*, with the As atom in the center. All the atoms in AsF_3 lie in the same plane, and there is only 1 unique angle—120°—between adjacent As–F bonds (see Figure 2).

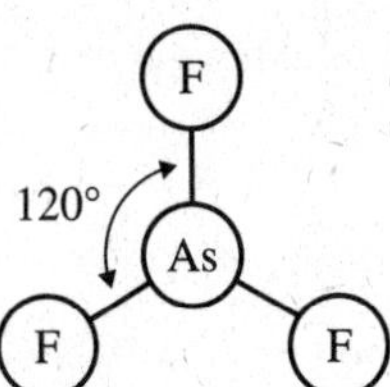

Figure 2

The As atom does not have a lone pair. The 3 As–F bonds repel each other equally, resulting in the 1 unique bond angle of 120°.

$AsCl_3$, $AsBr_3$, and AsI_3 are also trigonal planar.

Student 3

The shape of an AsF_3 molecule is *trigonal pyramidal*, with the As atom in the center. All the atoms in AsF_3 do not lie in the same plane, and there is only 1 unique angle—109°—between adjacent As–F bonds (see Figure 3).

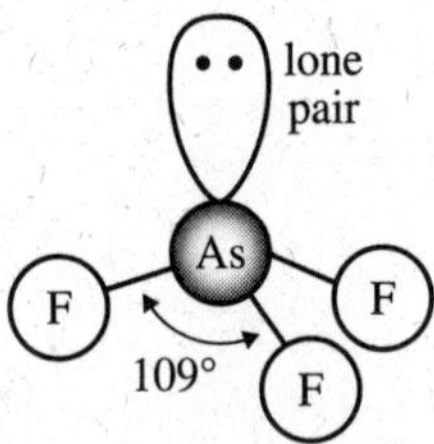

Figure 3

The As atom has a lone pair. The lone pair and the 3 As–F bonds repel each other equally, resulting in the 1 unique bond angle of 109°.

$AsCl_3$, $AsBr_3$, and AsI_3 are also trigonal pyramidal.

GO ON TO THE NEXT PAGE.

4 ○ ○ ○ ○ ○ ○ ○ ○ ○ 4

Student 4

Student 3 is correct that, due to the lone pair, AsF_3, $AsCl_3$, $AsBr_3$, and AsI_3 molecules are all trigonal pyramidal. AsF_3, $AsCl_3$, $AsBr_3$, and AsI_3 each have only 1 unique bond angle, but that bond angle is different for each of the 4 molecules. The bond angle depends on the size of the atom that is bound to the As atom: the larger the atom that is bound to the As atom, the larger the bond angle. The atoms bound to the As atom, listed by size from smallest to largest, are F, Cl, Br, and I.

After the 4 descriptions were offered, the teacher used a computer program that (1) determined that in each of the 4 molecules, there is only 1 unique bond angle and (2) calculated the bond angle for each molecule (see Table 1).

Table 1

Molecule	Calculated bond angle
AsF_3	100°
$AsCl_3$	101°
$AsBr_3$	103°
AsI_3	111°

Table adapted from Ian J. McNaught, "Testing and Extending VSEPR with WebMO and MOPAC or GAMESS." ©2011 by Division of Chemical Education, Inc., American Chemical Society.

1. The table below gives the atomic mass (in atomic mass units, amu) of the elements F, Cl, Br, and I.

Element	Atomic mass (amu)
F	19.00
Cl	35.45
Br	79.90
I	126.9

Based on Student 4's description, among the elements listed in the table, as atomic mass increases, *atomic radius*:

A. increases only.
B. decreases only.
C. increases, then decreases.
D. decreases, then increases.

2. Which of the students claimed that the As atom in an AsF_3 molecule has a lone pair?

F. Students 1 and 2 only
G. Students 3 and 4 only
H. Students 1, 3, and 4 only
J. Students 2, 3, and 4 only

3. Which of the students would be likely to agree with the statement "All 4 atoms in an AsF_3 molecule lie in the same plane"?

A. Student 1 only
B. Student 3 only
C. Students 1 and 2 only
D. Students 3 and 4 only

4. Consider the claim that there are 3 unique bond angles in an AsF_3 molecule. This claim is consistent with the description(s) given by which student(s), if any?

F. Student 2 only
G. Students 1 and 2 only
H. Students 3 and 4 only
J. None of the students

5. Based on the descriptions given by Students 1, 2, and 3, which of these students would be likely to agree that the sum of the 3 bond angles in an AsI_3 molecule is equal to 360° ?

A. Students 1 and 2 only
B. Students 1 and 3 only
C. Students 2 and 3 only
D. Students 1, 2, and 3

6. A molecule of ammonia (NH_3) has only 1 unique bond angle, and that bond angle is 107°. The N atom also has a lone pair that strongly repels the 3 N–H bonds. Based on the descriptions given by Students 2 and 3, is the molecular shape of NH_3 more likely trigonal planar or trigonal pyramidal?

F. Trigonal planar; the bond angle is more consistent with Student 2's description.
G. Trigonal planar; the bond angle is more consistent with Student 3's description.
H. Trigonal pyramidal; the bond angle is more consistent with Student 2's description.
J. Trigonal pyramidal; the bond angle is more consistent with Student 3's description.

7. The data in Table 1 are most consistent with the description given by which student?

A. Student 1
B. Student 2
C. Student 3
D. Student 4

GO ON TO THE NEXT PAGE.

4 ○ ○ ○ ○ ○ ○ ○ ○ ○ 4

Passage II

Each dog in a particular population has a black, brown, or yellow coat. In this population, coat color is determined by 2 unlinked genes: Gene B and Gene E. Gene B has 2 alleles: *B* and *b*. Gene E also has 2 alleles: *E* and *e*. Table 1 shows the possible genotypes for Gene B and Gene E and the resulting coat color phenotypes.

Table 1	
Genotype	Coat color
BBEE	black
BBEe	black
BBee	yellow
BbEE	black
BbEe	black
Bbee	yellow
bbEE	brown
bbEe	brown
bbee	yellow

Two of the dogs with black coats were crossed 3 times (Crosses 1–3). The coat colors of the offspring produced in each cross are shown in Table 2.

Table 2			
	Number of offspring with a:		
Cross	black coat	brown coat	yellow coat
1	8	0	0
2	6	1	2
3	2	2	2

8. After Cross 1 but before Cross 2, a student hypothesized that each of the parents in Cross 1 had the genotype *BBEE*. Was this hypothesis consistent with the results of Cross 1 ?

F. Yes, because all the offspring of Cross 1 had black coats.
G. Yes, because all the offspring of Cross 1 had yellow coats.
H. No, because all the offspring of Cross 1 had black coats.
J. No, because all the offspring of Cross 1 had yellow coats.

9. What was the Gene B and Gene E genotype of the offspring of Cross 2 that had a brown coat?

A. *bbee*
B. *BBEE*
C. *BbEE* or *BbEe*
D. *bbEE* or *bbEe*

10. Based on Tables 1 and 2, what fraction of the offspring of Cross 3 had 1 or more copies of the *E* allele of Gene E ?

F. $\frac{1}{4}$
G. $\frac{1}{3}$
H. $\frac{2}{3}$
J. $\frac{15}{16}$

GO ON TO THE NEXT PAGE.

4 ○ ○ ○ ○ ○ ○ ○ ○ ○ 4

11. Consider the offspring of each of the 3 crosses. Based on Tables 1 and 2, some of the offspring of which of the crosses, if any, could have had only recessive alleles of Gene B and Gene E ?

A. Cross 1 only
B. Crosses 2 and 3 only
C. Crosses 1, 2, and 3
D. None of the crosses

12. Suppose 2 of the offspring from Cross 3 with yellow coats are crossed. What percent of the resulting offspring will have yellow coats?

F. 0%
G. 25%
H. 50%
J. 100%

13. Approximately what percent of the normal gametes produced by a dog with the genotype *BbEE* will contain the *B* allele?

A. 0%
B. 25%
C. 50%
D. 100%

GO ON TO THE NEXT PAGE.

4 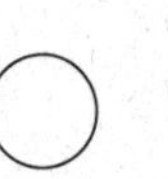 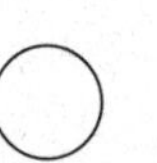       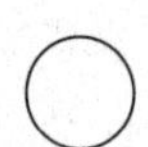 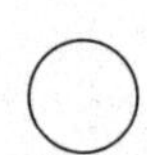 4

Passage III

The *tensile strength* of a paper towel (PT) is the force per unit width required to break the PT when it is clamped and stretched (see diagram).

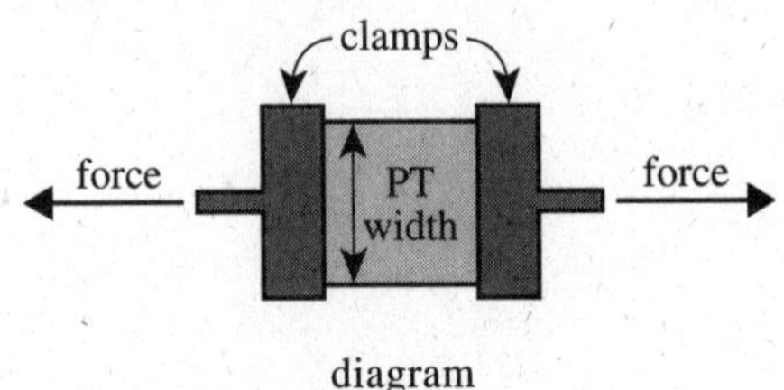

diagram

Dry strength is the tensile strength of a dry PT, and *wet strength* is the tensile strength of a PT that has been submerged in water. The wet strength can be increased by treating the PT with certain chemicals.

Students conducted 2 experiments to study the wet strengths of identical PTs, each 20 cm × 20 cm, treated with glutaraldehyde (GLA) or with GLA and zinc nitrate.

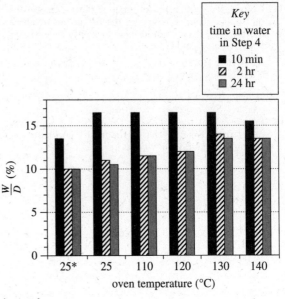

Experiment 1

First, the dry strengths of 5 PTs were measured, in newtons per meter (N/m), and the average of the measurements, D, was calculated. Then, Steps 1–5 were performed on each of 100 other PTs:

1. A PT was submerged for 30 sec in water (if the PT was to be a control) or in a test solution containing GLA.
2. The PT was dried on a hot plate at 85°C for 4 min.
3. The PT was heated in an oven for 3 min at a certain temperature—25°C for a control PT and 25°C, 110°C, 120°C, 130°C, or 140°C for a treated PT.
4. The PT was submerged in water for 10 min, 2 hr, or 24 hr.
5. The wet strength of the PT was measured in N/m.

The wet strengths of PTs that had been subjected to identical conditions were averaged. Each average wet strength, W, was divided by D and then multiplied by 100. The resulting $\frac{W}{D}$ values are shown in Figure 1.

Key
time in water in Step 4
10 min
2 hr
24 hr

$\frac{W}{D}$ (%)
oven temperature (°C)
25* 25 110 120 130 140

*controls

Figure 1

Experiment 2

Steps 1–5 were repeated with 100 other PTs, except that the test solution contained both GLA and zinc nitrate (see Figure 2).

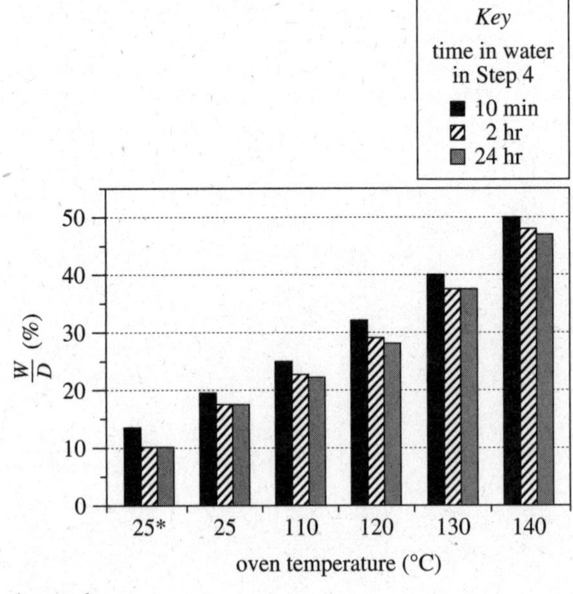

Figure 2

GO ON TO THE NEXT PAGE.

4 ○ ○ ○ ○ ○ ○ ○ ○ ○ 4

Figures 1 and 2 adapted from Gordon Guozhong Xu, Charles Qixiang Yang, and Yulin Deng, "Applications of Bifunctional Aldehydes to Improve Paper Wet Strength." ©2002 by John Wiley & Sons, Inc.

14. In Experiment 2, the greatest average wet strength was observed for the PTs that were submerged in water for 10 min after having been heated in an oven at what temperature?

F. 110°C
G. 120°C
H. 130°C
J. 140°C

15. In Experiment 2, for PTs that were submerged in water for 2 hr, as the oven temperature increased from 110°C through 140°C, the $\frac{W}{D}$ value:

A. increased only.
B. decreased only.
C. remained the same.
D. varied, but with no general trend.

16. In Step 1 of Experiment 1, the PTs that would become controls were submerged in what liquid, and in Step 3 of Experiment 1, these control PTs were heated in an oven at what temperature?

	liquid	temperature
F.	water	25°C
G.	water	85°C
H.	GLA solution	25°C
J.	GLA solution	85°C

17. In which of Experiments 1 and 2, if either, did the students measure the wet strengths of PTs that had been submerged in water for a total of 18 hr ?

A. Experiment 1 only
B. Experiment 2 only
C. Both Experiment 1 and Experiment 2
D. Neither Experiment 1 nor Experiment 2

18. Which of the following statements comparing the $\frac{W}{D}$ value of the PTs that were submerged in water for 2 hr with the $\frac{W}{D}$ value of the PTs that were submerged in water for 10 min is supported by the results of Experiment 1 ?

F. For all the oven temperatures, the $\frac{W}{D}$ value at 2 hr was greater than the $\frac{W}{D}$ value at 10 min.
G. For all the oven temperatures, the $\frac{W}{D}$ value at 2 hr was less than the $\frac{W}{D}$ value at 10 min.
H. For all the oven temperatures, the $\frac{W}{D}$ value at 2 hr was the same as the $\frac{W}{D}$ value at 10 min.
J. For some of the oven temperatures, the $\frac{W}{D}$ value at 2 hr was greater than the $\frac{W}{D}$ value at 10 min; at the other oven temperatures, the $\frac{W}{D}$ value at 2 hr was less than the $\frac{W}{D}$ value at 10 min.

19. One of the students predicted that the wet strengths of PTs would NOT increase after treating the PTs with a solution containing both GLA and zinc nitrate. The results of which experiment better refute or support this prediction? The results of:

A. Experiment 1 better refute this prediction.
B. Experiment 1 better support this prediction.
C. Experiment 2 better refute this prediction.
D. Experiment 2 better support this prediction.

20. Based on the results of the experiments, is the dry strength of a paper towel greater than or less than the wet strength of the paper towel?

F. Greater; each average wet strength, *W*, was greater than 100% of *D*.
G. Greater; each average wet strength, *W*, was less than 100% of *D*.
H. Less; each average wet strength, *W*, was greater than 100% of *D*.
J. Less; each average wet strength, *W*, was less than 100% of *D*.

GO ON TO THE NEXT PAGE.

4 ○ ○ ○ ○ ○ ○ ○ ○ ○ 4

Passage IV

The tiger frog, *Rana rugulosa*, is a species of frog that is commercially farmed. A farmer conducted 2 experiments to help determine the optimum diet for the growth of *R. rugulosa*.

Prior to the experiments, 10 diets (Diets 1–10) were prepared. The diets differed in the percent by mass of protein, the number of calories per gram (cal/g), or both (see Table 1).

Table 1

Diet	Percent by mass of protein	Calories per gram (cal/g)
1	30.0	5,300
2	32.5	5,300
3	35.0	5,300
4	37.5	5,300
5	40.0	5,300
6	37.0	4,500
7	37.0	4,700
8	37.0	4,900
9	37.0	5,300
10	37.0	5,700

Experiment 1

Each of 5 identical outdoor 1 m^3 tanks was prepared as follows: First, the tank was filled with water to a depth of 20 cm. Next, 30 adult *R. rugulosa*, each with a mass of 3.3 g, were placed into the tank. Then the tank was covered with a fine wire mesh.

Each tank of frogs was assigned a different diet: Diet 1, Diet 2, Diet 3, Diet 4, or Diet 5. Each frog was fed 1,000 mg of its assigned diet, twice per day, for the next 12 weeks. At the end of 12 weeks, the average final mass of the frogs was determined for each diet (see Table 2).

Table 2

Diet	Average final mass (g)
1	54.0
2	69.3
3	80.1
4	86.2
5	90.4

Experiment 2

Five more of the outdoor 1 m^3 tanks were prepared as in Experiment 1, except that each of the *R. rugulosa* had an initial mass of 7.9 g instead of 3.3 g. Each tank of frogs was assigned a different diet: Diet 6, Diet 7, Diet 8, Diet 9, or Diet 10. Each frog was fed 2,000 mg of its assigned diet, once per day, for the next 12 weeks. At the end of 12 weeks, the average final mass of the frogs was determined for each diet (see Table 3).

Table 3

Diet	Average final mass (g)
6	126.9
7	135.1
8	143.0
9	132.0
10	129.5

Tables adapted from P. Somsueb and M. Boonyaratpalin, "Optimum Protein and Energy Levels for the Thai Native Frog, *Rana rugulosa* Weigmann." ©2001 by Blackwell Science Ltd.

21. The values that were averaged to obtain the data in Tables 2 and 3 were most likely read from which of the following instruments?

A. Graduated cylinder
B. Electronic balance
C. Metric ruler
D. Calorimeter

22. In Experiment 1, as the percent by mass of protein increased, the average final mass of the frogs:

F. increased only.
G. decreased only.
H. increased, then decreased.
J. decreased, then increased.

GO ON TO THE NEXT PAGE.

4 ○ ○ ○ ○ ○ ○ ○ ○ ○ 4

23. The fine wire mesh was most likely intended to function in which of the ways described below?

I. To prevent predators of frogs from entering each tank
II. To place the frogs into each tank
III. To keep the frogs from leaving each tank

A. I and II only
B. I and III only
C. II and III only
D. I, II, and III

24. In Experiment 2, as the number of calories per gram increased, the average final mass of the frogs:

F. increased only.
G. decreased only.
H. increased, then decreased.
J. decreased, then increased.

25. Which of the statements about the frogs involved in the experiments given below, if either, is(are) consistent with the information in the passage?

I. All the frogs belonged to the same genus.
II. All the frogs belonged to the same species.

A. I only
B. II only
C. Both I and II
D. Neither I nor II

26. Experiment 2 differed from Experiment 1 in which of the following ways?

F. The initial mass of each frog was greater in Experiment 1 than in Experiment 2.
G. The initial mass of each frog was greater in Experiment 2 than in Experiment 1.
H. The quantity of food that each frog was fed per day was greater in Experiment 1 than in Experiment 2.
J. The quantity of food that each frog was fed per day was greater in Experiment 2 than in Experiment 1.

27. To determine whether the number of calories per gram in the diet of *R. rugulosa* affects the growth of *R. rugulosa*, would the farmer more likely have compared the results of Diets 1–5 or the results of Diets 6–10 ?

A. Diets 1–5, because those diets varied in the percent by mass of protein but not in the number of calories per gram.
B. Diets 1–5, because those diets varied in the number of calories per gram but not in the percent by mass of protein.
C. Diets 6–10, because those diets varied in the percent by mass of protein but not in the number of calories per gram.
D. Diets 6–10, because those diets varied in the number of calories per gram but not in the percent by mass of protein.

GO ON TO THE NEXT PAGE.

4 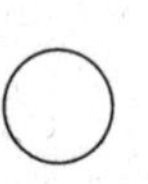 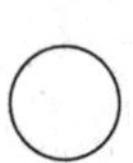   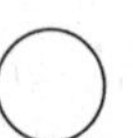 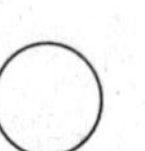 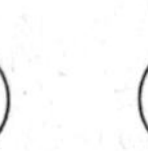  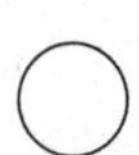 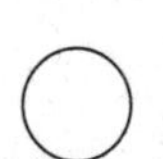 4

Passage V

In soil, CO_2 is produced through 2 processes—respiration in plant roots and bacterial decomposition of organic matter. A study was done in an oak forest to examine the CO_2 content of soil gas as well as the water content of the soil. The study was done during an 8-week period that began just as the growing season ended.

Study

On October 12, 5 evenly spaced locations in the forest were marked along a 120 m long straight line, starting at one end. At each location, 5 sets of 2 instruments each—a *diffusion well* and a *moisture sensor*—were positioned so that soil gas could be collected and soil water content could be measured at each of 5 soil depths: 10 cm, 30 cm, 60 cm, 100 cm, and 140 cm. The slots near one end of the steel pipe of the diffusion well allowed only soil gas to enter the pipe. The soil gas could be sampled by inserting the needle of a syringe through the airtight seal on the aboveground end of the pipe. See Figure 1.

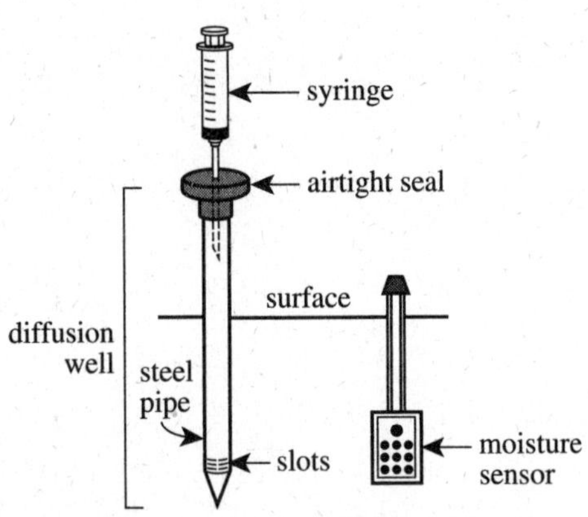

Note: Drawing is not to scale.

Figure 1

At noon on each of 4 dates—October 26, November 9, November 23, and December 7—a 0.5 mL sample of soil gas was collected from each diffusion well and the water content of the soil was read from each moisture sensor. Each soil gas sample was analyzed to determine its CO_2 content. Figure 2 shows the averaged results for CO_2 content of the soil gas, expressed in percent by volume, and Figure 3 shows the averaged results for water content of the soil, expressed in percent by mass.

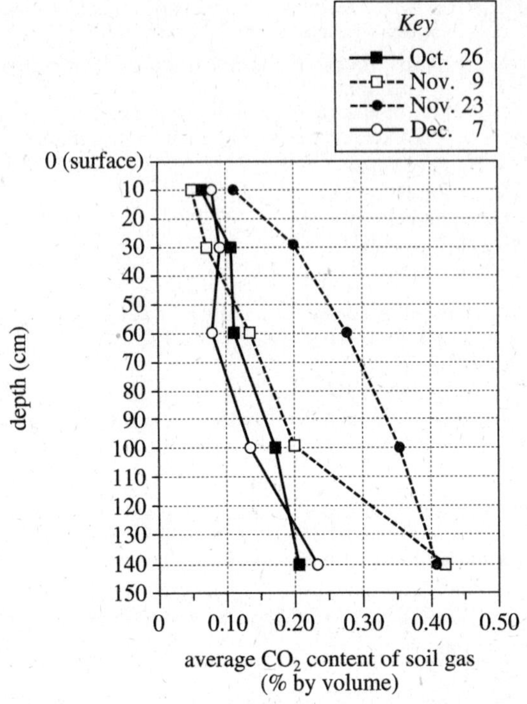

Figure 2

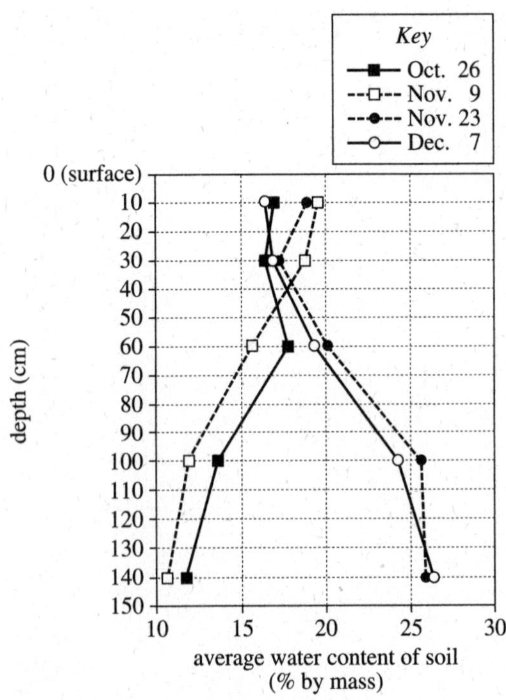

Figure 3

GO ON TO THE NEXT PAGE.

4 ○ ○ ○ ○ ○ ○ ○ ○ ○ 4

28. According to Figure 3, at what depth were the average water content values for the 4 dates closest in value?

F. 30 cm
G. 60 cm
H. 100 cm
J. 140 cm

29. The slots at the bottom of a diffusion well's pipe were designed to allow the passage of:

A. soil gas but not soil or water.
B. soil and water but not soil gas.
C. water but not soil or soil gas.
D. soil gas as well as soil and water.

30. What percent of the CO_2 in each soil gas sample was due to bacterial decomposition of organic matter and not due to respiration in plant roots?

F. 10%
G. 25%
H. 50%
J. Cannot be determined from the given information

31. In the study, one step in the determination of CO_2 content was to divide a volume of CO_2 by another volume. That other volume was the volume of a:

A. sample of soil.
B. sample of soil gas.
C. sample of water.
D. steel pipe of a diffusion well.

32. Which of the following statements describing how the average water content generally varied over the 140 cm of soil depth is consistent with Figure 3 ?

F. On each of the 4 dates, the average water content generally increased with depth.
G. On each of the 4 dates, the average water content generally decreased with depth.
H. On October 26 and November 9, the average water content generally increased with depth, whereas on November 23 and December 7, the average water content generally decreased with depth.
J. On October 26 and November 9, the average water content generally decreased with depth, whereas on November 23 and December 7, the average water content generally increased with depth.

33. Suppose that at each of the 5 locations a diffusion well had been positioned at a depth of 145 cm. Based on Figure 2, on November 23, the average CO_2 content of the soil gas at that depth would most likely have been determined to be:

A. less than 0.30% by volume.
B. between 0.30% by volume and 0.35% by volume.
C. between 0.35% by volume and 0.40% by volume.
D. greater than 0.40% by volume.

34. Suppose that a 10 g sample of soil had been collected on November 23 at a depth of 60 cm. Based on Figure 3, what mass of water would most likely have been present in the sample?

F. 1 g
G. 2 g
H. 5 g
J. 10 g

GO ON TO THE NEXT PAGE.

4 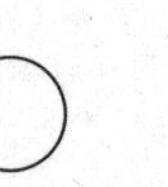 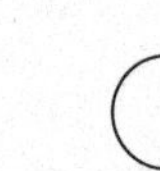  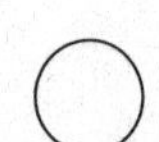 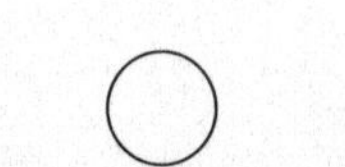 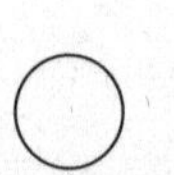 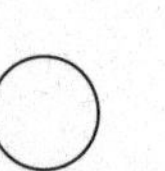 4

Passage VI

An object falling through a liquid has 3 forces acting on it: gravity, a buoyant force, and *drag* (a force that opposes motion). If the net upward force on the object is equal in magnitude to the net downward force on the object, then the object will fall at *terminal speed.*

A steel ball was dropped from rest into a column of motor oil and into a column of glycerin. Figures 1 and 2 show how the speed of the ball and the drag on the ball varied with time as the ball fell through the oil and through the glycerin, respectively. Figure 3 shows how the depth of the ball varied with time for each case.

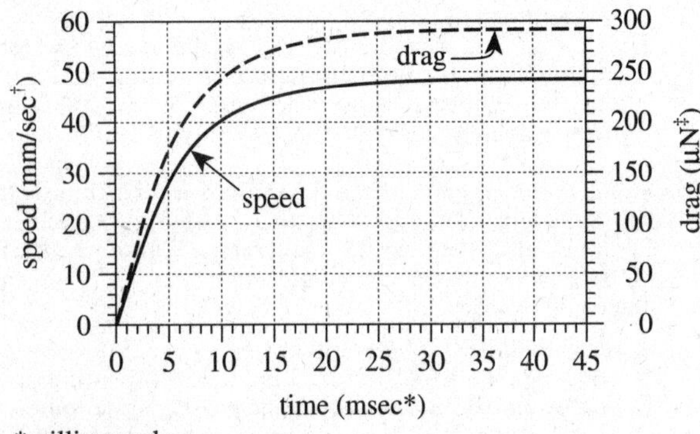

*milliseconds
†millimeters per second
‡micronewtons

Figure 1

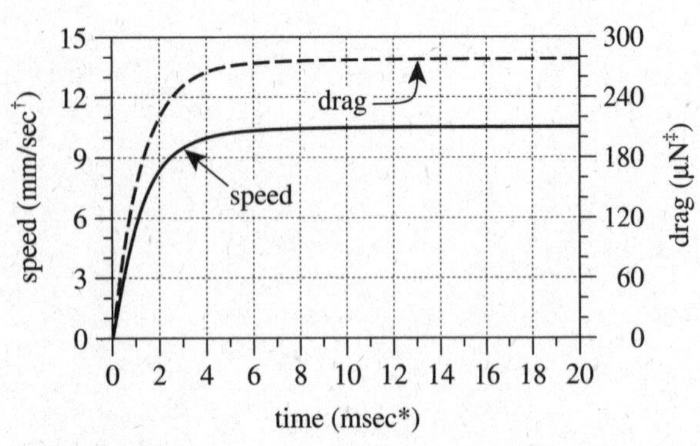

*milliseconds
†millimeters per second
‡micronewtons

Figure 2

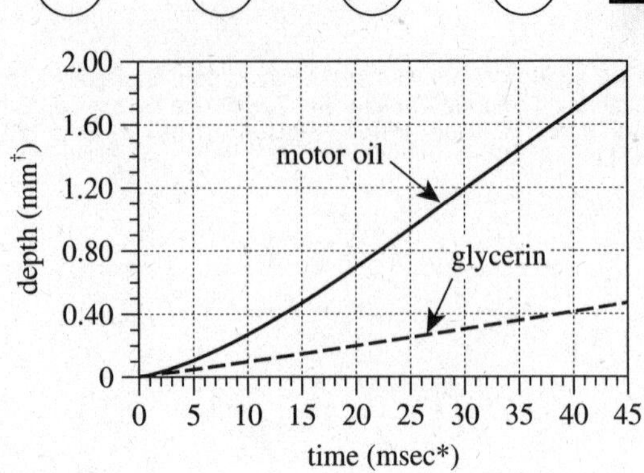

*milliseconds
†millimeters

Figure 3

35. Based on Figure 3, the depth of the steel ball in the motor oil at time = 50 msec would most likely have been closest to which of the following?

A. 0.50 mm
B. 0.60 mm
C. 1.90 mm
D. 2.10 mm

36. Which of the following diagrams best represents the 3 forces that acted on the steel ball—gravity (*G*), the buoyant force (*B*), and drag (*D*)—as it moved through either liquid?

(Note: Assume that down is toward the bottom of the page.)

F.
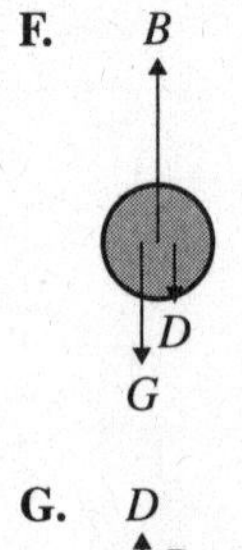

H.
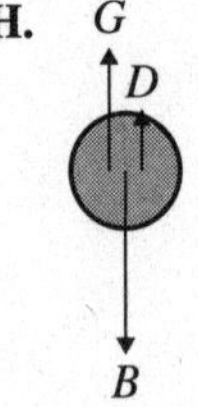

G.
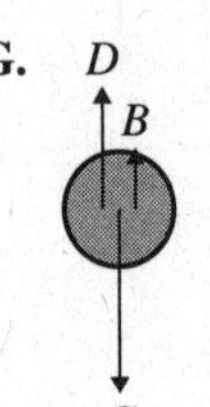

J.

GO ON TO THE NEXT PAGE.

4 ○ ○ ○ ○ ○ ○ ○ ○ ○ 4

37. The steel ball required *less* time to reach terminal speed in which liquid?

A. Motor oil; the ball took less than 10 msec in motor oil but more than 25 msec in glycerin to reach terminal speed.
B. Motor oil; the ball took more than 25 msec in motor oil but less than 10 msec in glycerin to reach terminal speed.
C. Glycerin; the ball took less than 10 msec in glycerin but more than 25 msec in motor oil to reach terminal speed.
D. Glycerin; the ball took more than 25 msec in glycerin but less than 10 msec in motor oil to reach terminal speed.

38. According to Figures 1 and 2, the steel ball's terminal speed was greater in which liquid?

F. Motor oil; the terminal speed was about 48 mm/sec in motor oil and about 10.5 mm/sec in glycerin.
G. Motor oil; the terminal speed was about 240 mm/sec in motor oil and about 210 mm/sec in glycerin.
H. Glycerin; the terminal speed was about 48 mm/sec in glycerin and about 10.5 mm/sec in motor oil.
J. Glycerin; the terminal speed was about 240 mm/sec in glycerin and about 210 mm/sec in motor oil.

39. Based on Figures 1, 2, and 3, is it reasonable to conclude that the drag on the steel ball was directly proportional to the depth of the ball?

A. Yes; both the depth and the drag increased only.
B. Yes; both the depth and the drag increased and then gradually approached a constant value.
C. No; the depth increased only, whereas the drag increased and then approached a constant value.
D. No; the depth increased and then approached a constant value, whereas the drag increased only.

40. Based on Figures 1 and 3, at a depth of 0.50 mm in the motor oil, what was the approximate drag exerted on the steel ball?

F. 230 μN
G. 250 μN
H. 270 μN
J. 290 μN

END OF TEST 4

STOP! DO NOT RETURN TO ANY OTHER TEST.

You may wish to photocopy these sample answer document pages to respond to the practice ACT Writing Test.

Please enter the information at the right before beginning the writing test.

Use a soft lead No. 2 pencil only. Do NOT use a mechanical pencil, ink, ballpoint, or felt-tip pen.

WRITING TEST BOOKLET NUMBER

Print your 6-digit **Booklet Number** in the boxes at the right.

WRITING TEST FORM

Print your 5-character **Test Form** in the boxes above and fill in the corresponding oval at the right.

- ○ 16W1A
- ○ 16W2A
- ○ 16W3A
- ○ 18W4A
- ○ 19WT5

Begin WRITING TEST here.

If you need more space, please continue on the next page.

WRITING TEST

If you need more space, please continue on the back of this page.

WRITING TEST

If you need more space, please continue on the next page.

WRITING TEST

STOP here with the writing test.

072953

Practice Writing Test Prompt 4

Your Signature: ______________________
(Do not print.)

Print Your Name Here: ______________________

Your Date of Birth:
[ ][ ] - [ ][ ] - [ ][ ][ ][ ]
Month Day Year

Form 18W4A

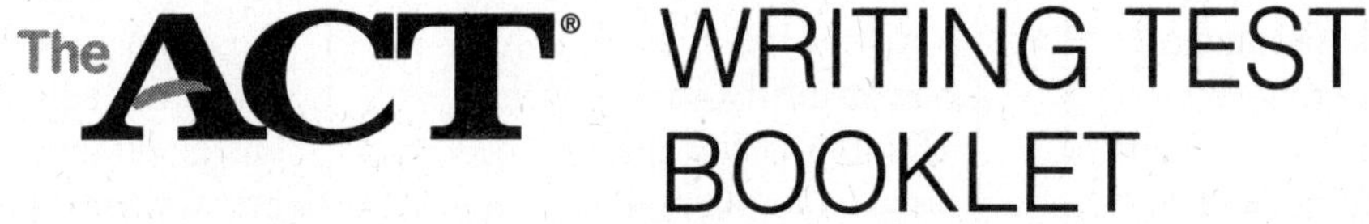

You must take the multiple-choice tests before you take the writing test.

Directions

This is a test of your writing skills. You will have **forty** (40) minutes to read the prompt, plan your response, and write an essay in English. Before you begin working, read all material in this test booklet carefully to understand exactly what you are being asked to do.

You will write your essay on the lined pages in the **answer document** provided. Your writing on those pages will be scored. You may use the unlined pages in this test booklet to plan your essay. Your work on these pages will not be scored.

Your essay will be evaluated based on the evidence it provides of your ability to:

- clearly state your own perspective on a complex issue and analyze the relationship between your perspective and at least one other perspective
- develop and support your ideas with reasoning and examples
- organize your ideas clearly and logically
- communicate your ideas effectively in standard written English

Lay your pencil down immediately when time is called.

DO NOT OPEN THIS BOOKLET UNTIL TOLD TO DO SO.

PO Box 168
Iowa City, IA 52243-0168

Celebrities and Privacy

Many people believe that celebrities must give up some of their privacy in exchange for the wealth and fame that celebrity status affords. After all, to become a celebrity, one must seek public attention and recognition, and a loss of privacy, some say, is an unavoidable trade-off. But should being a celebrity mean having no right to privacy? Should people who are well known for their work or skill be expected to share details about their home life, family, and loved ones? In a culture that lavishes attention on celebrities, it is worth examining celebrities' right to privacy.

Read and carefully consider these perspectives. Each suggests a particular way of thinking about celebrities' right to privacy.

Perspective One

Our belief that celebrities must lose their right to privacy is the product of jealousy and envy. We resent celebrities for their wealth and fame, and so we punish them by intruding into their private lives.

Perspective Two

Celebrities do give up some of their rights to privacy when they pursue a career that makes them famous. They can't expect to maintain a private life when the only way to become famous is to capture the imagination of the public.

Perspective Three

Most people claim that privacy is important, but these days everyone with a social media account has given up some privacy for the sake of attention. We're not doing anything to celebrities that we aren't already doing to ourselves.

Essay Task

Write a unified, coherent essay about celebrities' right to privacy. In your essay, be sure to:

- clearly state your own perspective on the issue and analyze the relationship between your perspective and at least one other perspective
- develop and support your ideas with reasoning and examples
- organize your ideas clearly and logically
- communicate your ideas effectively in standard written English

Your perspective may be in full agreement with any of those given, in partial agreement, or completely different.

Planning Your Essay

Your work on these prewriting pages will not be scored.

Use the space below and on the back cover to generate ideas and plan your essay. You may wish to consider the following as you think critically about the task:

Strengths and weaknesses of different perspectives on the issue

- What insights do they offer, and what do they fail to consider?
- Why might they be persuasive to others, or why might they fail to persuade?

Your own knowledge, experience, and values

- What is your perspective on this issue, and what are its strengths and weaknesses?
- How will you support your perspective in your essay?

If you need more space to plan, please continue on the back of this page.

Planning Your Essay

Use this page to continue planning your essay. Your work on this page will not be scored.

Scoring Your Practice Tests

Scoring Practice Practice Tests 2, 3, 4, and 5 is covered in chapter 11.

Explanatory Answers

Passage I

Question 1. The best answer is A because it clearly and succinctly indicates that the young woman arrived at the same location where the narrator was waiting.

The best answer is NOT:

B because it unnecessarily repeats the first part of the sentence, explaining again that the narrator is waiting in a veterinarian's office.

C because it unnecessarily repeats that the narrator is waiting in the office. This information has already been established in the first part of the sentence, "I was waiting in the veterinarian's office."

D because it unnecessarily repeats that the narrator is there in the office. This information is already established in the first part of the sentence, "I was waiting in the veterinarian's office."

Question 2. The best answer is G because the verb *scuttling* provides a vivid description of the iguana's movement. This choice also provides a description of the iguana's rain forest environment, "dank undergrowth."

The best answer is NOT:

F because "walking on the ground" does not satisfy the requirement in the question that the choice be a vivid description. "Walking on the ground" indicates what the iguana does but is not a vivid description of the iguana's action or environment.

H because "living underneath the treetops" states an obvious point about iguanas and nearly restates the next part of the sentence, "resting high in the trees." No vivid modifiers or verbs are used.

J because the words "down low" are repetitive and the expression "moving about down low" is vague and imprecise.

ENGLISH • PRACTICE TEST 4 • EXPLANATORY ANSWERS

Question 3. The best answer is C because the comma after *trees* indicates that the iguanas, not the canopy itself, are hidden in the trees.

The best answer is NOT:

A because it is nonsensical given the context of the sentence. The comma after *trees* followed by "which are hidden in the canopy" indicates that the trees themselves are hidden in the canopy.

B because it is a comma splice. "They're . . . trees" is an independent clause. "They are hidden in the canopy" is another independent clause. Two independent clauses cannot be joined using only a comma.

D because the semicolon is incorrectly placed between an independent clause and an explanatory phrase in a simple sentence. Semicolons are used to join two independent clauses.

Question 4. The best answer is G because the contrast between the narrator's desire to be polite and the narrator's reluctance emphasizes the narrator's feelings toward the iguana. If the phrase were removed, the following sentence would suggest the narrator is ambivalent about the iguana's presence, which contrasts with the beginning of the third paragraph when the narrator "guardedly" examines the iguana. The phrase is critical to establishing the narrator's negative feelings toward the iguana.

The best answer is NOT:

F because "wishing to be polite, but with reluctance in my voice" describes an action taking place at the time the woman asked permission to take the iguana out of its carrier. This does not offer any suggestion that the narrator had a previous experience with iguanas out of their carriers at veterinary offices.

H because the narrator's overall attitude toward the iguana is negative. She "guardedly" examines the iguana. She is amazed that the woman "tenderly caresses" the animal and initially feels pity for the woman who gives love to an animal the narrator initially feels can't love the woman back. The phrase "with reluctance in my voice" is consistent with this negative attitude.

J because the purpose of the paragraph is not to provide background information on iguanas in general; it is a continuation of the narrative about the narrator's encounter with an iguana at the veterinarian's office.

Question 5. The best answer is D because the *rows* specified in the response indicate the pattern of spikes that appear on the reptile. The word *lined* also indicates the position and pattern of the spikes.

The best answer is NOT:

A because "it had a spine with tiny spikes" indicates the size of the spikes but not the pattern of the spikes.

B because the spikes "just beginning to develop again" indicates the potential size of the spikes and their development but not the arrangement or pattern of the spikes as stipulated in the stem.

C because "there were small spikes on its armored back" indicates the size of the spikes and provides a visual description of the appearance and texture of the reptile's back but does not indicate the pattern of the spikes.

Question 6. The best answer is G because it creates a clear, logical, and parallel sentence (the verbs *caressed* and *watched* are parallel in form). The pronoun *it* later in the sentence also has a clear and logical antecedent, *pet*.

The best answer is NOT:

F because it is overly wordy and does not fit with the rest of the sentence. The underlined text is not parallel with the phrase "and watched it" later in the sentence, and the pronoun *it* has no clear antecedent.

H because the verb *caressing* is in the ongoing present tense, which is inconsistent with the past tense *watched* later in the sentence. This creates a confusing sequence of time when part of the action is an ongoing present action, *caressing*, and part of the action occurred in the past, *watched*.

J because it results in an illogical and ungrammatical transition to the rest of the sentence. The pronoun *it* in the remaining sentence also has no clear antecedent.

ENGLISH • PRACTICE TEST 4 • EXPLANATORY ANSWERS

Question 7. The best answer is B because the word *woman* clarifies the meaning of the sentence by indicating who is lavishing attention on the iguana and serves as a clear antecedent to the pronoun *her* used later in the sentence.

The best answer is NOT:

A because there is an incorrect shift in pronouns from *us* to *her* in the same sentence. There is also no antecedent for the word *us* in this sentence or the preceding sentence (the narrator does not join the young woman in lavishing affection on the iguana).

C because the plural noun *people* is not a logical antecedent for the singular pronoun *her.* There is no mention in the sentence or in the rest of the essay of a wider audience lavishing attention on the iguana.

D because the pronoun *you* is an incorrect pronoun shift. The essay is a narrative written in the first person, and there aren't any logical or stylistic reasons for the narrator to shift to the second person *you* at this point. *You* does not serve as a logical antecedent for the pronoun *her* used later in the sentence.

Question 8. The best answer is J because no comma is needed to separate the modifiers describing the iguana's eyes and how they shone and the prepositional phrase.

The best answer is NOT:

F because there is an unnecessary comma between a modifier and a prepositional phrase. No comma is needed to set off the prepositional phrase "from its scaly face."

G because there is an unnecessary comma between a preposition (*from*) and its object ("its scaly face").

H because there is an unnecessary comma between modifiers joined by the conjunction *and.* No comma is needed here because *and* is joining two adjectives, not two independent clauses.

ENGLISH • PRACTICE TEST 4 • EXPLANATORY ANSWERS

Question 9. The best answer is B because the word *supposed* means to assume. This word does not match the context of the iguana staring steadily and fixedly like a judge, nor is it a reasonable alternative for the word *regarded. Supposed* also does not track with the object, *me,* and creates the nonsensical idea that the iguana is assessing the narrator like a judge.

The best answer is NOT:

A because the word *scrutinized* means to study closely. This word matches the context of the rest of the sentence, which compares the iguana to a judge delivering a verdict.

C because the word *appraised* means to survey and evaluate. This word matches the context of the rest of the sentence, which compares the iguana to a judge delivering a verdict.

D because the word *considered* means to look attentively at someone or something. This word matches the context of the rest of the sentence, which states the iguana stares "steadily and fixedly" at the narrator.

Question 10. The best answer is F because it clearly indicates that the narrator is comparing the iguana's actions to a judge delivering (or giving) the verdict.

The best answer is NOT:

G because the phrase "having a delivery of a verdict" is awkward and wordy, and it does not make sense in the given context. Without an explanation, it's hard to imagine how an iguana's actions could be like a judge *having* a delivery of a verdict.

H because the phrase "in deliverance with a verdict" does not make sense in this context (a judge delivers a verdict; she does not deliver the verdict with the verdict). The intended meaning of this action is unclear, especially when likened to the actions of the iguana.

J because the plural verb form *deliver* does not agree with the singular noun *judge.*

ENGLISH • PRACTICE TEST 4 • EXPLANATORY ANSWERS

Question 11. The best answer is D because the sentence is complex (containing an independent and a dependent clause), so commas aren't needed to separate two independent clauses. There also isn't any nonessential information in the portion that needs to be set apart by punctuation.

The best answer is NOT:

A because there is an unnecessary comma between *cat* and the conjunction *and.* The phrase "cat and me" functions as a compound object in this sentence and should not be interrupted by a comma.

B because there are unnecessary commas around words that are essential to the meaning of the sentence ("and me from the hallway"). Setting these words apart with commas indicates that they are not crucial to understanding the sentence, but without them the sentence would state that the cat, not the hallway, leads to the examination room.

C because there is an unnecessary comma between the independent clause ending with *hallway* and the dependent clause beginning with *that.*

Question 12. The best answer is F because the word *looking* offers a concise and effective choice to indicate the comparison between the appearance of the iguana and the appearance of a kitten.

The best answer is NOT:

G because the phrase "like as if it was" offers a wordy and repetitive description of the iguana. This repetition is distracting and unnecessary. It is also overly informal given the style and tone of the rest of the essay.

H because the phrase "appearing something like" is wordy and vague. The phrase also does a poor job of setting up the comparison in the sentence "appearing something like as content as a kitten, and close its eyes again." The meaning here is unclear.

J because the phrase "sort of like it was" is wordy and vague, which makes the comparison in the sentence less clear. The phrase is also overly informal for the style and tone of the essay.

ENGLISH • PRACTICE TEST 4 • EXPLANATORY ANSWERS

Question 13. The best answer is B because placing the sentence at Point B further explains the young woman's statement that the iguana liked being held. The sentence is a logical extension of the preceding sentence.

The best answer is NOT:

A because neither the woman nor her pet iguana have entered the office yet, so placing the sentence at Point A is incorrect. The pronoun *she* in the added sentence would have no antecedent, so it would be unclear who is speaking.

C because placing the sentence at Point C interrupts the logical flow between the narrator's statement that she dislikes iguanas and her reasons for disliking the creatures.

D because placing the sentence at Point D interrupts the narrative flow between the iguana opening its eyes and it staring at the narrator.

Question 14. The best answer is F because the essay focuses on the narrator's surprise that the iguana is pampered and loved by its owner. The iguana is lovingly caressed by its owner, which the narrator finds both amazing and unsettling.

The best answer is NOT:

G because there is no indication in the essay that the narrator believes the woman is impolite. The woman politely asks the narrator if she can let the reptile out of its carrier, and the narrator gives her approval. The narrator's guarded response comes from her awe at the relationship between owner and pet, not from annoyance.

H because the essay makes it clear that the narrator does not like iguanas, but it does not tell the story of why the narrator dislikes the creatures. The essay is primarily about the narrator's observation of a bond between the iguana and its owner on a particular day at the veterinary clinic.

J because the essay focuses on the narrator's observations of one iguana in a veterinary clinic. Only a brief mention is given to where iguanas live. Any physical descriptions in the essay focus on one pet iguana, not iguanas in general or as a species.

ENGLISH • PRACTICE TEST 4 • EXPLANATORY ANSWERS

Passage II

Question 15. The best answer is A because the conjunction *but* contrasts the achievement of qualifying for the Olympics with the fact that Mills was not expected to do well. This choice also correctly coordinates two independent clauses by joining them with a comma and a coordinating conjunction.

The best answer is NOT:

B because the conjunctive adverb *nonetheless* introduces a second independent clause. Using a comma and no coordinating conjunction between the independent clause ending with *Olympics* and *nevertheless* creates a comma splice. A semicolon after the word *Olympics* would be one option for making this construction correct.

C because it introduces an illogical transition. The fact that Mills qualified but was a long shot establishes a contrast, not an intensification of the first action as "in fact" implies. Furthermore, this option introduces a comma splice by joining two independent clauses with a comma. A semicolon is needed after the word *Olympics* to make this construction correct.

D because it creates a comma splice by joining two independent clauses with a comma. This choice also provides no transitional word indicating a contrast between the ideas that Mills qualified and that he was a long shot.

Question 16. The best answer is F because no comma is needed between the object, *medal,* and the prepositional phrase "for the United States in the event."

The best answer is NOT:

G because no comma is needed between the object, *medal,* and the prepositional phrase that follows.

H because *gold* and *medal* are not coordinating adjectives that require a comma between them. Placing a comma between them indicates that the order of the adjectives can be reversed, but logically, gold must come before medal. Also, no comma is needed between the object, *medal,* and the prepositional phrase that follows.

J because *Olympic* and *gold* are not coordinating adjectives that require a comma between them.

Question 17. The best answer is C because the verb *lagged* earlier in the sentence indicates that the qualifying time was slower than that of Ron Clarke. The word *behind* is the only choice that is idiomatic in this context ("lagged behind"), and it also creates the most logical sentence.

The best answer is NOT:

A because the verb *lagged* earlier in the sentence indicates that the qualifying time was slower than that of Ron Clarke. The word *above* does not fit logically with *lagging* (describing Mills's time as both "falling behind" and *above* is confusing). The phrase "lag above" is also not idiomatic.

B because the adverb *around* does not fit logically with the verb *lagged* earlier in the sentence. It is not clear what "lagged around" would mean in this context. "Lagged around" is also not idiomatic.

D because the preposition *from* does not pair logically with the verb *lagged*. The phrase "lagged from" is also not idiomatic.

Question 18. The best answer is G because placing Sentence 3 before Sentence 2 presents events in a logical, chronological order. For example, Sentence 3, which describes Mills as having a qualifying time that was one minute slower than the world record holder's, explains Sentence 2's assertion that Mills was a "long shot."

The best answer is NOT:

F because the information about the qualifying times of the runners is interrupted by the result of the Olympic race itself. The sentences create an unnecessary shift in time and are out of chronological order.

H because placing Sentence 2 before Sentence 1 presents a statement that purposefully contrasts with the information that Mills was a "long shot" before the essay has even established that Mills was unlikely to win. The transition word *however* would be unexplained if Sentence 2 were to start the paragraph.

J because this order places the information about Mills winning the gold medal before information about Mills qualifying for the race. Also, this order does not clearly establish up front who Mills is and what race is being discussed.

ENGLISH • PRACTICE TEST 4 • EXPLANATORY ANSWERS

Question 19. The best answer is A because it correctly places commas around the appositive "an Oglala Lakota," which further identifies Mills.

The best answer is NOT:

B because commas are needed to separate the subject of the sentence, *Mills,* from the appositive, which further identifies the subject ("an Oglala Lakota").

C because it does not correctly set off the appositive "an Oglala Lakota" from the rest of the sentence.

D because it does not correctly set off the appositive "an Oglala Lakota" from the rest of the sentence.

Question 20. The best answer is H because it follows logically from the information given about Mills's desire to be a boxer and transitions to information that follows about Mills pursuing running.

The best answer is NOT:

F because despite extending the idea from the previous sentence, it does not transition to the next paragraph in the essay, which describes Mills's accomplishments as a runner.

G because despite extending the idea from the previous sentence, it does not transition to the next paragraph in the essay, which describes Mills's accomplishments as a runner. This choice also says that Mills did not make it as a boxer but leaves the reader wondering why.

J because it gives the reader more information about the various sports Mills tried, which doesn't connect with the information about boxing and running in the paragraph. It also doesn't connect well with the information in the next paragraph about Mills as a runner.

Question 21. The best answer is C because it clearly establishes that while in the Marines, Mills, rather than his talent, began racing again.

The best answer is NOT:

A because the phrase "races became part of his life again" is a misplaced modifier. This construction indicates that it's the races that are in the Marines, not Mills.

B because the phrase "his talent raced back to him" is a misplaced modifier. In this construction, it's Mills's talent that is in the Marines, which is illogical. Also, the idea that Mill's talent raced back to him is an awkward use of personification that's inconsistent with the tone of the rest of the essay.

D because the phrase "racing was in his life again" is a misplaced modifier. In this construction, it's *racing* that is in the Marines, which is illogical.

Question 22. The best answer is H because it refers directly to the 1964 Olympics, the time and place that were established in the first paragraph. It also refers to Mills's training before the Olympics, which effectively introduces the paragraph's focus on Mills's preparations.

The best answer is NOT:

F because it is vague and therefore a weak introduction to the paragraph. It also doesn't reference the topic of the first paragraph.

G because although it hints at Mills's success after the Olympics, it does not effectively introduce the paragraph, which focuses on Mills's preparations and the fact that Mills was a long shot.

J because it is vague and therefore a weak introduction. It also doesn't reference the topic of the first paragraph.

Question 23. The best answer is A because in the phrase "rather unknown," *rather* indicates that at least some people knew of Mills's talent before the 1964 Olympics.

The best answer is NOT:

B because the word *rather* in the sentence qualifies *unknown* by indicating that at least some people knew Mills was talented. Removing *rather* indicates Mills was completely unknown, but it does not lose a description of the approach Mills used to motivate himself.

C because removing the word *rather* in the sentence and stating that Mills was entirely unknown does not explain why Mills decided to run in the Olympics. The sentence merely states that Mills was determined to win after qualifying.

D because there is no indication in the sentence that Mills required more training because he was unknown or "rather unknown."

ENGLISH • PRACTICE TEST 4 • EXPLANATORY ANSWERS

Question 24. The best answer is H because the word *undeterred* indicates that Mills did not allow the fact that the Olympic shoe sponsor did not send him shoes to prevent him from racing. Mills borrowed shoes so he can compete.

The best answer is NOT:

F because the word *luckily* implies that it was simple chance that Mills was able to borrow a pair of shoes, not that it was the result of Mills's commitment to winning.

G because the word *eventually* implies that at a later time Mills was able to borrow a pair of shoes. No indication of the role of commitment is indicated here. The word *eventually* is an indication of when, not how.

J because the word *concentrating* here is vague. The reader doesn't know if Mills is concentrating on the race or on borrowing the shoes. There is no suggestion of commitment on Mills's part to borrowing the shoes, merely the suggestion that he is concentrating on an unknown objective.

Question 25. The best answer is D because adding the sentence would interrupt the transition between Mills being ready to hit the starting line and the description of the actual race in the following paragraph.

The best answer is NOT:

A because the sentence adds information about only one gold medalist in the 1964 Olympics. Also, this statement is only tangentially related to the topic of the essay and interrupts the transition between Mills being ready to hit the starting line and the description of the actual race in the following paragraph.

B because the sentence is only tangentially related to the topic of the essay and interrupts the transition between Mills being ready to hit the starting line and the actual race described in the following paragraph.

C because it implies that the essay is focused on the US track team. The essay is focused only on one member of the US track team, Mills. Furthermore, only two US runners' shoes are mentioned, not the shoes of all the members as implied in this choice.

ENGLISH • PRACTICE TEST 4 • EXPLANATORY ANSWERS

Question 26. The best answer is J because it is clear from the context of the essay that the people mentioned in the sentence are in first place and second place at the start of the last lap. Referring to Gammoudi and Clarke as *leaders* is the most logical, idiomatic choice given the sentence.

The best answer is NOT:

F because an *overseer* is one who has authority over others. It is clear from the context of the essay that the people mentioned in the sentence are on their last lap of a race. Therefore, they are runners in the race and not overseers who have authority over the other racers.

G because a *ruler* is one who has authority over others. It is clear from the context of the essay that the people mentioned in the sentence are on their last lap of a race. Therefore, they are runners in the race and not rulers who have authority over the other racers.

H because it is clear from the context of the essay that the people mentioned in the sentence are on their last lap of a race. Therefore, they are runners in the race rather than authorities who may be outside of the race itself.

Question 27. The best answer is A because "who had been in third place" is a clause that adds nonessential information to the main idea of the sentence. Interrupters or nonessential clauses are set off with commas.

The best answer is NOT:

B because two commas are needed to set off a nonessential clause from the rest of the sentence.

C because two commas are needed to set off a nonessential clause from the main sentence. Using one comma creates confusion here because it looks as if Mills is being directly addressed, and there is no antecedent for the pronoun *who.*

D because "who had been in third place" is nonessential information. It is a nonessential clause that needs to be set apart from the main idea of the sentence.

Question 28. The best answer is F because the use of the auxiliary verb *had* requires the use of the participle *run.*

The best answer is NOT:

G because the use of the auxiliary verb *has* requires the use of the participle *run,* not the past tense *ran.* The present *has* also is not appropriate here in the context. The race was completed.

H because the race is completed, requiring the use of the past tense. Using present tense here shifts the verb tense in the paragraph from past to present and creates an illogical sequence of time.

J because the use of the auxiliary verb *had* requires the use of the participle *run,* not the past tense *ran.*

ENGLISH • PRACTICE TEST 4 • EXPLANATORY ANSWERS

Question 29. The best answer is C because **it has already been stated that Mills won the race, beating Gammoudi and Clarke, in the same paragraph as the underlined portion. The information is not needed for emphasis and is therefore unnecessarily repetitious.**

The best answer is NOT:

A because who Mills finished ahead of is not mentioned in the opening paragraph of the essay. Therefore, the underlined portion does not connect in a meaningful way to the opening paragraph of the essay.

B because it has already been stated that Mills won (and therefore beat the former leaders in the race). It merely repeats the fact unnecessarily, without adding additional details.

D because the information is repetitious and not needed, not because it strays from the main point.

Passage III

Question 30. The best answer is H because placing a period after the word *unfolds* separates the two independent clauses into two complete sentences.

The best answer is NOT:

F because placing a comma after the word *unfolds* creates a comma splice between two independent clauses.

G because placing a comma after the word *boy* indicates that the movie scene unfolds a boy, which doesn't make sense. It also could be read that the scene, not the boy, is out exploring.

J because a semicolon or a period is needed to separate the independent clauses. Without punctuation, the sentence becomes a run-on, and the logic of the sentence is hard to follow.

Question 31. The best answer is D because the sentence clearly introduces information about what draws an audience into a movie scene, which sets up the examples in the next sentence and introduces the topic of the essay.

The best answer is NOT:

A because the pronoun *that* has no clear antecedent, and the expression does not work logically with the rest of the sentence.

B because the expression "for the time being" provides a vague sense of how long the audience might be drawn into a scene by sound, but this information is irrelevant to the rest of the sentence and the essay.

C because *nevertheless* indicates that the information provided in this sentence contrasts with information provided earlier in the essay. This sentence does not, however, provide a contrast; it introduces new information about what draws audience members into scenes like this.

ENGLISH • PRACTICE TEST 4 • EXPLANATORY ANSWERS

Question 32. The best answer is F because the verb *swept* implies that the action was swift and dramatic.

The best answer is NOT:

G because it suggests that silent movies had a gradual exit. Talkies "invited the beginning of what would one day . . ." implies that the transition from silent movies occurred over time, not swiftly or dramatically.

H because it does not mention silent movies or the role that talkies played in their demise.

J because it does not mention silent movies or the role that talkies played in their demise.

Question 33. The best answer is C because the pronoun *who* correctly functions as the subject of the verb *figured* (*who* refers to the predicate noun *Foley*).

The best answer is NOT:

A because *whom* functions as the object of a verb or a preposition (the person or thing that receives the action of the verb). Because the action "figured out" in this sentence is done *by* Foley, not *to* Foley, the subject pronoun *who* is required, not the objective pronoun *whom.*

B because *whom* functions as the object of a verb or a preposition (the person or thing that receives the action of the verb). Because the action "figured out" in this sentence is done *by* Foley, not *to* Foley, the subject pronoun *who* is required, not the objective pronoun *whom.* The reflexive pronoun *himself* becomes part of the noun that *who* refers to (Foley himself).

D because the pronoun *he* creates a run-on sentence (two independent clauses are joined without punctuation).

ENGLISH • PRACTICE TEST 4 • EXPLANATORY ANSWERS

Question 34. The best answer is H because it completes the sentence by clearly and grammatically connecting the act of squeezing a sock of cornstarch with its result ("produces a sound like that of footsteps in the snow").

The best answer is NOT:

F because the phrase "a sound like that of . . ." dangles in the sentence, seeming to describe cornstarch as the sound of footsteps in the snow. The sentence is also incomplete; it doesn't state what Foley figured out about squeezing a bag full of cornstarch.

G because the comma after cornstarch and the pronoun *which* indicates that "which makes a sound like that of footsteps in the snow" is an appositive that describes cornstarch itself, not the act of squeezing a sock full of cornstarch. This results in an incomplete sentence.

J because although "to get" connects the phrase "a sound like that of footsteps in the snow" to the act of squeezing a sock full of cornstarch, the sentence as constructed does not represent a complete thought. (*What* did Foley figure out about squeezing a sock full of cornstarch to get a sound like walking in the snow?)

Question 35. The best answer is C because an *illusion* is perceiving something in a way that misinterprets the thing's true nature. Foley is misleading the audience into perceiving the sound of the cane as many people walking.

The best answer is NOT:

A because an *allusion* is a reference to a historical event in literature or a reference to something in passing. Foley is not creating a reference to history here or a reference to something in passing. The context of the sentence indicates that Foley wants to create the impression that people are walking on foot.

B because *elude* means to evade. Foley is using a cane to create the impression that people are walking on foot, not to avoid people on foot.

D because an *allusion* is a reference to a historical event in literature or a reference to something in passing. Foley is not creating a reference to history here or a reference to something in passing. The context of the sentence indicates that Foley wants to create the impression that people are walking on foot.

ENGLISH • PRACTICE TEST 4 • EXPLANATORY ANSWERS

Question 36. The best answer is J because it results in a clear, logical sentence. *Eventually* functions as an adverb modifying the verb *earned.* This indicates when Foley earned the status of Hollywood legend.

The best answer is NOT:

F because the use of the word *that* in the underlined portion creates an incomplete sentence that lacks a clear subject and verb.

G because it creates an incoherent sentence that lacks a clear subject and verb. It is also unnecessarily wordy.

H because it creates an incoherent sentence that lacks a clear subject and a clear connection between the subject and verb. The phrase "that eventually even so" is also vague and unnecessarily wordy.

Question 37. The best answer is D because **ending the sentence with information about Foley's status as a "Hollywood legend" creates a logical transition to the next paragraph, which further explains the process Foley pioneered.**

The best answer is NOT:

A because this information is not directly related to the discussion of Foley's contributions, and it unnecessarily states a fact that has already been clearly established (movies with sound had not been around for long).

B because it unnecessarily repeats information provided earlier about how Foley used a cane as a prop.

C because the fact that sound editing takes place after the action has been filmed has already been explained in the first sentence of the paragraph, "sounds are recorded after the cameras have stopped rolling."

Question 38. The best answer is F because "arises from" means to originate from a source or to begin to occur or exist. The Foley process was created in response to the need for absolute quiet when capturing dialogue. (Foley artists add in the "sound clutter of real life" later.)

The best answer is NOT:

G because "aroused from" means to evoke or awaken. "The need for 'Foley'" was not evoked or awakened by the sound clutter of real life; the need didn't even exist until sound was introduced in movies.

H because without the preposition *from,* the sentence suggests that Foley was the source of the "sound clutter of real life," which is illogical.

J because the singular subject "The need for 'Foley'" requires the singular verb *arises.* The form *arise* is used with plural words. The sentence is also lacking the preposition *from* between *arise* and "the sound."

ENGLISH • PRACTICE TEST 4 • EXPLANATORY ANSWERS

Question 39. The best answer is D because the underlined portion draws a distinction between a Foley artist and a sound artist. This reduces the chance that a reader will assume that the terms "sound technician" and "Foley artist" refer to the same role.

The best answer is NOT:

A because the underlined portion indicates that there is a distinction between a Foley artist and a sound artist without explaining the role of either occupation.

B because the underlined portion indicates that there is a distinction between a Foley artist and a sound artist without explaining the origin of the term "Foley artist." The origin of the term is explained in the first sentence of the second paragraph of the essay.

C because the underlined portion indicates that there is a distinction between a Foley artist and a sound artist without indicating the degree to which a sound technician is influenced by the work of John Foley.

Question 40. The best answer is J because it continues the subject-verb pattern established in the paragraph: "An airplane flying, a phone ringing, a door slamming."

The best answer is NOT:

F because it breaks the subject-verb pattern established in the paragraph. Only a subject is provided: "An airplane flying, a phone ringing, a door ___________?"

G because the clause, "which is not part of the scene," is wordy and unnecessary. This choice also breaks the subject-verb pattern by using the word *slamming* as an adjective, not a verb.

H because it breaks the subject-verb pattern established in the paragraph. Only a subject is provided: "An airplane flying, a phone ringing, a sound of a door."

Question 41. The best answer is B because it uses two dashes to correctly set off a nonessential phrase.

The best answer is NOT:

A because it incorrectly sets off a nonessential phrase with a colon and a dash.

C because it incorrectly sets off a nonessential phrase with a comma and a dash.

D because the phrase "a small room with a screen, a microphone, and countless props" interrupts the main clause in the sentence and must be set off with a pair of commas or dashes.

Question 42. The best answer is F because *untold* means too many to count or measure. Here, the amount of money being saved is emphasized. It is so much that the actual amount is unknown.

The best answer is NOT:

G because the sentence implies that the movie's budget was cut drastically, which was positive. The word *unspeakable* suggests that the cut was something negative, which is illogical given the context of the essay.

H because it adds an illogical personification to the essay. To describe the money itself as *speechless* implies that at other times the money spoke.

J because the movie's budget was cut by thousands of dollars, a limited sum. *Endless* implies that the amount that was cut from the movie was infinite.

Question 43. The best answer is C because "an army's worth" is nonessential and therefore needs to be set off with commas. The commas clarify that "an army's worth" refers to the actors and horses.

The best answer is NOT:

A because "an army's worth" is nonessential and needs to be set off with punctuation. Without punctuation, it's difficult to determine who would be headed overseas.

B because it results in a comma splice between two independent clauses.

D because "an army's worth" is nonessential and needs to be set off with punctuation. Without punctuation, the sentence is ungrammatical and illogical.

Question 44. The best answer is G because the sentence emphasizes how Foley's work impacted on both the filmmakers and the audience. It reveals that the actors and horses were able to stay home rather than embark on an expensive journey and that the audience didn't know the difference between the actual sounds of a battlefield and the sounds created using Foley's techniques.

The best answer is NOT:

F because the sentence does not indicate that the audience ever learned about Foley's work.

H because the sentence does not mention the movie's director; therefore, there's no shift in focus from Foley to the director.

J because the sentence does not argue that his work was insignificant to the public; it just states the audience wasn't aware that the sounds were not the actual sounds of a battlefield.

ENGLISH • PRACTICE TEST 4 • EXPLANATORY ANSWERS

Passage IV

Question 45. The best answer is C because **the comma after the word University correctly separates the introductory clause "in her lab at Princeton University" from the sentence's main clause.**

The best answer is NOT:

A because if the description "molecular biologist" is treated as nonessential and set aside by commas, it is unclear whether it describes Princeton University or Bonnie Bassler.

B because it incorrectly separates with a comma the subject "Bonnie Bassler" from the verb *leans.*

D because a comma is needed after the word *University* in order to separate the introductory clause "in her lab at Princeton University" from the sentence's main clause.

Question 46. The best answer is J because **it correctly uses a comma to separate the main idea of the sentence from an aside that provides additional details.**

The best answer is NOT:

F because a semicolon is used to combine two independent clauses. "Her face illuminated by an aquamarine glow" is not an independent clause.

G because the coordinating conjunction *and* must be preceded by a comma in order to correctly join the two independent clauses.

H because the comma between *dishes* and "her face" must be followed by a coordinating conjunction such as *and* in order to avoid a comma splice.

Question 47. The best answer is C because the comma after *bacteria* paired with the comma after *glow* accurately signals that the nonessential phrase "caused by a particular species of bacteria" describes "the glow."

The best answer is NOT:

A because the prepositional phrase "of bacteria" modifies the word *species.* Prepositional phrases cannot be separated from what they modify by a comma.

B because the prepositional phrase "of bacteria" is essential to the meaning of the sentence and should not be set aside with commas, nor should "of bacteria" be separated from the noun it modifies, *species.*

D because a comma is needed after *bacteria* in order to enclose the entire nonessential phrase "caused by a particular species of bacteria" in commas, signaling that this phrase describes "the glow."

ENGLISH • PRACTICE TEST 4 • EXPLANATORY ANSWERS

Question 48. The best answer is H because it correctly uses the plural possessive form of *researcher,* resulting in a sentence that is both understandable and grammatical.

The best answer is NOT:

F because the text "and their discoveries" requires the noun *researchers* to be nonpossessive. As worded, this sentence describes Bassler as being intrigued not only with the researchers' inventions but also with the researchers themselves.

G because the wording in this option requires *researcher* to be nonpossessive. Also, the singular possessive form *researcher's* does not agree in number with the plural pronoun *their.*

J because as worded, the sentence requires a possessive form of *researcher.* Note that the words "and their," found in two of the other choices, have been removed. The sentence now states that Bassler was intrigued only by the researchers' discoveries, not by the researchers themselves. Only a possessive form of *researcher* in this context would be grammatical.

Question 49. The best answer is C because **the phrase "a luminescent marine bacteria" is an appositive renaming *Vibrio fischeri.* This phrase is nonessential and must be set off with a comma.**

The best answer is NOT:

A because it incorrectly uses a semicolon to separate the main part of an independent clause from an appositive phrase. A semicolon is used to join independent clauses.

B because the phrase that follows "a luminescent marine bacteria" is nonessential to the sentence and must be set off with a comma. The words "which is" are also unnecessarily wordy.

D because the phrase "a luminescent marine bacteria" is an appositive renaming *Vibrio fischeri.* This phrase is nonessential and must be set off with a comma.

ENGLISH • PRACTICE TEST 4 • EXPLANATORY ANSWERS

Question 50. The best answer is J because **the present tense *allows* is consistent with the use of the present tense in this paragraph.**

The best answer is NOT:

F because it shifts the established verb tense in the paragraph from present to past. The sentence uses present tense verbs to describe the actions of the bacteria: they *assemble, begin,* and *release.* The use of the past tense *allowed* here would create an illogical pattern, with one step in the process of glowing inexplicably happening in the past.

G because the use of the past conditional tense in this series of present tense descriptions suggests an essential step in the glowing may or may not have occurred in the past. The bacteria must, however, *hear* the message to release a high concentration of autoinducer.

H because the shift from the present to the present perfect tense results in an ambiguous, confusing sequence of events.

Question 51. The best answer is A because **a comma is needed to separate the dependent clause from the independent clause in the sentence.**

The best answer is NOT:

B because dashes are used to indicate an abrupt break in thought. There is not an abrupt change in thought between the dependent clause and the independent clause in this sentence; the clauses express a sequence of events that are closely related.

C because it creates a sentence fragment. The words "once the bacteria have released a high enough concentration of autoinducer" create a dependent clause that must be attached to an independent clause to make a complete sentence.

D because it creates a run-on sentence by not using a comma between the dependent clause that begins the sentence and the independent clause that follows.

ENGLISH • PRACTICE TEST 4 • EXPLANATORY ANSWERS

Question 52. The best answer is G because **it logically indicates that after some time, Bassler discovered a similar process of glowing occurring in a related species of bacteria.**

The best answer is NOT:

F because "On the contrary" signals a contrast. There is no contrast between the discovery of the process of glowing in one species of bacteria and the discovery of a similar process in another species of bacteria.

H because the fact that Bassler made an important scientific discovery suggests that this is a significant event. *Ordinarily* suggests that the discovery was common and ongoing. This *ongoing* discovery does not work with the simple past tense verb *found,* which indicates that the discovery was a one-time event.

J because the word *namely* is used to introduce a specific example of or specific, detailed information about something that has already been discussed. Bassler's *discovery* of the process of glowing in another species of bacteria has not yet been mentioned in the essay; therefore, the use of this transition word is not logical.

Question 53. The best answer is A because **the words "related bacterial species" in the underlined portion are essential to the meaning of the sentence and should not be set off by commas.**

The best answer is NOT:

B because the words *related* and *bacterial* are not coordinating adjectives. A comma between the words indicates they are coordinating and can be reversed without affecting the meaning, but if these two words were reversed the sentence would not make sense. Also, the words "bacterial species" are essential to the sentence and should not be set off by commas.

C because the words *related* and *bacterial* are not coordinating adjectives. The order of the words cannot be reversed, and a comma between the words would incorrectly indicate that they can be.

D because no comma is needed between the word *called* and *Vibrio harveyi.* In this case, there is no need for a comma between a verb and its object.

Question 54. The best answer is J because **it conveys that bacteria can communicate with other bacteria nearby. This choice is not repetitive and does not create an odd or informal image of bacteria within the paragraph.**

The best answer is NOT:

F because it is overly informal for the academic tone of the essay.

G because it is unnecessarily repetitive. Both *neighboring* and *proximity* mean "nearby."

H because it is unnecessarily repetitive. *Locale* means "in the area." To say "surrounding locale" is to repeat the concept of "in the area."

ENGLISH • PRACTICE TEST 4 • EXPLANATORY ANSWERS

Question 55. The best answer is D because ***them* is an object pronoun, a pronoun that refers to a person or thing that receives the action of a verb. A demonstrative pronoun, a pronoun that points to a specific thing, is needed in this part of the sentence to refer back to the word *species*.**

The best answer is NOT:

A because "the kinds" refers back to the bacteria that live in humans.

B because *species* clearly refers to a type of bacteria that live in humans.

C because *those* has a clear antecedent in the sentence: *species*.

Question 56. The best answer is F because **the verb form *communicate* correctly agrees with the plural subject "virulent strains" in the sentence.**

The best answer is NOT:

G because *has* is a singular verb, which does not agree with the plural subject "virulent strains."

H because in this sentence *is* is a singular verb, which does not agree with the plural subject "virulent strains."

J because in this sentence *communicates* is a singular verb, which does not agree with the plural subject "virulent strains."

Question 57. The best answer is D because **the words "these bacteria" help the reader understand that the bacteria in the preceding sentence are the bacteria being discussed in this sentence. "These bacteria" also establishes the subject without being redundant.**

The best answer is NOT:

A because it unnecessarily repeats the idea that the bacteria are "disease spreading." The reader has already been told that the bacteria are *virulent,* and this idea is further established later in this sentence with "spreading disease."

B because it has already been established in the paragraph and in the essay that Bassler has studied the bacteria. To repeat the idea here is unnecessary and redundant.

C because it has already been established at the end of the preceding sentence that the bacteria are found in humans. To repeat the idea here is unnecessary and redundant.

ENGLISH • PRACTICE TEST 4 • EXPLANATORY ANSWERS

Question 58. The best answer is G because **it correctly uses the object pronoun *her* as the object of the verb *enable*. The words "her team" also clearly refer to the other scientists with whom Bassler is working.**

The best answer is NOT:

F because an object pronoun is required to receive the action of the verb *enable*. The pronoun *she* functions as a subject, not an object.

H because *herself* is a reflexive pronoun, which is ungrammatical in this sentence. The context calls for an object pronoun (*her*). Also, the pronoun *them* has no clear antecedent.

J because the pronoun *them* has no clear antecedent.

Question 59. The best answer is B because **the information would clearly communicate why Bassler and her team study bacteria and what they hope the result of disrupting quorum sensing will be for humans.**

The best answer is NOT:

A because the paragraph has already clearly established that Bassler is working to understand "bacteria found in humans." The proposed information would not serve this function.

C because it is not important to the meaning of the sentence for the reader to know which particular strains of the bacteria attack humans' immune systems.

D because the focus of the essay was on Bassler's discovery of the fact that bacteria in humans use quorum processing, not on how Bassler and her team plan to disrupt that processing. This information would be an inappropriate conclusion because it would require more explanation.

Passage V

Question 60. The best answer is G because *subterranean* refers to something below the surface of the earth, and *routes* refers to different lines the subway system runs. This is a logical and precise choice of words given the context.

The best answer is NOT:

F because it suggests the subway is *creeping* beneath the ground, which doesn't make sense on either a literal or a metaphorical level. The word *vicinity,* meaning "nearby," is also an odd word choice; the system doesn't exist nearby but within the city limits.

H because the word *submerged* typically refers to something pushed below the surface of water. The London subway is not located entirely beneath water, nor does the passage suggest that it is. This description introduces an inaccuracy.

J because the subway is described in the essay as being below the city streets, rather than in alleys that are "low down," which is a vague and confusing description.

ENGLISH • PRACTICE TEST 4 • EXPLANATORY ANSWERS

Question 61. The best answer is D because **the essay begins by establishing that a system of mapping was needed after the subway system was built. It follows logically that the next sentence would be about the early mapping system, so no transition word is needed.**

The best answer is NOT:

A because the words "as a result" are not logical here. Building the subway did not require the early maps to "superimpose the subway lines over standard maps of London." This is just the technique these maps happened to use.

B because the information that this word introduces is *not* one example of many different types of early maps that were developed; it is the only type that the passage discusses. Therefore, "to provide an example" is incorrect.

C because *secondly* indicates that what follows is the second event, idea, or step in a process or series. However, the information provided in the paragraph is not framed as a series (there is no *firstly*). The transition word *secondly* creates a logical inconsistency.

Question 62. The best answer is H because ***indecipherable*** **indicates that the maps were not able to be read at all, suggesting the highest degree of failure for a map—it was unusable.**

The best answer is NOT:

F because *obscured* suggests that the routes were difficult, but not impossible, to read. It does not eliminate the possibility that the map could be read and used by subway riders.

G because *disappointing* does not suggest the "highest degree of failure." It indicates that the maps did not live up to expectations but does not say they were not able to serve their function.

J because "didn't fully capture" the subway indicates that the maps at least partially captured the routes.

ENGLISH • PRACTICE TEST 4 • EXPLANATORY ANSWERS

Question 63. **The best answer is C** because **this information is only tangentially related to the information in the paragraph. The focus of the first paragraph is on the method of mapping the subway that was devised in the 1800s. Details about the modern subway system distract from the focus on these early maps.**

The best answer is NOT:

A because providing details about the modern subway is not essential information in a paragraph that focuses on early subway mapping systems. Adding the sentence would also interrupt the transition from a discussion of the first attempts to map the subway to the discussion of a later (more effective) method of mapping.

B because the modern name of the subway does not suggest the need for a clear, accurate map. Such a map already exists, according to the essay (thanks to Beck).

D because the first paragraph does not focus on recent maps of the London Underground; it is about the mapping of the Underground in the 1800s.

Question 64. **The best answer is G** because **the stylistic outline is being compared to the sketch. The construction "more . . . than" works syntactically and creates a clear, precise comparison.**

The best answer is NOT:

F because *besides* means "other than" or "in addition to," neither of which makes sense within the sentence. The "more a" at the beginning of the sentence does not connect logically with *besides.*

H because *instead* creates a sentence with faulty syntax. The construction "more . . . instead" does suggest a comparison, but the preposition *of* would be needed after *instead* to avoid faulty sentence structure. A "more . . . than" construction captures the main idea more precisely.

J because *into* here suggests a transformation from one thing to another. The words "more . . . than" at the beginning of the sentence signal that the sentence will make a comparison, not describe a transformation.

ENGLISH • PRACTICE TEST 4 • EXPLANATORY ANSWERS

Question 65. The best answer is C because **the beginning of the sentence contains an introductory phrase that requires a comma between it and the main part of the sentence.**

The best answer is NOT:

A because the phrase before the semicolon lacks a verb and therefore is not an independent clause. Semicolons are used to separate independent clauses; a semicolon is not needed and is incorrect.

B because the conjunction *and* suggests that two ideas are being coordinated. Here, there is no coordination between two independent clauses. The beginning of the sentence is an introductory phrase that sets up a comparison to follow.

D because it creates a fragment by placing a period after the introductory phrase that begins the sentence. This phrase lacks a verb and cannot be an independent clause.

Question 66. The best answer is J because **it correctly combines the two adjective phrases "grid-like structure" and "color-coded routes" with the conjunction *and*, making it clear that these were both features of Beck's map.**

The best answer is NOT:

F because it creates an ambiguity that makes the meaning of the sentence unclear: Did the map have a color-coded route, or was it the grid-like structures that had a color-coded route? In the context of the sentence, the phrase "having also" creates a faulty construction.

G because it creates an ambiguity that makes the meaning of the sentence unclear: Did the map have a color-coded route, or was it the grid-like structures that had a color-coded route? It also creates a structurally faulty sentence.

H because it creates an ambiguity that makes the meaning of the sentence unclear: Did the map have a color-coded route, or was it the grid-like structures that had a color-coded route? It also creates a structurally faulty sentence.

Question 67. The best answer is A because "to show" makes the first clause in this sentence a dependent introductory clause, which creates a sentence with grammatically appropriate subordination.

The best answer is NOT:

B because "would show" creates a comma splice by making the introductory phrase at the beginning of the sentence an independent clause.

C because "had shown" creates a comma splice by transforming an introductory phrase into an independent clause.

D because *showed* creates a comma splice by making the introductory phrase at the beginning of the sentence an independent clause.

ENGLISH • PRACTICE TEST 4 • EXPLANATORY ANSWERS

Question 68. The best answer is F because **it provides a specific example of how Beck simplified the map by deleting the references to the city streets that had obscured some of the Underground routes.**

The best answer is NOT:

G because it merely indicates Beck's annoyance at the curving lines on the map. It does not provide an example of how Beck simplified the existing maps for subway passengers.

H because it indicates that Beck knew the maps had to be simple, but it does not give an example of how Beck created his "simplest possible schema."

J because it indicates the map's iconic status, but it does not provide an example of the map's simple schema.

Question 69. The best answer is B because to *increase* means to become larger or greater in size, amount, or number. This is the correct word given the context, because it's the number of riders (ridership) the Transport Board hoped to increase.

The best answer is NOT:

A because *rise* is an intransitive verb that means to move upward. The subway ridership itself would not literally move upward; rather, the number of riders would increase.

C because *enlarge* means to increase in size rather than number. The subway ridership would not increase in physical size; rather, the number of riders would increase.

D because *upend* means to cause something to be upside down or to fall down. The number of subway riders is increasing; the group is not being turned upside down or caused to fall down.

Question 70. The best answer is G because **"the board" makes it clear that it was the Transport Board that was desperate to increase subway ridership and revenues.**

The best answer is NOT:

F because as written, the sentence indicates it was the limited number of copies that were "willing to try anything to increase subway ridership and therefore revenues." The sentence fails to name "the board" as the group that is printing the copies, which makes this misreading possible.

H because as written, the sentence indicates it was the copies that were "willing to try anything to increase subway ridership and therefore revenues." The sentence fails to name "the board" as the group that is printing the copies, which makes this misreading possible.

J because as written, the sentence indicates it was the copies that were "willing to try anything to increase subway ridership and therefore revenues." The sentence fails to name "the board" as the group that is printing the copies, which makes this misreading possible. In addition, the lack of a verb in this phrase creates a sentence fragment.

ENGLISH • PRACTICE TEST 4 • EXPLANATORY ANSWERS

Question 71. The best answer is B because **Sentence 1 discusses the fact that the Transport Board initially resisted the map, and Sentence 5 explains why the board resisted the map. This is a logical way to present this information and provides a smooth transition to the rest of the paragraph.**

The best answer is NOT:

A because Sentence 5, which explains why the Transport Board resisted Beck's map, is out of place in the middle of a discussion about the map's success.

C because placing Sentence 5 after Sentence 2 breaks the logical progression from the board's resistance to the map to the reasons for the resistance. This placement is also not logical because it mentions the creation of copies of the map before mention of the board's initial resistance to the idea.

D because placing Sentence 5 after Sentence 3 breaks the logical progression from the board's resistance to the map to the reasons for the resistance. This placement is also not logical because it explains the board's resistance to the map after mentioning the later copying of the map and the map's success.

Question 72. The best answer is H because *its* is a singular possessive pronoun referring to the word *map.* Because map is singular, the pronoun and antecedent agree in number. Also, a possessive is needed because the sentence is referring to the basic elements that are features of the map.

The best answer is NOT:

F because *it's* is a contraction for "it is." Saying that "he retained it is basic elements" creates a nonsensical, ungrammatical sentence. At this point, the sentence also requires a possessive pronoun to refer back to the map. The contraction *it's* is not possessive.

G because *their* is a plural possessive pronoun. The antecedent of the pronoun in the sentence is *map,* which is singular. A pronoun and its antecedent must agree in number.

J because *its'* is not the correct possessive form of *it.* The correct possessive for it is *its,* without an apostrophe.

ENGLISH • PRACTICE TEST 4 • EXPLANATORY ANSWERS

Question 73. The best answer is C because **a comma should not separate any of the elements in the noun phrase "approach to mapping," nor should there be a comma between the noun phrase and the verb remains.**

The best answer is NOT:

A because a comma should not separate the noun phrase "approach to mapping" from the verb *remains.*

B because a comma should not separate the adjective *diagrammatic* from the noun phrase "approach to mapping." The comma separating this phrase from the verb *remains* is also incorrect.

D because the comma separates the prepositional phrase "to mapping" from the noun *approach,* which incorrectly breaks up the noun phrase that serves as the subject of the sentence: "[Beck's] approach to mapping."

Question 74. The best answer is J because **it clearly and concisely identifies Beck's mapping method as what other urban transit maps model. This also works as a suitable conclusion for the sentence and the essay because it is a fitting description of Beck's approach as described in the essay.**

The best answer is NOT:

F because the use of the pronoun *this* creates an ambiguous pronoun reference. *This* could refer to the approach, to the field of information, to the map's basic elements, to the world, and so on, which makes the meaning of the sentence unclear.

G because "this means" creates an ambiguous pronoun reference. This option is also redundant because it has already been stated that Beck's approach is "standard in the field."

H because this option is redundant; it has already been stated that Beck's approach is "deceptively simple."

ENGLISH • PRACTICE TEST 4 • EXPLANATORY ANSWERS

Question 75. The best answer is B because **it places the added sentence, which explains why Beck left out the actual distances between points, immediately after the sentence that reveals Beck left out the distances. This creates a logical progression from Beck's decision to the reasoning behind his decision.**

The best answer is NOT:

A because Point A occurs during a discussion of early versions of subway maps. The added sentence refers to Beck's maps, which have not been introduced yet. The sentence does not make sense without the information about Beck and his mapping that are provided in Paragraph 2.

C because the sentence immediately before Point C refers to the refinements that Beck made to his map after it had already become a success. The essay makes it clear that even Beck's first maps left out actual distances; therefore, leaving out the distances was not a refinement but part of the original diagram. The added sentence does not logically fit at Point C because this placement suggests Beck's reasons for not including the distances are related to later refinements to the map.

D because the sentence immediately before Point D discusses how Beck's approach to mapping has been widely adopted. The added sentence, however, explains a specific statement made about the map's features in Paragraph 2. This placement for the added sentence not only puts the sentence too far away from the point it is meant to explain but also it interferes with the last paragraph's attempt to describe the broader impact Beck's map has had on the world.

MATHEMATICS • PRACTICE TEST 4 • EXPLANATORY ANSWERS

Question 1. The correct answer is C. The area of a rectangle is equal to the product of its width and length, $A = WL$. Because the top surface of the rectangular table has an area of 100 square feet and a width of 5 feet, $100 = 5L$ and $20 = L$. If you chose **E**, you may have set up the equation incorrectly and calculated the area for a length of 100 feet and a width of 5 feet.

Question 2. The correct answer is J. The number of possible outcomes (that is, the total number of bills in the wallet) is $2 + 9 + 5 = 16$, and the number of favorable outcomes (choosing a twenty-dollar bill) is 5. The probability of a favorable outcome is equal to $\frac{\text{the number of favorable outcomes}}{\text{the number of possible outcomes}}$. So, the probability of a twenty-dollar bill being randomly selected from the wallet is $\frac{5}{16}$. If you chose **F**, you could have overlooked how many possible favorable outcomes there are.

Question 3. The correct answer is E. In order to determine how many combinations of clown costumes Elmo can make, multiply the number of items in each category that makes up a complete costume (noses, pairs of lips, and wigs), $4 \cdot 3 \cdot 2 = 24$. If you chose **B**, you may have added the number of items Elmo has in each category to find the total number of items rather than the number of combinations of items that make a complete costume.

Question 4. The correct answer is F. The remaining materials for care packages are 30 pens (3 boxes with 10 pens each, $3 \cdot 10 = 30$), which can fill 6 care packages at 5 pens each ($\frac{30}{5} = 6$); 20 notebooks (4 boxes with 5 notebooks each, $4 \cdot 5 = 20$), which can fill 10 care packages at 2 notebooks each ($\frac{20}{2} = 10$); 24 envelopes (2 boxes with 12 envelopes each, $2 \cdot 12 = 24$), which can fill 8 care packages at 3 envelopes each ($\frac{24}{3} = 8$); 84 cookies, which can fill 7 care packages at 12 cookies each ($\frac{84}{12} = 7$); and 45 bars of candy (4.5 boxes with 10 candy bars each, $4.5 \cdot 10 = 45$), which can fill 9 care packages at 5 candy bars each ($\frac{45}{5} = 9$). Because the remaining pens can create the least number of care packages, 6, that is the additional number of complete care packages Esteban and his family can make with the remaining materials. If you chose **J**, you may have failed to realize that every care package must be complete.

Question 5. The correct answer is C. A right circular cone with a height of 28 inches and a radius of 6 inches would have an approximate volume of 1,056 cubic inches: $V = \frac{1}{3}\pi r^2 h = \frac{1}{3}\left(\frac{22}{7}\right)(6^2)(28) = 1{,}056$.

Question 6. The correct answer is G. Because $\overline{AD}$ is perpendicular to $\overline{BE}$, the measure of $\angle BEA$ is $90°$. The measure of $\angle ABE$ is $62°$ because the sum of the measures of the angles in a triangle is $180°$, and $180° - 28° - 90° = 62°$. Because $\angle ABE$ and $\angle CBE$ create a straight line, the measure of $\angle CBE$ is $118°$ because $180° - 62° = 118°$.

MATHEMATICS • PRACTICE TEST 4 • EXPLANATORY ANSWERS

Question 7. The correct answer is B. The sum of the two expressions can be found algebraically by combining like terms, $(0.1x^2+3x+80)+(0.5x^2-2x+60)=(0.1x^2+0.5x^2)+(3x-2x)+(80+60)=0.6x^2+x+140$. If you chose **A**, you may have calculated the difference of the expressions.

Question 8. The correct answer is H. The slope-intercept form, $y=mx+b$ where m is the slope and b is the y-intercept, can be used to write the equation of a line that represents the relationship between y and x. The slope of the line that represents the relationship between d and t is the rate at which the cart is rolling, which is $\frac{\text{the change in distance}}{\text{the change in time}}=\frac{30-15}{5-0}=3$. When you substitute the value of the slope into the slope-intercept form and use d and t in place of y and x, you get $d=3t+b$. To determine b, the d-intercept of the line, substitute a given ordered pair in the table for d and t in the equation and solve for b. $15=3(0)+b \Leftrightarrow 15=b$. Therefore the equation that represents the relationship between d and t is $d=3t+15$. If you chose **J**, you could have mixed up the values of the slope and d-intercept in the equation.

Question 9. The correct answer is C. The original price of the pants was \$40 but Dmitry bought them at the discounted price of \$30 which is \$10 less than the original price because \$40 – \$30 = \$10. The percent of the discount is $\left(\frac{10}{40}\right)(100)=25\%$ of the original price. If you chose **E**, you could have calculated the percent the discounted price is of the original price.

Question 10. The correct answer is G. The absolute value of a number is its magnitude. The magnitude of –6 is 6 and the magnitude of (7 – 41) is 34. Therefore, $|-6|-|7-41|=6-34=-28$. If you chose **J**, you may have added 6 and 34.

Question 11. The correct answer is C. The total number of shares of stock owned by Samantha, Nyla, and Jerry is $70+50+40=160$. The value of each single share of stock is $\frac{\text{combined value of the shares of stock}}{\text{total number of the shares of stock}}=\frac{\$6{,}880}{160 \text{ shares}}=\$43$ per share. Therefore, the value of the shares of stock that Samantha owns is $\$43\times70=\$3{,}010$. If you chose **A**, you may have divided the combined value of the shares of stock by the number of shares of stock owned by Samantha only and rounded to the nearest dollar: $\frac{6{,}880}{70}\approx98$. If you chose **B**, you may have erroneously computed $43\times7=301$. If you chose **D**, you may have thought the value of the shares of stock that Samantha owns is 70% of the combined value of the shares of stock or $0.70(6{,}880)=4{,}816$. If you chose **E**, you may divided the combined value of the shares of stock by the number of shares of stock owned by Nyla and Jerry and then multiplied by the value of the shares of stock that Samantha owns: $\frac{6{,}880}{50+40}\cdot70\approx5{,}351$.

Taking Additional Practice Tests

Question 12. The correct answer is G. Customers who are at least 18 years of age are represented on the number line by a closed dot on 18 to indicate 18 is part of the solution and shading of the number line to the right of 18. Customers who are less than 30 years of age are represented on the number line by an open dot on 30 to indicate 30 is NOT part of the solution and shading of the number line to the left of 30. As a result, the number line that illustrates the required age range of at least 18 but less than 30 years of age has a line segment with a closed dot on18, shading between 18 and 30, and an open dot on 30. If you chose **F**, you chose the number line that represents customers who were between 18 and 30 years of age, inclusive. If you chose **H**, you chose the number line that represents customers who were 30 years of age or younger. If you chose **J**, you chose the number line that represents customers who were younger than 30 years of age. If you chose **K**, you chose the number line that represents customers who were younger than 18 years of age or older than 30 years of age.

Question 13. The correct answer is D. The Triangle Proportionality Theorem states that if a line parallel to one side of a triangle intersects the other two sides of the triangle, then the line divides these two sides proportionally. Therefore, because $\overline{DE} \cdot \overline{FG}$, then $\frac{AD}{DF} = \frac{AE}{EG} \Leftrightarrow \frac{6}{5} = \frac{12}{EG} \Leftrightarrow 6(EG) = 5(12) \Leftrightarrow 6(EG) = 60 \Leftrightarrow EG = 10$. Similarly, because $\overline{FG} \cdot \overline{BC}$, then $\frac{AF}{FB} = \frac{AG}{GC} \Leftrightarrow \frac{6+5}{4} = \frac{12+10}{GC} \Leftrightarrow \frac{11}{4} = \frac{22}{GC} \Leftrightarrow 11(GC) = 4(22) \Leftrightarrow 11(GC) = 88 \Leftrightarrow GC = 8$. Thus, $AC = AE + EG + GC = 12 + 10 + 8 = 30$. If you chose **B**, you may have found the sum of EG and GC only: $10 + 8 = 18$. If you chose **A**, you may have multiplied the sum of EG and GC by $\frac{AD}{AE}$: $18\left(\frac{6}{12}\right) = 9$. If you chose **E**, you may have multiplied the sum of EG and GC by $\frac{AE}{AD}$: $18\left(\frac{12}{6}\right) = 36$. If you chose **C**, you may have added AE, DF and FB: $12 + 5 + 4 = 21$.

Question 14. The correct answer is G. First, set up an inequality with the closest perfect square integer values below and above the integer 50: $49 < 50 < 64$. Next, take the square root of all three parts: $\sqrt{49} < \sqrt{50} < \sqrt{64} \Leftrightarrow 7 < \sqrt{50} < 8$. Finally, divide all three parts by 2: $\frac{7}{2} < \frac{\sqrt{50}}{2} < \frac{8}{2} \Leftrightarrow 3.5 < \frac{\sqrt{50}}{2} < 4$. Now, $\frac{\sqrt{50}}{2}$ is greater than 3.5 and less than 4, which makes 4 the closest integer to $\frac{\sqrt{50}}{2}$. If you chose **F**, you may have used 36 as the closest perfect square integer value below 50 and neglected to find the closest perfect square integer value above 50: $36 < 50 \Leftrightarrow \frac{\sqrt{36}}{2} < \frac{\sqrt{50}}{2} \Leftrightarrow \frac{6}{2} < \frac{\sqrt{50}}{2} \Leftrightarrow 3 < \frac{\sqrt{50}}{2}$. Similarly, if you chose **H**, you may have used 100 as the closest perfect square integer value above 50 and neglected to find the closest perfect square integer value below 50: $50 < 100 \Leftrightarrow \frac{\sqrt{50}}{2} < \frac{\sqrt{100}}{2} \Leftrightarrow \frac{\sqrt{50}}{2} < \frac{10}{2} \Leftrightarrow \frac{\sqrt{50}}{2} < 5$. If you chose **K**, you may have found that $\sqrt{49} < \sqrt{50} \Leftrightarrow 7 < \sqrt{50}$ and then doubled the value on the left.

MATHEMATICS • PRACTICE TEST 4 • EXPLANATORY ANSWERS

Question 15. The correct answer is D. Let x represent a factor of the sum of Jane's age and her daughter's age. Then, we have $9x+2x=44 \Leftrightarrow 11x=44 \Leftrightarrow x=4$. Therefore, Jane's age is $9(x)=9(4)=36$. If you chose **A**, you may have multiplied 4 by the average of the 9 and $2: 4\cdot\frac{9+2}{2}=4\cdot\frac{11}{2}=22$. If you chose **B**, you may have subtracted 9 and 2 from the sum of their ages: $44-9-2=33$. If you chose **C**, you may have subtracted 9 from the sum of their ages: $44-9=35$. If you chose **E**, you may have subtracted 4 from the sum of their ages: $44-4=40$.

Question 16. The correct answer is H. First, we compute the fraction of the operating budget that is allocated to library books and scholarships. This is the sum of the fractions for each allocation: $\frac{1}{9}+\frac{1}{6}=\frac{2}{18}+\frac{3}{18}=\frac{5}{18}$. To compute the fraction of the operating budget that remains for other uses, we subtract the previous sum from the whole of the operating budget: $1-\frac{5}{18}=\frac{18}{18}-\frac{5}{18}=\frac{13}{18}$. If you chose **F**, you may have subtracted the fraction of the operating budget that is allocated to library books from the fraction of the operating budget that is allocated to scholarships. If you chose **G**, you selected the fraction of the operating budget that is allocated to library books and scholarships only. If you chose **K**, you selected the fraction of the operating budget that is NOT allocated to library books.

Question 17. The correct answer is A. The second fraction in the proportion may be simplified to $\frac{5}{6}$, so that we have $\frac{10}{10+x}=\frac{5}{6}$. We may use the multiplication property of equality to solve the proportion. We multiply both sides of the equation by the product $6(10+x)$:

$$\left(\frac{10}{10+x}\right)\cdot 6(10+x)=\left(\frac{5}{6}\right)\cdot 6(10+x) \Leftrightarrow 10(6)=5(10+x) \Leftrightarrow 60=50+5x$$

Next, we solve the resulting linear equation for $x: 60=50+5x \Leftrightarrow 10=5x \Leftrightarrow x=2$.

If you chose **B**, you may have subtracted the numerator of the second fraction from the denominator of the second fraction. If you chose **C**, you selected the value of $10+x$, which is $10+2=12$. If you chose **D**, you may have subtracted the numerator of the second fraction from the denominator of the second fraction and then added $10: 42-35+10=17$. If you chose **E**, you selected the value of x for which the denominator of the first fraction will be equal to the denominator of the second fraction. However, $\frac{10}{10+32}=\frac{10}{42}\neq\frac{35}{42}$.

Question 18. The correct answer is J. The total area of the 2 shaded triangles can be found by subtracting the area of the unshaded triangle from the area of the rectangle. The area of the rectangle is $8(10)=80$ square inches. The area of the unshaded triangle is $\frac{1}{2}(10)(8)=40$ square inches. Thus, the total area of the 2 shaded triangles is $80-40=40$ square inches. If you chose **F**, you may have thought that the total area of the 2 shaded triangles is $\frac{1}{2}$ the area of the unshaded triangle. If you chose **H**, you may have subtracted 2 times the area of the larger shaded triangle from the area of the rectangle: $80-2\left(\frac{1}{2}\right)(6)(8)=80-48=32$. If you chose **K**, you may have found the area of the rectangle only.

MATHEMATICS • PRACTICE TEST 4 • EXPLANATORY ANSWERS

Question 19. The correct answer is C. We need to find the ordered pair that satisfies all three of the inequalities in the given system. Therefore, the x-coordinate of the ordered pair must be greater than 2, the y-coordinate of the ordered pair must be greater than 0, and the sum of the x-coordinate and the y-coordinate of the ordered pair must be less than 5. The only ordered pair that satisfies all three of the inequalities is (3,1). If you chose **A**, you may have chosen (1,3) because it satisfies the second and third inequalities; however, it does not satisfy the first inequality. Similarly, if you chose **B**, you may have chosen (2,2) because it satisfies the second and third inequalities; however, it does not satisfy the first inequality. If you chose **D**, you may have chosen (3,2) because it satisfies the first and second inequalities; however, it does not satisfy the third inequality. If you chose **E**, you may have chosen (4,0) because it satisfies the first and third inequalities; however, it does not satisfy the second inequality.

Question 20. The correct answer is H. For real numbers b and c, the range of any sine function of the form $y = \sin(bx + c)$ is $-1 \le y \le 1$. Thus, the range of the function $y = \sin(x - \pi)$ is $-1 \le y \le 1$. It follows that $y = 3 - 5\sin(x - \pi)$ will have y-values such that $3 - 5(1) \le y \le 3 + 5(1)$. Thus, the range of $y = 3 - 5\sin(x - \pi)$ is $-2 \le y \le 8$. If you chose **F**, you may have ignored the 3 in the given function and instead found the range of the function $y = -5\sin(x - \pi): -5(1) \le y \le 5(1) \Leftrightarrow -5 \le y \le 5$. If you chose **G**, you may have computed the range as $3 - 5(1) \le y \le 5(1) - 3 \Leftrightarrow -2 \le y \le 2$. If you chose **J**, you may have thought $0 \le y \le 1$ was the range of the function $y = \sin(x - \pi)$, and then found the range of the function $y = 3 - 5\sin(x - \pi)$ to be $3 - 5(0) \le y \le 3 + 5(1) \Leftrightarrow 3 \le y \le 8$.

Question 21. The correct answer is D. In the composition $f(g(-3))$, first replace each x found in $g(x)$, the inside function, with the input –3. Next, replace each x found in $f(x)$ with the value $g(-3)$. First of all, $g(x) = x^2 - 4$, so $g(-3) = (-3)^2 - 4 = 9 - 4 = 5$. Accordingly, $f(x) = 2x + 1$, so $f(g(-3)) = f(5) = 2(5) + 1 = 10 + 1 = 11$. If you chose **A**, you may have thought $(-5)^2 = -25$ and attempted to compute $g(f(-3))$: $f(-3) = 2(-3) + 1 = -5$, and so $g(f(-3)) = g(-5) = (-5)^2 - 4 \Rightarrow -25 - 4 = -29$. If you chose **B**, you may have thought $(-3)^2 = -9$, so that $g(-3) = -9 - 4 = -13$, and $f(g(-3)) = f(-13) = 2(-13) + 1 = -25$. If you chose **C**, you may have attempted to compute $f(-3) + g(-3)$. However, you may have dropped the constant from the function $f(x) = 2x + 1$, so that $f(-3) = -2(3) = -6$. In addition, you may have thought $(-3)^2 = -9$, so that $g(-3) = -9 - 4 = -13$. Then $f(-3) + g(-3) = -19$. If you chose **E**, you may have found $(f(-3))$: $f(-3) = 2(-3) + 1 = -5$, and so $g(f(-3)) = g(-5) = (-5)^2 - 4 = 21$.

MATHEMATICS • PRACTICE TEST 4 • EXPLANATORY ANSWERS

Question 22. The correct answer is G. We may set up a system of two equations in two variables to model the dollar amounts that Joan and Chris each paid for the fabrics. Let x be the price, in dollars, of 1 yard of flannel fabric. Let y be the price, in dollars, of 1 yard of calico fabric. Then we have $\begin{matrix} 3x+4y=25\,(\text{Joan}) \\ x+2y=11\,(\text{Chris}) \end{matrix}$. To solve this system, multiply the second equation by −3, and add it to the first equation. $\begin{matrix} 3x+4y=25 \\ -3(x+2y=11) \end{matrix} \Leftrightarrow \begin{matrix} 3x+4y=25 \\ -3x-6y=-33 \end{matrix} \Leftrightarrow -2y=-8$.

Then, solve for y: $-2y=-8 \Leftrightarrow y=4$. The price, in dollars, of 1 yard of calico fabric is \$4. If you chose **F**, you may have solved the system for x, the price, in dollars, of 1 yard of flannel fabric. If you chose **H**, you may have divided the total number of yards of fabric bought by Joan and Chris in half: $\frac{3+4+1+2}{2}=\frac{10}{2}=5$. If you chose **J**, you may have divided the sum of the dollar amounts that Joan and Chris each paid by the total number of yards of calico fabric bought: $\frac{25+11}{4+2}=\frac{36}{6}=6$. If you chose **K**, you may have found how much more Joan paid and then divided it by how much more calico fabric she bought: $\frac{25-11}{4-2}=\frac{14}{2}=7$.

Question 23. The correct answer is C. To find the median of a data set, arrange the data values in order from least to greatest. The median is the value separating the upper half of the data from the lower half. When a data set has an odd number of values, the median is the exact middle value. When a data set has an even number of values, there are two middlemost values. Average them to find the median. In order from least to greatest, the scores in this data set are $71, 77, 78, 80, 86, 88, 88, 94, 94, 94$. The two middlemost scores are 86 and 88, which makes the key $\frac{86+88}{2}=87$. If you chose **A**, you may have found the mean of the ten scores: $\frac{\textit{sum of the scores}}{\textit{number of scores}}=\frac{850}{210}=85$. If you chose **B**, you selected the average of the mean and the median: $\frac{85+87}{2}=86$. If you chose **D**, you may have chosen the least of the two middlemost scores of the unordered ten scores: $\min\{88,94\}=88$. If you chose **E**, you may have found the mean of the two middlemost scores of the unordered ten scores: $\frac{88+94}{2}=91$.

Question 24. The correct answer is H. Opposite sides of a parallelogram are congruent. Thus, the side of the parallelogram that measures 16 inches has a side opposite to it that also measures 16 inches. It follows that the sum of the measures of the parallelogram's remaining two sides is equal to $84-2(16)=84-32=52$ inches. Therefore, each of the two sides must measure $\frac{52}{2}=26$ inches. If you chose **F**, you may have subtracted the given side from the perimeter and then selected three side lengths whose sum was the value of that difference: $84-16=68$ and $16+16+36=68$. However, sides of length 16, 16, 16, and 36 inches do not form a parallelogram. If you chose **G**, you have selected a parallelogram with a perimeter of $16+16+18+18=68$ inches. If you chose **J**, you may have subtracted the given side from the perimeter before dividing by 2: $\frac{84-16}{2}=34$. However, the perimeter of the parallelogram would then be $16+16+34+34=100$ inches.

MATHEMATICS • PRACTICE TEST 4 • EXPLANATORY ANSWERS

Question 25. The correct answer is E. First, note that the shaded region is also a rectangle and that each of its dimensions is a fraction of the corresponding dimension of rectangle *ABCD*. Now, let the area of rectangle *ABCD* be given by $A = LW$, where L is the length and W is the width. Each row in rectangle *ABCD* has 6 squares, and each row in the shaded region has 5 squares. Thus, the length of the shaded region is $\frac{5}{6}L$. Each column in rectangle *ABCD* has 4 squares, and each column in the shaded region has 3 squares. Thus, the width of the shaded region is $\frac{3}{4}W$. It follows that the area, in square units, of the shaded region is $\left(\frac{5}{6}L\right)\left(\frac{3}{4}W\right) = \frac{5}{6}\cdot\frac{3}{4}LW = \frac{5}{6}\cdot\frac{3}{4}\cdot(1) = \frac{5}{6}\cdot\frac{3}{4}$. If you chose **A**, you may have computed the area of a single small square only, neglecting the fact that there are 5 small squares in a row and 3 small squares in a column. If you chose **B**, you may have first computed the area of a single small square and also noticed that there are 3 small squares in a column, but you neglected the fact that there are 5 small squares in a row. If you chose **C**, you may have found that the length of the shaded rectangle is $\frac{5}{6}$ the length of rectangle *ABCD*. As a result, you may have multiplied this fraction by the length of a single small square. If you chose **D**, you may have first computed the area of a single small square and also noticed that there are 5 small squares in a row, but you neglected the fact that there are 3 small squares in a column.

Question 26. The correct answer is G. We can set up a proportion where each side represents the probability of randomly drawing a red marble; that is, $\frac{\text{number of red marbles}}{\text{total marbles}}$. Let x be the number of additional red marbles added to the 42 marbles. It follows that $\frac{3}{5} = \frac{16+x}{42+x}$. We can use the multiplication property of equality to solve the proportion. We multiply both sides of the equation by the product $5(42+x)$: $5(42+x)\left(\frac{3}{5}\right) = 5(42+x)\left(\frac{16+x}{42+x}\right) \Leftrightarrow 3(42+x) = 5(16+x) \Leftrightarrow 126+3x = 80+5x$. Next, we solve the resulting linear equation for x: $126+3x = 80+5x \Leftrightarrow 46 = 2x \Leftrightarrow x = 23$. If you chose **F**, you may have computed $\frac{3(42)}{5(16)}+16 = 17.575$ and rounded up. If you chose **K**, you may have solved the proportion $\frac{3}{5} = \frac{x}{16} \Leftrightarrow x = 9.6$, rounded the solution up to the nearest integer, and added to 42.

Question 27. The correct answer is E. Negative exponents signify multiplicative inverses and thus are the reciprocal of positive exponents. This means that a base raised to a negative exponent is equivalent to 1 divided by the base raised to the positive of the exponent. Therefore, $a^{-2} = \frac{1}{a^2}$. If you chose **A**, you may have multiplied the exponent by the base. If you chose **D**, you may have used the reciprocal of the positive of the exponent in the denominator: $a^{-2} \Rightarrow \frac{1}{\frac{1}{a^2}} \Rightarrow \frac{1}{\sqrt{a}}$.

MATHEMATICS • PRACTICE TEST 4 • EXPLANATORY ANSWERS

Question 28. The correct answer is F. Jamie's claim is a conditional statement in the form of a hypothesis followed by a conclusion. The hypothesis of Jamie's claim is "a triangle is in set *A*," and the conclusion of the claim is "it is not isosceles." Now, the only way for a conditional statement to be false is for the hypothesis to be true and the conclusion to be false. Because ΔMNP is a counterexample that proves Jamie's claim is false, it must be true that ΔMNP is a triangle in set *A* and that ΔMNP is isosceles. If you chose **G**, you selected the statement for which the hypothesis is true and the conclusion is true. If you chose **H**, you neglected the fact that obtuse triangles may be isosceles or scalene, so you selected the statement for which the hypothesis is false and the conclusion may be true or false. If you chose **J**, you selected the statement for which the hypothesis is false and the conclusion is true. If you chose **K**, you selected the statement for which the hypothesis is false and the conclusion is false.

Question 29. The correct answer is D. The area of a parallelogram is given by the formula $A = bh$ where *b* is the base and *h* is the height of the parallelogram. Side $\overline{AD}$ is a base of parallelogram *ABCD*, and the height of parallelogram *ABCD* is equal to the distance between $\overline{AD}$ and $\overline{BC}$. Therefore, the area, in square coordinate units, of parallelogram *ABCD* is given by $A = bh = 5(3) = 15$. If you chose **B**, you may have used the formula for the area of a triangle: $A = \frac{1}{2}bh = \frac{1}{2}(5)(3)$. If you chose **E**, you may have used the formula for the perimeter of a square: $A = 4s = 4(5)$.

Question 30. The correct answer is H. To find the distance between two points (x_1, y_1) and (x_2, y_2), we can use the distance formula, $d = \sqrt{(x_2 - x_1)^2 + (y_2 - y_1)^2}$. It follows that the distance between *B*(0,4) and *D*(4,1) is given y $d = \sqrt{(4-1)^2 + (0-4)^2} = \sqrt{(3)^2 + (-4)^2} = \sqrt{9+16} = \sqrt{25} = 5$ coordinate units. If you chose **F**, you may have switched the plus and minus signs in the distance formula: $\sqrt{(4+1)^2 - (0+4)^2} \Rightarrow \sqrt{25-16} \Rightarrow \sqrt{9} \Rightarrow 3$. If you chose **J**, you may have incorrectly computed the distance as $\left|(4-1)^2 - (0-4)^2\right| \Rightarrow |9-16| \Rightarrow 7$.

Question 31. The correct answer is A. To find the slope of a line containing two points (x_1, y_1) and (x_2, y_2), use the slope formula $m = \frac{y_2 - y_1}{x_2 - x_1}$. Line $\overleftrightarrow{BC}$ contains the points *B*(0,4) and *C*(5,4). It follows that the slope of $\overleftrightarrow{BC}$ is given by $m = \frac{y_2 - y_1}{x_2 - x_1} = \frac{4-4}{5-0} = 0$. If you chose **B**, you may have computed the difference in the *x*-coordinate and *y*-coordinate of point *C*(5,4): $5 - 4 = 1$. If you chose **D**, you may have computed the difference in the *x*-coordinates of *B*(0,4) and *C*(5,4): $5 - 0 = 5$. If you chose **E**, you may have computed the slope as $\frac{run}{rise} = \frac{\text{change in } x}{\text{change in } y}$.

MATHEMATICS • PRACTICE TEST 4 • EXPLANATORY ANSWERS

Question 32. The correct answer is J. When we reflect a point over the y-axis, the y-coordinate remains the same, but the x-coordinate is transformed into its opposite (its sign is changed). Therefore, the coordinates of the image of $A(-1,1)$ after reflection over the y-axis are $(1,1)$. If you chose **F**, you selected the image of point $D(4,1)$ after reflection over the y-axis. If you chose **G**, you selected the image of point $A(-1,1)$ after reflection over the x-axis, where the x-coordinate remains the same, but the y-coordinate is transformed into its opposite. If you chose **H**, you selected the image of point $A(-1,1)$ after reflection over the origin $(0,0)$, where both the x- and y-coordinates are transformed into their opposites. If you chose **K**, you selected the image of point $D(4,1)$ after reflection over the x-axis.

Question 33. The correct answer is A. First, rewrite the product $8^2 \cdot 4^{0.5}$ so that each factor has the same base: $(2^3)^2 \cdot (2^2)^{0.5}$. Next, apply the power rule for exponents, $(a^m)^n = a^{mn}$, to each factor. Therefore, we have $(2^3)^2 \cdot (2^2)^{0.5} = 2^{3(2)} \cdot 2^{2(0.5)} = 2^6 \cdot 2^1 s$. Finally, apply the product rule for exponents, $a^m \cdot a^n = a^{m+n}$, to combine the 2 factors. Thus, we have $2^6 \cdot 2^1 = 2^{6+1} = 2^7$. If you chose **B**, you may have rewritten the base of the first factor as $4 \cdot 2$ and then incorrectly applied the power rule for exponents: $8^2 \cdot 4^{0.5} \Rightarrow (4 \cdot 2)^2 \cdot (4)^{0.5} \Rightarrow (4)^{2(2)} \cdot (4)^{0.5} \Rightarrow 4^{4+0.5}$. If you chose **C**, you may have used the greater of the bases together with the sum of the exponents: $8^2 \cdot 4^{0.5} \Rightarrow 8^{2+0.5} \Rightarrow 8^{2.5}$. If you chose **D**, you may have simplified the second factor and then multiplied it by the base of the first factor: $8^2 \cdot 4^{0.5} \Rightarrow 8^2 \cdot 2 \Rightarrow (8 \cdot 2)^2 \Rightarrow 16^2$. If you chose **E**, you may have multiplied the bases and multiplied the exponents: $8^2 \cdot 4^{0.5} \Rightarrow (8 \cdot 4)^{2 \cdot 0.5} \Rightarrow 32^1$.

Question 34. The correct answer is K. The school admissions office accepts 2 of every 7 applicants. That means that 5 of every 7 applicants are NOT accepted. Let x be the number of applicants that were not accepted. We may set up a proportion where each side represents the ratio $\frac{\text{number of applicants NOT accepted}}{\text{total number of applicants}}$. It follows that $\frac{5}{7} = \frac{x}{x+630}$. We may use the multiplication property of equality to solve the proportion. We multiply both sides of the equation by the product $7(x+630)$: $7(x+630) \cdot \left(\frac{5}{7}\right) = 7(x+630) \cdot \left(\frac{x}{x+630}\right) \Leftrightarrow 5(x+630) = 7x \Leftrightarrow 5x + 3{,}150 = 7x$. Then, we solve the linear equation for x: $5x + 3{,}150 = 7x \Leftrightarrow 2x = 3{,}150 \Leftrightarrow x = 1{,}575$. If you chose **F**, you may have divided the total number of applicants into $2+7=9$ parts and then computed $\frac{2}{9}(630) = 140$. If you chose **G**, you may have solved the proportion $\frac{2}{7} = \frac{x}{630} \Leftrightarrow x = 180$. If you chose **H**, you may have divided the total number of applicants into 9 parts and then computed $\frac{7}{9}(630) = 490$. If you chose **J**, you may have doubled the number of applicants that were accepted: $2(630) = 1{,}260$.

MATHEMATICS • PRACTICE TEST 4 • EXPLANATORY ANSWERS

Question 35. The correct answer is B. First, note that by the properties of exponents, $\sqrt{8}=\sqrt{2^3}=(2^3)^{1/2}=2^{3/2}$. Next, note that because the functions $y=\log_2 x$ and $y=2^x$ are inverse functions, then $\log_2(2^x)=x$. It follows that $\log_2\sqrt{8}=\log_2 2^{3/2}=\frac{3}{2}$. If you chose **A**, you may have simplified the radical but then incorrectly applied the product property of logarithms: $\log_2\sqrt{8}=\log_2 2\sqrt{2}\Rightarrow(\log_2 2)(\log_2\sqrt{2})\Rightarrow(1)(\log_2 2^{1/2})\Rightarrow\frac{1}{2}$. If you chose **C**, you may have simplified the radical but then incorrectly applied the inverse property, $\log_2(2^x)=x$, and thought that $\log_2\sqrt{8}=\log_2 2\sqrt{2}\Rightarrow\sqrt{2}$. If you chose **E**, you may have dropped the square root when simplifying: $\log_2\sqrt{8}=\log_2 2^3\Rightarrow 3$.

Question 36. The correct answer is F. In a circle graph, each different sector represents a proportion of a total. Moreover, the measure of each central angle of a circle graph is proportional to the quantity it represents. Because there are 360° in a circle, Jie must represent each part of the data as a proportion of 360. First, we note that apples, bananas, and strawberries were each chosen as favorites by an equal number of the $90-15=75$ remaining students. Thus, bananas were chosen as the favorite fruit of $\frac{75}{3}=25$ students out of the 90 students in the survey. It follows that Jie will represent bananas on the circle graph as a sector with a central angle that measures $\frac{25}{90}\cdot 360°=100°$. If you chose **G**, you may have thought the central angle in the circle for the 15 students who chose peaches represented 15% and computed $\frac{360-0.15(360)}{3}=\frac{306}{3}=102°$. If you chose **H**, you may have thought the central angle in the circle for the 15 students who chose peaches was $\frac{90}{2}=45$ and computed $\frac{360-45}{3}=\frac{315}{3}=105°$. If you chose **J**, you may have thought the central angle in the circle for the 15 students who chose peaches was $\frac{90}{4}=22.5$ and computed $\frac{360-22.5}{3}=\frac{337.5}{3}=112.5°$. If you chose **K**, you may have thought the central angle in the circle for the 15 students who chose peaches measured 15° and computed $\frac{360-15}{3}=\frac{345}{3}=115°$.

Question 37. The correct answer is E. The denominators of the two fractions are unlike. We may rewrite each fraction with a new denominator that is equal to the least common multiple of their denominators: $5x$. We do this by multiplying each of the two fractions by additional fractions that are equivalent to 1. Then we may finally add the numerators of the rewritten fractions. Thus, we have $\frac{x}{x}\cdot\frac{4}{5}+\frac{5}{5}\cdot\frac{7}{x}=\frac{4x}{5x}+\frac{35}{5x}=\frac{4x+35}{5x}$. If you chose **A**, you may have placed the sum of the numerators over the product of the denominators: $\frac{4}{5}+\frac{7}{x}\Rightarrow\frac{4+7}{5x}$. If you chose **B**, you may have placed the product of the numerators over the product of the denominators: $\frac{4}{5}+\frac{7}{x}\Rightarrow\frac{4(7)}{5x}$. If you chose **C**, you may have added the numerators and added the denominators: $\frac{4}{5}+\frac{7}{x}\Rightarrow\frac{4+7}{5+x}$. If you chose **D**, you may have multiplied the numerator and denominator of each fraction and put the sum over the sum of the denominators: $\frac{4}{5}+\frac{7}{x}\Rightarrow\frac{4(5)+7(x)}{5+x}$.

Taking Additional Practice Tests

MATHEMATICS • PRACTICE TEST 4 • EXPLANATORY ANSWERS

Question 38. The correct answer is K. The total number of nonstudent residents who replied to the survey was $85+353+47=485$. The number of nonstudent residents who replied that they disapproved of the change in hours was 353. Thus, $\frac{353}{485}$ of the nonstudent residents replied that they disapproved of the change in hours. If you chose **F**, you selected the fraction of college students who replied that they disapproved: $\frac{10}{14+10+6}$. If you chose **G**, you selected the fraction of high school students who replied that they disapproved: $\frac{4}{30+4+11}$. If you chose **H**, you selected the fraction of high school and college students who replied that they disapproved: $\frac{4+10}{30+45}$. If you chose **J**, you selected the fraction for which the denominator is the total number of residents who replied with disapproval, including high school and college students, and not the total number of nonstudent residents: $\frac{353}{367}$.

Question 39. The correct answer is D. The total number of college student and nonstudent residents who replied either approve or disapprove is $14+10+85+353=462$ residents. This is the total number of residents who were NOT high school students and did NOT reply with no opinion. It follows that the probability that the person chosen will NOT be a high school student and will NOT have replied with no opinion is $\frac{462}{560}=0.825\approx0.83$. If you chose **A**, you may have computed the probability that the person chosen will be a high school student who replied either approve or disapprove: $\frac{30+4}{560}\approx0.06$. If you chose **B**, you may have computed the probability that the person chosen will be a college student or a nonstudent who replied with no opinion: $\frac{6+47}{560}\approx0.09$. If you chose **C**, you may have attempted to compute the probability that the person chosen will be a nonstudent who replied approve. However, you may have divided by the total number of residents who replied either approve or with no opinion: $\frac{85}{129+64}=\frac{85}{193}\approx0.44$. If you chose **E**, you may have computed the probability that the person chosen will NOT be a high school student who replied with no opinion: $1-\frac{11}{560}\approx0.98$.

MATHEMATICS • PRACTICE TEST 4 • EXPLANATORY ANSWERS

Question 40. The correct answer is H. Of the 15 incorrectly classified residents, some are college students who approved, and some are high school students who approved. We may first set up a linear equation involving the 60% of the college students who approved. Let x be the number of incorrectly classified college students who approved. We know that there are 14 correctly classified college students who approved. Thus, $14+x=0.60(14+10+6+x)$, or $14+x=0.60(30+x)$. Now we solve for x. We distribute on the right-hand side to get $14+x=18+0.60x$. Next we subtract the constant term 14 from both sides: $x=4+0.60x$. Then we subtract the variable term $0.60x$ from both sides: $0.40x=4$. After dividing, we have $x=10$ college students. This means that the remaining 5 incorrectly classified residents are high school students. Finally, the percent of high school students who replied that they approved is $\frac{30+5}{30+4+11+5}=\frac{35}{50}=0.70$, or 70%. If you chose **F**, you may have used the table values to find 60% of the total number of college students: $0.60(30)=18$. Next, you may have computed $\frac{30-(18-15)}{45}=\frac{27}{45}=0.60$, or 60%. If you chose **G**, you may have used the table values to find the percentage of high school students who replied that they approved: $\frac{30}{45}\approx 0.67$, or 67%. If you chose **J**, you may have used the table values and added 15 to the total number of high school students who replied that they approved: $\frac{30+15}{45+15}=\frac{45}{60}=0.75$, or 75%. If you chose **K**, you may have used the table values to find the percentage of high school students who replied that they approved and then added 15%. Thus, $\frac{30}{45}\approx 0.67$, and so $67\%+15\%=82\%$.

Question 41. The correct answer is A. Let Set A be the set of $\{a,b,c,d,e\}$ where $a<b<c<d<e$. Set B is then $\{x,b,c,d,e\}$ where $a<x<b$. The mean of Set A is $\frac{a+b+c+d+e}{5}$, and the mean of Set B is $\frac{x+b+c+d+e}{5}$. Because $x>a$, $\frac{x+b+c+d+e}{5}>\frac{a+b+c+d+e}{5}$. Thus, the mean of Set B is greater than the mean of Set A. The median of both Set A and Set B is c; thus **B**, **D**, and **E** are not correct answers. Set A and Set B each consists of 5 distinct numbers, so there is no mode for either set. This means that **C** and **E** are not correct answers.

Question 42. The correct answer is G. Because the function $f(x)=\sin x$ is an odd function, $\sin(-x)=-\sin x$. For example, $\sin 30°=\frac{1}{2}$, and $\sin(-30°)=-\frac{1}{2}$. Thus, $\sin(-x°)\neq \sin x°$, so **G** is the correct answer. It is true that $-\sin(-x°)=-(-\sin x°)=\sin x°$, so **F** is not the correct answer. By the cofunction identity, $\cos(90-x)°=\sin x°$, so **H** is not the correct answer. If you picked **J**, you might not have remembered $\cos(x-90)°=\cos(-(90-x)°)$. Because the function $g(\theta)=\cos\theta$ is even, $\cos(-\theta)=\cos(\theta)$. This means that $\cos(x-90)°=\cos(-(90-x)°)=\cos(90-x)°=\sin x°$. Thus, **J** is not the correct answer. If

MATHEMATICS • PRACTICE TEST 4 • EXPLANATORY ANSWERS

you chose **K**, you might have forgotten the identity, $\sin^2 x + \cos^2 x = 1$. Solving for $\sin x$ gives $\sin x = \pm\sqrt{1-\cos^2 x}$. Because $0 \le x \le 90$, $\sin x° \ge 0$. Thus, $\sin x° = \sqrt{1-(\cos x°)^2}$, so **K** is not the correct answer.

Question 43. The correct answer is D. The smallest square that will fit a circle with a diameter of 8 inches is a square with side lengths 8 inches. The box will thus have a base that is a square with side length 8 inches. Because the height of the box is 3 inches, the volume is $3(8^2)$, or 192 cubic inches. If you selected **A**, you might have multiplied the side length of the base by the height of the box, 3(8), instead of multiplying the area of the base by the height of the box. If you selected **B**, you might have found the area of the base, instead of the volume of the box. If you selected **C**, you might have confused the height of the box with the side length of the base and found $8(3^2)$ instead of $3(8^2)$. If you selected **E**, you might have found the volume of a cube with side length 8.

Question 44. The correct answer is G. Draw diagonal $\overline{DB}$. Triangle ΔBCD is a right triangle with $BC = 4$ and $CD = 3$, so $BD^2 = 3^2 + 4^2 = 5^2$. Because $5^2 + 12^2 = 13^2$, $BD^2 + AD^2 = AB^2$, and ΔBDA is a right triangle with right angle D. The tangent of an angle in a right triangle, is the ratio of the lengths of the side opposite the angle and the side adjacent to the angle. Thus, $\tan A$ is $\frac{BD}{AD} = \frac{5}{12}$. If you chose **F**, you might have found $\frac{BC}{AD}$. If you chose **H**, you might have found $\frac{BC}{AB}$. If you chose **J**, you might have found $\sin A = \frac{BD}{AB}$. If you chose **K**, you might have found $\cos A = \frac{AD}{AB}$.

Question 45. The correct answer is D. There are 7 days in a week. Because $28(7) = 196$, 196 days ago it was Tuesday. This means that 197 days ago was a Monday, 198 days ago was a Sunday, 199 days ago was a Saturday, and 200 days ago was a Friday. If you picked an answer other than **D**, you might have not realized that the remainder when 200 is divided by 7 is equal to 4, or you might not have known to count back 4 days from Tuesday.

Question 46. The correct answer is G. Because $\angle 1$ and $\angle 2$ are vertical angles, they are congruent. This means that $3x - 10 = 2x + 10 \rightarrow x = 20$. Substituting $x = 20$ back into the equation tells us $m\angle 2 = (2(20)+10)° = 50°$. Because line *m* is perpendicular to line *n*, $m\angle 2 + m\angle 3 = 90°$. Because $m\angle 2 = 50°$, $50° + m\angle 3 = 90° \rightarrow m\angle 3 = 40°$. If you selected **F**, you might have thought that $\angle 1$ and $\angle 2$ were supplementary and found the value of *x* in the equation $3x - 10 + 2x + 10 = 180$. If you selected **H**, you might have estimated from the diagram that $m\angle 3$ was slightly less than $m\angle 2$ but didn't know how to calculate the value exactly. If you selected **J**, you might have thought that line *q* bisected the angle, making $\angle 2$ and $\angle 3$ congruent. If you selected **K**, you might have found the value of *x* in the equation $3x - 10 + 2x + 10 = 180$. You might have thought that $m\angle 2 = x° = 36°$ and then found the angle complementary to 36°: $(90 - 36)°$.

MATHEMATICS • PRACTICE TEST 4 • EXPLANATORY ANSWERS

Question 47. The correct answer is E. Because $30 = 2(3)(5)$ and $40 = 2^3(5)$, the greatest common factor (GCF) of 30 and 40 is $2(5) = 10$, and the least common multiple (LCM) is $2^3(3)(5) = 120$. If you selected **A,** you may not have realized that the GCF of 6 and 20 is 2 and the LCM is 60. If you selected **B,** you may not have realized that the GCF of 10 and 12 is 2 and the LCM is 60. If you selected **C,** you may not have realized that the LCM of 10 and 20 is 20. If you selected **D,** you may not have realized that the GCF of 20 and 60 is 20 and the LCM is 60.

Question 48. The correct answer is H. Because all the sides are different lengths, the triangle is scalene. Because the length of the longest side squared is greater than the sum of the squares of the lengths of the other two sides ($7^2 > 4^2 + 5^2$), the triangle is obtuse. If you selected **F,** you may not have known that in an acute triangle, the length of the longest side squared is less than the sum of the squares of the lengths of the other two sides: $c^2 < a^2 + b^2$. If you selected **G,** you may not have known that in a right triangle, the length of the hypotenuse squared is equal to the sum of the squares of the lengths of the other two sides: $c^2 = a^2 + b^2$. If you selected **J** or **K,** you may not have known that an isosceles triangle has at least two congruent sides.

Question 49. The correct answer is D. Because the team has a 60% chance of winning on Saturday, the probability that they will lose on Saturday is $1 - 0.6 = 0.4$. Because the team has a 35% chance of winning on Sunday, the probability that they will lose on Sunday is $1 - 0.35 = 0.65$. The probability of them losing both games is thus $0.4(0.65) = 0.26$ or 26%. If you selected **A,** you may have found the probability that they will lose on Saturday but win on Sunday: $0.4(0.35) = 0.14$. If you selected **B,** you may have found the probability that they will win both games: $0.6(0.35) = 0.21$. If you selected **C,** you may have found the difference between the given probabilities: $0.6 - 0.35 = 0.25$. If you selected **E,** you may have found the probability that they will win on Saturday but lose on Sunday: $0.6(0.65) = 0.39$.

Question 50. The correct answer is J. The domain of a rational function, like *f*, excludes any *x*-values that make the denominator 0. This includes both removable points of discontinuity (holes) and nonremovable points of discontinuity (vertical asymptotes). Solving $0 = x^2 - 2x - 3 = (x-3)(x+1)$ gives us solutions $x = 3$ and $x = -1$. The domain of *f* is thus $\{x | x \neq -1 \text{ and } x \neq 3\}$. If you selected **F,** you might not have known that removable points of discontinuity (like 3 for *f*) are also domain restrictions. If you selected **G,** you might have incorrectly factored $0 = x^2 - 2x - 3 \rightarrow (x-2)(x-3)$ and then found only the nonremovable points of discontinuity for the incorrect function: $f(x) = \dfrac{x-3}{(x-2)(x-3)}$. If you selected **H,** you might not have known that nonremovable points of discontinuity (like -1 for *f*) are also domain restrictions. If you selected **K,** you might have incorrectly simplified *f* by canceling the 3s: $f(x) = \dfrac{x-3}{x^2 - 2x - 3} \rightarrow \dfrac{x}{x^2 - 2x}$. You might have then found the domain restrictions of the incorrect function.

Taking Additional Practice Tests

MATHEMATICS • PRACTICE TEST 4 • EXPLANATORY ANSWERS

Question 51. The correct answer is E. The first three numbers are set and do NOT affect the number of possible phone numbers. The choices for possible phone numbers have the form 555-XXXX. We note that each X in a phone number may be any of the 10 digits allowed (0 through 9). Therefore, we have $10 \cdot 10 \cdot 10 \cdot 10 = 10^4$ possible phone numbers. If you chose **C**, you selected the case where each of the first three digits of a phone number has 5 choices: $5 \cdot 5 \cdot 5 \cdot 10 \cdot 10 \cdot 10 \cdot 10 = 5^3(10^4)$. If you chose **D**, you may not have included 0 in the number of digits allowed: $9 \cdot 9 \cdot 9 \cdot 9 = 9^4$. If you chose **A**, you selected the case where only 1 of the first 3 digits of a phone number has 5 choices, $5 \cdot 1 \cdot 1$ or $1 \cdot 5 \cdot 1$ or $1 \cdot 1 \cdot 5$, and each of the last 4 digits of the phone number has 9 choices, 9^4. Thus, $5(9^4)$.

Question 52. The correct answer is F. A circle is the set of all points whose distance from the center is equal to the radius. Therefore, the measure of the radius of the given circle is equal to the distance between the center, (1,3) and the given point on the circle,(4,7). The distance between any two points (x_1, y_1) and (x_2, y_2) is given by $\sqrt{(x_2 - x_1)^2 + (y_2 - y_1)^2}$. It follows that the radius of the given circle has a measure of $\sqrt{(4-1)^2 + (7-3)^2} = \sqrt{3^2 + 4^2} = \sqrt{9+16} = \sqrt{25} = 5$ coordinate units. Thus, the given circle is the set of all points that are 5 coordinate units from the center (1,3). If you chose **G**, you selected the intersection of circles with radii of 5 coordinate units centered at (1,3) and (4,7). If you chose **H**, you selected the parallel line segments above and below the line segment from (1,3) to (4,7). If you chose **J**, you selected the perpendicular bisector of the line segment with endpoints (1,3) and (4,7). If you chose **K**, you selected the closed region composed of a rectangle whose endpoints are capped off with semicircles. The length of the rectangle is formed by two parallel line segments above and below the line segment from (1,3) to (4,7), and the two semicircles are centered at each of the endpoints (1,3) and (4,7).

Question 53. The correct answer is B. To find the *x*-coordinate of the point of intersection of the two graphs, we set the right-hand side of the two equations equal to each other and solve for *x*. First, we have $7 = \ln(x-2)+3$. Next, we subtract 3 from both sides to get $4 = \ln(x-2)$. Now, we note that the exponent property of logarithms states that $e^{lnx} = e^{\log_e x} = x$. It follows from this property that if we have $e^4 = e^{\ln(x-2)}$, then we will have $e^4 = x-2$. Thus, $x = e^4 + 2$. If you chose **A**, you may have dropped the *ln* and solved the equation $7 = (x-2)+3$. If you chose **C**, you may have moved the exponent down from the expression e^4 and to the front as multiplication: $e^4 = e^{\ln(x-2)} \Rightarrow 4e = x-2$. If you chose **D**, you may have incorrectly thought $\ln(\ln x) = x$ and attempted to solve using this erroneous property: $\ln(4) = \ln(\ln(x-2)) \Rightarrow \ln(4) = x-2$.

MATHEMATICS • PRACTICE TEST 4 • EXPLANATORY ANSWERS

Question 54. The correct answer is F. The three machines copy at the same rate. Thus, as long as they are running together, the number of copies will increase at the same rate, *r*. When a machine breaks down the rate is reduced by $\frac{1}{3}r$. A rate will correspond to the slope of a line segment on the graph of *n* versus *t*. There will be 5 connected line segments on the graph due to the machine break downs. From 8:00 a.m. to 10:00 a.m., the first line segment has slope *r*. From 10:00 a.m. to 12:00 p.m., the breakdown of Machine A makes the second line segment have slope $\frac{2}{3}r$. From 12:00 p.m. to 1:00 p.m., the intersection of the breakdowns of Machines A and B makes the third line segment have slope $\frac{1}{3}r$. From 1:00 p.m. to 3:00 p.m., the breakdown of Machine B makes the fourthline segment have slope $\frac{2}{3}r$. Finally, from 3:00 p.m. to 5:00 p.m., the slope of the fifth line segment is *r*. The graph that matches these conditions has the first and fifth line segments with equal and greatest incline, followed by the second and fourth line segments with equal slope, and last, by the third line segment with the least incline. If you chose **G**, you selected the graph for which the number of copies will increase at the greatest rate between 12:00 p.m. and 1:00 p.m.; however, the breakdowns of Machines A and B during this time frame make this impossible. If you chose **H**, you selected the graph for which there are only three connected line segments, which does not match the scenario. If you chose **K**, you selected the graph for which the number of copies will increase at the same rate.

Question 55. The correct answer is E. Let *p* be the number of \$1 decreases in the price of the caps. If $p=0$, there are 40 caps sold per week. For each \$1 decrease in *p*, 4 more caps are sold. It follows that the number of caps sold for 1 week will be $40+4p$. Moreover, the price per cap for 1 week will be $22-p$. Now, from the given note we know that the revenue, *R*, for 1 week is $R=(22-p)(40+4p)$. After multiplying the two binomials, we have $R=-4p^2+48p+880$, which is a quadratic function in terms of *p*. Therefore, the maximum value of *R* will occur at the vertex. For a given quadratic function $y=ax^2+bx+c$, the vertex is found by computing $x=-\frac{b}{2a}$ and then evaluating *y* at $x=-\frac{b}{2a}$ to find the maximum value. It follows that for $R=-4p^2+48p+880$, $p=-\frac{b}{2a}=-\frac{48}{2(-4)}=6$. Then, evaluating at $p=6$, we find that $R=(22-6)(40+4(6))=16(64)=\$1{,}024$. If you chose **A**, you may have thought the maximum revenue equals the given number of caps sold times the given price per cap: $40(22)=\$880$. If you chose **C**, you may have thought the maximum revenue equals 4 more than the given number of caps sold times \$1 less than the given price per cap: $(40+4)(22-1)=44(21)=\$924$. If you chose **D**, you may have thought the maximum revenue equals 8 more than the given number of caps sold times \$2 less than the given price per cap: $(40+8)(22-2)=48(20)=\$960$.

MATHEMATICS • PRACTICE TEST 4 • EXPLANATORY ANSWERS

Question 56. The correct answer is K. First, we may write the linear inequality in slope-intercept form $y \le -\frac{a}{b}x + \frac{c}{b}$. From the condition $0 < a < b < c$, we know that the boundary line has a negative slope, $m = -\frac{a}{b}$. Moreover, we know that the boundary line has a y-intercept, $\left(0, \frac{c}{b}\right)$, located on the positive y-axis. Finally, $y \le -\frac{a}{b}x + \frac{c}{b}$ indicates that all the (x,y) coordinates on the boundary line and in the half-pane below the boundary line satisfy the inequality. If you chose **F**, you have selected a graph that has a boundary line with a positive slope. If you chose **G**, you have selected a graph that has (x,y) coordinates in the half-plane above the boundary line for which the inequality is NOT true. If you chose **H** or **J**, you have selected a graph that has a boundary line with a y-intercept $\left(0, \frac{c}{b}\right)$ located on the negative y-axis.

Question 57. The correct answer is A. First, we note that to make the 500 banners, the club needed to purchase a minimum of $500\left(\frac{1}{4}\right) = 125$ yards of blue material and a minimum of $500\left(\frac{3}{8}\right) = 187\frac{1}{2}$ yards of white material. Next, we note that each 10-yard bolt of blue material can be used to make $\frac{10}{1/4} = 40$ banners, and each 12-yard bolt of white material can be used to make $\frac{12}{3/8} = 32$ banners. Moreover, $10(13) = 130$ is the closest multiple of 10 that is greater than 125, and $12(16) = 192$ is the closest multiple of 12 that is greater than $187\frac{1}{2}$. It follows that the club purchased 130 yards of blue material and 192 yards of white material. The 130 yards of blue material could make $\frac{130}{1/4} = 520$ banners, and the 192 yards of white material could make $\frac{192}{3/8} = 512$ banners. Therefore, the club was able to make a total of $min(520,512) = 512$ banners, which included 12 extra banners. If you chose **B**, you may have divided the 130 yards of blue material by the number of yards in a bolt of blue material: $\frac{130}{10} = 13$. If you chose **C**, you may have divided the total number of yards of each material that was purchased by the sum of the yards of material needed to make each banner: $\frac{130+192}{\frac{1}{4}+\frac{3}{8}} = \frac{322}{0.625} = 515.2 \Rightarrow 515 - 500 = 15$. If you chose **D**, you may have divided the 192 yards of white material by the number of yards in a bolt of white material: $\frac{160}{10} = 16$. If you chose **E**, you may have calculated the overage from the blue material only: $\frac{130}{1/4} = 520$ banners with 20 extra banners possible.

MATHEMATICS • PRACTICE TEST 4 • EXPLANATORY ANSWERS

Question 58. The correct answer is F. We note that to find the expanded form of$(x-3i)^3$, we may use the cube of a binomial formula: $(a-b)^3 = a^3 - 3a^2b + 3ab^2 - b^3$. There are four terms in the result. The exponents of a decrease in each term, while the exponents of b increase in each term. The middle terms contain a factor of 3, and the second and fourth terms are negative. For the case of $(x-3i)^3$, we have $(x-3i)^3 = (x)^3 - 3(x)^2(3i) + 3(x)(3i)^2 - (3i)^3 = x^3 - 9x^2i + 27xi^2 - 27i^3$. Now, for the imaginary number $i, i^2 = -1$. It follows that $(x-3i)^3 = x^3 - 9x^2i - 27x + 27i$. If you chose **G**, you may have computed $+(3i)^3$ for the last term: $+(3i)^3 = 27(i)^2 i = -27i$. If you chose **J**, you have selected the expression where the middle terms do NOT contain a factor of 3. If you chose **K**, you have selected the expression where the two middle terms are missing.

Question 59. The correct answer is D. First, we note that the graph rises to the left and rises to the right, or $f(x) \to +\infty$, as $x \to -\infty$, and $f(x) \to +\infty$, as $x \to +\infty$. Thus, the degree of the function is even, and the leading coefficient is positive. The graph of the function has zeros located at $x = -4$, $x = 0$, and $x = 6$. These correspond to the polynomial factors $(x+4)$, x, and $(x-6)$. Next, we find the multiplicity of each zero, that is, how many times a particular number is a zero for a given polynomial function. We note that the sign of $f(x)$ does NOT change from one side of $x = 0$ to the other side because the graph touches the x-axis at 0 and turns around. This means that a zero of even multiplicity occurs at $x = 0$. We also note that the sign of $f(x)$ changes from one side of $x = -4$ to the other side and the sign of $f(x)$ changes from one side of $x = 6$ to the other side. That is, the graph crosses the x-axis at -4 and 6. This means that the zero at $x = -4$ and the zero at $x = 6$ are of odd multiplicity. Therefore, the only function that satisfies all the above conditions is $p(x) = x^2(x-6)^3(x+4)$. If you chose **A**, you have selected a function with an odd degree. If you chose **B** or **C**, you have selected a function that has zeros located at $x = -6$, $x = 0$, and $x = 4$. If you chose **E**, you have selected a function that has a zero of odd multiplicity at $x = 0$ and a zero of even multiplicity at $x = 6$.

Question 60. The correct answer is K. We can only multiply two matrices if the number of columns in the first matrix is the same as the number of rows in the second matrix. Matrix A has n columns, and Matrix C has k rows. Therefore, the matrix product AC is NOT possible. If you chose **F**, Matrix E has m columns, and Matrix D has m rows, so the matrix product ED is possible. If you chose **G**, Matrix D has k columns, and Matrix C has k rows, so the matrix product DC is possible. If you chose **H**, Matrix C has n columns, and Matrix E has n rows, so the matrix product CE is possible. If you chose **J**, Matrix A has n columns, and Matrix E has n rows, so the matrix product AE is possible.

READING • PRACTICE TEST 4 • EXPLANATORY ANSWERS

Passage I

Question 1. The best answer is B because lines 21–22 clearly state why the blond woman is traveling to Palm Beach: "she's taking the bus to see" a man who "left for a construction job" there.

The best answer is NOT:

A because the passage does not address why the character "you" is leaving Memphis.

C because the blond woman turns away from the character "you" at the end of the passage, so there is no indication of what she is thinking.

D because the passage does not address where the blond woman is from originally.

Question 2. The best answer is H because lines 22–25 state that the man in Palm Beach thinks the blond woman's eyes are "as blue as" the Atlantic Ocean, and he cannot bear to look at "the thing" (the Atlantic Ocean) one more time if the blond woman isn't there with him.

The best answer is NOT:

F because the man in Palm Beach works in a construction job; it is not the thing he cannot bear to look at.

G because the blond woman's blue eyes are mentioned as a point of comparison with the Atlantic Ocean; they are not the thing the man in Palm Beach cannot bear to look at.

J because a bus is the setting where the scene in the passage takes place; it is not the thing the man in Palm Beach cannot bear to look at.

Question 3. The best answer is D because the word *occasional* is modifying *home,* not porch lights or fireflies. The "you" character is watching homes as the bus moves along, and those homes are not close together.

The best answer is NOT:

A because Lines 34–35 state that the porch lights are "perched, fat and throbbing" outside *every* home.

B because Lines 34–35 state that the porch lights are "perched, fat and throbbing" outside *every* home.

C because firefly porch lights are described; actual fireflies are not mentioned.

Question 4. The best answer is F because the girl does not acknowledge the narrator in any way.

The best answer is NOT:

G because the girl never speaks.

H because the passage provides no indication of how the girl perceives the narrator or whether she even notices his presence on the train.

J because the girl does not express any reaction to the narrator's presence.

READING • PRACTICE TEST 4 • EXPLANATORY ANSWERS

Question 5. The best answer is B because lines 88–89 reveal that the narrator had been in a dark frame of mind before he watched the girl toss the oranges to her brothers, so when he wants her to fail at opening the window, he is feeling "unspeakable fatigue" with his "tedious life."

The best answer is NOT:

A because the passage never suggests that the girl is helpless or has an uncertain future; she struggles with the window but eventually opens it.

C because the narrator doesn't notice the boys until after the window is open.

D because the train conductor is not around when the girl attempts to open the window.

Question 6. The best answer is F because lines 84–85 indicate that the girl needed to open the window to toss oranges "to her younger brothers as a token of gratitude."

The best answer is NOT:

G because there is no evidence in the passage that suggests the girl had to prove anything.

H because the girl never acknowledges the narrator, so there is no support for her needing to create space between the two of them.

J because there is no evidence in the passage that suggests the girl feels a need to freshen the air in the train.

Question 7. The best answer is C because lines 44–46 state that the narrator heard the conductor cursing and the "clattering of dry-weather clogs" coming from the ticket gate. These sounds and the direction from which they emanate provide strong cues that someone is about to board the train at the last minute.

The best answer is NOT:

A because the passage does not reference the screech of the train's brakes.

B because the passage does not reference the rustle of paper parcels.

D because the young girl in the passage does not shout.

Question 8. The best answer is J because the situation described in both passages involves an encounter between two characters traveling in close quarters. In both passages, the encounter has a strong impact on the main character, whose state of mind is shifted by the second character's words or actions.

The best answer is NOT:

F because only Passage A uses the second person point of view.

G because the time period in which these passages are set is never clearly indicated.

H because there is no dialogue in Passage B.

READING • PRACTICE TEST 4 • EXPLANATORY ANSWERS

Question 9. The best answer is D because the only character in either passage who shows interest in having a conversation is the blond woman in Passage A. The first paragraph in Passage A clearly shows that the "you" character does not want to talk, and neither character in Passage B shows any interest in conversing.

The best answer is NOT:

A because the "you" character's actions in lines 5–11 (pulling lips tight, staring at the floor, motioning to an open novel) are all clear indications that this character has no interest in communicating with the blond woman.

B because the girl is intent on opening the window and shows no interest in communicating with the narrator.

C because lines 52–59 reveal that the narrator is repelled by the girl and even attempts to "blot her existence."

Question 10. The best answer is F because in Passage A, the "you" character describes the blond woman as having teased hair and "sad, neglected teeth" (lines 13–14). In Passage B, the narrator describes the girl as having "lusterless hair"; chapped, red cheeks; and "a grimy woolen scarf" (lines 52–56).

The best answer is NOT:

G because Passage A does not suggest that the blond woman delayed the bus's departure.

H because when the "you" character in Passage A and the narrator of Passage B first see the blond woman and the young girl, respectively, neither knows the reason the other character is traveling.

J because both the "you" character in Passage A and the narrator of Passage B use disparaging language to describe the blond woman and the young girl, respectively. There is no evidence in either passage to support the idea that the blond woman and the young girl are envied or that life seems easy to them.

Passage II

Question 11. The best answer is D because lines 3–5 make it clear that Stevenson "turned his back on the Victorian idol, progress," and instead steered toward the "rougher fringes." The phrase "skirts of civilization" in lines 69–70 conveys the same idea: Stevenson preferred the gas lamp over any "technological miracle of the future" (line 62).

The best answer is NOT:

A because the phrase "fire of adventure" describes the theme of Stevenson's novels, which is not directly related to his reluctance to embrace progress.

B because the phrase "an epic ocean voyage" refers to a literal sea journey; it is not synonymous with the "rougher fringes" of civilization.

C because the phrase "a glittering hieroglyph" refers to electric lights, which represent progress, something Stevenson objects to.

READING • PRACTICE TEST 4 • EXPLANATORY ANSWERS

Question 12. The best answer is F because lines 48–60 describe the places the author visited in order to gather information about Stevenson.

The best answer is NOT:

G because there is no evidence in the passage to suggest that Stevenson's novels contain biographical information about Stevenson.

H because the passage contains no evidence to support the idea that the author worked for D. & T. Stevenson, Engineers.

J because where the author "comes from" is not addressed in the passage.

Question 13. The best answer is D because the paragraph's focus is on Stevenson's family; lines 14–15 state that Stevenson was "born into a Scottish family of civil engineers, esteemed for its technological genius."

The best answer is NOT:

A because the paragraph never mentions that Stevenson's grandfather insisted on anything.

B because Stevenson's desire to be a writer is not mentioned in the second paragraph.

C because the paragraph does not include a comparison between Stevenson's grandfather's lighthouses and his father's screens.

Question 14. The best answer is G because lines 60–64 capture the main idea of the fifth paragraph with the author's description of Stevenson imagining a future London flashing with electric lights.

The best answer is NOT:

F because the paragraph does not mention the plot of any of Stevenson's books.

H because the opposite is true: Stevenson preferred the gas lamps, which is evidenced by the statement "Not for him improvements in optics" (line 68).

J because the main focus of the paragraph is Stevenson's prediction and not his father's engineering feats.

Question 15. The best answer is C because line 50 ("he tried his hand at being an apprentice engineer"), lines 87–88 ("Stevenson . . . became a mariner himself"), and lines 6–8 ("his most popular novels . . .") provide evidence that Stevenson was an engineer, a mariner, and a writer.

The best answer is NOT:

A because the passage provides evidence that Stevenson had also been an engineer and a mariner.

B because the passage provides no evidence that Stevenson was a lamplighter.

D because the passage provides no evidence that Stevenson was a builder.

READING • PRACTICE TEST 4 • EXPLANATORY ANSWERS

Question 16. The best answer is H because the image of telephone wires in line 11 suggests progress, which Stevenson was not interested in; he preferred "the sound of clashing swords" (line 10), which, in the context of the paragraph, represents the opposite of progress.

The best answer is NOT:

F because lines 15–22 provide evidence that technological progress did, in fact, occur in Stevenson's lifetime.

G because lines 1–3 provide evidence that, in fact, Stevenson preferred to avoid civilization's "increasing reliance on contraptions."

J because the passage provides no evidence that Stevenson was a sword fighter.

Question 17. The best answer is A because lines 23–25 state that Stevenson had been expected to join the family business. The phrase "a great wringing of hands" is used to describe the family's implied dismay at Stevenson's announcement that he would not, in fact, be following their expectations.

The best answer is NOT:

B because the passage provides no evidence that the family criticized Stevenson's diet.

C because the passage provides no evidence that the family was humiliated; rather, they were greatly disappointed.

D because the family's consternation in line 28 is presented as a possible result of the pleas Stevenson makes in his letters for his family to accept him as he is; it happens later, *after* the wringing of hands over Stevenson's announcement about not joining the family business.

Question 18. The best answer is J because lines 35–36 provide a quote from Stevenson revealing that he preferred to travel without a set itinerary: "I travel not to go anywhere, but to go." Lines 37–38 suggest that Stevenson found happiness in open-ended travel: "I travel for travel's sake. The great affair is to move."

The best answer is NOT:

F because Stevenson's own words in lines 35–38 indicate that the destination was not important to him.

G because lines 34–35 indicate that Stevenson provided "the template for generations of college-educated adventurers"; they do not say that traveling should replace education.

H because the only mention of the character David Balfour is in line 52, and there is no indication that Stevenson's travels were a model for Balfour.

READING • PRACTICE TEST 4 • EXPLANATORY ANSWERS

Question 19. The best answer is A because the meaning of the idiomatic phrase "stumbled across" is "found by accident," and this is the only option that logically fits the context of the sentence. The narrator found Abernethy House by accident.

The best answer is NOT:

B because the passage provides no evidence that the author staggered.

C because the passage provides no evidence that the author "unearthed" a building.

D because the passage provides no evidence that the author "tripped over" a building.

Question 20. The best answer is J because lines 83–85 directly state that "Thomas Stevenson's name may not have been widely known," but "his lights were in every part of the world."

The best answer is NOT:

F because the passage provides no evidence that Robert Louis Stevenson and his father, Thomas, were estranged.

G because lines 15–20 explain how Thomas Stevenson's father was "Britain's greatest builder of lighthouses" and how Thomas "followed him into the profession." Clearly, Thomas Stevenson would not have been unaware that his name would become associated with lighthouses.

H because the passage provides no evidence that Thomas was more famous than his son, Robert.

Passage III

Question 21. The best answer is B because lines 71–85 suggest that the author's cultural intuition, which she acquired on her reservation, gives her the knowledge to know that "kivas are safe places" and not the "frightening places" described in Gerald McDermott's book. In lines 71–72, the author directly states that she draws upon her cultural intuition when reading a book about Pueblo Indians.

The best answer is NOT:

A because the reference to Bruchac is about storytelling, not about the author's cultural intuition.

C because the passage does not mention where the author has presented her research.

D because the passage provides no evidence that the author and Silko discussed anything.

READING • PRACTICE TEST 4 • EXPLANATORY ANSWERS

Question 22. The best answer is G because lines 1–13 explain the value and functions of traditional stories: to pass "religious beliefs, customs, history, lifestyle, language, [and] values" from one generation to another and to transmit "an entire culture, a worldview complete with strategies for survival."

The best answer is NOT:

F because there is no mention of stories changing as they are passed from one generation to the next.

H because the paragraph states that traditional stories *include* folktales, myths, and legends; these are not compared or contrasted.

J because there is no mention of a culture's worldview changing over time.

Question 23. The best answer is D because lines 41–44 directly state that "in order for it to be acceptable . . . [the story] should remain true to the spirit and content of the original."

The best answer is NOT:

A because lines 33–41 make it clear that it is acceptable for storytellers to add and change details in the stories they are telling.

B because lines 39–40 state that "a storyteller may revise a story according to his or her own interpretation."

C because lines 35–38 suggest that it is acceptable for audience members to offer new details.

Question 24. The best answer is G because the author's statement that her home pueblo is different from other pueblos (lines 67–69) precedes her discussion of McDermott's book and provides support for her critique that his book fails to show the differences among the many pueblos in New Mexico (lines 74–78).

The best answer is NOT:

F because the culture and traditions of her home pueblo are not specifically described in the passage; rather, the author discusses the traditions of the Pueblo people as a whole.

H because the author never compares her tribe's stories with the stories of other tribal nations.

J because the passage does not contain a list of criteria the author uses when evaluating books marketed as "Native American folktales."

READING • PRACTICE TEST 4 • EXPLANATORY ANSWERS

Question 25. The best answer is C because lines 86–88 clearly state that "depictions that are culturally acceptable at one Pueblo are not necessarily acceptable at a different Pueblo." Elders take the cultural values of their *specific* community (or *audience,* line 92) into account when determining whether books are culturally acceptable for children of that community.

The best answer is NOT:

A because the passage does not address the entertainment value of books, comparatively or otherwise.

B because the passage does not address the popularity of books among tribal members.

D because elders are concerned with the appropriateness of books for their *specific communities* (lines 86–92); there is no mention of elders being concerned with the way books represent the worldviews of many groups.

Question 26. The best answer is H because lines 16–17 state that the hunting stories contain information "about the behavior and migration patterns of mule deer."

The best answer is NOT:

F because Silko never mentions rescuing hunters from other tribes.

G because there is no mention of documenting the number of successful hunts.

J because Silko mentions locations of fresh water and lost piñon-nut gatherers, but she does not state that hunting stories help people find caches of food.

Question 27. The best answer is A because lines 65–67 directly state this: "As a scholar in American Indian studies, I know there are great distinctions between and across American Indian tribal nations."

The best answer is NOT:

B because there is no evidence to suggest that the author and McDermott were friends.

C because there is no evidence to suggest that the author is an editor for picture books.

D because there is no evidence to suggest that the author is an elder.

Question 28. The best answer is G because in lines 66–67 the author is making the point that there are "great distinctions" between and across American Indian tribal nations. In this context, *great* is synonymous with *significant.*

The best answer is NOT:

F because *excessive* does not logically fit the context of the paragraph.

H because *exuberant* does not logically fit the context of the paragraph.

J because *splendid* does not logically fit the context of the paragraph.

Question 29. The best answer is D because lines 67–70 directly state that one of the differences among the pueblos in New Mexico is that "there are several different language groups."

The best answer is NOT:

A because the Pueblo communities mentioned are all in New Mexico, so the geographic differences cannot be *vast.*

B because a disparity of resources is never discussed.

C because approaches to parenting are not discussed.

Question 30. The best answer is J because lines 84–85 directly state that the author knows kivas as "safe places of worship and instruction."

The best answer is NOT:

F because the author says that for her, kivas are "safe places," not places of fear and trial.

G because kivas are never described by the author as mysterious or exciting.

H because kivas are not mentioned in relation to rest or healing.

Passage IV

Question 31. The best answer is B because the passage begins with a discussion of "the spontaneous vegetation that dominates the neglected interstices" (lines 3–5), goes on to define weeds (lines 24–25), and then discusses how weeds "survive in derelict urban wastelands" and are "famous (or infamous) for their ability to grow under extremely harsh conditions" (lines 49–51).

The best answer is NOT:

A because the passage never presents an argument for eradicating weeds.

C because the passage is not a *report*, and it does not mention a need for more vegetation in urban environments.

D because the passage does not mention the work or opinions of environmentalists.

READING • PRACTICE TEST 4 • EXPLANATORY ANSWERS

Question 32. The best answer is H because the author's perspective throughout the passage best fits the biological one described in the second paragraph: "weeds are opportunistic plants that are adapted to disturbance" (lines 26–27). Support for this perspective is found in a number of places in the passage: "The plants that grow and survive in derelict urban wastelands are famous . . . for their ability to grow under extremely harsh conditions" (lines 49–51); a successful urban plant is "*opportunistic* in its ability to take advantage of locally abundant resources" (lines 73–75); urban plants are "*tolerant* of the stressful growing conditions" (line 76).

The best answer is NOT:

F because the idea that weeds grow in places where people don't want them is only summarized; it is not developed enough to represent the author's own perspective.

G because the problem of weeds in agriculture is only summarized; it is not developed enough to represent the author's own perspective.

J because the city dweller's notion that weeds are "perceived as ugly" or a potential security hazard is only summarized; it is not developed enough to represent the author's own perspective.

Question 33. The best answer is B because based on lines 31–33, economic crops are agricultural plants, which compete with "spontaneous vegetation," or weeds.

The best answer is NOT:

A because ragweed is a type of "spontaneous vegetation," or weed.

C because urban plants are described as spontaneous plants in the first paragraph.

D because calcium-loving grasses are described as an example of urban weeds (lines 63–70).

Question 34. The best answer is G because lines 28–31 state that weed "pervasiveness in the urban environment is simply a reflection of the continual disruption that characterizes that habitat—they are not its cause."

The best answer is NOT:

F because the process of removing weeds is not discussed in the passage.

H because there is no evidence in the passage to suggest that there is a pervasive acceptance of weeds in urban areas.

J because the passage does not provide a comparison of the life cycle of weeds with the life cycle of other plants.

READING • PRACTICE TEST 4 • EXPLANATORY ANSWERS

Question 35. The best answer is C because the word *greenery* refers to the "spontaneous vegetation," or weeds, introduced in lines 4–5 and further defined and discussed throughout the first paragraph.

The best answer is NOT:

A because in the context of the paragraph, *greenery* refers to "spontaneous vegetation," not to cultivated plants.

B because in the context of the paragraph, *greenery* refers to "spontaneous vegetation," not to landscapes that are protected.

D because in the context of the paragraph, *greenery* refers to "spontaneous vegetation," not to crops.

Question 36. The best answer is F because both sources cite specific examples that support the passage author's statement that weeds, "through a quirk of evolutionary fate, . . . developed traits in their native habitats that . . . 'preadapted' them to flourish in cities" (lines 51–54). The transitional word *similarly* (line 63) further establishes the complementary relationship between the study and the book.

The best answer is NOT:

G because the conclusions are similar, so they could not be contrasting.

H because the passage provides no evidence to suggest that Lundholm used Gilbert's book.

J because the paragraph clearly establishes that Lundholm and Marlin's study and Gilbert's book are *not* irrelevant to each other: both sources drew similar conclusions about weeds that originated in limestone-rich habitats.

Question 37. The best answer is D because lines 78–80 state that so-called weeds "managed to survive the transition from one land use to another as cities developed." This statement, and especially the author's use of the word *managed,* makes it clear that the author is appreciative and respectful of urban plants' adaptability and resilience.

The best answer is NOT:

A because the paragraph provides no suggestion of alarm.

B because the paragraph provides no indication that the author fears for weeds' survival; rather, he is impressed by their ability to survive.

C because the paragraph provides no evidence to suggest that the author is ever annoyed about anything.

READING • PRACTICE TEST 4 • EXPLANATORY ANSWERS

Question 38. The best answer is F because lines 11–13 directly state that Norway maple was among the plants "brought in intentionally or unintentionally by people."

The best answer is NOT:

G because the passage does not indicate that the Norway maple was brought by wind.

H because the passage does not indicate that the Norway maple was brought by water.

J because the passage does not indicate that the Norway maple was brought by birds.

Question 39. The best answer is B because lines 15–16 make it clear that "on their own" refers to "dispersed by wind, water, or wild animals," which indicates people were not involved.

The best answer is NOT:

A because the passage provides no evidence that any of the plants being discussed were brought to urban environments one at a time.

C because the passage directly states that the plants were brought by "wind, water, or wild animals"; they were, therefore, not self-propelled.

D because the word *voluntarily* suggests that the plants had a choice, which would be impossible given that plants do not have the ability to choose whether they are relocated or not.

Question 40. The best answer is J because lines 20–21 directly state that "if left undisturbed long enough," weeds "may even develop into mature woodlands."

The best answer is NOT:

F because the passage provides no evidence to suggest that weeds would eventually compete for space and die out.

G because the passage provides no evidence to suggest that weeds might eventually enhance landscaped gardens.

H because the passage provides no evidence to suggest that weeds might eventually dry out the soil.

SCIENCE • PRACTICE TEST 4 • EXPLANATORY ANSWERS

Passage I

1. **The best answer is A.** According to Student 4, the atoms from smallest to largest are F, Cl, Br, and I. The table shows that the atoms from smallest to largest atomic mass are F, Cl, Br, and I. As atomic mass increases, atomic radius also increases. **A** is correct. **B, C,** and **D** are incorrect: as atomic mass increases, atomic radius increases.

2. **The best answer is H.** According to the passage, only Student 2 states that As does not have a lone pair. Students 1, 3, and 4 all state that As has a lone pair. **F, G,** and **J** are incorrect: Students 1, 3, and 4 state that As has a lone pair. **H** is correct.

3. **The best answer is C.** Students 1 and 2 both propose planar structures for AsF_3 in which all the atoms lie in the same plane. Students 3 and 4 both propose pyramidal structures in which the As lies above the plane of the three F. Only Students 1 and 2 would agree with the statement. **A, B,** and **D** are incorrect: Students 3 and 4 propose structures for AsF_3 that are not planar, and therefore they are not likely to agree with the statement. **C** is correct.

4. **The best answer is J.** Student 1 claims that there are 2 unique angles in the AsF_3 molecule, and Students 2, 3, and 4 claim that there is only 1 unique angle in the AsF_3 molecule. None of the students would agree that there are 3 unique bond angles in the molecule. **F, G,** and **H** are incorrect: none of the students would agree with the claim. **J** is correct.

5. **The best answer is A.** According to the passage, the sum of the angles in Student 1's model is $180+90+90=360$. The sum of the angles in Student 2's model is $120+120+120=360$. The sum of the angles in Student 3's model is $109+109+109=327$. The sum of the angles in Student 4's model ranges from $100+100+100=300$ to $111+111+111=333$. Only Students 1 and 2 are likely to agree that the sum of the bond angles is equal to 360°. A is correct. **B, C,** and **D** are incorrect: only Students 1 and 2 would agree that the sum of the bond angles is 360°.

6. **The best answer is J.** According to the passage, Student 2 claims that As has no lone pair and the molecule is trigonal planar. Student 3 claims that As has a lone pair and, because of this, the molecule is trigonal pyramidal. Because N has a lone pair, it is more likely that it will adopt the trigonal pyramid conformation. F and G are incorrect: because of the lone pair, it is not likely that the ammonia molecule will adopt a trigonal planar conformation. **H** is incorrect: the bond angle is more consistent with Student 3's description. **J** is correct.

7. **The best answer is D.** According to Table 1, the bond angles vary depending on the type of atom bonded to As. Only Student 4 claimed that the bond angles would vary, and therefore the data is most consistent with Student 4's description. **A, B,** and **C** are incorrect: Students 1, 2, and 3 all claimed that the bond angles would be the same for the different molecules. **D** is correct.

SCIENCE • PRACTICE TEST 4 • EXPLANATORY ANSWERS

Passage II

8. **The best answer is F.** According to Table 2, all the offspring from Cross 1 had a black coat. If both of the parents were *BBEE,* then all the offspring would have also been *BBEE.* According to Table 1, the genotype *BBEE* corresponds to a black coat. The hypothesis is consistent with the results of Cross 1. **F** is correct. **G** is incorrect: the offspring of Cross 1 had black coats. **H** and **J** are incorrect: the hypothesis is consistent with the results of Cross 1.

9. **The best answer is D.** According to Table 2, the genotypes *bbEE* and *bbEe* resulted in brown coats. The offspring from Cross 2 with a brown coat must have been either *bbEE* or *bbEe.* **A** is incorrect: *bbee* would have a yellow coat. **B** is incorrect: *BBEE* would have a black coat. **C** is incorrect: *BbEE* or *BbEe* would have a black coat. **D** is correct: both *bbEE* and *bbEe* would have a brown coat.

10. **The best answer is H.** According to Table 1, offspring with one or more copies of the *E* allele of Gene E would have a black coat or a brown coat. Table 2 shows that 2 of the Cross 3 offspring had a black coat, and 2 of the offspring had a brown coat. There were 6 offspring total. Four out of 6, or 2/3, of the offspring had one or more copies of the *E* allele of Gene E. **F, G,** and **J** are incorrect: 2/3 of the offspring had one or more copies of the *E* allele of Gene E. **H** is correct.

11. **The best answer is B.** To answer this item, the examinee must be familiar with dominant-recessive gene nomenclature. Capital letter for dominant and lowercase letter for recessive. According to Table 1, the genotype *bbee* with all recessive alleles corresponds to a yellow coat. According to Table 2, only Crosses 2 and 3 had offspring with a yellow coat, and therefore only Crosses 2 and 3 could have had only recessive alleles of Gene B and Gene E. **A** is incorrect: Cross 1 had no offspring with yellow coats. **B** is correct. **C** is incorrect: Cross 1 had no offspring with yellow coats. **D** is incorrect: Crosses 2 and 3 both had offspring with yellow coats that could have had the genotype *bbee.*

12. **The best answer is J.** According to Table 1, the *EE* genotype results in a black or brown coat color, and the *ee* genotype results in a yellow coat color. The observation that the *ee* genotype always corresponds to a yellow coat color indicates that the Gene E phenotypic expression is not affected by Gene B. **F** and **G** are incorrect: the data are not consistent with the hypothesis. **H** is incorrect: *EE* does not always result in a black coat. **J** is correct.

13. **The best answer is C.** To answer this item, the examinee must understand the segregation of chromosomes into gametes. For a dog with the genotype *BbEE,* half of the gametes will contain the *B* allele and the other half will contain the *b* allele. **A, B,** and **D** are incorrect: 50% will contain the *B* allele. **C** is correct.

SCIENCE • PRACTICE TEST 4 • EXPLANATORY ANSWERS

Passage III

14. **The best answer is J.** According to Figure 2, the highest $\frac{W}{D}$%, corresponding to the greatest average wet strength, was observed for the PTs submerged in water for 10 min and heated in the 140°C oven with a $\frac{W}{D} = 50\%$. **F** is incorrect: the PTs heated in the 110°C oven had a $\frac{W}{D}$ value less than 25%. **G** is incorrect: the PTs heated in the 120°C oven had a $\frac{W}{D}$ value less than 35%. **H** is incorrect: the PTs heated in the 130°C oven had a $\frac{W}{D}$ value of 40%. **J** is correct.

15. **The best answer is A.** According to Figure 2, as the oven temperature increased from 110°C to 140°C, the $\frac{W}{D}$ value for PTs submerged in water for 2 hr increased from approximately 23% to 48%. **A** is correct. **B, C,** and **D** are incorrect: the $\frac{W}{D}$ value increased steadily as the temperature increased.

16. **The best answer is F.** According to the passage, in Step 1 the control PTs were submerged in water, and in Step 3 the control PTs were heated in an oven at 25°C. F is correct. **G** is incorrect: the oven temperature was 25°C. **H** and **J** are incorrect: the PTs were submerged in water.

17. **The best answer is D.** According to the passage, the PTs in both Experiments 1 and 2 were soaked in water for 10 min, 2 hr, or 24 hr. None of the PTs was soaked in water for 18 hr. **A, B,** and **C** are incorrect: PTs were not soaked for 18 hr in either experiment. **D** is correct.

18. **The best answer is G.** According to Figure 1, the PTs submerged in water for 10 min had a higher $\frac{W}{D}$ value at all oven temperatures than did the PTs submerged in water for 2 hr. **F** is incorrect: the $\frac{W}{D}$ value at 2 hr was less than the $\frac{W}{D}$ value at 10 min. **G** is correct. **H** is incorrect: the $\frac{W}{D}$ values were not the same. **J** is incorrect: the $\frac{W}{D}$ value at 10 min was always greater than the $\frac{W}{D}$ value at 2 hr.

19. **The best answer is C.** The results of Experiment 2 show that wet strength of PTs treated with both GLA and zinc nitrate was greater than the wet strength of PTs treated with water. Because the results show that treatment with GLA and zinc nitrate did increase the wet strength of the PTS, the results of Experiment 2 refute the prediction. **A** and **B** are incorrect: Experiment 1 did not investigate the effect of treating the PTs with GLA and zinc nitrate. **C** is correct. **D** is incorrect: Experiment 2 does not support the prediction.

20. **The best answer is G.** In both experiments, the wet strength of the PTs is expressed as a percentage of the dry strength. Because this percentage is less than 100%, the dry strength is greater than the wet strength. **F** is incorrect: the wet strength was less than 100% of the dry strength. **G** is correct. **H** and **J** are incorrect: the dry strength was greater than the wet strength.

SCIENCE • PRACTICE TEST 4 • EXPLANATORY ANSWERS

Passage IV

21. **The best answer is B.** To answer this item, the examinee must be familiar with basic scientific instruments and know that an electronic balance is used to measure mass. Tables 2 and 3 list the average final mass of the adult frogs that would have been measured with an electronic balance. **A** is incorrect: a graduated cylinder is used to measure volume. **C** is incorrect: a metric ruler is used to measure length. **D** is incorrect: a calorimeter is used to measure changes in heat during a chemical reaction or process. **B** is correct: an electronic balance is used to measure mass.

22. **The best answer is F.** According to Table 1, the percent by mass of protein increased in Diets 1–5. Table 2 shows that the average final mass of the frogs also increased for the frogs fed Diets 1–5. **F** is correct. **G, H,** and **J** are incorrect: as the percent by mass of protein increased, the average final mass of the frogs also increased.

23. **The best answer is B.** According to the passage, the frogs were placed in outdoor tanks. It is most likely that the wire mesh was used to keep the frogs in the tanks and to keep predators out of the tanks. The tanks were covered after the frogs were placed in the tanks, so the mesh was not used to place the frogs in the tanks. **A, C,** and **D** are incorrect: the mesh was used to prevent predators from entering the tanks and keep the frogs from leaving the tanks. **B** is correct.

24. **The best answer is H.** According to Table 1, the number of calories per gram increased in Diets 6–10. Table 3 shows that the average final mass of the frogs increased as the frogs were fed Diets 6–8, but then decreased for the frogs fed Diets 8–10. **F, G,** and **J** are incorrect: the average final mass of the frogs increased and then decreased. **H** is correct.

25. **The best answer is C.** To answer this item, the examinee must know that organisms that belong to the same species also belong to the same genus. According to the passage, the species *Rana rugulosa* was studied. All the frogs were the same species and genus. **A, B,** and **D** are incorrect: the frogs belonged to the same genus and the same species. **C** is correct.

26. **The best answer is G.** According to the passage, in Experiment 1 the starting mass of the frogs was 3.3 g, and each frog was fed 1,000 mg of food twice a day for a total of 2,000 mg. In Experiment 2, the starting mass of the frogs was 7.9 g, and each frog was fed 2,000 mg of food once a day. **F** is incorrect: the initial mass of each frog was less in Experiment 1 than in Experiment 2. **G** is correct: the initial mass of each frog in Experiment 2 was 7.9 g, and the initial mass of each frog in Experiment 1 was 3.3 g. **H** and **J** are incorrect: the frogs in both experiments were fed 2,000 mg of food per day.

27. **The best answer is D.** According to Table 1, Diets 1–5 all contained the same number of calories per gram, and the number of calories per gram was varied in Diets 6–10. To determine whether the number of calories per gram in the diet affected the growth, the farmer should have compared the results of Diets 6–10. **A** and **B** are incorrect: the percent by mass of protein was varied in Diets 1–5, and this would give no information about the effect of the number of calories per gram in the diet. **C** is incorrect: Diets 6–10 varied in the number of calories per gram. The percent by mass of protein was held constant. **D** is correct.

SCIENCE • PRACTICE TEST 4 • EXPLANATORY ANSWERS

Passage V

28. **The best answer is F.** According to Figure 3, the average water content of soil values for the 4 dates were closest to one another, differing by less than 5%, at a depth of 30 cm. F is correct. **G** is incorrect: the values were slightly more spread out at a depth of 60 cm. **H** is incorrect: the values had a range that was greater than 10% at a depth of 100 cm. **J** is incorrect: the values had a range of approximately 15% at a depth of 140 cm.

29. **The best answer is A.** According to the passage, the slots near the end of the steel pipe allowed only soil gas to enter the pipe. **A** is correct. **B, C,** and **D** are incorrect: only soil gas entered the pipe.

30. **The best answer is J.** According to the passage, CO_2 is produced through 2 processes, but the experimental procedure does not provide any way of determining how much of the gas is produced by either process. **F, G,** and **H** are incorrect. **J** is correct: there is no way of knowing what percentage of the gas is produced by respiration in plant roots and how much is produced through decomposition of organic matter in this experiment.

31. **The best answer is B.** According to Figure 2, the percentage recorded is the average CO_2 content of soil gas by volume. To calculate this amount, one would divide the volume of CO_2 by the total volume of the gas sample. **A** is incorrect: to determine the percentage of CO_2 in the gas, one would have to divide by the volume of the gas sample. **B** is correct. **C** is incorrect: the percentage of CO_2 in the gas sample is being calculated, not the percentage of CO_2 in the water sample. **D** is incorrect: not all the gas collected in the steel pipe was analyzed for its CO_2 content, and therefore only the volume of the gas removed from the steel pipe via the syringe should be used in the percentage calculation.

32. **The best answer is J.** According to Figure 3, the average water content of the soil increased for the samples collected on November 23 and December 7, and the average water content decreased for the samples collected on October 26 and November 9. **F** is incorrect: the average water content increased only on November 23 and December 7. **G** is incorrect: the average water content decreased only on October 26 and November 9. **H** is incorrect: the average water content increased on November 23 and December 7 and decreased on October 26 and November 9. **J** is correct.

33. **The best answer is D.** According to Figure 2, for the samples collected on November 23, as the depth increased, the average CO_2 content also increased. At a depth of 140 cm, the average CO_2 content was approximately 0.41% by volume. If another diffusion well was positioned at a depth of 145 cm, then the average CO_2 content of the soil gas would have been greater than 0.40% by volume. **A, B,** and **C** are incorrect: the CO_2 content would have been greater than 0.40%. **D** is correct.

34. **The best answer is G.** According to Figure 3, on November 23 at a depth of 60 cm, the soil had an average water content of 20% by mass. A 10 g sample of soil would have contained 2 g of water (20% of 10 g = 2 g). **F** is incorrect: the mass of water would be 1 g if the average water content was 10% by mass. **G** is correct. **H** is incorrect: the mass of water would be 5 g if the average water content was 50% by mass. **J** is incorrect: if 10 g of water was in the sample, then the sample was 100% water and contained no soil.

SCIENCE • PRACTICE TEST 4 • EXPLANATORY ANSWERS

Passage VI

35. **The best answer is D.** According to Figure 3, as time increased, the depth in motor oil also increased. At a time of 45 msec, the depth of the steel ball in motor oil was approximately 1.9 mm. The depth at time = 50 msec would most likely have been slightly greater than 1.9 mm. **A, B,** and **C** are incorrect: the depth would have been greater than 1.9 mm. **D** is correct.

36. **The best answer is G.** To answer this item, the examinee must know that buoyant forces are always directed upward and the gravitational force is directed downward. According to the passage, drag is a force that opposes motion. Because the ball is moving downward, drag is an upward force. **F** is incorrect: *D* should be an upward force. **G** is correct. **H** and **J** are incorrect: *G* is a downward force and *B* is an upward force.

37. **The best answer is C.** According to Figure 1, the steel ball in motor oil reaches terminal speed, where the speed remains constant, after approximately 25 msec. Figure 2 shows that the steel ball in glycerin reaches terminal speed after approximately 10 msec. It required less time for the steel ball to reach terminal speed in glycerin. **A** and **B** are incorrect: it took more time to reach terminal speed in motor oil. **C** is correct. **D** is incorrect: it took approximately 25 msec in motor oil and only 10 msec in glycerin.

38. **The best answer is F.** According to Figure 1, the terminal speed of the steel ball in motor oil was approximately 48 mm/sec. Figure 2 shows that the terminal speed of the steel ball in glycerin was approximately 10 mm/sec. The terminal speed was greater in motor oil. **F** is correct. **G** is incorrect: the terminal speed was approximately 48 mm/sec in motor oil and 10 mm/sec in glycerin. **H** and **J** are incorrect: the steel ball's terminal speed was greater in motor oil.

39. **The best answer is C.** According to Figure 3, in both motor oil and glycerin, the depth of the steel ball increased over time. According to Figures 2 and 3, over time the draw increased and then leveled off. The drag on the steel ball was not proportional to the depth of the ball because as the depth increased, the drag increased and then remained roughly constant. **A** and **B** are incorrect: it is not reasonable to conclude that the drag on the steel ball was directly proportional to the depth of the ball. **C** is correct. **D** is incorrect: the drag increased and then remained roughly constant.

40. **The best answer is H.** According to Figure 3, the steel ball reached a depth of 0.50 mm in motor oil after approximately 16 msec. Figure 1 shows that, after 16 msec in motor oil, the drag on the steel ball was approximately 270 μN. **F** is incorrect: the drag reached 230 μN after approximately 9 msec, and at this time the steel ball was at a depth of only about 0.20 mm. **G** is incorrect: the drag reached 250 μN after approximately 11 msec, and at this time the steel ball was at a depth of only about 0.25 mm. **H** is correct: the drag reached 270 μN after approximately 14 msec, and the steel ball at this time was at a depth of about 0.50 mm. **J** is incorrect: the drag reached 290 μN after approximately 30 msec, and the steel ball at this time was at a depth of about 1.20 mm.

PAGE 1

The ACT® *Sample Answer Sheet*

EXAMINEE STATEMENT, CERTIFICATION, AND SIGNATURE

1. Read the following **Statement:** By submitting this answer document, I agree to comply with and be bound by the *Terms and Conditions: Testing Rules and Policies for the ACT® Test* provided in the ACT registration materials for this test, including those concerning test security, score cancellation, examinee remedies, binding arbitration, and consent to the processing of my personally identifying information, including the collection, use, transfer, and disclosure of information as described in the ACT Privacy Policy (www.act.org/privacy.html).

   I understand that ACT owns the test questions and responses and affirm that I will not share any test questions or responses with anyone by any form of communication before, during, or after the test administration. I understand that assuming anyone else's identity to take this test is strictly prohibited and may violate the law and subject me to legal penalties.

   International Examinees: By my signature, I am also providing my consent to ACT to transfer my personally identifying information to the United States to ACT, or a third-party service provider for processing, where it will be subject to use and disclosure under the laws of the United States. I acknowledge and agree that it may also be accessible to law enforcement and national security authorities in the United States.

2. Copy the **Certification** shown below (only the text in italics) on the lines provided. Write in your normal handwriting.

Certification: *I agree to the Statement above and certify that I am the person whose name and address appear on this answer document.*

Your Signature

Today's Date

Do NOT mark in this shaded area.

USE A SOFT LEAD NO. 2 PENCIL ONLY.
(Do NOT use a mechanical pencil, ink, ballpoint, correction fluid, or felt-tip pen.)

A **NAME, MAILING ADDRESS, AND TELEPHONE**
(Please print.)

Last Name | First Name | MI (Middle Initial)

House Number & Street (Apt. No.); or PO Box & No.; or RR & No.

City | State/Province | ZIP/Postal Code

Area Code / Number | Country

ACT, Inc.—Confidential Restricted when data present

ALL examinees must complete block A – please print.

Blocks B, C, and D are required for all examinees. Find the MATCHING INFORMATION on your ticket. Enter it EXACTLY the same way, even if any of the information is missing or incorrect. Fill in the corresponding ovals. If you do not complete these blocks to match your previous information EXACTLY, your scores will be **delayed up to 8 weeks.**

ACT

PO BOX 168, IOWA CITY, IA 52243-0168

B **MATCH NAME**
(First 5 letters of last name)

A B C D E F G H I J K L M N O P Q R S T U V W X Y Z

C **MATCH NUMBER**

1 2 3 4 5 6 7 8 9 0

D **DATE OF BIRTH**

Month	Day	Year
January		
February		
March	1	1
April	2	2
May	3	3
June	4	4
July	5	5
August	6	6
September	7	7
October	8	8
November	9	9
December	0	0

A011 215 190 Rev 1

IM-(A)199526-001:654321 Printed in the US.

PAGE 2

Marking Directions: Mark only **one** oval for each question. Fill in response completely. Erase errors cleanly without smudging.

Correct mark:

Do NOT use these *incorrect* **or** *bad* **marks.**

Incorrect marks:
Overlapping mark:
Cross-out mark:
Smudged erasure:
Mark is too light:

BOOKLET NUMBER

1	1	1	1	1	1
2	2	2	2	2	2
3	3	3	3	3	3
4	4	4	4	4	4
5	5	5	5	5	5
6	6	6	6	6	6
7	7	7	7	7	7
8	8	8	8	8	8
9	9	9	9	9	9
0	0	0	0	0	0

FORM

Print your 5-character **Test Form** in the boxes above and fill in the corresponding oval at the right.

BE SURE TO FILL IN THE CORRECT FORM OVAL.

- 16MC1
- 16MC2
- 16MC3
- 18MC4
- 19MC5

TEST 1

1 A B C D	14 F G H J	27 A B C D	40 F G H J	53 A B C D	66 F G H J
2 F G H J	15 A B C D	28 F G H J	41 A B C D	54 F G H J	67 A B C D
3 A B C D	16 F G H J	29 A B C D	42 F G H J	55 A B C D	68 F G H J
4 F G H J	17 A B C D	30 F G H J	43 A B C D	56 F G H J	69 A B C D
5 A B C D	18 F G H J	31 A B C D	44 F G H J	57 A B C D	70 F G H J
6 F G H J	19 A B C D	32 F G H J	45 A B C D	58 F G H J	71 A B C D
7 A B C D	20 F G H J	33 A B C D	46 F G H J	59 A B C D	72 F G H J
8 F G H J	21 A B C D	34 F G H J	47 A B C D	60 F G H J	73 A B C D
9 A B C D	22 F G H J	35 A B C D	48 F G H J	61 A B C D	74 F G H J
10 F G H J	23 A B C D	36 F G H J	49 A B C D	62 F G H J	75 A B C D
11 A B C D	24 F G H J	37 A B C D	50 F G H J	63 A B C D	
12 F G H J	25 A B C D	38 F G H J	51 A B C D	64 F G H J	
13 A B C D	26 F G H J	39 A B C D	52 F G H J	65 A B C D	

TEST 2

1 A B C D E	11 A B C D E	21 A B C D E	31 A B C D E	41 A B C D E	51 A B C D E
2 F G H J K	12 F G H J K	22 F G H J K	32 F G H J K	42 F G H J K	52 F G H J K
3 A B C D E	13 A B C D E	23 A B C D E	33 A B C D E	43 A B C D E	53 A B C D E
4 F G H J K	14 F G H J K	24 F G H J K	34 F G H J K	44 F G H J K	54 F G H J K
5 A B C D E	15 A B C D E	25 A B C D E	35 A B C D E	45 A B C D E	55 A B C D E
6 F G H J K	16 F G H J K	26 F G H J K	36 F G H J K	46 F G H J K	56 F G H J K
7 A B C D E	17 A B C D E	27 A B C D E	37 A B C D E	47 A B C D E	57 A B C D E
8 F G H J K	18 F G H J K	28 F G H J K	38 F G H J K	48 F G H J K	58 F G H J K
9 A B C D E	19 A B C D E	29 A B C D E	39 A B C D E	49 A B C D E	59 A B C D E
10 F G H J K	20 F G H J K	30 F G H J K	40 F G H J K	50 F G H J K	60 F G H J K

TEST 3

1 A B C D	8 F G H J	15 A B C D	22 F G H J	29 A B C D	36 F G H J
2 F G H J	9 A B C D	16 F G H J	23 A B C D	30 F G H J	37 A B C D
3 A B C D	10 F G H J	17 A B C D	24 F G H J	31 A B C D	38 F G H J
4 F G H J	11 A B C D	18 F G H J	25 A B C D	32 F G H J	39 A B C D
5 A B C D	12 F G H J	19 A B C D	26 F G H J	33 A B C D	40 F G H J
6 F G H J	13 A B C D	20 F G H J	27 A B C D	34 F G H J	
7 A B C D	14 F G H J	21 A B C D	28 F G H J	35 A B C D	

TEST 4

1 A B C D	8 F G H J	15 A B C D	22 F G H J	29 A B C D	36 F G H J
2 F G H J	9 A B C D	16 F G H J	23 A B C D	30 F G H J	37 A B C D
3 A B C D	10 F G H J	17 A B C D	24 F G H J	31 A B C D	38 F G H J
4 F G H J	11 A B C D	18 F G H J	25 A B C D	32 F G H J	39 A B C D
5 A B C D	12 F G H J	19 A B C D	26 F G H J	33 A B C D	40 F G H J
6 F G H J	13 A B C D	20 F G H J	27 A B C D	34 F G H J	
7 A B C D	14 F G H J	21 A B C D	28 F G H J	35 A B C D	

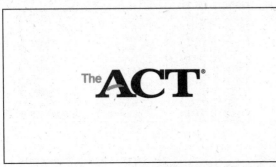

PAGE 1

The ACT® *Sample Answer Sheet*

EXAMINEE STATEMENT, CERTIFICATION, AND SIGNATURE

1. Read the following **Statement:** By submitting this answer document, I agree to comply with and be bound by the *Terms and Conditions: Testing Rules and Policies for the ACT® Test* provided in the ACT registration materials for this test, including those concerning test security, score cancellation, examinee remedies, binding arbitration, and consent to the processing of my personally identifying information, including the collection, use, transfer, and disclosure of information as described in the ACT Privacy Policy (www.act.org/privacy.html).

   I understand that ACT owns the test questions and responses and affirm that I will not share any test questions or responses with anyone by any form of communication before, during, or after the test administration. I understand that assuming anyone else's identity to take this test is strictly prohibited and may violate the law and subject me to legal penalties.

   International Examinees: By my signature, I am also providing my consent to ACT to transfer my personally identifying information to the United States to ACT, or a third-party service provider for processing, where it will be subject to use and disclosure under the laws of the United States. I acknowledge and agree that it may also be accessible to law enforcement and national security authorities in the United States.

2. Copy the **Certification** shown below (only the text in italics) on the lines provided. Write in your normal handwriting.

Certification: *I agree to the Statement above and certify that I am the person whose name and address appear on this answer document.*

Your Signature

Today's Date

Do NOT mark in this shaded area.

USE A SOFT LEAD NO. 2 PENCIL ONLY.
(Do NOT use a mechanical pencil, ink, ballpoint, correction fluid, or felt-tip pen.)

A NAME, MAILING ADDRESS, AND TELEPHONE (Please print.)

Last Name | First Name | MI (Middle Initial)

House Number & Street (Apt. No.); or PO Box & No.; or RR & No.

City | State/Province | ZIP/Postal Code

Area Code / Number | Country

ACT, Inc.—Confidential Restricted when data present

ALL examinees must complete block A – please print.

Blocks B, C, and D are required for all examinees. Find the MATCHING INFORMATION on your ticket. Enter it EXACTLY the same way, even if any of the information is missing or incorrect. Fill in the corresponding ovals. If you do not complete these blocks to match your previous information EXACTLY, your scores will be **delayed up to 8 weeks.**

ACT®

PO BOX 168, IOWA CITY, IA 52243-0168

B MATCH NAME (First 5 letters of last name)

C MATCH NUMBER

D DATE OF BIRTH

Month | Day | Year

- January
- February
- March
- April
- May
- June
- July
- August
- September
- October
- November
- December

 A011 215 190 Rev 1 IM-(A)199526-001:654321 Printed in the US.

PAGE 2

Marking Directions: Mark only **one** oval for each question. Fill in response completely. Erase errors cleanly without smudging.

Correct mark:

Do NOT use these *incorrect* or *bad* marks.

Incorrect marks:
Overlapping mark:
Cross-out mark:
Smudged erasure:
Mark is too light:

BOOKLET NUMBER

1	1	1	1	1	1
2	2	2	2	2	2
3	3	3	3	3	3
4	4	4	4	4	4
5	5	5	5	5	5
6	6	6	6	6	6
7	7	7	7	7	7
8	8	8	8	8	8
9	9	9	9	9	9
0	0	0	0	0	0

FORM

Print your 5-character **Test Form** in the boxes above and fill in the corresponding oval at the right.

BE SURE TO FILL IN THE CORRECT FORM OVAL.

○ 16MC1 ○ 18MC4
○ 16MC2 ○ 19MC5
○ 16MC3

TEST 1

1 Ⓐ Ⓑ Ⓒ Ⓓ	14 Ⓕ Ⓖ Ⓗ Ⓙ	27 Ⓐ Ⓑ Ⓒ Ⓓ	40 Ⓕ Ⓖ Ⓗ Ⓙ	53 Ⓐ Ⓑ Ⓒ Ⓓ	66 Ⓕ Ⓖ Ⓗ Ⓙ
2 Ⓕ Ⓖ Ⓗ Ⓙ	15 Ⓐ Ⓑ Ⓒ Ⓓ	28 Ⓕ Ⓖ Ⓗ Ⓙ	41 Ⓐ Ⓑ Ⓒ Ⓓ	54 Ⓕ Ⓖ Ⓗ Ⓙ	67 Ⓐ Ⓑ Ⓒ Ⓓ
3 Ⓐ Ⓑ Ⓒ Ⓓ	16 Ⓕ Ⓖ Ⓗ Ⓙ	29 Ⓐ Ⓑ Ⓒ Ⓓ	42 Ⓕ Ⓖ Ⓗ Ⓙ	55 Ⓐ Ⓑ Ⓒ Ⓓ	68 Ⓕ Ⓖ Ⓗ Ⓙ
4 Ⓕ Ⓖ Ⓗ Ⓙ	17 Ⓐ Ⓑ Ⓒ Ⓓ	30 Ⓕ Ⓖ Ⓗ Ⓙ	43 Ⓐ Ⓑ Ⓒ Ⓓ	56 Ⓕ Ⓖ Ⓗ Ⓙ	69 Ⓐ Ⓑ Ⓒ Ⓓ
5 Ⓐ Ⓑ Ⓒ Ⓓ	18 Ⓕ Ⓖ Ⓗ Ⓙ	31 Ⓐ Ⓑ Ⓒ Ⓓ	44 Ⓕ Ⓖ Ⓗ Ⓙ	57 Ⓐ Ⓑ Ⓒ Ⓓ	70 Ⓕ Ⓖ Ⓗ Ⓙ
6 Ⓕ Ⓖ Ⓗ Ⓙ	19 Ⓐ Ⓑ Ⓒ Ⓓ	32 Ⓕ Ⓖ Ⓗ Ⓙ	45 Ⓐ Ⓑ Ⓒ Ⓓ	58 Ⓕ Ⓖ Ⓗ Ⓙ	71 Ⓐ Ⓑ Ⓒ Ⓓ
7 Ⓐ Ⓑ Ⓒ Ⓓ	20 Ⓕ Ⓖ Ⓗ Ⓙ	33 Ⓐ Ⓑ Ⓒ Ⓓ	46 Ⓕ Ⓖ Ⓗ Ⓙ	59 Ⓐ Ⓑ Ⓒ Ⓓ	72 Ⓕ Ⓖ Ⓗ Ⓙ
8 Ⓕ Ⓖ Ⓗ Ⓙ	21 Ⓐ Ⓑ Ⓒ Ⓓ	34 Ⓕ Ⓖ Ⓗ Ⓙ	47 Ⓐ Ⓑ Ⓒ Ⓓ	60 Ⓕ Ⓖ Ⓗ Ⓙ	73 Ⓐ Ⓑ Ⓒ Ⓓ
9 Ⓐ Ⓑ Ⓒ Ⓓ	22 Ⓕ Ⓖ Ⓗ Ⓙ	35 Ⓐ Ⓑ Ⓒ Ⓓ	48 Ⓕ Ⓖ Ⓗ Ⓙ	61 Ⓐ Ⓑ Ⓒ Ⓓ	74 Ⓕ Ⓖ Ⓗ Ⓙ
10 Ⓕ Ⓖ Ⓗ Ⓙ	23 Ⓐ Ⓑ Ⓒ Ⓓ	36 Ⓕ Ⓖ Ⓗ Ⓙ	49 Ⓐ Ⓑ Ⓒ Ⓓ	62 Ⓕ Ⓖ Ⓗ Ⓙ	75 Ⓐ Ⓑ Ⓒ Ⓓ
11 Ⓐ Ⓑ Ⓒ Ⓓ	24 Ⓕ Ⓖ Ⓗ Ⓙ	37 Ⓐ Ⓑ Ⓒ Ⓓ	50 Ⓕ Ⓖ Ⓗ Ⓙ	63 Ⓐ Ⓑ Ⓒ Ⓓ	
12 Ⓕ Ⓖ Ⓗ Ⓙ	25 Ⓐ Ⓑ Ⓒ Ⓓ	38 Ⓕ Ⓖ Ⓗ Ⓙ	51 Ⓐ Ⓑ Ⓒ Ⓓ	64 Ⓕ Ⓖ Ⓗ Ⓙ	
13 Ⓐ Ⓑ Ⓒ Ⓓ	26 Ⓕ Ⓖ Ⓗ Ⓙ	39 Ⓐ Ⓑ Ⓒ Ⓓ	52 Ⓕ Ⓖ Ⓗ Ⓙ	65 Ⓐ Ⓑ Ⓒ Ⓓ	

TEST 2

1 Ⓐ Ⓑ Ⓒ Ⓓ Ⓔ	11 Ⓐ Ⓑ Ⓒ Ⓓ Ⓔ	21 Ⓐ Ⓑ Ⓒ Ⓓ Ⓔ	31 Ⓐ Ⓑ Ⓒ Ⓓ Ⓔ	41 Ⓐ Ⓑ Ⓒ Ⓓ Ⓔ	51 Ⓐ Ⓑ Ⓒ Ⓓ Ⓔ
2 Ⓕ Ⓖ Ⓗ Ⓙ Ⓚ	12 Ⓕ Ⓖ Ⓗ Ⓙ Ⓚ	22 Ⓕ Ⓖ Ⓗ Ⓙ Ⓚ	32 Ⓕ Ⓖ Ⓗ Ⓙ Ⓚ	42 Ⓕ Ⓖ Ⓗ Ⓙ Ⓚ	52 Ⓕ Ⓖ Ⓗ Ⓙ Ⓚ
3 Ⓐ Ⓑ Ⓒ Ⓓ Ⓔ	13 Ⓐ Ⓑ Ⓒ Ⓓ Ⓔ	23 Ⓐ Ⓑ Ⓒ Ⓓ Ⓔ	33 Ⓐ Ⓑ Ⓒ Ⓓ Ⓔ	43 Ⓐ Ⓑ Ⓒ Ⓓ Ⓔ	53 Ⓐ Ⓑ Ⓒ Ⓓ Ⓔ
4 Ⓕ Ⓖ Ⓗ Ⓙ Ⓚ	14 Ⓕ Ⓖ Ⓗ Ⓙ Ⓚ	24 Ⓕ Ⓖ Ⓗ Ⓙ Ⓚ	34 Ⓕ Ⓖ Ⓗ Ⓙ Ⓚ	44 Ⓕ Ⓖ Ⓗ Ⓙ Ⓚ	54 Ⓕ Ⓖ Ⓗ Ⓙ Ⓚ
5 Ⓐ Ⓑ Ⓒ Ⓓ Ⓔ	15 Ⓐ Ⓑ Ⓒ Ⓓ Ⓔ	25 Ⓐ Ⓑ Ⓒ Ⓓ Ⓔ	35 Ⓐ Ⓑ Ⓒ Ⓓ Ⓔ	45 Ⓐ Ⓑ Ⓒ Ⓓ Ⓔ	55 Ⓐ Ⓑ Ⓒ Ⓓ Ⓔ
6 Ⓕ Ⓖ Ⓗ Ⓙ Ⓚ	16 Ⓕ Ⓖ Ⓗ Ⓙ Ⓚ	26 Ⓕ Ⓖ Ⓗ Ⓙ Ⓚ	36 Ⓕ Ⓖ Ⓗ Ⓙ Ⓚ	46 Ⓕ Ⓖ Ⓗ Ⓙ Ⓚ	56 Ⓕ Ⓖ Ⓗ Ⓙ Ⓚ
7 Ⓐ Ⓑ Ⓒ Ⓓ Ⓔ	17 Ⓐ Ⓑ Ⓒ Ⓓ Ⓔ	27 Ⓐ Ⓑ Ⓒ Ⓓ Ⓔ	37 Ⓐ Ⓑ Ⓒ Ⓓ Ⓔ	47 Ⓐ Ⓑ Ⓒ Ⓓ Ⓔ	57 Ⓐ Ⓑ Ⓒ Ⓓ Ⓔ
8 Ⓕ Ⓖ Ⓗ Ⓙ Ⓚ	18 Ⓕ Ⓖ Ⓗ Ⓙ Ⓚ	28 Ⓕ Ⓖ Ⓗ Ⓙ Ⓚ	38 Ⓕ Ⓖ Ⓗ Ⓙ Ⓚ	48 Ⓕ Ⓖ Ⓗ Ⓙ Ⓚ	58 Ⓕ Ⓖ Ⓗ Ⓙ Ⓚ
9 Ⓐ Ⓑ Ⓒ Ⓓ Ⓔ	19 Ⓐ Ⓑ Ⓒ Ⓓ Ⓔ	29 Ⓐ Ⓑ Ⓒ Ⓓ Ⓔ	39 Ⓐ Ⓑ Ⓒ Ⓓ Ⓔ	49 Ⓐ Ⓑ Ⓒ Ⓓ Ⓔ	59 Ⓐ Ⓑ Ⓒ Ⓓ Ⓔ
10 Ⓕ Ⓖ Ⓗ Ⓙ Ⓚ	20 Ⓕ Ⓖ Ⓗ Ⓙ Ⓚ	30 Ⓕ Ⓖ Ⓗ Ⓙ Ⓚ	40 Ⓕ Ⓖ Ⓗ Ⓙ Ⓚ	50 Ⓕ Ⓖ Ⓗ Ⓙ Ⓚ	60 Ⓕ Ⓖ Ⓗ Ⓙ Ⓚ

TEST 3

1 Ⓐ Ⓑ Ⓒ Ⓓ	8 Ⓕ Ⓖ Ⓗ Ⓙ	15 Ⓐ Ⓑ Ⓒ Ⓓ	22 Ⓕ Ⓖ Ⓗ Ⓙ	29 Ⓐ Ⓑ Ⓒ Ⓓ	36 Ⓕ Ⓖ Ⓗ Ⓙ
2 Ⓕ Ⓖ Ⓗ Ⓙ	9 Ⓐ Ⓑ Ⓒ Ⓓ	16 Ⓕ Ⓖ Ⓗ Ⓙ	23 Ⓐ Ⓑ Ⓒ Ⓓ	30 Ⓕ Ⓖ Ⓗ Ⓙ	37 Ⓐ Ⓑ Ⓒ Ⓓ
3 Ⓐ Ⓑ Ⓒ Ⓓ	10 Ⓕ Ⓖ Ⓗ Ⓙ	17 Ⓐ Ⓑ Ⓒ Ⓓ	24 Ⓕ Ⓖ Ⓗ Ⓙ	31 Ⓐ Ⓑ Ⓒ Ⓓ	38 Ⓕ Ⓖ Ⓗ Ⓙ
4 Ⓕ Ⓖ Ⓗ Ⓙ	11 Ⓐ Ⓑ Ⓒ Ⓓ	18 Ⓕ Ⓖ Ⓗ Ⓙ	25 Ⓐ Ⓑ Ⓒ Ⓓ	32 Ⓕ Ⓖ Ⓗ Ⓙ	39 Ⓐ Ⓑ Ⓒ Ⓓ
5 Ⓐ Ⓑ Ⓒ Ⓓ	12 Ⓕ Ⓖ Ⓗ Ⓙ	19 Ⓐ Ⓑ Ⓒ Ⓓ	26 Ⓕ Ⓖ Ⓗ Ⓙ	33 Ⓐ Ⓑ Ⓒ Ⓓ	40 Ⓕ Ⓖ Ⓗ Ⓙ
6 Ⓕ Ⓖ Ⓗ Ⓙ	13 Ⓐ Ⓑ Ⓒ Ⓓ	20 Ⓕ Ⓖ Ⓗ Ⓙ	27 Ⓐ Ⓑ Ⓒ Ⓓ	34 Ⓕ Ⓖ Ⓗ Ⓙ	
7 Ⓐ Ⓑ Ⓒ Ⓓ	14 Ⓕ Ⓖ Ⓗ Ⓙ	21 Ⓐ Ⓑ Ⓒ Ⓓ	28 Ⓕ Ⓖ Ⓗ Ⓙ	35 Ⓐ Ⓑ Ⓒ Ⓓ	

TEST 4

1 Ⓐ Ⓑ Ⓒ Ⓓ	8 Ⓕ Ⓖ Ⓗ Ⓙ	15 Ⓐ Ⓑ Ⓒ Ⓓ	22 Ⓕ Ⓖ Ⓗ Ⓙ	29 Ⓐ Ⓑ Ⓒ Ⓓ	36 Ⓕ Ⓖ Ⓗ Ⓙ
2 Ⓕ Ⓖ Ⓗ Ⓙ	9 Ⓐ Ⓑ Ⓒ Ⓓ	16 Ⓕ Ⓖ Ⓗ Ⓙ	23 Ⓐ Ⓑ Ⓒ Ⓓ	30 Ⓕ Ⓖ Ⓗ Ⓙ	37 Ⓐ Ⓑ Ⓒ Ⓓ
3 Ⓐ Ⓑ Ⓒ Ⓓ	10 Ⓕ Ⓖ Ⓗ Ⓙ	17 Ⓐ Ⓑ Ⓒ Ⓓ	24 Ⓕ Ⓖ Ⓗ Ⓙ	31 Ⓐ Ⓑ Ⓒ Ⓓ	38 Ⓕ Ⓖ Ⓗ Ⓙ
4 Ⓕ Ⓖ Ⓗ Ⓙ	11 Ⓐ Ⓑ Ⓒ Ⓓ	18 Ⓕ Ⓖ Ⓗ Ⓙ	25 Ⓐ Ⓑ Ⓒ Ⓓ	32 Ⓕ Ⓖ Ⓗ Ⓙ	39 Ⓐ Ⓑ Ⓒ Ⓓ
5 Ⓐ Ⓑ Ⓒ Ⓓ	12 Ⓕ Ⓖ Ⓗ Ⓙ	19 Ⓐ Ⓑ Ⓒ Ⓓ	26 Ⓕ Ⓖ Ⓗ Ⓙ	33 Ⓐ Ⓑ Ⓒ Ⓓ	40 Ⓕ Ⓖ Ⓗ Ⓙ
6 Ⓕ Ⓖ Ⓗ Ⓙ	13 Ⓐ Ⓑ Ⓒ Ⓓ	20 Ⓕ Ⓖ Ⓗ Ⓙ	27 Ⓐ Ⓑ Ⓒ Ⓓ	34 Ⓕ Ⓖ Ⓗ Ⓙ	
7 Ⓐ Ⓑ Ⓒ Ⓓ	14 Ⓕ Ⓖ Ⓗ Ⓙ	21 Ⓐ Ⓑ Ⓒ Ⓓ	28 Ⓕ Ⓖ Ⓗ Ⓙ	35 Ⓐ Ⓑ Ⓒ Ⓓ	

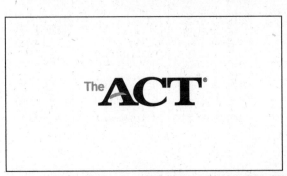

080662

Practice Test 5

EXAMINEE STATEMENT, CERTIFICATION, AND SIGNATURE

1. Read the following **Statement:** By opening this test booklet, I agree to comply with and be bound by the *Terms and Conditions: Testing Rules and Policies for the ACT® Test* provided in the ACT registration materials for this test, including those concerning test security, score cancellation, examinee remedies, binding arbitration, and consent to the processing of my personally identifying information, including the collection, use, transfer, and disclosure of information as described in the ACT Privacy Policy (www.act.org/privacy.html).

   I understand that ACT owns the test questions and responses and affirm that I will not share any test questions or responses with anyone by any form of communication before, during, or after the test administration. I understand that assuming anyone else's identity to take this test is strictly prohibited and may violate the law and subject me to legal penalties.

   International Examinees: By my signature, I am also providing my consent to ACT to transfer my personally identifying information to the United States to ACT, or a third-party service provider for processing, where it will be subject to use and disclosure under the laws of the United States. I acknowledge and agree that it may also be accessible to law enforcement and national security authorities in the United States.

2. Copy the **Certification** shown below (only the text in italics) on the lines provided. Write in your normal handwriting.

   Certification: *I agree to the Statement above and certify that I am the person whose name appears on this form.*

   ____

   ____

3. Sign your name as you would any official document, enter today's date, and print your name in the spaces provided.

Your Signature	Today's Date	Print Your Name

Form 19MC5

2019 | 2020

Directions

This booklet contains tests in English, mathematics, reading, and science. These tests measure skills and abilities highly related to high school course work and success in college. **Calculators may be used on the mathematics test only.**

The questions in each test are numbered, and the suggested answers for each question are lettered. On the answer document, the rows of ovals are numbered to match the questions, and the ovals in each row are lettered to correspond to the suggested answers.

For each question, first decide which answer is best. Next, locate on the answer document the row of ovals numbered the same as the question. Then, locate the oval in that row lettered the same as your answer. Finally, fill in the oval completely. Use a soft lead pencil and make your marks heavy and black. **Do not use ink or a mechanical pencil.**

Mark only one answer to each question. If you change your mind about an answer, erase your first mark thoroughly before marking your new answer. For each question, make certain that you mark in the row of ovals with the same number as the question.

Only responses marked on your answer document will be scored. Your score on each test will be based only on the number of questions you answer correctly during the time allowed for that test. You will **not** be penalized for guessing. **It is to your advantage to answer every question even if you must guess.**

You may work on each test **only** when the testing staff tells you to do so. If you finish a test before time is called for that test, you should use the time remaining to reconsider questions you are uncertain about in that test. You may **not** look back to a test on which time has already been called, and you may **not** go ahead to another test. To do so will disqualify you from the examination.

Lay your pencil down immediately when time is called at the end of each test. You may **not** for any reason fill in or alter ovals for a test after time is called for that test. To do so will disqualify you from the examination.

Do not fold or tear the pages of your test booklet.

DO NOT OPEN THIS BOOKLET UNTIL TOLD TO DO SO.

1 ■ ■ ■ ■ ■ ■ ■ ■ ■ 1

ENGLISH TEST

45 Minutes—75 Questions

DIRECTIONS: In the five passages that follow, certain words and phrases are underlined and numbered. In the right-hand column, you will find alternatives for the underlined part. In most cases, you are to choose the one that best expresses the idea, makes the statement appropriate for standard written English, or is worded most consistently with the style and tone of the passage as a whole. If you think the original version is best, choose "NO CHANGE." In some cases, you will find in the right-hand column a question about the underlined part. You are to choose the best answer to the question.

You will also find questions about a section of the passage, or about the passage as a whole. These questions do not refer to an underlined portion of the passage, but rather are identified by a number or numbers in a box.

For each question, choose the alternative you consider best and fill in the corresponding oval on your answer document. Read each passage through once before you begin to answer the questions that accompany it. For many of the questions, you must read several sentences beyond the question to determine the answer. Be sure that you have read far enough ahead each time you choose an alternative.

PASSAGE I

Ukulele Life

My older sister was a guitar buff and my idol [1] when I was growing up. She would teach me songs on her acoustic guitar now and then after school and on long family road trips to the beach. In those moments, my sister and I were the closest we've ever been. And my guitar itself felt like, well, family.

When my sister left Chicago for college in California, I began carting my guitar around everywhere: [2] to school, to work, to friends houses. [3] Years later, my guitar accompanied me on business trips. No matter where I was, [4] playing it made me feel a little bit closer to home.

1. If the writer were to delete the underlined portion, the paragraph would primarily lose:
   - A. an indication that the narrator learned to play guitar at a relatively young age.
   - B. an indication of why the narrator became interested in playing the guitar.
   - C. a detail that specifies how much older the sister is compared to the narrator.
   - D. a detail that reveals the amount of musical talent the narrator's sister had.

2. F. NO CHANGE
   G. around. Everywhere,
   H. around everywhere;
   J. around everywhere

3. A. NO CHANGE
   B. friend's house's.
   C. friends' houses.
   D. friend's houses.

4. F. NO CHANGE
   G. trips and no matter where I was
   H. trips. No matter where I was
   J. trips, no matter where I was,

GO ON TO THE NEXT PAGE.

But one day, after landing in Honolulu, Hawaii, for an extended trip, I couldn't locate my guitar on the luggage carousel. Panicked, I assailed[5] airport personnel, who assured myself[6] that they would try to recover my beloved instrument. At that moment of my extended trip,[7] continuing the trip without it seemed impossible.

My worries began to dissipate, otherwise,[8] as I walked out of the airport and upon[9] the balmy Hawaiian air. In front of me, a man was playing what looked like a miniature guitar. Warm, mellow tones accrued[10] from the instrument, complementing the lyrical rhythm of the Hawaiian words he sang. It was a ukulele.

As soon as I could, I bought a ukulele of my own. I began to linger on[11] the beach, where several native Hawaiians often played. I watched them for hours, my ukulele in my hands, and practiced. Unlike the guitar, which has six strings, my ukulele had four; to make the same chords with the uke, I had to learn completely different finger positions. I also had trouble with dexterity at first because the neck of the uke is much narrower then that of a guitar.[12] I had to retrain my fingers to make smaller movements in order to shape the chords.

5. Which choice best illustrates the fervor with which the narrator communicated with the airport personnel?
   A. NO CHANGE
   B. approached
   C. questioned
   D. contacted

6. F. NO CHANGE
   G. whom assured myself
   H. whom assured me
   J. who assured me

7. A. NO CHANGE
   B. moment, due to the fact that I was on an extended trip,
   C. very moment during my time in Honolulu,
   D. moment,

8. F. NO CHANGE
   G. therefore,
   H. though,
   J. instead,

9. A. NO CHANGE
   B. amid
   C. onto
   D. into

10. F. NO CHANGE
    G. distributed
    H. appeared
    J. issued

11. A. NO CHANGE
    B. Beginning to linger on
    C. Lingering on
    D. On

12. F. NO CHANGE
    G. than that of a guitar.
    H. than it.
    J. then it.

GO ON TO THE NEXT PAGE.

1 ■ ■ ■ ■ ■ ■ ■ ■ ■ 1

When I wasn't working, I was on the beach, losing myself in the bright notes of the uke. Eventually, I began playing music[13] like "He'eia" as[14] the locals. And the sound of the ukulele is synonymous with the romance and beauty of Hawaii's beaches.[15]

13. Which choice best specifies the type of songs the narrator played on the ukulele?
   A. NO CHANGE
   B. Hawaiian classics
   C. tropical tunes
   D. things

14. F. NO CHANGE
   G. through
   H. with
   J. along

15. Which choice best concludes the essay by emphasizing the central point made in the first and second paragraphs?
   A. NO CHANGE
   B. And I couldn't think of a better way to spend my guitarless time in Honolulu.
   C. And although I was guitarless and far from family, I felt like I was home.
   D. And even though I was on a business trip, I didn't want to leave.

PASSAGE II

Hedy Lamarr, Across the Spectrum

In 1940, Hedy Lamarr was becoming a Hollywood star, but she was bored. On set for only three months of the year, she filled her spare time with an unusual hobby: inventing. World War II was underway in Europe, where Lamarr had grown up, and she hoped to invent something to help the Allied cause. Because Lamarr's former husband had often discussed his work in munitions, the actress knew about weaponry.

GO ON TO THE NEXT PAGE.

She had ideas of her own, including <u>an idea of hers</u> [16] for a torpedo with a sophisticated radio-controlled guidance system. [17] Lamarr knew that radio signals on one frequency <u>is easy to jam</u> [18] by anyone sending a competing signal on the same <u>frequency. She envisioned a</u> [19] system that used dozens of frequencies to transmit a signal to guide torpedoes. To protect the signal further, transmitters and receivers would jump from frequency to frequency in a predetermined order that would seem random to an outsider. Such a signal <u>like that would be</u> [20] hard to detect and nearly impossible to disrupt.

[1] In August 1940, Lamarr met composer George Antheil, and the two began collaborating. [2] Antheil, who had synchronized player pianos for his compositions, had the mechanical knowledge that Lamarr needed to <u>instigate</u> [21] her idea. [3] Then in 1942, the inventors heard that the Navy had rejected their idea. [4] They submitted the "Secret Communication System" to the military in June 1941. [5] In the decades after the <u>war, however,</u> [22] the US military discovered the value of Lamarr's idea, which came to be called "spread spectrum," and used it in guidance, radio, and navigation systems. [23]

16. F. NO CHANGE
G. one idea that she had
H. her own idea
J. one

17. At this point, the writer is considering dividing the paragraph into two. Making this change would help organize the essay by separating:
A. an analysis of Lamarr's first invention from details about another one she later developed.
B. information about the origin of Lamarr's idea from details about how the invention would work.
C. an overview of Lamarr's film career from an account of how she conceived of her invention.
D. details about Lamarr's childhood from general information about radio signals.

18. F. NO CHANGE
G. has been easy to jam
H. are easily jammed
J. is easily jammed

19. A. NO CHANGE
B. frequency she envisioned. A
C. frequency, she envisioned a
D. frequency she envisioned; a

20. F. NO CHANGE
G. similar to that would be
H. would be difficult and
J. would be

21. A. NO CHANGE
B. implement
C. discharge
D. uphold

22. F. NO CHANGE
G. war; however,
H. war, however
J. war however

23. For the sake of logic and cohesion, Sentence 3 should be placed:
A. where it is now.
B. before Sentence 1.
C. after Sentence 4.
D. after Sentence 5.

GO ON TO THE NEXT PAGE.

1 ■ ■ ■ ■ ■ ■ ■ ■ ■ 1

In 1978, spread spectrum was declassified, and it made a difference.[24] Devices that operate wirelessly, cellular phones, wireless Internet networks,[25] the Global Positioning System—functioning[26] because of Lamarr's idea. It[27] wasn't until 1996 that Lamarr and Antheil, they were finally given[28] credit for spread spectrum. However, they[29] were awarded the Pioneer Award from the Electronic Frontier Foundation. Upon hearing of her award, Lamarr said, "It's about time."

24. Which choice most strongly and specifically emphasizes that the declassification of spread spectrum was a turning point in the history of communication technology?

F. NO CHANGE
G. transformed the communication landscape.
H. had an impact on communications.
J. revolutionized things.

25. A. NO CHANGE
B. wirelessly—cellular phones,
C. wirelessly: cellular phones,
D. wirelessly, cellular phones

26. F. NO CHANGE
G. to function
H. function
J. DELETE the underlined portion.

27. A. NO CHANGE
B. Such
C. This
D. That

28. F. NO CHANGE
G. Antheil—both finally got
H. Antheil finally to receive
J. Antheil finally received

29. A. NO CHANGE
B. Conversely, they
C. Anyway, they
D. They

Question 30 asks about the preceding passage as a whole.

30. Suppose the writer's primary purpose had been to give an overview of the history of an important invention. Would this essay accomplish that purpose?

F. Yes, because it recounts the story of Lamarr and Antheil's invention of spread spectrum and the invention's significance.
G. Yes, because it shows how Lamarr and Antheil changed the course of World War II by inventing spread spectrum.
H. No, because although it describes Lamarr and Antheil's invention, it does not establish the importance of spread spectrum.
J. No, because it instead focuses on Lamarr, Antheil, and their collaborations in the film industry.

GO ON TO THE NEXT PAGE.

PASSAGE III

Climbing Mt. Windmill

[1]

They're some 45,000 electricity-generating wind turbines in the United States, and the task of repairing and maintaining these huge machines have represented a substantial undertaking. Ladders inside the towers simplify access to the generators and controllers within the turbine housing. In contrast, servicing the turbine blades those long fiberglass vanes that slice through the air, is a serious challenge.

[2]

[A] Rock climbers are comfortable in high places and capable, equipped with rope and other simple gear, of scaling almost anything. After completing specialized training, rock climbers become ideal "rope technicians."

[3]

When the rope technicians arrive across a turbine, they first lock the blades into a "bunny ears" position, in which two blades angle up and one blade points straight down. The technicians climb the ladder inside the tower, secure themselves with ropes and harnesses, open a hatch in the turbine's housing, and rappel down the vertical blade.

[4]

Certainly, turbine blades withstand severe stress. The blades zip through the elements as fast as 200 miles

31. A. NO CHANGE
B. There are
C. Their is
D. There's

32. F. NO CHANGE
G. are representing
H. represents
J. represent

33. A. NO CHANGE
B. Likewise,
C. Instantly,
D. First,

34. F. NO CHANGE
G. blades—those long fiberglass vanes that slice through the air—
H. blades—those long fiberglass vanes that slice through the air,
J. blades, those long fiberglass vanes that slice through the air

35. A. NO CHANGE
B. climbing nearly anything—something they're able to do.
C. ascending just about anything by climbing it.
D. using rope to climb almost anything.

36. F. NO CHANGE
G. old skills and new knowledge turn rock climbers into ideal "rope technicians."
H. new careers as "rope technicians" open up for rock climbers.
J. ideal "rope technicians" can be made out of rock climbers.

37. A. NO CHANGE
B. with
C. via
D. at

GO ON TO THE NEXT PAGE.

1 ■ ■ ■ ■ ■ ■ ■ ■ ■ 1

per hour, braving heat, hail, blizzards, and more. Yet despite enduring such harsh conditions, most turbine blades that rope technicians service only need a thorough cleaning or other basic upkeep, such as a new coat of paint. [B] Sometimes, the task can be more complicated: patching fiberglass damage from a lightning strike, for example.

[5]

The largest wind turbine blades are over 270 feet long.[38] Technicians work in pairs; while[39] they don't climb in high winds, extreme temperatures, or precipitation. Whether[40] there's lightning within thirty miles, the technicians stay on the ground. [C] Precautions such as these—along[41] with rigorous procedures and training, make[42] the job quite safe.

[6]

For many rock climbers, being a rope technician is a dream job. [D] Fresh air, great vistas, to practice climbing daily,[43] and ample time off to scale actual rocks—it's not a typical job description, is it?[44]

38. Given that all the choices are true, which one would provide the most effective introduction to the paragraph?
F. NO CHANGE
G. The number of wind turbine–related jobs has doubled in five years.
H. A typical wind turbine has about 8,000 parts.
J. Whatever the job, safety is the first priority.

39. A. NO CHANGE
B. pairs, and
C. pairs,
D. pairs

40. F. NO CHANGE
G. So that
H. Unless
J. If

41. A. NO CHANGE
B. these;
C. these,
D. these

42. F. NO CHANGE
G. is making
H. has made
J. makes

43. A. NO CHANGE
B. they practice climbing regularly,
C. while often practicing climbing,
D. plenty of climbing practice,

44. The writer wants to end this sentence by emphasizing that rock climbers in particular may find being a rope technician an appealing occupation. Which choice best accomplishes that goal?
F. NO CHANGE
G. what inspires rock climbers to reach such heights?
H. what more could a climber want?
J. ready to sign up yet?

GO ON TO THE NEXT PAGE.

Question 45 asks about the preceding passage as a whole.

45. The writer wants to add the following sentence to the essay:

Enter rock climbers.

The sentence would most logically be placed at:

A. Point A in Paragraph 2.
B. Point B in Paragraph 4.
C. Point C in Paragraph 5.
D. Point D in Paragraph 6.

PASSAGE IV

The following paragraphs may or may not be in the most logical order. Each paragraph is numbered in brackets, and question 59 will ask you to choose where Paragraph 3 should most logically be placed.

Christy's Constitution

[1]

From shoes to chandelier, *Scene at the Signing of the Constitution of the United States* blend [46] accuracy with artistic license to achieve the artist's vision of an event that took place in Philadelphia's Independence Hall. [47] The artist, Howard Chandler Christy, was born in 1873, long after George Washington presided—[48] over the momentous event that in 1787 served the final role of ending [49] the Constitutional Convention.

46. **F.** NO CHANGE
G. have blended
H. are blending
J. blends

47. Which choice best indicates where the painting is on display?
A. NO CHANGE
B. in a way that is not immediately apparent to all who see it on display.
C. in one of the most famous paintings in Washington, DC.
D. on a canvas that has been on display for many decades.

48. **F.** NO CHANGE
G. presided,
H. presided
J. presided;

49. **A.** NO CHANGE
B. ended in the conclusion of
C. finished off
D. concluded

GO ON TO THE NEXT PAGE.

1 ■ ■ ■ ■ ■ ■ ■ ■ ■ 1

[2]

[1] The group portrait, as big as a billboard, hangs in the US Capitol building, where it was installed in 1940. [2] Christy's <u>prior preparations in advance of</u> [50] the work included a visit to Philadelphia to study how the light falls through the windows in Independence Hall. [3] Christy arranged to see the inkwells <u>into which</u> [51] the quills would have been dipped as the delegates prepared to make history. [4] He scoured countless drawings of period furniture and fabrics, <u>noting</u> [52] color, texture, design. [5] <u>Hunting</u> [53] down portraits of the signers and scrutinized them. [54]

50. F. NO CHANGE
G. preparation work leading up to
H. advance preparations preceding
J. preparations for

51. A. NO CHANGE
B. which
C. of
D. DELETE the underlined portion.

52. F. NO CHANGE
G. of which were noted
H. because they were noted
J. DELETE the underlined portion.

53. A. NO CHANGE
B. While hunting
C. As he hunted
D. He hunted

54. The writer wants to add the following statement to the paragraph:

> He deliberately timed his trip for September, the month in which the thirty-nine signers had put their names on the revered document.

This statement would most logically be placed after:

F. Sentence 1.
G. Sentence 2.
H. Sentence 3.
J. Sentence 4.

[3]

Such measures may seem standard in the making of historical paintings, but that is not the case. For example, in Emanuel Luetze's *Washington Crossing the Delaware*, the president strikes a noble pose on a <u>boat. Experts</u> [55] now agree could not have been the vessel that carried the revolutionary leader across the river. In <u>another, painting of the signing</u> [56] of the US Constitution, artist Barry Faulkner places the figures in a Roman ruin.

55. A. NO CHANGE
B. boat experts
C. boat; experts
D. boat, experts

56. F. NO CHANGE
G. another painting of the signing,
H. another painting of the signing
J. another painting, of the signing

[4]

Accurate in many respects, Christy's painting also plays with the truth to suggest the grandeur of the moment. For instance, Washington benefits from more

GO ON TO THE NEXT PAGE.

than his share of natural light, which singles him out in Christy's famous painting. [57] Many of the assembled men, luminaries as [58] Benjamin Franklin and James Madison, improbably stare the viewer squarely in the eye. Their expressions suggest they are well aware of their own importance but even more aware of the viewer's, almost as if one more signature will give the document its full meaning.

57. Which choice both supports the claim the writer makes in the preceding sentence about the grandeur of the moment and best emphasizes that Christy deliberately presents Washington as having a special status among the signers?
   A. NO CHANGE
   B. as a hero among heroes.
   C. with visual effects.
   D. in the group.

58. **F.** NO CHANGE
   G. including such luminaries as
   H. who are luminaries
   J. DELETE the underlined portion.

Questions 59 and 60 ask about the preceding passage as a whole.

59. For the sake of logic and cohesion, Paragraph 3 should be placed:
   A. where it is now.
   B. before Paragraph 1.
   C. after Paragraph 1.
   D. after Paragraph 4.

60. Suppose the writer's primary purpose had been to examine how a work of art changed the direction of an artist's career. Would this essay accomplish that purpose?
   F. Yes, because it indicates that Christy led a trend in striving for authenticity in historical paintings.
   G. Yes, because it reveals that a single painting put Christy in the national spotlight.
   H. No, because it focuses on Christy's approach to a particular painting but does not discuss the painting's effect on Christy's career.
   J. No, because it indicates that Christy consistently focused on historical subject matter throughout his career.

PASSAGE V

The Artful Stitch of *Paj Ntaub*

She depicts flowers with layers of petals, intricate spirals and rosettes, teardrops bending within circles, and dizzying mazes of lines— [61] embroidering them in vibrant reds, blues, pinks, yellows, and greens on fabric of delicate silk or cotton. Pang Xiong Sirirathasuk Sikoun is a master of *paj ntaub*, or "flower cloth" embroidery, the most difficult of the century's-oldest [62] Hmong needlework arts.

61. Which choice best maintains the stylistic pattern of descriptions established earlier in the sentence?
   A. NO CHANGE
   B. something with a dizzying effect—
   C. mazes that she creates—
   D. so many lines—

62. **F.** NO CHANGE
   G. centuries-old
   H. centuries'-old
   J. century's-old

GO ON TO THE NEXT PAGE.

Taking Additional Practice Tests

1 ■ ■ ■ ■ ■ ■ ■ ■ ■ 1

Paj ntaub is increasingly made in lighter, softer shades today. [63] She's been creating stitched textiles since she was a young woman, and lived in northern Laos. For the past several decades, she's been designing *paj ntaub* in Philadelphia, Pennsylvania, where she also teaches her craft.

63. The writer is considering deleting the preceding sentence. Should the sentence be kept or deleted?
 A. Kept, because it compares Pang Xiong's embroidery style with that of modern *paj ntaub*.
 B. Kept, because it places the subject of the essay in a modern context.
 C. Deleted, because it detracts from the paragraph's focus on the various styles of ancient Hmong needlework arts.
 D. Deleted, because it adds a detail that is irrelevant to the paragraph's introduction of Pang Xiong's connection to *paj ntaub*.

64. F. NO CHANGE
 G. woman living
 H. woman, who lives
 J. woman, having lived

Flower cloth (commonly as a shirt, dress, coat, or collar) is made to be worn as clothing and, depending on the amount of needlework on the piece, is designed either for everyday wear or for a special occasion. With pattern names such as "elephant's foot" and "snail house" and images of animals framed by geometric designs, *paj ntaub* patterns are versatile. What distinguishes *paj ntaub* from other Hmong needlework arts is the artist's use of tiny, tight stitches, and several complex techniques. One technique is reverse appliqué, in which shapes are cut out from, rather than adding on top of, the embroidered fabric.

65. The best placement for the underlined portion would be:
 A. where it is now.
 B. after the word *made*.
 C. after the word *clothing*.
 D. after the word *needlework*.

66. F. NO CHANGE
 G. have been designed
 H. are designed
 J. design

67. Which choice most clearly builds on the information provided earlier in the sentence about a common theme in *paj ntaub* patterns and images?
 A. NO CHANGE
 B. only a master artist is able to create *paj ntaub* clothing for special occasions.
 C. *paj ntaub* patterns are extraordinarily colorful.
 D. *paj ntaub* celebrates the natural world.

68. F. NO CHANGE
 G. tiny tight, stitches
 H. tiny, tight stitches
 J. tiny tight stitches,

69. A. NO CHANGE
 B. appliqué which
 C. appliqué and
 D. appliqué,

70. F. NO CHANGE
 G. as an addition
 H. to add them
 J. added

GO ON TO THE NEXT PAGE.

Another is elaborate overstitching: thousands of layered stitches are applied to its surface. [71]

71. A. NO CHANGE
B. the surface of the fabric.
C. the surface of it.
D. their surface.

Pang Xiong regrets that most people she knows today wear only regular [72] clothes. When she was growing up in Laos, she explains, she had few items of clothing, but each garment she owned was handcrafted *paj ntaub*.

72. The writer is considering revising the underlined portion to the following:

mass-produced

Should the writer make this revision?

F. Yes, because the revision creates a clearer contrast between the homogeneous styles of clothing that are popular today and the handcrafted *paj ntaub*.
G. Yes, because the revision emphasizes Pang Xiong's desire for her handcrafted *paj ntaub* to be sold on a large scale in stores.
H. No, because the original word reinforces the idea that although *paj ntaub* clothing can be used for everyday wear, it should be saved for special occasions.
J. No, because the original word more specifically describes the type of clothing Pang Xiong disapproves of.

However, she [73] still wears flower cloth every day and would like to inspire others to do so. [74] Pang Xiong teaches *paj ntaub* in art museums—including at the Smithsonian Institution, where some of her textiles are on permanent display—and in community settings around Philadelphia. [75] Pang Xiong is showing a new generation the joys of *paj ntaub* and beautiful handcrafted clothing.

73. A. NO CHANGE
B. For example, she
C. Besides, she
D. She

74. Which choice most clearly and concisely indicates that Pang Xiong wants other people to wear and appreciate handcrafted clothing?
F. NO CHANGE
G. people to also attempt that approach.
H. people she knows.
J. others.

75. Which of the following true statements, if added here, would best build on the ideas presented in this paragraph and connect to the final sentence of the essay?
A. She loves when people, no matter what their ethnicity, wear traditional clothing every day.
B. She often teaches *paj ntaub* to Hmong adults her age who want to learn new techniques.
C. Recently, she worked with nine young Hmong women in a formal apprenticeship.
D. One of her own favorite pieces tells the story of her family.

END OF TEST 1

STOP! DO NOT TURN THE PAGE UNTIL TOLD TO DO SO.

2 △ △ △ △ △ △ △ △ △ 2

MATHEMATICS TEST

60 Minutes—60 Questions

DIRECTIONS: Solve each problem, choose the correct answer, and then fill in the corresponding oval on your answer document.

Do not linger over problems that take too much time. Solve as many as you can; then return to the others in the time you have left for this test.

You are permitted to use a calculator on this test. You may use your calculator for any problems you choose, but some of the problems may best be done without using a calculator.

Note: Unless otherwise stated, all of the following should be assumed.

1. Illustrative figures are NOT necessarily drawn to scale.
2. Geometric figures lie in a plane.
3. The word *line* indicates a straight line.
4. The word *average* indicates arithmetic mean.

DO YOUR FIGURING HERE.

1. A marble will be randomly selected from a bag of solid-colored marbles. The probability of selecting a red marble is $\frac{5}{19}$. The probability of selecting a blue marble is $\frac{4}{19}$. What is the probability of selecting a red marble *or* a blue marble?

A. $\frac{1}{19}$

B. $\frac{9}{19}$

C. $\frac{9}{38}$

D. $\frac{20}{38}$

E. $\frac{20}{361}$

2. The graph below shows the number of students who were present on Thursday from each of the 5 groups in Ms. Meagan's class. What is the probability that a student selected at random from the class on Thursday is in Group 4 ?

F. $\frac{1}{28}$

G. $\frac{1}{14}$

H. $\frac{1}{5}$

J. $\frac{1}{4}$

K. $\frac{1}{2}$

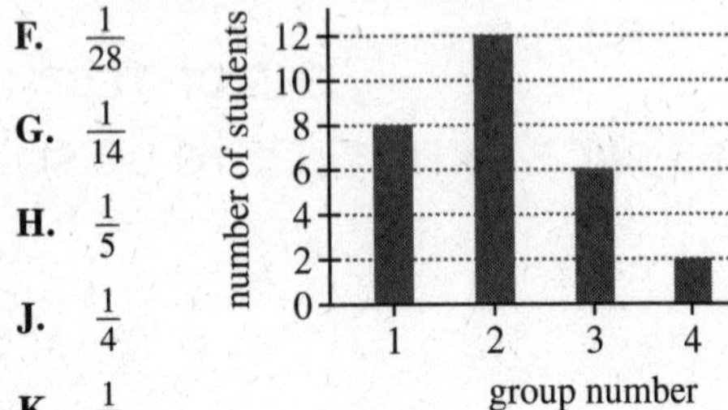

GO ON TO THE NEXT PAGE.

2 △ △ △ △ △ △ △ △ △ 2

DO YOUR FIGURING HERE.

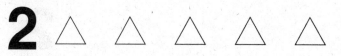

3. Consider the equation $k = \frac{7}{5}j + 54$. For what value of j is the value of k equal to 40 ?

A. -10

B. $-\frac{98}{5}$

C. $\frac{178}{7}$

D. $\frac{200}{7}$

E. 56

4. What is $|3 - x|$ when $x = 8$?

F. -11
G. -5
H. 5
J. 8
K. 11

5. When Tyrese fell asleep one night, the temperature was 24°F. When Tyrese awoke the next morning, the temperature was −16°F. Letting + denote a rise in temperature and − denote a drop in temperature, what was the change in temperature from the time Tyrese fell asleep until the time he awoke?

A. −40°F
B. −8°F
C. +4°F
D. +8°F
E. +40°F

6. Ming purchased a car that had a purchase price of $5,400, which included all other costs and tax. She paid $1,000 as a down payment and got a loan for the rest of the purchase price. Ming paid off the loan by making 28 payments of $200 each. The total of all her payments, including the down payment, was how much more than the car's purchase price?

F. $ 200
G. $1,200
H. $4,400
J. $5,600
K. $6,600

7. Shown below is a regular hexagon inscribed in a circle whose radius is 4 inches. What is the perimeter, in inches, of the hexagon?

A. 8π
B. $12\sqrt{3}$
C. 18
D. 20
E. 24

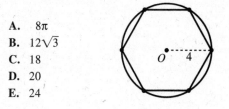

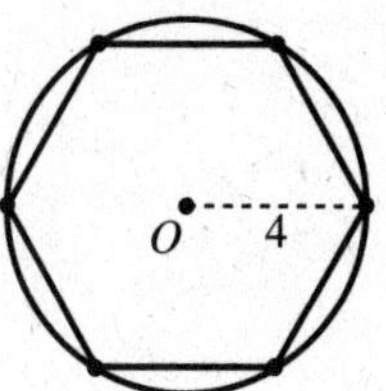

GO ON TO THE NEXT PAGE.

Taking Additional Practice Tests

2 △ △ △ △ △ △ △ △ △ 2

DO YOUR FIGURING HERE.

8. The floor plan for an L-shaped storage building is shown below with distances marked in feet. What is the floor area of the building, in square feet?

(Note: Walls in this building meet only at right angles.)

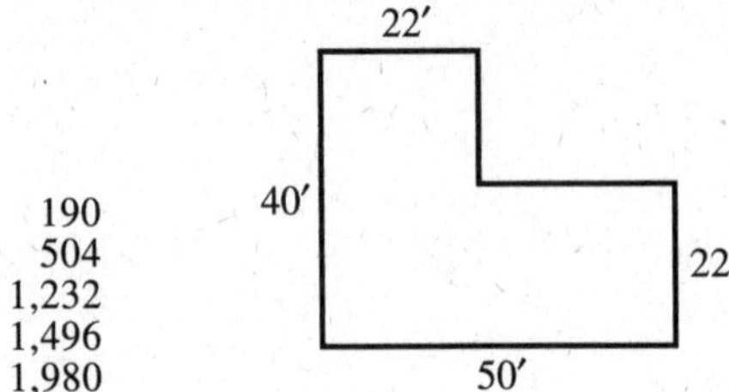

F. 190
G. 504
H. 1,232
J. 1,496
K. 1,980

9. Quadrilateral $ABCD$ with vertices $A(-2,0)$, $B(0,4)$, $C(5,5)$, and $D(8,2)$ will be graphed in the standard (x,y) coordinate plane below.

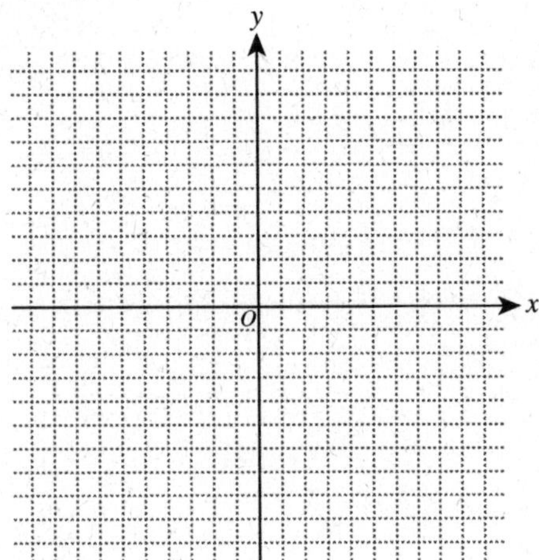

Which of the following is a type of quadrilateral determined by these vertices?

A. Kite
B. Parallelogram
C. Trapezoid
D. Rectangle
E. Square

10. Given that $f(x) = 3x + 7$ and $g(x) = \frac{x^2}{2}$, what is the value of $f(g(4))$?

F. 8
G. 19
H. 31
J. 152
K. 180.5

GO ON TO THE NEXT PAGE.

2 △ △ △ △ △ △ △ △ △ 2

DO YOUR FIGURING HERE.

11. At her hot dog stand, Julie sells hot dogs for \$2 each. Purchasing hot dogs and other supplies costs \$200 per month. The solution of which of the following inequalities models the numbers of hot dogs, h, Julie can sell per month and make a profit?

A. $h - 200 > 0$
B. $h - 200 < 0$
C. $h + 200 > 0$
D. $2h - 200 < 0$
E. $2h - 200 > 0$

12. In the standard (x,y) coordinate plane, what is the slope of the line $3x + 8y = 5$?

F. -3

G. $-\frac{3}{8}$

H. $\frac{3}{5}$

J. 3

K. 5

13. Which of the following (x,y) pairs is the solution for the system of equations $x + 2y = 2$ and $-2x + y = 16$?

A. $(-6,4)$
B. $(-1,1.5)$
C. $(\ 1,0.5)$
D. $(\ 0,1)$
E. $(\ 2,0)$

14. On a map, $\frac{1}{4}$ inch represents 16 actual miles. Two towns that are $2\frac{3}{4}$ inches apart on this map are how many actual miles apart?

F. 11
G. 16
H. 44
J. 64
K. 176

15. Which of the following matrices is equal to $4\begin{bmatrix} -1 & 2 \\ 0 & -4 \end{bmatrix}$?

A. $\begin{bmatrix} -4 & -8 \end{bmatrix}$

B. $\begin{bmatrix} 4 \\ -16 \end{bmatrix}$

C. $\begin{bmatrix} 3 & 6 \\ 4 & 0 \end{bmatrix}$

D. $\begin{bmatrix} -\frac{1}{4} & \frac{1}{2} \\ 0 & -1 \end{bmatrix}$

E. $\begin{bmatrix} -4 & 8 \\ 0 & -16 \end{bmatrix}$

GO ON TO THE NEXT PAGE.

2          2

DO YOUR FIGURING HERE.

16. What is the value of tan A in right triangle $\triangle ABC$ below?

A
17
8
C
15
B

F. $\frac{8}{17}$

G. $\frac{8}{15}$

H. $\frac{15}{17}$

J. $\frac{15}{8}$

K. $\frac{17}{8}$

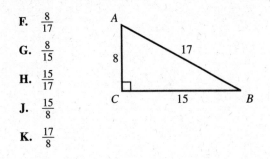

17. Tina runs at a rate of 8 miles per hour. At that rate, how many miles will she run in 12 minutes?

A. $\frac{5}{8}$

B. $\frac{2}{3}$

C. $1\frac{1}{2}$

D. $1\frac{3}{5}$

E. 2

18. A function $f(x)$ is defined as $f(x) = -6x^2$. What is $f(-3)$?

F. −324
G. −54
H. 54
J. 108
K. 324

19. In the figure below, A is on $\overleftrightarrow{BE}$ and C is on $\overleftrightarrow{BD}$. What is the measure of $\angle ABC$?

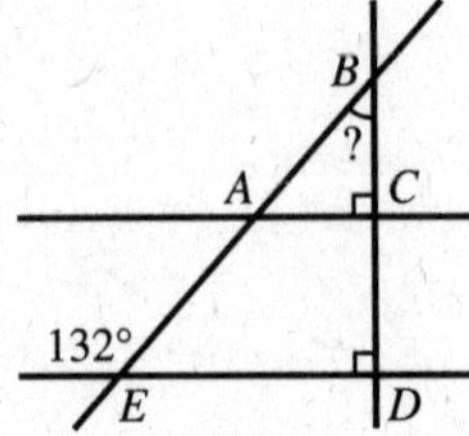

A. 24°
B. 42°
C. 45°
D. 48°
E. 66°

GO ON TO THE NEXT PAGE.

2 △ △ △ △ △ △ △ △ △ 2

20. Marcos programs his calculator to evaluate a linear function, but he doesn't say what the function is. When 5 is entered, the calculator displays the value 2. When 15 is entered, the calculator displays the value 6. Which of the following expressions explains what the calculator will display when any number, n, is entered?

F. $\frac{2}{5}n$

G. $\frac{5}{2}n$

H. $n - 3$

J. $n - 9$

K. $\frac{5}{2}n - \frac{21}{2}$

DO YOUR FIGURING HERE.

21. On Friday, the temperature at 8:00 a.m. was 49°F and rose at a constant rate of $\frac{1}{2}$°F per hour until noon. A cold front passed through at noon, and the temperature then fell at a constant rate of 1°F per hour. The temperature first fell below 49°F between:

A. noon and 1 p.m.
B. 1 p.m. and 2 p.m.
C. 2 p.m. and 3 p.m.
D. 3 p.m. and 4 p.m.
E. 4 p.m. and 5 p.m.

22. Letter grades in Hugo's math class are based on the percent of the total possible points on 4 unit exams (each worth 100 points) and the final exam (worth 200 points) and are assigned according to the chart below.

Range	Course grade
At least 90%	A
80%–89%	B
70%–79%	C
60%–69%	D
Less than 60%	F

The number of points Hugo scored on the unit exams this term were 82, 88, 91, and 83. When course grades were posted, Hugo's course grade was listed as a B. Which of the following could NOT have been the number of points he scored on the final exam?

F. 136
G. 156
H. 166
J. 176
K. 196

Taking Additional Practice Tests

GO ON TO THE NEXT PAGE.

2 △ △ △ △ △ △ △ △ △ 2

DO YOUR FIGURING HERE.

Use the following information to answer questions 23–25.

Halle is bowling a series of 3 games. She has bowled 2 of 3 games with scores of 148 and 176. The figure below is a top view of the bowling lane. The dimensions for the bowling lane are given in the figure. The *pin deck* is the rectangular area within the bowling lane where the 10 bowling pins are set up.

(Note: The figure is not drawn to scale.)

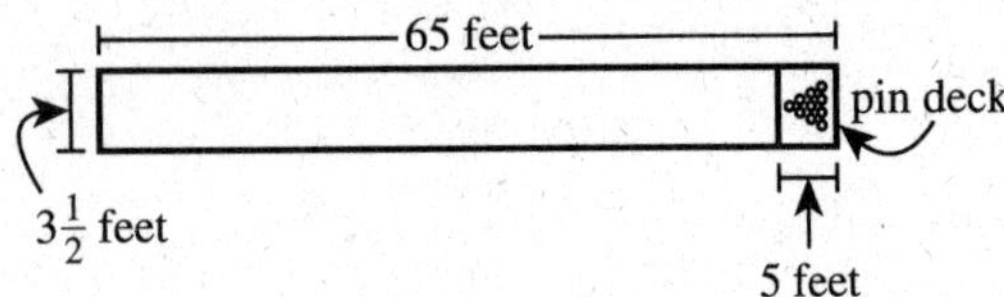

23. The diameter of each pin at its base is 2.25 in. When all of the pins are set up, which of the following values is closest to the area, in square inches, that is covered by the bases of the pins?

A. 40
B. 71
C. 111
D. 125
E. 159

24. What is the ratio of the total area of the bowling lane to the area of the pin deck?

F. 12:1
G. 13:1
H. 13:12
J. 127:17
K. 137:17

25. What score will Halle need to earn in her 3rd game to have an average score of 172 for the 3 games?

A. 165
B. 172
C. 182
D. 192
E. 200

---

26. The area of a rectangle is 300 square meters, and its length is 3 times its width. How many meters wide is the rectangle?

F. 10
G. 30
H. 50
J. 100
K. 150

GO ON TO THE NEXT PAGE.

2 △ △ △ △ △ △ △ △ △ 2

27. A parallelogram has a perimeter of 96 inches, and 1 of its sides measures 16 inches. If it can be determined, what are the lengths, in inches, of the other 3 sides?

A. 16, 16, 48
B. 16, 24, 24
C. 16, 32, 32
D. 16, 40, 40
E. Cannot be determined from the given information

DO YOUR FIGURING HERE.

28. Elmhurst Street is a two-way street. In each direction, it has one 12-foot-wide lane for car traffic, one 6-foot-wide bike lane, and one 8-foot-wide parking lane. How many feet wide is Elmhurst Street?

F. 26
G. 38
H. 52
J. 60
K. 80

29. At Central High School, 4 out of every 10 students ride the bus to and from school, and 3 out of every 8 who ride the bus are freshmen. If there are 2,500 students at Central, how many of the students are freshmen who ride the bus?

A. 375
B. 412
C. 428
D. 561
E. 705

30. If $90° < \theta < 180°$ and $\sin \theta = \frac{20}{29}$, then $\cos \theta = ?$

F. $\frac{29}{20}$
G. $\frac{20}{21}$
H. $-\frac{21}{29}$
J. $-\frac{29}{21}$
K. $-\frac{29}{20}$

31. Given $f(x) = \frac{2}{x+1}$, what is(are) the real value(s) of t for which $f(t) = t$?

A. -1 only
B. 2 only
C. -2 and 1 only
D. -1 and 2 only
E. 1 and 2 only

GO ON TO THE NEXT PAGE.

2 △ △ △ △ △ △ △ △ △ 2

DO YOUR FIGURING HERE.

Use the following information to answer questions 32–35.

In the figure below, a highway rest area (at D) and radar stations (at A and B) lie on a level east-west line; A is 9,000 feet due west of D. An airplane (at C) is shown directly above the rest area, flying due west at a constant speed of 300 feet per second and at a constant altitude of 12,000 feet. The airplane is located at a straight-line distance of 15,000 feet from the radar station at A and 13,000 feet from the radar station at B.

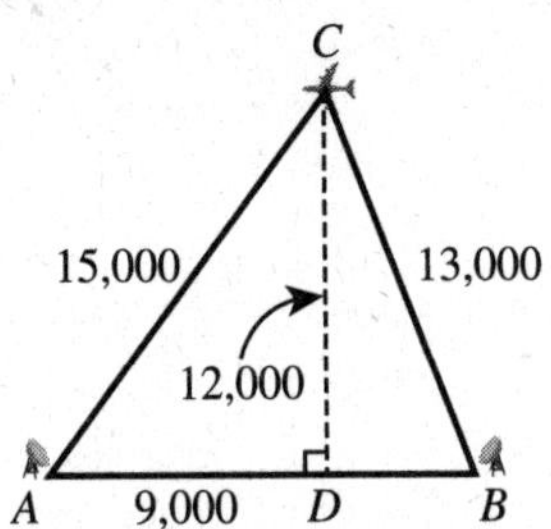

32. Which of the following values is closest to the distance, in feet, between the 2 radar stations?

F. 5,000
G. 10,000
H. 10,500
J. 14,000
K. 15,000

33. Let A, C, and D lie in the standard (x,y) coordinate plane such that A is at (0,0) and D is at (9,000, 0). Which of the following equations represents the line along which the airplane is flying?

A. $x = 9{,}000$
B. $x = 15{,}000$
C. $y = 12{,}000$
D. $y = 13{,}000$
E. $y = 15{,}000$

34. Which of the following values is closest to the number of seconds it will take for the airplane to fly from C to the point directly above the radar station at A ?

F. 17
G. 30
H. 40
J. 43
K. 50

GO ON TO THE NEXT PAGE.

2 △ △ △ △ △ △ △ △ △ 2

35. When considering the changing triangle formed by A, B, and the moving airplane (C), which of the angles below increases in measure as the airplane flies due west beyond the point directly above A ?

I. $\angle A$
II. $\angle B$
III. $\angle C$

A. I only
B. II only
C. I and II only
D. I and III only
E. II and III only

---

36. Troy made a rectangular poster that is 4 feet long and 2 feet wide. The poster is too large to fit in the available display space, so Troy is going to make a new poster that will have an area that is 50% of the area of the original poster. The length of Troy's new poster will be $\frac{3}{4}$ the length of the original poster. How many feet wide will the new poster be?

F. $\frac{3}{4}$
G. $1\frac{1}{3}$
H. $1\frac{1}{2}$
J. 3
K. 6

37. What is the solution set of the equation $x + 6 = 2(x + 3) - x$?

A. The empty set (no solution)
B. {0}
C. {2}
D. {3}
E. The set of all real numbers

38. Steve plans to use 28 feet of fencing to enclose a region of his yard for a pen for his pet rabbit. What is the area, in square feet, of the largest rectangular region Steve can enclose?

F. 40
G. 45
H. 48
J. 49
K. 196

DO YOUR FIGURING HERE.

Taking Additional Practice Tests

GO ON TO THE NEXT PAGE.

2 △ △ △ △ △ △ △ △ △ 2

DO YOUR FIGURING HERE.

39. There are exactly 5 people in a bookstore at 12:00 p.m. Each person earns an annual income that is between \$30,000 and \$35,000. No one enters or leaves the bookstore until 12:15 p.m., when a professional athlete with an annual income of more than \$1,000,000 enters the bookstore and joins the other 5 people. The mean, median, range, and standard deviation of the annual incomes of the 5 people in the bookstore at 12:00 p.m. are calculated and compared to the same 4 statistics of the annual incomes of the 6 people in the bookstore at 12:15 p.m. If it can be determined, which of the 4 statistics changed the least?

A. Range
B. Mean
C. Median
D. Standard deviation
E. Cannot be determined from the given information

40. Ana and Amy started a landscaping job together. When Ana stopped, she had completed $\frac{2}{5}$ of the job. When Amy stopped, she had completed $\frac{1}{3}$ of the job. Then Ruben completed the rest of the job in 2 hours. Assume that Ana, Amy, and Ruben all worked at the same rate. Which of the following values is closest to the number of hours it would have taken 1 of them to complete the entire job alone?

F. 0.37
G. 1.27
H. 2.73
J. 5.00
K. 7.50

41. If a and b are positive real numbers, which of the following is equivalent to $\frac{(2a^{-1}\sqrt{b})^4}{ab^{-3}}$?

A. $8a^2b^4$

B. $\frac{8b^6}{a^4}$

C. $\frac{16b^5}{a^5}$

D. $\frac{16b^4}{a^5}$

E. $\frac{16b}{a^3}$

GO ON TO THE NEXT PAGE.

2 △ △ △ △ △ △ △ △ △ 2

DO YOUR FIGURING HERE.

42. To become a contestant on a quiz show, a person must correctly order 4 rock stars by age, from youngest to oldest. The contestant knows which one is the oldest rock star, but randomly guesses at the order of the other 3 rock stars. What is the probability the contestant will get all 4 in the correct order?

F. $\frac{1}{24}$

G. $\frac{1}{6}$

H. $\frac{1}{4}$

J. $\frac{1}{3}$

K. $\frac{1}{2}$

43. Which of the following expressions is equivalent to $\dfrac{\frac{x}{3}+\frac{1}{2}}{\frac{2}{3}-\frac{1}{4}}$?

A. $\frac{-x-1}{5}$

B. $\frac{2x+6}{5}$

C. $\frac{4x+3}{5}$

D. $\frac{4x+6}{5}$

E. $4x+6$

44. An automobile license plate number issued by a certain state has 6 character positions. Each of the first 3 positions contains a single digit from 0 through 9. Each of the last 3 positions contains 1 of the 26 letters of the alphabet. Digits and letters of the alphabet can be repeated on a license plate. How many different such license plate numbers can be made?

F. 36
G. 46,656
H. 1,000,000
J. 12,812,904
K. 17,576,000

GO ON TO THE NEXT PAGE.

2   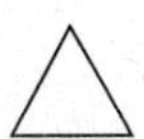       2

DO YOUR FIGURING HERE.

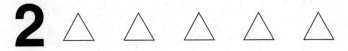

45. The function $y = f(x)$ is graphed in the standard (x,y) coordinate plane below.

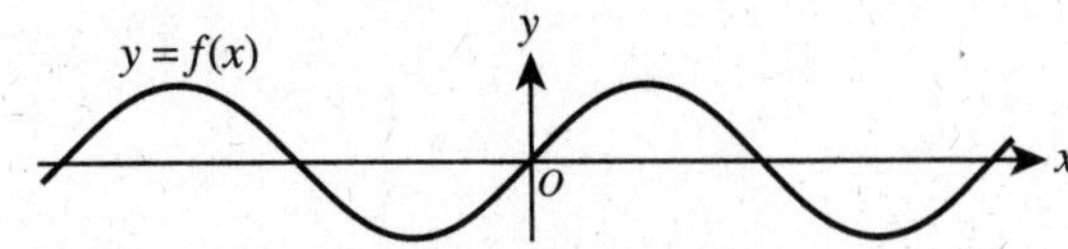

The points on the graph of the function $y = 3 + f(x - 1)$ can be obtained from the points on $y = f(x)$ by a shift of:

A. 1 unit to the right and 3 units up.
B. 1 unit to the right and 3 units down.
C. 3 units to the right and 1 unit up.
D. 3 units to the right and 1 unit down.
E. 3 units to the left and 1 unit down.

46. When $\log_5 x = -2$, what is x ?

F. -32

G. -25

H. -10

J. $\frac{1}{10}$

K. $\frac{1}{25}$

47. Which of the following lists those integer values of D for which the fraction $\frac{2}{D}$ lies between $\frac{1}{5}$ and $\frac{1}{3}$?

A. 4 only
B. 3, 4, and 5
C. 8 only
D. 7, 8, and 9
E. 16 only

48. For all real numbers a, b, and c such that $a > b$ and $c < 0$, which of the following inequalities *must* be true?

F. $\frac{a}{c} < \frac{b}{c}$

G. $\frac{a}{c} > \frac{b}{c}$

H. $ac > bc$

J. $a + c < b + c$

K. $a < b - c$

GO ON TO THE NEXT PAGE.

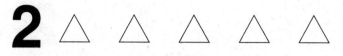

2 △ △ △ △ △ △ △ △ △ 2

DO YOUR FIGURING HERE.

49. The triangle shown below has side lengths 37, 38, and 39 inches. Which of the following expressions gives the measure of the largest angle of the triangle?

(Note: For every triangle with sides of length a, b, and c that are opposite $\angle A$, $\angle B$, and $\angle C$, respectively, $c^2 = a^2 + b^2 - 2ab\cos C$.)

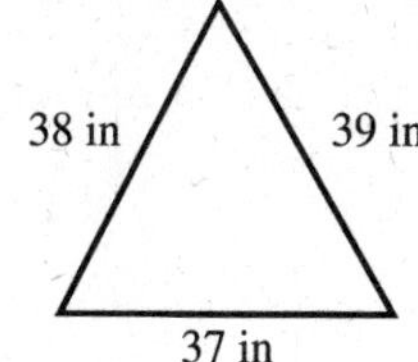

A. $\cos^{-1}\left(-\frac{37^2 - 38^2 - 39^2}{2(38)(39)}\right)$

B. $\cos^{-1}\left(-\frac{39^2 - 37^2 - 38^2}{2(37)(38)}\right)$

C. $\cos^{-1}\left(37^2 - 38^2 - 39^2 + 2(38)(39)\right)$

D. $\cos^{-1}\left(38^2 - 37^2 - 39^2 + 2(37)(39)\right)$

E. $\cos^{-1}\left(39^2 - 37^2 - 38^2 + 2(37)(38)\right)$

50. Pete has an average score of exactly x points on 4 equally weighted tests. How many points higher than x must Pete score on the 5th equally weighted test to raise his average score after the 5th test to $x + 2$ points?

F. 2
G. 4
H. 5
J. 8
K. 10

51. The intersection of lines l and m forms the 4 angles $\angle A$, $\angle B$, $\angle C$, and $\angle D$. The measure of $\angle B$ is $3\frac{1}{2}$ times the measure of $\angle A$. Which of the following values is closest to the measure of $\angle A$?

A. 20°
B. 26°
C. 35°
D. 40°
E. 51°

52. A sequence is defined for all positive integers by $s_n = 2s_{(n-1)} + n + 1$ and $s_1 = 3$. What is s_4 ?

F. 9
G. 18
H. 22
J. 49
K. 111

Taking Additional Practice Tests

GO ON TO THE NEXT PAGE.

2 △ △ △ △ △ △ △ △ △ 2

DO YOUR FIGURING HERE.

53. If a is an integer less than -1, which of the following orders the expressions $|a|$, $-a^2$, and $-\frac{1}{a}$ from least value to greatest value?

A. $-\frac{1}{a} < -a^2 < |a|$

B. $-\frac{1}{a} < |a| < -a^2$

C. $|a| < -\frac{1}{a} < -a^2$

D. $-a^2 < |a| < -\frac{1}{a}$

E. $-a^2 < -\frac{1}{a} < |a|$

54. At the school carnival, Ann is playing a game involving a stack of 10 index cards. Each card has a single number written on it: 1 card has a 1, 2 cards have a 2, 3 cards have a 3, and 4 cards have a 4. Ann will choose 1 card at random, and she will be awarded the number of points equal to the number written on the card. Let the random variable X represent the number of points Ann receives on any 1 draw. What is the expected value of X ?

F. 0.4
G. 1
H. 2.5
J. 3
K. 4

55. Which of the following is equivalent to the sum of any 3 consecutive odd integers, x, y, and z, such that $x < y < z$?

A. $3z$

B. $3y$

C. $3x$

D. $3x + 2$

E. $\frac{x+y+z}{3}$

56. The mean of the set of 5 numbers $\{42, 3, 11, 27, x\}$ is 24, and the median of the set of 4 numbers $\{53, 8, 29, y\}$ is 38. If it can be determined, which of the following values is equal to $x - y$?

F. -38
G. -10
H. 10
J. 38
K. Cannot be determined from the given information

GO ON TO THE NEXT PAGE.

2 △ △ △ △ △ △ △ △ △ 2

57. Consider all rectangles such that the rectangle's length is greater than the rectangle's width and the length and width are whole numbers of inches. Which of the following perimeters, in inches, is NOT possible for such a rectangle with an area of 144 square inches?

A. 48
B. 60
C. 80
D. 102
E. 148

DO YOUR FIGURING HERE.

58. The equation $(x-7)^2+(y-8)^2=10$ is that of a circle that lies in the standard (x,y) coordinate plane. One endpoint of a diameter of the circle has y-coordinate 11. What is the y-coordinate of the other endpoint of that diameter?

F. 1
G. 3
H. 4
J. 5
K. 8

59. The plans for a diving pool call for a rectangular prism that has a length of 30 meters, a width of 25 meters, and a depth of 5 meters. If the plans are changed to increase both the length and the width of the pool by 10%, what will be the increase, to the nearest 1%, in the volume of the pool?

A. 10%
B. 17%
C. 20%
D. 21%
E. 33%

60. One solution of the equation $4x^3-2x^2+x+7=0$ is $x=-1$. Which of the following describes the other 2 solutions?

F. Both are negative real numbers.
G. One is a negative real number, and the other is a positive real number.
H. Both are positive real numbers.
J. One is a positive real number, and the other is a complex number that is not real.
K. Both are complex numbers that are not real.

END OF TEST 2

STOP! DO NOT TURN THE PAGE UNTIL TOLD TO DO SO.

DO NOT RETURN TO THE PREVIOUS TEST.

3 3

READING TEST

35 Minutes—40 Questions

DIRECTIONS: There are several passages in this test. Each passage is accompanied by several questions. After reading a passage, choose the best answer to each question and fill in the corresponding oval on your answer document. You may refer to the passages as often as necessary.

Passage I

LITERARY NARRATIVE: This passage is adapted from the short story "Pride" by Alice Munro (©2011 by Alice Munro).

Oneida didn't go to school with the rest of us. She went to a girls' school, a private school. Even in the summers she was not around much. I believe the family had a place on Lake Simcoe.

Oneida was an unusual name. Her father, I believe, called her Ida. Ida's father ran the bank. Even in those days bankers came and went, I suppose to keep them from ever getting too cozy with the customers. But the Jantzens had been having their way in town for too long for any regulations to matter, or that was how it seemed. Horace Jantzen had certainly the look of a man born to be in power. A heavy white beard and a ponderous expression.

In the hard times of the Thirties people were still coming up with ideas. You can be sure, men were nursing a notion bound to make them a million dollars. A million dollars in those days was a million dollars.

It wasn't any railway bum, however, who got into the bank to talk to Horace Jantzen. Who knows if it was a single person or a cohort. Maybe a stranger or some friends of friends. Well dressed and plausible looking, you may be sure. Horace set store by appearances. He wasn't a fool, though maybe not as quick as he should have been to smell a rat.

The idea was the resurrection of the steam-driven car, such as had been around at the turn of the century. Horace Jantzen may have had one himself and had a fondness for them. This new model would be an improved version, of course, and have the advantages of being economical and not making a racket.

I'm not acquainted with the details, having been in high school at the time. But I can imagine the leak of talk and the scoffing and enthusiasm and the news getting through of some entrepreneurs from Toronto or Windsor or Kitchener getting ready to set up locally. Some hotshots, people would say. And others would ask if they had the backing.

They did indeed, because the bank had put up the loan. It was Jantzen's decision and there was some confusion that he had put in his own money. He may have done so, but he had also dipped improperly into bank funds, thinking no doubt that he could pay it back with nobody the wiser. Maybe the laws were not so tight then. There were actually men hired and the old Livery Stable was cleared out to be their place of operations. And here my memory grows shaky, because I graduated from high school, and I had to think about earning a living if that was possible. I settled for bookkeeping, and that meant going out of town to apprentice to an outfit in Goderich. By the time I got back home the steam-car operation was spoken of with scorn by the people who had been against it and not at all by those who had promoted it. The visitors to town who promoted it had disappeared.

The bank had lost a lot of money. There was talk not of cheating but of mismanagement. Somebody had to be punished. Any ordinary manager would have been out on his ear, but given that it was Horace Jantzen this was avoided. What happened to him was almost worse. He was switched to the job of bank manager in the little village of Hawksburg, about six miles up the highway. Prior to this there had been no manager there at all, because they didn't need one. There had just been a head cashier and an underling cashier, both women.

Surely he could have refused, but pride, as it was thought, chose otherwise. Pride chose that he be driven every morning those six miles to sit behind a partial wall of cheap varnished boards, no proper office at all. There he sat and did nothing until it was time for him to be driven home. The person who drove him was his daughter. Sometime in these years of driving she made the transition from Ida to Oneida. At last she had something to do.

If I picture Oneida and her father on these journeys to and from Hawksburg, I see him riding in the back seat, and her in front, like a chauffeur. It may have been that he was too bulky to ride up beside her. I don't see Oneida looking downtrodden or unhappy at the arrangement, nor her father looking actually unhappy. Dignity was what he had, and plenty of it. She had something different. When she went into a store or even walked on the street there seemed to be a little space cleared around her, made ready for whatever she might want or greetings she might spread. She seemed then a bit flustered but gracious, ready to laugh a little at herself or the situation. Of course she had her good bones and

GO ON TO THE NEXT PAGE.

3 3

bright looks, all that fair dazzle of skin and hair. So it might seem strange that I could feel sorry for her, the way she was all on the surface of things, trusting.

1. Based on the passage, it could be assumed that the narrator gained the knowledge to tell this story about Jantzen by:
   A. piecing the story together out of hearsay and his own recollections.
   B. learning the details directly from Jantzen.
   C. fabricating the entire story because it didn't really happen.
   D. being a participant in the events as they unfolded.

2. In the context of the passage, which of the following statements most strongly foreshadows Jantzen's downfall?
   F. "Ida's father ran the bank" (line 6).
   G. "In the hard times of the Thirties people were still coming up with ideas" (lines 14–15).
   H. "He wasn't a fool, though maybe not as quick as he should have been to smell a rat" (lines 23–24).
   J. "Horace Jantzen may have had one himself and had a fondness for them" (lines 27–28).

3. The passage suggests that in considering who convinced Jantzen to invest in manufacturing steam-driven cars, most people in town:
   A. could list everyone who was involved.
   B. believed some were friends of friends while others were complete strangers.
   C. figured it had been an old cohort of Jantzen's who had fallen on hard times.
   D. indulged in speculation, but didn't know for sure who it had been.

4. Which of the following is true of people's behavior when the narrator returned to town after his apprenticeship?
   I. Visitors who promoted steam cars had left town.
   II. People in town blamed the loss of money on Jantzen having cheated.
   III. People in town who had favored the plan to bring back steam cars stopped speaking of the cars.
   IV. People who had been against the plan to bring back steam cars spoke of the cars scornfully.

   F. I and II only
   G. III and IV only
   H. I, III, and IV only
   J. II, III, and IV only

5. Which of the following best paraphrases the narrator's comments in lines 14–16?
   A. People in their thirties had the best ideas for making money.
   B. Because times were hard, people were trying to find new money-making schemes.
   C. Men were making as much as a million dollars a year in the 1930s.
   D. Everyone was sure that they should take their money-making plans to Jantzen.

6. As it is used in line 16, the word *nursing* most nearly means:
   F. rearing.
   G. educating.
   H. healing.
   J. fostering.

7. The narrator speculates that whoever convinced Jantzen to invest in a steam-driven car must have been:
   A. well dressed; Jantzen would have been impressed by someone who looked affluent.
   B. wealthy; otherwise, Jantzen wouldn't have risked loaning the money.
   C. elderly; Jantzen would have trusted someone who could remember the original steam-driven cars.
   D. intelligent; it would have taken someone clever to convince Jantzen to invest.

8. Based on the passage, it's most logical to conclude that the original steam-driven cars were:
   F. expensive and noisy.
   G. reliable and fast.
   H. unattractive and impractical.
   J. luxurious and durable.

9. According to the passage, the majority of the investment money to manufacture a steam-driven car came from:
   A. some of Jantzen's wealthy friends.
   B. Jantzen's entire life savings.
   C. the bank Jantzen was managing.
   D. entrepreneurs from Toronto, Windsor, or Kitchener.

10. The narrator states that people assumed it was pride that drove Jantzen to:
   F. invest in steam-driven cars.
   G. agree to manage the Hawksburg bank.
   H. look miserable while Oneida drove him to work.
   J. create a makeshift office out of varnished boards.

GO ON TO THE NEXT PAGE.

3 3

Passage II

SOCIAL SCIENCE: Passage A is adapted from *Plastic: A Toxic Love Story* by Susan Freinkel (©2011 by Susan Freinkel). Passage B is adapted from *American Plastic: A Cultural History* by Jeffrey L. Meikle (©1995 by Jeffrey L. Meikle).

Passage A by Susan Freinkel

Designers were enthralled by the universe of possibility from plastics' earliest days. They loved the design freedom that synthetics offered and the spirit of modernity the materials embodied. To furniture designer Paul T. Frankl, a material like Bakelite, the world's first synthetic plastic, spoke "in the vernacular of the twentieth century . . . the language of invention, of synthesis," and he urged his fellow designers to use their full imaginative powers to explore the new materials' frank artificiality. As interpreted by Frankl and other designers working with Bakelite in the '30s and '40s, that was the language of streamlining, a lingo of curves and dashes and teardrop shapes that created a feeling of speed and motion in everyday objects. Streamline a fountain pen and even that stolid item declared: we're hurtling toward the future here!

There was another reason designers embraced plastics. From the mid-twentieth century on, modern design has been guided by an egalitarian gospel, a belief that good design needn't cost a lot of money, that even the most mundane items could be things of beauty. "Get the most of the best to the most for the least" was the way Ray and Charles Eames put it in their famous tongue-twisting credo. Plastics were the ideal medium for that mission: malleable, relatively inexpensive, and made for mass manufacture.

Yet, as in any new relationship, there were risks. It was all too easy to exploit plastics' powers of mimicry to produce the kinds of imitations—pseudo-wood cabinets and faux-leather recliners—that contributed to the growing reputation of plastic as an inferior material. Plastics' adaptability and glibness undermined their capacity to achieve "dignity" as legitimate materials worthy of being taken seriously, one critic wrote.

This impression was exacerbated by people's unfortunate experiences with plastics in the immediate postwar years. There were plastic plates that melted in hot water, plastic toys that cracked on Christmas morning, plastic raincoats that grew clammy and fell apart in the rain. Polymer technology improved during the 1950s as manufacturers figured out how to make better plastics and, even more important, how to match the right polymer with the right application. But the damage to plastic's reputation had been done.

Passage B by Jeffrey L. Meikle

Worrying about the image of plastic made sense in 1945 when unfamiliar new materials confronted wary consumers. By the mid-1950s, however, no one was ignorant of plastic because it surrounded everyone. Sidney Gross, who joined *Modern Plastics* in 1952 and became editor in 1968, recalled that he had "agitated a lot" over the years to get SPI, the trade association for the plastics industry, to quit trying to convince people "that plastic is not bad." It was a waste of money because plastic's image—good or bad—did not really matter. The key to plastic's success, as he saw it, was always "selling the manufacturer." Once plastic products filled the stores, people had no choice but to consume what they were offered. Most of the time, Gross maintained, after the industry had solved postwar quality problems, plastic objects did work better. Things made of plastic were better designed and lasted longer. People intuitively recognized that fact even if they retained an intellectual notion that plastic was bad or shoddy. In short, nothing succeeded like success.

Often plastic did offer a significant improvement on whatever it replaced. A sleepy householder had to watch only once in disbelief as a polyethylene juice pitcher bounced off the kitchen floor to begin accepting plastic in a practical way no matter how strong the conceptual disdain for it. Even plastic toys, despite the brittle polystyrene items that broke on Christmas morning, proved superior in many ways. A toy soldier of molded polyethylene could not scratch the furniture as readily as an old-fashioned lead soldier. Most people who expressed negative attitudes about plastic used it anyway without thinking about it, either because a particular use had proven itself or because an inexpensive trouble-free alternative no longer existed. As *House Beautiful* observed in 1955, "The news is not that plastics exist, but [that] they have already been so assimilated into our lives." The average person was "conditioned to plastics." They had penetrated so far into the material fabric of everyday life that their presence could not be denied no matter how many people considered them second-rate substitutes or a sad commentary on modern times.

Questions 11–14 ask about Passage A.

11. In the context of Passage A, the author uses the description of a fountain pen (lines 15–16) most nearly to:

A. lament the way that unique objects began to look identical after the advent of streamlining.
B. critique designers for creating items that were beautiful rather than functional.
C. illustrate how even everyday items could be designed to appear modern.
D. exemplify the kind of item that remained largely unaffected by new design trends.

GO ON TO THE NEXT PAGE.

3 3

12. The main idea of the second paragraph (lines 17–26) is that plastics:
   F. appealed to a prevailing philosophy of providing great design to many people for a low cost.
   G. quickly became popular enough to inspire a number of famous credos and advertising slogans.
   H. created a challenge for designers, who were not used to working with such a malleable material.
   J. inspired an artistic movement whose members prized mundane objects rather than beautiful ones.

13. According to Passage A, one reason for designers' early interest in plastics was that:
   A. the materials' ability to be freely shaped encouraged inventiveness.
   B. consumers' demand for attractively designed items was high.
   C. a person creating everyday items out of plastics was seen as a bold risk taker.
   D. older materials like Bakelite were difficult to work with.

14. It can reasonably be inferred from Passage A that before the 1950s, plastics manufacturers had not yet figured out:
   F. how to mold plastics to create the impression of streamlining.
   G. which plastics were best suited to specific purposes.
   H. whether consumers would buy everyday items made of plastics.
   J. whether designers would embrace working with plastics.

Questions 15–17 ask about Passage B.

15. In the context of Passage B, the statement "They had penetrated so far into the material fabric of everyday life" (lines 82–83) most nearly refers to the way that plastics came to be:
   A. considered a symbol of increased consumerism.
   B. preferred by most consumers to more conventional materials.
   C. perceived as a threat to traditional ways of life.
   D. pervasive to the extent that they were integral to people's routines.

16. In Passage B, the primary purpose of the details about the polyethylene juice pitcher (lines 66–70) is to:
   F. describe an advertisement created by the plastic industry in an attempt to improve plastic's image.
   G. show how people might be persuaded by plastic's durability despite disliking plastic in general.
   H. demonstrate how dramatically plastic's quality improved between 1945 and the mid-1950s.
   J. provide an example of the kinds of mishaps that biased people against plastic.

17. Passage B most nearly suggests that compared to toys made of traditional materials, toys made of plastic were often:
   A. more flexible and more detailed.
   B. less costly and sturdier.
   C. less durable but also less destructive.
   D. more popular with kids but less popular with parents.

Questions 18–20 ask about both passages.

18. To support their claims about the public's perception of plastics during the time periods discussed in the passages, both passage authors:
   F. quote people who used or wrote about plastics.
   G. analyze publications that promoted plastics.
   H. define key concepts used to market plastics.
   J. personify artwork or objects made of plastics.

19. Both passages suggest that one bias the public held in the postwar years was that items made of plastic were:
   A. unattractive in design.
   B. unnervingly artificial.
   C. expensive novelties.
   D. inferior substitutes.

20. Which of the following statements best compares the ways the authors of Passage A and Passage B use details about plastic toys on Christmas morning?
   F. Passage A uses the toys as an example of good design, while Passage B uses the toys as proof that plastic items were superior to what they replaced.
   G. Passage A uses the toys to illustrate plastic's popularity, while Passage B uses the toys to illustrate the lack of practical plastic goods.
   H. Both passages use the toys to show the variety of plastic items produced during the postwar era.
   J. Both passages use the toys as an example of early problems with plastic's quality.

GO ON TO THE NEXT PAGE.

3 3

Passage III

HUMANITIES: This passage is adapted from the article "The Myth of Gabriel García Márquez: How the Colombian Writer Really Changed Literature" by Michael Wood (©2009 by Washington Post.Newsweek Interactive Co. LLC).

Many years later, and many times over, the writer Gabriel García Márquez was to remember the day he discovered how to set about writing his great novel. He was driving from Mexico City to Acapulco when the illumination hit him. He turned the car around, went home, and locked himself away for 18 months. When he reappeared, he had the manuscript of *One Hundred Years of Solitude* in his hands.

When Gerald Martin, around the middle of his rich and resourceful biography of García Márquez, starts to tell this story, the reader may be a little surprised, even disappointed. "He had not been driving long that day when . . . García Márquez, as if in a trance, turned the Opel around, and drove back in the direction of Mexico City. And then . . ." Up to this point, Martin has not been challenging what he calls his subject's "mythomania"—how could he, since it's the basis of the writer's art and fame—but he has not been retelling the myths, either. He has been grounding them, laying out the pieces of what became the puzzles. And that's what he's doing here, too.

After "and then," Martin writes in mock apology, "It seems a pity to intervene in the story at this point but the biographer feels constrained to point out that there have been many versions of this story . . . and that the one just related cannot be true." The truth was no doubt less "miraculous," to use Martin's word. The writer probably continued to Acapulco. He didn't live in total seclusion for 18 months. And García Márquez wasn't starting a new book; he was reviving an old one.

What García Márquez found was a way of telling it. He would combine, as he frequently said, the narrative tone of his grandmother with that of the author Franz Kafka. She told fantastic stories as if they were true, because for her, they were true. Kafka told them that way because he was Kafka. After his moment of illumination García Márquez came more and more to look for (and often to find) the truth in the fantastic, to pursue whatever truth was lurking in the nonliteral reading of literally presented events.

Just because the miracle didn't happen as the story says it did doesn't mean there wasn't a miracle. *One Hundred Years of Solitude* changed García Márquez's life entirely, and it changed literature. When he got into the car to set out for Acapulco, he was a gifted and hardworking writer, certainly. When he got out of the car, he was on his way to the Nobel Prize, which he won in 1982.

García Márquez made many jokes about his fame over the years. These jokes are witty and complicated acts of gratitude for a destiny the writer was sure could have been quite different. One of his finest sentences, written in an article in 1983, concerns a dream of the life he might have led if he had stayed in his isolated birthplace of Aracataca, Colombia. "I would not perhaps be the same person I am now but maybe I would have been something better: just a character in one of the novels I would never have written."

The term "mythomania" certainly covers García Márquez's stories about his life and plenty of his journalism. But his fiction is different. It takes pieces of already thoroughly mythified reality—there is scarcely an extravagant incident in his novels and stories that doesn't have some sort of basis in specific, local fact or legend—and finds the perfect, unforgettable literary home for them. But García Márquez neither copies nor further mythifies these facts and legends. He honors them, to borrow a well-placed word from Martin:

> [O]ver the dark story of conquest and violence, tragedy and failure, he laid the other side of the continent, the carnival spirit, the music and the art of the Latin American people, the ability to honor life even in its darkest corners.

To honor life, I take Martin as saying, is to celebrate dignity, courage, and style wherever they are found and in whatever forms they take. It is not to deny darkness or even to believe it has its compensations.

Martin's biography is itself rather a dark affair—appropriately, since he is telling the life of a man whose autobiography is an elaborate historical myth. In García Márquez's own accounts, his life is both hard and magical. But it's never sad, and Martin evokes the sorrow that must lurk in such a life. There is perhaps a slight imbalance in Martin's insistence on the writer's sadness, an excess of melancholy; but it's a good corrective to García Márquez's own joking cheerfulness and elaborate ironies, and we can return to the master if we get too depressed.

21. The primary function of the first paragraph is to:

A. correct misconceptions about how long it took García Márquez to write *One Hundred Years of Solitude*.
B. describe García Márquez's approach to writing novels.
C. relate a story about García Márquez that Martin discusses in his biography.
D. provide background information about García Márquez's childhood.

GO ON TO THE NEXT PAGE.

3 3

22. Based on the passage, which of the following best describes the passage author's opinion of García Márquez's writing?

F. He considers García Márquez to be a gifted writer.
G. He prefers García Márquez's journalism to García Márquez's novels.
H. He thinks García Márquez's novels borrow too heavily from local facts and legends.
J. He believes that García Márquez's writing contains excessive melancholy.

23. The "illumination" mentioned in lines 5 and 37 most nearly refers to:

A. the realization García Márquez had concerning the approach he should take in writing *One Hundred Years of Solitude*.
B. Martin's discovery that García Márquez modeled his writing after Franz Kafka's.
C. the passage author's discovery that García Márquez based his stories on local facts and legends.
D. the awareness by García Márquez of how miraculous it was that he completed *One Hundred Years of Solitude*.

24. The passage most strongly suggests that a reader might "be a little surprised, even disappointed" (lines 11–12) while reading Martin's book because Martin:

F. is critical of García Márquez's preference for writing in seclusion.
G. focuses on analyzing the novels of García Márquez rather than discussing his development as a writer.
H. interrupts a familiar story about García Márquez to claim that it's not true.
J. fails to adequately explain why García Márquez drove back to Mexico City.

25. As it is used in line 24, the word *constrained* most nearly means:

A. restrained.
B. compelled.
C. coerced.
D. limited.

26. According to García Márquez, his grandmother told fantastic stories as if they were true because she:

F. was imitating Kafka.
G. believed they were true.
H. hoped to become a successful author.
J. had learned the technique from García Márquez.

27. The passage indicates that the comments García Márquez makes about his fame demonstrate his:

A. hope that his best work has yet to be written.
B. concern that his accomplishments are distorted by others.
C. gratitude that his life has unfolded the way it has.
D. belief that he deserves more credit for his wit and the complexity of his writing.

28. According to García Márquez, he might have become "something better" (line 57) if he had:

F. written *One Hundred Years of Solitude* sooner.
G. completed his journey to Acapulco.
H. taken his fame less seriously.
J. stayed in Aracataca, Colombia.

29. The passage author indicates that Martin's biography helps balance García Márquez's:

A. denial that fiction writing is worthy of merit.
B. joking cheerfulness and elaborate ironies.
C. belief that darkness has its compensations.
D. refusal to write about life's tragedies.

30. As it is used in line 87, the word *master* refers to:

F. the passage author.
G. Martin.
H. Kafka.
J. García Márquez.

GO ON TO THE NEXT PAGE.

Passage IV

NATURAL SCIENCE: This passage is adapted from the essay "Our Place in the Universe" by Alan Lightman (©2012 by Harper's Magazine Foundation).

One measure of the progress of human civilization is the increasing scale of our maps. A clay tablet dating from about the twenty-fifth century B.C. found near what is now the Iraqi city of Kirkuk depicts a river valley with a plot of land labeled as being 354 *iku* (about thirty acres) in size. In the earliest recorded cosmologies, such as the Babylonian *Enuma Elish*, from around 1500 B.C., the oceans, the continents, and the heavens were considered finite, but there were no scientific estimates of their dimensions. The early Greeks, including Homer, viewed Earth as a circular plane with the ocean enveloping it and Greece at the center, but there was no understanding of scale. In the early sixth century B.C., the Greek philosopher Anaximander, whom historians consider the first mapmaker, and his student Anaximenes proposed that the stars were attached to a giant crystalline sphere. But again there was no estimate of its size.

The first large object ever accurately measured was Earth, accomplished in the third century B.C. by Eratosthenes, a geographer who ran the Library of Alexandria. From travelers, Eratosthenes had heard the intriguing report that at noon on the summer solstice, in the town of Syene, due south of Alexandria, the sun casts no shadow at the bottom of a deep well. Evidently the sun is directly overhead at that time and place. (Before the invention of the clock, noon could be defined at each place as the moment when the sun was highest in the sky, whether that was exactly vertical or not.) Eratosthenes knew that the sun was not overhead at noon in Alexandria. In fact, it was tipped 7.2 degrees from the vertical, or about one fiftieth of a circle—a fact he could determine by measuring the length of the shadow cast by a stick planted in the ground. That the sun could be directly overhead in one place and not another was due to the curvature of Earth. Eratosthenes reasoned that if he knew the distance from Alexandria to Syene, the full circumference of the planet must be about fifty times that distance. Traders passing through Alexandria told him that camels could make the trip to Syene in about fifty days, and it was known that a camel could cover one hundred stadia (almost eleven and a half miles) in a day. So the ancient geographer estimated that Syene and Alexandria were about 570 miles apart. Consequently, the complete circumference of Earth he figured to be about 50 × 570 miles, or 28,500 miles. This number was within 15 percent of the modern measurement, amazingly accurate considering the imprecision of using camels as odometers.

As ingenious as they were, the ancient Greeks were not able to calculate the size of our solar system. That discovery had to wait for the invention of the telescope, nearly two thousand years later. In 1672, the French astronomer Jean Richer determined the distance from Earth to Mars by measuring how much the position of the latter shifted against the background of stars from two different observation points on Earth. The two points were Paris and Cayenne, French Guiana. Using the distance to Mars, astronomers were also able to compute the distance from Earth to the sun, approximately 100 million miles.

A few years later, Isaac Newton managed to estimate the distance to the nearest stars. (Only someone as accomplished as Newton could have been the first to perform such a calculation and have it go almost unnoticed among his other achievements.) If one assumes that the stars are similar objects to our sun, equal in intrinsic luminosity, Newton asked, how far away would our sun have to be in order to appear as faint as nearby stars? Writing his computations in a spidery script, with a quill dipped in the ink of oak galls, Newton correctly concluded that the nearest stars are about 100,000 times the distance from Earth to the sun, about 10 trillion miles away. Newton's calculation is contained in a short section of his *Principia* titled simply "On the distance of the stars."

Newton's estimate of the distance to nearby stars was larger than any distance imagined before in human history. Even today, nothing in our experience allows us to relate to it. The fastest most of us have traveled is about 500 miles per hour, the cruising speed of a jet. If we set out for the nearest star beyond our solar system at that speed, it would take us about 5 million years to reach our destination. If we traveled in the fastest rocket ship ever manufactured on Earth, the trip would last 100,000 years, at least a thousand human life spans.

31. The overall organization of the passage is best described as a:

A. chronological account of scientists' attempts to determine the distance of the stars from Earth.
B. series of historical examples explaining how increasingly large distances were measured.
C. step-by-step explanation of the calculations used to measure Earth's circumference.
D. collection of anecdotes describing how maps of the universe have changed over time.

32. The main function of the first paragraph is to:

F. list the distances and measurements that were known when Eratosthenes made his calculations.
G. explain what led early geographers to conclude that Earth was curved.
H. demonstrate how humans' sense of their surroundings has expanded over time.
J. summarize contributions the ancient Greeks made to astronomy.

GO ON TO THE NEXT PAGE.

3 3

33. Based on the passage, one similarity among the ancient models of the universe described in lines 6–18 is that:

A. they were based on the assumption that the universe was infinite.
B. they provided no scientific estimates of the size or scale of the objects they identified.
C. their depictions of geographical features were surprisingly accurate according to modern maps.
D. the people who developed them positioned their homelands as the center of the universe.

34. The main idea of the last paragraph is that:

F. nothing in our experience allows us to relate to the distance from Earth to the nearest stars.
G. recent advancements in space travel make the distance from Earth to the nearest stars seem small.
H. the time it would take to travel the distance from Earth to the nearest stars has been calculated only recently.
J. the nearest stars are more distant from Earth than Newton predicted.

35. According to the passage, the early Greeks imagined Earth as a:

A. circular plane with the ocean enveloping it and Greece at the center.
B. giant crystalline sphere to which the stars were attached.
C. planet tilted 7.2 degrees from the vertical.
D. plot of land 354 *iku* in size.

36. Based on the passage, to calculate the distance between Syene and Alexandria, Eratosthenes required information about the:

F. curvature of Earth and the angle of the sun in each city.
G. number of miles in one hundred stadia and the complete circumference of Earth.
H. height of the sun at noon in each city and the length of shadows cast on the ground.
J. time it took camels to travel between the cities and the distance camels could cover in one day.

37. The passage indicates that astronomers could not calculate the distance from Earth to other points in the solar system until:

A. they had identified proper observation points.
B. they applied ancient Greek calculations.
C. the telescope was invented.
D. Earth and Mars aligned.

38. The passage suggests that compared to his other work, Newton's calculation of the distance to the nearest stars was:

F. more important.
G. more speculative.
H. less complete.
J. less acknowledged.

39. It can reasonably be inferred from the passage that the author includes the description of Newton's handwriting and writing tools (lines 70–74) primarily to:

A. highlight how advanced Newton's calculation was by contrasting it with Newton's old-fashioned writing method.
B. suggest one reason Newton's calculation took so long to decipher.
C. describe the artistic flourishes of the section of *Principia* in which Newton's calculation appears.
D. illustrate the number of mistakes Newton made before arriving at the correct calculation.

40. As it is used in line 82, the phrase *set out* most nearly means:

F. described a vision.
G. stated a purpose.
H. started a journey.
J. created an arrangement.

END OF TEST 3

STOP! DO NOT TURN THE PAGE UNTIL TOLD TO DO SO.

DO NOT RETURN TO A PREVIOUS TEST.

4  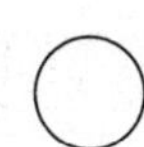     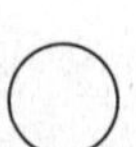   4

SCIENCE TEST

35 Minutes—40 Questions

DIRECTIONS: There are several passages in this test. Each passage is followed by several questions. After reading a passage, choose the best answer to each question and fill in the corresponding oval on your answer document. You may refer to the passages as often as necessary.

You are NOT permitted to use a calculator on this test.

Passage I

If a gum is added to water (such as the water in a food product), the *viscosity* (resistance to flow) of the resulting aqueous mixture changes. Table 1 shows, for each of 4 gums (Gums W, X, Y, and Z), the viscosity, in centipoise (cP), of a 1.0% by mass aqueous mixture of the gum at 3 temperatures and at 3 resting times. A *resting time* is a period of time an aqueous mixture of a gum sits at rest just after having been prepared.

Table 1

Gum	Temperature (°C)	Viscosity (cP) of a 1.0% aqueous gum mixture at a resting time of:		
		30 min	75 min	120 min
W	25	4,826	8,300	11,288
	45	3,250	6,825	9,282
	65	2,549	3,849	5,158
X	25	2,562	4,058	5,534
	45	2,100	3,462	4,686
	65	1,640	2,509	3,387
Y	25	1,201	1,994	2,771
	45	781	1,639	2,279
	65	531	802	1,075
Z	25	1,064	1,879	2,668
	45	512	1,562	2,233
	65	384	626	864

Figure 1 shows, for a certain temperature and a certain resting time, how the viscosity of aqueous mixtures of each of the 4 gums varies with gum concentration in percent by mass.

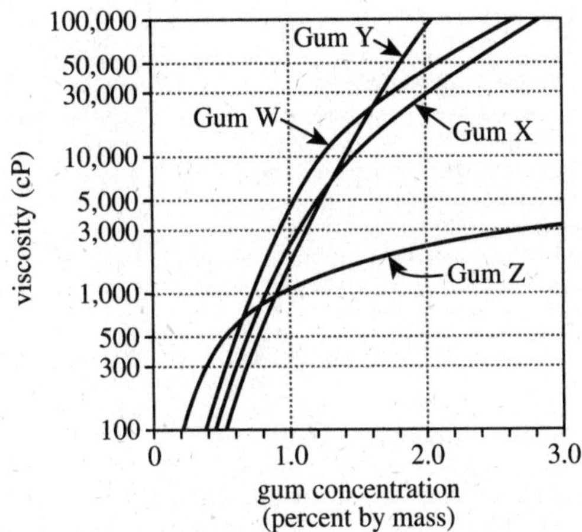

Figure 1

Table and figure adapted from G. O. Phillips and P. A. Williams, eds., *Handbook of Hydrocolloids*, 2nd ed. ©2009 by CRC Press and Woodhead Publishing, Ltd.

GO ON TO THE NEXT PAGE.

4 ○ ○ ○ ○ ○ ○ ○ ○ ○ 4

1. Based on Table 1, which of the following graphs best compares the viscosities of 1.0% aqueous mixtures of Gums W, X, Y, and Z at 45°C and a resting time of 75 min ?

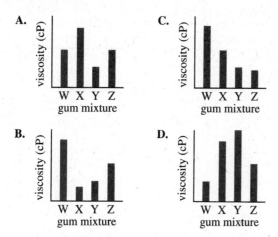

A.

viscosity (cP)

W X Y Z
gum mixture

C.

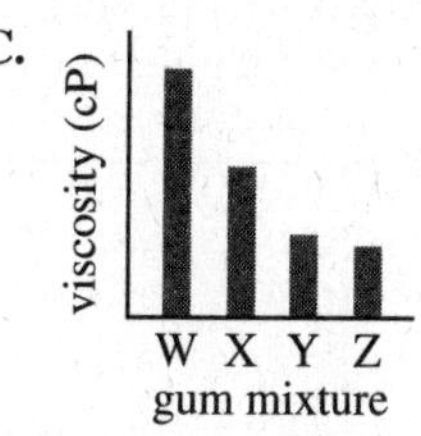

B.

viscosity (cP)

W X Y Z
gum mixture

D.

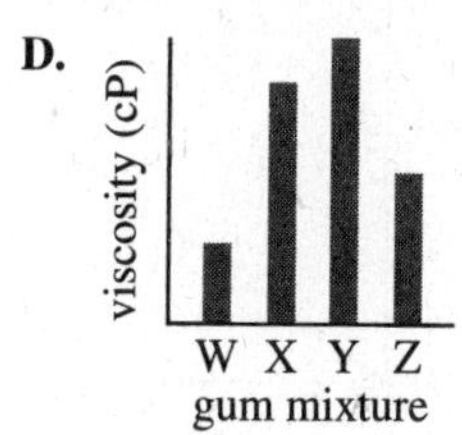

2. Based on Table 1, if a just-prepared 1.0% aqueous mixture of Gum Y is allowed to sit at rest for 100 min at 65°C, its viscosity will most likely be:

F. less than 500 cP.
G. between 500 cP and 800 cP.
H. between 800 cP and 1,100 cP.
J. greater than 1,100 cP.

3. Consider the viscosities shown in Figure 1 for a gum concentration of 2.0%. What is the order of the gums corresponding to those viscosities, from lowest viscosity to highest viscosity?

A. Gum W, Gum Y, Gum X, Gum Z
B. Gum W, Gum Z, Gum X, Gum Y
C. Gum Z, Gum X, Gum W, Gum Y
D. Gum Z, Gum Y, Gum W, Gum X

4. Under the conditions that are the basis for Figure 1, a 1.3% aqueous mixture of which gum has the highest viscosity?

F. Gum W
G. Gum X
H. Gum Y
J. Gum Z

5. Based on Table 1, a 1.0% aqueous mixture of Gum Z at 30°C and a resting time of 75 min would most likely have a viscosity closest to which of the following?

A. 1,250 cP
B. 1,750 cP
C. 2,050 cP
D. 2,350 cP

6. Under the conditions that are the basis for Figure 1, an aqueous mixture of which gum has a viscosity of 100,000 cP at a *lower* concentration than any of the other 3 gums?

F. Gum W
G. Gum X
H. Gum Y
J. Gum Z

GO ON TO THE NEXT PAGE.

4 ○ ○ ○ ○ ○ ○ ○ ○ ○ 4

Passage II

Biodiesel (BD) is a renewable alternative to traditional petroleum diesel (PD). BD is typically prepared by reacting soybean oil with methanol in the presence of a catalyst, forming compounds called *fatty acid methyl esters* (FAMEs). In contrast, PD contains no FAMEs. The presence of FAMEs in BD causes BD to absorb infrared light differently than does PD. This difference allows pure BD, pure PD, and mixtures of BD and PD to be distinguished by analyzing the absorbance of infrared light.

Students performed 3 studies in which they determined the infrared absorbance characteristics of pure BD, pure PD, and mixtures of BD and PD.

Study 1

The students measured the absorbance, *A*, of a sample of pure BD and a sample of pure PD at *wavenumbers* from 600 cm^{-1} through 1,800 cm^{-1}. The wavenumber corresponding to a given wavelength is defined as $\frac{1}{\text{the wavelength}}$, where the wavelength is given in cm and the resulting wavenumber is given in cm^{-1}. They plotted the results for each sample (see Figure 1).

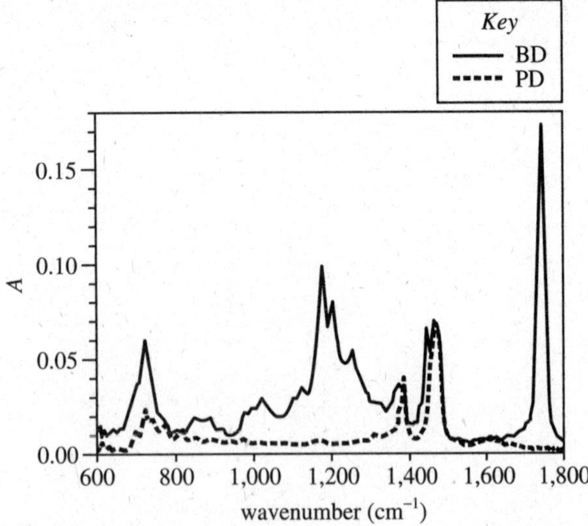

Figure 1

Study 2

The students prepared 7 different mixtures of BD and PD, each containing a different percent by volume of BD. Then, they measured *A* at 1,746 cm^{-1} for a sample of each of the 7 mixtures, a sample of pure BD, and a sample of pure PD (see Figure 2).

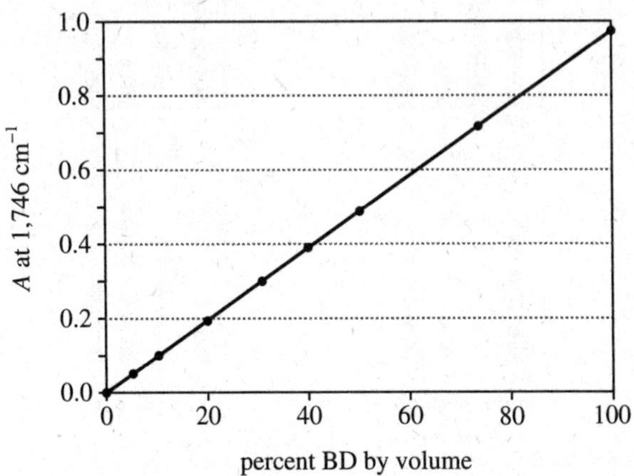

Figure 2

Figures 1 and 2 adapted from A. P. Ault and R. Pomery, "Quantitative Investigations of Biodiesel Fuel Using Infrared Spectroscopy: An Instrumental Analysis Experiment for Undergraduate Chemistry Students." ©2011 by Division of Chemical Education, Inc., American Chemical Society.

Study 3

The students obtained 4 different samples of commercial fuel blends of BD and PD (Samples W–Z). They measured *A* at 1,746 cm^{-1} for each sample, and then used Figure 2 to calculate the percent BD by volume of each sample (see Table 1).

Table 1

Sample	Percent BD by volume
W	4.0
X	6.0
Y	4.8
Z	4.7

Table 1 adapted from Z. V. Feng and J. T. Buchman, "Instrumental Analysis of Biodiesel Content in Commercial Diesel Blends: An Experiment for Undergraduate Analytical Chemistry." ©2012 by Division of Chemical Education, Inc., American Chemical Society.

GO ON TO THE NEXT PAGE.

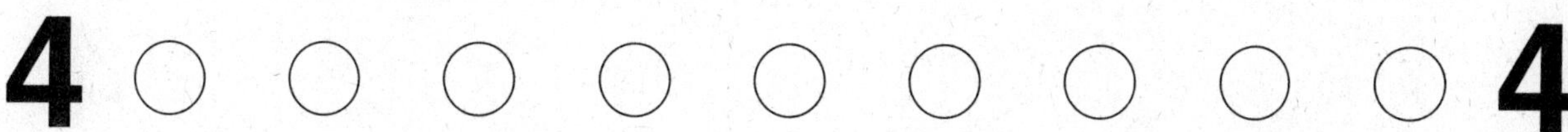

7. If the students had tested a 60% BD by volume sample in Study 2, A at 1,746 cm^{-1} would most likely have been:

   A. less than 0.45.
   B. between 0.45 and 0.55.
   C. between 0.55 and 0.65.
   D. greater than 0.65.

8. In Study 2, among the samples tested, as the percent by volume of BD increased, A at 1,746 cm^{-1}:

   F. increased only.
   G. decreased only.
   H. increased and then decreased.
   J. decreased and then increased.

9. Based on the results of Study 2, which fuel sample in Study 3 most likely had the smallest A at 1,746 cm^{-1} ?

   A. Sample W
   B. Sample X
   C. Sample Y
   D. Sample Z

10. The production of BD as described in the passage is best represented by which of the following chemical equations?

   F. FAMEs + catalyst → soybean oil + methanol
   G. FAMEs + methanol → soybean oil + catalyst
   H. Soybean oil + methanol $\xrightarrow{\text{catalyst}}$ FAMEs
   J. Soybean oil + FAMEs $\xrightarrow{\text{catalyst}}$ methanol

11. Suppose that in Study 1 the students had measured the absorbance at wavenumbers from 600 cm^{-1} through only 1,600 cm^{-1} (instead of through 1,800 cm^{-1}). Based on Figure 1, would the students more likely have measured the absorbance in Study 2 at a wavenumber of 1,172 cm^{-1} or at a wavenumber of 1,464 cm^{-1} ?

   A. A wavenumber of 1,172 cm^{-1}, because PD, but not BD, absorbs strongly at this wavenumber.
   B. A wavenumber of 1,172 cm^{-1}, because BD, but not PD, absorbs strongly at this wavenumber.
   C. A wavenumber of 1,464 cm^{-1}, because PD, but not BD, absorbs strongly at this wavenumber.
   D. A wavenumber of 1,464 cm^{-1}, because BD, but not PD, absorbs strongly at this wavenumber.

12. Consider a sample that contains only FAMEs. Based on the results of Study 1, would the sample more strongly absorb light at a wavenumber of 900 cm^{-1} or light at a wavenumber of 1,250 cm^{-1} ?

   F. A wavenumber of 900 cm^{-1}; PD contains FAMEs, and PD absorbed more strongly at 900 cm^{-1} than it did at 1,250 cm^{-1}.
   G. A wavenumber of 900 cm^{-1}; BD contains FAMEs, and BD absorbed more strongly at 900 cm^{-1} than it did at 1,250 cm^{-1}.
   H. A wavenumber of 1,250 cm^{-1}; PD contains FAMEs, and PD absorbed more strongly at 1,250 cm^{-1} than it did at 900 cm^{-1}.
   J. A wavenumber of 1,250 cm^{-1}; BD contains FAMEs, and BD absorbed more strongly at 1,250 cm^{-1} than it did at 900 cm^{-1}.

13. Consider the percent BD by volume listed in Table 1 for Sample Y. A 10 liter (L) volume of Sample Y would contain approximately what volume of BD, in liters and in milliliters (mL) ?

	L	mL
A.	0.5	500
B.	0.5	5,000
C.	5	500
D.	5	5,000

GO ON TO THE NEXT PAGE.

4 ○ ○ ○ ○ ○ ○ ○ ○ ○ 4

Passage III

Earth's gravitational field extends both above and below Earth's surface. In Figure 1, both the value of this field, g_E, and the average density, ρ, of matter within Earth are graphed versus distance, r, from Earth's center. In addition, Figure 1 identifies 5 regions, each of which is located either above or below Earth's surface.

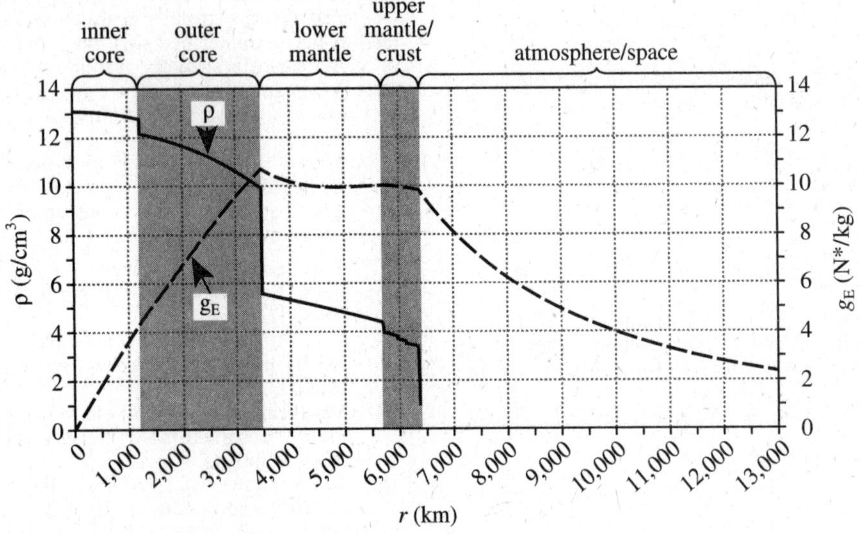

*newtons, a unit of force

Figure 1

Figure 2 shows the percent of Earth's mass located within a given distance r from Earth's center. For example, 10% of Earth's mass is located within 2,300 km of Earth's center, 20% of Earth's mass is located within 2,900 km of Earth's center, and so on.

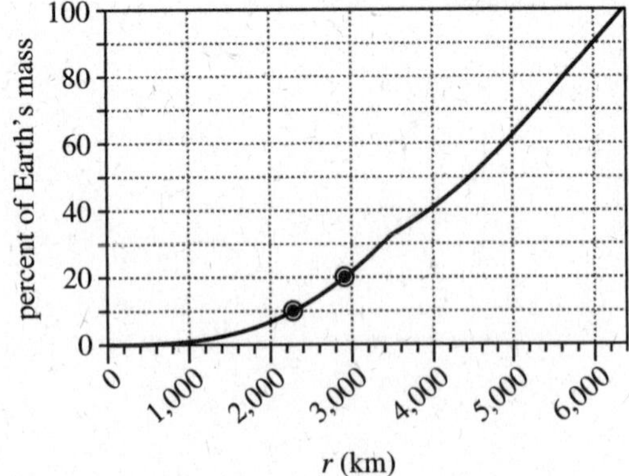

Figure 2

Figures adapted from A. M. Dziewonski and D. L. Anderson, "Preliminary Reference Earth Model." ©1981 by Elsevier B.V.

GO ON TO THE NEXT PAGE.

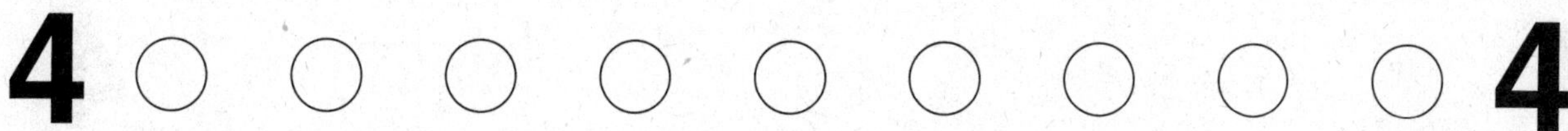

14. According to Figure 1, which 2 regions are most similar in thickness?

F. The inner core and the outer core
G. The inner core and the upper mantle/crust
H. The outer core and the lower mantle
J. The outer core and the upper mantle/crust

15. According to Figure 2, the innermost 30% of Earth's mass is located between $r = 0$ km and:

A. $r = 3{,}400$ km.
B. $r = 3{,}900$ km.
C. $r = 4{,}500$ km.
D. $r = 5{,}300$ km.

16. Figures 1 and 2 indicate that Earth's radius is approximately:

F. 1,400 km.
G. 3,500 km.
H. 5,700 km.
J. 6,400 km.

17. Based on Figure 1, the approximate value of Earth's gravitational field at $r = 14{,}000$ km is most likely:

A. less than 0.5 N/kg.
B. between 0.5 N/kg and 1.5 N/kg.
C. between 1.5 N/kg and 2.5 N/kg.
D. greater than 2.5 N/kg.

18. On average, Earth's crust is about 30 km thick. Based on Figure 2, the crust accounts for approximately what percent of Earth's mass?

F. 1%
G. 10%
H. 90%
J. 99%

19. Consider 2 hypothetical 1 kg rocks: one located at $r = 2{,}000$ km and the other located at $r = 4{,}000$ km. Based on Figure 1, which of these 2 rocks, if either, more likely weighs *less* ?

A. The rock located at $r = 2{,}000$ km; the value of g_E is less at that location so the rock there has a smaller gravitational force exerted on it.
B. The rock located at $r = 4{,}000$ km; the value of ρ is less at that location so the rock there has a smaller mass.
C. Neither rock; the rocks have identical masses so they have the same weight.
D. Neither rock; the value of g_E is the same for both rocks so they have the same weight.

GO ON TO THE NEXT PAGE.

4 ○ ○ ○ ○ ○ ○ ○ ○ ○ 4

Passage IV

Biological aging is the process by which the functions within an animal cell gradually decline, causing the cell to age. Four students each proposed an explanation for how this process occurs.

Student 1

Biological aging is caused solely by the *reactive oxygen species* (ROS) produced by cellular respiration. ROS are molecules that damage the proteins and lipids in a cell. A cell produces antioxidants, which eliminate ROS before they cause cell damage. However, the amount of antioxidants produced by a cell is always less than what is needed to eliminate all the ROS produced by that cell. Therefore, ROS damage accumulates in a cell, causing it to age.

Student 2

Biological aging is caused solely by the formation of *cross-links* (a type of chemical bond) between the proteins in a cell, causing these proteins to form clumps. These clumps accumulate in a cell, interfering with the cell's functions, causing it to age. Although ROS is damaging to proteins and lipids, this damage never occurs in a cell because the amount of antioxidants produced by a cell is always greater than what is needed to eliminate all the ROS produced by that cell.

Student 3

Biological aging is caused solely by the DNA damage that results from cell exposure to certain environmental agents. The extent of DNA damage caused by these agents eventually exceeds the cell's ability to repair this damage. Therefore, DNA damage accumulates in a cell, causing it to age. Although cells do produce ROS, ROS damage never accumulates in a cell. While cross-linked proteins do form clumps in a cell, these clumps never affect cell function.

Student 4

Biological aging is caused solely by the *lipofuscin* (a brown pigment made of oxidized lipids) produced by cellular respiration. Lipofuscin forms clumps that accumulate in a cell, interfering with the cell's functions, causing it to age. Although cells do produce ROS, ROS damage never accumulates in a cell. Because protein cross-links are short-lived, protein clumps never accumulate in a cell. The extent of DNA damage that occurs in a cell never exceeds the cell's ability to repair that damage.

20. Which of the students, if any, claimed that biological aging is caused by a substance produced by cellular respiration?

F. Student 1 only
G. Students 1 and 4 only
H. Students 2 and 3 only
J. None of the students

21. Suppose it were determined that the rate of biological aging in an animal cell is directly proportional to the number of chemical bonds formed between the proteins in that cell. This finding would be most consistent with the explanation given by:

A. Student 1.
B. Student 2.
C. Student 3.
D. Student 4.

22. Based on Student 2's explanation, the substances present in cells that are most directly involved with biological aging are composed of what type of subunits?

F. Amino acids
G. Fatty acids
H. Monosaccharides
J. Nucleotides

23. *Carnosine* is a substance that prevents protein cross-linking in animal cells. Which student would be most likely to predict that the average concentration of carnosine in the cells of young adults would be greater than the average concentration of carnosine in the cells of elderly adults?

A. Student 1
B. Student 2
C. Student 3
D. Student 4

24. Which of the students claimed that biological aging occurs because a substance accumulates into clumps that interfere with cellular function?

F. Students 1 and 2 only
G. Students 2 and 4 only
H. Students 1, 3, and 4 only
J. Students 1, 2, 3, and 4

GO ON TO THE NEXT PAGE.

4 ○ ○ ○ ○ ○ ○ ○ ○ ○ 4

25. Student 1's explanation would be most strongly supported if which of the following observations were made?

A. Increasing the number of protein cross-links in animal cells increases the rate at which those cells age.
B. Decreasing the number of protein cross-links in animal cells increases the rate at which those cells age.
C. Increasing the antioxidant concentration in animal cells increases the rate at which those cells age.
D. Decreasing the antioxidant concentration in animal cells increases the rate at which those cells age.

26. *Compound X* is a chemical that causes genetic mutations in human cells. Suppose it were determined that human neurons grown in the presence of Compound X age at the same rate as human neurons grown in the absence of Compound X. This finding would *weaken* the explanation(s) given by which of the students?

F. Student 2 only
G. Student 3 only
H. Students 1 and 3 only
J. Students 2 and 4 only

GO ON TO THE NEXT PAGE.

4  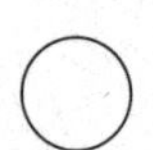 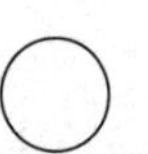  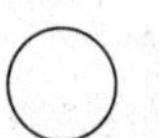  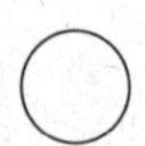 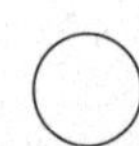  4

Passage V

In a lake, water *leaches* (dissolves out) soluble organic compounds from decaying tree leaves, producing *dissolved organic carbon* (DOC). DOC is subsequently removed from the water if it is *adsorbed* by (becomes adhered to the surface of) clay mineral particles that are suspended in the water. Three studies done at a lake examined DOC adsorption by 3 clay minerals—CM1, CM2, and CM3—found in the lake's sediment.

Green leaves were collected from 5 types of trees around the lake (maple, oak, pine, magnolia, and rhododendron). A 5 L volume of lake water was filtered to remove all solid particles. The following procedures were performed for each type of leaf: A 100 g sample of the leaves was mixed with a 1 L volume of the filtered lake water. The mixture was then placed in the dark for 10 weeks at 4°C while leaching occurred. At 10 weeks, the mixture was filtered to remove all solid particles. The resulting liquid (the *leachate*) was analyzed for DOC.

Study 1

The following procedures were performed for each leachate: A 100 mL volume of the leachate was mixed with 10 g of CM1. The mixture was stirred continuously for 2 hr, then filtered to remove all solid particles. The resulting liquid (the *filtrate*) was analyzed for DOC. The percent of the leachate DOC that had been adsorbed by CM1 was calculated (see Figure 1).

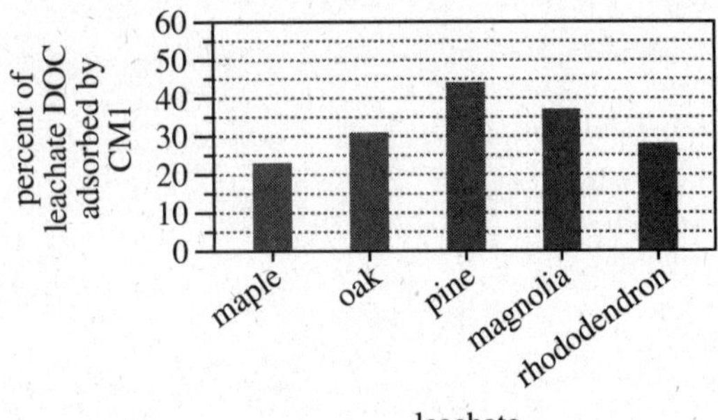

Figure 1

Study 2

Study 1 was repeated, substituting CM2 for CM1 (see Figure 2).

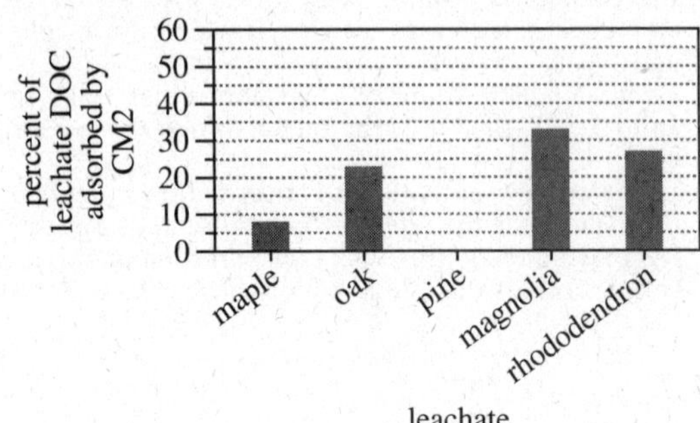

Figure 2

Study 3

Study 1 was repeated, substituting CM3 for CM1 (see Figure 3).

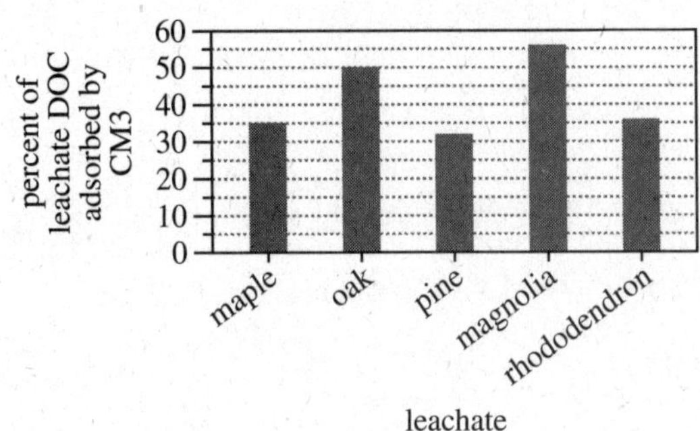

Figure 3

GO ON TO THE NEXT PAGE.

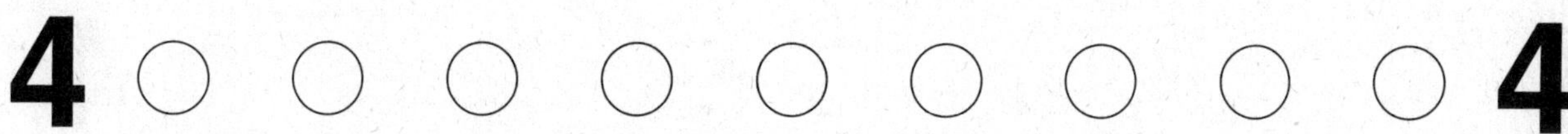

27. According to the results of the studies, from which of the 5 leachates was the greatest percent of DOC adsorbed by CM1, CM2, and CM3, respectively?

	CM1	CM2	CM3
A.	maple	maple	rhododendron
B.	oak	pine	magnolia
C.	pine	magnolia	rhododendron
D.	pine	magnolia	magnolia

28. According to the results of Study 3, the percent of leachate DOC adsorbed by CM3, averaged across the 5 types of leaves, is closest to which of the following?

F. 10%
G. 20%
H. 30%
J. 40%

29. Is the statement "CM2 adsorbed a greater percent of the DOC in the maple leachate than did CM3" supported by the results of Studies 2 and 3 ?

A. Yes; CM2 adsorbed 35% of the leachate DOC, whereas CM3 adsorbed 7%.
B. Yes; CM2 adsorbed 55% of the leachate DOC, whereas CM3 adsorbed 17%.
C. No; CM2 adsorbed 7% of the leachate DOC, whereas CM3 adsorbed 35%.
D. No; CM2 adsorbed 17% of the leachate DOC, whereas CM3 adsorbed 55%.

30. What was the independent (manipulated) variable in each of the 3 studies and what was the independent variable across the 3 studies?

	in each study	across the studies
F.	type of lake water	type of clay mineral
G.	type of leaf leachate	type of clay mineral
H.	volume of leaf leachate	mass of clay mineral
J.	volume of filtrate	mass of leaves

31. According to the results of the studies, which of the 3 clay minerals, if any, reduced the DOC in the oak leachate by more than 50% ?

A. CM1 only
B. CM2 only
C. CM1 and CM3 only
D. None of the 3 clay minerals

32. Is a mixture of any one of the leachates and any one of the clay minerals properly considered a solution?

F. Yes, because the clay mineral particles are dissolved in the leachate.
G. Yes, because the clay mineral particles are not dissolved in the leachate.
H. No, because the clay mineral particles are dissolved in the leachate.
J. No, because the clay mineral particles are not dissolved in the leachate.

33. In lake water, DOC is broken down into simpler compounds by electromagnetic energy in the visible wavelength range. What action was taken in the studies to prevent this process from occurring?

A. Each mixture of leaves and filtered lake water was placed in the dark.
B. Each mixture of filtrate and clay mineral was placed in the dark.
C. Each mixture of leaves and lake water was filtered.
D. Each mixture of leachate and clay mineral was filtered.

GO ON TO THE NEXT PAGE.

4 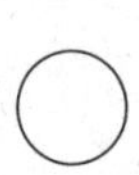 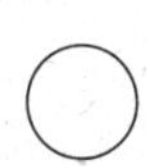        4

Passage VI

Plant roots can respond to a stimulus. Response to light is *phototropism*; response to gravity is *gravitropism*. Growth toward a stimulus is a *positive tropism*; growth away from a stimulus is a *negative tropism*.

For 2 experiments with *wild-type* (WT) and *mutant* (M) *Arabidopsis* seeds, nutrient agar was put into each of 8 petri dishes (PD1–PD8).

Experiment 1

Six WT *Arabidopsis* seeds were placed in each of PD1 and PD2. Six M *Arabidopsis* seeds were placed in each of PD3 and PD4. Then, PD1 and PD3 were placed in the dark for 70 hr, and PD2 and PD4 were exposed to light from above for 70 hr. Figure 1 shows the growth of the *hypocotyls* (seedling stems) above the surface of the nutrient agar and the growth of the *radicles* (seedling roots) below the surface of the nutrient agar in each dish at 70 hr.

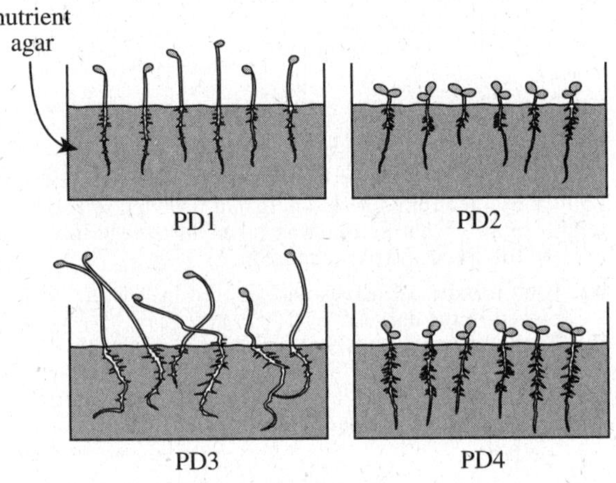

Figure 1

Experiment 2

Six WT *Arabidopsis* seeds were placed in each of PD5 and PD6. Six M *Arabidopsis* seeds were placed in each of PD7 and PD8. Then, PD5–PD8 were exposed to light from above for 70 hr. After 70 hr, each petri dish was turned 90° such that each dish was vertical and the seedlings in each dish were approximately horizontal (see Figure 2).

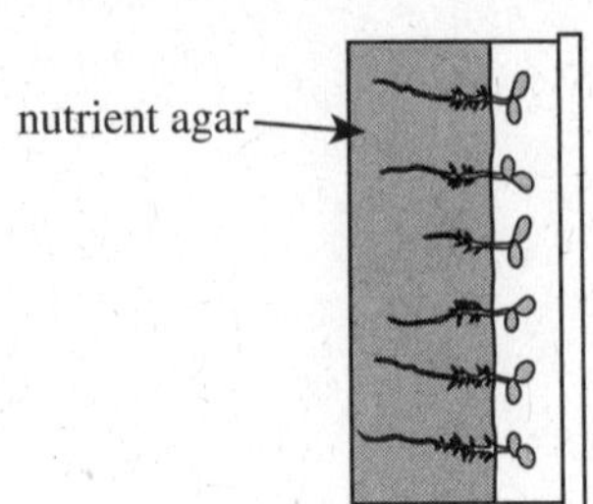

Figure 2

Then, PD5 and PD7 were exposed to light from above for 25 hr while PD6 and PD8 were exposed to light from below for 25 hr. At various times during the 25 hr, the downward curvature, in degrees (°), of the radicle (relative to its starting position) of each seedling in each dish was measured. The average downward curvature of the radicles in each dish at each measurement time is shown in Figure 3.

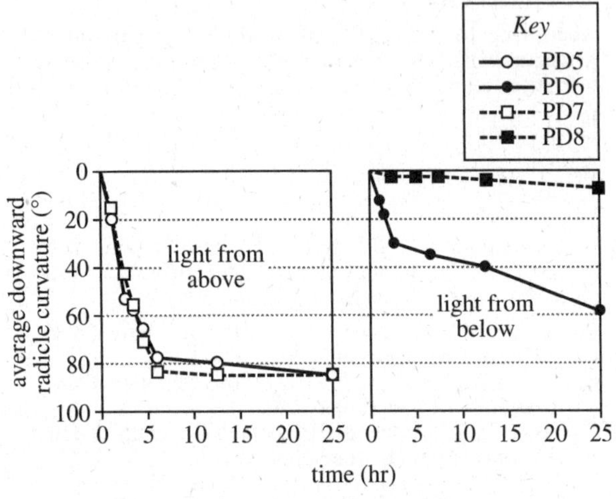

Figure 3

Figures adapted from Stanislav Vitha, Liming Zhao, and Fred David Sack, "Interaction of Root Gravitropism and Phototropism in Arabidopsis Wild-Type and Starchless Mutants." ©2000 by American Society of Plant Physiologists.

34. Which of the following figures best shows the orientation of PD5 before the petri dish was turned 90° ?

F. 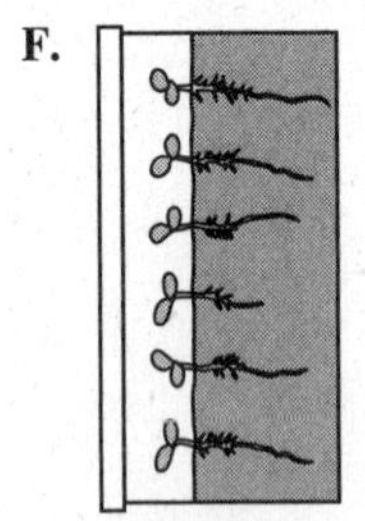

H. 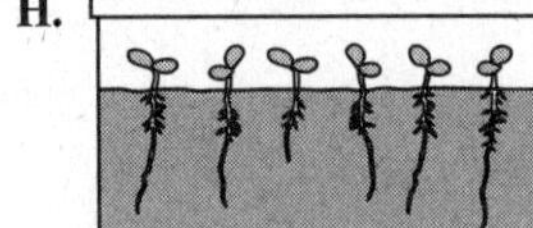

G. 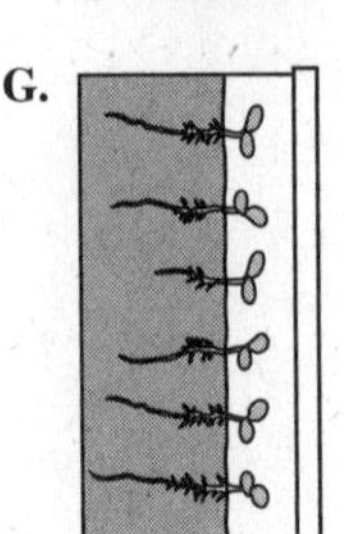

J. 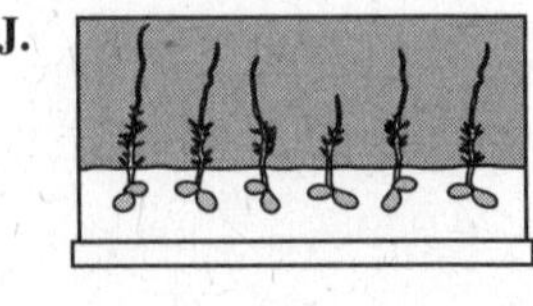

GO ON TO THE NEXT PAGE.

4 ○ ○ ○ ○ ○ ○ ○ ○ ○ 4

35. PD8 contained the same type of seeds, and was subject to the same growth conditions before being turned 90°, as which petri dish in Experiment 1 ?

A. PD1
B. PD2
C. PD3
D. PD4

36. Based on the results of Experiment 1, in the absence of light, did the radicles of the M *Arabidopsis* seedlings have the same response to gravity as did the radicles of the WT seedlings?

F. No; the variation in the orientation of the radicles in PD3 was greater than that of the radicles in PD1.
G. No; the variation in the orientation of the radicles in PD4 was greater than that of the radicles in PD2.
H. Yes; the variation in the orientation of the radicles in PD3 was the same as that of the radicles in PD1.
J. Yes; the variation in the orientation of the radicles in PD4 was the same as that of the radicles in PD2.

37. During the 25 hr in Experiment 2 that WT *Arabidopsis* seedlings were exposed to light from below, did the hypocotyls of the seedlings more likely exhibit positive phototropism or negative phototropism?

A. Positive, because seedling hypocotyls typically grow away from a light stimulus.
B. Positive, because seedling hypocotyls typically grow toward a light stimulus.
C. Negative, because seedling hypocotyls typically grow away from a light stimulus.
D. Negative, because seedling hypocotyls typically grow toward a light stimulus.

38. Based on the results shown in Figure 1 for PD2, is *Arabidopsis* a monocot or a dicot?

F. Monocot; seedlings have 1 cotyledon.
G. Monocot; seedlings have 2 cotyledons.
H. Dicot; seedlings have 1 cotyledon.
J. Dicot; seedlings have 2 cotyledons.

39. In Experiment 2, each petri dish had how many different orientations?

A. 1
B. 2
C. 3
D. 4

40. To evaluate the effect of light on the growth of WT *Arabidopsis* seedlings, the results for which 2 petri dishes in Experiment 1 should be compared?

F. PD1 and PD2
G. PD1 and PD3
H. PD2 and PD3
J. PD2 and PD4

END OF TEST 4

STOP! DO NOT RETURN TO ANY OTHER TEST.

You may wish to photocopy these sample answer document pages to respond to the practice ACT Writing Test.

Please enter the information at the right before beginning the writing test.

Use a soft lead No. 2 pencil only. Do NOT use a mechanical pencil, ink, ballpoint, or felt-tip pen.

WRITING TEST BOOKLET NUMBER

Print your 6-digit **Booklet Number** in the boxes at the right.

WRITING TEST FORM

Print your 5-character **Test Form** in the boxes above and fill in the corresponding oval at the right.

- 16W1A
- 16W2A
- 16W3A
- 18W4A
- 19WT5

Begin WRITING TEST here.

If you need more space, please continue on the next page.

WRITING TEST

If you need more space, please continue on the back of this page.

WRITING TEST

If you need more space, please continue on the next page.

WRITING TEST

STOP here with the writing test.

072954

Practice Writing Test Prompt 5

Your Signature: ______________________________
(Do not print.)

Print Your Name Here: ______________________________

Your Date of Birth:

☐☐ – ☐☐ – ☐☐☐☐
Month Day Year

Form 19WT5

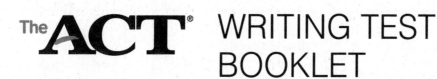

The ACT® WRITING TEST BOOKLET

You must take the multiple-choice tests before you take the writing test.

Directions

This is a test of your writing skills. You will have **forty** (40) minutes to read the prompt, plan your response, and write an essay in English. Before you begin working, read all material in this test booklet carefully to understand exactly what you are being asked to do.

You will write your essay on the lined pages in the **answer document** provided. Your writing on those pages will be scored. You may use the unlined pages in this test booklet to plan your essay. Your work on these pages will not be scored.

Your essay will be evaluated based on the evidence it provides of your ability to:

- clearly state your own perspective on a complex issue and analyze the relationship between your perspective and at least one other perspective
- develop and support your ideas with reasoning and examples
- organize your ideas clearly and logically
- communicate your ideas effectively in standard written English

Lay your pencil down immediately when time is called.

DO NOT OPEN THIS BOOKLET UNTIL TOLD TO DO SO.

PO Box 168
Iowa City, IA 52243-0168

Winning

"It's not whether you win or lose, it's how you play the game." This popular expression, often repeated by coaches, parents, and competitors alike, encourages us to ignore victories and defeats and to focus instead on our effort. Yet we all know how good winning can feel. Not only does it offer a sense of pride and accomplishment, but we are often rewarded and praised for our victories in athletics, academics, the arts, and so on. Even when we've worked hard and performed well, there can be a sense of emptiness if our best efforts do not lead to a win. To what extent, then, is it true that effort in competition is more important than the final result? Given these contradictory views, it is worth considering the importance of winning.

Read and carefully consider these perspectives. Each suggests a particular way of thinking about the importance of winning.

Perspective One	Perspective Two	Perspective Three
People are programmed to compete. We can tell ourselves that effort is more important than the end result, but in truth, we are naturally inclined to strive for victory.	In any competition, victory depends on a number of factors outside our control—talent and luck, for example. Our effort is the only thing we *can* control and thus is more important than the final result.	An emphasis on winning teaches us to see others as enemies to defeat. As a result, our world becomes a more hostile, less cooperative place.

Essay Task

Write a unified, coherent essay about the importance of winning. In your essay, be sure to:

- clearly state your own perspective on the issue and analyze the relationship between your perspective and at least one other perspective
- develop and support your ideas with reasoning and examples
- organize your ideas clearly and logically
- communicate your ideas effectively in standard written English

Your perspective may be in full agreement with any of those given, in partial agreement, or completely different.

Planning Your Essay

Your work on these prewriting pages will not be scored.

Use the space below and on the back cover to generate ideas and plan your essay. You may wish to consider the following as you think critically about the task:

Strengths and weaknesses of different perspectives on the issue

- What insights do they offer, and what do they fail to consider?
- Why might they be persuasive to others, or why might they fail to persuade?

Your own knowledge, experience, and values

- What is your perspective on this issue, and what are its strengths and weaknesses?
- How will you support your perspective in your essay?

If you need more space to plan, please continue on the back of this page.

Planning Your Essay

Use this page to continue planning your essay. Your work on this page will not be scored.

Scoring Your Practice Tests

Scoring Practice Practice Tests 2, 3, 4, and 5 is covered in chapter 11.

Explanatory Answers

ENGLISH • PRACTICE TEST 5 • EXPLANATORY ANSWERS

Question 1. The best answer is B because it correctly identifies the rhetorical impact of losing the phrase "and my idol." An idol is greatly admired, so it is logical to conclude that if the narrator idolized her sister—"a guitar buff"—she would want to learn to play the guitar, too.

The best answer is NOT:

A because it fails to correctly identify the rhetorical impact of the phrase "and my idol." This phrase indicates nothing about the narrator's age when she learned to play the guitar.

C because it fails to correctly identify the rhetorical impact of the phrase "and my idol." This phrase suggests nothing about the age difference between the narrator and her sister.

D because it fails to correctly identify the rhetorical impact of the phrase "and my idol." This phrase suggests nothing about degree of musical talent.

Question 2. The best answer is F because it provides the appropriate punctuation (a colon) to precede a list (the places the narrator took her guitar).

The best answer is NOT:

G because it introduces unnecessary punctuation that makes the narrator's point less clear and creates an ungrammatical sentence. Placing the period after the word *around* creates a vague statement that loses the emphatic point that the narrator carried the guitar around everywhere (not just around). In addition, the unnecessary punctuation creates an ungrammatical sentence (a fragment in this case) beginning with the word *Everywhere.*

H because it uses grammatically incorrect punctuation (a semicolon) to introduce a list.

J because it fails to provide any punctuation to precede the list. The statement ending with the word *everywhere* is a complete sentence that requires punctuation to precede the list.

Question 3. The best answer is C because it correctly distinguishes between possessives and plurals by using an apostrophe to form the plural possessive *friends'* and no apostrophe in the plural noun *houses*.

The best answer is NOT:

A because it incorrectly provides the plural noun *friends* where the plural possessive *friends'* is needed.

B because it incorrectly provides the singular possessive *friend's* where a plural is needed and incorrectly provides the singular possessive *house's* where the plural noun *houses* is needed.

D because it incorrectly provides the singular possessive *friend's*.

ENGLISH • PRACTICE TEST 5 • EXPLANATORY ANSWERS

Question 4. The best answer is F because it provides the appropriate punctuation and capitalization for the two complete sentences and supplies the necessary comma after the introductory clause "No matter where I was" to avoid ambiguity in terms of whether the writer is saying "No matter where I was" or "No matter where I was playing."

The best answer is NOT:

G because it lacks a comma after the word *and*, creating a run-on sentence.

H because it lacks a comma after the word *was*, creating ambiguity in terms of whether the writer is saying "No matter where I was" or "No matter where I was playing."

J because it incorrectly uses commas to join two complete statements without any connector words.

Question 5. The best answer is A because it provides the most precise expression of the idea described in the stem. The word *assailed* best illustrates "the fervor with which the narrator communicated with the airport personnel" because it figuratively conveys the narrator's energy in the interaction.

The best answer is NOT:

B because it provides a word choice that fails to precisely describe the idea identified in the stem; the neutral word *approached* does not adequately illustrate fervor.

C because it provides a word choice that fails to precisely describe the idea identified in the stem; the neutral word *questioned* does not adequately illustrate fervor.

D because it provides a word choice that fails to precisely describe the idea identified in the stem; the neutral word *contacted* does not adequately illustrate fervor.

Question 6. The best answer is J because it provides the appropriate pronouns for this sentence. The subjective pronoun case *who* is needed here because the word *who* serves as the subject of the dependent clause, and the pronoun *me* is the object.

The best answer is NOT:

F because it inappropriately uses a reflexive pronoun. The object is not the same person as the subject, so the reflexive pronoun *myself* is grammatically incorrect.

G because it incorrectly provides the objective pronoun case *whom* where the subjective pronoun case is needed. In addition, the object is not the same person as the subject, so the reflexive pronoun *myself* is grammatically incorrect.

H because it incorrectly provides the objective pronoun case *whom* where the subjective pronoun case is needed.

Question 7. The best answer is D because it eliminates redundancy and unnecessary wordiness.

The best answer is NOT:

A because it fails to eliminate redundancy at the paragraph level; the idea that this is an extended trip is mentioned earlier in the paragraph.

B because it fails to eliminate wordiness and redundancy at the paragraph level; the phrase "due to the fact that I was on an extended trip" contains a redundant reference to the extended trip and lacks concision.

C because it fails to eliminate redundancy at the paragraph level; the idea that the narrator is in Hawaii is mentioned earlier in the paragraph.

Question 8. The best answer is H because it provides the most logical transition based on the surrounding context. The word *though* logically conveys the shift from the narrator feeling upset in the preceding paragraph to the narrator's worries dissipating.

The best answer is NOT:

F because it provides an illogical transition word; the word *otherwise* provides no logical meaning in this context.

G because it provides an illogical transition word; the word *therefore* suggests a cause-effect relationship between ideas that does not exist here.

J because it provides an illogical transition word; the word *instead* means "alternatively," which makes no sense in this context.

Question 9. The best answer is D because it provides the idiomatically correct preposition in context. The phrase "into the . . . air" is consistent with standard English usage.

The best answer is NOT:

A because it provides the preposition *upon*, which creates an idiomatically nonstandard expression.

B because it provides the preposition *amid*, which creates an idiomatically nonstandard expression.

C because it provides the preposition *onto*, which creates an idiomatically nonstandard expression.

ENGLISH • PRACTICE TEST 5 • EXPLANATORY ANSWERS

Question 10. The best answer is J because it is the most precise word for the context. The word *issued* correctly and logically conveys the idea that the tones came from an instrument.

The best answer is NOT:

F because it supplies an imprecise word choice for the context; the word *accrued* conveys the idea of accumulating, which does not make sense for describing musical tones.

G because it supplies an imprecise word choice for the context; the word *distributed* conveys the idea of something being passed out or delivered, which does not make sense for describing musical tones.

H because it supplies an imprecise word choice for the context; the word *appeared* conveys the idea of something becoming visible, which does not make sense for describing musical tones.

Question 11. The best answer is A because it is a complete statement, preventing the introduction of a rhetorically ineffective fragment.

The best answer is NOT:

B because it creates a sentence fragment.

C because it creates a sentence fragment.

D because it creates a sentence fragment.

Question 12. The best answer is G because it uses the appropriate conjunction for indicating a comparison (the word *than*), and the phrase "that of a guitar" clearly indicates that the comparison is between the guitar and the ukulele.

The best answer is NOT:

F because it uses the adverb *then* instead of the conjunction *than*.

H because it contains the pronoun *it*, which has no clear antecedent here, making the sentence unclear in terms of what is being compared.

J because it incorrectly supplies the adverb *then* where the conjunction *than* is needed. In addition, it contains the pronoun *it*, which has no clear antecedent here, making the sentence unclear in terms of what is being compared.

ENGLISH • PRACTICE TEST 5 • EXPLANATORY ANSWERS

Question 13. The best answer is B because it provides the most specific description of the music the narrator played, as defined in the stem.

The best answer is NOT:

A because it uses the general word *music*, which lacks the specificity of the term "Hawaiian classics."

C because it uses the general term "tropical tunes," which lacks the specificity of the term "Hawaiian classics."

D because it uses the general word *things*, which is too vague to have any specific meaning.

Question 14. The best answer is H because it provides the idiomatically correct preposition in context. The phrase "playing . . . with the locals" is clear and consistent with standard English usage.

The best answer is NOT:

F because it creates the phrase "playing . . . as the locals," which is unclear in meaning and is inconsistent with standard English usage.

G because it creates the phrase "playing . . . through the locals," which creates an illogical meaning and is inconsistent with standard English usage.

J because it creates the phrase "playing . . . along the locals," which is unclear in meaning and is inconsistent with standard English usage.

Question 15. The best answer is C because it best expresses the idea specified in the stem by referring to the narrator's closeness to her sister and love of playing the guitar. These are key points in the first two paragraphs.

The best answer is NOT:

A because it fails to fulfill the goal specified in the stem; neither the ukulele nor Hawaii is mentioned in the first two paragraphs.

B because it fails to fulfill the goal specified in the stem; the narrator's time in Hawaii is not discussed in the first two paragraphs.

D because it fails to fulfill the goal specified in the stem; the narrator's business trip is not the central focus of the first two paragraphs.

ENGLISH • PRACTICE TEST 5 • EXPLANATORY ANSWERS

Question 16. The best answer is J because it eliminates redundancy and unnecessary wordiness.

The best answer is NOT:

F because it fails to eliminate redundancy at the sentence level; the sentence already mentions that she had ideas.

G because it fails to eliminate redundancy at the sentence level; the sentence already mentions that she had ideas.

H because it fails to eliminate redundancy at the sentence level; the sentence already mentions that she had ideas, so we know the ideas were her own.

Question 17. The best answer is B because it provides the most accurate description of how the paragraph break would create two separate but cohesive paragraphs. The information that precedes this point focuses on why and how Lamarr came up with the idea for "a sophisticated radio-controlled guidance system." But the information that follows this point has a different focus; it explains how Lamarr's invention would work.

The best answer is NOT:

A because it provides an inaccurate description of the two paragraphs that would be created; it suggests that two inventions are discussed here when only one is mentioned.

C because it provides an inaccurate description of the essay's focus here; the section preceding this point in the essay does not provide an overview of Lamarr's film career.

D because it provides an inaccurate description of the two paragraphs that would be created; except for mentioning where she grew up, the section preceding this point in the essay does not include details about Lamarr's childhood, and the section that follows focuses on Lamarr's work in particular rather than on general information about radio signals.

Question 18. The best answer is H because it ensures correct subject-verb agreement. The plural verb form *are jammed* agrees with the plural subject *radio signals.*

The best answer is NOT:

F because it lacks subject-verb agreement; the singular verb form *is* does not agree with the plural subject *radio signals.*

G because it lacks subject-verb agreement; the singular verb form *has been* does not agree with the plural subject *radio signals.*

J because it lacks subject-verb agreement; the singular verb form *is jammed* does not agree with the plural subject *radio signals.*

ENGLISH • PRACTICE TEST 5 • EXPLANATORY ANSWERS

Question 19. The best answer is A because it correctly separates two distinct statements into two sentences with correct punctuation.

The best answer is NOT:

B because it incorrectly places a period after the word *envisioned*, creating a sentence fragment beginning with the word *A*.

C because it incorrectly uses a comma to join two independent clauses.

D because it incorrectly places a semicolon after the word *envisioned*. A semicolon must be followed by an independent clause rather than a fragment.

Question 20. The best answer is J because it eliminates redundancy and unnecessary wordiness.

The best answer is NOT:

F because it fails to eliminate redundancy at the sentence level; the phrase "like that" is redundant because the word *such* is used earlier in the sentence.

G because it fails to eliminate redundancy at the sentence level; the phrase "similar to that" is redundant because the word *such* is used earlier in the sentence.

H because it fails to eliminate redundancy at the sentence level; the word *difficult* is redundant because the word *hard* is used later in the sentence.

Question 21. The best answer is B because it provides the most precise wording for the context; the word *implement* suggests putting something into action, which precisely describes what Lamarr was trying to do.

The best answer is NOT:

A because it is illogical in this context; the word *instigate* suggests provoking or inciting, which is not something one does to an idea.

C because it is illogical in this context; the word *discharge* suggests the idea of unloading something, which makes no sense in this context.

D because it is illogical in this context; the word *uphold* suggests supporting or defending something. Lamarr wanted to put her idea into practice; she did not need to defend it.

ENGLISH • PRACTICE TEST 5 • EXPLANATORY ANSWERS

Question 22. The best answer is F because it provides appropriate and consistent punctuation (commas) to set off the nonessential element (the word *however*).

The best answer is NOT:

G because it fails to provide appropriate and consistent punctuation to set off the nonessential element by substituting a semicolon for the comma after the word *war*.

H because it fails to provide appropriate and consistent punctuation to set off the nonessential element by omitting the comma after the word *however*.

J because it lacks any punctuation to set off the nonessential element.

Question 23. The best answer is C because it is the most effective placement of the statement in terms of logic and cohesion. Placing Sentence 3 after Sentence 4 ensures that the paragraph discusses the events in chronological order.

The best answer is NOT:

A because it creates a sequence of events that is not chronological; the event in Sentence 3 occurs after the event in Sentence 4.

B because it creates a sequence of events that is not chronological; the event in Sentence 3 occurs after the event in Sentence 1.

D because it creates a sequence of events that is not chronological; the event in Sentence 3 occurs before the event in Sentence 5.

Question 24. The best answer is G because it best expresses the idea specified in the stem by strongly and specifically emphasizing that the declassification of spread spectrum was a turning point in the history of communication. The word *transformed* indicates a dramatic change in communications, and the phrase "communications landscape" indicates that the change affected many facets of communication.

The best answer is NOT:

F because it is a less effective choice based on the goal specified in the stem; the phrase "made a difference" is too general to suggest a turning point.

H because it is a less effective choice based on the goal specified in the stem; even though the phrase "had an impact on communications" suggests that the declassification of spread spectrum had a strong effect on communications, the phrase fails to clearly indicate a turning point in the history of communication technology.

J because it is a less effective choice based on the goal specified in the stem; the phrase "revolutionized things" is imprecise and unclear.

ENGLISH • PRACTICE TEST 5 • EXPLANATORY ANSWERS

Question 25. The best answer is B because it provides the appropriate punctuation (an em dash) to set off the nonessential element (the phrase "cellular phones, wireless Internet networks, the Global Positioning System"). The em dash that precedes the nonessential element is consistent with the em dash that follows the nonessential element.

The best answer is NOT:

A because it fails to use appropriate and consistent punctuation to set off the nonessential element; a comma rather than an em dash precedes the nonessential element.

C because it fails to use appropriate and consistent punctuation to set off the nonessential element; a colon rather than an em dash precedes the nonessential element.

D because it fails to use appropriate and consistent punctuation to set off the nonessential element; a comma rather than an em dash precedes the nonessential element. In addition, it fails to include the comma after the word *phones* to appropriately separate items in a list.

Question 26. The best answer is H because it corrects the introduction of a rhetorically ineffective fragment by providing the appropriate verb form *function* to make this a complete sentence.

The best answer is NOT:

F because it creates a sentence fragment; it lacks a predicate.

G because it creates a sentence fragment; it lacks a predicate.

J because it creates a sentence fragment; it lacks a predicate.

Question 27: The best answer is A because it creates an expression consistent with standard English usage. The idiom "It wasn't until" is used to emphasize that a relatively lengthy period passed before Lamarr and Antheil were given credit for spread spectrum.

The best answer is NOT:

B because it is an idiomatically nonstandard and vague expression; the word *Such* has no clear antecedent.

C because it introduces a vague pronoun; the pronoun *This* has no clear antecedent.

D because it introduces a vague pronoun; the pronoun *That* has no clear antecedent.

ENGLISH • PRACTICE TEST 5 • EXPLANATORY ANSWERS

Question 28. The best answer is J because it corrects the introduction of an error in coordination and subordination.

The best answer is NOT:

F because it contains an error in coordination created by adding a comma and the word *they* after the name *Antheil*, making the relationship between what comes before and after the comma unclear.

G because it contains an error in coordination created by adding an em dash and the word *both* after the name *Antheil*; the em dash serves no clear purpose here and therefore makes the relationship between what comes before and after the em dash unclear.

H because it contains an error in coordination. The compound subject *Lamarr and Antheil* is incorrectly followed by the infinitive verb form *to receive*, failing to provide a predicate for the sentence.

Question 29. The best answer is D because it eliminates the illogical and confusing transition word. The link between this sentence and the preceding one is obvious; no other transition is needed.

The best answer is NOT:

A because it provides an illogical transition word for the context; the word *However* suggests two opposing ideas, which is not the case here.

B because it provides an illogical transition word for the context; the word *Conversely* suggests two opposing ideas, which is not the case here.

C because it provides an unnecessary transition word for the context; there is no clear rhetorical purpose for the word *Anyway* in this context.

Question 30. The best answer is F because it offers a clear and convincing reason the essay accomplishes the purpose identified in the stem. This essay gives an overview of the history of Lamarr's invention. The essay begins with Lamarr's idea and then goes on to explain how the invention was developed and why it was important.

The best answer is NOT:

G because it identifies an incorrect reason the essay has accomplished the specified purpose; Lamarr and Antheil could not have changed the course of World War II with spread spectrum because, according to the essay, spread spectrum was not fully developed until after World War II.

H because it indicates that the essay hasn't accomplished the specified primary purpose when it has; the second half of the essay explains the importance of spread spectrum.

J because it indicates that the essay hasn't accomplished the specified primary purpose when it has and identifies a reason that does not accurately describe the essay; the essay gives very little attention to the film industry.

ENGLISH • PRACTICE TEST 5 • EXPLANATORY ANSWERS

Question 31. The best answer is B because it properly distinguishes among pronouns, contractions, and possessives by providing the phrase "There are" to correctly set up the independent clause and agree with plural noun *turbines*.

The best answer is NOT:

A because it incorrectly provides the contraction *They're*, which means "They are." This phrase creates an ungrammatical sentence.

C because it incorrectly substitutes the possessive *Their*, creating an ungrammatical sentence.

D because it incorrectly substitutes the contraction *There's*, which means "There is." This phrase creates an ungrammatical sentence and fails to agree with the plural noun *turbines*.

Question 32. The best answer is H because it ensures correct subject-verb agreement. The subject of this part of the sentence is the singular word *task*. The singular verb form *represents* agrees with the singular subject *task*.

The best answer is NOT:

F because it lacks subject-verb agreement; the plural verb form *have represented* does not agree with the singular subject *task*.

G because it lacks subject-verb agreement; the plural verb form *are representing* does not agree with the singular subject *task*.

J because it lacks subject-verb agreement; the plural verb form *represent* does not agree with the singular subject *task*.

Question 33. The best answer is A because it correctly signals a contrast between this sentence and the preceding sentence. The idea that servicing the turbine blades "that slice through the air is a serious challenge" contrasts with the preceding idea that "ladders inside the tower simplify access to the generators and controllers."

The best answer is NOT:

B because it signals a similarity rather than a contrast between the ideas in these two sentences.

C because it signals a time marker that is illogical; there is nothing in the essay to suggest servicing the turbine blades happens instantly.

D because it incorrectly signals a transition to an order of steps.

ENGLISH • PRACTICE TEST 5 • EXPLANATORY ANSWERS

Question 34. The best answer is G because it provides appropriate and consistent punctuation (em dashes) before and after the nonessential element ("those long fiberglass vanes that slice through the air").

The best answer is NOT:

F because it lacks appropriate punctuation after the word *blades* to correctly set off the nonessential element.

H because it uses inconsistent punctuation (an em dash after the word *blades* and a comma after the word *air*) to set off the nonessential element.

J because it lacks appropriate punctuation after the word *air* to correctly set off the nonessential element.

Question 35. The best answer is A because it prevents the introduction of redundant or unnecessary wording.

The best answer is NOT:

B because it introduces redundancy at the sentence level; the phrase "something they're able to do" is redundant because the sentence already says "Rock climbers are . . . capable."

C because it contains an internal redundancy; ascending and climbing indicate the same action.

D because it introduces redundancy at the sentence level; the phrase "using rope" is redundant because the use of rope has already been mentioned in the sentence.

Question 36. The best answer is F because it prevents the introduction of a squinting modifier. It correctly places the subject ("rock climbers") after the comma so that the introductory clause "After completing specialized training" correctly modifies "rock climbers."

The best answer is NOT:

G because it creates a squinting modifier; it incorrectly makes "old skills and new knowledge" the subject, which suggests that "old skills and new knowledge" have completed specialized training.

H because it creates a squinting modifier; it incorrectly makes "new careers" the subject, which suggests that "new careers" have completed specialized training.

J because it shifts to the passive voice, making it unclear who has completed specialized training.

ENGLISH • PRACTICE TEST 5 • EXPLANATORY ANSWERS

Question 37. The best answer is D because it correctly provides the appropriate preposition for the standard English phrase "arrive at."

The best answer is NOT:

A because it incorrectly provides the preposition *across*, which creates a nonstandard and illogical phrase; technicians could not arrive by being across the turbine.

B because it incorrectly substitutes the preposition *with*, which creates a nonstandard and illogical phrase; the word *with* suggests that the technicians already had the turbine with them when they arrived.

C because it incorrectly substitutes the preposition *via*, which creates a nonstandard and illogical phrase; the word *via* suggests that the technicians reached a new location by using a turbine.

Question 38. The best answer is J because it provides the most effective introduction to the paragraph. "Whatever the job, safety is the first priority" correctly introduces the main topic of the paragraph: safety.

The best answer is NOT:

F because it provides a detail (the length of the blades) that is not clearly connected to the main topic of the paragraph: safety.

G because it provides a detail (the rise in the number of turbine-related jobs) that is not clearly connected to the main topic of the paragraph: safety.

H because it provides a detail (the number of parts) that is not clearly connected to the main topic of the paragraph: safety.

Question 39. The best answer is B because it correctly punctuates two independent clauses with a comma and the word *and*.

The best answer is NOT:

A because it incorrectly uses a semicolon to separate an independent clause and a dependent clause.

C because it incorrectly uses a comma to join two independent clauses, which creates a run-on sentence.

D because it fails to provide any punctuation between two independent clauses.

ENGLISH • PRACTICE TEST 5 • EXPLANATORY ANSWERS

Question 40. The best answer is J because it uses the most logical subordinate conjunction for the context. The word *If* correctly introduces a conditional clause that explains when technicians stay on the ground.

The best answer is NOT:

F because it provides an imprecise word choice; the word *Whether* incorrectly indicates that the sentence will present two options, which it does not do.

G because it provides an imprecise word choice; the phrase "So that" illogically suggests the intention of creating lightning.

H because it provides an imprecise word choice; the word *Unless* illogically suggests that the technicians do not stay on the ground when there's lightning, which contradicts the idea that the technicians take safety precautions.

Question 41. The best answer is C because it ensures appropriate and consistent punctuation (commas) before and after the nonessential element ("along with rigorous procedures and training").

The best answer is NOT:

A because it uses punctuation (an em dash) that is inconsistent with the punctuation used later in the sentence (a comma after the word *training*) to set off the nonessential element.

B because it substitutes punctuation (a semicolon) that is inconsistent with the punctuation used later in the sentence (a comma after the word *training*) to set off the nonessential element.

D because it lacks appropriate punctuation after the word *these* to correctly set off the nonessential element.

Question 42. The best answer is F because it ensures correct subject-verb agreement. The subject of the sentence is the plural word *Precautions*. The plural verb form *make* agrees with the plural subject *Precautions*.

The best answer is NOT:

G because it lacks subject-verb agreement; the singular verb form *is making* does not agree with the plural subject *Precautions*.

H because it lacks subject-verb agreement; the singular verb form *has made* does not agree with the plural subject *Precautions*.

J because it lacks subject-verb agreement; the singular verb form *makes* does not agree with the plural subject *Precautions*.

ENGLISH • PRACTICE TEST 5 • EXPLANATORY ANSWERS

Question 43. The best answer is D because it corrects the introduction of an error in parallelism regarding the noun phrases. The noun phrase "plenty of climbing practice" correctly parallels the structure of the other noun phrases in the sentence ("fresh air," "great vistas," and "ample time off").

The best answer is NOT:

A because it disrupts the parallel structure by interrupting the series of noun phrases with the infinitive phrase "to practice climbing daily."

B because it disrupts the parallel structure by interrupting the series of noun phrases with the independent clause "they practice climbing regularly."

C because it disrupts the parallel structure by interrupting the series of noun phrases with the conditional phrase "while often practicing climbing."

Question 44. The best answer is H because it best expresses the idea specified in the stem that "rock climbers in particular may find being a rope technician an appealing occupation." The question "what more could a climber want?" suggests that the elements identified earlier in the sentence would appeal to rock climbers; rock climbers could want nothing more.

The best answer is NOT:

F because it is an ineffective choice based on the goal specified in the stem; it poses a question about the job of a rope technician in general rather than expressing the idea specified in the stem.

G because it is an ineffective choice based on the goal specified in the stem; it poses a question about rock climbers in general rather than expressing the idea specified in the stem.

J because it is an ineffective choice based on the goal specified in the stem; it poses a question directly to the reader (who may or may not be a rock climber) rather than expressing the idea specified in the stem.

Question 45. The best answer is A because the statement "Enter rock climbers" introduces rock climbers, the main subject of the essay. Point A correctly places this sentence where it would introduce rock climbers prior to any other reference to rock climbers in the essay.

The best answer is NOT:

B because it would interrupt the paragraph by reintroducing rock climbers. At this point in the essay, it is already clear that rope technicians are often rock climbers.

C because it would interrupt the paragraph by reintroducing rock climbers. At this point in the essay, it is already clear that rope technicians are often rock climbers.

D because it would interrupt the paragraph by reintroducing rock climbers. At this point in the essay, it is already clear that rope technicians are often rock climbers.

ENGLISH • PRACTICE TEST 5 • EXPLANATORY ANSWERS

Question 46. The best answer is J because it ensures correct subject-verb agreement. The singular verb form *blends* agrees with the singular subject *Scene at the Signing of the Constitution of the United States* (the title of the painting).

The best answer is NOT:

F because it lacks subject-verb agreement; the plural verb form *blend* does not agree with the singular subject.

G because it lacks subject-verb agreement; the plural verb form *have blended* does not agree with the singular subject.

H because it lacks subject-verb agreement; the plural verb form *are blending* does not agree with the singular subject.

Question 47. The best answer is C because it provides the clearest and most specific information asked for in the stem by indicating where the painting is on display (Washington, DC).

The best answer is NOT:

A because it fails to indicate what the stem asks for; it gives the location of the event characterized in the painting rather than where the painting is on display.

B because it fails to indicate what the stem asks for; it mentions the experience of those who see the painting on display but gives no indication of the location.

D because it fails to indicate what the stem asks for; it mentions that the painting has been on display but gives no indication of the location.

Question 48. The best answer is H because it eliminates the unnecessary punctuation between the verb and the preposition.

The best answer is NOT:

F because it provides unnecessary punctuation; the em dash after the word *presided* creates an unclear sentence with an illogical interruption of the phrase "presided over."

G because it introduces unnecessary punctuation; the comma after the word *presided* creates an unclear sentence with an illogical interruption of the phrase "presided over."

J because it introduces unnecessary punctuation; the semicolon after the word *presided* creates an unclear sentence with an illogical interruption of the phrase "presided over." In addition, the phrase following the semicolon forms an incomplete statement.

ENGLISH • PRACTICE TEST 5 • EXPLANATORY ANSWERS

Question 49. The best answer is D because it eliminates redundancy by providing the most precise and concise wording. In addition, it maintains a tone that is consistent with the rest of the essay.

The best answer is NOT:

A because it contains an internal redundancy; the phrase "final role" and the word *ending* mean the same thing.

B because it contains an internal redundancy; the word *ended* and the phrase "in the conclusion of" mean the same thing.

C because it provides a phrase that is imprecise in meaning and creates a tone that is too informal for the essay.

Question 50. The best answer is J because it eliminates redundancy by providing the most precise and concise wording.

The best answer is NOT:

F because it contains an internal redundancy; the word *prior* and the phrase "in advance of" mean the same thing.

G because it contains an internal redundancy; the word *preparation* and the phrase "leading up to" mean the same thing.

H because it contains an internal redundancy; the words *advance* and *preceding* mean the same thing.

Question 51. The best answer is A because it prevents the introduction of an error in subordination in the sentence structure. The phrase "into which" most clearly and correctly establishes that the quills would have been dipped into the inkwells.

The best answer is NOT:

B because it introduces an error in subordination; it inaccurately reads as though the inkwells are being dipped into something rather than the quills being dipped into the inkwells.

C because it introduces an error in subordination; it creates a sentence with unclear meaning in terms of the relationship between or actions with the inkwells and quills.

D because it introduces an error in subordination; it creates a sentence with unclear meaning in terms of the relationship between or actions with the inkwells and quills.

ENGLISH • PRACTICE TEST 5 • EXPLANATORY ANSWERS

Question 52. The best answer is F because it prevents the introduction of an error in subordination in sentence structure. The sentence clearly and correctly establishes that Christy was "noting color, texture, design" while scouring countless drawings.

The best answer is NOT:

G because it introduces an error in subordination; it creates a sentence with unclear meaning in terms of what was noted and by whom.

H because it introduces an error in subordination; it creates a sentence with unclear meaning in terms of what was noted.

J because it introduces an error in subordination; it creates a sentence with unclear meaning in terms of the nature of the drawings Christy scoured.

Question 53. The best answer is D because it corrects the introduction of a rhetorically ineffective fragment. The phrase "He hunted" provides both the subject and verb for the sentence.

The best answer is NOT:

A because it creates a rhetorically ineffective sentence fragment.

B because it introduces a rhetorically ineffective sentence fragment.

C because it introduces a rhetorically ineffective sentence fragment.

Question 54. The best answer is G because it is the most effective placement of the sentence in terms of logic and cohesion. Sentence 2 informs the reader about Christy's trip "to Philadelphia to study how the light falls through the windows." The added sentence provides more information about the reason for the trip, logically following Sentence 2. Sentences 3 and 4 should follow the added sentence because Sentences 3 and 4 focus on more specific aspects of Christy's preparations for creating the painting.

The best answer is NOT:

F because it is an illogical placement of the sentence within the paragraph. The added sentence expands on why and when Christy traveled to Philadelphia, so it would be illogical to place it after Sentence 1, which gives information about where and when the painting was installed and precedes any reference to Christy's trip to Philadelphia. The references to "He" and "his trip" in the added sentence would have no clear meaning.

H because it is an illogical placement of the sentence within the paragraph. The added sentence expands on why and when Christy traveled to Philadelphia, so it would be illogical to place it after Sentence 3, which focuses more specifically on the inkwells and quills.

J because it is an illogical placement of the sentence within the paragraph. The added sentence expands on why and when Christy traveled to Philadelphia, so it would be illogical to place it after Sentence 4, which focuses more specifically on Christy's research involving drawings of period furniture and fabrics.

ENGLISH • PRACTICE TEST 5 • EXPLANATORY ANSWERS

Question 55. The best answer is B because it correctly eliminates the punctuation separating the word *boat* from the description that tells us about that boat (one that "experts now agree could not have been the vessel that carried the revolutionary leader across the river").

The best answer is NOT:

A because it provides unnecessary punctuation; it incorrectly provides a period separating the word *boat* from the description that tells us about that boat and creates a rhetorically ineffective fragment starting with the word *Experts*.

C because it introduces unnecessary punctuation; it incorrectly provides a semicolon separating the word *boat* from the description that tells us about that boat. In addition, it incorrectly creates a fragment following the semicolon.

D because it introduces unnecessary punctuation; it incorrectly provides a comma separating the word *boat* from the description that tells us about that boat.

Question 56. The best answer is H because it correctly eliminates unnecessary punctuation in the phrase "another painting of the signing."

The best answer is NOT:

F because it provides unnecessary punctuation; the comma after the word *another* incorrectly sets off the phrase "painting of the signing of the US Constitution" as a nonessential element.

G because it provides unnecessary punctuation; the comma after the word *signing* incorrectly sets off the phrase "of the US Constitution" as a nonessential element.

J because it provides unnecessary punctuation; the comma after the word *painting* incorrectly sets off the phrase "of the signing of the US Constitution" as a nonessential element.

Question 57. The best answer is B because it best expresses the idea specified in the stem by supporting the claim about the grandeur of the moment and emphasizing that Christy gave Washington a special status. The phrase "a hero among heroes" emphasizes the grandeur by characterizing all the signers as heroic and singling out Washington's special status as the most heroic of the group.

The best answer is NOT:

A because it fails to express the idea specified in the stem; it references the fame of Christy's painting but says nothing about Washington's special status.

C because it fails to express the idea specified in the stem; it mentions that Christy used visual techniques to single Washington out, but it does nothing to support the claim about the grandeur of the moment.

D because it fails to express the idea specified in the stem; it mentions that Christy did single Washington out, but does nothing to support the claim about the grandeur of the moment.

ENGLISH • PRACTICE TEST 5 • EXPLANATORY ANSWERS

Question 58. The best answer is G because it eliminates an error in subordination in the sentence structure. The correct sentence structure makes clear that Franklin and Madison are examples of the many luminaries depicted in the painting.

The best answer is NOT:

F because it contains an error in subordination; the faulty sentence structure makes it unclear whether Franklin and Madison are in the painting or are absent but are being compared to the figures who are in the painting.

H because it introduces an error in subordination; the faulty sentence structure illogically suggests that only Franklin and Madison are being referred to by the phrase "many of the assembled men."

J because it introduces an error in subordination; the faulty sentence structure illogically suggests that only Franklin and Madison are being referred to by the phrase "many of the assembled men."

Question 59. The best answer is A because it creates the most logical ordering of paragraphs within the essay. Paragraph 2 describes the measures Christy took to prepare for the work on his famous painting. Paragraph 3 then logically begins with the phrase "Such measures may seem standard," which directly refers to the measures described in Paragraph 2.

The best answer is NOT:

B because it creates an illogical ordering of the paragraphs within the essay; Paragraph 3 begins with "Such measures may seem standard," which would make no sense as the first paragraph of the essay. The reader would not know to whom or what the essay is referring.

C because it creates an illogical ordering of the paragraphs within the essay; Paragraph 3 begins with "Such measures may seem standard," which has no clear connection to Paragraph 1. Paragraph 1 introduces the painting rather than the measures Christy took to produce it.

D because it creates an illogical ordering of the paragraphs within the essay; Paragraph 3 begins with "Such measures may seem standard," which has no clear connection to Paragraph 4. Rather, Paragraph 4 logically follows Paragraph 3 because Paragraph 3 refers to a painting that is not historically accurate, and Paragraph 4 begins with the statement "Christy's painting also plays with the truth."

ENGLISH • PRACTICE TEST 5 • EXPLANATORY ANSWERS

Question 60. The best answer is H because it offers a clear and convincing reason the essay does not accomplish the purpose identified in the stem. Rather than explaining how Christy's painting changes the direction of his career, the essay focuses on Christy's approach to creating *Scene at the Signing of the Constitution of the United States*.

The best answer is NOT:

F because it indicates that the essay has accomplished the primary purpose identified in the stem when it hasn't and gives an inaccurate description of the essay. The essay does not indicate that Christy's painting led a trend in historical art.

G because it indicates that the essay has accomplished the primary purpose identified in the stem when it hasn't and gives an inaccurate description of the essay. The essay does not discuss the impact of *Scene at the Signing of the Constitution of the United States* on Christy's career.

J because it fails to offer a clear and convincing reason the essay does not accomplish the purpose identified in the stem. The essay does not indicate or address Christy's subject matter throughout his career; it focuses on only one painting.

Question 61. The best answer is A because it best maintains the stylistic pattern established earlier in the sentence. The phrase "dizzying mazes of lines" contains a detailed image that most closely matches the pattern of detailed images created by the adjectives and nouns in the phrases "layers of petals, intricate spirals and rosettes, teardrops bending within circles."

The best answer is NOT:

B because it fails to maintain the stylistic pattern; the phrase "something with a dizzying effect" is too vague to match the level of detail established in the preceding phrases in the series.

C because it fails to maintain the stylistic pattern; the phrase "mazes that she creates" disrupts the pattern because it has significantly less detail and specificity and reintroduces the subject.

D because it fails to maintain the stylistic pattern; the phrase "so many lines" disrupts the pattern because it has significantly less detail and specificity than preceding phrases in the series.

ENGLISH • PRACTICE TEST 5 • EXPLANATORY ANSWERS

Question 62. The best answer is G because it correctly distinguishes between plurals and possessives. The term *centuries-old* is correctly written as a compound adjective (to convey that *paj ntaub* has been practiced for many centuries) rather than a possessive noun.

The best answer is NOT:

F because it inaccurately substitutes the singular possessive *century's* for the plural noun *centuries*. In addition, it substitutes the superlative *oldest* for the word *old* when there is no clear context to indicate a comparison with other forms of Hmong needlework.

H because it inaccurately substitutes the plural possessive *centuries'* for the plural noun *centuries*.

J because it inaccurately substitutes the singular possessive *century's* for the plural noun *centuries*.

Question 63. The best answer is D because it deletes irrelevant information. The first paragraph is mainly about Pang Xiong as a master of *paj ntaub*, but the sentence in question describes recent trends in *paj ntaub* in general. Details about recent trends in *paj ntaub* are irrelevant at this point in the essay.

The best answer is NOT:

A because it retains irrelevant information and inaccurately describes the relationship between the sentence in question and the surrounding text. The sentence in question offers no connection to Pang Xiong's embroidery style.

B because it retains irrelevant information and inaccurately describes the relationship between the sentence in question and the surrounding text. Pang Xiong's work with *paj ntaub* is the main subject of the essay. The sentence in question offers no connection to Pang Xiong, so its reference to recent trends fails to place the subject of the essay in a modern context.

C because it offers an incorrect reason to delete information and inaccurately describes the relationship between the sentence in question and the surrounding text. The paragraph focuses on Pang Xiong as a master of a single style of Hmong needlework: *paj ntaub*. The paragraph does not describe the various styles of ancient Hmong needlework arts.

Question 64. The best answer is G because it eliminates an error in coordination in sentence structure. The participial phrase "living in northern Laos" modifies the word *woman* and accurately explains that Pang Xiong lived in northern Laos when she was a young woman.

The best answer is NOT:

F because it creates an error in coordination; the comma after the word *woman* separates two coordinate elements, creating an ungrammatical sentence that is unclear in terms of the relationship between the details about when Pang Xiong was a young woman and when she lived in northern Laos.

H because it introduces an error in coordination; it creates an ungrammatical shift in verb tense that makes the meaning of the sentence unclear.

J because it introduces an error in coordination; it creates an ungrammatical sentence that is unclear in terms of the relationship between the detail about living in northern Laos and how long Pang Xiong has been creating stitched textiles.

Question 65. The best answer is C because it corrects the introduction of a misplaced modifier. The parenthetical phrase offers examples of types of clothing, so it would most logically be placed after the word *clothing* to modify it and offer clarification about how flower cloth is "worn as clothing."

The best answer is NOT:

A because it creates a misplaced modifier; the placement of the parenthetical phrase after the term "flower cloth" suggests that flower cloth is defined by the phrase "commonly as a shirt, dress, coat, or collar," which is inaccurate based on the information given in the essay.

B because it introduces a misplaced modifier; the placement of the parenthetical phrase after the word *made* suggests that the parenthetical phrase explains or defines how flower cloth is made, which it does not.

D because it introduces a misplaced modifier; the placement of the parenthetical phrase after the word *needlework* suggests that the parenthetical phrase explains or defines something about needlework, which it does not.

ENGLISH • PRACTICE TEST 5 • EXPLANATORY ANSWERS

Question 66. The best answer is F because it ensures subject-verb agreement; the singular verb form *is designed* agrees with the singular subject *Flower cloth.*

The best answer is NOT:

G because it lacks subject-verb agreement; the plural verb form *have been designed* does not agree with the singular subject *Flower cloth.*

H because it lacks subject-verb agreement; the plural verb form *are designed* does not agree with the singular subject *Flower cloth.*

J because it lacks subject-verb agreement; the plural verb form *design* does not agree with the singular subject *Flower cloth.*

Question 67. The best answer is D because it best expresses the idea specified in the stem by building on the information provided earlier in the sentence about a common theme in *paj ntaub* patterns and images. The sentence refers to animals, which leads to a common theme of celebrating the natural world.

The best answer is NOT:

A because it fails to express the idea specified in the stem; the idea of versatile patterns is too vague and broad to build on the theme of animals or the natural word.

B because it fails to express the idea specified in the stem; the detail about master artists creating *paj ntaub* clothing for special occasions has no clear connection to the common animal patterns referred to earlier in the sentence.

C because it fails to express the idea specified in the stem; the idea that *paj ntaub* patterns are colorful has no clear connection to the common animal patterns referred to earlier in the sentence.

Question 68. The best answer is H because it correctly separates two coordinate adjectives (*tiny* and *tight*) with a comma while omitting unnecessary punctuation after the words *tight* (between the adjective and the noun) and *stitches* (clearly indicating that the artist makes use of two key features: "tiny, tight stitches" and "several complex techniques").

The best answer is NOT:

F because it contains unnecessary punctuation; the comma after the word *stitches* inappropriately separates the two features the artist makes use of: "tiny, tight stitches" and "several complex techniques."

G because it contains unnecessary punctuation; it inaccurately separates the adjective *tight* from the noun it needs to modify: *stitches.*

J because it both fails to include necessary punctuation and contains unnecessary punctuation; it fails to separate the two coordinate adjectives (*tight* and *tiny*) with a comma, and it places a comma after the word *stitches*, which inappropriately separates the two features the artist makes use of: "tiny, tight stitches" and "several complex techniques."

Question 69. The best answer is A because it prevents the introduction of an error in coordination and subordination in the sentence structure. The preposition *in* is needed before the relative pronoun *which* to indicate that what follows in the sentence describes "reverse appliqué."

The best answer is NOT:

B because it introduces an error in subordination; it creates an ungrammatical sentence with an unclear meaning in terms of the relationship between the term "reverse appliqué" and the information that follows.

C because it introduces an error in coordination; it creates both a run-on sentence and an unclear statement in terms of the relationship between the term "reverse appliqué" and the information about the shapes being cut out.

D because it introduces an error in coordination; the comma after the word *appliqué* inappropriately creates two complete statements joined by a comma. This introduces an ungrammatical and unclear statement in terms of the relationship between the term "reverse appliqué" and the information about the shapes being cut out.

Question 70. The best answer is J because it eliminates an error in parallelism in the sentence structure. It provides the appropriate passive voice form *added* to parallel the passive voice form *are cut*, which is used earlier in the sentence.

The best answer is NOT:

F because it contains an error in parallelism; it incorrectly uses the present participle *adding* rather than the passive voice form *added.*

G because it introduces an error in parallelism; it incorrectly uses the phrase "as an addition" rather than the passive voice form *added.*

H because it introduces an error in parallelism; it incorrectly uses the phrase "to add them" rather than the passive voice form *added.*

Question 71. The best answer is B because it corrects the use of a vague pronoun. The phrase "the surface of the fabric" clearly identifies where the stitches are layered: on the fabric.

The best answer is NOT:

A because it uses a vague pronoun; the possessive pronoun *its* has no clear antecedent, making it unclear which object's surface is being referred to.

C because it introduces a vague pronoun; the pronoun *it* has no clear antecedent, making it unclear which object's surface is being referred to.

D because it introduces a vague pronoun; the pronoun *their* has no clear antecedent, making it unclear which object's surface is being referred to.

ENGLISH • PRACTICE TEST 5 • EXPLANATORY ANSWERS

Question 72. The best answer is F because it correctly identifies that the writer should make the revision and accurately states the rhetorical impact of doing so. The adjective *regular* is vague; the more specific adjective *mass-produced* creates a clearer contrast between the homogeneous styles of clothing that are popular today and handcrafted *paj ntaub*.

The best answer is NOT:

G because it inaccurately states the rhetorical impact of making the revision. Although the adjective *mass-produced* describes the clothing that Pang Xiong is not fond of, it does nothing to indicate how or where Pang Xiong wants her work sold.

H because it incorrectly indicates that the writer should not make the revision. In addition, it inaccurately states the rhetorical impact of the original word. The word *regular* applies to clothing most people wear today; it does not refer to *paj ntaub* clothing at all.

J because it incorrectly indicates that the writer should not make the revision. In addition, it inaccurately states the rhetorical impact of the original word. The adjective *mass-produced* is more specific than the vague adjective *regular*.

Question 73. The best answer is D because it accurately eliminates the use of unnecessary transition words. No transition word or phrase is needed to clarify the connection between the ideas in this sentence and the preceding one.

The best answer is NOT:

A because it provides a transition word that is illogical for the context; the word *However* suggests that this sentence will present a contrast to what came before, which is not the case here.

B because it introduces a transition word that is illogical for the context; the transition phrase "For example" suggests that the sentence will provide an example, which is not the case here.

C because it introduces a transition word that is illogical for the context; the word *Besides* fails to provide a logical transition from the discussion of Pang Xiong's clothing when she was young to the discussion of Pang Xiong's clothing today and how she would like to inspire others. It is unclear what the word *Besides* would mean in this context.

ENGLISH • PRACTICE TEST 5 • EXPLANATORY ANSWERS

Question 74. The best answer is F because it provides the clearest and most precise wording based on the stem. The phrase "to do so" clearly refers to wearing flower cloth, which is precisely what Pang Xiong wants to inspire others to do. This wording best indicates that Pang Xiong wants others to share her appreciation of *paj ntaub* by wearing it.

The best answer is NOT:

G because it is unnecessarily wordy and imprecise. The phrase "attempt that approach" is less precise because it does not clearly refer to the specific action of wearing flower cloth.

H because it does not offer precise wording to indicate that Pang Xiong wants others to share her appreciation of *paj ntaub* by wearing it. It vaguely states that Pang Xiong wants to inspire people she knows, but it doesn't indicate what she wants to inspire them to do.

J because it does not offer precise wording to indicate that Pang Xiong wants others to share her appreciation of *paj ntaub* by wearing it. Instead, it vaguely indicates that she wants to inspire others in general.

Question 75. The best answer is C because it is the most effective sentence to connect the ideas in the paragraph based on the criteria in the stem. By explaining that Pang Xiong has recently worked with nine young Hmong women in a formal apprenticeship, the sentence builds on the ideas mentioned earlier in the paragraph: that Pang Xiong wants to inspire an appreciation of *paj ntaub* in others and teaches the skill. The sentence also connects to the final sentence of the essay because it refers to nine young Hmong apprentices who are examples of the "new generation" mentioned in the final sentence.

The best answer is NOT:

A because it offers little connection to ideas presented earlier in the paragraph and fails to connect to the final sentence in the essay; this sentence mentions Pang Xiong's appreciation of others wearing traditional clothing in general (not only *paj ntaub*) but offers no connection to her "showing a new generation the joys of *paj ntaub*."

B because it builds on one idea presented earlier in the paragraph (teaching) but fails to connect to the final sentence in the essay; this sentence focuses on Hmong adults who are Pang Xiong's age rather than on the "new generation" referred to in the final sentence.

D because it offers no connection to the ideas presented earlier in the paragraph or to the final sentence of the essay; this sentence refers to Pang Xiong's family's story, but her family is not discussed elsewhere in the paragraph.

MATHEMATICS • PRACTICE TEST 5 • EXPLANATORY ANSWERS

Question 1. The correct answer is B. The probability of selecting either a red marble or a blue marble is calculated by adding the probability of selecting a red marble and the probability of selecting a blue marble: $\frac{5}{19}+\frac{4}{19}=\frac{9}{19}$. If you chose **A**, you may have thought the probability is the positive difference between the probability of selecting a red marble and the probability of selecting a blue marble. If you chose **C**, you may have added the values in the numerator and the values in the denominator. If you chose **D**, you may have multiplied the numerators and added the denominators. If you chose **E**, you may have multiplied the probabilities.

Question 2. The correct answer is G. The graph shows that, of the students who were present on Thursday, 8 were in Group 1, 12 were in Group 2, 6 were in Group 3, 2 were in Group 4, and 0 were in Group 5. The probability that a student from Group 4 is selected at random from the class on Thursday can be calculated by taking the number of students present on Thursday who were in Group 4 and dividing it by the total number of students present on Thursday in the class: $\frac{2}{8+12+6+2+0}=\frac{2}{28}=\frac{1}{14}$. If you chose **F**, you may have incorrectly identified the number of students present on Thursday who were in Group 4 as 1 instead of 2. If you chose **H**, you may have found the probability of selecting Group 4 from the 5 groups. If you chose **J**, you may have found the probability of selecting Group 4 from the 4 nonempty groups. If you chose **K**, you may have found the probability of selecting 1 student from Group 4.

Question 3. The correct answer is A. To solve for the value of j given a value of k, substitute the value of k into the equation to get $40=\frac{7}{5}j+54$; subtract 54 from both sides of the equation, $40-54=\frac{7}{5}j+54-54$, to get $-14=\frac{7}{5}j$; and multiply both sides of the equation by $\frac{5}{7}$, $\left(\frac{5}{7}\right)(-14)=\left(\frac{5}{7}\right)\left(\frac{7}{5}\right)j$, to get $-10=j$. If you chose **B**, you may have multiplied by $\frac{7}{5}$ instead of its reciprocal: $\left(\frac{7}{5}\right)(-14)=\frac{-98}{5}$. If you chose **C**, you may have multiplied 40 by $\frac{5}{7}$ and then subtracted from 54: $54-40\left(\frac{5}{7}\right)=\frac{178}{7}$. If you chose **D**, you may have forgotten the 54 and solved $40=\frac{7}{5}j$: $40\left(\frac{5}{7}\right)=\frac{200}{7}$. If you chose **E**, you may have forgotten the 54 and attempted to solve $40=\frac{7}{5}j$ but multiplied by $\frac{7}{5}$ instead of its reciprocal: $40\left(\frac{7}{5}\right)=56$.

Question 4. The correct answer is H. First, substitute the value of x into the expression: $|3-8|$. Next, subtract 8 from 3: $|3-8|=|-5|$. Finally, because the absolute value of a number is its distance from 0, and because distance is positive, the absolute value of -5 is 5. If you chose **F**, you may have thought the absolute value bars change the – sign to +, calculated 3 + 8, and then changed the sign of 11 to -11. If you chose **G**, you may have subtracted 8 from 3 but neglected to calculate the absolute value. If you chose **J**, you may have simply chosen the value of x. If you chose **K**, you may have thought the absolute value bars change the – sign to + and calculated 3 + 8.

Question 5. The correct answer is A. The change in temperature can be determined by subtracting the starting temperature from the ending temperature: $-16-24=-40$. If you chose **B**, you may have added instead of subtracting, $-16+24$, and made the result negative

MATHEMATICS • PRACTICE TEST 5 • EXPLANATORY ANSWERS

because the temperature dropped. If you chose **D**, you may have added instead of subtracting: $-16+24$. If you chose **E**, you may have subtracted in the wrong order or considered the starting temperature to be −16°F and the ending temperature to be 24°F: $24-(-16)=40$.

Question 6. The correct answer is G. The amount of money Ming paid for the car after the \$1,000 down payment and 28 payments of \$200 each is $\$1,000+28(\$200)=\$6,600$. Because the car had a purchase price of \$5,400, the total she paid was \$1,200 more than the purchase price: $\$6,600-\$5,400=\$1,200$. If you chose **F**, you may have subtracted the purchase price of the car from only the total Ming paid in the 28 payments: $28(\$200)-\$5,400=\$200$. If you chose **H**, you may have subtracted the down payment from the purchase price of the car: $\$5,400-\$1,000=\$4,400$. If you chose **J**, you may have calculated the total Ming paid in the 28 payments: $28(\$200)=\$5,600$. If you chose **K**, you may calculated the total Ming paid for the car and neglected to calculate how much more that was than the purchase price: $\$1,000+28(\$200)=\$6,600$.

Question 7. The correct answer is E. When a regular hexagon is inscribed in a circle, the radius of the circle is the same value as each side length of the hexagon because the diagonals of a hexagon form 6 congruent equilateral triangles. Because all the side lengths of a regular hexagon are the same and there are 6 sides in a hexagon, multiply the side length by 6 to find the perimeter: $4(6)=24$. If you chose **A**, you may have calculated the circumference of the circle: $2(4)\pi=8\pi$. If you chose **B**, you may have thought that diagonals of the hexagon form 6 congruent 30-60-90 triangles and used $\frac{4\sqrt{3}}{2}$ as a side length: $\left(\frac{4\sqrt{3}}{2}\right)(6)=12\sqrt{3}$. If you chose **C**, you may have thought that the side lengths of the hexagon were each 1 less than the radius of the circle: $(4-1)(6)=18$. If you chose **D**, you may have correctly determined that the side lengths were 4 but multiplied by 5 sides instead of 6: $4(5)=20$.

Question 8. The correct answer is J. The L-shaped floor plan is a composite shape. Find the missing horizontal length by subtracting the given horizontal lengths: 50 – 22 = 28. Find the missing vertical length by subtracting the given vertical lengths: 40 – 22 = 18. One possible method to find the area of the composite shape is to find the area that remains when a 28-by-18 rectangle is subtracted from a 50-by-40 rectangle: $(50)(40)-(28)(18)=2,000-504=1,496$. If you chose **F**, you may have thought both missing lengths were 28 and found the perimeter of the floor plan instead of the area: $22+28+28+22+50+40=190$. If you chose **G**, you may have calculated the area of the 28-by-18 rectangle that is not included in the floor plan: $28\times18=504$. If you chose **H**, you may have found a missing length to be 28 and thought the floor plan could be decomposed into two rectangles that are 22 by 28: $2(22)(28)=1,232$. If you chose **K**, you may have calculated the sum of the area of a 22-by-50 rectangle and a 22-by-40 rectangle, which represents an overlap: $22(50)+22(40)=1,980$.

Question 9. The correct answer is C. To classify the type of quadrilateral determined by the vertices, calculate the slopes of the sides to figure out which, if any, sides are parallel. The slope of $\overline{AB}$ is $\frac{4-0}{0-(-2)}=\frac{4}{2}=2$. The slope of $\overline{BC}$ is $\frac{5-4}{5-0}=\frac{1}{5}$. The slope of $\overline{CD}$ is $\frac{2-5}{8-5}=\frac{-3}{3}=-1$.

MATHEMATICS • PRACTICE TEST 5 • EXPLANATORY ANSWERS

The slope of $\overline{DA}$ is $\frac{0-2}{-2-8}=\frac{-2}{-10}=\frac{1}{5}$. There are two sides with a slope of $\frac{1}{5}$, $\overline{BC}$ and $\overline{DA}$. Because $\overline{BC}$ and $\overline{DA}$ have the same slope, they are parallel. The other sides are not parallel to each other. A trapezoid has exactly one pair of parallel sides. Therefore, Quadrilateral *ABCD* is a trapezoid. If you chose **A**, you may have thought the diagonals were perpendicular. If you chose **B**, **D**, or **E**, which are all parallelograms, you may have thought one pair of parallel sides was enough, or you may have miscalculated the slopes of the sides.

Question 10. The correct answer is H. Given that $f(x)=3x+7$ and $g(x)=\frac{x^2}{2}$, $f(g(x))=3\left(\frac{x^2}{2}\right)+7$. For $x=4$, $f(g(4))=3\left(\frac{4^2}{2}\right)+7=3\left(\frac{16}{2}\right)+7=3(8)+7=24+7=31$. If you chose **F**, you may have calculated $g(4)$: $g(4)=\frac{4^2}{2}=8$. If you chose **G**, you may have calculated $f(4)$: $f(4)=3(4)+7=19$. If you chose **J**, you may have calculated the product of $g(4)$ and $f(4)$: $\left(\frac{4^2}{2}\right)(3(4)+7)=\left(\frac{16}{2}\right)(12+7)=(8)(19)=152$. If you chose **K**, you may have calculated $g(f(4))$: $g(f(4))=\frac{(3(4)+7)^2}{2}=\frac{(12+7)^2}{2}=\frac{(19)^2}{2}=\frac{361}{2}=180.5$.

Question 11. The correct answer is E. Julie's profit is the product of the number of hot dogs she sells and the price she sells them for minus the cost of her supplies: $2h-200$. In order for her to make a profit, that value must be greater than 0: $2h-200>0$. If you chose **A**, you selected the inequality that models making a profit if each hot dog sells for \$1 each. If you chose **B**, you selected the inequality that models making no profit if each hot dog sells for \$1 each. If you chose **C**, you may have thought that the purchase of supplies increased the profit and selected the inequality that models a profit if each hot dog sells for \$1 each. If you chose **D**, you selected the inequality that models the number of hot dogs Julie can sell that keeps her from making a profit.

Question 12. The correct answer is G. To determine the slope of the line $3x+8y=5$, rewrite the equation of the line to its slope-intercept form, $y=mx+b$, where m is the slope of the line and b is the y-intercept. Subtract $3x$ from both sides of the equation to get $8y=-3x+5$, and then divide both sides of the equation by 8 to get $y=-\frac{3}{8}x+\frac{5}{8}$. Therefore, the slope is $-\frac{3}{8}$. If you chose **F**, you may have thought the slope was the coefficient of the x term when the equation was in this form: $8y=-3x+5$. If you chose **H**, you may have thought the slope was the coefficient of the x term when you divided by 5: $3x+8y=5$, $\frac{3}{5}x+\frac{8}{5}y=\frac{5}{5}$. If you chose **J**, you may have thought the slope was the coefficient of the x term in the given form of the equation: $3x+8y=5$. If you chose **K**, you may have thought the slope was the constant in the given form of the equation: $3x+8y=5$.

Question 13. The correct answer is A. The solution to the system of equations is the (x, y) pair that satisfies both equations in the system. One way to solve this system is by substitution. Begin by solving one of the equations for one of its variables. Then, substitute the solution from this first step into the other equation. If you solve the first equation

MATHEMATICS • PRACTICE TEST 5 • EXPLANATORY ANSWERS

for x, you have $x+2y=2$, $x=2-2y$. Next, substitute this expression for x into the second equation to get $-2x+y=16 \Leftrightarrow -2(2-2y)+y=16$. Now, solve this new equation for y: $-2(2-2y)+y=16 \Leftrightarrow -4+4y+y=16 \Leftrightarrow -4+5y=16 \Leftrightarrow 5y=20 \Leftrightarrow y=4$. You can substitute this y-value into either equation to solve for the x value: $-2x+y=16 \Leftrightarrow -2x+4=16 \Leftrightarrow -2x=12 \Leftrightarrow x=-6$. Thus, the solution to the system is $(-6,4)$. If you chose **B**, you may have selected a value for x and used it to solve the first equation for y: $x=-1 \Rightarrow -1+2y=2 \Rightarrow 2y=3 \Rightarrow y=1.5$. If you chose **C**, you may have selected a value for x and used it to solve the first equation for y: $x=1 \Rightarrow 1+2y=2 \Rightarrow 2y=1 \Rightarrow y=0.5$. If you chose **D**, you may have selected a value for y and used it to solve the first equation for x: $y=1 \Rightarrow x+2(1)=2 \Rightarrow x=0$. If you chose **E**, you may have selected a value for y and used it to solve the first equation for x: $y=0 \Rightarrow x+2(0)=2 \Rightarrow x=2$.

Question 14. The correct answer is K. Convert the $2\frac{3}{4}$ inches on the map to the number of miles apart the towns are by multiplying $2\frac{3}{4}$ inches ($2\frac{3}{4}=\frac{11}{4}$) by 16 miles per $\frac{1}{4}$ of an inch. The inches cancel out, leaving the number of miles apart the towns are: $\frac{11}{4}\ \cancel{\text{in}} \times \dfrac{16 \text{ miles}}{\frac{1}{4}\ \cancel{\text{in}}} = 176$ miles. If you chose **F**, you may have calculated $\dfrac{\frac{11}{4}}{\frac{1}{4}} = 11$. If you chose **G**, you selected the number of miles that are represented by $\frac{1}{4}$ inch, not $2\frac{3}{4}$ inches. If you chose **H**, you may have calculated $\frac{11}{4}(16) = 44$. If you chose **J**, you may have calculated $\dfrac{16}{\frac{1}{4}} = 64$, which is how many miles are represented by 1 inch.

Question 15. The correct answer is E. To multiply a matrix by a scalar, you multiply each term in the matrix by the scalar: $4\begin{bmatrix}-1 & 2\\ 0 & -4\end{bmatrix}=\begin{bmatrix}4(-1) & 4(2)\\ 4(0) & 4(-4)\end{bmatrix}=\begin{bmatrix}-4 & 8\\ 0 & -16\end{bmatrix}$. If you chose **A**, you may have been thinking of matrix multiplication and multiplied each term in the matrix by the scalar and then added the terms of each column: $\begin{bmatrix}4(-1)+4(0) & 4(2)+4(-4)\end{bmatrix}=\begin{bmatrix}-4 & -8\end{bmatrix}$. If you chose **B**, you may have multiplied each term in the matrix by the scalar and then added the terms of each row: $\begin{bmatrix}4(-1)+4(2)\\ 4(0)+4(-4)\end{bmatrix}=\begin{bmatrix}4\\ -16\end{bmatrix}$. If you chose **C**, you may have added the scalar to each term in the matrix: $\begin{bmatrix}4+(-1) & 4+2\\ 4+0 & 4+(-4)\end{bmatrix}=\begin{bmatrix}3 & 6\\ 4 & 0\end{bmatrix}$. If you chose **D**, you may have divided each term in the matrix by the scalar: $\begin{bmatrix}\frac{-1}{4} & \frac{2}{4}\\ \frac{0}{4} & \frac{-4}{4}\end{bmatrix}=\begin{bmatrix}-\frac{1}{4} & \frac{1}{2}\\ 0 & -1\end{bmatrix}$.

Question 16. The correct answer is J. The tangent of an angle in a right triangle is equal to the ratio of the length of the leg opposite that angle to the length of the leg adjacent to that angle: $\tan A = \frac{BC}{AC} = \frac{15}{8}$. If you chose **F**, you might have found $\cos A$. If you chose **G**, you may have found $\cot A$. If you chose **H**, you may have found $\sin A$. If you chose **K**, you may have found the reciprocal of $\cos A$, $\sec A$.

MATHEMATICS • PRACTICE TEST 5 • EXPLANATORY ANSWERS

Question 17. The correct answer is D. Observe that 8 miles per hour is equal to $\frac{8 \text{ miles}}{60 \text{ minutes}} = \frac{2}{15}$ miles per minute. Because distance is equal to the product of rate and time, it will take12 minutes for Tina to run $\frac{2}{15}(12) = \frac{8}{5} = 1\frac{3}{5}$ miles. If you chose **A**, you may have divided the rate in minutes per mile by the time in minutes: $\frac{\left(\frac{60 \text{ minutes}}{8 \text{ miles}}\right)}{12 \text{ minutes}} = \left(\frac{60 \text{ minutes}}{8 \text{ miles}}\right)\left(\frac{1}{12 \text{ minutes}}\right) = \frac{3}{8}\left(\frac{1}{\text{mile}}\right)$. Notice that this is the reciprocal of the key. If you chose **B**, you may have divided the rate, in miles per hour, by the time, in minutes: $\frac{8}{12} = \frac{2}{3}$. If you chose **C**, you may have divided the time, in minutes, by the rate, in miles per hour: $\frac{12}{8} = \frac{3}{2}$.

Question 18. The correct answer is G. $f(-3) = -6(-3)^2 = -6(9) = -54$. If you chose **F**, you may have multiplied the 6 by -3 before squaring it: $-(6 \cdot -3)^2 = -324$. If you chose **H**, you may have squared 3 instead of -3: $-6\left(-(3)^2\right) = -6(-9) = 54$. If you chose **J**, you may have squared 6 instead of -3: $-6^2(-3) = 108$. If you chose **K**, you may have multiplied the -6 by -3 before squaring it: $(-6 \cdot -3)^2 = 324$.

Question 19. The correct answer is B. Because $\overleftrightarrow{BC}$ is perpendicular to both $\overleftrightarrow{AC}$ and $\overleftrightarrow{DE}$, $\overleftrightarrow{AC}$ is parallel to $\overleftrightarrow{DE}$. Because $\overleftrightarrow{AC}$ and $\overleftrightarrow{DE}$ are two parallel lines cut by transversal $\overleftrightarrow{BE}$, alternate interior angles are congruent. Thus, $m\angle CAE = 132°$. Angles $\angle CAE$ and $\angle BAC$ form a straight line; thus they are supplementary: $m\angle BAC = 180° - 132° = 48°$. Because $\angle BAC$ and $\angle ABC$ are the acute angles of right triangle ΔABC, they are complementary: $m\angle ABC = 90° - 48° = 42°$. If you chose **A**, you may have computed $90 - \frac{132}{2}$. If you chose **C**, you may have thought ΔABC was isosceles and computed $\frac{90}{2}$. If you chose **D**, you may have found $m\angle BAC$ instead of $m\angle ABC$. If you chose **E**, you may have computed $\frac{132}{2}$.

Question 20. The correct answer is F. Because the function value at 5 is 2, and the function value at 15 is 6, the rate of change of the function is $\frac{6-2}{15-5} = \frac{4}{10} = \frac{2}{5}$. Because the function is linear, you can use the point-slope formula $y - y_1 = m(x - x_1)$ where m is the rate of change, $x_1$is a specific input of the function, and y_1 is the respective output. Substituting $m = \frac{2}{5}$, $x_1 = 5$, and $y_1 = 2$ gives you the equation $y - 2 = \frac{2}{5}(x - 5) \rightarrow y = \frac{2}{5}x$. If you chose **B**, you may have switched the input and output values: $m = \frac{15-5}{6-2} = \frac{5}{2} \rightarrow y - 5 = \frac{5}{2}(x - 2) \rightarrow y = \frac{5}{2}x$. If you chose **C**, you may have selected an expression that was true for an input of 5 only: $n - 3 \rightarrow 5 - 3 = 2$. If you chose **D**, you may have selected the expression that was true for an input of 15 only: $n - 9 \rightarrow 15 - 9$. If you chose **E**, you may have selected an expression that was true for an input of 5 only: $\frac{5}{2}(n - 5) + 2 \rightarrow \frac{5}{2}(5 - 5) + 2 = 2$.

Question 21. The correct answer is C. The first table lists the temperatures at each hour between 8:00 a.m. and noon. The second table lists the temperatures at each hour between noon and 4:00 p.m. Because the temperature fell at a constant rate, it first fell below 49°F sometime between 2:00 p.m. and 3:00 pm.

Taking Additional Practice Tests

MATHEMATICS • PRACTICE TEST 5 • EXPLANATORY ANSWERS

Temperature rose $\frac{1}{2}$°F each hour		Temperature fell 1°F each hour	
Time	Temperature in °F	Time	Temperature in °F
8:00 a.m.	49°F	Noon	51°F
9:00 a.m.	$49\frac{1}{2}$°F	1:00 p.m.	50°F
10:00 a.m.	50°F	2:00 p.m.	49°F
11:00 a.m.	$50\frac{1}{2}$°F	3:00 p.m.	48°F
Noon	51°F	4:00 p.m.	47°F

If you chose **A**, you may have thought the temperature at noon was $49\frac{1}{2}$°F. If you chose **B**, you picked the option that would be true if the temperature had fallen at 2°F each hour. If you chose **D**, you did not consider non-integer degree values between 49°F and 48°F. If you chose **E**, you picked the option that would be true if the temperature had fallen at $\frac{1}{2}$°F each hour.

Question 22. The correct answer is K. The 4 unit exams and the final exam were worth a total of 600 points. The lowest number of points that earned a grade of B was 600(0.80) = 480 points. The lowest number of points that earned a grade of A was 600(0.90) = 540 points. Therefore, students with scores ranging from 480 points to 539 points earned a grade of B. On the 4 unit exams, Hugo earned a total of 82 + 88 + 91 + 83 = 344 points. Thus, his final exam score was between 480 – 344 = 136 points and 539 – 344 = 195 points. If you chose **F**, **G**, **H**, or **J**, you picked a score on the final exam that is in the range 136–195 and, thus, results in a grade of B.

Question 23. The correct answer is A. The base of each of the 10 bowling pins shown in the figure is represented by a circle. The area of a circle with radius r is πr^2. Therefore, when all of the pins are set up, the total area, in square inches, that is covered by the bases of the 10 pins is $10 \cdot \pi \left(\frac{2.25}{2}\right)^2 \approx 39.8$ or 40 square inches. If you chose **B**, you may have chosen the value closest to 10 times the circumference (πd) of a single bowling pin: $10 \cdot \pi(2.25) \approx 71$. If you chose **C**, you may have chosen the value closest to the sum of the area of 10 pins and 10 times the circumference of a single bowling pin: 40 + 71 = 111. If you chose **D**, you may have squared the number of pins and dropped the pi, $10^2 \cdot \left(\frac{2.25}{2}\right)^2 \approx 127$, which is closest to 125. If you chose **E**, you may have used the diameter instead of the radius: $10 \cdot \pi(2.25)^2 \approx 159$.

Question 24. The correct answer is G. In the figure, the bowling area and the pin deck are each in the shape of a rectangle. The area of a rectangle with length L and width W is LW. Therefore, the total area of the bowling lane is 65(3.5) = 227.5 square feet. Similarly, the area of the pin deck is 5(3.5) = 17.5 square feet. Therefore, the ratio of the total area of the bowling lane to the area of the pin deck is $\frac{227.5}{17.5} = \frac{13}{1} \Rightarrow 13:1$. If you chose **F**, you may have chosen the ratio of the area of the non-pin deck bowling lane to the area of the pin deck: $\frac{(65-5) \cdot 3.5}{5 \cdot 3.5} \Rightarrow \frac{60}{5} \Rightarrow 12:1$. If you chose **H**, you may have chosen the ratio of the total area of the bowling lane

MATHEMATICS • PRACTICE TEST 5 • EXPLANATORY ANSWERS

to the area of the non-pin deck bowling lane: $\frac{65 \cdot 3.5}{(60-5) \cdot 3.5} \Rightarrow \frac{65}{60} \Rightarrow$ 13:12. If you chose **J**, you may have chosen the ratio of the perimeter of the non-pin deck bowling lane to the perimeter of the pin deck: $\frac{2(65-5)+2(3.5)}{2(5)+2(3.5)} \Rightarrow \frac{127}{17} \Rightarrow$ 127:17. If you chose **K**, you may have chosen the ratio of the total perimeter of the bowling lane to the perimeter of the pin deck: $\frac{2(65)+2(3.5)}{2(5)+2(3.5)} \Rightarrow \frac{137}{17} \Rightarrow$ 137:17.

Question 25. The correct answer is D. Let x represent the score Halle needs to earn in her 3rd game. Then, to find this unknown score, solve the equation $\frac{148+176+x}{3} = 172$. First, add the numbers in the numerator of the fraction on the left side of the equation: $\frac{324+x}{3} = 172$. Next, multiply by 3 on both sides of the equation: $3\left(\frac{324+x}{3}\right) = 3(172) \Leftrightarrow 324 + x = 516$. Therefore, $x = 516 - 324 = 192$. So, Halle needs to earn 192 points in her 3rd game to have an average score of 172 points. If you chose **A**, you may have computed $\frac{148+176+172}{3} \approx 165$. If you chose **B**, you may have thought the unknown score was equal to the given average. If you chose **C**, you may have computed $2(172) - \frac{324}{2} = 182$. If you chose **E**, you picked the option that would earn Halle an average greater than 172, because $\frac{148+176+200}{3} \approx 175$.

Question 26. The correct answer is F. The area of a rectangle is equal to the product of its width and length: $A = WL$. You can call the unknown width x and the unknown length $3x$ because the length is 3 times the width. Then, $300 = x(3x)$. To solve for x, you divide both sides by 3 and then take the square root. 300 divided by 3 is 100. The positive square root of 100 is 10. So the width, x, is 10. If you chose **G**, you found the length instead of the width; you should have chosen the shorter of 10 and 30. If you chose **H**, you may have divided 300 by 3 to get 100 but then took half of 100 instead of taking the square root. If you chose **J**, you may have divided 300 by 3 and then stopped. If you chose **K**, you may have divided 300 by 3 to get 100, but then you took half of 100 to get 50 and then multiplied by 3 to get the length.

Question 27. The correct answer is C. Every parallelogram has 2 pairs of congruent sides. So if 1 of its sides measures 16, then another side must measure 16, and there must be 2 more sides of unknown length. Call that unknown length x. The perimeter is the sum of all the side lengths; we have $96 = 16 + 16 + x + x$, or $96 = 32 + 2x$. Subtract 32 and divide by 2, and you get $x = 32$. If you chose **A**, you may have solved $96 = 16 + 16 + 16 + x$, using 16 as 3 side lengths. If you chose **B**, you may have solved the equation $96 = 16 + 2(x + 16)$ for x. If you chose **D**, you may have solved the equation $96 = 16 + x + x$ for x.

Question 28. The correct answer is H. Each of two directions has three lanes. You can add the widths of the lanes, 12 + 6 + 8, and then multiply by 2 to account for both directions: 2(12 + 6 + 8) = 52. If you chose **F**, you may have forgotten to multiply by 2. If you chose **G**, you may have doubled the 12 but not the 6 or 8: (12 + 12 + 6 + 8).

Question 29. The correct answer is A. If there are 2,500 students and 4 out of every 10 students ride the bus, then the number of students who ride the bus, x, can be found by solving $\frac{4}{10} = \frac{x}{2{,}500}$. The number of students who ride the bus is 1,000. If 3 out of every 8 who ride the bus are freshman, then the number of students who are freshman and ride the bus, y, can be found by solving $\frac{3}{8} = \frac{y}{1{,}000}$. Alternatively, you can find $\frac{3}{8}$ of $\frac{4}{10}$ of 2,500 by multiplying $\frac{3}{8} \cdot \frac{4}{10} \cdot 2{,}500 = 375$.

Taking Additional Practice Tests

Question 30. The correct answer is H. Using the Pythagorean identity, $\sin^2\theta + \cos^2\theta = 1$, we have $\left(\frac{20}{29}\right)^2 + \cos^2\theta = 1$, which is equivalent to $\cos^2\theta = \frac{441}{841}$, which is equivalent to $\cos\theta = \pm\frac{21}{29}$. Because 90 degrees < $\cos\theta$ < 180 degrees, $\cos\theta$ must be negative. If you chose **F**, you may have found cosecant instead of cosine. If you chose **G**, you may have found tangent instead of cosine and forgot to consider the quadrant. If you chose **J**, you may have found secant instead of cosine. If you chose **K**, you may have found cosecant instead of cosine and changed the sign to negative.

Question 31. The correct answer is C. To find $f(t)=t$, solve the equation $t=\frac{2}{t+1}$ by multiplying both sides by $(t + 1)$. This gives you $t(t+1)=2 \rightarrow t^2+t-2=0 \rightarrow (t+2)(t-1)=0 \rightarrow t=-2$ or $t=1$. Because the function $f(t)=\frac{2}{t+1}$ is undefined only when both −2 and 1 are values for which $f(t)=t$. If you chose **A**, you may have found the value for which $f(x)$ is undefined. If you chose **B** or **D**, you may have factored incorrectly: $(t-2)(t+1)=0$. If you chose **E**, you may have incorrectly factored $t^2+t-2=0$ to be $(t-2)(t-1)=0$.

Question 32. The correct answer is J. To find the distance between the 2 radar stations, you have to find AB in the given figure. Using the Pythagorean Theorem, $BD^2+CD^2=BC^2$; thus, $BD^2+12{,}000^2=13{,}000^2 \rightarrow BD=5{,}000$. Alternatively, you could recognize that this triangle is similar to the triangle that represents the Pythagorean triple: 5-12-13. Because $BD=5{,}000$ and $AD=9{,}000$, $AB=5{,}000+9{,}000=14{,}000$. If you chose **F**, you may have found BD instead of AB. If you chose **G**, you may have thought BD = 13,000 – 12,000 and then added 1,000 + 9,000. If you chose **K**, you may have thought triangle ΔABC was isosceles.

Question 33. The correct answer is C. Because the airplane is flying due west and point A is due west of point D, the airplane is flying on a path parallel to $\overleftrightarrow{AD}$. In the standard (x,y) coordinate plane, both A and D are on the x-axis, so the airplane is flying on a line parallel to the x-axis. Because the airplane is 12,000 feet above D(9,000, 0), the airplane is currently at (9,000, 12,000). The line that is parallel to the x-axis and goes through (9,000, 12,000) is y = 12,000. If you chose **A**, you may have chosen the vertical line that goes through (9,000, 12,000) instead of the horizontal line. If you chose **D**, you may have used the straight-line distance the plane was from B instead of the distance the plane was from $\overleftrightarrow{AD}$. If you chose **E**, you may have used the straight-line distance the plane was from A instead of the distance the plane was from $\overleftrightarrow{AD}$.

Question 34. The correct answer is G. Because the airplane is currently directly above D and flying on a path parallel to $\overleftrightarrow{AD}$ to get to a point directly above A, it will travel this distance: AD = 9,000 feet. Because the airplane is traveling at a rate of 300 feet per second, the time it will take the airplane is $\frac{9{,}000 \text{ feet}}{300 \text{ feet/sec}}$ = 30 seconds. If you chose **F**, you may have confused Station B and Station A and divided 5,000 (the distance from D to B) by 300. If you chose **H**, you may have divided 12,000 by 300. If you chose **J**, you may have divided 13,000 by 300. If you chose **K**, you may have divided 15,000 by 300.

MATHEMATICS • PRACTICE TEST 5 • EXPLANATORY ANSWERS

Question 35. The correct answer is A. When the airplane is directly above point A, it forms the right triangle ΔABC shown in Figure 1. From question 32, you know that $AB = 14{,}000$. You also know that $m\angle A$ is 90°, and you can estimate that $m\angle B$ and $m\angle C$ are both between 40° and 50°. Figure 2 shows the new triangle at a certain point in time after the plane has flown due west. Notice that $\angle A$ in Figure 2 is larger than in Figure 1 and $\angle B$ and $\angle C$ are smaller than in Figure 1. You can estimate $m\angle A$ to be greater than 90° and both $m\angle B$ and $m\angle C$ to be less than 40°. This shows that $m\angle A$ is increasing, and $m\angle B$ and $m\angle C$ are decreasing. Therefore, "I only" is the correct answer.

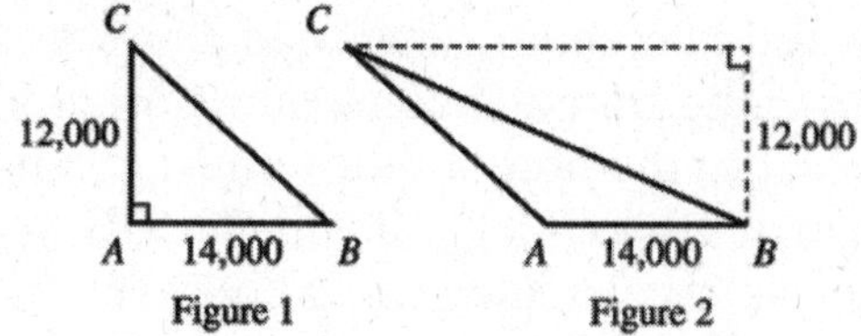

Figure 1 Figure 2

Question 36. The correct answer is G. The area of the original poster is 4(2) = 8 square feet. The area of the new poster will be 0.5(8) = 4 square feet. The length of the new poster will be $\frac{3}{4}(4) = 3$ feet. Therefore, the width of the new poster will be $\frac{\text{Area of the new poster}}{\text{Length of the new poster}} = \frac{4 \text{ square feet}}{3 \text{ feet}} = 1\frac{1}{3}$ feet. If you chose **F**, you may have chosen the given fraction or you may have found the reciprocal of the width of the new poster: $\frac{\text{Length of the new poster}}{\text{Area of the new poster}}$. If you chose **H**, you selected the value that is $\frac{3}{4}$ of the width of the original poster: $\frac{3}{4}(2)$. If you chose **J**, you selected the value that is $\frac{3}{4}$ of the area of the new poster: $\frac{3}{4}(4)$. If you chose **K**, you selected the value that is $\frac{3}{4}$ of the area of the original poster: $\frac{3}{4}(8)$.

Question 37. The correct answer is E. To find the solution set, simplify the right side of the equation. Multiply the 2 and the binomial $(x + 3)$ to get $x + 6 = 2x + 6 - x$. Next, combine like terms to get $x + 6 = x + 6$. Observe that the resulting equation will be true for any real number x. If you chose **A**, you may have multiplied the 2 by the first term in the binomial only and then solved: $x + 6 = 2x + 3 - x \Rightarrow x + 6 = x + 3 \Rightarrow 6 = 3$. If you chose **B**, **C**, or **D**, you may have verified that the given equation was satisfied with the value in the set.

Question 38. The correct answer is J. Let L be the length of the region. Let W be the width of the region. The perimeter, in feet, of the region will be $2L + 2W = 28$. To express the width W in terms of the length L, rewrite the equation as $2W = 28 - 2L$ or $W = 14 - L$. The area, in square feet, of the region is $A = LW$. Use the fact that $W = 14 - L$ to rewrite the area as $A = L(14 - L)$ or $A = 14L - L^2$. This quadratic equation represents a function of L where the maximum value occurs at the vertex. Thus, the maximum value occurs for $L = -\frac{14}{2(-1)} = 7$, and the maximum value is $A = 7(14 - 7) = 49$. So, the area of the largest rectangular region Steve can enclose is 49 square feet. If you chose **F**, you may have thought the dimensions 4 and 10 yield the greatest area. If you chose **G**, you may have thought the dimensions 5 and 9 yield the greatest area. If you chose **H**, you may have thought 6 and 8 yield the greatest area and didn't

MATHEMATICS • PRACTICE TEST 5 • EXPLANATORY ANSWERS

consider that a square is a rectangle. If you chose **K**, you may have mistaken the width as $28 - L$ and the area as $A = L(28 - L)$, which yields $L = 14$ and $W = 14$.

Question 39. The correct answer is C. The addition of the professional athlete's annual income will not change the median significantly. The median is calculated using the middle 1 or 2 values in a data set, written in numeric order, so it will not be influenced by an extreme outlier. The median annual income of the original group of 5 people is between \$30,000 and \$35,000 and so is the median annual income of the new group of 6 people. If you chose **A**, you picked a measure that is not resistant to outliers. Because the range is based on the minimum and maximum values in a data set, it will be influenced by the extreme outlier. The range of the annual income of the original group of 5 people is roughly \$35,000 – \$30,000 = \$5,000, but the range of the annual income of the new group of 6 people is roughly \$1,000,000 – \$30,000 = \$970,000. If you chose **B**, you picked a measure that is not resistant to outliers. The mean is calculated using every value in the data set. Thus, it will be influenced by the extreme outlier. If you chose **D**, you picked a measure that is not resistant to outliers. The standard deviation is roughly the typical distance that the values in a data set fall from the mean. In the original group of 5 people, all of the values are reasonably close to the mean, so the standard deviation is small. But because there is an outlier of \$1,000,000 in the new group of 6 people, the typical distance of the values from the mean is much higher, so the standard deviation is much higher.

Question 40. The correct answer is K. Ana and Amy completed $\frac{2}{5} + \frac{1}{3} = \frac{6+5}{15} = \frac{11}{15}$ of the job. Ruben finished the remaining $1 - \frac{11}{15} = \frac{4}{15}$ of the job in 2 hours. Because all 3 worked at the same rate, each person completed $\frac{4/15}{2} = \frac{4}{30}$ of the job per hour. It follows that it would have taken 1 person, working alone, $\frac{1}{\frac{4}{30}} = \frac{30}{4} = 7.5$ hours to complete the entire job. If you chose **F**, you may have solved $\frac{2}{5}x + \frac{1}{3}x + 2x = 1$. If you chose **G**, you may have computed $2 - \frac{1}{3} - \frac{2}{5}$. If you chose **H**, you may have computed $\frac{2}{5} + \frac{1}{3} + 2$. If you chose **J**, you may have thought Ana worked 2 hours so you computed $\frac{2/5}{2} = \frac{2}{10} \Rightarrow \frac{1}{\frac{10}{2}} \Rightarrow \frac{10}{2}$.

Question 41. The correct answer is C. Applying the exponent of 4 to all factors in the numerator gives $\frac{16a^{-4}b^2}{ab^{-3}}$. Rewriting this expression gives $16a^{-5}b^5$, which is equivalent to $\frac{16b^5}{a^5}$. If you chose **B**, you may have multiplied the coefficient 2 by the exponent 4 and combined the exponents -1 and 4 to get $\frac{8a^{-3}b^3}{ab^{-3}}$. If you chose **D**, you may have mistaken the square root symbol for a 4th root. If you chose **E**, you may have ignored the square root symbol and thought $\frac{b^4}{b^{-3}}$ equals b^{4-3} and also thought $\frac{a^{-4}}{a^1}$ equals a^{-4+1}.

Question 42. The correct answer is G. The contestant knows the oldest, so the probability of getting the oldest correct is 1. The contestant guesses the 2nd oldest from the other 3 rock stars, so the probability of getting the 2nd oldest correct is $\frac{1}{3}$. Assuming the first 2 are correct, the probability of guessing the 3rd oldest is $\frac{1}{2}$, which leaves only 1 person for the 4th oldest. Multiplying these probabilities, $1 \cdot \frac{1}{3} \cdot \frac{1}{2} \cdot 1$, you get $\frac{1}{6}$. If you chose **F**, you may have thought

MATHEMATICS • PRACTICE TEST 5 • EXPLANATORY ANSWERS

the contestant guessed all 4 and multiplied $\frac{1}{4}\cdot\frac{1}{3}\cdot\frac{1}{2}\cdot 1$. If you chose **H**, you may have chosen the denominator 4 because there were 4 rock stars. If you chose **J**, you may have chosen the denominator 3 because there were 3 positions the contestant didn't know. If you chose **K**, you may have thought the contestant could be either correct or incorrect with equal probability.

Question 43. The correct answer is D. Here is one course of simplification.

Rewrite the given expression with two pairs of common denominators: $\dfrac{\frac{2x}{6}+\frac{3}{6}}{\frac{8}{12}-\frac{3}{12}}$

Combine fractions with like denominators: $\dfrac{\frac{2x+3}{6}}{\frac{5}{12}}$

Rewrite, using multiplication of the reciprocal: $\frac{2x+3}{6}\cdot\frac{12}{5}$

Reduce the 12 and 6 to 2 and 1: $\frac{2x+3}{1}\cdot\frac{2}{5}$

Multiply numerators, using distribution, and multiply denominators: $\dfrac{2\cdot 2x+2\cdot 3}{5\cdot 1}$

If you chose **A**, you may have neglected to get common denominators and added numerators and denominators to get $\dfrac{\frac{x+1}{5}}{\frac{1}{-1}}$. If you chose **B**, you may have neglected to distribute the factor 2 to the $2x$ in the last step. If you chose **C**, you may have neglected to distribute the factor 2 to the 3 in the last step. If you chose **E**, you may have thought that $\frac{2}{3}-\frac{1}{4}$ in the first step was $\frac{1}{12}$.

Question 44. The correct answer is K. The fundamental counting principle allows us to multiply the number of ways to fill each position to get the total number of unique strings of characters. There are 10 digits that could fill each of the first 3 positions and 26 letters that could fill each of the last 6 positions, so the number of license plates is $10\cdot10\cdot10\cdot26\cdot26\cdot26$. If you chose **F**, you may have added 10 and 26. If you chose **G**, you may have thought there were only 6 possible characters for each of the 6 positions. If you chose **H**, you may have thought that no letters and only digits were being used. If you chose **J**, you may have thought there were only 9 digits instead of 10.

Question 45. The correct answer is A. The function $y=3+f(x-1)$ is equivalent to $(y-3)=f(x-1)$. To turn $(y-3)=f(x-1)$ into $y=f(x)$, we'd have to add 1 to x and add 3 to y. So the graph of $(y-3)=f(x-1)$ will be shifted 1 unit to the right and 3 units up. For example, the point (0,0) satisfies $y=f(x)$, and the point (1,3) satisfies $(y-3)=f(x-1)$. If you chose **B**, you may have thought $y=3+f(x-1)$ was equivalent to $(y+3)=f(x-1)$. If you chose **C**, you may have confused the directions right and up. If you chose **D**, you may have thought the positive 3 and negative 1 meant there must be some shift in a positive direction (right) and some shift in a negative direction (down). If you chose **E**, you may have thought $y=3+f(x-1)$ was equivalent to $(y-3)=f(x-1)$ but then mixed up the x and y axes and didn't realize the shift on each axis should be in the positive direction.

MATHEMATICS • PRACTICE TEST 5 • EXPLANATORY ANSWERS

Question 46. The correct answer is K. The logarithmic equation $\log_5 x = -2$ is equivalent to the exponential equation $5^{-2} = x$. Because $5^{-2} = \frac{1}{5^2}$, it follows that $x = \frac{1}{25}$. If you chose **F**, you might have thought the logarithmic equation $\log_5 x = -2$ was equivalent to the exponential equation $(-2)^5 = x$. If you chose **G**, you might have thought the logarithmic equation $\log_5 x = -2$ was equivalent to the exponential equation $-5^2 = x$. If you chose **H**, you might have thought the logarithmic equation $\log_5 x = -2$ was equivalent to the equation $-2(5) = x$. If you chose **J**, you might have thought $5^{-2} = \frac{1}{2(5)}$.

Question 47. The correct answer is D. The fraction $\frac{1}{5} = \frac{2}{10}$ and $\frac{1}{3} = \frac{2}{6}$. Because $\frac{2}{10} < \frac{2}{9} < \frac{2}{8} < \frac{2}{7} < \frac{2}{6}$, it follows that $\frac{2}{D}$ is between $\frac{1}{5}$ and $\frac{1}{3}$ for $D = 7, 8,$ and 9. If you chose **A**, you might have ignored the 2 in $\frac{2}{D}$. If you chose **B**, you might have ignored the 2 in $\frac{2}{D}$ and included the denominators of the given fractions as well as $\frac{1}{4}$. If you chose **C**, you might have known $\frac{1}{4}$ was between $\frac{1}{5}$ and $\frac{1}{3}$ and converted $\frac{1}{4}$ to $\frac{2}{8}$ but didn't consider other values for D. If you chose **E**, you might have added the denominators of $\frac{2}{10}$ and $\frac{2}{6}$.

Question 48. The correct answer is F. Whenever you multiply or divide both sides of an inequality by a negative number, you must reverse the inequality symbol. The inequality $a > b$ is equivalent to $\frac{a}{c} < \frac{b}{c}$. If you chose **G** or **H**, then you might not have realized that when you multiply or divide both sides of an inequality by a negative number, you must reverse the inequality symbol. Notice that the inequality $8 > 2$ is true, but both inequalities $\frac{8}{-2} > \frac{2}{-2}$ and $8(-2) > 2(-2)$ are false. If you chose **J**, you might not have remembered the additive property of inequality that says if $a > b$, then $a + c > b + c$. Thus, it is false that $a + c < b + c$. Adding or subtracting a negative number from both sides of the inequality does not require reversing the inequality symbol. If you chose **K**, you might not have realized that this inequality is not true for all values of *a*, *b*, and *c*. Notice that the inequality $8 > 2$, but $8 < 2 - (-1)$ is not true.

Question 49. The correct answer is B. Subtracting $a^2 + b^2$ from both sides of the equation $c^2 = a^2 + b^2 - 2ab\cos C$ gives $c^2 - a^2 - b^2 = -2ab\cos C$. Dividing that equation by $-2ab$ and then taking the inverse cosine of both sides gives $\cos^{-1}\left(-\frac{c^2 - a^2 - b^2}{2ab}\right) = C$. Let $\angle C$ be the largest angle in the triangle. Because the largest angle, C, is opposite the longest side, define $c = 39$. Plugging in the values $c = 39$, $a = 37$, and $b = 38$ gives the equation $\cos^{-1}\left(-\frac{39^2 - 37^2 - 38^2}{2(37)(38)}\right) = C$. If you chose **A**, you might have thought the largest angle was opposite the shortest side. If you chose **C**, **D**, or **E**, you might have added $2ab$ instead of dividing by $2ab$.

Question 50. The correct answer is K. If Pete's average score on 4 tests is x points, then the sum of his scores on those 4 tests is $4x$ points. Let y be Pete's score on the 5th test. His average score on all 5 tests is $\frac{4x+y}{5} = x + 2$. Multiplying both sides of this equation by 5 gives $4x + y = 5x + 10$. Subtracting $4x$ from both sides gives $y = x + 10$. His average score on the 5th test must be 10 greater than x. If you chose **F**, you might have thought the question

MATHEMATICS • PRACTICE TEST 5 • EXPLANATORY ANSWERS

asked how many points higher than x is $x + 2$. If you chose **G**, you might have thought that $x + 2$ was the average of 2 scores (old test and new test) instead of 5 scores. If you chose **H**, you might have chosen a number equal to the total number of tests. If you chose **J**, you might have multiplied the change in average, 2, by the number of tests already taken, 4.

Question 51. The correct answer is D. Two intersecting lines form pairs of adjacent angles, called *linear pairs,* which are supplementary. Also, two intersecting lines form pairs of congruent angles, called *vertical angles.* Because the measure of ∠B is $3\frac{1}{2}$ times the measure of ∠A, the angles are not congruent angles. Therefore, ∠B and ∠A must be adjacent angles that form a linear pair, and so they are supplementary. Let x be the measure of ∠A in degrees. Then, $x + 3.5x = 180$ and so $4.5x = 180 \Leftrightarrow x = 40$. Hence, the measure of ∠A is 40°. If you chose **A**, you may have thought the angles were complementary, $x + 3.5x = 90$. If you chose **B**, you may have computed $\frac{90}{3.5} \approx 26$. If you chose **E**, you may have computed $\frac{180}{3.5} \approx 51$.

Question 52. The correct answer is J. The sequence is defined recursively, so begin with the given initial value of $s_1 = 3$ and compute the values of s_2, s_3, and s_4. Each calculation is shown in the table.

n	$s_n = 2s_{(n-1)} + n + 1$
1	$s_1 = 3$
2	$s_2 = 2s_{(2-1)} + 2 + 1 = 2s_1 + 2 + 1 = 2(3) + 2 + 1 = 9$
3	$s_3 = 2s_{(3-1)} + 3 + 1 = 2s_2 + 3 + 1 = 2(9) + 3 + 1 = 22$
4	$s_4 = 2s_{(4-1)} + 4 + 1 = 2s_3 + 4 + 1 = 2(22) + 4 + 1 = 49$

If you chose **F**, you may have stopped at s_2. If you chose **G**, you may have multiplied 2 times the value of s_2. If you chose **H**, you may have stopped at s_3.

Question 53. The correct answer is E. If a is an integer less than −1, then $|a|$ is greater than 1. Also, if a is an integer less than −1, then a^2 is an integer greater than 1, and thus, $-a^2$ is an integer less than −1. Finally, if a is an integer less than −1, then $\frac{1}{a}$ is a negative number greater than −1, and thus, $-\frac{1}{a}$ is a positive number less than 1. So $-a^2 < -1 < -\frac{1}{a} < 1 < |a|$. Therefore, the expressions ordered from least to greatest are $-a^2 < -\frac{1}{a} < |a|$. If you chose **A** or **B**, you may not have noticed that $-\frac{1}{a}$ is a positive number and $-a^2$ is a negative number. If you chose **C**, you may have ordered the expressions from greatest to least. If you chose **D**, you may not have noticed that $-\frac{1}{a}$ is less than 1 and $|a|$ is greater than 1.

Question 54. The correct answer is J. First create the probability distribution for the random variable X. There are 10 equally likely outcomes in the sample space: 1, 2, 2, 3, 3, 3, 4, 4, 4, 4. Each value of X and its associated probability, $P(X)$, is listed in the table. The expected value of X, $E(X)$, is calculated by adding all $X \cdot P(X)$ products. Thus, $E(X) = \Sigma XP(X) = 1(0.1) + 2(0.2) + 3(0.3) + 4(0.4) = 3$. If you chose **F**, you may have divided the number of distinct cards by the total number of cards: $\frac{4}{10} = 0.4$. If you chose **G**, you may have chosen the sum of all the probabilities, $\Sigma P(X) = 1$. If you chose **H**, you may have found

Taking Additional Practice Tests

MATHEMATICS • PRACTICE TEST 5 • EXPLANATORY ANSWERS

the mean of 1, 2, 3, and 4. If you chose **K**, you may have thought "expected value" meant the value of X that is associated with the greatest probability.

X	P(X)
1	$\frac{1}{10} = 0.1$
2	$\frac{2}{10} = 0.2$
3	$\frac{3}{10} = 0.3$
4	$\frac{4}{10} = 0.4$

Question 55. The correct answer is B. Define 3 consecutive odd integers x, y, and z such that $x < y < z$ with the expressions $x = 2n + 1$, $y = 2n + 3$, and $z = 2n + 5$ where n is an integer. The sum of x, y, and z is, therefore, $2n + 1 + 2n + 3 + 2n + 5 = 6n + 9 = 3(2n + 3) = 3y$. If you chose **A** or **C**, you may have chosen an expression that represents the sum if x, y, and z are the same number. If you chose **D**, you may have rewritten $x + y + z$ as $x + x + 2 + x + 2 + 2$ and then incorrectly simplified to $3x + 2$. If you chose **E**, you may have chosen the expression that represents the average of the 3 consecutive odd integers rather than the sum.

Question 56. The correct answer is G. Because the mean of the 5 numbers is 24, the sum of the 5 numbers must be 5(24). Solving $42+3+11+27+x=120$ gives $x = 37$. Because the median of the 4 numbers is 38, the arithmetic mean of the middle 2 numbers (2nd and 3rd greatest numbers) must be 38. One of the middle numbers must be 29 because 8 is less and 53 is greater. Solving $\frac{29+y}{2}=38$ gives $y = 47$. Therefore, $x-y=37-47$. If you chose **F**, you may have taken the additive inverse of the given median. If you chose **H**, you may have calculated $47-37$. If you chose **J**, you may have chosen the given median. If you chose **K**, you may have thought the value of y couldn't be determined because the order of the 4 numbers wasn't given.

Question 57. The correct answer is A. Let the length and width of such a rectangle be l inches and w inches. It is given that the area is 144 square inches, so $lw = 144$. If we assume **A** is true, the perimeter is 48 inches, and $l + w = 24$ inches. Solving the system $\begin{cases} lw=144 \\ l+w=24 \end{cases}$, we get only one solution: $l = w = 12$. But this doesn't meet the condition that the rectangle's length is greater than the width. Therefore, 48 inches cannot be the perimeter for such a rectangle. Alternatively, you can write all lw factor pairs of 144 (where $l \neq w$) and double each $l + w$ sum to get possible $2(l + w)$ perimeters. If you chose **B**, you didn't realize that $l = 24$ and $w = 6$ satisfy the conditions. If you chose **C**, you didn't realize that $l = 36$ and $w = 4$ satisfy the conditions. If you chose **D**, you didn't realize that $l = 48$ and $w = 3$ satisfy the conditions. If you chose **E**, you didn't realize that $l = 72$ and $w = 2$ satisfy the conditions.

MATHEMATICS • PRACTICE TEST 5 • EXPLANATORY ANSWERS

Question 58. The correct answer is J. The y-coordinate of the center of the circle is 8. One endpoint of a diameter has a y-coordinate of 11, which is 3 greater than 8. So the other endpoint must have a y-coordinate that is 3 less than 8. If you chose **F**, you may have subtracted 11 – 10. If you chose **G**, you may have used the x-coordinate of the center, 7, and subtracted the difference of 11 and 7 from 7; or you may have subtracted the y-coordinate of the center from 11. If you chose **H**, you may have subtracted the x-coordinate of the center from 11. If you chose **K**, you may have chosen the y-coordinate of the center.

Question 59. The correct answer is D. For any values of length, width, and depth, the volume reflecting the increase in length and width can be represented by $(1.1l)(1.1w)(d)$, which is equivalent to $1.21(lwd)$. The value 1.21 represents a 21% increase. If you chose **A**, you may have thought the percent increase in volume would equal the percent increase in length and width. If you chose **B**, you may have rounded the result of $\frac{1.21-1}{1.21}$ to the nearest 1%. If you chose **C**, you may have added 10% + 10%. If you chose **E**, you may have thought all three dimensions were increased by 10%.

Question 60. The correct answer is K. Because $x = -1$ is a solution, $x + 1$ is a linear factor. Dividing $4x^3 - 2x^2 + x + 7$ by $x + 1$ gives $4x^2 - 6x + 7$. The discriminant of the quadratic formula is $b^2 - 4ac$, which for $4x^2 - 6x + 7$ is equal to $(-6)^2 - 4(4)(7)$. If you chose **F**, you may have thought a negative discriminant meant the solutions are both negative.

Passage I

Question 1. The best answer is A because the narrator makes clear that he does not know or remember all the details of the story he relates about Jantzen. The narrator states, "I'm not acquainted with the details, having been in high school at the time. But I can imagine" (lines 31–32). Later, the narrator points out that his memory "grows shaky" (line 46) because he had graduated from high school and moved out of town. When the narrator returned, "the steam-car operation was spoken of with scorn by the people who had been against it" (lines 50–52), which suggests hearsay.

The best answer is NOT:

B because the passage does not mention the narrator ever having spoken with Jantzen. Instead, the narrator states that he was "not acquainted with the details" (line 31).

C because the passage does not indicate that the entire story is fabricated. The narrator frames the story as if it actually happened, providing details about Jantzen and enough information about the events to strongly suggest that the story did happen.

D because the passage makes clear that the narrator was not a participant in the events. "I'm not acquainted with the details. . . . But I can imagine" (lines 31–32).

Question 2. The best answer is H because the phrase "though maybe not as quick as he should have been to smell a rat" (lines 23–24) suggests that Jantzen was not sensitive to the possibility that someone might try to take advantage of him. For the narrator to bring up Jantzen's not being quick to "smell a rat" hints that Jantzen, ultimately, was tricked in some way.

The best answer is NOT:

F because, as it is presented in the passage, the fact that Jantzen ran the bank does not in itself foreshadow his downfall more strongly than response H does. This detail is used to help establish Jantzen's position.

G because the passage does not make a clear connection between people coming up with ideas in the Thirties and Jantzen's downfall. This detail provides context for the story rather than strongly foreshadowing Jantzen's downfall.

J because, though the passage mentions that Jantzen might have had a steam-driven car, and that he may have had a fondness for them, the detail does not provide foreshadowing. It suggests one reason Jantzen might have been interested in the idea to resurrect the steam-driven car.

READING • PRACTICE TEST 5 • EXPLANATORY ANSWERS

Question 3. The best answer is D because the passage suggests that people in town didn't know who convinced Jantzen to invest in steam-driven cars. Lines 19–21: "Who knows if it was a single person or a cohort. Maybe a stranger or some friends of friends."

The best answer is NOT:

A because the passage does not indicate that the townspeople knew who was involved in the investment scheme. Instead, lines 19–21 suggest that they could only speculate about this.

B because although strangers and friends of friends are mentioned as people who hypothetically could have convinced Jantzen to invest (lines 20–21), their involvement is portrayed as speculation only. The suggestion is that the townspeople didn't know, not that some people believed it was strangers and others believed it was friends of friends.

C because although an undescribed cohort is mentioned as possibly convincing Jantzen to invest (line 20), any involvement is portrayed as speculation only.

Question 4. The best answer is H because the passage presents options I, III, and IV as being true of the townspeople's behavior, as conveyed in lines 50–54. "By the time I got back home the steam-car operation was spoken of with scorn by the people who had been against it and not at all by those who had promoted it. The visitors to town who promoted it had disappeared."

The best answer is NOT:

F because it includes option II, "People in town blamed the loss of money on Jantzen having cheated." This contradicts the point made in lines 55–56: "There was talk not of cheating but of mismanagement."

G because it does not include option I, "Visitors who promoted steam cars had left town," which is made clear in lines 53–54.

J because it includes option II, "People in town blamed the loss of money on Jantzen having cheated." This contradicts information provided in lines 55–56: "There was talk not of cheating but of mismanagement."

READING • PRACTICE TEST 5 • EXPLANATORY ANSWERS

Question 5. The best answer is B because lines 14–16 state that times were hard in the Thirties and that people were coming up with ideas to make money. "In the hard times of the Thirties people were still coming up with ideas. You can be sure, men were nursing a notion bound to make them a million dollars." "In the hard times of the Thirties" indicates that times were hard. "Men were nursing a notion bound to make them a million dollars" indicates that people were trying to come up with money-making schemes.

The best answer is NOT:

A because lines 14–16 refer to the 1930s, not to people in their thirties. This is supported by the reference to "those days" in line 17.

C because the lines suggest that men wanted to make a million dollars ("nursing a notion bound to make them a million dollars"), not that they were actually making as much as a million dollars a year.

D because the lines do not indicate or suggest that people felt that they should take their money-making plans to Jantzen. The lines instead capture a general trend in the 1930s, according to the narrator.

Question 6. The best answer is J because *fostering,* a synonym for *nursing,* makes sense in the context of people coming up with new money-making schemes (lines 14–17). In this context, *fostering* means "to promote the growth and development of," which is similar to the meaning of *nursing* as the word is used in the sentence.

The best answer is NOT:

F because *rearing* is not a contextually appropriate synonym for *nursing* as the word is used in the sentence. "To rear" means to support until maturity, usually in the context of people or animals, or to erect by building, which does not make sense in context.

G because *educating* is not a contextually appropriate synonym for *nursing* as the word is used in the sentence. *Educating* usually refers to teaching or informing, which does not make sense in context.

H because *healing* is not a contextually appropriate synonym for *nursing* as the word is used in the sentence. *Healing* typically means *curing,* which does not make sense in context.

READING • PRACTICE TEST 5 • EXPLANATORY ANSWERS

Question 7. The best answer is A because as the narrator speculates about who might have convinced Jantzen to invest, he notes Jantzen's admiration of appearances. Lines 21–22: "Well dressed and plausible looking, you may be sure. Horace set store by appearances."

The best answer is NOT:

B because the narrator does not suggest that Jantzen would not have loaned money to someone who wasn't wealthy. The passage implies that the person would have been "well dressed and plausible looking," but the focus is on appearances, not wealth or risk.

C because the narrator does not mention age as a factor Jantzen would have considered, nor does the passage indicate that Jantzen would have trusted someone who had once owned a steam-driven car.

D because the narrator does not indicate the person who convinced Jantzen to invest needed to be intelligent. Instead, the narrator suggests Jantzen would have relied on appearances. "Well dressed and plausible looking, you may be sure. Horace set store by appearances" (lines 21–22). Jantzen himself may not have been "as quick as he should have been to smell a rat" (lines 23–24), which implies he may have been fooled rather easily.

Question 8. The best answer is F because the passage makes clear that the new version of the steam-driven car would be an improved version of earlier models. The passage states that the new model would be less expensive and quiet, which suggests that the earlier cars were expensive and noisy. "This new model would be an improved version, of course, and have the advantages of being economical and not making a racket" (lines 28–30).

The best answer is NOT:

G because there is no indication in the passage that the original steam-driven cars were reliable or fast.

H because the passage does not indicate that the original steam-driven cars were unattractive and impractical. Impracticality may be implied since economy is mentioned as a benefit of the new model, but attractiveness is never mentioned.

J because the passage does not indicate that the original steam-driven cars were luxurious or durable.

READING • PRACTICE TEST 5 • EXPLANATORY ANSWERS

Question 9. The best answer is C because the passage makes clear in lines 38–39 that "the bank had put up the loan." It goes on: "It was Jantzen's decision and there was some confusion that he had put in his own money. He may have done so, but he had also dipped improperly into bank funds, thinking no doubt that he could pay it back with nobody the wiser" (lines 39–43).

The best answer is NOT:

A because the passage does not mention any involvement of "some of Jantzen's wealthy friends."

B because the passage states in lines 40–41 that Jantzen may have invested his own money but does not indicate that this definitely occurred or that it was his entire life savings. The passage bluntly states, however, that he did use bank funds. "But he had also dipped improperly into bank funds, thinking no doubt that he could pay it back with nobody the wiser" (lines 41–43).

D because the passage does not make clear that the entrepreneurs from Toronto, Windsor, or Kitchener referred to in lines 34–35 invested any money. The passage states that "others would ask if they [the entrepreneurs] had backing," and goes on to say that "they did indeed, because the bank had put up the loan" (lines 36–39).

Question 10. The best answer is G because lines 65–68 state that it was pride that led Jantzen to agree to take the job at the Hawksburg bank. "Surely he could have refused, but pride, as it was thought, chose otherwise. Pride chose that he be driven every morning those six miles to sit behind a partial wall of cheap varnished boards, no proper office at all."

The best answer is NOT:

F because pride is not presented as a possible reason for Jantzen's decision to invest in steam-driven cars. The narrator speculates that Jantzen may have been swayed by someone plausible looking and also suggests that Jantzen may have had a steam-driven car himself and may have "had a fondness for them" (lines 27–28).

H because the narrator makes it clear that Jantzen did not look unhappy when Oneida drove him to work. Lines 77–80: "I don't see Oneida looking downtrodden or unhappy at the arrangement, nor her father looking actually unhappy. Dignity was what he had, and plenty of it."

J because although the passage notes that Jantzen had to sit in an office made out of varnished boards, the passage does not indicate that Jantzen himself created the office.

READING • PRACTICE TEST 5 • EXPLANATORY ANSWERS

Passage II

Question 11. The best answer is C because the paragraph in which the description of the fountain pen appears is about the ways in which plastic allowed designers to embrace "the spirit of modernity" (lines 3–4). In addition, the lines before the mention of the fountain pen suggest that everyday objects, when created out of plastic, could seem exciting. Lines 12–16: ". . . a lingo of curves and dashes and teardrop shapes that created a feeling of speed and motion in everyday objects. Streamline a fountain pen and even that stolid item declared: we're hurtling toward the future here!"

The best answer is NOT:

A because the passage does not mention plastic items looking identical as a result of being streamlined.

B because the passage does not indicate that designers were critiqued for creating items that were beautiful rather than functional.

D because it contradicts the suggestion in the passage that fountain pens were in fact changed by new design trends. Lines 15–16: "Streamline a fountain pen and even that stolid item declared: we're hurtling toward the future here!"

Question 12. The best answer is F because the paragraph notes that plastics allowed designers to create quality designs at lower prices. "There was another reason designers embraced plastics. From the mid-twentieth century on, modern design has been guided by an egalitarian gospel, a belief that good design needn't cost a lot of money" (lines 17–20).

The best answer is NOT:

G because the paragraph mentions only one slogan that was associated with plastics, and the slogan supports the main idea that plastics could be used to create appealing products at low prices.

H because the paragraph does not mention that plastics were challenging to work with.

J because the paragraph does not indicate that designers who embraced plastics prized the mundane over the beautiful. Rather, the idea was that mundane things could be made beautiful.

READING • PRACTICE TEST 5 • EXPLANATORY ANSWERS

Question 13. The best answer is A because a number of points in the passage suggest that designers felt that plastics encouraged inventiveness. Lines 2–4: "They loved the design freedom that synthetics offered and the spirit of modernity the materials embodied." Lines 5–10: "Bakelite, the world's first synthetic plastic, spoke 'in the vernacular of the twentieth century . . . the language of invention, of synthesis,' and he [Frankl] urged his fellow designers to use their full imaginative powers to explore the new materials' frank artificiality."

The best answer is NOT:

B because the passage does not mention that consumers demanded attractively designed items.

C because the passage does not indicate that people who created items out of plastics were seen as risk takers.

D because the passage does not suggest or indicate that Bakelite was difficult to work with.

Question 14. The best answer is G because the passage lists a number of examples of items made from plastics that didn't work for the purposes for which they were made. The passage also states that during the 1950s, plastic technology improved, in turn improving the objects that were made from plastics. Lines 37–43: "There were plastic plates that melted in hot water, plastic toys that cracked on Christmas morning, plastic raincoats that grew clammy and fell apart in the rain. Polymer technology improved during the 1950s as manufacturers figured out how to make better plastics and, even more important, how to match the right polymer with the right application."

The best answer is NOT:

F because the passage notes that even in the 1930s and 1940s, plastics could be made to appear streamlined. Lines 10–12: "As interpreted by Frankl and other designers working with Bakelite in the '30s and '40s, that was the language of streamlining."

H because there is no indication that manufacturers had not figured out whether consumers would buy plastics. In fact, the examples listed in the last paragraph (plastic plates, plastic toys, plastic raincoats) suggest that consumers did buy everyday items made of plastics.

J because the first paragraph of the passage notes that designers loved to work with plastics. Lines 1–4: "Designers were enthralled by the universe of possibility from plastics' earliest days. They loved the design freedom that synthetics offered and the spirit of modernity the materials embodied."

READING • PRACTICE TEST 5 • EXPLANATORY ANSWERS

Question 15. The best answer is D because the lines that come before this statement make it clear that plastics had become part of people's everyday routines. "As *House Beautiful* observed in 1955, 'The news is not that plastics exist, but [that] they have already been so assimilated into our lives.' The average person was 'conditioned to plastics'" (lines 78–82).

The best answer is NOT:

A because the passage does not mention that the production and use of plastics represented increased consumerism.

B because the passage does not indicate that people preferred to buy things made out of plastics over things made out of other materials. The passages stresses that consumers didn't really have a choice because plastic "surrounded everyone" (line 48). "Once plastic products filled the stores, people had no choice but to consume what they were offered" (lines 56–58). "The average person was 'conditioned to plastics'" (lines 81–82).

C because the passage does not indicate that people found plastics to be a threat to traditional ways of life.

Question 16. The best answer is G because the passage asserts that "a sleepy householder had to watch only once in disbelief as a polyethylene juice pitcher bounced off the kitchen floor to begin accepting plastic in a practical way no matter how strong the conceptual disdain for it" (lines 66–70). The juice pitcher provides a specific example of plastic's durability, which was enough to overcome "disdain" for the material.

The best answer is NOT:

F because the passage does not indicate that the juice pitcher was part of an advertisement.

H because the paragraph in which the quoted lines appear is not about how plastics improved, but rather about the effects of improvements. As noted in response G, the lines serve as an example of plastic's durability.

J because the lines show how plastic could win people over, not bias people against it. "A sleepy householder had to watch only once in disbelief as a polyethylene juice pitcher bounced off the kitchen floor to begin accepting plastic in a practical way no matter how strong the conceptual disdain for it" (lines 66–70).

READING • PRACTICE TEST 5 • EXPLANATORY ANSWERS

Question 17. The best answer is C because the passage specifically describes toys that were made out of plastic as being both less durable and less destructive. Lines 70–74: "Even plastic toys, despite the brittle polystyrene items that broke on Christmas morning, proved superior in many ways. A toy soldier of molded polyethylene could not scratch the furniture as readily as an old-fashioned lead soldier."

The best answer is NOT:

A because the passage does not mention that plastic toys were more flexible and detailed.

B because the passage does not indicate that plastic toys were less costly, and, as noted in response C, they were often less sturdy than nonplastic toys. Lines 70–71: "Even plastic toys, despite the brittle polystyrene items that broke on Christmas morning."

D because the passage does not discuss the relative popularity of plastic toys among kids and parents.

Question 18. The best answer is F because both passages include quotations about plastics, either from designers who used plastics or from publications writing about plastics. Passage A: "To furniture designer Paul T. Frankl, a material like Bakelite, the world's first synthetic plastic, spoke 'in the vernacular of the twentieth century . . . the language of invention, of synthesis'" (lines 4–8). "Plastics' adaptability and glibness undermined their capacity to achieve 'dignity' as legitimate materials worthy of being taken seriously, one critic wrote" (lines 32–34). Passage B: "Sidney Gross, who joined *Modern Plastics* in 1952 and became editor in 1968, recalled that he had 'agitated a lot' over the years to get SPI, the trade association for the plastics industry, to quit trying to convince people 'that plastic is not bad'" (lines 49–53). "As *House Beautiful* observed in 1955, 'The news is not that plastics exist, but [that] they have already been so assimilated into our lives.' The average person was 'conditioned to plastics'" (lines 78–82).

The best answer is NOT:

G because although Passage B refers to *Modern Plastics* and *House Beautiful*, it does not analyze these publications or assert that they promoted plastics. Passage A does not mention publications that promoted plastics.

H because neither passage defines the key concepts that were used to market plastics.

J because neither passage personifies artwork or objects that were made of plastics.

READING • PRACTICE TEST 5 • EXPLANATORY ANSWERS

Question 19. The best answer is D because both passages indicate that the public believed plastic was interior. Passage A, lines 30–31: "The growing reputation of plastic as an inferior material." Lines 35–40: "This impression was exacerbated by people's unfortunate experiences with plastics in the immediate postwar years. There were plastic plates that melted in hot water, plastic toys that cracked on Christmas morning, plastic raincoats that grew clammy and fell apart in the rain." In Passage B, lines 58–64 indicate that after the plastics industry solved postwar quality problems and plastics worked better, people still held on to the idea that plastic was inferior. "Things made of plastic were better designed and lasted longer. People intuitively recognized that fact even if they retained an intellectual notion that plastic was bad or shoddy."

The best answer is NOT:

A because there is no indication in either passage that people found plastics unattractive in design. In fact, Passage A suggests that items made from plastics could be beautiful. Lines 18–21: "From the mid-twentieth century on, modern design has been guided by an egalitarian gospel, a belief that good design needn't cost a lot of money, that even the most mundane items could be things of beauty." Passage B does not discuss plastics' aesthetic qualities.

B because although plastics' artificiality is mentioned in Passage A, it is not suggested that this is unnerving, but rather that it is something to be embraced. Lines 8–10: "He urged his fellow designers to use their full imaginative powers to explore the new materials' frank artificiality." Passage B does not discuss plastics' artificiality.

C because Passage A notes that plastics were relatively inexpensive. Lines 24–26: "Plastics were the ideal medium for that mission: malleable, relatively inexpensive, and made for mass manufacture." Passage B does not discuss the cost of plastics. Moreover, neither passage indicates that the public believed items made of plastics were "novelties."

Question 20. The best answer is J because both passages use toys as an example of problems with the quality of plastics. In Passage A, the example follows a paragraph that asserts plastic's reputation as an inferior material. Lines 35–40: "This impression [that plastics were inferior] was exacerbated by people's unfortunate experiences with plastics in the immediate postwar years. There were plastic plates that melted in hot water, plastic toys that cracked on Christmas morning, plastic raincoats that grew clammy and fell apart in the rain." The passage goes on to assert that technology improved during the 1950s, but "the damage to plastic's reputation had been done" (lines 43–44). In Passage B, toys also provide an example of a flaw. Lines 70–72: "Even plastic toys, despite the brittle polystyrene items that broke on Christmas morning, proved superior in many ways." In this case, despite the problem with quality ("brittle polystyrene items that broke on Christmas morning"), plastic could be superior in other ways ("not scratch the furniture").

The best answer is NOT:

F because although Passage B notes that plastic items could be superior to what they replaced ("Even plastic toys, despite the brittle polystyrene items that broke on Christmas morning, proved superior in many ways"), Passage A uses toys as an example of bad design, not good design. Lines 35–40: "This impression was exacerbated by people's unfortunate experiences with plastics in the immediate postwar years. There were plastic plates that melted in hot water, plastic toys that cracked on Christmas morning, plastic raincoats that grew clammy and fell apart in the rain."

G because Passage A does not mention that plastic toys were particularly popular, and the example of toys in Passage B is used to demonstrate both quality problems and plastics' superiority.

H because, in both passages, the example of toys is provided to show problems with plastics, not the variety of plastic items that were produced. Passage A: "This impression was exacerbated by people's unfortunate experiences with plastics in the immediate postwar years. There were . . . plastic toys that cracked on Christmas morning" (lines 35–39). Passage B: ". . . plastic toys, despite the brittle polyethylene items that broke on Christmas morning" (lines 70–71).

READING • PRACTICE TEST 5 • EXPLANATORY ANSWERS

Passage III

Question 21. The best answer is C because the paragraph tells a story that is narrated in a biography of García Márquez. The author of the passage specifically notes this at the beginning of the second paragraph. "When Gerald Martin, around the middle of his rich and resourceful biography of García Márquez, starts to tell this story" (lines 9–11).

The best answer is NOT:

A because as noted in response C, the paragraph tells the story of García Márquez's writing the novel. The paragraph does not mention misconceptions about how long it took to write *One Hundred Years of Solitude.*

B because the paragraph describes only the circumstances surrounding García Márquez's writing one particular novel, not novels in general.

D because the paragraph does not discuss García Márquez's childhood at all.

Question 22. The best answer is F because the author of the passage specifically states that he believes García Márquez to be a gifted writer. Lines 44–46: "When he got into the car to set out for Acapulco, he was a gifted and hardworking writer, certainly."

The best answer is NOT:

G because although the passage mentions García Márquez's journalism, there is no mention in the passage that the author preferred his journalism to his novels.

H because although the author of the passage notes that García Márquez's novels borrow from local facts and legends, there is no indication that he thinks García Márquez does so too much. Lines 61–66: "It takes pieces of already thoroughly mythified reality—there is scarcely an extravagant incident in his novels and stories that doesn't have some sort of basis in specific, local fact or legend—and finds the perfect, unforgettable literary home for them."

J because the author of the passage refers to Martin's insistence on excessive melancholy, not García Márquez's. Lines 83–87: "There is perhaps a slight imbalance in Martin's insistence on the writer's sadness, an excess of melancholy; but it's a good corrective to García Márquez's own joking cheerfulness and elaborate ironies."

READING • PRACTICE TEST 5 • EXPLANATORY ANSWERS

Question 23. The best answer is A because in the first paragraph of the passage, it is made clear that the "illumination" is referring to García Márquez's writing of the novel. "Many years later, and many times over, the writer Gabriel García Márquez was to remember the day he discovered how to set about writing his great novel. He was driving from Mexico City to Acapulco when the illumination hit him" (lines 1–5). When the word is used again in line 37, it is in reference to the story that is first told in the first paragraph.

The best answer is NOT:

B because the passage notes that García Márquez directly stated that he modeled an aspect of his writing after Kafka's, not that Martin discovered this. Lines 31–34: "What García Márquez found was a way of telling it. He would combine, as he frequently said, the narrative tone of his grandmother with that of the author Franz Kafka."

C because the reference to "illumination" occurs well before the passage author notes that García Márquez based his stories on local facts and legends, and also because the use of "illumination," as noted in response A, is in reference to García Márquez, not the passage's author.

D because there is no indication in the passage that García Márquez considered his completion of *One Hundred Years of Solitude* miraculous. As noted in response A, the use of "illumination" refers to García Márquez's discovery of "how to set about writing his great novel" (line 3).

Question 24. The best answer is H because Martin interrupts the story about García Márquez to claim that it is not true. Lines 9–12: "When Gerald Martin, around the middle of his rich and resourceful biography of García Márquez, starts to tell this story, the reader may be a little surprised, even disappointed." Lines 22–26: "After 'and then,' Martin writes in mock apology, 'It seems a pity to intervene in the story at this point but the biographer feels constrained to point out that there have been many versions of this story . . . and that the one just related cannot be true.'"

The best answer is NOT:

F because there is no indication in the passage that García Márquez preferred to write in seclusion.

G because the passage does not indicate that Martin's biography of García Márquez focuses on analyzing his novels rather than on discussing the author's development as a writer.

J because, as noted in response H, the disappointment the reader might feel is in reference to the story not being true, not to the lack of information about why García Márquez drove back to Mexico City. In addition, later in the passage Martin notes that García Márquez probably did not drive back to Mexico City. Lines 27–28: "The writer probably continued to Acapulco."

READING • PRACTICE TEST 5 • EXPLANATORY ANSWERS

Question 25. The best answer is B because *compelled* means "urged forcefully or irresistibly," which makes it a contextually appropriate synonym of *constrained* here. Martin feels as if he must point out that the story cannot be true.

The best answer is NOT:

A because *restrain* means to hold back from, and the author is not holding back from pointing out that "there have been many versions of this story . . . and that the one just related cannot be true" (lines 25–26).

C because *coerced* implies being persuaded by outside forces, and there is no indication in the passage that Martin had to be persuaded by someone else to share the truth about García Márquez's story.

D because *limited* means confined or restricted, and there is no indication in the passage that Martin felt that his options were restricted.

Question 26. The best answer is G because the passage specifically notes that García Márquez's grandmother believed the stories she told were true. Lines 32–35: "He would combine, as he frequently said, the narrative tone of his grandmother with that of the author Franz Kafka. She told fantastic stories as if they were true, because for her, they were true."

The best answer is NOT:

F because the passage notes that García Márquez imitated Kafka, not that his grandmother did. Lines 32–34: "He would combine, as he frequently said, the narrative tone of his grandmother with that of the author Franz Kafka."

H because there is no indication in the passage that García Márquez's grandmother hoped to become a successful author.

J because the passage states that García Márquez learned from his grandmother, not that his grandmother learned from him. Lines 32–34: "He would combine, as he frequently said, the narrative tone of his grandmother with that of the author Franz Kafka."

Question 27. The best answer is C because the passage notes that García Márquez made jokes that indicated his gratitude for his life. "García Márquez made many jokes about his fame over the years. These jokes are witty and complicated acts of gratitude for a destiny the writer was sure could have been quite different" (lines 49–52).

The best answer is NOT:

A because there is no mention in the passage that García Márquez ever hoped that his best work had yet to be written.

B because there is no mention in the passage that García Márquez was ever concerned that his accomplishments had been distorted by others.

D because there is no mention in the passage that García Márquez ever believed that he deserved more credit for his wit and the complexity of his writing.

READING • PRACTICE TEST 5 • EXPLANATORY ANSWERS

Question 28. The best answer is J because the passage cites a quotation by García Márquez that suggests he believed he might have been a better person if he had stayed in Aracataca. "One of his finest sentences, written in an article in 1983, concerns a dream of the life he might have led if he had stayed in his isolated birthplace of Aracataca, Colombia. 'I would not perhaps be the same person I am now but maybe I would have been something better: just a character in one of the novels I would never have written'" (lines 52–58).

The best answer is NOT:

F because there is no indication in the passage that García Márquez ever stated that he should have written *One Hundred Years of Solitude* sooner.

G because there is no indication in the passage that García Márquez ever stated that he wished he had completed his journey to Acapulco. In addition, the passage suggests that García Márquez did complete his journey. Lines 27–28: "The writer probably continued to Acapulco."

H because there is no indication in the passage that García Márquez ever wished he had taken his fame less seriously.

Question 29. The best answer is B because the passage author directly states that the biography helps balance García Márquez's joking cheerfulness and elaborate ironies. Lines 83–88: "There is perhaps a slight imbalance in Martin's insistence on the writer's sadness, an excess of melancholy; but it's a good corrective to García Márquez's own joking cheerfulness and elaborate ironies, and we can return to the master if we get too depressed."

The best answer is NOT:

A because, as noted in response B, the author directly states that the biography helps balance García Márquez's joking cheerfulness and elaborate ironies.

C because, as noted in response B, the author directly states that the biography helps balance García Márquez's joking cheerfulness and elaborate ironies.

D because, as noted in response B, the author directly states that the biography helps balance García Márquez's joking cheerfulness and elaborate ironies.

READING • PRACTICE TEST 5 • EXPLANATORY ANSWERS

Question 30. The best answer is J because in this context, *master* refers to García Márquez, who is referenced earlier in the sentence. Lines 83–88: "There is perhaps a slight imbalance in Martin's insistence on the writer's sadness, an excess of melancholy; but it's a good corrective to García Márquez's own joking cheerfulness and elaborate ironies, and we can return to the master if we get too depressed." The passage author is asserting that we can return to the master himself, García Márquez, when Martin's biography seems too dark.

The best answer is NOT:

F because, as noted in response J, in this context, *master* refers to García Márquez, who is referenced earlier in the sentence. Lines 83–88: "There is perhaps a slight imbalance in Martin's insistence on the writer's sadness, an excess of melancholy; but it's a good corrective to García Márquez's own joking cheerfulness and elaborate ironies, and we can return to the master if we get too depressed." If the passage author were referring to himself here, it would not make sense in context.

G because, as noted in response J, in this context, *master* refers to García Márquez, who is referenced earlier in the sentence. Lines 83–88: "There is perhaps a slight imbalance in Martin's insistence on the writer's sadness, an excess of melancholy; but it's a good corrective to García Márquez's own joking cheerfulness and elaborate ironies, and we can return to the master if we get too depressed." García Márquez's joking cheerfulness is in contrast to Martin's melancholy.

H because, as noted in response J, in this context, *master* refers to García Márquez, who is referenced earlier in the sentence. Lines 83–88: "There is perhaps a slight imbalance in Martin's insistence on the writer's sadness, an excess of melancholy; but it's a good corrective to García Márquez's own joking cheerfulness and elaborate ironies, and we can return to the master if we get too depressed." The reference to Kafka comes much earlier in the passage, and therefore does not make sense in this context.

READING • PRACTICE TEST 5 • EXPLANATORY ANSWERS

Passage IV

Question 31. The best answer is B because the passage explains how increasingly large distances were measured throughout history. The first sentence of the passage helps establish the overall organization: "One measure of the progress of human civilization is the increasing scale of our maps." What follows is a series of historical examples to illustrate this idea. The first paragraph describes a map from the twenty-fifth century B.C. showing a thirty-acre plot of land; the second paragraph describes Eratosthenes's process for measuring the circumference of Earth in the third century B.C.; the third paragraph describes Richer's measurement of the distance between Earth and Mars in 1672; the fourth paragraph describes Newton's measurement of the distance between Earth and the nearest stars. Each example is of an increasingly large distance.

The best answer is NOT:

A because the passage is about more than just attempts to determine the distance of stars from Earth. As noted in response B, the passage describes attempts to measure distance on Earth as well as distances from Earth to other objects in the universe.

C because although the passage does include an explanation of the calculations used by Eratosthenes to measure Earth's circumference, this is limited to one paragraph. It does not describe the passage as a whole.

D because "collection of anecdotes" doesn't capture how the passage moves through historical examples of increasingly large distances. Response B more accurately captures the passage's overall organization.

Question 32. The best answer is H because the paragraph presents examples of the ways in which humans' understanding of their surroundings expanded over time. The first sentence of the paragraph, "One measure of the progress of human civilization is the increasing scale of our maps" (lines 1–2), suggests that the paragraph will discuss this expansion. The paragraph begins with an example of a relatively small scale and proceeds with examples that show how this scale broadened.

The best answer is NOT:

F because the paragraph does not discuss Eratosthenes or the time period in which he made his calculations.

G because there is no discussion in the paragraph of early geographers concluding that Earth was curved.

J because although the paragraph acknowledges the ancient Greeks, it does not summarize all of their contributions to astronomy. Instead, the information is included to show how humans' understanding of their surroundings expanded over time, as noted in response H.

READING • PRACTICE TEST 5 • EXPLANATORY ANSWERS

Question 33. The best answer is B because the passage notes that these models of the universe did not include size or scale of objects. Lines 6–10: "In the earliest recorded cosmologies, such as the Babylonian *Enuma Elish*, from around 1500 B.C., the oceans, the continents, and the heavens were considered finite, but there were no scientific estimates of their dimensions." Lines 10–13: "The early Greeks, including Homer, viewed Earth as a circular plane with the ocean enveloping it and Greece at the center, but there was no understanding of scale." Lines 13–18: "In the early sixth century B.C., the Greek philosopher Anaximander, whom historians consider the first mapmaker, and his student Anaximenes proposed that the stars were attached to a giant crystalline sphere. But again there was no estimate of its size."

The best answer is NOT:

A because the passage notes that in at least one of the models, the universe was considered finite. "In the earliest recorded cosmologies, such as the Babylonian *Enuma Elish*, from around 1500 B.C., the oceans, the continents, and the heavens were considered finite, but there were no scientific estimates of their dimensions" (lines 6–10).

C because there is no mention in these lines of any similarities between ancient models of the universe and modern maps.

D because only one of the examples of the ancient models of the universe is noted to have positioned the citizens' homelands at the center of the universe. "The early Greeks, including Homer, viewed Earth as a circular plane with the ocean enveloping it and Greece at the center, but there was no understanding of scale" (lines 10–13).

Question 34. The best answer is F because the passage notes that we do not have sufficient experience to relate to the distance from Earth to the nearest stars. "Newton's estimate of the distance to nearby stars was larger than any distance imagined before in human history. Even today, nothing in our experience allows us to relate to it" (lines 77–80). The examples that follow in the paragraph help illustrate this point.

The best answer is NOT:

G because it contradicts the paragraph's point that even advancements in space travel would not make the distance from Earth to the nearest stars seem small. In fact, the passage notes that "if we traveled in the fastest rocket ship ever manufactured on Earth, the trip would last 100,000 years, at least a thousand human life spans" (lines 84–86).

H because the last paragraph is not about when the distance was calculated. Rather, the paragraph is about how far this distance is—so far that nothing in our experience allows us to relate to it.

J because the paragraph does not indicate that Newton's estimate of the distance between Earth and the nearest stars was incorrect.

READING • PRACTICE TEST 5 • EXPLANATORY ANSWERS

Question 35. The best answer is A according to lines 10–13: "The early Greeks, including Homer, viewed Earth as a circular plane with the ocean enveloping it and Greece at the center, but there was no understanding of scale."

The best answer is NOT:

B because it was Anaximander and Anaximenes who described Earth as a giant crystalline sphere with stars attached. "In the early sixth century B.C., the Greek philosopher Anaximander, whom historians consider the first mapmaker, and his student Anaximenes proposed that the stars were attached to a giant crystalline sphere" (lines 13–17).

C because the passage mentions 7.2 degrees in relation to Eratosthenes's work to calculate the circumference of Earth. "Eratosthenes knew that the sun was not overhead at noon in Alexandria. In fact, it was tipped 7.2 degrees from the vertical, or about one fiftieth of a circle" (lines 30–32).

D because the measurement of a plot of land 354 *iku* in size was recorded well before the time of the ancient Greeks. "A clay tablet dating from about the twenty-fifth century B.C. found near what is now the Iraqi city of Kirkuk depicts a river valley with a plot of land labeled as being 354 *iku* (about thirty acres) in size" (lines 2–6).

Question 36. The best answer is J because the passage states, "Eratosthenes reasoned that if he knew the distance from Alexandria to Syene, the full circumference of the planet must be about fifty times that distance. Traders passing through Alexandria told him that camels could make the trip to Syene in about fifty days, and it was known that a camel could cover one hundred stadia (almost eleven and a half miles) in a day" (lines 36–43). This information suggests that Eratosthenes needed to know the time it took camels to travel between the cities and how far they could travel in a day.

The best answer is NOT:

F because the passage notes that Eratosthenes used information about the curvature of Earth and the angle of the sun to calculate the circumference of Earth, not the distance between Syene and Alexandria.

G because the passage notes that Eratosthenes used his knowledge of the distance between Syene and Alexandria to calculate the circumference of Earth. Lines 36–39: "Eratosthenes reasoned that if he knew the distance from Alexandria to Syene, the full circumference of the planet must be about fifty times that distance." He could not know Earth's circumference until he knew the distance between these cities.

H because, as noted in response F, Eratosthenes used information about the height of the sun at noon in each city and the length of shadows cast on the ground to calculate the circumference of Earth, not to calculate the distance between Syene and Alexandria.

READING • PRACTICE TEST 5 • EXPLANATORY ANSWERS

Question 37. The best answer is C because the passage suggests that the distance from Earth to other points in the solar system could not be calculated until the telescope was invented. "As ingenious as they were, the ancient Greeks were not able to calculate the size of our solar system. That discovery had to wait for the invention of the telescope, nearly two thousand years later" (lines 50–53).

The best answer is NOT:

A because there is no mention in the passage that astronomers needed to find proper observation points before they could determine the distance between Earth and other points in the solar system.

B because there is no mention in the passage of astronomers using ancient Greek calculations to determine the distance between Earth and other objects in the solar system.

D because there is no mention in the passage that Earth and Mars had to align for astronomers to calculate the distance from Earth to other points in the solar system.

Question 38. The best answer is J because the passage indicates that Newton's calculation of the distance to the nearest stars was less acknowledged than his other work. "Only someone as accomplished as Newton could have been the first to perform such a calculation and have it go almost unnoticed among his other achievements" (lines 63–66). "Almost unnoticed among his other achievements" suggests that this calculation was less acknowledged than other achievements.

The best answer is NOT:

F because the passage indicates that Newton's calculation was "almost unnoticed among his other achievements" (lines 65–66). This suggests that his other achievements were considered more important.

G because there's no indication in the passage that this work was speculative or that it was more speculative than Newton's other work.

H because there's no indication in the passage that this work was not complete or that it was less complete than Newton's other work.

Question 39. The best answer is A because the language used to describe how Newton wrote his calculation emphasizes the time period in which he worked and how old-fashioned his tools seemed, particularly in the context of describing an advanced, complicated calculation: "Writing his computations in a spidery script, with a quill dipped in the ink of oak galls" (lines 70–71). Newton was calculating the distance of stars ten trillion miles away while using a rudimentary writing tool.

The best answer is NOT:

B because there is no indication in the passage of how long Newton's calculation took, much less that it took a long time to decipher.

C because there is no description in the passage of the artistic flourishes in the section of Newton's *Principia* in which the calculation appears.

D because there is no mention in the passage of the mistakes Newton made when calculating the distance between Earth and the nearest stars.

Question 40. The best answer is H because the paragraph is about travel and distance. The lines before *set out* help make this clear. "The fastest most of us have traveled is about 500 miles per hour, the cruising speed of a jet. If we set out for the nearest star beyond our solar system at that speed, it would take us about 5 million years to reach our destination" (lines 80–84).

The best answer is NOT:

F because the sentence is about travel, not about a vision. "Described a vision" doesn't make sense in this context.

G because the sentence is about travel, not about stating a purpose. "Stated a purpose" doesn't make sense in this context.

J because the sentence is about travel, not about creating an arrangement. "Created an arrangement" doesn't make sense in this context.

SCIENCE • PRACTICE TEST 5 • EXPLANATORY ANSWERS

Passage I

1. **The best answer is C.** According to Table 1, at 45°C after a 75 min resting time, a 1.0% aqueous mixture of Gum W has a viscosity of 6,825 cP, an aqueous mixture of Gum X has a viscosity of 3,462 cP, an aqueous mixture of Gum Y has a viscosity of 1,639 cP, and an aqueous mixture of Gum Z has a viscosity of 1,562 cP. The viscosity decreases from Gum W to X to Y to Z. **A, B,** and **D** are incorrect; these graphs do not show the correct trend of decreasing viscosity. **C** is correct.

2. **The best answer is H.** According to Table 1, for a given temperature, the viscosity of a gum mixture increased as the rest time increased. A 1.0% mixture of Gum Y at 65°C had a viscosity of 802 cP after a resting time of 75 min and a viscosity of 1,075 cP after a resting time of 102 min. One would predict that after a resting time of 100 min, the viscosity would most likely be between 802 cP and 1,075 cP. **F** and **G** are incorrect; the viscosity would be greater than 800 cP. **H** is correct. **J** is incorrect; the viscosity would be less than 1,100 cP.

3. **The best answer is C.** According to Figure 1, for a gum concentration of 2.0%, Gum Z had the lowest viscosity, followed by Gum X, then Gum W. Gum Y had the highest viscosity. **A** and **B** are incorrect; the 2.0% mixture of Gum Z had the lowest viscosity. **C** is correct. **D** is incorrect; the 2.0% mixture of Gum Y had the highest viscosity.

4. **The best answer is F.** According to Figure 1, a 1.3% aqueous mixture of Gum W had the highest viscosity, greater than 10,000 cP. **F** is correct. **G** is incorrect; the viscosity of a 1.3% aqueous mixture of Gum X was less than 10,000 cP. **H** is incorrect; the viscosity of a 1.3% aqueous mixture of Gum Y was less than 10,000 cP. **J** is incorrect; the viscosity of a 1.3% aqueous mixture of Gum Z was less than 10,000 cP.

5. **The best answer is B.** According to Table 1, the viscosity of the aqueous gum mixtures decreased as the temperature increased. A 1.0% aqueous mixture of Gum Z at 25°C and a resting time of 75 min had a viscosity of 1,879 cP, and a similar solution at 45°C had a viscosity of 1,562 cP. One would predict that a 1.0% aqueous mixture of Gum Z at 30°C and a resting time of 75 min would have a viscosity between 1,562 cP and 1,879 cP. **A** is incorrect; the viscosity would be greater than 1,562 cP. **B** is correct. **C** and **D** are incorrect; the viscosity would be less than 1,879 cP.

6. **The best answer is H.** According to Figure 1, Gum Y had a viscosity of 100,000 cP at a gum concentration of approximately 2.2%. Gums X and Y did not have a viscosity of 100,000 cP until their concentrations were greater than 2.5%. The viscosity of Gum Z did not reach 100,000 cP even at a gum concentration of 3.0%. Gum Y had a viscosity of 100,000 cP at a lower concentration than any of the other 3 gums. **F** is incorrect; Gum W had a viscosity of 100,000 cP at a concentration greater than 2.5%. **G** is incorrect; Gum X had a viscosity of 100,000 cP at a concentration greater than 2.5%. **H** is correct; Gum Y had a viscosity of 100,000 cP at a concentration of approximately 2.25%. **J** is incorrect; Gum Z did not have a viscosity of 100,000 cP at any concentration.

SCIENCE • PRACTICE TEST 5 • EXPLANATORY ANSWERS

Passage II

7. **The best answer is C.** According to Figure 1, a 60% BD by volume sample would have an *A* of approximately 0.6 at 1,746 cm^{-1}. **A** and **B** are incorrect; *A* would be greater than 0.55. **C** is correct. **D** is incorrect; *A* would be less than 0.65.

8. **The best answer is F.** According to Figure 2, as the percent by volume of BD increased, *A* at 1,746 cm^{-1} also increased. **F** is correct. **G, H,** and **J** are incorrect; *A* increased only.

9. **The best answer is A.** According to Figure 2, as the percent BD by volume decreased, *A* at 1,746 cm^{-1} also decreased. The fuel sample in Study 3 with the smallest *A* would be that with the lowest percent BD by volume. Sample W had the lowest percent BD by volume. **A** is correct; the percent BD by volume for Sample W was 4.0%. **B** is incorrect; the percent BD by volume for Sample X was 6.0%. **C** is incorrect; the percent BD by volume for Sample Y was 4.8%. **D** is incorrect; the percent BD by volume for Sample Z was 4.7%.

10. **The best answer is H.** In order to answer this item, the examinee must know that a catalyst is not a reactant or a product and how to write a chemical equation. According to the passage, soybean oil and methanol react in the presence of a catalyst to form FAMEs. Soybean oil and methanol are the reactants, and FAMEs are the products. **F, G,** and **J** are incorrect; FAMEs should appear on the product side of the equation. **H** is correct.

11. **The best answer is B.** In order to gain useful information from the absorbance data for Study 2, the students had to measure the absorbance at a wavenumber at which either BD or PD, but not both, absorbed strongly. According to Figure 1, BD absorbed strongly at 1,172 cm^{-1} and PD did not, while both BD and PD absorbed at 1,464 cm^{-1}. The students would most likely have measured the absorbance in Study 2 at 1,172 cm^{-1}. **A** is incorrect; BD absorbed strongly at 1,172 cm^{-1}, and PD did not. **B** is correct. **C** and **D** are incorrect; a wavenumber of 1,172 cm^{-1} would have been a better choice.

12. **The best answer is J.** According to the passage, BD contained FAMEs and PD did not. Figure 1 shows that BD did not strongly absorb light at a wavenumber of 900 cm^{-1} but did absorb at 1,250 cm^{-1}. A sample that contained only FAMEs would show the same absorbance behavior. **F** and **G** are incorrect; the sample would more strongly absorb at a wavenumber of 1,250 cm^{-1}. **H** is incorrect; PD does not contain FAMEs. **J** is correct.

13. **The best answer is A.** In order to answer this item, the examinee must know that there are 1,000 mL in 1 L. According to Table 1, Sample Y is 4.8% BD by volume. A 10 L sample would therefore contain approximately $0.05 \times 10 \text{ L} = 0.5 \text{ L}$ of BD, which is equal to $0.5 \text{ L} \times \frac{1000 \text{ mL}}{1 \text{ L}} = 500 \text{ mL}$. **A** is correct. **B** is incorrect; 0.5 L = 500 mL. **C** and **D** are incorrect; the sample would contain 0.5 L of BD.

SCIENCE • PRACTICE TEST 5 • EXPLANATORY ANSWERS

Passage III

14. **The best answer is H.** According to Figure 1, the inner core is approximately 1,200 km thick, the outer core is approximately 2,300 km thick, the lower mantle is approximately 2,200 km thick, and the upper mantle/crust is approximately 600 km thick. The outer core and lower mantle are most similar in thickness. **F, G,** and **J** are incorrect; the outer core and lower mantle are most similar, with thicknesses of approximately 2,300 km and 2,200 km, respectively. **H** is correct.

15. **The best answer is A.** Figure 2 shows that the innermost 30% of Earth's mass is located between $r = 0$ km and $r = 3{,}400$ km. **A** is correct. **B** is incorrect; just under 40% of Earth's mass is located between $r = 0$ km and $r = 3{,}900$ km. **C** is incorrect; approximately 50% of Earth's mass is located between $r = 0$ km and $r = 4{,}500$ km. **D** is incorrect; 70% of Earth's mass is located between $r = 0$ km and $r = 5{,}300$ km.

16. **The best answer is J.** According to Figure 1, the crust ends and the atmosphere begins at $r = 6{,}400$ km. Figure 2 shows that 100% of Earth's mass is located within 6,400 km of the center of Earth. From both figures, it can be concluded that Earth's radius is approximately 6,400 km. **F** is incorrect; 1,400 km is the radius of the inner core. **G** is incorrect; 3,500 km is the distance from the center of Earth to the edge of the outer core. **H** is incorrect; 5,700 km is the distance from the center of Earth to the edge of the lower mantle. **J** is correct; 6,400 km is the distance from the center of Earth to Earth's surface.

17. **The best answer is C.** According to Figure 2, throughout the atmosphere and into space, as the distance from the center of Earth increases, the strength of the gravitational field decreases. At $r = 13{,}000$ km, $g_E =$ approximately 2.4 N/kg. Based on the rate at which g_E was decreasing, at $r = 14{,}000$ km, g_E would most likely be close to 2.0 N/kg. **A** and **B** are incorrect; g_E would most likely be greater than 1.5 N/kg. **C** is correct. **D** is incorrect; g_E would most likely be less than 2.5 N/kg.

18. **The best answer is F.** According to Figure 2, the outermost 400 km contains 10% of Earth's mass. Earth's crust, the outermost 30 km, therefore contains much less than 10% of Earth's mass. **F** is correct. **G** is incorrect; the outermost 400 km contains 10% of Earth's mass. **H** is incorrect; the outermost 4,000 km contains 90% of Earth's mass. **J** is incorrect; 99% of Earth's mass in contained in the outermost 5,400 km.

19. **The best answer is A.** In order to answer this item, the examinee must know that weight is directly proportional to gravitational field strength. According to Figure 1, at $r = 2{,}000$ km, $g_E = 7$ N/kg, and at $r = 4{,}000$ km, $g_E = 10.2$ N/kg. Because the strength of the gravitational field is less at $r = 2{,}000$ km, the rock will weigh less at $r = 2{,}000$ km than at $r = 4{,}000$ km. **A** is correct. **B** is incorrect; the rock located at $r = 4{,}000$ km will weigh more. **C** is incorrect; because the rocks have identical masses, the rock in the stronger gravitational field will weigh more. **D** is incorrect; the value of g_E is not the same at both locations.

Passage IV

20. **The best answer is G.** According to the passage, Student 1 stated that biological aging is caused by ROS produced by cellular respiration. Student 4 stated that biological aging is caused by lipofuscin produced by cellular respiration. Neither Student 2 nor Student 3 claimed that the cause of biological aging is related to cellular respiration. **F** is incorrect; Student 4 also claimed that biological aging is caused by a substance produced by cellular respiration. **G** is correct; Students 1 and 4 claimed that biological aging is caused by a substance produced by cellular respiration. **H** is incorrect; Students 2 and 3 did not claim that the cause of biological aging is related to cellular respiration. **J** is incorrect; Students 1 and 4 made the claim about cellular respiration.

21. **The best answer is B.** Student 2 claimed that biological aging is caused by cross-links formed between proteins in the cell. Cross-links are a type of chemical bond. None of the other students' explanations involved the formation of chemical bonds between proteins. The finding would be most consistent with the explanation given by Student 2. **A** is incorrect; Student 1 claimed that biological aging is caused by ROS. **B** is correct. **C** is incorrect; Student 3 claimed that biological aging is caused by DNA damage and that cross-linked proteins do not affect cell function. **D** is incorrect; Student 4 claimed that biological aging is caused by lipofuscin and that cross-linked proteins do not accumulate in the cell.

22. **The best answer is F.** In order to answer this item, the examinee must know that proteins are composed of amino acids. Student 2 claimed that biological aging is caused by cross-linking between proteins. **F** is correct. **G** is incorrect; fatty acids are not found in proteins. **H** is incorrect; monosaccharides are not found in proteins. **J** is incorrect; nucleotides are found in DNA, not proteins.

23. **The best answer is B.** Student 2 claimed that the accumulation of protein clumps formed by cross-linking of the proteins causes biological aging. Student 2 would most likely predict that a substance that prevents cross-linking would be present in a greater concentration in the cells of young adults where less cross-linking is found. **A** is incorrect; Student 1 did not address cross-linking of proteins in their explanation. **B** is correct. **C** is incorrect; Student 3 claimed that cross-linked proteins do not affect cell function. **D** is incorrect; Student 4 claimed that protein clumps do not accumulate in the cell.

24. **The best answer is G.** According to the passage, Student 2 claimed that biological aging is due to protein cross-linking that forms clumps of protein. Student 4 claimed that biological aging is due to lipofuscin that forms clumps. **F** is incorrect; Student 1 claimed that biological aging is due to ROS that damage proteins and lipids in a cell. **G** is correct. **H** and **J** are incorrect; Student 1 claimed that biological aging is due to ROS that damage proteins and lipids in a cell, and Student 3 claimed that biological aging is due to DNA damage.

SCIENCE • PRACTICE TEST 5 • EXPLANATORY ANSWERS

25. **The best answer is D.** According to the passage, Student 1 claimed that biological aging is due to ROS that damage proteins and lipids in the cell. Antioxidants eliminate ROS before they cause damage; however, the cell does not produce enough antioxidants to eliminate all the ROS. **A** and **B** are incorrect; Student 1's explanation did not involve cross-linked proteins. **C** is incorrect; this observation would weaken Student 1's explanation. **D** is correct.

26. **The best answer is G.** In order to answer this item, the examinee must know that genetic mutations are caused by DNA damage. According to the passage, only Student 3 claimed that damage to the DNA is responsible for biological aging. The finding that a mutagen does not affect aging would weaken Student 3's explanation. **F** is incorrect; Student 2 claimed that biological aging is caused by cross-linked proteins, and the finding would not weaken their explanation. **G** is correct. **H** is incorrect; Student 1 claimed that biological aging is caused by ROS, and the finding would not weaken their explanation. **J** is incorrect; Student 2 claimed that biological aging is caused by cross-linked proteins, and Student 4 claimed that DNA damage is not a factor in biological aging. The finding would weaken neither Student 2's nor Student 4's explanation.

Passage V

27. **The best answer is D.** According to Figure 1, the greatest percent of DOC adsorbed by CM1 was adsorbed from the pine leachate. According to Figure 2, the greatest percent of DOC adsorbed by CM2 was adsorbed from the magnolia leachate. Figure 3 shows that the greatest percent of DOC adsorbed by CM3 was adsorbed from the magnolia leachate. **A** and **B** are incorrect; the greatest percent of DOC from the pine leachate was adsorbed by CM1. **C** is incorrect; the greatest percent of DOC from the magnolia leachate was adsorbed by CM3. **D** is correct.

28. **The best answer is J.** According to Figure 3, the percent of leachate DOC adsorbed by CM3 varied from 32% to 56%. The average was 42%, but one can estimate that it must have been between 30% and 56%. **F, G,** and **H** are incorrect; the average was greater than 30%. **J** is correct.

29. **The best answer is C.** According to Figure 2, CM2 adsorbed 7% of the DOC in the maple leachate. Figure 3 shows that CM3 adsorbed 35% of the DOC in the maple leachate. The results of Studies 2 and 3 do not support the statement. A greater percentage of DOC in the maple leachate was adsorbed by CM3 than by CM2. **A** and **B** are incorrect; the results do not support the statement. **C** is correct. **D** is incorrect; CM2 adsorbed 7% and CM3 adsorbed 35% of the DOC in the maple leachate.

30. **The best answer is G.** In each study, 5 different types of leaf leachate were used. Each study used 1 type of clay mineral, but a different type of clay mineral was used in each study. **F** is incorrect; the type of lake water used was the same in all studies. **G** is correct. **H** is incorrect; the volume of leaf leachate was the same in all studies. **J** is incorrect; the volume of filtrate was not varied in each study.

SCIENCE • PRACTICE TEST 5 • EXPLANATORY ANSWERS

31. **The best answer is D.** According to Figure 1, CM1 reduced the DOC in the oak leachate by 31%. Figure 2 shows that CM2 reduced the DOC in the oak leachate by 23%, and Figure 3 shows that CM3 reduced the DOC in the oak leachate by 50%. None of the clay minerals reduced the DOC in the oak leachate by more than 50%. **A, B,** and **C** are incorrect; all clay minerals reduced the DOC in the oak leachate by 50% or less. **D** is correct.

32. **The best answer is J.** In order to answer this item, the examinee must be able to distinguish between a suspension and a solution. According to the passage, in each of the studies, the leachate was prepared by mixing filtered lake water with a sample of leaves. After time was allowed for leaching, the mixture was filtered to remove all solid particles. The leachate was then mixed with the clay mineral. After 2 hours of stirring, the mixture was filtered to remove all solid particles. The presence of solid particles in the mixture indicated that the mixture was a suspension and not a solution. **F** and **G** are incorrect; the mixture was not a solution. **H** is incorrect; the clay mineral particles were not dissolved in the leachate. **J** is correct.

33. **The best answer is A.** According to the passage, the leachate was prepared by allowing the mixture of lake water and leaves to sit for 10 weeks at 4°C in the dark. Keeping the mixture in the dark ensured that none of the DOC would be broken down by electromagnetic energy in the visible wavelength range (i.e., light). **A** is correct. **B** is incorrect; the filtrate and clay mineral were not placed in the dark. **C** is incorrect; filtering the mixture of leaves and lake water would not prevent the breakdown of DOC by visible light. **D** is incorrect; filtering the leachate and clay mineral would not prevent the breakdown of DOC by visible light.

Passage VI

34. **The best answer is H.** According to the passage, all eight Petri dishes were set up in the same way. PD5 was turned 90° so that the dish was vertical. **F** and **G** are incorrect; the Petri dishes shown are both in a vertical orientation, indicating that they have been turned and are not in their original orientation. **H** is correct. **J** is incorrect; the Petri dish would have to be right side up when the experiment was set up, and at no time was the dish inverted.

35. **The best answer is D.** According to Experiment 2, PD8 contained M *Arabidopsis* seeds and was exposed to light from above for 70 hr. **A** is incorrect; PD1 contained WT *Arabidopsis* seeds and was placed in the dark for 70 hr. **B** is incorrect; PD2 contained WT *Arabidopsis* seeds. **C** is incorrect; PD3 was placed in the dark for 70 hr. **D** is correct; PD4 contained M *Arabidopsis* seeds and was exposed to light from above for 70 hr.

SCIENCE • PRACTICE TEST 5 • EXPLANATORY ANSWERS

36. **The best answer is F.** According to Experiment 1, PD1 contained WT *Arabidopsis* seeds and was placed in the dark. PD3 contained M *Arabidopsis* seeds and was placed in the dark. Figure 1 shows that the radicles in PD1 extended straight down, and the radicles in PD3 had more random growth. The radicles did not have the same response to gravity. **F** is correct. **G** is incorrect; PD2 and PD4 were exposed to light. **H** and **J** are incorrect; the radicles did not have the same response to gravity.

37. **The best answer is B.** In order to answer this item, the examinee must know that above-ground plant growth typically exhibits positive phototropism. **A** is incorrect; hypocotyls typically grow toward a light stimulus. **B** is correct. **C** and **D** are incorrect; the hypocotyls most likely exhibited positive phototropism.

38. **The best answer is J.** In order to answer this item, the examinee must know that cotyledons are embryonic leaves. Plants having embryos with one seed leaf are monocots. Plants having embryos with two seed leaves are dicots. Figure 2 shows that each seedling had 2 leaves, and therefore *Arabidopsis* is a dicot. **F** and **G** are incorrect; *Arabidopsis* is a dicot. **H** is incorrect; the seedlings had 2 cotyledons. **J** is correct.

39. **The best answer is B.** According to the passage, the Petri dishes were set up with the agar and seeds and were turned 90° after being exposed to light for 70 hr. The orientation of the Petri dishes was changed one time, and therefore each Petri dish had 2 different orientations. **A, C,** and **D** are incorrect; the Petri dishes had 2 different orientations. **B** is correct.

40. **The best answer is F.** In order to determine the effect of light on the growth of WT *Arabidopsis* seedlings, the results for the Petri dish with WT *Arabidopsis* placed in the dark (PD1) and the Petri dish with WT *Arabidopsis* exposed to light (PD2) should be compared. **F** is correct. **G** and **H** are incorrect; PD3 contained M *Arabidopsis* seeds. **J** is incorrect; PD4 contained M *Arabidopsis* seeds.

11 Chapter 11: Scoring the Additional Practice Tests

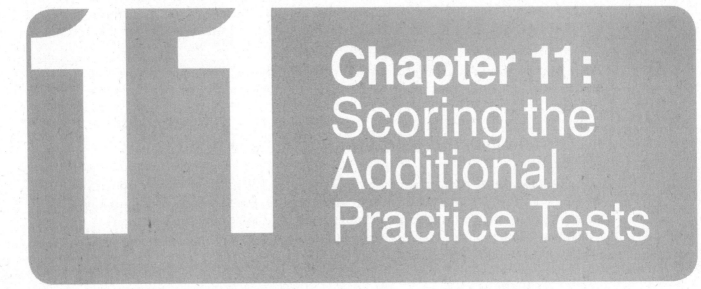

After taking the ACT practice tests 2, 3, 4, or 5, you are ready to score the test to see how you did. In this chapter, you learn how to determine your raw score, convert raw scores to scale scores, compute your Composite score, determine your estimated percentile ranks for each of your scale scores, and score your practice writing test essay. Assuming you already scored practice test 1 (see chapter 3), you should be familiar with the scoring procedures.

When scoring each practice test and reviewing your scores, remember that your scores on the practice tests are only estimates of the scores that you will obtain on the ACT. If your score isn't as high as you expected, the cause could be related to any number of factors. Maybe you need to review important content and skills. Maybe you should work a little faster, or more slowly and carefully, when taking the test. Perhaps you simply weren't doing your best work on the test. Or maybe you need to take more challenging courses to be better prepared. Keep in mind that a test score is just one indicator of your level of academic knowledge and skills. You know your own strengths and weaknesses better than anyone else, so keep them in mind as you evaluate your performance.

Scoring Your Practice Tests

For the multiple-choice tests (English, mathematics, reading, and science), the number of questions you answer correctly is called a *raw* score. To figure out your raw scores for the practice tests in this book count the number of correct answers for each test using the scoring keys provided in the following sections. Then you can convert your raw scores into *scale* scores. Scale scores are the scores that ACT reports to students, high schools, colleges, and scholarship agencies. Raw scores are converted to a common scale score to enhance score interpretation and allow comparability across different forms. After you've converted your raw scores for the practice tests to scale scores, you'll want to convert your scale scores to percentile ranks. Percentile ranks, which are explained in the following pages, are useful for interpreting your scores relative to the scores of others who have taken the ACT.

If you took the optional practice writing test, use the analytic rubric in chapter 3 to evaluate your essay and estimate your writing test score. Being objective about one's own work is difficult, and you have not had the extensive training provided to actual readers of the ACT writing test. However, it is to your advantage to read your own writing critically. Becoming your own editor helps you grow as a writer and as a reader, so it makes sense for you to evaluate your own practice essay. That having been said, it may also be helpful for you to give your practice essay to another reader to get another perspective: perhaps that of a classmate, a parent, or an English teacher, for example. To rate your essay, you and your reader should be familiar with the analytic rubric in chapter 3 and the sample essays and scoring explanations in chapter 9, and then assign your practice essay a score of 1 (low) through 6 (high) in each of the four writing domains (Ideas and Analysis, Development and Support, Organization, and Language Use and Conventions).

Your writing test should be based on two ratings, so you may either multiply your own rating times two, or sum your rating and another reader's rating to calculate your domain scores (2–12 for each domain). Your raw score is the average of your domain scores and will be in a range of 2–12.

Scoring Practice Test 2

Scoring the Multiple-Choice Tests

To score each of your multiple-choice practice tests, starting with the English test, follow these six steps:

STEP 1. Write a "1" in the blank for each question that you answered correctly. An example is provided in the following box:

	Key		Your answer was
1.	A	–	Incorrect
2.	J	1	Correct
3.	B	1	Correct
4.	G	–	Incorrect

English ■ Scoring Key ■ Practice Test 2

	Key			Key			Key	
1.	B	______	26.	J	______	51.	D	______
2.	F	______	27.	C	______	52.	J	______
3.	C	______	28.	H	______	53.	A	______
4.	G	______	29.	B	______	54.	G	______
5.	D	______	30.	J	______	55.	B	______
6.	G	______	31.	A	______	56.	H	______
7.	A	______	32.	J	______	57.	A	______
8.	F	______	33.	B	______	58.	F	______
9.	A	______	34.	G	______	59.	A	______
10.	J	______	35.	C	______	60.	G	______
11.	C	______	36.	H	______	61.	D	______
12.	J	______	37.	D	______	62.	G	______
13.	D	______	38.	F	______	63.	B	______
14.	J	______	39.	B	______	64.	H	______
15.	C	______	40.	H	______	65.	D	______
16.	H	______	41.	A	______	66.	J	______
17.	D	______	42.	J	______	67.	B	______
18.	G	______	43.	C	______	68.	G	______
19.	A	______	44.	J	______	69.	C	______
20.	G	______	45.	A	______	70.	J	______
21.	D	______	46.	H	______	71.	C	______
22.	G	______	47.	A	______	72.	F	______
23.	C	______	48.	H	______	73.	C	______
24.	F	______	49.	C	______	74.	F	______
25.	D	______	50.	J	______	75.	B	______

STEP 2. Add the numbers you entered in Step 1 and write this total in the following shaded box. This is your raw score.

Number Correct (Raw Score) for:	
English Test (75 questions)	_______

STEP 3. Repeat Steps 1 and 2 for the ACT mathematics, reading, and science tests using the scoring keys on the following pages.

Mathematics ■ Scoring Key ■ Practice Test 2

	Key			Key			Key	
1.	C	____	21.	D	____	41.	C	____
2.	H	____	22.	H	____	42.	F	____
3.	D	____	23.	A	____	43.	D	____
4.	H	____	24.	K	____	44.	F	____
5.	D	____	25.	B	____	45.	C	____
6.	F	____	26.	F	____	46.	J	____
7.	C	____	27.	D	____	47.	D	____
8.	G	____	28.	F	____	48.	J	____
9.	A	____	29.	B	____	49.	A	____
10.	F	____	30.	K	____	50.	K	____
11.	B	____	31.	E	____	51.	D	____
12.	K	____	32.	G	____	52.	F	____
13.	E	____	33.	D	____	53.	D	____
14.	J	____	34.	F	____	54.	K	____
15.	D	____	35.	B	____	55.	D	____
16.	H	____	36.	F	____	56.	K	____
17.	D	____	37.	B	____	57.	E	____
18.	H	____	38.	G	____	58.	J	____
19.	E	____	39.	E	____	59.	A	____
20.	G	____	40.	G	____	60.	F	____

Number Correct (Raw Score) for:	
Mathematics Test (60 questions)	_______

Reading ■ Scoring Key ■ Practice Test 2

	Key			Key			Key	
1.	A	______	15.	A	______	29.	C	______
2.	H	______	16.	J	______	30.	G	______
3.	B	______	17.	B	______	31.	D	______
4.	F	______	18.	F	______	32.	G	______
5.	D	______	19.	C	______	33.	C	______
6.	G	______	20.	F	______	34.	G	______
7.	C	______	21.	B	______	35.	D	______
8.	H	______	22.	F	______	36.	F	______
9.	A	______	23.	B	______	37.	D	______
10.	H	______	24.	J	______	38.	F	______
11.	D	______	25.	C	______	39.	B	______
12.	J	______	26.	F	______	40.	G	______
13.	B	______	27.	B	______			
14.	H	______	28.	J	______			

Number Correct (Raw Score) for:

Reading Test (40 questions) ______

Science ■ Scoring Key ■ Practice Test 2

	Key			Key			Key	
1.	B	______	15.	A	______	29.	A	______
2.	G	______	16.	F	______	30.	J	______
3.	D	______	17.	D	______	31.	C	______
4.	H	______	18.	F	______	32.	H	______
5.	D	______	19.	C	______	33.	B	______
6.	J	______	20.	J	______	34.	G	______
7.	A	______	21.	B	______	35.	C	______
8.	G	______	22.	F	______	36.	G	______
9.	A	______	23.	D	______	37.	D	______
10.	H	______	24.	H	______	38.	F	______
11.	B	______	25.	B	______	39.	A	______
12.	G	______	26.	J	______	40.	F	______
13.	D	______	27.	C	______			
14.	H	______	28.	J	______			

Number Correct (Raw Score) for:

Science Test (40 questions) ______

STEP 4. On each of the four tests, the total number of correct responses yields a raw score. Use the conversion table on the following page to convert your raw scores to scale scores. For each of the four tests, locate and circle your raw score or the range of raw scores that includes it in the conversion table. Then, read across to either outside column of the table and circle the scale score that corresponds to that raw score. As you determine your scale scores, enter them in the blanks provided below. The highest possible scale score for each test is 36. The lowest possible scale score for any of the four tests is 1.

	Your Scale Scores
English	________
Mathematics	________
Reading	________
Science	________
Sum of Scores	________

STEP 5. Compute your Composite score by averaging the four scale scores. To do this, add your four scale scores and divide the sum by 4. If the resulting number ends in a fraction, round it off to the nearest whole number. (Round down any fraction less than one-half; round up any fraction that is one-half or more.) Enter this number in the appropriate blank below. This is your Composite score. The highest possible Composite score is 36. The lowest possible Composite score is 1.

	Your Scale Scores
English	________
Mathematics	________
Reading	________
Science	________
Sum of Scores	________
Composite Score (sum ÷ 4)	________

Scale Score Conversion Table: Practice Test 2

Scale Score	Raw Score				Scale Score
	English	Mathematics	Reading	Science	
36	74–75	58–60	39–40	39–40	**36**
35	72–73	56–57	38	38	**35**
34	71	54–55	37	37	**34**
33	69–70	53	36	36	**33**
32	68	51–52	34–35	–	**32**
31	67	49–50	33	35	**31**
30	66	47–48	32	34	**30**
29	65	46	–	33	**29**
28	63–64	43–45	31	32	**28**
27	61–62	41–42	30	31	**27**
26	59–60	39–40	29	29–30	**26**
25	57–58	37–38	28	27–28	**25**
24	55–56	35–36	26–27	25–26	**24**
23	52–54	33–34	25	23–24	**23**
22	50–51	32	23–24	21–22	**22**
21	47–49	30–31	22	20	**21**
20	44–46	28–29	20–21	18–19	**20**
19	42–43	26–27	19	17	**19**
18	40–41	24–25	17–18	15–16	**18**
17	37–39	21–23	16	14	**17**
16	34–36	18–20	15	12–13	**16**
15	31–33	15–17	13–14	11	**15**
14	28–30	12–14	12	10	**14**
13	26–27	11	10–11	9	**13**
12	24–25	9–10	8–9	8	**12**
11	21–23	7–8	7	7	**11**
10	18–20	6	6	6	**10**
9	15–17	5	5	5	**9**
8	13–14	4	4	4	**8**
7	11–12	3	–	3	**7**
6	8–10	–	3	–	**6**
5	7	2	–	2	**5**
4	5–6	–	2	–	**4**
3	3–4	1	1	1	**3**
2	2	–	–	–	**2**
1	0–1	0	0	0	**1**

STEP 6. Use the table on page 893 to determine your estimated percentile ranks (percent at or below) for each of your scale scores. In the far left column of the table, circle your scale score for the English test (from page 891). Then read across to the percentile rank column for that test; circle or put a checkmark beside the corresponding percentile rank. Use the same procedure for the other three tests (from page 891). Using the right-hand column of scale scores for your science test and Composite scores may be easier. As you mark your percentile ranks, enter them in the blanks provided. You may also find it helpful to compare your performance with the national mean (average) score for each of the four tests and the Composite as shown at the bottom of the table.

National Distributions of Cumulative Percents for ACT Test Scores
ACT-Tested High School Graduates from 2016, 2017, and 2018

Score	ENGLISH	MATHEMATICS	READING	SCIENCE	COMPOSITE	STEM	Score
36	100	100	100	100	100	100	36
35	99	99	99	99	99	99	35
34	97	99	97	99	99	99	34
33	95	98	95	97	98	98	33
32	93	97	93	96	97	97	32
31	92	96	90	95	95	96	31
30	91	95	88	94	93	94	30
29	88	93	85	92	91	93	29
28	87	91	83	91	89	91	28
27	85	88	80	88	86	88	27
26	82	83	77	86	82	84	26
25	79	79	74	82	78	80	25
24	75	74	71	77	74	75	24
23	70	68	66	70	69	69	23
22	64	64	60	64	63	64	22
21	59	60	54	56	58	58	21
20	53	56	48	49	51	52	20
19	47	52	43	42	45	45	19
18	43	47	37	36	39	38	18
17	39	40	31	29	32	30	17
16	35	30	27	23	26	23	16
15	29	18	22	17	20	15	15
14	23	9	17	13	14	9	14
13	18	3	12	9	8	4	13
12	14	1	8	6	4	2	12
11	10	1	4	4	1	1	11
10	6	1	2	2	1	1	10
9	3	1	1	1	1	1	9
8	2	1	1	1	1	1	8
7	1	1	1	1	1	1	7
6	1	1	1	1	1	1	6
5	1	1	1	1	1	1	5
4	1	1	1	1	1	1	4
3	1	1	1	1	1	1	3
2	1	1	1	1	1	1	2
1	1	1	1	1	1	1	1
Mean	20.2	20.6	21.3	20.8	20.9	20.9	
S.D.	6.9	5.5	6.6	5.6	5.7	5.3	

Note: These national norms are the source of U.S. ranks, for multiple-choice tests, displayed on ACT reports during the 2018-2019 testing year.

These norms with a sample size of 6,035,197, are based on 2016, 2017, and 2018 graduates.

Scoring Your Practice Writing Test 2 Essay

To score your practice writing test essay, follow these steps:

STEP 1. Use the guidelines from the writing test analytic rubric in chapter 3 to score your essay. Because many essays do not fit the exact description at each score point, read each description and try to determine which paragraph in the rubric best describes most of the characteristics of your essay.

STEP 2. Because your writing test domain scores are the sum of two readers' ratings of your essay, multiply your own 1–6 rating from step 1 by 2. Or, have both you and someone else read and score your practice essay, add those ratings together, and record the total in the Domain Score column in step 3.

STEP 3. Enter your writing test domain scores in the following box:

			Domain Score
Ideas and Analysis	______________	x 2 =	______________
Development and Support	______________	x 2 =	______________
Organization	______________	x 2 =	______________
Language Use and Conventions	______________	x 2 =	______________

STEP 4. Enter the sum of the second-column scores here _______.

STEP 5. Divide sum by 4† (range 2–12). This is your Writing Subject score.

†Round value to the nearest whole number. Round down any fraction less than one-half; round up any fraction that is one-half or more.

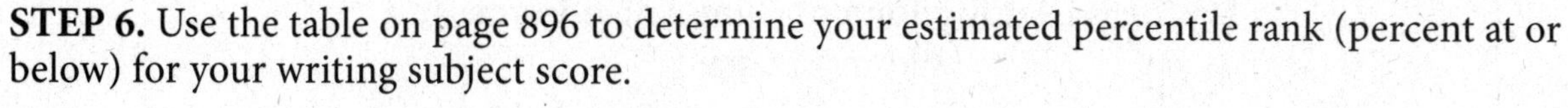
STEP 6. Use the table on page 896 to determine your estimated percentile rank (percent at or below) for your writing subject score.

National Distributions of Cumulative Percents
Writing Score

ACT-Tested High School Graduates
from 2016, 2017, and 2018

Score	Writing
12	22
11	18
10	15
9	12
8	7
7	5
6	4
5	3
4	3
3	2
2	2
1	1
Mean	17.8
S.D.	6.4

Note: The norms for the ACT ELA and 2–12 Writing scores are the source of U.S. and state ranks printed on ACT score reports during the 2018–2019 testing year. The norms for the ACT 1–36 Writing scores are the source of U.S. and state ranks printed on ACT supplemental score reports for test events between September 2015 and June 2017.
These norms with a sample size of 2,839,108, are based on 2016, 2017, and 2018 graduates.

Scoring Practice Test 3

Scoring the Multiple-Choice Tests

To score each of your multiple-choice practice tests, starting with the English test, follow these six steps:

STEP 1. Write a “1” in the blank for each question that you answered correctly. An example is provided in the following box:

	Key		Your answer was
1.	A	–	Incorrect
2.	J	1	Correct
3.	B	1	Correct
4.	G	–	Incorrect

English ■ Scoring Key ■ Practice Test 3

	Key			Key			Key	
1.	C	______	26.	J	______	51.	B	______
2.	F	______	27.	B	______	52.	G	______
3.	D	______	28.	H	______	53.	A	______
4.	J	______	29.	D	______	54.	H	______
5.	A	______	30.	F	______	55.	C	______
6.	G	______	31.	B	______	56.	H	______
7.	A	______	32.	F	______	57.	B	______
8.	J	______	33.	C	______	58.	F	______
9.	C	______	34.	F	______	59.	C	______
10.	F	______	35.	D	______	60.	F	______
11.	A	______	36.	H	______	61.	C	______
12.	G	______	37.	D	______	62.	H	______
13.	D	______	38.	J	______	63.	B	______
14.	J	______	39.	B	______	64.	G	______
15.	A	______	40.	F	______	65.	C	______
16.	H	______	41.	C	______	66.	H	______
17.	D	______	42.	J	______	67.	A	______
18.	F	______	43.	D	______	68.	F	______
19.	C	______	44.	G	______	69.	B	______
20.	J	______	45.	B	______	70.	F	______
21.	C	______	46.	G	______	71.	D	______
22.	F	______	47.	B	______	72.	J	______
23.	B	______	48.	J	______	73.	D	______
24.	J	______	49.	C	______	74.	G	______
25.	A	______	50.	F	______	75.	D	______

STEP 2. Add the numbers you entered in step 1 and write this total in the following shaded box. This is your raw score.

Number Correct (Raw Score) for:	
English Test (75 questions)	________

STEP 3. Repeat steps 1 and 2 for the ACT mathematics, reading, and science tests using the scoring keys on the following pages.

Mathematics ■ Scoring Key ■ Practice Test 3

	Key			Key			Key	
1.	E	________	21.	E	________	41.	B	________
2.	K	________	22.	G	________	42.	F	________
3.	A	________	23.	C	________	43.	C	________
4.	K	________	24.	H	________	44.	F	________
5.	E	________	25.	B	________	45.	E	________
6.	G	________	26.	H	________	46.	G	________
7.	B	________	27.	C	________	47.	E	________
8.	J	________	28.	J	________	48.	H	________
9.	E	________	29.	A	________	49.	D	________
10.	J	________	30.	G	________	50.	F	________
11.	C	________	31.	B	________	51.	E	________
12.	J	________	32.	F	________	52.	H	________
13.	E	________	33.	D	________	53.	B	________
14.	G	________	34.	J	________	54.	G	________
15.	A	________	35.	B	________	55.	B	________
16.	J	________	36.	H	________	56.	H	________
17.	E	________	37.	E	________	57.	E	________
18.	K	________	38.	G	________	58.	K	________
19.	A	________	39.	E	________	59.	B	________
20.	J	________	40.	H	________	60.	K	________

Number Correct (Raw Score) for:	
Mathematics Test (60 questions)	________

Reading ■ Scoring Key ■ Practice Test 3

	Key			Key			Key	
1.	A	______	15.	B	______	29.	B	______
2.	G	______	16.	H	______	30.	H	______
3.	A	______	17.	C	______	31.	D	______
4.	H	______	18.	G	______	32.	G	______
5.	C	______	19.	D	______	33.	C	______
6.	G	______	20.	J	______	34.	G	______
7.	B	______	21.	A	______	35.	D	______
8.	F	______	22.	H	______	36.	G	______
9.	A	______	23.	D	______	37.	D	______
10.	J	______	24.	F	______	38.	G	______
11.	A	______	25.	C	______	39.	C	______
12.	J	______	26.	H	______	40.	F	______
13.	D	______	27.	D	______			
14.	F	______	28.	J	______			

Number Correct (Raw Score) for:

Reading Test (40 questions) ______

Science ■ Scoring Key ■ Practice Test 3

	Key			Key			Key	
1.	B	______	15.	C	______	29.	D	______
2.	F	______	16.	F	______	30.	J	______
3.	A	______	17.	A	______	31.	A	______
4.	G	______	18.	H	______	32.	J	______
5.	A	______	19.	D	______	33.	D	______
6.	J	______	20.	G	______	34.	J	______
7.	B	______	21.	B	______	35.	C	______
8.	G	______	22.	H	______	36.	G	______
9.	A	______	23.	C	______	37.	A	______
10.	H	______	24.	G	______	38.	J	______
11.	D	______	25.	D	______	39.	D	______
12.	J	______	26.	F	______	40.	J	______
13.	B	______	27.	C	______			
14.	G	______	28.	H	______			

Number Correct (Raw Score) for:

Science Test (40 questions) ______

STEP 4. On each of the four tests, the total number of correct responses yields a raw score. Use the conversion table on the following page to convert your raw scores to scale scores. For each of the four tests, locate and circle your raw score or the range of raw scores that includes it in the conversion table. Then, read across to either outside column of the table and circle the scale score that corresponds to that raw score. As you determine your scale scores, enter them in the blanks provided below. The highest possible scale score for each test is 36. The lowest possible scale score for any of the four tests is 1.

	Your Scale Scores
English	________
Mathematics	________
Reading	________
Science	________
Sum of Scores	________

STEP 5. Compute your Composite score by averaging the four scale scores. To do this, add your four scale scores and divide the sum by 4. If the resulting number ends in a fraction, round it off to the nearest whole number. (Round down any fraction less than one-half; round up any fraction that is one-half or more.) Enter this number in the appropriate blank below. This is your Composite score. The highest possible Composite score is 36. The lowest possible Composite score is 1.

	Your Scale Scores
English	________
Mathematics	________
Reading	________
Science	________
Sum of Scores	________
Composite Score (sum ÷ 4)	________

Scale Score Conversion Table: Practice Test 3

Scale Score	Raw Score English	Mathematics	Reading	Science	Scale Score
36	75	58–60	40	39–40	36
35	73–74	56–57	–	38	35
34	72	54–55	39	–	34
33	71	52–53	38	37	33
32	70	50–51	37	36	32
31	69	49	–	35	31
30	68	47–48	36	34	30
29	66–67	46	35	33	29
28	65	44–45	34	32	28
27	63–64	41–43	33	31	27
26	61–62	39–40	32	30	26
25	58–60	37–38	31	28–29	25
24	56–57	35–36	30	26–27	24
23	53–55	33–34	29	24–25	23
22	50–52	31–32	27–28	23	22
21	47–49	30	26	21–22	21
20	44–46	28–29	24–25	18–20	20
19	42–43	26–27	22–23	16–17	19
18	40–41	24–25	21	15	18
17	37–39	21–23	19–20	13–14	17
16	35–36	17–20	17–18	12	16
15	32–34	14–16	15–16	11	15
14	30–31	10–13	13–14	10	14
13	28–29	8–9	11–12	9	13
12	26–27	7	9–10	8	12
11	24–25	5–6	8	7	11
10	22–23	4	6–7	6	10
9	19–21	–	–	5	9
8	16–18	3	5	4	8
7	13–15	–	4	–	7
6	11–12	2	3	3	6
5	8–10	–	–	2	5
4	6–7	1	2	–	4
3	4–5	–	–	1	3
2	3	–	1	–	2
1	0–2	0	0	0	1

STEP 6. Use the table on page 893 to determine your estimated percentile ranks (percent at or below) for each of your scale scores. In the far left column of the table, circle your scale score for the English test (from page 900). Then read across to the percentile rank column for that test; circle or put a checkmark beside the corresponding percentile rank. Use the same procedure for the other three tests (from page 900). Using the right-hand column of scale scores for your science test and Composite scores may be easier. As you mark your percentile ranks, enter them in the blanks provided. You may also find it helpful to compare your performance with the national mean (average) score for each of the four tests and the Composite as shown at the bottom of the table.

Scoring Your Practice Writing Test 3 Essay

To score your practice writing test essay, follow these steps:

STEP 1. Use the guidelines from the writing test analytic rubric in chapter 3 to score your essay. Because many essays do not fit the exact description at each score point, read each description and try to determine which paragraph in the rubric best describes most of the characteristics of your essay.

STEP 2. Because your writing test domain scores are the sum of two readers' ratings of your essay, multiply your own 1–6 rating from step 1 by 2. Or, have both you and someone else read and score your practice essay, add those ratings together, and record the total in the Domain Score column in step 3.

STEP 3. Enter your writing test domain scores in the following box:

			Domain Score
Ideas and Analysis	________	x 2 =	________
Development and Support	________	x 2 =	________
Organization	________	x 2 =	________
Language Use and Conventions	________	x 2 =	________

STEP 4. Enter the sum of the second-column scores here ______.

STEP 5. Divide sum by 4† (range 2–12). This is your Writing Subject score.

†Round value to the nearest whole number. Round down any fraction less than one-half; round up any fraction that is one-half or more.

STEP 6. Use the table on page 896 to determine your estimated percentile rank (percent at or below) for your writing subject score.

Scoring Practice Test 4

Scoring the Multiple-Choice Tests

To score each of your multiple-choice practice tests, starting with the English test, follow these six steps:

STEP 1. Write a "1" in the blank for each question that you answered correctly. An example is provided in the following box:

	Key		Your answer was
1.	A	–	Incorrect
2.	J	1	Correct
3.	B	1	Correct
4.	G	–	Incorrect

English ■ Scoring Key ■ Practice Test 4

	Key			Key			Key	
1.	A	______	26.	J	______	51.	A	______
2.	G	______	27.	A	______	52.	G	______
3.	C	______	28.	F	______	53.	A	______
4.	G	______	29.	C	______	54.	J	______
5.	D	______	30.	H	______	55.	D	______
6.	G	______	31.	D	______	56.	F	______
7.	B	______	32.	F	______	57.	D	______
8.	J	______	33.	C	______	58.	G	______
9.	B	______	34.	H	______	59.	B	______
10.	F	______	35.	C	______	60.	G	______
11.	D	______	36.	J	______	61.	D	______
12.	F	______	37.	D	______	62.	H	______
13.	B	______	38.	F	______	63.	C	______
14.	F	______	39.	D	______	64.	G	______
15.	A	______	40.	J	______	65.	C	______
16.	F	______	41.	B	______	66.	J	______
17.	C	______	42.	F	______	67.	A	______
18.	G	______	43.	C	______	68.	F	______
19.	A	______	44.	G	______	69.	B	______
20.	H	______	45.	C	______	70.	G	______
21.	C	______	46.	J	______	71.	B	______
22.	H	______	47.	C	______	72.	H	______
23.	A	______	48.	H	______	73.	C	______
24.	H	______	49.	C	______	74.	J	______
25.	D	______	50.	J	______	75.	B	______

STEP 2. Add the numbers you entered in step 1 and write this total in the following shaded box. This is your raw score.

Number Correct (Raw Score) for:	
English Test (75 questions)	________

STEP 3. Repeat steps 1 and 2 for the ACT mathematics, reading, and science tests using the scoring keys on the following pages.

Mathematics ■ Scoring Key ■ Practice Test 4

	Key			Key			Key	
1.	C	________	21.	D	________	41.	A	________
2.	J	________	22.	G	________	42.	G	________
3.	E	________	23.	C	________	43.	D	________
4.	F	________	24.	H	________	44.	G	________
5.	C	________	25.	E	________	45.	D	________
6.	G	________	26.	G	________	46.	G	________
7.	B	________	27.	E	________	47.	E	________
8.	H	________	28.	F	________	48.	H	________
9.	C	________	29.	D	________	49.	D	________
10.	G	________	30.	H	________	50.	J	________
11.	C	________	31.	A	________	51.	E	________
12.	G	________	32.	J	________	52.	F	________
13.	D	________	33.	A	________	53.	B	________
14.	G	________	34.	K	________	54.	F	________
15.	D	________	35.	B	________	55.	E	________
16.	H	________	36.	F	________	56.	K	________
17.	A	________	37.	E	________	57.	A	________
18.	J	________	38.	K	________	58.	F	________
19.	C	________	39.	D	________	59.	D	________
20.	H	________	40.	H	________	60.	K	________

Number Correct (Raw Score) for:	
Math Test (60 questions)	________

Reading ■ Scoring Key ■ Practice Test 4

	Key			Key			Key	
1.	B	______	15.	C	______	29.	D	______
2.	H	______	16.	H	______	30.	J	______
3.	D	______	17.	A	______	31.	B	______
4.	F	______	18.	J	______	32.	H	______
5.	B	______	19.	A	______	33.	B	______
6.	F	______	20.	J	______	34.	G	______
7.	C	______	21.	B	______	35.	C	______
8.	J	______	22.	G	______	36.	F	______
9.	D	______	23.	D	______	37.	D	______
10.	F	______	24.	G	______	38.	F	______
11.	D	______	25.	C	______	39.	B	______
12.	F	______	26.	H	______	40.	J	______
13.	D	______	27.	A	______			
14.	G	______	28.	G	______			

Number Correct (Raw Score) for:

Reading Test (40 questions) ______

Science ■ Scoring Key ■ Practice Test 4

	Key			Key			Key	
1.	A	______	15.	A	______	29.	A	______
2.	H	______	16.	F	______	30.	J	______
3.	C	______	17.	D	______	31.	B	______
4.	J	______	18.	G	______	32.	J	______
5.	A	______	19.	C	______	33.	D	______
6.	J	______	20.	G	______	34.	G	______
7.	D	______	21.	B	______	35.	D	______
8.	F	______	22.	F	______	36.	G	______
9.	D	______	23.	B	______	37.	C	______
10.	H	______	24.	H	______	38.	F	______
11.	B	______	25.	C	______	39.	C	______
12.	J	______	26.	G	______	40.	H	______
13.	C	______	27.	D	______			
14.	J	______	28.	F	______			

Number Correct (Raw Score) for:

Science Test (40 questions) ______

STEP 4. On each of the four tests, the total number of correct responses yields a raw score. Use the conversion table on the following page to convert your raw scores to scale scores. For each of the four tests, locate and circle your raw score or the range of raw scores that includes it in the conversion table. Then, read across to either outside column of the table and circle the scale score that corresponds to that raw score. As you determine your scale scores, enter them in the blanks provided below. The highest possible scale score for each test is 36. The lowest possible scale score for any of the four tests is 1.

	Your Scale Scores
English	________
Mathematics	________
Reading	________
Science	________
Sum of Scores	________

STEP 5. Compute your Composite score by averaging the four scale scores. To do this, add your four scale scores and divide the sum by 4. If the resulting number ends in a fraction, round it off to the nearest whole number. (Round down any fraction less than one-half; round up any fraction that is one-half or more.) Enter this number in the appropriate blank below. This is your Composite score. The highest possible Composite score is 36. The lowest possible Composite score is 1.

	Your Scale Scores
English	________
Mathematics	________
Reading	________
Science	________
Sum of Scores	________
Composite Score (sum ÷ 4)	________

Scale Score Conversion Table: Practice Test 4

Scale Score	Raw Score				Scale Score
	English	Mathematics	Reading	Science	
36	73–75	59–60	40	39–40	**36**
35	71–72	57–58	39	38	**35**
34	69–70	55–56	37–38	37	**34**
33	68	54	36	–	**33**
32	67	53	35	36	**32**
31	66	52	34	35	**31**
30	65	50–51	33	34	**30**
29	64	48–49	32	33	**29**
28	63	46–47	31	32	**28**
27	61–62	42–45	30	31	**27**
26	59–60	40–41	29	30	**26**
25	57–58	37–39	28	28–29	**25**
24	54–56	35–36	27	27	**24**
23	51–53	32–34	25–26	25–26	**23**
22	48–50	31	23–24	23–24	**22**
21	45–47	29–30	22	22	**21**
20	42–44	27–28	21	20–21	**20**
19	40–41	25–26	19–20	19	**19**
18	38–39	23–24	18	17–18	**18**
17	36–37	20–22	17	16	**17**
16	33–35	16–19	15–16	14–15	**16**
15	30–32	13–15	14	13	**15**
14	27–29	10–12	12–13	11–12	**14**
13	25–26	8–9	11	10	**13**
12	23–24	6–7	10	9	**12**
11	20–22	5	8–9	8	**11**
10	18–19	4	7	7	**10**
9	15–17	–	6	6	**9**
8	13–14	3	5	5	**8**
7	11–12	–	4	4	**7**
6	8–10	2	–	3	**6**
5	7	–	3	2	**5**
4	5–6	1	2	–	**4**
3	3–4	–	–	1	**3**
2	2	–	1	–	**2**
1	0–1	0	0	0	**1**

STEP 6. Use the table on page 893 to determine your estimated percentile ranks (percent at or below) for each of your scale scores. In the far left column of the table, circle your scale score for the English test (from page 907). Then read across to the percentile rank column for that test; circle or put a checkmark beside the corresponding percentile rank. Use the same procedure for the other three tests (from page 907). Using the right-hand column of scale scores for your science test and Composite scores may be easier. As you mark your percentile ranks, enter them in the blanks provided. You may also find it helpful to compare your performance with the national mean (average) score for each of the four tests and the Composite as shown at the bottom of the table.

Scoring Your Practice Writing Test 4 Essay

To score your practice writing test essay, follow these steps:

STEP 1. Use the guidelines from the writing test analytic rubric in chapter 3 to score your essay. Because many essays do not fit the exact description at each score point, read each description and try to determine which paragraph in the rubric best describes most of the characteristics of your essay.

STEP 2. Because your writing test domain scores are the sum of two readers' ratings of your essay, multiply your own 1–6 rating from step 1 by 2. Or, have both you and someone else read and score your practice essay, add those ratings together, and record the total in the Domain Score column in step 3.

STEP 3. Enter your writing test domain scores in the following box:

			Domain Score
Ideas and Analysis	____________	x 2 =	____________
Development and Support	____________	x 2 =	____________
Organization	____________	x 2 =	____________
Language Use and Convention	____________	x 2 =	____________

STEP 4. Enter the sum of the second-column scores here ______.

STEP 5. Divide sum by 4† (range 2–12). This is your Writing Subject score.

†Round value to the nearest whole number. Round down any fraction less than one-half; round up any fraction that is one-half or more.

STEP 6. Use the table on page 896 to determine your estimated percentile rank (percent at or below) for your writing subject score.

Scoring Practice Test 5

Scoring the Multiple-Choice Tests

To score your multiple-choice practice tests, starting with the English test, follow these six steps:

STEP 1. Write a "1" in the blank for each question that you answered correctly. An example is provided in the following box:

	Key		Your answer was
1.	A	–	Incorrect
2.	J	1	Correct
3.	B	1	Correct
4.	G	–	Incorrect

English ■ Scoring Key ■ Practice Test 5

	Key			Key			Key	
1.	B	______	26.	H	______	51.	A	______
2.	F	______	27.	A	______	52.	F	______
3.	C	______	28.	J	______	53.	D	______
4.	F	______	29.	D	______	54.	G	______
5.	A	______	30.	F	______	55.	B	______
6.	J	______	31.	B	______	56.	H	______
7.	D	______	32.	H	______	57.	B	______
8.	H	______	33.	A	______	58.	G	______
9.	D	______	34.	G	______	59.	A	______
10.	J	______	35.	A	______	60.	H	______
11.	A	______	36.	F	______	61.	A	______
12.	G	______	37.	D	______	62.	G	______
13.	B	______	38.	J	______	63.	D	______
14.	H	______	39.	B	______	64.	G	______
15.	C	______	40.	J	______	65.	C	______
16.	J	______	41.	C	______	66.	F	______
17.	B	______	42.	F	______	67.	D	______
18.	H	______	43.	D	______	68.	H	______
19.	A	______	44.	H	______	69.	A	______
20.	J	______	45.	A	______	70.	J	______
21.	B	______	46.	J	______	71.	B	______
22.	F	______	47.	C	______	72.	F	______
23.	C	______	48.	H	______	73.	D	______
24.	G	______	49.	D	______	74.	F	______
25.	B	______	50.	J	______	75.	C	______

STEP 2. Add the numbers you entered in step 1 and write this total in the following shaded box. This is your raw score.

Number Correct (Raw Score) for:	
English Test (75 questions)	________

STEP 3. Repeat steps 1 and 2 for the ACT mathematics, reading, and science tests using the scoring keys on the following pages.

Mathematics ■ Scoring Key ■ Practice Test 5

	Key			Key			Key	
1.	B	________	21.	C	________	41.	C	________
2.	G	________	22.	K	________	42.	G	________
3.	A	________	23.	A	________	43.	D	________
4.	H	________	24.	G	________	44.	K	________
5.	A	________	25.	D	________	45.	A	________
6.	G	________	26.	F	________	46.	K	________
7.	E	________	27.	C	________	47.	D	________
8.	J	________	28.	H	________	48.	F	________
9.	C	________	29.	A	________	49.	B	________
10.	H	________	30.	H	________	50.	K	________
11.	E	________	31.	C	________	51.	D	________
12.	G	________	32.	J	________	52.	J	________
13.	A	________	33.	C	________	53.	E	________
14.	K	________	34.	G	________	54.	J	________
15.	E	________	35.	A	________	55.	B	________
16.	J	________	36.	G	________	56.	G	________
17.	D	________	37.	E	________	57.	A	________
18.	G	________	38.	J	________	58.	J	________
19.	B	________	39.	C	________	59.	D	________
20.	F	________	40.	K	________	60.	K	________

Number Correct (Raw Score) for:	
Mathematics Test (60 questions)	________

Reading ■ Scoring Key ■ Practice Test 5

	Key			Key			Key	
1.	A	______	15.	D	______	29.	B	______
2.	H	______	16.	G	______	30.	J	______
3.	D	______	17.	C	______	31.	B	______
4.	H	______	18.	F	______	32.	H	______
5.	B	______	19.	D	______	33.	B	______
6.	J	______	20.	J	______	34.	F	______
7.	A	______	21.	C	______	35.	A	______
8.	F	______	22.	F	______	36.	J	______
9.	C	______	23.	A	______	37.	C	______
10.	G	______	24.	H	______	38.	J	______
11.	C	______	25.	B	______	39.	A	______
12.	F	______	26.	G	______	40.	H	______
13.	A	______	27.	C	______			
14.	G	______	28.	J	______			

Number Correct (Raw Score) for:

Reading Test (40 questions) ______

Science ■ Scoring Key ■ Practice Test 5

	Key			Key			Key	
1.	C	______	15.	A	______	29.	C	______
2.	H	______	16.	J	______	30.	G	______
3.	C	______	17.	C	______	31.	D	______
4.	F	______	18.	F	______	32.	J	______
5.	B	______	19.	A	______	33.	A	______
6.	H	______	20.	G	______	34.	H	______
7.	C	______	21.	B	______	35.	D	______
8.	F	______	22.	F	______	36.	F	______
9.	A	______	23.	B	______	37.	B	______
10.	H	______	24.	G	______	38.	J	______
11.	B	______	25.	D	______	39.	B	______
12.	J	______	26.	G	______	40.	F	______
13.	A	______	27.	D	______			
14.	H	______	28.	J	______			

Number Correct (Raw Score) for:

Science Test (40 questions) ______

STEP 4. On each of the four tests, the total number of correct responses yields a raw score. Use the conversion table on the following page to convert your raw scores to scale scores. For each of the four tests, locate and circle your raw score or the range of raw scores that includes it in the conversion table. Then, read across to either outside column of the table and circle the scale score that corresponds to that raw score. As you determine your scale scores, enter them in the blanks provided below. The highest possible scale score for each test is 36. The lowest possible scale score for any of the four tests is 1.

	Your Scale Scores
English	__________
Mathematics	__________
Reading	__________
Science	__________
Sum of Scores	__________

STEP 5. Compute your Composite score by averaging the four scale scores. To do this, add your four scale scores and divide the sum by 4. If the resulting number ends in a fraction, round it off to the nearest whole number. (Round down any fraction less than one-half; round up any fraction that is one-half or more.) Enter this number in the appropriate blank below. This is your Composite score. The highest possible Composite score is 36. The lowest possible Composite score is 1.

	Your Scale Scores
English	__________
Mathematics	__________
Reading	__________
Science	__________
Sum of Scores	__________
Composite Score (sum ÷ 4)	__________

Scale Score Conversion Table: Practice Test 5

Scale Score	Raw Score: English	Mathematics	Reading	Science	Scale Score
36	73–75	59–60	39–40	39–40	36
35	71–72	56–58	38	38	35
34	70	54–55	37	37	34
33	69	53	36	36	33
32	68	52	34–35	35	32
31	67	50–51	33	34	31
30	66	49	32	–	30
29	65	47–48	31	33	29
28	64	44–46	30	32	28
27	62–63	42–43	29	31	27
26	61	39–41	28	30	26
25	58–60	37–38	27	28–29	25
24	55–57	35–36	26	27	24
23	52–54	33–34	24–25	25–26	23
22	50–51	31–32	23	24	22
21	47–49	30	21–22	22–23	21
20	44–46	28–29	20	21	20
19	42–43	26–27	19	19–20	19
18	40–41	24–25	17–18	18	18
17	38–39	20–23	16	16–17	17
16	35–37	17–19	15	15	16
15	32–34	13–16	13–14	13–14	15
14	29–31	10–12	12	12	14
13	26–28	8–9	11	10–11	13
12	24–25	6–7	9–10	9	12
11	21–23	5	8	8	11
10	17–20	4	7	7	10
9	15–16	–	6	6	9
8	13–14	3	5	5	8
7	10–12	–	4	4	7
6	8–9	2	–	3	6
5	6–7	–	3	–	5
4	5	1	2	2	4
3	3–4	–	–	1	3
2	2	–	1	–	2
1	0–1	0	0	0	1

STEP 6. Use the table on page 893 to determine your estimated percentile ranks (percent at or below) for each of your scale scores. In the far left column of the table, circle your scale score for the English test (from page 914). Then read across to the percentile rank column for that test; circle or put a checkmark beside the corresponding percentile rank. Use the same procedure for the other four tests (from page 914). Using the right-hand column of scale scores for your science test and Composite scores may be easier. As you mark your percentile ranks, enter them in the blanks provided. You may also find it helpful to compare your performance with the national mean (average) score for each of the five tests and the Composite as shown at the bottom of the table.

Scoring Your Practice Writing Test 5 Essay

To score your practice writing test essay, follow these steps:

STEP 1. Use the guidelines from the writing test analytic rubric in chapter 3 to score your essay. Because many essays do not fit the exact description at each score point, read each description and try to determine which paragraph in the rubric best describes most of the characteristics of your essay.

STEP 2. Because your writing test domain scores are the sum of two readers' ratings of your essay, multiply your own 1–6 rating from step 1 by 2. Or, have both you and someone else read and score your practice essay, add those ratings together, and record the total in the Domain Score column in step 3.

STEP 3. Enter your writing test domain scores in the following box:

			Domain Score
Ideas and Analysis	______	x 2 =	______
Development and Support	______	x 2 =	______
Organization	______	x 2 =	______
Language Use and Convention	______	x 2 =	______

STEP 4. Enter the sum of the second-column scores here ______.

STEP 5. Divide sum by 4† (range 2–12). This is your Writing Subject score.

†Round value to the nearest whole number. Round down any fraction less than one-half; round up any fraction that is one-half or more.

STEP 6. Use the table on page 896 to determine your estimated percentile rank (percent at or below) for your writing subject score.

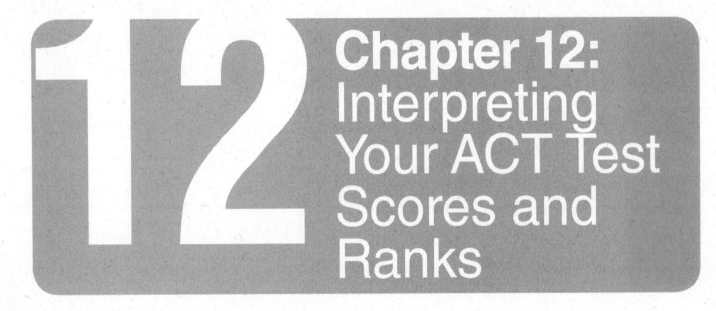

Chapter 12: Interpreting Your ACT Test Scores and Ranks

After taking any test, students are eager to see how they've done. Assuming you took and scored ACT practice test 1 in chapter 3 or took other practice tests in chapter 10 and scored them in chapter 11, you have a great deal of information to consider when determining how well you did.

- **Raw scores:** ACT does not provide raw scores, but you have raw scores for the practice tests in this book.
- **Scale scores** are the scores that ACT reports to students, high schools, colleges, and scholarship agencies.
- **Composite score** is a scale score that reflects your overall performance on *all* of the multiple choice tests—English, math, reading, and science.
- **Ranks** indicate the approximate percentage of ACT-tested students who scored at or below each of your scores; for example, if your mathematics rank is 85%, then you scored as well or better than 85% of the other students who took the mathematics test.

If you take the ACT you receive the *ACT Student Report*, which includes scale scores, the Composite score, and the rank for each score. You can visit www.act.org to view samples of this report as well as the High School and College reports.

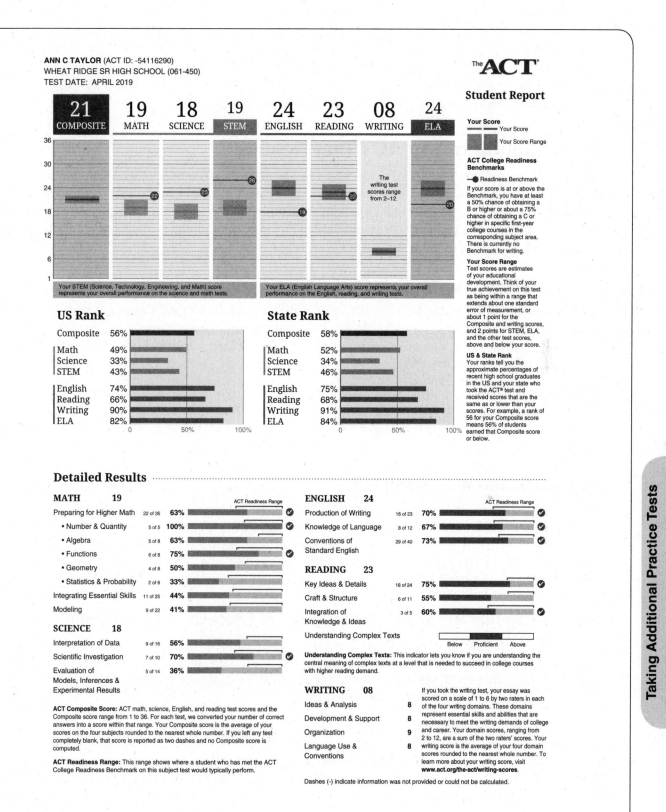

ANN C TAYLOR (ACT ID: -54116290)
WHEAT RIDGE SR HIGH SCHOOL (061-450)
TEST DATE: APRIL 2019

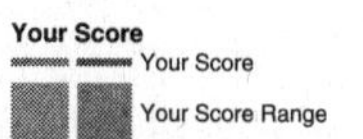

Student Report

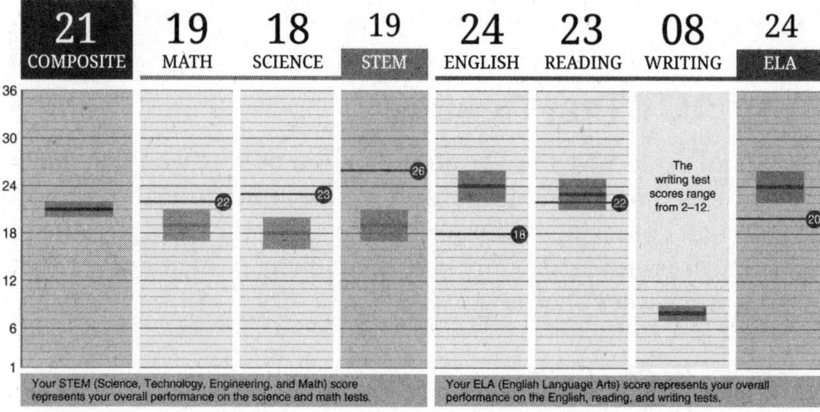

Your Score

Your Score

Your Score Range

ACT College Readiness Benchmarks

Readiness Benchmark

If your score is at or above the Benchmark, you have at least a 50% chance of obtaining a B or higher or about a 75% chance of obtaining a C or higher in specific first-year college courses in the corresponding subject area. There is currently no Benchmark for writing.

Your Score Range

Test scores are estimates of your educational development. Think of your true achievement on this test as being within a range that extends about one standard error of measurement, or about 1 point for the Composite and writing scores, and 2 points for STEM, ELA, and the other test scores, above and below your score.

US & State Rank

Your ranks tell you the approximate percentages of recent high school graduates in the US and your state who took the ACT® test and received scores that are the same as or lower than your scores. For example, a rank of 56 for your Composite score means 56% of students earned that Composite score or below.

US Rank

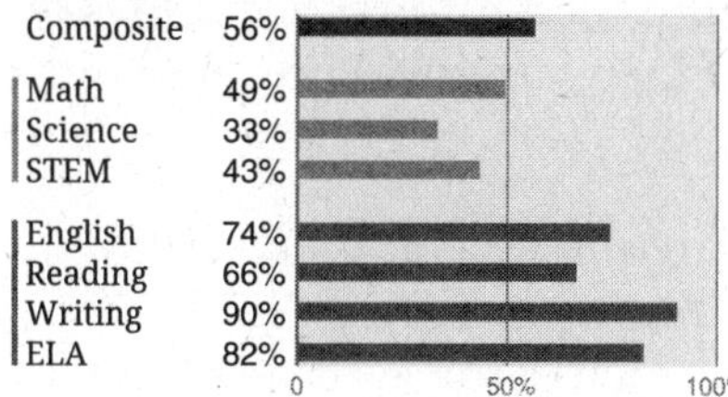

State Rank

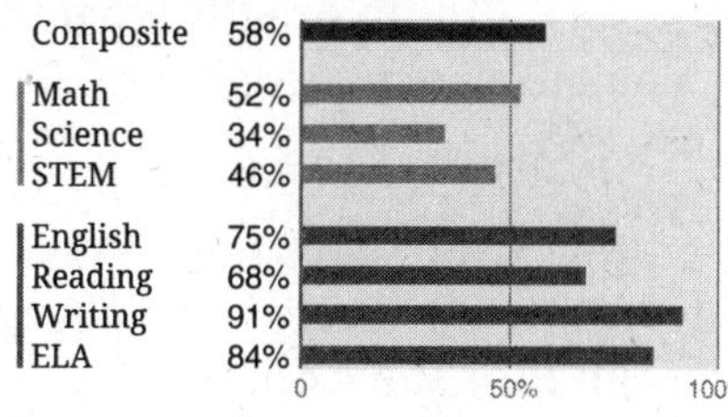

Detailed Results

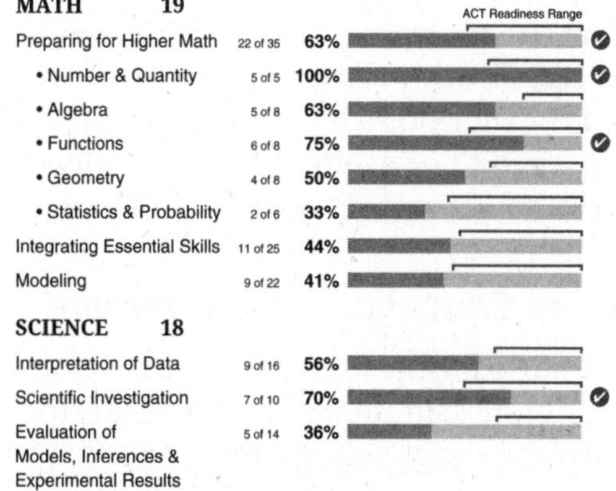

MATH 19
ACT Readiness Range
Preparing for Higher Math 22 of 35 63%
• Number & Quantity 5 of 5 100%
• Algebra 5 of 8 63%
• Functions 6 of 8 75%
• Geometry 4 of 8 50%
• Statistics & Probability 2 of 6 33%
Integrating Essential Skills 11 of 25 44%
Modeling 9 of 22 41%
SCIENCE 18
Interpretation of Data 9 of 16 56%
Scientific Investigation 7 of 10 70%
Evaluation of Models, Inferences & Experimental Results 5 of 14 36%

ACT Composite Score: ACT math, science, English, and reading test scores and the Composite score range from 1 to 36. For each test, we converted your number of correct answers into a score within that range. Your Composite score is the average of your scores on the four subjects rounded to the nearest whole number. If you left any test completely blank, that score is reported as two dashes and no Composite score is computed.

ACT Readiness Range: This range shows where a student who has met the ACT College Readiness Benchmark on this subject test would typically perform.

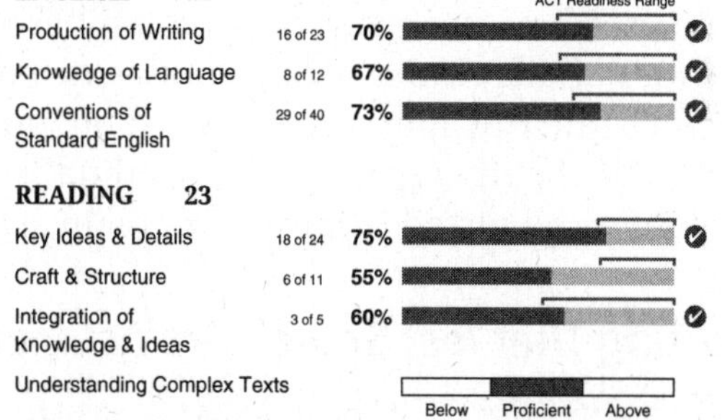

ENGLISH 24
ACT Readiness Range
Production of Writing 16 of 23 70%
Knowledge of Language 8 of 12 67%
Conventions of Standard English 29 of 40 73%
READING 23
Key Ideas & Details 18 of 24 75%
Craft & Structure 6 of 11 55%
Integration of Knowledge & Ideas 3 of 5 60%
Understanding Complex Texts
Below
Proficient
Above

Understanding Complex Texts: This indicator lets you know if you are understanding the central meaning of complex texts at a level that is needed to succeed in college courses with higher reading demand.

WRITING 08

Ideas & Analysis	8
Development & Support	8
Organization	9
Language Use & Conventions	8

If you took the writing test, your essay was scored on a scale of 1 to 6 by two raters in each of the four writing domains. These domains represent essential skills and abilities that are necessary to meet the writing demands of college and career. Your domain scores, ranging from 2 to 12, are a sum of the two raters' scores. Your writing score is the average of your four domain scores rounded to the nearest whole number. To learn more about your writing score, visit **www.act.org/the-act/writing-scores**.

Dashes (-) indicate information was not provided or could not be calculated.

In this chapter, we explain how to interpret your scores and use them as a tool to help inform your education and career decisions. We encourage you to look at your ACT test scores and ranks with additional information to help guide your future education and career planning.

Understanding Your ACT Test Results

Your scores, composite score, and ranks provide a good indication of how well you did on the test, but you can interpret these scores on a deeper level to find out more about how well prepared you are to tackle a certain course of studies or pursue a specific career. In the following sections, we help you put your scores and ranks in perspective to make them more meaningful and relevant to your education and career planning.

How ACT Scores Your Multiple-Choice Tests

ACT scores the multiple-choice tests the same way you scored your ACT practice tests in chapters 3 and 11. The first step is to do exactly what you did for your practice tests: count the number of questions you answered correctly to determine your raw score. No points are deducted for incorrect answers.

The raw score is converted to a scale score to enhance score interpretation and allow comparability across different forms. Scale scores range from 1 (low) to 36 (high) for each of the four individual tests and for the Composite score, which is the average of the four test scores.

How ACT Scores Your Writing Test

Two trained readers score each writing test based on the analytic rubric presented on pages 109–110. Each reader scores your essay on a scale from 1 (low) to 6 (high) on each domain. If their scores differ by more than 1 point on any of the four domains, a third reader scores your essay to resolve the discrepancy. This method is designed to be as impartial as possible. The writing score is calculated from your domain scores and is reported on a 2-to-12 scale.

Recognizing That Test Scores Are Estimates of Educational Achievement

No test, including the ACT, is an exact measure of your educational achievement. We estimate the amount of imprecision using the "standard error of measurement." On the ACT, the standard error of measurement (SEM) is 2 points for each of the multiple-choice tests, 4 points for the writing test, and 1 point for the Composite score.

Because no test score is an exact measure of your achievement, think of each of your ACT scores as a range of scores rather than as a precise number. The SEM can be used to estimate ranges for your scores. To do this, just add the SEM to, and subtract it from, each of your scores. For example, if your score on the English test is 22, your true achievement is likely in the score range of 20 to 24 (22 plus or minus 2 points).

Using Ranks to Interpret Your Scores

The US and state ranks for a score tell you how your scores compare to those earned by recent high school graduates who took the ACT. The numbers indicate the cumulative percent of students who scored at or below a given score. For example, if your rank is 63%, then 63% of recent high school graduates who took the ACT scored at or below your score.

Comparing Your Test Scores to Each Other

Another way to interpret your ACT test scores is by comparing them to each other using the ranks. You may find it interesting, for example, to compare your ranks for the science and mathematics tests to your ranks for the reading and English tests. Perhaps you felt more comfortable and successful in some subject areas than in others. Making comparisons among your ACT test ranks can be especially helpful as you make decisions about the courses you will take in high school and college. A high rank in a particular area indicates that you compare well to other ACT test-takers in that subject. A low rank may indicate that you need to develop your skills more in that area.

Keep in mind, however, that scale scores from the different individual tests can't be directly compared to each other. Scoring 23 on the ACT English and mathematics tests, for example, doesn't necessarily mean that your levels of skill and knowledge in English are the same as they are in mathematics. The percentile ranks corresponding to the scores—not the scores themselves—are probably best for making comparisons among subject areas.

Comparing Your Scores and Ranks to Your High School Grades

After you take the ACT and receive your student report, compare your scores and ranks to your high school grades. Are your highest grades and highest ACT test scores and ranks in the same content areas? If so, you might want to consider college majors that would draw on your areas of greatest strength or seek to improve your knowledge and skills in weaker subject areas. However, if your grades and scores differ significantly, talk with your counselor about possible reasons for the differences.

Comparing Your Scores to Those of Enrolled First-Year College Students

Another way to understand your ACT test scores and ranks is by comparing them to those of students enrolled at colleges or universities you're interested in attending. This information can be very useful as you make decisions about applying for college. Keep in mind that admissions offices use a number of measures—including high school grades, recommendations, and extracurricular activities—to determine how students are likely to perform at their schools. Still, knowing that your ACT test scores are similar to those of students already enrolled at a college or university you're considering may make you more confident in applying for admission there.

Using ACT College and Career Readiness Standards to Help You Understand Your ACT Scores

After you calculate your scores, you may wonder what your test scores mean regarding how well you are prepared to tackle college-level courses. In other words, what do your test scores tell you about your knowledge and skills in English, math, reading, and science? One way to understand this is to consider your scores from the perspective of what students who have that score are likely to know and be able to do. ACT developed the College and Career Readiness Standards to tell you exactly that.

What Are the ACT College and Career Readiness Standards?

The ACT College and Career Readiness Standards are sets of statements that describe what students are *likely* to know and be able to do in each content area based on their scores on each of the tests (English, mathematics, reading, science, and writing). The statements serve as score descriptors and reflect a progression of skills and knowledge in a particular content area. The College and Career Readiness Standards are reported in terms of score range, so that the statements describe the knowledge and skills that students *typically* demonstrate who score in these different ranges on the multiple-choice tests: 13–15, 16–19, 20–23, 24–27, 28–32, 33–36. A score of 1–12 indicates the student is most likely beginning to develop the knowledge and skills described in the 13–15 score range for that particular test. All the College and Career Readiness Standards are cumulative, meaning that students typically can also demonstrate the skills and knowledge described in the score ranges below the range in which they scored.

How Can the ACT College and Career Readiness Standards Help You?

The purpose of the ACT College and Career Readiness Standards is to help you and others better understand what your ACT scores indicate about the knowledge and skills you likely have and what areas might need further development for you to be better prepared for college.

Because the ACT College and Career Readiness Standards provide statements that describe what you are *likely* to know and be able to do, you can use that information to help zero in on what specific steps you should take to further develop your college readiness. If, for example, you scored in the 16–19 range on the English test, you might infer that you are likely able to do and know the skills and knowledge described in the 13–15 and in the 16–19 range. You might choose to take a closer look at the standards in the 20–23 and higher score ranges to see what courses to take, or what instruction you might need, to develop those particular areas in order to be better prepared for college. In other words, you can use the ACT College and Career Readiness Standards to help you select courses and instruction that will focus on preparing you for college.

ACT College Readiness Benchmarks

ACT has identified the minimum score needed on each ACT test to indicate a 50% chance of obtaining a B or higher or about a 75% chance of obtaining a C or higher in the corresponding first-year college course. Your score report will have a visual representation of where you scored compared to the ACT College Readiness Benchmark.

ACT Test	ACT Benchmark Score	College Course
English	18	English Composition
Mathematics	22	Algebra
Reading	22	Social Sciences/Humanities
Science	23	Biology

To increase your college readiness, consider taking additional rigorous course work before you enter college. When you meet with your academic advisor to plan your first-year college courses, select courses that are appropriate for your academic background and reflect your planned curriculum.

Planning Your Education and Career

The *ACT Student Report* includes a College and Career Planning section that helps you explore college majors and occupations, consider your options, and develop plans. The information in this section is all about you. Majors and occupations you may want to explore have been listed here, because they are related to the interests you expressed or occupations you said you were considering.

Seeking Additional Information and Guidance

Your *ACT Student Report* will provide additional information to help you understand your ACT test results and use them to make important decisions about college and to explore possible future careers.

As you approach decisions about college and careers, be sure to take advantage of all the assistance you can find. Talk to your parents, counselors, and teachers; visit your local library; and talk directly to personnel at colleges in which you're interested. The more you can find out about all the educational options available to you and the level of your academic skills and knowledge (using such information as your ACT test results), the better prepared you'll be to make informed college and career choices.

ACT College and Career Readiness Standards—English

These standards describe what students who score in specific score ranges on the English test are likely to know and be able to do.

- Students who score in the 1–12 range are most likely beginning to develop the knowledge and skills assessed in the other ranges.
- The ACT College Readiness Benchmark for English is 18. Students who achieve this score on the ACT English test have a 50% likelihood of achieving a B or better in a first-year English composition course at a typical college. The knowledge and skills highly likely to be demonstrated by students who meet the benchmark are shaded.

Production of Writing

Score Range	Production of Writing: Topic Development in Terms of Purpose and Focus (TOD)
13–15	TOD 201. Delete material because it is obviously irrelevant in terms of the topic of the essay
16–19	TOD 301. Delete material because it is obviously irrelevant in terms of the focus of the essay TOD 302. Identify the purpose of a word or phrase when the purpose is simple (e.g., identifying a person, defining a basic term, using common descriptive adjectives) TOD 303. Determine whether a simple essay has met a straightforward goal
20–23	TOD 401. Determine relevance of material in terms of the focus of the essay TOD 402. Identify the purpose of a word or phrase when the purpose is straightforward (e.g., describing a person, giving examples) TOD 403. Use a word, phrase, or sentence to accomplish a straightforward purpose (e.g., conveying a feeling or attitude)
24–27	TOD 501. Determine relevance of material in terms of the focus of the paragraph TOD 502. Identify the purpose of a word, phrase, or sentence when the purpose is fairly straightforward (e.g., identifying traits, giving reasons, explaining motivations) TOD 503. Determine whether an essay has met a specified goal TOD 504. Use a word, phrase, or sentence to accomplish a fairly straightforward purpose (e.g., sharpening an essay's focus, illustrating a given statement)

18

Score Range	Production of Writing: Topic Development in Terms of Purpose and Focus (TOD) (*continued*)
28–32	TOD 601. Determine relevance when considering material that is plausible but potentially irrelevant at a given point in the essay TOD 602. Identify the purpose of a word, phrase, or sentence when the purpose is subtle (e.g., supporting a later point, establishing tone) or when the best decision is to delete the text in question TOD 603. Use a word, phrase, or sentence to accomplish a subtle purpose (e.g., adding emphasis or supporting detail, expressing meaning through connotation)
33–36	TOD 701. Identify the purpose of a word, phrase, or sentence when the purpose is complex (e.g., anticipating a reader's need for background information) or requires a thorough understanding of the paragraph and essay TOD 702. Determine whether a complex essay has met a specified goal TOD 703. Use a word, phrase, or sentence to accomplish a complex purpose, often in terms of the focus of the essay

Score Range	Production of Writing: Organization, Unity, and Cohesion (ORG)
13–15	ORG 201. Determine the need for transition words or phrases to establish time relationships in simple narrative essays (e.g., *then*, *this time*)
16–19	ORG 301. Determine the most logical place for a sentence in a paragraph ORG 302. Provide a simple conclusion to a paragraph or essay (e.g., expressing one of the essay's main ideas)
20–23	ORG 401. Determine the need for transition words or phrases to establish straightforward logical relationships (e.g., *first*, *afterward*, *in response*) ORG 402. Determine the most logical place for a sentence in a straightforward essay ORG 403. Provide an introduction to a straightforward paragraph ORG 404. Provide a straightforward conclusion to a paragraph or essay (e.g., summarizing an essay's main idea or ideas) ORG 405. Rearrange the sentences in a straightforward paragraph for the sake of logic

18

(*continued*)

Score Range	Production of Writing: Organization, Unity, and Cohesion (ORG) (*continued*)
24–27	ORG 501. Determine the need for transition words or phrases to establish subtle logical relationships within and between sentences (e.g., *therefore*, *however*, *in addition*) ORG 502. Provide a fairly straightforward introduction or conclusion to or transition within a paragraph or essay (e.g., supporting or emphasizing an essay's main idea) ORG 503. Rearrange the sentences in a fairly straightforward paragraph for the sake of logic ORG 504. Determine the best place to divide a paragraph to meet a particular rhetorical goal ORG 505. Rearrange the paragraphs in an essay for the sake of logic
28–32	ORG 601. Determine the need for transition words or phrases to establish subtle logical relationships within and between paragraphs ORG 602. Determine the most logical place for a sentence in a fairly complex essay ORG 603. Provide a subtle introduction or conclusion to or transition within a paragraph or essay (e.g., echoing an essay's theme or restating the main argument) ORG 604. Rearrange the sentences in a fairly complex paragraph for the sake of logic and coherence
33–36	ORG 701. Determine the need for transition words or phrases, basing decisions on a thorough understanding of the paragraph and essay ORG 702. Provide a sophisticated introduction or conclusion to or transition within a paragraph or essay, basing decisions on a thorough understanding of the paragraph and essay (e.g., linking the conclusion to one of the essay's main images)

Score Range	Production of Writing: Knowledge of Language (KLA)
13–15	KLA 201. Revise vague, clumsy, and confusing writing that creates obvious logic problems
16–19	KLA 301. Delete obviously redundant and wordy material KLA 302. Revise expressions that deviate markedly from the style and tone of the essay
20–23	KLA 401. Delete redundant and wordy material when the problem is contained within a single phrase (e.g., "alarmingly startled," "started by reaching the point of beginning") KLA 402. Revise expressions that deviate from the style and tone of the essay KLA 403. Determine the need for conjunctions to create straightforward logical links between clauses KLA 404. Use the word or phrase most appropriate in terms of the content of the sentence when the vocabulary is relatively common
24–27	KLA 501. Revise vague, clumsy, and confusing writing KLA 502. Delete redundant and wordy material when the meaning of the entire sentence must be considered KLA 503. Revise expressions that deviate in subtle ways from the style and tone of the essay KLA 504. Determine the need for conjunctions to create logical links between clauses KLA 505. Use the word or phrase most appropriate in terms of the content of the sentence when the vocabulary is uncommon
28–32	KLA 601. Revise vague, clumsy, and confusing writing involving sophisticated language KLA 602. Delete redundant and wordy material that involves fairly sophisticated language (e.g., "the outlook of an aesthetic viewpoint") or that sounds acceptable as conversational English KLA 603. Determine the need for conjunctions to create subtle logical links between clauses KLA 604. Use the word or phrase most appropriate in terms of the content of the sentence when the vocabulary is fairly sophisticated
33–36	KLA 701. Delete redundant and wordy material that involves sophisticated language or complex concepts or where the material is redundant in terms of the paragraph or essay as a whole KLA 702. Use the word or phrase most appropriate in terms of the content of the sentence when the vocabulary is sophisticated

18

Score Range	Conventions of Standard English Sentence Structure and Formation (SST)
13–15	SST 201. Determine the need for punctuation or conjunctions to join simple clauses SST 202. Recognize and correct inappropriate shifts in verb tense between simple clauses in a sentence or between simple adjoining sentences
16–19	SST 301. Determine the need for punctuation or conjunctions to correct awkward-sounding fragments and fused sentences as well as obviously faulty subordination and coordination of clauses SST 302. Recognize and correct inappropriate shifts in verb tense and voice when the meaning of the entire sentence must be considered
20–23	SST 401. Recognize and correct marked disturbances in sentence structure (e.g., faulty placement of adjectives, participial phrase fragments, missing or incorrect relative pronouns, dangling or misplaced modifiers, lack of parallelism within a simple series of verbs)
24–27	SST 501. Recognize and correct disturbances in sentence structure (e.g., faulty placement of phrases, faulty coordination and subordination of clauses, lack of parallelism within a simple series of phrases) SST 502. Maintain consistent and logical verb tense and pronoun person on the basis of the preceding clause or sentence
28–32	SST 601. Recognize and correct subtle disturbances in sentence structure (e.g., danglers where the intended meaning is clear but the sentence is ungrammatical, faulty subordination and coordination of clauses in long or involved sentences) SST 602. Maintain consistent and logical verb tense and voice and pronoun person on the basis of the paragraph or essay as a whole
33–36	SST 701. Recognize and correct very subtle disturbances in sentence structure (e.g., weak conjunctions between independent clauses, run-ons that would be acceptable in conversational English, lack of parallelism within a complex series of phrases or clauses)

18

Score Range	Conventions of Standard English Usage Conventions (USG)
13–15	USG 201. Form the past tense and past participle of irregular but commonly used verbs USG 202. Form comparative and superlative adjectives
16–19	USG 301. Determine whether an adjective form or an adverb form is called for in a given situation USG 302. Ensure straightforward subject-verb agreement USG 303. Ensure straightforward pronoun-antecedent agreement USG 304. Use idiomatically appropriate prepositions in simple contexts USG 305. Use the appropriate word in frequently confused pairs (e.g., *there* and *their*, *past* and *passed*, *led* and *lead*)
20–23	USG 401. Use the correct comparative or superlative adjective or adverb form depending on context (e.g., "He is the oldest of my three brothers") USG 402. Ensure subject-verb agreement when there is some text between the subject and verb USG 403. Use idiomatically appropriate prepositions, especially in combination with verbs (e.g., *long for*, *appeal to*) USG 404. Recognize and correct expressions that deviate from idiomatic English
24–27	USG 501. Form simple and compound verb tenses, both regular and irregular, including forming verbs by using *have* rather than *of* (e.g., "would have gone," not "would of gone") USG 502. Ensure pronoun-antecedent agreement when the pronoun and antecedent occur in separate clauses or sentences USG 503. Recognize and correct vague and ambiguous pronouns
28–32	USG 601. Ensure subject-verb agreement in some challenging situations (e.g., when the subject-verb order is inverted or when the subject is an indefinite pronoun) USG 602. Correctly use reflexive pronouns, the possessive pronouns *its* and *your*, and the relative pronouns *who* and *whom* USG 603. Use the appropriate word in less-common confused pairs (e.g., *allude* and *elude*)
33–36	USG 701. Ensure subject-verb agreement when a phrase or clause between the subject and verb suggests a different number for the verb USG 702. Use idiomatically and contextually appropriate prepositions in combination with verbs in situations involving sophisticated language or complex concepts

18

Score Range	Conventions of Standard English Conventions (PUN)
13–15	PUN 201. Delete commas that create basic sense problems (e.g., between verb and direct object)
16–19	PUN 301. Delete commas that markedly disturb sentence flow (e.g., between modifier and modified element) PUN 302. Use appropriate punctuation in straightforward situations (e.g., simple items in a series)
20–23	PUN 401. Delete commas when an incorrect understanding of the sentence suggests a pause that should be punctuated (e.g., between verb and direct object clause) PUN 402. Delete apostrophes used incorrectly to form plural nouns PUN 403. Use commas to avoid obvious ambiguity (e.g., to set off a long introductory element from the rest of the sentence when a misreading is possible) PUN 404. Use commas to set off simple parenthetical elements
24–27	PUN 501. Delete commas in long or involved sentences when an incorrect understanding of the sentence suggests a pause that should be punctuated (e.g., between the elements of a compound subject or compound verb joined by *and*) PUN 502. Recognize and correct inappropriate uses of colons and semicolons PUN 503. Use punctuation to set off complex parenthetical elements PUN 504. Use apostrophes to form simple possessive nouns
28–32	PUN 601. Use commas to avoid ambiguity when the syntax or language is sophisticated (e.g., to set off a complex series of items) PUN 602. Use punctuation to set off a nonessential/nonrestrictive appositive or clause PUN 603. Use apostrophes to form possessives, including irregular plural nouns PUN 604. Use a semicolon to link closely related independent clauses
33–36	PUN 701. Delete punctuation around essential/restrictive appositives or clauses PUN 702. Use a colon to introduce an example or an elaboration

18

ACT College and Career Readiness Standards—Mathematics

These standards describe what students who score in specific score ranges on the math test are likely to know and be able to do. For more information about the ACT College and Career Readiness Standards in mathematics, go to www.act.org/standard/planact/math/mathnotes.html.

- Students who score in the 1–12 range are most likely beginning to develop the knowledge and skills assessed in the other ranges.
- The ACT College Readiness Benchmark for mathematics is 22. Students who achieve this score on the ACT mathematics test have a 50% likelihood of achieving a B or better in a first-year college algebra course at a typical college. The knowledge and skills highly likely to be demonstrated by students who meet the benchmark are shaded.

Score Range	Number and Quantity (N)
13–15	N 201. Perform one-operation computation with whole numbers and decimals N 202. Recognize equivalent fractions and fractions in lowest terms N 203. Locate positive rational numbers (expressed as whole numbers, fractions, decimals, and mixed numbers) on the number line
16–19	N 301. Recognize one-digit factors of a number N 302. Identify a digit's place value N 303. Locate rational numbers on the number line Note: A matrix as a representation of data is treated here as a basic table.
20–23	N 401. Exhibit knowledge of elementary number concepts such as rounding, the ordering of decimals, pattern identification, primes, and greatest common factor N 402. Write positive powers of 10 by using exponents N 403. Comprehend the concept of length on the number line, and find the distance between two points N 404. Understand absolute value in terms of distance N 405. Find the distance in the coordinate plane between two points with the same *x*-coordinate or *y*-coordinate N 406. Add two matrices that have whole number entries
24–27	N 501. Order fractions N 502. Find and use the least common multiple N 503. Work with numerical factors N 504. Exhibit some knowledge of the complex numbers N 505. Add and subtract matrices that have integer entries

22

(continued)

Taking Additional Practice Tests

Score Range	Number and Quantity (N) (*continued*)
28–32	N 601. Apply number properties involving prime factorization N 602. Apply number properties involving even/odd numbers and factors/multiples N 603. Apply number properties involving positive/negative numbers N 604. Apply the facts that π is irrational and that the square root of an integer is rational only if that integer is a perfect square N 605. Apply properties of rational exponents N 606. Multiply two complex numbers N 607. Use relations involving addition, subtraction, and scalar multiplication of vectors and of matrices
33–36	N 701. Analyze and draw conclusions based on number concepts N 702. Apply properties of rational numbers and the rational number system N 703. Apply properties of real numbers and the real number system, including properties of irrational numbers N 704. Apply properties of complex numbers and the complex number system N 705. Multiply matrices N 706. Apply properties of matrices and properties of matrices as a number system

Because algebra and functions are closely connected, some standards apply to both categories.

Score Range	Algebra (A)	Functions (F)
13–15	AF 201. Solve problems in one or two steps using whole numbers and using decimals in the context of money	
	A 201. Exhibit knowledge of basic expressions (e.g., identify an expression for a total as $b + g$) A 202. Solve equations in the form $x + a = b$, where a and b are whole numbers or decimals	F 201. Extend a given pattern by a few terms for patterns that have a constant increase or decrease between terms
16–19	AF 301. Solve routine one-step arithmetic problems using positive rational numbers, such as single-step percent AF 302. Solve some routine two-step arithmetic problems AF 303. Relate a graph to a situation described qualitatively in terms of familiar properties such as before and after, increasing and decreasing, higher and lower AF 304. Apply a definition of an operation for whole numbers (e.g., $a \bullet b = 3a - b$)	

<table>
<tr><th>Score Range</th><th>Algebra (A)</th><th>Functions (F)</th></tr>
<tr><td></td><td>A 301. Substitute whole numbers for unknown quantities to evaluate expressions
A 302. Solve one-step equations to get integer or decimal answers
A 303. Combine like terms (e.g., $2x + 5x$)</td><td>F 301. Extend a given pattern by a few terms for patterns that have a constant factor between terms</td></tr>
<tr><td>20–23</td><td colspan="2">AF 401. Solve routine two-step or three-step arithmetic problems involving concepts such as rate and proportion, tax added, percentage off, and estimating by using a given average value in place of actual values
AF 402. Perform straightforward word-to-symbol translations
AF 403. Relate a graph to a situation described in terms of a starting value and an additional amount per unit (e.g., unit cost, weekly growth)</td></tr>
<tr><td></td><td>A 401. Evaluate algebraic expressions by substituting integers for unknown quantities
A 402. Add and subtract simple algebraic expressions
A 403. Solve routine first-degree equations
A 404. Multiply two binomials
A 405. Match simple inequalities with their graphs on the number line (e.g., $x > -3$)
A 406. Exhibit knowledge of slope</td><td>F 401. Evaluate linear and quadratic functions, expressed in function notation, at integer values</td></tr>
<tr><td>24–27</td><td colspan="2">AF 501. Solve multistep arithmetic problems that involve planning or converting common derived units of measure (e.g., feet per second to miles per hour)
AF 502. Build functions and write expressions, equations, or inequalities with a single variable for common pre-algebra settings (e.g., rate and distance problems and problems that can be solved by using proportions)
AF 503. Match linear equations with their graphs in the coordinate plane</td></tr>
</table>

22

(*continued*)

(*continued*)

Score Range	Algebra (A)	Functions (F)
	A 501. Recognize that when numerical quantities are reported in real-world contexts, the numbers are often rounded A 502. Solve real-world problems by using first-degree equations A 503. Solve first-degree inequalities when the method does not involve reversing the inequality sign A 504. Match compound inequalities with their graphs on the number line (e.g., $-10.5 < x < 20.3$) A 505. Add, subtract, and multiply polynomials A 506. Identify solutions to simple quadratic equations A 507. Solve quadratic equations in the form $(x + a)(x + b) = 0$, where a and b are numbers or variables A 508. Factor simple quadratics (e.g., the difference of squares and perfect square trinomials) A 509. Work with squares and square roots of numbers A 510. Work with cubes and cube roots of numbers A 511. Work with scientific notation A 512. Work problems involving positive integer exponents A 513. Determine when an expression is undefined A 514. Determine the slope of a line from an equation	F 501. Evaluate polynomial functions, expressed in function notation, at integer values F 502. Find the next term in a sequence described recursively F 503. Build functions and use quantitative information to identify graphs for relations that are proportional or linear F 504. Attend to the difference between a function modeling a situation and the reality of the situation F 505. Understand the concept of a function as having a well-defined output value at each valid input value F 506. Understand the concept of domain and range in terms of valid input and output, and in terms of function graphs F 507. Interpret statements that use function notation in terms of their context F 508. Find the domain of polynomial functions and rational functions F 509. Find the range of polynomial functions F 510. Find where a rational function's graph has a vertical asymptote F 511. Use function notation for simple functions of two variables

Score Range	Algebra (A)	Functions (F)
28–32	AF 601. Solve word problems containing several rates, proportions, or percentages AF 602. Build functions and write expressions, equations, and inequalities for common algebra settings (e.g., distance to a point on a curve and profit for variable cost and demand) AF 603. Interpret and use information from graphs in the coordinate plane AF 604. Given an equation or function, find an equation or function whose graph is a translation by a specified amount up or down	
	A 601. Manipulate expressions and equations A 602. Solve linear inequalities when the method involves reversing the inequality sign A 603. Match linear inequalities with their graphs on the number line A 604. Solve systems of two linear equations A 605. Solve quadratic equations A 606. Solve absolute value equations	F 601. Relate a graph to a situation described qualitatively in terms of faster change or slower change F 602. Build functions for relations that are inversely proportional F 603. Find a recursive expression for the general term in a sequence described recursively F 604. Evaluate composite functions at integer values
33–36	AF 701. Solve complex arithmetic problems involving percent of increase or decrease or requiring integration of several concepts (e.g., using several ratios, comparing percentages, or comparing averages) AF 702. Build functions and write expressions, equations, and inequalities when the process requires planning and/or strategic manipulation AF 703. Analyze and draw conclusions based on properties of algebra and/or functions AF 704. Analyze and draw conclusions based on information from graphs in the coordinate plane AF 705. Identify characteristics of graphs based on a set of conditions or on a general equation such as $y = ax^2 + c$ AF 706. Given an equation or function, find an equation or function whose graph is a translation by specified amounts in the horizontal and vertical directions	

(*continued*)

(*continued*)

Score Range	Algebra (A)	Functions (F)
	A 701. Solve simple absolute value inequalities A 702. Match simple quadratic inequalities with their graphs on the number line A 703. Apply the remainder theorem for polynomials, that $P(a)$ is the remainder when $P(x)$ is divided by $(x - a)$	F 701. Compare actual values and the values of a modeling function to judge model fit and compare models F 702. Build functions for relations that are exponential F 703. Exhibit knowledge of geometric sequences F 704. Exhibit knowledge of unit circle trigonometry F 705. Match graphs of basic trigonometric functions with their equations F 706. Use trigonometric concepts and basic identities to solve problems F 707. Exhibit knowledge of logarithms F 708. Write an expression for the composite of two simple functions

Score Range	Geometry (G)
13–15	G 201. Estimate the length of a line segment based on other lengths in a geometric figure G 202. Calculate the length of a line segment based on the lengths of other line segments that go in the same direction (e.g., overlapping line segments and parallel sides of polygons with only right angles) G 203. Perform common conversions of money and of length, weight, mass, and time within a measurement system (e.g., dollars to dimes, inches to feet, and hours to minutes)
16–19	G 301. Exhibit some knowledge of the angles associated with parallel lines G 302. Compute the perimeter of polygons when all side lengths are given G 303. Compute the area of rectangles when whole number dimensions are given G 304. Locate points in the first quadrant

Score Range	Geometry (G) (*continued*)
20–23	G 401. Use properties of parallel lines to find the measure of an angle G 402. Exhibit knowledge of basic angle properties and special sums of angle measures (e.g., 90°, 180°, and 360°) G 403. Compute the area and perimeter of triangles and rectangles in simple problems G 404. Find the length of the hypotenuse of a right triangle when only very simple computation is involved (e.g., 3–4–5 and 6–8–10 triangles) G 405. Use geometric formulas when all necessary information is given G 406. Locate points in the coordinate plane G 407. Translate points up, down, left, and right in the coordinate plane
24–27	G 501. Use several angle properties to find an unknown angle measure G 502. Count the number of lines of symmetry of a geometric figure G 503. Use symmetry of isosceles triangles to find unknown side lengths or angle measures G 504. Recognize that real-world measurements are typically imprecise and that an appropriate level of precision is related to the measuring device and procedure G 505. Compute the perimeter of simple composite geometric figures with unknown side lengths G 506. Compute the area of triangles and rectangles when one or more additional simple steps are required G 507. Compute the area and circumference of circles after identifying necessary information G 508. Given the length of two sides of a right triangle, find the third when the lengths are Pythagorean triples G 509. Express the sine, cosine, and tangent of an angle in a right triangle as a ratio of given side lengths G 510. Determine the slope of a line from points or a graph G 511. Find the midpoint of a line segment G 512. Find the coordinates of a point rotated 180° around a given center point

22

(*continued*)

Taking Additional Practice Tests

Score Range	Geometry (G) (*continued*)
28–32	G 601. Use relationships involving area, perimeter, and volume of geometric figures to compute another measure (e.g., surface area for a cube of a given volume and simple geometric probability) G 602. Use the Pythagorean theorem G 603. Apply properties of 30°–60°–90°, 45°–45°–90°, similar, and congruent triangles G 604. Apply basic trigonometric ratios to solve right-triangle problems G 605. Use the distance formula G 606. Use properties of parallel and perpendicular lines to determine an equation of a line or coordinates of a point G 607. Find the coordinates of a point reflected across a vertical or horizontal line or across $y = x$ G 608. Find the coordinates of a point rotated 90° about the origin G 609. Recognize special characteristics of parabolas and circles (e.g., the vertex of a parabola and the center or radius of a circle)
33–36	G 701. Use relationships among angles, arcs, and distances in a circle G 702. Compute the area of composite geometric figures when planning and/or visualization is required G 703. Use scale factors to determine the magnitude of a size change G 704. Analyze and draw conclusions based on a set of conditions G 705. Solve multistep geometry problems that involve integrating concepts, planning, and/or visualization

Score Range	Statistics and Probability (S)
13–15	S 201. Calculate the average of a list of positive whole numbers S 202. Extract one relevant number from a basic table or chart, and use it in a single computation
16–19	S 301. Calculate the average of a list of numbers S 302. Calculate the average given the number of data values and the sum of the data values S 303. Read basic tables and charts S 304. Extract relevant data from a basic table or chart and use the data in a computation S 305. Use the relationship between the probability of an event and the probability of its complement

Score Range	Statistics and Probability (S) (*continued*)
20–23	S 401. Calculate the missing data value given the average and all data values but one S 402. Translate from one representation of data to another (e.g., a bar graph to a circle graph) S 403. Determine the probability of a simple event S 404. Describe events as combinations of other events (e.g., using *and*, *or*, and *not*) S 405. Exhibit knowledge of simple counting techniques
24–27	S 501. Calculate the average given the frequency counts of all the data values S 502. Manipulate data from tables and charts S 503. Compute straightforward probabilities for common situations S 504. Use Venn diagrams in counting S 505. Recognize that when data summaries are reported in the real world, results are often rounded and must be interpreted as having appropriate precision S 506. Recognize that when a statistical model is used, model values typically differ from actual values
28–32	S 601. Calculate or use a weighted average S 602. Interpret and use information from tables and charts, including two-way frequency tables S 603. Apply counting techniques S 604. Compute a probability when the event and/or sample space are not given or obvious S 605. Recognize the concepts of conditional and joint probability expressed in real-world contexts S 606. Recognize the concept of independence expressed in real-world contexts
33–36	S 701. Distinguish among mean, median, and mode for a list of numbers S 702. Analyze and draw conclusions based on information from tables and charts, including two-way frequency tables S 703. Understand the role of randomization in surveys, experiments, and observational studies S 704. Exhibit knowledge of conditional and joint probability S 705. Recognize that part of the power of statistical modeling comes from looking at regularity in the differences between actual values and model values

22

ACT College and Career Readiness Standards—Reading

These standards describe what students who score in specific score ranges on the reading test are likely to know and be able to do.

- Students who score in the 1–12 range are most likely beginning to develop the knowledge and skills assessed in the other ranges.
- The ACT College Readiness Benchmark for reading is 22. Students who achieve this score on the ACT reading test have a 50% likelihood of achieving a B or better in a first-year social science course at a typical college. The knowledge and skills highly likely to be demonstrated by students who meet the benchmark are shaded.

Score Range	Close Reading (CLR)
13–15	CLR 201. Locate basic facts (e.g., names, dates, events) clearly stated in a passage CLR 202. Draw simple logical conclusions about the main characters in somewhat challenging literary narratives
16–19	CLR 301. Locate simple details at the sentence and paragraph level in somewhat challenging passages CLR 302. Draw simple logical conclusions in somewhat challenging passages
20–23	CLR 401. Locate important details in somewhat challenging passages CLR 402. Draw logical conclusions in somewhat challenging passages CLR 403. Draw simple logical conclusions in more challenging passages CLR 404. Paraphrase some statements as they are used in somewhat challenging passages
24–27	CLR 501. Locate and interpret minor or subtly stated details in somewhat challenging passages CLR 502. Locate important details in more challenging passages CLR 503. Draw subtle logical conclusions in somewhat challenging passages CLR 504. Draw logical conclusions in more challenging passages CLR 505. Paraphrase virtually any statement as it is used in somewhat challenging passages CLR 506. Paraphrase some statements as they are used in more challenging passages

22

Score Range	Close Reading (CLR) (*continued*)
28–32	CLR 601. Locate and interpret minor or subtly stated details in more challenging passages CLR 602. Locate important details in complex passages CLR 603. Draw subtle logical conclusions in more challenging passages CLR 604. Draw simple logical conclusions in complex passages CLR 605. Paraphrase virtually any statement as it is used in more challenging passages
33–36	CLR 701. Locate and interpret minor or subtly stated details in complex passages CLR 702. Locate important details in highly complex passages CLR 703. Draw logical conclusions in complex passages CLR 704. Draw simple logical conclusions in highly complex passages CLR 705. Draw complex or subtle logical conclusions, often by synthesizing information from different portions of the passage CLR 706. Paraphrase statements as they are used in complex passages

Score Range	Central Ideas, Themes, and Summaries (IDT)
13–15	IDT 201. Identify the topic of passages and distinguish the topic from the central idea or theme
16–19	IDT 301. Identify a clear central idea in straightforward paragraphs in somewhat challenging literary narratives
20–23	IDT 401. Infer a central idea in straightforward paragraphs in somewhat challenging literary narratives IDT 402. Identify a clear central idea or theme in somewhat challenging passages or their paragraphs IDT 403. Summarize key supporting ideas and details in somewhat challenging passages
24–27	IDT 501. Infer a central idea or theme in somewhat challenging passages or their paragraphs IDT 502. Identify a clear central idea or theme in more challenging passages or their paragraphs IDT 503. Summarize key supporting ideas and details in more challenging passages

(*continued*)

22

Taking Additional Practice Tests

Score Range	Central Ideas, Themes, and Summaries (IDT) (*continued*)
28–32	IDT 601. Infer a central idea or theme in more challenging passages or their paragraphs IDT 602. Summarize key supporting ideas and details in complex passages
33–36	IDT 701. Identify or infer a central idea or theme in complex passages or their paragraphs IDT 702. Summarize key supporting ideas and details in highly complex passages

Score Range	Relationships (REL)
13–15	REL 201. Determine when (e.g., *first, last, before, after*) an event occurs in somewhat challenging passages REL 202. Identify simple cause-effect relationships within a single sentence in a passage
16–19	REL 301. Identify clear comparative relationships between main characters in somewhat challenging literary narratives REL 302. Identify simple cause-effect relationships within a single paragraph in somewhat challenging literary narratives
20–23	REL 401. Order simple sequences of events in somewhat challenging literary narratives REL 402. Identify clear comparative relationships in somewhat challenging passages REL 403. Identify clear cause-effect relationships in somewhat challenging passages
24–27	REL 501. Order sequences of events in somewhat challenging passages REL 502. Understand implied or subtly stated comparative relationships in somewhat challenging passages REL 503. Identify clear comparative relationships in more challenging passages REL 504. Understand implied or subtly stated cause-effect relationships in somewhat challenging passages REL 505. Identify clear cause-effect relationships in more challenging passages

22

Score Range	Relationships (REL) (*continued*)
28–32	REL 601. Order sequences of events in more challenging passages REL 602. Understand implied or subtly stated comparative relationships in more challenging passages REL 603. Identify clear comparative relationships in complex passages REL 604. Understand implied or subtly stated cause-effect relationships in more challenging passages REL 605. Identify clear cause-effect relationships in complex passages
33–36	REL 701. Order sequences of events in complex passages REL 702. Understand implied or subtly stated comparative relationships in complex passages REL 703. Identify clear comparative relationships in highly complex passages REL 704. Understand implied or subtly stated cause-effect relationships in complex passages REL 705. Identify clear cause-effect relationships in highly complex passages

Score Range	Craft and Structure: Word Meanings and Word Choice (WME)
13–15	WME 201. Understand the implication of a familiar word or phrase and of simple descriptive language
16–19	WME 301. Analyze how the choice of a specific word or phrase shapes meaning or tone in somewhat challenging passages when the effect is simple WME 302. Interpret basic figurative language as it is used in a passage
20–23	WME 401. Analyze how the choice of a specific word or phrase shapes meaning or tone in somewhat challenging passages WME 402. Interpret most words and phrases as they are used in somewhat challenging passages, including determining technical, connotative, and figurative meanings

(*continued*)

Score Range	Craft and Structure: Word Meanings and Word Choice (WME) (*continued*)
24–27	WME 501. Analyze how the choice of a specific word or phrase shapes meaning or tone in somewhat challenging passages when the effect is subtle WME 502. Analyze how the choice of a specific word or phrase shapes meaning or tone in more challenging passages WME 503. Interpret virtually any word or phrase as it is used in somewhat challenging passages, including determining technical, connotative, and figurative meanings WME 504. Interpret most words and phrases as they are used in more challenging passages, including determining technical, connotative, and figurative meanings
28–32	WME 601. Analyze how the choice of a specific word or phrase shapes meaning or tone in complex passages WME 602. Interpret virtually any word or phrase as it is used in more challenging passages, including determining technical, connotative, and figurative meanings WME 603. Interpret words and phrases in a passage that makes consistent use of figurative, general academic, domain-specific, or otherwise difficult language
33–36	WME 701. Analyze how the choice of a specific word or phrase shapes meaning or tone in passages when the effect is subtle or complex WME 702. Interpret words and phrases as they are used in complex passages, including determining technical, connotative, and figurative meanings WME 703. Interpret words and phrases in a passage that makes extensive use of figurative, general academic, domain-specific, or otherwise difficult language

Score Range	Craft and Structure: Text Structure (TST)
13–15	TST 201. Analyze how one or more sentences in passages relate to the whole passage when the function is stated or clearly indicated
16–19	TST 301. Analyze how one or more sentences in somewhat challenging passages relate to the whole passage when the function is simple TST 302. Identify a clear function of straightforward paragraphs in somewhat challenging literary narratives

Score Range	Craft and Structure: Text Structure (TST) (*continued*)
20–23	TST 401. Analyze how one or more sentences in somewhat challenging passages relate to the whole passage TST 402. Infer the function of straightforward paragraphs in somewhat challenging literary narratives TST 403. Identify a clear function of paragraphs in somewhat challenging passages TST 404. Analyze the overall structure of somewhat challenging passages
24–27	TST 501. Analyze how one or more sentences in somewhat challenging passages relate to the whole passage when the function is subtle TST 502. Analyze how one or more sentences in more challenging passages relate to the whole passage TST 503. Infer the function of paragraphs in somewhat challenging passages TST 504. Identify a clear function of paragraphs in more challenging passages TST 505. Analyze the overall structure of more challenging passages
28–32	TST 601. Analyze how one or more sentences in complex passages relate to the whole passage TST 602. Infer the function of paragraphs in more challenging passages TST 603. Analyze the overall structure of complex passages
33–36	TST 701. Analyze how one or more sentences in passages relate to the whole passage when the function is subtle or complex TST 702. Identify or infer the function of paragraphs in complex passages TST 703. Analyze the overall structure of highly complex passages

22

Score Range	Craft and Structure: Purpose and Point of View (PPV)
13–15	PPV 201. Recognize a clear intent of an author or narrator in somewhat challenging literary narratives
16–19	PPV 301. Recognize a clear intent of an author or narrator in somewhat challenging passages
20–23	PPV 401. Identify a clear purpose of somewhat challenging passages and how that purpose shapes content and style PPV 402. Understand point of view in somewhat challenging passages

22

(*continued*)

Taking Additional Practice Tests

Score Range	Craft and Structure: Purpose and Point of View (PPV) (*continued*)
24–27	PPV 501. Infer a purpose in somewhat challenging passages and how that purpose shapes content and style PPV 502. Identify a clear purpose of more challenging passages and how that purpose shapes content and style PPV 503. Understand point of view in more challenging passages
28–32	PPV 601. Infer a purpose in more challenging passages and how that purpose shapes content and style PPV 602. Understand point of view in complex passages
33–36	PPV 701. Identify or infer a purpose in complex passages and how that purpose shapes content and style PPV 702. Understand point of view in highly complex passages

Score Range	Integration of Knowledge and Ideas: Arguments (ARG)
13–15	ARG 201. Analyze how one or more sentences in passages offer reasons for or support a claim when the relationship is clearly indicated
16–19	ARG 301. Analyze how one or more sentences in somewhat challenging passages offer reasons for or support a claim when the relationship is simple
20–23	ARG 401. Analyze how one or more sentences in somewhat challenging passages offer reasons for or support a claim ARG 402. Identify a clear central claim in somewhat challenging passages
24–27	ARG 501. Analyze how one or more sentences in more challenging passages offer reasons for or support a claim ARG 502. Infer a central claim in somewhat challenging passages ARG 503. Identify a clear central claim in more challenging passages
28–32	ARG 601. Analyze how one or more sentences in complex passages offer reasons for or support a claim ARG 602. Infer a central claim in more challenging passages
33–36	ARG 701. Analyze how one or more sentences in passages offer reasons for or support a claim when the relationship is subtle or complex ARG 702. Identify or infer a central claim in complex passages ARG 703. Identify a clear central claim in highly complex passages

22

Score Range	Integration of Knowledge and Ideas: Multiple Texts (SYN)
13–15	SYN 201. Make simple comparisons between two passages
16–19	SYN 301. Make straightforward comparisons between two passages
20–23	SYN 401. Draw logical conclusions using information from two literary narratives
24–27	SYN 501. Draw logical conclusions using information from two informational texts
28–32	SYN 601. Draw logical conclusions using information from multiple portions of two literary narratives
33–36	SYN 701. Draw logical conclusions using information from multiple portions of two informational texts

22

Text Complexity Rubric—Reading

This rubric describes reading passages for ACT Aspire™ Grade 8, ACT Aspire Early High School, and the ACT.

Literary Narratives: Stories and Literary Nonfiction

	Somewhat Challenging Literary Narratives	**More Challenging Literary Narratives**	**Complex Literary Narratives**	**Highly Complex Literary Narratives**
Purpose/Levels of Meaning	• Have a largely straightforward purpose (chiefly literary nonfiction) • Contain literal and inferential levels of meaning (chiefly stories)	• Have a largely straightforward to somewhat complex purpose (chiefly literary nonfiction) • Contain literal, inferential, and interpretive levels of meaning (chiefly stories)	• Have a somewhat complex to complex purpose; apparent purpose may differ from real purpose (chiefly literary nonfiction) • Contain literal, inferential, and interpretive levels of meaning (chiefly stories)	• Have a complex purpose; apparent purpose may differ from real purpose (chiefly literary nonfiction) • Contain literal, inferential, and interpretive levels of meaning (chiefly stories)

(*continued*)

Taking Additional Practice Tests

(continued)

	Somewhat Challenging Literary Narratives	More Challenging Literary Narratives	Complex Literary Narratives	Highly Complex Literary Narratives
Structure	• Use a mostly straightforward structure and a wide range of transitions (chiefly literary nonfiction) • Offer insights into people, situations, and events (e.g., motives) • May contain subplots, flashbacks, and flash-forwards (chiefly stories) • Explore largely straightforward conflicts that may be internal or external (chiefly stories) • May have multiple narrators, with switches clearly signaled; main characters exhibit growth and change (chiefly stories)	• Use a somewhat complex structure and a full range of transitions (chiefly literary nonfiction) • Offer deep insights into people, situations, and events (e.g., motives in conflict) • May contain numerous subplots, flashbacks, and flash-forwards as well as parallel and nonlinear plots; may lack clear resolution (chiefly stories) • Explore subtle conflicts that may be internal or external (chiefly stories) • May have multiple narrators; main characters are well rounded (chiefly stories)	• Use a complex structure (chiefly literary nonfiction) • Offer sophisticated and profound insights into people, situations, and events (e.g., philosophical commentary) • May contain numerous subplots, flashbacks, and flash-forwards as well as parallel and nonlinear plots; may lack clear resolution (chiefly stories) • Explore complex conflicts that are largely internal and lack an obvious or easy resolution (e.g., moral dilemmas) (chiefly stories) • May have multiple and/or unreliable narrator(s); main characters are well rounded (chiefly stories)	• Use a highly complex structure (chiefly literary nonfiction) • Offer sophisticated and profound insights into people, situations, and events (e.g., philosophical commentary) • Contain plots that are intricate, nonlinear, and/or difficult to discern; may lack resolution or may not be plot driven (chiefly stories) • Explore complex conflicts that are largely internal and lack an obvious or easy resolution (e.g., moral dilemmas) (chiefly stories) • May have multiple and/or unreliable narrator(s); main characters are well rounded (chiefly stories)

	Somewhat Challenging Literary Narratives	More Challenging Literary Narratives	Complex Literary Narratives	Highly Complex Literary Narratives
Language	• Use some uncommon words and phrases (e.g., general academic [tier 2] words, archaic words, dialect) • Use varied sentence structures significantly more or less formal than in everyday language • Use some somewhat challenging nonliteral and figurative language and literary devices (e.g., symbols, irony) • Observe language conventions (e.g., standard paragraph breaks) (chiefly stories)	• Use some uncommon words and phrases (e.g., general academic [tier 2] words, archaic words, dialect) • Use varied, often complex, and formal sentence structures, with texts from earlier time periods containing structures uncommon in more modern reading • Consistently use somewhat challenging nonliteral and figurative language and literary devices (e.g., symbols, irony) • Largely observe language conventions, with some unconventional elements possible (e.g., dialogue marked with dashes) (chiefly stories)	• Consistently use uncommon words and phrases (e.g., general academic [tier 2] words, archaic words, dialect) • Use varied, often complex, and formal sentence structures, with texts from earlier time periods containing structures uncommon in more modern reading • Consistently use challenging nonliteral and figurative language and literary devices (e.g., extended metaphors, satire, parody) • May use unconventional language structures (e.g., stream-of-consciousness)	• Extensively use uncommon words and phrases (e.g., general academic [tier 2] words, archaic words, dialect) • Use varied, often complex, and formal sentence structures, with texts from earlier time periods containing structures uncommon in more modern reading • Extensively use challenging nonliteral and figurative language and literary devices (e.g., extended metaphors, satire, parody) • Use unconventional language structures (e.g., stream-of-consciousness)

(*continued*)

(*continued*)

	Somewhat Challenging Literary Narratives	More Challenging Literary Narratives	Complex Literary Narratives	Highly Complex Literary Narratives
Abstractness (chiefly literary nonfiction)	• Depict some abstract ideas and concepts that may be important to understanding the text	• Depict several abstract ideas and concepts that are essential to understanding the text	• Depict numerous abstract ideas and concepts that are essential to understanding the text	• Depict numerous abstract ideas and concepts that are essential to understanding the text
Density (chiefly literary nonfiction)	• Have moderate information/ concept density	• Have moderately high information/ concept density	• Have high information/ concept density	• Have very high information/ concept density
Knowledge Demands: Textual Analysis, Life Experiences, Cultural and Literary Knowledge	• Assume readers can read on literal and inferential levels • Assume readers can handle somewhat challenging themes and subject matter with some maturity and objectivity • Assume readers can relate to experiences outside of their own • Call on cultural or literary knowledge to some extent	• Assume readers can read on literal, inferential, and interpretive levels • Assume readers can handle somewhat challenging themes and subject matter with some maturity and objectivity • Assume readers can relate to experiences distinctly different from their own	• Assume readers can read on literal, inferential, and interpretive levels • Assume readers can handle challenging themes and subject matter with maturity and objectivity • Assume readers can relate to experiences distinctly different from their own • Call on cultural or literary knowledge to some extent	• Assume readers can read on literal, inferential, and interpretive levels • Assume readers can handle complex themes and subject matter with maturity and objectivity • Assume readers can relate to experiences distinctly different from their own • Require cultural or literary knowledge for full comprehension

	Somewhat Challenging Literary Narratives	More Challenging Literary Narratives	Complex Literary Narratives	Highly Complex Literary Narratives
	• Have low intertextuality (i.e., make no/few or unimportant connections to other texts); drawing connections between texts at the level of theme may enhance understanding and appreciation	• Call on cultural or literary knowledge to some extent • Have moderate intertextuality (i.e., make some important connections to other texts); drawing connections between texts may enhance understanding and appreciation	• Have moderate intertextuality (i.e., make some important connections to other texts); drawing connections between texts may enhance understanding and appreciation	• Have high intertextuality (i.e., make many important connections to other texts); drawing connections between texts is essential for full understanding and appreciation

Informational Texts: Social Science, Humanities, and Natural Science

	Somewhat Challenging Informational Texts	More Challenging Informational Texts	Complex Informational Texts	Highly Complex Informational Texts
Purpose	• Have a largely straightforward purpose	• Have a largely straightforward to somewhat complex purpose	• Have a somewhat complex to complex purpose; apparent purpose may differ from real purpose	• Have a complex purpose; apparent purpose may differ from real purpose

(*continued*)

(continued)

	Somewhat Challenging Informational Texts	More Challenging Informational Texts	Complex Informational Texts	Highly Complex Informational Texts
Structure	• Use a mostly straightforward structure and a wide range of transitions • Exhibit norms and conventions of a general discipline (e.g., natural science)	• Use a somewhat complex structure and a full range of transitions • Exhibit norms and conventions of a general discipline (e.g., natural science	• Use a complex structure • Exhibit norms and conventions of a general discipline (e.g., natural science)	• Use a highly complex and possibly highly formalized structure (e.g., journal article) • Exhibit norms and conventions of a specific discipline (e.g., biology)
Language	• Use some general academic [tier 2] and domain-specific [tier 3] words and phrases • Use varied and some long and complicated sentence structures	• Consistently use general academic [tier 2] and domain-specific [tier 3] words and phrases • Use varied and often complex sentence structures, with consistent use of long and complicated structures	• Consistently use general academic [tier 2] and domain-specific [tier 3] words and phrases • Use varied and often complex sentence structures, with consistent use of long and complicated structures	• Extensively use general academic [tier 2] and domain-specific [tier 3] words and phrases • Use varied and often complex sentence structures, with consistent use of long and complicated structures
Abstractness	• Depict some abstract ideas and concepts that may be important to understanding the text	• Depict several abstract ideas and concepts that are essential to understanding the text	• Depict numerous abstract ideas and concepts that are essential to understanding the text	• Depict numerous abstract ideas and concepts that are essential to understanding the text
Density	• Have moderate information/concept density	• Have moderately high information/concept density	• Have high information/concept density	• Have very high information/concept density

	Somewhat Challenging Informational Texts	More Challenging Informational Texts	Complex Informational Texts	Highly Complex Informational Texts
Knowledge Demands: Textual Analysis, Life Experiences, Content and Discipline Knowledge	• Assume readers can read on literal and inferential levels • Assume readers can handle somewhat challenging subject matter, including perspectives, values, and ideas unlike their own, with some maturity and objectivity • Assume readers have everyday knowledge and some broad content knowledge, with texts at the high end of the range assuming some content knowledge • Have low intertextuality (i.e., make no/few or unimportant connections to other texts); drawing connections between texts at the level of general concept may enhance understanding	• Assume readers can read on literal, inferential, and evaluative levels • Assume readers can handle somewhat challenging subject matter, including perspectives, values, and ideas unlike their own, with some maturity and objectivity • Assume readers have some content knowledge, with texts at the high end of the range assuming some discipline-specific content knowledge • Have moderate intertextuality (i.e., make some important connections to other texts); drawing connections between texts may enhance understanding	• Assume readers can read on literal, inferential, and evaluative levels • Assume readers can handle challenging subject matter, including perspectives, values, and ideas in opposition to their own, with maturity and objectivity • Assume readers have some discipline-specific content knowledge • Have moderate intertextuality (i.e., make some important connections to other texts); drawing connections between texts may enhance understanding	• Assume readers can read on literal, inferential, and evaluative levels • Assume readers can handle complex subject matter, including perspectives, values, and ideas in opposition to their own, with maturity and objectivity • Assume readers have extensive discipline-specific content knowledge, often in specialized subjects or areas • Have high intertextuality (i.e., make many important connections to other texts); drawing connections between texts is essential for full understanding

ACT College and Career Readiness Standards—Science

These standards describe what students who score in specific score ranges on the science test are likely to know and be able to do.

- Students who score in the 1–12 range are most likely beginning to develop the knowledge and skills assessed in the other ranges.
- The ACT College Readiness Benchmark for science is 23. Students who achieve this score on the ACT science test have a 50% likelihood of achieving a B or better in a first-year biology course at a typical college. The knowledge and skills highly likely to be demonstrated by students who meet the benchmark are shaded.

Score Range	Interpretation of Data (IOD)
13–15	IOD 201. Select one piece of data from a simple data presentation (e.g., a simple food web diagram) IOD 202. Identify basic features of a table, graph, or diagram (e.g., units of measurement) IOD 203. Find basic information in text that describes a simple data presentation
16–19	IOD 301. Select two or more pieces of data from a simple data presentation IOD 302. Understand basic scientific terminology IOD 303. Find basic information in text that describes a complex data presentation IOD 304. Determine how the values of variables change as the value of another variable changes in a simple data presentation
20–23	IOD 401. Select data from a complex data presentation (e.g., a phase diagram) IOD 402. Compare or combine data from a simple data presentation (e.g., order or sum data from a table) IOD 403. Translate information into a table, graph, or diagram IOD 404. Perform a simple interpolation or simple extrapolation using data in a table or graph
24–27	IOD 501. Compare or combine data from two or more simple data presentations (e.g., categorize data from a table using a scale from another table) IOD 502. Compare or combine data from a complex data presentation IOD 503. Determine how the values of variables change as the value of another variable changes in a complex data presentation IOD 504. Determine and/or use a simple (e.g., linear) mathematical relationship that exists between data IOD 505. Analyze presented information when given new, simple information

23

Score Range	Interpretation of Data (IOD) (*continued*)
28–32	IOD 601. Compare or combine data from a simple data presentation with data from a complex data presentation IOD 602. Determine and/or use a complex (e.g., nonlinear) mathematical relationship that exists between data IOD 603. Perform a complex interpolation or complex extrapolation using data in a table or graph
33–36	IOD 701. Compare or combine data from two or more complex data presentations IOD 702. Analyze presented information when given new, complex information

Score Range	Scientific Investigation (SIN)
13–15	SIN 201. Find basic information in text that describes a simple experiment SIN 202. Understand the tools and functions of tools used in a simple experiment
16–19	SIN 301. Understand the methods used in a simple experiment SIN 302. Understand the tools and functions of tools used in a complex experiment SIN 303. Find basic information in text that describes a complex experiment
20–23	SIN 401. Understand a simple experimental design SIN 402. Understand the methods used in a complex experiment SIN 403. Identify a control in an experiment SIN 404. Identify similarities and differences between experiments SIN 405. Determine which experiments used a given tool, method, or aspect of design
24–27	SIN 501. Understand a complex experimental design SIN 502. Predict the results of an additional trial or measurement in an experiment SIN 503. Determine the experimental conditions that would produce specified results
28–32	SIN 601. Determine the hypothesis for an experiment SIN 602. Determine an alternate method for testing a hypothesis
33–36	SIN 701. Understand precision and accuracy issues SIN 702. Predict the effects of modifying the design or methods of an experiment SIN 703. Determine which additional trial or experiment could be performed to enhance or evaluate experimental results

23

Score Range	Evaluation of Models, Inferences, and Experimental Results (EMI)
13–15	EMI 201. Find basic information in a model (conceptual)
16–19	EMI 301. Identify implications in a model EMI 302. Determine which models present certain basic information
20–23	EMI 401. Determine which simple hypothesis, prediction, or conclusion is, or is not, consistent with a data presentation, model, or piece of information in text EMI 402. Identify key assumptions in a model EMI 403. Determine which models imply certain information EMI 404. Identify similarities and differences between models
24–27	EMI 501. Determine which simple hypothesis, prediction, or conclusion is, or is not, consistent with two or more data presentations, models, and/or pieces of information in text EMI 502. Determine whether presented information, or new information, supports or contradicts a simple hypothesis or conclusion, and why EMI 503. Identify the strengths and weaknesses of models EMI 504. Determine which models are supported or weakened by new information EMI 505. Determine which experimental results or models support or contradict a hypothesis, prediction, or conclusion
28–32	EMI 601. Determine which complex hypothesis, prediction, or conclusion is, or is not, consistent with a data presentation, model, or piece of information in text EMI 602. Determine whether presented information, or new information, supports or weakens a model, and why EMI 603. Use new information to make a prediction based on a model
33–36	EMI 701. Determine which complex hypothesis, prediction, or conclusion is, or is not, consistent with two or more data presentations, models, and/or pieces of information in text EMI 702. Determine whether presented information, or new information, supports or contradicts a complex hypothesis or conclusion, and why

23

ACT College and Career Readiness Standards for science are measured in rich and authentic contexts based on science content that students encounter in science courses. This content includes the following:

Life Science/Biology

- Animal behavior
- Animal development and growth
- Body systems
- Cell structure and processes
- Ecology
- Evolution
- Genetics
- Homeostasis
- Life cycles
- Molecular basis of heredity
- Origin of life
- Photosynthesis
- Plant development, growth, structure
- Populations
- Taxonomy

Physical Science/Chemistry, Physics

- Atomic structure
- Chemical bonding, equations, nomenclature, reactions
- Electrical circuits
- Elements, compounds, mixtures
- Force and motions
- Gravitation
- Heat and work
- Kinetic and potential energy
- Magnetism
- Momentum
- The periodic table
- Properties of solutions
- Sound and light
- States, classes, and properties of matter
- Waves

Earth and Space Science

- Earthquakes and volcanoes
- Earth's atmosphere
- Earth's resources
- Fossils and geological time
- Geochemical cycles
- Groundwater
- Lakes, rivers, oceans
- Mass movements
- Plate tectonics
- Rocks, minerals
- Solar system
- Stars, galaxies, and the universe
- Water cycle
- Weather and climate
- Weathering and erosion

5 Part Five: Moving Forward to Test Day

In This Part

Even when you are fully prepared, mentally and physically, to take the ACT, you may need additional guidance to handle the logistics of arriving at the test center on time and with the necessary items. This part helps you avoid any unpleasant surprises on test day that might cause confusion and anxiety, which could negatively affect your performance. Specifically, in this part, you learn how to do the following:

- Register for a convenient test date and test center in plenty of time to have your scores reported to the colleges and scholarship agencies of your choice by their deadlines.
- Map a route and choose a means of travel that ensure you arrive at the test center on time.
- Dress for comfort to ensure that you are not too hot or too cold when taking the test.
- Pack everything you need for test day, so you are admitted to the testing room and have the items you need to take the test.
- Find out what to expect at the test center in terms of check-in procedures, rules, and maintaining your composure and energy.
- Obtain additional information you may need, including how to void your test on test day, retake the test, and gather additional information.

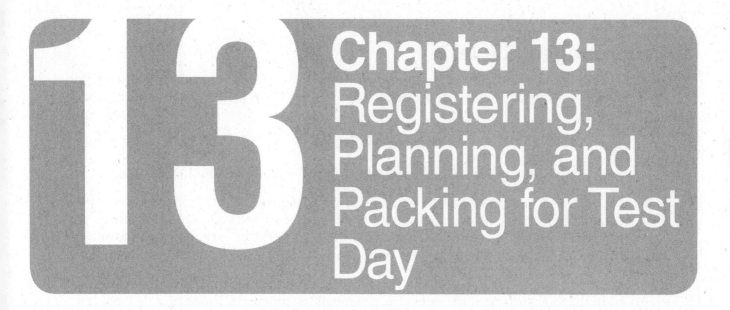

Chapter 13: Registering, Planning, and Packing for Test Day

When you feel ready to take the actual ACT, the time has come to register, plan, and pack for the upcoming day. Your goal is to avoid any unpleasant surprises on test day, such as getting lost on the way to the test center, showing up without a valid ID, or wearing the wrong clothing and being physically uncomfortable during the entire test. Such surprises distract you from what should be your sole focus on test day—doing your very best on the test.

In this chapter, we help you register for the ACT, avoid the most common pitfalls that test-takers encounter leading up to test day, offer guidance on how to dress and what to pack for test day, explain what you can expect at the test center, and give you a heads up about posttest concerns, such as voiding your test on test day, retaking the test, and reporting your scores.

National Testing Program versus State and District Testing

ACT makes the test available via national testing centers and through certain school districts or states. Registration for and administration of the test varies accordingly. For example, if your district or state offers the test, you do not need to register for that test. Instead, your district or state registers for the test and chooses a school day on which to administer it. If you want to take the test at a national test center on a Saturday, you will need to register yourself for that test. Check with your counselor to find out whether your school offers the ACT or whether you must register individually to take the ACT at a national testing center.

Registering for the ACT

If your district or state offers the ACT for your grade level test, you can skip ahead to the section "Planning and Packing for Test Day." Your district or state will take the first two registration steps for you:

- Selects a test date (typically a school day)
- Chooses whether students will take the ACT with or without the writing test

Note: If you have a diagnosed disability or are an English language learner, and have documentation of receiving an accommodation or support in school, you *may* be eligible to take the ACT with that accommodation or support. Work with your school counselor or accommodations coordinator to determine if they have submitted the required documentation.

If your school does not offer the ACT, you must register for it through the ACT national testing program. In the following sections, we lead you through the process of choosing a national test date and test option (ACT with or without the writing test) and registering for the test. We also address special circumstances that could affect your registration.

Selecting a National Testing Date and Location

Prior to registering for the ACT through the ACT national testing program, choose the date on which you want to take the test. When choosing a date, consider the following:

- Available test dates and test centers near you
- College and scholarship application deadlines
- Where you stand in your high school course work
- Whether you may want to take the ACT more than once

Let's look at each of these considerations in turn.

Checking Available Test Dates and Test Centers

The ACT is offered nationally and internationally several times a year. However, it's not offered at every test center on each test date. If you need to take the ACT on a day other than Saturday (for religious reasons), you'll want to be especially attentive in selecting a test date when a test center near you is open on a non-Saturday date.

One of the first things you should find out, then, is where and when the ACT is being offered in your area. A quick and easy way to access available test dates and find test centers is to visit ACT's website at www.actstudent.org. Search for **test dates and deadlines** to find test dates and registration deadlines. You can also look at nearby ACT test centers by searching for **ACT test centers**.

Note: You may *not* receive scores from more than one test taken on a scheduled national or international test date *and* one of the alternate test dates associated with that date. For example, suppose you take the test on Saturday *and* then again on the non-Saturday date associated with that Saturday. We will report only the scores from the first test. The second set of scores will be cancelled without refund.

Considering College and Scholarship Application Deadlines

Colleges and scholarship agencies may require that ACT test scores be submitted sometime during your junior year of high school. Find out what these deadlines are and then make absolutely sure that you take the test early enough to ensure that the colleges and scholarship agencies you're applying to receive your ACT test scores by those deadlines.

Score reports are usually ready about 2 to 8 weeks after the test date. To be on the safe side, consider taking your ACT at least 10 weeks prior to the earliest deadline.

You may not be certain yet which school or program you'll decide on. That's okay. Just be sure you're doing everything, including taking the ACT, early enough to keep all options open.

Gauging Where You Stand in Your High School Course Work and Whether You May Want to Take the ACT More Than Once

Another consideration in deciding when to take the ACT is where you stand in your high school course work. If you're in a college-prep program and taking a lot of courses in English, mathematics, and science in your sophomore and junior years, taking the ACT in your junior year, while those subjects are still fresh in your memory, is probably best.

Perhaps you'll decide to take the ACT more than once, in hopes of improving your score. In that case, it's better to take the exam early in the spring of your junior year to allow time for a second try. If you find you're studying a significant amount of material covered on the ACT during your senior year, you may plan on retaking the ACT in your senior year, based on the reasonable assumption that your scores will reflect your improved knowledge and skills.

Taking the ACT in your junior year has several advantages:

- You probably will have completed much of the course work corresponding to the material covered on the ACT.
- You will have your ACT scores and other information in time to help make decisions about your final year of high school course work. (For example, you may decide to take additional classes in an area in which your test score was lower than you wanted it to be.)
- Colleges will know of your interest and have your scores in time to contact you during the summer before your senior year, when many of them like to send information about admissions, scholarships, advanced placement, and special programs to prospective students.
- You'll have your ACT scores and information from colleges in time to make decisions about visiting campuses or contacting schools.
- You'll have the opportunity to take the ACT again if you feel your scores don't accurately reflect your achievement.

Selecting a Test Option

When you register, you must choose one of two test options—the ACT (which includes the four multiple-choice tests: English, mathematics, reading, and science), or the ACT with the optional writing test (which includes the four multiple-choice tests plus a 40-minute writing test). Taking the writing test does not affect your composite score.

Not all institutions require the ACT writing test. Check directly with the institutions you are considering to find out their requirements, or ask your high school counselor which test option you should take.

Registering

The fastest and easiest way to register to take the ACT through its national testing program is online at www.actstudent.org. When you register on the web, you will know immediately if your preferred test center has space for you, and you can print your admission ticket. Read all the information on your admission ticket carefully to make sure it is correct.

You are guaranteed a seat and test booklet at a test center only if you register by the deadline for a test date. If you miss the late registration deadline, you can try to test as a "standby" examinee. Testing as a standby costs more and does not guarantee you a seat or test booklet. If you decide to take your chance as a standby, be sure to follow the instructions for standby testing on the ACT website. You must bring acceptable identification to be admitted. Standby examinees will be admitted only after all registered students have been seated for their test option.

However you register, you are encouraged to create your free ACT web account. You can use your ACT web account to do several things:

- View your scores and score report on the web at no charge.
- Send your scores to additional colleges.
- Receive e-mail updates from ACT about changes to your registration.
- Make changes to your student profile.
- Print your admission ticket.

Registering Under Special Circumstances

See the website or our online registration brochure for instructions if special circumstances apply to you—for example, if your religious beliefs prevent you from taking the exam on Saturday and no test centers in your area offer non-Saturday test dates or if you have a diagnosed disability or are an English language learner and require accommodations or supports.

If you have a diagnosed disability, or are an English language learner, and have documentation of receiving an accommodation or support in school, you *may* be eligible to take the ACT with that accommodation or support. Details about the procedures for applying to test with accommodations and supports are provided on the ACT website.

Planning and Packing for Test Day

At least one week before your scheduled test date, start planning and packing for test day. You need to know where you're going, how you're getting there, how much time the trip will take you, how to dress, and what to pack. In the following sections, we help you plan and pack for test day.

Getting to the Test Center

If your school is administering the ACT on a school day, you simply need to arrive at your school at the start of the school day. Testing will be the first activity of the day.

Under no circumstances will you be admitted to the test after the test booklets have been distributed, so be sure to arrive on time.

If you registered to take the test through the ACT national testing program, you'll be asked to report to the test center by 8:00 AM on your test date. Under no circumstances will you be admitted after the test booklets have been distributed so be sure to arrive on time by 8:00 AM.

You may need to walk a few blocks to get to the test center or drive several hours, perhaps to an unfamiliar city. Whatever your situation, be certain to allow plenty of time. We recommend that you plan to arrive 15 to 30 minutes early just in case you experience an unexpected delay.

Test centers vary considerably. You may be taking the ACT in your own high school, at a local community college, or in a large building on a nearby university campus. Your surroundings may be quite familiar or they may be new. If they're new, allow yourself a few extra minutes to get acclimated. Then try to forget about your surroundings so that you can concentrate on the test.

To ensure that you arrive on time, map your route to the test center and choose a means of travel—car, train, bus, taxi, bicycle, carpool with a friend . . . whatever works best for you.

One week prior to test day, travel to the testing center using the selected means of travel. By doing a test run on the same day and at the same time (but a week early), you gain a better sense of what traffic will be like, what your parking options will be, whether the buses are running during those times, and so on.

Dressing for Test Day

The night before the test, set out the clothes you want to wear. Dress in layers so that you can adjust to the temperature in your testing room.

Keep in mind that you're going to be sitting in the same place for more than three hours. Wearing something you're especially comfortable in may make you better able to relax and concentrate on the test. For many people, what they're wearing can make a difference in how they feel about themselves. Picking something you like and feel good wearing may boost your confidence.

Packing for Test Day: What to Bring

Bring with you only what you'll need that morning, because other materials will be in your way and may be prohibited in the test room. Be sure to bring these:

- **Your paper admission ticket** (if you are taking the test on a national or international ACT test date). Failure to bring your admission ticket will delay your scores. If your district or state is administering the test, you will not receive (or need) an admission ticket.
- **Acceptable photo identification.** Examples of acceptable identification include current identification issued by your city/state/federal government or school, on which both your name and current photograph appear (for example, driver's license or passport). Without acceptable identification, you will not be allowed to take the test. (See www.actstudent.org for details on what constitutes acceptable and unacceptable identification.)
- Several sharpened **soft-lead no. 2 pencils with good erasers** (no mechanical pencils or ink pens). Test the erasers to make sure they erase cleanly without leaving any residue.

- **A watch *without* an alarm function** to pace yourself. If your watch has an alarm function and the alarm goes off, it will disturb the other students, you will be dismissed, and your answer document will not be scored. Although the test supervisor will announce when 5 minutes remain on each test, not all test rooms have wall clocks for pacing yourself in the meantime.
- A **permitted calculator** if you wish to use one *on the mathematics test only* (for a list of permitted and prohibited calculators, visit www.actstudent.org). You are solely responsible for knowing whether a particular calculator is permitted.
- **A snack and a drink** to consume outside the test room only during the break.

Obtaining Additional Test Details

On certain national test dates, if you test at a national test center, you may request and pay for a copy of the multiple-choice test questions used to determine your scores, a list of your answers, and the answer key. If you take the writing test, you will also receive a copy of the writing prompt, scoring guidelines, and the scores assigned to your essay. You'll also get information about requesting a photocopy of your answer document for an additional fee. These services are not offered for all test dates, so if you're interested in receiving any of these services, you'll need to check the dates on ACT's website (www.actstudent.org) to be sure you're choosing a test date on which the desired service is available.

At the Test Center

Knowing ahead of time what to expect at the test center can alleviate any anxiety you may feel, ensure that you do everything ACT requires in terms of checking in and obeying the rules, and help you maintain your composure. In the following sections, we describe the check-in procedure, present the rules, encourage you to communicate with the testing staff (if necessary), and provide tips on maintaining your composure and energy level.

Checking In

The way **check-in procedures** are handled may vary from location to location. You may find that all students are met at a central location and directed from there to different classrooms. Signs may be posted, telling you that everyone whose last name falls between certain letters should report directly to a particular room. However this part of the check-in is handled at your location, you can anticipate that certain check-in procedures will be performed, including verification of your identity.

In the room you'll be directed to a seat by a member of the testing staff. If you are left-handed, let the testing staff know so that an appropriate desk or table may be made available to you.

Following the Rules

The below text was pulled from the Terms and Conditions: Testing Rules and Policies for the ACT® Test at the time of publishing.

The following behaviors are prohibited. You may be dismissed and/or your test may not be scored, at ACT's sole discretion, if you are found:

- Filling in or altering responses or continuing to write the essay after time has been called on that test section; this means that you cannot make any changes to a test section outside of the designated time for that section, even to fix a stray mark or accidental keystroke
- Looking back at a test section on which time has already been called
- Looking ahead in the test
- Looking at another person's test or answers
- Giving or receiving assistance by any means
- Discussing or sharing test content, test form identification numbers, or answers during test administration, during breaks, after the test, or on social media
- Using a prohibited calculator
- Using a calculator on any test section other than mathematics
- Sharing a calculator with another person
- Using a watch with recording, internet, communication, or calculator capabilities (e.g., a smart watch or fitness band)
- Accessing any electronic device other than an approved calculator or watch; **all** other electronic devices, including cell phones and other wearable devices, must be powered off and stored out of sight from the time you are admitted to test until you leave the test center
- Attempting to photograph, copy, or memorize test-related information or remove test materials, including questions or answers, from the test room in any way, including through social media
- Using highlight pens, colored pens or pencils, notes, dictionaries, or other aids
- Using scratch paper
    - If you are taking the ACT online, some use of ACT-provided scratch paper or an ACT-provided white board may be permitted; all such use must be in accordance with ACT policies and procedures
- Not following instructions or abiding by the rules of the test center
- Exhibiting confrontational, threatening, or unruly behavior, or violating any laws; if ACT suspects you are engaging in criminal activities, such activities may be reported to law enforcement agencies
- Allowing an alarm to sound in the test room or creating any other disturbance

ACT may restrict the items you bring into the test center. All items brought into the test center, such as hats, purses, backpacks, cell phones, calculators, watches, and other electronic devices, may be searched at the discretion of ACT and its testing staff. Searches may include the use of tools, such as handheld metal detectors, that detect prohibited devices. ACT and its testing staff may confiscate and retain for a reasonable period of time any item suspected of having been used, or capable of being used, in violation of these prohibited behaviors. ACT may also provide such items to and permit searches by third parties in connection with an investigation conducted by ACT or others. ACT and its testing staff shall not be responsible for lost, stolen, or damaged items that you bring to a test center. Your test center may also have additional procedures with which you must comply.

Dismissal for Prohibited Behavior

Examinees who are dismissed because of prohibited behavior forfeit their registration for that test date. There are no options for refunds or appeals in situations involving prohibited behavior.

Eating, drinking, and the use of tobacco are not allowed in the test room. You may bring a snack to eat or drink before the test or during the break, but any food or beverage you bring must be put away during testing and must be consumed outside the test room.

Communicating with the Testing Staff

Although you are required to work silently during the test, you may need to communicate with the testing staff under certain circumstances, such as the following:

- **If you have problems with the testing environment, let the testing staff know immediately.** Possible problems include being seated below, over, or next to a heating or cooling vent that is making you too warm or too cold; having a defective chair or desk; poor lighting that makes reading difficult; or excessive noise.
- **If any aspect of the test-taking procedure is not perfectly clear to you, request clarification.** Testing staff will be available throughout the exam. In fact, they'll be moving quietly around the room while you're working. If you have a question about the administration of the test (not about any of the test questions), raise your hand and quietly ask for information.
- **If you need to use the restroom, ask.** Bathroom breaks are permitted during the test or between tests, but you're not allowed to make up the lost time.
- **If you become ill during the test, you may turn in your test materials and leave, if necessary.** Let the testing staff know that you are ill and whether you wish to have your answer document scored. One caution: Once you leave the test center, you won't be allowed to return and continue—so be sure that leaving is what you want to do. You might try closing your eyes or putting your head on the desk for a minute first; then if you feel better, you'll be able to continue.

Maintaining Your Composure and Energy

While you're waiting for the test to begin, you may find yourself getting anxious or jittery. That's perfectly normal. Most of us get nervous in new situations. People handle this nervousness in different ways.

Some people find it helpful to practice **mental and physical relaxation techniques.** If this appeals to you, try alternately flexing and relaxing your muscles, beginning at your toes and moving up through your shoulders, neck, and arms. Meanwhile, imagine yourself in a quiet, peaceful place: at the beach, in the mountains, or just in your favorite lounge chair. Breathe deeply and evenly.

Other people like to **redirect that nervous energy** and turn it to their advantage. For them, concentrating on the task at hand and shutting everything else out of their minds is the most helpful strategy. If this is your style, you may even want to close your eyes and imagine yourself already working on the exam, thinking about how it will feel to move confidently and smoothly through the tests.

If you have the chance, try out the two approaches on some classroom tests and see which one works better for you. The important thing is to keep the ACT in perspective. Try not to let it become larger than life. Remember, it's just one part of a long academic and professional career. If you begin to feel tired during the test, check your posture to make sure you're sitting up straight. Getting enough air in your lungs is difficult when you're slouching. You'll stay more alert and confident if your brain receives a steady supply of oxygen.

You might want to practice those relaxation techniques again, too, because tension contributes to fatigue. As you start a new test, you might find it helpful to stretch your neck and shoulder muscles, rotate your shoulders, stretch back in your chair and take some long, deep breaths.

You can expect a short break (approximately 10 to 15 minutes) after the second test. During this break, it's a good idea to stand up, walk around a little, stretch, and relax. You may wish to get a drink, have a snack, or use the restroom. Keep in mind, though, that you still have work ahead of you that requires concentrated effort. Eat lightly and return to the room quickly. The third test will start promptly, and you'll need to be back at your desk and ready to go on time.

Voiding Your Answer Documents on Test Day

If you have to leave before completing all tests, you must decide whether you want your answer document scored and then inform your supervisor if you do *not* want your answer document scored; otherwise, your answer document will be scored.

Once you break the seal on your multiple-choice test booklet, you cannot request a test date change. If you do not complete all your tests and want to test again, you will have to pay the full fee for your test option again. If you want to take the ACT again, see www.actstudent.org for your options. Once you begin filling out your answer document, you cannot change from one test option to another.

Testing More Than Once

If you think you can improve your scores, you can retake the ACT. ACT may limit the number of times you take the ACT. The current retest limit can be found at www.actstudent.org. Many students take the test twice, once as a junior and again as a senior. Of the students who took the ACT more than once:

- 57% increased their Composite score
- 21% had no change in their Composite score
- 22% decreased their Composite score

You determine which set of scores are sent to colleges or scholarship programs. ACT will release only the scores from the test date (month and year) and test location (e.g., national or state) you designate. This protects you and ensures that you direct the reporting of your scores.

However, you cannot mix and match scores. For example, ACT will not send your mathematics test results from one test and your English test results from another.

Our mission is helping people achieve education and workplace success. Thank you for allowing ACT to be a part of your journey and good luck on test day.

NOTES

NOTES

NOTES

NOTES

NOTES

NOTES

NOTES

NOTES

NOTES

NOTES

NOTES

NOTES

NOTES

NOTES

NOTES

NOTES

NOTES

NOTES

NOTES

NOTES

NOTES

NOTES

NOTES